THE PEPIN PRESS | AGILE RABBIT EDITIONS

WEB DESIGN INDEX BY CONTENT

COMPILED BY GÜNTER BEER

Layout by Günter Beer & Sigurd Buchberger (www.webdesignindex.org)
Cover and book design by Pepin van Roojen
CD Master by Sigurd Buchberger

Front cover illustration by Alice Chan (www.asterialand.com)
Illustration pages 4-5 by Philippe Delvigne (www.filigrif.com)

Introduction by Pepin van Roojen
Translations by LocTeam, Barcelona (German, Spanish, Italian, French and Portuguese), and The Big Word (Chinese, Japanese, Korean, Arabic and Russian). With special thanks to Magda Garcia Masana, Naoko Yamasaki and Vladimir Nazarov.

ISBN 90 5768 069 6
The Pepin Press | Agile Rabbit Editions
Amstedam & Singapore

The Pepin Press BV
P.O. Box 10349
1001 EH Amsterdam
The Netherlands

Tel +31 20 4202021
Fax +31 20 4201152
mail@pepinpress.com
www.pepinpress.com

10 9 8 7 6 5 4 3 2 1
2010 2009 2008 2007 2006 2005

Manufactured in Singapore

CV
Portfolio
Sean O'Riada

Ou ?
act
Liens
Livre d'or

Web Design By Content contains a selection of 500 websites, arranged by subject. Of each site, two pages are included: one opening page and one page representative of the nature of the site. Enclosed is a CD-ROM containing a browser and one-click facility to view and access the selected sites. Together, book and CD offer a comprehensive overview of the standard of web design in any particular field.

With each site in the book, the URL is indicated. The Names of those involved in the design and programming of the sites are stated as follows:

D design
C coding
P production
A agency
M designer's email address

submissions & recommendations

Each year, brand new editions of all The Pepin Press' web design books are published. Should you wish to submit or recommend designs for consideration, please access the submissions form at www.webdesignindex.org.

The Pepin Press / Agile Rabbit Editions

For more information about The Pepin Press' many publications on design, fashion, popular culture, visual reference and ready-to-use images, please visit www.pepinpress.com.

Web Design By Content (Diseño de páginas web por contenidos) presenta una selección de 500 sitios web organizados por temas. De cada sitio se incluyen dos páginas: una página inicial y una página representativa de la naturaleza del sitio. Además, se adjunta un CD-ROM que contiene un navegador con una función «de un solo clic» que permite ver dichos sitios y acceder a ellos. Juntos, el libro y el CD ofrecen un panorama exhaustivo de los patrones utilizados en el campo del diseño web en numerosos ámbitos.

Se indica la URL de cada sitio que aparece en el libro. Asimismo, el nombre de las personas que han participado en el diseño y la programación de dichos sitios se recoge del modo siguiente:

D diseño
C codificación
P producción
A agencia
M dirección de correo electrónico del diseñador

Propuestas y recomendaciones
Cada año, se publican nuevas ediciones de todos los libros de diseño de páginas web de The Pepin Press. Si desea proponer o recomendar un diseño para que se tenga en cuenta para próximas ediciones, rellene el formulario que figura en www.webdesignindex.org.

The Pepin Press / Agile Rabbit Editions
Para obtener más información acerca de las numerosas publicaciones de The Pepin Press sobre diseño, moda, cultura popular, referencia visual e imágenes listas para utilizar, visite www.pepinpress.com.

Web Design By Content (Webdesign nach Thema) enthält eine thematisch gegliederte Auswahl von 500 Websites. Jede Website ist mit zwei Seiten vertreten: mit der Startseite und einer für die Website repräsentativen Seite. Beiliegend finden Sie eine CD-ROM mit einem Browser und einer 1-Klick-Funktion zum Anzeigen und Aufrufen der ausgewählten Websites. Gemeinsam bieten das Buch und die CD einen umfassenden Überblick über die Webdesign-Standards vieler unterschiedlicher Bereiche.

Für jede im Buch genannte Website ist die URL angegeben. Die Namen der an Design und Programmierung der Websites beteiligten Personen sind wie folgt gekennzeichnet:

D Design
C Codierung
P Produktion
A Agentur
M E-Mail-Adresse des Designers

Einsendungen & Empfehlungen
Jedes Jahr werden brandaktuelle Neuausgaben aller Websdesign-Bücher von The Pepin Press herausgebracht. Sollten Sie Designs einreichen oder empfehlen wollen, füllen Sie bitte das entsprechende Einsendeformular unter www.webdesignindex.org aus.

The Pepin Press / Agile Rabbit Editions
Weitere Informationen über die zahlreichen Publikationen von The Pepin Press zu den Themen Design, Mode, Kultur, visuelle Referenz und Bilder zur direkten Verwendung finden Sie auf unserer Website unter www.pepinpress.com.

Web Design By Content (Disegno Web per contenuto) è una selezione di 500 siti ripartiti per argomento. Per ogni sito sono presentate l'home page e una pagina interna per dare un'idea della sua natura. L'accluso CD-ROM contiene il browser e un sistema che consente di visualizzare e accedere al sito desiderato con un semplice clic. Il libro e il CD insieme offrono una panoramica dello standard del web design in alcuni settori specifici.

Per ogni sito è indicato l'URL corrispondente. I nomi delle persone che hanno collaborato al design e alla programmazione di ogni sito sono riportati secondo i seguenti criteri:

D design
C codificazione
P produzione
A agenzia
M indirizzo e-mail del designer

Segnalazioni
Ogni anno The Pepin Press pubblica un'edizione aggiornata di tutte le opere che hanno come oggetto il web design. Se desiderate portare alla nostra attenzione un progetto di design, potete scaricare l'apposito modulo sul sito www.webdesignindex.org.

The Pepin Press / Agile Rabbit Editions
Per ulteriori informazioni sulle numerose opere inserite nel nostro catalogo che hanno come oggetto design, moda, cultura popolare, banca immagini e consultazione grafica potete visitare il sito www.pepinpress.com.

Web Design By Content (Modèles de sites Web par contenu) comprend une sélection de 500 sites Web classés par sujet. Deux pages sont consacrées à chaque site : une page d'ouverture et une page représentative du site. Un CD-ROM est inclus : il contient un navigateur et offre la possibilité de voir et d'accéder aux sites sélectionnés par simple clic. Livre et CD donnent un aperçu global des designs web standard dans chacun des domaines spécifiques.

L'URL de chaque site est indiquée. Les noms des personnes ayant participé à sa conception et à sa programmation sont indiqués comme suit :

D conception
C codage
P production
A agence
M adresse e-mail du concepteur

Suggestions et recommandations
Chaque année, de nouvelles éditions des ouvrages de design Web de The Pepin Press sont éditées. Si vous avez des designs à nous suggérer ou à nous recommander, vous pouvez accéder au formulaire de suggestion qui se trouve à l'adresse www.webdesignindex.org.

The Pepin Press / Agile Rabbit Editions
Pour en savoir plus sur les nombreuses publications de The Pepin Press consacrées au design, à la mode, à la culture pop, aux références visuelles et aux images prêtes à l'emploi, veuillez visiter le site Web www.pepinpress.com.

Web Design By Content (Web Design por Conteúdo) contém uma selecção de 500 sítios na Web, organizados por assunto. Foram incluídas duas páginas de cada sítio na Web: uma página de abertura e uma página representativa da natureza do sítio na Web. O CD-ROM anexo contém um programa de navegação e está estruturado de modo a permitir a visualização e o acesso aos sítios na Web seleccionados com um clique. Em conjunto, o livro e o CD proporcionam uma perspectiva abrangente do nível de Web design em qualquer área específica.

É indicado o URL de cada sítio na Web presente no livro. Os nomes das pessoas envolvidas na concepção e programação dos sítios na Web são indicados da seguinte forma:

D design
C codificação
P produção
A agência
M endereço de correio electrónico do designer

Propostas e recomendações
Todos os anos, The Pepin Press publica edições novas de todos os seus livros sobre Web design. Para propor ou recomendar designs à nossa avaliação, aceda ao formulário de propostas em www.webdesignindex.org.

The Pepin Press/Agile Rabbit Editions
Para obter mais informações sobre as diversas publicações de The Pepin Press sobre design, moda, cultura popular, referências visuais e imagens prontas a usar, visite www.pepinpress.com.

Книга «**Веб-дизайн по содержанию**» содержит выборку из 500 веб-сайтов, сгруппированных по темам. Каждый сайт представлен двумя страницами: заглавной и содержательной. К книге прилагается компакт-диск с браузером и утилитой, позволяющей загрузить и просмотреть выбранный сайт одним щелчком мыши. Книга и компакт-диск вместе содержат полный обзор стандартов веб-дизайна во всех приведенных областях.

Для каждого сайта, приведенного в книге, указывается его адрес (URL). Фамилии людей, принимавших участие в проектировании и создании сайтов, отмечены следующим образом:

D дизайн
C программирование
P производство
A агентство
M адрес электронной почты дизайнера

Подача на рассмотрение заявок и рекомендации

Новые издания книг по веб-дизайну издательства The Pepin Press публикуются каждый год. Если вы желаете подать на рассмотрение заявку или порекомендовать какой-либо дизайн, заполните, пожалуйста, бланк заявки на сайте www.webdesignindex.org.

Издательство The Pepin Press / Agile Rabbit Editions

За дополнительной информацией об основных публикациях издательства The Pepin Press по дизайну, моде, современной культуре, визуальным справочникам и библиотекам высококачественных изображений, готовых к непосредственному использованию, обращайтесь на сайт www.pepinpress.com.

Web Design By Content 包括 500 個精選網站，依主題分類。每個網站都包括兩個網頁：首頁與另一個代表網站內容的網頁。內附的光碟片有瀏覽器和單擊設備，方便您瀏覽並訪問所選網站。有了書跟光碟片，您就可以對任何領域標準網站的設計有個總體上的把握。

本書將每個網站都梓出 URL。參與網站設計和編程的人員名單分類別列出：

D 設計
C 編碼
P 生成
A 代理商
M 設計者的電子郵件地址

提交與推薦

每年都會有新的 The Pepin Press 網站設計書版本出版。如果您有想提交或推薦的設計，請到 www.webdesignindex.org 下載提交表。

The Pepin Press / Agile Rabbit Editions

如需更多有關 The Pepin Press 在設計、流行、大眾文化、設計參考與即用圖片上的出版品訊息，請瀏覽 www.pepinpress.com。

Web Design By Content には、カテゴリー別にまとめられた選りすぐりのウェブサイトが 500 以上収録されています。本書ではすべてのサイトについてオープニング・ページ、およびサイトの特徴をよく表していると思われるページを紹介しています。さらに付属の CD-ROM には、ブラウザとワンクリックで簡単にサイトにアクセスできる機能がついていますので、本と CD の双方を参照することで、今どんなウェブサイトがポピュラーなのか手軽に知ることができます。

本書では、各サイトの URL だけでなく、デザイナー、プログラマーの名前を表記しています。表記方法は以下の通りです。

D デザイン
C コーディング
P プロダクション
A エージェンシー
M デザイナーの電子メール アドレス

ウェブサイトの推薦
Pepin Press では、ウェブデザイン・ブックの改訂版を毎年出版しています。新たに収録したらよさそうな推薦サイトなどありましたら、www.webdesignindex.org までアクセスしてください。

ペピン・プレス/アジャイル・ラビット・エディション
Pepin Press では、デザイン、ポップカルチャー、ビジュアルといった多様な出版物を出版しています。すぐに使える画像などもありますので、出版物および画像についてさらに詳しい情報を知りたい方は、www.pepinpress.com までどうぞ。

Web Design By Content (내용별 웹 디자인)에는 주제별로 정렬된 500 여개의 웹사이트 디자인이 들어 있습니다. 각 사이트는 첫 페이지와 사이트의 특징을 잘 나타내는 기본 페이지 등 두 페이지로 구성되어 있습니다. 동봉된 CD-ROM 에는 브라우저와 선택한 사이트를 보고 액세스할 수 있는 원 클릭 기능이 들어 있습니다. 또한 책과 CD 에는 특정 분야의 표준 웹 디자인에 대해 알기 쉽게 설명되어 있습니다.

책에는 각 사이트의 URL 이 표시되어 있습니다. 각 사이트의 디자인 및 프로그래밍 관련 이름은 다음과 같이 표기되어 있습니다.

D 디자인
C 코딩
P 제작
A 대행사
M 디자이너의 전자 메일 주소

제안 및 추천

해마다 Pepin Press 의 모든 웹 디자인 책이 새로운 버전으로 출판됩니다. 생각하고 있는 디자인을 제안하거나 추천하시려면 www.webdesignindex.org 의 제출 양식에 액세스하시기 바랍니다.

The Pepin Press / Agile Rabbit Editions

디자인, 패션, 대중문화, 영상 자료 및 기성 이미지와 관련된 수많은 Pepin Press 의 출판물에 대한 자세한 내용은 www.pepinpress.com 을 방문하시기 바랍니다.

يحتوي وب ديزاين باي كونتنت Web Design By Content على 500 من المواقع المختارة على شبكة الإنترنت، مرتبة حسب الموضوع. وهو يتضمن صفحتين من كل موقع: صفحة افتتاح وصفحة تمثل طبيعة الموقع. وتجد مرفقاً قرص مدمج يحتوي على مستعرض للبحث عن المعلومات يعمل بنقرة واحدة لعرض المواقع المنتخبة والوصول إليها. كما أن الكتاب والقرص المدمج يقدمان معاً نظرة شاملة عن مستوى تصميم الموقع في أي مجال من المجالات المختلفة.

مع كل موقع في الكتاب، يشار إلى معرّف الموارد الموحّد URL. أما أسماء الموضوعات ذات العلاقة بتصميم المواقع وبرمجتها فإنها مذكورة على الشكل التالي:

D	design	التصميم
C	coding	الترميز
P	production	الإنتاج
A	agency	الوكالة
M	designer's email address	العنوان الإلكتروني للمصمم

العروض والمقترحات

في كل سنة، يتم نشر طبعات جديدة من كافة كتب بيبين برس The Pepin Press لتصميم المواقع على شبكة الإنترنت المعروفة بالاسم. إذا كنت ترغب في عرض أو اقتراح تصاميم للنظر فيها، يرجى الحصول على نموذج الاقتراح من الموقع www.webdesignindex.org.

طبعات The Pepin Press/ Agile Rabbit

لمزيد من المعلومات عن منشورات The Pepin Press حول مواضيع التصميم، الأزياء، الثقافة الشعبية، مرجعية الصور والصور الجاهزة للاستعمال، يرجى زيارة الموقع www.pepinpress.com.

home
john st.
Portfolio
john st. mission
Book of john
Jobs
Dumpster
People
Contact us
Featured work
Browse Clients
Use our Clientlist
Arrow
Fuji Film
Gay Lea
GlaxoSmithKline
Harvey's
John Hall
K&G
Love Craft
Marketing Awards
Moores
Mount Sinai
Rolling Rampage
Scot Towels
Summit Karate
Tetley Tea
Viewers Choice

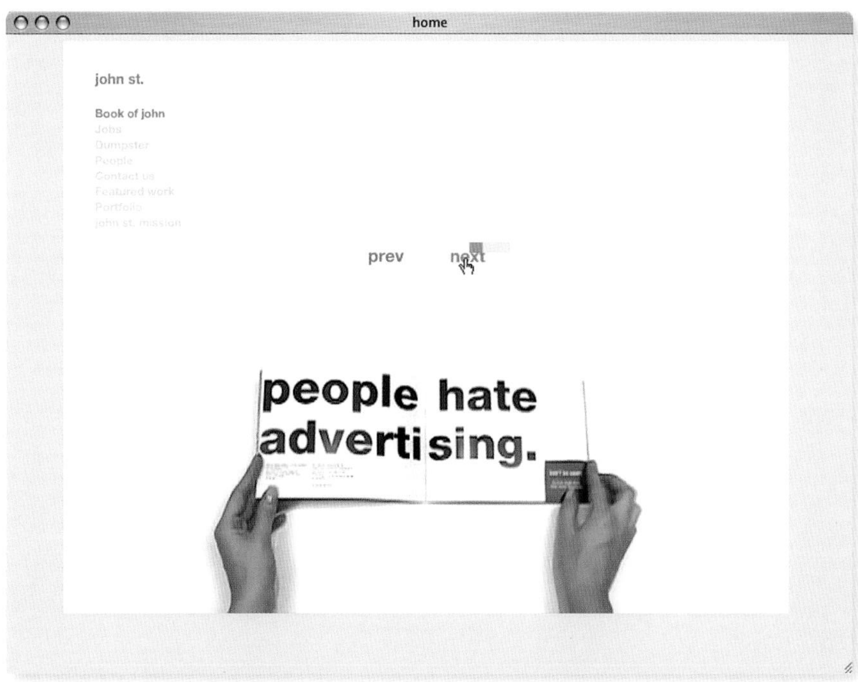
home
john st.
Book of john
Jobs
Dumpster
People
Contact us
Featured work
Portfolio
john st. mission
prev
next
people hate advertising.

www.johnst.com
D: thierry loa **C:** thierry loa **P:** thierry loa, stephen jurisic
A: hellohello world design etc. **M:** www.hellohello.bz

KC&D is een full service reclamebureau dat zich on...int presentaties | advertenties en mediaplanningen

KC&D bureau voor communicatie & design

02 | 03 | 04 | 05 | 06 | 01 profiel

VISIE

Profiel // KC&D~zonderkapsones

De creatieve vertaling van een boodschap naar functioneel design. Een sterke visuele identiteit. Innovatieve concepten die waarde toevoegen. Daar houdt KC&D zich mee bezig.

KC&D. Full-service reclamebureau. Nuchter, met een hoog creatief gehalte. Wij werken vanuit het belang van onze opdrachtgevers. Snel, flexibel en doelmatig. Steeds toekomstgericht. Doelstellingen realiseren én overtreffen. Werken aan verdergaande oplossingen. Vanuit de kracht van onze verbeelding.

KC&D heeft in 10 jaar een brede klantenkring opgebouwd. Toch zijn we niet veranderd. Dienstbaar aan onze opdrachtgevers, ongeacht hun omvang. En nuchter. Want van kapsones houden we niet.

KC&D is een full service reclamebureau dat zich on...int presentaties | advertenties en mediaplanningen

KC&D bureau voor communicatie & design

01 | 02 | 04 | 05 | 06 | 03 mensen

VISIE

krachten in beeld

Dit zijn de jonge, gedreven professionals achter KC&D.
Teamspelers met verbeeldingskracht. Zonder kapsones.

Fleur Suijten
Ontwerper

Fran

www.kc-d.nl
D: fleur suijten
A: kc&d **M:** frank@kc-d.nl

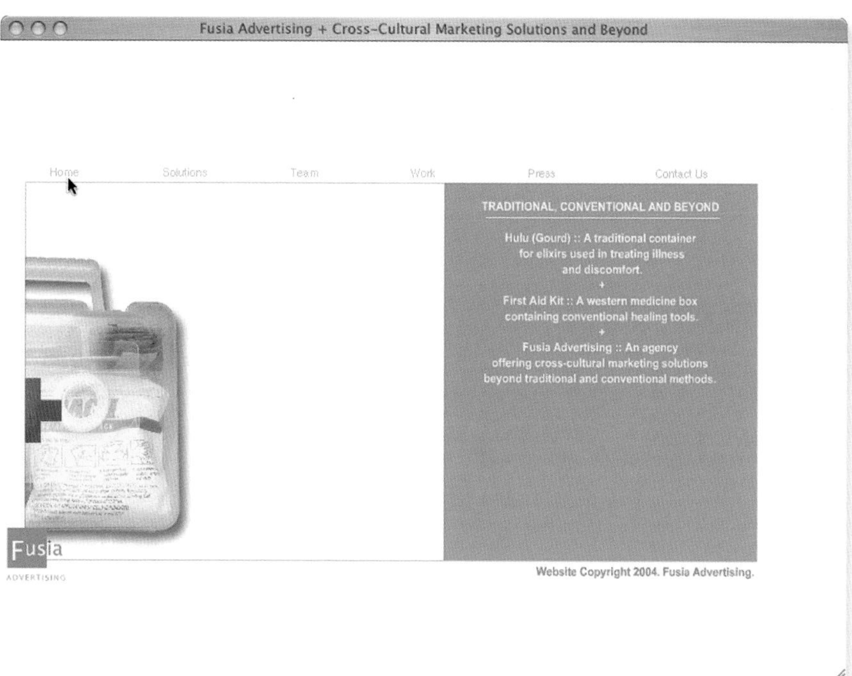
Fusia Advertising + Cross-Cultural Marketing Solutions and Beyond
Home
Solutions
Team
Work
Press
Contact Us
TRADITIONAL, CONVENTIONAL AND BEYOND
Hulu (Gourd) :: A traditional container for elixirs used in treating illness and discomfort.
First Aid Kit :: A western medicine box containing conventional healing tools.
Fusia Advertising :: An agency offering cross-cultural marketing solutions beyond traditional and conventional methods.
Fusia
ADVERTISING
Website Copyright 2004. Fusia Advertising.

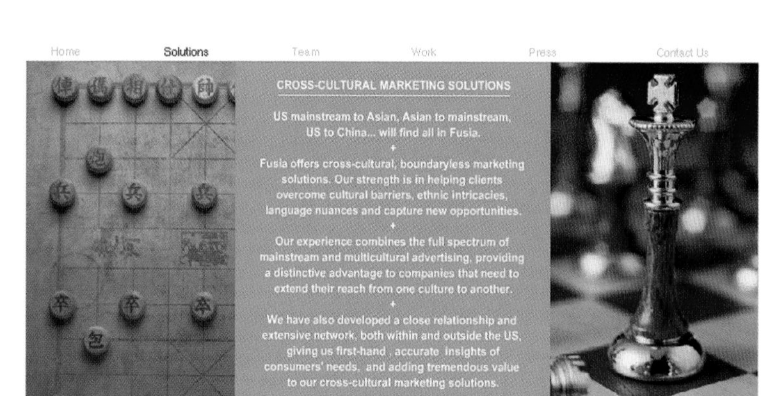
Fusia Advertising + Cross-Cultural Marketing Solutions and Beyond
Home
Solutions
Team
Work
Press
Contact Us
CROSS-CULTURAL MARKETING SOLUTIONS
US mainstream to Asian, Asian to mainstream, US to China... will find all in Fusia.
Fusia offers cross-cultural, boundaryless marketing solutions. Our strength is in helping clients overcome cultural barriers, ethnic intricacies, language nuances and capture new opportunities.
Our experience combines the full spectrum of mainstream and multicultural advertising, providing a distinctive advantage to companies that need to extend their reach from one culture to another.
We have also developed a close relationship and extensive network, both within and outside the US, giving us first-hand , accurate insights of consumers' needs, and adding tremendous value to our cross-cultural marketing solutions.
>> Next
Fusia
ADVERTISING
Website Copyright 2004. Fusia Advertising.

www.fusia.net
D: andrew lau **C:** elizabeth kay
A: fusia advertising **M:** ekay@fusia.net

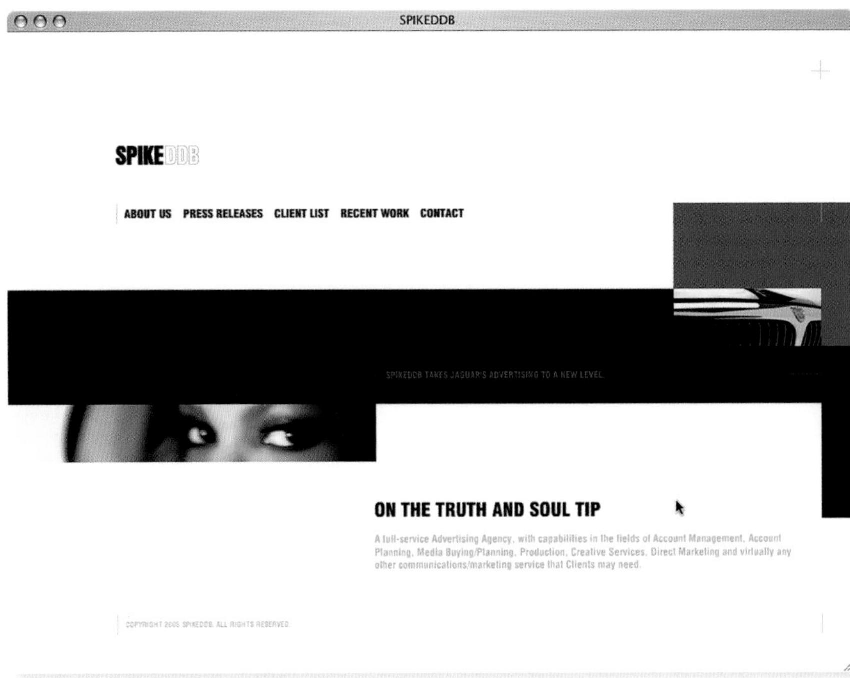
SPIKEDDB
SPIKEDDB
ABOUT US PRESS RELEASES CLIENT LIST RECENT WORK CONTACT
SPIKEDDB TAKES JAGUAR'S ADVERTISING TO A NEW LEVEL.
ON THE TRUTH AND SOUL TIP
A full-service Advertising Agency, with capabilities in the fields of Account Management, Account Planning, Media Buying/Planning, Production, Creative Services, Direct Marketing and virtually any other communications/marketing service that Clients may need.
COPYRIGHT 2005 SPIKEDDB. ALL RIGHTS RESERVED.

SPIKEDDB
RECENT WORK BROADCAST PRINT RADIO
ABOUT US PRESS RELEASES CLIENT LIST CONTACT
STATE FARM MOUNTAIN DEW PAPER MAGAZINE
SPIKEDDB
FASHION IS THE VICTIM
PAPER MAGAZINE FASHION VICTIM
COPYRIGHT 2005 SPIKEDDB. ALL RIGHTS RESERVED.

www.spikeddb.com
D: joon yong park **C:** joon yong park **P:** jeremy berg
A: firstborn

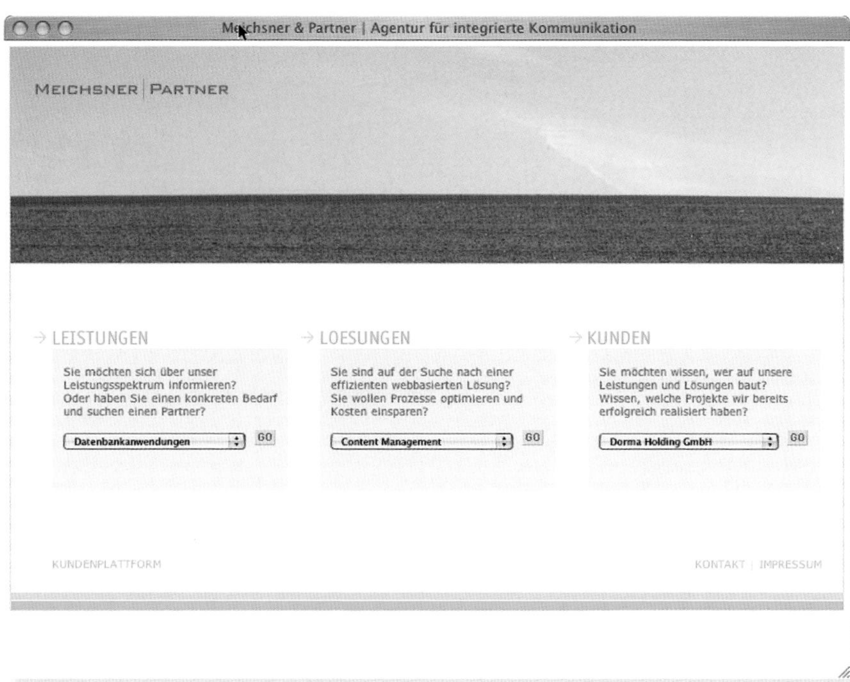
Meichsner & Partner | Agentur für integrierte Kommunikation
MEICHSNER | PARTNER
LEISTUNGEN
Sie möchten sich über unser Leistungsspektrum informieren? Oder haben Sie einen konkreten Bedarf und suchen einen Partner?
Datenbankanwendungen
GO
LOESUNGEN
Sie sind auf der Suche nach einer effizienten webbasierten Lösung? Sie wollen Prozesse optimieren und Kosten einsparen?
Content Management
GO
KUNDEN
Sie möchten wissen, wer auf unsere Leistungen und Lösungen baut? Wissen, welche Projekte wir bereits erfolgreich realisiert haben?
Dorma Holding GmbH
GO
KUNDENPLATTFORM
KONTAKT | IMPRESSUM

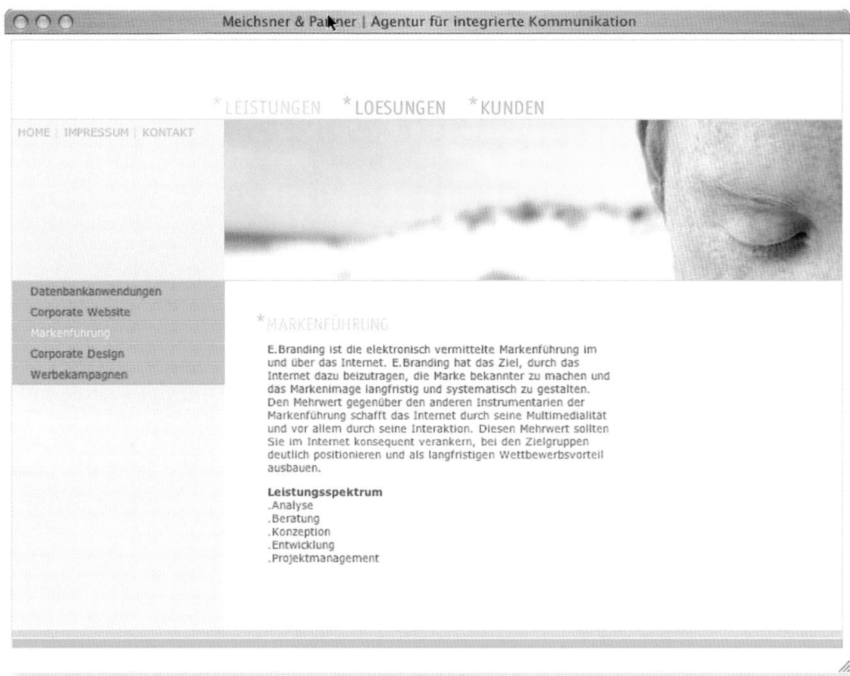
Meichsner & Partner | Agentur für integrierte Kommunikation
*LEISTUNGEN *LOESUNGEN *KUNDEN
HOME | IMPRESSUM | KONTAKT
Datenbankanwendungen
Corporate Website
Markenführung
Corporate Design
Werbekampagnen
*MARKENFÜHRUNG
E.Branding ist die elektronisch vermittelte Markenführung im und über das Internet. E.Branding hat das Ziel, durch das Internet dazu beizutragen, die Marke bekannter zu machen und das Markenimage langfristig und systematisch zu gestalten. Den Mehrwert gegenüber den anderen Instrumentarien der Markenführung schafft das Internet durch seine Multimedialität und vor allem durch seine Interaktion. Diesen Mehrwert sollten Sie im Internet konsequent verankern, bei den Zielgruppen deutlich positionieren und als langfristigen Wettbewerbsvorteil ausbauen.
Leistungsspektrum
.Analyse
.Beratung
.Konzeption
.Entwicklung
.Projektmanagement

www.meichsner-partner.de
D: dominik meichsner
A: meichsner & partner **M:** info@meichsner-partner.de

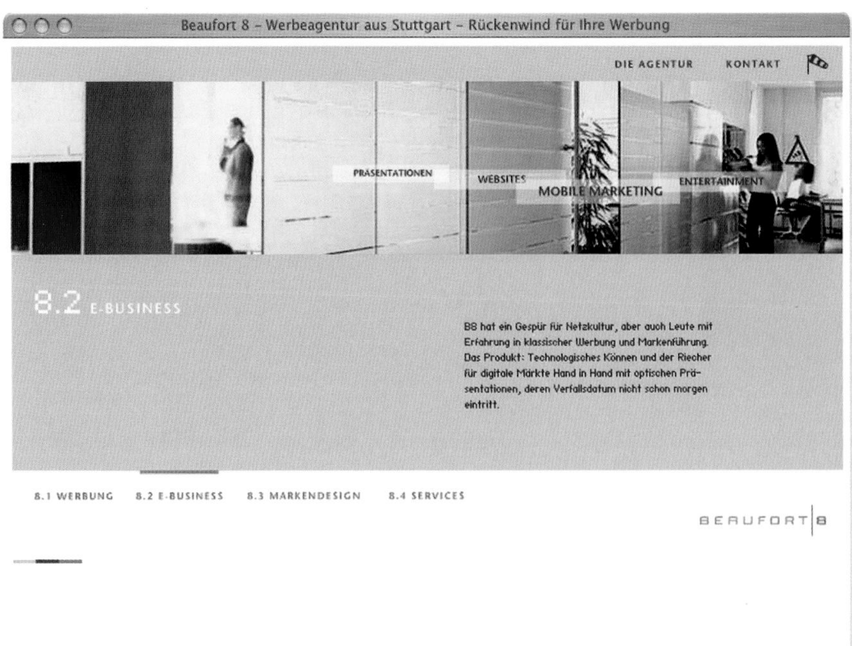
Beaufort 8 - Werbeagentur aus Stuttgart - Rückenwind für Ihre Werbung
DIE AGENTUR
KONTAKT
PRÄSENTATIONEN
WEBSITES
MOBILE MARKETING
ENTERTAINMENT
8.2 E-BUSINESS
B8 hat ein Gespür für Netzkultur, aber auch Leute mit Erfahrung in klassischer Werbung und Markenführung. Das Produkt: Technologisches Können und der Riecher für digitale Märkte Hand in Hand mit optischen Präsentationen, deren Verfallsdatum nicht schon morgen eintritt.
8.1 WERBUNG
8.2 E-BUSINESS
8.3 MARKENDESIGN
8.4 SERVICES
BEAUFORT 8

Beaufort 8 - Werbeagentur aus Stuttgart - Rückenwind für Ihre Werbung - beaufort8
DIE AGENTUR
KONTAKT
MEDIA
PRODUKTION
REPRODUKTION
PUBLIC RELATIONS
8.4.4 PUBLIC RELATIONS
Unsere PR-Profis sorgen für die Bekanntheit Ihrer Marke. Im Sinne integrierter Kommunikation pflegen wir Kontakte zu Journalisten, organisieren Roundtable-Gespräche, stoßen ungewöhnliche Medienkooperationen an und vieles mehr.
8.1 WERBUNG
8.2 E-BUSINESS
8.3 MARKENDESIGN
8.4 SERVICES
BEAUFORT 8

www.beaufort8.de
D: sonja hölzle **C:** jens hennings
A: beaufort 8 **M:** hoelzle@beaufort8.de

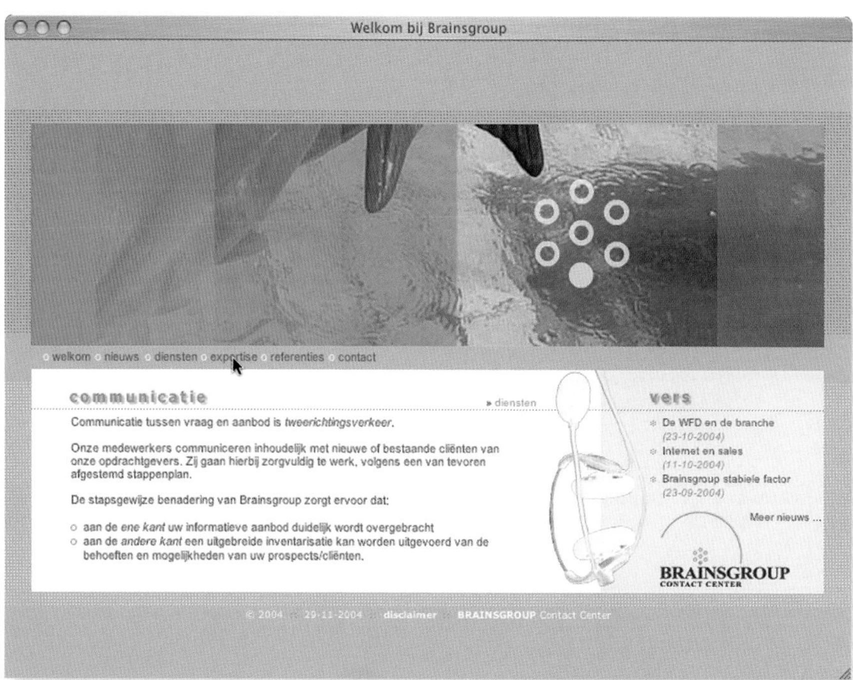
Welkom bij Brainsgroup
welkom nieuws diensten expertise referenties contact
communicatie
» diensten
Communicatie tussen vraag en aanbod is tweerichtingsverkeer.
Onze medewerkers communiceren inhoudelijk met nieuwe of bestaande cliënten van onze opdrachtgevers. Zij gaan hierbij zorgvuldig te werk, volgens een van tevoren afgestemd stappenplan.
De stapsgewijze benadering van Brainsgroup zorgt ervoor dat:
aan de ene kant uw informatieve aanbod duidelijk wordt overgebracht
aan de andere kant een uitgebreide inventarisatie kan worden uitgevoerd van de behoeften en mogelijkheden van uw prospects/cliënten.
vers
De WFD en de branche
(23-10-2004)
Internet en sales
(11-10-2004)
Brainsgroup stabiele factor
(23-09-2004)
Meer nieuws ...
BRAINSGROUP
CONTACT CENTER
© 2004 29-11-2004 disclaimer BRAINSGROUP Contact Center

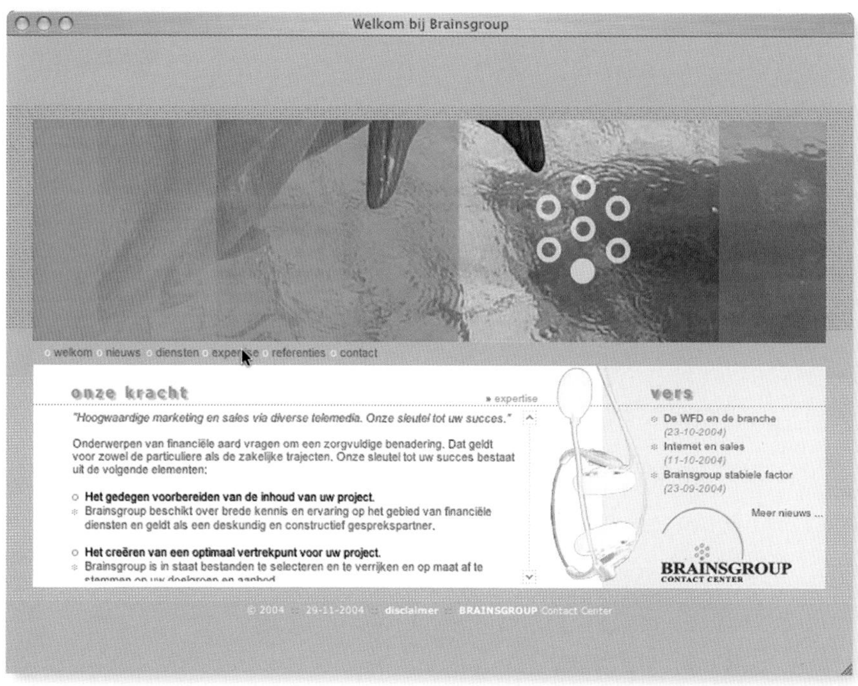
Welkom bij Brainsgroup
welkom nieuws diensten expertise referenties contact
onze kracht
» expertise
"Hoogwaardige marketing en sales via diverse telemedia. Onze sleutel tot uw succes."
Onderwerpen van financiële aard vragen om een zorgvuldige benadering. Dat geldt voor zowel de particuliere als de zakelijke trajecten. Onze sleutel tot uw succes bestaat uit de volgende elementen:
Het gedegen voorbereiden van de inhoud van uw project.
Brainsgroup beschikt over brede kennis en ervaring op het gebied van financiële diensten en geldt als een deskundig en constructief gesprekspartner.
Het creëren van een optimaal vertrekpunt voor uw project.
Brainsgroup is in staat bestanden te selecteren en te verrijken en op maat af te
vers
De WFD en de branche
(23-10-2004)
Internet en sales
(11-10-2004)
Brainsgroup stabiele factor
(23-09-2004)
Meer nieuws ...
BRAINSGROUP
CONTACT CENTER
© 2004 29-11-2004 disclaimer BRAINSGROUP Contact Center

www.brainsgroup.com
D: ronald kuijper
A: roquin e-solutions **M:** ronald@roquin.nl

Trendbüro - Beratungsunternehmenfür gesellschaftlichen Wandel
AKTUELLES
UNTERNEHMEN
LEISTUNGEN
PUBLIKATIONEN
TREND®
BÜRO
Trendstudien
Trendletter
Vorträge
Markenberatung
Innovations-beratung
WIE NAGELT MAN EINEN PUDDING AN DIE WAND ?
ANTWORT: MIT SEINER VERPACKUNG.
Ihr Ansprechpartner für Markenberatung ist Oliver Perzborn
MARKENSTRATEGIEN STEUERN DIE EVOLUTION EINER MARKE
Trendbüro entwickelt ganzheitliche Marken-, Produkt- und Kommunikationsstrategien entlang gesellschaftlicher Veränderungen. Dazu betrachten wir Marken, Produkte und Unternehmenspersönlichkeiten nicht nur in ihrem unmittelbaren Wettbewerbsumfeld, sondern immer auch in ihrem kulturellen Kontext. Im Zentrum steht die Frage, wie sehr sich eine Marke oder ein Unternehmen verändern muss und kann, um sich selber treu zu bleiben. Oder anders ausgedrückt: Welche Trends sollten berücksichtigt und welche sollten ignoriert werden, um sich zukunftsgerecht auszurichten. Zur Beantwortung dieser Frage nutzen wir u.a. folgende Methoden und Tools:

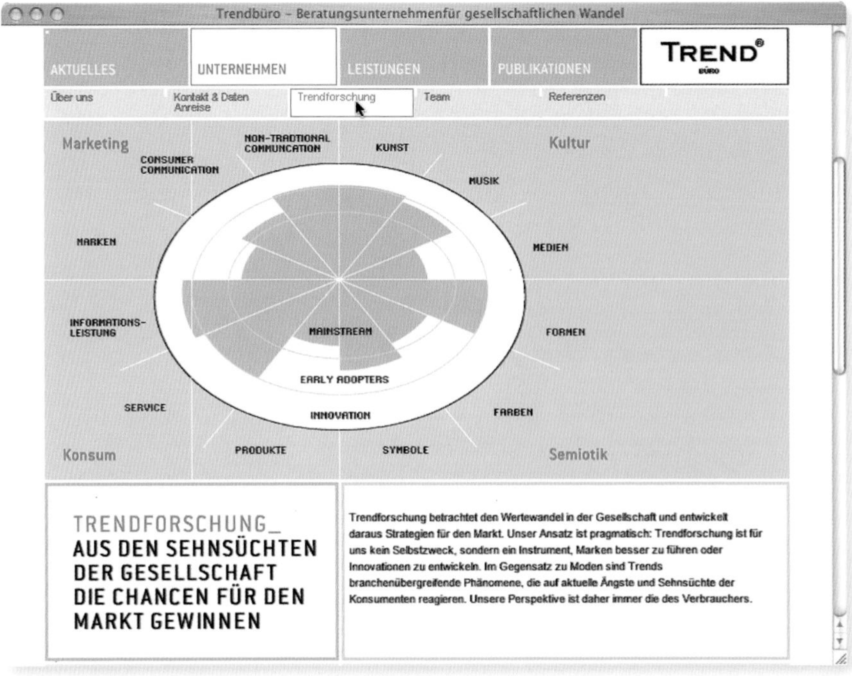
Trendbüro - Beratungsunternehmenfür gesellschaftlichen Wandel
AKTUELLES
UNTERNEHMEN
LEISTUNGEN
PUBLIKATIONEN
TREND®
BÜRO
Über uns
Kontakt & Daten Anreise
Trendforschung
Team
Referenzen
Marketing
Kultur
Konsum
Semiotik
CONSUMER COMMUNICATION
NON-TRADTIONAL COMMUNCATION
KUNST
MUSIK
MARKEN
MEDIEN
INFORMATIONS-LEISTUNG
MAINSTREAM
FORMEN
EARLY ADOPTERS
SERVICE
INNOVATION
FARBEN
PRODUKTE
SYMBOLE
TRENDFORSCHUNG_
AUS DEN SEHNSÜCHTEN DER GESELLSCHAFT DIE CHANCEN FÜR DEN MARKT GEWINNEN
Trendforschung betrachtet den Wertewandel in der Gesellschaft und entwickelt daraus Strategien für den Markt. Unser Ansatz ist pragmatisch: Trendforschung ist für uns kein Selbstzweck, sondern ein Instrument, Marken besser zu führen oder Innovationen zu entwickeln. Im Gegensatz zu Moden sind Trends branchenübergreifende Phänomene, die auf aktuelle Ängste und Sehnsüchte der Konsumenten reagieren. Unsere Perspektive ist daher immer die des Verbrauchers.

www.trendbuero.de
D: stefan landrock **C:** sebastian deutsch
A: v2a **M:** lw@v2a.net

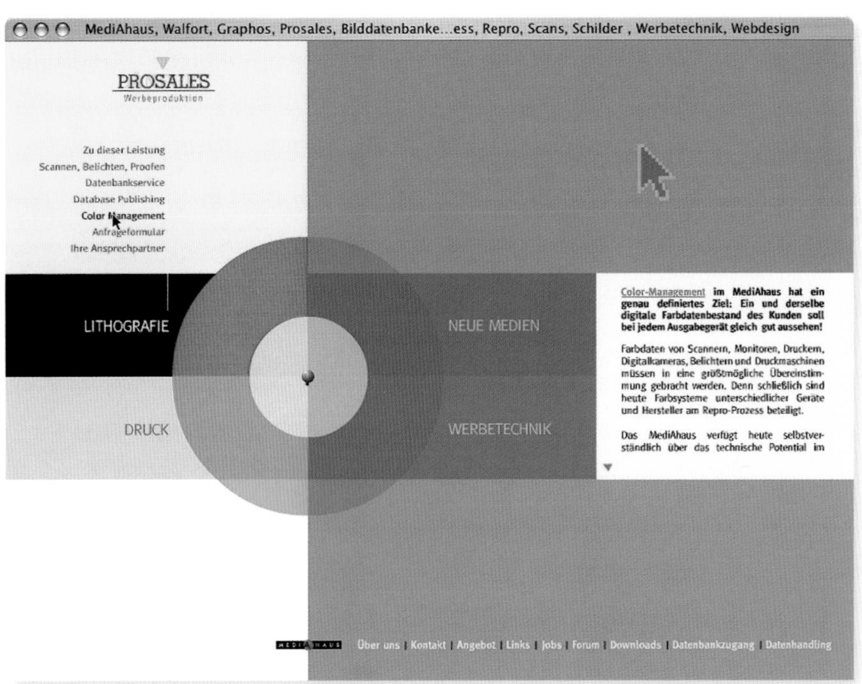
MediAhaus, Walfort, Graphos, Prosales, Bilddatenbanke...ess, Repro, Scans, Schilder , Werbetechnik, Webdesign
PROSALES
Werbeproduktion
Zu dieser Leistung
Scannen, Belichten, Proofen
Datenbankservice
Database Publishing
Color Management
Anfrageformular
Ihre Ansprechpartner
LITHOGRAFIE
NEUE MEDIEN
DRUCK
WERBETECHNIK
Color-Management im MediAhaus hat ein genau definiertes Ziel: Ein und derselbe digitale Farbdatenbestand des Kunden soll bei jedem Ausgabegerät gleich gut aussehen!
Farbdaten von Scannern, Monitoren, Druckern, Digitalkameras, Belichtern und Druckmaschinen müssen in eine größtmögliche Übereinstimmung gebracht werden. Denn schließlich sind heute Farbsysteme unterschiedlicher Geräte und Hersteller am Repro-Prozess beteiligt.
Das MediAhaus verfügt heute selbstverständlich über das technische Potential im
Über uns | Kontakt | Angebot | Links | Jobs | Forum | Downloads | Datenbankzugang | Datenhandling

Dänecke Label and More
Wer macht aus der Wurst die echte Herta?

www.mediahaus.de
D: thomas rickert **C:** roy oonk
A: prosales gmbh **M:** j.ebbing@mediahaus.de

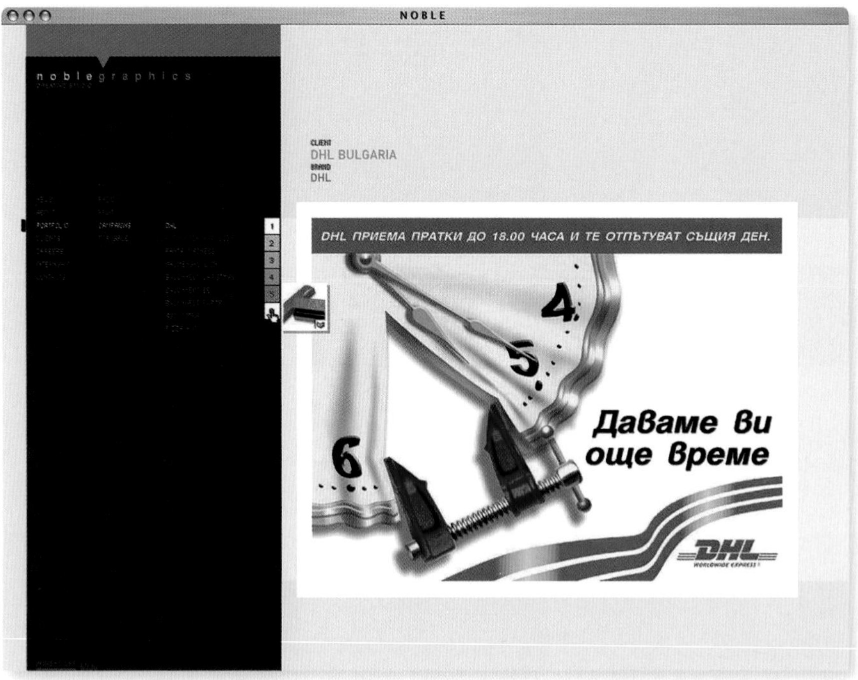
NOBLE
noblegraphics
CLIENT
DHL BULGARIA
BRAND
DHL
DHL ПРИЕМА ПРАТКИ ДО 18.00 ЧАСА И ТЕ ОТПЪТУВАТ СЪЩИЯ ДЕН.
Даваме ви
още време
DHL
WORLDWIDE EXPRESS

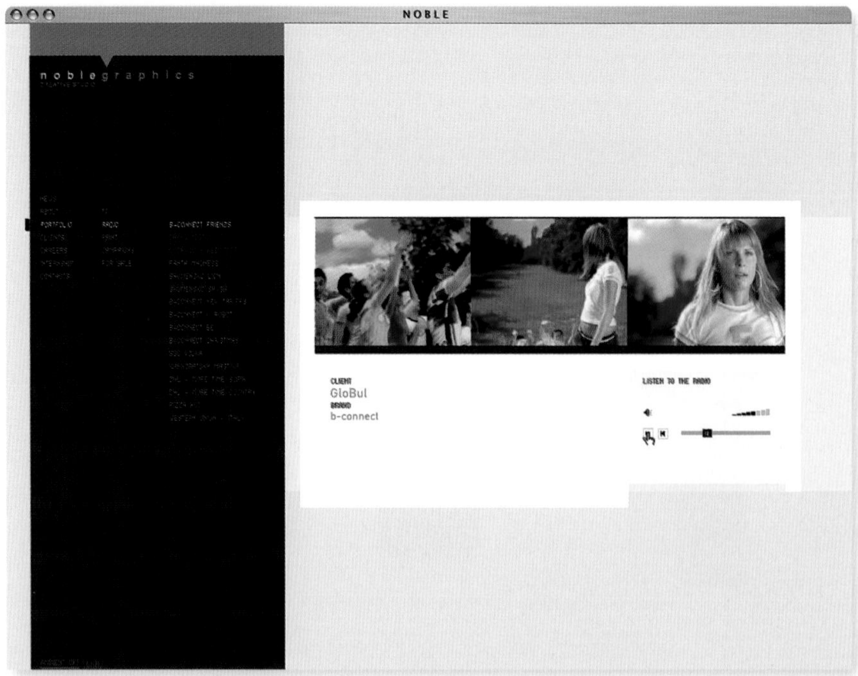
NOBLE
noblegraphics
CLIENT
GloBul
BRAND
b-connect
LISTEN TO THE RADIO

www.allnoble.org
D: gueorgui vassilev **C:** ventsislav dimitrov **P:** gueorgui vassilev
A: noble graphics creative studio **M:** joro@orjo.com

mm+a design:clienting - empresa
empresa | serviços | portfolio | notícias | referências | contactos
mm+a
design e clienting
empresa
A mm +a define-se pela sua dedicação ao cliente.
Desde o início, pretendemos que a mm+a fosse diferente das demais. Uma empresa nacional com visão mundial, que trabalha para construir uma equipa respeitável e respeitada, de qualidade, altamente criativa e inteligente.
A nossa responsabilidade é apoiar os nossos Clientes na relação com os seus Clientes!
A nossa missão
+ Ajudar os nossos Clientes e Colaboradores a atingirem Resultados Extraordinários, com base no Empenho e Compromisso da nossa actuação, no Rigor e Objectividade dos nossos métodos e na Inovação e Fiabilidade das nossas soluções.
Principais metas
+ Oferecer aos nossos clientes a excelência em soluções que agreguem valor e gerem resultados concretos.
+ Promover o máximo enriquecimento profissional e pessoal de todos os nossos colaboradores, através da criação de oportunidades, aperfeiçoamento contínuo e vivência de novos desafios.
EXPOGuimarães |+|
mm+a |+|

mm+a design:clienting - serviços
empresa | serviços | portfolio | notícias | referências | contactos
mm+a
design e clienting
serviços
A mm +a baseia o seu método no IMA (image and marketing analysis), um estudo que tem como principal função analisar a empresa-cliente sobre 3 perspectivas fundamentais: a perspectiva interna, a de mercado e concorrência.
01 Design
+ Gráfico | Identidade Corporativa
- Estacionário-Base
- Suportes Informativos e Promocionais
- Embalagem
- Expositores
- Fotografia
+ Multimédia e Audiovisual
- Site Institucional
- CD-R de Apresentação institucional e/ou produtos da empresa
- DVD de Apresentação institucional e/ou produtos da empresa
- Animação Digital 3D
- Produção de conteúdos
02 Clienting
+ Treino e Formação
- Atendimento ao Cliente
- Estratégias de Relacionamento
- Fidelização de Clientes
- Estudos de Caso
+ Marketing
- Estudos de Marketing
- Estudos de Imagem
mm+a |+|
mm+a |+|

www.mma.pt
D: ricardo mena
A: mm +a **M:** info@mma.pt

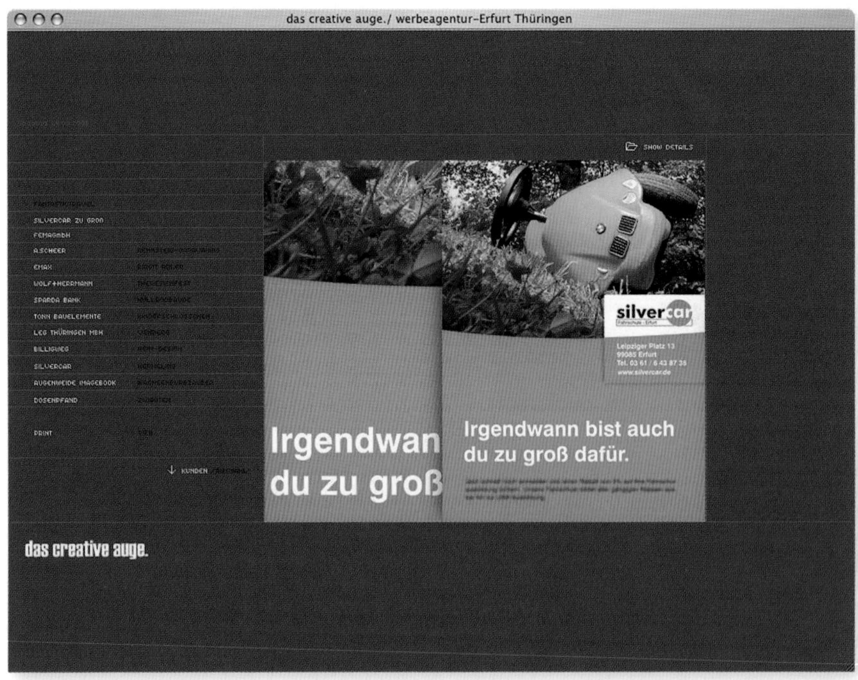
das creative auge./ werbeagentur-Erfurt Thüringen
SHOW DETAILS
silvercar
Leipziger Platz 13
99085 Erfurt
www.silvercar.de
Irgendwan
du zu groß
Irgendwann bist auch
du zu groß dafür.
das creative auge.

das creative auge./ werbeagentur-Erfurt Thüringen
SHOW DETAILS
das creative auge.
AGENTUR
KREATION
PRESSE
KONTAKT
3rd AWARD

www.das-creative-auge.de
D: alexander senf
A: das creative auge.|design agency **M:** info@das-creative-auge.de

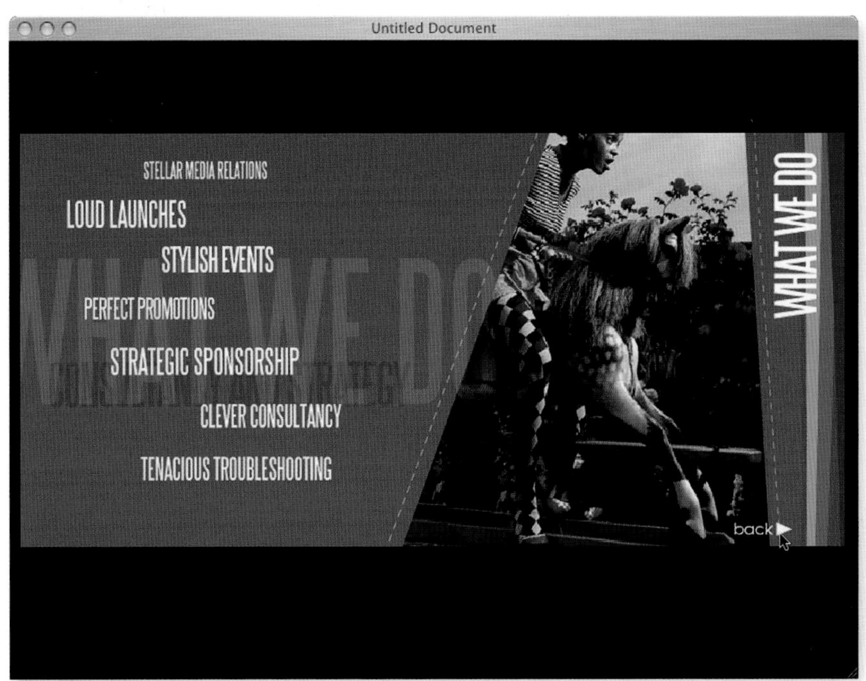
Untitled Document
STELLAR MEDIA RELATIONS
LOUD LAUNCHES
STYLISH EVENTS
PERFECT PROMOTIONS
STRATEGIC SPONSORSHIP
CLEVER CONSULTANCY
TENACIOUS TROUBLESHOOTING
WHAT WE DO
back

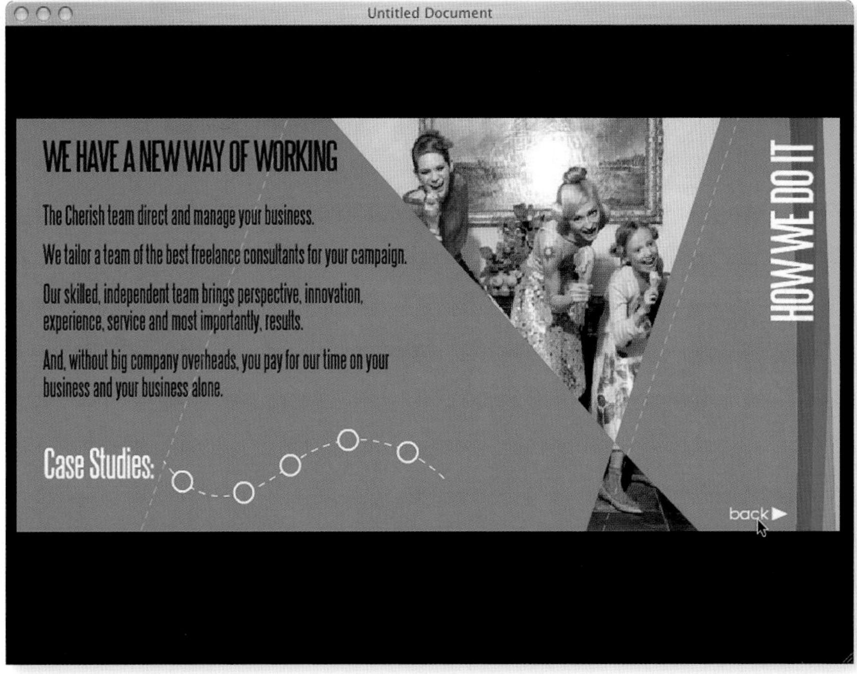
Untitled Document
WE HAVE A NEW WAY OF WORKING
The Cherish team direct and manage your business.
We tailor a team of the best freelance consultants for your campaign.
Our skilled, independent team brings perspective, innovation, experience, service and most importantly, results.
And, without big company overheads, you pay for our time on your business and your business alone.
Case Studies:
HOW WE DO IT
back

www.cherishpr.com
D: robert jennings
A: fraction associates M: robert@fraction.co.uk

AgencyNet Interactive, Inc.
agencynet
CLIENT LIST
PORTFOLIO
DEMO REEL
CAPABILITIES
NEWS
AGENCYNET DIFFERENCE
AgencyNet awarded the redesign of Bacardi DJ
agencynet
Interested in working together?
bizdev@agencynet.com | 954.524.8800

AgencyNet Interactive, Inc.
FEATURED PROJECTS
BACARDI DJ
STILL IN THE DOGHOUSE
INHD CENTER STAGE
OLN WINTER REVOLUTION
BOMBAY SAPPHIRE
MARTINI PUNTOS
IN DEMAND PAY-PER-VIEW
BUDWEISER
NHL CENTER ICE
HBO
NBA LEAGUE PASS
CLARINEX
NASCAR IN CAR
MLB EXTRA INNINGS
NOVARTIS
MCA UNIVERSAL
contact us for a complete agency portfolio
agencynet
CORE SERVICES
INTERNET/EXTRANET
CUSTOM APPLICATION DEV
CD ROM
INTERACTIVE GAMES
VIDEO DEMOS/ COMPRESSION
WEB MARKETING/BRANDING
ECRM/ADMIN TOOLS
CONSULTING
VIDEO PRODUCTION
VIDEO POST PRODUCTION
INDUSTRIES OF FOCUS
MEDIA/ BROADCAST
SPORTS
SPIRITS / CONSUMER BRANDS
PHARMACEUTICALS
BUSINESS TO BUSINESS
CLIENT LIST
PORTFOLIO
DEMO REEL
CAPABILITIES
NEWS
AGENCYNET DIFFERENCE
AgencyNet awarded the Bristoff Vodka online account
agencynet
Interested in working together?
bizdev@agencynet.com | 954.524.8800

www.agencynet.com
D: agencynet interactive
A: interactive **M:** info@agencynet.com

Hondo Digital
HONDO DIGITAL TOUCH'
べんきょうする
てきようする
さがす
さいはっけんする
GUERLAIN
PARIS

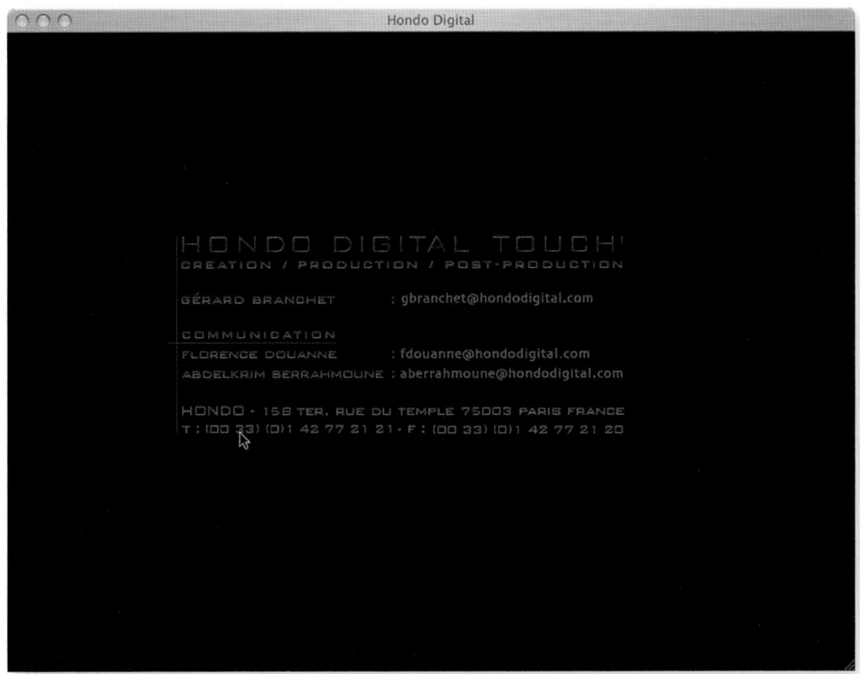
Hondo Digital
HONDO DIGITAL TOUCH'
CREATION / PRODUCTION / POST-PRODUCTION
GÉRARD BRANCHET : gbranchet@hondodigital.com
COMMUNICATION
FLORENCE DOUANNE : fdouanne@hondodigital.com
ABDELKRIM BERRAHMOUNE : aberrahmoune@hondodigital.com
HONDO - 158 TER, RUE DU TEMPLE 75003 PARIS FRANCE
T : (00 33) (0)1 42 77 21 21 - F : (00 33) (0)1 42 77 21 20

www.hondodigital.com
D: rachel saïdani **C:** hervé borredon **P:** hondo digital touch'
M: rsaidani@club-internet.fr

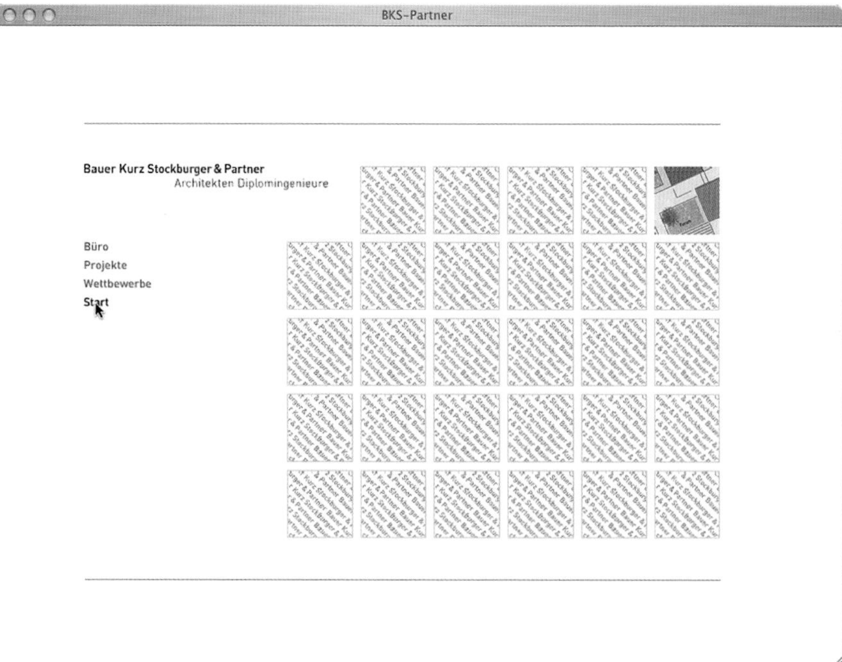
BKS-Partner
Bauer Kurz Stockburger & Partner
Architekten Diplomingenieure
Büro
Projekte
Wettbewerbe
Start

BKS-Partner

Bauer Kurz Stockburger & Partner
Architekten Diplomingenieure

Büro

- **Büroprofil**
- Partner
- Preise & Publikationen
- Mitarbeiter
- Projektliste
- Kontakt

Projekte
Wettbewerbe
Start

Das Büro Bauer Kurz Rauch Stockburger, gegründet 1974, entstand als Zusammenschluss von leitenden Mitarbeitern des Planungsteams der olympischen Sportbauten in München. Seit 2002 firmiert es jetzt als Partnerschaft Bauer Kurz Stockburger & Partner. Im Durchschnitt beschäftigt das Büro 15 Mitarbeiter.

Neben dem Schwerpunkt unserer Arbeit, wie Bauten für Lehre und Forschung, Verwaltungsbauten und Wohngebäude für behinderte und alte Menschen wird in unserem Büro das gesamte Spektrum bearbeitet, vom Einfamilienhaus über Industrie- und Verkehrsbauten bis zur Renovierung historischer Gebäude. Dabei ist überwiegend die öffentliche Hand der Bauherr. Die beauftragten Projekte werden im Team bearbeitet. Einer der Partner ist dabei von de Konzeptphase über die Planung bis zur Ausführung und Fertigstellung in das Projekt aktiv eingebunden.

Unsere Arbeit sehen wir in Verantwortung für die gebaute Umwelt und in dem Wissen, wie gute Gestaltung die Qualität unseres Lebens positiv beeinflussen kann. Die Gestalt unserer Bauten ist Ergebnis der Auseinandersetzung mit der Aufgabenstellung und den Besonderheiten des Ortes, wobei letztlich der Mensch, der in diesen Gebäuden lebt, im Mittelpunkt unserer Planung steht.

Um Häuser aus einer ganzheitlichen Sicht heraus zu entwerfen, ist für uns die enge fachliche Zusammenarbeit aller an der Planung beteiligten Ingenieure wichtig.
Wir sind der Überzeugung, dass gute Bauten nur im intensiven Dialog mit dem Bauherrn und de Nutzern des Gebäudes entstehen können. Sie sind eine Synthese von schlüssigem, funktionalem Design und erlebnisreicher und einprägsamer Gestalt.

www.bks-partner.de
D: alexander bauer **C:** christian leitschuh **P:** maryam monschizada
A: 812 networks **M:** mary@812networks.com

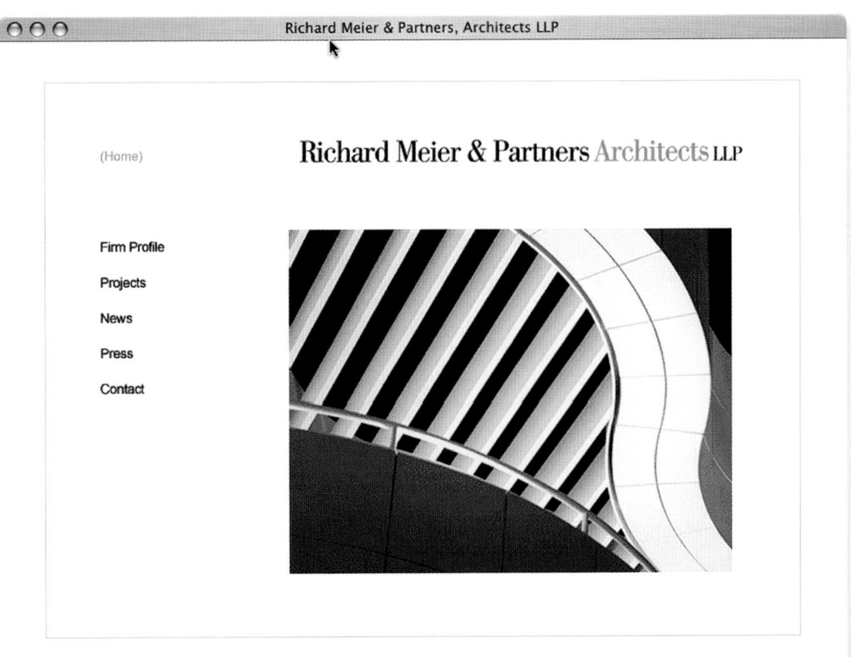
Richard Meier & Partners, Architects LLP
(Home)
Richard Meier & Partners Architects LLP
Firm Profile
Projects
News
Press
Contact

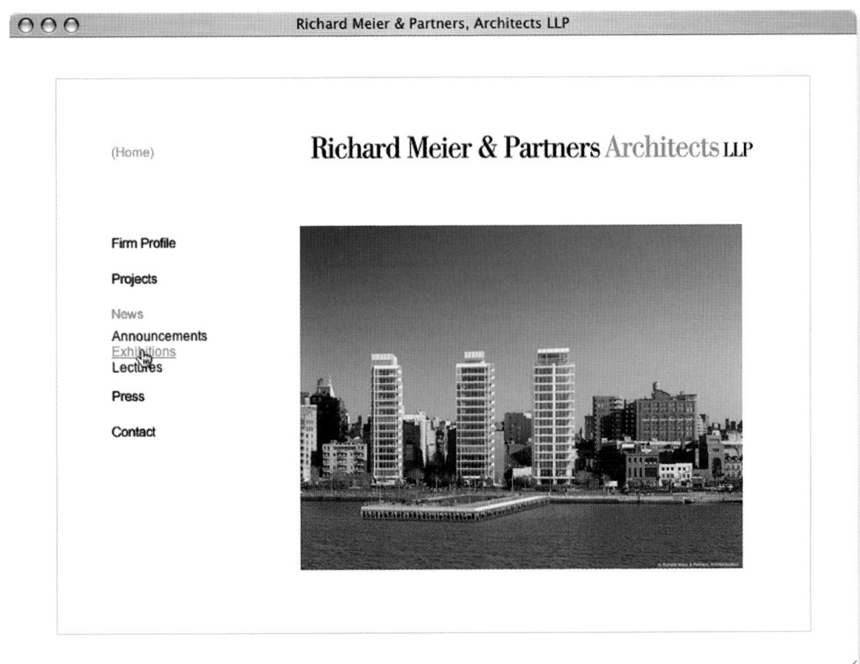
Richard Meier & Partners, Architects LLP
(Home)
Richard Meier & Partners Architects LLP
Firm Profile
Projects
News
Announcements
Exhibitions
Lectures
Press
Contact

www.richardmeier.com
D: lisetta koe **C:** stella lee
A: richard meier & partners architects **M:** l.koe@richardmeier.com

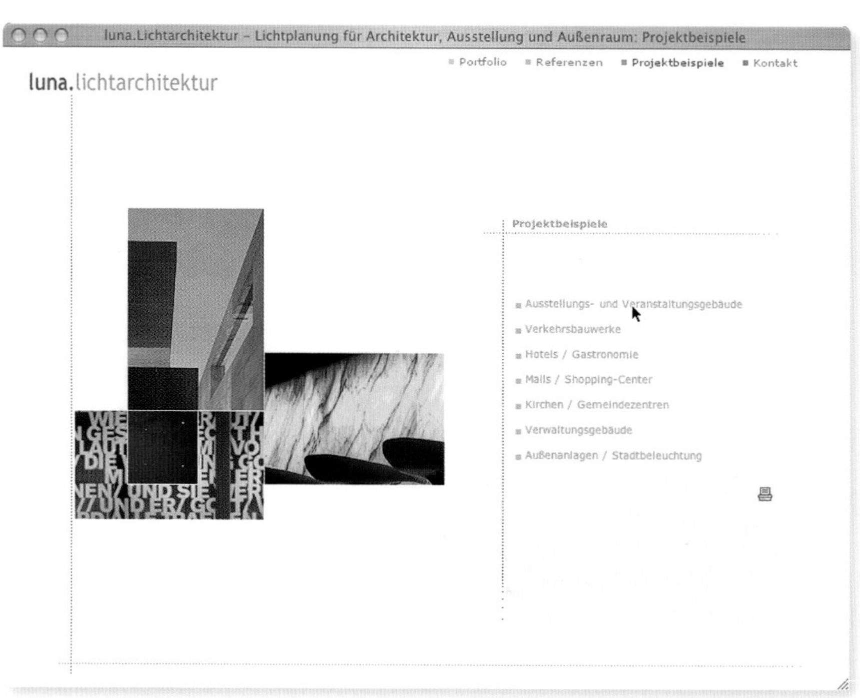
luna.Lichtarchitektur – Lichtplanung für Architektur, Ausstellung und Außenraum: Projektbeispiele
Portfolio
Referenzen
Projektbeispiele
Kontakt
luna.lichtarchitektur
Projektbeispiele
Ausstellungs- und Veranstaltungsgebäude
Verkehrsbauwerke
Hotels / Gastronomie
Malls / Shopping-Center
Kirchen / Gemeindezentren
Verwaltungsgebäude
Außenanlagen / Stadtbeleuchtung

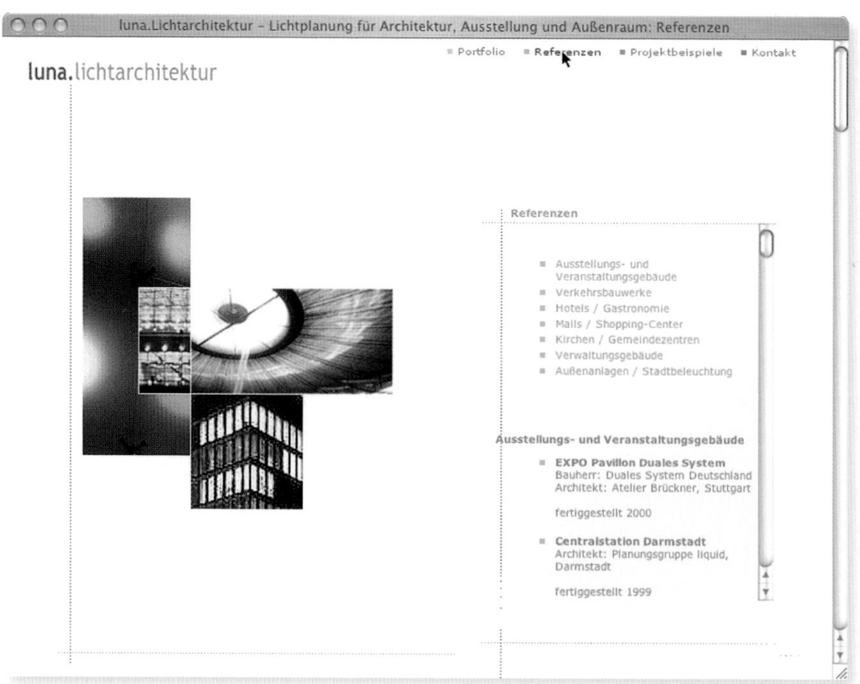
luna.Lichtarchitektur – Lichtplanung für Architektur, Ausstellung und Außenraum: Referenzen
Portfolio
Referenzen
Projektbeispiele
Kontakt
luna.lichtarchitektur
Referenzen
Ausstellungs- und Veranstaltungsgebäude
Verkehrsbauwerke
Hotels / Gastronomie
Malls / Shopping-Center
Kirchen / Gemeindezentren
Verwaltungsgebäude
Außenanlagen / Stadtbeleuchtung
Ausstellungs- und Veranstaltungsgebäude
EXPO Pavillon Duales System
Bauherr: Duales System Deutschland
Architekt: Atelier Brückner, Stuttgart
fertiggestellt 2000
Centralstation Darmstadt
Architekt: Planungsgruppe liquid, Darmstadt
fertiggestellt 1999

www.lunalicht.de
D: pia danner **C:** wolfgang becker
A: macina **M:** pd@macina.com

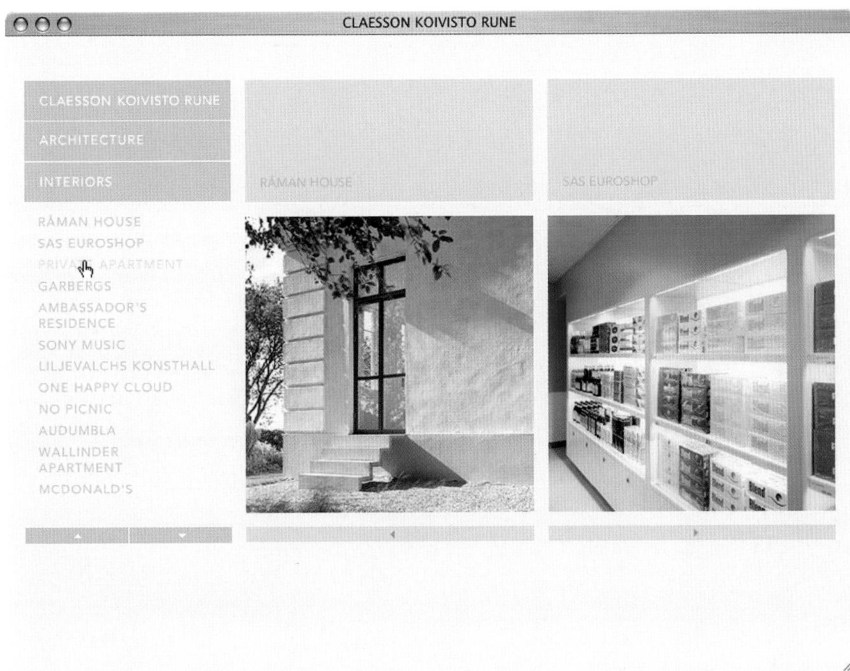
CLAESSON KOIVISTO RUNE
CLAESSON KOIVISTO RUNE
ARCHITECTURE
INTERIORS
RÅMAN HOUSE
SAS EUROSHOP
RÅMAN HOUSE
SAS EUROSHOP
PRIVATE APARTMENT
GARBERGS
AMBASSADOR'S RESIDENCE
SONY MUSIC
LILJEVALCHS KONSTHALL
ONE HAPPY CLOUD
NO PICNIC
AUDUMBLA
WALLINDER APARTMENT
MCDONALD'S

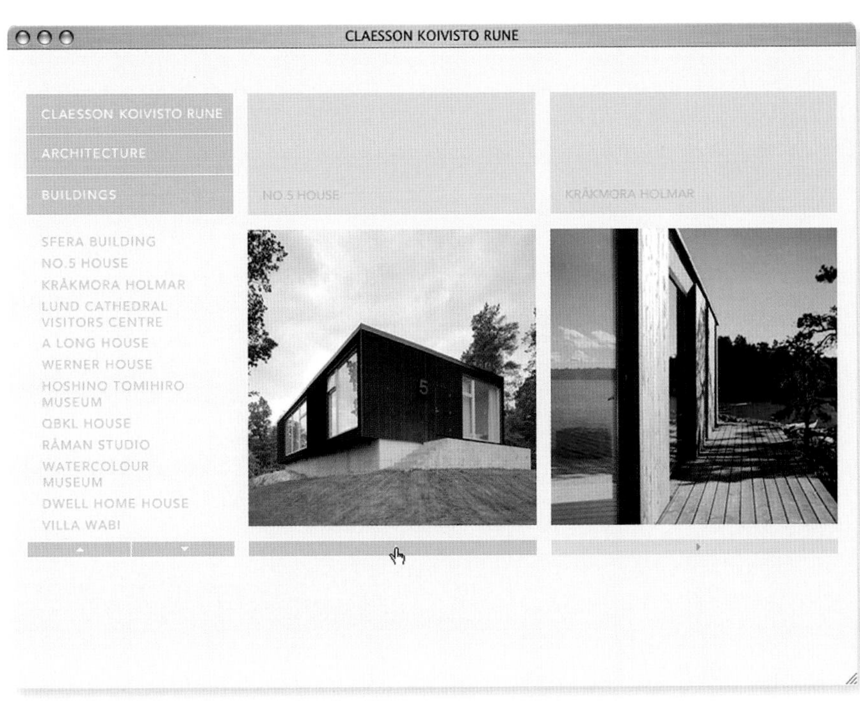
CLAESSON KOIVISTO RUNE
CLAESSON KOIVISTO RUNE
ARCHITECTURE
BUILDINGS
NO.5 HOUSE
KRÅKMORA HOLMAR
SFERA BUILDING
NO.5 HOUSE
KRÅKMORA HOLMAR
LUND CATHEDRAL VISITORS CENTRE
A LONG HOUSE
WERNER HOUSE
HOSHINO TOMIHIRO MUSEUM
OBKL HOUSE
RÅMAN STUDIO
WATERCOLOUR MUSEUM
DWELL HOME HOUSE
VILLA WABI

www.claesson-koivisto-rune.se
D: fredrik nilsson **C:** johan nilsson, kj vogelius
A: superhype **M:** fredrik@superhype.com

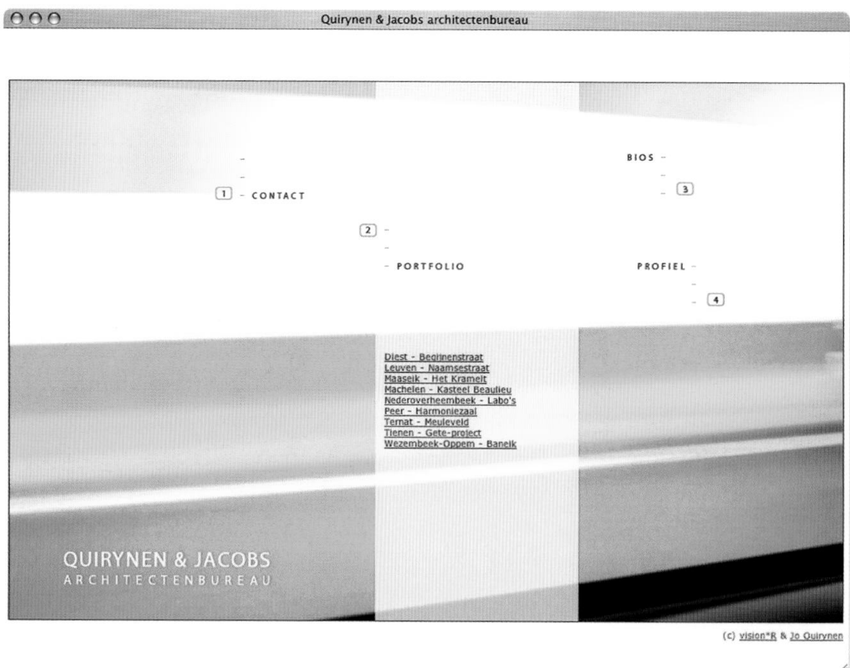
Quirynen & Jacobs architectenbureau
BIOS
1 CONTACT
3
2
PORTFOLIO
PROFIEL
4
Diest - Begijnenstraat
Leuven - Naamsestraat
Maaseik - Het Krameit
Machelen - Kasteel Beaulieu
Nederoverheembeek - Labo's
Peer - Harmoniezaal
Ternat - Meuleveld
Tienen - Gete-project
Wezembeek-Oppem - Baneik
QUIRYNEN & JACOBS
ARCHITECTENBUREAU
(c) vision*R & Jo Quirynen

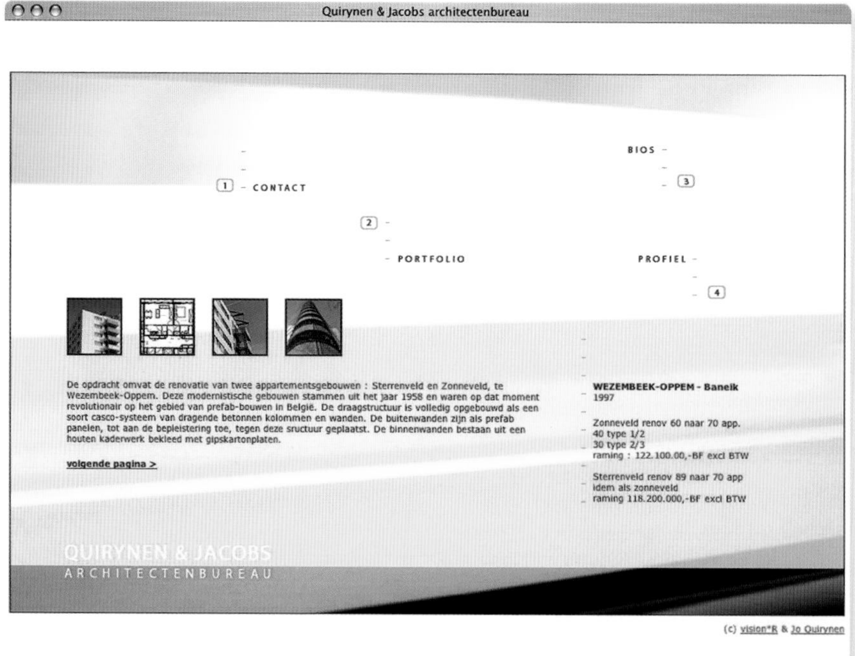
Quirynen & Jacobs architectenbureau
BIOS
1 CONTACT
3
2
PORTFOLIO
PROFIEL
4
De opdracht omvat de renovatie van twee appartementsgebouwen : Sterrenveld en Zonneveld, te Wezembeek-Oppem. Deze modernistische gebouwen stammen uit het jaar 1958 en waren op dat moment revolutionair op het gebied van prefab-bouwen in België. De draagstructuur is volledig opgebouwd als een soort casco-systeem van dragende betonnen kolommen en wanden. De buitenwanden zijn als prefab panelen, tot aan de bepleistering toe, tegen deze sructuur geplaatst. De binnenwanden bestaan uit een houten kaderwerk bekleed met gipskartonplaten.
volgende pagina >
WEZEMBEEK-OPPEM - Baneik
1997
Zonneveld renov 60 naar 70 app.
40 type 1/2
30 type 2/3
raming : 122.100.00,-BF excl BTW
Sterrenveld renov 89 naar 70 app
idem als zonneveld
raming 118.200.000,-BF excl BTW
QUIRYNEN & JACOBS
ARCHITECTENBUREAU
(c) vision*R & Jo Quirynen

www.qj-architecten.be
D: ruben luyten
A: vision* **M:** ruben@visionr.be

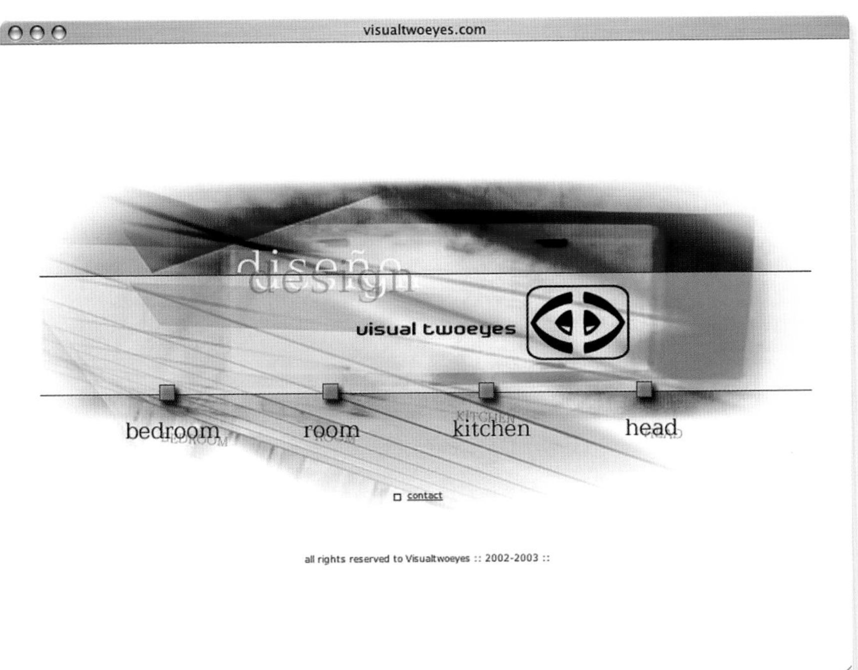
visualtwoeyes.com
diseño
design
visual twoeyes
bedroom
room
kitchen
head
contact
all rights reserved to Visualtwoeyes :: 2002-2003 ::

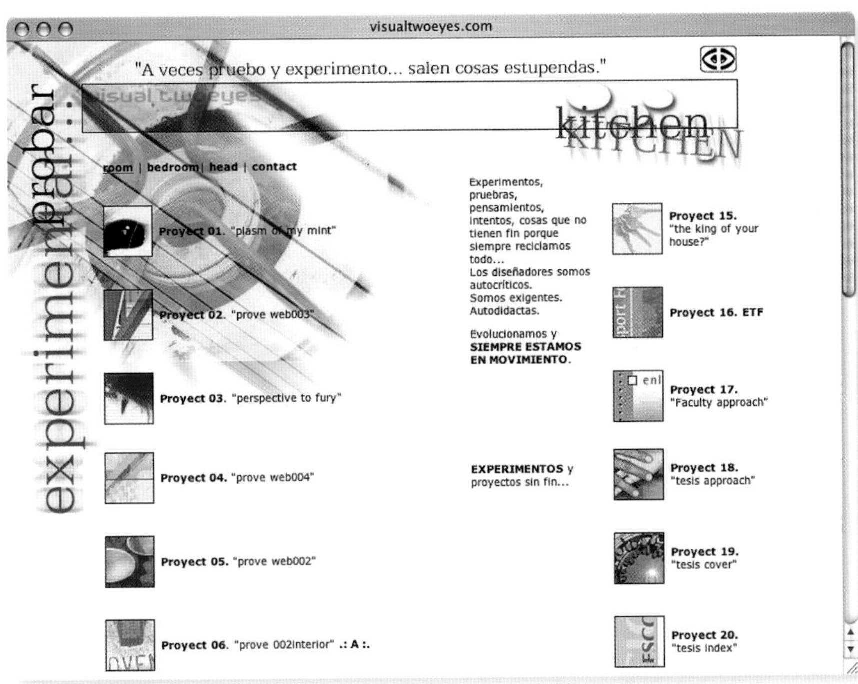
visualtwoeyes.com
"A veces pruebo y experimento... salen cosas estupendas."
experimentar... probar
kitchen
room | bedroom | head | contact
Proyect 01. "plasm of my mint"
Proyect 02. "prove web003"
Proyect 03. "perspective to fury"
Proyect 04. "prove web004"
Proyect 05. "prove web002"
Proyect 06. "prove 002interior" .: A :.
Experimentos, pruebras, pensamientos, intentos, cosas que no tienen fin porque siempre reciclamos todo...
Los diseñadores somos autocríticos.
Somos exigentes.
Autodidactas.
Evolucionamos y SIEMPRE ESTAMOS EN MOVIMIENTO.
EXPERIMENTOS y proyectos sin fin...
Proyect 15. "the king of your house?"
Proyect 16. ETF
Proyect 17. "Faculty approach"
Proyect 18. "tesis approach"
Proyect 19. "tesis cover"
Proyect 20. "tesis index"

www.visualtwoeyes.com
D: m. jose castañer navarro
M: mjcndsgn@ono.com

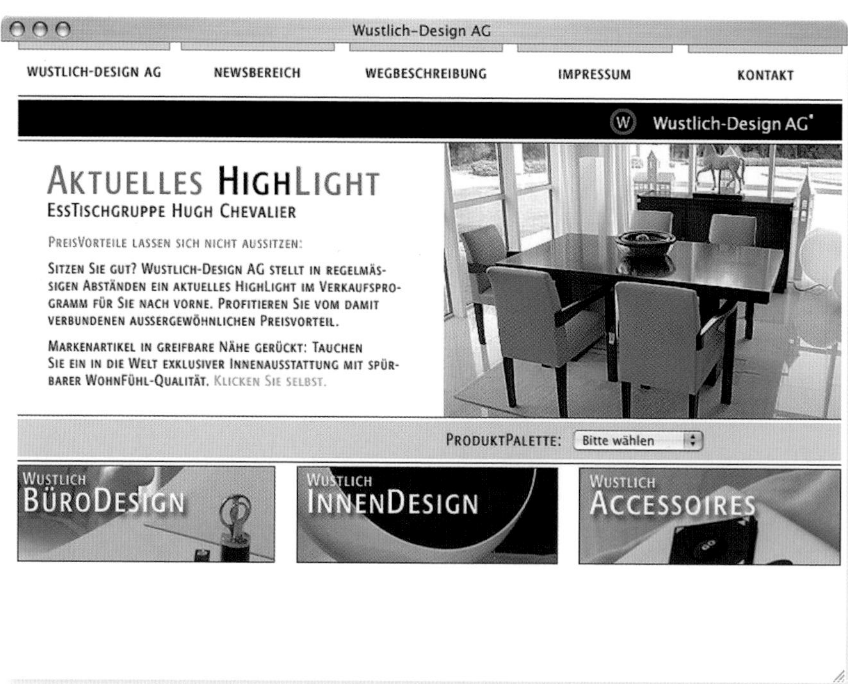
Wustlich-Design AG
WUSTLICH-DESIGN AG
NEWSBEREICH
WEGBESCHREIBUNG
IMPRESSUM
KONTAKT
Wustlich-Design AG
Aktuelles HighLight
EssTischgruppe Hugh Chevalier
PreisVorteile lassen sich nicht aussitzen:
Sitzen Sie gut? Wustlich-Design AG stellt in regelmäs-sigen Abständen ein aktuelles HighLight im Verkaufspro-gramm für Sie nach vorne. Profitieren Sie vom damit verbundenen aussergewöhnlichen Preisvorteil.
Markenartikel in greifbare Nähe gerückt: Tauchen Sie ein in die Welt exklusiver Innenausstattung mit spür-barer WohnFühl-Qualität. Klicken Sie selbst.
ProduktPalette: Bitte wählen
Wustlich BüroDesign
Wustlich InnenDesign
Wustlich Accessoires

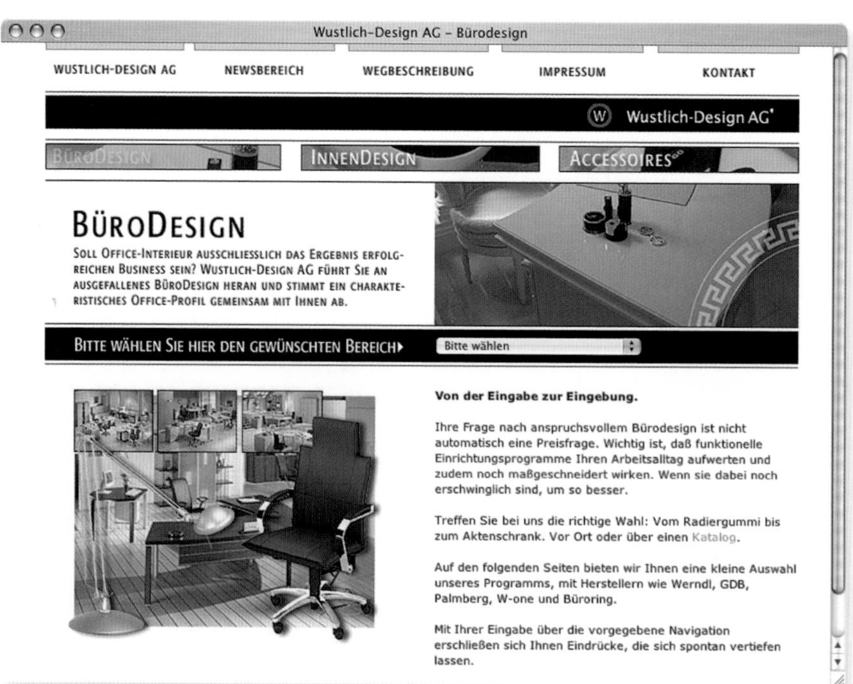
Wustlich-Design AG - Bürodesign
WUSTLICH-DESIGN AG
NEWSBEREICH
WEGBESCHREIBUNG
IMPRESSUM
KONTAKT
Wustlich-Design AG
BüroDesign
InnenDesign
Accessoires
BüroDesign
Soll Office-Interieur ausschliesslich das Ergebnis erfolg-reichen Business sein? Wustlich-Design AG führt Sie an ausgefallenes BüroDesign heran und stimmt ein charakte-ristisches Office-Profil gemeinsam mit Ihnen ab.
Bitte wählen Sie hier den gewünschten Bereich
Bitte wählen
Von der Eingabe zur Eingebung.
Ihre Frage nach anspruchsvollem Bürodesign ist nicht automatisch eine Preisfrage. Wichtig ist, daß funktionelle Einrichtungsprogramme Ihren Arbeitsalltag aufwerten und zudem noch maßgeschneidert wirken. Wenn sie dabei noch erschwinglich sind, um so besser.
Treffen Sie bei uns die richtige Wahl: Vom Radiergummi bis zum Aktenschrank. Vor Ort oder über einen Katalog.
Auf den folgenden Seiten bieten wir Ihnen eine kleine Auswahl unseres Programms, mit Herstellern wie Werndl, GDB, Palmberg, W-one und Büroring.
Mit Ihrer Eingabe über die vorgegebene Navigation erschließen sich Ihnen Eindrücke, die sich spontan vertiefen lassen.

www.wustlich-design.de
D: andreas feldmann **C:** richard zelzer
A: pixelemotion **M:** richard.zelzer@t-online.de

David Lisle - Furniture makers - Interior decorators

Print This Page

DAVID LISLE

— furniture makers & interior designers —

About us | Portfolio | The Process | Contact | Home

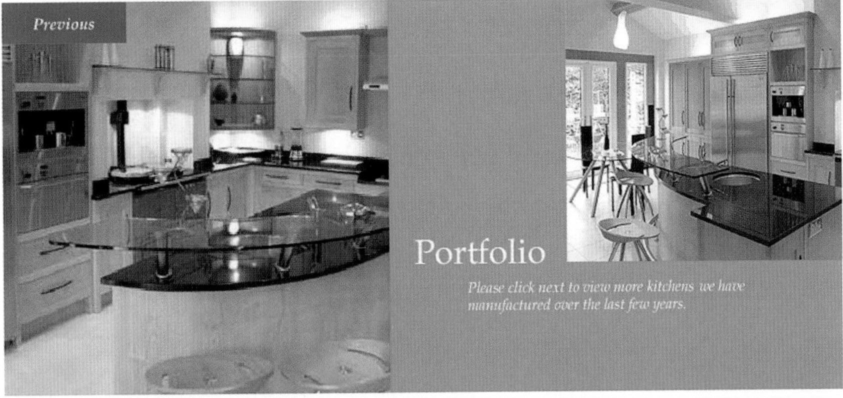
Previous
Portfolio
Please click next to view more kitchens we have manufactured over the last few years.

Beech Lane Chapel, Beech Lane, Macclesfield, Cheshire SK10 2DR tel 01625 503092 fax 01625 503098

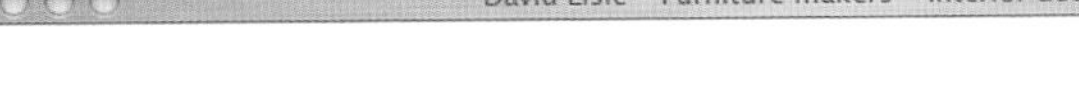

David Lisle - Furniture makers - Interior decorators

Print This Page

DAVID LISLE

— furniture makers & interior designers —

About us | Portfolio | The Process | Contact | Home

Welcome...
Consultation
Relax and let us develop ideas for your kitchen.
Interior Design
See your kitchen's development through detailed drawings.
Workshop
See your kitchen being built here on site.
Installation
Skilled installers fit your handmade kitchen with care.
High quality
hand painted bespoke kitchen projects
developed entirely within our historic chapel.

Beech Lane Chapel, Beech Lane, Macclesfield, Cheshire SK10 2DR tel 01625 503092 fax 01625 503098

www.davidlisle.co.uk

D: marc malone **C:** andrew mullett **P:** mark garner

A: 2m media **M:** catdesign2000@yahoo.co.uk

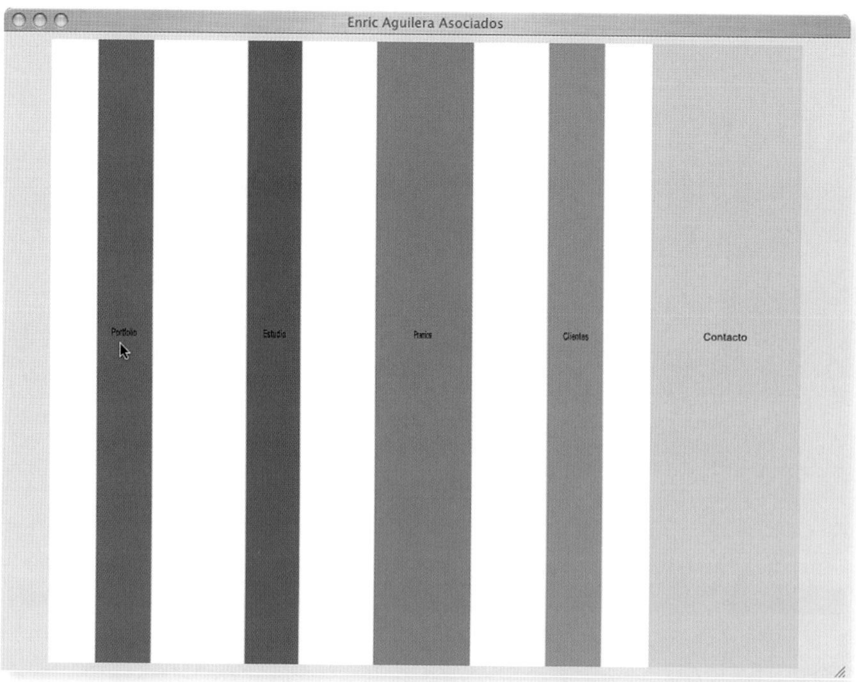
Enric Aguilera Asociados
Portfolio
Estudio
Clientes
Contacto

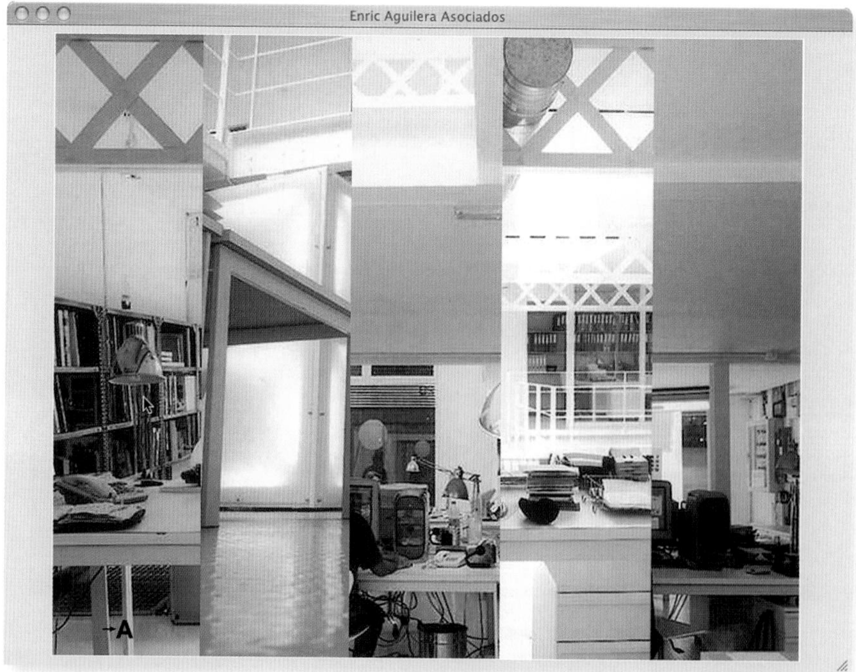
Enric Aguilera Asociados
A

www.enricaguilera.com
D: diego fernández **P:** enric aguilera
A: excèntric comunicació **M:** diego@excentric-bcn.com

VDVDP
VDVDP
VAN DOLDEREN VAN DER PRIJT ARCHITECTEN
E-MAIL
BOLLENSTREEK . DE PAREL EN DE POOL . DE WITTE OLIFANT . HEK
DIERENKLINIEK67 . ICT . SANTO DOMINGO . NSO . StPETERSBURG
BALDAKIJN . ZANDDWARSSTRAAT . RECHTBOOMSLOOT . ANTARIS
WORDEN MET ELKAAR VERBONDEN DOOR CONTRASTRIJKE KLEUR

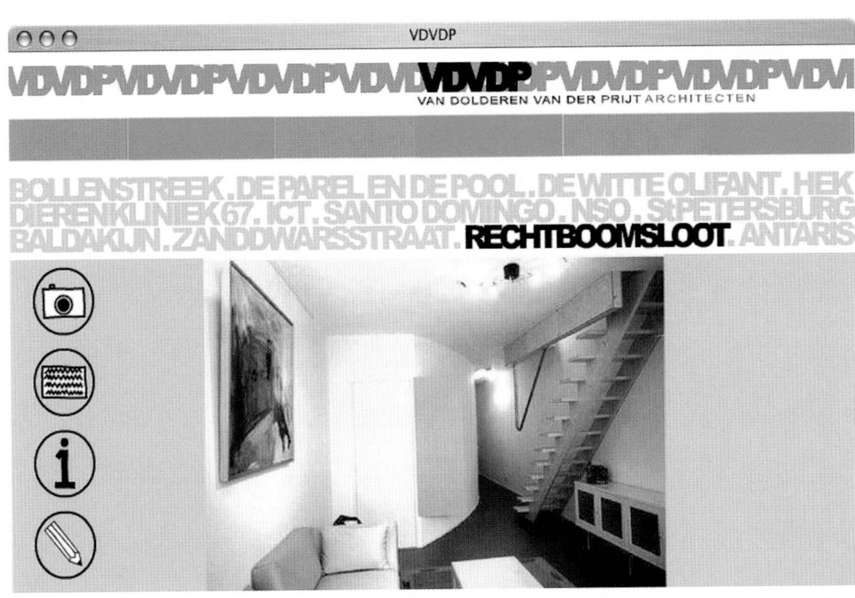
VDVDP
VDVDP
VAN DOLDEREN VAN DER PRIJT ARCHITECTEN
BOLLENSTREEK . DE PAREL EN DE POOL . DE WITTE OLIFANT . HEK
DIERENKLINIEK67 . ICT . SANTO DOMINGO . NSO . StPETERSBURG
BALDAKIJN . ZANDDWARSSTRAAT . RECHTBOOMSLOOT . ANTARIS
HORIZONTALE EN

www.vdvdp.nl

D: yves van dieren P: martijn bakker

A: click internet concepts M: martijn@click-ic.nl

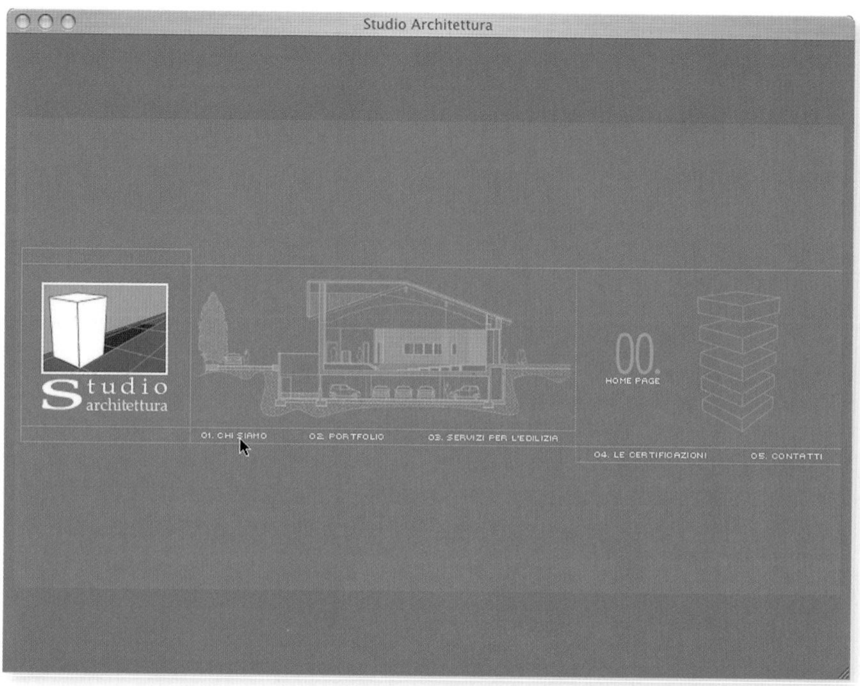
Studio Architettura
studio architettura
00.
HOME PAGE
01. CHI SIAMO
02. PORTFOLIO
03. SERVIZI PER L'EDILIZIA
04. LE CERTIFICAZIONI
05. CONTATTI

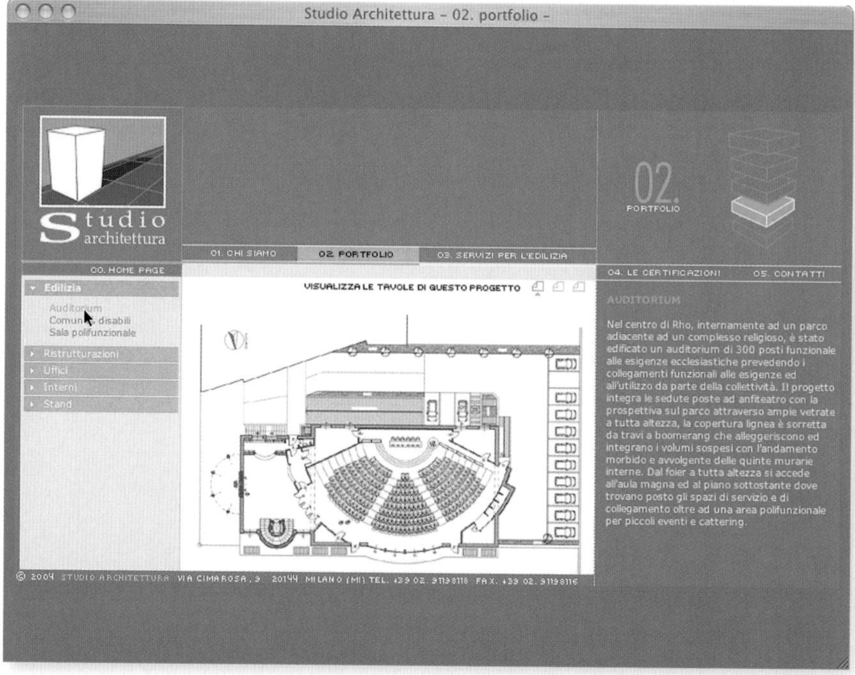
Studio Architettura - 02. portfolio -
studio architettura
02.
PORTFOLIO
01. CHI SIAMO
02. PORTFOLIO
03. SERVIZI PER L'EDILIZIA
00. HOME PAGE
04. LE CERTIFICAZIONI
05. CONTATTI
Edilizia
Sala polifunzionale
Ristrutturazioni
Uffici
Interni
Stand
VISUALIZZA LE TAVOLE DI QUESTO PROGETTO
AUDITORIUM
Nel centro di Rho, internamente ad un parco adiacente ad un complesso religioso, è stato edificato un auditorium di 300 posti funzionale alle esigenze ecclesiastiche prevedendo i collegamenti funzionali alle esigenze ed all'utilizzo da parte della collettività. Il progetto integra le sedute poste ad anfiteatro con la prospettiva sul parco attraverso ampie vetrate a tutta altezza, la copertura lignea è sorretta da travi a boomerang che alleggeriscono ed integrano i volumi sospesi con l'andamento morbido e avvolgente delle quinte murarie interne. Dal foier a tutta altezza si accede all'aula magna ed al piano sottostante dove trovano posto gli spazi di servizio e di collegamento oltre ad una area polifunzionale per piccoli eventi e cattering.

www.studioarchitettura.biz

D: alessandro di lelio **C:** matteo casati

A: overlaps **M:** a.dilelio@overlaps.it

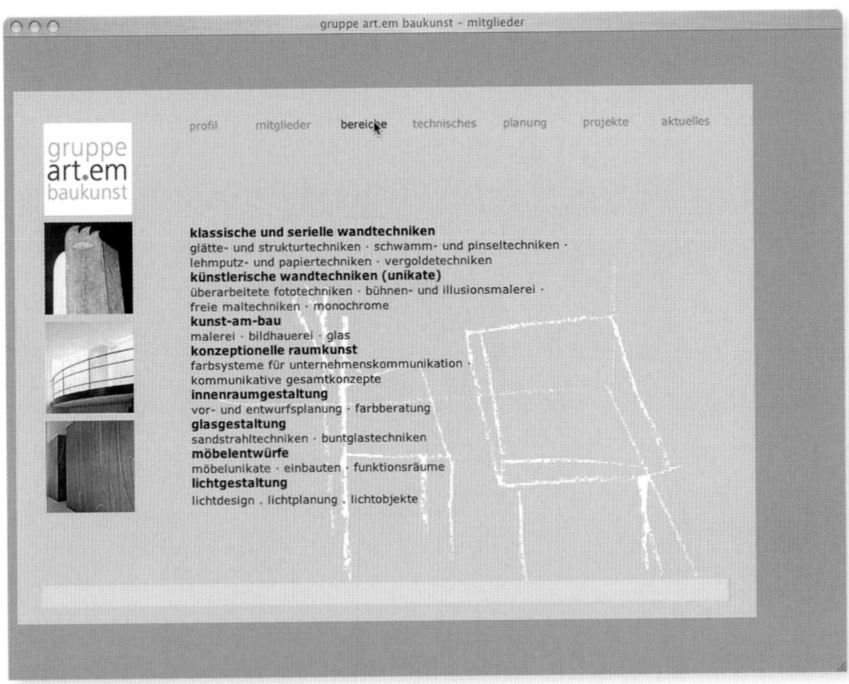
gruppe art.em baukunst – mitglieder
profil
mitglieder
bereiche
technisches
planung
projekte
aktuelles
gruppe art.em baukunst
klassische und serielle wandtechniken
glätte- und strukturtechniken · schwamm- und pinseltechniken ·
lehmputz- und papiertechniken · vergoldetechniken
künstlerische wandtechniken (unikate)
überarbeitete fototechniken · bühnen- und illusionsmalerei ·
freie maltechniken · monochrome
kunst-am-bau
malerei · bildhauerei · glas
konzeptionelle raumkunst
farbsysteme für unternehmenskommunikation ·
kommunikative gesamtkonzepte
innenraumgestaltung
vor- und entwurfsplanung · farbberatung
glasgestaltung
sandstrahltechniken · buntglastechniken
möbelentwürfe
möbelunikate · einbauten · funktionsräume
lichtgestaltung
lichtdesign . lichtplanung . lichtobjekte

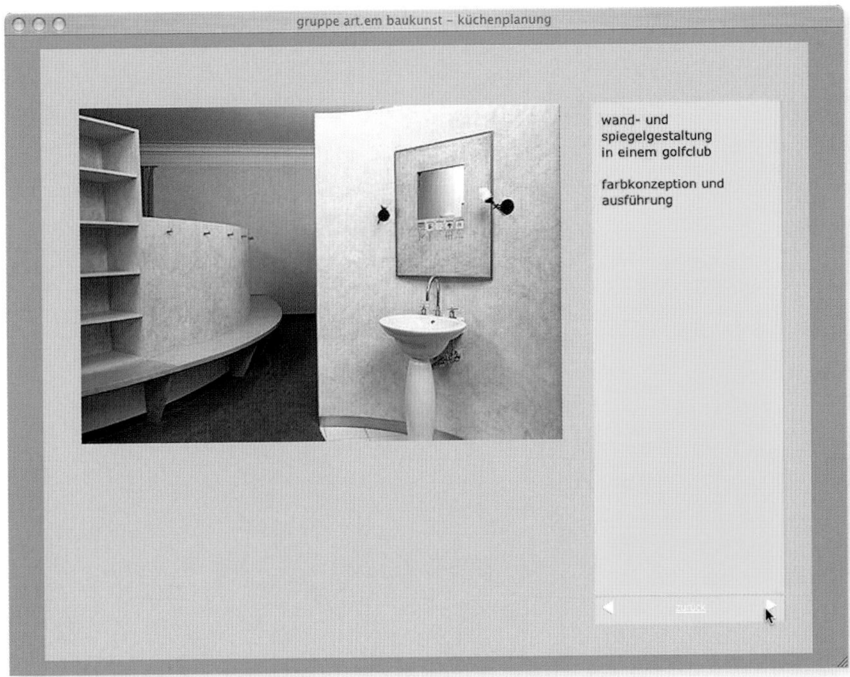
gruppe art.em baukunst – küchenplanung
wand- und
spiegelgestaltung
in einem golfclub
farbkonzeption und
ausführung

www.art-em.de
D: pit kinzer
M: kunstprojekte@pitkinzer.de

DHP Architecten
DHP
architecten
PUBLIEK
BEURSSCHOUWBURG
WONEN
KANTOOR
INFO
BEURSSCHOUWBURG
Verbouwing & renovatie
August Ortsstraat 20-28
1000 Brussel
ontwerp: 1997
uitvoering: 1999-2003
PRIJZEN
eerste prijs architectuurwedstrijd
eerste prijs RenoScripto
BOUWHEER
Vlaamse Gemeenschap
ARCHITECTEN
DHP architecten
B-architecten
englisch version
site by www.concrete.be

DHP Architecten

DHP
architecten

PUBLIEK
WONEN
MEIR 80
KANTOOR
INFO

APPARTEMENTEN
STADSFEESTZAAL
renovatie appartementen
Meir 80 - 2000 Antwerpen
ontwerp: 1995
uitvoering: 1997-1998

BOUWHEER
Pensioenfonds vzw

PROJECTONTWIKKELAAR
Erasme nv

ARCHITECTEN
Architectenbureel Fuyen
DHP architecten

englisch version
site by www.concrete.be

www.dhp-architecten.be
D: pieter lesage
A: concrete **M:** pieter@concrete.be

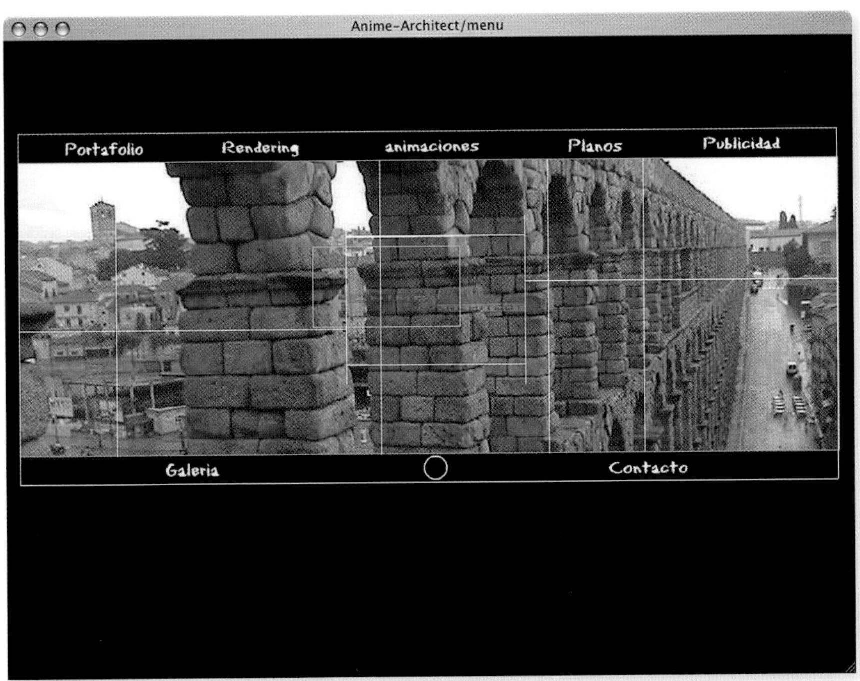
Anime-Architect/menu
Portafolio
Rendering
animaciones
Planos
Publicidad
Galeria
Contacto

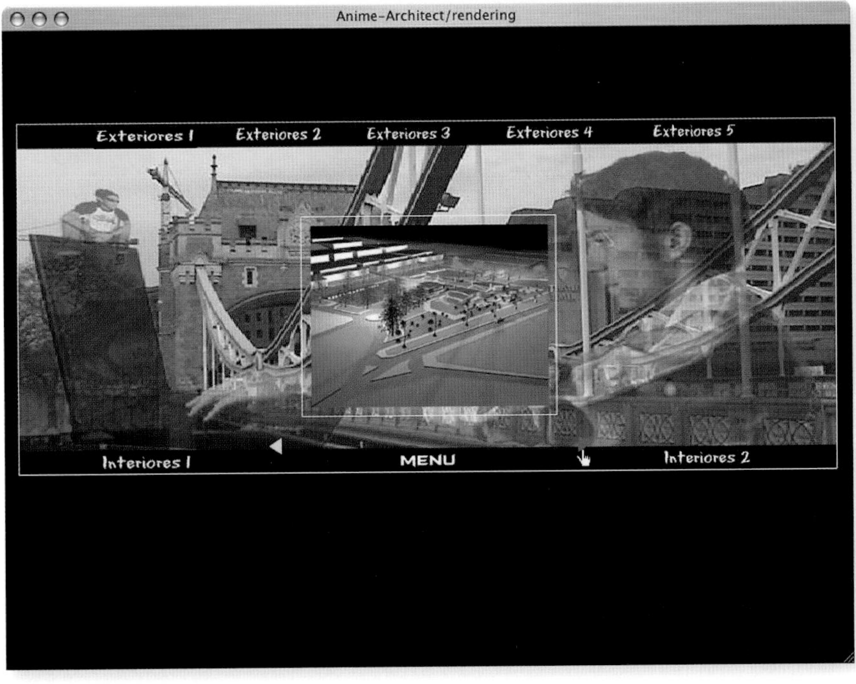
Anime-Architect/rendering
Exteriores 1
Exteriores 2
Exteriores 3
Exteriores 4
Exteriores 5
Interiores 1
MENU
Interiores 2

www.anime-architect.com
D: daniel godoy
A: anime architect **M:** laujara@hotmail.com

CBA : Christian Bauer et Associes Architectes
christian bauer & associés architectes
Außenansicht mit Stahlfassade
Lukas Roth
Jean Schmit Immobilière
Rotarex
Seniorenresidenz Strassen
Europaschule
Jean Schmit Immobilière
Haus in Luxemburg
Haus in Bridel
Museum
SES-ASTRA
Expo 2000
Projekte
in Arbeit
Städtebau
Referenz
Team
Kontakt
Veröffentlichungen

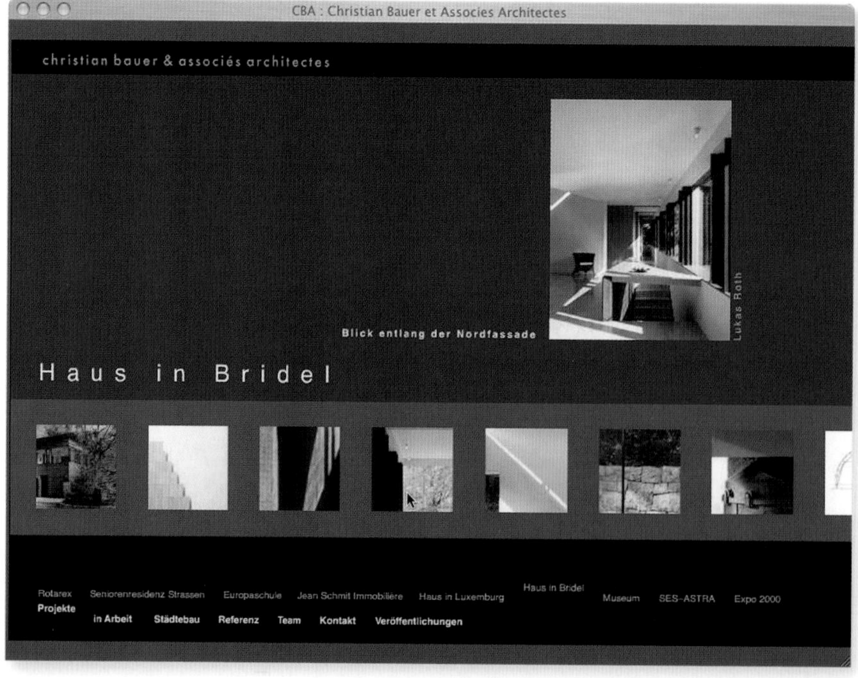
CBA : Christian Bauer et Associes Architectes
christian bauer & associés architectes
Blick entlang der Nordfassade
Lukas Roth
Haus in Bridel
Rotarex
Seniorenresidenz Strassen
Europaschule
Jean Schmit Immobilière
Haus in Luxemburg
Haus in Bridel
Museum
SES-ASTRA
Expo 2000
Projekte
in Arbeit
Städtebau
Referenz
Team
Kontakt
Veröffentlichungen

www.cba.lu
D: christian bauer
A: studio 42 **M:** cba@cba.lu

foster architects limited
foster architects limited
White house
02
02
Philosophy
Contact

foster architects limited
foster architects limited
Black box
01
Black box. a series of black boxes stacked together form the ten storey grid of the museum apartments - a hotel complex with apartments to the four corners of the structure : the building borrows its form and function for the neighboring building - the museum hotel - completing the parkin grid. the black box is due for completion in 2005.
01
Philosophy
Contact

www.fosterarchitects.co.nz
D: rikki campbell, steve le marquand **C:** matt halford **P:** steve le marquand
A: resn **M:** hello@resn.co.nz

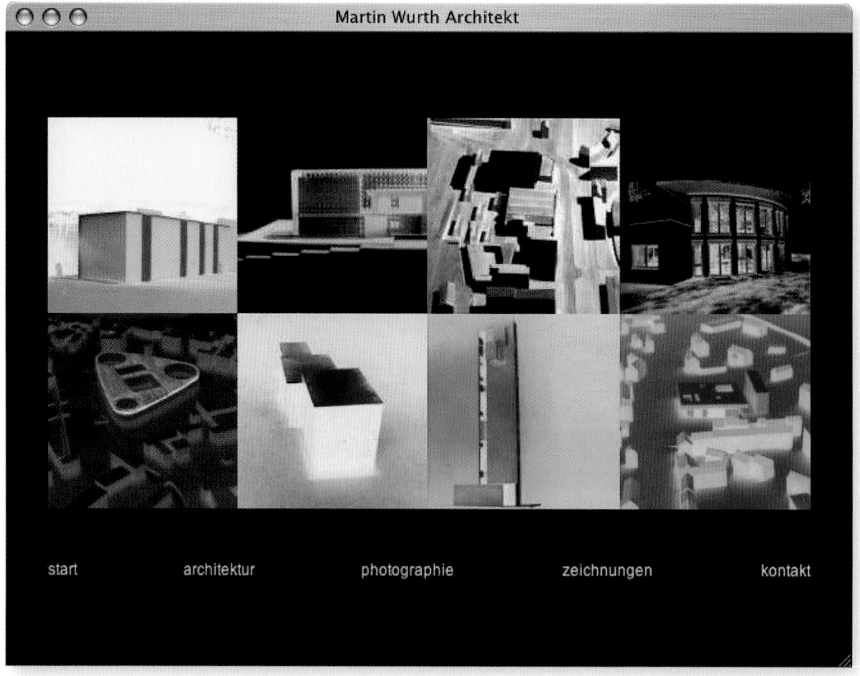
Martin Wurth Architekt
start
architektur
photographie
zeichnungen
kontakt

Martin Wurth Architekt
start
architektur
photographie
zeichnungen
kontakt

www.buero-m.net
D: michael kleber
A: artalacarte **M:** michael@artalacarte.de

gussmann + valentien atelier. architekturbüro
Startseite | Portfolio | Atelier
PORTFOLIO
ATELIER
AUSGEWÄHLTE PROJEKTE. 1996-2004.
Büro für Architektur, Städtebau und Innenraumplanung mit aktuellen Arbeiten im Wohnungsbau.
GUSSMANN + VALENTIEN ATELIER . FÜR ARCHITEKTUR UND STÄDTEBAU
Winter 2004 / 14:11:32

gussmann + valentien atelier. architekturbüro
Startseite | Portfolio | Atelier
GUSSMANN + VALENTIEN ATELIER
PARTNER
MITARBEITER
PUBLIKATIONEN
BÜROPROFIL
KONTAKT
Als eine untrennbare Einheit wird von ihnen Architektur und Städtebau definiert, die jedoch nicht in homogenen, sondern im heterotopen Raum erfahren werden will. Ganz bewusst setzen sie dafür auf städtebauliche Maßstabssprünge, definieren sie unmissverständliche Raumgrenzen, um sie dann umso verblüffender durch gewagte Schnitte und schwindende Materialitäten wieder aufzulösen. Es ist eine Architektur der Zwischenräume, die daraus hervorgeht, ein Städtebau, der sehr zwanglos Großmaßstäbliches mit kleinteiligen Körpern und Nischen zusammenführt.
Sehr körperlich ist ihre Architektur, orthogonal oftmals ihre Ordnungssysteme, die mit unterschiedlich durchlässigen Raumfassungen unterschiedliche Grade an Kommunikation mit dem öffentlichen Raum herzustellen versuchen. Denn um Vermittlung zur Stadt und ihrer Öffentlichkeit geht es ihnen, die sich als kontextuelle Architekten verstehen, die ihre Architektur stets in Relation zum Vorgefundenen entwickeln.
Als Raumplastizismus lässt sich so wohl ihre architektonische Sprache am Präzisesten bezeichnen. Als
GUSSMANN + VALENTIEN ATELIER . FÜR ARCHITEKTUR UND STÄDTEBAU
Winter 2004 / 14:12:07

www.gussmann-valentien.de
D: dirk müller
A: snoep **M:** post@snoep.de

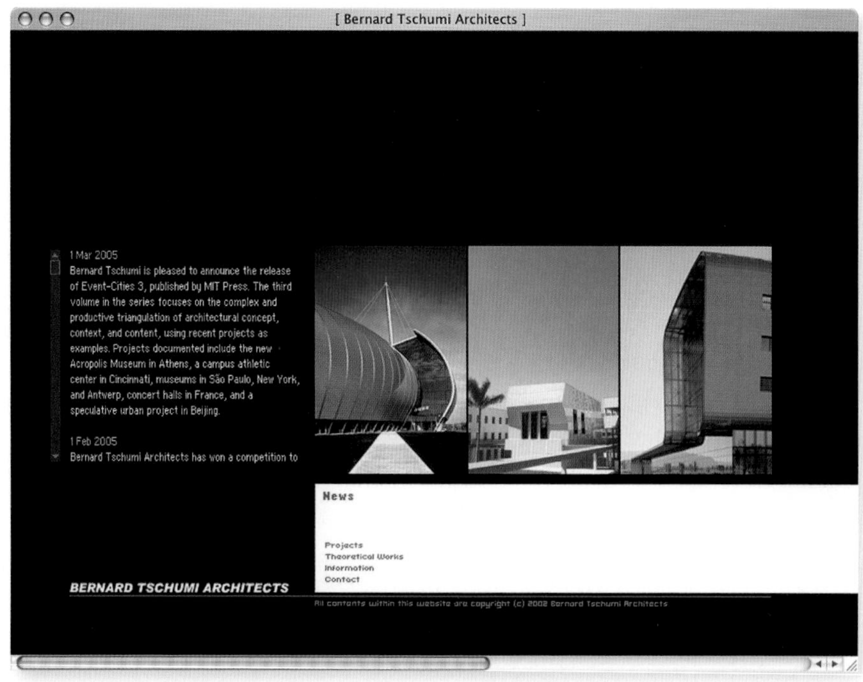
[Bernard Tschumi Architects]
1 Mar 2005
Bernard Tschumi is pleased to announce the release of Event-Cities 3, published by MIT Press. The third volume in the series focuses on the complex and productive triangulation of architectural concept, context, and content, using recent projects as examples. Projects documented include the new Acropolis Museum in Athens, a campus athletic center in Cincinnati, museums in São Paulo, New York, and Antwerp, concert halls in France, and a speculative urban project in Beijing.
1 Feb 2005
Bernard Tschumi Architects has won a competition to
News
Projects
Theoretical Works
Information
Contact
BERNARD TSCHUMI ARCHITECTS
All contents within this website are copyright (c) 2002 Bernard Tschumi Architects

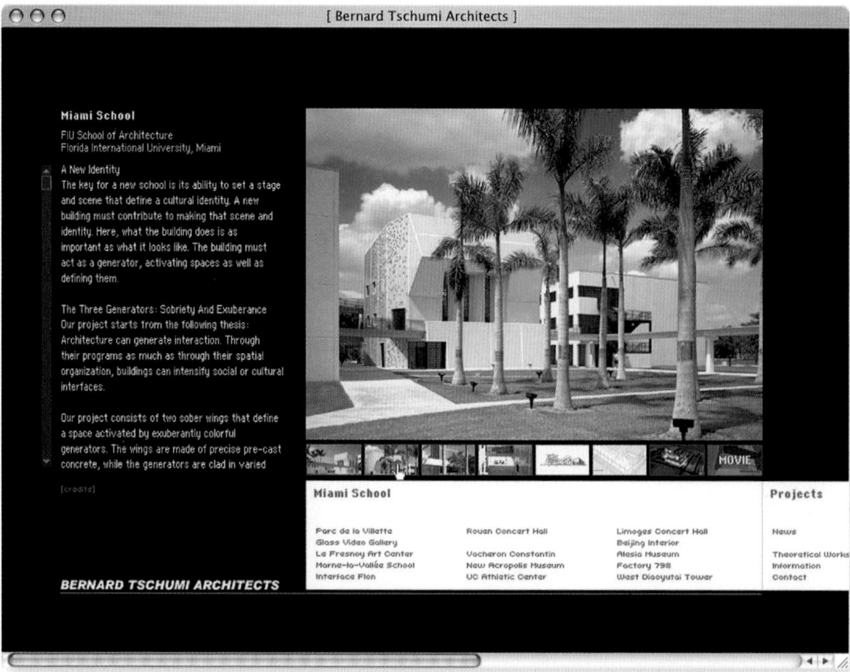
[Bernard Tschumi Architects]
Miami School
FIU School of Architecture
Florida International University, Miami
A New Identity
The key for a new school is its ability to set a stage and scene that define a cultural identity. A new building must contribute to making that scene and identity. Here, what the building does is as important as what it looks like. The building must act as a generator, activating spaces as well as defining them.
The Three Generators: Sobriety And Exuberance
Our project starts from the following thesis: Architecture can generate interaction. Through their programs as much as through their spatial organization, buildings can intensify social or cultural interfaces.
Our project consists of two sober wings that define a space activated by exuberantly colorful generators. The wings are made of precise pre-cast concrete, while the generators are clad in varied
[credits]
MOVIE
Miami School
Parc de la Villette
Glass Video Gallery
Le Fresnoy Art Center
Marne-la-Vallée School
Interface Flon
Rouen Concert Hall
Vacheron Constantin
New Acropolis Museum
UC Athletic Center
Limoges Concert Hall
Beijing Interior
Alesia Museum
Factory 798
West Diaoyutai Tower
Projects
News
Theoretical Works
Information
Contact
BERNARD TSCHUMI ARCHITECTS

www.tschumi.com
D: john szot, philip ryan, brian lenond
A: brooklyn digital foundry **M:** www.brooklynfoundry.com

Studio Granda Architects
Contact
About
Works
In Progress
Projects
Competitions
Exhibitions
Publications
Awards
News & Events
People
Search
Studio Granda
Skrudás
residence

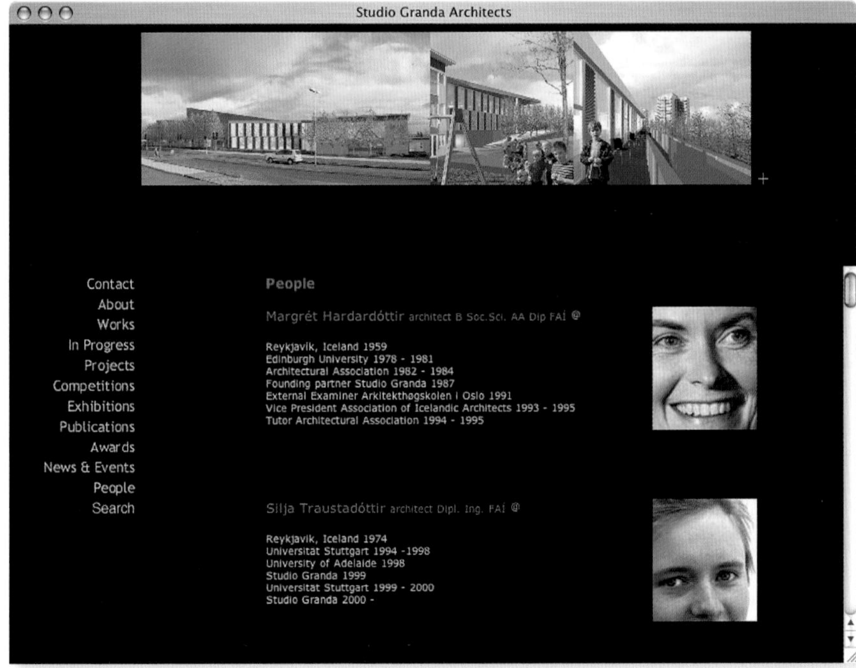
Studio Granda Architects
Contact
About
Works
In Progress
Projects
Competitions
Exhibitions
Publications
Awards
News & Events
People
Search
People
Margrét Hardardóttir architect B Soc.Sci. AA Dip FAÍ
Reykjavik, Iceland 1959
Edinburgh University 1978 - 1981
Architectural Association 1982 - 1984
Founding partner Studio Granda 1987
External Examiner Arkitekthøgskolen i Oslo 1991
Vice President Association of Icelandic Architects 1993 - 1995
Tutor Architectural Association 1994 - 1995
Silja Traustadóttir architect Dipl. Ing. FAÍ
Reykjavik, Iceland 1974
Universitat Stuttgart 1994 -1998
University of Adelaide 1998
Studio Granda 1999
Universitat Stuttgart 1999 - 2000
Studio Granda 2000 -

studiogranda.is
D: studio granda
M: studiogranda@studiogranda.is

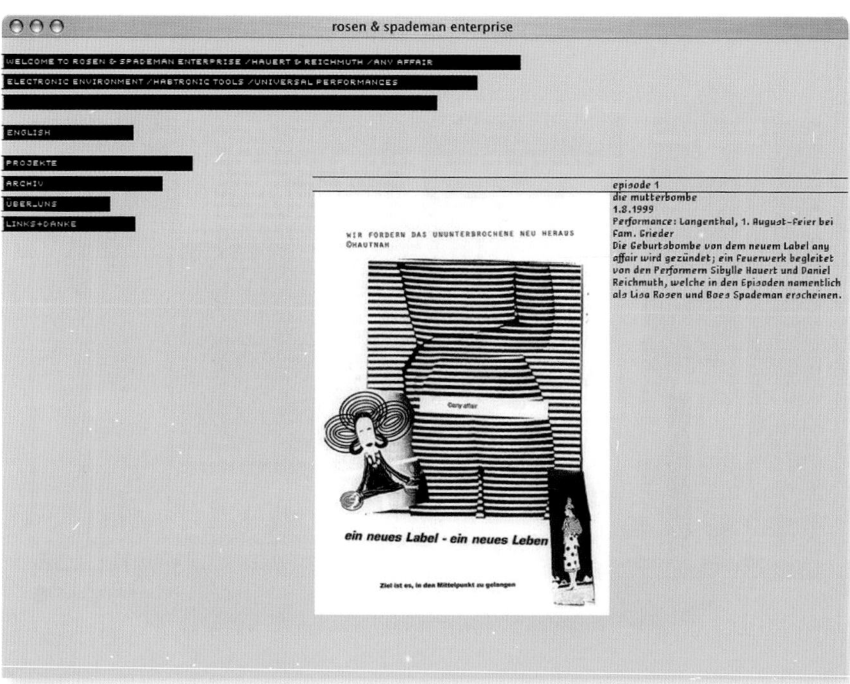
rosen & spademan enterprise
WELCOME TO ROSEN & SPADEMAN ENTERPRISE /HAUERT & REICHMUTH /ANY AFFAIR
ELECTRONIC ENVIRONMENT /HABTRONIC TOOLS /UNIVERSAL PERFORMANCES
ENGLISH
PROJEKTE
ARCHIV
ÜBER_UNS
LINKS+DANKE
WIR FORDERN DAS UNUNTERBROCHENE NEU HERAUS
OHAUTNAH
any affair
ein neues Label - ein neues Leben
Ziel ist es, in den Mittelpunkt zu gelangen
episode 1
die mutterbombe
1.8.1999
Performance: Langenthal, 1. August-Feier bei Fam. Grieder
Die Geburtsbombe von dem neuem Label any affair wird gezündet; ein Feuerwerk begleitet von den Performern Sibylle Hauert und Daniel Reichmuth, welche in den Episoden namentlich als Lisa Rosen und Boes Spademan erscheinen.

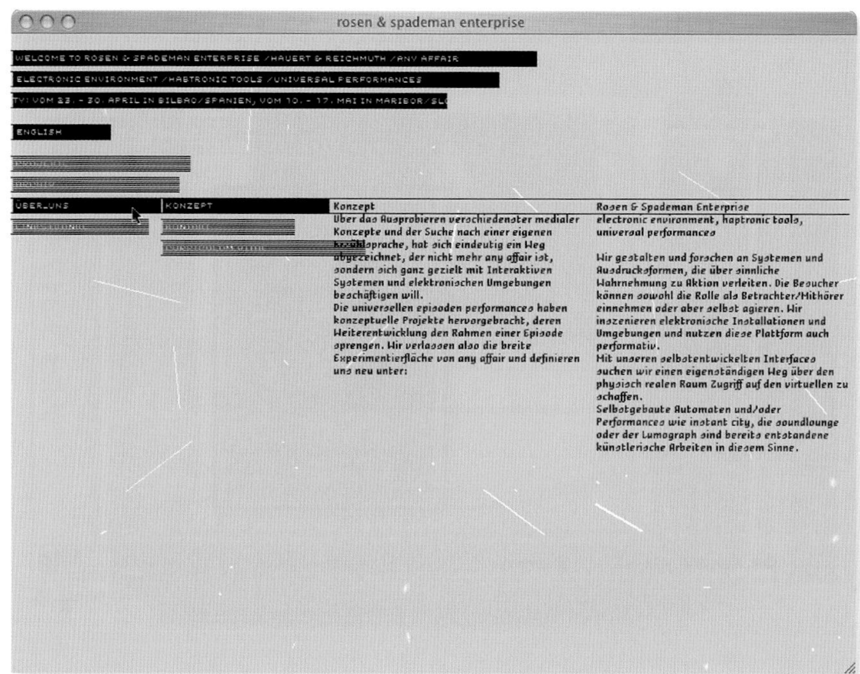
rosen & spademan enterprise
WELCOME TO ROSEN & SPADEMAN ENTERPRISE /HAUERT & REICHMUTH /ANY AFFAIR
ELECTRONIC ENVIRONMENT /HABTRONIC TOOLS /UNIVERSAL PERFORMANCES
TY: VOM 23. - 30. APRIL IN BILBAO/SPANIEN, VOM 10. - 17. MAI IN MARIBOR/SL
ENGLISH
ÜBER_UNS
KONZEPT
Konzept
Über das Ausprobieren verschiedenster medialer Konzepte und der Suche nach einer eigenen sprache, hat sich eindeutig ein Weg abgezeichnet, der nicht mehr any affair ist, sondern sich ganz gezielt mit Interaktiven Systemen und elektronischen Umgebungen beschäftigen will.
Die universellen episoden performances haben konzeptuelle Projekte hervorgebracht, deren Weiterentwicklung den Rahmen einer Episode sprengen. Wir verlassen also die breite Experimentierfläche von any affair und definieren uns neu unter:
Rosen & Spademan Enterprise
electronic environment, haptronic tools, universal performances
Wir gestalten und forschen an Systemen und Ausdrucksformen, die über sinnliche Wahrnehmung zu Aktion verleiten. Die Besucher können sowohl die Rolle als Betrachter/Mithörer einnehmen oder aber selbst agieren. Wir inszenieren elektronische Installationen und Umgebungen und nutzen diese Plattform auch performativ.
Mit unseren selbstentwickelten Interfaces suchen wir einen eigenständigen Weg über den physisch realen Raum Zugriff auf den virtuellen zu schaffen.
Selbstgebaute Automaten und/oder Performances wie instant city, die soundlounge oder der Lumograph sind bereits entstandene künstlerische Arbeiten in diesem Sinne.

www.rosen-spademan.net
D: jan voellmy
M: info@enpassant.net

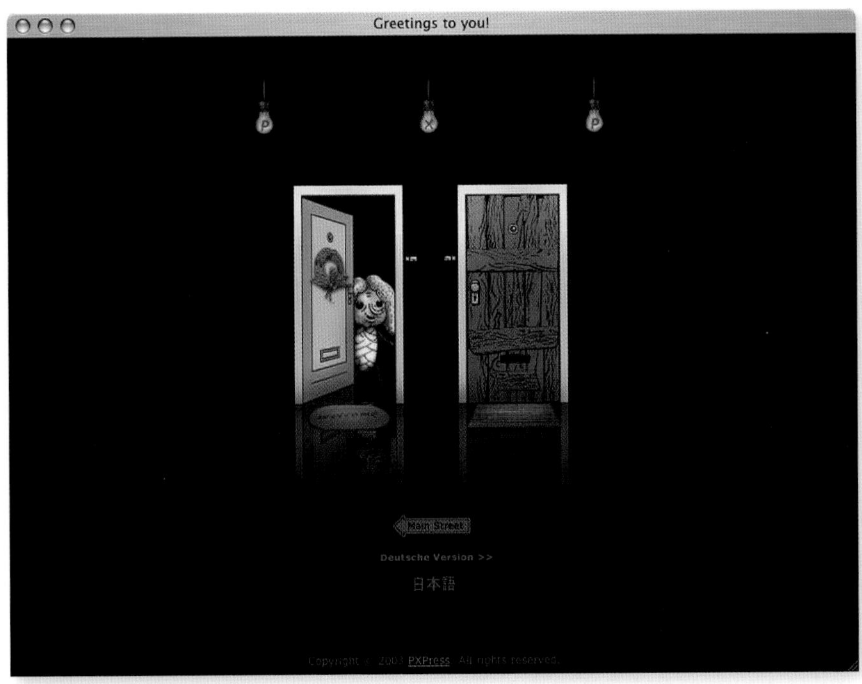
Greetings to you!
Main Street
Deutsche Version >>
日本語

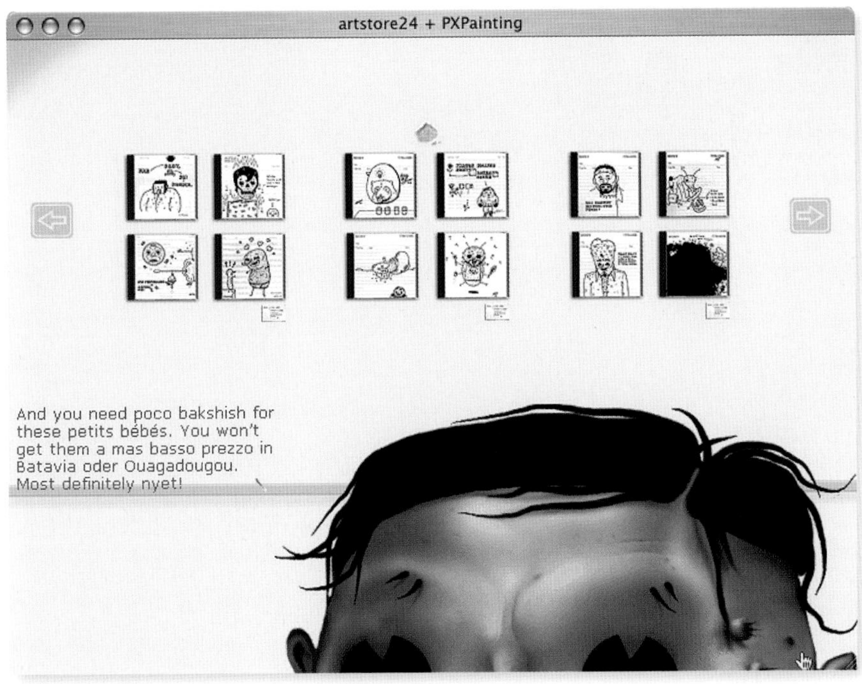
artstore24 + PXPainting
And you need poco bakshish for these petits bébés. You won't get them a mas basso prezzo in Batavia oder Ouagadougou. Most definitely nyet!

www.pxp2000.com
D: heiko kiendl-müller
A: pxpress

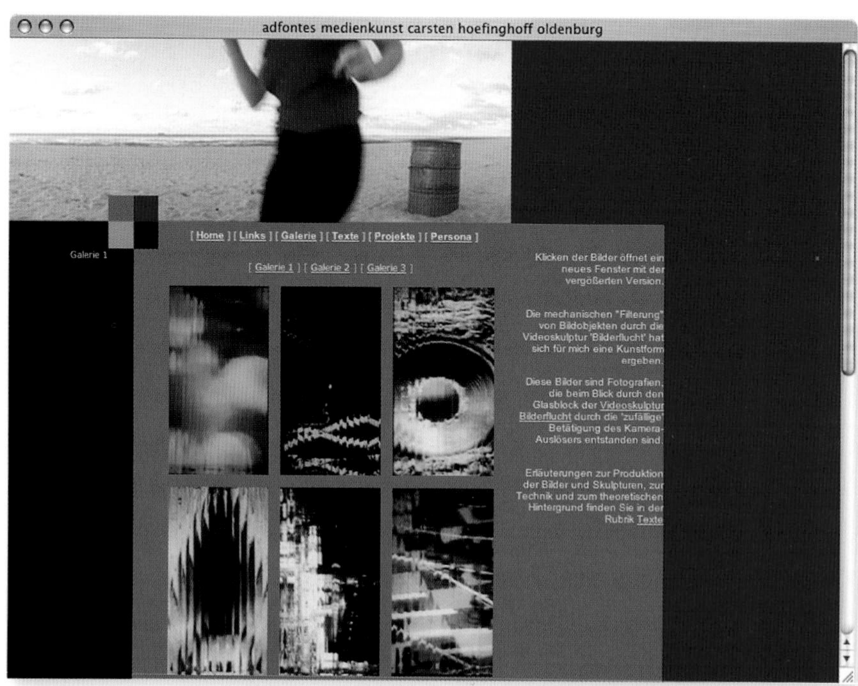
adfontes medienkunst carsten hoefinghoff oldenburg
[Home] [Links] [Galerie] [Texte] [Projekte] [Persona]
Galerie 1
[Galerie 1] [Galerie 2] [Galerie 3]
Klicken der Bilder öffnet ein neues Fenster mit der vergößerten Version.
Die mechanischen "Filterung" von Bildobjekten durch die Videoskulptur 'Bilderflucht' hat sich für mich eine Kunstform ergeben.
Diese Bilder sind Fotografien, die beim Blick durch den Glasblock der Videoskulptur Bilderflucht durch die 'zufällige' Betätigung des Kamera-Auslösers entstanden sind.
Erläuterungen zur Produktion der Bilder und Skulpturen, zur Technik und zum theoretischen Hintergrund finden Sie in der Rubrik Texte

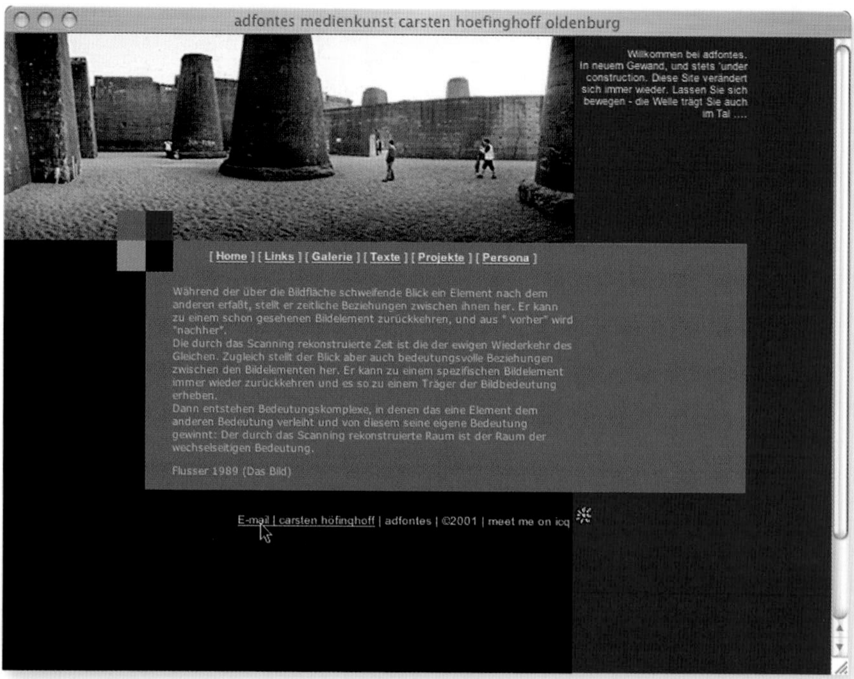
adfontes medienkunst carsten hoefinghoff oldenburg
Willkommen bei adfontes. In neuem Gewand, und stets 'under construction. Diese Site verändert sich immer wieder. Lassen Sie sich bewegen - die Welle trägt Sie auch im Tal ....
[Home] [Links] [Galerie] [Texte] [Projekte] [Persona]
Während der über die Bildfläche schweifende Blick ein Element nach dem anderen erfaßt, stellt er zeitliche Beziehungen zwischen ihnen her. Er kann zu einem schon gesehenen Bildelement zurückkehren, und aus " vorher" wird "nachher".
Die durch das Scanning rekonstruierte Zeit ist die der ewigen Wiederkehr des Gleichen. Zugleich stellt der Blick aber auch bedeutungsvolle Beziehungen zwischen den Bildelementen her. Er kann zu einem spezifischen Bildelement immer wieder zurückkehren und es so zu einem Träger der Bildbedeutung erheben.
Dann entstehen Bedeutungskomplexe, in denen das eine Element dem anderen Bedeutung verleiht und von diesem seine eigene Bedeutung gewinnt: Der durch das Scanning rekonstruierte Raum ist der Raum der wechselseitigen Bedeutung.
Flusser 1989 (Das Bild)
E-mail | carsten höfinghoff | adfontes | ©2001 | meet me on icq

www.adfontes.net
D: carsten höfinghoff
A: adfontes **M:** hoefinghoff@adfontes.net

[gabriele dell'otto official web site]
ENLARGE
CORRIDOR WELL COMICS TALES FRAMES SKETCHES PROJECTS HOME > NAVIGATION

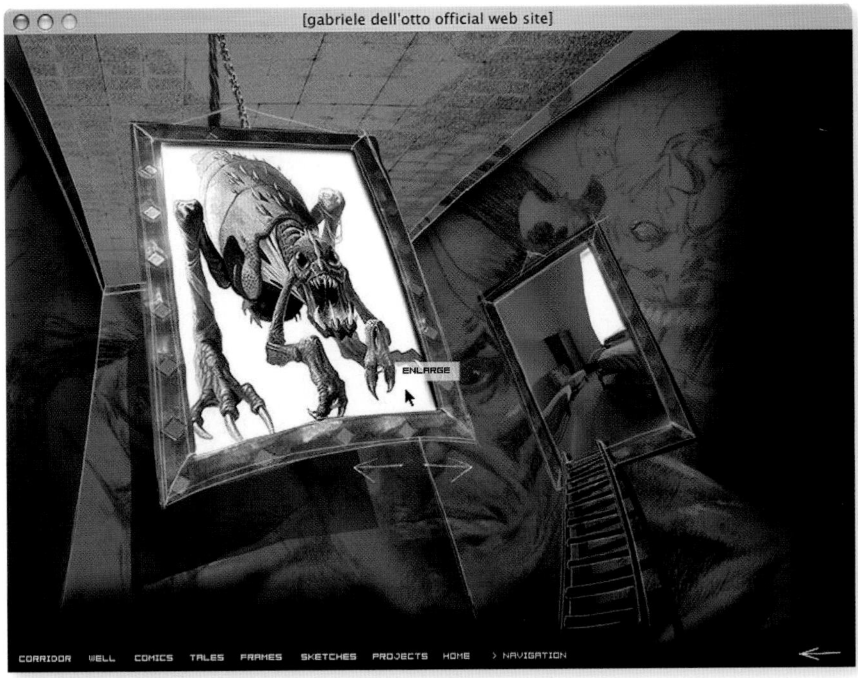
[gabriele dell'otto official web site]
ENLARGE
CORRIDOR WELL COMICS TALES FRAMES SKETCHES PROJECTS HOME > NAVIGATION

www.dellotto.it
D: gabriele dell'otto **C:** andrea ciavattini
A: interzona art studio **M:** izn@interzona.it

PPUPPY
about
vision
contacts
PPUPPY
FASHION CABINET

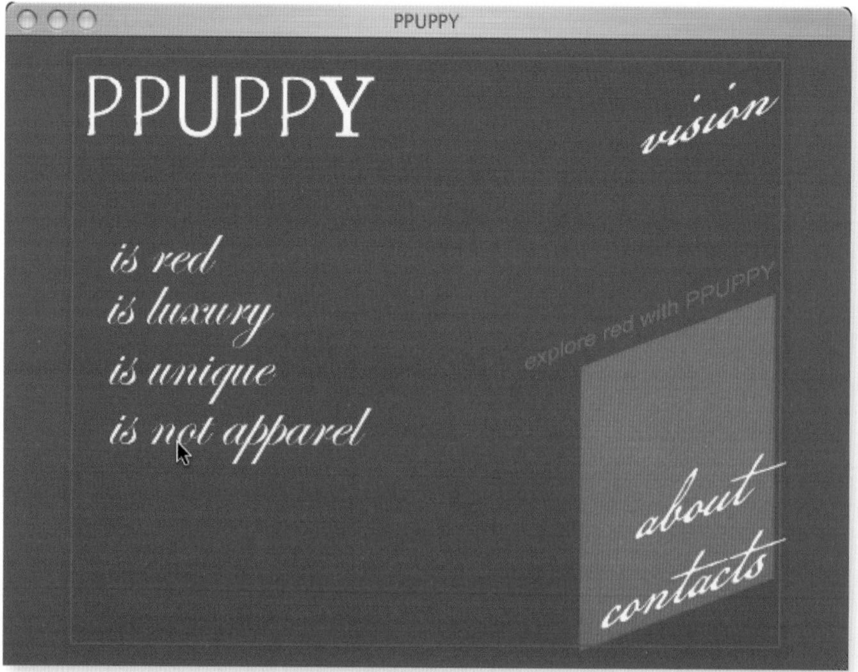
PPUPPY
PPUPPY
vision
is red
is luxury
is unique
is not apparel
explore red with PPUPPY
about
contacts

www.ppuppy.info
D: algy jaft
M: info@ppuppy.info

Cracking Art
mostre-eventi-bio/bibliografia
cracking art

„Cracking Art – Il Centro" wird geladen
< home >
Veduta del centro negli anni '40
IL CENTRO
NEL QUARTIERE STORICO DI BIELLA RIVA (VIA COSTA DI RIVA 8) E' STATO RIPORTATO A NUOVA VITA UN FABBRICATO INDUSTRIALE ABBANDONATO, RISALENTE AI PRIMI ANNI DEL SECOLO SCORSO.
NELL'IMMOBILE CHE E' ORA LA SEDE DEL CENTRO STUDI E DOCUMENTAZIONI CRACKING ART SI SVOLGONO NUMEROSE ATTIVITA' CULTURALI, CONFERENZE E DIBATTITI APERTI AL PUBBLICO, AGLI APPASSIONATI D'ARTE ED AGLI AMICI DEGLI ARTISTI CRACKING.
OMAR RONDA - WILLIAM SWEETLOVE - RENZO NUCARA
MARCO VERONESE - ALEX ANGI - CARLO RIZZETTI - KICCO

www.crackingart.com
D: simone casaliggi
M: simone@casaliggi.com

http://www.visual0.de/part1.swf

printed image representation and size
of the cutout at 100%

L 01

title: 50yb
format: 265 cm X 175 cm
technique: photo rework / digital / -print on cloth
creation: 2000

@
landscape L
S

http://www.visual0.de/artsite1.swf

artsite I

werk

norbert coors
jg. 1953
objektkünstler
bbk
lebt in düsseldorf
seit 1979 diverse ausstellungen

arbeiten bis 1985
architektur & metapher
konstruktive studien
& kommunikative szenarien /
drahtobjekte

arbeiten bis 1995
kinetik & transfer I
dreidimensionale kinetische objekte /
metall & fiberglasgewebe

arbeiten bis 1998
kinetik & transfer II
visuelle kommunikation /
bewegte scheiben

arbeiten bis 1999
kinetik & transfer III
visuelle interaktion /
bewegte röhren

arbeiten bis 2000
virtualität I
zweidimensionale objekte,
dreidimensionale flächen /
objektanimationen

arbeiten bis 2001
virtualität II
prospektive visuelle objekte
animationen & clips /
großbild projektion

arbeiten bis 2002
virtualität III
bild ton kompositionen
clips & trailer /
großbild projektion

aktuelle arbeiten
strukturen
simultankontraste & interferenzen /
großbild projektion

intro portrait contact works extro artsite II distance sitedesign -sitemap-

werk kommunikation transfer / kinetik information -clip multimedia -clip

www.visual0.de
D: norbert coors
M: norbert_coors@web.de

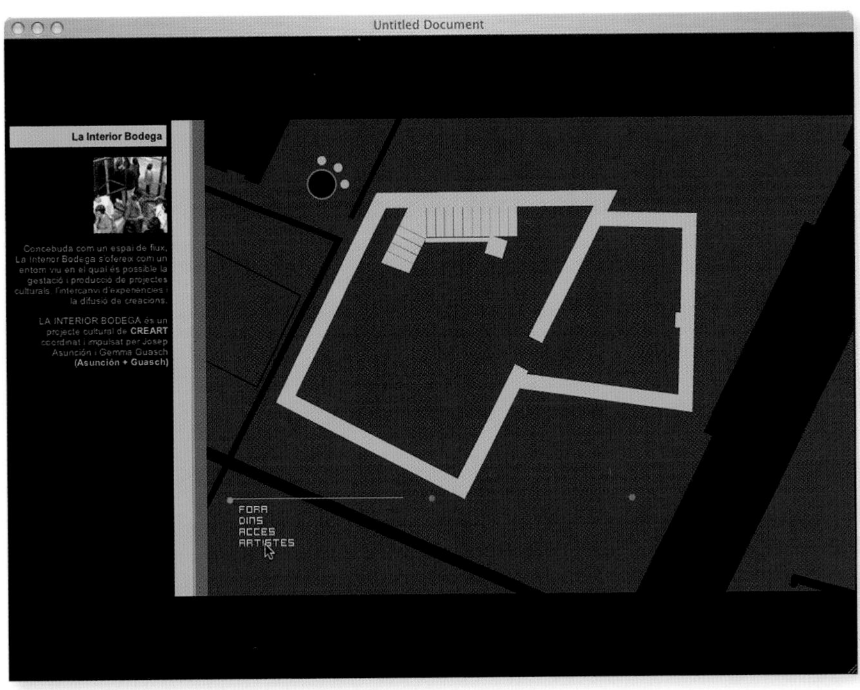
Untitled Document
La Interior Bodega
Concebuda com un espai de flux, La Interior Bodega s'oferex com un entorn viu en el qual és possible la gestació i producció de projectes culturals, l'intercanvi d'experiències i la difusió de creacions.
LA INTERIOR BODEGA és un projecte cultural de CREART coordinat i impulsat per Josep Asunción i Gemma Guasch (Asunción + Guasch)
FORA
DINS
ACCES
ARTISTES

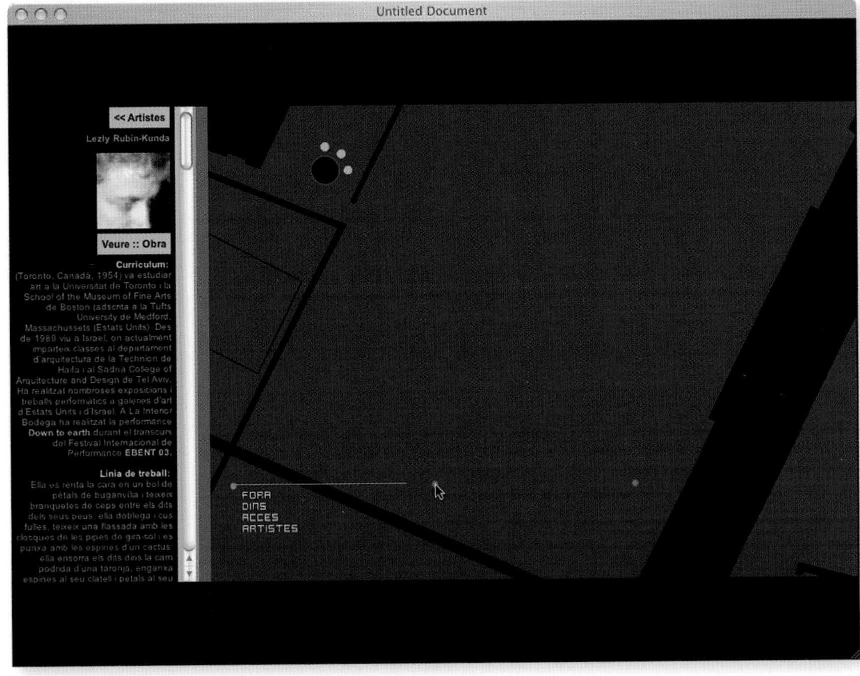
Untitled Document
<< Artistes
Lezly Rubin-Kunda
Veure :: Obra
Curriculum:
(Toronto, Canadà, 1954) va estudiar art a la Universitat de Toronto i la School of the Museum of Fine Arts de Boston (adscrita a la Tufts University de Medford, Massachussets (Estats Units). Des de 1989 viu a Israel, on actualment imparteix classes al departament d'arquitectura de la Technion de Haifa i al Sadna College of Arquitecture and Design de Tel Aviv. Ha realitzat nombroses exposicions i treballs performàtics a galeries d'art d'Estats Units i d'Israel. A La Interior Bodega ha realitzat la performance Down to earth durant el transcurs del Festival Internacional de Performance EBENT 03.
Linia de treball:
Ella es renta la cara en un bol de pètals de buganvilla i teixeix branquetes de ceps entre els dits dels seus peus; ella doblega i cus fulles, teixeix una flassada amb les closques de les pipes de gira-sol i es punxa amb les espines d'un cactus; ella ensorra els dits dins la carn podrida d'una taronja, enganxa espines al seu clatell i pètals al seu
FORA
DINS
ACCES
ARTISTES

lainteriorbodega.org
D: rodrigo mendoza
A: s3 design **M:** rodrigomendoza@onesourcecreative.com

Artificialduck Studios

PRESS PROGRAMM ~~PROJECTS~~ PEOPLE PRIZES CONTACT
~~/ H.J. SCHLIEKER~~ FDGG ~~DRAWINGS DH~~ GRIFFELKUNST NETWORK SITE DAVIDOFF

// DE version

LEADING AN AUDIENCE THROUGH TIME.

THE AIM OF THIS PROJECT WAS TO CREATE A DIGITAL RECORD AND INTERACTIVE CATALOGUE OF INFORMEL ARTIST, HANS-JÜRGEN SCHLIEKER'S (1924 - 2004), EXTENSIVE BODY OF WORK. AND, IN CREATING A MODERN, DIGITAL RETROSPECTIVE WE HAVE ENABLED NEW LEVELS OF INTERACTION THAT EVEN THE ORIGINAL WORKS THEMSELVES COULD NOT OFFER. THE SITE USES A HORIZONTAL NAVIGATION SYSTEM FLOATING ATOP A VERTICAL GRID OF CONTENT. EACH OF THESE PLANES DIVIDES AND CONTRACTS ACCORDING TO WINDOWS SIZE AND REQUIREMENTS OF CONTENT DISPLAY; COMING TO EQUILIBRIUM IN THE 'GOLDEN CUT'. THIS FORMAL STRUCTURE BOTH CHANNELS THE VIEWER'S ATTENTION AND MAKES THE INFORMATIONAL PROGRESSION FROM TOP-LEVEL TO DETAIL NATURAL AND EFFORTLESS. AS A FORM OF META-CATALOGUE, THE PAGE MERGES DIFFERENT APPROACHES AND PERSPECTIVES: SERVING AS A MONOGRAPH OF THE LIFE AND WORK OF THE ARTIST WHILE ALSO OFFERING SUMMARIES ARRANGED ACCORDING TO ERA AND ARTISTIC TECHNIQUE.

HTTP://WWW.HJSCHLIEKER.COM

Artificialduck Studios

PRESS PROGRAMM PROJECTS ~~PEOPLE~~ PRIZES CONTACT

// DE version

PARTICULARS.

ARTIFICIALDUCK WAS FOUNDET BY DIRK HOFFMANN AND PATRIK DE JONG IN 2005.

PATRIK DE JONG
SHORTLY AFTER GRADUATING FROM HIGH SCHOOL IN 1998, PATRIK DE JONG (BORN IN 1979), TOOK UP A POSITION AS FLASH DESIGNER AT I-D MEDIA AG; HAMBURG. AFTER 2 YEARS IN THE ROLE HE BRANCHED OUT AS A FREELANCE ART DIRECTOR AND WORKED ACROSS THE HAMBURG AND BERLIN REGION WHILE STUDING COMMUNICATION DESIGN AT THE HAW HAMBURG. IN 2002, HE CO- FOUNDED THE PUNKTX NETWORK THAT WAS TO BECOME ARTIFICIALDUCK STUDIO IN 2005. PATRIK DE JONG ALSO TEACHES AT THE MACROMEDIA ACADEMY AND AT THE SAE IN HAMBURG

PDJ@ARTIFICIALDUCK.NET

DIRK HOFFMANN
AFTER COMPLETING HIS STUDIES IN VISUAL COMMUNICATIONS AT THE HAMBURG DESIGN COLLEGE IN 1993, DIRK HOFFMANN (BORN IN 1966) WORKED AS FREELANCE PAINTER FOR SEVERAL YEARS. IN 1999, AFTER INCREASING ENGAGEMENT IN MULTIMEDIA, HE TOOK UP A POSITION AS ART DIRECTOR AT ID-MEDIA AG; HAMBURG. IN 2002 HE RETURNED TO FREELANCE CONTRACTING, WORKING FOR VARIOUS AGENCIES; WHILE HE BUILT UP THE PUNKTX NETWORK. IN 2005, PUNKTX WAS DISSOLVED AND REBORN AS ARTIFICIALDUCK STUDIO. DIRK HOFFMANN IS LECTURER FOR DIGITAL DESIGN AT, AMONG OTHER PLACES,THE BILDKUNST ACADEMY IN HAMBURG.

DH@ARTIFICIALDUCK.NET

■

ARTIFICIALDUCK WOULD NOT EXIST WITHOUT THE SUPPORT AND LOVE OF THE FOLLOWING PEOPLE:
BRITTA PETERS, NINIK VOGELSANG, WOLFGANG MÜLLER, GESINE WIERER

www.artificialduck.net
D: dirk hoffmann, patrik de jong **C:** patrik de jong **P:** dirk hoffmann
A: artificialduck studio **M:** contact@artificialduck.net

Ty Lettau

Ty Lettau

Index

+ = Recent

Last Update: March, '04

Shop

Type Foundry

Work

Archive

Play

Born Magazine - "Instructions"
Range
360
Chaos Attractors
Order Generators
Cymbal
VectorLounge - "Process"
Born Magazine - "Core"
Lab

Information

Curriculum Vitae
Client List

Inquiries

ty@soundofdesign.com

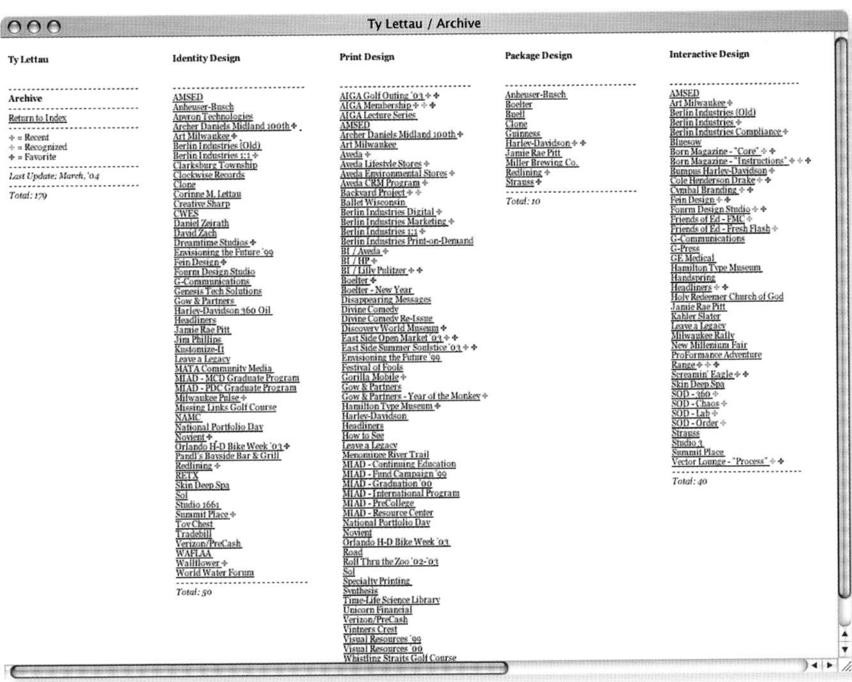
Ty Lettau / Archive
Ty Lettau
Archive
Return to Index
+ = Recent
+ = Recognized
+ = Favorite
Last Update: March, '04
Total: 179
Identity Design
AMSED
Anheuser-Busch
Apyron Technologies
Archer Daniels Midland 100th
Art Milwaukee
Berlin Industries (Old)
Berlin Industries 1:1
Clarksburg Township
Clockwise Records
Clone
Corinne M. Lettau
Creative Sharp
CWES
Daniel Zeirath
David Zach
Dreamtime Studios
Envisioning the Future '99
Fein Design
Fourm Design Studio
G-Communications
Genesis Tech Solutions
Gow & Partners
Harley-Davidson 360 Oil
Headliners
Jamie Rae Pitt
Jim Phillips
Kustomize-It
Leave a Legacy
MATA Community Media
MIAD - MCD Graduate Program
MIAD - PDC Graduate Program
Milwaukee Pulse
Missing Links Golf Course
NAMC
National Portfolio Day
Novient
Orlando H-D Bike Week '03
Pandl's Bayside Bar & Grill
Redlining
RETX
Skin Deep Spa
Sol
Studio 1661
Summit Place
Toy Chest
Tradebill
Verizon/PreCash
WAFLAA
Wallflower
World Water Forum
Total: 50
Print Design
AIGA Golf Outing '03
AIGA Membership
AIGA Lecture Series
AMSED
Archer Daniels Midland 100th
Art Milwaukee
Aveda
Aveda Lifestyle Stores
Aveda Environmental Stores
Aveda CRM Program
Backyard Project
Ballet Wisconsin
Berlin Industries Digital
Berlin Industries Marketing
Berlin Industries 1:1
Berlin Industries Print-on-Demand
BI / Aveda
BI / HP
BI / Lilly Pulitzer
Boelter
Boelter - New Year
Disappearing Messages
Divine Comedy
Divine Comedy Re-Issue
Discovery World Museum
East Side Open Market '03
East Side Summer Soulstice '03
Envisioning the Future '99
Festival of Fools
Gorilla Mobile
Gow & Partners
Gow & Partners - Year of the Monkey
Hamilton Type Museum
Harley-Davidson
Headliners
How to See
Leave a Legacy
Menominee River Trail
MIAD - Continuing Education
MIAD - Fund Campaign '99
MIAD - Graduation '00
MIAD - International Program
MIAD - PreCollege
MIAD - Resource Center
National Portfolio Day
Novient
Orlando H-D Bike Week '03
Road
Roll Thru the Zoo '02-'03
Sol
Specialty Printing
Synthesis
Time-Life Science Library
Unicorn Financial
Verizon/PreCash
Vintners Crest
Visual Resources '99
Visual Resources '00
Whistling Straits Golf Course
Package Design
Anheuser-Busch
Boelter
Buell
Clone
Guinness
Harley-Davidson
Jamie Rae Pitt
Miller Brewing Co.
Redlining
Strauss
Total: 10
Interactive Design
AMSED
Art Milwaukee
Berlin Industries (Old)
Berlin Industries
Berlin Industries Compliance
Bluesow
Born Magazine - "Core"
Born Magazine - "Instructions"
Bumpus Harley-Davidson
Cole Henderson Drake
Cymbal Branding
Fein Design
Fourm Design Studio
Friends of Ed - FMC
Friends of Ed - Fresh Flash
G-Communications
G-Press
GE Medical
Hamilton Type Museum
Handspring
Headliners
Holy Redeemer Church of God
Jamie Rae Pitt
Kahler Slater
Leave a Legacy
Milwaukee Rally
New Millenium Fair
ProFormance Adventure
Range
Screamin' Eagle
Skin Deep Spa
SOD - 360
SOD - Chaos
SOD - Lab
SOD - Order
Strauss
Studio 3
Summit Place
Vector Lounge - "Process"
Total: 40

www.soundofdesign.com
D: ty lettau
A: soundofdesign **M:** info@soundofdesign.com

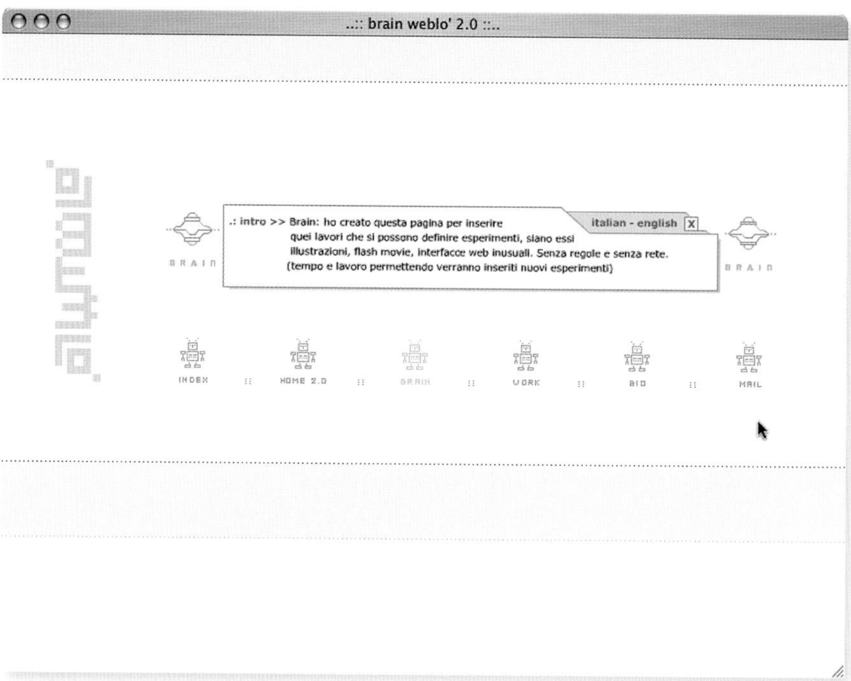
..:: brain weblo' 2.0 ::..
.: intro >> Brain: ho creato questa pagina per inserire quei lavori che si possono definire esperimenti, siano essi illustrazioni, flash movie, interfacce web inusuali. Senza regole e senza rete. (tempo e lavoro permettendo verranno inseriti nuovi esperimenti)
italian - english
BRAIN
INDEX :: HOME 2.0 :: BRAIN :: WORK :: BIO :: MAIL

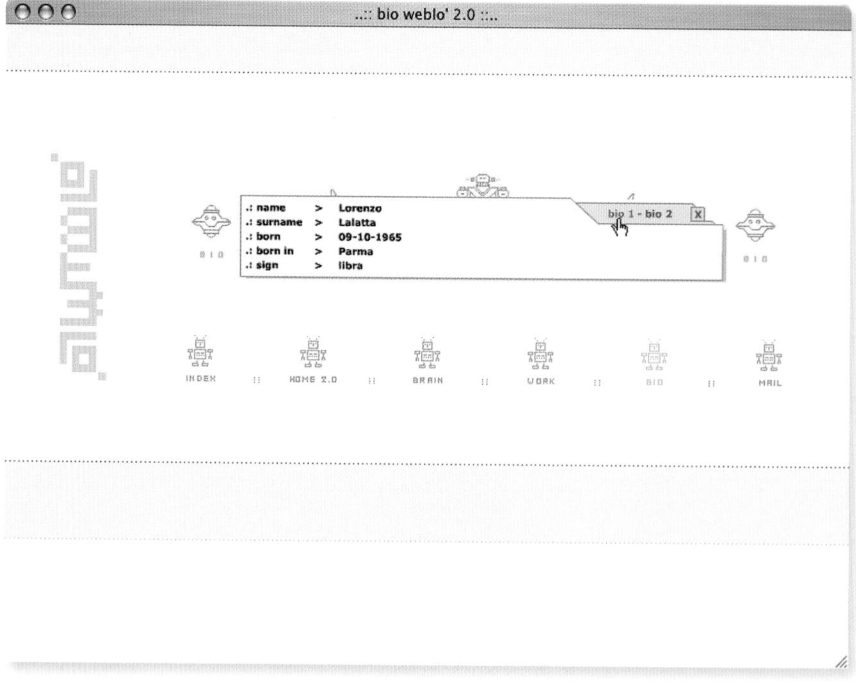
..:: bio weblo' 2.0 ::..
.: name > Lorenzo
.: surname > Lalatta
.: born > 09-10-1965
.: born in > Parma
.: sign > libra
bio 1 - bio 2
BIO
INDEX :: HOME 2.0 :: BRAIN :: WORK :: BIO :: MAIL

www.lalatta.it
D: lorenzo lalatta
M: lorenzo@lalatta.it

LG&F

LE
MENU
S.V.P.
LG&F
EN DIGITAL
08 Apr.

yes,

Today is the day.
The day we like to call...

YOU HAVE
00 NEW
MESSAGES
CLICK

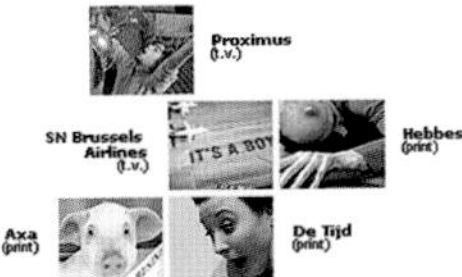
I ❤ NEW WORK

Proximus (t.v.)

SN Brussels Airlines (t.v.)

Hebbes (print)

Axa (print)

De Tijd (print)

LG&F

LE
MENU
S.V.P.
LG&F
EN DIGITAL

NUCLEAR PHYSICS IS SOMETHING WE KNOW NOTHING
ABOUT

LG&F
VISION

We're fairly pragmatic people at LG&F. We don't have a mission statement full of important sounding phrases. What we have instead is a single-minded obsession about one thing: the work and nothing but the work. We judge ourselves by the success of our campaigns. But far from having no mission, we have many. As many as we have brands to work for. Each brand has its own mission (and if it doesn't, that's one of

LG&F
HISTORY

Comedy version — Classic version — Cowboy version

LG&F
THE GROUP

In 2002, some LG&F clients and prospects wanted LG&F to solve more than their advertising problems. Perhaps it was time to expand beyond a single discipline. There were two options: hire experienced DM and promotion specialists in -house, or simply claim we'd been experts in DM and promotion all along. Fortunately for our clients, LG&F did neither of the above - and instead started a separate, dedicated company

I DO Pride

www.lgf.be

D: pauwels stijn **C:** peter ginneberge **P:** tim siaens

A: www.milkandcookies.be **M:** tim@milkandcookies.be

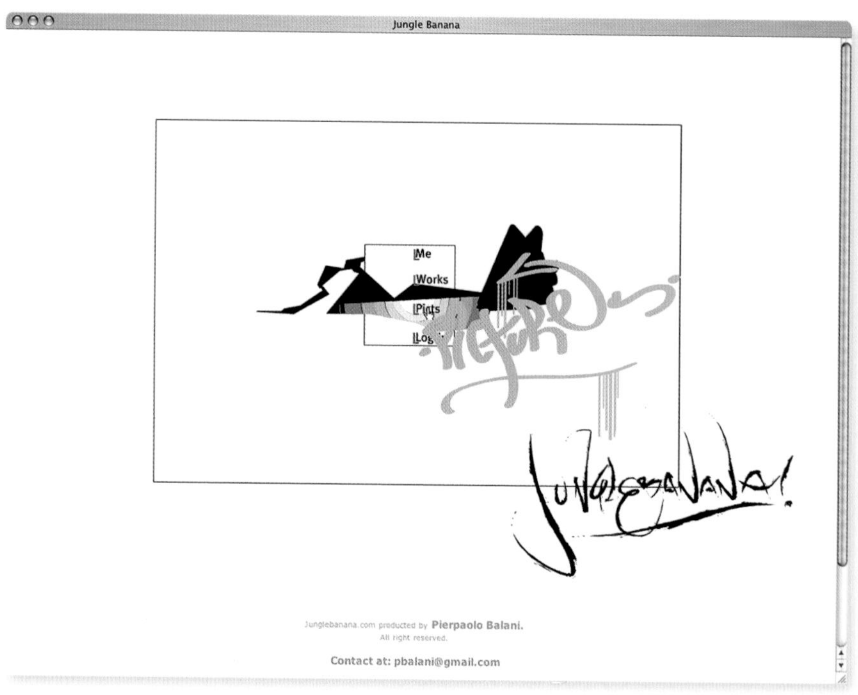
Jungle Banana
Me
Works
Prints
Junglebanana.com produced by Pierpaolo Balani.
All right reserved.
Contact at: pbalani@gmail.com

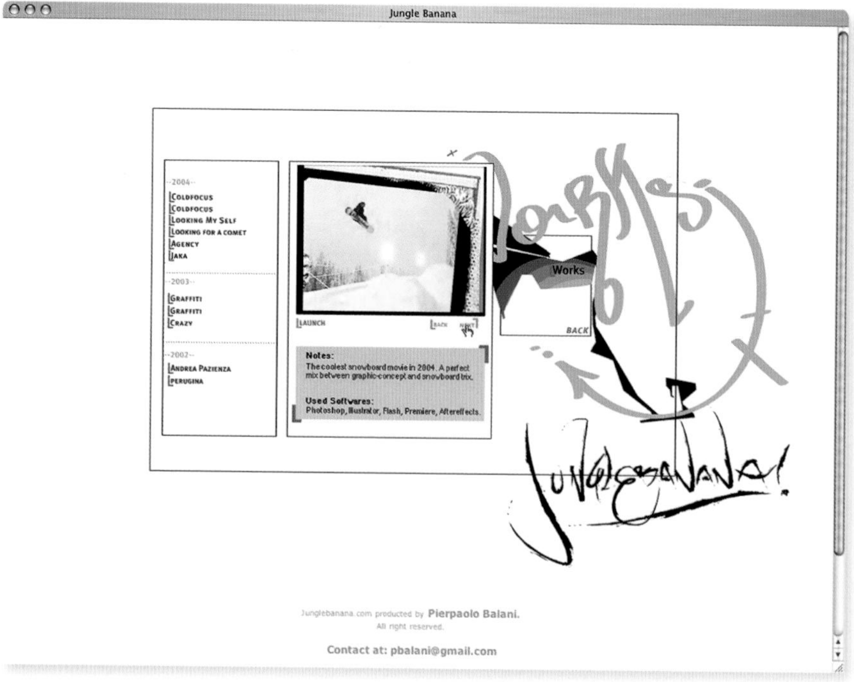
Jungle Banana
2004
Coldfocus
Coldfocus
Looking My Self
Looking for a comet
Agency
Jaka
2003
Graffiti
Graffiti
Crazy
2002
Andrea Pazienza
Perugina
Launch
Back
Notes:
The coolest snowboard movie in 2004. A perfect mix between graphic-concept and snowboard trix.
Used Softwares:
Photoshop, Illustrator, Flash, Premiere, Aftereffects.
Works
BACK
Junglebanana.com produced by Pierpaolo Balani.
All right reserved.
Contact at: pbalani@gmail.com

www.junglebanana.com
D: pierpaolo balani
M: pbalani@libero.it

artboxx

about
Konzeption & Entwurf
Typografie
Webdesign

| menue |

artboxx

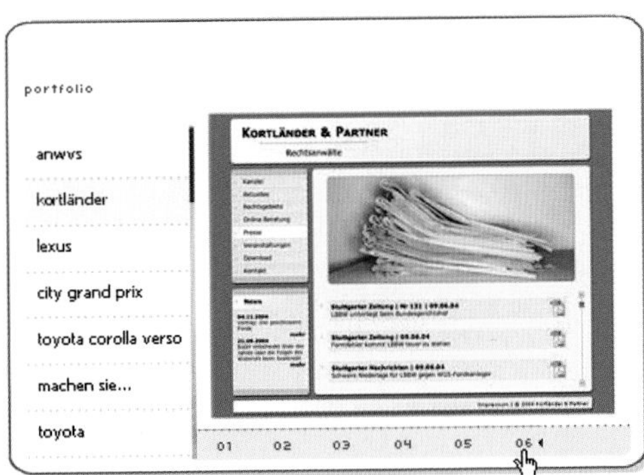
portfolio
anwvs
kortländer
lexus
city grand prix
toyota corolla verso
machen sie...
toyota
Kortländer & Partner
Rechtsanwälte
01 02 03 04 05 06

| menue |

www.artboxx.net
D: guido eichhoff
A: artboxx **M:** guido@artboxx.net

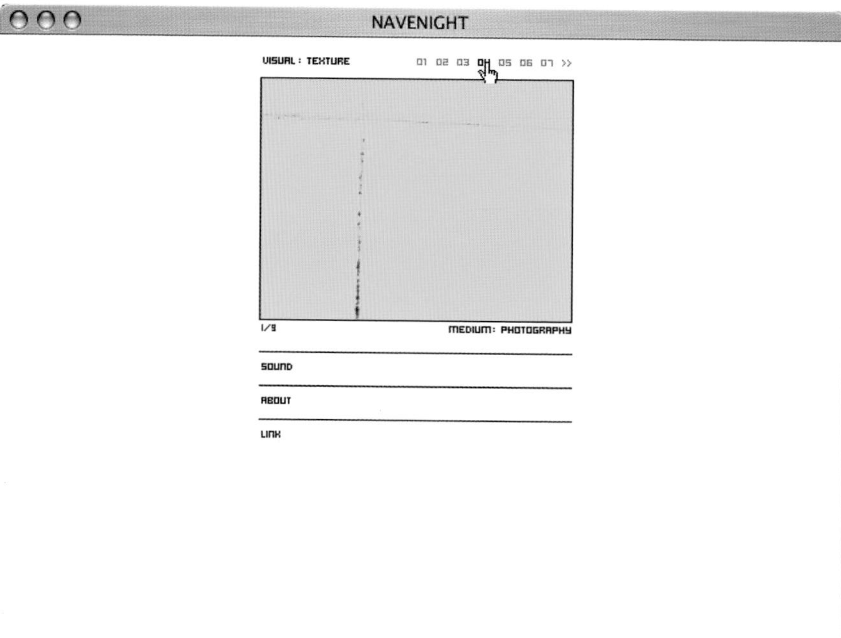
NAVENIGHT
VISUAL : TEXTURE
01 02 03 04 05 06 07 >>
1/9
MEDIUM: PHOTOGRAPHY
SOUND
ABOUT
LINK

NAVENIGHT

VISUAL

SOUND

LOOP SERIES
MP 3
REVIEWS

20-07-2005
NEW RELEASE
ESA: SIGN.SILENCE. SINE3PM ||| S3P016 |||. AVAILABLE FROM HTTP://WWW.SINEWAVES.IT

ABOUT

LINK

www.navenight.com
D: luigi turra
M: luigi@navenight.com

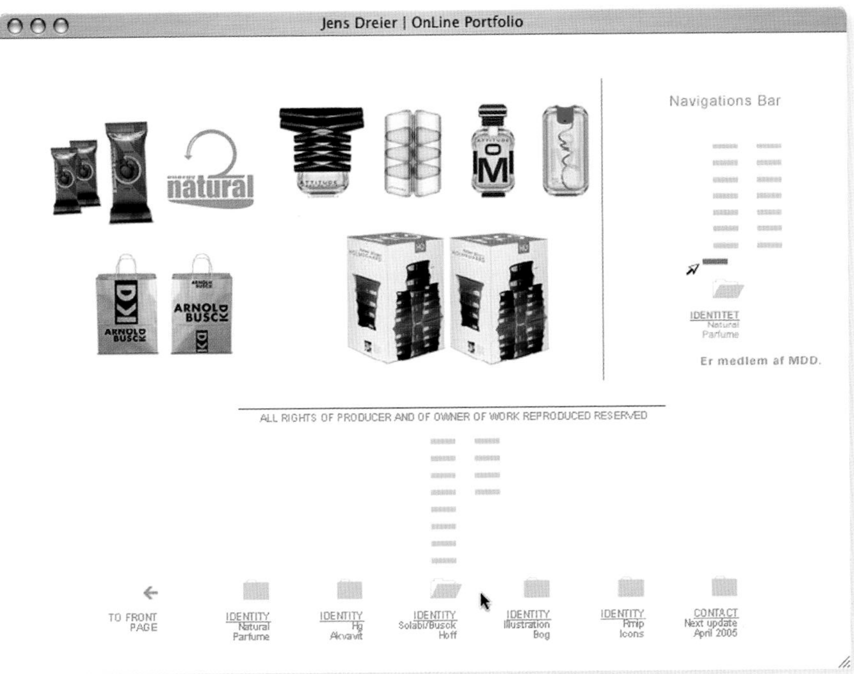
Jens Dreier | OnLine Portfolio
Navigations Bar
IDENTITET
Natural
Parfume
Er medlem af MDD.
ALL RIGHTS OF PRODUCER AND OF OWNER OF WORK REPRODUCED RESERVED
TO FRONT PAGE
IDENTITY Natural Parfume
IDENTITY Hg Akvavit
IDENTITY Solabi/Busck Hoff
IDENTITY Illustration Bog
IDENTITY Rmip Icons
CONTACT Next update April 2005

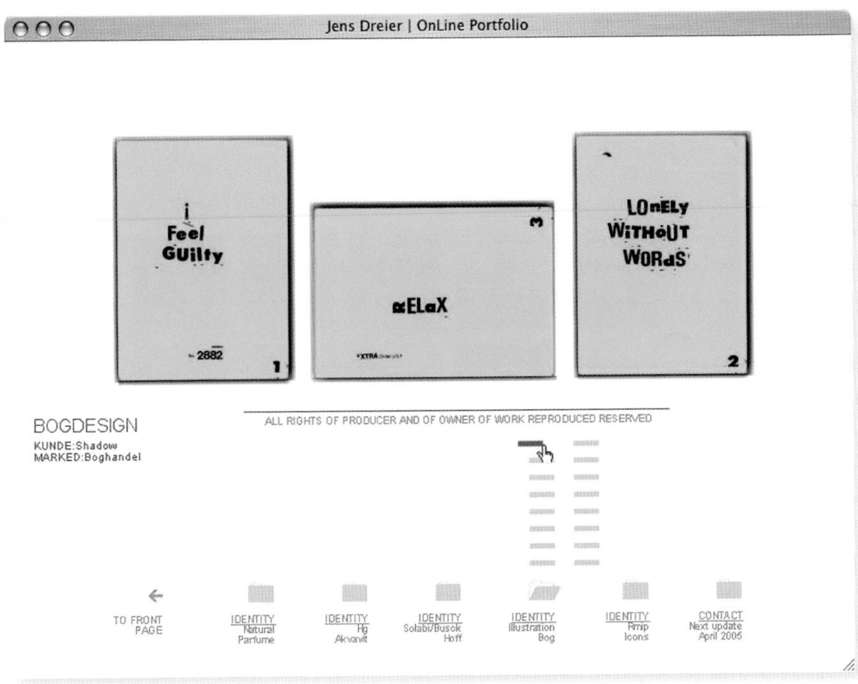
Jens Dreier | OnLine Portfolio
i Feel GUilty
RELAX
LOnELy WiTHoUT WORdS
BOGDESIGN
KUNDE:Shadow
MARKED:Boghandel
ALL RIGHTS OF PRODUCER AND OF OWNER OF WORK REPRODUCED RESERVED
TO FRONT PAGE
IDENTITY Natural Parfume
IDENTITY Hg Akvavit
IDENTITY Solabi/Busck Hoff
IDENTITY Illustration Bog
IDENTITY Rmip Icons
CONTACT Next update April 2005

www.jensdreier.dk
D: jens dreier
A: grafisk designer mdd **M:** info@jensdreier.dk

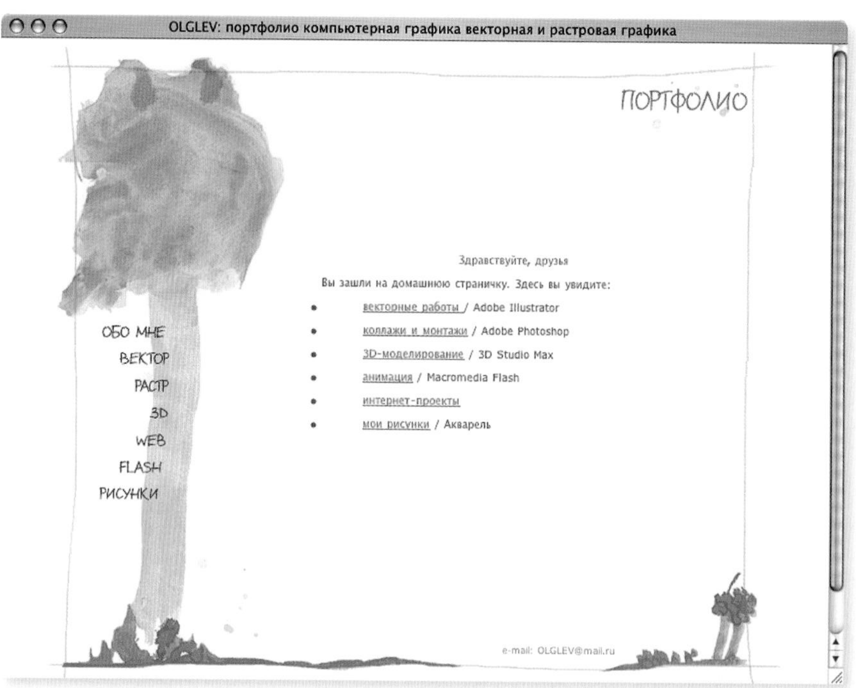
OLGLEV: портфолио компьютерная графика векторная и растровая графика
ПОРТФОЛИО
Здравствуйте, друзья
Вы зашли на домашнюю страничку. Здесь вы увидите:
векторные работы / Adobe Illustrator
коллажи и монтажи / Adobe Photoshop
3D-моделирование / 3D Studio Max
анимация / Macromedia Flash
интернет-проекты
мои рисунки / Акварель
ОБО МНЕ
ВЕКТОР
РАСТР
3D
WEB
FLASH
РИСУНКИ
e-mail: OLGLEV@mail.ru

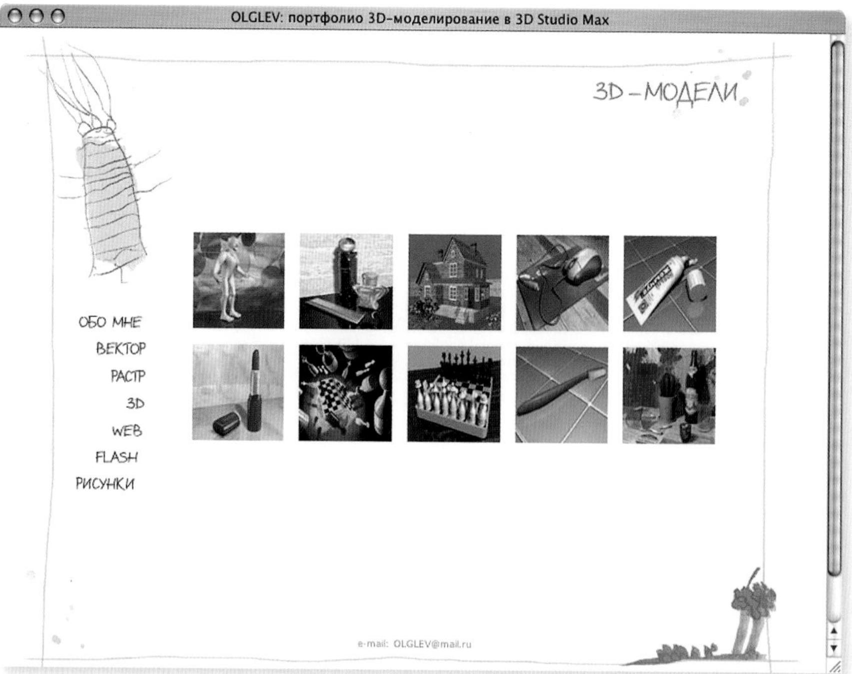
OLGLEV: портфолио 3D-моделирование в 3D Studio Max
3D-МОДЕЛИ
ОБО МНЕ
ВЕКТОР
РАСТР
3D
WEB
FLASH
РИСУНКИ
e-mail: OLGLEV@mail.ru

www.olglev.front.ru
D: olga levkina
M: olglev@mail.ru

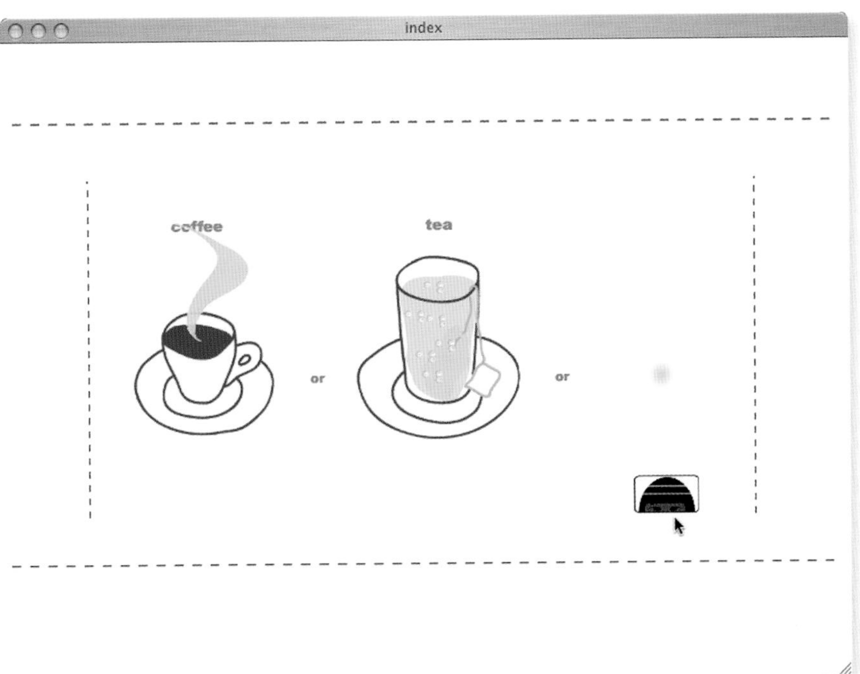
index
coffee
tea
or
or

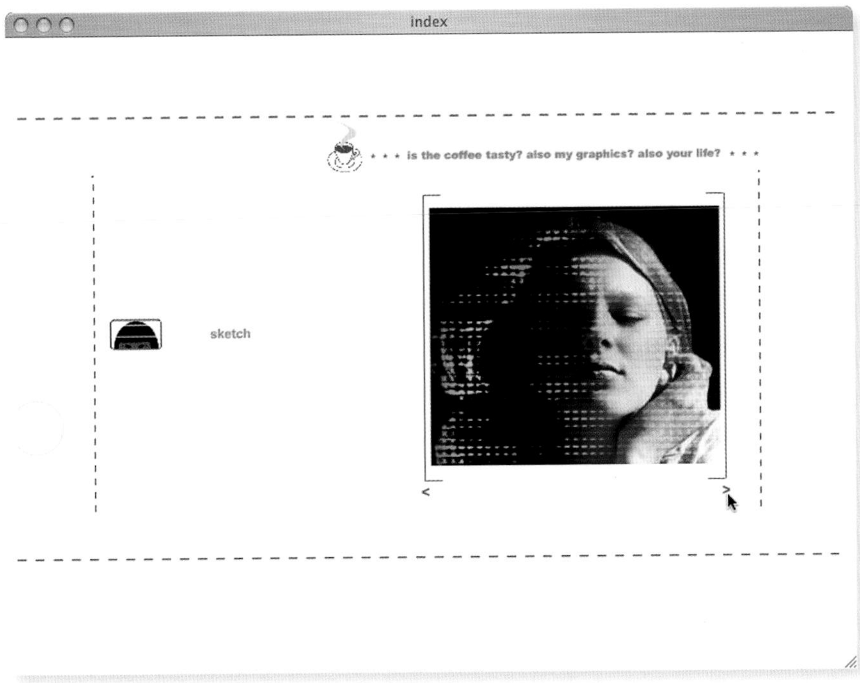
index
is the coffee tasty? also my graphics? also your life?
sketch

www.cocoluu.com

D: lu wang
M: cocoluu@hotmal.com

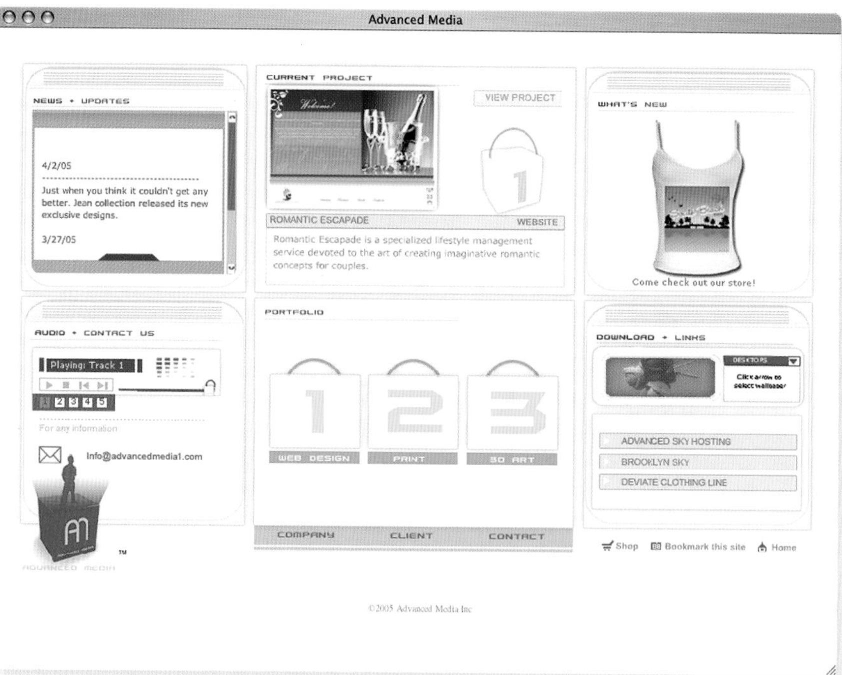
Advanced Media
NEWS + UPDATES
4/2/05
Just when you think it couldn't get any better. Jean collection released its new exclusive designs.
3/27/05
CURRENT PROJECT
VIEW PROJECT
ROMANTIC ESCAPADE
WEBSITE
Romantic Escapade is a specialized lifestyle management service devoted to the art of creating imaginative romantic concepts for couples.
WHAT'S NEW
Come check out our store!
AUDIO + CONTACT US
Playing: Track 1
For any information
Info@advancedmedia1.com
PORTFOLIO
WEB DESIGN
PRINT
3D ART
DOWNLOAD + LINKS
ADVANCED SKY HOSTING
BROOKLYN SKY
DEVIATE CLOTHING LINE
COMPANY
CLIENT
CONTACT
Shop
Bookmark this site
Home
©2005 Advanced Media Inc

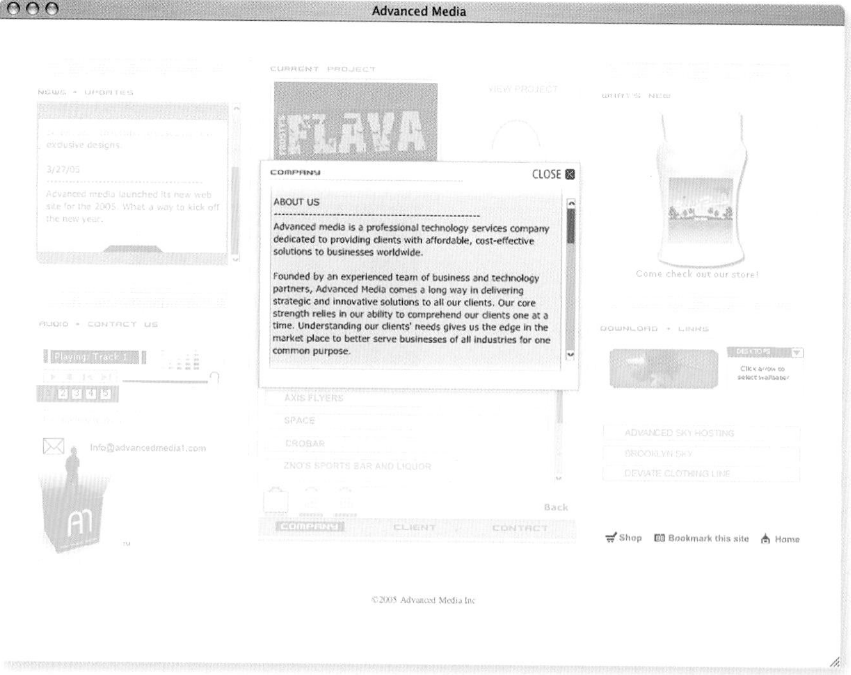
Advanced Media
FLAVA
COMPANY
CLOSE
ABOUT US
Advanced media is a professional technology services company dedicated to providing clients with affordable, cost-effective solutions to businesses worldwide.
Founded by an experienced team of business and technology partners, Advanced Media comes a long way in delivering strategic and innovative solutions to all our clients. Our core strength relies in our ability to comprehend our clients one at a time. Understanding our clients' needs gives us the edge in the market place to better serve businesses of all industries for one common purpose.
Shop
Bookmark this site
Home
©2005 Advanced Media Inc

www.advancedmedia1.com
D: jean r. delcin
A: advanced media inc. **M:** info@advancedmedia1.com

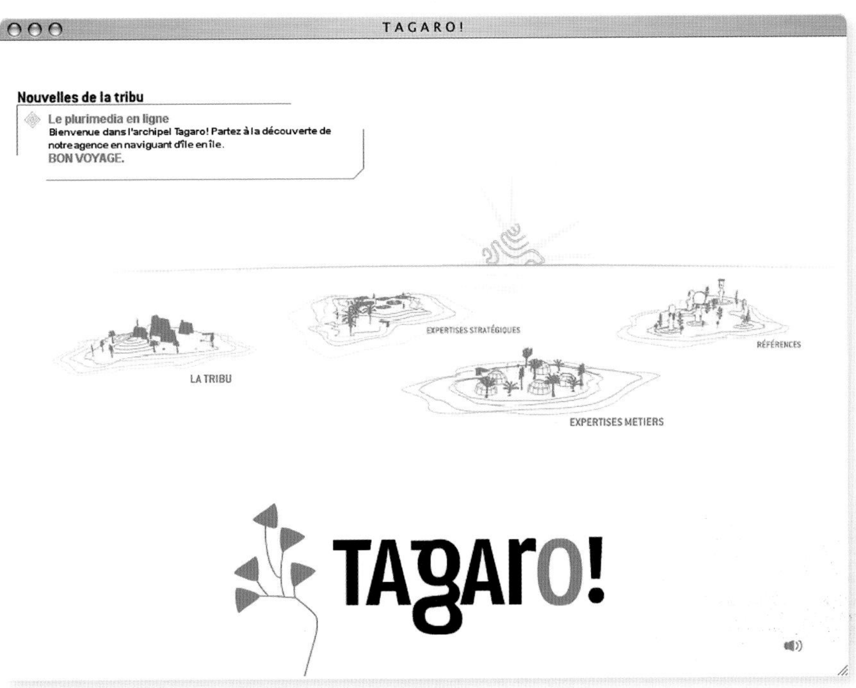
TAGARO!
Nouvelles de la tribu
Le plurimedia en ligne
Bienvenue dans l'archipel Tagaro! Partez à la découverte de notre agence en naviguant d'île en île.
BON VOYAGE.
EXPERTISES STRATÉGIQUES
RÉFÉRENCES
LA TRIBU
EXPERTISES METIERS
TAgArO!

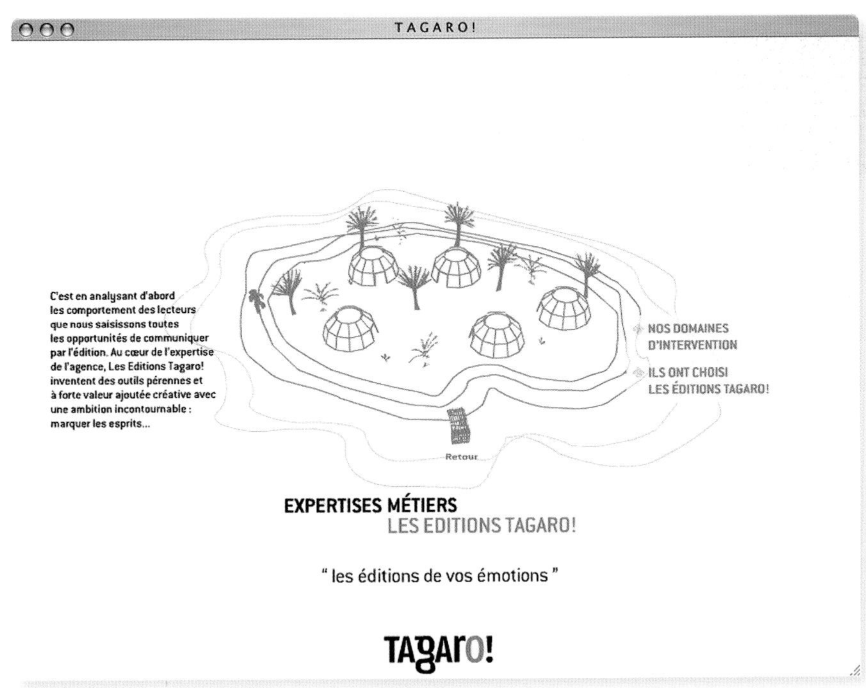
TAGARO!
C'est en analysant d'abord les comportement des lecteurs que nous saisissons toutes les opportunités de communiquer par l'édition. Au cœur de l'expertise de l'agence, Les Editions Tagaro! inventent des outils pérennes et à forte valeur ajoutée créative avec une ambition incontournable : marquer les esprits...
NOS DOMAINES D'INTERVENTION
ILS ONT CHOISI LES ÉDITIONS TAGARO!
Retour
EXPERTISES MÉTIERS
LES EDITIONS TAGARO!
" les éditions de vos émotions "
TAgArO!

www.tagaro.fr

D: jean-philippe maigret **C:** alexandre koch **P:** laurent malvaux
A: tagaro **M:** jean-philippe.maigret@tagaro.fr

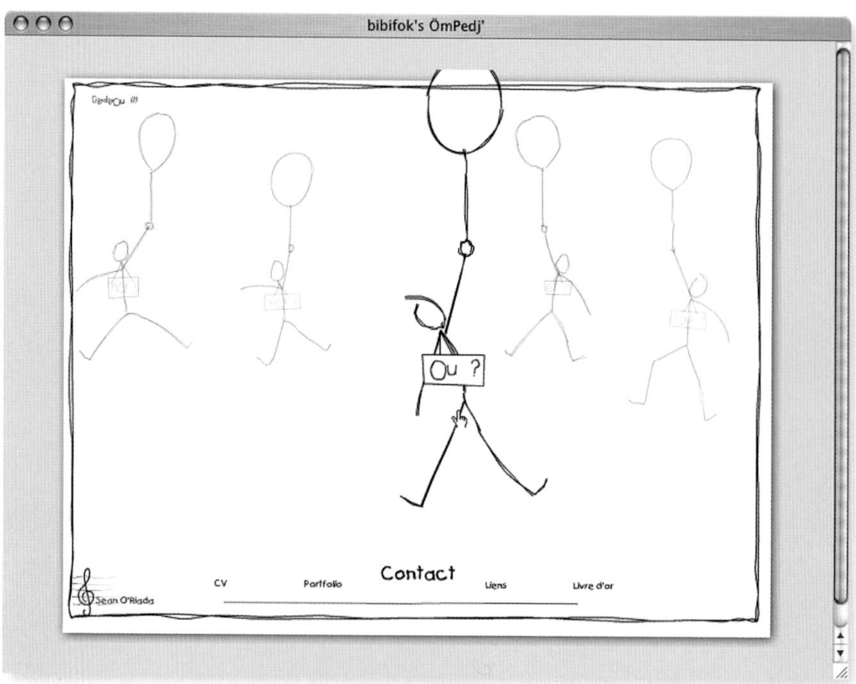
bibifok's ÖmPedj'
Ou ?
Contact
CV
Portfolio
Liens
Livre d'or
Sean O'Riada

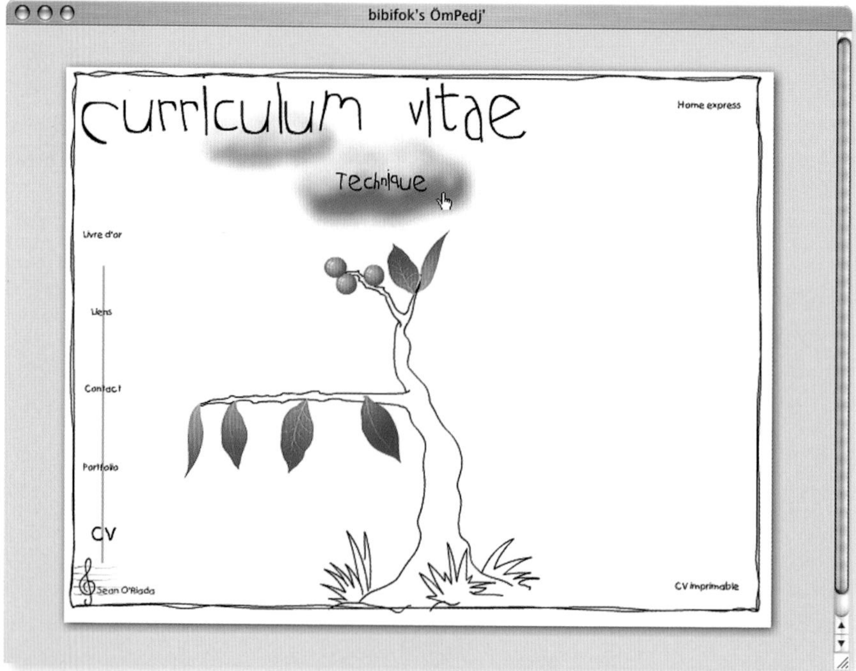
bibifok's ÖmPedj'
curriculum vitae
Home express
Technique
Livre d'or
Liens
Contact
Portfolio
CV
Sean O'Riada
CV imprimable

www.filigrif.com
D: philippe delvigne
A: filigrif **M:** pdelvigne@nerim.fr

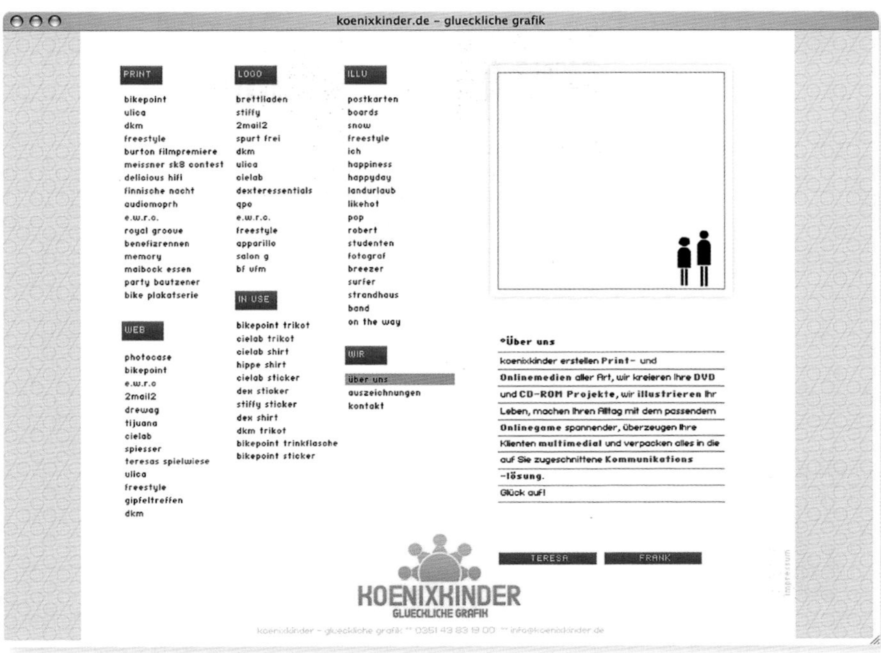
koenixkinder.de – glueckliche grafik
PRINT
bikepoint
ulica
dkm
freestyle
burton filmpremiere
meissner sk8 contest
delicious hifi
finnische nacht
audiomoprh
e.w.r.c.
royal groove
benefizrennen
memory
malbeck essen
party bautzener
bike plakatserie
WEB
photocase
bikepoint
e.w.r.c
2mail2
drewag
tijuana
cielab
spiesser
teresas spielwiese
ulica
freestyle
gipfeltreffen
dkm
LOGO
brettlladen
stiffy
2mail2
spurt frei
dkm
ulica
cielab
dexteressentials
qpo
e.w.r.c.
freestyle
apparillo
salon g
bf ufm
IN USE
bikepoint trikot
cielab trikot
cielab shirt
hippe shirt
cielab sticker
dex sticker
stiffy sticker
dex shirt
dkm trikot
bikepoint trinkflasche
bikepoint sticker
ILLU
postkarten
boards
snow
freestyle
ich
happiness
happyday
landurlaub
likehot
pop
robert
studenten
fotograf
breezer
surfer
strandhaus
band
on the way
WIR
über uns
auszeichnungen
kontakt
°Über uns
koenixkinder erstellen Print- und
Onlinemedien aller Art, wir kreieren Ihre DVD
und CD-ROM Projekte, wir illustrieren Ihr
Leben, machen Ihren Alltag mit dem passendem
Onlinegame spannender, überzeugen Ihre
Klienten multimedial und verpacken alles in die
auf Sie zugeschnittene Kommunikations
-lösung.
Glück auf!
TERESA
FRANK
KOENIXKINDER
GLUECKLICHE GRAFIK
impressum

koenixkinder.de – glueckliche grafik
PRINT
bikepoint
ulica
dkm
freestyle
burton filmpremiere
meissner sk8 contest
delicious hifi
finnische nacht
audiomoprh
e.w.r.c.
royal groove
benefizrennen
memory
malbeck essen
party bautzener
bike plakatserie
WEB
photocase
bikepoint
e.w.r.c
2mail2
drewag
tijuana
cielab
spiesser
teresas spielwiese
ulica
freestyle
gipfeltreffen
dkm
LOGO
brettlladen
stiffy
2mail2
spurt frei
dkm
ulica
cielab
dexteressentials
qpo
e.w.r.c.
freestyle
apparillo
salon g
bf ufm
IN USE
bikepoint trikot
cielab trikot
cielab shirt
hippe shirt
cielab sticker
dex sticker
stiffy sticker
dex shirt
dkm trikot
bikepoint trinkflasche
bikepoint sticker
ILLU
postkarten
boards
snow
ich
happiness
happyday
landurlaub
likehot
pop
robert
studenten
fotograf
breezer
surfer
strandhaus
band
on the way
WIR
über uns
auszeichnungen
kontakt
Free style
°Freestyle
Citycard zur Bewerbung der Nichtraucher-
kampagne für Jugendliche in Sachsen.
GROSSE ANSICHT
KOENIXKINDER
GLUECKLICHE GRAFIK
impressum

www.koenixkinder.de
D: frank erler, teresa schebiella
A: koenixkinder - glueckliche grafik **M:** teresa@koenixkinder.de

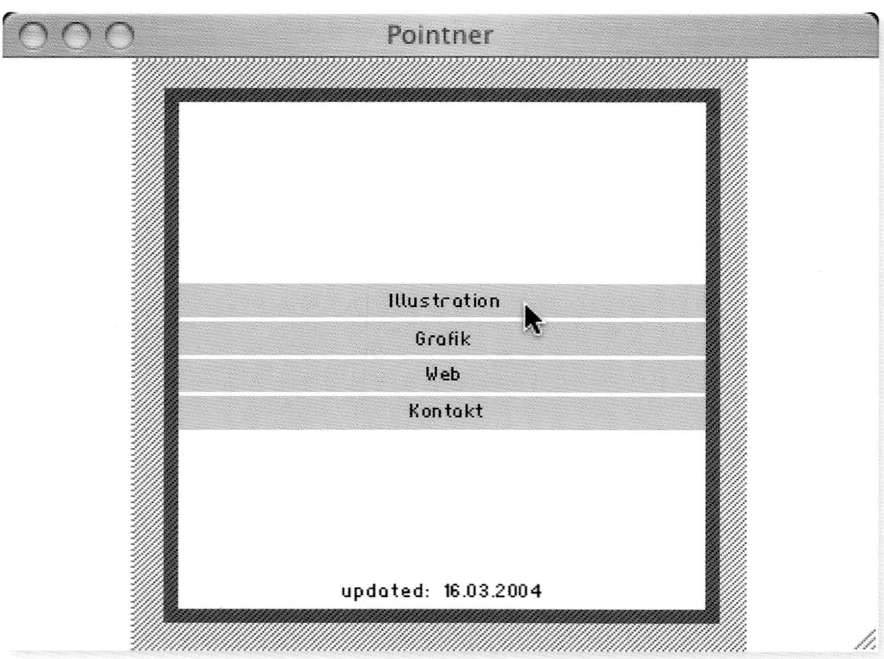
Pointner
Illustration
Grafik
Web
Kontakt
updated: 16.03.2004

Pointner

www.mindwarp.at/pointner
D: michael pointner
A: loop + logo **M:** bounty@mindwarp.at

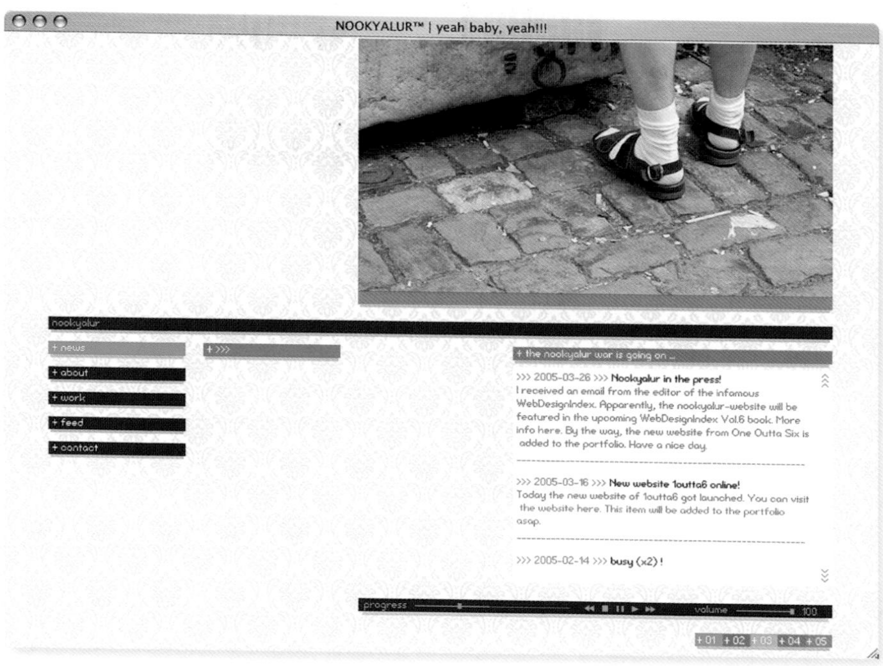
NOOKYALUR™ | yeah baby, yeah!!!
nookyalur
+ news
+ about
+ work
+ feed
+ contact
+ >>>
+ the nookyalur war is going on ...
>>> 2005-03-26 >>> Nookyalur in the press!
I received an email from the editor of the infamous WebDesignIndex. Apparently, the nookyalur-website will be featured in the upcoming WebDesignIndex Vol.6 book. More info here. By the way, the new website from One Outta Six is added to the portfolio. Have a nice day.
>>> 2005-03-16 >>> New website 1outta6 online!
Today the new website of 1outta6 got launched. You can visit the website here. This item will be added to the portfolio asap.
>>> 2005-02-14 >>> busy (x2)!
progress
volume
100
+ 01 + 02 + 03 + 04 + 05

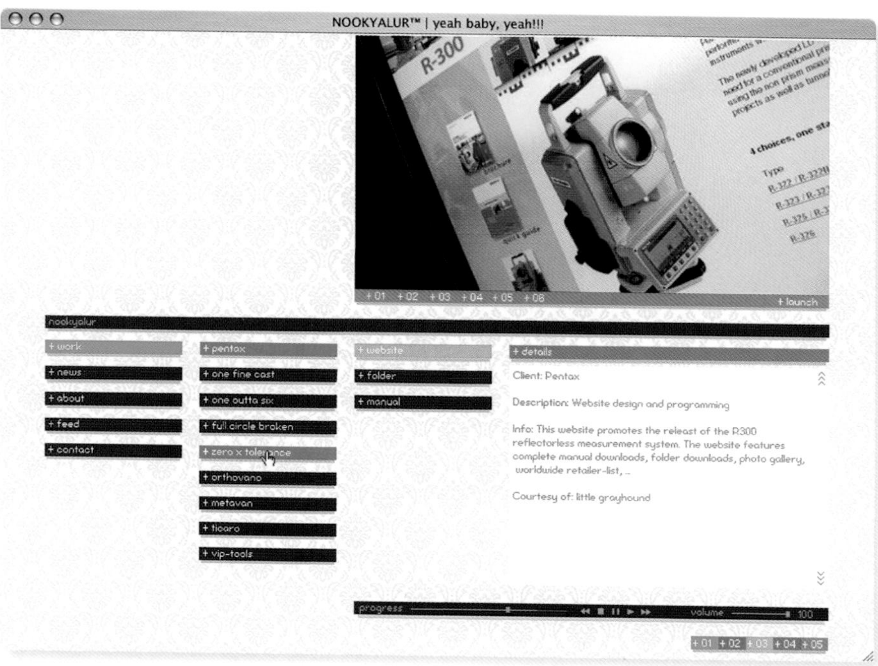
NOOKYALUR™ | yeah baby, yeah!!!
R-300
+ 01 + 02 + 03 + 04 + 05 + 06
+ launch
nookyalur
+ work
+ news
+ about
+ feed
+ contact
+ pentax
+ one fine cast
+ one outta six
+ full circle broken
+ zero x tolerance
+ orthovano
+ metavan
+ ticaro
+ vip-tools
+ website
+ folder
+ manual
+ details
Client: Pentax
Description: Website design and programming
Info: This website promotes the release of the R300 reflectorless measurement system. The website features complete manual downloads, folder downloads, photo gallery, worldwide retailer-list, ...
Courtesy of: little grayhound
progress
volume
100
+ 01 + 02 + 03 + 04 + 05

www.nookyalur.com
D: laurent lampaert
A: nookyalur **M:** info@nookyalur.com

PagePlay.com - publishing and design services for everyone.
pageplay.
pageplay
1) evolving story
2) editorial services
3) design services
4) publishing solutions
RESOURCES
* customer comments
speak to us?
© PagePlay. All Rights Reserved 2004.
Speak.

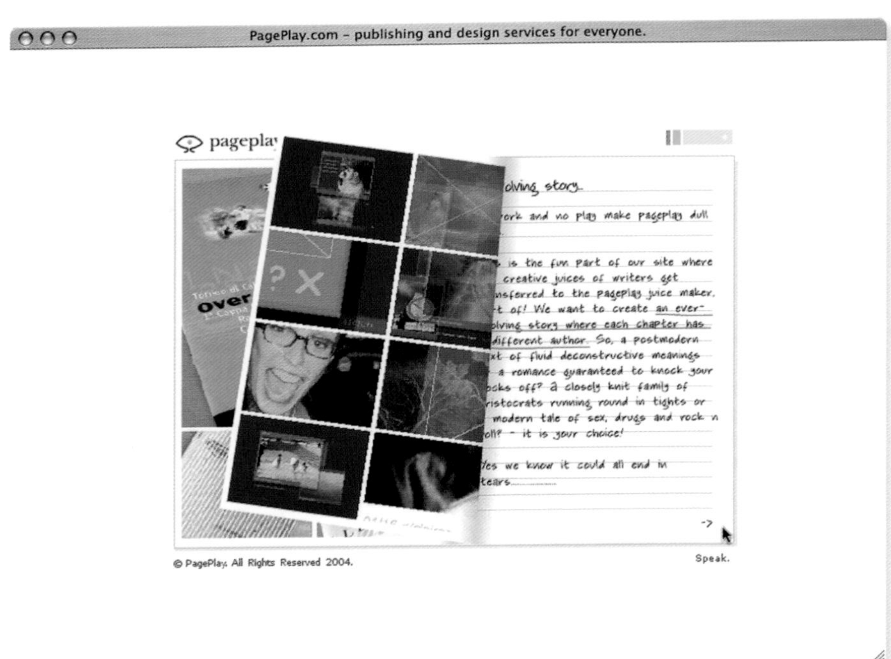
PagePlay.com - publishing and design services for everyone.
© PagePlay. All Rights Reserved 2004.
Speak.

www.pageplay.com
D: anthony la pusata
A: pageplay **M:** republika04@tiscali.it

the site of yooco

works
(c) 2004 yooco tanimoto
art direction & design : nem visual concept : yooco

the site of yooco

Still Lifes

back

www.yooco.com
D: yooco tanimoto, shinji nemoto **C:** shinji nemoto **P:** yooco tanimoto
A: yooco tanimoto **M:** web@yooco.com

cg.
home
chameleongraphics.
Chameleon Graphics – kurz cg. – bietet Ihnen kreative Grafik- und Weblösungen. Wir sind der richtige Partner für Printdesign, Corporate Design und Webdesign. In der Verbindung von grafischem Können und technischem Know-how liegt die Stärke unseres Unternehmens.
© 2005 chameleon graphics | letzte Aktualisierung 4/05

cg.
das team
chameleongraphics.
JAMAICA
UNIV.
PRINCESS
68
© 2005 chameleon graphics | letzte Aktualisierung 4/05

www.chameleongraphics.ch
D: michel seeliger
A: chameleon graphics **M:** info@chameleongraphics.ch

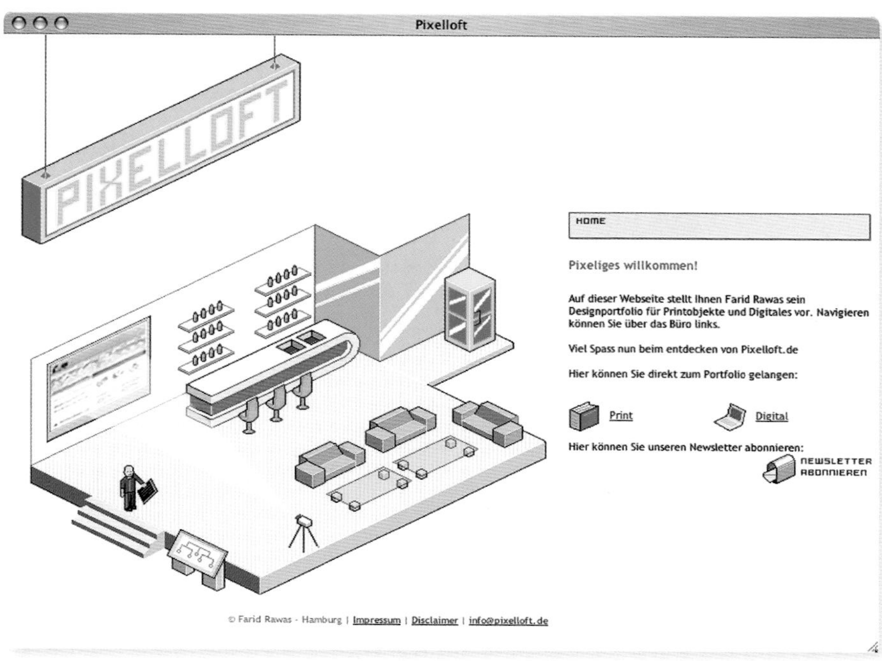
Pixelloft
PIXELLOFT
HOME
Pixeliges willkommen!
Auf dieser Webseite stellt Ihnen Farid Rawas sein Designportfolio für Printobjekte und Digitales vor. Navigieren können Sie über das Büro links.
Viel Spass nun beim entdecken von Pixelloft.de
Hier können Sie direkt zum Portfolio gelangen:
Print
Digital
Hier können Sie unseren Newsletter abonnieren:
NEWSLETTER ABONNIEREN
© Farid Rawas - Hamburg | Impressum | Disclaimer | info@pixelloft.de

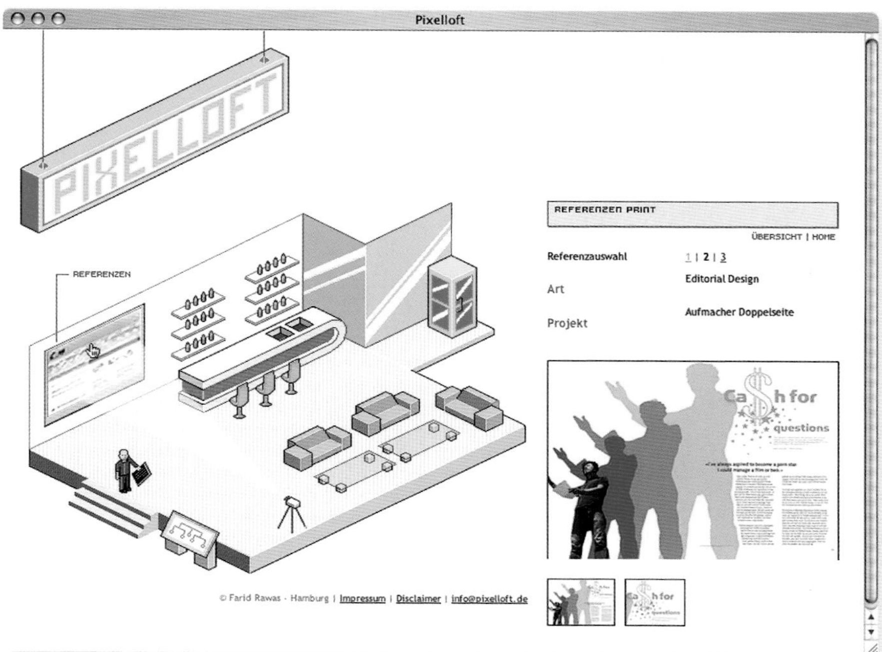
Pixelloft
PIXELLOFT
REFERENZEN
REFERENZEN PRINT
ÜBERSICHT | HOME
Referenzauswahl
1 | 2 | 3
Art
Editorial Design
Projekt
Aufmacher Doppelseite
Ca$h for questions
© Farid Rawas - Hamburg | Impressum | Disclaimer | info@pixelloft.de

www.pixelloft.de
D: mohamed rawas
A: pixelloft **M:** info@pixelloft.de

G31D kreatívna agentúra - webdesign / marketing solutions / direct mail / design outsourcing

There are only several things important in life. We found design at first place

filozofia naša práca kontakt

[G31D] KREATÍVNA AGENTÚRA

V ŽIVOTE JE LEN NIEKOĽKO DÔLEŽITÝCH VECÍ.
PRE NÁS JE NA PRVOM MIESTE DESIGN.

↗ VITAJTE

Kľúčom je kreativita. Nie sme kreatívna agentúra len preto že to máme napísané v claime, ale kôli kvalite produktov, ktoré ponúkame. Vieme že moderné design riešenia nemusia byť len divoké krivky a nerozpoznateľné obrázky. Pozrite si naše práce a pochopíte.

mapa serveru
F.A.Q.
povedzte nám Váš názor

© 2005 G31D; Všetky práva vyhradené. právne informácie

G31D kreatívna agentúra - webdesign / marketing solutions / direct mail / design outsourcing

Choose your advertising partner as good as your company is.

filozofia ▸ naša práca kontakt

[G31D] KREATÍVNA AGENTÚRA

V ŽIVOTE JE LEN NIEKOĽKO DÔLEŽITÝCH VECÍ.
PRE NÁS JE NA PRVOM MIESTE DESIGN.

↗ NAŠA PRÁCA

Potrebujete novú identitu? Radi Vám s tým pomôžeme. Vaša nová identita Vás však nezachráni pred zákonom, ale pomôže Vám pri prezentovaní Vašej spoločnosti. Vytvoríme pre Vás riešenie, ktoré sa pre Vás stane skutočnou identitou.

Na profesionálnej úrovni pre klientov pripravujeme nie len logá, design manuály, internetové prezentácie, inzercie, katalógy, ale aj menšie kampane, direct mailingy, alebo súťaže a vernostné programy. Neza-budnite si pozrieť naše referencie, ktoré Vám o našej práci povedia viac ako tisíce slov.

+ referencie

+ viac o internetových riešeniach
+ design outsourcing

mapa serveru
F.A.Q.
povedzte nám Váš názor

© 2005 G31D; Všetky práva vyhradené. právne informácie

www.g31d.com
D: vitkor kovac
A: g31d **M:** info@g31d.com

Nikola Krajačić | blackshtef.org

blackshtef.orgportfolio of Nikola Krajačić

hostingplus.hr

Taking a day off

I must say that there will be no updates on the site since I'm taking my computer to Bjelovar, where I will have no internet connection :o(
Also, I'm currently working on new blackshtef.org site, which will have totally different concept than this one...
cya

I'm a driver now :o)

Finnaly, I got my own driving licence :D
No more need to play NFS Underground now :o)

R-on3

Here's one interesting portfolrio with very cool navigation, check it.
R-On3

/me returns :o)

Hello friends!
Sorry for this, non-update interval, but I really don't have time for my computer, since I go home once a month :o(
I have some new works for portfolio, but don't have time to put them on-line. As soon as I get 5 minutes free, you'll see it.

Allow me to introduce myself to you. As you already may noticed, my real name is **Nikola Krajačić**, I'm 17, and I attend the Techincal school in Bjelovar. I am situated in small town in Croatia, named Grubišno Polje. Small town, small, but cute... I started designig somewhere in 2001., but I don't have any work from then, lost them all, unfortunatley.
blackshtef.org was on-line for the first time on **August, 17th 2003. at 15:00h**. That week I got sponsored hosting service from great guys at **plus.hr**. Pay them a visit or two!
In my freetime, I listen to music (techno/house/dance), ride a bike or drink coffee with my parents. I must say I like to sleep for a long time

Currently, I'm in a relationship with one very special girl, **A.P. (15)**, and I wolud like to thank her for very big support during my hard time at school. **Thanks, Milka!** Well, that's about it...if you have any questions, send me a message, drop me an SMS, call if you want

Enjoy the site!

Nikola Krajačić | blackshtef
freelance designer
Cellular phone : +38598/540-048
Icq UIN : 98362380
Current Icq status :
Your name :
Your e-mail address :
Message :
Send enquiry
Clear everything

NEWS ABOUT CONTACT

1 HOME | 2 PRINT | 3 PHOTO | 4 SCREEN | 5 WEB | 6 BLOG

Nikola Krajačić | blackshtef.org
blackshtef.orgportfolio of Nikola Krajačić
hostingplus.hr
Type of work | personal bussines card
Created in | Adobe Photoshop
Printed | Yes
NIKOLA KRAJAČIĆ | BLACKSHTEF.ORG
PREVIEW
INFO
1
HOME
2
PRINT
3
PHOTO
4
SCREEN
5
WEB
6
BLOG

blackshtef.org
D: nikola kraja
M: contact@blackshtef.org

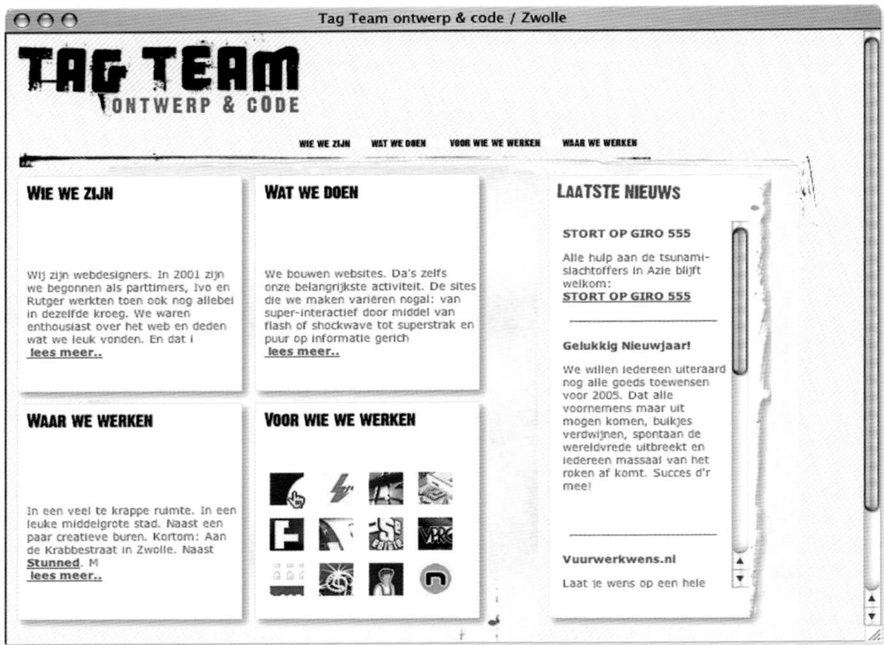

Tag Team ontwerp & code / Zwolle
TAG TEAM
ONTWERP & CODE
WIE WE ZIJN
WAT WE DOEN
VOOR WIE WE WERKEN
WAAR WE WERKEN
WIE WE ZIJN
Wij zijn webdesigners. In 2001 zijn we begonnen als parttimers, Ivo en Rutger werkten toen ook nog allebei in dezelfde kroeg. We waren enthousiast over het web en deden wat we leuk vonden. En dat i
lees meer..
WAT WE DOEN
We bouwen websites. Da's zelfs onze belangrijkste activiteit. De sites die we maken variëren nogal: van super-interactief door middel van flash of shockwave tot superstrak en puur op informatie gerich
lees meer..
LAATSTE NIEUWS
STORT OP GIRO 555
Alle hulp aan de tsunami-slachtoffers in Azie blijft welkom:
STORT OP GIRO 555
Gelukkig Nieuwjaar!
We willen iedereen uiteraard nog alle goeds toewensen voor 2005. Dat alle voornemens maar uit mogen komen, buikjes verdwijnen, spontaan de wereldvrede uitbreekt en iedereen massaal van het roken af komt. Succes d'r mee!
Vuurwerkwens.nl
Laat je wens op een hele
WAAR WE WERKEN
In een veel te krappe ruimte. In een leuke middelgrote stad. Naast een paar creatieve buren. Kortom: Aan de Krabbestraat in Zwolle. Naast Stunned. M
lees meer..
VOOR WIE WE WERKEN

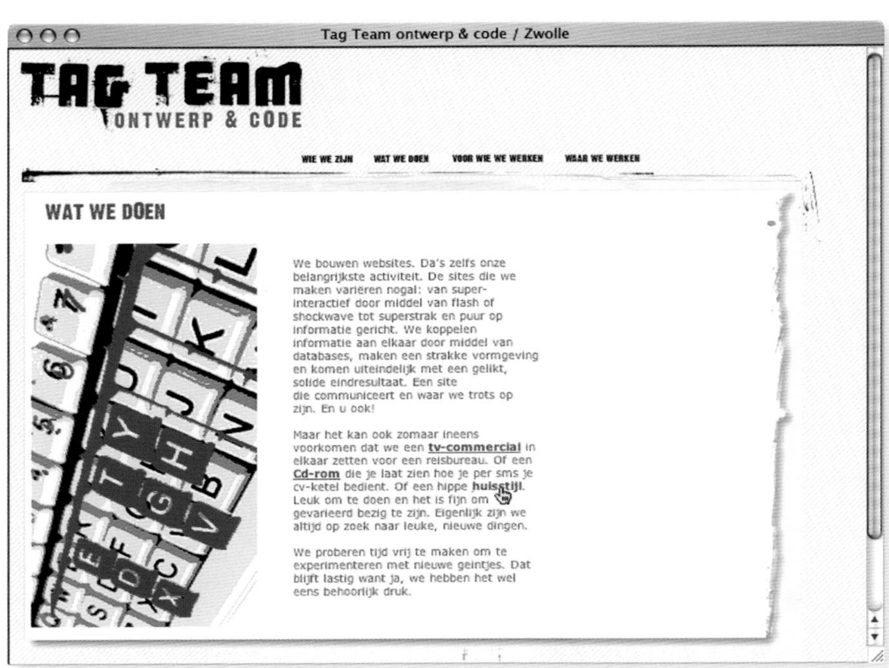

Tag Team ontwerp & code / Zwolle
TAG TEAM
ONTWERP & CODE
WIE WE ZIJN
WAT WE DOEN
VOOR WIE WE WERKEN
WAAR WE WERKEN
WAT WE DOEN
We bouwen websites. Da's zelfs onze belangrijkste activiteit. De sites die we maken variëren nogal: van super-interactief door middel van flash of shockwave tot superstrak en puur op informatie gericht. We koppelen informatie aan elkaar door middel van databases, maken een strakke vormgeving en komen uiteindelijk met een gelikt, solide eindresultaat. Een site die communiceert en waar we trots op zijn. En u ook!
Maar het kan ook zomaar ineens voorkomen dat we een tv-commercial in elkaar zetten voor een reisbureau. Of een Cd-rom die je laat zien hoe je per sms je cv-ketel bedient. Of een hippe huisstijl. Leuk om te doen en het is fijn om gevarieerd bezig te zijn. Eigenlijk zijn we altijd op zoek naar leuke, nieuwe dingen.
We proberen tijd vrij te maken om te experimenteren met nieuwe geintjes. Dat blijft lastig want ja, we hebben het wel eens behoorlijk druk.

www.tag-team.nl
D: ivo boerdam
A: tag team **M:** ivo@tag-team.nl

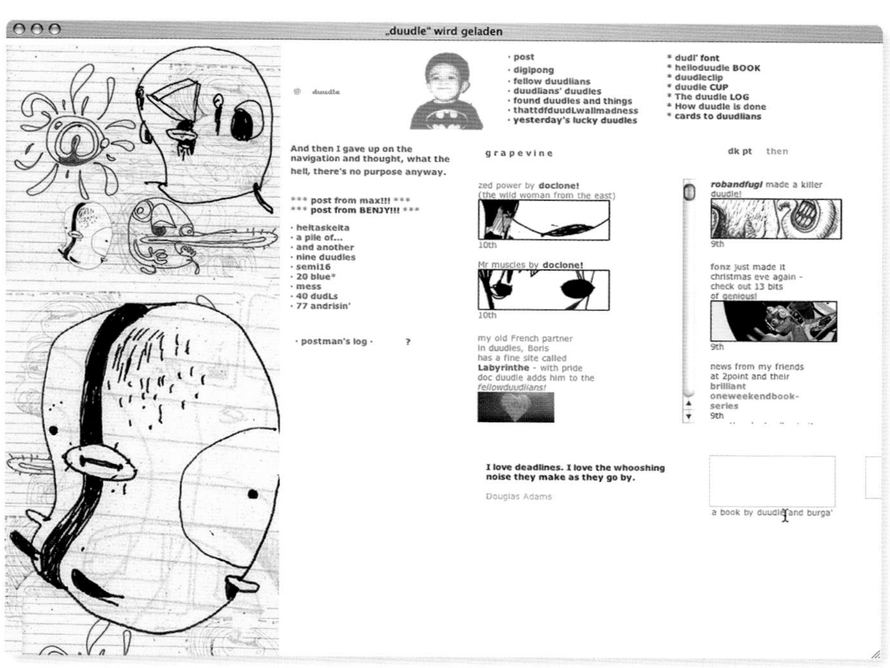

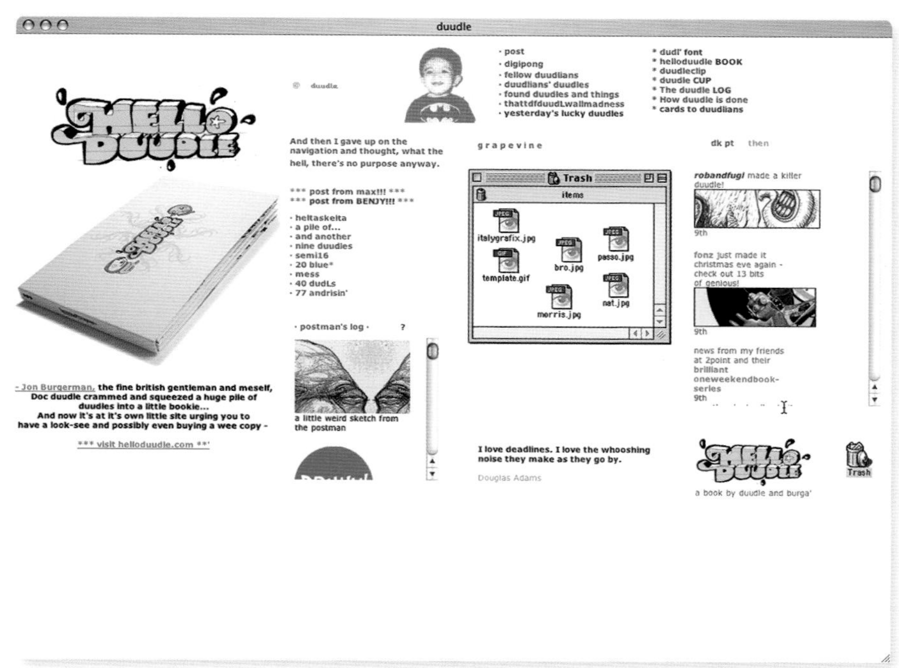

www.duudle.dk
D: sune ehlers
A: duudle M: ehlers@zilo.dk

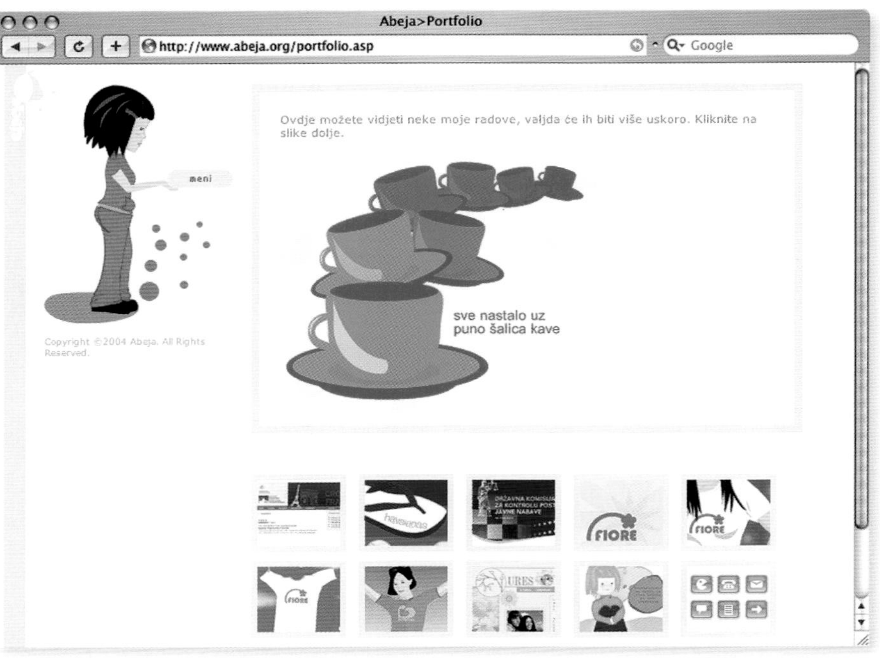
Abeja>Portfolio
http://www.abeja.org/portfolio.asp
Google
meni
Copyright ©2004 Abeja. All Rights Reserved.
Ovdje možete vidjeti neke moje radove, valjda će ih biti više uskoro. Kliknite na slike dolje.
sve nastalo uz
puno šalica kave

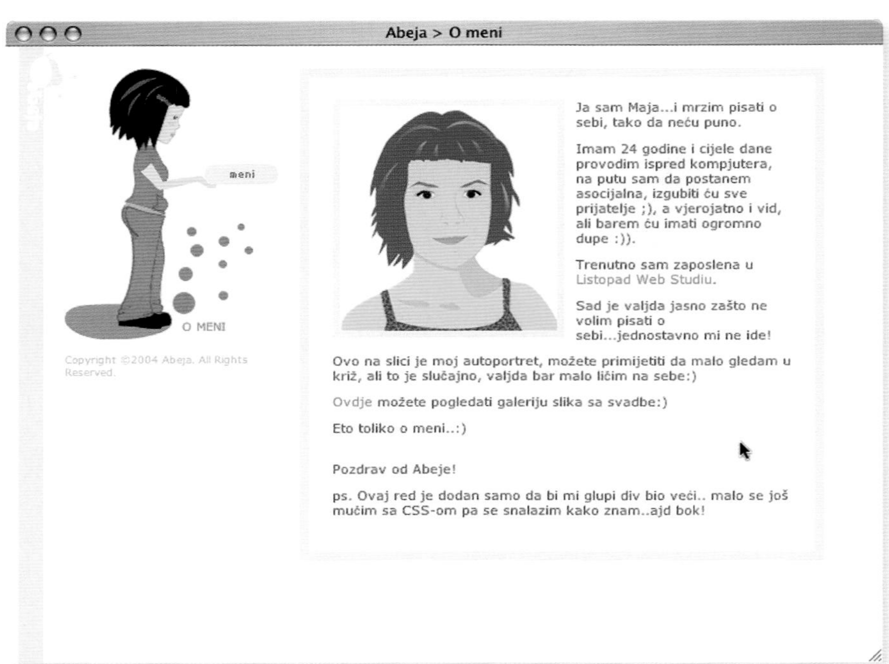
Abeja > O meni
meni
O MENI
Copyright ©2004 Abeja. All Rights Reserved.
Ja sam Maja...i mrzim pisati o sebi, tako da neću puno.
Imam 24 godine i cijele dane provodim ispred kompjutera, na putu sam da postanem asocijalna, izgubiti ću sve prijatelje ;), a vjerojatno i vid, ali barem ću imati ogromno dupe :)).
Trenutno sam zaposlena u Listopad Web Studiu.
Sad je valjda jasno zašto ne volim pisati o sebi...jednostavno mi ne ide!
Ovo na slici je moj autoportret, možete primijetiti da malo gledam u križ, ali to je slučajno, valjda bar malo ličim na sebe:)
Ovdje možete pogledati galeriju slika sa svadbe:)
Eto toliko o meni..:)
Pozdrav od Abeje!
ps. Ovaj red je dodan samo da bi mi glupi div bio veći.. malo se još mučim sa CSS-om pa se snalazim kako znam..ajd bok!

www.abeja.cosmosart.org
D: maja bencic
M: maja.bencic@pu.htnet.hr

subfuse studios | made with computers

subfuse studios
AMSTERDAM | BERLIN

1.PORTFOLIO 2.FREEWORK 3.INFO 4.CONTACT 5.PROJECTS 6.DOWNLOADS

046.WTFF MENU2 GFX
045.FIOD ILLUSTRATION
044.SUPERMEN
043.WTFF DELETED
042.MACHI SITE
041.GAME ILLUSTRATION
040.SWAAB ILLUSTRATION
039.LAURA ILLUSTRATION
038.MCGREGOR ILLUSTRATION
037.OIL ILLUSTRATIONS
036.BATTLE ILLUSTRATIONS
035.WTFF SHIRTS
034.RICHE TEST
033.DE STILLE MACHT
032.WTFF STUFF
031.CLUBIT CONCEPT
030.ONEILL DESIGN
029.SINNERS ID AND SITE
028.COMMERCIAL 01 RDD
027.FAMILY ILLUSTRATIONS

<< PREV | NEXT >>

039.LAURA ILLUSTRATION
ILLUSTRATION FOR A CLIENT FROM HOT-DNA (ALLSPORTS). THIS ONE APPEARS ON A POSTCARD WHICH ALLSPORTS (FITNESS / GYM) SENDS OUT TO THEIR CLIENTS WHO HAVE A BIRTDAY. BASICALLY SAYING THAT IT'S OK TO EAT A BIRTHDAY CAKE SINCE YOU'RE GOING BACK TO THE GYM TO LOSE SOME WEIGHT ANYWAYS. CONCEPT BY HOT-DNA. SEE EXTRA OPTIONS FOR A FULL VIEW.

HTTP://WWW.HOT-DNA.COM

EXTRA OPTIONS:
ILLUSTRATION.GIF

<< LEFT | RIGHT >>

subfuse studios | made with computers

subfuse studios
AMSTERDAM | BERLIN

1.PORTFOLIO 2.FREEWORK 3.INFO 4.CONTACT 5.PROJECTS 6.DOWNLOADS

051.LANDMARK ILL NEW
050.SOCCER ANIMATION NEW
049.PAUW ILL NEW
048.ACHTEN ILL NEW
047.MATRYOSHKAS ILL
046.WTFF MENU2 GFX
045.FIOD ILLUSTRATION
044.SUPERMEN
043.WTFF DELETED
042.MACHI SITE
041.GAME ILLUSTRATION
040.SWAAB ILLUSTRATION
039.LAURA ILLUSTRATION
038.MCGREGOR ILLUSTRATION
037.OIL ILLUSTRATIONS
036.BATTLE ILLUSTRATIONS
035.WTFF SHIRTS
034.RICHE TEST
033.DE STILLE MACHT
032.WTFF STUFF

<< PREV | NEXT >>

051.LANDMARK ILL
ILLUSTRATIONS FOR QUOTE MAGAZINE. THE FEATURE IS ABOUT AN ORGANIZATION WHO IS A BIT SCIENTOLOGY-ESQUE. NOT RELIGIOUS AT ALL THOUGH. WHAT STRUCK US MOST WAS THE WAY HOW THEY PUSHED THE PEOPLE WHO WENT TO THEIR MEETINGS TO ENROLL MORE PEOPLE. FRIENDS, FAMILY AND COLLEAGUES, IT DOESN'T MATTER. AND YOU COULD ONLY BE HAPPY IF YOU WOULD HAVE ENROLLED A LOT OF PEOPLE. THE TACTIC THEY USE IS TO WEAR YOU DOWN PSYCHOLOGICALLY SO THAT YOU'LL SAY OR DO ANYTHING THEY SAY. HENCE COMPUTERHEADS AND ALL THE ENROLLING CONNECTIONS. PUBLISHED IN JUNE 2004. ALL THE STUFF YOU WANT TO SEE IS OVER AT THE RIGHT.

IT'S SIMPLE...

ENROLL...

EXTRA OPTIONS:
DETAIL_1.GIF
DETAIL_2.GIF
LANDMARK.SWF

<< LEFT | RIGHT >>

www.subfuse.net
D: eike menijn
A: subfuse **M:** eike@subfuse.net

#sEr
нумера
www
номера
растры и векторы
намера
повествования
номер ноль
не суждено быть
#sEr 2003, 2004
e-mail ser007@mail.ru
icq 172862569
grafika.com.ua

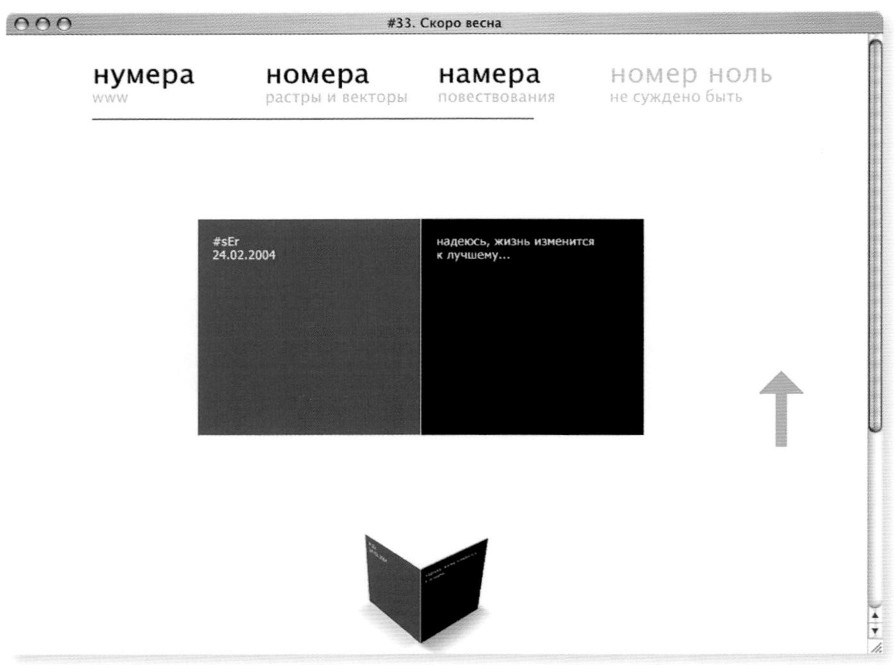
#33. Скоро весна
нумера
www
номера
растры и векторы
намера
повествования
номер ноль
не суждено быть
#sEr
24.02.2004
надеюсь, жизнь изменится
к лучшему...

www.grafika.com.ua
D: sergei kononenko
A: #ser **M:** ser007@yandex.ru

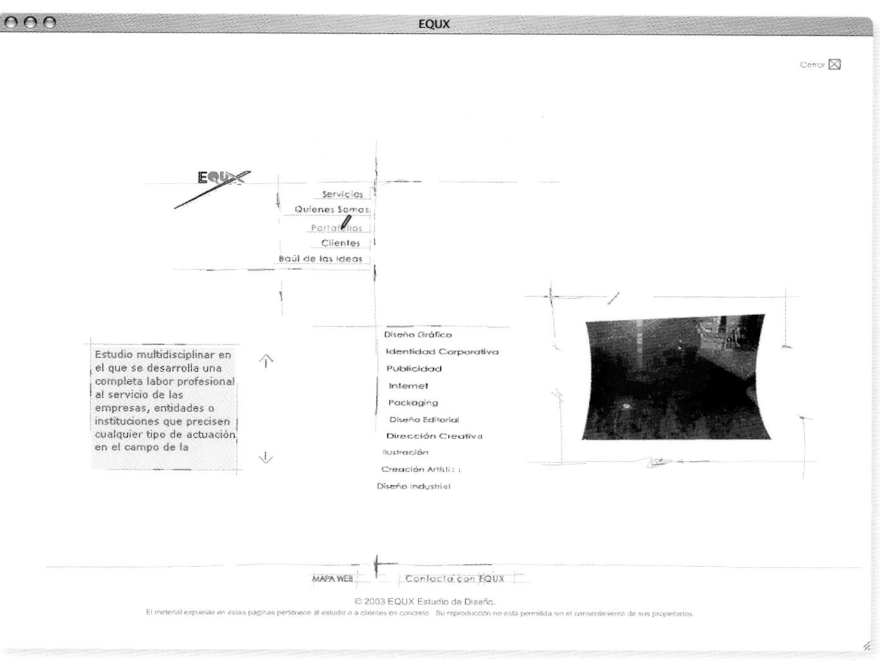
EQUX
Servicios
Quienes Somos
Portafolios
Clientes
Baúl de las Ideas
Estudio multidisciplinar en el que se desarrolla una completa labor profesional al servicio de las empresas, entidades o instituciones que precisen cualquier tipo de actuación en el campo de la
Diseño Gráfico
Identidad Corporativa
Publicidad
Internet
Packaging
Diseño Editorial
Dirección Creativa
Ilustración
Diseño Industrial
MAPA WEB
Contacta con EQUX
© 2003 EQUX Estudio de Diseño.

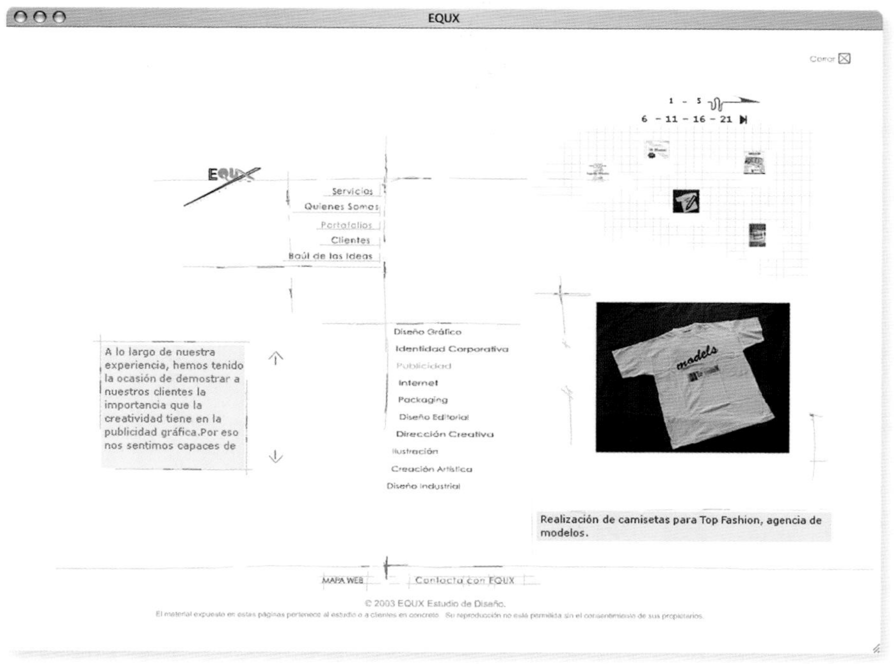
EQUX
1 - 5
6 - 11 - 16 - 21
Servicios
Quienes Somos
Portafolios
Clientes
Baúl de las Ideas
A lo largo de nuestra experiencia, hemos tenido la ocasión de demostrar a nuestros clientes la importancia que la creatividad tiene en la publicidad gráfica.Por eso nos sentimos capaces de
Diseño Gráfico
Identidad Corporativa
Publicidad
Internet
Packaging
Diseño Editorial
Dirección Creativa
Ilustración
Creación Artística
Diseño Industrial
Realización de camisetas para Top Fashion, agencia de modelos.
MAPA WEB
Contacta con EQUX
© 2003 EQUX Estudio de Diseño.

www.cesaraugusta.com/equx
D: miguel sanza pilas **C:** alfredo piqueras lasa
A: equx **M:** equx@cesaraugusta.com

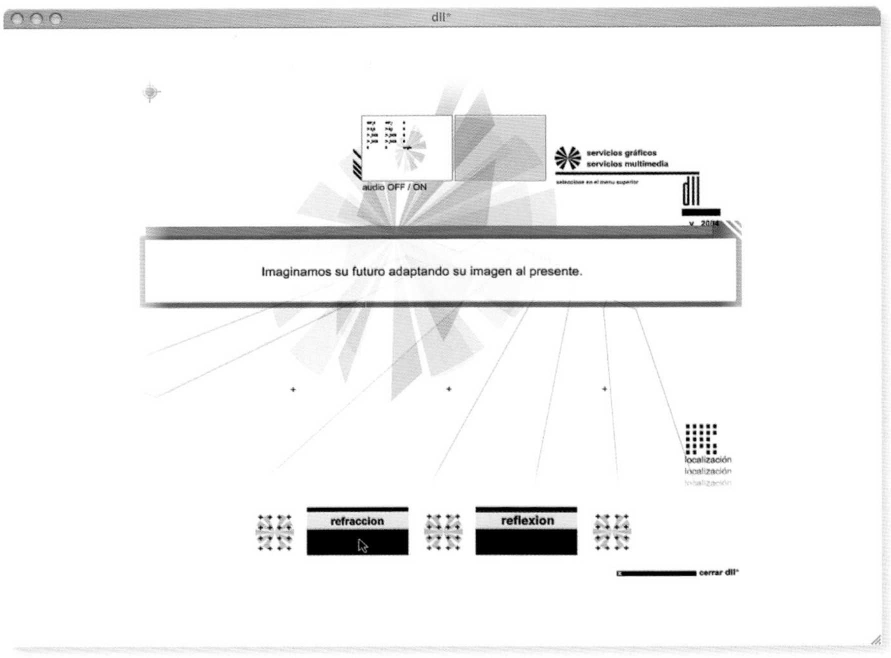
dll*
audio OFF / ON
servicios gráficos
servicios multimedia
dll
Imaginamos su futuro adaptando su imagen al presente.
localización
refraccion
reflexion
cerrar dll*

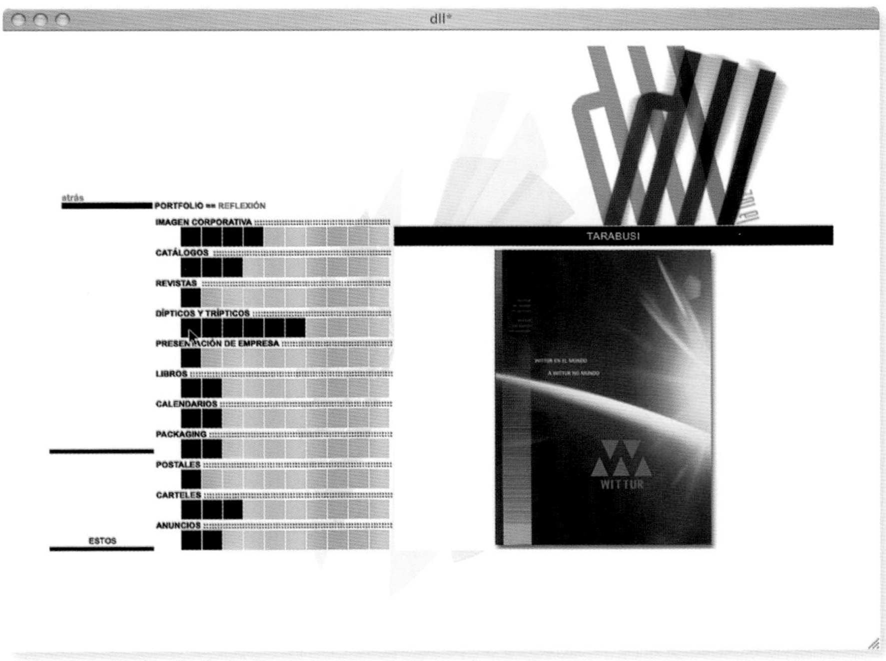
dll*
atrás
PORTFOLIO == REFLEXIÓN
IMAGEN CORPORATIVA
CATÁLOGOS
REVISTAS
DÍPTICOS Y TRÍPTICOS
PRESENTACIÓN DE EMPRESA
LIBROS
CALENDARIOS
PACKAGING
POSTALES
CARTELES
ANUNCIOS
ESTOS
TARABUSI
WITTUR

www.delaluz.org
D: angel j. lalana **P:** paco medina
A: delaluz **M:** alalana@delaluz.org

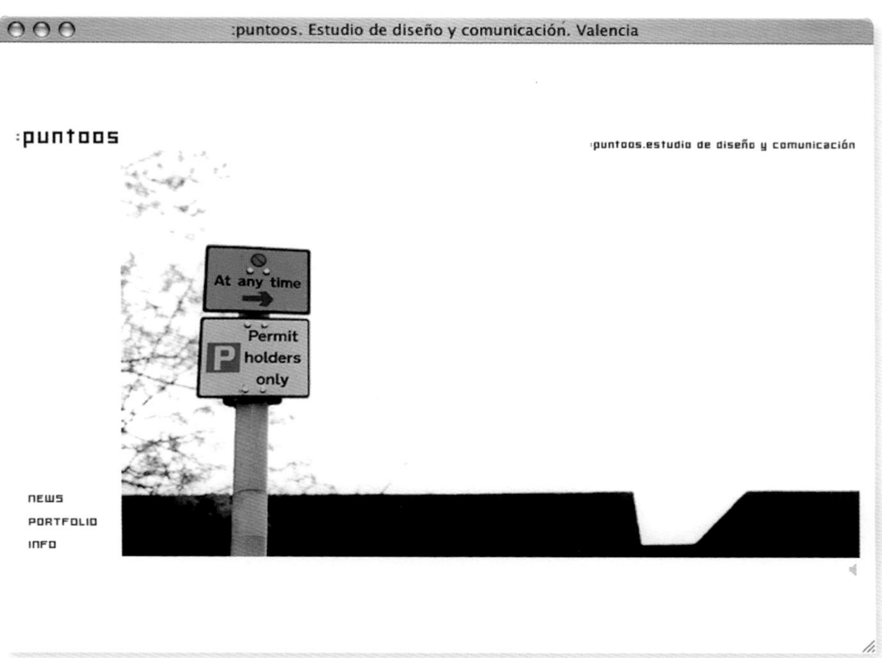
:puntoos. Estudio de diseño y comunicación. Valencia
:puntoos
:puntoos.estudio de diseño y comunicación
At any time
Permit holders only
news
PORTFOLIO
info

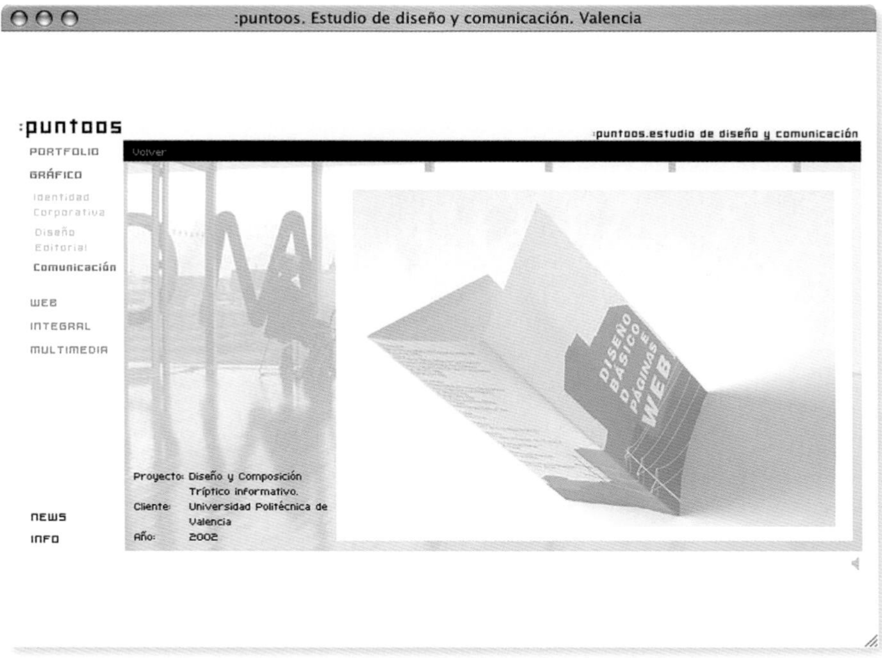
:puntoos. Estudio de diseño y comunicación. Valencia
:puntoos
:puntoos.estudio de diseño y comunicación
PORTFOLIO
GRÁFICO
Identidad Corporativa
Diseño Editorial
Comunicación
WEB
INTEGRAL
MULTIMEDIA
news
info
Volver
Proyecto: Diseño y Composición Tríptico informativo.
Cliente: Universidad Politécnica de Valencia
Año: 2002

www.puntoos.com
D: miguel ángel moya, cristina muñoz
A: puntoos **M:** miguel@puntoos.com

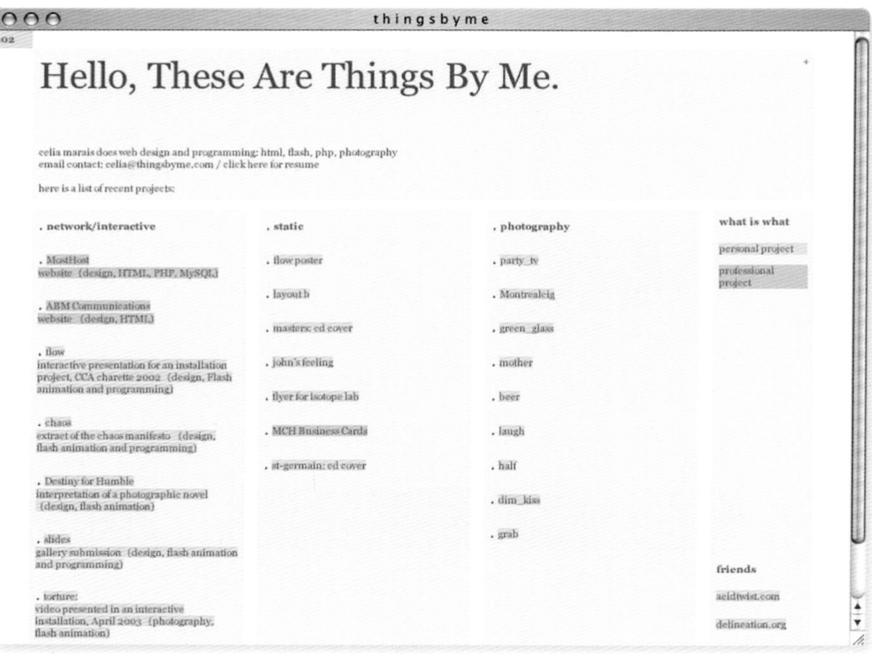
thingsbyme
Hello, These Are Things By Me.
celia marais does web design and programming: html, flash, php, photography
email contact: celia@thingsbyme.com / click here for resume
here is a list of recent projects:
. network/interactive
. MostHost
website (design, HTML, PHP, MySQL)
. ABM Communications
website (design, HTML)
. flow
interactive presentation for an installation project, CCA charette 2002 (design, Flash animation and programming)
. chaos
extract of the chaos manifesto (design, flash animation and programming)
. Destiny for Humble
interpretation of a photographic novel (design, flash animation)
. slides
gallery submission (design, flash animation and programming)
. torture:
video presented in an interactive installation, April 2003 (photography, flash animation)
. static
. flow poster
. layout b
. masters: cd cover
. john's feeling
. flyer for isotope lab
. MCH Business Cards
. st-germain: cd cover
. photography
. party_tv
. Montrealcig
. green_glass
. mother
. beer
. laugh
. half
. dim_kiss
. grab
what is what
personal project
professional project
friends
acidtwist.com
delineation.org

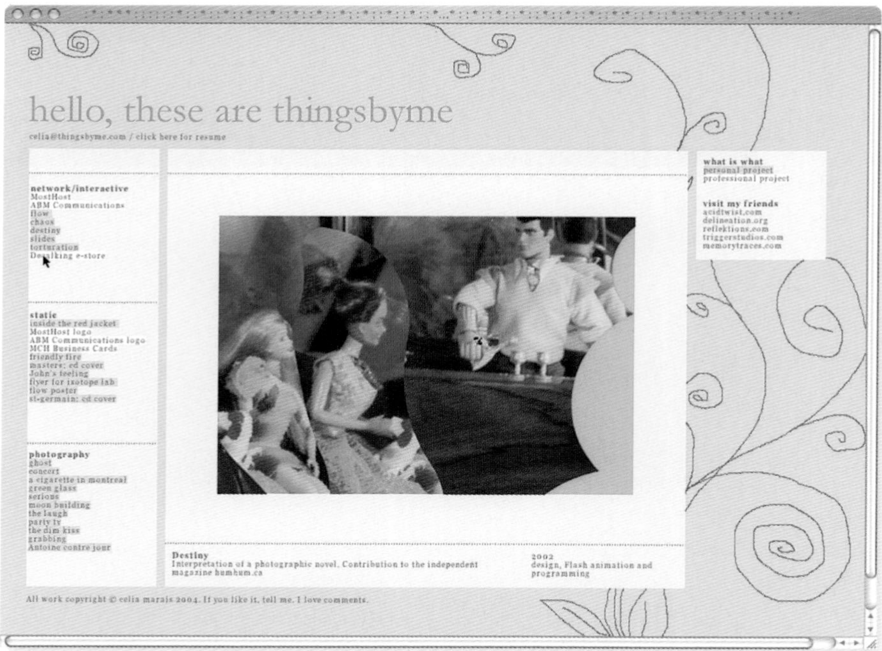
hello, these are thingsbyme
celia@thingsbyme.com / click here for resume
network/interactive
MostHost
ABM Communications
flow
chaos
destiny
slides
torturation
static
inside the red jacket
MostHost logo
ABM Communications logo
MCH Business Cards
friendly fire
masters: cd cover
John's feeling
flyer for isotope lab
flow poster
st-germain: cd cover
photography
ghost
concert
a cigarette in montreal
green glass
serious
moon building
the laugh
party tv
the dim kiss
grabbing
Antoine contre jour
what is what
personal project
professional project
visit my friends
acidtwist.com
delineation.org
reflektions.com
triggerstudios.com
memorytraces.com
Destiny
Interpretation of a photographic novel. Contribution to the independent magazine humhum.ca
2002
design, Flash animation and programming
All work copyright © celia marais 2004. If you like it, tell me. I love comments.

www.thingsbyme.com
D: celia marais
A: thingsbyme **M:** celia@thingsbyme.com

bubble
News
Who is bubble?
Portfolio
Guestbook
Jobs
Downloads
Contact
bubble
EEN DINER VOOR 10 BIJ
APRIKACHIPS
Aardappel
Everything you've always wanted to know about the delectable spud but never dared to ask.
Read more
Loading

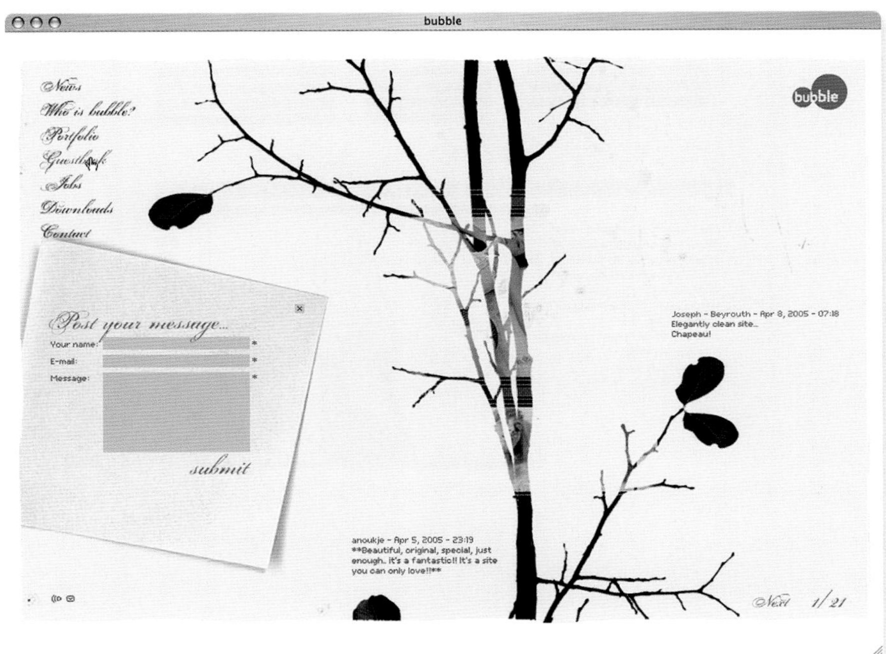
bubble
News
Who is bubble?
Portfolio
Guestbook
Jobs
Downloads
Contact
bubble
Post your message...
Your name:
E-mail:
Message:
submit
Joseph - Beyrouth - Apr 8, 2005 - 07:18
Elegantly clean site..
Chapeau!
anoukje - Apr 5, 2005 - 23:19
Beautiful, original, special, just enough.. it's a fantastic!! It's a site you can only love!!
Next 1/21

www.bubble.be
D: peter dekens **C:** mathias baert **P:** peter dekens
A: bubble **M:** info@bubble.be

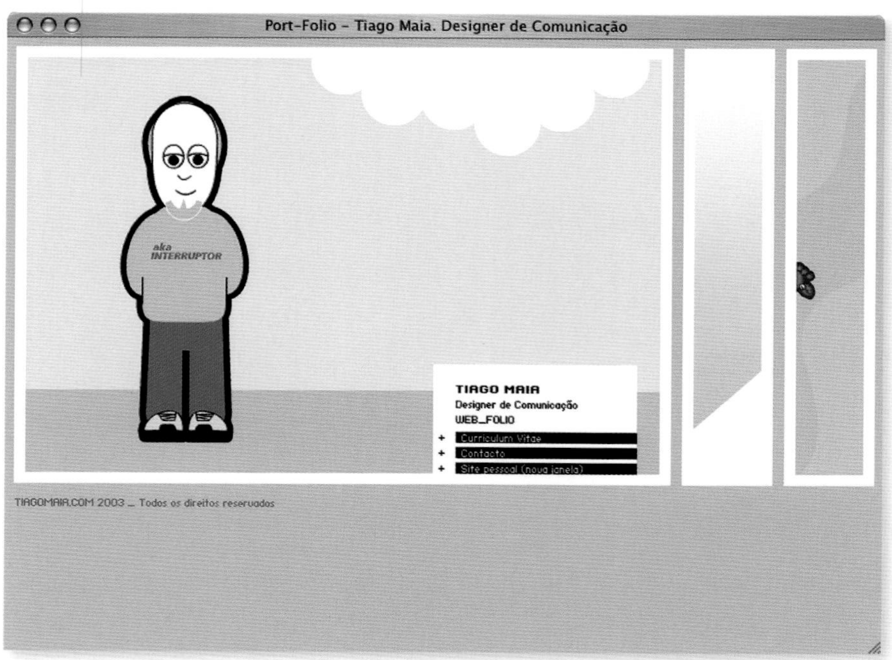
Port-Folio - Tiago Maia. Designer de Comunicação
aka INTERRUPTOR
TIAGO MAIA
Designer de Comunicação
WEB_FOLIO
Curriculum Vitae
Contacto
Site pessoal (nova janela)
TIAGOMAIA.COM 2003 _ Todos os direitos reservados

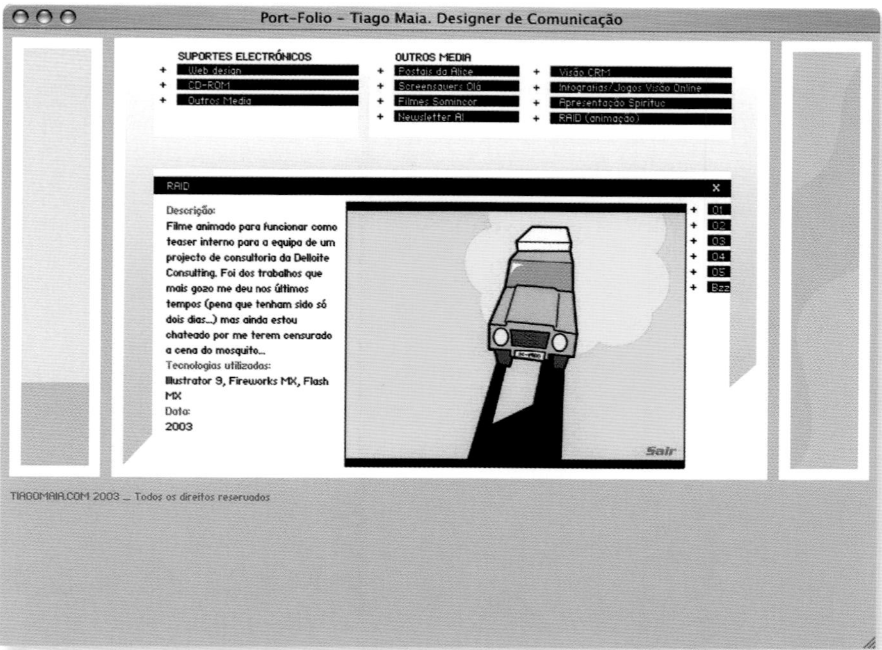
Port-Folio - Tiago Maia. Designer de Comunicação
SUPORTES ELECTRÓNICOS
Web design
CD-ROM
Outros Media
OUTROS MEDIA
Postais da Alice
Screensavers Olá
Filmes Somincor
Newsletter AI
Visão CRM
Infografias/Jogos Visão Online
Apresentação Spirituc
RAID (animação)
RAID
Descrição:
Filme animado para funcionar como teaser interno para a equipa de um projecto de consultoria da Delloite Consulting. Foi dos trabalhos que mais gozo me deu nos últimos tempos (pena que tenham sido só dois dias...) mas ainda estou chateado por me terem censurado a cena do mosquito...
Tecnologias utilizadas:
Illustrator 9, Fireworks MX, Flash MX
Data:
2003
01
02
03
04
05
Sair
TIAGOMAIA.COM 2003 _ Todos os direitos reservados

www.tiagomaia.com
D: tiago maia
M: tiago@tiagomaia.com

meSTUDIO
mestudio
HOME | WEB | 3D | MOBILE | PRINT | TV | PHOTO | CV | CONTACT
webdesign
mobiledesign
3ddesign
printdesign
tvdesign
photodesign
contact
COPYRIGHT 2005 FRANCIS HERNANDEZ
LEAVE ME A NOTE

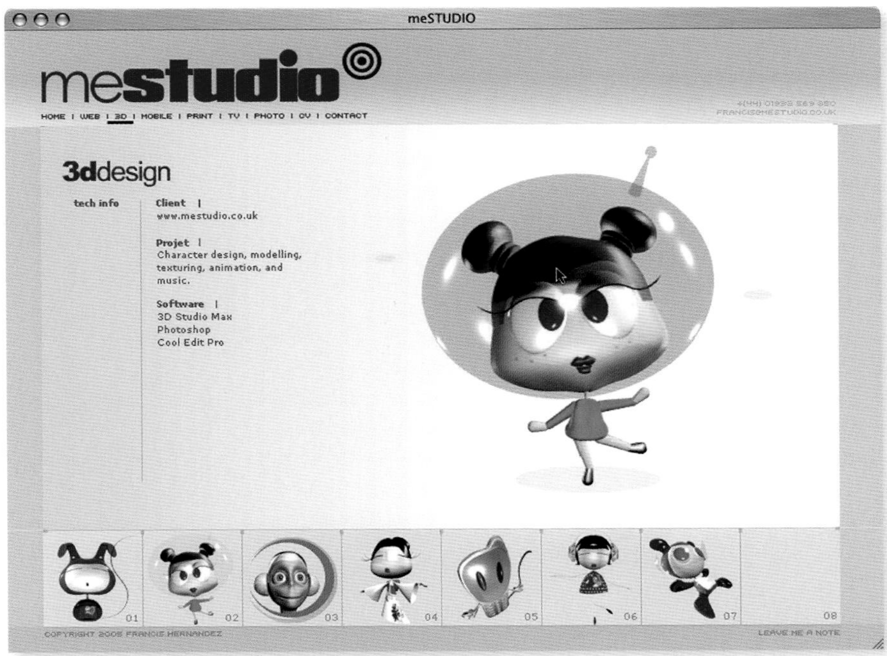
meSTUDIO
mestudio
HOME | WEB | 3D | MOBILE | PRINT | TV | PHOTO | CV | CONTACT
3ddesign
tech info
Client |
www.mestudio.co.uk
Projet |
Character design, modelling, texturing, animation, and music.
Software |
3D Studio Max
Photoshop
Cool Edit Pro
01
02
03
04
05
06
07
08
COPYRIGHT 2005 FRANCIS HERNANDEZ
LEAVE ME A NOTE

www.mestudio.co.uk
D: francisco hernandez
A: mecompany **M:** francis@mestudio.co.uk

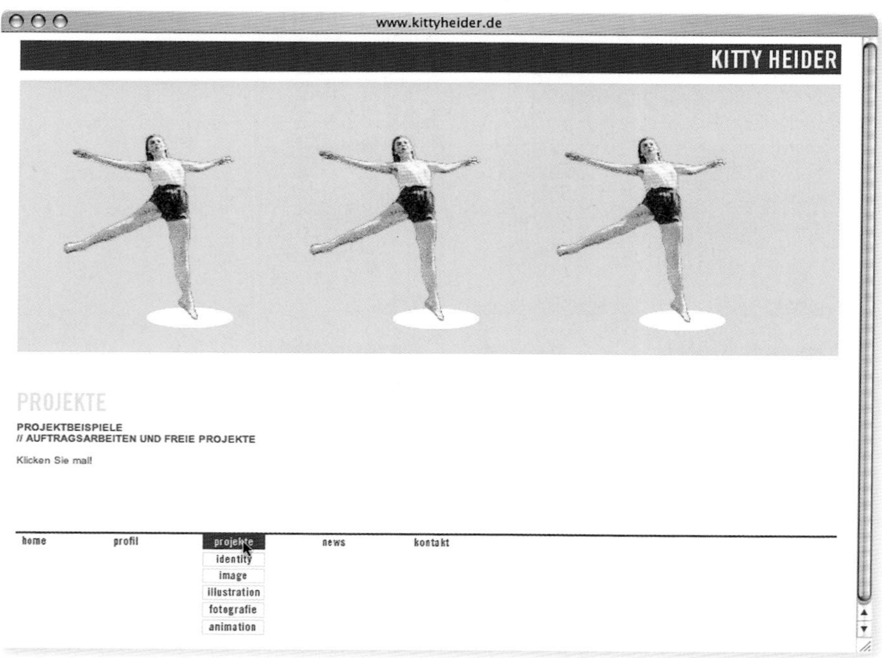
www.kittyheider.de
KITTY HEIDER
PROJEKTE
PROJEKTBEISPIELE
// AUFTRAGSARBEITEN UND FREIE PROJEKTE
Klicken Sie mal!
home
profil
projekte
identity
image
illustration
fotografie
animation
news
kontakt

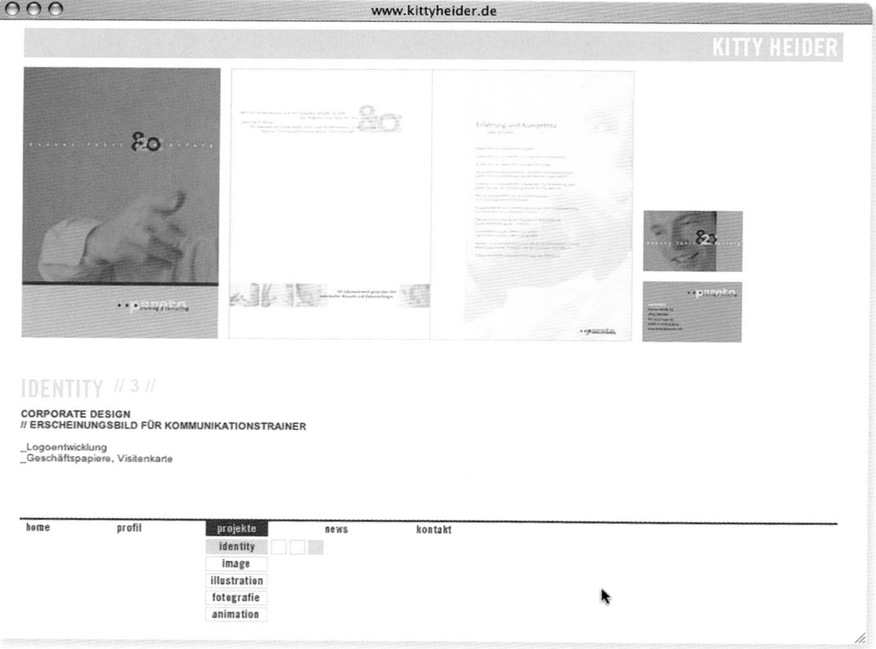
www.kittyheider.de
KITTY HEIDER
IDENTITY // 3 //
CORPORATE DESIGN
// ERSCHEINUNGSBILD FÜR KOMMUNIKATIONSTRAINER
_Logoentwicklung
_Geschäftspapiere, Visitenkarte
home
profil
projekte
identity
image
illustration
fotografie
animation
news
kontakt

www.kittyheider.de
D: kitty heider
M: mail@kittyheider.de

Terri Pecora
TERRI PECORA. design studio.

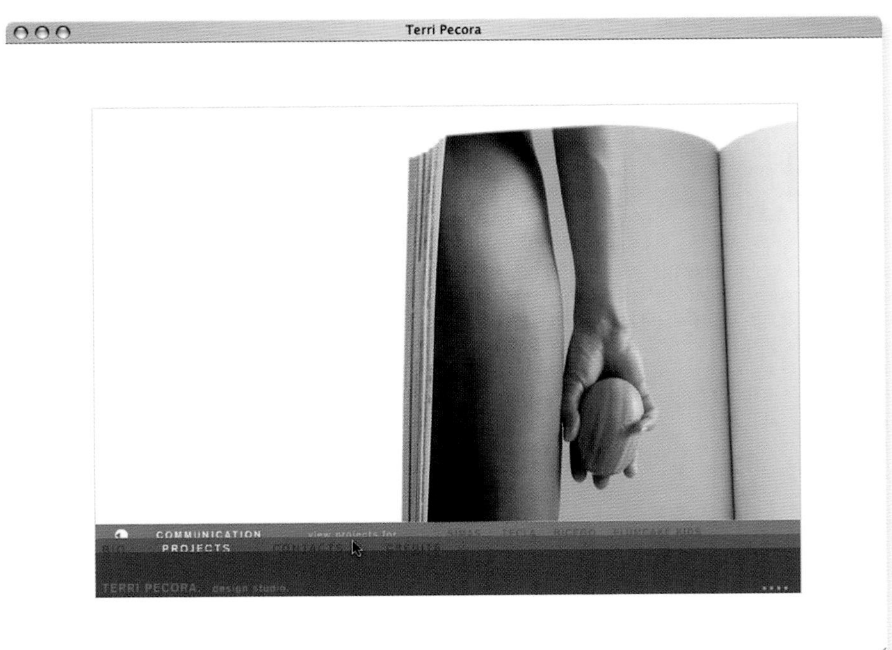
Terri Pecora
COMMUNICATION
PROJECTS
TERRI PECORA. design studio.

www.terripecora.net
D: antonio mangialardi
A: amd **M:** amd@fastwebnet.it

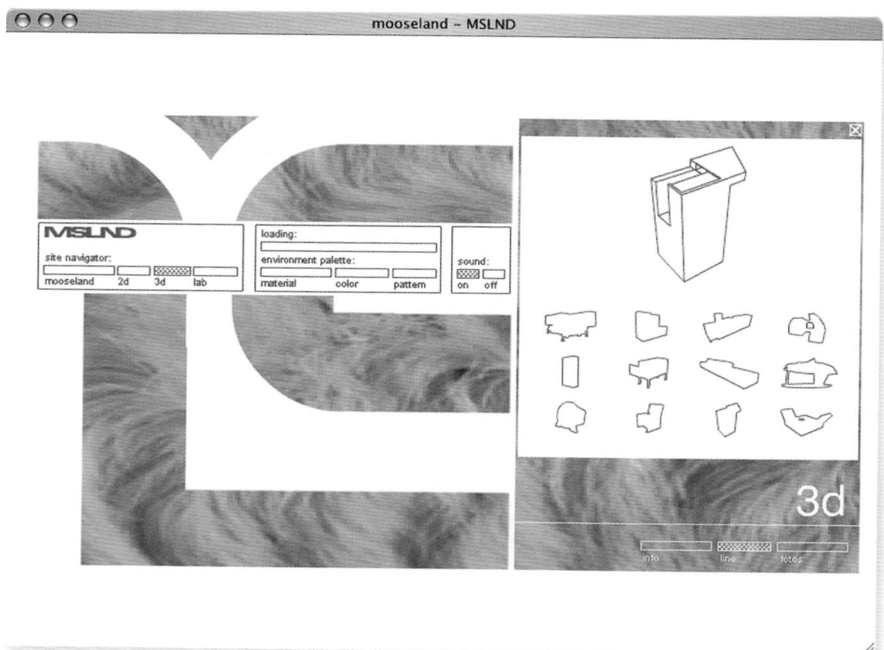
mooseland – MSLND
MSLND
site navigator:
mooseland 2d 3d lab
loading:
environment palette:
material color pattern
sound:
on off
3d
info line fotos

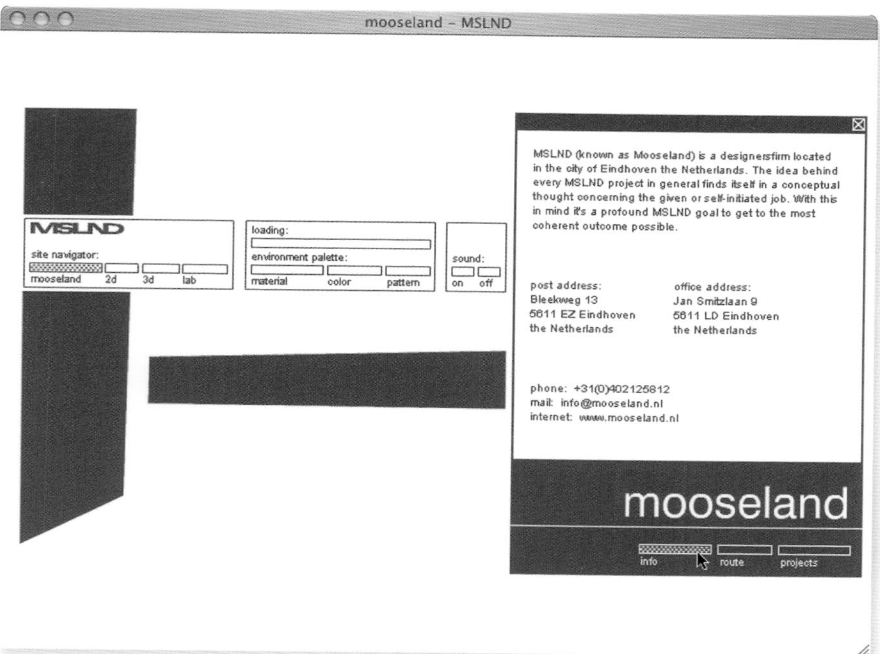
mooseland – MSLND
MSLND
site navigator:
mooseland 2d 3d lab
loading:
environment palette:
material color pattern
sound:
on off
MSLND (known as Mooseland) is a designersfirm located in the city of Eindhoven the Netherlands. The idea behind every MSLND project in general finds itself in a conceptual thought concerning the given or self-initiated job. With this in mind it's a profound MSLND goal to get to the most coherent outcome possible.
post address:
Bleekweg 13
5611 EZ Eindhoven
the Netherlands
office address:
Jan Smitzlaan 9
5611 LD Eindhoven
the Netherlands
phone: +31(0)402125812
mail: info@mooseland.nl
internet: www.mooseland.nl
mooseland
info route projects

www.mooseland.nl
D: jasper den dekker
A: mooseland **M:** info@mooseland.nl

:::BAGTRIP:::
CONTENTS :
PHOTO BOOK
GRAFFITI PICT.
SAN FRANCISCO PICT.
T-SHIRTS SHOP
AND MANY MORE..
M_CHAIX@BAGTRIP.ORG
GRAPHIC WORK BY
MIAMY.BIZ
BAGTRIP.ORG
PHOTO GALLERY BY M. CHAIX

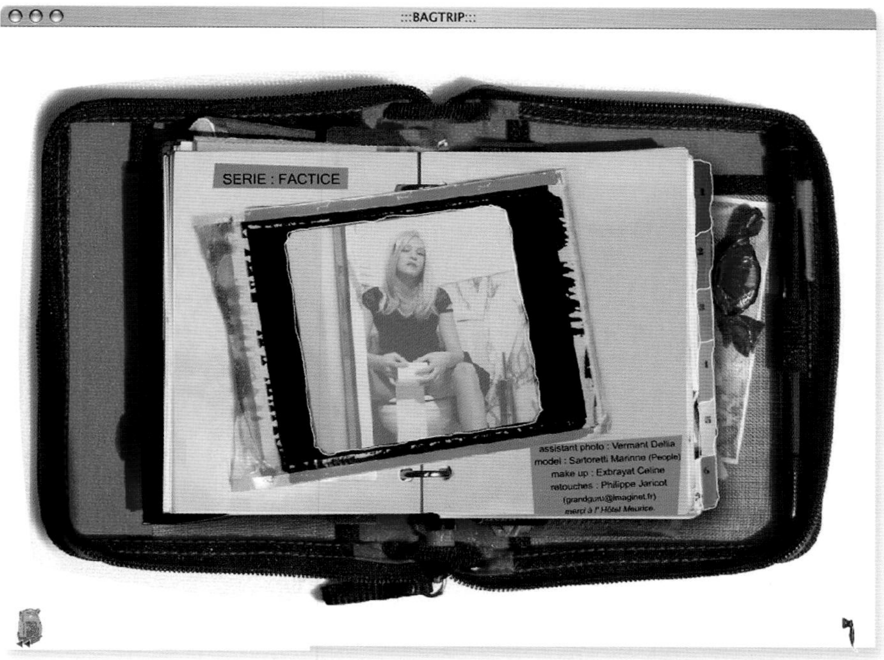
:::BAGTRIP:::
SERIE : FACTICE
assistant photo : Vermant Della
model : Sartoretti Marinne (People)
make up : Exbrayat Celine
retouches : Philippe Jaricot
(grandguru@imaginet.fr)
merci à l'Hôtel Meurice.

a.masure.free.fr/bagtrip
D: antoine masure
A: miamy **M:** a.masure@free.fr

Untitled Document

ESTUDIO
PROYECTOS
CONTACTA

ESTUDI CARAVACA ES UN ESTUDIO DE DISEÑO GRÁFICO PARA DAR SOLUCIÓN A LOS PROBLEMAS DE COMUNICACIÓN QUE TIENEN LAS EMPRESAS Y ENTIDADES PARA LLEVAR A CABO SUS PROYECTOS EMPRESARIALES E INSTITUCIONALES.

Untitled Document

ESTUDIO
PROYECTOS
CONTACTA

LA CALIDAD, ORIGINALIDAD Y LA EFECTIVIDAD EN LOS PROYECTOS HAN ABALADO EL TRABAJO DEL ESTUDIO, CONSIGUIENDO QUE CADA UNO DE NUESTROS CLIENTES SE SIENTA IDENTIFICADO CON EL RESULTADO FINAL Y SATISFECHO DE LLEGAR A UN PÚBLICO OBJETIVO.

PROYECTOS

Justo 50
87€
CONÉCTATE!
PROMO
90 €
AB
Limpiezas Generales

www.estudicaravaca.com
D: alex caravaca ponce
A: estudi caravaca **M:** info@estudicaravaca.com

: Andy Titus :

andy titus | portfolio of interactive design

heavy

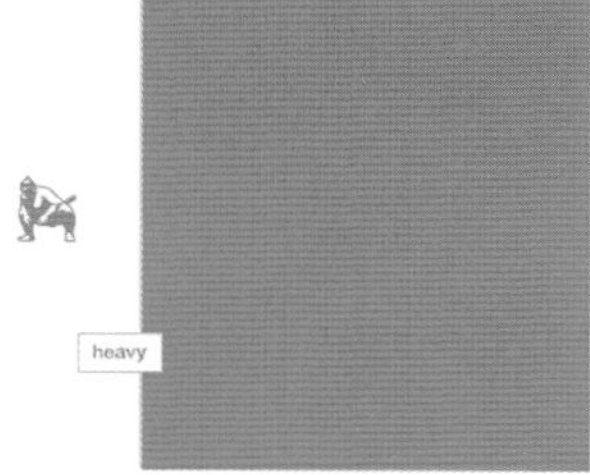

: Andy Titus :

FOOD
STORY
COMMENT
LOCATE
chop't
SALADS
SANDWICHES
DRESSINGS
TECHNIQUE

heavy

STORY
LOCATE
DEAR SALAD LOVER,

chop't view 1 launch

Chop't is a creative salad company on the rise with multiple locations in New York City. They sought after a site that simply communicated the core components of their restaurants: freshness, summertime vibes, and a fierce double-bladed mezzaluna chopper.

info@andytitus.com

www.andytitus.com
D: andy titus **C:** joe mease
A: andy titus **M:** at@andytitus.com

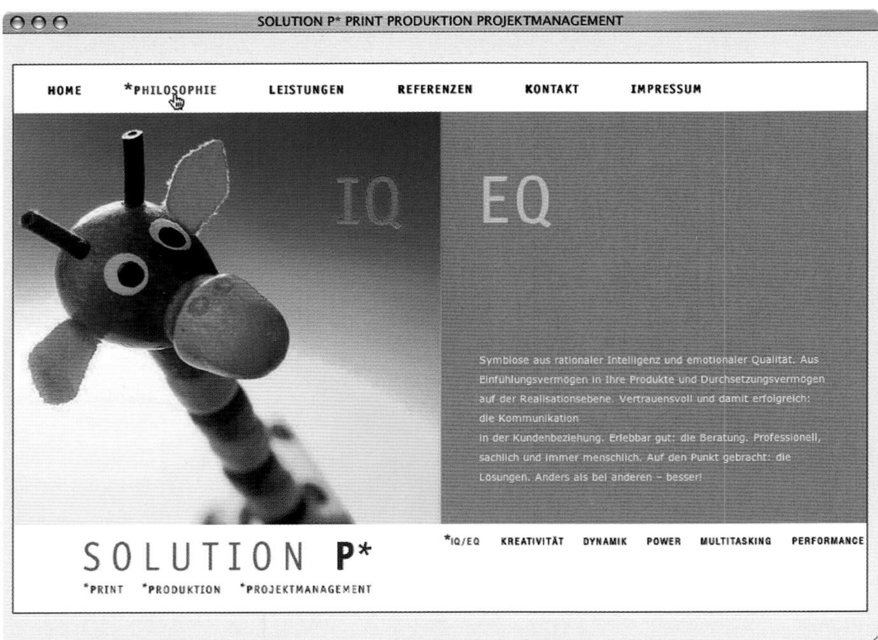
SOLUTION P* PRINT PRODUKTION PROJEKTMANAGEMENT
HOME
*PHILOSOPHIE
LEISTUNGEN
REFERENZEN
KONTAKT
IMPRESSUM
IQ
EQ
Symbiose aus rationaler Intelligenz und emotionaler Qualität. Aus Einfühlungsvermögen in Ihre Produkte und Durchsetzungsvermögen auf der Realisationsebene. Vertrauensvoll und damit erfolgreich: die Kommunikation
in der Kundenbeziehung. Erlebbar gut: die Beratung. Professionell, sachlich und immer menschlich. Auf den Punkt gebracht: die Lösungen. Anders als bei anderen – besser!
SOLUTION P*
*PRINT *PRODUKTION *PROJEKTMANAGEMENT
*IQ/EQ
KREATIVITÄT
DYNAMIK
POWER
MULTITASKING
PERFORMANCE

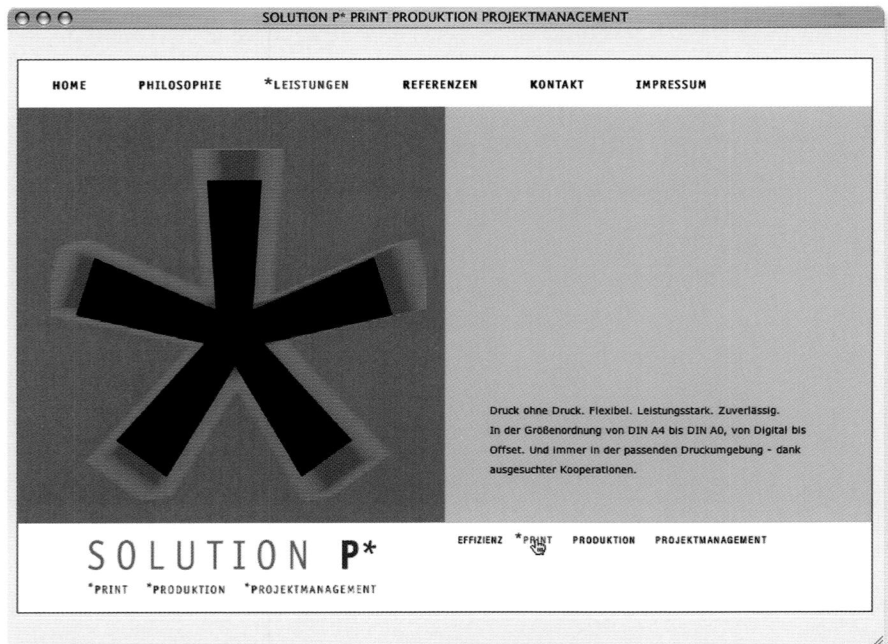
SOLUTION P* PRINT PRODUKTION PROJEKTMANAGEMENT
HOME
PHILOSOPHIE
*LEISTUNGEN
REFERENZEN
KONTAKT
IMPRESSUM
Druck ohne Druck. Flexibel. Leistungsstark. Zuverlässig.
In der Größenordnung von DIN A4 bis DIN A0, von Digital bis Offset. Und immer in der passenden Druckumgebung - dank ausgesuchter Kooperationen.
SOLUTION P*
*PRINT *PRODUKTION *PROJEKTMANAGEMENT
EFFIZIENZ
*PRINT
PRODUKTION
PROJEKTMANAGEMENT

www.solutionp.de
D: sylvia trautmann
A: das tagewerk **M:** sylvia.trautmann@das-tagewerk.de

Vectorized Me - The Portfolio of Tema Semenov
ABOUT
PERSONAL INFORMATION
WORK
PERSONAL / CLIENT WORK
CONTACT
FOR JOB OR ANYTHING ELSE

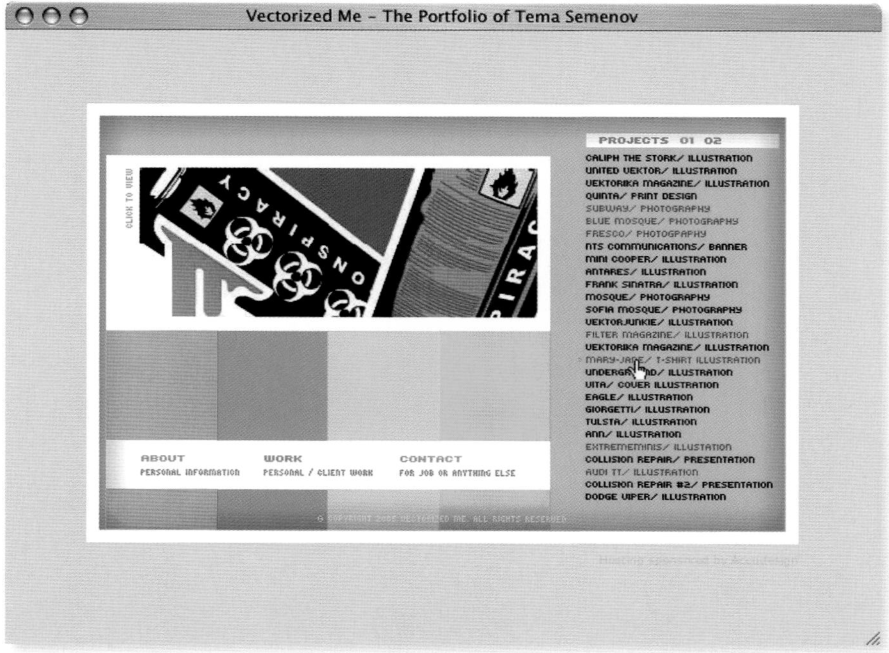
Vectorized Me - The Portfolio of Tema Semenov
PROJECTS 01 02
CALIPH THE STORK/ ILLUSTRATION
UNITED VEKTOR/ ILLUSTRATION
VEKTORIKA MAGAZINE/ ILLUSTRATION
QUINTA/ PRINT DESIGN
SUBWAY/ PHOTOGRAPHY
BLUE MOSQUE/ PHOTOGRAPHY
FRESCO/ PHOTOGRAPHY
NTS COMMUNICATIONS/ BANNER
MINI COOPER/ ILLUSTRATION
ANTARES/ ILLUSTRATION
FRANK SINATRA/ ILLUSTRATION
MOSQUE/ PHOTOGRAPHY
SOFIA MOSQUE/ PHOTOGRAPHY
VEKTORJUNKIE/ ILLUSTRATION
FILTER MAGAZINE/ ILLUSTRATION
VEKTORIKA MAGAZINE/ ILLUSTRATION
T-SHIRT ILLUSTRATION
ILLUSTRATION
VITA/ COVER ILLUSTRATION
EAGLE/ ILLUSTRATION
GIORGETTI/ ILLUSTRATION
TULSTA/ ILLUSTRATION
ANN/ ILLUSTRATION
EXTREMEMINIS/ ILLUSTRATION
COLLISION REPAIR/ PRESENTATION
AUDI TT/ ILLUSTRATION
COLLISION REPAIR #2/ PRESENTATION
DODGE VIPER/ ILLUSTRATION
CLICK TO VIEW
ABOUT
PERSONAL INFORMATION
WORK
PERSONAL / CLIENT WORK
CONTACT
FOR JOB OR ANYTHING ELSE

www.vectorizedme.com
D: tema semenov
A: vectorized me **M:** tema@vectorizedme.com

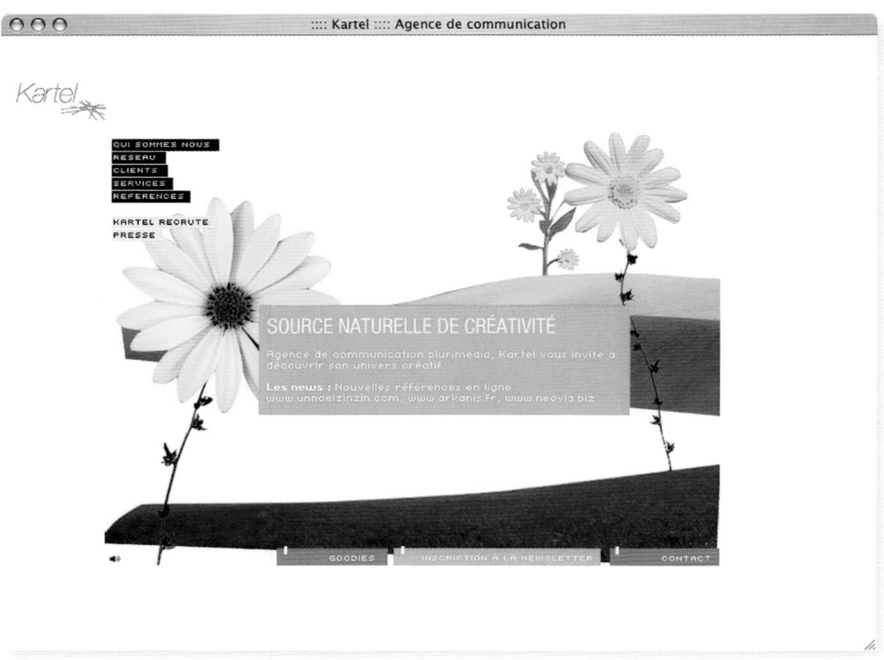
:::: Kartel :::: Agence de communication
Kartel
QUI SOMMES NOUS
RESEAU
CLIENTS
SERVICES
REFERENCES
KARTEL RECRUTE
PRESSE
SOURCE NATURELLE DE CRÉATIVITÉ
Agence de communication plurimedia, Kartel vous invite à découvrir son univers créatif.
Les news : Nouvelles références en ligne : www.unnoelzinzin.com, www.arkanis.fr, www.neovia.biz
GOODIES
INSCRIPTION À LA NEWSLETTER
CONTACT

:::: Kartel :::: Agence de communication
Kartel
QUI SOMMES NOUS
RESEAU
CLIENTS
SERVICES
REFERENCES
KARTEL RECRUTE
PRESSE
NOS RACINES C'EST LA COM, MAIS NOS BRANCHES POUSSENT PARTOUT
Solutionner les problématiques de communication... c'est notre vocation.
Conseiller, définir, créer, développer des outils media, hors media, multimedia... notre expertise.
GOODIES
INSCRIPTION À LA NEWSLETTER
CONTACT

www.kartel.fr
D: team kartel **C:** m. zylberait, g.savanne
A: kartel **M:** damaro@kartel.fr

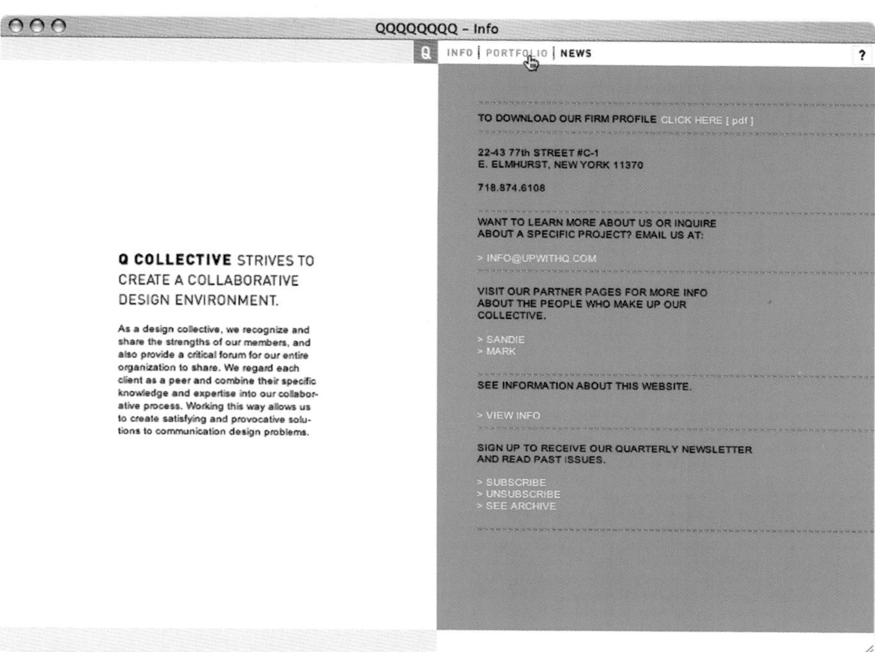
QQQQQQQQ - Info
INFO | PORTFOLIO | NEWS
?
Q COLLECTIVE STRIVES TO CREATE A COLLABORATIVE DESIGN ENVIRONMENT.
As a design collective, we recognize and share the strengths of our members, and also provide a critical forum for our entire organization to share. We regard each client as a peer and combine their specific knowledge and expertise into our collaborative process. Working this way allows us to create satisfying and provocative solutions to communication design problems.
TO DOWNLOAD OUR FIRM PROFILE CLICK HERE [pdf]
22-43 77th STREET #C-1
E. ELMHURST, NEW YORK 11370
718.874.6108
WANT TO LEARN MORE ABOUT US OR INQUIRE ABOUT A SPECIFIC PROJECT? EMAIL US AT:
> INFO@UPWITHQ.COM
VISIT OUR PARTNER PAGES FOR MORE INFO ABOUT THE PEOPLE WHO MAKE UP OUR COLLECTIVE.
> SANDIE
> MARK
SEE INFORMATION ABOUT THIS WEBSITE.
> VIEW INFO
SIGN UP TO RECEIVE OUR QUARTERLY NEWSLETTER AND READ PAST ISSUES.
> SUBSCRIBE
> UNSUBSCRIBE
> SEE ARCHIVE

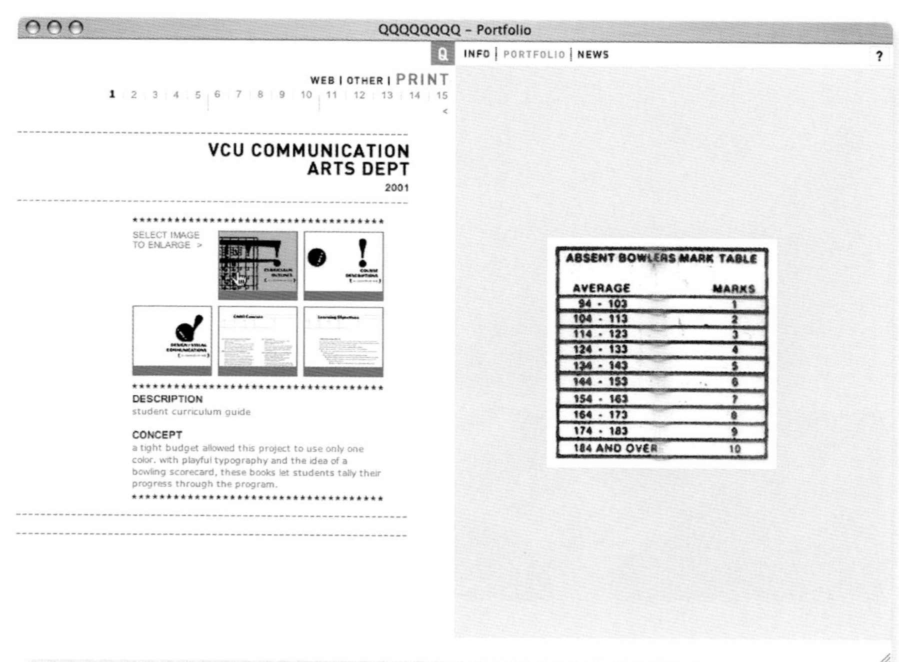
QQQQQQQQ - Portfolio
INFO | PORTFOLIO | NEWS
?
WEB | OTHER | PRINT
1 | 2 | 3 | 4 | 5 | 6 | 7 | 8 | 9 | 10 | 11 | 12 | 13 | 14 | 15
VCU COMMUNICATION ARTS DEPT
2001
SELECT IMAGE TO ENLARGE >
DESCRIPTION
student curriculum guide
CONCEPT
a tight budget allowed this project to use only one color. with playful typography and the idea of a bowling scorecard, these books let students tally their progress through the program.
ABSENT BOWLERS MARK TABLE
AVERAGE
MARKS
94 - 103
1
104 - 113
2
114 - 123
3
124 - 133
4
134 - 143
5
144 - 153
6
154 - 163
7
164 - 173
8
174 - 183
9
184 AND OVER
10

www.upwithq.com
D: mark sanders
A: q collective **M:** mark@upwithq.com

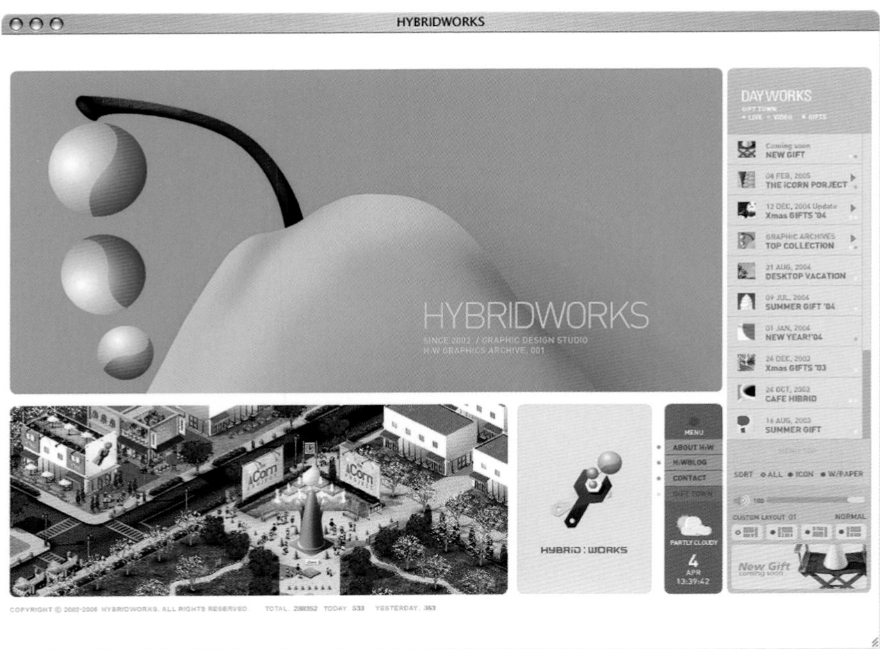
HYBRIDWORKS
DAYWORKS
NEW GIFT
THE ICORN PORJECT
Xmas GIFTS '04
TOP COLLECTION
DESKTOP VACATION
SUMMER GIFT '04
NEW YEAR!'04
Xmas GIFTS '03
CAFE HIBRID
SUMMER GIFT
HYBRIDWORKS
SINCE 2002 / GRAPHIC DESIGN STUDIO
H/W GRAPHICS ARCHIVE, 001
MENU
ABOUT H/W
H/WBLOG
CONTACT
HYBRID : WORKS
SORT ALL ICON W/PAPER
New Gift

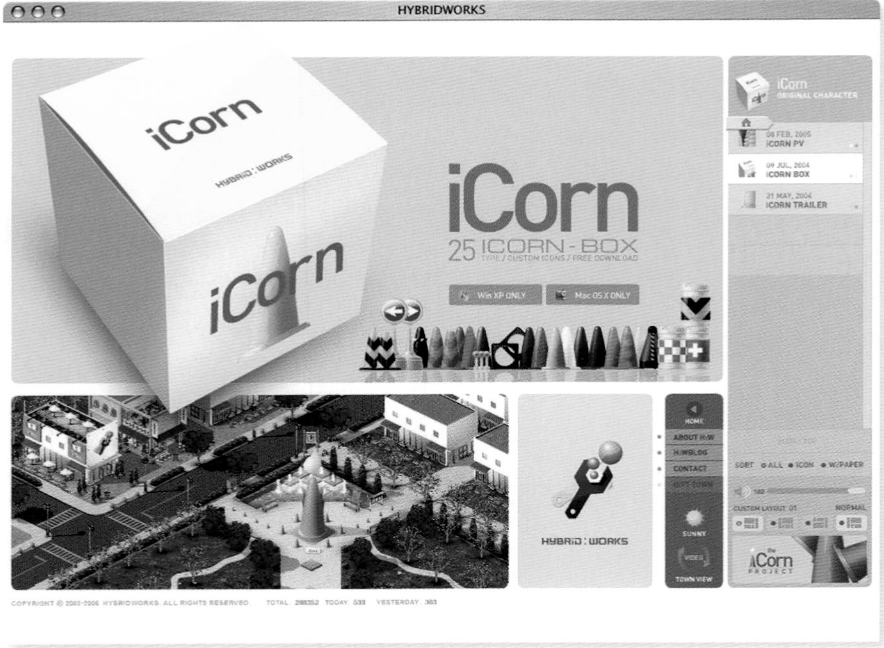
HYBRIDWORKS
iCorn
HYBRID : WORKS
iCorn
iCorn
25 ICORN - BOX
Win XP ONLY
Mac OS X ONLY
ICORN PV
ICORN BOX
ICORN TRAILER
HOME
ABOUT H/W
H/WBLOG
CONTACT
SUNNY
HYBRID : WORKS
SORT ALL ICON W/PAPER

www.hybridworks.jp

D: masaki hoshino **C:** masaki hoshino
A: hybridworks inc. **M:** mhoshino@hybridworks.jp

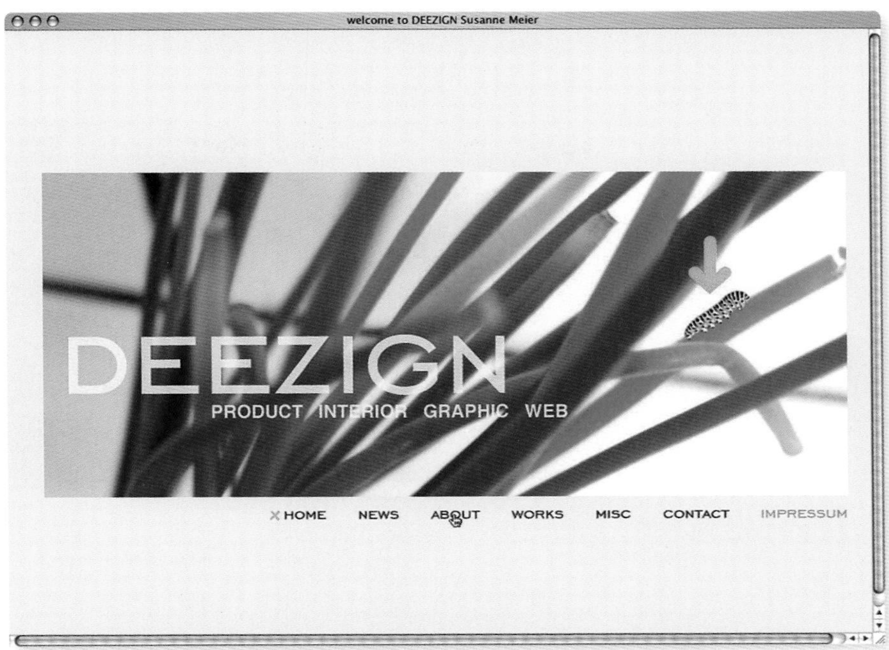
welcome to DEEZIGN Susanne Meier
DEEZIGN
PRODUCT INTERIOR GRAPHIC WEB
HOME NEWS ABOUT WORKS MISC CONTACT IMPRESSUM

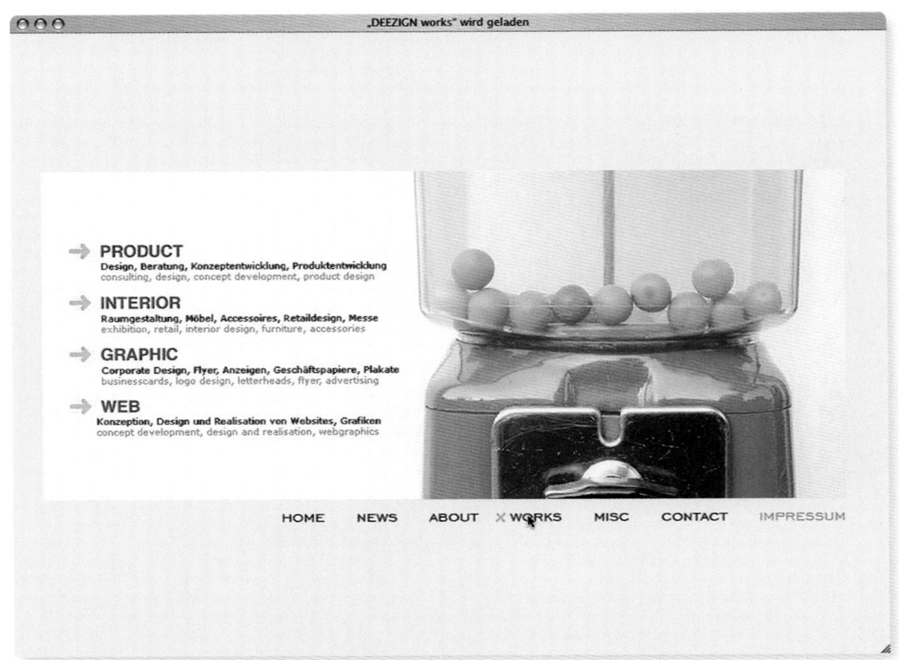
„DEEZIGN works" wird geladen
PRODUCT
Design, Beratung, Konzeptentwicklung, Produktentwicklung
consulting, design, concept development, product design
INTERIOR
Raumgestaltung, Möbel, Accessoires, Retaildesign, Messe
exhibition, retail, interior design, furniture, accessories
GRAPHIC
Corporate Design, Flyer, Anzeigen, Geschäftspapiere, Plakate
businesscards, logo design, letterheads, flyer, advertising
WEB
Konzeption, Design und Realisation von Websites, Grafiken
concept development, design and realisation, webgraphics
HOME NEWS ABOUT WORKS MISC CONTACT IMPRESSUM

www.deezign.de
D: susanne meier
A: deezign **M:** susanne.meier@email.de

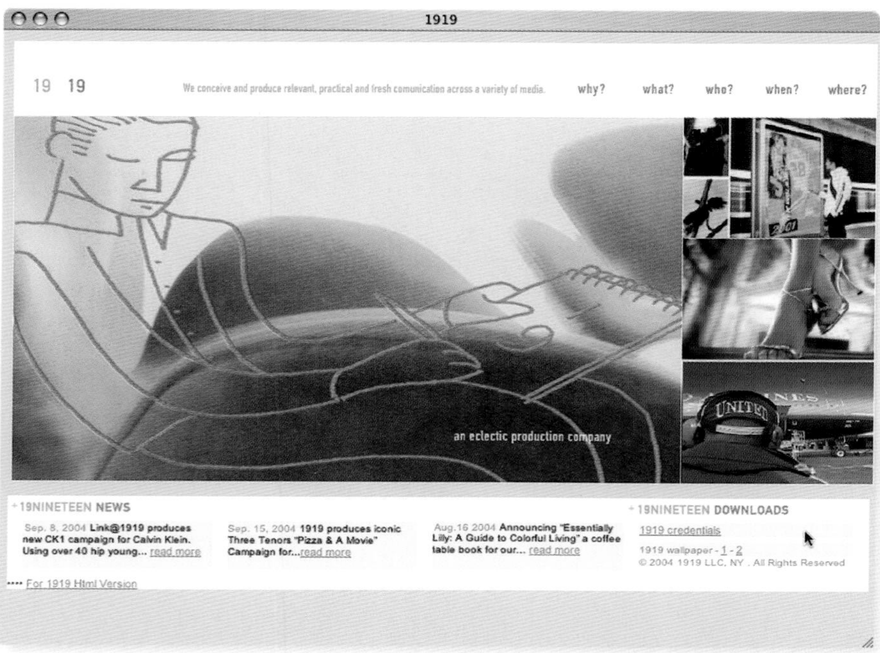
1919
19 19
We conceive and produce relevant, practical and fresh comunication across a variety of media.
why? what? who? when? where?
an eclectic production company
19NINETEEN NEWS
Sep. 8, 2004 Link@1919 produces new CK1 campaign for Calvin Klein. Using over 40 hip young... read more
Sep. 15, 2004 1919 produces iconic Three Tenors "Pizza & A Movie" Campaign for...read more
Aug.16 2004 Announcing "Essentially Lilly: A Guide to Colorful Living" a coffee table book for our... read more
19NINETEEN DOWNLOADS
1919 credentials
1919 wallpaper - 1 - 2
© 2004 1919 LLC, NY . All Rights Reserved
For 1919 Html Version

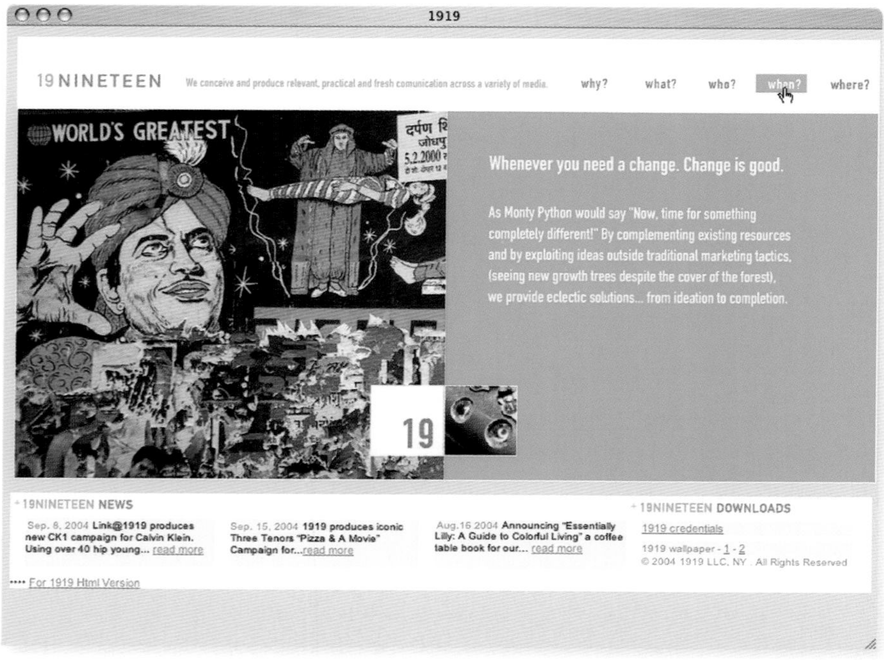
1919
19 NINETEEN
We conceive and produce relevant, practical and fresh comunication across a variety of media.
why? what? who? when? where?
WORLD'S GREATEST
Whenever you need a change. Change is good.
As Monty Python would say "Now, time for something completely different!" By complementing existing resources and by exploiting ideas outside traditional marketing tactics, (seeing new growth trees despite the cover of the forest), we provide eclectic solutions... from ideation to completion.
19
19NINETEEN NEWS
Sep. 8, 2004 Link@1919 produces new CK1 campaign for Calvin Klein. Using over 40 hip young... read more
Sep. 15, 2004 1919 produces iconic Three Tenors "Pizza & A Movie" Campaign for...read more
Aug.16 2004 Announcing "Essentially Lilly: A Guide to Colorful Living" a coffee table book for our... read more
19NINETEEN DOWNLOADS
1919 credentials
1919 wallpaper - 1 - 2
© 2004 1919 LLC, NY . All Rights Reserved
For 1919 Html Version

www.1919.com
D: peter klueger
A: 1919 **M:** info@1919.com

Webdesign Düsseldorf Flash-Garden - Html, Homepag...et. Design in Kombination mit der von Ihnen selbs
WEBDESIGN WITH STYLE
STUDIO FÜR INTERNETGESTALTUNG
VOLL KRASS
FLASH-GARDEN - Villa Flora - Oberkasseler Str. 26 40545 Düsseldorf - Tel: 0211 99 44 389 - Fax: -92 INFO

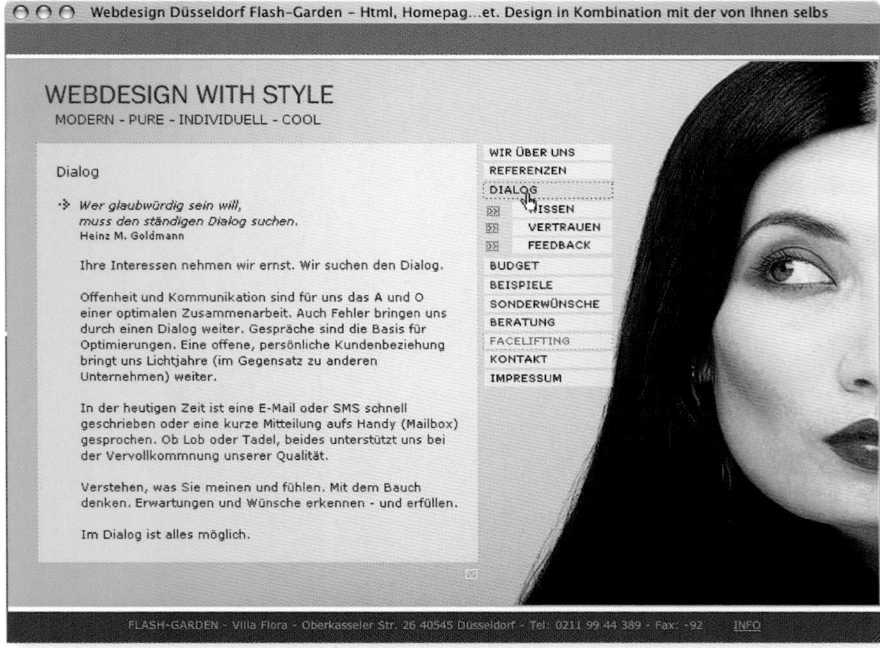
Webdesign Düsseldorf Flash-Garden - Html, Homepag...et. Design in Kombination mit der von Ihnen selbs
WEBDESIGN WITH STYLE
MODERN - PURE - INDIVIDUELL - COOL
Dialog
Wer glaubwürdig sein will, muss den ständigen Dialog suchen.
Heinz M. Goldmann
Ihre Interessen nehmen wir ernst. Wir suchen den Dialog.
Offenheit und Kommunikation sind für uns das A und O einer optimalen Zusammenarbeit. Auch Fehler bringen uns durch einen Dialog weiter. Gespräche sind die Basis für Optimierungen. Eine offene, persönliche Kundenbeziehung bringt uns Lichtjahre (im Gegensatz zu anderen Unternehmen) weiter.
In der heutigen Zeit ist eine E-Mail oder SMS schnell geschrieben oder eine kurze Mitteilung aufs Handy (Mailbox) gesprochen. Ob Lob oder Tadel, beides unterstützt uns bei der Vervollkommnung unserer Qualität.
Verstehen, was Sie meinen und fühlen. Mit dem Bauch denken. Erwartungen und Wünsche erkennen - und erfüllen.
Im Dialog ist alles möglich.
WIR ÜBER UNS
REFERENZEN
DIALOG
VERTRAUEN
FEEDBACK
BUDGET
BEISPIELE
SONDERWÜNSCHE
BERATUNG
FACELIFTING
KONTAKT
IMPRESSUM
FLASH-GARDEN - Villa Flora - Oberkasseler Str. 26 40545 Düsseldorf - Tel: 0211 99 44 389 - Fax: -92 INFO

www.flash-garden.de
D: rene unruh
A: flash-garden **M:** info@flash-garden.de

feed
Press Space Bar to Next Graphic...
back

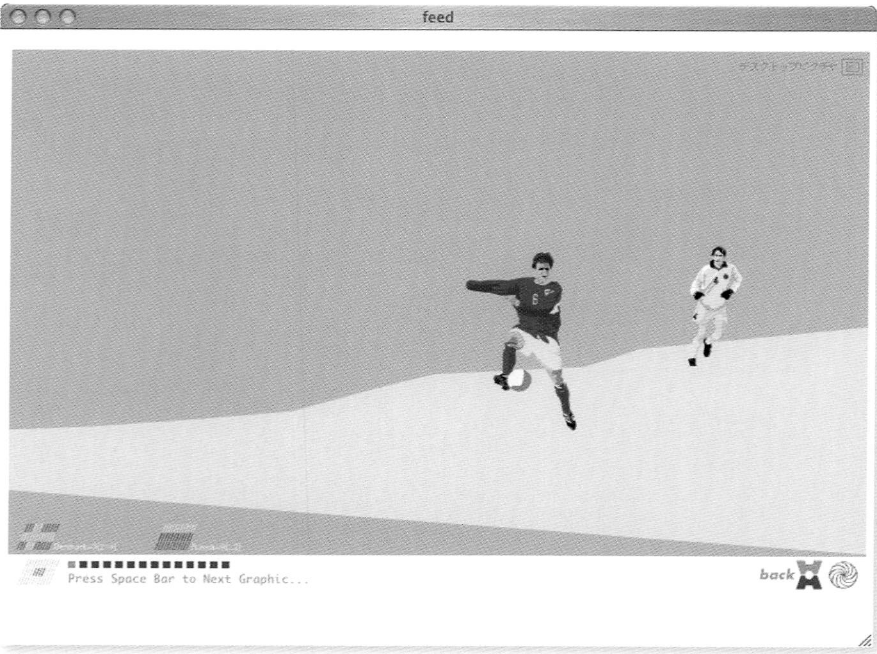
feed
Press Space Bar to Next Graphic...
back

www.marble-co.net/feed/
D: hiroaki ohta
A: marble.co **M:** mail@marble-co.net

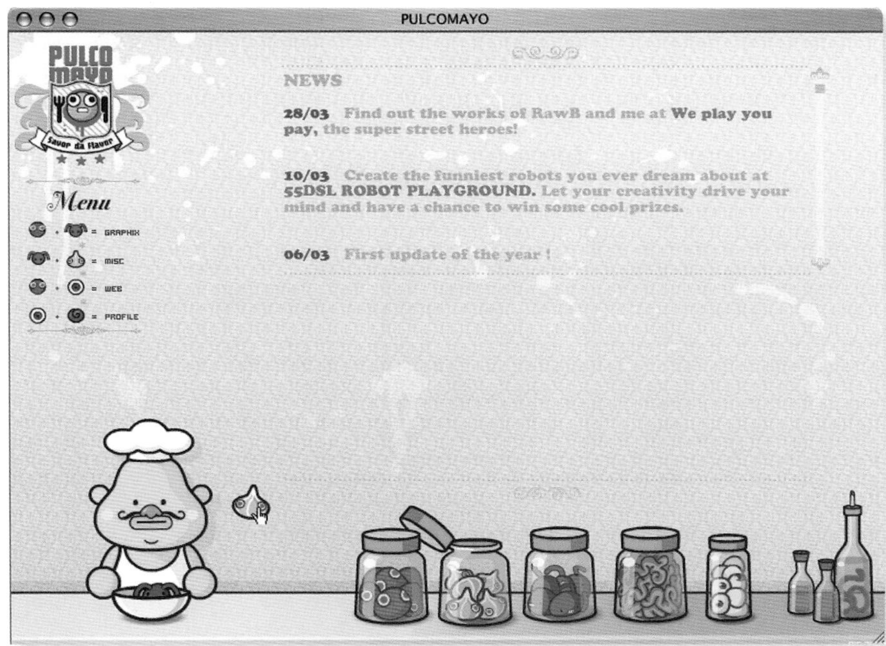
PULCOMAYO
PULCO MAYO
Savor da Flavor
Menu
GRAPHIX
MISC
WEB
PROFILE
NEWS
28/03 Find out the works of RawB and me at We play you pay, the super street heroes!
10/03 Create the funniest robots you ever dream about at 55DSL ROBOT PLAYGROUND. Let your creativity drive your mind and have a chance to win some cool prizes.
06/03 First update of the year !

PULCOMAYO
PULCO MAYO
Savor da Flavor
Graphix
VECTO
PAINT
STREET
SKETCH
BACK TO MENU
PREVIOUS
NEXT
Character design for a skateboard project with WE PLAY YOU PAY
Janv 2005

www.pulcomayo.com
D: vincent bechet **C:** patrice fournet, julien fauveau **P:** vincent bechet
A: pulco mayo **M:** bechetvincent@hotmail.com

255 Design Studio | Handcrafted Websites since 2001
twofivefive
255 DESIGN STUDIO
03
01HOME | 02ABOUT | 03PORTFOLIO | 04CONTACT
PORTFOLIO
WEBSITES
STUFF
LOGOS
HORNY WEDNESDAY
CELEBRATE A HORNY CHRISTMAS
HORNY WEDNESDAY FLYERS
Screenshot 1 · 2 · 3 · 4
2005 | 255 DESIGN STUDIO
HANDCRAFTED WEBSITES SINCE 2001

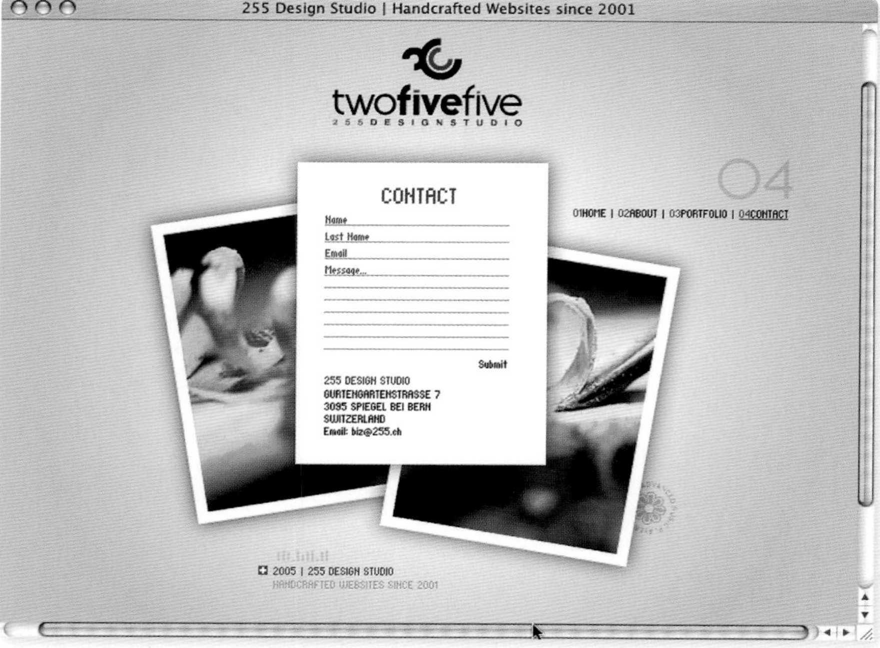
255 Design Studio | Handcrafted Websites since 2001
twofivefive
255 DESIGN STUDIO
04
01HOME | 02ABOUT | 03PORTFOLIO | 04CONTACT
CONTACT
Name
Last Name
Email
Message...
Submit
255 DESIGN STUDIO
GURTENGARTENSTRASSE 7
3095 SPIEGEL BEI BERN
SWITZERLAND
Email: biz@255.ch
2005 | 255 DESIGN STUDIO
HANDCRAFTED WEBSITES SINCE 2001

www.255.ch
D: kai reusser **C:** kai reusser
A: 255 design studio **M:** biz@255.ch

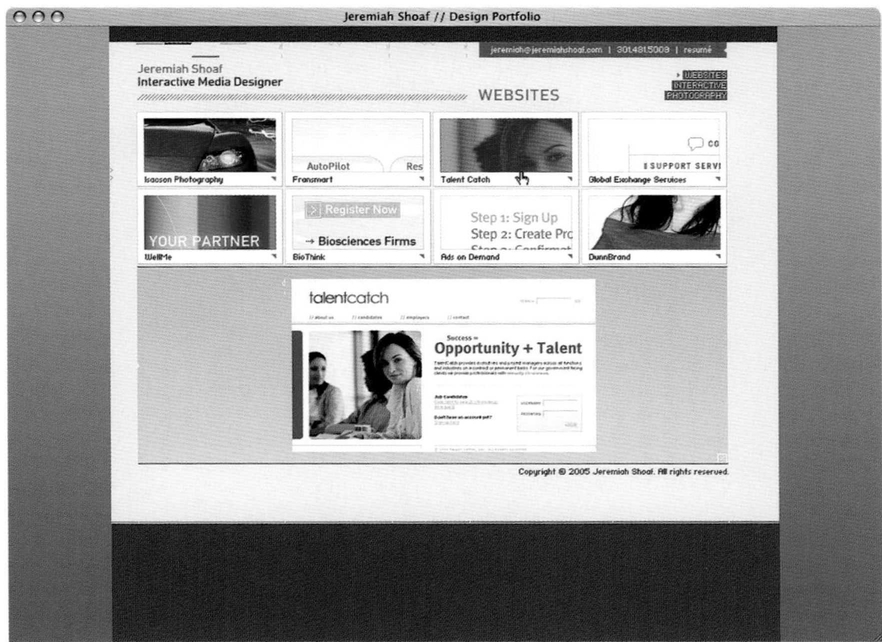
Jeremiah Shoaf // Design Portfolio
Jeremiah Shoaf
Interactive Media Designer
WEBSITES
Isaacson Photography
Fransmart
Talent Catch
Global Exchange Services
WellMe
BioThink
Ads on Demand
DunnBrand
talentcatch
Opportunity + Talent
Copyright © 2005 Jeremiah Shoaf. All rights reserved.

Jeremiah Shoaf // Design Portfolio
Jeremiah Shoaf
Interactive Media Designer
PHOTOGRAPHY
WEBSITES
INTERACTIVE
PHOTOGRAPHY
THREE
FOUR
FIVE
SEVEN
EIGHT
NINE
TEN
ELEVEN
TWELVE
Copyright © 2005 Jeremiah Shoaf. All rights reserved.

jeremiahshoaf.com
D: jeremiah shoaf
A: jeremiah shoaf **M:** jeremiah@jeremiahshoaf.com

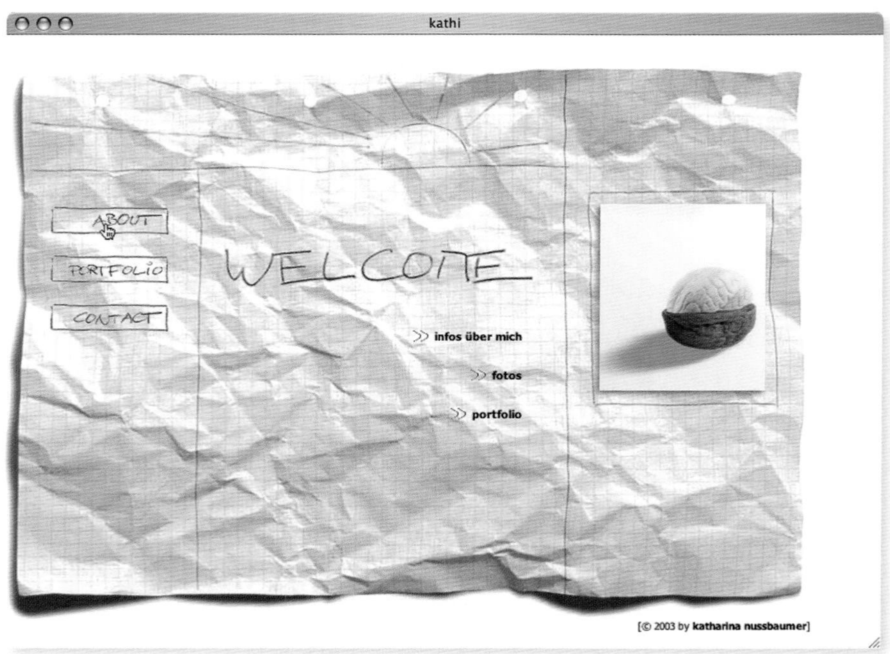
kathi
ABOUT
PORTFOLIO
CONTACT
WELCOME
>> infos über mich
>> fotos
>> portfolio
[© 2003 by katharina nussbaumer]

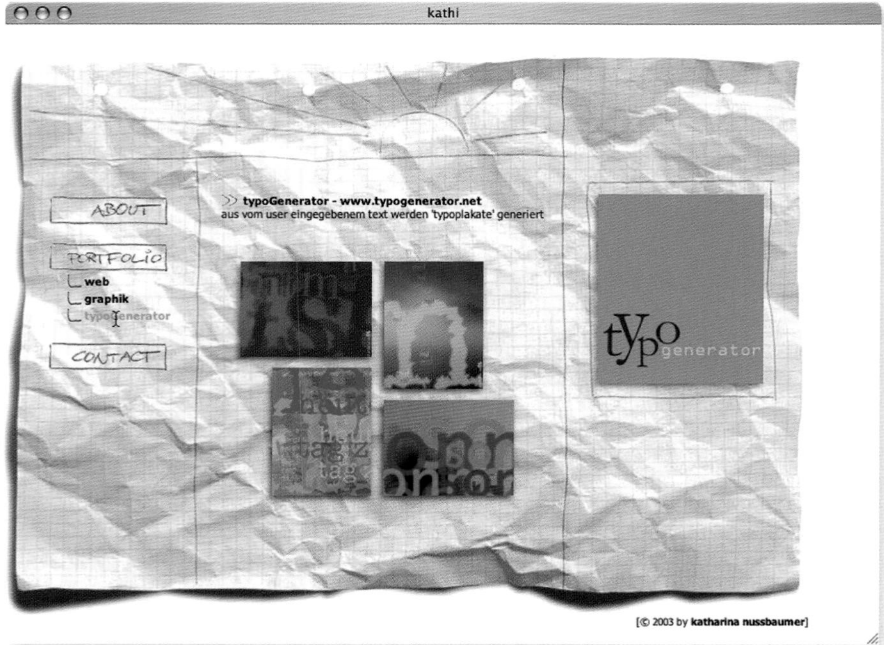
kathi
ABOUT
PORTFOLIO
web
graphik
typoGenerator
CONTACT
>> typoGenerator - www.typogenerator.net
aus vom user eingegebenem text werden 'typoplakate' generiert
typo generator
[© 2003 by katharina nussbaumer]

kathi.nussnet.at

D: katharina nussbaumer

M: kathi@nussnet.at

mg@

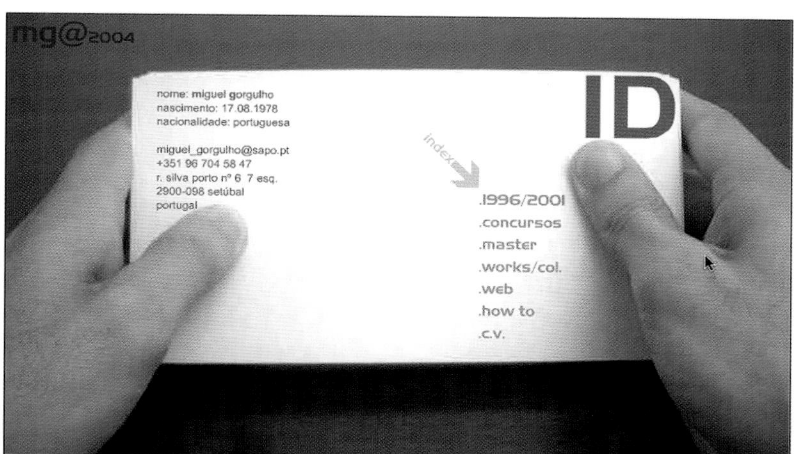
mg@2004
nome: miguel gorgulho
nascimento: 17.08.1978
nacionalidade: portuguesa
miguel_gorgulho@sapo.pt
+351 96 704 58 47
r. silva porto nº 6 7 esq.
2900-098 setúbal
portugal
ID
index
.1996/2001
.concursos
.master
.works/col.
.web
.how to
.c.v.

design by: miguel gorgulho

mg@

mg@2004
> vic
.stop .play
Concurso restrito para a elaboração de um projecto de urbanização de 3600 fogos e
zonas de equipamento com vista a criar um novo limite da cidade de Vic.
Vic, Barcelona, Espanha.
Responsável pelo concurso
1º prémio
back to works/col
back

design by: miguel gorgulho

www.miguelgorgulho.no.sapo.pt
D: miguel gorgulho
M: miguel_gorgulho@portugalmail.pt

Portfolio Bob Corporaal

PORTFOLIO BOB CORPORAAL v2 fugu mei 2004

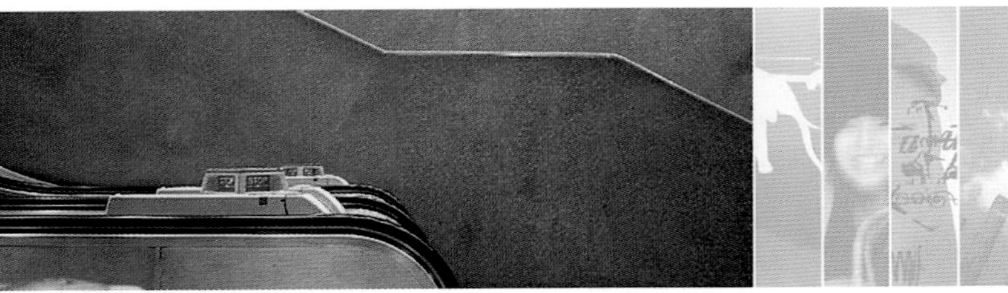

BOB CORPORAAL - FREELANCE VORMGEVING & INTERACTIE ONTWERP

HOME
INFORMATIE
CONTACT
ENGLISH

Een collectie van recente projecten en informatie. Oftewel mijn portfolio.

Als vormgever en interactie ontwerper heb ik de afgelopen 8 jaar ruime ervaring opgedaan met een grote verscheidenheid aan projecten. Websites, fotografie, posters, t-shirts, drukwerk, logo's en projecties.

info@reefscape.net

andere sites:
reefscape.net
latenightnoodles.net

Portfolio Bob Corporaal

PORTFOLIO BOB CORPORAAL v2 fugu mei 2004

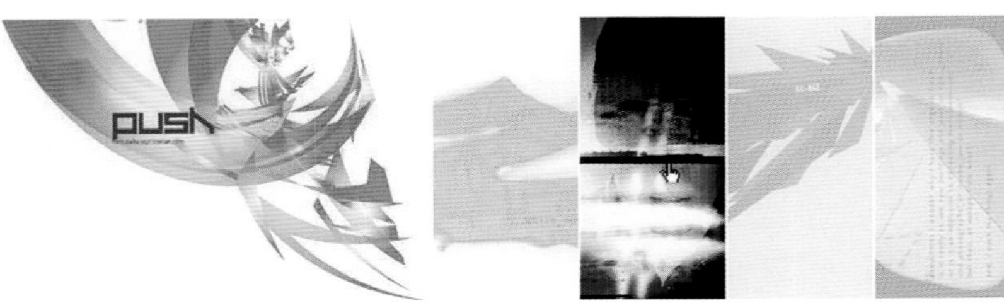
push

INFORMATIE

HOME
INFORMATIE
PROJECTEN
CONTACT
ENGLISH

Na een groot aantal projecten waaronder mijn eigen site reefscape.net, heb ik bijna twee jaar gewerkt bij het communicatie bureau PLAYcollective. Hier was ik als interactie ontwerper verantwoordelijk voor de vormgeving, functioneel ontwerp en de ontwikkeling van websites.

Sinds begin 2004 werk ik als freelance vormgever en interactie ontwerper. Als ontwerper maak ik graag dingen die de gebruiker boeien door een sterke combinatie van vormgeving en interactiviteit zonder daarbij de bruikbaarheid te vergeten.

Ook ben ik betrokken bij Magic Marketing, een netwerk van ontwerp en marketing professionals. Voor Naar Voren heb ik een artikel geschreven over Flash Actionscript. Een andere kijk op mijn interesses is te lezen in het interview van Annedien Hoen van Impulsant.

Als aanvulling op reefscape.net ben ik in 2004 begonnen met latenightnoodles.net. Deze site bevat persoonlijk flash en processing projecten.

andere sites:
reefscape.net
latenightnoodles.net
Magic Marketing
Naar voren artikel
interview Annedien

portfolio.reefscape.net
D: bob corporaal
A: reefscape **M:** info@reefscape.net

christopher luxton dot com
NEWS!
Work
Scrap Paper
Resume
Contact

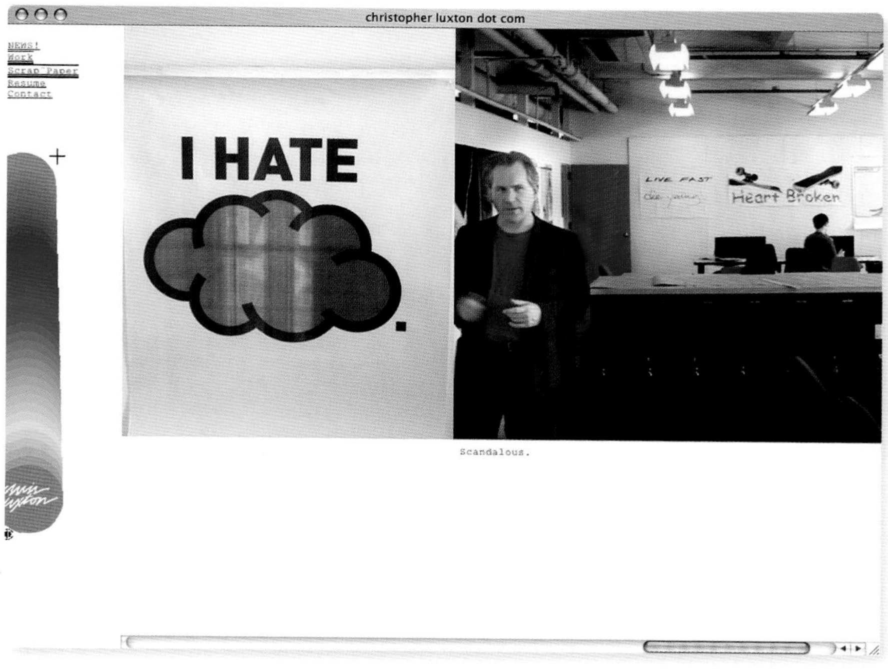
christopher luxton dot com
NEWS!
Work
Scrap Paper
Resume
Contact
I HATE
LIVE FAST
Heart Broken
Scandalous.

www.christopherluxton.com
D: christopher luxton
M: cluxton@gmail.com

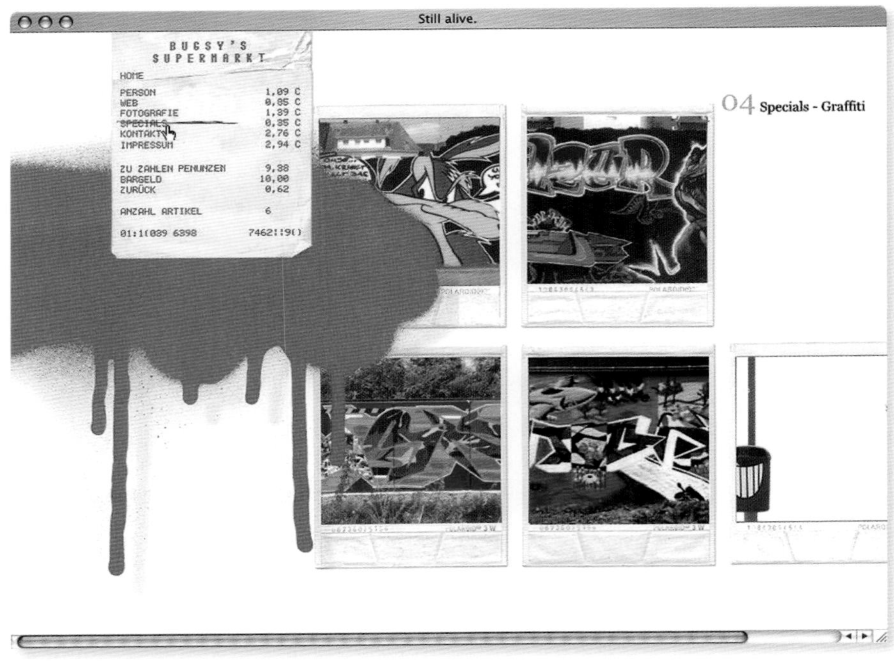
Still alive.
BUGSY'S
SUPERMARKT
HOME
PERSON 1,09 C
WEB 0,85 C
FOTOGRAFIE 1,39 C
SPECIALS 0,35 C
KONTAKT 2,76 C
IMPRESSUM 2,94 C
ZU ZAHLEN PENUNZEN 9,38
BARGELD 10,00
ZURÜCK 0,62
ANZAHL ARTIKEL 6
04 Specials - Graffiti

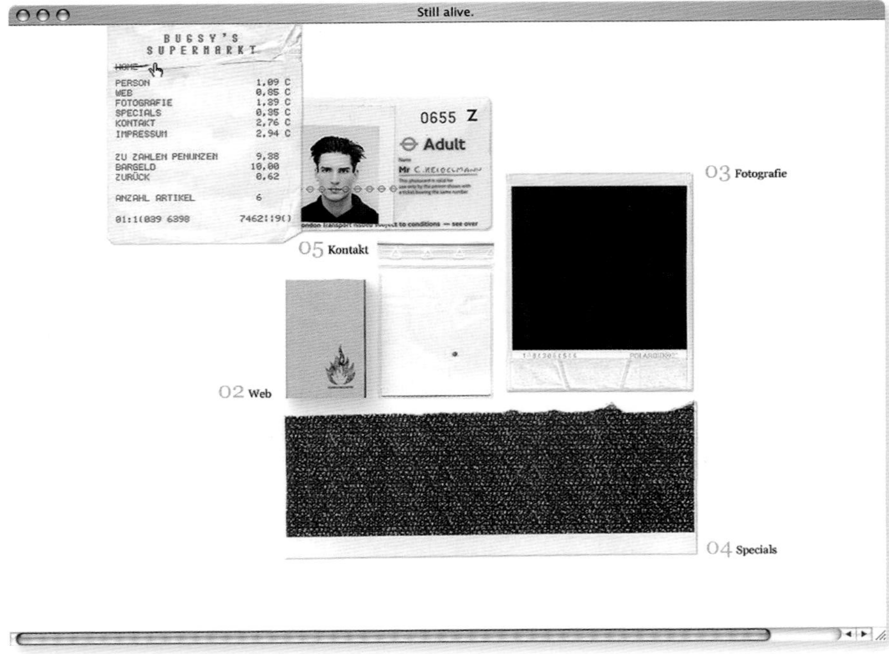
Still alive.
BUGSY'S
SUPERMARKT
HOME
PERSON 1,09 C
WEB 0,85 C
FOTOGRAFIE 1,39 C
SPECIALS 0,35 C
KONTAKT 2,76 C
IMPRESSUM 2,94 C
ZU ZAHLEN PENUNZEN 9,38
BARGELD 10,00
ZURÜCK 0,62
ANZAHL ARTIKEL 6
0655 Z
Adult
05 Kontakt
03 Fotografie
02 Web
04 Specials

www.still-alive.de
D: christian heidemann
M: mail@still-alive.de

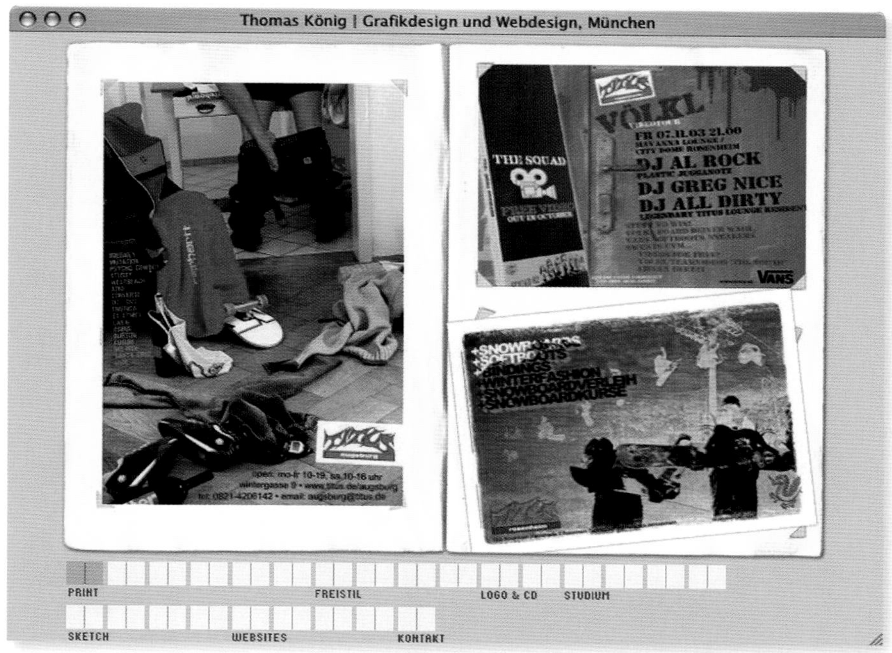
Thomas König | Grafikdesign und Webdesign, München
VÖLKL
THE SQUAD
DJ AL ROCK
DJ GREG NICE
DJ ALL DIRTY
VANS
+SNOWBOARDS
+SOFTBOOTS
+BINDINGS
+WINTERFASHION
+SNOWBOARDVERLEIH
+SNOWBOARDKURSE
PRINT
FREISTIL
LOGO & CD
STUDIUM
SKETCH
WEBSITES
KONTAKT

Thomas König | Grafikdesign und Webdesign, München
PRINT
LOGO & CD
STUDIUM
SKETCH
WEBSITES
KONTAKT

www.thomaskoenig.de
D: thomas koenig
M: thomas@thomaskoenig.de

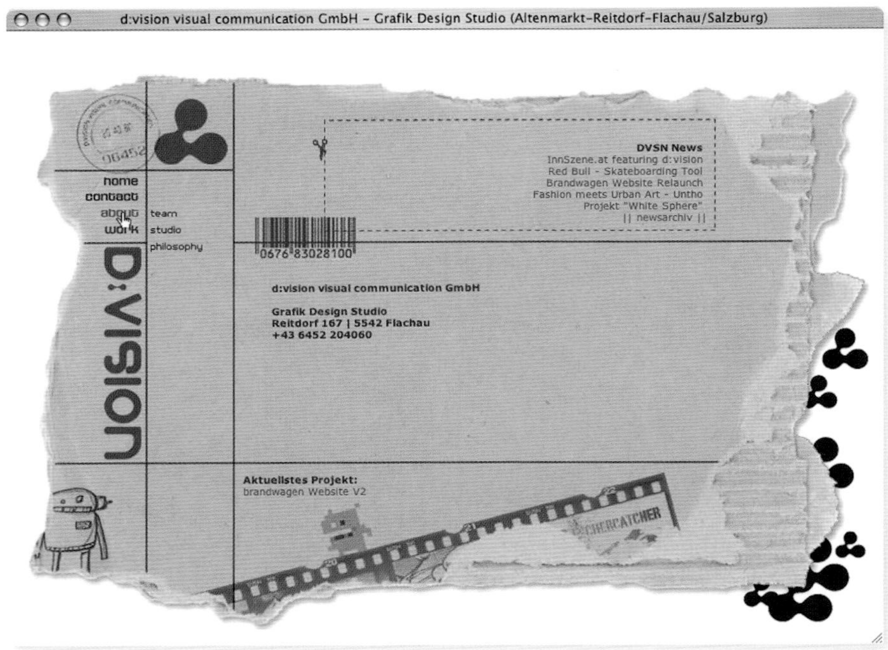
d:vision visual communication GmbH - Grafik Design Studio (Altenmarkt-Reitdorf-Flachau/Salzburg)
home
contact
about
work
team
studio
philosophy
D:VISION
DVSN News
InnSzene.at featuring d:vision
Red Bull - Skateboarding Tool
Brandwagen Website Relaunch
Fashion meets Urban Art - Untho
Projekt "White Sphere"
|| newsarchiv ||
0676 83028100
d:vision visual communication GmbH
Grafik Design Studio
Reitdorf 167 | 5542 Flachau
+43 6452 204060
Aktuellstes Projekt:
brandwagen Website V2

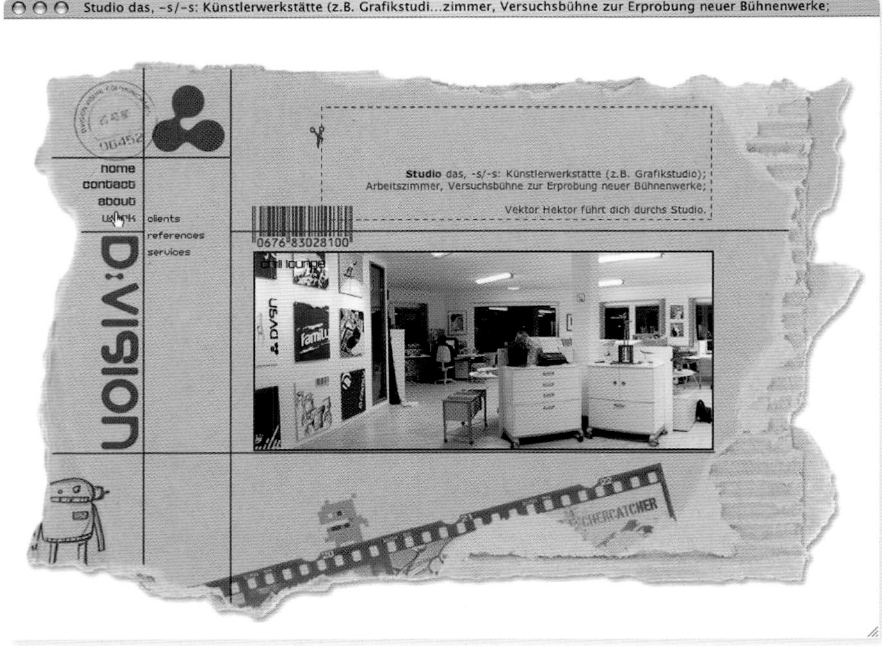
Studio das, -s/-s: Künstlerwerkstätte (z.B. Grafikstudi...zimmer, Versuchsbühne zur Erprobung neuer Bühnenwerke;
home
contact
about
work
clients
references
services
D:VISION
Studio das, -s/-s: Künstlerwerkstätte (z.B. Grafikstudio);
Arbeitszimmer, Versuchsbühne zur Erprobung neuer Bühnenwerke;
Vektor Hektor führt dich durchs Studio.
0676 83028100

www.dvsn.at
D: kathi macheiner **C:** mac krebernik
A: d:vision **M:** studio@dvsn.at

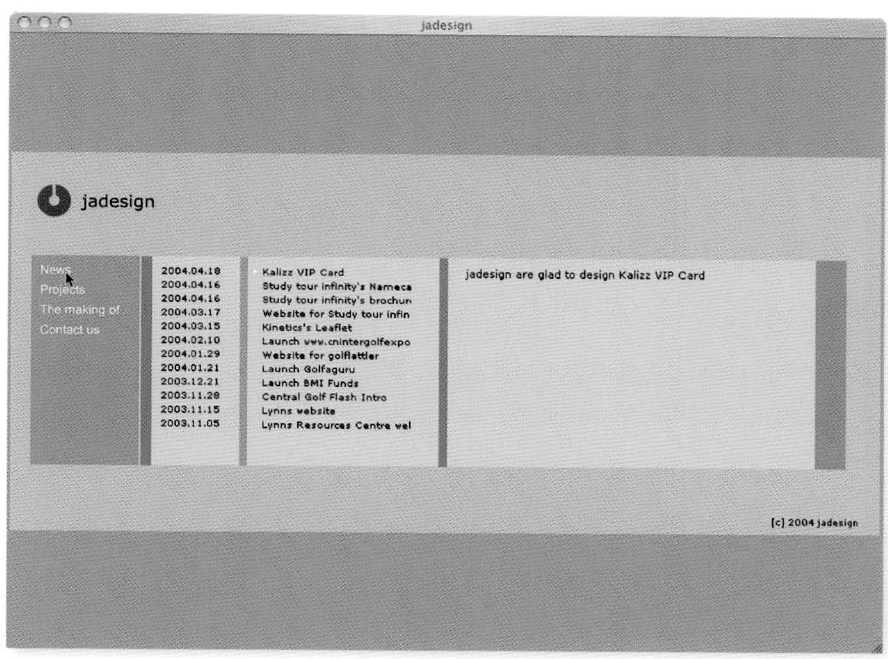
jadesign
jadesign
News
Projects
The making of
Contact us
2004.04.18 Kalizz VIP Card
2004.04.16 Study tour infinity's Nameca
2004.04.16 Study tour infinity's brochur
2004.03.17 Website for Study tour infin
2004.03.15 Kinetics's Leaflet
2004.02.10 Launch www.cnintergolfexpo
2004.01.29 Website for golflattler
2004.01.21 Launch Golfaguru
2003.12.21 Launch BMI Funds
2003.11.28 Central Golf Flash Intro
2003.11.15 Lynns website
2003.11.05 Lynns Resources Centre wel
jadesign are glad to design Kalizz VIP Card
[c] 2004 jadesign

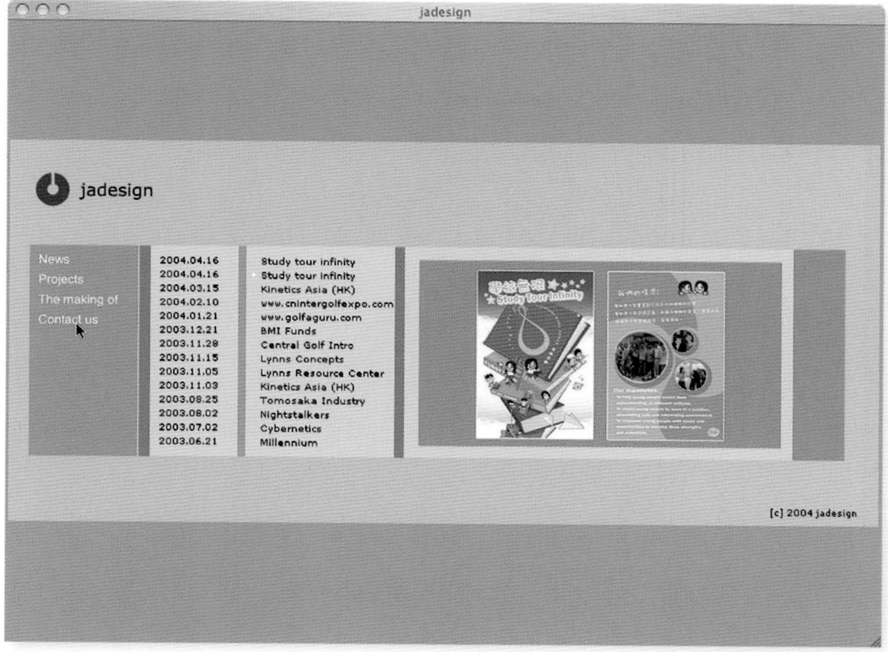
jadesign
jadesign
News
Projects
The making of
Contact us
2004.04.16 Study tour infinity
2004.04.16 Study tour infinity
2004.03.15 Kinetics Asia (HK)
2004.02.10 www.cnintergolfexpo.com
2004.01.21 www.golfaguru.com
2003.12.21 BMI Funds
2003.11.28 Central Golf Intro
2003.11.15 Lynns Concepts
2003.11.05 Lynns Resource Center
2003.11.03 Kinetics Asia (HK)
2003.08.25 Tomosaka Industry
2003.08.02 Nightstalkers
2003.07.02 Cybernetics
2003.06.21 Millennium
Study Tour Infinity
[c] 2004 jadesign

nightstalkers.jadesign.com.hk
D: arnold chan
A: jadesign **M:** arnold@jadesign.com.hk

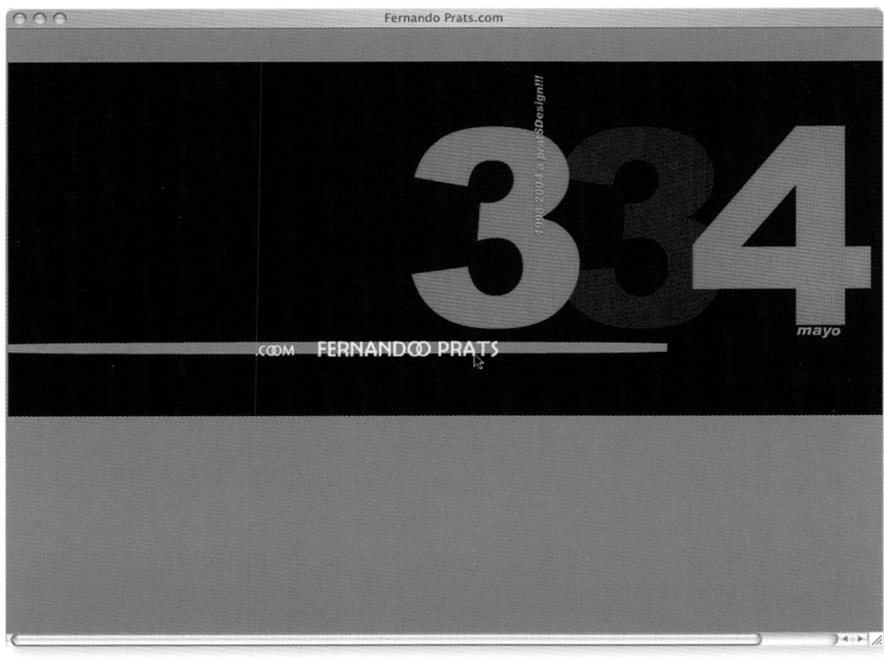
Fernando Prats.com
1998-2004 a pratsDesign!!!
334
mayo
.COOM FERNANDOO PRATS

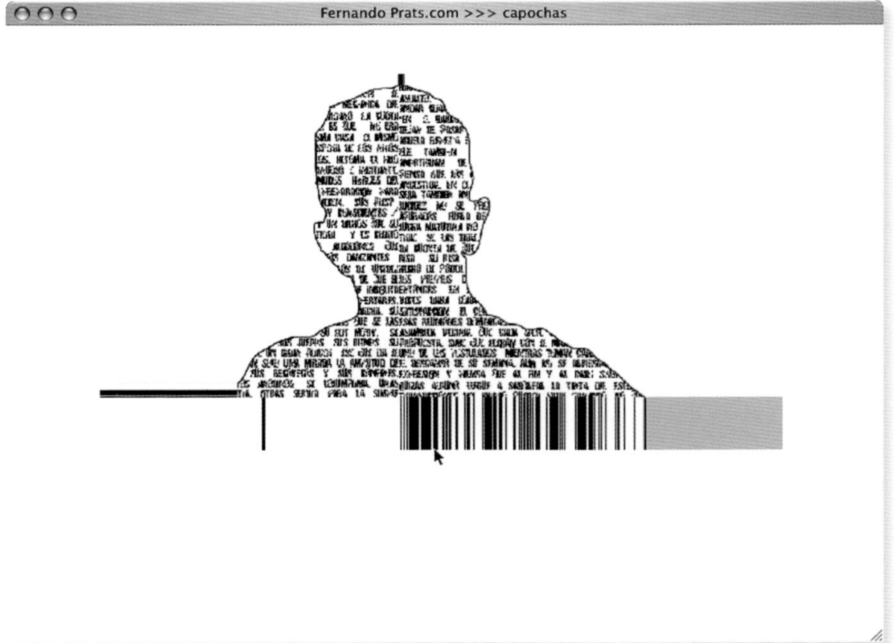
Fernando Prats.com >>> capochas

www.fernandoprats.com
D: fernando prats
A: pratsdesign **M:** info@fernandoprats.com

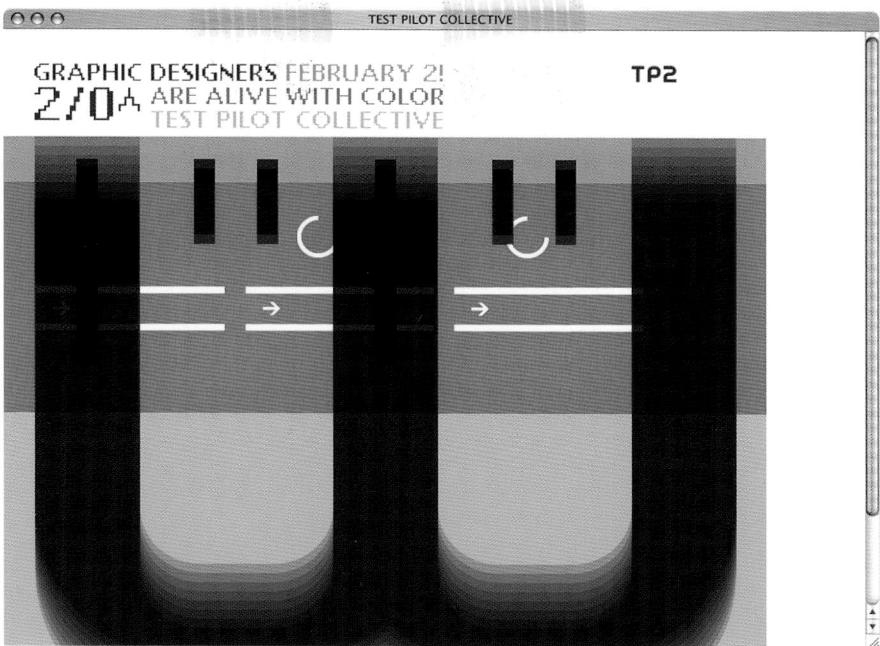
TEST PILOT COLLECTIVE
GRAPHIC DESIGNERS FEBRUARY 2!
2/04 ARE ALIVE WITH COLOR
TEST PILOT COLLECTIVE
TP2

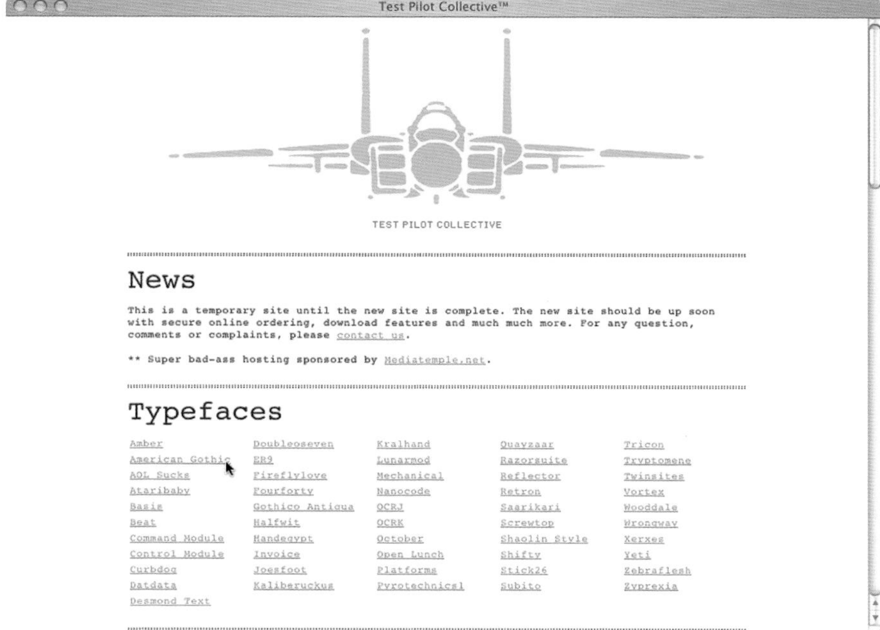
Test Pilot Collective™
TEST PILOT COLLECTIVE
News
This is a temporary site until the new site is complete. The new site should be up soon with secure online ordering, download features and much much more. For any question, comments or complaints, please contact us.
** Super bad-ass hosting sponsored by Mediatemple.net.
Typefaces
Amber
American Gothic
AOL Sucks
Ataribaby
Basis
Beat
Command Module
Control Module
Curbdog
Datdata
Desmond Text
Doubleoseven
ER9
Fireflylove
Fourforty
Gothico Antiqua
Halfwit
Handegypt
Invoice
Joesfoot
Kaliberuckus
Kralhand
Lunarmod
Mechanical
Nanocode
OCRJ
OCRK
October
Open Lunch
Platforms
Pyrotechnics1
Quayzaar
Razorsuite
Reflector
Retron
Saarikari
Screwtop
Shaolin Style
Shifty
Stick26
Subito
Tricon
Tryptomene
Twinsites
Vortex
Wooddale
Wrongway
Xerxes
Yeti
Zebraflesh
Zyprexia

www.testpilotcollective.com
D: joseph kral **C:** matt desmond
A: test pilot **M:** info@testpilotcollective.com

Анимация. Иллюстрации. Фирменный стиль. Дизайн студия Тундра.
TOONDRA
animation studio
новости портфолио услуги контакт о нас ссылки заставка
ПОРТФОЛИО/
В этом разделе представлены некоторые работы нашей студии.
АНИМАЦИЯ
анимация 3D веб-дизайн иллюстрации фирменный стиль
Активный десктоп для сети спортивных клубов "Sport Life"
Скринсейвер для сети спортивных клубов "Sport Life"
Рабочая версия игры "Разбей свою мышь" для рекламной акции компании "Defender"
(просто движок для игры)

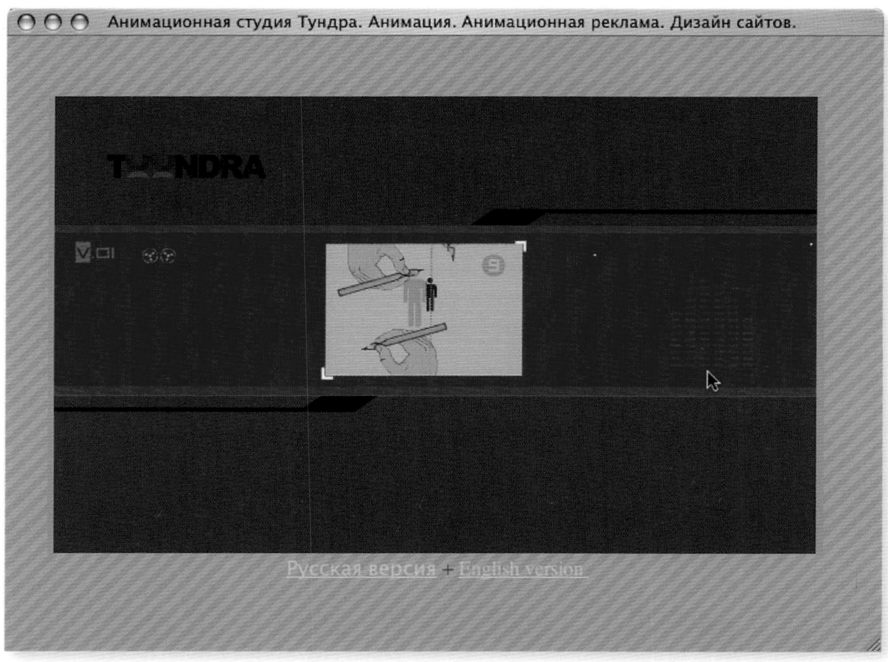
Анимационная студия Тундра. Анимация. Анимационная реклама. Дизайн сайтов.
TOONDRA
Русская версия + English version

www.toondra.ru
D: alexander satim
A: toondra animation-studio **M:** info@toondra.ru

doismaisdois.com
8.04.2004 READY TO GO
site pessoal de Diogo Melo (in English).
19.02.2004 o bom M
mini-site para a curta metragem "o bom M" de Miguel Uhlfelder.
12.02.2004 WEB DESIGN INDEX 4
Estamos presentes no Catálogo de Web Design anual, "uma das publicações + importantes da área".
15.01.2004 www.lajjarecordings.com
"as Pure as it Gets" o conceito chave por trás da visão de Maurel & Fauvrelle para a editora lajjarecordings. Foi e é um prazer trabalhar com
MY FAVOURITE CONFERENCE 2004 / SINGAPORE
NEXT SLIDE
22 EXTRAS
04 QUEM SOMOS
03 LIGAÇÕES
02 CONTACTO
01 PORTFOLIO
00 INDEX

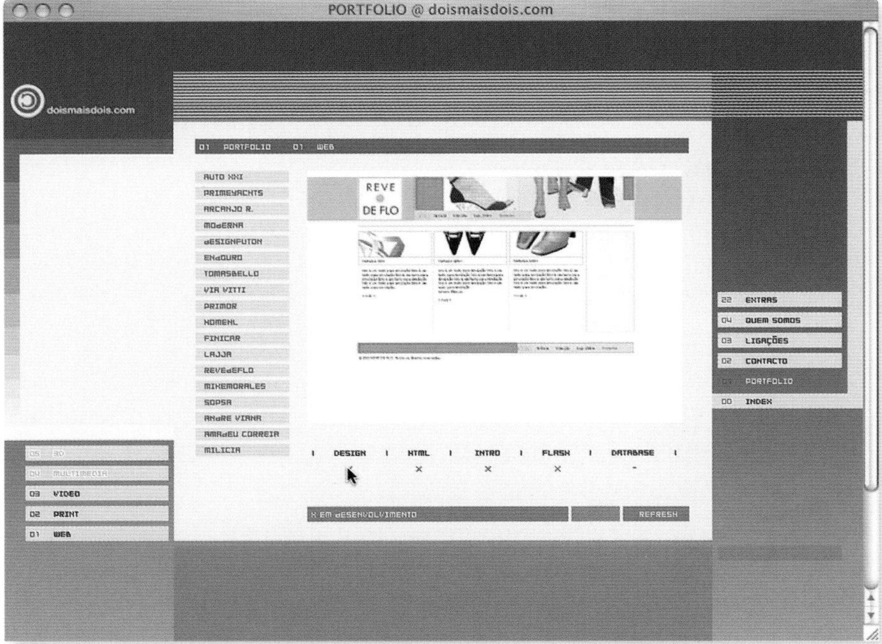
PORTFOLIO @ doismaisdois.com
doismaisdois.com
01 PORTFOLIO 01 WEB
AUTO XXI
PRIMEYACHTS
ARCANJO R.
MOdERNA
dESIGNFUTON
ENdOURO
TOMASBELLO
VIA VITTI
PRIMOR
HOMEHL
FINICAR
LAJJA
REVEdEFLO
MIKEMORALES
SOPSA
ANdRE VIANA
AMAdEU CORREIA
MILICIA
REVE DE FLO
DESIGN
HTML
INTRO
FLASH
DATABASE
X EM dESENVOLVIMENTO
REFRESH
22 EXTRAS
04 QUEM SOMOS
03 LIGAÇÕES
02 CONTACTO
01 PORTFOLIO
00 INDEX
05 3D
04 MULTIMEDIA
03 VIDEO
02 PRINT
01 WEB

www.doismaisdois.com
D: diogo melo
A: doismaisdois **M:** dmelo@netcabo.pt

++++ MOO ++++ productora de vídeo, diseño gráfico y diseño web
moo
{impresiona} + {edita} + {interactiva} + {crea}
{comoonicación}
MOO es una productora que une a realizadores y diseñadores gráficos en este estudio, a las afueras de Madrid, para ofrecer un servicio íntegro de imagen y comunicación. Bienvenido al moondo MOO.
MOODRIGUERA
{mooestras} + {comoonidad} + {termoometro} + {curriculumoo} + {mooralla} + {moosica}
MOO invitado por el Festival de Málaga para participar en la sección ART TV (22-30 abril)
MOO y 24 PRODUCCIONES empiezan el rodaje del documental sobre el diseñador de moda "Davidelfin".
El diario 'El País' en su suplemento 'Ciberpaís', recomienda nuestra web moo.es Gracias
© Decollage MOO S.L. - Todos los derechos reservados - Datos legales

++++ MOO ++++ productora de vídeo, diseño gráfico y diseño web
moo
{impresiona} + {edita} + {interactiva} + {crea}
{comoonicación}
arte digital
creaciones
{mooestras} + {comoonidad} + {termoometro} + {curriculumoo} + {mooralla} + {moosica}
MOO invitado por el Festival de Málaga para participar en la sección ART TV (22-30 abril)
MOO y 24 PRODUCCIONES empiezan el rodaje del documental sobre el diseñador de moda "Davidelfin".
El diario 'El País' en su suplemento 'Ciberpaís', recomienda nuestra web moo.es Gracias
© Decollage MOO S.L. - Todos los derechos reservados - Datos legales

www.moo.es
D: pilar vazquez-pena **P:** nesto
A: moo **M:** pilar@moo.es

::: Aridient : Where Creativity Means Business :::
ambience on
10th Apr 2005, Sun 19:12:24
aridient
the aridient approach
If your company is serious about growing your business by leveraging design and communications technologies, then Aridient is the right outsource for you. We promise to strive to become "your trusted creative partner." We will work hard to understand the challenges your company or organization is facing and will help you bridge the gap between where you are today and where you want to be.
About us | Expertise | Approach | Portfolio | Insights | Contact
where creativity means business
news
20/07/2004 : Aridient launches its revamped website with more interactivity.
12/06/2004 : Aridient featured in July issue of Marketing Magazine - Singapore's Marketing
LEARN : Strap on your Thinking Cap
Learn
Work
Play
Home | Privacy Policy | © Copyright 2004 Aridient Pte Ltd
client login

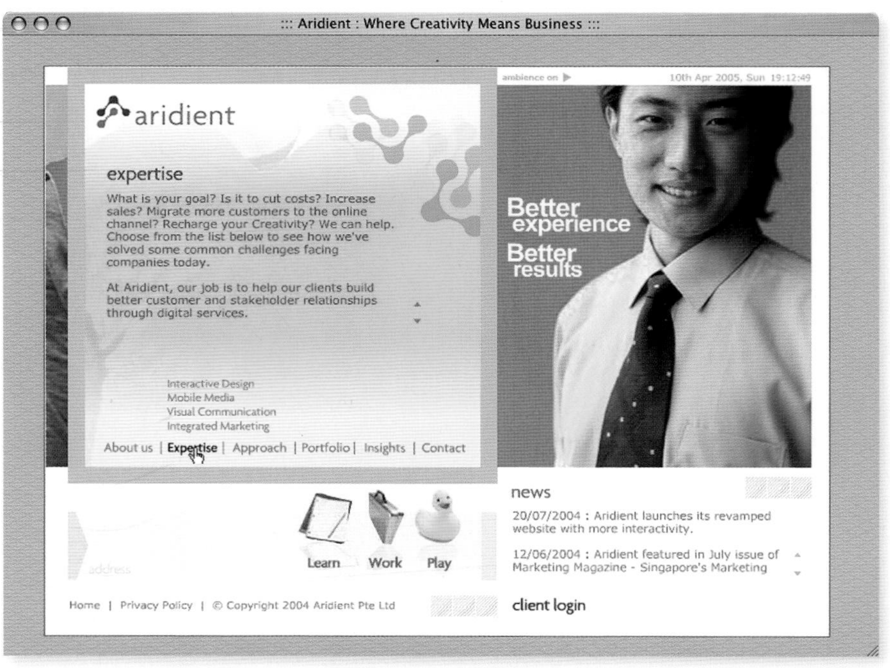
::: Aridient : Where Creativity Means Business :::
ambience on
10th Apr 2005, Sun 19:12:49
aridient
expertise
What is your goal? Is it to cut costs? Increase sales? Migrate more customers to the online channel? Recharge your Creativity? We can help. Choose from the list below to see how we've solved some common challenges facing companies today.
At Aridient, our job is to help our clients build better customer and stakeholder relationships through digital services.
Interactive Design
Mobile Media
Visual Communication
Integrated Marketing
About us | Expertise | Approach | Portfolio | Insights | Contact
Better experience
Better results
news
20/07/2004 : Aridient launches its revamped website with more interactivity.
12/06/2004 : Aridient featured in July issue of Marketing Magazine - Singapore's Marketing
Learn
Work
Play
Home | Privacy Policy | © Copyright 2004 Aridient Pte Ltd
client login

www.aridient.com
D: alan leong
A: aridient **M:** info@aridient.com

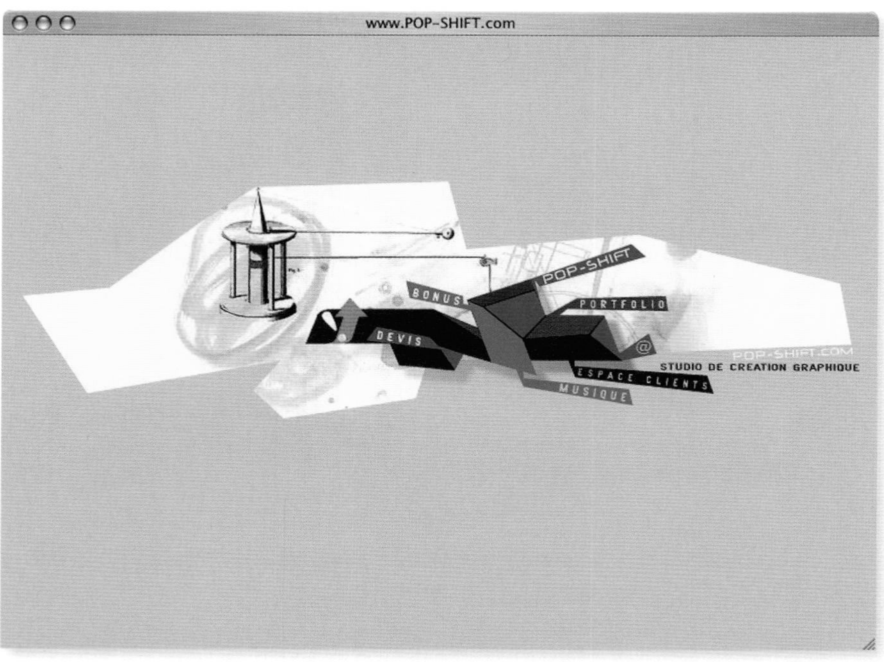
www.POP-SHIFT.com
POP-SHIFT
BONUS
PORTFOLIO
DEVIS
@
POP-SHIFT.COM
STUDIO DE CREATION GRAPHIQUE
ESPACE CLIENTS
MUSIQUE

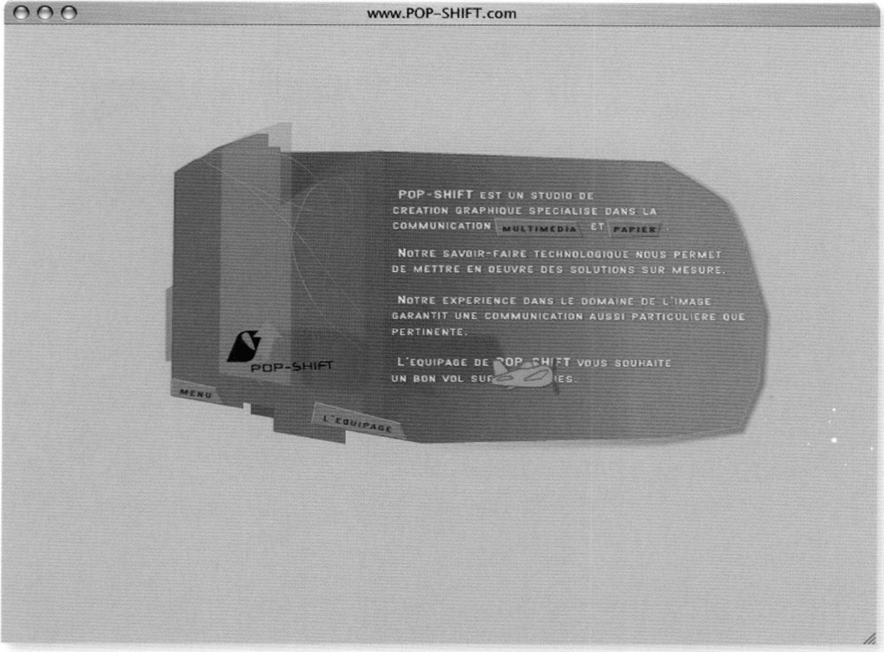
www.POP-SHIFT.com
POP-SHIFT EST UN STUDIO DE
CREATION GRAPHIQUE SPECIALISE DANS LA
COMMUNICATION MULTIMEDIA ET PAPIER.
NOTRE SAVOIR-FAIRE TECHNOLOGIQUE NOUS PERMET
DE METTRE EN OEUVRE DES SOLUTIONS SUR MESURE.
NOTRE EXPERIENCE DANS LE DOMAINE DE L'IMAGE
GARANTIT UNE COMMUNICATION AUSSI PARTICULIERE QUE
PERTINENTE.
POP-SHIFT
MENU
L'EQUIPAGE

www.pop-shift.com
D: jean-christophe lantier **C:** nicolas brignol
A: pop-shift **M:** jlantier@pop-shift.com

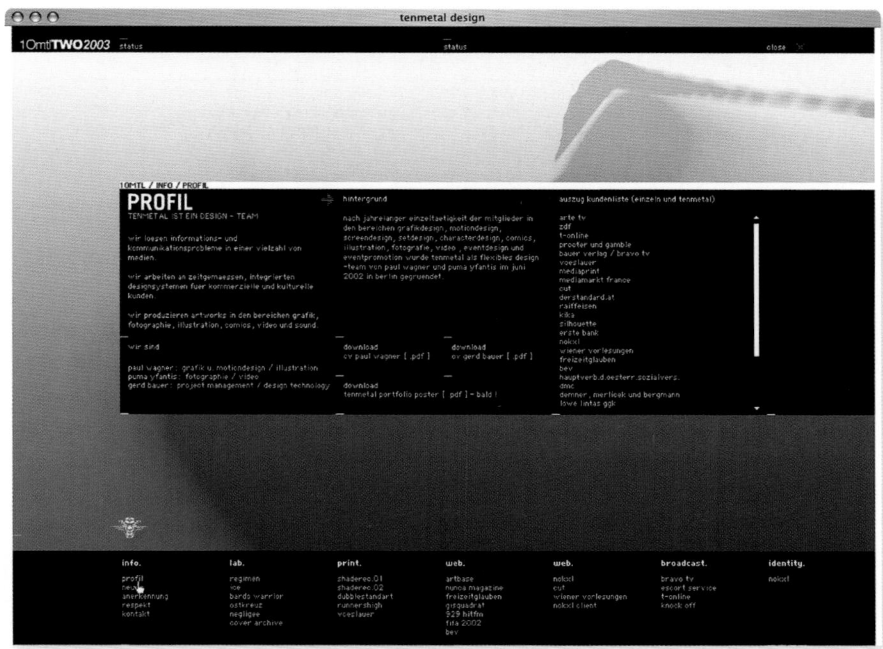
tenmetal design
1OmtlTWO2003 status
status
close
10MTL / INFO / PROFIL
PROFIL
TENMETAL IST EIN DESIGN - TEAM
wir loesen informations- und kommunikationsprobleme in einer vielzahl von medien.
wir arbeiten an zeitgemaessen, integrierten designsystemen fuer kommerzielle und kulturelle kunden.
wir produzieren artworks in den bereichen grafik, fotographie, illustration, comics, video und sound.
wir sind
paul wagner : grafik u. motiondesign / illustration
puma yfantis : fotographie / video
gerd bauer : project management / design technology
hintergrund
nach jahrelanger einzeltaetigkeit der mitglieder in den bereichen grafikdesign, motiondesign, screendesign, setdesign, characterdesign, comics, illustration, fotografie, video , eventdesign und eventpromotion wurde tenmetal als flexibles design -team von paul wagner und puma yfantis im juni 2002 in berlin gegruendet.
download
cv paul wagner [.pdf]
download
cv gerd bauer [.pdf]
download
tenmetal portfolio poster [.pdf] - bald !
auszug kundenliste (einzeln und tenmetal)
arte tv
zdf
t-online
procter und gamble
bauer verlag / bravo tv
voeslauer
mediaprint
mediamarkt france
cut
derstandard.at
raiffeisen
kika
silhouette
erste bank
nokxl
wiener vorlesungen
freizeitglauben
bev
hauptverb.d.oesterr.sozialvers.
dmc
demner , merlicek und bergmann
lowe lintas ggk
info.
profil
neues
anerkennung
respekt
kontakt
lab.
regimen
ice
bardo warrior
ostkreuz
negligee
cover archive
print.
shaderec.01
shaderec.02
dubblestandart
runnershigh
voeslauer
web.
artbase
nunca magazine
freizeitglauben
gisquadrat
929 hitfm
fifa 2002
bev
web.
nokxl
cut
wiener vorlesungen
nokxl client
broadcast.
bravo tv
escort service
t-online
knock off
identity.
nokxl

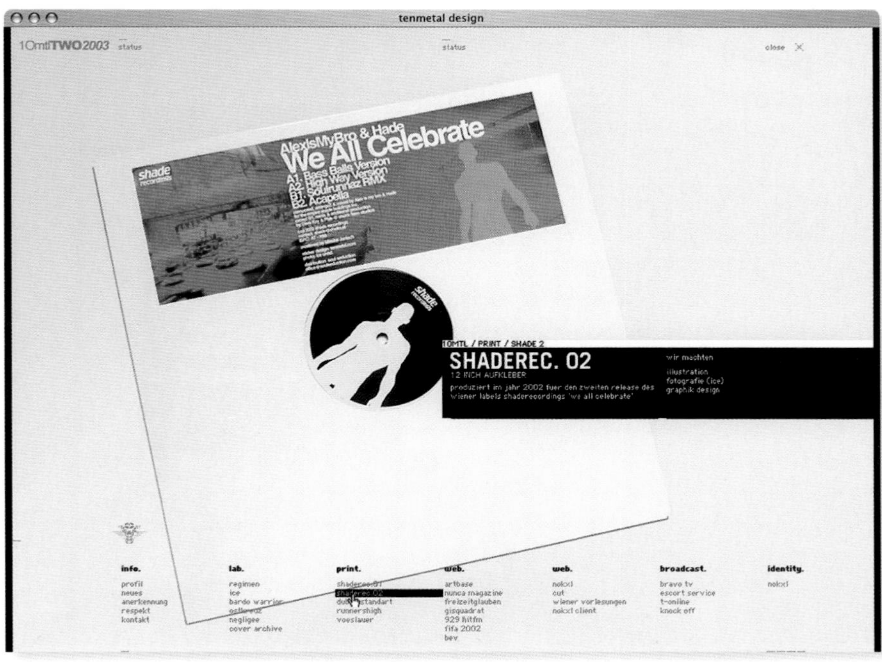
tenmetal design
1OmtlTWO2003 status
status
close
shade recordings
AlexIsMyBro & Hade
We All Celebrate
A1. Bass Balls Version
A2. High Way Version
B2. Acapella
10MTL / PRINT / SHADE 2
SHADEREC. 02
12 INCH AUFKLEBER
produziert im jahr 2002 fuer den zweiten release des wiener labels shaderecordings 'we all celebrate'
wir machten
illustration
fotografie (ice)
graphik design
info.
profil
neues
anerkennung
respekt
kontakt
lab.
regimen
ice
negligee
cover archive
print.
shaderec.02
runnershigh
voeslauer
web.
artbase
nunca magazine
freizeitglauben
gisquadrat
929 hitfm
fifa 2002
bev
web.
nokxl
cut
wiener vorlesungen
nokxl client
broadcast.
bravo tv
escort service
t-online
knock off
identity.
nokxl

www.tenmetal.com
D: paul wagner **C:** gerd bauer
A: tenmetal design **M:** pw@tenmetal.com

honey production || a freelancing multimedia artist..
Honey the toilet experience..
info
Honey is a freelancing multimedia artist. He does web, print, illustration, id, clothes (streetstyle).His speciality are flash produced web applications.. you will find more information on page 3. ENJOY..
contact
info@honeys.se
+46 704384485 (0704384485)
news
170105 STRANGEFRUITS..
Honey production marches on.
yet an another AWARD!!
081204 e-CREATIVE AWARD!!!
those which give insperation...
fredrik hörnström
love / a honey
FREEDOM
Honey
fly away
the online experience
goto
contents

honey production || a freelancing multimedia artist..
FREEDOM
display
place: apelviken sweden
A cold day in paradise
photo: honey crew
surfer: Don cavalli
goto
contents

www.honeys.se
D: fredrik hörnström **C:** fredrik hörnström
A: honeys **M:** info@honeys.se

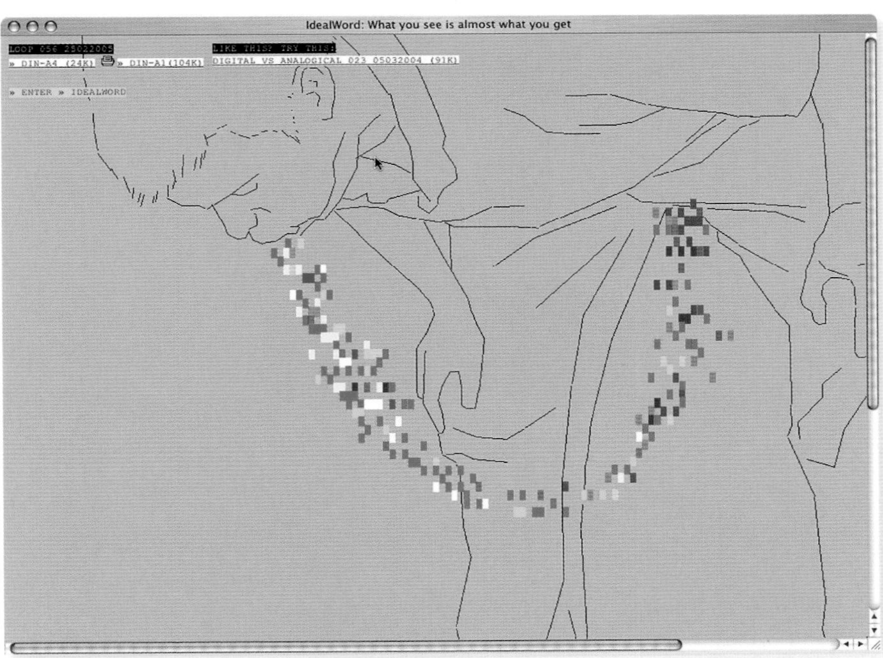
IdealWord: What you see is almost what you get
LOOP 056 25022005
» DIN-A4 (24K) » DIN-A1(104K)
LIKE THIS? TRY THIS:
DIGITAL VS ANALOGICAL 023 05032004 (91K)
» ENTER » IDEALWORD

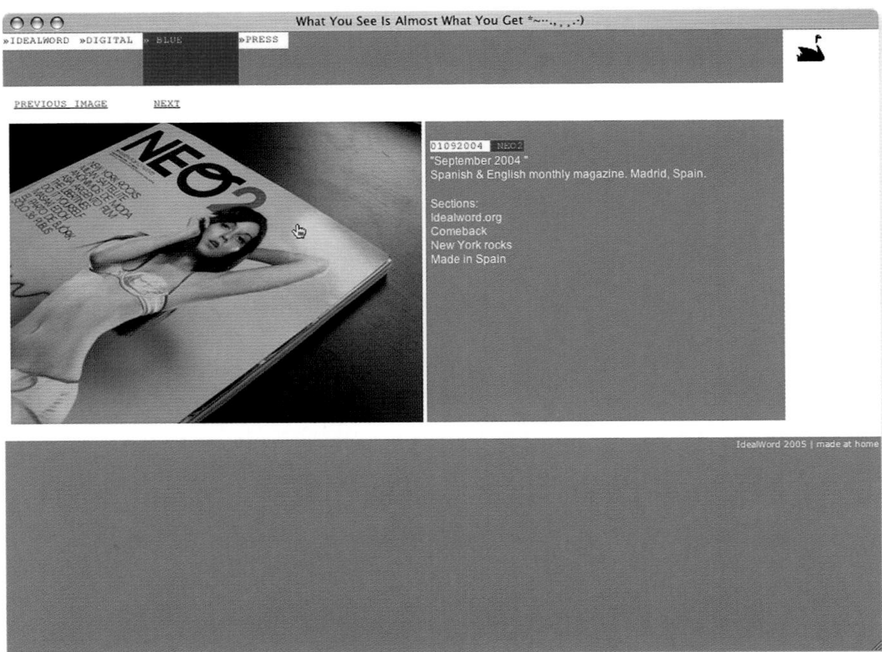
What You See Is Almost What You Get
»IDEALWORD »DIGITAL » BLUE »PRESS
PREVIOUS IMAGE NEXT
01092004 NEO2
"September 2004 "
Spanish & English monthly magazine. Madrid, Spain.
Sections:
Idealword.org
Comeback
New York rocks
Made in Spain
IdealWord 2005 | made at home

www.idealword.org
D: enrique radigales
A: enrichment **M:** perla@idealword.org

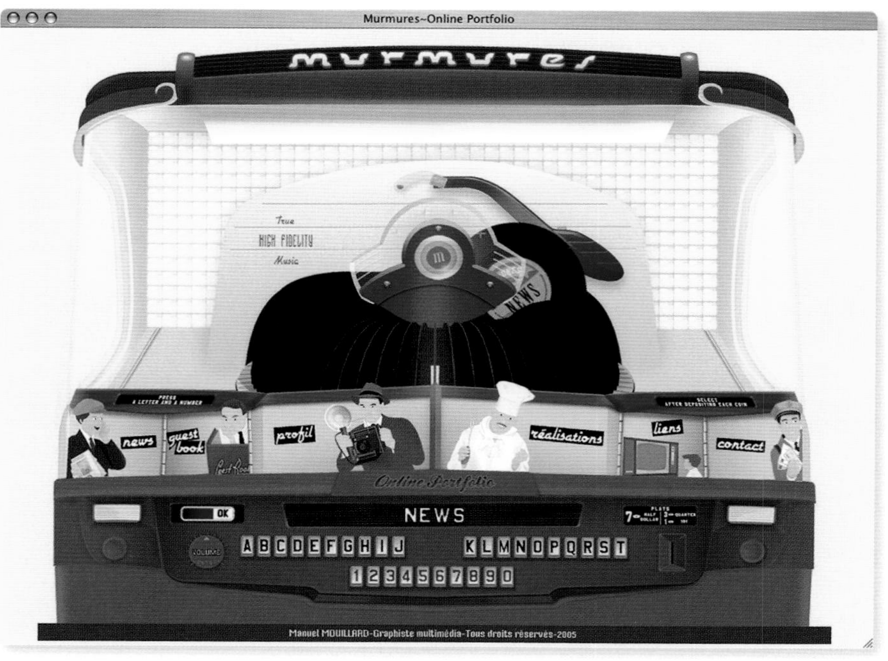
Murmures~Online Portfolio
murmures
True
HIGH FIDELITY
Music
news
guest book
profil
réalisations
liens
contact
Online Portfolio
OK
NEWS
VOLUME
ABCDEFGHIJ
KLMNOPQRST
1234567890
Manuel MOUILLARD-Graphiste multimédia-Tous droits réservés-2005

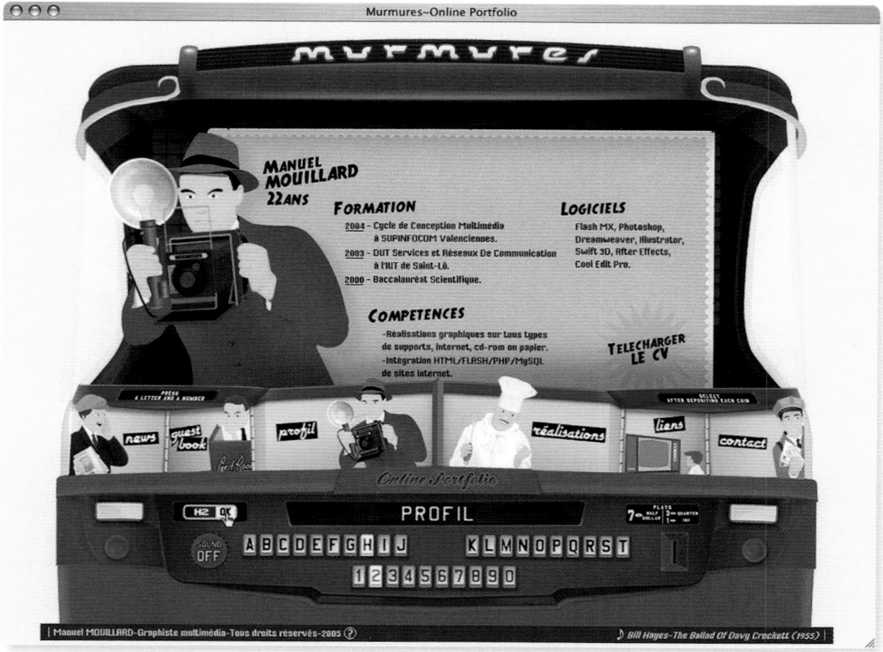
Murmures~Online Portfolio
murmures
MANUEL MOUILLARD
22ANS
FORMATION
2004 - Cycle de Conception Multimédia à SUPINFOCOM Valenciennes.
2003 - DUT Services et Réseaux De Communication à l'IUT de Saint-Lô.
2000 - Baccalauréat Scientifique.
LOGICIELS
Flash MX, Photoshop, Dreamweaver, Illustrator, Swift 3D, After Effects, Cool Edit Pro.
COMPETENCES
-Réalisations graphiques sur tous types de supports, internet, cd-rom ou papier.
-Intégration HTML/FLASH/PHP/MySQL de sites internet.
TELECHARGER LE CV
news
guest book
profil
réalisations
liens
contact
Online Portfolio
HZ OK
PROFIL
SOUND OFF
ABCDEFGHIJ
KLMNOPQRST
1234567890
Manuel MOUILLARD-Graphiste multimédia-Tous droits réservés-2005
Bill Hayes-The Ballad Of Davy Crockett (1955)

www.murmures.tk
D: manuel mouillard
M: contact@murmures.tk

RESN v1
RESN
Resn
Makers of fine websites
Mailing list
Wallpapers
Respect

RESN v2
RESN
Resn
Makers of web sushi
1024
1152
1280
1600
Wallpapers
GUEST BOOK
Mailing list
Wallpapers
Respect

www.resn.co.nz
D: rikki campbell, steve le marquand **C:** matt halford **P:** steve le marquand
A: resn **M:** hello@resn.co.nz

->SAMOURAI<-
DEMENAGEMENT
132 rue du Faubourg St-Denis
75010 Paris
75010 PARIS
01-44-89-85-00
numéros de téléphone inchangés
www.agence-samourai.com
SAMOURAI
FRAGILE
CLOSE
SAMOURAI, AGENCE DE CREATION VISUELLE
ACCUEIL
CAMPAGNES
CONTACTS
SAMOURAÏ
NEWSLETTER
GO

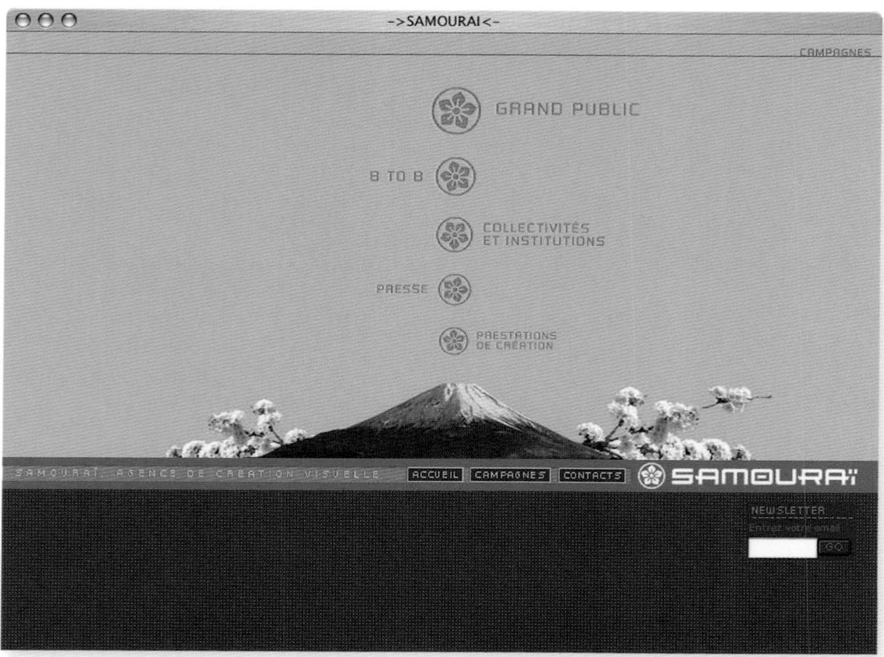
->SAMOURAI<-
CAMPAGNES
GRAND PUBLIC
B TO B
COLLECTIVITÉS
ET INSTITUTIONS
PRESSE
PRESTATIONS
DE CRÉATION
SAMOURAI, AGENCE DE CREATION VISUELLE
ACCUEIL
CAMPAGNES
CONTACTS
SAMOURAÏ
NEWSLETTER
GO

www.agence-samourai.com
D: matthieu corgnet **P:** breysse
A: gazole-production **M:** webmaster@tagence-samourai.com

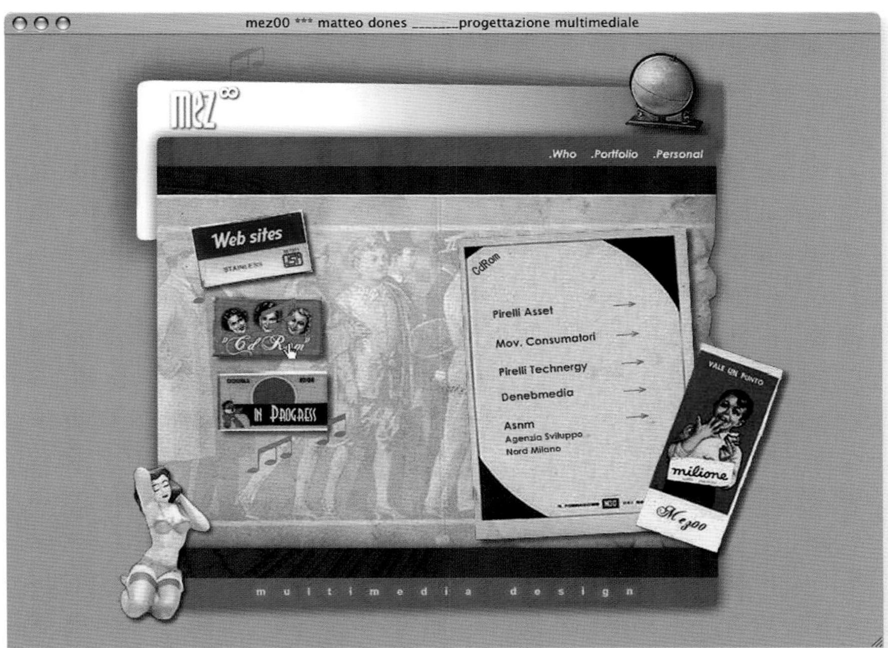
mez00 *** matteo dones _______progettazione multimediale
.Who .Portfolio .Personal
Web sites
CdRom
Pirelli Asset
Mov. Consumatori
Pirelli Technergy
Denebmedia
Asnm
Agenzia Sviluppo
Nord Milano
milione
m u l t i m e d i a d e s i g n

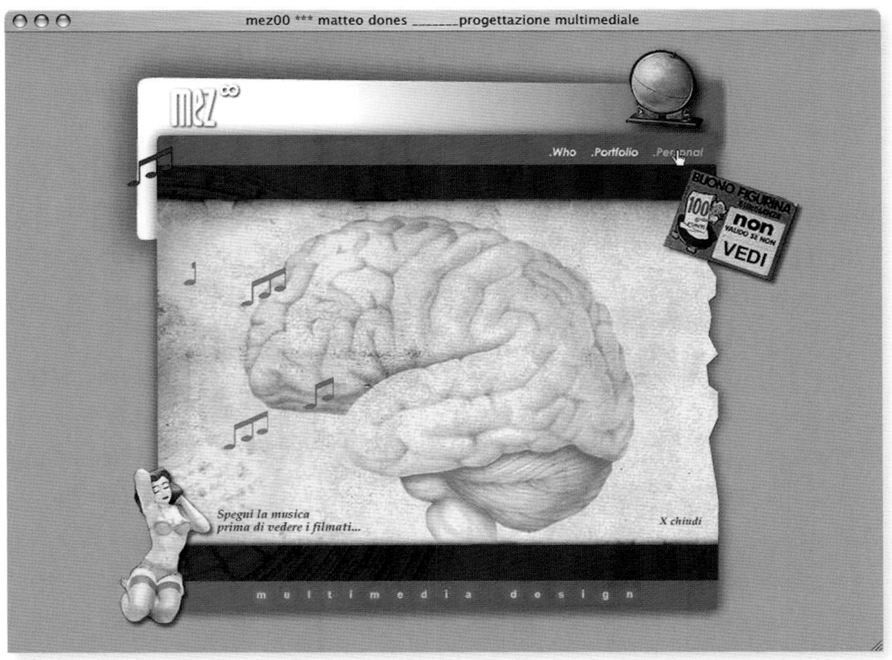
mez00 *** matteo dones _______progettazione multimediale
.Who .Portfolio .Personal
BUONO FIGURINA
non
VEDI
Spegni la musica
prima di vedere i filmati...
X chiudi
m u l t i m e d i a d e s i g n

www.mez00.net
D: matteo dones
M: matteo.dones@bastard.it

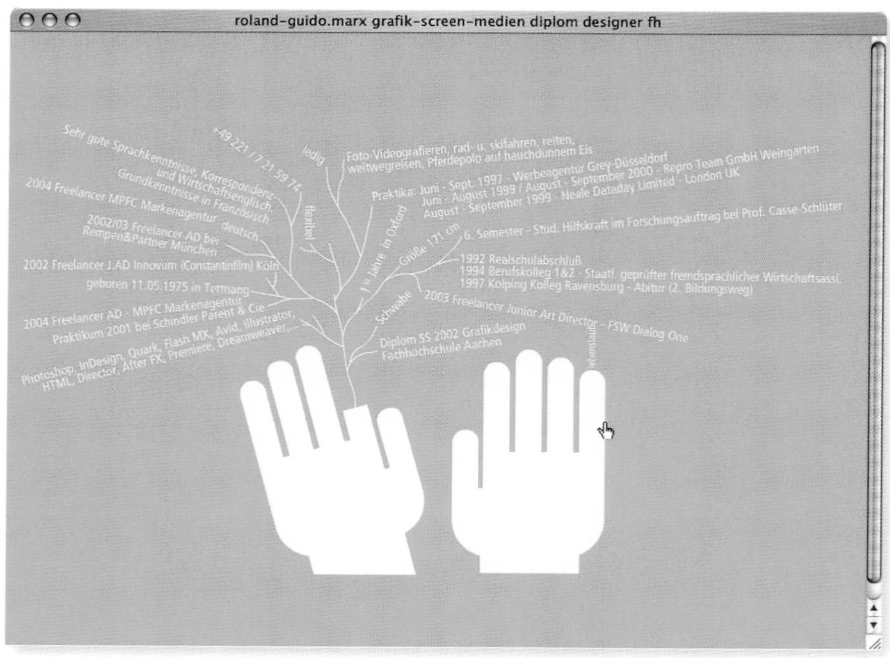
roland-guido.marx grafik-screen-medien diplom designer fh
Sehr gute Sprachkenntnisse, Korrespondenz- und Wirtschaftsenglisch, Grundkenntnisse in Französisch
+49 221 / 7 21 59 74
ledig
Foto Videografieren, rad- u. skifahren, reiten, weitwegreisen, Pferdepolo auf hauchdünnem Eis
2004 Freelancer MPFC Markenagentur
deutsch
flexibel
Praktika: Juni - Sept. 1997 - Werbeagentur Grey-Düsseldorf
Juni - August 1999 / August - September 2000 - Repro Team GmbH Weingarten
August - September 1999 - Neale Dataday Limited - London UK
2002/03 Freelancer AD bei Rempen&Partner München
1 ½ Jahre in Oxford
Größe 171 cm
6. Semester - Stud. Hilfskraft im Forschungsauftrag bei Prof. Casse-Schlüter
2002 Freelancer J.AD Innovum (Constantinfilm) Köln
1992 Realschulabschluß
1994 Berufskolleg 1&2 - Staatl. geprüfter fremdsprachlicher Wirtschaftsassi.
1997 Kolping Kolleg Ravensburg - Abitur (2. Bildungsweg)
geboren 11.05.1975 in Tettnang
Schwabe
2003 Freelancer Junior Art Director - FSW Dialog One
2004 Freelancer AD - MPFC Markenagentur
Praktikum 2001 bei Schindler Parent & Cie
Photoshop, InDesign, Quark, Flash MX, Avid, Illustrator, HTML, Director, After FX, Premiere, Dreamweaver,...
Diplom SS 2002 Grafikdesign Fachhochschule Aachen
lebenslauf

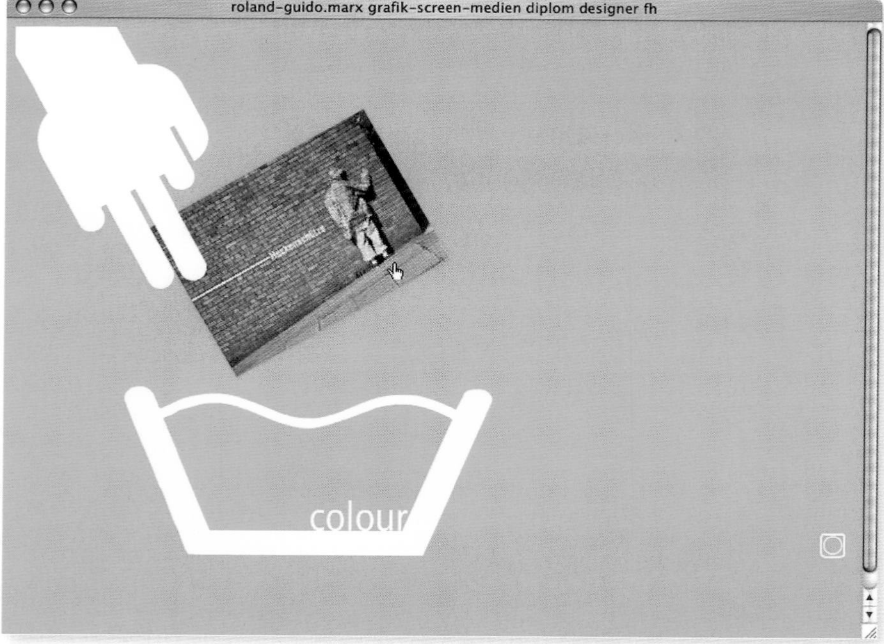
roland-guido.marx grafik-screen-medien diplom designer fh
colour

www.rgmarx.de
D: roland-guido marx
M: dsein@netcologne.de

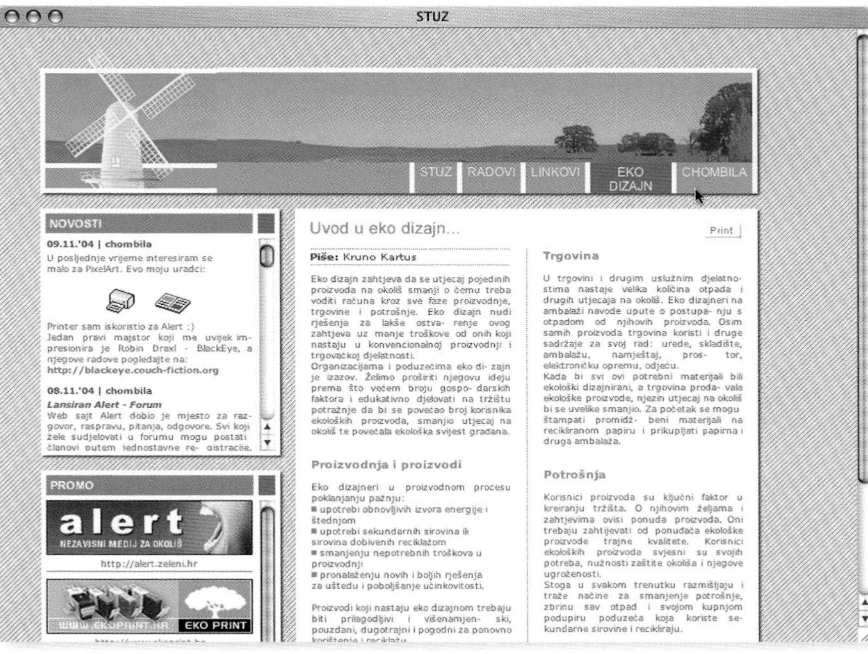
STUZ
STUZ
RADOVI
LINKOVI
EKO DIZAJN
CHOMBILA
NOVOSTI
09.11.'04 | chombila
08.11.'04 | chombila
Lansiran Alert - Forum
PROMO
alert
NEZAVISNI MEDIJ ZA OKOLIŠ
http://alert.zeleni.hr
WWW.EKOPRINT.HR
EKO PRINT
Uvod u eko dizajn...
Print
Piše: Kruno Kartus
Trgovina
Proizvodnja i proizvodi
Potrošnja

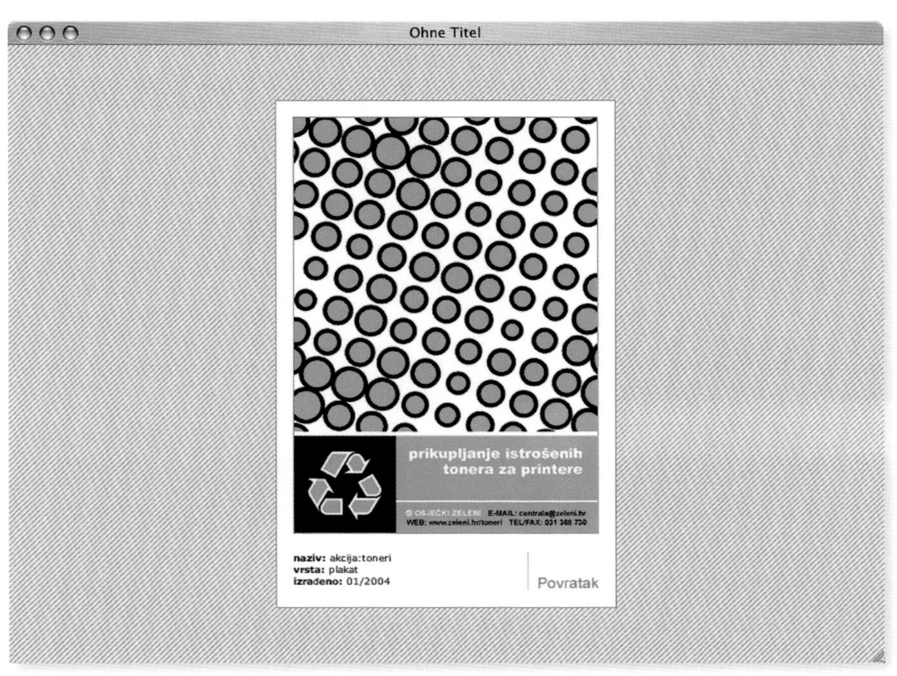
Ohne Titel
prikupljanje istrošenih
tonera za printere
naziv: akcija:toneri
vrsta: plakat
izrađeno: 01/2004
Povratak

www.zeleni.hr/stuz
D: vjenceslav svoboda
A: stuz - studio zeleni **M:** stuz@zeleni.hr

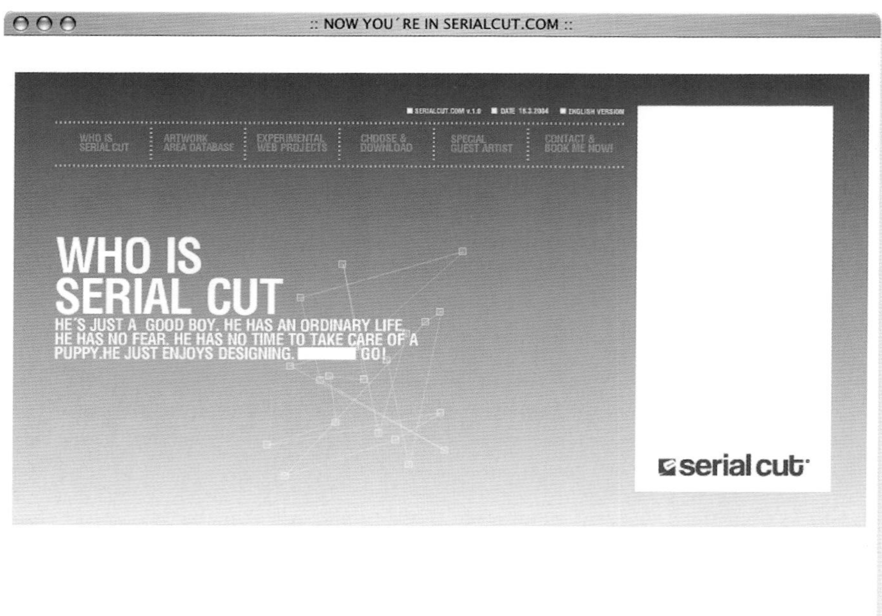
:: NOW YOU´RE IN SERIALCUT.COM ::
WHO IS SERIAL CUT
ARTWORK AREA DATABASE
EXPERIMENTAL WEB PROJECTS
CHOOSE & DOWNLOAD
SPECIAL GUEST ARTIST
CONTACT & BOOK ME NOW!
WHO IS
SERIAL CUT
HE'S JUST A GOOD BOY. HE HAS AN ORDINARY LIFE.
HE HAS NO FEAR. HE HAS NO TIME TO TAKE CARE OF A
PUPPY.HE JUST ENJOYS DESIGNING. GO!
serial cut

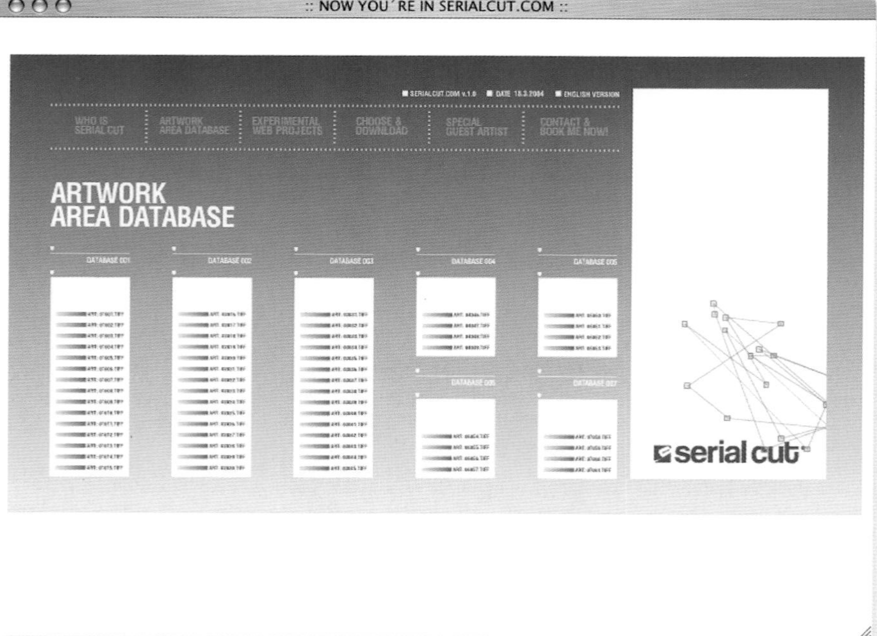
:: NOW YOU´RE IN SERIALCUT.COM ::
WHO IS SERIAL CUT
ARTWORK AREA DATABASE
EXPERIMENTAL WEB PROJECTS
CHOOSE & DOWNLOAD
SPECIAL GUEST ARTIST
CONTACT & BOOK ME NOW!
ARTWORK
AREA DATABASE
serial cut

www.serialcut.com

D: sergio del puerto
A: serial cut **M:** serialcut@serialcut.com

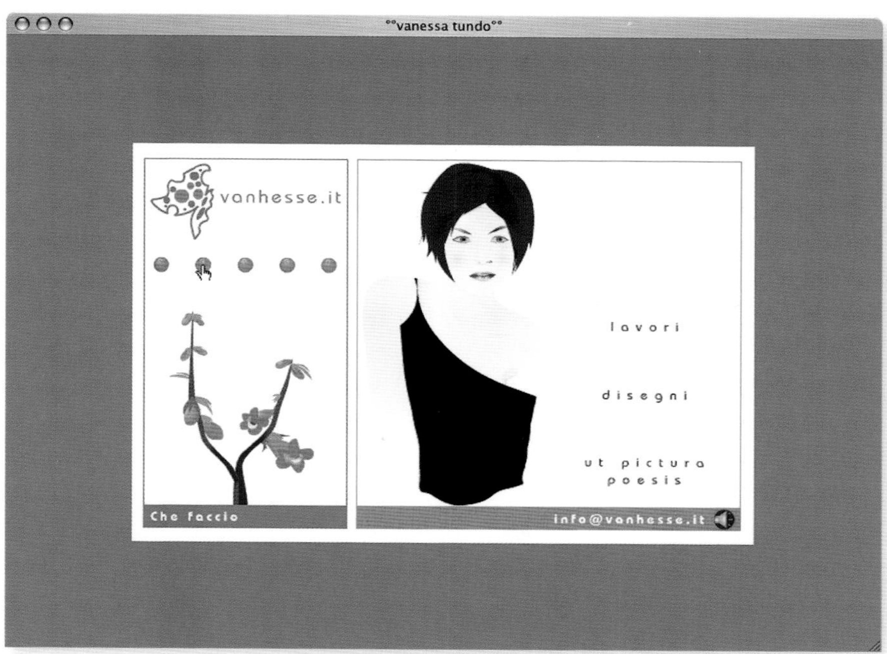
°°vanessa tundo°°
vanhesse.it
lavori
disegni
ut pictura
poesis
Che faccio
info@vanhesse.it

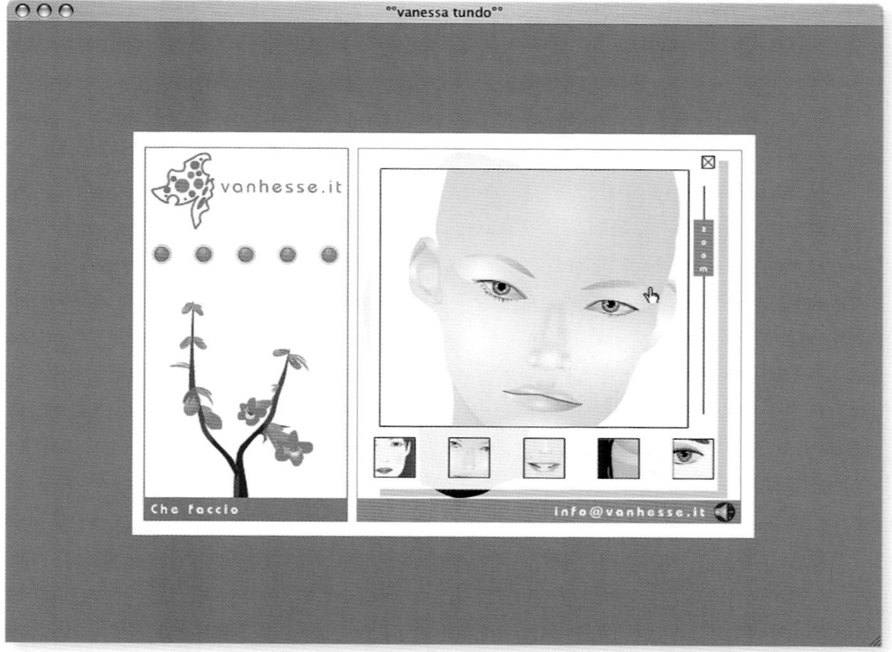
°°vanessa tundo°°
vanhesse.it
zoom
Che faccio
info@vanhesse.it

www.vanhesse.it
D: vanessa tundo
M: vanessatundo@vanhesse.it

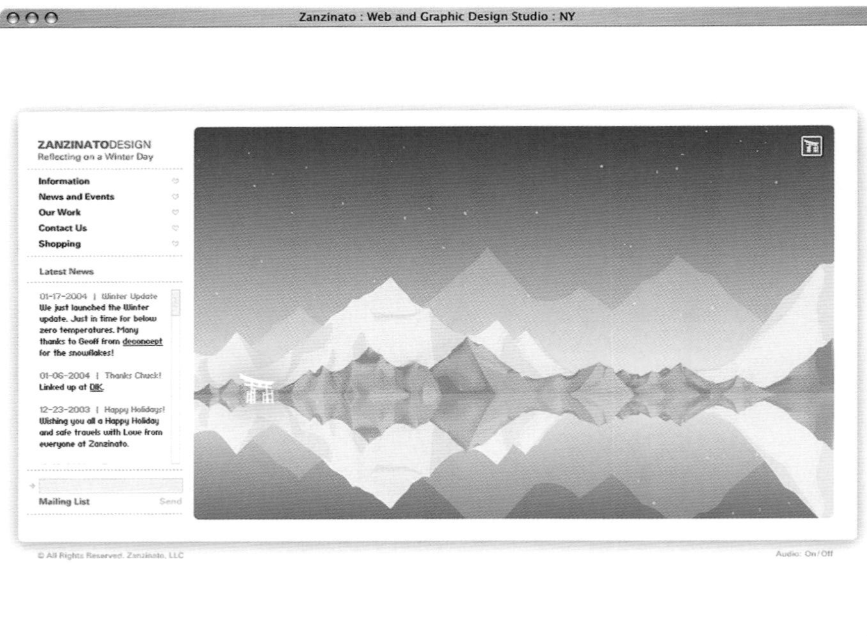
Zanzinato : Web and Graphic Design Studio : NY
ZANZINATODESIGN
Reflecting on a Winter Day
Information
News and Events
Our Work
Contact Us
Shopping
Latest News
01-17-2004 | Winter Update
We just launched the Winter update. Just in time for below zero temperatures. Many thanks to Geoff from deconcept for the snowflakes!
01-06-2004 | Thanks Chuck!
Linked up at DIK.
12-23-2003 | Happy Holidays!
Wishing you all a Happy Holiday and safe travels with Love from everyone at Zanzinato.
Mailing List
Send
© All Rights Reserved. Zanzinato, LLC
Audio: On/Off

Zanzinato : Web and Graphic Design Studio : NY
ZANZINATODESIGN
Reflecting on a Winter Day
Information
News and Events
Our Work
Contact Us
Shopping
Latest News
Our Work
Aduion BioSciences
Alden Design
Christopher Morgan Loy
Clarity Consulting
Drink Exchange
Emissarius Records
Environmental Toxicology
Eudora
Cornell Hotel School
JBF Glass Studio
Johnson Business School
Mr. Downstairs
Pamboo
Qualcomm
Smith Marketing
San Diego Yacht Club
Tag CD
TenEleven
Toxics Targeting
Windgarth House
Working Woman Network
www.mrdownstairs.com
Mailing List
Send
© All Rights Reserved. Zanzinato, LLC
Audio: On/Off

www.zanzinato.com
D: serge isaacson
A: zanzinato **M:** serge@zanzinato.com

Web Designers Graphic Designers Denver Colorado USA Brian Wilson
brian wilson
visual ideas
HELLO@BRIANWILSON.INFO
ENTER PORTFOLIO >
OR
ENTER BLOG >
THIS SITE FEATURED ON

Web Designers Graphic Designers Denver Colorado USA Brian Wilson

PORTFOLIO www.brianwilson.info/archives/ © copyright 2004, brian wilson

Problem Employees at local Starbucks were awarded for excellent performance (100%) and excellent store performance (5 stars). The manager wanted more than a certificate on the wall to mark this achievement. The solution needed to be cheap, and needed to attach to the employees apron during work.

Solution After brainstorming we decided to create buttons. My friend has a button making machine, and we knew the price would be reasonable. The designs were simple and reflected the name of the award.

www.brianwilson.info
D: brian wilson
A: brian wilson visual ideas **M:** hello@brianwilson.info

Changethethought™
Amer. Dream Tee
Being Watched Illus.
Bleeds it Leads Tee
Comp. Love Poster
Consumer Illus.
CTT Site Ver. 2
CTT Promo. Illus.
Dog Eat Dog Tee
Eradicate Illus.
american dreams
time to wise up, tee
This design was originally created for Fake clothing. The idea was rejected for another design from ctt.
This design is currently available for sale, please contact us for details and price quotes.
click for image 2
this is my
AMERICAN
DREAM
NO MORE LIES ITS TIME TO WISE UP
ctt
LAST UPDATE*
02.15.05
WORK
NEWS
ABOUT
CONTACT
LINKS

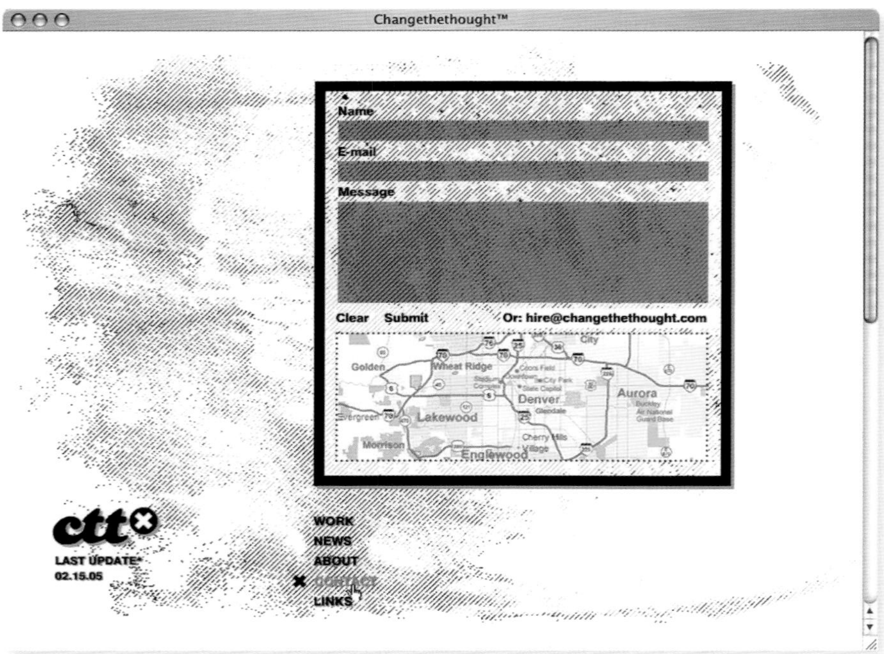
Changethethought™
Name
E-mail
Message
Clear Submit
Or: hire@changethethought.com
Golden
Wheat Ridge
Denver
Aurora
Lakewood
Evergreen
Morrison
Englewood
ctt
LAST UPDATE*
02.15.05
WORK
NEWS
ABOUT
CONTACT
LINKS

www.changethethought.com
D: christopher cox
A: changethethought **M:** hire@changethethought.com

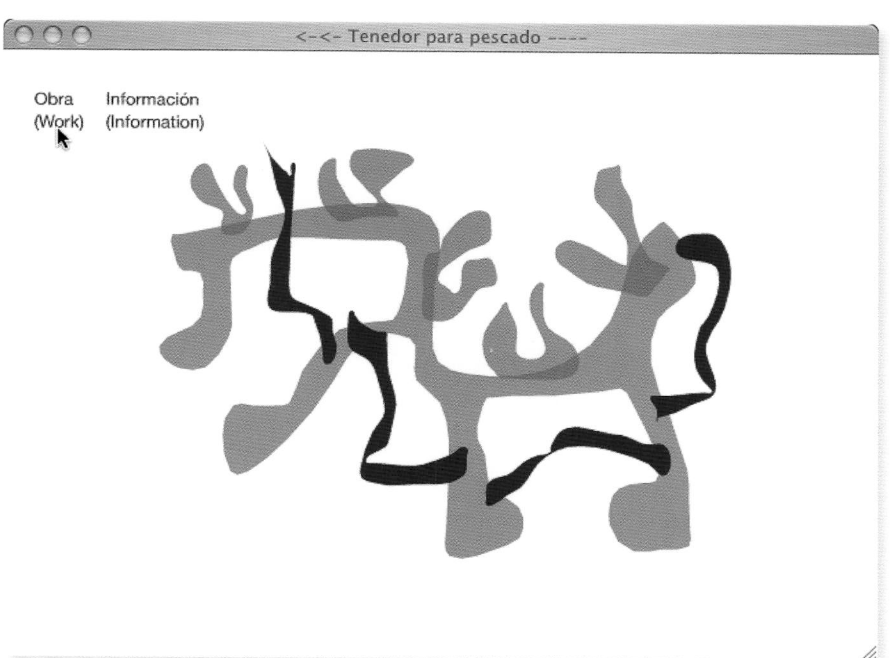
<-<- Tenedor para pescado ----
Obra
(Work)
Información
(Information)

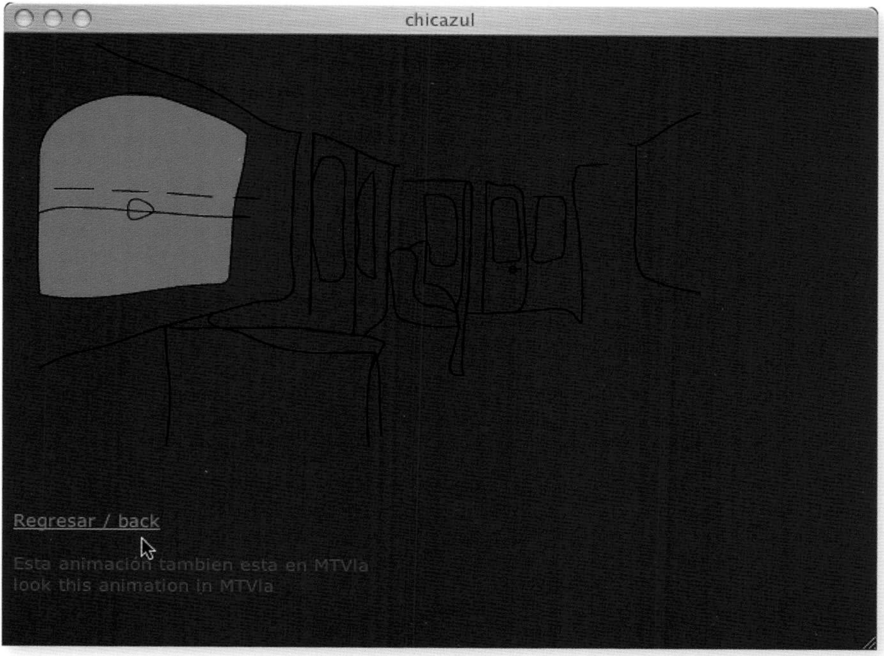
chicazul
Regresar / back
Esta animacion tambien esta en MTVla
look this animation in MTVla

www.tenedorparapescado.com
D: mejia ivan fabela
A: bcomsulting **M:** imejia32@prdogy.net.mx

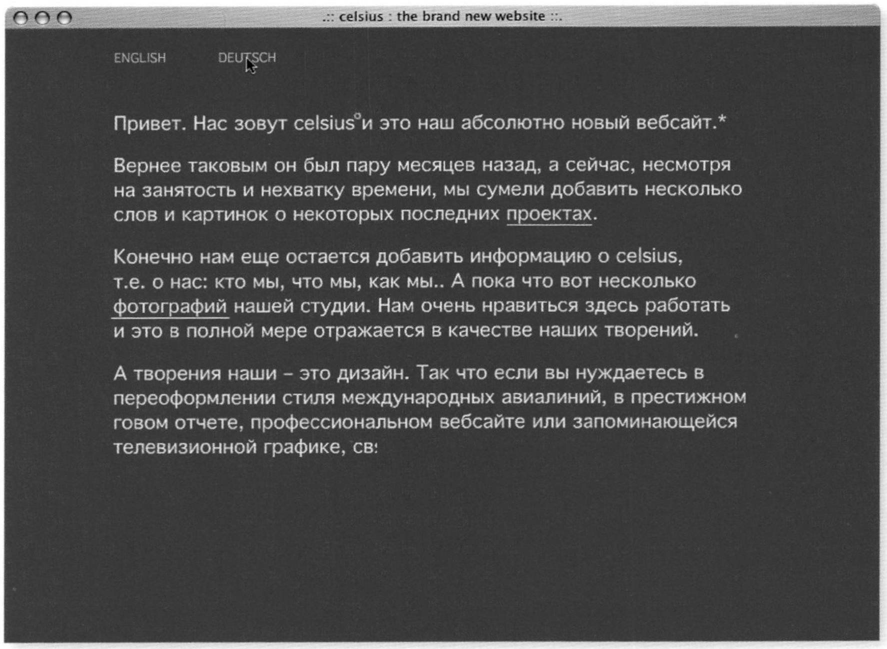
.:: celsius : the brand new website ::.
ENGLISH
DEUTSCH
Привет. Нас зовут celsius°и это наш абсолютно новый вебсайт.*
Вернее таковым он был пару месяцев назад, а сейчас, несмотря на занятость и нехватку времени, мы сумели добавить несколько слов и картинок о некоторых последних проектах.
Конечно нам еще остается добавить информацию о celsius, т.е. о нас: кто мы, что мы, как мы.. А пока что вот несколько фотографий нашей студии. Нам очень нравиться здесь работать и это в полной мере отражается в качестве наших творений.
А творения наши – это дизайн. Так что если вы нуждаетесь в переоформлении стиля международных авиалиний, в престижном говом отчете, профессиональном вебсайте или запоминающейся телевизионной графике, св:

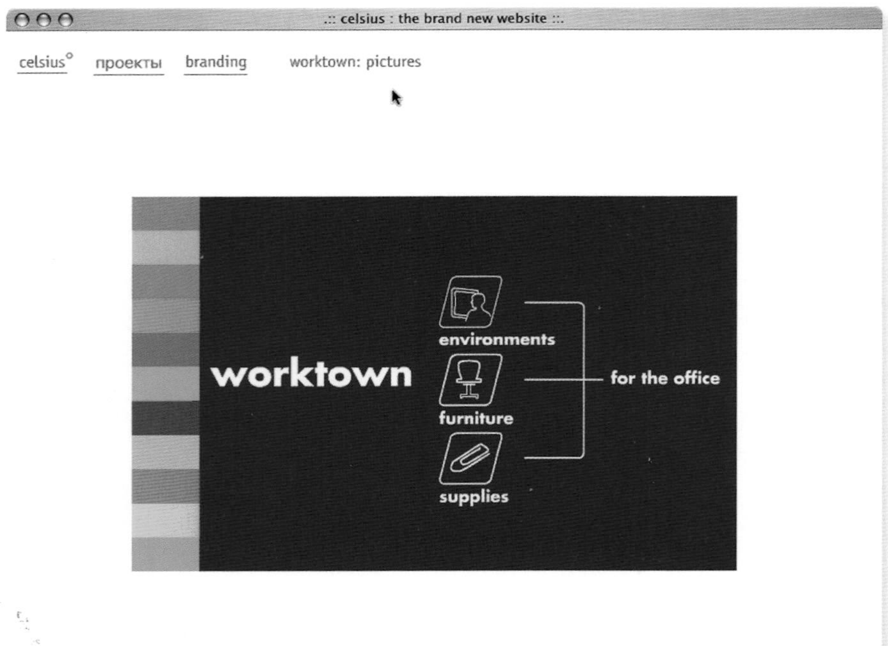
.:: celsius : the brand new website ::.
celsius°
проекты
branding
worktown: pictures
worktown
environments
furniture
supplies
for the office

www.celsius.eu.com
D: david hyde
A: celsius **M:** david@celsius.eu.com

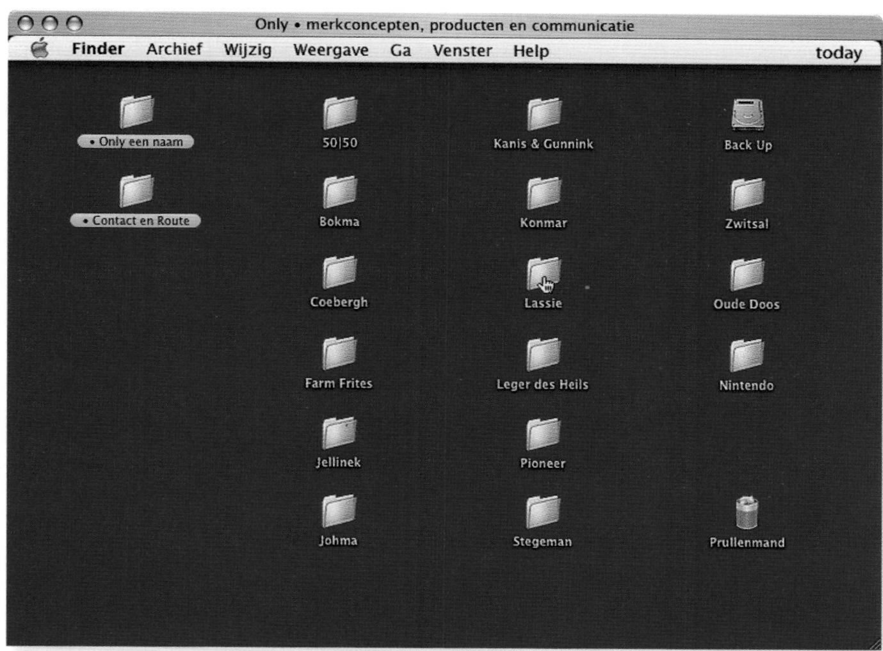
Only • merkconcepten, producten en communicatie
Finder Archief Wijzig Weergave Ga Venster Help today
• Only een naam
• Contact en Route
50|50
Bokma
Coebergh
Farm Frites
Jellinek
Johma
Kanis & Gunnink
Konmar
Lassie
Leger des Heils
Pioneer
Stegeman
Back Up
Zwitsal
Oude Doos
Nintendo
Prullenmand

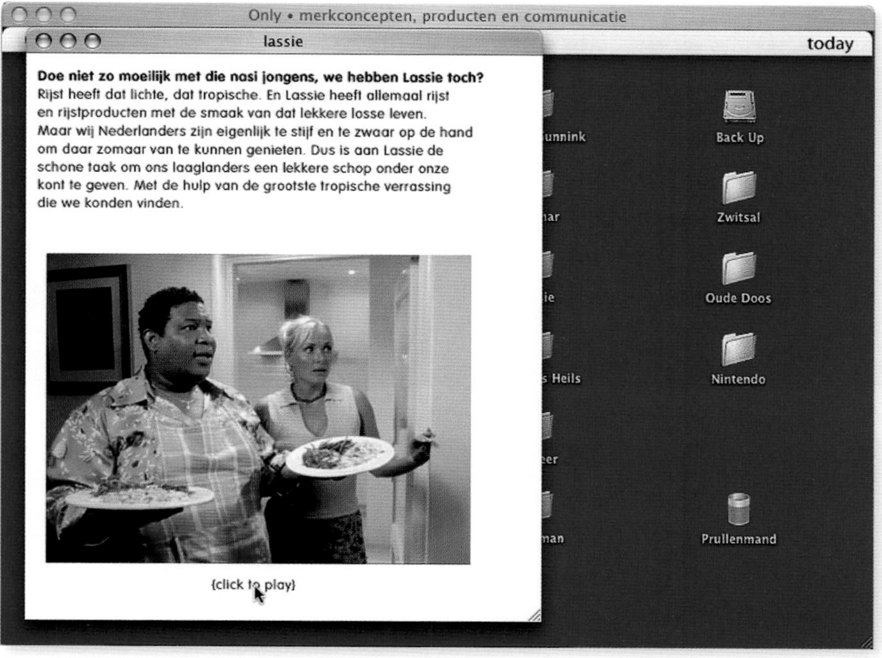
Only • merkconcepten, producten en communicatie
lassie
today
Doe niet zo moeilijk met die nasi jongens, we hebben Lassie toch?
Rijst heeft dat lichte, dat tropische. En Lassie heeft allemaal rijst en rijstproducten met de smaak van dat lekkere losse leven. Maar wij Nederlanders zijn eigenlijk te stijf en te zwaar op de hand om daar zomaar van te kunnen genieten. Dus is aan Lassie de schone taak om ons laaglanders een lekkere schop onder onze kont te geven. Met de hulp van de grootste tropische verrassing die we konden vinden.
{click to play}
Back Up
Zwitsal
Oude Doos
Nintendo
Prullenmand

www.only.nl
D: dennis van den brink
A: only M: dennis@only.nl

terotero inc
CLOSE
MENU'
Welcome to TEROTERO
21-03-2005 - WOW! TEROTERO COULD GET A BUNCH OF AWARDS! THANX EVERYBODY WHO SUPPORT US! TEROTERO NOW IS WORKING ON A PROJECT FOR TERRAZZAMARE.COM
27-01-2005 - SUPPORT EXTENDED. WE INSTALLED I-SIGHT, SO WE CAN EASLY GET IN TOUCH WITH OUR CLIENTS. CHECK CONTACT PAGE FOR OUR I-CHAT NICK
AUDIO

terotero inc
CLOSE
HOME ▸
ABOUT WORKS PRODUCTS LINKS CONTACTS
WEB
GRAPHIC
T-SHIRT
MUSIC
T-SHIRT 02
2 colori
cotone
VIEW DETAIL
#03
www.terotero.com
AUDIO

www.terotero.com
D: kyoko yamamoto, dario perissutti **C:** dario perissutti
A: terotero international **M:** a we allow

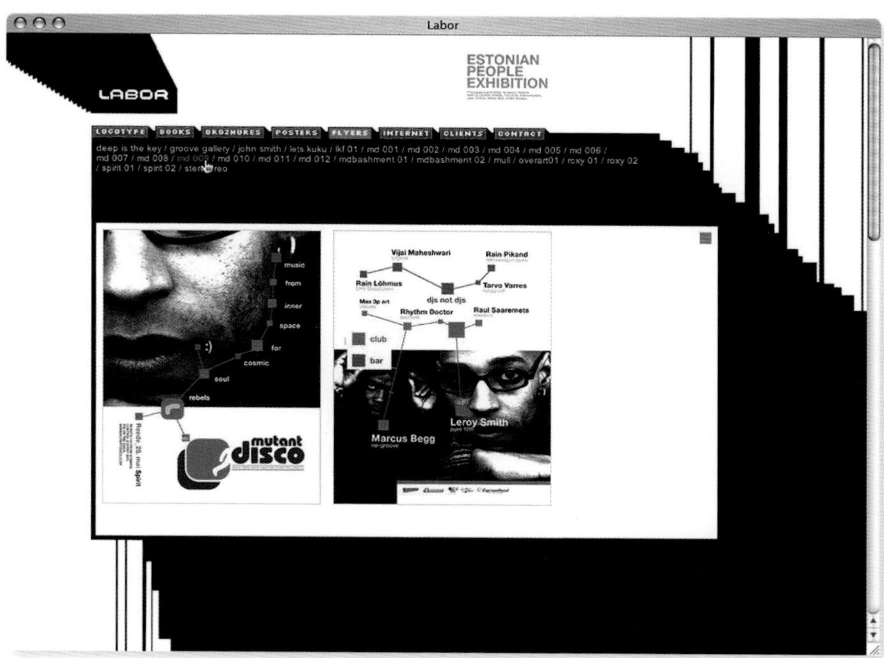
Labor
LABOR
ESTONIAN PEOPLE EXHIBITION
LOGOTYPE BOOKS BROCHURES POSTERS FLYERS INTERNET CLIENTS CONTACT
deep is the key / groove gallery / john smith / lets kuku / lkf 01 / md 001 / md 002 / md 003 / md 004 / md 005 / md 006 / md 007 / md 008 / md 009 / md 010 / md 011 / md 012 / mdbashment 01 / mdbashment 02 / mull / overart01 / roxy 01 / roxy 02 / spirit 01 / spirit 02 / stereo
music from inner space for cosmic soul rebels
mutant disco
Vijai Maheshwari
Rain Pikand
Rain Lõhmus
Tarvo Varres
djs not djs
Rhythm Doctor
Raul Saaremets
club
bar
Leroy Smith
Marcus Begg

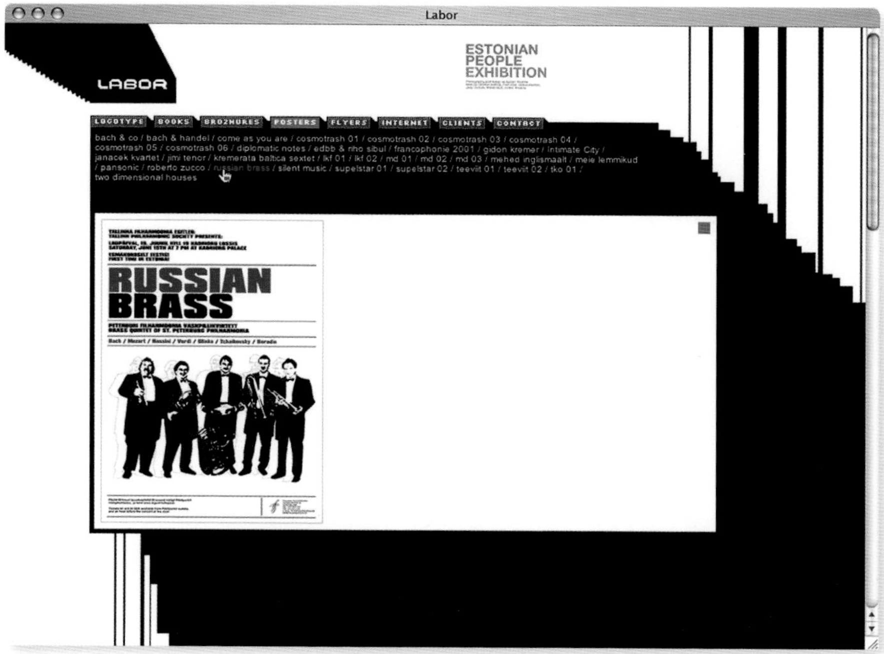
Labor
LABOR
ESTONIAN PEOPLE EXHIBITION
LOGOTYPE BOOKS BROCHURES POSTERS FLYERS INTERNET CLIENTS CONTACT
bach & co / bach & handel / come as you are / cosmotrash 01 / cosmotrash 02 / cosmotrash 03 / cosmotrash 04 / cosmotrash 05 / cosmotrash 06 / diplomatic notes / edbb & riho sibul / francophonie 2001 / gidon kremer / intimate City / janacek kvartet / jimi tenor / kremerata baltica sextet / lkf 01 / lkf 02 / md 01 / md 02 / md 03 / mehed inglismaalt / meie lemmikud / pansonic / roberto zucco / russian brass / silent music / supelstar 01 / supelstar 02 / teevitt 01 / teevitt 02 / tko 01 / two dimensional houses
RUSSIAN BRASS

www.labor.ee
D: martin pedanik **C:** martin salo **P:** martin pedanik
A: labor **M:** labor@labor.ee

ITOMI
ITOMI
CREATIVE DPT.
EST.1978
/ ABOUT
/ PORTFOLIO
/ WORDS
/ CONTACT
/ NEWS
/ CLOSE
REPLAY.
QUARTA
DIMENSIONE

ITOMI
ITOMI
CREATIVE DPT.
EST.1978
WORDS
Ho scritto e scrivo per varie riviste on e off-line. Qui un compendio delle ultime parole uscite dalla mia tastiera, a proposito di design, webdesign, comunicazione
// PROSPETTIVE: ZERO
// PIU' DESIGN, MENO WEB
// LIBERTA'
// INTERVISTA A CG&P
PIU' DESIGN,-
MENO WEB.
Forse è ora di cambiare atteggiamento quando si comincia ad avvicinarsi alla professione di WebDesigner. Pensare a quali sono le cose più importanti da imparare può essere vitale nella propria formazione
Come faccio a fare la tal cosa con i css? Xml, xtml, xhtkhl, jspthsl tutte domande tecniche che girano sulle mailing list, insieme ad una serie infinita di "guarda il mio sito", "guarda il tal sito", "aiutami con questo script", ecc. Tutte domande fondamentalmente tecniche che spessissimo riguardano aspetti che influiscono sull'utente in piccolissima parte.
Tutte domande legittime e utili, ma che nella mia modesta opinione riguardano argomenti che per un webdesigner dovrebbero essere secondari rispetto ad altri più importanti di cui ci si dimentica sempre più spesso.

www.itomi.it
D: antonio moro
A: itomi **M:** antonio@itomi.it

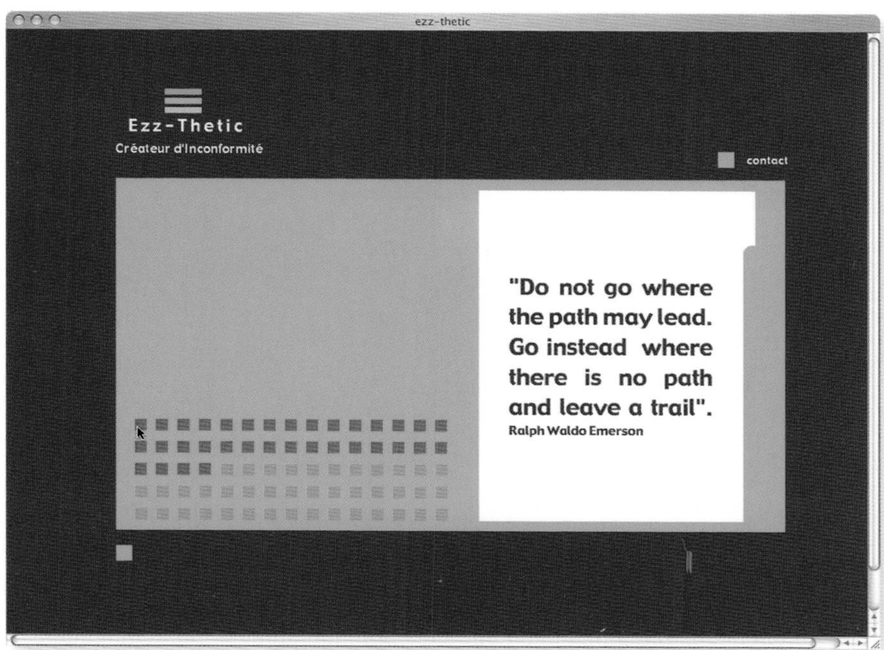
ezz-thetic
Ezz-Thetic
Créateur d'Inconformité
contact
"Do not go where the path may lead. Go instead where there is no path and leave a trail".
Ralph Waldo Emerson

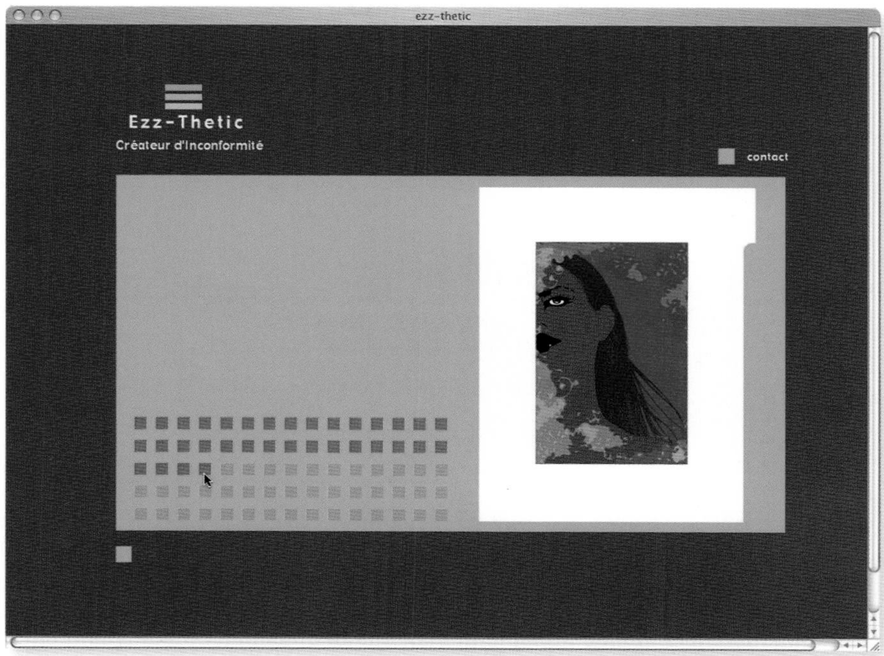
ezz-thetic
Ezz-Thetic
Créateur d'Inconformité
contact

www.ezz-thetic.net
D: erwann gauthier
A: ezz-thetic **M:** ezz.thetic@wanadoo.fr

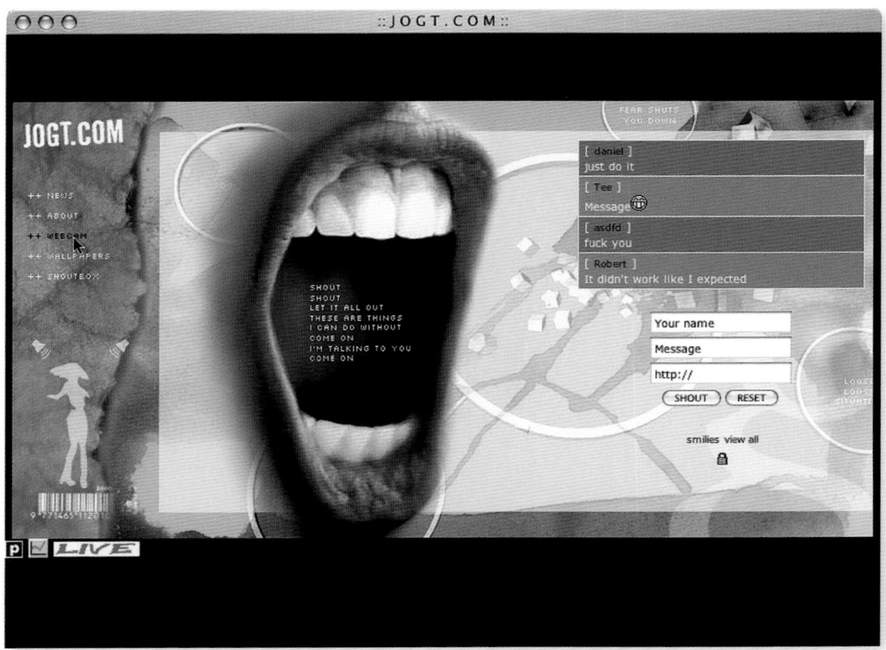
::JOGT.COM::
JOGT.COM
++ NEWS
++ ABOUT
++ WEBCAM
++ WALLPAPERS
++ SHOUTBOX
SHOUT
SHOUT
LET IT ALL OUT
THESE ARE THINGS
I CAN DO WITHOUT
COME ON
I'M TALKING TO YOU
COME ON
FEAR SHUTS
YOU DOWN
[daniel]
just do it
[Tee]
Message
[asdfd]
fuck you
[Robert]
It didn't work like I expected
Your name
Message
http://
SHOUT
RESET
smilies view all
LIVE

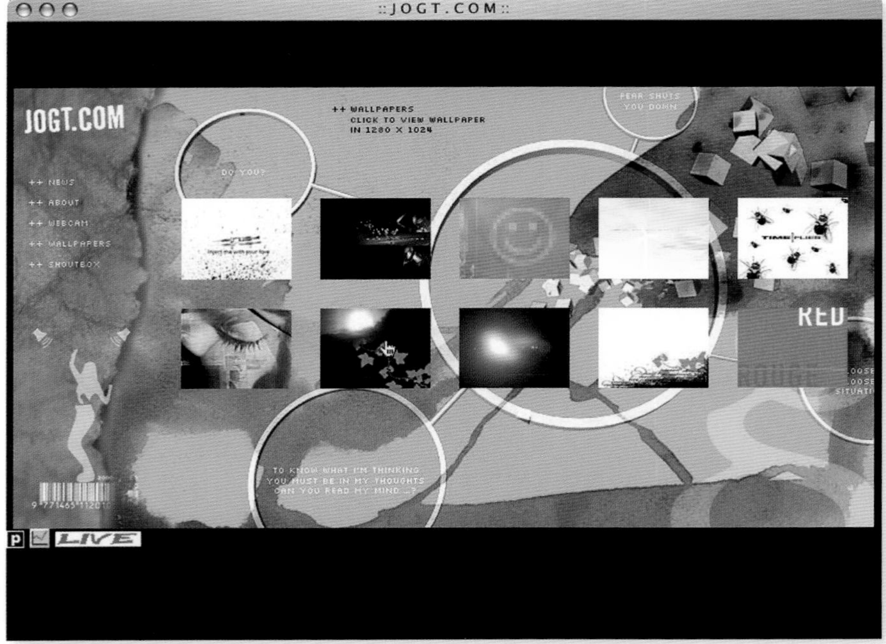
::JOGT.COM::
JOGT.COM
++ WALLPAPERS
CLICK TO VIEW WALLPAPER
IN 1280 X 1024
FEAR SHUTS
YOU DOWN
DO YOU?
++ NEWS
++ ABOUT
++ WEBCAM
++ WALLPAPERS
++ SHOUTBOX
TO KNOW WHAT I'M THINKING
YOU MUST BE IN MY THOUGHTS
CAN YOU READ MY MIND ...?
LIVE

www.jogt.com
D: thomas petersen
M: thomas@jogt.com

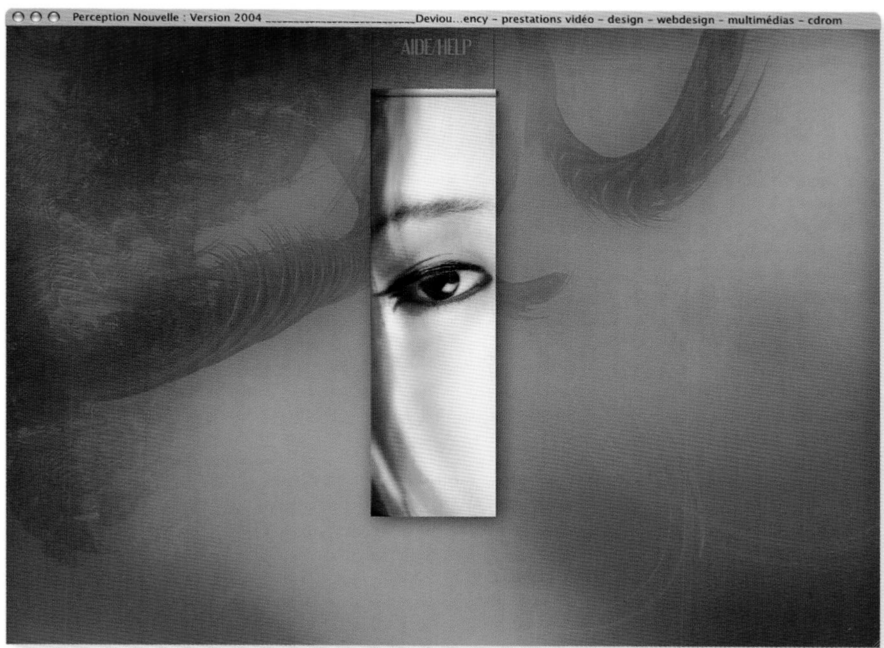
Perception Nouvelle : Version 2004 ___Deviou...ency - prestations vidéo - design - webdesign - multimédias - cdrom
AIDE/HELP

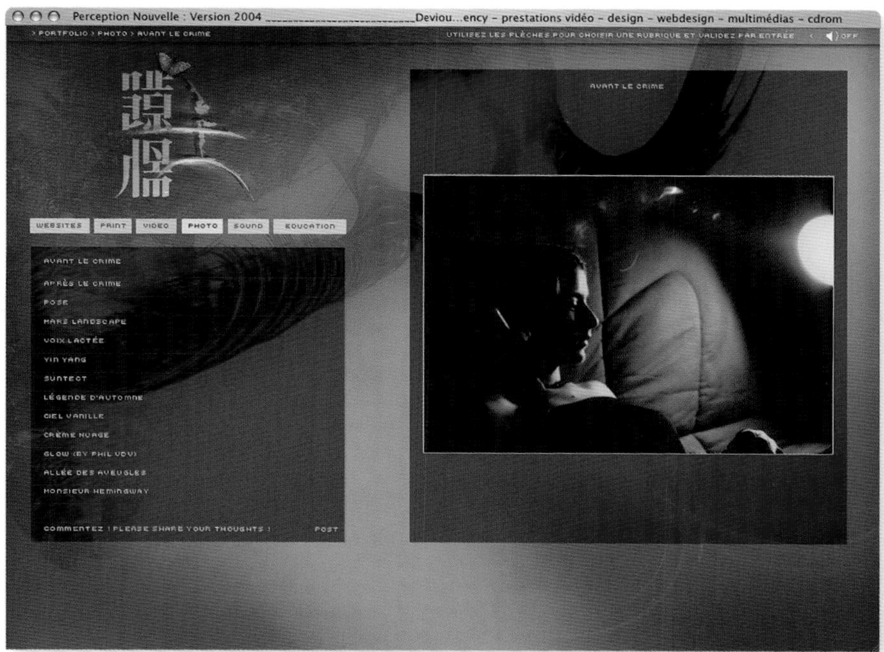
Perception Nouvelle : Version 2004 ___Deviou...ency - prestations vidéo - design - webdesign - multimédias - cdrom
> PORTFOLIO > PHOTO > AVANT LE CRIME
UTILISEZ LES FLÈCHES POUR CHOISIR UNE RUBRIQUE ET VALIDEZ PAR ENTRÉE
WEBSITES
PRINT
VIDEO
PHOTO
SOUND
EDUCATION
AVANT LE CRIME
APRÈS LE CRIME
POSE
MARS LANDSCAPE
VOIX LACTÉE
YIN YANG
SUNTECT
LÉGENDE D'AUTOMNE
CIEL VANILLE
CRÈME NUAGE
GLOW (BY PHIL VOV)
ALLÉE DES AVEUGLES
MONSIEUR HEMINGWAY
COMMENTEZ ! PLEASE SHARE YOUR THOUGHTS !
POST
AVANT LE CRIME

www.perception-nouvelle.com
D: julien pons
A: perception nouvelle **M:** j.pons@perception-nouvelle.com

indigo 6 pure digital
CLOSE
indigo 6 pure digital
Depart
from the ordinary
Indigo 6 is an "idea-first", interactive agency based in Norwalk (NLK), CT with routes servicing the continental United States and Puerto Rico. We believe that every success is built upon a great creative idea. That's how we fly.
So what do we do?
We create cool stuff. Engaging stuff that is different, compelling, usable and actionable. The stuff that exceeds expectations and builds brands.
Gates 1-6
CREW DESTINATIONS TICKETING

indigo 6 pure digital
CLOSE
indigo 6 pure digital
Flight-plan
To get you to the right destination, we use a very simple flight-plan. We listen to what you have to say and what you need to do; think a lot about the brand and then create the kind of work that gets you where you need to go.
Plan Build Manage
We uncover everything we need to know about brands to deliver our best possible work. We walk through the stores, read the literature, play with the product, wear hard hats in the plant... and eat it, if it's food.
Featured Destination
Mike and Ike
Original Fruits
Mike and Ike® Candies
Indigo 6 launches the first-ever Mike and Ike Brand website for Pennsylvania-based candy barrons, Just Born Inc. An online advertising campaign on MTV.com and "Instant Win!" site features drove kids to FlavUp in hordes.
>> WATCH THE EXCITING TRAILER
>> GO TO MIKE AND IKE.COM
CREW DESTINATIONS TICKETING

www.indigo6.com
D: charles silverman **C:** john packes **P:** ryan jennings
A: indigo 6 **M:** charles@indigo6.com

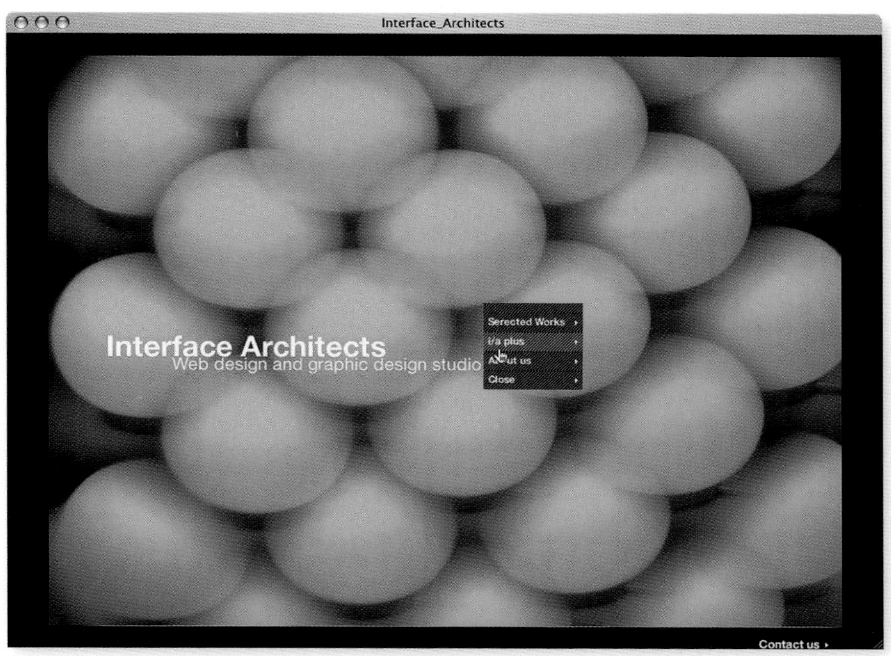
Interface_Architects
Interface Architects
Web design and graphic design studio
Serected Works
i/a plus
About us
Close
Contact us

Interface_Architects
Adaptation
2003
View this site
映画「アダプテーション」のオフィシャルサイト。
スパイク・ジョーンズ監督の新作。1本の映画脚本をめぐって、
脚本家本人をはじめ、多くの実在人物を演じる役者が劇中に登場
する、虚実入り交じった奇妙な映画。過剰な期待の中、混乱して
いる脚本家の机上を再現すべく、机に散らばる書類がインター
フェイスになっている。この書類は実際に画面いっぱいに散らか
すことも、片付けることもできる。配給はアスミックエース。
AD/D:Shinichi Tateyama Flash:Kenji Inokuchi
アダプテーション
Back to Serected Works
Contact us

www.interfacearchitects.jp
D: shinichi tateyama
A: interface architects **M:** info@interfacearchitects.jp

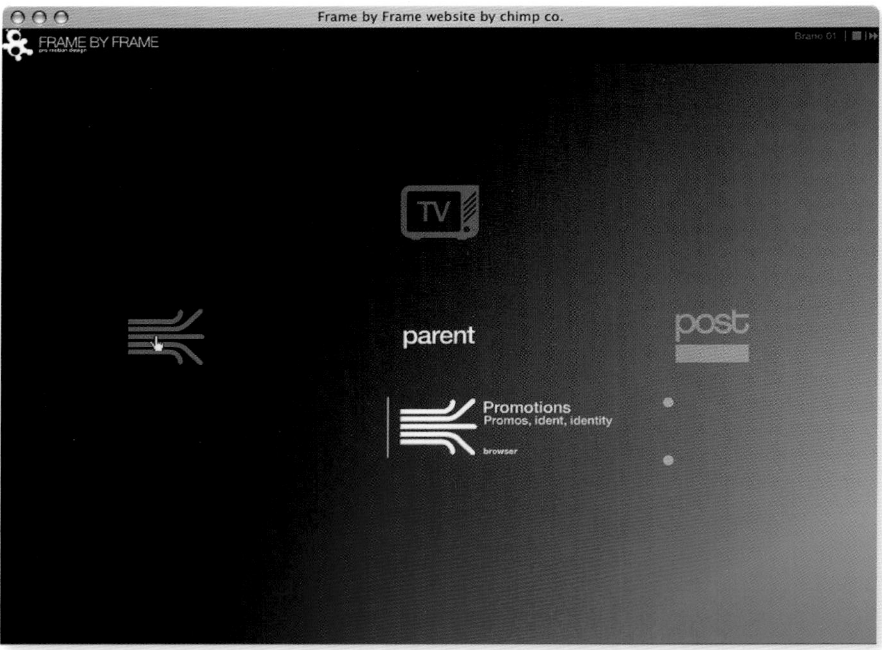
Frame by Frame website by chimp co.
FRAME BY FRAME
TV
parent
post
Promotions
Promos, ident, identity
browser

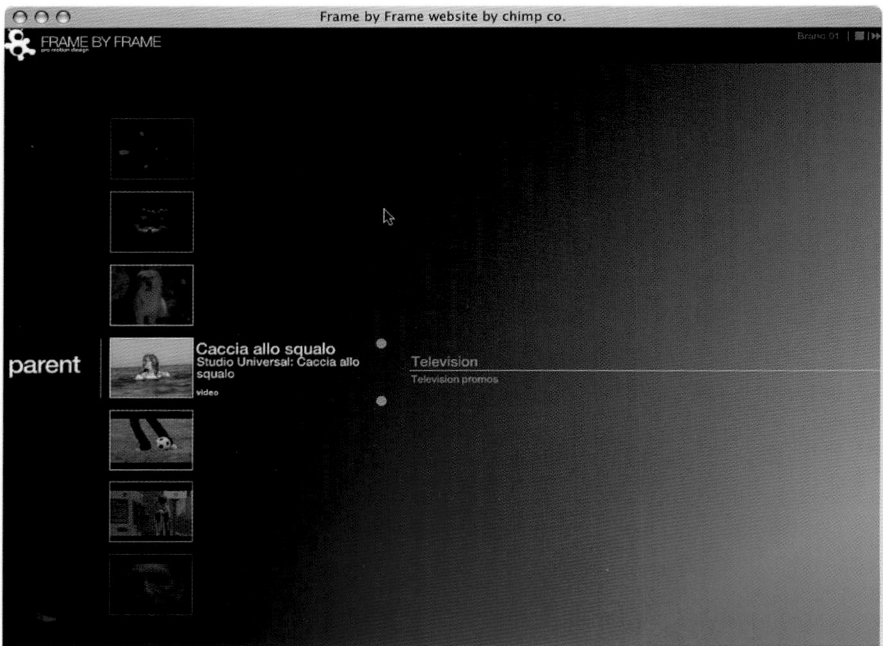
Frame by Frame website by chimp co.
FRAME BY FRAME
parent
Caccia allo squalo
Studio Universal: Caccia allo squalo
video
Television
Television promos

www.frame.it
D: lorenzo ceccotti, gianluca abbate **C:** mauro staci **P:** lorenzo ceccotti
A: chimp **M:** info@chimp.it

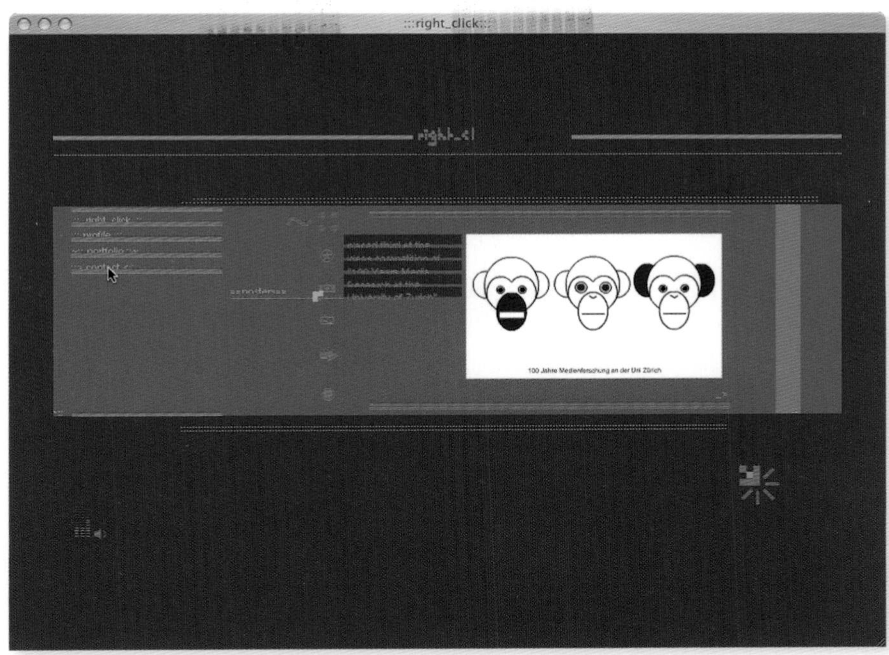
:::right_click:::
100 Jahre Medienforschung an der Uni Zürich

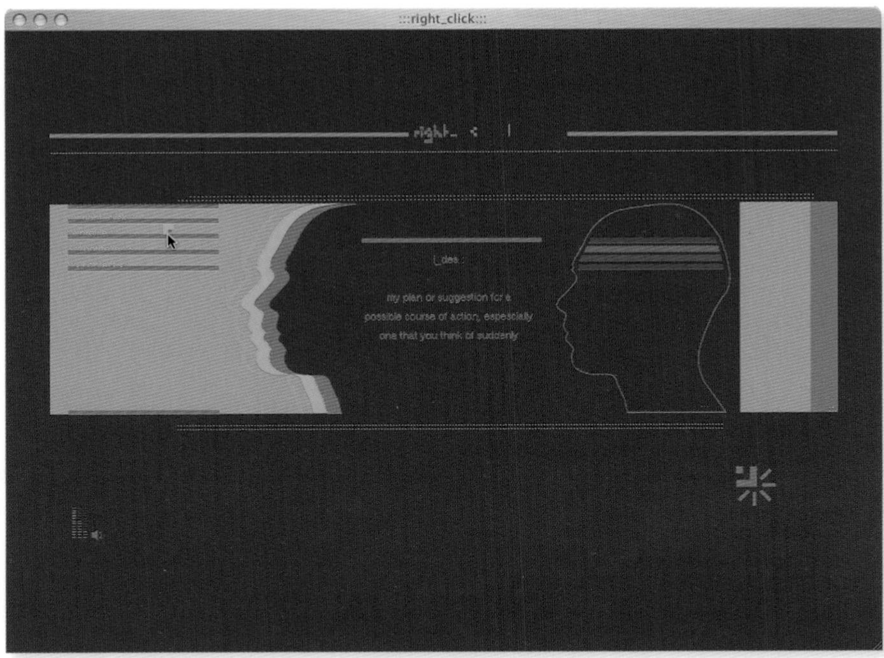
:::right_click:::
my plan or suggestion for a
possible course of action, especially
one that you think of suddenly

www.right-click.ch
D: fera ferrarelli
A: right-click **M:** fera@right-click.ch

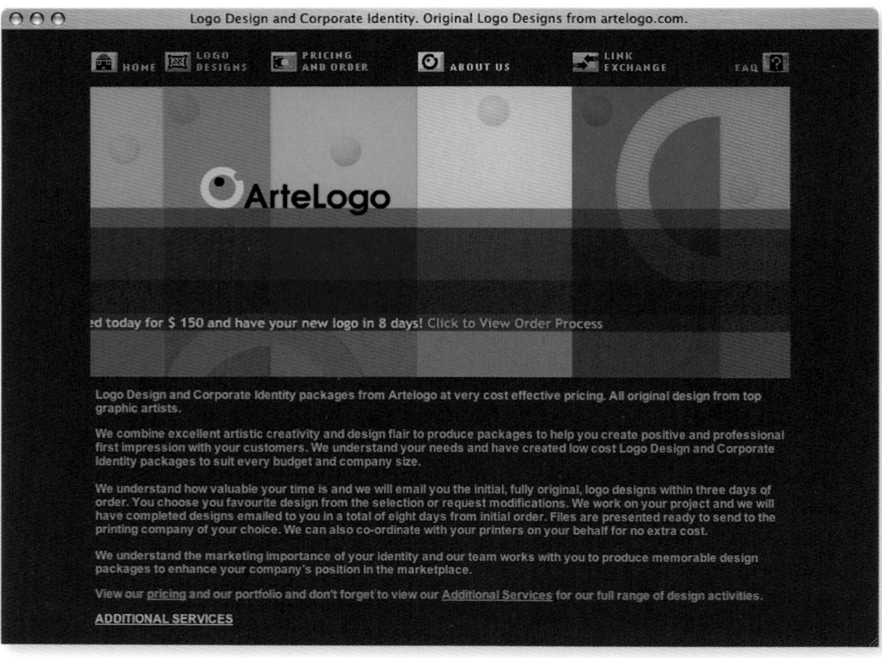
Logo Design and Corporate Identity. Original Logo Designs from artelogo.com.
HOME
LOGO DESIGNS
PRICING AND ORDER
ABOUT US
LINK EXCHANGE
FAQ
ArteLogo
ed today for $ 150 and have your new logo in 8 days! Click to View Order Process
Logo Design and Corporate Identity packages from Artelogo at very cost effective pricing. All original design from top graphic artists.
We combine excellent artistic creativity and design flair to produce packages to help you create positive and professional first impression with your customers. We understand your needs and have created low cost Logo Design and Corporate Identity packages to suit every budget and company size.
We understand how valuable your time is and we will email you the initial, fully original, logo designs within three days of order. You choose you favourite design from the selection or request modifications. We work on your project and we will have completed designs emailed to you in a total of eight days from initial order. Files are presented ready to send to the printing company of your choice. We can also co-ordinate with your printers on your behalf for no extra cost.
We understand the marketing importance of your identity and our team works with you to produce memorable design packages to enhance your company's position in the marketplace.
View our pricing and our portfolio and don't forget to view our Additional Services for our full range of design activities.
ADDITIONAL SERVICES

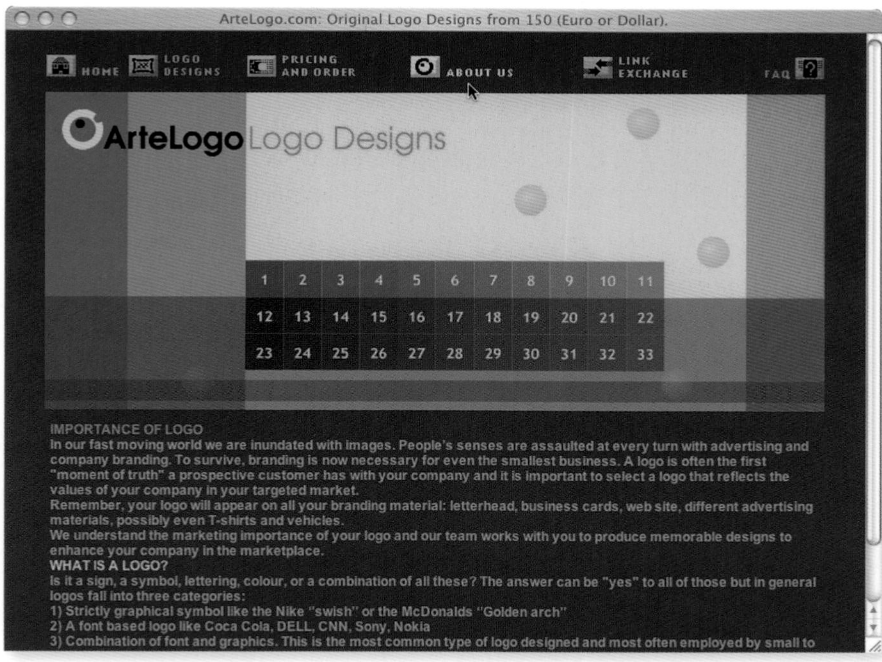
ArteLogo.com: Original Logo Designs from 150 (Euro or Dollar).
HOME
LOGO DESIGNS
PRICING AND ORDER
ABOUT US
LINK EXCHANGE
FAQ
ArteLogo Logo Designs
1 2 3 4 5 6 7 8 9 10 11
12 13 14 15 16 17 18 19 20 21 22
23 24 25 26 27 28 29 30 31 32 33
IMPORTANCE OF LOGO
In our fast moving world we are inundated with images. People's senses are assaulted at every turn with advertising and company branding. To survive, branding is now necessary for even the smallest business. A logo is often the first "moment of truth" a prospective customer has with your company and it is important to select a logo that reflects the values of your company in your targeted market.
Remember, your logo will appear on all your branding material: letterhead, business cards, web site, different advertising materials, possibly even T-shirts and vehicles.
We understand the marketing importance of your logo and our team works with you to produce memorable designs to enhance your company in the marketplace.
WHAT IS A LOGO?
Is it a sign, a symbol, lettering, colour, or a combination of all these? The answer can be "yes" to all of those but in general logos fall into three categories:
1) Strictly graphical symbol like the Nike "swish" or the McDonalds "Golden arch"
2) A font based logo like Coca Cola, DELL, CNN, Sony, Nokia
3) Combination of font and graphics. This is the most common type of logo designed and most often employed by small to

www.artelogo.com

D: ivanova desislava **C:** javor kozarev

A: artelogo **M:** desi@artelogo.com

FunnelDesignGroup
funnel
design group
Funnel's website is awarded a plastic pilots award - plasticpilots.com
November 16, 2004 Funnel begins updating site content.
September 17, 2004 Funnel's website is awarded 5 stars and a golden site on
0 3 / 1 7
Smokin' Hot Ash Cigars
SMOKIN'
HOT ASH
PRINT
INTERACTIVE
EXHIBITION
IDENTITY
INTERIOR
EXTERIOR
OPEN
FUNNEL DESIGN GROUP
6531-A
N. Classen Blvd.
Oklahoma City, OK 73116
405.840.7006
email
audio

„FunnelDesignGroup" wird geladen
funnel
design group
Funnel's website is awarded a plastic pilots award - plasticpilots.com
November 16, 2004 Funnel begins updating site content.
September 17, 2004 Funnel's website is awarded 5 stars and a golden site on
0 1 / 1 3
Oklahoma Center for Neuroscience Invitation
we provide tools to make our clients more profitable
PRINT
INTERACTIVE
EXHIBITION
IDENTITY
INTERIOR
EXTERIOR
OPEN
FUNNEL DESIGN GROUP
6531-A
N. Classen Blvd.
Oklahoma City, OK 73116
405.840.7006
email
audio

www.funneldesigngroup.com
D: phil glofcheskie **P:** bryan ellison, sean cobb
A: funnel design group **M:** email@funneldesigngroup.com

== Asterialand ==
asteria
About Me
News
Gallery
Shop
Contact Me
Link
Comic
2004 Calendar
Download
Join Asteria mailing list :
GOLDEN WEB AWARDS
PLASTICPILOT AWARD
=== Last Update: 13th March, 2004 ===

== Asterialand == aboutme
asteria
About Me
News
Gallery
Shop
Contact Me
Link
About Me
I'm Alice Chan. I Studied and Worked Design for over 17 years specializing in Mode Illustration, Multimedia applications and Design. Started as an illustrator around 2000. Have been active in design and illustration for Advertisements, Graphics and Websites. Created a unforgettable image series for calendars, postcards, pin buttons and T-shirts.
Comic
Download

www.asterialand.com
D: alice chan **C:** asteria
M: info@asterialand.com

www.chrisgaillard.com
_home
Membre du collectif: www.beautifulscreen.tv +33476484352+33620374090
> autres :
_interface dvd
_encodage/conversion
_localisation
_qui suis-je ?
_contact
_liens
_credits
_vidéo _web _cd-rom
News
Dernières réalisations
_Titrage pour 2 spots diffusés dans les cinémas de l'Isére pour le SDIS 38.
_ Site Web Ploto : Chanteur en Bâtiment.
En cours et projets
_Film de présentation de la société N.A.D
_Site web Nikodem -artiste peintre-
_Site web www.madeindesign.com
—DVD lutin bleu "live"
_DVD beautifulscreen.tv
eKo - Burnin'
chris@chrisgaillard.com
audiovisuels interactifs

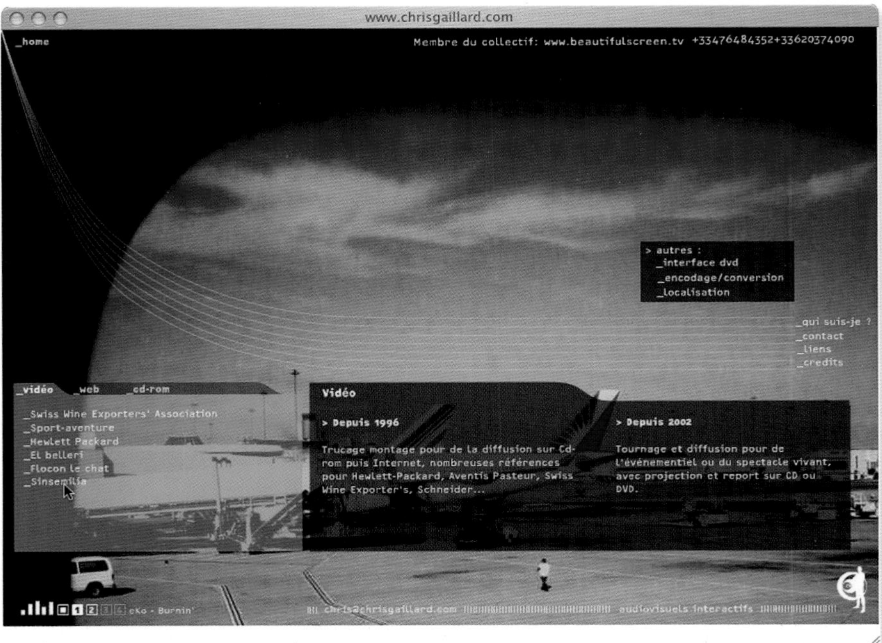
www.chrisgaillard.com
_home
Membre du collectif: www.beautifulscreen.tv +33476484352+33620374090
> autres :
_interface dvd
_encodage/conversion
_localisation
_qui suis-je ?
_contact
_liens
_credits
_vidéo _web _cd-rom
_Swiss Wine Exporters' Association
_Sport-aventure
_Hewlett Packard
_El belleri
_Flocon le chat
_Sinsemilia
Vidéo
> Depuis 1996
Trucage montage pour de la diffusion sur Cd-rom puis Internet, nombreuses références pour Hewlett-Packard, Aventis Pasteur, Swiss Wine Exporter's, Schneider...
> Depuis 2002
Tournage et diffusion pour de l'événementiel ou du spectacle vivant, avec projection et report sur CD ou DVD.
eKo - Burnin'
chris@chrisgaillard.com
audiovisuels interactifs

www.chrisgaillard.com
D: chris gaillard
A: wake up **M:** chris@chrisgaillard.com

-------Sixsidia------------
ANIMATIONS
OVER THE LAST YEAR OR SO, THE PONKA CHARACTERS HAVE STARTED TO DEVELOP THEIR OWN DISTINCT IDENTITIES.
THE THREE ORIGINAL PONKAS NOW HAVE FIVE NEW PONKAS TO CONTEND WITH. ALL THIS MEANS THAT AS EACH ANIMATION DEVELOPS I GET TO HAVE GREAT FUN DECIDING HOW EACH PONKA WILL REACT AND WHAT THEY'LL DO NEXT.
PETER O'DWYER
1 2 3 4 5
PONKA GOD FIGHTS THE POWER
IN THIS SHORT ANIMATION PONKA GOD IS OUT FOR A WALK WITH HER DOG GRRR. SHE COMES ACROSS HER RIVAL TOUGH GIRLS, THE POWERPUFFS, AND DECIDES THAT IT'S TIME TO SET THOSE GIRLS STRAIGHT.
FILE SIZE: 24Kb
DURATION: 0:21
SIXSIDIA デザイン ©2002
BACK
MUSIC ON / OFF
©MARK MURPHY
SIXSIDIA NEWS
09-05-03 JUST BACK FROM OFFF IN BARCELONA. HAD A GREAT TIME AND MET SOME AMAZING PEOPLE.
29-04-03 GO OUT AND BUY THIS MONTHS COMPUTER ARTS SPECIAL ON CHARACTER ANIMATION, IT'S GOT A FOUR PAGE FEATURE ON SIXSIDIA. THE PONKAS ARE REALLY CHUFFED.
06-04-03 THANKS TO AVCAN OF WOW WEB DESIGNS FOR MAKING ME HIS CHOICE OF THE MONTH ON WELLVETTED #9

-------Sixsidia------------
SIXSIDIA デザイン ©2002
WEB SITES
ANIMATIONS
PROFILE
SICKBAGS
ICE PHOTO'S
DESKTOPS
LINKS
MAIL
MUSIC ON / OFF
©MARK MURPHY
SIXSIDIA NEWS
09-05-03 JUST BACK FROM OFFF IN BARCELONA. HAD A GREAT TIME AND MET SOME AMAZING PEOPLE.
29-04-03 GO OUT AND BUY THIS MONTHS COMPUTER ARTS SPECIAL ON CHARACTER ANIMATION, IT'S GOT A FOUR PAGE FEATURE ON SIXSIDIA. THE PONKAS ARE REALLY CHUFFED.
06-04-03 THANKS TO AVCAN OF WOW WEB DESIGNS FOR MAKING ME HIS CHOICE OF THE MONTH ON WELLVETTED #8

www.sixsidia.com
D: peter o'dwyer
A: sixsidia **M:** peter@sixsidia.com

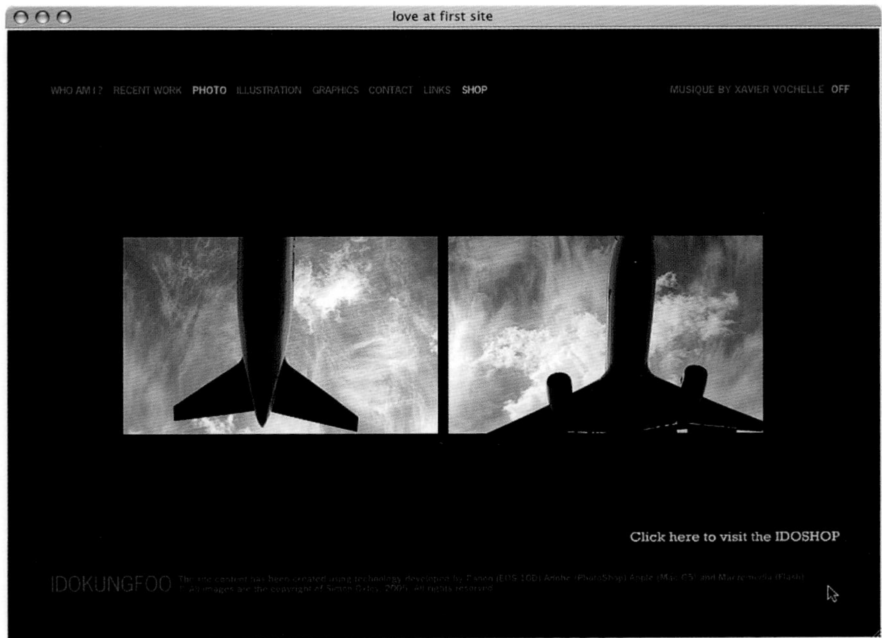
love at first site
WHO AM I ? RECENT WORK PHOTO ILLUSTRATION GRAPHICS CONTACT LINKS SHOP
MUSIQUE BY XAVIER VOCHELLE OFF
Click here to visit the IDOSHOP
IDOKUNGFOO

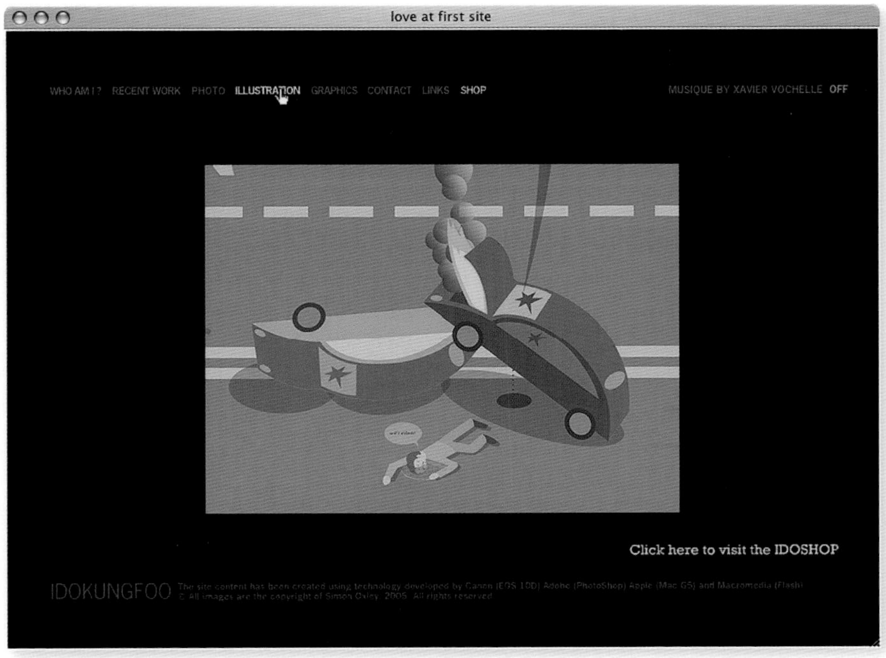
love at first site
WHO AM I ? RECENT WORK PHOTO ILLUSTRATION GRAPHICS CONTACT LINKS SHOP
MUSIQUE BY XAVIER VOCHELLE OFF
Click here to visit the IDOSHOP
IDOKUNGFOO

www.idokungfoo.com
D: simon oxley
A: idokungfoo **M:** simonox@jcom.home.ne.jp

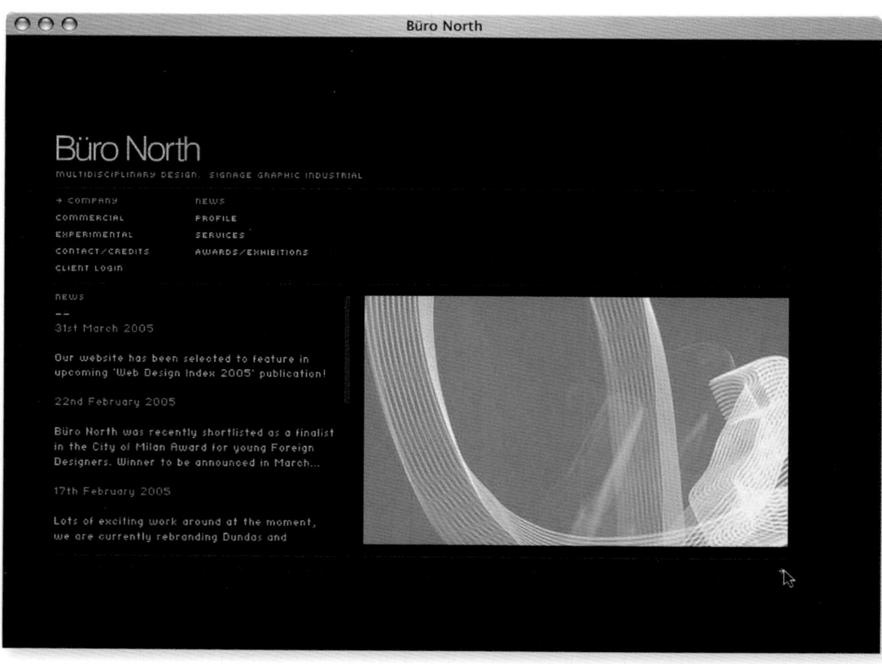
Büro North
Büro North
multidisciplinary design. signage graphic industrial
→ company
commercial
experimental
contact/credits
client login
news
profile
services
awards/exhibitions
news
31st March 2005
Our website has been selected to feature in upcoming 'Web Design Index 2005' publication!
22nd February 2005
Büro North was recently shortlisted as a finalist in the City of Milan Award for young Foreign Designers. Winner to be announced in March...
17th February 2005
Lots of exciting work around at the moment, we are currently rebranding Dundas and

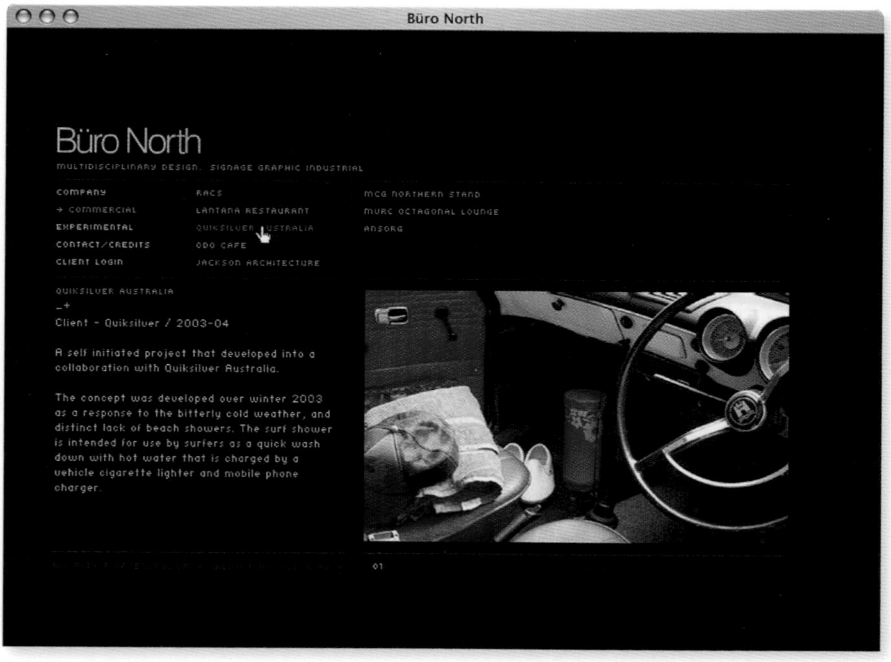
Büro North
Büro North
multidisciplinary design. signage graphic industrial
company
→ commercial
experimental
contact/credits
client login
racs
lantana restaurant
odo cafe
jackson architecture
mcg northern stand
murc octagonal lounge
ansorg
quiksilver australia
Client - Quiksilver / 2003-04
A self initiated project that developed into a collaboration with Quiksilver Australia.
The concept was developed over winter 2003 as a response to the bitterly cold weather, and distinct lack of beach showers. The surf shower is intended for use by surfers as a quick wash down with hot water that is charged by a vehicle cigarette lighter and mobile phone charger.
01

www.buronorth.com
D: martin konrad, soren luckins
A: www.octoc.com **M:** www.octoc.com

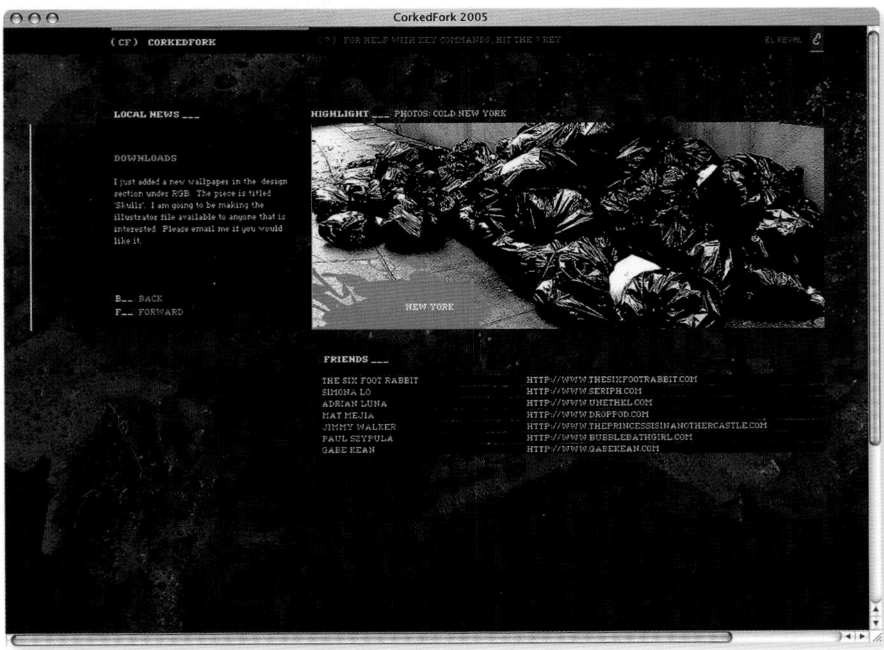
CorkedFork 2005
(CF) CORKEDFORK
LOCAL NEWS ___
HIGHLIGHT ___ PHOTOS: COLD NEW YORK
DOWNLOADS
I just added a new wallpaper in the design section under RGB. The piece is titled 'Skulls'. I am going to be making the illustrator file available to anyone that is interested. Please email me if you would like it.
B__ BACK
F__ FORWARD
NEW YORK
FRIENDS ___
THE SIX FOOT RABBIT HTTP://WWW.THESIXFOOTRABBIT.COM
SIMONA LO HTTP://WWW.SERIPH.COM
ADRIAN LUNA HTTP://WWW.UNETHEL.COM
MAT MEJIA HTTP://WWW.DROPPOD.COM
JIMMY WALKER HTTP://WWW.THEPRINCESSISINANOTHERCASTLE.COM
PAUL SZYPULA HTTP://WWW.BUBBLEBATHGIRL.COM
GABE KEAN HTTP://WWW.GABEKEAN.COM

CorkedFork 2005
NAVIGATION
UPDATES
DESIGN
PHOTOS
CONTACT
HTTP
HTTP
CMYK
RGB
MOTION
OTHER
INFECTED LOGIC
JOHN JOHNSON
CINGULAR WIRELESS
CORKEDFORK 2003
45RPM SESSIONS
INFECTED LOGIC
KOBAY FINANCIAL
SPANGLISH
DARREN CHRISTIAN
INFECTED LOGIC
MUSIC ADVANCED
Save the drama for your mama...
Oakie gives up!!
tweedle-dee finds long lost brother...
CONTACT
Current Poll
DESC__ INFECTED LOGIC WEBSITE
CLIENT__ INFECTED LOGIC
DATE__ 03/2003
EXTRAS__

www.corkedfork.com
D: scott baggett
A: corkedfork M: contact@corkedfork.com

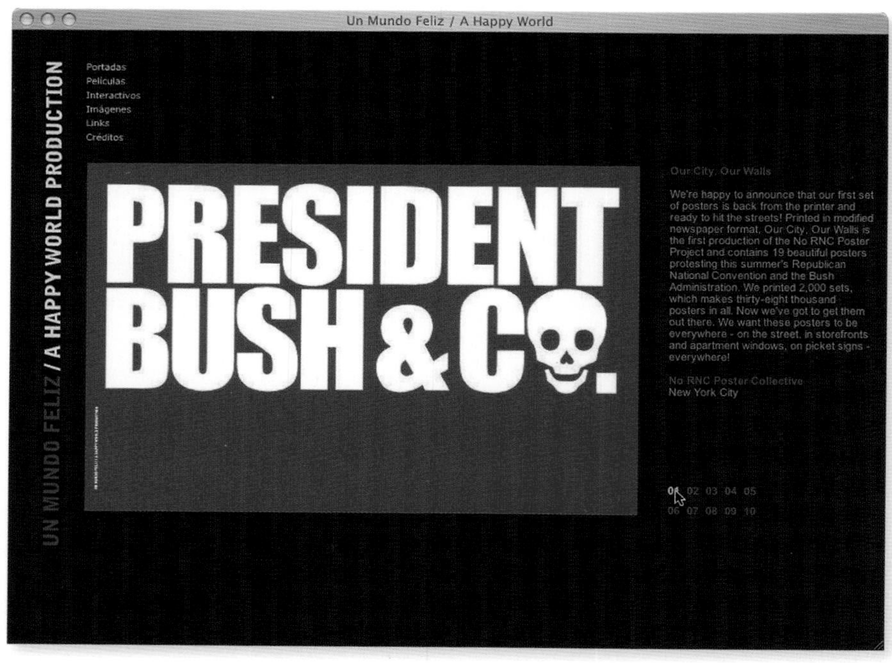
Un Mundo Feliz / A Happy World
UN MUNDO FELIZ / A HAPPY WORLD PRODUCTION
Portadas
Películas
Interactivos
Imágenes
Links
Créditos
PRESIDENT BUSH & CO.
Our City, Our Walls
We're happy to announce that our first set of posters is back from the printer and ready to hit the streets! Printed in modified newspaper format, Our City, Our Walls is the first production of the No RNC Poster Project and contains 19 beautiful posters protesting this summer's Republican National Convention and the Bush Administration. We printed 2,000 sets, which makes thirty-eight thousand posters in all. Now we've got to get them out there. We want these posters to be everywhere - on the street, in storefronts and apartment windows, on picket signs - everywhere!
No RNC Poster Collective
New York City
01 02 03 04 05
06 07 08 09 10

Un Mundo Feliz / A Happy World
UN MUNDO FELIZ / A HAPPY WORLD PRODUCTION
Portadas
Películas
Interactivos
Imágenes
Links
Créditos
Missing
Endangered Missing
BRITTNEY BEERS
Child's photo is shown aged to 10 years.
Brittney

www.unmundofeliz.org
D: gabriel freeman
A: un mundo feliz **M:** gabriel@unmundofeliz.org

« Quidante . Valentijn Destoop »
the past . present . future
the work of valentijn
QUIDANTE.COM

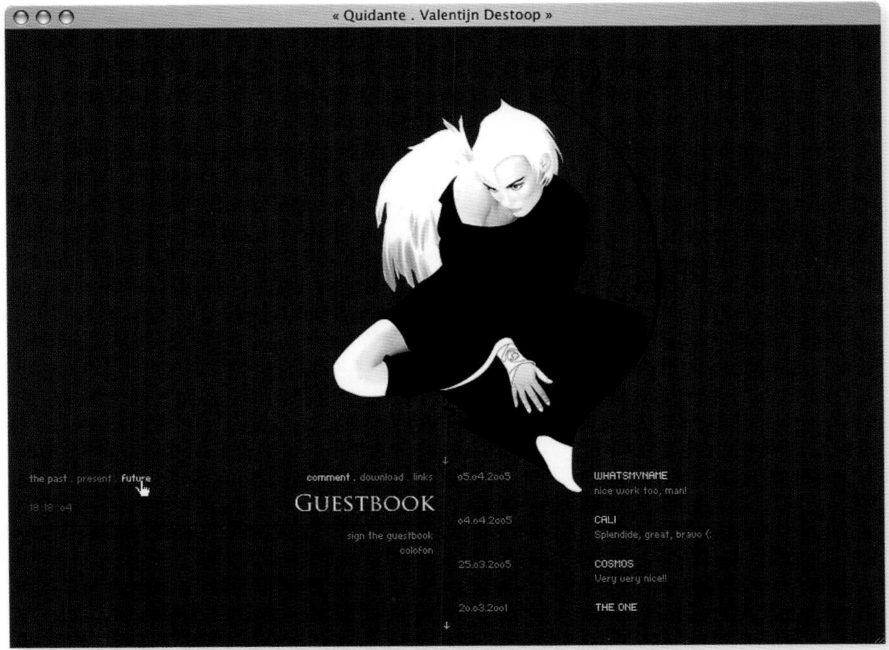
« Quidante . Valentijn Destoop »
the past . present . future
comment . download . links
GUESTBOOK
sign the guestbook
colofon
05.04.2005
WHATSMYNAME
nice work too, man!
04.04.2005
CALI
Splendide, great, bravo (:
25.03.2005
COSMOS
Very very nice!!
20.03.2001
THE ONE

www.quidante.com
D: valentijn destoop **C:** vic rau, stefan colins, thomas spiessens
A: quidante **M:** valentijn@quidante.com

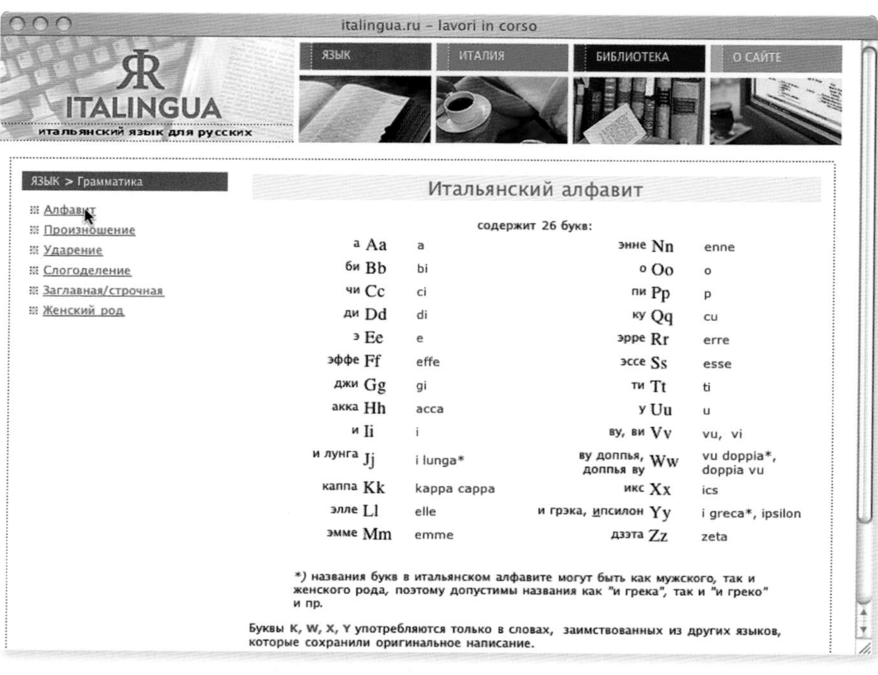
italingua.ru – lavori in corso
ЯЗЫК
ИТАЛИЯ
БИБЛИОТЕКА
О САЙТЕ
ITALINGUA
итальянский язык для русских
ЯЗЫК > Грамматика
Алфавит
Произношение
Ударение
Слогоделение
Заглавная/строчная
Женский род
Итальянский алфавит
содержит 26 букв:
а Aa a
би Bb bi
чи Cc ci
ди Dd di
э Ee e
эффе Ff effe
джи Gg gi
акка Hh acca
и Ii i
и лунга Jj i lunga*
каппа Kk kappa cappa
элле Ll elle
эмме Mm emme
энне Nn enne
о Oo o
пи Pp p
ку Qq cu
эрре Rr erre
эссе Ss esse
ти Tt ti
у Uu u
ву, ви Vv vu, vi
ву доппья, доппья ву Ww vu doppia*, doppia vu
икс Xx ics
и грэка, ипсилон Yy i greca*, ipsilon
дзэта Zz zeta
*) названия букв в итальянском алфавите могут быть как мужского, так и женского рода, поэтому допустимы названия как "и грека", так и "и греко" и пр.
Буквы K, W, X, Y употребляются только в словах, заимствованных из других языков, которые сохранили оригинальное написание.

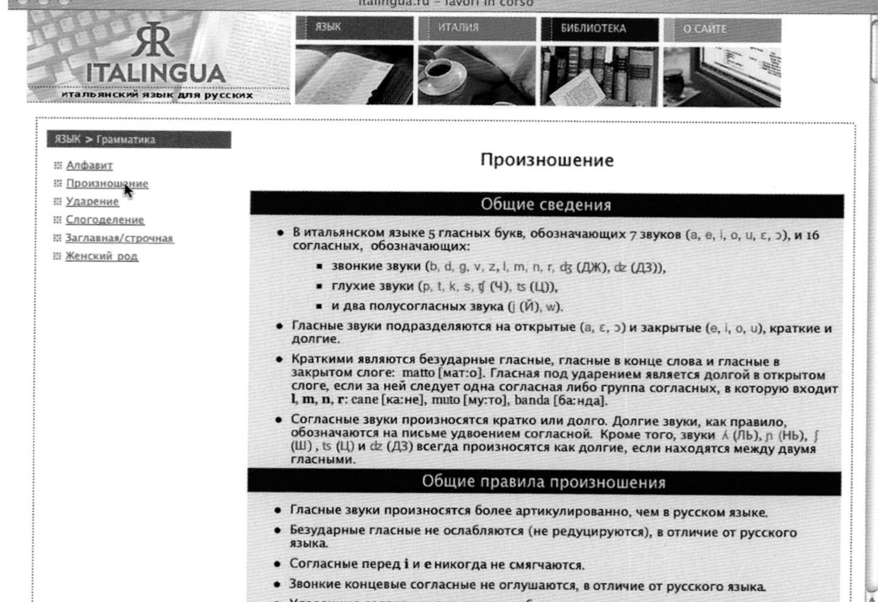
italingua.ru – lavori in corso
ЯЗЫК
ИТАЛИЯ
БИБЛИОТЕКА
О САЙТЕ
ITALINGUA
итальянский язык для русских
ЯЗЫК > Грамматика
Алфавит
Произношение
Ударение
Слогоделение
Заглавная/строчная
Женский род
Произношение
Общие сведения
В итальянском языке 5 гласных букв, обозначающих 7 звуков (a, e, i, o, u, ɛ, ɔ), и 16 согласных, обозначающих:
звонкие звуки (b, d, g, v, z, l, m, n, r, ʤ (ДЖ), ʣ (ДЗ)),
глухие звуки (p, t, k, s, ʧ (Ч), ʦ (Ц)),
и два полусогласных звука (j (Й), w).
Гласные звуки подразделяются на открытые (a, ɛ, ɔ) и закрытые (e, i, o, u), краткие и долгие.
Краткими являются безударные гласные, гласные в конце слова и гласные в закрытом слоге: matto [мат:о]. Гласная под ударением является долгой в открытом слоге, если за ней следует одна согласная либо группа согласных, в которую входит l, m, n, r: cane [ка:не], muto [му:то], banda [ба:нда].
Согласные звуки произносятся кратко или долго. Долгие звуки, как правило, обозначаются на письме удвоением согласной. Кроме того, звуки ʎ (ЛЬ), ɲ (НЬ), ʃ (Ш), ʦ (Ц) и ʣ (ДЗ) всегда произносятся как долгие, если находятся между двумя гласными.
Общие правила произношения
Гласные звуки произносятся более артикулированно, чем в русском языке.
Безударные гласные не ослабляются (не редуцируются), в отличие от русского языка.
Согласные перед i и e никогда не смягчаются.
Звонкие концевые согласные не оглушаются, в отличие от русского языка.
Удвоенные согласные произносятся более четко, чем в русском языке.

www.italingua.ru
D: pavel maximov
M: maximov@inwind.it

·· Santillana en Red ··
Santillana en Red
Inicio Contenidos Plataforma Servicio Integral Contacto
Enseñar y aprender con tecnología:
una realidad
Santillana en Red nace con el objetivo de impulsar la utilización de las Tecnologías de la Información y la Comunicación (TIC) en el proceso de enseñanza-aprendizaje.
Ofrecemos una solución integral dirigida a los Centros Educativos y de la que pueden beneficiarse todos los miembros de la comunidad educativa: docentes, alumnado, familias y gestores.
Hemos desarrollado unos productos y servicios concebidos por y para el mundo educativo: flexibles, de diseño sencillo y fácil manejo.
Contenidos curriculares multimedia
Plataforma educativa
Acceso a clientes
Clave
Contraseña
© 2004 Santillana en Red · Edificio Apot · Avda Ribera del Sena s/n · 28042 Madrid
créditos

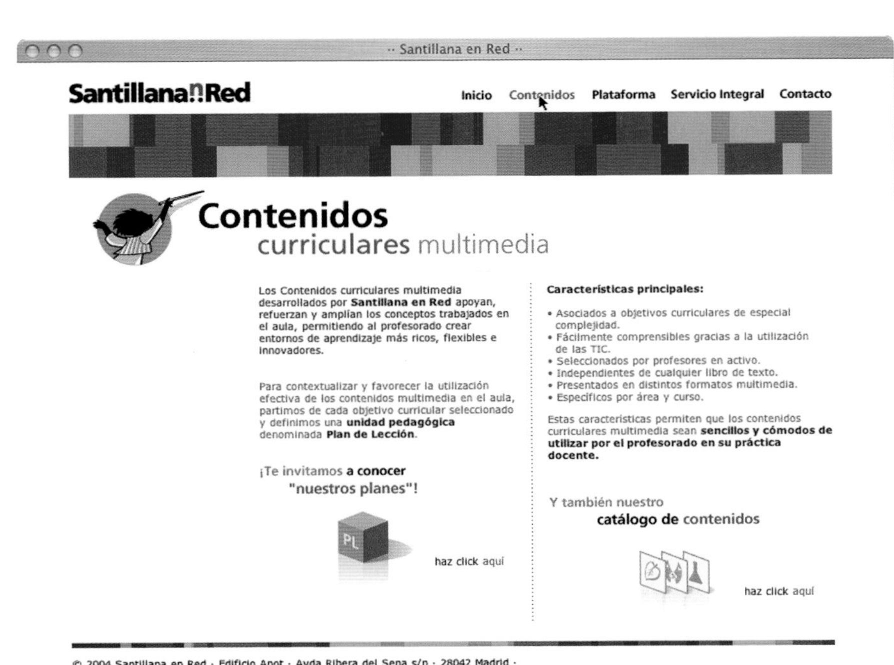
·· Santillana en Red ··
Santillana en Red
Inicio Contenidos Plataforma Servicio Integral Contacto
Contenidos
curriculares multimedia
Los Contenidos curriculares multimedia desarrollados por Santillana en Red apoyan, refuerzan y amplían los conceptos trabajados en el aula, permitiendo al profesorado crear entornos de aprendizaje más ricos, flexibles e innovadores.
Para contextualizar y favorecer la utilización efectiva de los contenidos multimedia en el aula, partimos de cada objetivo curricular seleccionado y definimos una unidad pedagógica denominada Plan de Lección.
¡Te invitamos a conocer
"nuestros planes"!
PL
haz click aquí
Características principales:
• Asociados a objetivos curriculares de especial complejidad.
• Fácilmente comprensibles gracias a la utilización de las TIC.
• Seleccionados por profesores en activo.
• Independientes de cualquier libro de texto.
• Presentados en distintos formatos multimedia.
• Específicos por área y curso.
Estas características permiten que los contenidos curriculares multimedia sean sencillos y cómodos de utilizar por el profesorado en su práctica docente.
Y también nuestro
catálogo de contenidos
haz click aquí
© 2004 Santillana en Red · Edificio Apot · Avda Ribera del Sena s/n · 28042 Madrid ·

www.santillanaenred.com
D: patricia fuentes
A: blue planet **M:** info@blplanet.com

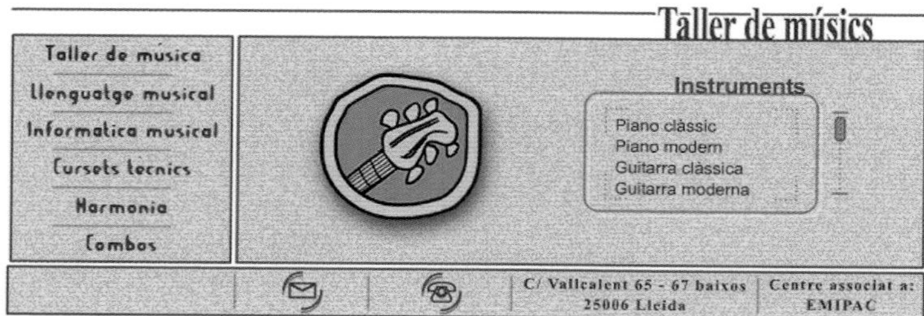
MÚSICS taller de música
Taller de músics
Taller de musica
Llenguatge musical
Informatica musical
Cursets tecnics
Harmonia
Combos
Instruments
Piano clàssic
Piano modern
Guitarra clàssica
Guitarra moderna
C/ Vallcalent 65 - 67 baixos
25006 Lleida
Centre associat a:
EMIPAC

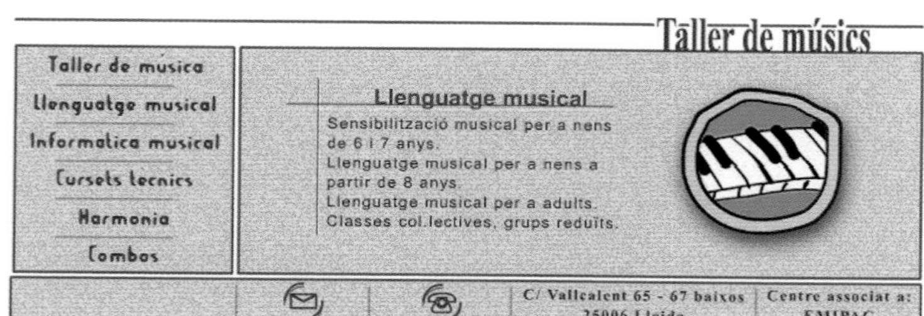
MÚSICS taller de música
Taller de músics
Taller de musica
Llenguatge musical
Informatica musical
Cursets tecnics
Harmonia
Combos
Llenguatge musical
Sensibilització musical per a nens de 6 i 7 anys.
Llenguatge musical per a nens a partir de 8 anys.
Llenguatge musical per a adults.
Classes col.lectives, grups reduïts.
C/ Vallcalent 65 - 67 baixos
25006 Lleida
Centre associat a:
EMIPAC

www.maatmedia.com/musics
D: jordi barrero alba
M: pcmejo@terra.es

(the cry) ------ existentialism
search engine
site map
guestbook
@
phenomenology
art
forums
chat
exquisite corpse
mail-list
(the cry)
a cry towards the absurd
(existentialism::home)
the authors
kierkegaard dostoevsky allen sartre jaspers camus nietzsche kafka heidegger descartes de beauvoir rilke
the philosophy
- Definition
- Roots
- History
- Beyond
- Social and historical practices
- Further reading
best web sites
- Existentialism: A Primer
- Realm of Existentialism
- Kierkegaard, Soren - D. Anthony Storm
- The Nietzsche Page
- Glossary of Existential Terms
more links..
(the cry)is the home to the
Existentialism
Philosophy, philosophers, readings, articles
Wait a minute, there's a snag somewhere; something disagreeable. Why, now, should it be disagreeable?...Ah,I see; it's life without a break. (Jean Paul Sartre - huis clos)
Existentialism is a philosophical movement which emphasizes on individual existence, freedom, and choice.
There are several philosophical positions all related to existential philosophy but the main identifiable common proposition, is that existence precedes essence. By this, existentialism states that man exists and in that existence man defines himself and the world in his own subjectivity, and wanders between choice, freedom, and existential angst.
The first philosopher to use the term was Soren Kierkegaard (1813 - 1855), who reacted against systematic rational philosophy, specially Hegel, and grasped the notion of a truth inside of the evolving self.
Deriving from this stress on existence there are other main subjects and images that have been developed by the existentialists.
Becoming a Being (existential ontology):
We are what we can become. Ours is a process, and our becoming is our ontic possibility of becoming. Human existence is a project, in which past and present are subordinate to future, is the main residence of our existence, because it is the north of our projection of

(the cry) existentialism sartre nietzsche kafka kier... beauvoir allen dostoievsky marcel camus zarathustra
search engine
site map
guestbook
@
phenomenology
art
forums
chat
exquisite corpse
mail-list
(the cry)
a cry towards the absurd
(existentialism::Friedrich Nietzsche
the authors
kierkegaard dostoevsky allen sartre jaspers camus nietzsche kafka heidegger descartes de beauvoir rilke
the philosophy
- Definition
- Roots
- History
- Beyond
- Social and historical practices
- Further reading
- existentialism discussion board
-general philosophy discussion board
best web sites
- Existentialism: A Primer
- Realm of Existentialism
- Kierkegaard, Soren - D. Anthony Storm
- The Nietzsche Page
- Glossary of Existential Terms
more links..
Existentialism
Friedrich Nietzsche (1844 - 1900)
A sublime one saw I today, a solemn one, a penitent of the spirit: Oh, how my soul laughed at his ugliness! (thus spake zarathustra)
Friedrich Nietzsche
- biography
- quotes
- his work
- pictures
- links on Niezsche
On-line works:
- zarathustra
- poems
- why am I so clever
- the problem of socrates
- the "improvers" of mankind
- gay science section 109
Why do I know more than other people? Why, in general, am I so clever? I have never pondered over questions that are not really questions. I have never wasted my strength. I have no experience, for instance, of actual religious difficulties. I am quite unfamiliar with the feeling of "sinfulness." Similarly I lack a reliable criterion for determining a prick of conscience: from what one hears, a prick of conscience does not seem to me anything very worthy of veneration. . . . I dislike to leave an action of mine in the lurch; I prefer to omit utterly the bad result, the consequences, from any problem involving values. In the face of evil . consequences it is too easy to lose the proper standpoint from which to view an action. A prick of conscience seems to me a sort of "evil eye." Something that has failed should be all the more honored just because it has failed-this agrees much better with my morality.-"God," "the immortality of the soul," tcsalvation," a "beyond"-these are mere notions, to which I paid no attention, on which I never wasted any time, even as a child-though perhaps I was never enough of a child for that-I am quite unacquainted with atheism as a result, and still less as an event: with me it is instinctive. I am too inquisitive, too skeptical, too arrogant ', to let myself be satisfied with an obvious and crass solution of things. God is such an obvious and crass solution; a solution which is a sheer indelicacy to us thinkers-at bottom He is really nothing but a coarse commandment

www.thecry.com
D: indira montoya
M: simbolososcuros@yahoo.com

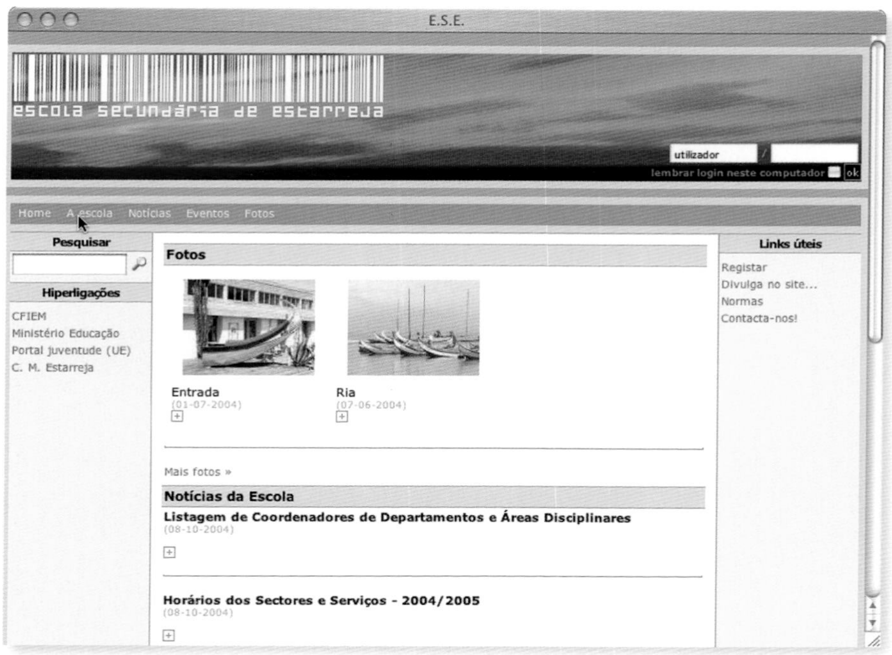
E.S.E.
escola secundária de estarreja
utilizador
lembrar login neste computador
ok
Home
A escola
Notícias
Eventos
Fotos
Pesquisar
Hiperligações
CFIEM
Ministério Educação
Portal juventude (UE)
C. M. Estarreja
Fotos
Entrada
(01-07-2004)
Ria
(07-06-2004)
Mais fotos »
Notícias da Escola
Listagem de Coordenadores de Departamentos e Áreas Disciplinares
(08-10-2004)
Horários dos Sectores e Serviços - 2004/2005
(08-10-2004)
Links úteis
Registar
Divulga no site...
Normas
Contacta-nos!

E.S.E.
escola secundária de estarreja
utilizador
lembrar login neste computador
ok
Home
A escola
Notícias
Eventos
Fotos
Pesquisar
Hiperligações
CFIEM
Ministério Educação
Portal juventude (UE)
C. M. Estarreja
Notícias
Listagem de Coordenadores de Departamentos e Áreas Disciplinares
(08-10-2004)
Horários dos Sectores e Serviços - 2004/2005
(08-10-2004)
90 mil imigrantes nas escolas portuguesas
(20-09-2004)
O relatório do Eurydice sobre os imigrantes que frequentam o sistema de ensino português revela que existem, em Portugal, quase noventa mil estudantes de outras (...)
Horários 2004/2005
(16-09-2004)
Os horários deste ano lectivo já estão disponíveis. Mas atenção, ainda não são definitivos. Os horários definitivos deverão ser disponibilizados a partir do f (...)
Links úteis
Registar
Divulga no site...
Normas
Contacta-nos!

www.esestarreja.net
D: pedro piedade
A: sinergias **M:** pedro@nitrogenio.net

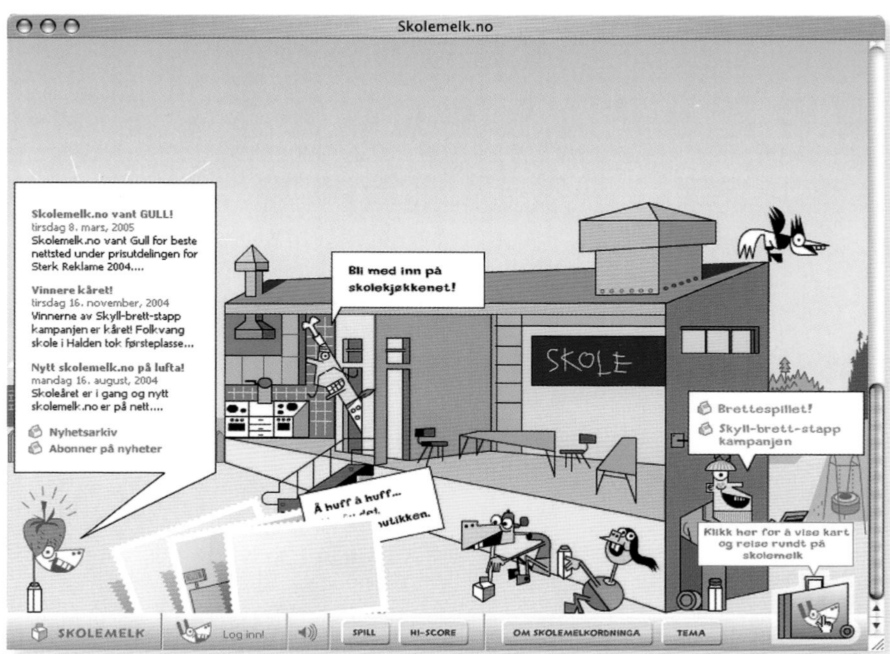
Skolemelk.no
Skolemelk.no vant GULL!
tirsdag 8. mars, 2005
Skolemelk.no vant Gull for beste nettsted under prisutdelingen for Sterk Reklame 2004....
Vinnere kåret!
tirsdag 16. november, 2004
Vinnerne av Skyll-brett-stapp kampanjen er kåret! Folkvang skole i Halden tok førsteplasse...
Nytt skolemelk.no på lufta!
mandag 16. august, 2004
Skoleåret er i gang og nytt skolemelk.no er på nett....
Nyhetsarkiv
Abonner på nyheter
Bli med inn på skolekjøkkenet!
SKOLE
Brettespillet!
Skyll-brett-stapp kampanjen
Klikk her for å vise kart og reise rundt på skolemelk
SKOLEMELK
Log inn!
SPILL
HI-SCORE
OM SKOLEMELKORDNINGA
TEMA

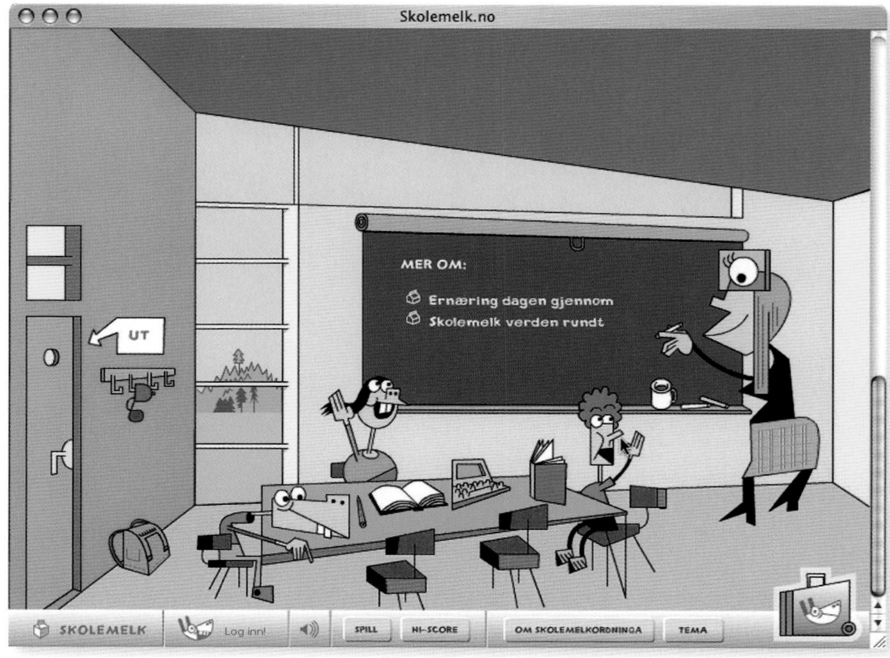
Skolemelk.no
MER OM:
Ernæring dagen gjennom
Skolemelk verden rundt
UT
SKOLEMELK
Log inn!
SPILL
HI-SCORE
OM SKOLEMELKORDNINGA
TEMA

www.skolemelk.no
D: eiliv gunnleiksrud **C:** almir busevac
A: klapp media **M:** havardg@klapp.no

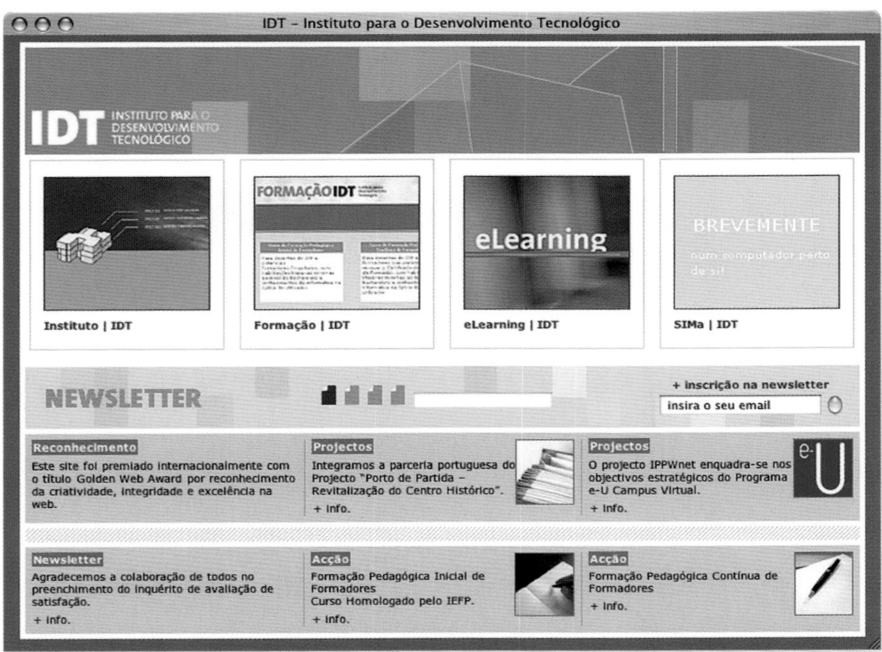
IDT - Instituto para o Desenvolvimento Tecnológico
IDT INSTITUTO PARA O DESENVOLVIMENTO TECNOLÓGICO
FORMAÇÃO IDT
eLearning
BREVEMENTE
Instituto | IDT
Formação | IDT
eLearning | IDT
SIMa | IDT
NEWSLETTER
+ inscrição na newsletter
insira o seu email
Reconhecimento
Este site foi premiado internacionalmente com o título Golden Web Award por reconhecimento da criatividade, integridade e excelência na web.
Projectos
Integramos a parceria portuguesa do Projecto "Porto de Partida – Revitalização do Centro Histórico".
+ info.
Projectos
O projecto IPPWnet enquadra-se nos objectivos estratégicos do Programa e-U Campus Virtual.
+ info.
Newsletter
Agradecemos a colaboração de todos no preenchimento do inquérito de avaliação de satisfação.
+ info.
Acção
Formação Pedagógica Inicial de Formadores
Curso Homologado pelo IEFP.
+ info.
Acção
Formação Pedagógica Contínua de Formadores
+ info.

Instituto para o Desenvolvimento Tecnológico
INSTITUTO PARA O DESENVOLVIMENTO TECNOLÓGICO
MENU
IDT INSTITUTO PARA O DESENVOLVIMENTO TECNOLÓGICO
O Instituto para o Desenvolvimento Tecnológico é a Unidade de interface da Fundação Instituto Politécnico do Porto com a comunidade, vocacionada para a Prestação de Serviços no domínio da Gestão e Tecnologia, com actividades nas áreas da consultadoria, projecto, sistemas de informação e formação.
Formação Pedagógica Inicial de Formadores
english version
versão html

www.idt.ipp.pt
D: antónio cruz, paulo magalhães **C:** filipe murteira
A: idt multimédia **M:** paulom@ipp.pt

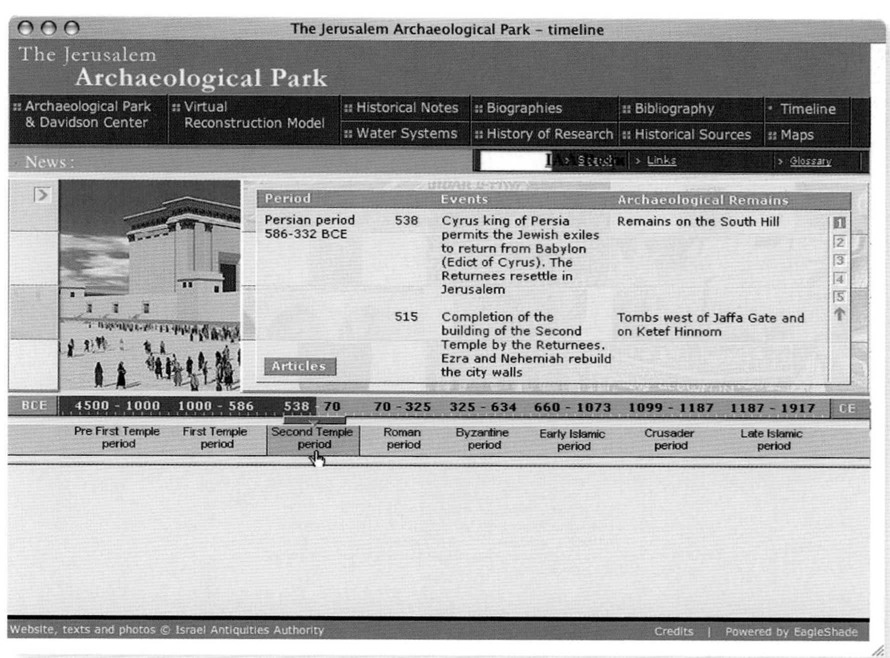
The Jerusalem Archaeological Park – timeline
The Jerusalem
Archaeological Park
Archaeological Park & Davidson Center
Virtual Reconstruction Model
Historical Notes
Water Systems
Biographies
History of Research
Bibliography
Historical Sources
Timeline
Maps
News :
Links
Glossary
Period
Events
Archaeological Remains
Persian period 586-332 BCE
538
Cyrus king of Persia permits the Jewish exiles to return from Babylon (Edict of Cyrus). The Returnees resettle in Jerusalem
Remains on the South Hill
515
Completion of the building of the Second Temple by the Returnees. Ezra and Nehemiah rebuild the city walls
Tombs west of Jaffa Gate and on Ketef Hinnom
Articles
BCE
4500 - 1000
1000 - 586
538 - 70
70 - 325
325 - 634
660 - 1073
1099 - 1187
1187 - 1917
CE
Pre First Temple period
First Temple period
Second Temple period
Roman period
Byzantine period
Early Islamic period
Crusader period
Late Islamic period
Website, texts and photos © Israel Antiquities Authority
Credits | Powered by EagleShade

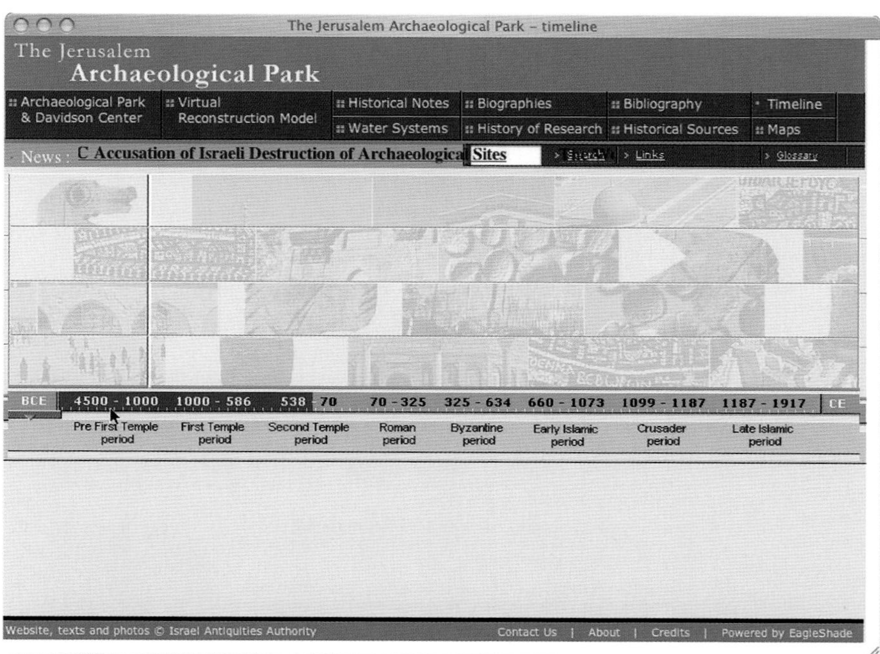
The Jerusalem Archaeological Park – timeline
The Jerusalem
Archaeological Park
Archaeological Park & Davidson Center
Virtual Reconstruction Model
Historical Notes
Water Systems
Biographies
History of Research
Bibliography
Historical Sources
Timeline
Maps
News : C Accusation of Israeli Destruction of Archaeological Sites
Links
Glossary
BCE
4500 - 1000
1000 - 586
538 - 70
70 - 325
325 - 634
660 - 1073
1099 - 1187
1187 - 1917
CE
Pre First Temple period
First Temple period
Second Temple period
Roman period
Byzantine period
Early Islamic period
Crusader period
Late Islamic period
Website, texts and photos © Israel Antiquities Authority
Contact Us | About | Credits | Powered by EagleShade

www.archpark.org.il
D: ilan dray **C:** tamir mordeau **P:** israel antiquities authority
M: ilan@eaglehsade.com

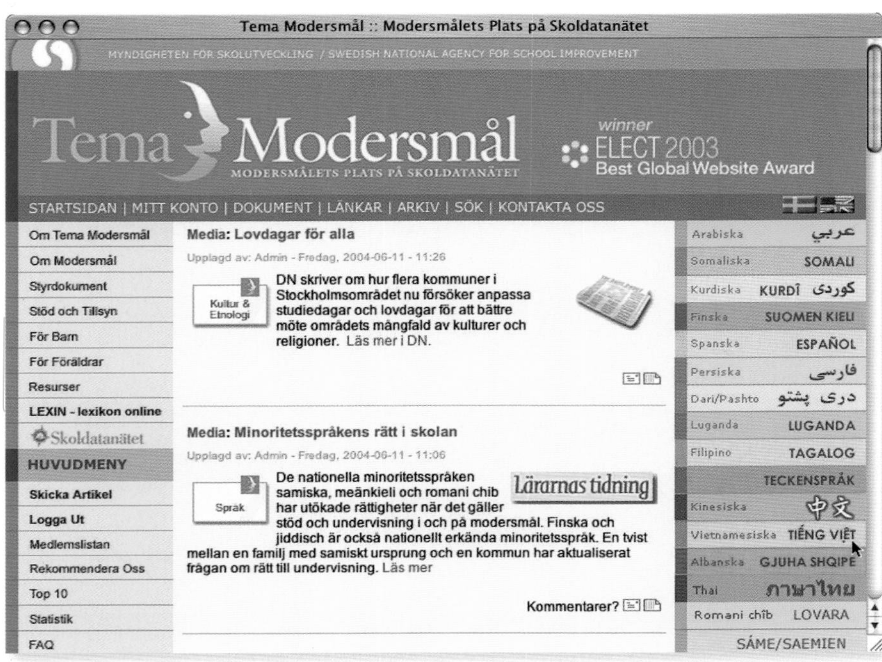
Tema Modersmål :: Modersmålets Plats på Skoldatanätet
MYNDIGHETEN FÖR SKOLUTVECKLING / SWEDISH NATIONAL AGENCY FOR SCHOOL IMPROVEMENT
Tema Modersmål
MODERSMÅLETS PLATS PÅ SKOLDATANÄTET
winner
ELECT 2003
Best Global Website Award
STARTSIDAN | MITT KONTO | DOKUMENT | LÄNKAR | ARKIV | SÖK | KONTAKTA OSS
Om Tema Modersmål
Om Modersmål
Styrdokument
Stöd och Tillsyn
För Barn
För Föräldrar
Resurser
LEXIN - lexikon online
Skoldatanätet
HUVUDMENY
Skicka Artikel
Logga Ut
Medlemslistan
Rekommendera Oss
Top 10
Statistik
FAQ
Media: Lovdagar för alla
Upplagd av: Admin - Fredag, 2004-06-11 - 11:26
Kultur & Etnologi
DN skriver om hur flera kommuner i Stockholmsområdet nu försöker anpassa studiedagar och lovdagar för att bättre möte områdets mångfald av kulturer och religioner. Läs mer i DN.
Media: Minoritetsspråkens rätt i skolan
Upplagd av: Admin - Fredag, 2004-06-11 - 11:06
Språk
Lärarnas tidning
De nationella minoritetsspråken samiska, meänkieli och romani chib har utökade rättigheter när det gäller stöd och undervisning i och på modersmål. Finska och jiddisch är också nationellt erkända minoritetsspråk. En tvist mellan en familj med samiskt ursprung och en kommun har aktualiserat frågan om rätt till undervisning. Läs mer
Kommentarer?
Arabiska عربي
Somaliska SOMALI
Kurdiska KURDÎ كوردى
Finska SUOMEN KIELI
Spanska ESPAÑOL
Persiska فارسی
Dari/Pashto دری پشتو
Luganda LUGANDA
Filipino TAGALOG
TECKENSPRÅK
Kinesiska 中文
Vietnamesiska TIẾNG VIỆT
Albanska GJUHA SHQIPE
Thai ภาษาไทย
Romani chib LOVARA
SÁME/SAEMIEN

Tema Modersmål :: Modersmålets Plats på Skoldatanätet
MYNDIGHETEN FÖR SKOLUTVECKLING / SWEDISH NATIONAL AGENCY FOR SCHOOL IMPROVEMENT
Tema Modersmål
MODERSMÅLETS PLATS PÅ SKOLDATANÄTET
winner
ELECT 2003
Best Global Website Award
STARTSIDAN | MITT KONTO | DOKUMENT | LÄNKAR | ARKIV | SÖK | KONTAKTA OSS
Om Tema Modersmål
Om Modersmål
Styrdokument
Stöd och Tillsyn
För Barn
För Föräldrar
Resurser
LEXIN - lexikon online
Skoldatanätet
HUVUDMENY
Skicka Artikel
Logga Ut
Medlemslistan
Rekommendera Oss
Top 10
Statistik
FAQ
Om Tema Modersmål
Välkommen!
Vi hoppas att Du som är intresserade av modersmålsstöd, modersmålundervisning och studiehandledning på modersmål uppskattar en samlad information och möjlighet till diskussion. Webbplatsen är i första hand formad som en resurs för de som arbetar inom barnomsorg och skola men alla besökare är givetvis lika välkomna!
De olika språkens temaplatser innehåller information och verktyg för kommunikation. Dessa drivs av aktiva modersmålslärare. Ambitionen är att lyfta fram bra pedagogiska resurser.
Temaplatsen innehåller just nu 23 språk. Arbete med jiddish pågår. Vi ser fram mot att starta arbete med fler språk. Vi siktar också på att utveckla stöd för distansundervisning och att utvidga internationella kontakter. Tema Modersmål tilldelades i november 2003 "The Best Global Website Award"

modersmal.skolutveckling.se
D: mats wennerholm

iCOM
icom
OVERVIEW MISSION DOWNLOADS CONTACT
Return Home
THE CENTER FOR MEDIA DESIGN
External Partnerships:
The Center for Media Design is fostering projects with industry partners ranging from R&D efforts to production of marketable digital products. A major focus of the R&D effort is the development of a testing and evaluation center for digital media - "Digital Middletown." The premise for the testing center is the prior existence of a body of sociological research that used Muncie, home of Ball State University, as a test bed that came to be known as "Middletown USA."
Goals
Model & demonstrate innovative technology methods, applications, and spatial environments.
Projects
Click Here to view past and future projects.
CENTER FOR MEDIA DESIGN
Redefining Collaboration
Learn More About CMD
View Projects
Browse CMD Projects
GET INVOLVED
Students
Virginia Ball Center For Creative Inquiry
Faculty
Tools, Procedures, and Forms
NEWS
CMD Headlines
Performance to blend digital sound, imagery at Artsgarden .
Download Radio Actualities
BALL STATE UNIVERSITY

iCOM
icom
OVERVIEW MISSION DOWNLOADS CONTACT
CMD
Redefining Collaboration
Learn More About CMD
View Projects
Browse CMD Projects
GET INVOLVED
Students
Virginia Ball Center For Creative Inquiry
Faculty
Tools, Procedures, and Forms
NEWS
CMD Headlines
Study finds TV viewers...
Download Media Studies Report
Download Radio Actualities
BALL STATE UNIVERSITY

www.bsu.edu/icommunication

D: brandon luhring
M: brandon@luhring-design.com

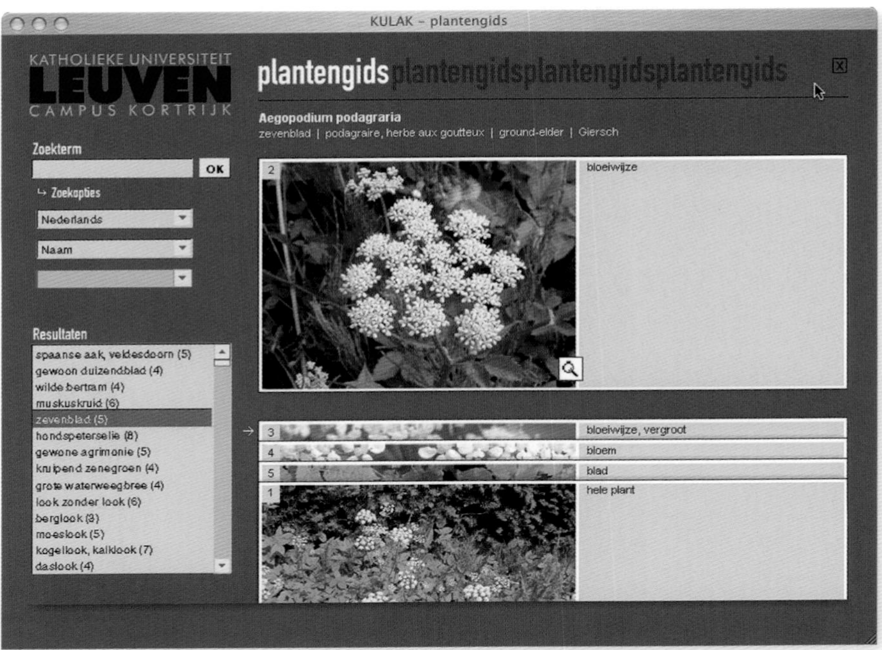
KULAK - plantengids
KATHOLIEKE UNIVERSITEIT
LEUVEN
CAMPUS KORTRIJK
plantengids plantengidsplantengidsplantengids
Aegopodium podagraria
zevenblad | podagraire, herbe aux goutteux | ground-elder | Giersch
Zoekterm
OK
Zoekopties
Nederlands
Naam
Resultaten
spaanse aak, veldesdoorn (5)
gewoon duizendblad (4)
wilde bertram (4)
muskuskruid (6)
zevenblad (5)
hondspeterselie (8)
gewone agrimonie (5)
kruipend zenegroen (4)
grote waterweegbree (4)
look zonder look (6)
berglook (3)
moeslook (5)
kogellook, kalklook (7)
daslook (4)
bloeiwijze
bloeiwijze, vergroot
bloem
blad
hele plant

KULAK - plantengids
KATHOLIEKE UNIVERSITEIT
LEUVEN
CAMPUS KORTRIJK
plantengids plantengidsplantengidsplantengids
Polygonatum multiflorum
gewone salomonszegel | sceau de Salomon commun | Solomon's-seal | Vielblütige Weißwurz
Zoekterm
OK
Zoekopties
Nederlands
Naam
Resultaten
gewone hennepnetel (10)
gewone hoornbloem (5)
gewone kattestaart (7)
gewone kropaar (2)
gewone melkdistel (6)
gewone ossentong (9)
gewone pastinaak (7)
gewone raket (6)
gewone reigersbek (6)
gewone rolklaver (6)
gewone salomonszegel (7)
gewone smeerwortel (7)
gewone spurrie (6)
gewone veldbies (4)
bloem
bloeiwijze
bloeiwijze, onderzijde
vrucht en blad
vrucht en blad
vrucht en blad
hele plant

www.kulak.ac.be/bioweb

D: laurence demedts **C:** christophe herreman **P:** kulak
A: telraam **M:** christophe.herreman@telraam.be

Keller Company
keller the school
Keller haircompany HAIR'N'MORE Keller the school TOP THEMA Jobs & Karriere Presse & Partner Impressum Schnellsuche...
ERFOLG KANN MAN LERNEN KELLER THE SCHOOL
Collectionen Modelle Vorteile Seminare Kalender Partnerkonzept AGB Kontakt
events
WILLKOMMEN BEI KELLER THE SCHOOL
Wer hoch hinaus will, braucht eine solide Grundlage. Wir vermitteln jungen Menschen, die sich für eine Karriere in unserer Branche entschlossen haben, Fachwissen aus erster Hand. Erfahrene Friseure und Saloninhaber schätzen die vielfältigen Seminarkonzepte, loben die Inspiration und Motivation die sie daraus mitnehmen.
Bei Keller the school entstehen die zahlreichen vorbildlichen Collectionen unseres Creativ Teams, die immer wieder internationale Fachleute und unsere Kunden begeistern. Wir suchen die Herausforderung, die in den Extremen steckt und setzen uns ein hohes Ziel: mit innovativen Konzepten visionäres Hairstyling erlebbar machen.
"NIGHT STYLE" zur Polarnacht
Große Fashion-Show in Reutlingens "färberei4"
Gewinner der L´Oréal Colour Trophy 2004 bei der Oscarverleihung für Friseure!
NEWS ARCHIV

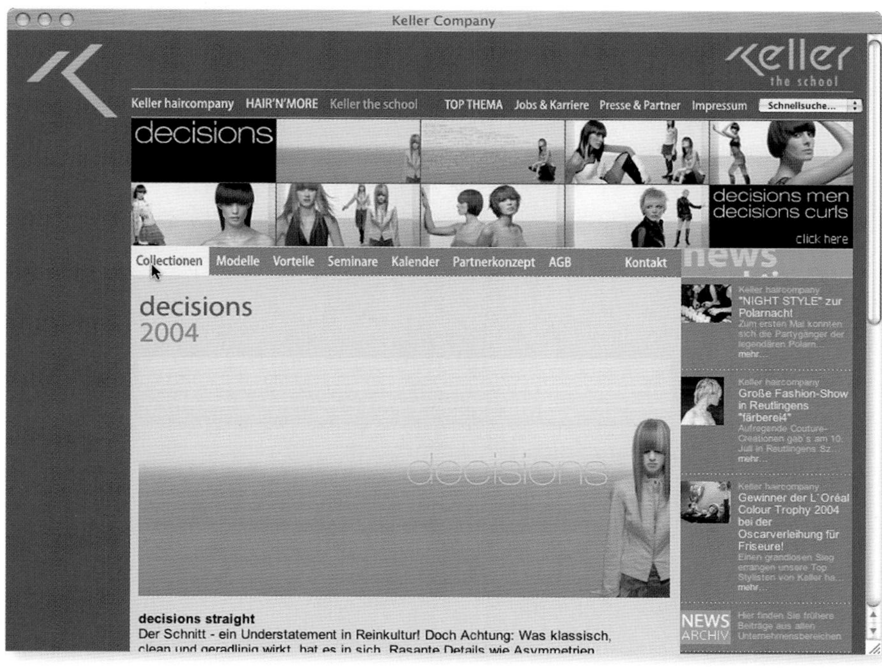
Keller Company
keller the school
Keller haircompany HAIR'N'MORE Keller the school TOP THEMA Jobs & Karriere Presse & Partner Impressum Schnellsuche...
decisions
decisions men
decisions curls
click here
Collectionen Modelle Vorteile Seminare Kalender Partnerkonzept AGB Kontakt
news
decisions 2004
decisions
"NIGHT STYLE" zur Polarnacht
Große Fashion-Show in Reutlingens "färberei4"
Gewinner der L´Oréal Colour Trophy 2004 bei der Oscarverleihung für Friseure!
NEWS ARCHIV
decisions straight
Der Schnitt - ein Understatement in Reinkultur! Doch Achtung: Was klassisch,

www.keller-the-school.de
D: stefan behringer **C:** jürgen wunderle
A: d:\sign **M:** behringer@dsign.de

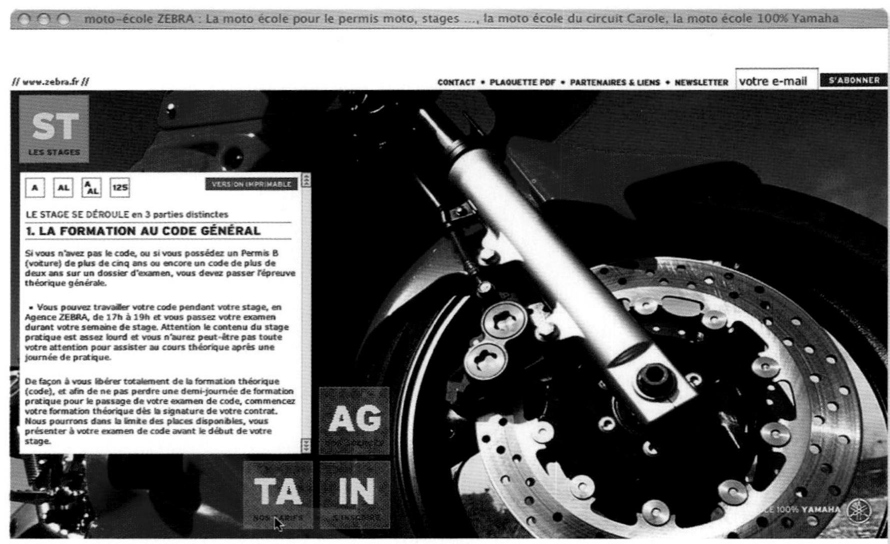
moto-école ZEBRA : La moto école pour le permis moto, stages ..., la moto école du circuit Carole, la moto école 100% Yamaha
// www.zebra.fr //
CONTACT • PLAQUETTE PDF • PARTENAIRES & LIENS • NEWSLETTER
votre e-mail
S'ABONNER
ST
LES STAGES
A
AL
A AL
125
VERSION IMPRIMABLE
LE STAGE SE DÉROULE en 3 parties distinctes
1. LA FORMATION AU CODE GÉNÉRAL
Si vous n'avez pas le code, ou si vous possédez un Permis B (voiture) de plus de cinq ans ou encore un code de plus de deux ans sur un dossier d'examen, vous devez passer l'épreuve théorique générale.
• Vous pouvez travailler votre code pendant votre stage, en Agence ZEBRA, de 17h à 19h et vous passez votre examen durant votre semaine de stage. Attention le contenu du stage pratique est assez lourd et vous n'aurez peut-être pas toute votre attention pour assister au cours théorique après une journée de pratique.
De façon à vous libérer totalement de la formation théorique (code), et afin de ne pas perdre une demi-journée de formation pratique pour le passage de votre examen de code, commencez votre formation théorique dès la signature de votre contrat. Nous pourrons dans la limite des places disponibles, vous présenter à votre examen de code avant le début de votre stage.
AG
TA
IN
YAMAHA
ZEBRA

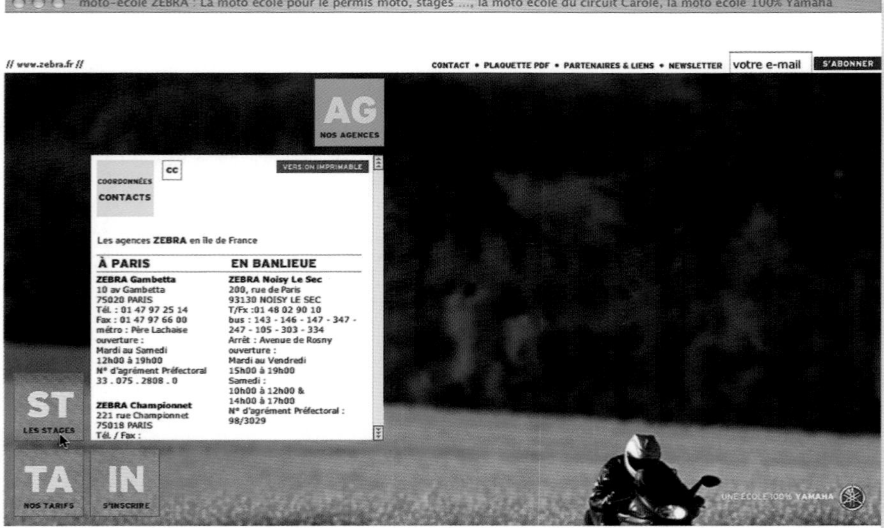
moto-école ZEBRA : La moto école pour le permis moto, stages ..., la moto école du circuit Carole, la moto école 100% Yamaha
// www.zebra.fr //
CONTACT • PLAQUETTE PDF • PARTENAIRES & LIENS • NEWSLETTER
votre e-mail
S'ABONNER
AG
NOS AGENCES
CC
VERSION IMPRIMABLE
COORDONNÉES
CONTACTS
Les agences ZEBRA en île de France
À PARIS
ZEBRA Gambetta
10 av Gambetta
75020 PARIS
Tél. : 01 47 97 25 14
Fax : 01 47 97 66 00
métro : Père Lachaise
ouverture :
Mardi au Samedi
12h00 à 19h00
N° d'agrément Préfectoral
33 . 075 . 2808 . 0
ZEBRA Championnet
221 rue Championnet
75018 PARIS
Tél. / Fax :
EN BANLIEUE
ZEBRA Noisy Le Sec
200, rue de Paris
93130 NOISY LE SEC
T/Fx :01 48 02 90 10
bus : 143 - 146 - 147 - 347 - 247 - 105 - 303 - 334
Arrêt : Avenue de Rosny
ouverture :
Mardi au Vendredi
15h00 à 19h00
Samedi :
10h00 à 12h00 &
14h00 à 17h00
N° d'agrément Préfectoral :
98/3029
ST
LES STAGES
TA
NOS TARIFS
IN
S'INSCRIRE
UNE ÉCOLE 100% YAMAHA
ZEBRA

www.zebra.fr
D: simon trabuc
A: snaap interactive M: simon@snaap.biz

FiloBytes
mijn naam is Socrates

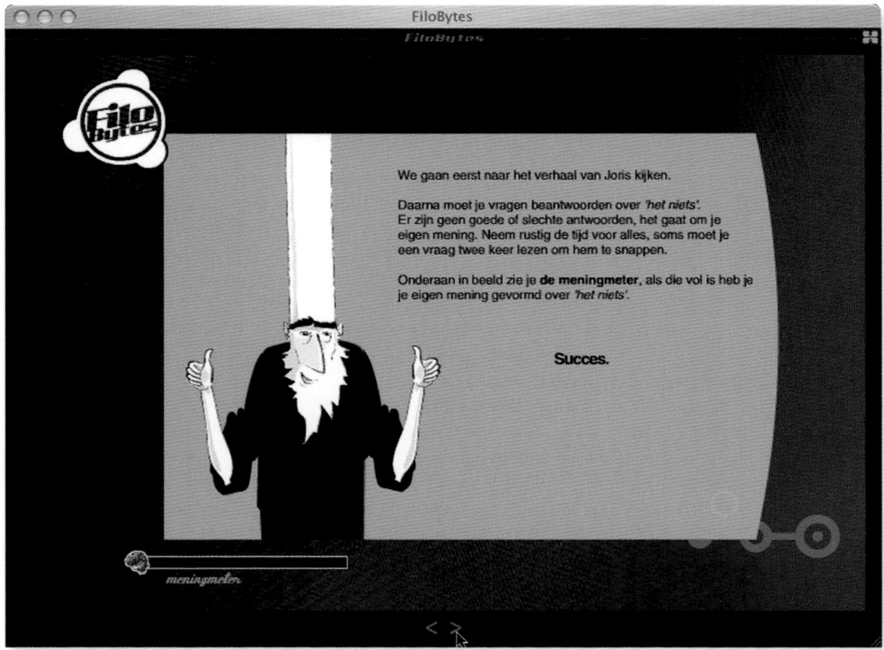
FiloBytes
Filo Bytes
We gaan eerst naar het verhaal van Joris kijken.
Daarna moet je vragen beantwoorden over 'het niets'.
Er zijn geen goede of slechte antwoorden, het gaat om je eigen mening. Neem rustig de tijd voor alles, soms moet je een vraag twee keer lezen om hem te snappen.
Onderaan in beeld zie je de meningmeter, als die vol is heb je je eigen mening gevormd over 'het niets'.
Succes.
meningmeter

www.filobytes.nl
D: michiel corten **C:** bart waalen
A: bruut ontwerp **M:** michiel@bruut.com

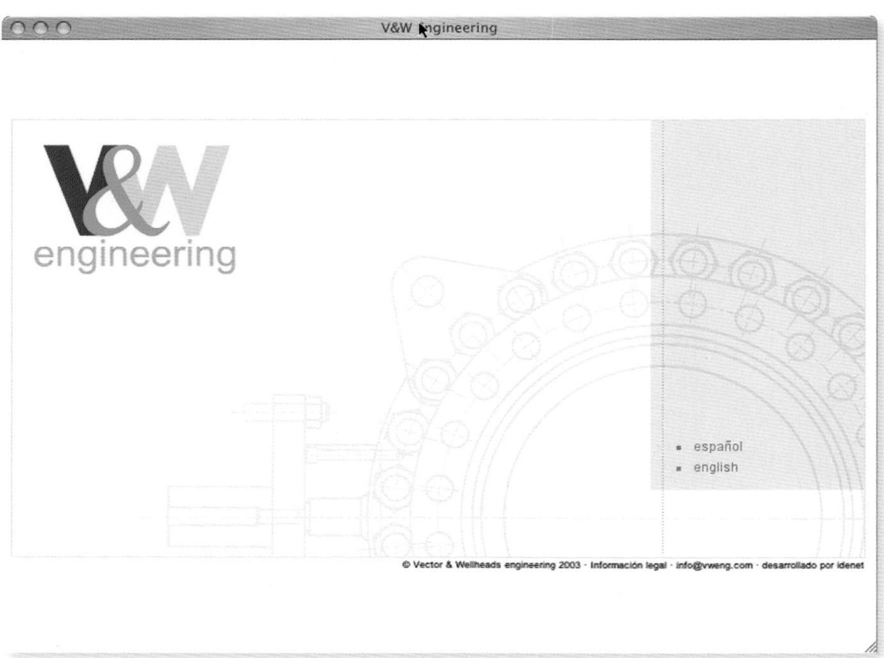
V&W Engineering
V&W
engineering
español
english
© Vector & Wellheads engineering 2003 · Información legal · info@vweng.com · desarrollado por idenet

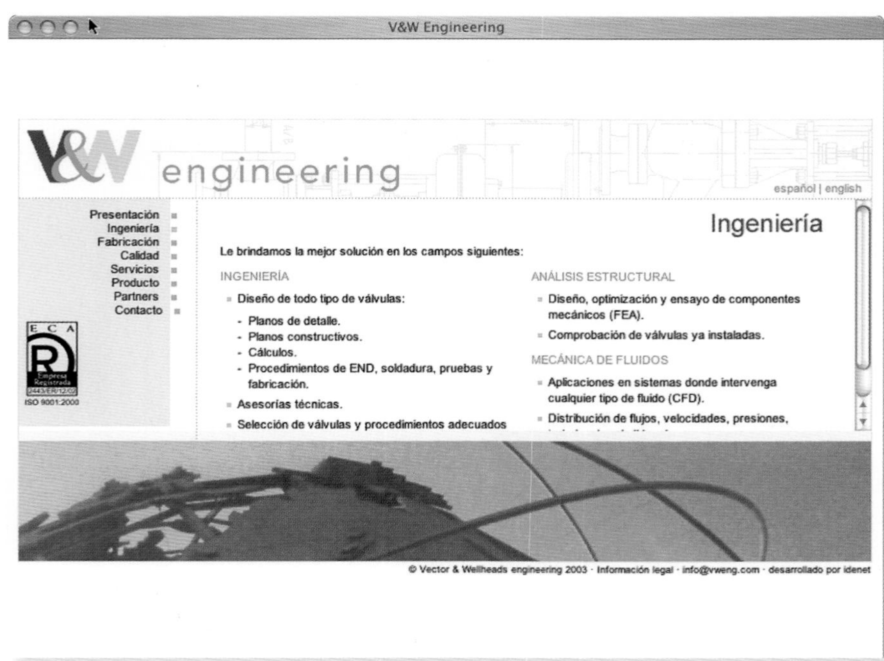
V&W Engineering
V&W engineering
español | english
Presentación
Ingeniería
Fabricación
Calidad
Servicios
Producto
Partners
Contacto
ISO 9001:2000
Ingeniería
Le brindamos la mejor solución en los campos siguientes:
INGENIERÍA
Diseño de todo tipo de válvulas:
- Planos de detalle.
- Planos constructivos.
- Cálculos.
- Procedimientos de END, soldadura, pruebas y fabricación.
Asesorías técnicas.
Selección de válvulas y procedimientos adecuados
ANÁLISIS ESTRUCTURAL
Diseño, optimización y ensayo de componentes mecánicos (FEA).
Comprobación de válvulas ya instaladas.
MECÁNICA DE FLUIDOS
Aplicaciones en sistemas donde intervenga cualquier tipo de fluido (CFD).
Distribución de flujos, velocidades, presiones,
© Vector & Wellheads engineering 2003 · Información legal · info@vweng.com · desarrollado por idenet

www.vweng.com
D: vanesa rubio **C:** alberto vicente
A: idenet **M:** info@idenet.net

·| OFIPACK |·
officeLINE
contactar
empresa
mailingSYSTEM
area privada
buscar
> Destructoras
> Cizallas
> Guillotinas
> Taladradoras
> Grapadoras
> Mesas de Presentaciones
> Colas
> Encuadernadoras
> Plastificadoras
> Consumibles
OFIPACK

·| OFIPACK |·
empresa
contactar
mailingSYSTEM
officeLINE
area privada
buscar
> Empresa
> Nuestras marcas
> Donde encontramos
> Servicio técnico
OFIPACK
2004
1974
OFIPACK es una empresa fundada en 1974 que mantiene el espíritu dinámico de sus inicios y sigue ofreciendo hoy, calidad e innovación en todos sus productos y servicios.
Cuenta con un grupo de profesionales que dedican su tiempo al conocimiento de las máquinas de oficina para que todos sus clientes tengan totalmente cubiertas las necesidades que requiere el tratamiento del papel y la seguridad de la información, así como la manipulación de la correspondencia en la oficina; incorporando a su catálogo distintas marcas: IDEAL, NEOPOST, etc..., todas ellas líderes en el mercado mundial; y siendo OFIPACK su único representante en España.

www.sole.es/test/ofipack
D: eduard sole
A: sole creativos, s.l. **M:** sole@sole.es

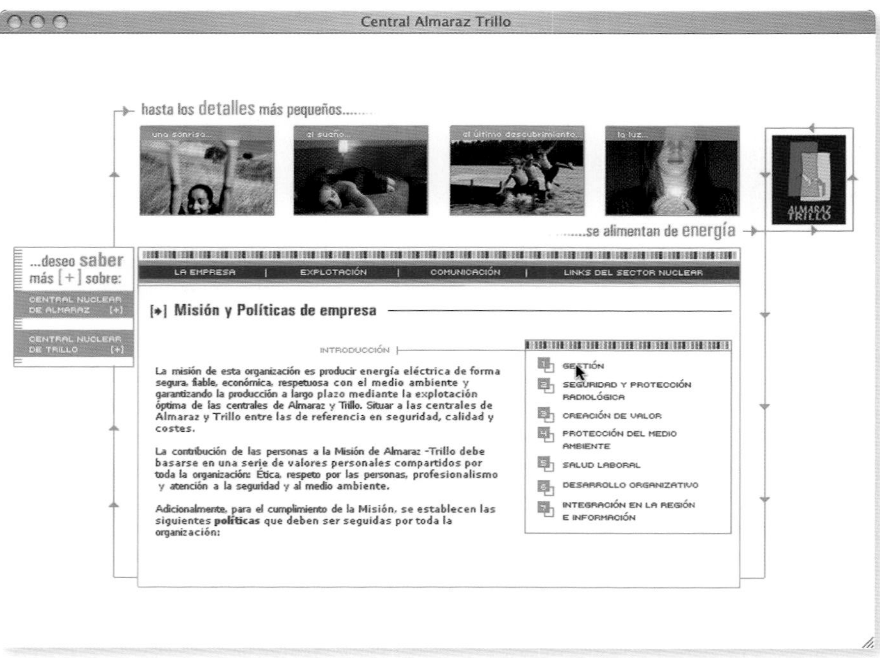
Central Almaraz Trillo
hasta los detalles más pequeños.......
...se alimentan de energía
ALMARAZ TRILLO
...deseo saber más [+] sobre:
CENTRAL NUCLEAR DE ALMARAZ [+]
CENTRAL NUCLEAR DE TRILLO [+]
LA EMPRESA | EXPLOTACIÓN | COMUNICACIÓN | LINKS DEL SECTOR NUCLEAR
[*] Misión y Políticas de empresa
INTRODUCCIÓN
La misión de esta organización es producir energía eléctrica de forma segura, fiable, económica, respetuosa con el medio ambiente y garantizando la producción a largo plazo mediante la explotación óptima de las centrales de Almaraz y Trillo. Situar a las centrales de Almaraz y Trillo entre las de referencia en seguridad, calidad y costes.
La contribución de las personas a la Misión de Almaraz -Trillo debe basarse en una serie de valores personales compartidos por toda la organización: Ética, respeto por las personas, profesionalismo y atención a la seguridad y al medio ambiente.
Adicionalmente, para el cumplimiento de la Misión, se establecen las siguientes políticas que deben ser seguidas por toda la organización:
GESTIÓN
SEGURIDAD Y PROTECCIÓN RADIOLÓGICA
CREACIÓN DE VALOR
PROTECCIÓN DEL MEDIO AMBIENTE
SALUD LABORAL
DESARROLLO ORGANIZATIVO
INTEGRACIÓN EN LA REGIÓN E INFORMACIÓN

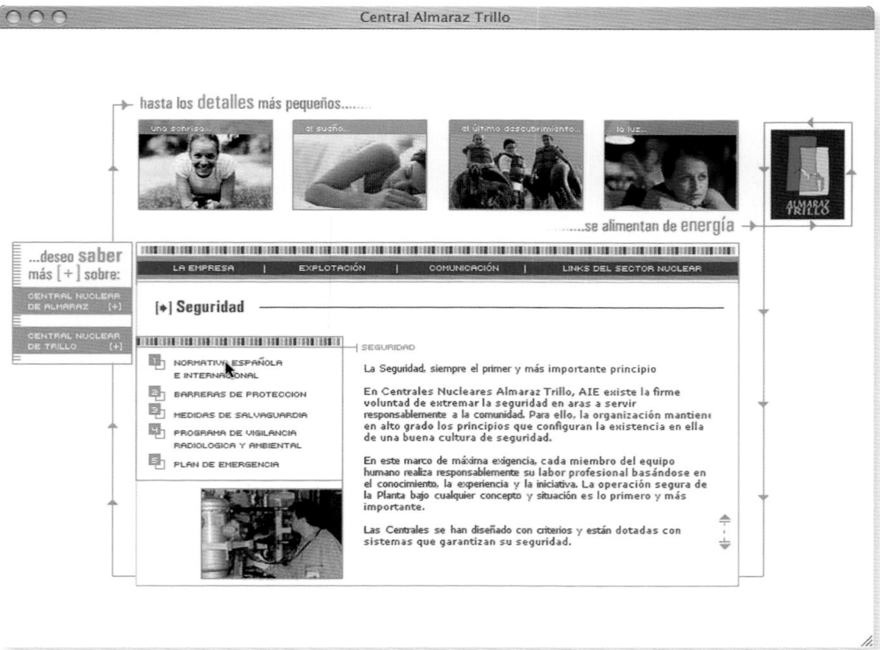
Central Almaraz Trillo
hasta los detalles más pequeños.......
...se alimentan de energía
ALMARAZ TRILLO
...deseo saber más [+] sobre:
CENTRAL NUCLEAR DE ALMARAZ [+]
CENTRAL NUCLEAR DE TRILLO [+]
LA EMPRESA | EXPLOTACIÓN | COMUNICACIÓN | LINKS DEL SECTOR NUCLEAR
[*] Seguridad
NORMATIVA ESPAÑOLA E INTERNACIONAL
BARRERAS DE PROTECCION
MEDIDAS DE SALVAGUARDIA
PROGRAMA DE VIGILANCIA RADIOLOGICA Y AMBIENTAL
PLAN DE EMERGENCIA
SEGURIDAD
La Seguridad, siempre el primer y más importante principio
En Centrales Nucleares Almaraz Trillo, AIE existe la firme voluntad de extremar la seguridad en aras a servir responsablemente a la comunidad. Para ello, la organización mantiene en alto grado los principios que configuran la existencia en ella de una buena cultura de seguridad.
En este marco de máxima exigencia, cada miembro del equipo humano realiza responsablemente su labor profesional basándose en el conocimiento, la experiencia y la iniciativa. La operación segura de la Planta bajo cualquier concepto y situación es lo primero y más importante.
Las Centrales se han diseñado con criterios y están dotadas con sistemas que garantizan su seguridad.

www.cnat.es
D: carlos esteban
A: avalora M: snowave@telefonica.net

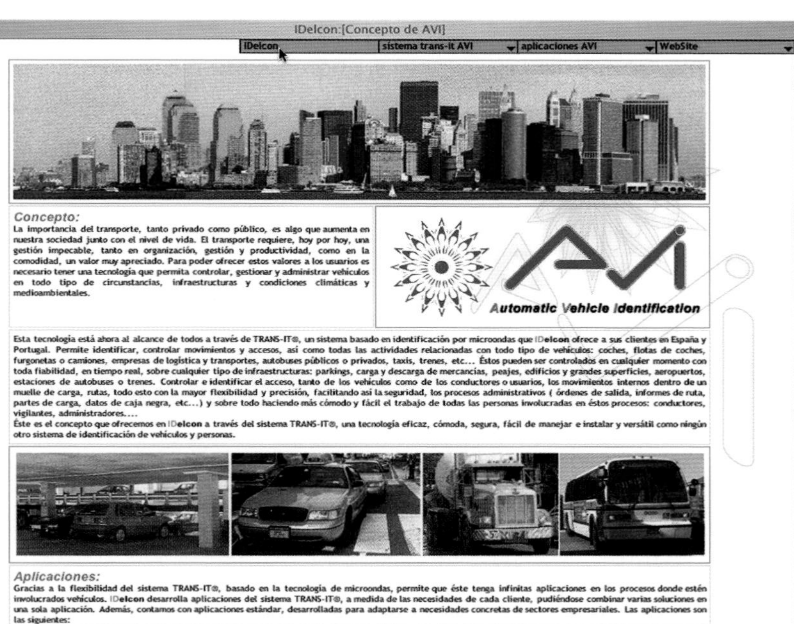
IDelcon:[Concepto de AVI]
IDelcon
sistema trans-it AVI
aplicaciones AVI
WebSite
Concepto:
La importancia del transporte, tanto privado como público, es algo que aumenta en nuestra sociedad junto con el nivel de vida. El transporte requiere, hoy por hoy, una gestión impecable, tanto en organización, gestión y productividad, como en la comodidad, un valor muy apreciado. Para poder ofrecer estos valores a los usuarios es necesario tener una tecnología que permita controlar, gestionar y administrar vehículos en todo tipo de circunstancias, infraestructuras y condiciones climáticas y medioambientales.
Automatic Vehicle Identification
Esta tecnología está ahora al alcance de todos a través de TRANS-IT®, un sistema basado en identificación por microondas que IDelcon ofrece a sus clientes en España y Portugal. Permite identificar, controlar movimientos y accesos, así como todas las actividades relacionadas con todo tipo de vehículos: coches, flotas de coches, furgonetas o camiones, empresas de logística y transportes, autobuses públicos o privados, taxis, trenes, etc... Éstos pueden ser controlados en cualquier momento con toda fiabilidad, en tiempo real, sobre cualquier tipo de infraestructuras: parkings, carga y descarga de mercancías, peajes, edificios y grandes superficies, aeropuertos, estaciones de autobuses o trenes. Controlar e identificar el acceso, tanto de los vehículos como de los conductores o usuarios, los movimientos internos dentro de un muelle de carga, rutas, todo esto con la mayor flexibilidad y precisión, facilitando así la seguridad, los procesos administrativos (órdenes de salida, informes de ruta, partes de carga, datos de caja negra, etc...) y sobre todo haciendo más cómodo y fácil el trabajo de todas las personas involucradas en éstos procesos: conductores, vigilantes, administradores....
Éste es el concepto que ofrecemos en IDelcon a través del sistema TRANS-IT®, una tecnología eficaz, cómoda, segura, fácil de manejar e instalar y versátil como ningún otro sistema de identificación de vehículos y personas.
Aplicaciones:
Gracias a la flexibilidad del sistema TRANS-IT®, basado en la tecnología de microondas, permite que éste tenga infinitas aplicaciones en los procesos donde estén involucrados vehículos. IDelcon desarrolla aplicaciones del sistema TRANS-IT®, a medida de las necesidades de cada cliente, pudiéndose combinar varias soluciones en una sola aplicación. Además, contamos con aplicaciones estándar, desarrolladas para adaptarse a necesidades concretas de sectores empresariales. Las aplicaciones son las siguientes:
Personalizadas: Realización de proyectos técnicos a la medida de las necesidades de cada cliente, obteniendo así el rendimiento óptimo del sistema.
Parkings: aplicación diseñada para la gestión integral de todo tipo de vehículos en zonas de aparcamiento, público, privado, grandes superficies o en zonas

IDelcon:[Concepto de trans-it]
IDelcon
sistema trans-it AVI
aplicaciones AVI
WebSite
trans-it
Identificación por microondas:
El rendimiento más exigente, la seguridad, la confianza y la comodidad son valores imprescindibles en los sistemas de control de accesos y vigilancia. Esto es exactamente lo que ofrecemos en IDelcon a través del sistema TRANS-IT®. Este sistema funciona mediante microondas, consta de uno o varios lectores que identifican una amplia gama de etiquetas y tarjetas personales. Es un producto de gran flexibilidad, permitiendo una total adaptación a las necesidades de cada cliente. TRANS-IT® posee una enorme versatilidad gracias a sus características, permitiendo una plena integración en todo tipo de infraestructuras y opera bajo cualquier condición climática o ambiental.
Trans-IT Automatic Vehicle Identification
Tecnología Microondas:
El sistema TRANS-IT® está basado en una tecnología funcional, fiable y probada, las microondas. Opera en banda ISM a 2,45 GHz. El sistema TRANS-IT® se diferencia de los sistemas tradicionales de identificación por radiofrecuencia, en el uso de la retrodispersión modulada "backscatter". En este método la etiqueta o tarjeta personal envía su código de identificación al lector TRANS-IT® reflejando y modulando la señal emitida por el lector o por el Booster (etiqueta activa, repetidora/amplificadora).
La mayoría de los materiales no metálicos son "transparentes" a las microondas, la nieve, el polvo, la lluvia o el hielo, no afectan al funcionamiento del sistema TRANS-IT®. Las etiquetas pueden montarse incluso sobre superficies metálicas sin que afecte a su funcionamiento.
dual.BAND
Tecnología dualBAND:
El sistema TRANS-IT® integra tecnología microondas e inductiva en una única solución, ofreciendo así la posibilidad de combinar ambas tecnologías sin tener que utilizar distintos componentes ni sistemas. Esto se traduce en una enorme flexibilidad y comodidad para el usuario, ya que el largo rango de lectura del sistema microondas, idoneo para la identificación de vehículos, y el corto alcance,

www.idelcon.biz
D: elena blanco lópez C: jaime bárcena
A: dsg-module M: idelcon@idelcon.biz

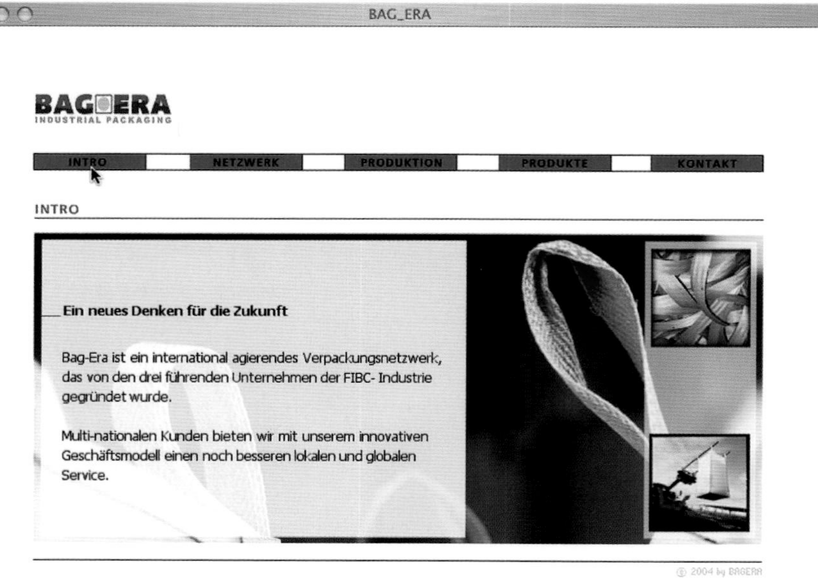
BAG_ERA
BAGERA
INDUSTRIAL PACKAGING
INTRO
NETZWERK
PRODUKTION
PRODUKTE
KONTAKT
INTRO
Ein neues Denken für die Zukunft
Bag-Era ist ein international agierendes Verpackungsnetzwerk, das von den drei führenden Unternehmen der FIBC- Industrie gegründet wurde.
Multi-nationalen Kunden bieten wir mit unserem innovativen Geschäftsmodell einen noch besseren lokalen und globalen Service.
© 2004 by BAGERA

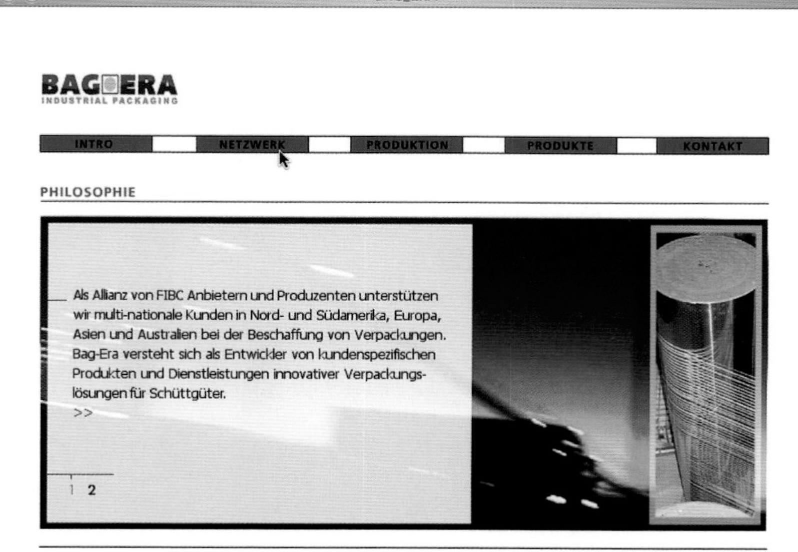
BAG_ERA
BAGERA
INDUSTRIAL PACKAGING
INTRO
NETZWERK
PRODUKTION
PRODUKTE
KONTAKT
PHILOSOPHIE
Als Allianz von FIBC Anbietern und Produzenten unterstützen wir multi-nationale Kunden in Nord- und Südamerika, Europa, Asien und Australien bei der Beschaffung von Verpackungen. Bag-Era versteht sich als Entwickler von kundenspezifischen Produkten und Dienstleistungen innovativer Verpackungs-lösungen für Schüttgüter.
>>
1 2
© 2004 by BAGERA

www.bagera.com
D: guido eichhoff
A: artboxx **M:** guido@artboxx.net

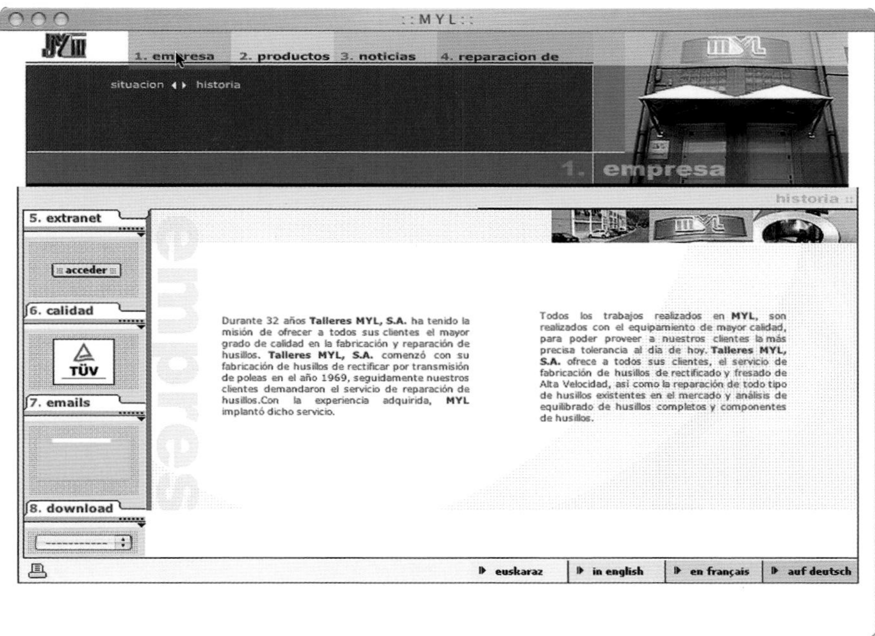
::MYL::
1. empresa
2. productos
3. noticias
4. reparacion de
situacion ◂ ▸ historia
1. empresa
historia ::
5. extranet
acceder
6. calidad
TÜV
7. emails
8. download
Durante 32 años Talleres MYL, S.A. ha tenido la misión de ofrecer a todos sus clientes el mayor grado de calidad en la fabricación y reparación de husillos. Talleres MYL, S.A. comenzó con su fabricación de husillos de rectificar por transmisión de poleas en el año 1969, seguidamente nuestros clientes demandaron el servicio de reparación de husillos.Con la experiencia adquirida, MYL implantó dicho servicio.
Todos los trabajos realizados en MYL, son realizados con el equipamiento de mayor calidad, para poder proveer a nuestros clientes la más precisa tolerancia al dia de hoy. Talleres MYL, S.A. ofrece a todos sus clientes, el servicio de fabricación de husillos de rectificado y fresado de Alta Velocidad, asi como la reparación de todo tipo de husillos existentes en el mercado y análisis de equilibrado de husillos completos y componentes de husillos.
euskaraz
in english
en français
auf deutsch

::MYL::
1. empresa
2. productos
3. noticias
4. reparacion de
husillos ◂ ▸ husillos especiales
equilibrados ◂ ▸ husillos neumáticos
rectificadoras ◂ ▸ husillos alta frecuencia
ejes principales ◂ ▸ sobretornos de rectificar
platos giratorios ◂ ▸ cabezal con motor integrado
2. productos
| CTI | CTC | CTCN | CTP |
husillos - transmisión de poleas ::
5. extranet
acceder
6. calidad
TÜV
7. emails
8. download
CTE
- Salida de cono exterior.
- Amplia gama de velocidad
- Orificios pequeños, grandes y medianos.
características
dimensiones
euskaraz
in english
en français
auf deutsch

www.myl.es
D: mariano carmona escudero
A: sansemedia **M:** mariano@sansemedia.com

Inkdigo – Innovative Materials Solution
contact us
innovative materials solution
standard card materials
about inkdigo
standard card materials
specialty card materials
other products
RIGID PVC MATERIAL
(1) Lamination Grade Card Materials include:
RICOPLUS
Material : Rigid PVC
Thickness : 0.20mm – 0.80mm
Surface Finish : Both side Matte
Colour : White / Transparent
Application: Credit cards, Magnetic Stripe Cards, Membership Cards.
RICOSMART
Material : PVC / ABS
Thickness : 0.20mm – 0.80mm
Surface Finish : Both sides Matte
Colour : White
Application : Contact / Contactless Cards, GSM Cards.
INKDIGO™ offers a wide range of Rigid PVC and ABS film in sheets and rolls formulated to use as card film for commercial cards, credit cards and ISO cards with matt surfaces for high quality printing on screen-printing, offset printing and UV drying process with good laminating and die cutting properties. There are various types of bonding strength and heat resistant grades available.
www.inkdigo.com

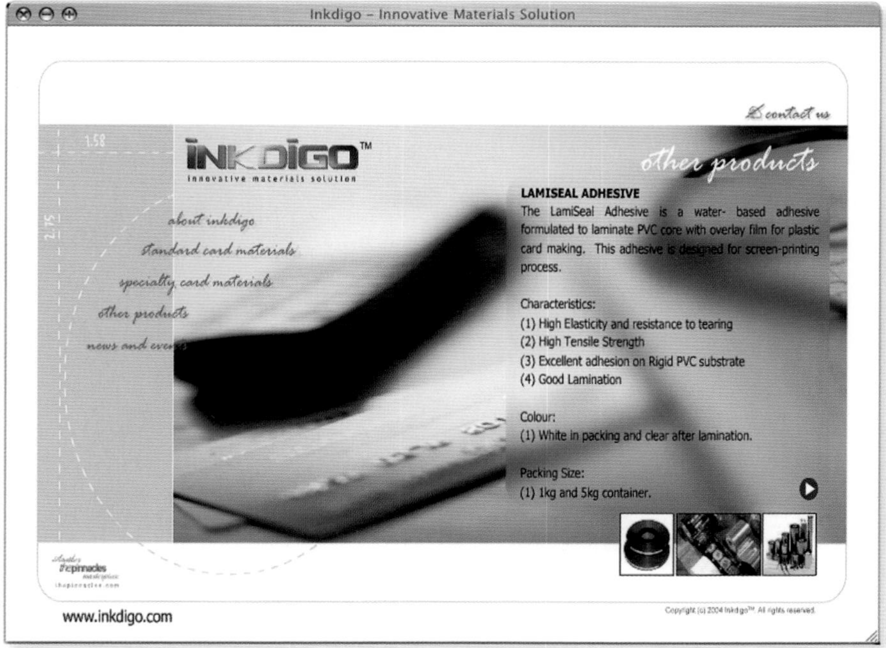
Inkdigo – Innovative Materials Solution
contact us
INKDIGO™
innovative materials solution
other products
about inkdigo
standard card materials
specialty card materials
other products
LAMISEAL ADHESIVE
The LamiSeal Adhesive is a water- based adhesive formulated to laminate PVC core with overlay film for plastic card making. This adhesive is designed for screen-printing process.
Characteristics:
(1) High Elasticity and resistance to tearing
(2) High Tensile Strength
(3) Excellent adhesion on Rigid PVC substrate
(4) Good Lamination
Colour:
(1) White in packing and clear after lamination.
Packing Size:
(1) 1kg and 5kg container.
www.inkdigo.com

www.inkdigo.com
D: charles yang
A: he pinnacles interactive **M:** charlesyang@thepinnacles.com

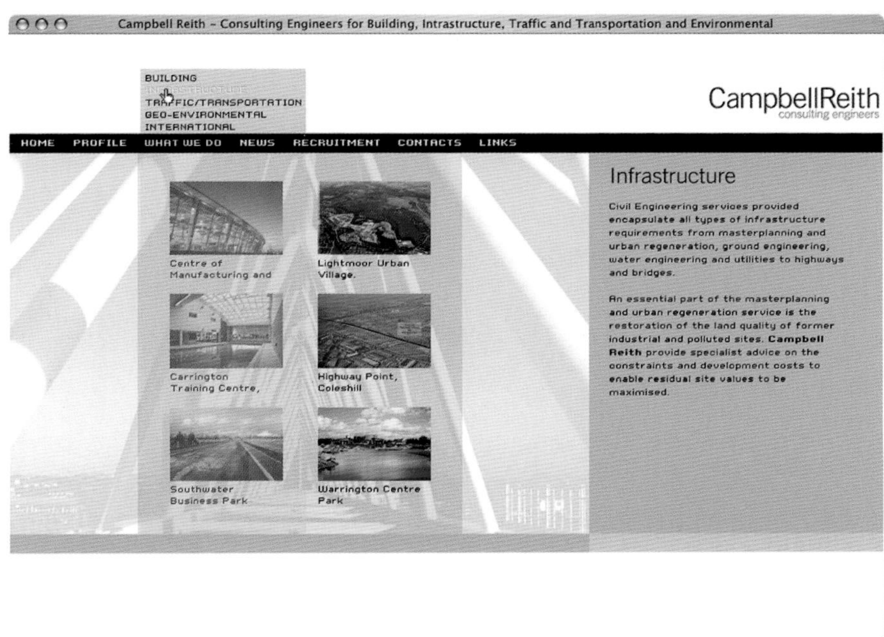
Campbell Reith - Consulting Engineers for Building, Intrastructure, Traffic and Transportation and Environmental
BUILDING
TRAFFIC/TRANSPORTATION
GEO-ENVIRONMENTAL
INTERNATIONAL
CampbellReith
consulting engineers
HOME PROFILE WHAT WE DO NEWS RECRUITMENT CONTACTS LINKS
Centre of Manufacturing and
Lightmoor Urban Village.
Carrington Training Centre,
Highway Point, Coleshill
Southwater Business Park
Warrington Centre Park
Infrastructure
Civil Engineering services provided encapsulate all types of infrastructure requirements from masterplanning and urban regeneration, ground engineering, water engineering and utilities to highways and bridges.
An essential part of the masterplanning and urban regeneration service is the restoration of the land quality of former industrial and polluted sites. Campbell Reith provide specialist advice on the constraints and development costs to enable residual site values to be maximised.

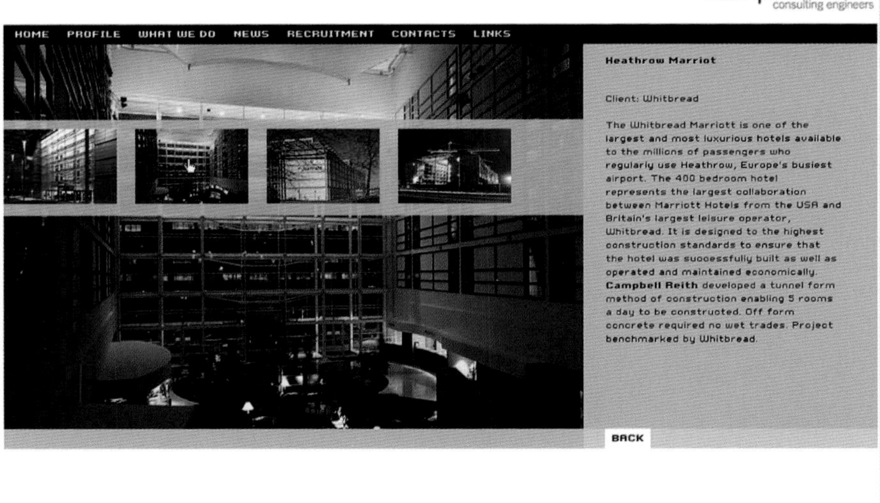
Campbell Reith - Consulting Engineers for Building, Intrastructure, Traffic and Transportation and Environmental
CampbellReith
consulting engineers
HOME PROFILE WHAT WE DO NEWS RECRUITMENT CONTACTS LINKS
Heathrow Marriot
Client: Whitbread
The Whitbread Marriott is one of the largest and most luxurious hotels available to the millions of passengers who regularly use Heathrow, Europe's busiest airport. The 400 bedroom hotel represents the largest collaboration between Marriott Hotels from the USA and Britain's largest leisure operator, Whitbread. It is designed to the highest construction standards to ensure that the hotel was successfully built as well as operated and maintained economically. Campbell Reith developed a tunnel form method of construction enabling 5 rooms a day to be constructed. Off form concrete required no wet trades. Project benchmarked by Whitbread.
BACK

www.campbellreith.com
D: deep
A: deep llp **M:** deeper@deep.co.uk

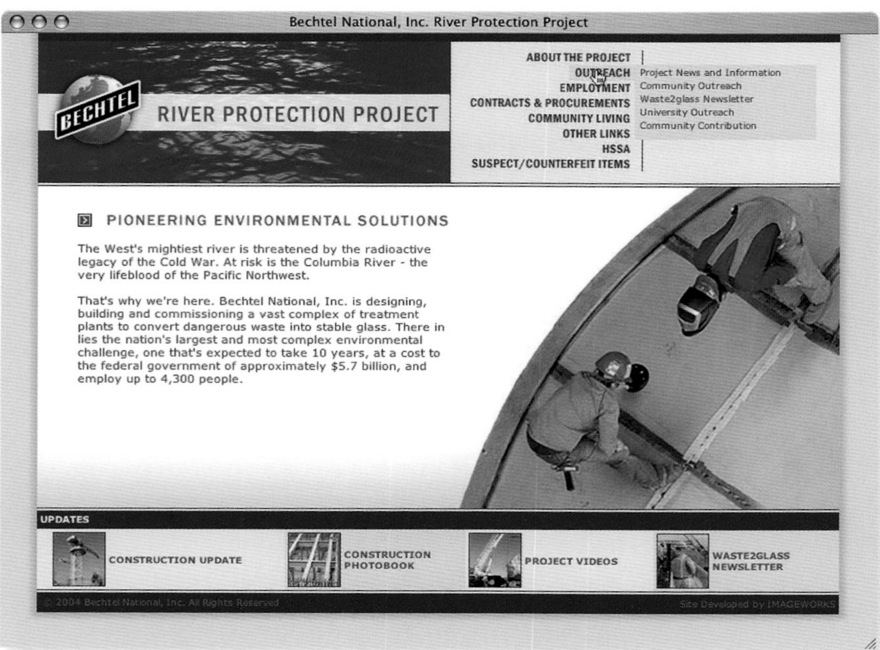
Bechtel National, Inc. River Protection Project
BECHTEL
RIVER PROTECTION PROJECT
ABOUT THE PROJECT
OUTREACH
EMPLOYMENT
CONTRACTS & PROCUREMENTS
COMMUNITY LIVING
OTHER LINKS
HSSA
SUSPECT/COUNTERFEIT ITEMS
Project News and Information
Community Outreach
Waste2glass Newsletter
University Outreach
Community Contribution
PIONEERING ENVIRONMENTAL SOLUTIONS
The West's mightiest river is threatened by the radioactive legacy of the Cold War. At risk is the Columbia River - the very lifeblood of the Pacific Northwest.
That's why we're here. Bechtel National, Inc. is designing, building and commissioning a vast complex of treatment plants to convert dangerous waste into stable glass. There in lies the nation's largest and most complex environmental challenge, one that's expected to take 10 years, at a cost to the federal government of approximately $5.7 billion, and employ up to 4,300 people.
UPDATES
CONSTRUCTION UPDATE
CONSTRUCTION PHOTOBOOK
PROJECT VIDEOS
WASTE2GLASS NEWSLETTER

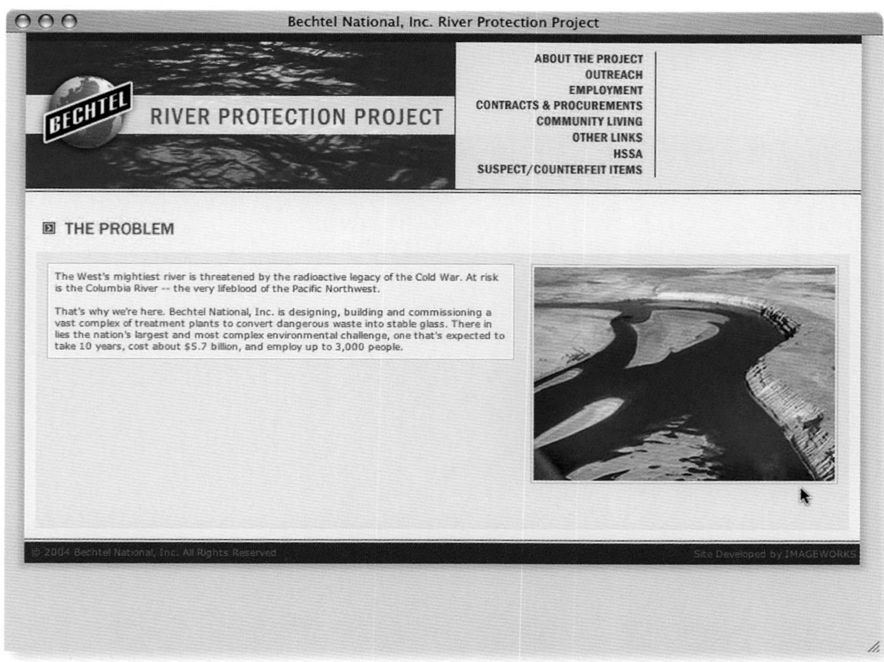
Bechtel National, Inc. River Protection Project
BECHTEL
RIVER PROTECTION PROJECT
ABOUT THE PROJECT
OUTREACH
EMPLOYMENT
CONTRACTS & PROCUREMENTS
COMMUNITY LIVING
OTHER LINKS
HSSA
SUSPECT/COUNTERFEIT ITEMS
THE PROBLEM
The West's mightiest river is threatened by the radioactive legacy of the Cold War. At risk is the Columbia River -- the very lifeblood of the Pacific Northwest.
That's why we're here. Bechtel National, Inc. is designing, building and commissioning a vast complex of treatment plants to convert dangerous waste into stable glass. There in lies the nation's largest and most complex environmental challenge, one that's expected to take 10 years, cost about $5.7 billion, and employ up to 3,000 people.

www.waste2glass.com
D: tyler goodro **C:** jeremy o'niel **P:** matt hammer
A: imageworks media group **M:** rachael@imageworksdigital.com

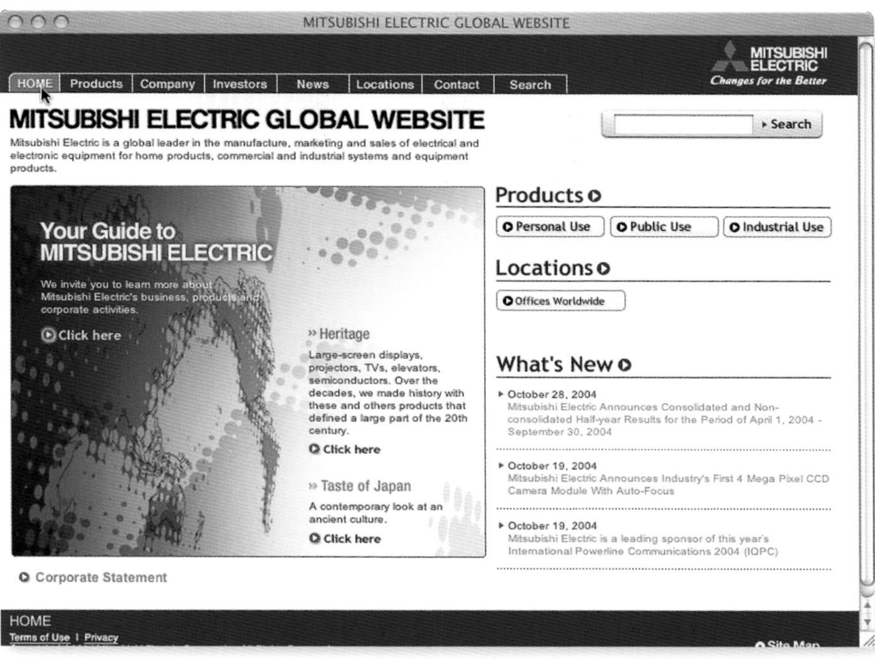
MITSUBISHI ELECTRIC GLOBAL WEBSITE
MITSUBISHI ELECTRIC
Changes for the Better
HOME
Products
Company
Investors
News
Locations
Contact
Search
MITSUBISHI ELECTRIC GLOBAL WEBSITE
Mitsubishi Electric is a global leader in the manufacture, marketing and sales of electrical and electronic equipment for home products, commercial and industrial systems and equipment products.
Search
Your Guide to MITSUBISHI ELECTRIC
Click here
Heritage
Large-screen displays, projectors, TVs, elevators, semiconductors. Over the decades, we made history with these and others products that defined a large part of the 20th century.
Click here
Taste of Japan
A contemporary look at an ancient culture.
Click here
Products
Personal Use
Public Use
Industrial Use
Locations
Offices Worldwide
What's New
October 28, 2004
October 19, 2004
October 19, 2004
Corporate Statement
HOME
Terms of Use | Privacy

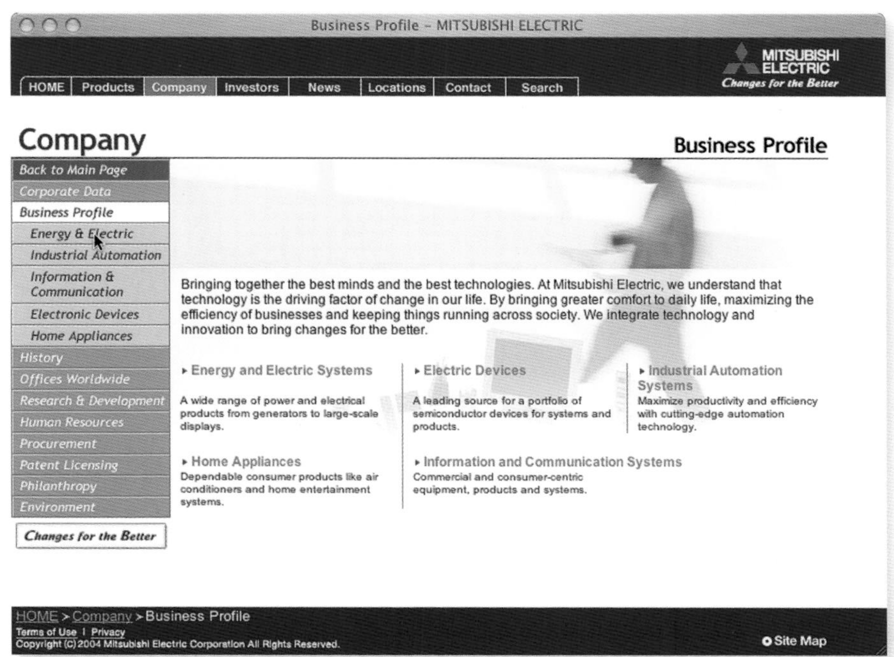
Business Profile – MITSUBISHI ELECTRIC
MITSUBISHI ELECTRIC
Changes for the Better
HOME
Products
Company
Investors
News
Locations
Contact
Search
Company
Business Profile
Back to Main Page
Corporate Data
Business Profile
Energy & Electric
Industrial Automation
Information & Communication
Electronic Devices
Home Appliances
History
Offices Worldwide
Research & Development
Human Resources
Procurement
Patent Licensing
Philanthropy
Environment
Changes for the Better
Bringing together the best minds and the best technologies. At Mitsubishi Electric, we understand that technology is the driving factor of change in our life. By bringing greater comfort to daily life, maximizing the efficiency of businesses and keeping things running across society. We integrate technology and innovation to bring changes for the better.
Energy and Electric Systems
A wide range of power and electrical products from generators to large-scale displays.
Electric Devices
A leading source for a portfolio of semiconductor devices for systems and products.
Industrial Automation Systems
Maximize productivity and efficiency with cutting-edge automation technology.
Home Appliances
Dependable consumer products like air conditioners and home entertainment systems.
Information and Communication Systems
Commercial and consumer-centric equipment, products and systems.
HOME > Company > Business Profile
Terms of Use | Privacy
Copyright (C) 2004 Mitsubishi Electric Corporation All Rights Reserved.
Site Map

global.mitsubishielectric.com
D: lorenzo lorefice **C:** richard archer
A: yosh **M:** info@yosh.com.au

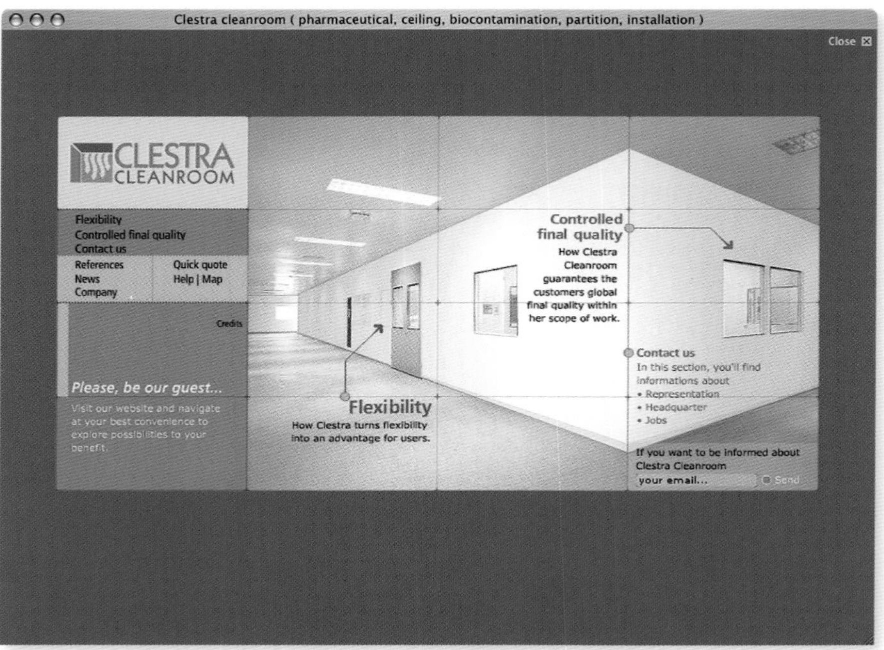
Clestra cleanroom (pharmaceutical, ceiling, biocontamination, partition, installation)
Close
CLESTRA CLEANROOM
Flexibility
Controlled final quality
Contact us
References
News
Company
Quick quote
Help | Map
Credits
Please, be our guest...
Visit our website and navigate at your best convenience to explore possibilities to your benefit.
Controlled final quality
How Clestra Cleanroom guarantees the customers global final quality within her scope of work.
Contact us
In this section, you'll find informations about
• Representation
• Headquarter
• Jobs
Flexibility
How Clestra turns flexibility into an advantage for users.
If you want to be informed about Clestra Cleanroom
your email...
Send

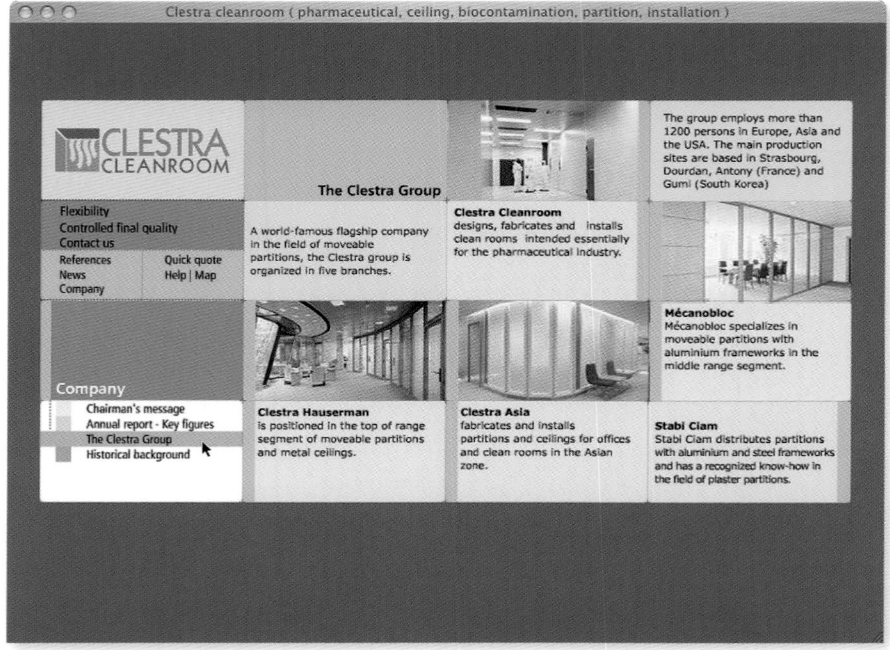
Clestra cleanroom (pharmaceutical, ceiling, biocontamination, partition, installation)
CLESTRA CLEANROOM
The Clestra Group
The group employs more than 1200 persons in Europe, Asia and the USA. The main production sites are based in Strasbourg, Dourdan, Antony (France) and Gumi (South Korea)
Flexibility
Controlled final quality
Contact us
References
News
Company
Quick quote
Help | Map
A world-famous flagship company in the field of moveable partitions, the Clestra group is organized in five branches.
Clestra Cleanroom
designs, fabricates and installs clean rooms intended essentially for the pharmaceutical industry.
Mécanobloc
Mécanobloc specializes in moveable partitions with aluminium frameworks in the middle range segment.
Company
Chairman's message
Annual report - Key figures
The Clestra Group
Historical background
Clestra Hauserman
is positioned in the top of range segment of moveable partitions and metal ceilings.
Clestra Asia
fabricates and installs partitions and ceilings for offices and clean rooms in the Asian zone.
Stabi Clam
Stabi Clam distributes partitions with aluminium and steel frameworks and has a recognized know-how in the field of plaster partitions.

www.clestra-cleanroom.com
D: tinsel frédéric **C:** galleano olivier
A: advisa **M:** ftinsel@advisa.fr

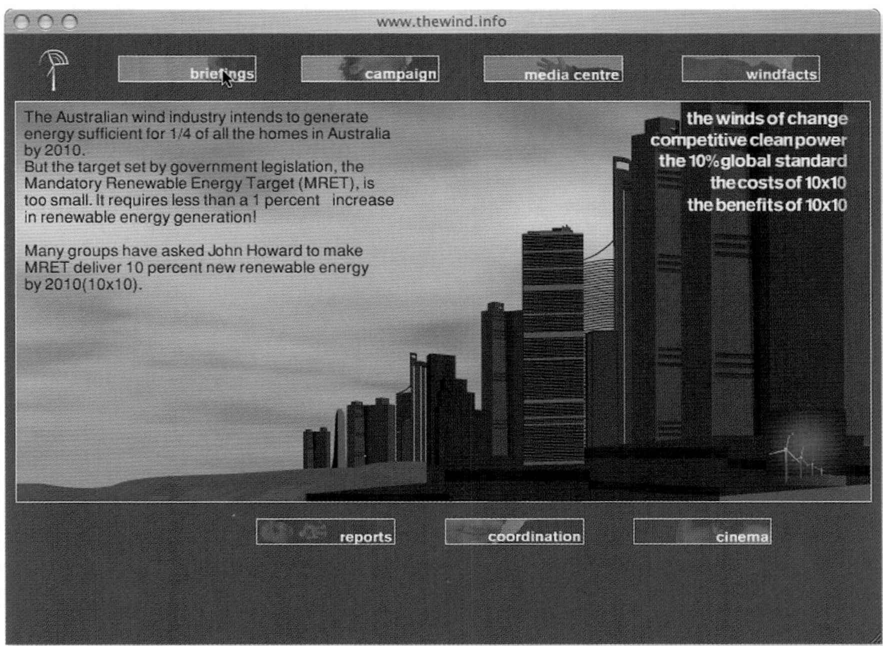
www.thewind.info
briefings
campaign
media centre
windfacts
The Australian wind industry intends to generate energy sufficient for 1/4 of all the homes in Australia by 2010.
But the target set by government legislation, the Mandatory Renewable Energy Target (MRET), is too small. It requires less than a 1 percent increase in renewable energy generation!
Many groups have asked John Howard to make MRET deliver 10 percent new renewable energy by 2010(10x10).
the winds of change
competitive clean power
the 10% global standard
the costs of 10x10
the benefits of 10x10
reports
coordination
cinema

www.thewind.info
briefings
campaign
media centre
windfacts
Your portal on the MRET debate...see who is saying what, links to key reports and background materials to help understand the issue.
thewind.info screensaver for PC
briefings
2010
reports
coordination
cinema

www.thewind.info
D: nicholas marshall
M: nick@nicholasmarshall.com.au

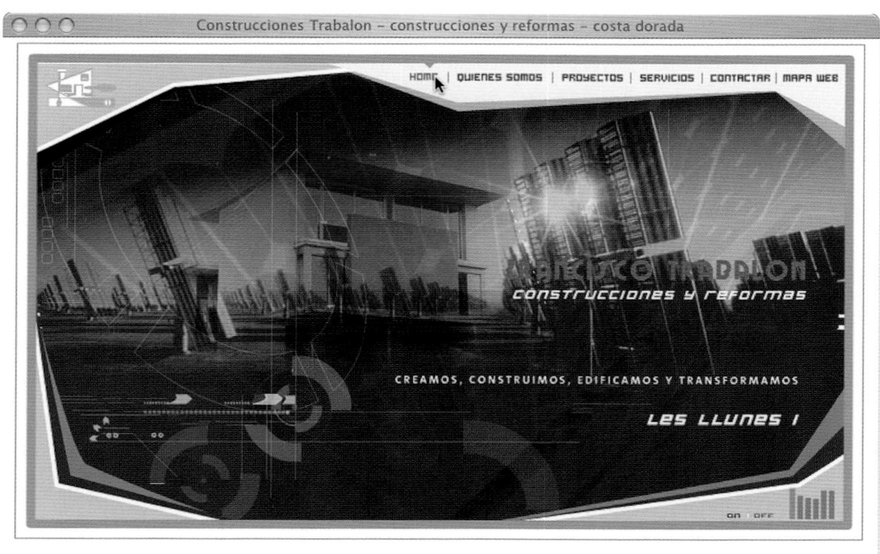
Construcciones Trabalon - construcciones y reformas - costa dorada
HOME | QUIENES SOMOS | PROYECTOS | SERVICIOS | CONTACTAR | MAPA WEB
construcciones y reformas
CREAMOS, CONSTRUIMOS, EDIFICAMOS Y TRANSFORMAMOS
LES LLUNES I
on | off

Construcciones Trabalon - construcciones y reformas - costa dorada
HOME | QUIENES SOMOS | PROYECTOS | SERVICIOS | CONTACTAR | MAPA WEB
PROYECTOS
LES LLUNES FASE I
OFICINAS TARRAGONA
SITUACIÓN
CARACTERÍSTICAS
PLANOS
GALERIA DE FOTOS
LES LLUNES FASE I
on | off

www.construccionestrabalon.com
D: asier lópez cabañas
M: asier@sherlockimage.com

JOURNAUX // Levage / Manutention
JOURNAUX
.Manutention
.Levage
01 | UNE NOUVELLE GENERATION
02 | L'EQUIPE JOURNAUX
03 | LE SERVICE CLIENT
04 | LEVAGE & MANUTENTION
05 | TYPOLOGIES DE CHANTIERS EFFECTUES
06 | LE MATERIEL ROULANT
07 | LE MATERIEL DE MANUTENTION
08 | REFERENCES
09 | CONTACT
01 | UNE NOUVELLE GENERATION
JOURNAUX MANUTENTION
Créée en 1973, notre société s'est spécialisée en manutention et en levage dans les domaines précis du chauffage, de la climatisation et de l'électricité.
Notre but est, et a toujours été, d'aider nos clients à la mise en place de leur matériel lourd à leur place définitive dans les meilleures conditions possibles et cela, malgré les aléas incontournables liés à nos métiers.
Yves JOURNAUX, le fondateur, a toujours été reconnu comme l'un des acteurs de ce secteur pendant de longues années. Ainsi il a cédé son entreprise depuis 1999 à une nouvelle équipe dont l'expérience de la manutention en milieu industriel est venue compléter celle, déjà importante, de l'entreprise.
C'est ainsi que Jean Michel PEROUX et Frédéric LECLERC apportent toute leur énergie à faire de JOURNAUX Manutention une référence dans son domaine.
Mentions légales - Conception/design : ntgraphx.com

JOURNAUX // Levage / Manutention
JOURNAUX
.Manutention
.Levage
01 | UNE NOUVELLE GENERATION
02 | L'EQUIPE JOURNAUX
03 | LE SERVICE CLIENT
04 | LEVAGE & MANUTENTION
05 | TYPOLOGIES DE CHANTIERS EFFECTUES
06 | LE MATERIEL ROULANT
07 | LE MATERIEL DE MANUTENTION
08 | REFERENCES
09 | CONTACT
07 | LE MATERIEL DE MANUTENTION
CHARIOTS ELEVATEURS
CHARIOTS ELEVATEURS
DANS CHAQUE VEHICULE
MATERIELS DE MANUTENTION SPECIAUX
type "Manitou"
capacité de levage : 2,5 T H = 1m90 hors tout
TRIPLEX
capacité de levage : 2,5 T Hauteur de levage 4300
DUPLEX
capacité de levage : 5 T Hauteur de levage 3400
Mentions légales - Conception/design : ntgraphx.com

www.journaux-manutention.com
D: frédéric than trong
A: ntropy graphx **M:** than@ntgraphx.com

Be. Luini35
Be. LUINI 35
whatever you want to Be.
COLLEZIONI
CONTATTI
whatever you want to be
Be. Luini35 :: via Bernardino Luini 35 :: Como :: tel. +39 031 262543 :: Email: info@be-luini35.it
Web Design & Photo sets by Eden Design

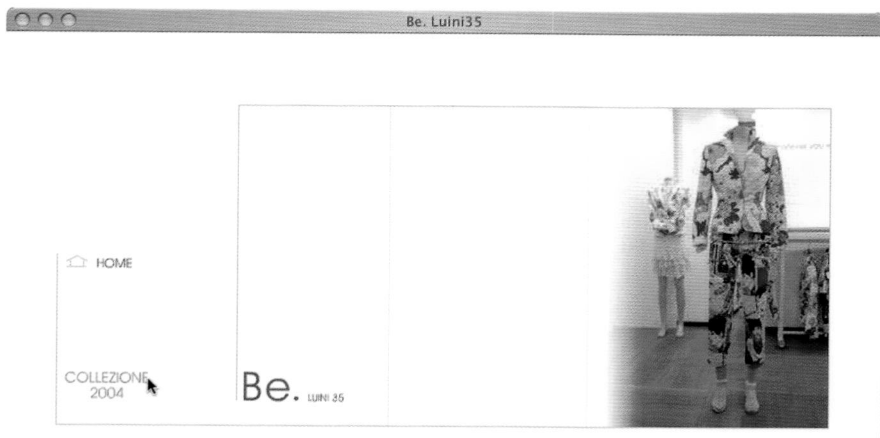
Be. Luini35
HOME
COLLEZIONE
2004
Be. LUINI 35
Be. Luini35 :: via Bernardino Luini 35 :: Como :: tel. +39 031 262543 :: Email: info@be-luini35.it
Web Design & Photo sets by Eden Design

www.be-luini35.it
D: giuseppe vitali
A: eden design **M:** info@edendesign.it

MODEHAUS WALZ
Walz
LIVING FASHION
ULM | NEU ULM | GÖPPINGEN
News
Über uns
Mode
Highlights
Homeaccessoires
Service
Kontakt
Mode
Women
Modern Women
Classic Women
Herren
Herren Boutique
Dessous
Les Jeunes
Kinder
WOMEN EG
LE TRICOT PERUGIA
Kollektionen
Cashmere Pullover
Cashmere Pullover
Cashmere Weste
Details

MODEHAUS WALZ
Walz
LIVING FASHION
ULM | NEU ULM | GÖPPINGEN
News
Über uns
Mode
Highlights
Homeaccessoires
Service
Kontakt
Service
Events
Galerie W
Cafebar W
Events 2005
... 2005
coming soon
Details
Unsere Eventsaison 2004 ist beendet
Wir bedanken uns bei Ihnen für ihr großes Interesse bei unseren diesjährigen Herbstevents und freuen uns, schon bald das neue Eventprogramm für das Frühjahr 2005 präsentieren zu können.
Ihr Walz Event Team
Newsletter Kontakt Impressum
© 2004 Modehaus Walz

www.modehaus-walz.com
D: alexander windisch
A: capeeshee **M:** a.windisch@capeeshee.com

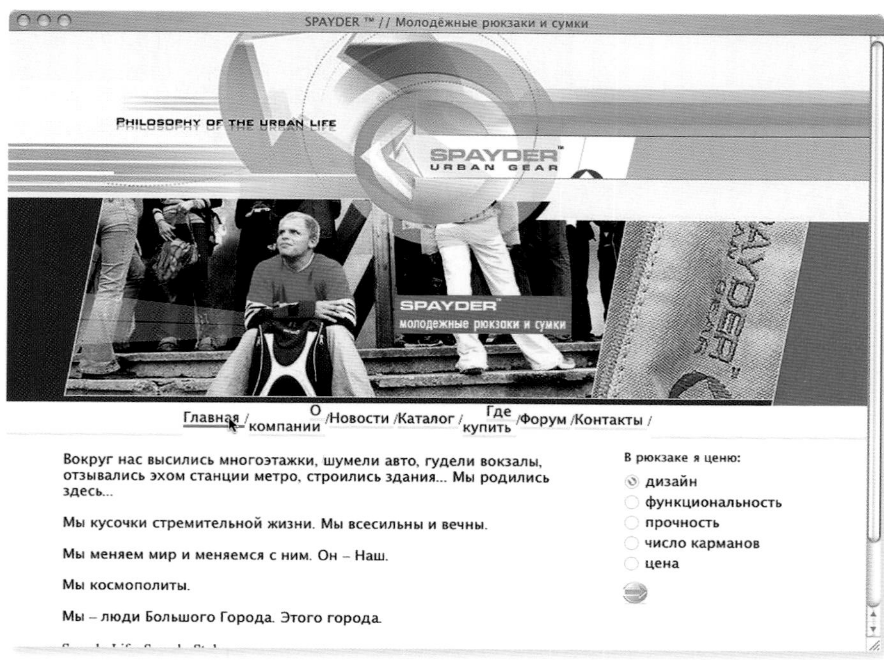
SPAYDER ™ // Молодёжные рюкзаки и сумки
PHILOSOPHY OF THE URBAN LIFE
SPAYDER
URBAN GEAR
SPAYDER
молодежные рюкзаки и сумки
Главная / О компании /Новости /Каталог / Где купить /Форум /Контакты /
Вокруг нас высились многоэтажки, шумели авто, гудели вокзалы, отзывались эхом станции метро, строились здания... Мы родились здесь...
Мы кусочки стремительной жизни. Мы всесильны и вечны.
Мы меняем мир и меняемся с ним. Он – Наш.
Мы космополиты.
Мы – люди Большого Города. Этого города.
В рюкзаке я ценю:
дизайн
функциональность
прочность
число карманов
цена

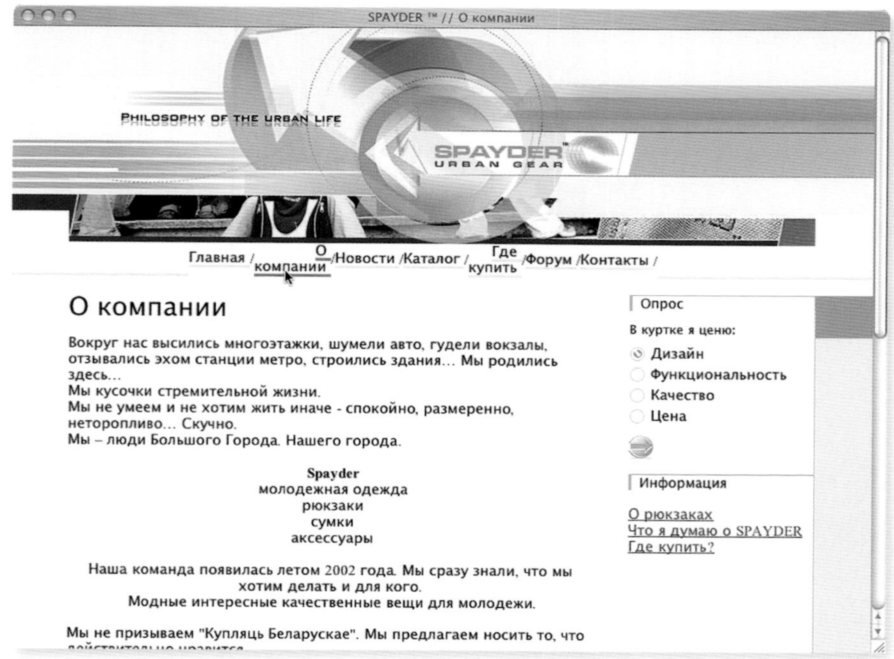
SPAYDER ™ // О компании
PHILOSOPHY OF THE URBAN LIFE
SPAYDER
URBAN GEAR
Главная / О компании /Новости /Каталог / Где купить /Форум /Контакты /
О компании
Вокруг нас высились многоэтажки, шумели авто, гудели вокзалы, отзывались эхом станции метро, строились здания... Мы родились здесь...
Мы кусочки стремительной жизни.
Мы не умеем и не хотим жить иначе - спокойно, размеренно, неторопливо... Скучно.
Мы – люди Большого Города. Нашего города.
Spayder
молодежная одежда
рюкзаки
сумки
аксессуары
Наша команда появилась летом 2002 года. Мы сразу знали, что мы хотим делать и для кого.
Модные интересные качественные вещи для молодежи.
Мы не призываем "Купляць Беларускае". Мы предлагаем носить то, что
Опрос
В куртке я ценю:
Дизайн
Функциональность
Качество
Цена
Информация
О рюкзаках
Что я думаю о SPAYDER
Где купить?

www.spayder.com
D: oleg tjagunov
A: activemedia M: denis@active.by

|| Suncorner ||
suncorner
MÚSICA ON / OFF
sunrise.01

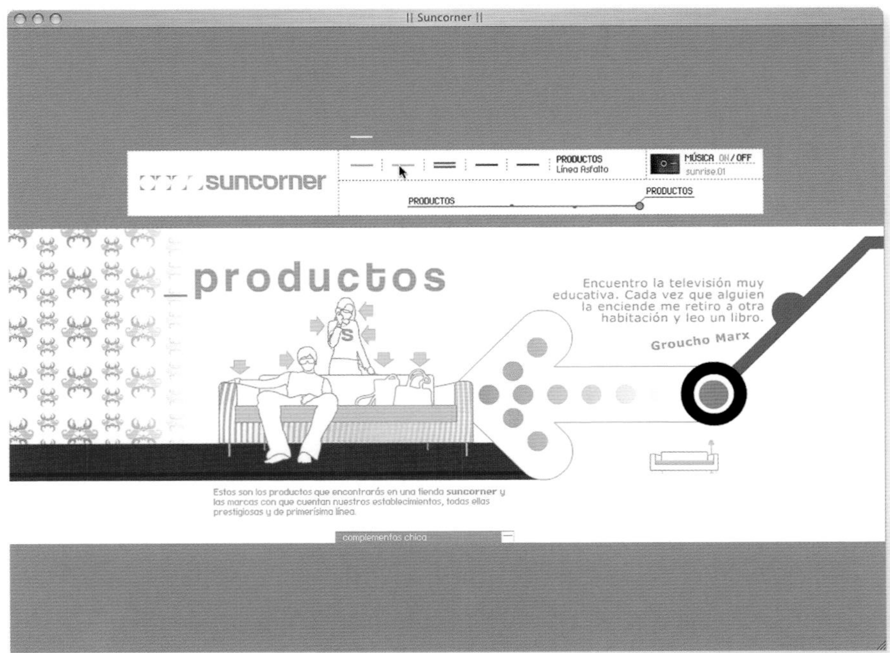
|| Suncorner ||
suncorner
PRODUCTOS
Línea Asfalto
MÚSICA ON / OFF
sunrise.01
PRODUCTOS
PRODUCTOS
_productos
Encuentro la televisión muy educativa. Cada vez que alguien la enciende me retiro a otra habitación y leo un libro.
Groucho Marx
Estos son los productos que encontrarás en una tienda suncorner y las marcas con que cuentan nuestros establecimientos, todas ellas prestigiosas y de primerísima línea.
complementos chica

www.suncorner.es
D: ángel antón svoboda
A: i am, i can **M:** design@iamican.com

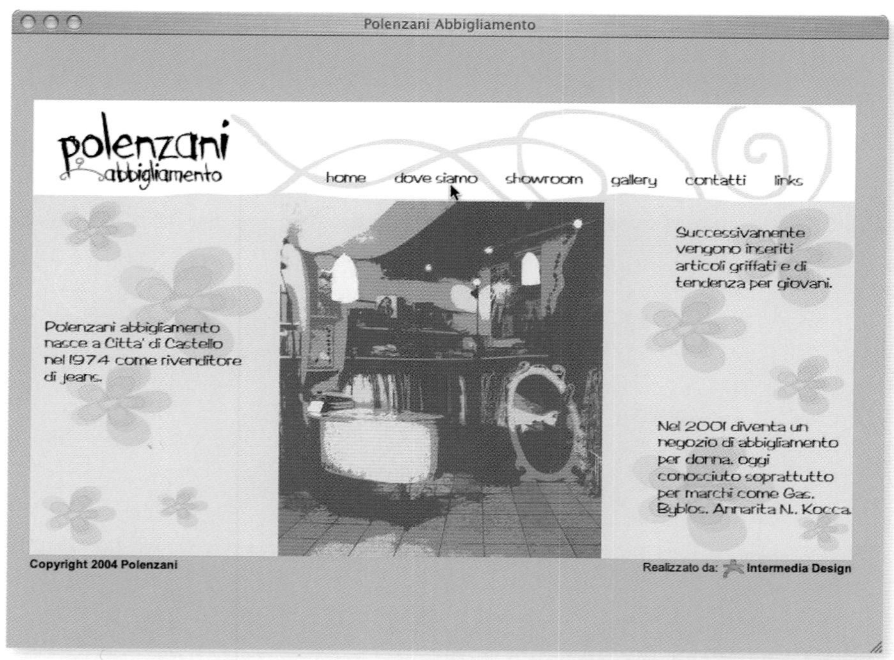
Polenzani Abbigliamento
polenzani abbigliamento
home
dove siamo
showroom
gallery
contatti
links
Successivamente vengono inseriti articoli griffati e di tendenza per giovani.
Polenzani abbigliamento nasce a Citta' di Castello nel 1974 come rivenditore di jeans.
Nel 2001 diventa un negozio di abbigliamento per donna, oggi conosciuto soprattutto per marchi come Gas, Byblos, Annarita N., Kocca.
Copyright 2004 Polenzani
Realizzato da: Intermedia Design

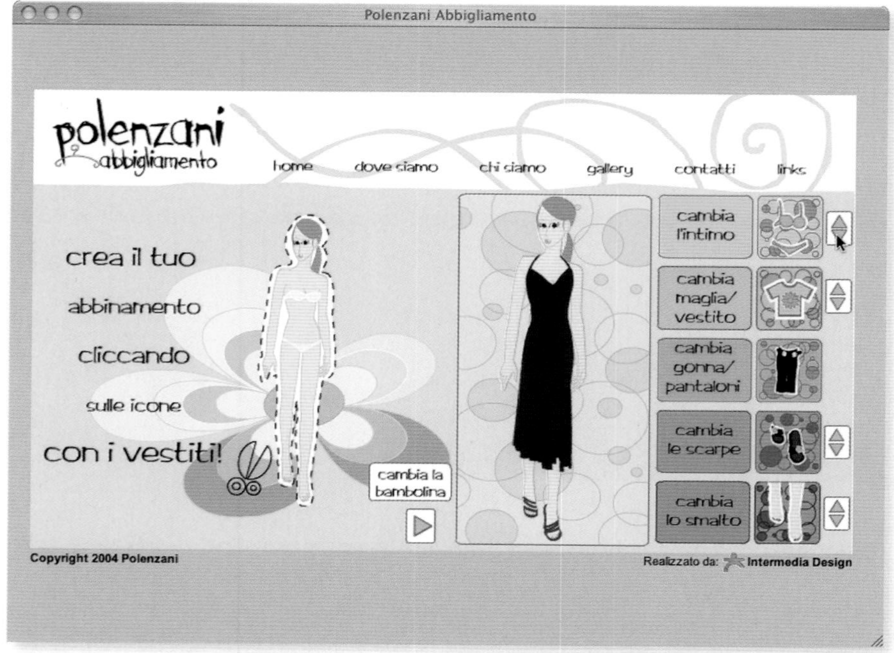
Polenzani Abbigliamento
polenzani abbigliamento
home
dove siamo
chi siamo
gallery
contatti
links
crea il tuo
abbinamento
cliccando
sulle icone
con i vestiti!
cambia la bambolina
cambia l'intimo
cambia maglia/ vestito
cambia gonna/ pantaloni
cambia le scarpe
cambia lo smalto
Copyright 2004 Polenzani
Realizzato da: Intermedia Design

www.polenzani.it
D: simona polenzani **C:** roberto serra
A: intermediadesign **M:** simona@intermediadesign.it

::::::::::RAFFINATO::::::::::
raffinato
empresa productos contacto
Raffinato, S.L. nace en el año 2001, para cubrir una necesidad en el mundo del complemento de moda de mujer.
Es un sistema nuevo e innovador pues con su apertura nace la primera tienda mayorista de complementos de moda de mujer en vigo, y con ella un nuevo concepto de venta.
empresa
Avda. Hispanidad 88, Apdo. Correos 716, 36203 VIGO, Tfno.986 494931 Fax.986 494932

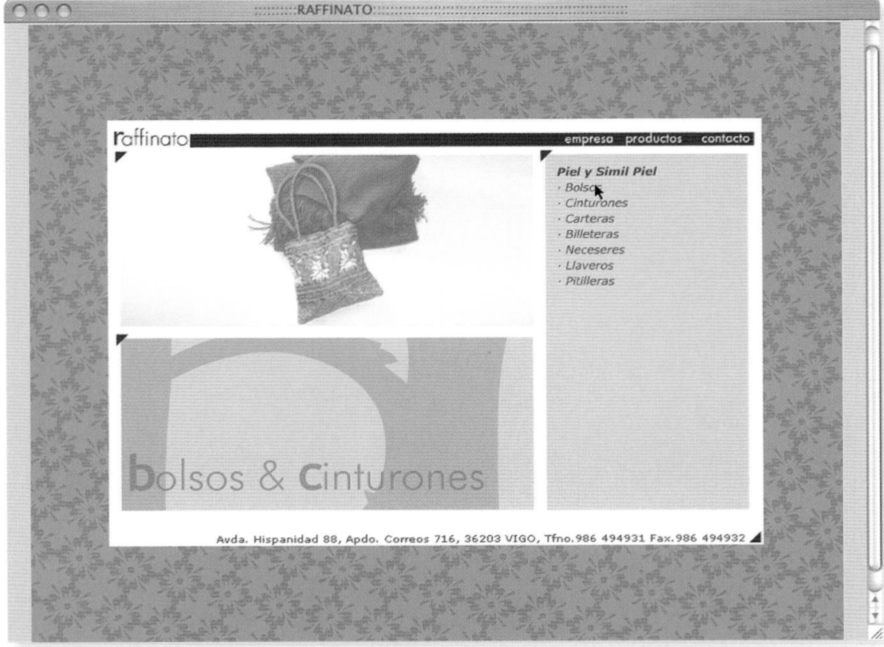
::::::::::RAFFINATO::::::::::
raffinato
empresa productos contacto
Piel y Simil Piel
· Bolsos
· Cinturones
· Carteras
· Billeteras
· Neceseres
· Llaveros
· Pitilleras
bolsos & Cinturones
Avda. Hispanidad 88, Apdo. Correos 716, 36203 VIGO, Tfno.986 494931 Fax.986 494932

www.raffinato.es
D: alberto garcia ariza
A: typognomics **M:** turuto@typognomics.com

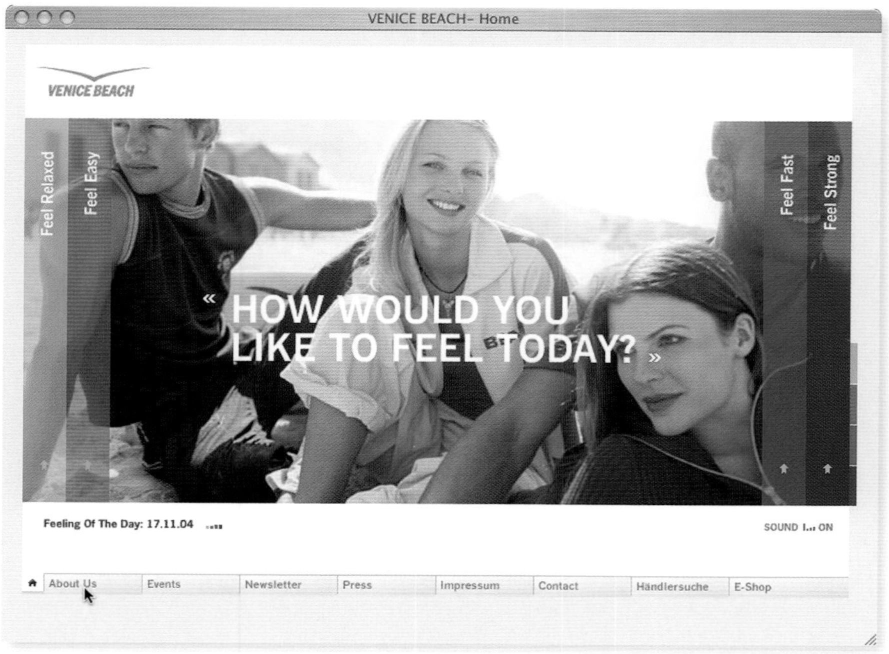
VENICE BEACH– Home
VENICE BEACH
Feel Relaxed
Feel Easy
Feel Fast
Feel Strong
« HOW WOULD YOU LIKE TO FEEL TODAY? »
Feeling Of The Day: 17.11.04
SOUND ON
About Us
Events
Newsletter
Press
Impressum
Contact
Händlersuche
E-Shop

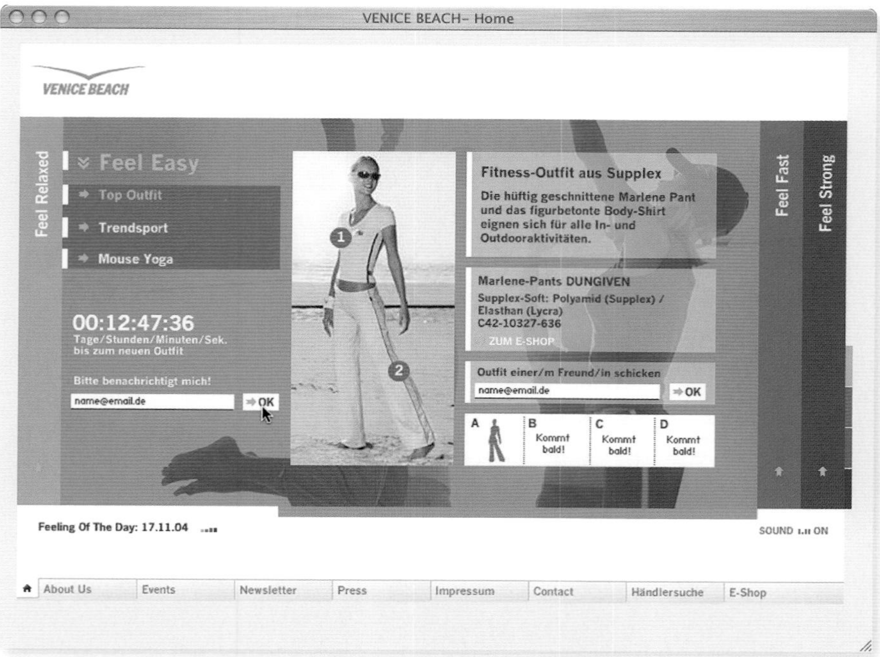
VENICE BEACH– Home
VENICE BEACH
Feel Relaxed
Feel Easy
Top Outfit
Trendsport
Mouse Yoga
00:12:47:36
Tage/Stunden/Minuten/Sek.
bis zum neuen Outfit
Bitte benachrichtigt mich!
name@email.de
OK
Fitness-Outfit aus Supplex
Die hüftig geschnittene Marlene Pant und das figurbetonte Body-Shirt eignen sich für alle In- und Outdooraktivitäten.
Marlene-Pants DUNGIVEN
Supplex-Soft: Polyamid (Supplex) / Elasthan (Lycra)
C42-10327-636
ZUM E-SHOP
Outfit einer/m Freund/in schicken
name@email.de
OK
A
B Kommt bald!
C Kommt bald!
D Kommt bald!
Feel Fast
Feel Strong
Feeling Of The Day: 17.11.04
SOUND ON
About Us
Events
Newsletter
Press
Impressum
Contact
Händlersuche
E-Shop

www.venice-beach.de
D: fork unstable media
A: fork unstable media **M:** svenja@fork.de

ringding
RING DING
ansteckend!
+ NEWS:
+ Jetzt auch mit Manschettenknöpfen...
+ RING ansehen...
+ RING anstecken...
+ OHRINGE ansehen...
+ OHRINGE bestellen...
+ MANSCHETTENKNÖPFE ansehen...
+ MANSCHETTENKNÖPFE bestellen...

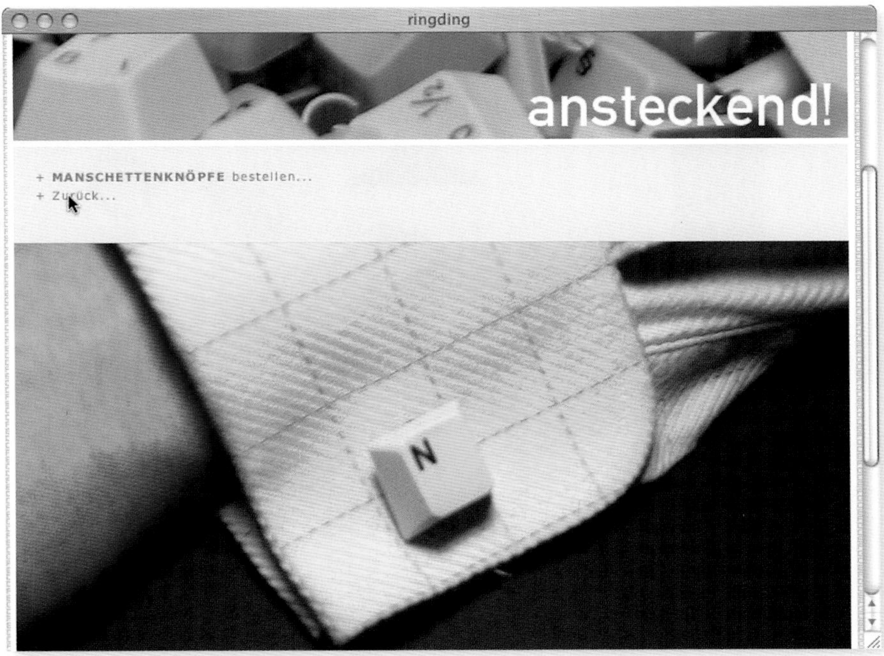
ringding
ansteckend!
+ MANSCHETTENKNÖPFE bestellen...
+ Zurück...

www.ring-ding.net
D: nico hensel
A: lichtpunkt // netzwerk für gestaltung M: nh@lichtpunkt.biz

Belén Bajo Joyas
belén bajo

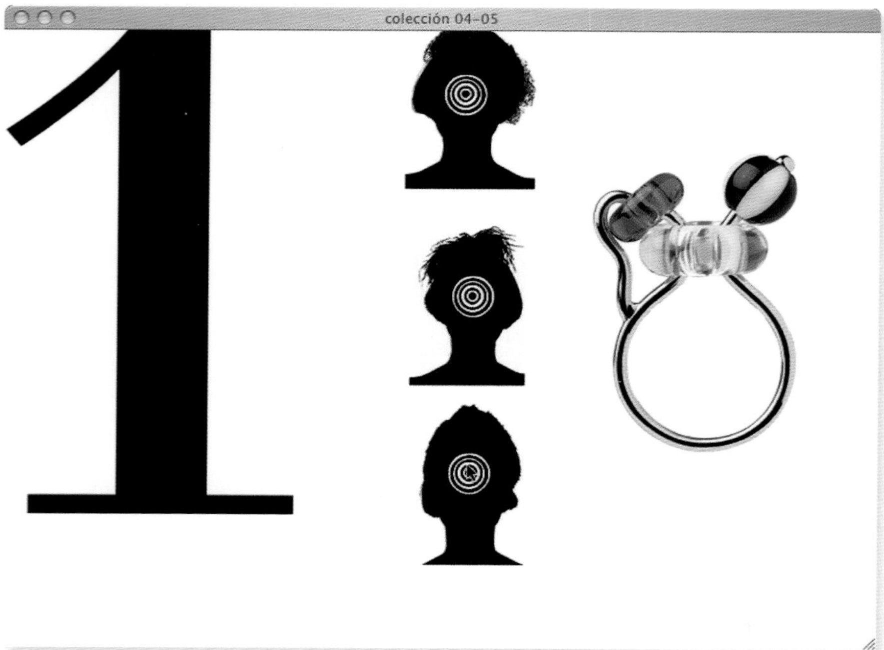
colección 04-05
1

www.belenbajo.com
D: elix fuentes **C:** susana fuentes **P:** maria garcia
A: la compañia grafica **M:** maria@co-grafica.com

ZONCHO
Las chemas | ¿Qué's esta vara?
Quiero mi camisetica | Pssst | Los compas
zonchó®

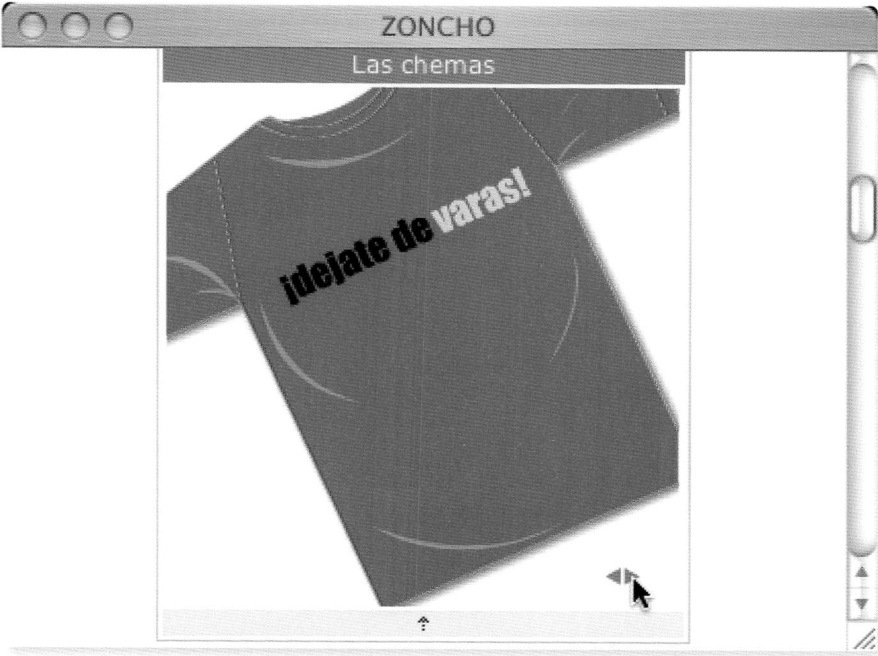
ZONCHO
Las chemas
¡dejate de varas!

www.zoncho.com/
D: carlos murillo hernández
M: carlos@rockcentro.com

< WELCOME TO STELLA McCARTNEY >

< WELCOME TO STELLA McCARTNEY >

STELLA McCARTNEY

AUTUMN '05 | ARCHIVE | ACCESSORIES | STELLA'S PAGE | STORES | SPECIAL EVENTS | NEWS UPDATES | REGISTER

SS '05 | AW '04 | SS '04 | AW '03 | SS '03 | AW '02 | SS '02

CONTACT US LEGAL/SITE CREDITS

www.stellamccartney.com
D: digit london ltd.
A: digit london ltd. **M:** info@digitlondon.com

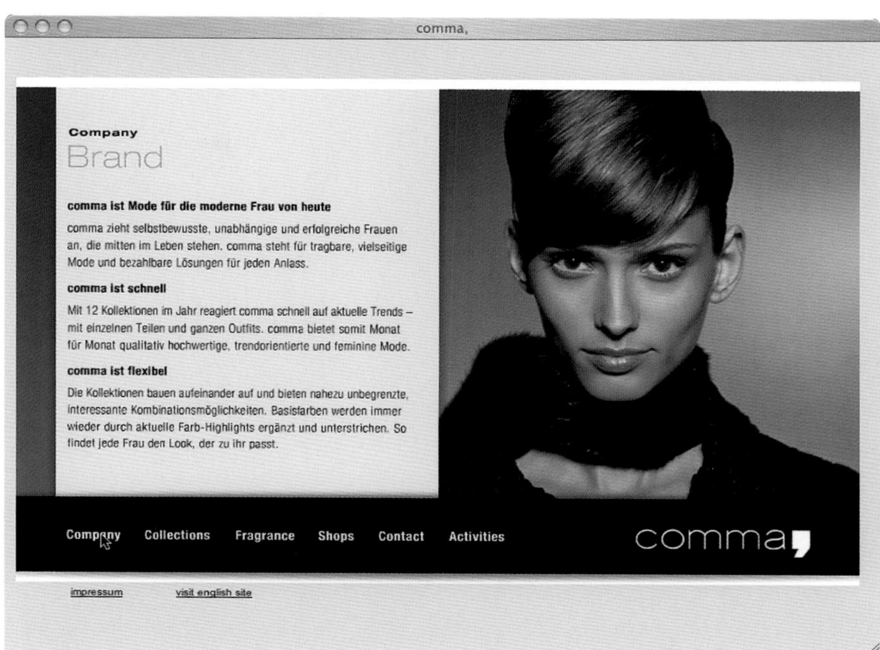
comma,
Company
Brand
comma ist Mode für die moderne Frau von heute
comma zieht selbstbewusste, unabhängige und erfolgreiche Frauen an, die mitten im Leben stehen. comma steht für tragbare, vielseitige Mode und bezahlbare Lösungen für jeden Anlass.
comma ist schnell
Mit 12 Kollektionen im Jahr reagiert comma schnell auf aktuelle Trends – mit einzelnen Teilen und ganzen Outfits. comma bietet somit Monat für Monat qualitativ hochwertige, trendorientierte und feminine Mode.
comma ist flexibel
Die Kollektionen bauen aufeinander auf und bieten nahezu unbegrenzte, interessante Kombinationsmöglichkeiten. Basisfarben werden immer wieder durch aktuelle Farb-Highlights ergänzt und unterstrichen. So findet jede Frau den Look, der zu ihr passt.
Company
Collections
Fragrance
Shops
Contact
Activities
comma,
impressum
visit english site

comma,
Collection
12/2004
Pullover
Art. 81.412.61.5417 € 49,95
Rock
Art. 81.412.78.8956 € 59,95
*(Unverbindliche Preisempfehlung. Preise gelten nur für Deutschland.)
Company
Collections
Fragrance
Shops
Contact
Activities
comma,
impressum
visit english site

www.comma-fashion.com
D: alex frank
A: lxfx **M:** alex@lxfx.de

WOMEN COLLECTION 2005

WOMEN COLLECTION 2005

www.isseymiyake.com
D: etienne mineur **C:** etienne mineur **P:** incandescence
A: incandescence **M:** www.incandescence.com

Battistoni
BATTISTONI
man| woman| perfumes| history | art | calendars | contacts
M A N
tailor-made
shirts
knitwear
sportswear
neckties
leather
gift items
M A N
BATTISTONI

Battistoni
BATTISTONI
man| woman| perfumes| history | art | calendars | contacts
W O M A N
tailor-made
shirts
knitwear
sportswear
leather
accessories
gift items
dresses
suits
jackets
trousers
skirts
overcoats
jacket 786
jacket 786
jacket 769
jacket 778
jacket 778
jacket 779
jacket 788
jacket 788
jacket mod.778 - nappa
JACKETS
W O M A N
BATTISTONI

www.battistoni.com
D: bahia bajja **C:** ubaldo ponzio
A: ubyweb&multimedia **M:** ubaldo@ponzio.it

Simply Mickey Rourke

Home | Profile | Articles | Quotes | Movies | Fans' Stuff | Notice Board | Links | Guestbook

Picture source:
(above) digitally edited by Tyk. Thank you Armin Osmancevic, for contributing this pic.

(Right: Carre Otis) from some fashion magazine

Profile mr

name
Philip Andre Rourke Jr.

birth place
Schenectady, New York, USA

birth date
16 July 1956

religion
Catholic

family members
- father, an Irish caretaker and amateur bodybuilder
- mom, Ann
- younger brother, Joey
- younger sister, Patti
- stepfather (a policeman)
- and five stepbrothers

spouses
- Debra Feuer, ex-wife
- Carre Otis, model/actress "Wild Orchid" co-star (I'm not sure about their current status)

before he started acting
- worked in whorehouses and transvestite night clubs
- laid linoleum on floors
- moved furniture
- trained attack dogs
- had a chestnut stand
- was an amateur boxer working out for several years at Miami's Fifth Street Gym

how he got into acting
A buddy in school informed him of an available role in the school play. While supporting himself with odd jobs, he studied with the distinguished coach, Sandra Seacat, who cast him as Eddie in a production of Arthur Miller's "A View From the Bridge."

his education in acting:
Actors Studio, New York City

The above info were extracted from the following sources:
·Interview with Joan Smallwood, M3 magazine
·Interview with Brandon Holey, In Fashion magazine
·Mr Showbiz Star Bio
'GROWING up in a poor, black Miami neighborhood, Mickey Rourke showed talent as a baseball player and boxer but, for the most part, was majoring in juvenile delinquency before he got into acting.'

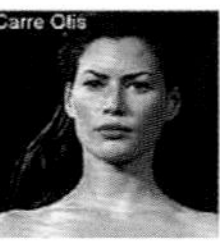
Carre Otis

If you feel that the info is inaccurate or would like to add on to it,

Simply Mickey Rourke

Home | Profile | Articles | Quotes | Movies | Fans' Stuff | Notice Board | Links | Guestbook

Picture source: internet
mr
Articles
archives

I'm sorry but I simply do not have the latest news and gossips on Mickey Rourke here. All I can show you are the few articles I chanced upon years ago. Thankyou, Chris for contributing one of the articles. Contributions from fans are all I can depend on.

full articles
- Fightin' Words (1994)
- Rebirth of the cool (1998)
- Call of the mild (2001)
- Mickey Rourke is Sorry (2004)

bits and pieces
- Falling Rourke
- Eye on the market
- Bright lights, big city (2001)
- Steve Buscemi Does Time (2000)

Simply Mickey Rourke Unofficial Tribute | about Tyk back to top

Steve Buscemi Does Time;
Directing "Animal Factory"
by Suzanne Ely, indieWIRE, 03 Nov 2000
Thanks to site visitor, Stefan Nylén for informing me!
Saturday, July 21, 2001 7:58 PM

Back to top

extract --

IW: The casting was also wonderful. Did you always imagine Mickey Rourke in the role of Jan the Actress?

Buscemi: He was the first one that we went to, but we didn't always imagine Mickey in that role. It was something that Sheila Jaffe thought about, who was my casting director. We knew that we wanted a really strong actor to play that role. We thought it would be a good opportunity for an actor. Once he signed on, I think he may have been a little sensitive at first, but once he committed, he really committed. He showed up on set practically in character. He did his own nails, he did his hair, he brought his own wardrobe. He even wrote that monologue when his character talks about becoming a

www.tykst.com/mickey
D: joan tan
A: zingee **M:** joan@zingee.com

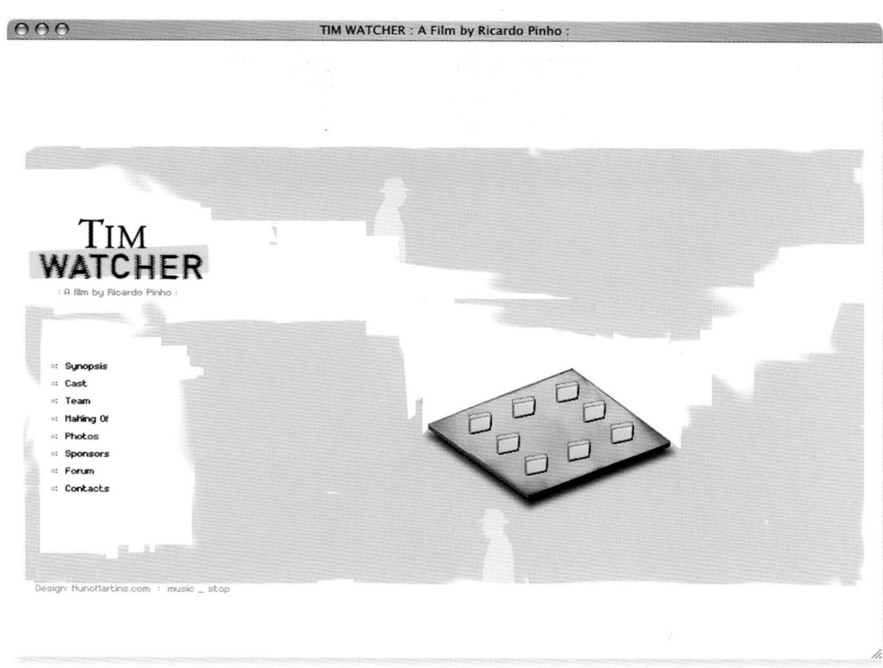
TIM WATCHER : A Film by Ricardo Pinho :
TIM
WATCHER
: A film by Ricardo Pinho :
Synopsis
Cast
Team
Making Of
Photos
Sponsors
Forum
Contacts
Design: NunoMartins.com : music _ stop

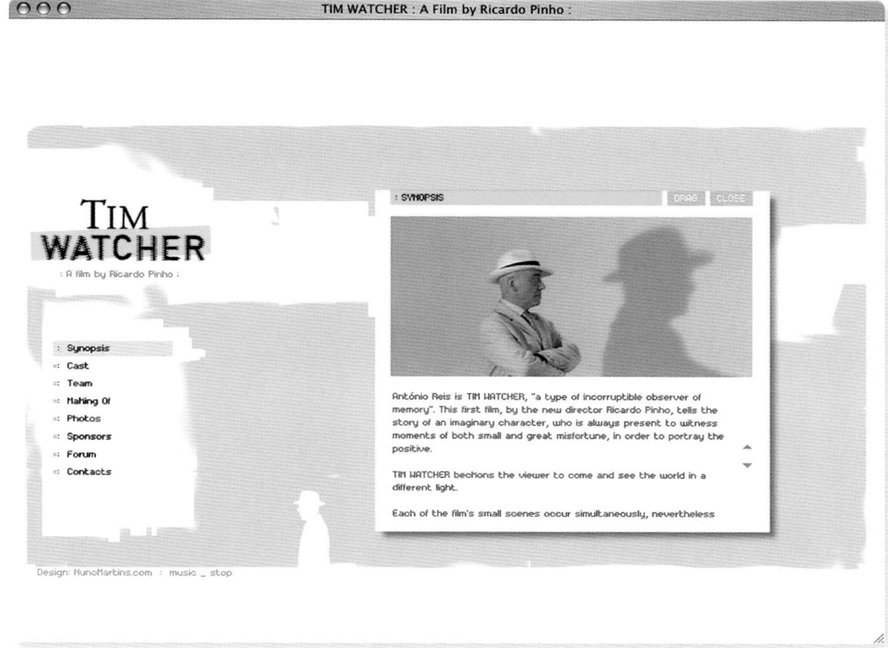
TIM WATCHER : A Film by Ricardo Pinho :
TIM
WATCHER
: A film by Ricardo Pinho :
Synopsis
Cast
Team
Making Of
Photos
Sponsors
Forum
Contacts
: SYNOPSIS
DRAG
CLOSE
António Reis is TIM WATCHER, "a type of incorruptible observer of memory". This first film, by the new director Ricardo Pinho, tells the story of an imaginary character, who is always present to witness moments of both small and great misfortune, in order to portray the positive.
TIM WATCHER beckons the viewer to come and see the world in a different light.
Each of the film's small scenes occur simultaneously, nevertheless
Design: NunoMartins.com : music _ stop

www.timwatchermovie.com
D: nuno martins
M: nuno@nunomartins.com

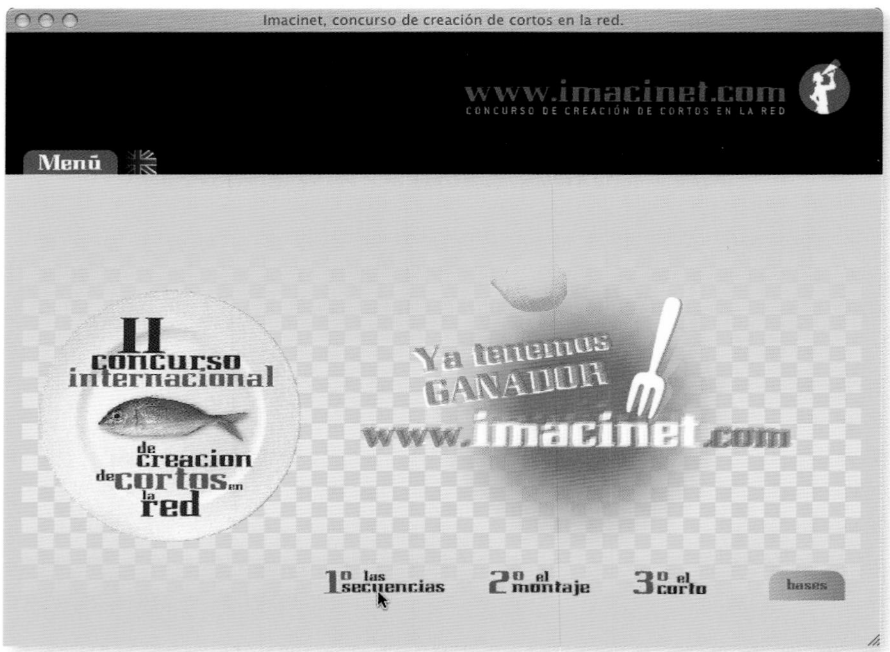
Imacinet, concurso de creación de cortos en la red.
www.imacinet.com
CONCURSO DE CREACIÓN DE CORTOS EN LA RED
Menú
II concurso internacional de creacion de cortos en la red
Ya tenemos GANADOR
www.imacinet.com
1º las secuencias
2º el montaje
3º el corto
bases

imacinet. Imacinet, concurso de creación de cortos en la red.
www.imacinet.com
CONCURSO DE CREACIÓN DE CORTOS EN LA RED
Menú
ingredientes
Título: Las viejitas
Descripción: Dos viejitas con la mirada en fuga
Título: La cosecha
Descripción: Calor en el ambiente
Título: La profesora
envia
Get QuickTime Free Download

www.imacinet.com
D: césar castañeyra P: imacinet
A: metro estudio M: info@metroestudio.com

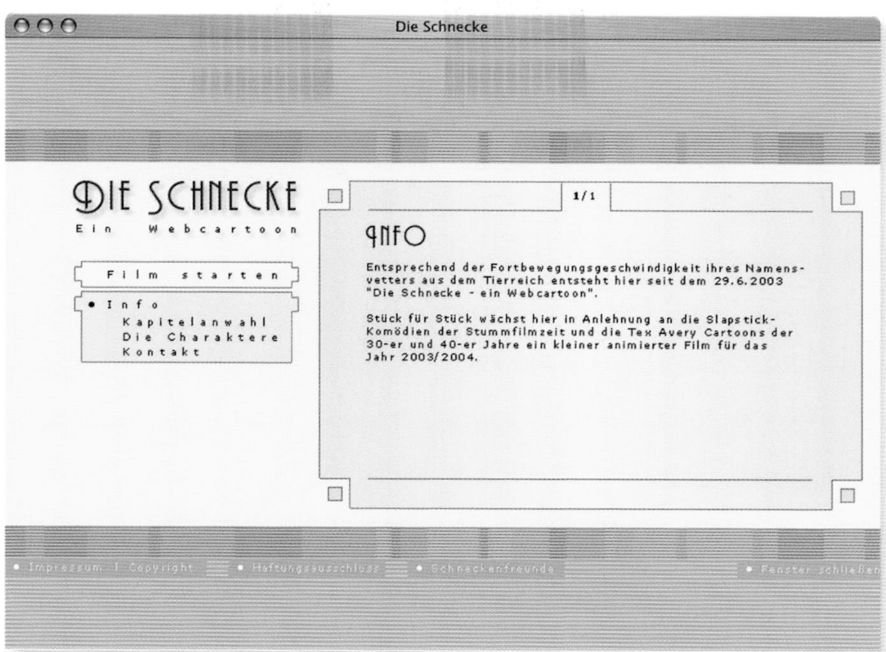
Die Schnecke
DIE SCHNECKE
Ein Webcartoon
Film starten
• Info
Kapitelanwahl
Die Charaktere
Kontakt
1/1
INFO
Entsprechend der Fortbewegungsgeschwindigkeit ihres Namensvetters aus dem Tierreich entsteht hier seit dem 29.6.2003 "Die Schnecke - ein Webcartoon".
Stück für Stück wächst hier in Anlehnung an die Slapstick-Komödien der Stummfilmzeit und die Tex Avery Cartoons der 30-er und 40-er Jahre ein kleiner animierter Film für das Jahr 2003/2004.
• Impressum | Copyright
• Haftungsausschluss
• Schneckenfreunde
• Fenster schließen

Die Schnecke
DIE SCHNECKE
Ein Webcartoon
• Film läuft
Info
• Impressum | Copyright
• Haftungsausschluss
• Schneckenfreunde
• Fenster schließen

www.die-webschnecke.de
D: rainer lieser
M: rainer.lieser@t-online.de

.:: Feng Shui Films ::.
feng Shui films
Feng Shui Films
Concepto
Equipo
Servicios
Videoclips
Publicidad
Videos Corporativos
Diseño
Making Of
Absolute Feng
Producciones Feng
Contacta
News
RODAJE
Feng Shui Films reactiva sus producciones propias con un cortometraje de título "ANONYMOUS".
CO-PRODUCCIÓN
Feng Shui Films participa como productora asociada en el cortometraje "BOTA DE ORO".
MAKING OF
Feng Shui Films entrega "LOBO" e
FENG SHUI FILMS REACTIVA SUS PRODUCCIONES PROPIAS CON UN CORTOMETRAJE DE TÍTULO PROVISIONAL "ANSIEDAD".
El rodaje, en formato HDCAM, está previsto para el mes de agosto de 2004 en localizaciones de Madrid y Lisboa y será dirigido por Cristian Pozo, el realizador de la productora. Los actores protagonistas son Alvaro Sanmiguel "El Tuli" y Luz Altamira. La producción corre a cargo de Francisco Ramos Escalada y Feng Shui Films.
Videoclips
Publicidad
Videos Corporativos
Making Of

.:: Feng Shui Films ::.
feng Shui films
Feng Shui Films
Concepto
Equipo
Servicios
Videoclips
Publicidad
Videos Corporativos
Diseño
Making Of
Absolute Feng
Producciones Feng
Contacta
Videoclips
La especialidad de la casa
Los videoclips son la madre de Feng Shui Films. Un montón de artistas han confiado en nuestro asesoramiento para sacar el concepto, la esencia o las sensaciones de sus canciones y plasmarlas en sus videos. La experiencia y la creatividad más desbordante desemboca en trabajos diferentes y resultados que siempre quitan el hipo.
Clips
Las hijas del Sol
Ay, ay, ay
Chenoa
7 pétalos
Soy lo que me dás
En tu cruz me clavaste
Pereza
Si quieres bailamos
Pienso en aquella tarde
Pienso en aquella tarde (acústico)
CLIPS
LAS HIJAS DEL SOL
Ay, Ay, Ay
BMG/ARIOLA
2004
DESCARGA VIDEO CLIP
descubre Absolute feng

www.fengshuifilms.com
D: fernando lago
M: fernandolago@fengshuifilsm.com

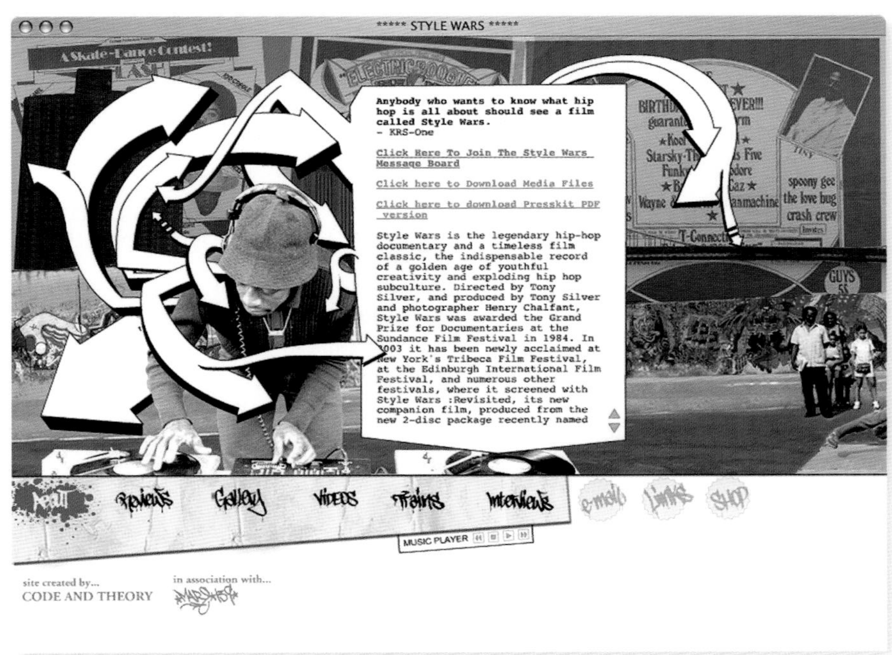
***** STYLE WARS *****
Anybody who wants to know what hip hop is all about should see a film called Style Wars.
- KRS-One
Click Here To Join The Style Wars Message Board
Click here to Download Media Files
Click here to download Presskit PDF version
Style Wars is the legendary hip-hop documentary and a timeless film classic, the indispensable record of a golden age of youthful creativity and exploding hip hop subculture. Directed by Tony Silver, and produced by Tony Silver and photographer Henry Chalfant, Style Wars was awarded the Grand Prize for Documentaries at the Sundance Film Festival in 1984. In 2003 it has been newly acclaimed at New York's Tribeca Film Festival, at the Edinburgh International Film Festival, and numerous other festivals, where it screened with Style Wars :Revisited, its new companion film, produced from the new 2-disc package recently named
MUSIC PLAYER
site created by...
CODE AND THEORY
in association with...

***** STYLE WARS *****
LIFESTYLE
BLACKBOOK
FASHION
MUSIC PLAYER
site created by...
CODE AND THEORY
in association with...

www.stylewars.com
D: brandon ralph, dan gardner **C:** arnie gullov-singh **P:** dave hartt
A: code and theory **M:** www.codeandtheory.com

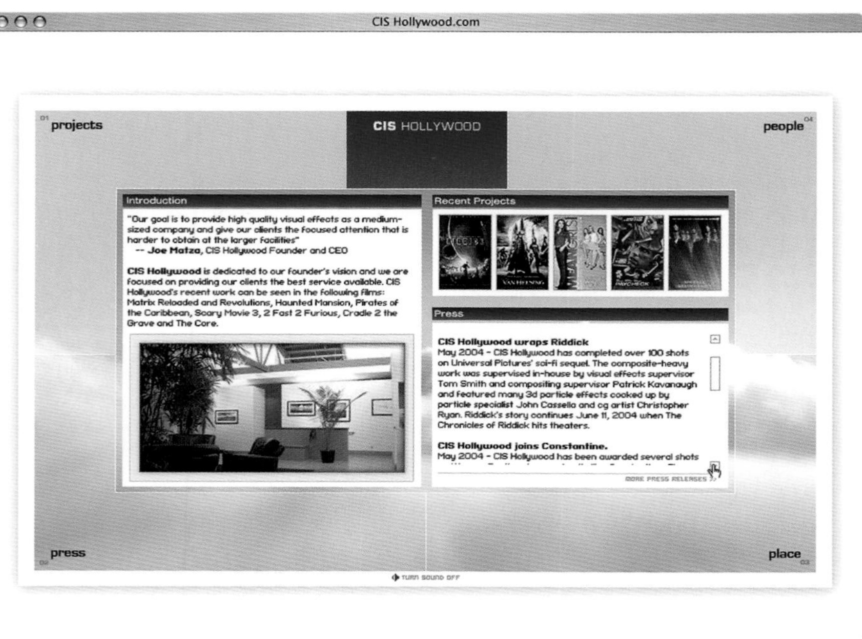
CIS Hollywood.com
projects
CIS HOLLYWOOD
people
Introduction
"Our goal is to provide high quality visual effects as a medium-sized company and give our clients the focused attention that is harder to obtain at the larger facilities"
-- Joe Matza, CIS Hollywood Founder and CEO
CIS Hollywood is dedicated to our founder's vision and we are focused on providing our clients the best service available. CIS Hollywood's recent work can be seen in the following films: Matrix Reloaded and Revolutions, Haunted Mansion, Pirates of the Caribbean, Scary Movie 3, 2 Fast 2 Furious, Cradle 2 the Grave and The Core.
Recent Projects
Press
CIS Hollywood wraps Riddick
May 2004 - CIS Hollywood has completed over 100 shots on Universal Pictures' sci-fi sequel. The composite-heavy work was supervised in-house by visual effects supervisor Tom Smith and compositing supervisor Patrick Kavanaugh and featured many 3d particle effects cooked up by particle specialist John Cassello and cg artist Christopher Ryan. Riddick's story continues June 11, 2004 when The Chronicles of Riddick hits theaters.
CIS Hollywood joins Constantine.
May 2004 - CIS Hollywood has been awarded several shots
press
place
TURN SOUND OFF

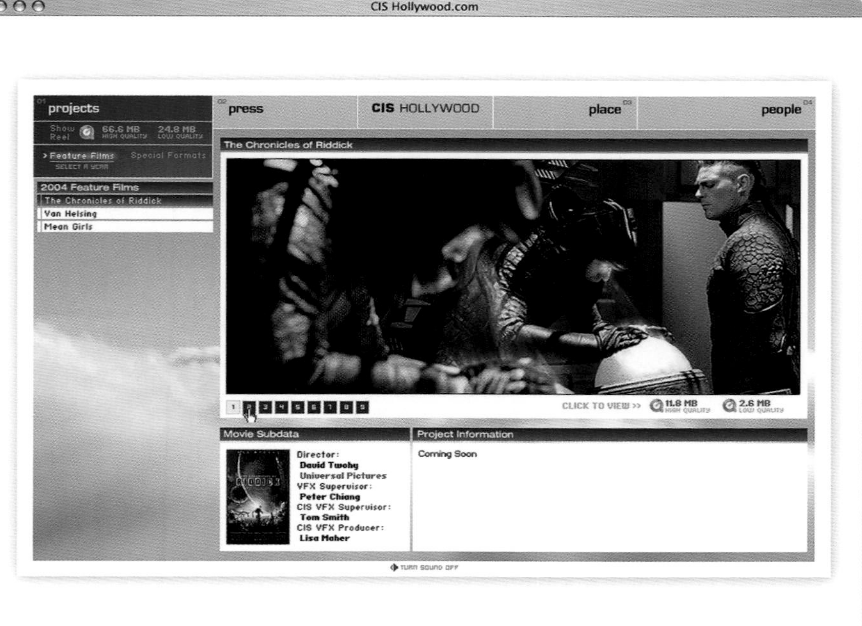
CIS Hollywood.com
projects
press
CIS HOLLYWOOD
place
people
Show Reel
66.6 MB HIGH QUALITY
24.8 MB LOW QUALITY
Feature Films
Special Formats
SELECT A YEAR
2004 Feature Films
The Chronicles of Riddick
Van Helsing
Mean Girls
The Chronicles of Riddick
CLICK TO VIEW >>
11.8 MB HIGH QUALITY
2.6 MB LOW QUALITY
Movie Subdata
Director:
David Twohy
Universal Pictures
VFX Supervisor:
Peter Chiang
CIS VFX Supervisor:
Tom Smith
CIS VFX Producer:
Lisa Maher
Project Information
Coming Soon
TURN SOUND OFF

www.cishollywood.com
D: shane seminole mielke
A: pixelranger **M:** www.pixelranger.com

Egolego - Festival de Brickfilms
Le 1er. Festival de Brickfilm européen
SÉLECTION DU MOMENT
ZeroGravity (par James Maduzia)
Un brickfilm d'une étonnante fluidité qui défie les lois de l'apesanteur
PRÉSENTATION DU FESTIVAL
LES BRICKFILMS EN COMPÉTITION
PARTENAIRES LIENS BRICKFILM
PRÉSENTATION DU FESTIVAL
25 / 26 / 27 Juin 2004
Les brickfilms se distinguent par leur réalisation en briques de Lego. Ils se sont largement développés au cours des 4 dernières années à travers des remakes de scènes célèbres, de blockbusters et de clips vidéo et connaissent actuellement une émergence en Europe.
Pour la première fois, un festival Brickfilm est organisé à Paris pour tous les fans de Legos et d'animations vidéos ! Pendant trois jours de folie vous pourrez venir découvrir une sélection des meilleurs Brickfilms internationaux du moment.
+ d'informations
Festival brickfilms egolego 25/26/27 Juin 2004
réservez vos tickets >>en ligne !
du 10 mai au 12 juin 2004
Projet fictif réalisé par krearoa.com | Tous droits réservés

Egolego - Festival de Brickfilms
Le 1er. Festival de Brickfilm européen
SÉLECTION DU MOMENT
ZeroGravity (par James Maduzia)
Un brickfilm d'une étonnante fluidité qui défie les lois de l'apesanteur
PRÉSENTATION DU FESTIVAL
LES BRICKFILMS EN COMPÉTITION
PARTENAIRES LIENS BRICKFILM
LES BRICKFILMS EN COMPÉTITION
StarWars Episode III
Categorie: Action, Sci-fi
Producteur: Jay Silver
Durée: 00:03:03
Date : 30 Juin 2002
Visionner un extrait
Zero Gravity
Categorie: Action, Sci-fi
Producteur: James Maduzia
Durée: 00:01:57
Date : 7 Octobre 2003
Visionner un extrait
A Space Odissey
Categorie: Comedi, Sci-fi
Producteur: Spite Your Face
Durée: 00:01:00
Date : 19 Février 2004
Visionner un extrait
réservez vos tickets >>en ligne !
du 10 mai au 12 juin 2004
Projet fictif réalisé par krearoa.com | Tous droits réservés

www.egolego.com
D: christophe grunenwald
A: 3gstudio **M:** contact@3gstudio.net

METROPOL spol. s r.o.
Info o společnosti
Nabídka prostor
Nabídka služeb
Kulturní program
Galerie Nahoře
Úvodní strana | Reference | Kontaktní informace | Podněty a připomínky
Úvodní strana
Aktuální zprávy
Vítáme Vás na internetových stránkách společnosti Metropol - víceúčelového kulturního a společenského zařízení v centru města Českých Budějovic.

METROPOL spol. s r.o.
Info o společnosti
Nabídka prostor
Nabídka služeb
Kulturní program
Galerie Nahoře
Úvodní strana | Reference | Kontaktní informace | Podněty a připomínky
Kulturní program
Plesová sezóna
Plesová sezóna
Hudební a zábavné pořady
Divadelní představení
7. 1. Maturitní ples Gymnázia Česká ul.
9. 1. 33.reprezentační ples Metropolu a jeho spoluuživatelů
10. 1. Reprezentační ples Lions Clubu České Budějovice
13. 1. Maturitní ples Integrované střední školy obchodu, služeb a podnikání

www.metropol-cb.cz
D: radek froulik
A: ing. radek froulik M: radek.froulik@dags.cz

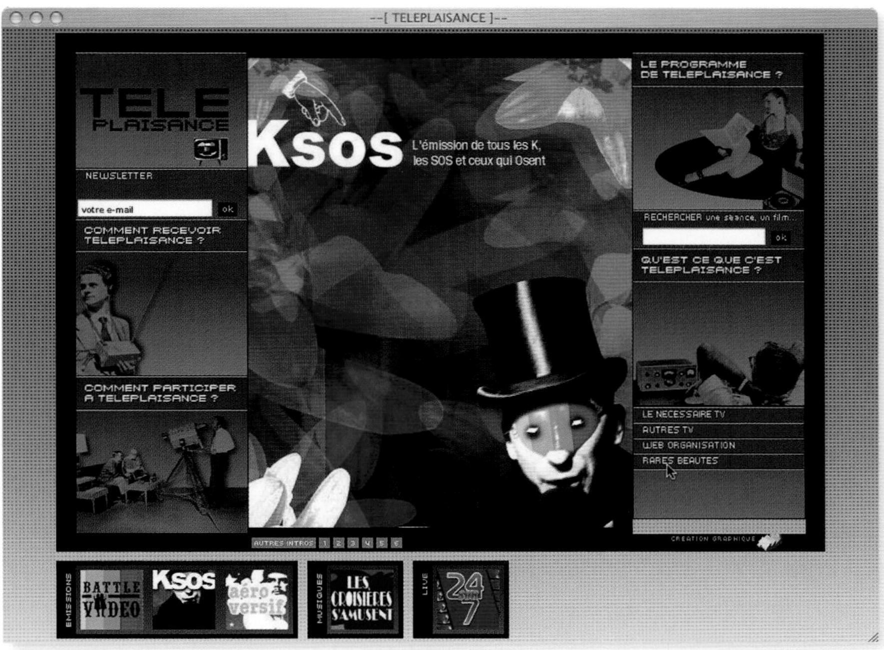
--[TELEPLAISANCE]--
TELE PLAISANCE
NEWSLETTER
votre e-mail
ok
COMMENT RECEVOIR TELEPLAISANCE ?
COMMENT PARTICIPER A TELEPLAISANCE ?
Ksos
L'émission de tous les K, les SOS et ceux qui Osent
LE PROGRAMME DE TELEPLAISANCE ?
RECHERCHER une séance, un film...
QU'EST CE QUE C'EST TELEPLAISANCE ?
LE NECESSAIRE TV
AUTRES TV
WEB ORGANISATION
RARES BEAUTES
AUTRES INTROS 1 2 3 4 5 6
EMISSIONS
BATTLE VIDEO
Ksos
aéro versif
MUSIQUES
LES CROISIÈRES S'AMUSENT
LIVE
24 7

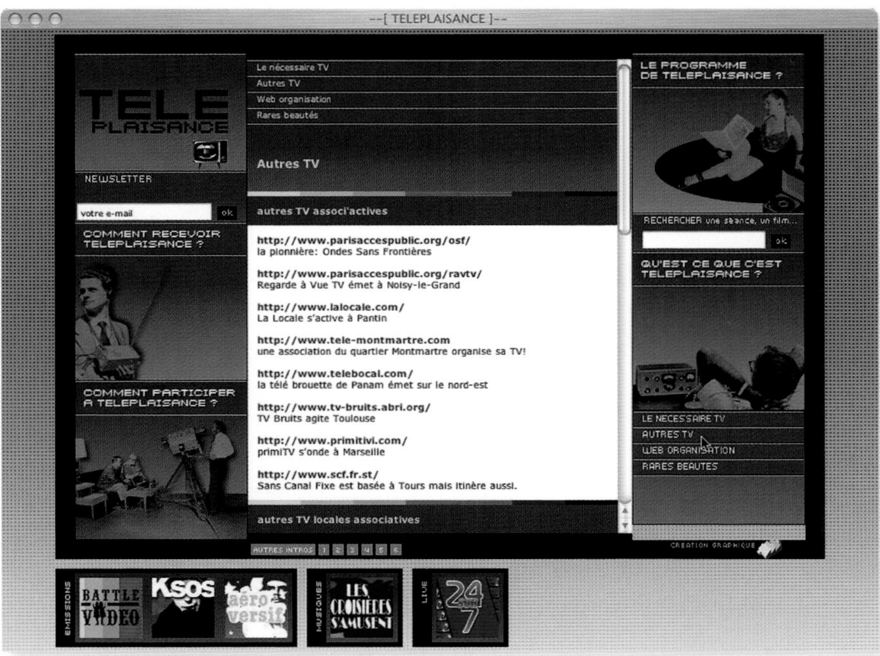
--[TELEPLAISANCE]--
Le nécessaire TV
Autres TV
Web organisation
Rares beautés
Autres TV
autres TV associ'actives
http://www.parisaccespublic.org/osf/
la pionnière: Ondes Sans Frontières
http://www.parisaccespublic.org/ravtv/
Regarde à Vue TV émet à Noisy-le-Grand
http://www.lalocale.com/
La Locale s'active à Pantin
http://www.tele-montmartre.com
une association du quartier Montmartre organise sa TV!
http://www.telebocal.com/
la télé brouette de Panam émet sur le nord-est
http://www.tv-bruits.abri.org/
TV Bruits agite Toulouse
http://www.primitivi.com/
primiTV s'onde à Marseille
http://www.scf.fr.st/
Sans Canal Fixe est basée à Tours mais itinère aussi.
autres TV locales associatives

www.teleplaisance.org
D: matthieu corgnet **P:** navarro
A: gazole-production **M:** webmaster@teleplaisance.org

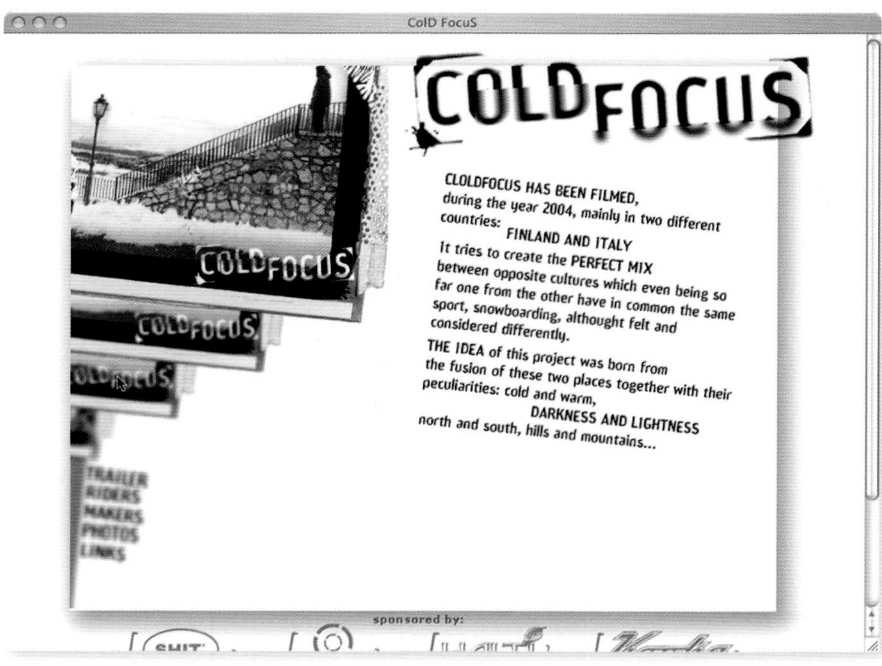
ColD FocuS
COLDFOCUS
CLOLDFOCUS HAS BEEN FILMED,
during the year 2004, mainly in two different
countries: FINLAND AND ITALY
It tries to create the PERFECT MIX
between opposite cultures which even being so
far one from the other have in common the same
sport, snowboarding, althought felt and
considered differently.
THE IDEA of this project was born from
the fusion of these two places together with their
peculiarities: cold and warm,
DARKNESS AND LIGHTNESS
north and south, hills and mountains...
TRAILER
RIDERS
MAKERS
PHOTOS
LINKS
sponsored by:

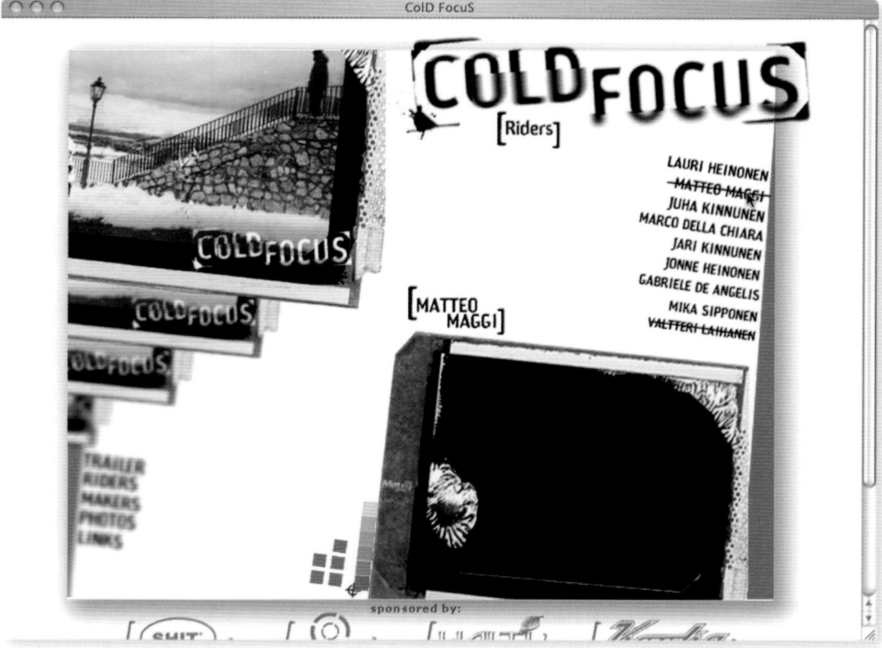
ColD FocuS
COLDFOCUS
[Riders]
LAURI HEINONEN
MATTEO MAGGI
JUHA KINNUNEN
MARCO DELLA CHIARA
JARI KINNUNEN
JONNE HEINONEN
GABRIELE DE ANGELIS
MIKA SIPPONEN
VALTTERI LAIHANEN
[MATTEO MAGGI]
TRAILER
RIDERS
MAKERS
PHOTOS
LINKS
sponsored by:

www.coldfocus.it
D: pierpaolo balani **C:** matteo maggi
M: pbalani@libero.it

AOEO
AOEO
IN AUSGEWÄHLTEN KINOS AB JUNI 2005
ENTER
ENTER ENGLISH VERSION
4030 CREW
AOEO
MARINA DELL MOUR ROLAND DELL MOUR JANINE HAID
IVA ZABKAR
DAVID WAGNER
SEBASTIAN WÖBER
JUNI '05
NEWSLETTER
GÄSTEBUCH
TRAILER ANSEHEN

AOEO
AOEO
DER FILM
DAS PROJEKT
TRAILER
ARTWORK
KONTAKT
IDEE
CREW
VERLAUF
SET-PHOTOS
PRESSE
LOCATIONS
BOCO >>
VERBRECHER >>
REGEN >>
AOEO INNEN >>
AOEO AUSSEN >>
SANDLER >>
GIRLIES >>
BULLETS >>
Während der 30 Drehtage im Zeitraum Juli / August '04 entstanden über 2000 Setphotos, welche die Arbeiten an AOEO festhalten.
Dies ist eine Auswahl der Photos, aufgeteilt auf die wichtigsten Locations der Dreharbeiten:
PRODUCTION AOEO
DIRECTOR
CAMERA BOCO.
DATE
SCENE
TAKE

www.aoeo.at
D: sebastian woeber
A: woeberland **M:** office@aoeo.at

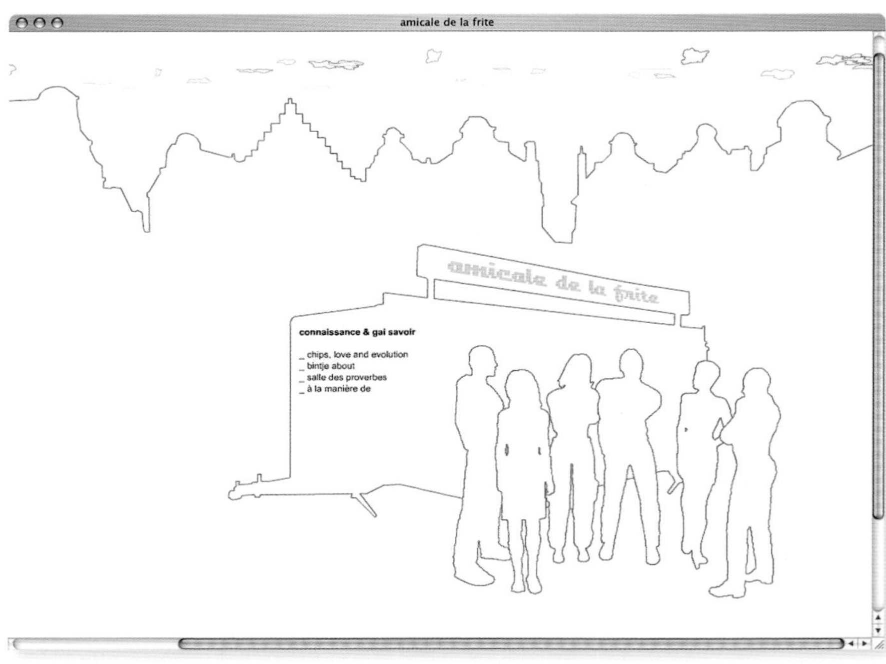
amicale de la frite
amicale de la frite
connaissance & gai savoir
_ chips, love and evolution
_ bintje about
_ salle des proverbes
_ à la manière de

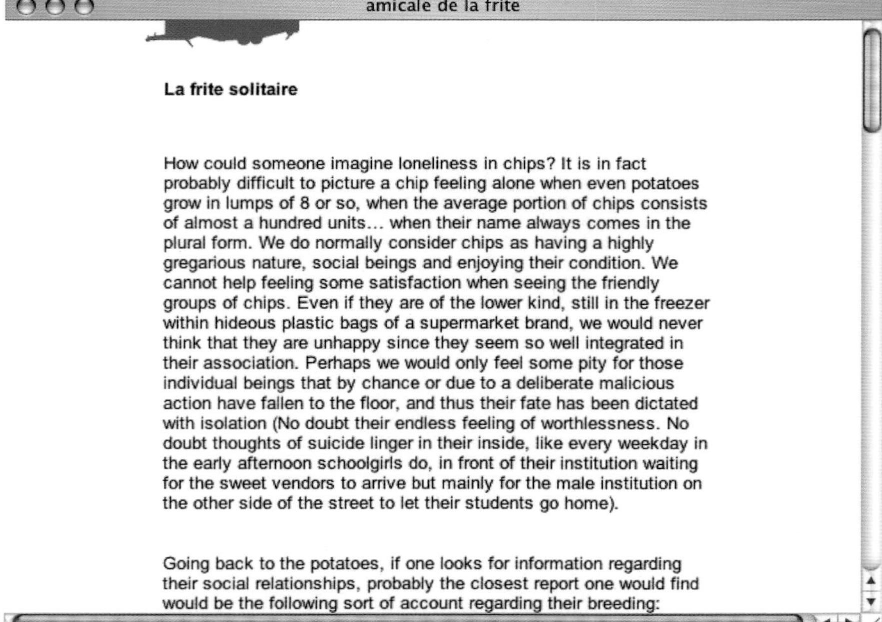
amicale de la frite

La frite solitaire

How could someone imagine loneliness in chips? It is in fact probably difficult to picture a chip feeling alone when even potatoes grow in lumps of 8 or so, when the average portion of chips consists of almost a hundred units... when their name always comes in the plural form. We do normally consider chips as having a highly gregarious nature, social beings and enjoying their condition. We cannot help feeling some satisfaction when seeing the friendly groups of chips. Even if they are of the lower kind, still in the freezer within hideous plastic bags of a supermarket brand, we would never think that they are unhappy since they seem so well integrated in their association. Perhaps we would only feel some pity for those individual beings that by chance or due to a deliberate malicious action have fallen to the floor, and thus their fate has been dictated with isolation (No doubt their endless feeling of worthlessness. No doubt thoughts of suicide linger in their inside, like every weekday in the early afternoon schoolgirls do, in front of their institution waiting for the sweet vendors to arrive but mainly for the male institution on the other side of the street to let their students go home).

Going back to the potatoes, if one looks for information regarding their social relationships, probably the closest report one would find would be the following sort of account regarding their breeding:

www.amicaledelafrite.org
D: stephane cauwel
A: hidden and too obvious **M:** s.cauwel@laposte.net

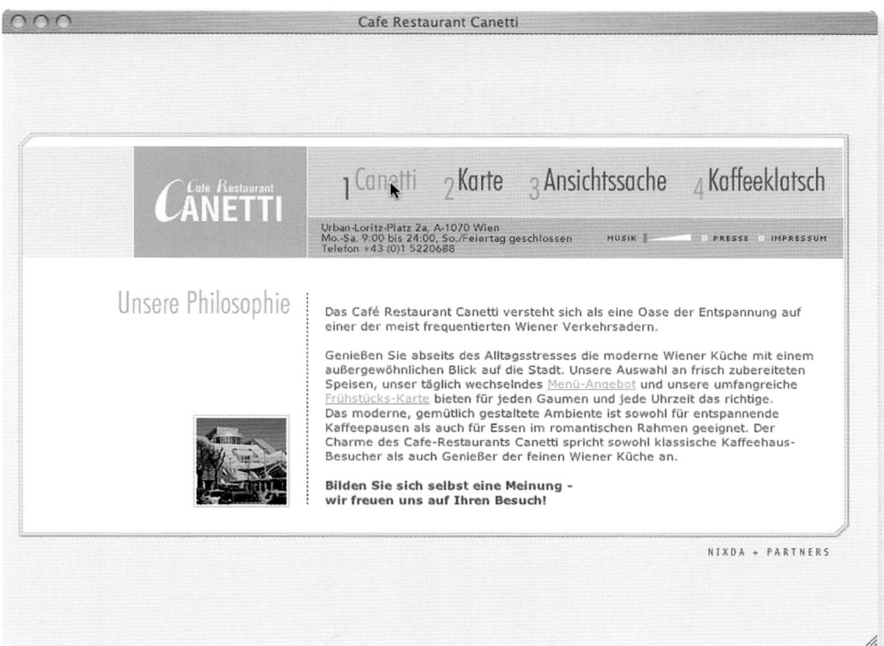
Cafe Restaurant Canetti
Café Restaurant CANETTI
1 Canetti 2 Karte 3 Ansichtssache 4 Kaffeeklatsch
Urban-Loritz-Platz 2a, A-1070 Wien
Mo.-Sa. 9:00 bis 24:00, So./Feiertag geschlossen
Telefon +43 (0)1 5220688
MUSIK PRESSE IMPRESSUM
Unsere Philosophie
Das Café Restaurant Canetti versteht sich als eine Oase der Entspannung auf einer der meist frequentierten Wiener Verkehrsadern.
Genießen Sie abseits des Alltagsstresses die moderne Wiener Küche mit einem außergewöhnlichen Blick auf die Stadt. Unsere Auswahl an frisch zubereiteten Speisen, unser täglich wechselndes Menü-Angebot und unsere umfangreiche Frühstücks-Karte bieten für jeden Gaumen und jede Uhrzeit das richtige.
Das moderne, gemütlich gestaltete Ambiente ist sowohl für entspannende Kaffeepausen als auch für Essen im romantischen Rahmen geeignet. Der Charme des Cafe-Restaurants Canetti spricht sowohl klassische Kaffeehaus-Besucher als auch Genießer der feinen Wiener Küche an.
Bilden Sie sich selbst eine Meinung - wir freuen uns auf Ihren Besuch!
NIXDA + PARTNERS

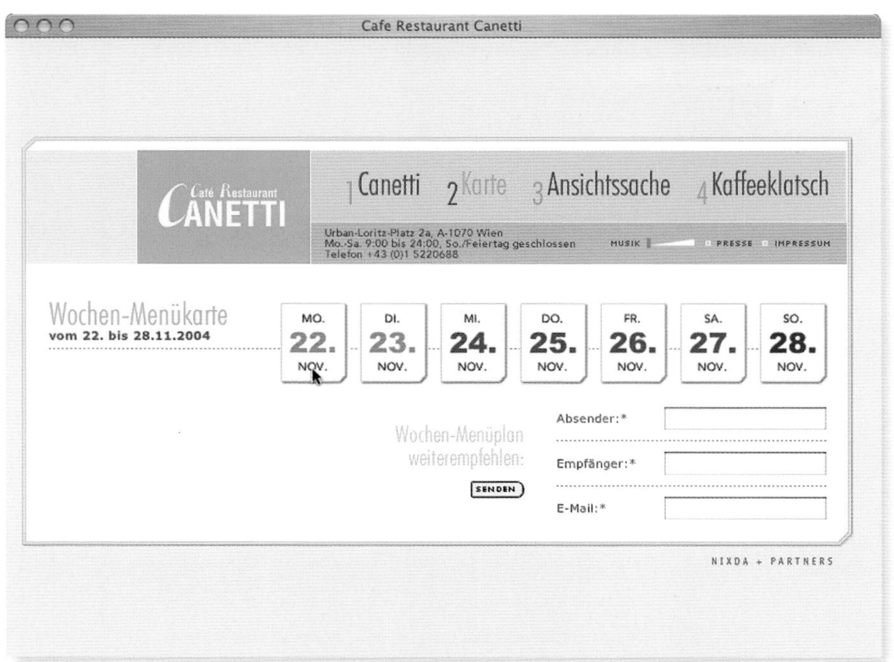
Cafe Restaurant Canetti
Café Restaurant CANETTI
1 Canetti 2 Karte 3 Ansichtssache 4 Kaffeeklatsch
Urban-Loritz-Platz 2a, A-1070 Wien
Mo.-Sa. 9:00 bis 24:00, So./Feiertag geschlossen
Telefon +43 (0)1 5220688
MUSIK PRESSE IMPRESSUM
Wochen-Menükarte
vom 22. bis 28.11.2004
MO. 22. NOV.
DI. 23. NOV.
MI. 24. NOV.
DO. 25. NOV.
FR. 26. NOV.
SA. 27. NOV.
SO. 28. NOV.
Wochen-Menüplan weiterempfehlen:
SENDEN
Absender:*
Empfänger:*
E-Mail:*
NIXDA + PARTNERS

www.cafe-canetti.at
D: jürgen oberguggenberger
A: nixda **M:** juergen@nixda.at

[OLUS]
<< accueil
cultivez la variété
Le bon
Le beau
L'utile
variétés
ressources
?
à propos
[OLUS]
Le beau >> Galerie de portraits
citation
Etre jardinier, c'est être comme le Bon Dieu, c'est donner vie et beauté avec de la terre, de l'eau et des graines
Jean Chalon
Galerie de portraits
Les mots tels que épurge, méum, arroche blonde, brune ou rouge, cougourde… ne font plus partie de notre vocabulaire quotidien.
La carotte et la laitue, onft toujours partie de notre vocabulaire, et pourtant… Qui sait qu'une carotte peut-être de Chantenay à coeur rouge ou Blanche de Kuttingen ou bien encore Jaune du Doubs. Les aubergines, parfois violettes pâles de Provence ont gardé pour certaines d'entre elles trace de leur première acclimatation en Italie, comme la Bianca di Imola Mezza lunga. Certains concombres, très anciens, sont consommés depuis des temps immémoriaux en Russie d'où leur nom charmant de concombre Vyaznikosky.
Un oignon peut être Jaune Pâle des Vertus… Enfin, c'est parmi les laitues que l'on trouve les dénominations les plus croustillantes et savoureuses. Ainsi on parle de Craquerelle du midi et de Cressonnette du Maroc, mais aussi de Passion Brune ou Blonde, d'Oreilles du diable, de Langue de Canari, de Merveille des quatre saisons et pour finir de Grosse Brune Têtue ou de Grosse Blonde Paresseuse.
Variété des couleurs et des formes [voir la mosaïque de photo]
Jardins potagers [voir la mosaïque de photo]

[OLUS]
<< accueil
cultivez la variété
Le bon
Le beau
L'utile
variétés
ressources
?
à propos
[OLUS]
L'utile >> Pourquoi tant de légumes oubliés ?
citation
Pourquoi tant de légumes oubliés ?
On pourrait penser que toutes ces variétés ont été abandonnées au cours du temps parce qu'elles étaient peu savoureuses ou encore difficiles à cuisiner, ou à cultiver, ou encore faiblement nutritives. Il n'en est rien. Alors pourquoi ?
Un axe d'explication est apporté par l'ethnobotanique (Elle s'intéresse à tout ce qui concerne les relations entre les plantes et les humains).
« Dans l'ethnobotanique nous traitons la culture, la récolte et l'utilisation possible et effective des plantes, les cultes autour de celles-ci ainsi que le rôle des plantes dans la vision du monde et la langue. La relation de l'humain avec les plantes sans utilité économique comme les plantes d'ornement ou les herbes dites mauvaises dans les champs sont également des sujets faisant partie de l'ethnobotanique. »
Source : Gereon Janzing
Ainsi, la consommation des légumes est un aspect caractéristique d'une culture dans un lieu donné à un moment déterminé de son histoire. Au Moyen-Âge en Europe non méditerranéenne par exemple, les légumes sont considérés comme proches de la terre et les classes supérieures préfèrent les fruits (plus « élevés »). Le résultat est que les recettes à base de légumes sont relativement rares à l'époque.
Le fait particulier de notre époque est économique et secondairement culturel. Industrialisation et production de masse impliquent : coûts de production minimaux, rendements maximaux, modernisation et surtout standardisation Toutes les espèces ne se prêtent pas à cette démarche, et variété et standardisation sont antinomiques.
Pourtant, la diversité possède en sa faveur non seulement des

olivier.richaud.free.fr/olus

D: olivier richaud

M: olivier.richaud.montpellier@wanadoo.fr

Latte - Un mondo di benessere

il latte

La guida completa per conoscere il latte

un mondo di benessere

Chi è Aprolat
Eventi
Ufficio stampa
Link utili

Conoscere il latte
Il latte, che cos'è e perché fa bene ad ogni età

I derivati del latte
Yogurt Formaggio Burro

Il latte in cucina
Ricette e golosità

Domande & Risposte
Tutti i quesiti più comuni

Area didattica

Potrete consultare ed eventualmente scaricare una lezione di educazione alimentare, completa di tutti i materiali per presentarla.

Sito promosso da:
aprolat
Associazione Produttori Latte Campania Molise

Programma realizzato con il contributo della Comunità Europea e dell'Italia

© 2003 Aprolat | Crediti | Webmaster | Versione accessibile solo testo

Latte - Un mondo di benessere

il latte

Homepage > I derivati del latte

Conoscere il latte
Il latte in cucina
Domande & Risposte

I derivati del latte

Chi è Aprolat
Eventi
Ufficio stampa
Link utili

Il latte si trasforma, pur mantenendo le caratteristiche che lo distinguono: questo prodotto straordinario offre una serie di "variazioni su tema", che rispondono alle esigenze più diverse e mantiene le sue doti di genuinità, di elevata qualità, rappresentando una fonte di elementi nutritivi essenziali.
Il mondo del latte è ricco di proposte, tra le quali è facile, e gradevole fare di volta in volta le proprie scelte.
Il latte e i suoi derivati sono un alimento ideale sia sul piano della salute, sia su quello, non meno importante, di un'alimentazione gustosa e variata.

Yogurt
Formaggi
Burro

© 2003 Aprolat

www.lattebenessere.it
D: stefano dominici **C:** francesco crisafi
A: tr e associati **M:** s.dominici@tr-associati.it

TINE
TINE
OM TINE
NYHETER/PRESSE
PRODUKTENE
FORBRUKERSENTER
SØK
Spør TINE Forbrukersenter
Jobb og utdanning
Nye produkter
Nyheter
Årets Hulda
24. nov 2004
Det var Lise Finckenhagen (28) fra Oslo som gikk av med seieren som årets kvinnelige kokk - Årets Hulda 2004.
Norges mest populære ildsjel er kåret
17. nov 2004
Svein Spjelkavik fra Andøya ble "Folkets Favoritt 2004"
For melkeprodusenter
Biola
TineMelk Smak
Tid for Ost
Registrer deg for daglige påminnelser
matglede fra TINE
finn oppskrift
SØK
AVANSERT
OPPSKRIFTER
MATNYTTIG
MINE FAVORITTER
5 PÅ TOPP
MITT KJØLESKAP
dagens
Jarlsberglimpe
Matnyttig
Ostepaier
Jarlsberg er en populær ingrediens
Chevre frå Haukeli
Tips om Ost og Vin
gode vaner
Hvorfor trenger vi kalsium?Kalsium styrker bein og tenner, men har også andre viktige roller i kroppen. Melk og meieriprodukter er de viktigste kildene i norsk kosthold.
Sans
En god vane

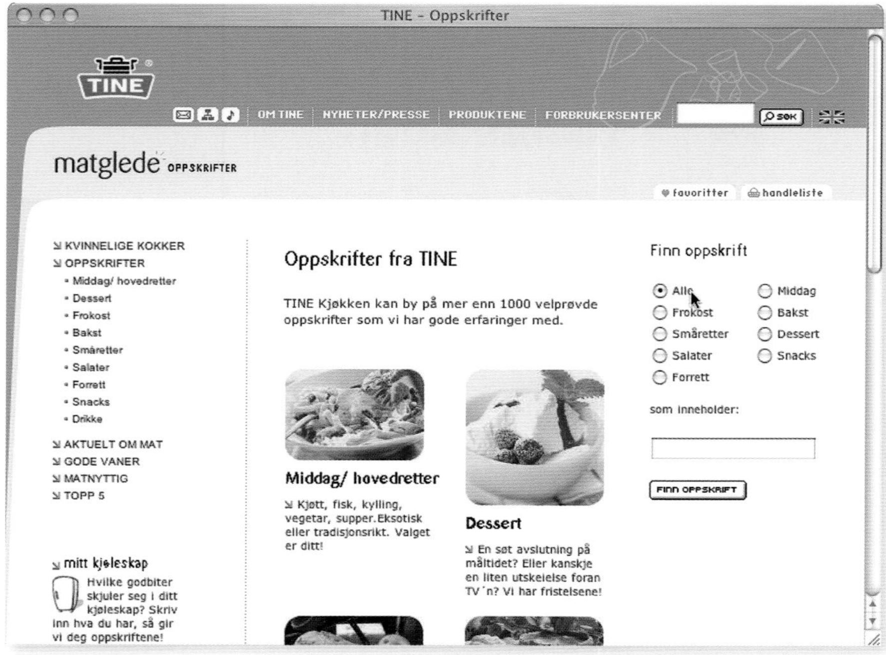
TINE - Oppskrifter
TINE
OM TINE
NYHETER/PRESSE
PRODUKTENE
FORBRUKERSENTER
SØK
matglede OPPSKRIFTER
favoritter
handleliste
KVINNELIGE KOKKER
OPPSKRIFTER
Middag/ hovedretter
Dessert
Frokost
Bakst
Småretter
Salater
Forrett
Snacks
Drikke
AKTUELT OM MAT
GODE VANER
MATNYTTIG
TOPP 5
mitt kjøleskap
Hvilke godbiter skjuler seg i ditt kjøleskap? Skriv inn hva du har, så gir vi deg oppskriftene!
Oppskrifter fra TINE
TINE Kjøkken kan by på mer enn 1000 velprøvde oppskrifter som vi har gode erfaringer med.
Middag/ hovedretter
Kjøtt, fisk, kylling, vegetar, supper.Eksotisk eller tradisjonsrikt. Valget er ditt!
Dessert
En søt avslutning på måltidet? Eller kanskje en liten utskeielse foran TV´n? Vi har fristelsene!
Finn oppskrift
Alle
Middag
Frokost
Bakst
Småretter
Dessert
Salater
Snacks
Forrett
som inneholder:
FINN OPPSKRIFT

www.tine.no
D: eiliv gunnleiksrund **C:** rune sandnes
A: klapp media **M:** havardg@klapp.no

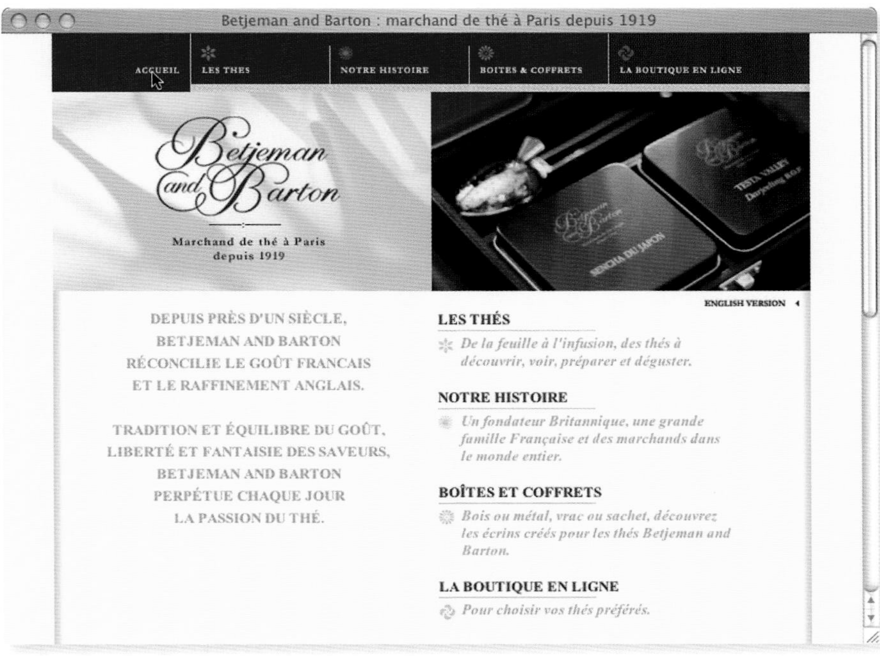
Betjeman and Barton : marchand de thé à Paris depuis 1919
ACCUEIL
LES THES
NOTRE HISTOIRE
BOITES & COFFRETS
LA BOUTIQUE EN LIGNE
Betjeman and Barton
Marchand de thé à Paris
depuis 1919
ENGLISH VERSION
DEPUIS PRÈS D'UN SIÈCLE,
BETJEMAN AND BARTON
RÉCONCILIE LE GOÛT FRANCAIS
ET LE RAFFINEMENT ANGLAIS.
TRADITION ET ÉQUILIBRE DU GOÛT,
LIBERTÉ ET FANTAISIE DES SAVEURS,
BETJEMAN AND BARTON
PERPÉTUE CHAQUE JOUR
LA PASSION DU THÉ.
LES THÉS
De la feuille à l'infusion, des thés à découvrir, voir, préparer et déguster.
NOTRE HISTOIRE
Un fondateur Britannique, une grande famille Française et des marchands dans le monde entier.
BOÎTES ET COFFRETS
Bois ou métal, vrac ou sachet, découvrez les écrins créés pour les thés Betjeman and Barton.
LA BOUTIQUE EN LIGNE
Pour choisir vos thés préférés.

Betjeman and Barton, les thés
ACCUEIL
LES THES
NOTRE HISTOIRE
BOITES & COFFRETS
LA BOUTIQUE EN LIGNE
Betjeman and Barton
Marchand de thé à Paris
depuis 1919
LA CARTE DES THÉS
UN THÉ A VOTRE GOÛT
LA MOSAÏQUE DES THÉS
PRÉPARER LE THÉ
Les Thés
LES PLUS BEAUX THÉS DU MONDE N'ONT AUCUNE VALEUR S'ILS NE SONT PAS A VOTRE GOÛT. NOTRE MÉTIER : TROUVER PARMI LES PLUS GRANDS JARDINS LE THÉ QUI VOUS EST DESTINÉ.
Une mesure de thé

www.betjemanandbarton.com
D: laurent chomette **C:** eric sokovision
M: eric.marillet@sokovision.com

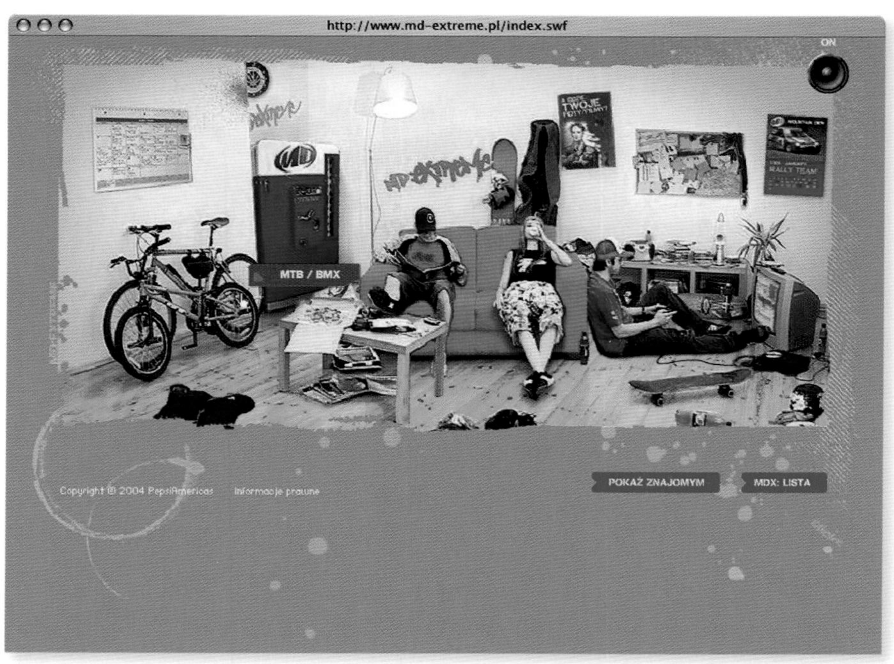
http://www.md-extreme.pl/index.swf
MTB / BMX
POKAŻ ZNAJOMYM
MDX: LISTA

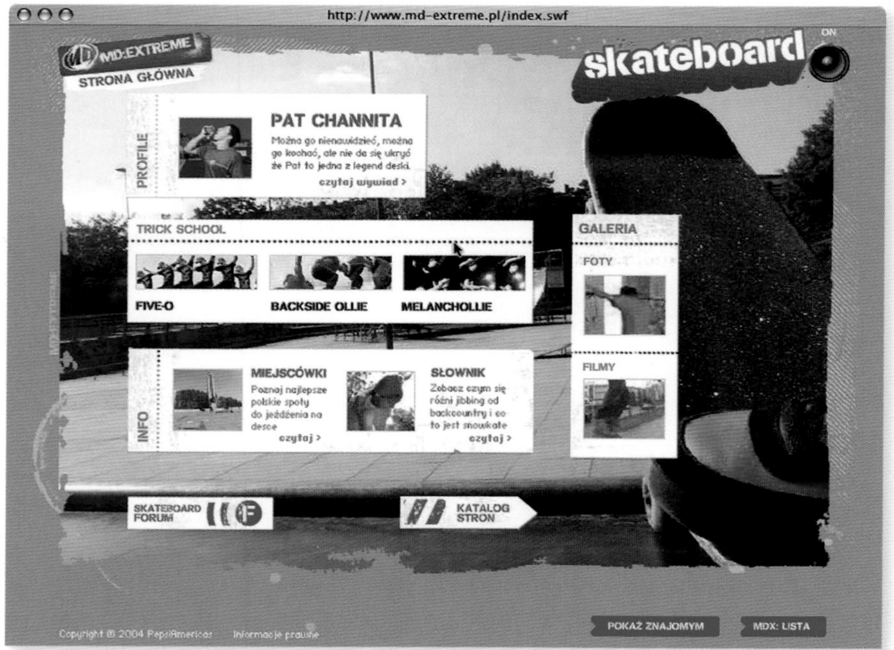
http://www.md-extreme.pl/index.swf
MD-EXTREME
STRONA GŁÓWNA
skateboard
PROFILE
PAT CHANNITA
Można go nienawidzieć, można go kochać, ale nie da się ukryć że Pat to jedna z legend deski.
czytaj wywiad >
TRICK SCHOOL
FIVE-O
BACKSIDE OLLIE
MELANCHOLLIE
GALERIA
FOTY
FILMY
INFO
MIEJSCÓWKI
Poznaj najlepsze polskie spoty do jeżdżenia na desce
czytaj >
SŁOWNIK
Zobacz czym się różni jibbing od backcountry i co to jest snowskate
czytaj >
SKATEBOARD FORUM
KATALOG STRON
POKAŻ ZNAJOMYM
MDX: LISTA

www.md-extreme.pl
D: bartek golebiowski **C:** adam nieszporek
A: click5 **M:** info@click5.pl

Yugamama
食得飯喇!
YUGAMAMA
虞家媽媽
FOOD WITH FRESH IDEAS

Yugamama
Breakfast Menu
玉桂丹麥甜包
Cinnamon Danish
藍莓鬆餅
Blueberry Muffin
意式雞蛋火腿三文治
Sandwiches with egg and ham
貝太必高
Bagel
返回
後面仲有

www.yugamama.com
D: henry chu
A: pill & pillow **M:** curious@pillandpillow.com

MENODICIOTTO GELATI – Chi siamo

CHI SIAMO

I NOSTRI PRODOTTI

FRANCHISING

NEWS E CURIOSITA'

PER COMUNICARE CON NOI

La Menodiciotto nasce a Torino nei primi anni ottanta come gelateria al minuto.
In breve tempo grazie al riscontro dell'affezionata clientela abbiamo iniziato a distribuire il nostro prodotto a bar e ristoranti che ne apprezzavano la qualità e la particolarità.
Tuttora produciamo gelati e sorbetti artigionali, utilizzando solo le migliori materie prime fresche, quali il latte, la panna, le uova, la frutta selezionata secondo le stagioni, reperendole nei migliori luoghi di origine e produzione. Garantiamo così sapori autentici che sono frutto di equilibrate ed armoniche miscelazioni fatte per ottenere un vero nettare di gelato.

MENODICIOTTO di Grassi Luca e Gallino Stefano & C. s.n.c.
Via Santagata, 50 - 10156 TORINO
Tel. (+39) 011.223.78.25 (r.a.) - Fax (+39) 011.223.92.79
e-mail: gelati@meno18.com

MENODICIOTTO GELATI – Prodotti / Gelatempo

PRODOTTI / GELATEMPO

GELATERIE E CREMERIE TOP

CHI SIAMO

I NOSTRI PRODOTTI

FRANCHISING

NEWS E CURIOSITA'

PER COMUNICARE CON NOI

GELATEMPO: PRODOTTO SEMILAVORATO PER GELATERIE

L'estrema semplicità e velocità d'uso, unita con l'ALTA QUALITA' e VARIETA' DI GUSTI, consente al gelatiere di RISPARMIARE MOLTO TEMPO, che potrà dedicare alla cura del prodotto.
Per ottenere la qualità, si utilizzano oltre che le materie prime selezionate, anche attrezzature avanzate come l'OMOGENEIZZATORE e l'IMPIANTO DI PASTORIZZAZIONE FLASH.
Infine, dopo il confezionamento in una BOTTIGLIA DA 3 KG, viene CONGELATO in un apposito tunnel, in modo che possa mantenere invariate le sue caratteristiche nel tempo.

GELATEMPO

Se vuoi conoscere tutte le caratteristiche tecniche, scarica la DOCUMENTAZIONE TECNICA in formato PDF qui a destra:

vai alla pagina dei gusti

www.meno18.com
D: paolo cagliero P: meno18
M: wbn@tiscali.it

http://www.birken-hof.de/
Birkenhof
Kontakt Wir über uns Links Impressum
Molkereiprodukte
Vorzugsmilch
Lieferservice
Hofladen
Highlights
Die Apfelsaison beginnt mit Elstar:
Ausserdem noch frische Zwiebeln aus der Pfalz!
mehr >>
Aktuell!
Wir haben unser Schulmilch Angebot erweitert ...
mehr >>
Molkereiprodukte und Vorzugsmilch vom Birkenhof
Das Hoffest 2004!
Endlich ist es wieder so weit! Das nächste Hoffest auf dem Birkenhof am 1. Mai 2004 steht vor der Tür!
mehr >>

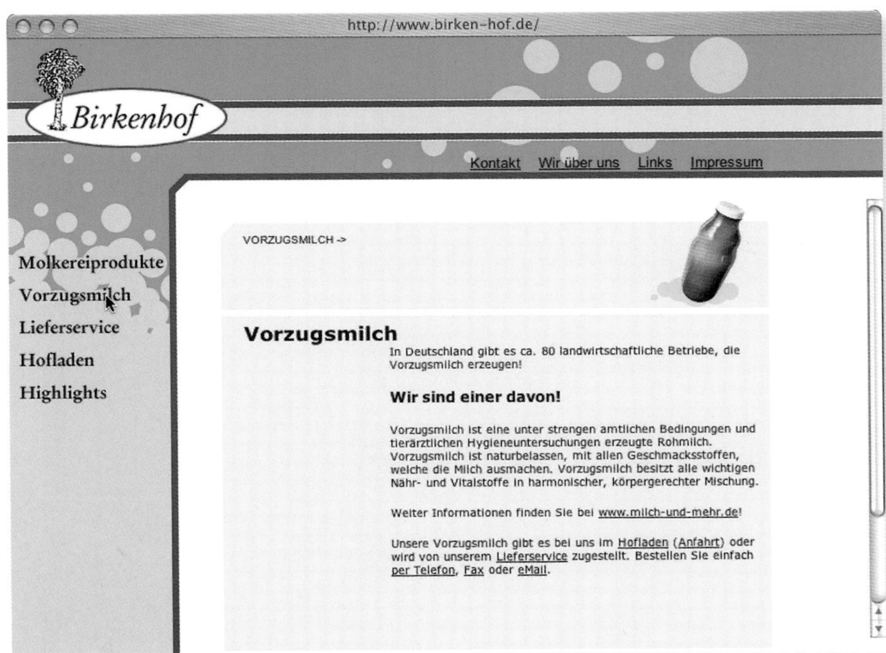
http://www.birken-hof.de/
Birkenhof
Kontakt Wir über uns Links Impressum
Molkereiprodukte
Vorzugsmilch
Lieferservice
Hofladen
Highlights
VORZUGSMILCH ->
Vorzugsmilch
In Deutschland gibt es ca. 80 landwirtschaftliche Betriebe, die Vorzugsmilch erzeugen!
Wir sind einer davon!
Vorzugsmilch ist eine unter strengen amtlichen Bedingungen und tierärztlichen Hygieneuntersuchungen erzeugte Rohmilch. Vorzugsmilch ist naturbelassen, mit allen Geschmacksstoffen, welche die Milch ausmachen. Vorzugsmilch besitzt alle wichtigen Nähr- und Vitalstoffe in harmonischer, körpergerechter Mischung.
Weiter Informationen finden Sie bei www.milch-und-mehr.de!
Unsere Vorzugsmilch gibt es bei uns im Hofladen (Anfahrt) oder wird von unserem Lieferservice zugestellt. Bestellen Sie einfach per Telefon, Fax oder eMail.

www.birken-hof.de
D: andreas schulz **P:** birkenhof bruchköbel
A: analog.eins **M:** andreas.schulz@analogeins.de

Succhi Yoga - Yoga Bar
Yoga
Yoga bar
OPEN
Con Smoo vai on air anche tu!
Il vellutato.
play Smoo
radio LatteMiele
© 2004 Conserve Italia Soc. Coop. a r.l. - Tutti i diritti riservati - Contatti - Credits

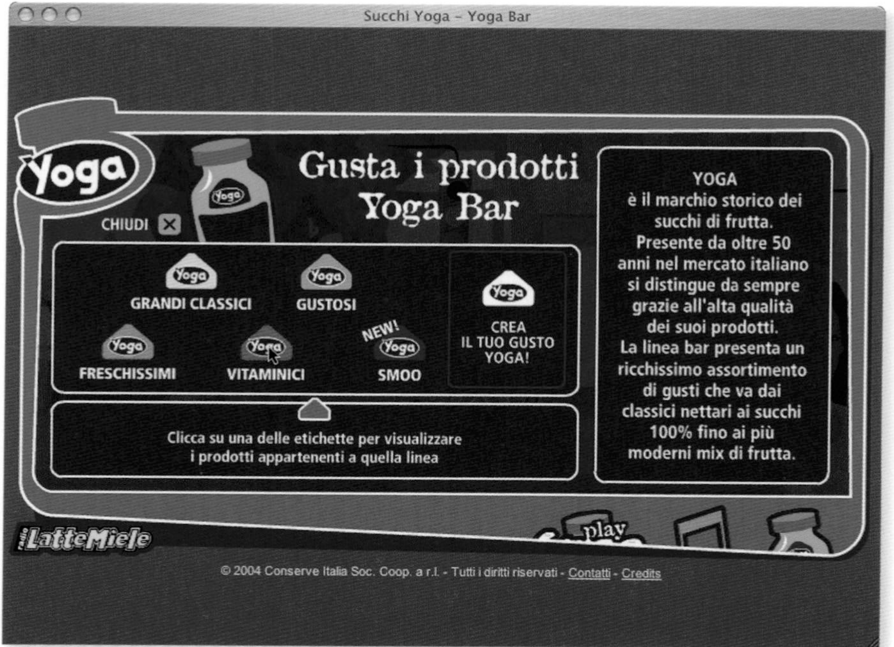
Succhi Yoga - Yoga Bar
Yoga
Gusta i prodotti Yoga Bar
CHIUDI
GRANDI CLASSICI
GUSTOSI
CREA IL TUO GUSTO YOGA!
FRESCHISSIMI
VITAMINICI
NEW! SMOO
Clicca su una delle etichette per visualizzare i prodotti appartenenti a quella linea
YOGA è il marchio storico dei succhi di frutta. Presente da oltre 50 anni nel mercato italiano si distingue da sempre grazie all'alta qualità dei suoi prodotti. La linea bar presenta un ricchissimo assortimento di gusti che va dai classici nettari ai succhi 100% fino ai più moderni mix di frutta.
play
radio LatteMiele
© 2004 Conserve Italia Soc. Coop. a r.l. - Tutti i diritti riservati - Contatti - Credits

www.succhiyoga.it
D: carlo rossi **C:** milo maneo **P:** kirio srl
M: pietro.lena@kirio.it

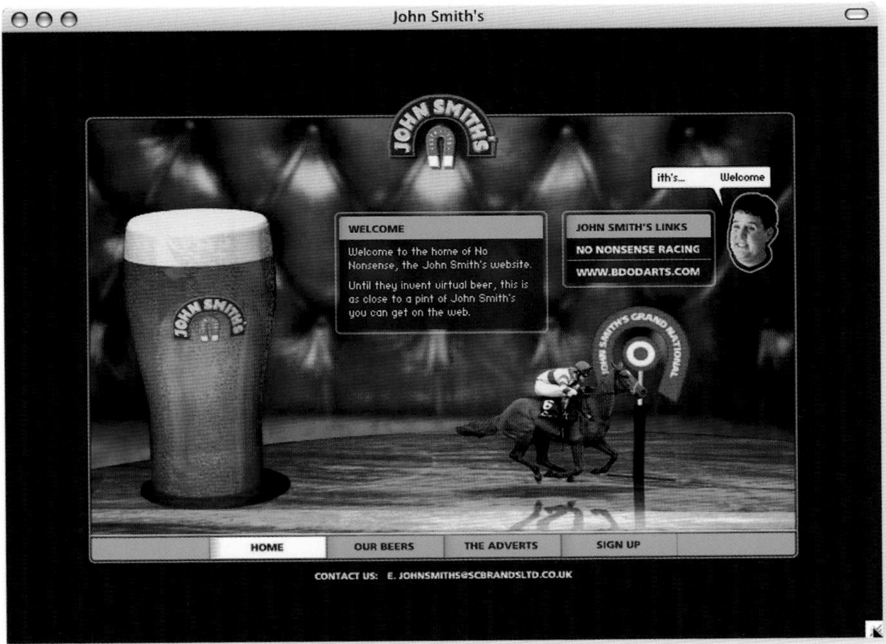
John Smith's
JOHN SMITH'S
ith's... Welcome
WELCOME
Welcome to the home of No Nonsense, the John Smith's website.
Until they invent virtual beer, this is as close to a pint of John Smith's you can get on the web.
JOHN SMITH'S LINKS
NO NONSENSE RACING
WWW.BDODARTS.COM
JOHN SMITH'S GRAND NATIONAL
HOME
OUR BEERS
THE ADVERTS
SIGN UP
CONTACT US: E. JOHNSMITHS@SCBRANDSLTD.CO.UK

John Smith's
JOHN SMITH'S
PRODUCTS
EXTRA SMOOTH
EXTRA COLD
BITTER
CASK
MAGNET
CARRY OUT
MAG
MAGNET
DETAILS
John Smith's Magnet is the Hear'Say of beer: full-bodied, initially sweet, but with a touch of bitterness.
HOME
OUR BEERS
THE ADVERTS
SIGN UP
CONTACT US: E. JOHNSMITHS@SCBRANDSLTD.CO.UK

www.johnsmiths.co.uk
D: chunk
M: donnie@chunk.co.uk

* * * KARLOVACKA PIVOVARA * * *
Karlovačka pivovara
Članica Heineken grupe
KONTAKT GLAZBA IMPRESUM
MEĐU SVOJIMA
POGLEDAJTE NOVI SPOT
JAČANJE POZICIJE NA TRŽIŠTU U 2004.
Ukupni udio u proizvodnji piva narastao u 2004. na 25,4 posto
OPŠIRNIJE
NOVI TV SPOT ZA KARLOVAČKO
Novi TV spot, Nostalgija, od danas počinje s emitiranjem
OPŠIRNIJE
POGLEDAJTE NOVI TV SPOT "NOSTALGIJA" >>>
NOVI RALLY WEB - NAGRADNA IGRA "SIGURNO DO CILJA">>>
OKRENI Karlovačko I OTVORI
O NAMA NOVOSTI POVIJEST PROIZVODI DISTRIBUCIJA IZVOZ KVALITETA KONTAKTI

* * * KARLOVACKA PIVOVARA * * *
Karlovačka pivovara
Članica Heineken grupe
KONTAKT GLAZBA IMPRESUM
NAŠI PROIZVODI: PIVO
Proizvodni asortiman Karlovačke pivovare čine Karlovačko svijetlo pivo (najpoznatiji i najprodavaniji proizvod Karlovačke pivovare), Rally bezalkoholno pivo (prvo hrvatsko pivo sa 0,0% alkohola), izrazito aromatično Karlovačko crno pivo te sezonsko Karlovačko zimsko pivo.
Kliknite na čep od svakog pojedinog branda kako bi se upoznali sa svim pakiranjima...
Karlovačko
Karlovačko CRNO
RALLY
Karlovačko ZIMSKO
O NAMA NOVOSTI POVIJEST PROIZVODI DISTRIBUCIJA IZVOZ KVALITETA KONTAKTI POČETNA

www.karlovacko.hr
D: boris bengez **C:** marjan burazer **P:** boris bengez
A: idea studio **M:** www.idea.hr

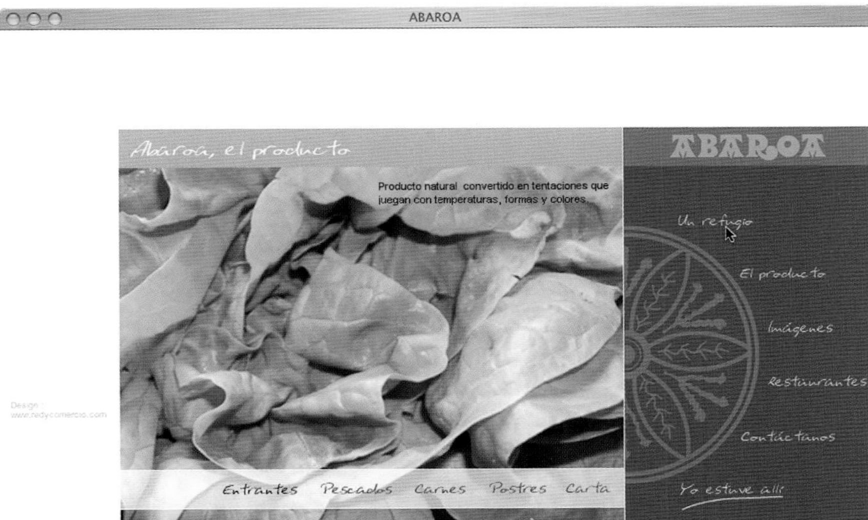
ABAROA
Abaroa, el producto
Producto natural convertido en tentaciones que juegan con temperaturas, formas y colores.
ABAROA
Un refugio
El producto
Imágenes
Restaurantes
Contáctanos
Yo estuve allí
Entrantes
Pescados
Carnes
Postres
Carta
Cocina Vasca
Euskera
English

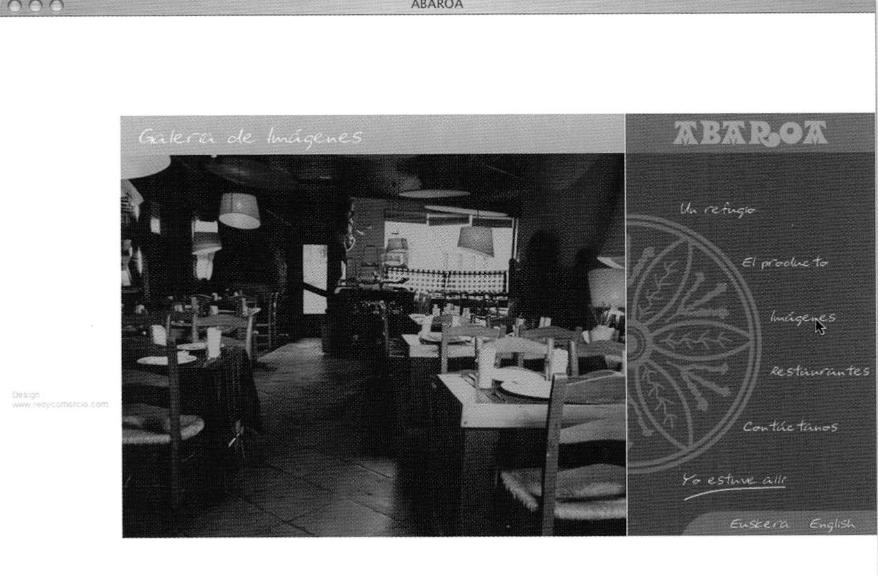
ABAROA
Galeria de Imágenes
ABAROA
Un refugio
El producto
Imágenes
Restaurantes
Contáctanos
Yo estuve allí
Euskera
English

www.abaroa.net
D: f.castañeda **C:** m. aguilera
A: red y comercio interactivos s.l. **M:** fcp@redycomercio.com

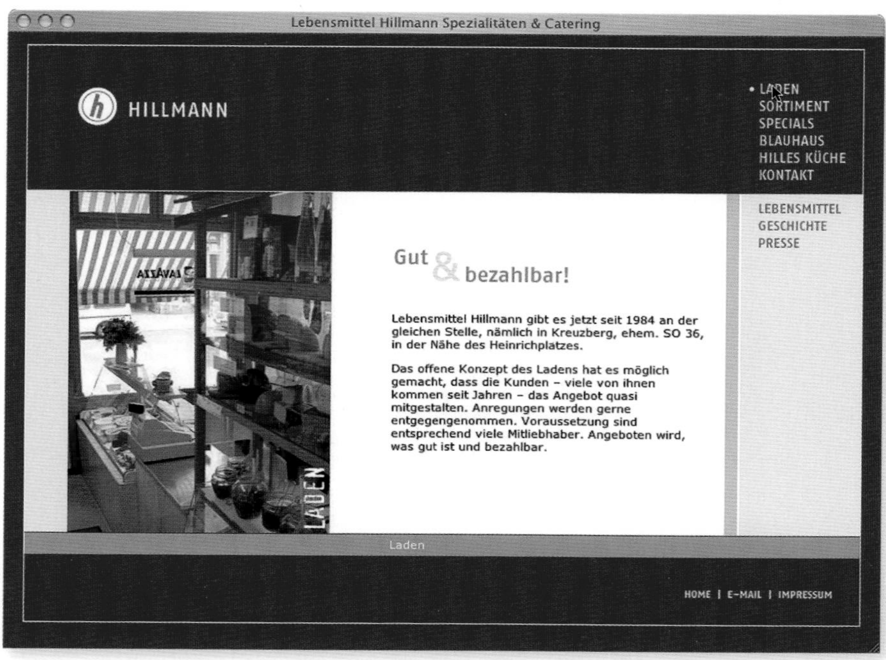
Lebensmittel Hillmann Spezialitäten & Catering
HILLMANN
• LADEN
SORTIMENT
SPECIALS
BLAUHAUS
HILLES KÜCHE
KONTAKT
LEBENSMITTEL
GESCHICHTE
PRESSE
Gut & bezahlbar!
Lebensmittel Hillmann gibt es jetzt seit 1984 an der gleichen Stelle, nämlich in Kreuzberg, ehem. SO 36, in der Nähe des Heinrichplatzes.
Das offene Konzept des Ladens hat es möglich gemacht, dass die Kunden – viele von ihnen kommen seit Jahren – das Angebot quasi mitgestalten. Anregungen werden gerne entgegengenommen. Voraussetzung sind entsprechend viele Mitliebhaber. Angeboten wird, was gut ist und bezahlbar.
LADEN
Laden
HOME | E-MAIL | IMPRESSUM

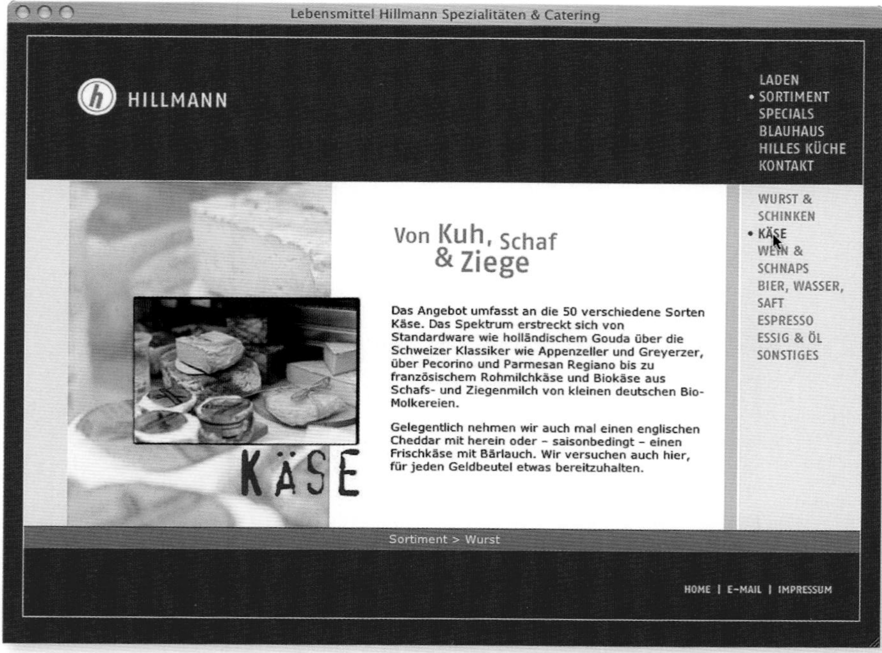
Lebensmittel Hillmann Spezialitäten & Catering
HILLMANN
LADEN
• SORTIMENT
SPECIALS
BLAUHAUS
HILLES KÜCHE
KONTAKT
WURST & SCHINKEN
• KÄSE
WEIN & SCHNAPS
BIER, WASSER, SAFT
ESPRESSO
ESSIG & ÖL
SONSTIGES
Von Kuh, Schaf & Ziege
Das Angebot umfasst an die 50 verschiedene Sorten Käse. Das Spektrum erstreckt sich von Standardware wie holländischem Gouda über die Schweizer Klassiker wie Appenzeller und Greyerzer, über Pecorino und Parmesan Regiano bis zu französischem Rohmilchkäse und Biokäse aus Schafs- und Ziegenmilch von kleinen deutschen Bio-Molkereien.
Gelegentlich nehmen wir auch mal einen englischen Cheddar mit herein oder – saisonbedingt – einen Frischkäse mit Bärlauch. Wir versuchen auch hier, für jeden Geldbeutel etwas bereitzuhalten.
KÄSE
Sortiment > Wurst
HOME | E-MAIL | IMPRESSUM

lebensmittel-hillmann.de

D: christine kühn **C:** jürgen temming
M: christine.kuehn@snafu.de

..:: Forest Pub ::..
Forest Pub
restaurant
Johnnie Walker.
Home
La Carta
Clientes
Happy Day
Galeria de Fotos
Contáctenos
Downloads
Forest Pub
restaurant
CARTA / MENÚ
ELIJA LA MEJOR OPCION
PARA DISFRUTAR
Happy Hour
Para Comer
Para Picar
Drink House
Forest Pub's
HappyHour
de Lunes a Viernes
POWERED BY CRON

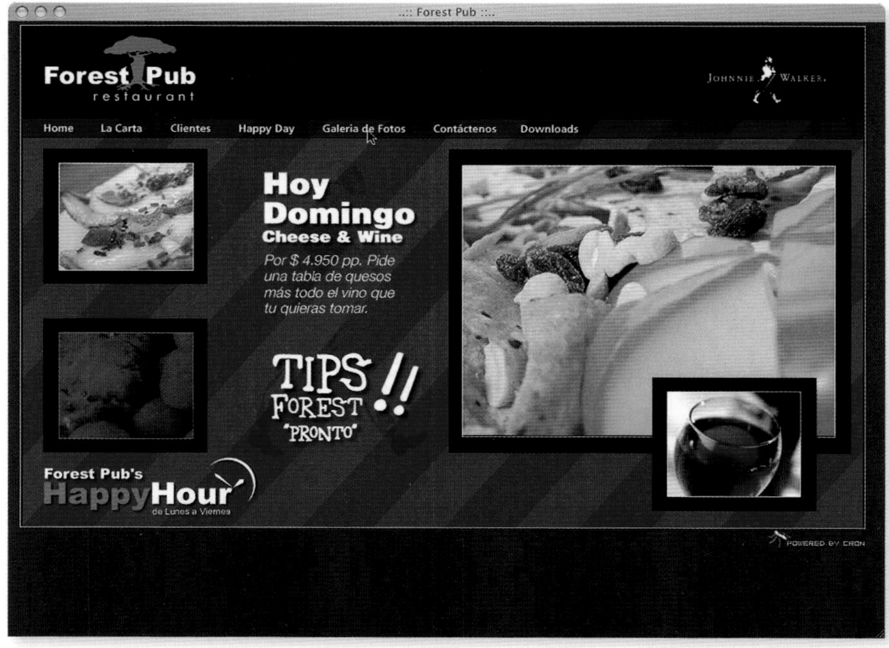
..:: Forest Pub ::..
Forest Pub
restaurant
Johnnie Walker.
Home
La Carta
Clientes
Happy Day
Galeria de Fotos
Contáctenos
Downloads
Hoy
Domingo
Cheese & Wine
Por $ 4.950 pp. Pide
una tabla de quesos
más todo el vino que
tu quieras tomar.
TIPS
FOREST !!
"PRONTO"
Forest Pub's
HappyHour
de Lunes a Viernes
POWERED BY CRON

www.forestpub.cl
D: alvaro caldera **C:** jordi nieto **P:** martin rodillo
A: cron **M:** acaldera@cron.cl

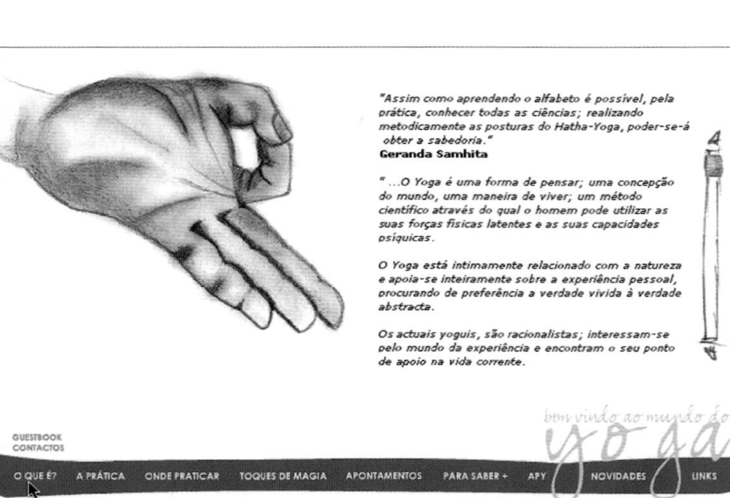

Bem Vindo ao Mundo do YOGA!
"Assim como aprendendo o alfabeto é possível, pela prática, conhecer todas as ciências; realizando metodicamente as posturas do Hatha-Yoga, poder-se-á obter a sabedoria."
Geranda Samhita
"...O Yoga é uma forma de pensar; uma concepção do mundo, uma maneira de viver; um método científico através do qual o homem pode utilizar as suas forças físicas latentes e as suas capacidades psíquicas.
O Yoga está intimamente relacionado com a natureza e apoia-se inteiramente sobre a experiência pessoal, procurando de preferência a verdade vivida à verdade abstracta.
Os actuais yoguis, são racionalistas; interessam-se pelo mundo da experiência e encontram o seu ponto de apoio na vida corrente.
GUESTBOOK
CONTACTOS
bem vindo ao mundo do yoga
O QUE É? A PRÁTICA ONDE PRATICAR TOQUES DE MAGIA APONTAMENTOS PARA SABER + APY NOVIDADES LINKS
Web-Design e Ilustrações JULIANA PINTO DA COSTA

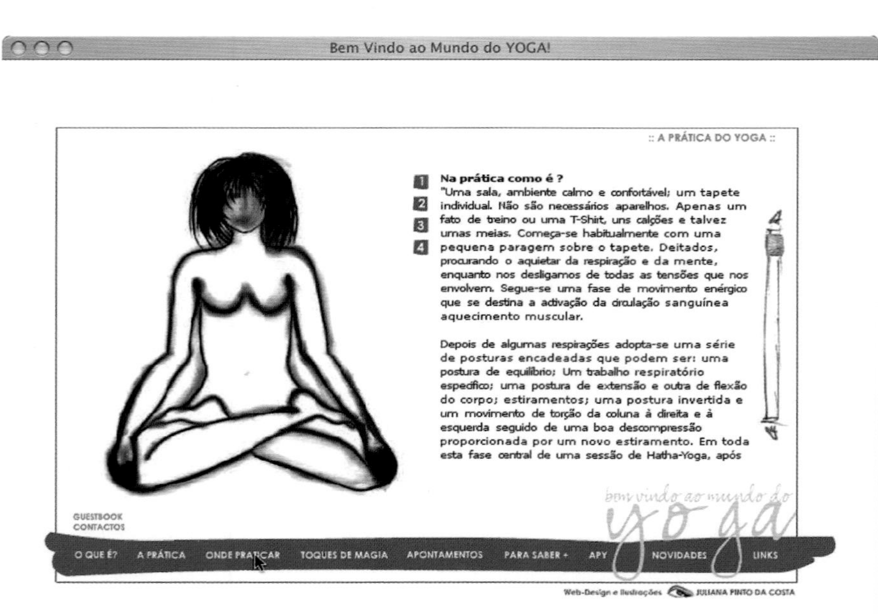

Bem Vindo ao Mundo do YOGA!
:: A PRÁTICA DO YOGA ::
1 2 3 4
Na prática como é ?
"Uma sala, ambiente calmo e confortável; um tapete individual. Não são necessários aparelhos. Apenas um fato de treino ou uma T-Shirt, uns calções e talvez umas meias. Começa-se habitualmente com uma pequena paragem sobre o tapete. Deitados, procurando o aquietar da respiração e da mente, enquanto nos desligamos de todas as tensões que nos envolvem. Segue-se uma fase de movimento enérgico que se destina a activação da circulação sanguínea aquecimento muscular.
Depois de algumas respirações adopta-se uma série de posturas encadeadas que podem ser: uma postura de equilíbrio; Um trabalho respiratório específico; uma postura de extensão e outra de flexão do corpo; estiramentos; uma postura invertida e um movimento de torção da coluna à direita e à esquerda seguido de uma boa descompressão proporcionada por um novo estiramento. Em toda esta fase central de uma sessão de Hatha-Yoga, após
GUESTBOOK
CONTACTOS
bem vindo ao mundo do yoga
O QUE É? A PRÁTICA ONDE PRATICAR TOQUES DE MAGIA APONTAMENTOS PARA SABER + APY NOVIDADES LINKS
Web-Design e Ilustrações JULIANA PINTO DA COSTA

www.yoga.loveslife.com

D: juliana pinto da costa
M: julianacosta@portugalmail.pt

Quality by Reborne - The Health Company

reBorne

THE HEALTH COMPANY

about us our products contact us

about us

Company Profile

Reborne's business is the brand development and marketing of health and lifestyle products.

Reborne only chooses to market products of the highest quality. Each product must be proven to be safe and effective and be backed by stringent scientific analysis.

In addition to scientific backing, each product is under strict controls on the production process to ensure quality and safety.

The company is committed to the highest standards of ethical behaviour

Quality by Reborne - The Health Company

Shi'Jäno
Shi'Jäno
Shi'Jäno

Shi'Jäno

about us our products contact us

Introduction
Scientific Data
Testimonials
Store Locations

Shi'Jäno™– a revolutionising result of Swedish research

What is Shi'Jäno™?
Shi'Jäno™ is a very effective method in reducing the appearance of wrinkles and other age associated changes of facial skin. **Shi'Jäno™** is based on a patent-protected composition which consists, for the most part, of three substances; Alpha-lipoic acid, Coenzyme Q10 and Acetyl-Carnitine. **Shi'Jäno™** has undergone extensive clinical tests under the supervision of Associate Professor Harry Beitner. The test plan and the information given to the test subjects were inspected and approved by the research committee at the Karolinska Hospital in Stockholm (one of the most renowned university hospitals in the world and from where the

www.rebornehealth.com
D: tay yi farn
A: w3eavers technologie **M:** yifarn@w3eavers.com

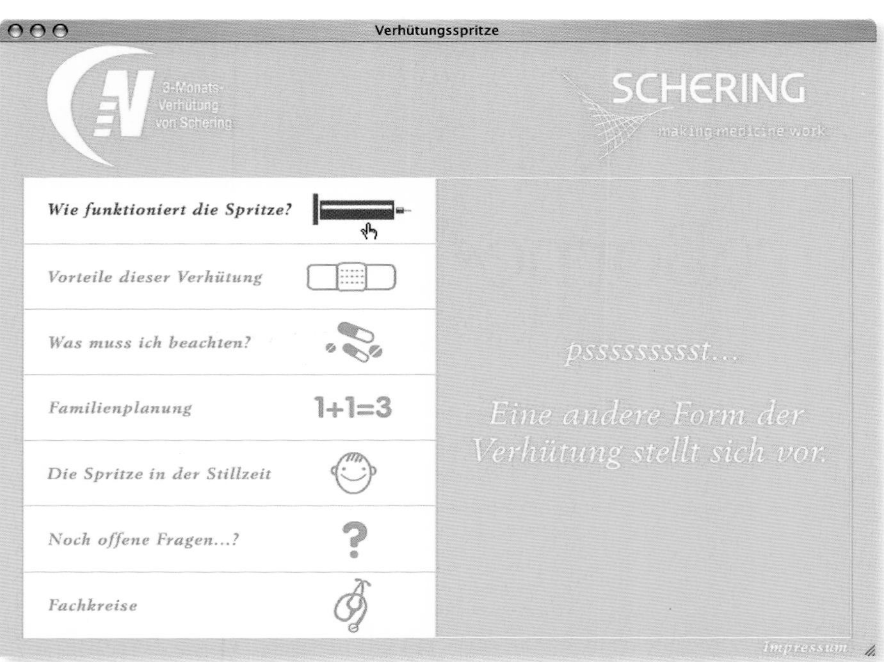
Verhütungsspritze
3-Monats-
Verhütung
von Schering
SCHERING
making medicine work
Wie funktioniert die Spritze?
Vorteile dieser Verhütung
Was muss ich beachten?
Familienplanung
1+1=3
Die Spritze in der Stillzeit
Noch offene Fragen...?
?
Fachkreise
psssssssst...
Eine andere Form der Verhütung stellt sich vor.
impressum

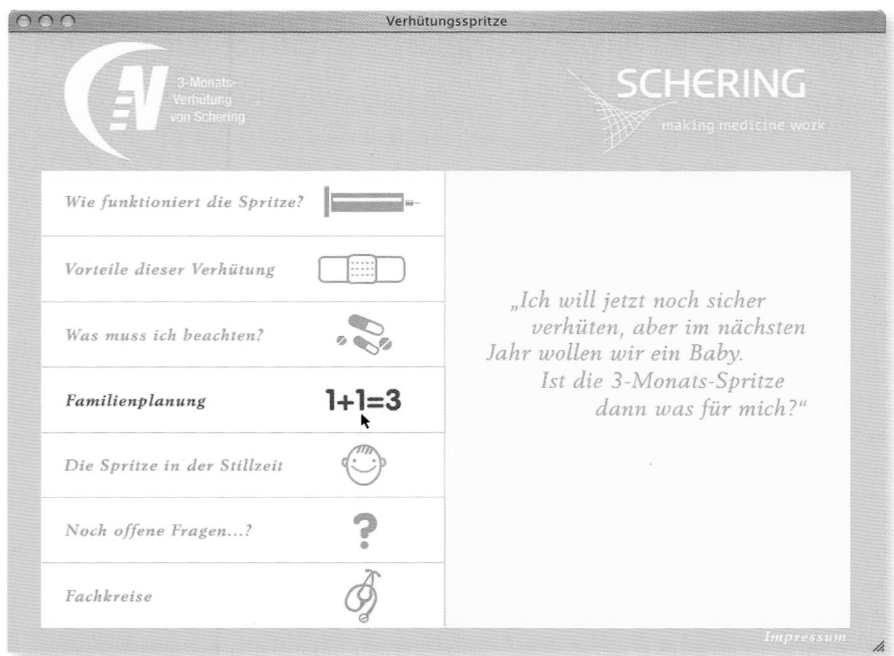
Verhütungsspritze
3-Monats-
Verhütung
von Schering
SCHERING
making medicine work
Wie funktioniert die Spritze?
Vorteile dieser Verhütung
Was muss ich beachten?
Familienplanung
1+1=3
Die Spritze in der Stillzeit
Noch offene Fragen...?
?
Fachkreise
„Ich will jetzt noch sicher verhüten, aber im nächsten Jahr wollen wir ein Baby. Ist die 3-Monats-Spritze dann was für mich?“
Impressum

www.noristerat.de
D: sebastian barz **C:** markus jahn
A: f3 multimedia **M:** barz@f-3.de

ABDA - Bundesvereinigung Deutscher Apothekerverbände
ABDA
- Bundesvereinigung Deutscher Apothekerverbände
herbst 04
HOME KONTAKT SITEMAP DATENSCHUTZ IMPRESSUM
LOGIN für...
Apotheker Kammern/Verbände
ÜBER DIE ABDA
ABDA POSITIONEN
PRESSE
PUBLIKATIONEN
SERVICES
THEMEN
++TOPTHEMA
Wechsel an der Spitze der Bundesapothekerkammer
Berlin (ABDA, 25. Nov. 2004) Die Delegierten der 17 Landesapothekerkammern haben heute in Berlin den neuen geschäftsführenden Vorstand der Bundesapothekerkammer (BAK) gewählt. Ab dem 1. Januar 2005 wird Magdalene Linz dem fünfköpfigen Gremium vorsitzen.
» Artikel lesen...
Arbeiten in der Apotheke – für Frauen besonders attraktiv
Berlin (ABDA, 19. Nov. 2004) Arbeitsplätze in Apotheken stehen bei Frauen hoch im Kurs. Bereits acht von zehn Beschäftigten sind weiblich. Dabei wird das Berufsfeld der pharmazeutisch-technischen Assistenten (PTA) mit 97 Prozent fast ausnahmslos von Frauen besetzt.
[19.11.2004] Artikel lesen
Erfolgsmodell Hausapotheke
Innerhalb kurzer Zeit hat sich das
hausapotheke
Hausapothekenkonzept bundesweit etabliert:
Berlin (ABDA, 29. Okt. 2004) Nach den ersten neun Monaten tragen bereits rund zwei Drittel der rund 21.400 deutschen Apotheken das Quali-tätssiegel „Hausapotheke".
[29.10.2004] Artikel lesen
Aktionswoche zum Weltdiabetestag erfolgreich abgeschlossen
Beratung zu den Themen Diabetes, gesunde Ernährung, Gewichtsreduktion bieten viele Apotheken das gesamte Jahr über an.
In unserer Bilddatenbank finden Sie 11 neue Fotos zum Thema Diabetes. Nutzen Sie die Suche oder klicken Sie auf die Box "Beratung". Außerdem wird noch bis zum 26. November 2004 auf Aponet.de täglich
Thema: Zuzahlungen
Online-Zuzahlungsrechner der ABDA
Zum 1. Januar 2004 wurde die Zuzahlung bei Medikamenten neu geregelt. Alle bisherigen Zuzahlungsbefreiungen haben zum Jahresbeginn ihre Gültigkeit verloren.
Artikel lesen
Neueste "Zahlen, Daten, Fakten"
Suche
» erweiterte Suche
ABDA Schnelleinstieg
Unser Informationsangebot für...
-Bitte wählen-
ABDA Terminkalender
16.01.2005 PHARMACON DAVOS 2005
16.06.2005 Tag der Apotheke 2005
22.-25.09.2005 EXPOPHARM in Köln
» weitere Termine
Newsletter-Abo
Hier E-Mail-Adresse eintragen:
Abonnieren » Abbestellen »
Newsletter-Archiv »
Diese Web-Seite gehört zu den 6.000 wichtigsten deutschen Internet-Adressen 2005
www.web-adressbuch.de
Gesundheitstipp aktuell
aponet.de
Zähne und Diabetes
(26.11.2004) Die Zahnpflege ist für Diabetiker besonders wichtig. Sie haben wegen der krankheitsbedingten ...
» weiter
Landesapothekerkammern
- Bitte wählen -

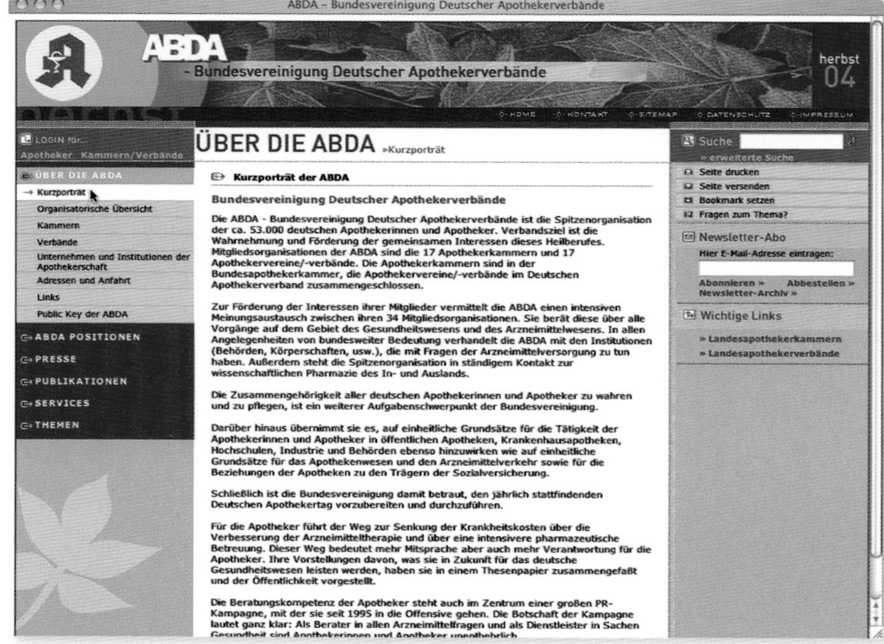
ABDA - Bundesvereinigung Deutscher Apothekerverbände
ABDA
- Bundesvereinigung Deutscher Apothekerverbände
herbst 04
HOME KONTAKT SITEMAP DATENSCHUTZ IMPRESSUM
LOGIN für...
Apotheker Kammern/Verbände
ÜBER DIE ABDA
Kurzporträt
Organisatorische Übersicht
Kammern
Verbände
Unternehmen und Institutionen der Apothekerschaft
Adressen und Anfahrt
Links
Public Key der ABDA
ABDA POSITIONEN
PRESSE
PUBLIKATIONEN
SERVICES
THEMEN
ÜBER DIE ABDA »Kurzporträt
Kurzporträt der ABDA
Bundesvereinigung Deutscher Apothekerverbände
Die ABDA - Bundesvereinigung Deutscher Apothekerverbände ist die Spitzenorganisation der ca. 53.000 deutschen Apothekerinnen und Apotheker. Verbandsziel ist die Wahrnehmung und Förderung der gemeinsamen Interessen dieses Heilberufes. Mitgliedsorganisationen der ABDA sind die 17 Apothekerkammern und 17 Apothekervereine/-verbände. Die Apothekerkammern sind in der Bundesapothekerkammer, die Apothekervereine/-verbände im Deutschen Apothekerverband zusammengeschlossen.
Zur Förderung der Interessen ihrer Mitglieder vermittelt die ABDA einen intensiven Meinungsaustausch zwischen ihren 34 Mitgliedsorganisationen. Sie berät diese über alle Vorgänge auf dem Gebiet des Gesundheitswesens und des Arzneimittelwesens. In allen Angelegenheiten von bundesweiter Bedeutung verhandelt die ABDA mit den Institutionen (Behörden, Körperschaften, usw.), die mit Fragen der Arzneimittelversorgung zu tun haben. Außerdem steht die Spitzenorganisation in ständigem Kontakt zur wissenschaftlichen Pharmazie des In- und Auslands.
Die Zusammengehörigkeit aller deutschen Apothekerinnen und Apotheker zu wahren und zu pflegen, ist ein weiterer Aufgabenschwerpunkt der Bundesvereinigung.
Darüber hinaus übernimmt sie es, auf einheitliche Grundsätze für die Tätigkeit der Apothekerinnen und Apotheker in öffentlichen Apotheken, Krankenhausapotheken, Hochschulen, Industrie und Behörden ebenso hinzuwirken wie auf einheitliche Grundsätze für das Apothekenwesen und den Arzneimittelverkehr sowie für die Beziehungen der Apotheken zu den Trägern der Sozialversicherung.
Schließlich ist die Bundesvereinigung damit betraut, den jährlich stattfindenden Deutschen Apothekertag vorzubereiten und durchzuführen.
Für die Apotheker führt der Weg zur Senkung der Krankheitskosten über die Verbesserung der Arzneimitteltherapie und über eine intensivere pharmazeutische Betreuung. Dieser Weg bedeutet mehr Mitsprache aber auch mehr Verantwortung für die Apotheker. Ihre Vorstellungen davon, was sie in Zukunft für das deutsche Gesundheitswesen leisten werden, haben sie in einem Thesenpapier zusammengefaßt und der Öffentlichkeit vorgestellt.
Die Beratungskompetenz der Apotheker steht auch im Zentrum einer großen PR-Kampagne, mit der sie seit 1995 in die Offensive gehen. Die Botschaft der Kampagne lautet ganz klar: Als Berater in allen Arzneimittelfragen und als Dienstleister in Sachen
Suche
» erweiterte Suche
Seite drucken
Seite versenden
Bookmark setzen
Fragen zum Thema?
Newsletter-Abo
Hier E-Mail-Adresse eintragen:
Abonnieren » Abbestellen »
Newsletter-Archiv »
Wichtige Links
» Landesapothekerkammern
» Landesapothekerverbände

www.abda.de
D: katrin brackmann **C:** jens conzel
A: oz design **M:** ka@oz-zone.de

:: o centro
Yoga
SAMKHYA
ASSOCIAÇÃO LUSA DE YOGA
CENTRO DE YOGA DE ALGÉS
"CONVIVA COM O MELHOR DE SI PRÓPRIO"
:: home
« o centro
:: horários
:: eventos
:: contactos
Centro de Yoga de Algés - Um novo espaço especialmente concebido e exclusivamente dedicado à prática do Yoga, a funcionar desde Novembro de 2003.
Venha desfrutar da serenidade e harmonia deste áshrama (Centro de Yoga).
[conheça os instrutores]
[localização do centro]

:: Ásana
Máyúrásana
Chakrásana
Vrshchikásana

www.centrosamtosha.com
D: paula melâneo
M: apmelaneo@yahoo.com

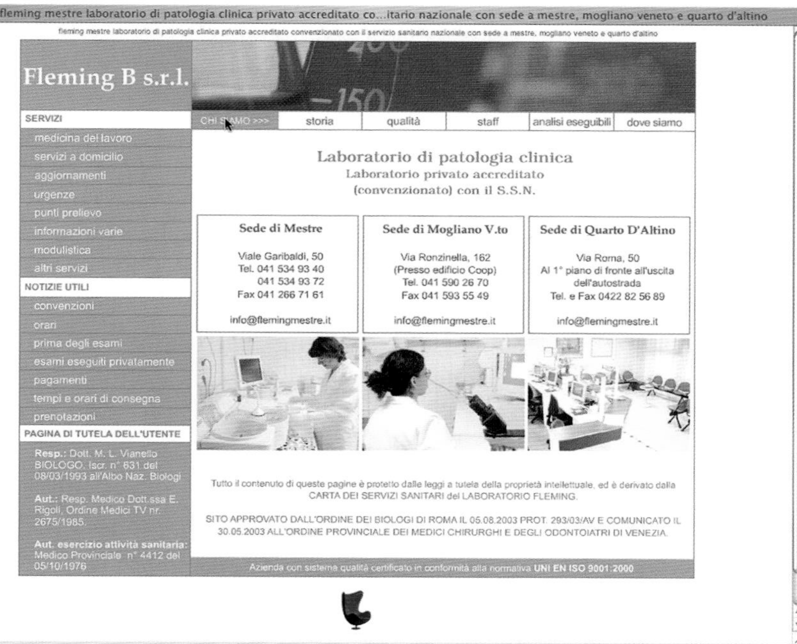
fleming mestre laboratorio di patologia clinica privato accreditato co...itario nazionale con sede a mestre, mogliano veneto e quarto d'altino
Fleming B s.r.l.
SERVIZI
medicina del lavoro
servizi a domicilio
aggiornamenti
urgenze
punti prelievo
informazioni varie
modulistica
altri servizi
NOTIZIE UTILI
convenzioni
orari
prima degli esami
esami eseguiti privatamente
pagamenti
tempi e orari di consegna
prenotazioni
PAGINA DI TUTELA DELL'UTENTE
Resp.: Dott. M. L. Vianello BIOLOGO, Iscr. n° 631 del 08/03/1993 all'Albo Naz. Biologi
Aut.: Resp. Medico Dott.ssa E. Rigoli, Ordine Medici TV nr. 2675/1985
Aut. esercizio attività sanitaria: Medico Provinciale n° 4412 del 05/10/1976
CHI SIAMO >>>
storia
qualità
staff
analisi eseguibili
dove siamo
Laboratorio di patologia clinica
Laboratorio privato accreditato
(convenzionato) con il S.S.N.
Sede di Mestre
Viale Garibaldi, 50
Tel. 041 534 93 40
041 534 93 72
Fax 041 266 71 61
info@flemingmestre.it
Sede di Mogliano V.to
Via Ronzinella, 162
(Presso edificio Coop)
Tel. 041 590 26 70
Fax 041 593 55 49
info@flemingmestre.it
Sede di Quarto D'Altino
Via Roma, 50
Al 1° piano di fronte all'uscita dell'autostrada
Tel. e Fax 0422 82 56 89
info@flemingmestre.it
Tutto il contenuto di queste pagine è protetto dalle leggi a tutela della proprietà intellettuale, ed è derivato dalla CARTA DEI SERVIZI SANITARI del LABORATORIO FLEMING.
SITO APPROVATO DALL'ORDINE DEI BIOLOGI DI ROMA IL 05.08.2003 PROT. 293/03/AV E COMUNICATO IL 30.05.2003 ALL'ORDINE PROVINCIALE DEI MEDICI CHIRURGHI E DEGLI ODONTOIATRI DI VENEZIA.
Azienda con sistema qualità certificato in conformità alla normativa UNI EN ISO 9001:2000

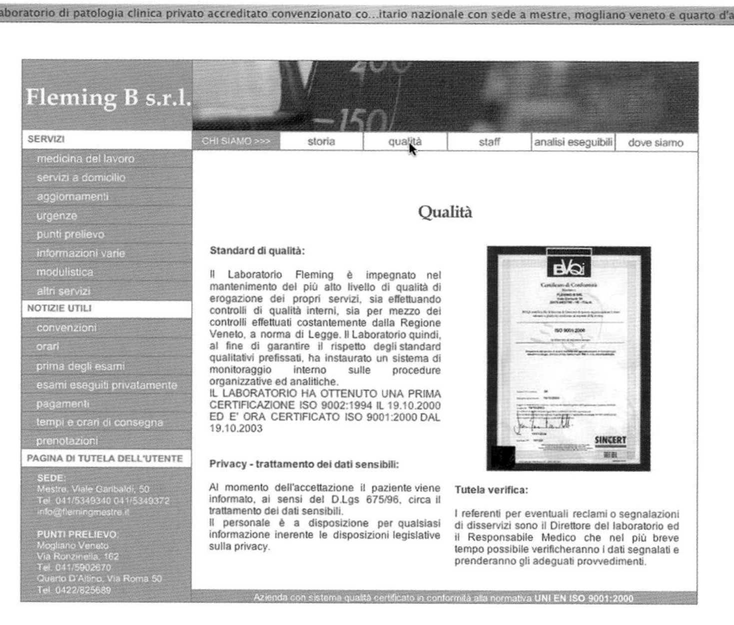
laboratorio di patologia clinica privato accreditato convenzionato co...itario nazionale con sede a mestre, mogliano veneto e quarto d'altino
Fleming B s.r.l.
SERVIZI
medicina del lavoro
servizi a domicilio
aggiornamenti
urgenze
punti prelievo
informazioni varie
modulistica
altri servizi
NOTIZIE UTILI
convenzioni
orari
prima degli esami
esami eseguiti privatamente
pagamenti
tempi e orari di consegna
prenotazioni
PAGINA DI TUTELA DELL'UTENTE
SEDE:
Mestre, Viale Garibaldi, 50
Tel. 041/5349340 041/5349372
info@flemingmestre.it
PUNTI PRELIEVO:
Mogliano Veneto
Via Ronzinella, 162
Tel. 041/5902670
Quarto D'Altino, Via Roma 50
Tel. 0422/825689
CHI SIAMO >>>
storia
qualità
staff
analisi eseguibili
dove siamo
Qualità
Standard di qualità:
Il Laboratorio Fleming è impegnato nel mantenimento del più alto livello di qualità di erogazione dei propri servizi, sia effettuando controlli di qualità interni, sia per mezzo dei controlli effettuati costantemente dalla Regione Veneto, a norma di Legge. Il Laboratorio quindi, al fine di garantire il rispetto degli standard qualitativi prefissati, ha instaurato un sistema di monitoraggio interno sulle procedure organizzative ed analitiche.
IL LABORATORIO HA OTTENUTO UNA PRIMA CERTIFICAZIONE ISO 9002:1994 IL 19.10.2000 ED E' ORA CERTIFICATO ISO 9001:2000 DAL 19.10.2003
Privacy - trattamento dei dati sensibili:
Al momento dell'accettazione il paziente viene informato, ai sensi del D.Lgs 675/96, circa il trattamento dei dati sensibili.
Il personale è a disposizione per qualsiasi informazione inerente le disposizioni legislative sulla privacy.
BVQi
SINCERT
Tutela verifica:
I referenti per eventuali reclami o segnalazioni di disservizi sono il Direttore del laboratorio ed il Responsabile Medico che nel più breve tempo possibile verificheranno i dati segnalati e prenderanno gli adeguati provvedimenti.
Azienda con sistema qualità certificato in conformità alla normativa UNI EN ISO 9001:2000

www.flemingmestre.it
D: beatrice susa
A: arte laguna **M:** beatrice@artelaguna.it

www.zahnarzt-biegert.de
zahnarztpraxis biegert
>>> Zahnarztpraxis Jörg Biegert
Denn Qualität darf kein Zufall sein
Deshalb haben wir in unserer Praxis ein Qualitäts– Management- System aufgebaut, das seit dem 5.8.2003 auch offiziell nach EN ISO 9001:2000 zertifiziert ist.
Sämtliche Praxisabläufe unterliegen damit einem international gültigen Standard, der regelmäßig von einer anerkannten Zertifizierungstelle überprüft wird.
praxis philosophie leistungsprofil kontakt so finden sie zu uns impressum
webdesign: www.grafikangelegenheiten.de

www.zahnarzt-biegert.de
zahnarztpraxis biegert
>>> Individualität durch Standardisierung
Auf den ersten Blick vielleicht ein Widerspruch.
Doch nur klare Regeln und für alle durchschaubare und verständliche Strukturen, lassen die Sicht frei auf das, was für uns immer im Mittelpunkt steht- den Menschen.
Ihm und seinen individuellen Bedürfnissen und Anforderungen fühlen wir uns verpflichtet. Mit modernster Technik, nach neuesten wissenschaftlichen Methoden und in einer angenehmen, menschlichen Atmosphäre, wollen wir seine Erwartungen erfüllen.
praxis philosophie leistungsprofil kontakt so finden sie zu uns impressum
webdesign: www.grafikangelegenheiten.de

www.zahnarzt-biegert.de
D: jens meier
A: meier grafikdesign **M:** j.meier@grafikangelegenheiten.de

Madison Healthcare
MADISON
HEALTHCARE
:: ABOUT US :: CLIENT / HOSPITAL :: HEALTHCARE PROFESSIONAL :: JOB SEARCH :: CONTACT US :: FAQ :: APPLY NOW :: NEWS :: HOME
APPLY NOW
JOB SEARCH
Welcome to Madison Healthcare
Where does your career take you next ....
As a leader in international healthcare staffing with more than 40 years of experience, Madison Healthcare offers comprehensive training & placement solutions to nursing professionals educated abroad. Through its customized and time-efficient migration program, Madison Healthcare assists each qualified, English speaking, healthcare professional in the process of credentialing, licensing, immigration, and selection of the most rewarding career in the United States.
To our valued healthcare providers – client facilities, we provide complete staffing solutions. We will tailor our recruitment, orientation, and the profile of the nurse recruits to fit your facility's needs.
:: ABOUT US :: CLIENT / HOSPITAL :: HEALTHCARE PROFESSIONAL :: JOB SEARCH :: CONTACT US :: FAQ :: APPLY NOW :: NEWS :: HOME

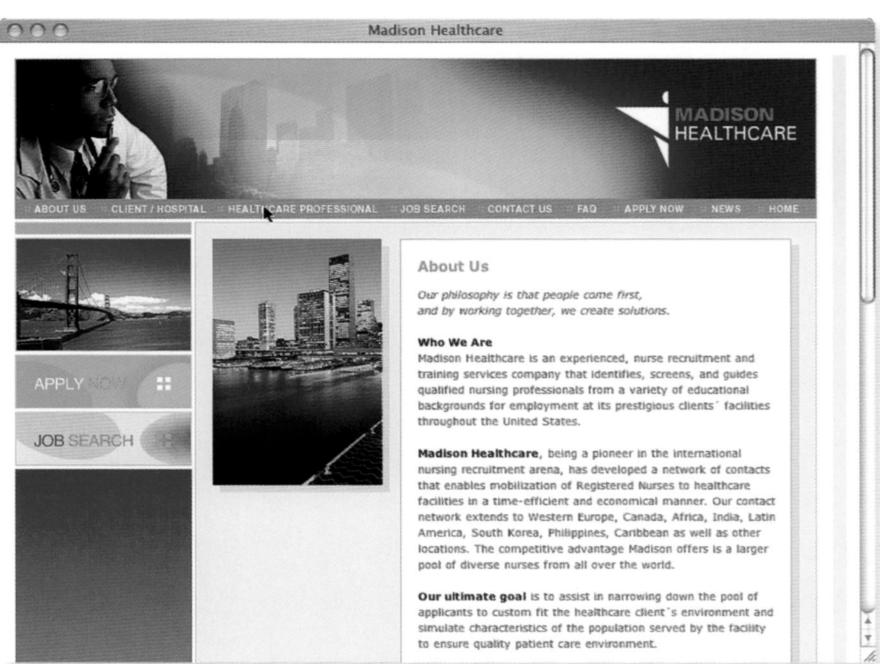
Madison Healthcare
MADISON
HEALTHCARE
:: ABOUT US :: CLIENT / HOSPITAL :: HEALTHCARE PROFESSIONAL :: JOB SEARCH :: CONTACT US :: FAQ :: APPLY NOW :: NEWS :: HOME
APPLY NOW
JOB SEARCH
About Us
Our philosophy is that people come first, and by working together, we create solutions.
Who We Are
Madison Healthcare is an experienced, nurse recruitment and training services company that identifies, screens, and guides qualified nursing professionals from a variety of educational backgrounds for employment at its prestigious clients' facilities throughout the United States.
Madison Healthcare, being a pioneer in the international nursing recruitment arena, has developed a network of contacts that enables mobilization of Registered Nurses to healthcare facilities in a time-efficient and economical manner. Our contact network extends to Western Europe, Canada, Africa, India, Latin America, South Korea, Philippines, Caribbean as well as other locations. The competitive advantage Madison offers is a larger pool of diverse nurses from all over the world.
Our ultimate goal is to assist in narrowing down the pool of applicants to custom fit the healthcare client's environment and simulate characteristics of the population served by the facility to ensure quality patient care environment.

www.madisonhealthcare.com
D: barbora kuklíková **C:** radek balkovsk
A: d-sign **M:** balkovsky@d-sign.cz

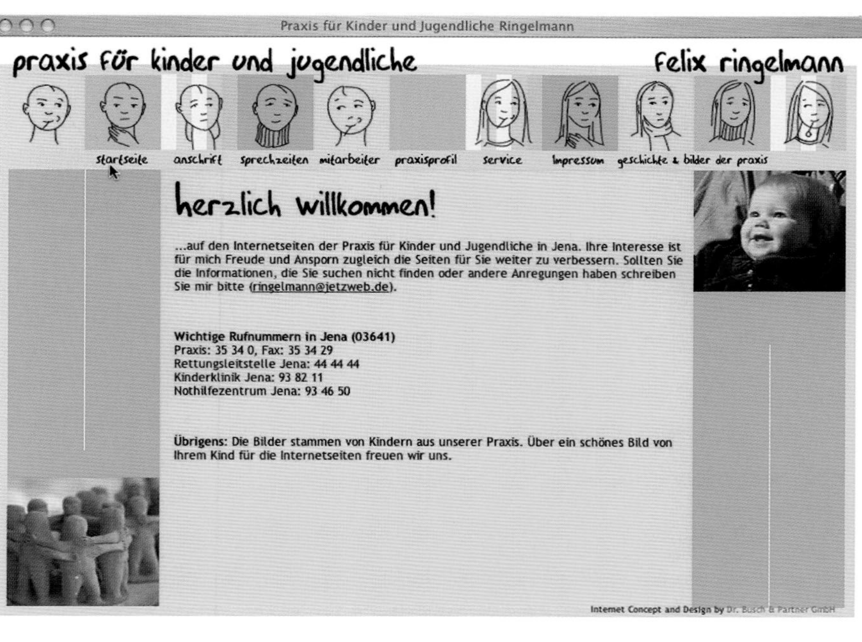
Praxis für Kinder und Jugendliche Ringelmann
praxis für kinder und jugendliche
felix ringelmann
startseite
anschrift
sprechzeiten
mitarbeiter
praxisprofil
service
impressum
geschichte & bilder der praxis
herzlich willkommen!
...auf den Internetseiten der Praxis für Kinder und Jugendliche in Jena. Ihre Interesse ist für mich Freude und Ansporn zugleich die Seiten für Sie weiter zu verbessern. Sollten Sie die Informationen, die Sie suchen nicht finden oder andere Anregungen haben schreiben Sie mir bitte (ringelmann@jetzweb.de).
Wichtige Rufnummern in Jena (03641)
Praxis: 35 34 0, Fax: 35 34 29
Rettungsleitstelle Jena: 44 44 44
Kinderklinik Jena: 93 82 11
Nothilfezentrum Jena: 93 46 50
Übrigens: Die Bilder stammen von Kindern aus unserer Praxis. Über ein schönes Bild von Ihrem Kind für die Internetseiten freuen wir uns.
Internet Concept and Design by Dr. Busch & Partner GmbH

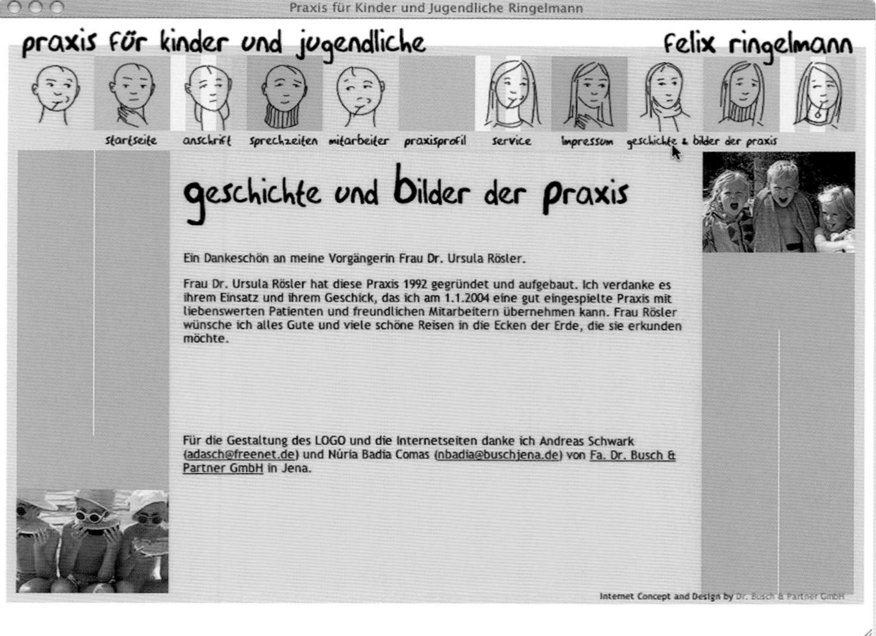
Praxis für Kinder und Jugendliche Ringelmann
praxis für kinder und jugendliche
felix ringelmann
startseite
anschrift
sprechzeiten
mitarbeiter
praxisprofil
service
impressum
geschichte & bilder der praxis
geschichte und bilder der praxis
Ein Dankeschön an meine Vorgängerin Frau Dr. Ursula Rösler.
Frau Dr. Ursula Rösler hat diese Praxis 1992 gegründet und aufgebaut. Ich verdanke es ihrem Einsatz und ihrem Geschick, das ich am 1.1.2004 eine gut eingespielte Praxis mit liebenswerten Patienten und freundlichen Mitarbeitern übernehmen kann. Frau Rösler wünsche ich alles Gute und viele schöne Reisen in die Ecken der Erde, die sie erkunden möchte.
Für die Gestaltung des LOGO und die Internetseiten danke ich Andreas Schwark (adasch@freenet.de) und Núria Badia Comas (nbadia@buschjena.de) von Fa. Dr. Busch & Partner GmbH in Jena.
Internet Concept and Design by Dr. Busch & Partner GmbH

www.ringelmann.de
D: núria badia comas **C:** robert häber
A: 3kon **M:** nbadia@buschjena.de

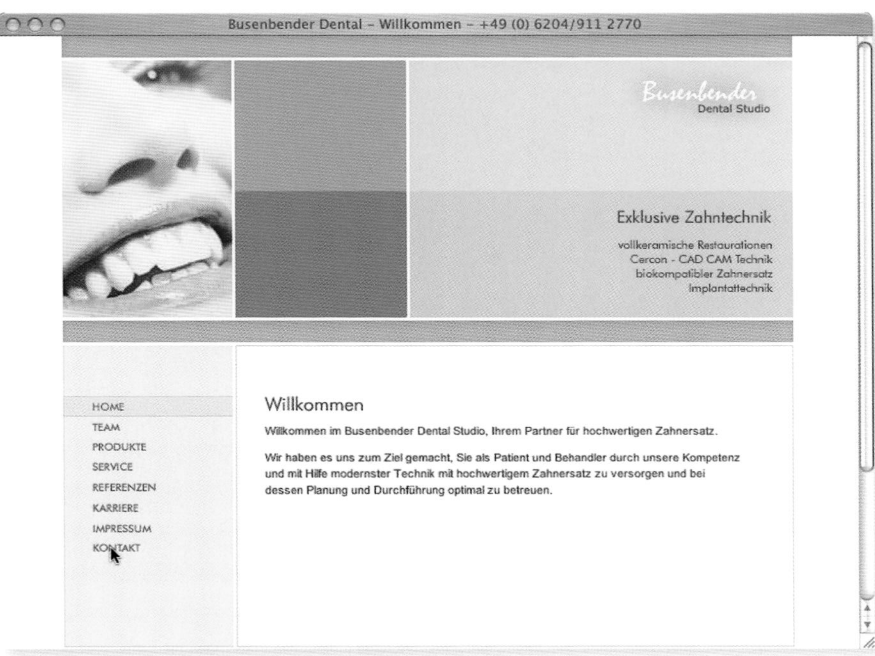
Busenbender Dental – Willkommen – +49 (0) 6204/911 2770
Busenbender
Dental Studio
Exklusive Zahntechnik
vollkeramische Restaurationen
Cercon - CAD CAM Technik
biokompatibler Zahnersatz
Implantattechnik
HOME
TEAM
PRODUKTE
SERVICE
REFERENZEN
KARRIERE
IMPRESSUM
KONTAKT
Willkommen
Willkommen im Busenbender Dental Studio, Ihrem Partner für hochwertigen Zahnersatz.
Wir haben es uns zum Ziel gemacht, Sie als Patient und Behandler durch unsere Kompetenz und mit Hilfe modernster Technik mit hochwertigem Zahnersatz zu versorgen und bei dessen Planung und Durchführung optimal zu betreuen.

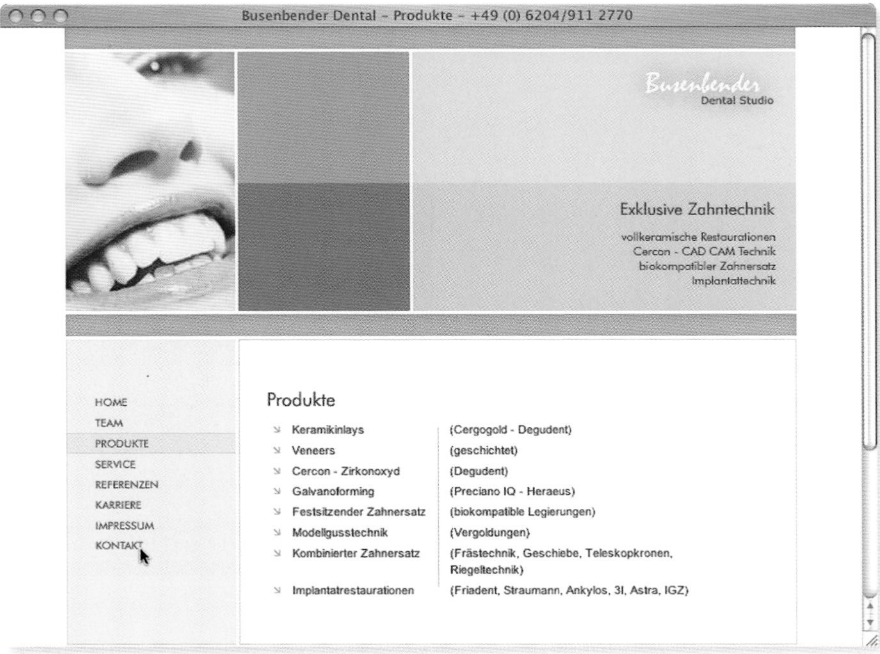
Busenbender Dental – Produkte – +49 (0) 6204/911 2770
Busenbender
Dental Studio
Exklusive Zahntechnik
vollkeramische Restaurationen
Cercon - CAD CAM Technik
biokompatibler Zahnersatz
Implantattechnik
HOME
TEAM
PRODUKTE
SERVICE
REFERENZEN
KARRIERE
IMPRESSUM
KONTAKT
Produkte
Keramikinlays (Cergogold - Degudent)
Veneers (geschichtet)
Cercon - Zirkonoxyd (Degudent)
Galvanoforming (Preciano IQ - Heraeus)
Festsitzender Zahnersatz (biokompatible Legierungen)
Modellgusstechnik (Vergoldungen)
Kombinierter Zahnersatz (Frästechnik, Geschiebe, Teleskopkronen, Riegeltechnik)
Implantatrestaurationen (Friadent, Straumann, Ankylos, 3I, Astra, IGZ)

www.busenbender-dental.com
D: heike stoecker
M: info@heikestoecker.com

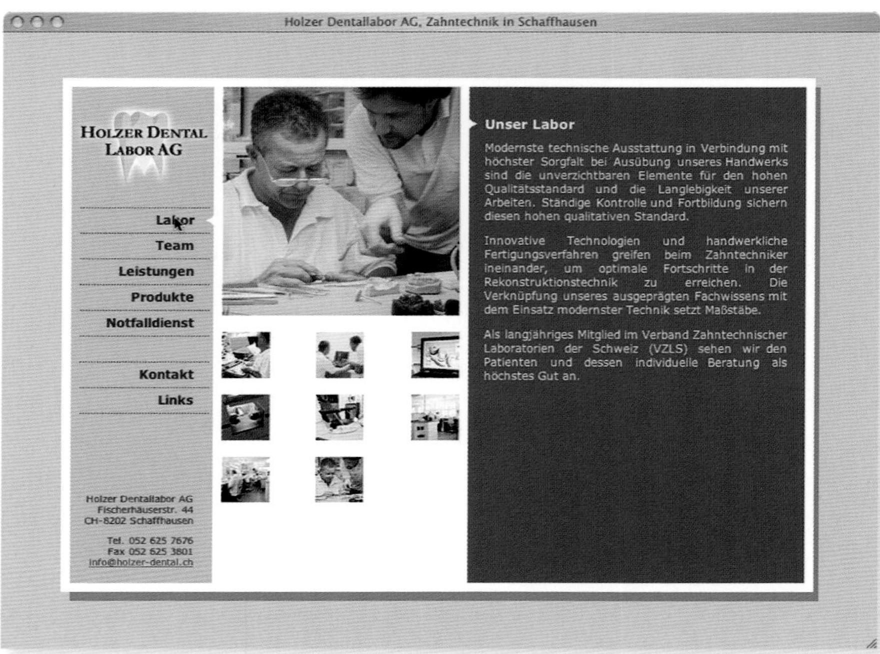
Holzer Dentallabor AG, Zahntechnik in Schaffhausen
Holzer Dental Labor AG
Labor
Team
Leistungen
Produkte
Notfalldienst
Kontakt
Links
Holzer Dentallabor AG
Fischerhäuserstr. 44
CH-8202 Schaffhausen
Tel. 052 625 7676
Fax 052 625 3801
info@holzer-dental.ch
Unser Labor
Modernste technische Ausstattung in Verbindung mit höchster Sorgfalt bei Ausübung unseres Handwerks sind die unverzichtbaren Elemente für den hohen Qualitätsstandard und die Langlebigkeit unserer Arbeiten. Ständige Kontrolle und Fortbildung sichern diesen hohen qualitativen Standard.
Innovative Technologien und handwerkliche Fertigungsverfahren greifen beim Zahntechniker ineinander, um optimale Fortschritte in der Rekonstruktionstechnik zu erreichen. Die Verknüpfung unseres ausgeprägten Fachwissens mit dem Einsatz modernster Technik setzt Maßstäbe.
Als langjähriges Mitglied im Verband Zahntechnischer Laboratorien der Schweiz (VZLS) sehen wir den Patienten und dessen individuelle Beratung als höchstes Gut an.

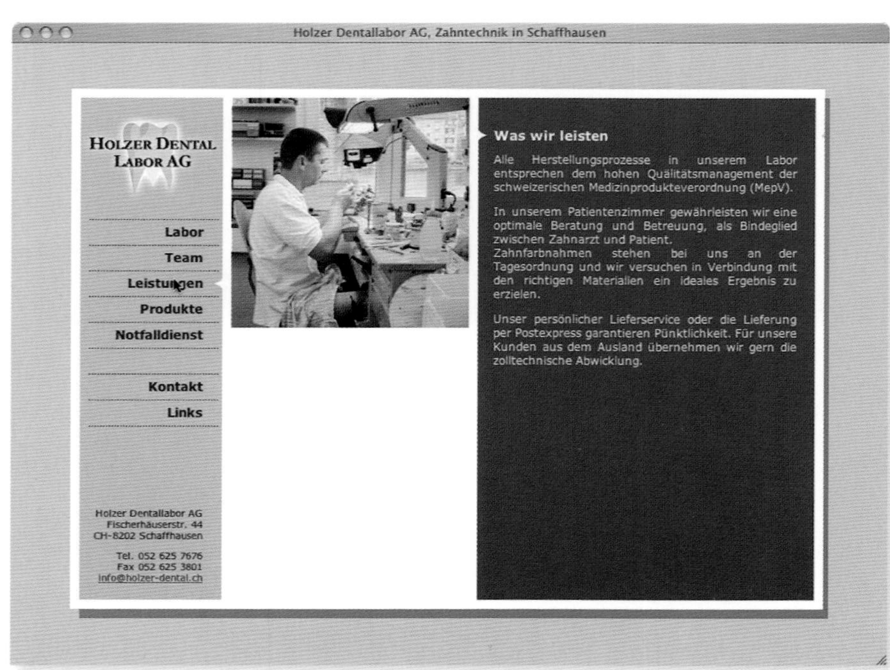
Holzer Dentallabor AG, Zahntechnik in Schaffhausen
Holzer Dental Labor AG
Labor
Team
Leistungen
Produkte
Notfalldienst
Kontakt
Links
Holzer Dentallabor AG
Fischerhäuserstr. 44
CH-8202 Schaffhausen
Tel. 052 625 7676
Fax 052 625 3801
info@holzer-dental.ch
Was wir leisten
Alle Herstellungsprozesse in unserem Labor entsprechen dem hohen Qualitätsmanagement der schweizerischen Medizinprodukteverordnung (MepV).
In unserem Patientenzimmer gewährleisten wir eine optimale Beratung und Betreuung, als Bindeglied zwischen Zahnarzt und Patient.
Zahnfarbnahmen stehen bei uns an der Tagesordnung und wir versuchen in Verbindung mit den richtigen Materialien ein ideales Ergebnis zu erzielen.
Unser persönlicher Lieferservice oder die Lieferung per Postexpress garantieren Pünktlichkeit. Für unsere Kunden aus dem Ausland übernehmen wir gern die zolltechnische Abwicklung.

www.holzer-dental.ch
D: simon habeck
M: info@like-sushi.de

IVI - Instituto Valenciano de Infertilidad
EQUIPO IVI
ENGLISH | DEUTSCH
NOTICIAS
MAPA WEB
BUSCAR
QUÉ ES EL IVI
CENTROS IVI
TRATAMIENTOS IVI
PACIENTES Y VISITANTES
PROFESIONAL
Centro de vida
DESTACADOS
TITULARES
PRIMERA VISITA VIRTUAL
Consultorio on-line del Equipo IVI
Charlas informativas
Infórmese sobre los temas que le interesan.
Fundación IVI
Investigación y docencia en Medicina Reproductiva.
Obstetricia-Ginecología
I Curso en Formación Continuada.
Atención Internacional
Si es usted extranjero/a y tiene previsto visitarnos.
Máster Reproducción
Enero-Diciembre 2003. Programa y Materiales.
Cita por Internet
Solicite hora para una visita en un Centro IVI.
El IVI Sevilla galardonado por su popularidad entre los sevillanos
Quinta Edición del Curso Práctico de Endoscopia Ginecológica
IVI México recibe el Laurel de Oro
Las parejas portadoras de atrofia
Diseño y Alojamiento: XL internet. © 2004 IVI. Todos los derechos reservados. ivi@ivi.es. Información Legal.

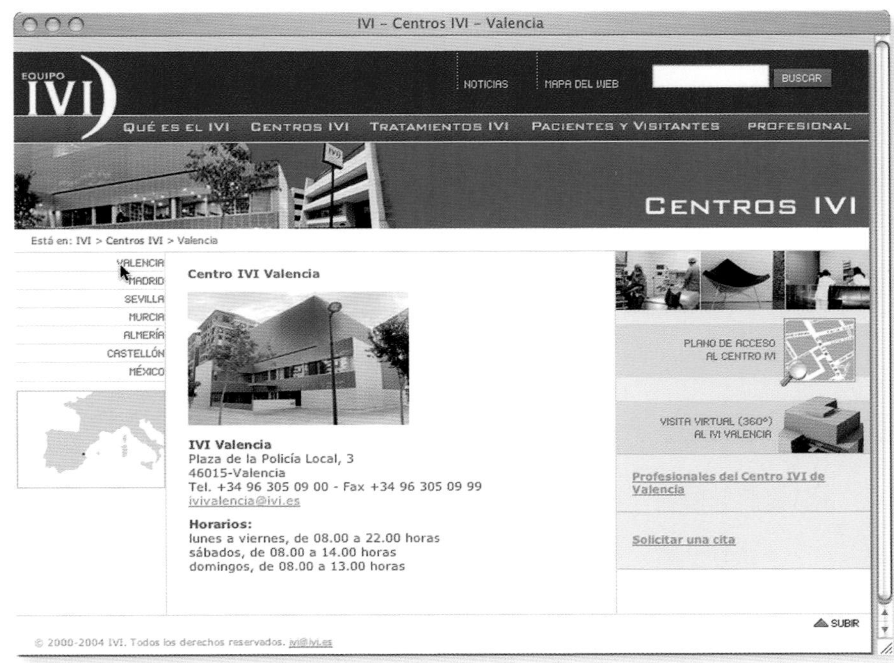
IVI - Centros IVI - Valencia
EQUIPO IVI
NOTICIAS
MAPA DEL WEB
BUSCAR
QUÉ ES EL IVI
CENTROS IVI
TRATAMIENTOS IVI
PACIENTES Y VISITANTES
PROFESIONAL
CENTROS IVI
Está en: IVI > Centros IVI > Valencia
VALENCIA
MADRID
SEVILLA
MURCIA
ALMERÍA
CASTELLÓN
MÉXICO
Centro IVI Valencia
IVI Valencia
Plaza de la Policía Local, 3
46015-Valencia
Tel. +34 96 305 09 00 - Fax +34 96 305 09 99
ivivalencia@ivi.es
Horarios:
lunes a viernes, de 08.00 a 22.00 horas
sábados, de 08.00 a 14.00 horas
domingos, de 08.00 a 13.00 horas
PLANO DE ACCESO AL CENTRO IVI
VISITA VIRTUAL (360°) AL IVI VALENCIA
Profesionales del Centro IVI de Valencia
Solicitar una cita
SUBIR
© 2000-2004 IVI. Todos los derechos reservados. ivi@ivi.es

www.ivi.es
D: daniel caballero
A: xl internet **M:** dcaballero@xli.net

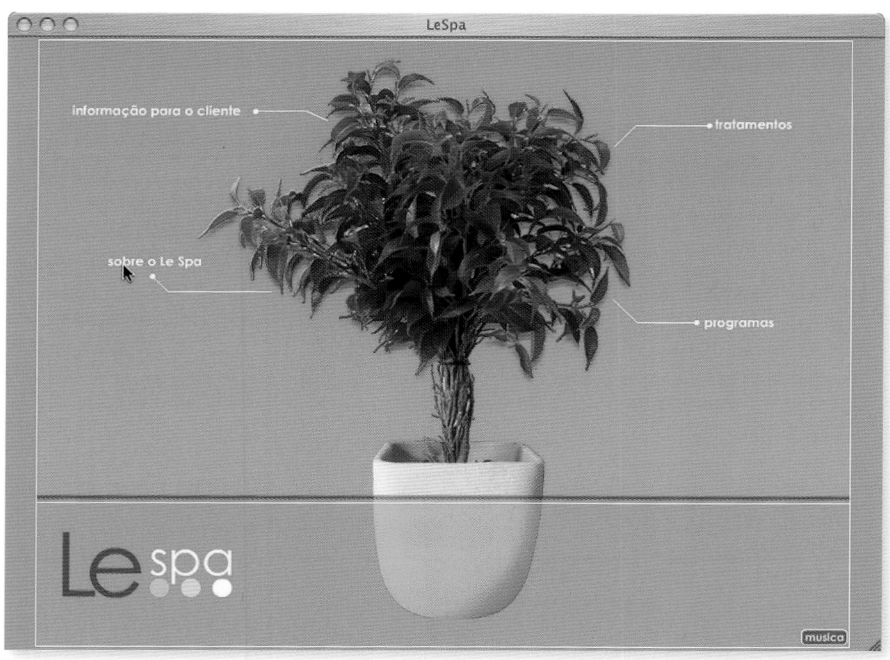
LeSpa
informação para o cliente
tratamentos
sobre o Le Spa
programas
Le spa
musica

LeSpa
informação para o cliente
tratamentos
Le spa
sobre o Le Spa
Sobre o
Lespa
Fuja ao stress do dia a dia e entre num mundo mais tranquilo
Deixe-se guiar pelos seus sentidos
Descubra o caminho para a paz interior e para o relaxamento total
No Le Spa poderá aceder a novos níveis de descoberta sobre o seu bem-estar pessoal de corpo e espírito, ao mesmo tempo que usufrui de um ambiente relaxante e totalmente exclusivo. É a melhor forma de se evadir da cidade e de se entregar a momentos de puro prazer.
O Le Spa dispõe de sete salas para tratamentos de rosto, corpo, massagens asiáticas, manicure e pedicure. Existe ainda um banho turco e uma sala de relaxamento para prolongar a sua experiência spa.
Aberto de 2ª a 6ª feira das 10h às 20h30 e sábados das 10h às 19 horas
R. Silva Carvalho 234 B 1250-024 Lisboa - Tel: 21 385 02 52 - lespa@sapo.pt
musica

www.lespa.info
D: almeida simão
A: s23 **M:** simao.c.almeida@netcabo.pt

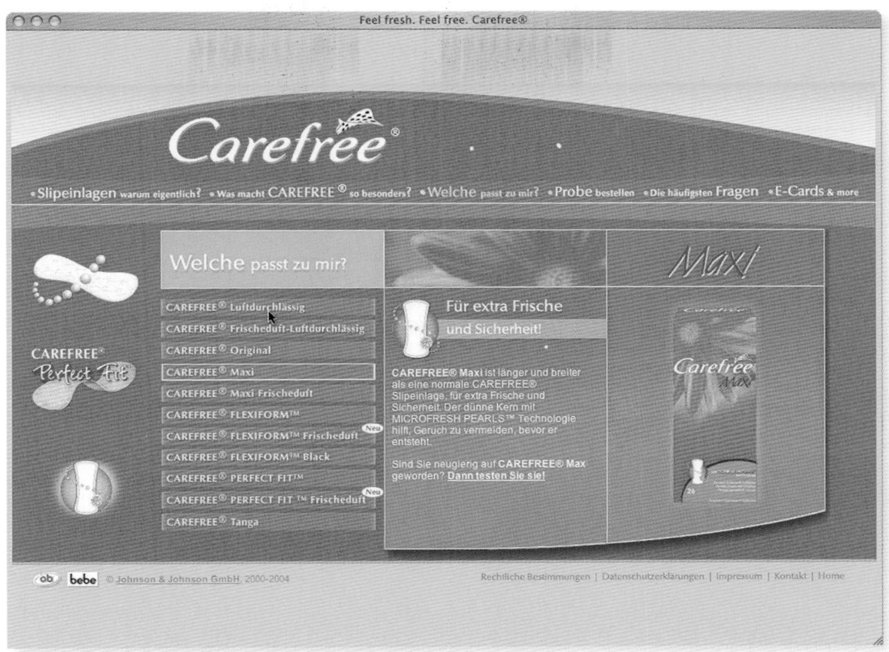
Feel fresh. Feel free. Carefree®
Carefree®
Slipeinlagen warum eigentlich? Was macht CAREFREE® so besonders? Welche passt zu mir? Probe bestellen Die häufigsten Fragen E-Cards & more
Welche passt zu mir?
Maxi
CAREFREE® Luftdurchlässig
CAREFREE® Frischeduft-Luftdurchlässig
CAREFREE® Original
CAREFREE® Maxi
CAREFREE® Maxi Frischeduft
CAREFREE® FLEXIFORM™
CAREFREE® FLEXIFORM™ Frischeduft Neu
CAREFREE® FLEXIFORM™ Black
CAREFREE® PERFECT FIT™
CAREFREE® PERFECT FIT™ Frischeduft Neu
CAREFREE® Tanga
CAREFREE® Perfect Fit
Für extra Frische und Sicherheit!
CAREFREE® Maxi ist länger und breiter als eine normale CAREFREE® Slipeinlage, für extra Frische und Sicherheit. Der dünne Kern mit MICROFRESH PEARLS™ Technologie hilft, Geruch zu vermeiden, bevor er entsteht.
Sind Sie neugierig auf CAREFREE® Max geworden? Dann testen Sie sie!
Carefree Maxi
ob bebe © Johnson & Johnson GmbH, 2000-2004
Rechtliche Bestimmungen | Datenschutzerklärungen | Impressum | Kontakt | Home

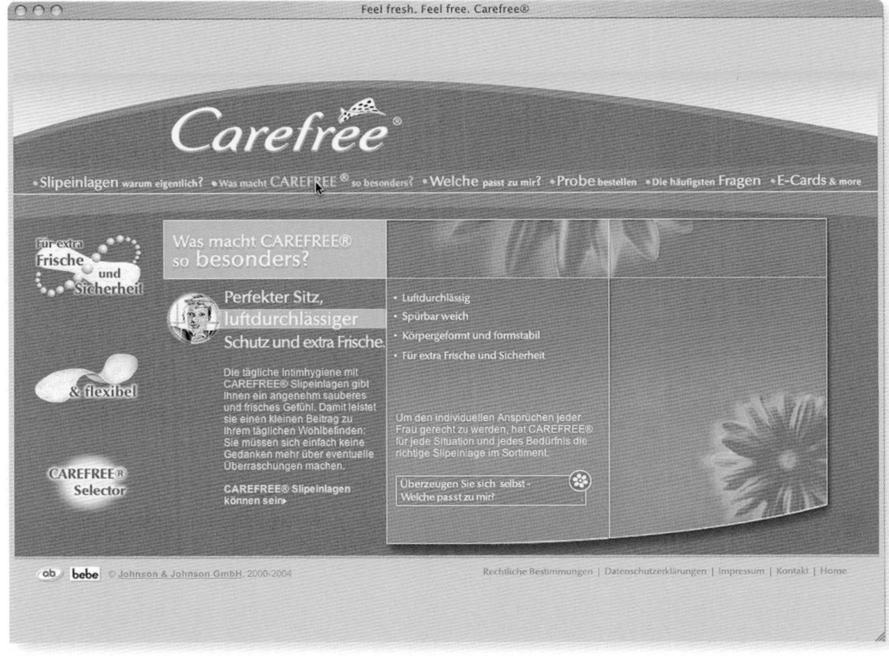
Feel fresh. Feel free. Carefree®
Carefree®
Slipeinlagen warum eigentlich? Was macht CAREFREE® so besonders? Welche passt zu mir? Probe bestellen Die häufigsten Fragen E-Cards & more
Für extra Frische und Sicherheit
& flexibel
CAREFREE® Selector
Was macht CAREFREE® so besonders?
Perfekter Sitz, luftdurchlässiger Schutz und extra Frische.
Die tägliche Intimhygiene mit CAREFREE® Slipeinlagen gibt Ihnen ein angenehm sauberes und frisches Gefühl. Damit leistet sie einen kleinen Beitrag zu Ihrem täglichen Wohlbefinden: Sie müssen sich einfach keine Gedanken mehr über eventuelle Überraschungen machen.
CAREFREE® Slipeinlagen können sein
Luftdurchlässig
Spürbar weich
Körpergeformt und formstabil
Für extra Frische und Sicherheit
Um den individuellen Ansprüchen jeder Frau gerecht zu werden, hat CAREFREE® für jede Situation und jedes Bedürfnis die richtige Slipeinlage im Sortiment.
Überzeugen Sie sich selbst - Welche passt zu mir?
ob bebe © Johnson & Johnson GmbH, 2000-2004
Rechtliche Bestimmungen | Datenschutzerklärungen | Impressum | Kontakt | Home

www.carefree.de

D: dirk heinemann **C:** christo zonnev

A: interactive marketing partner **M:** dirk.heinemann@impartner.de

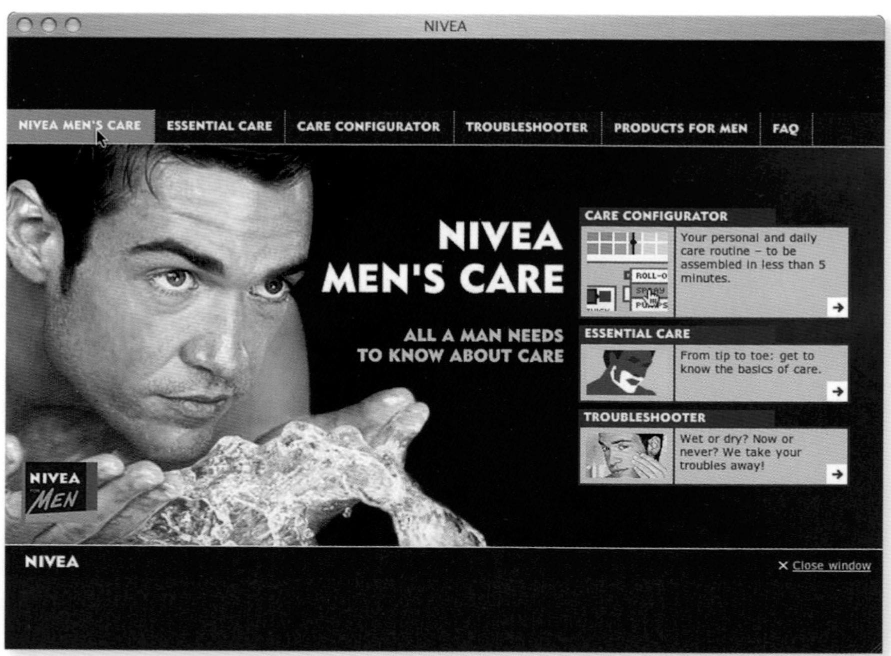
NIVEA
NIVEA MEN'S CARE
ESSENTIAL CARE
CARE CONFIGURATOR
TROUBLESHOOTER
PRODUCTS FOR MEN
FAQ
NIVEA
MEN'S CARE
ALL A MAN NEEDS
TO KNOW ABOUT CARE
CARE CONFIGURATOR
Your personal and daily care routine – to be assembled in less than 5 minutes.
ESSENTIAL CARE
From tip to toe: get to know the basics of care.
TROUBLESHOOTER
Wet or dry? Now or never? We take your troubles away!
NIVEA
MEN
NIVEA
Close window

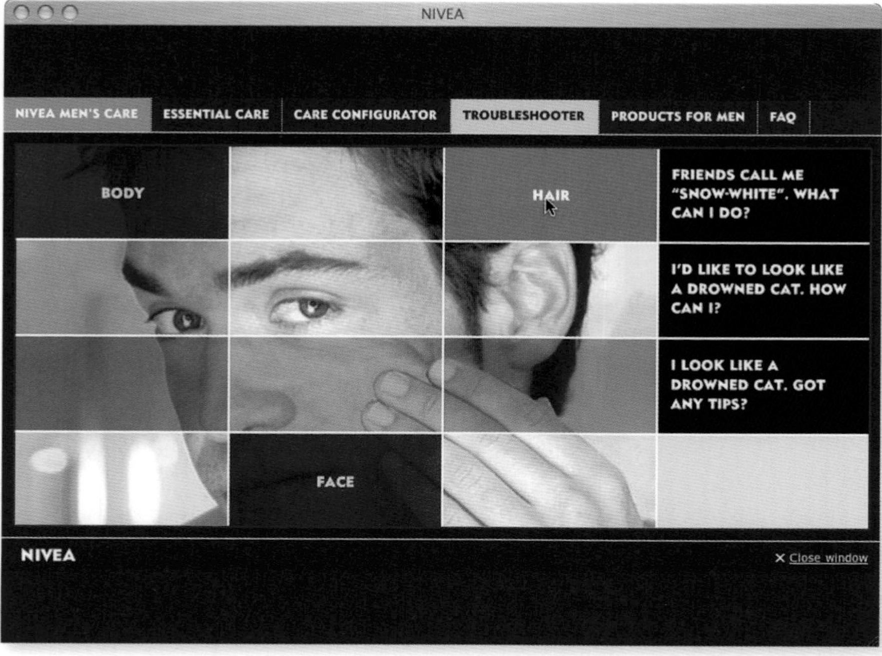
NIVEA
NIVEA MEN'S CARE
ESSENTIAL CARE
CARE CONFIGURATOR
TROUBLESHOOTER
PRODUCTS FOR MEN
FAQ
BODY
HAIR
FRIENDS CALL ME "SNOW-WHITE". WHAT CAN I DO?
I'D LIKE TO LOOK LIKE A DROWNED CAT. HOW CAN I?
I LOOK LIKE A DROWNED CAT. GOT ANY TIPS?
FACE
NIVEA
Close window

www.NIVEA.com/formen
D: christophe stoll
A: fork unstable media M: svenja@fork.de

www.doeamor.com.br
home
doeamor
quem somos
O Serviço de Hemoterapia dos Hospitais Santa Catarina e Cruz Azul de São Paulo, são administrados pela Takatu Serviços Médicos Especializados, empresa prestadora de serviços médicos com foco na área de hemoterapia. Tem como diretor geral o Dr. Pedro M. Takatu, um dos pioneiros da hemoterapia no Brasil, responsável pela implantação de vários avanços na área.
Temos como missão suprir toda a necessidade de sangue e hemocomponentes, com a máxima segurança e qualidade, nos serviços em que atuamos.
banco de
sangue
quem somos

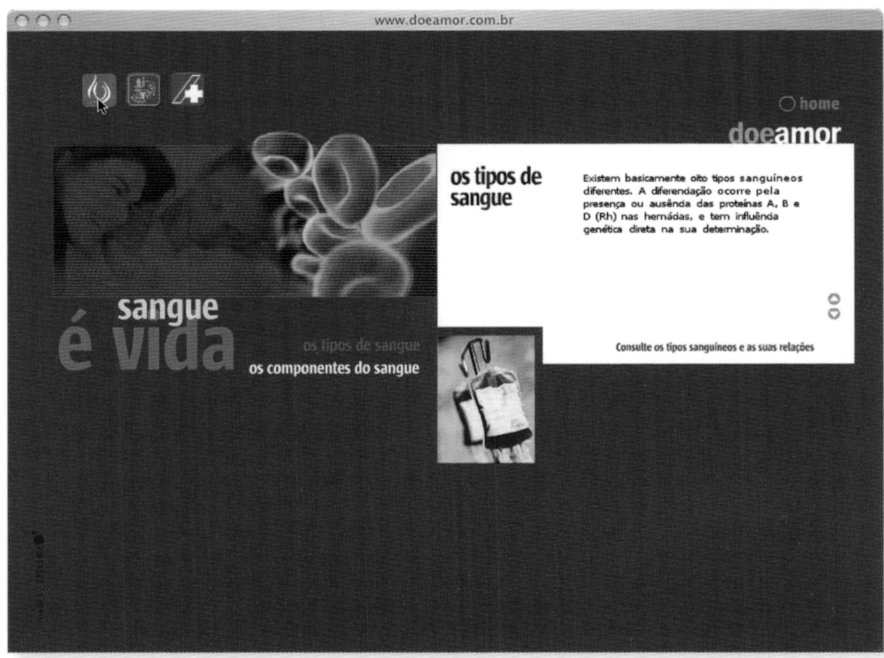
www.doeamor.com.br
home
doeamor
os tipos de sangue
Existem basicamente oito tipos sanguíneos diferentes. A diferenciação ocorre pela presença ou ausência das proteínas A, B e D (Rh) nas hemácias, e tem influência genética direta na sua determinação.
Consulte os tipos sanguíneos e as suas relações
sangue
é vida
os tipos de sangue
os componentes do sangue

www.doeamor.com.br
D: claudia sirera **C:** andré santocchi
A: choupana d'zain **M:** andre@achoupana.com

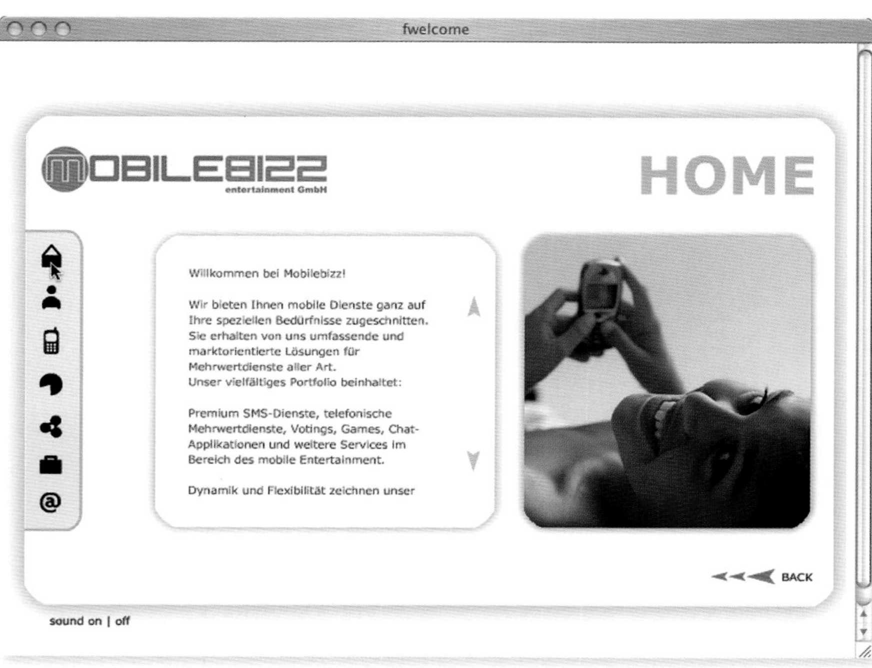
fwelcome
MOBILEBIZZ
entertainment GmbH
HOME
Willkommen bei Mobilebizz!
Wir bieten Ihnen mobile Dienste ganz auf Ihre speziellen Bedürfnisse zugeschnitten. Sie erhalten von uns umfassende und marktorientierte Lösungen für Mehrwertdienste aller Art.
Unser vielfältiges Portfolio beinhaltet:
Premium SMS-Dienste, telefonische Mehrwertdienste, Votings, Games, Chat-Applikationen und weitere Services im Bereich des mobile Entertainment.
Dynamik und Flexibilität zeichnen unser
BACK
sound on | off

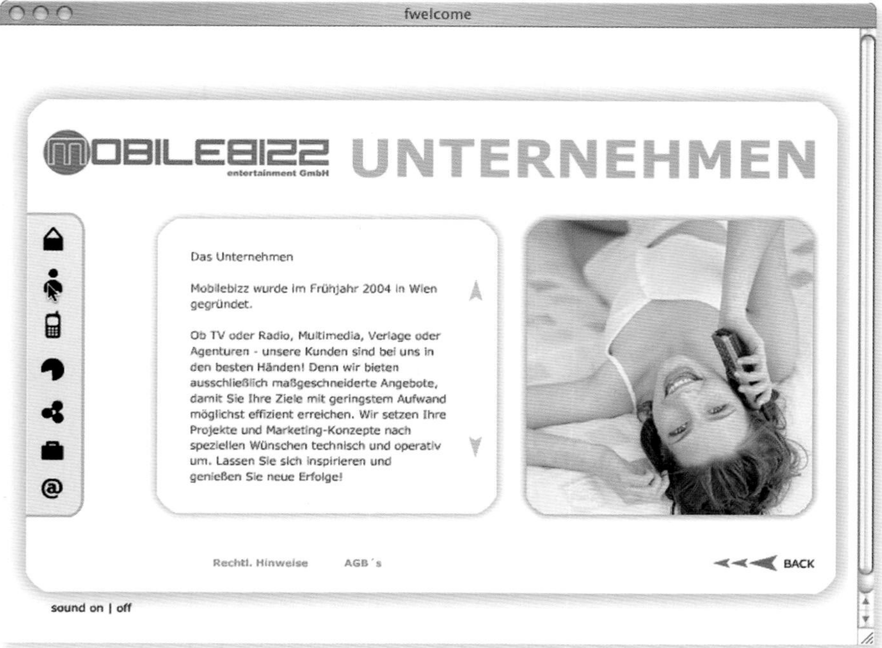
fwelcome
MOBILEBIZZ
entertainment GmbH
UNTERNEHMEN
Das Unternehmen
Mobilebizz wurde im Frühjahr 2004 in Wien gegründet.
Ob TV oder Radio, Multimedia, Verlage oder Agenturen - unsere Kunden sind bei uns in den besten Händen! Denn wir bieten ausschließlich maßgeschneiderte Angebote, damit Sie Ihre Ziele mit geringstem Aufwand möglichst effizient erreichen. Wir setzen Ihre Projekte und Marketing-Konzepte nach speziellen Wünschen technisch und operativ um. Lassen Sie sich inspirieren und genießen Sie neue Erfolge!
Rechtl. Hinweise
AGB´s
BACK
sound on | off

www.mobilebizz.biz
D: matthias spitzer
A: spitzerart **M:** webmaster@spitzerart.com

BEPESKOM :: Persatuan Bekas Pelajar Sains Komputer & Teknologi Maklumat UPM

bepeskom
persatuan bekas pelajar
sains komputer
& teknologi maklumat
universiti putra malaysia

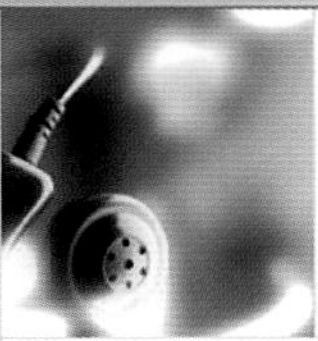

MENGENAI BEPESKOM

Wednesday, December 01, 2004

mengenai bepeskom
organisasi
aktiviti-aktiviti
pautan berkaitan
hubungi bepeskom

Teknologi maklumat dan komunikasi sedang berkembang dengan begitu pesat dan pantas di seluruh dunia. Perkembangan yang pesat ini turut memberi impak kepada negara Malaysia, di mana kepentingan teknologi maklumat semakin dititik beratkan oleh kerajaan. Bagi menyahut seruan ini, BEPESKOM yang telah ditubuhkan pada 20 Oktober 2000; menawarkan khidmat membantu mengadakan program melatih warga belia, pelajar dan warga luar bandar menguasai Teknologi Maklumat Berkomunikasi dengan cara tersendiri dan seterusnya akan dapat merapatkan jurang digital di antara golongan muda dan golongan dewasa.

No 4, Jalan 5/118C,
Desa Tun Razak
Industrial Park,
56000 Cheras,
Kuala Lumpur
Tel: 03-9172 2125
Fax: 03-9171 8152

Site by
Wahaza Extra Design

BEPESKOM :: Persatuan Bekas Pelajar Sains Komputer & Teknologi Maklumat UPM

bepeskom
persatuan bekas pelajar
sains komputer
& teknologi maklumat
universiti putra malaysia

ORGANISASI

Wednesday, December 01, 2004

mengenai bepeskom
organisasi
aktiviti-aktiviti
pautan berkaitan
hubungi bepeskom

Pengerusi Pengelola Kebangsaan:
YBhg. Tan Sri Dato' Ahmad Sabki Jahidin,

Penasihat:1
Y.Bhg Profesor Dato' Dr. Mohd. Zohadie Bardaie,
Naib Cancelor, Universiti Putra Malaysia.

Penasihat 2
Prof. Madya Abd. Azim Abd. Ghani
Dekan, Fakulti Sains Komputer & Teknologi Maklumat, UPM.

Presiden
Meor Hazlan bin Meor Hussin.

No 4, Jalan 5/118C,
Desa Tun Razak
Industrial Park,
56000 Cheras,
Kuala Lumpur
Tel: 03-9172 2125
Fax: 03-9171 8152

Site by
Wahaza Extra Design

www.bepeskom.com.my
D: mohd hisham saleh
A: wahaza extra design studio **M:** hisham@wahazaextra.com

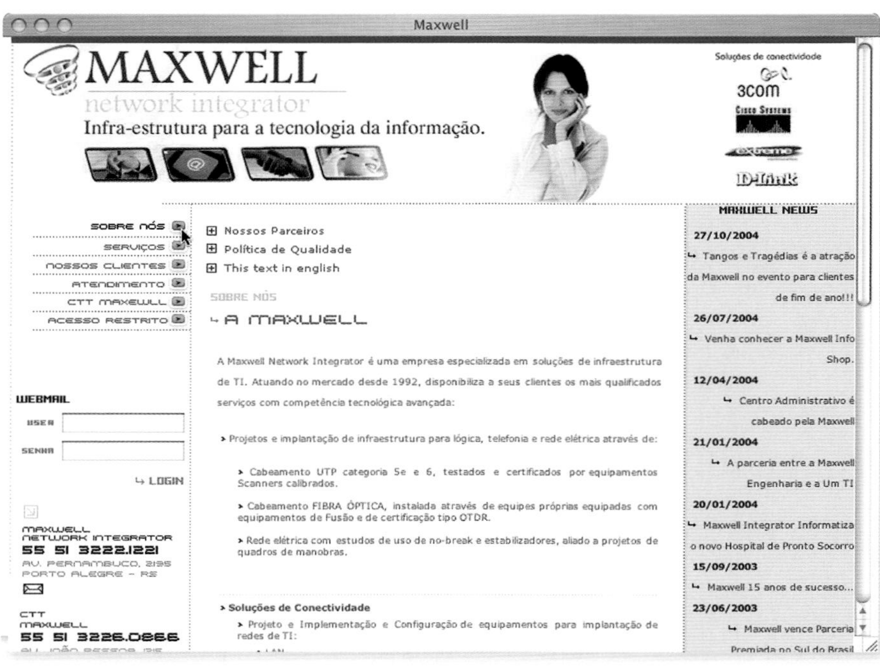
Maxwell
MAXWELL
network integrator
Infra-estrutura para a tecnologia da informação.
Soluções de conectividade
3com
Cisco Systems
D-Link
sobre nós
serviços
nossos clientes
atendimento
ctt maxwell
acesso restrito
Nossos Parceiros
Política de Qualidade
This text in english
SOBRE NÓS
A MAXWELL
A Maxwell Network Integrator é uma empresa especializada em soluções de infraestrutura de TI. Atuando no mercado desde 1992, disponibiliza a seus clientes os mais qualificados serviços com competência tecnológica avançada:
Projetos e implantação de infraestrutura para lógica, telefonia e rede elétrica através de:
Cabeamento UTP categoria 5e e 6, testados e certificados por equipamentos Scanners calibrados.
Cabeamento FIBRA ÓPTICA, instalada através de equipes próprias equipadas com equipamentos de Fusão e de certificação tipo OTDR.
Rede elétrica com estudos de uso de no-break e estabilizadores, aliado a projetos de quadros de manobras.
Soluções de Conectividade
Projeto e Implementação e Configuração de equipamentos para implantação de redes de TI:
MAXWELL NEWS
27/10/2004
Tangos e Tragédias é a atração da Maxwell no evento para clientes de fim de ano!!!
26/07/2004
Venha conhecer a Maxwell Info Shop.
12/04/2004
Centro Administrativo é cabeado pela Maxwell
21/01/2004
A parceria entre a Maxwell Engenharia e a Um TI
20/01/2004
Maxwell Integrator Informatiza o novo Hospital de Pronto Socorro
15/09/2003
Maxwell 15 anos de sucesso...
23/06/2003
Maxwell vence Parceria Premiada no Sul do Brasil
WEBMAIL
USER
SENHA
LOGIN
maxwell network integrator
55 51 3222.1221
av. pernambuco, 2195
porto alegre - rs
ctt maxwell
55 51 3226.0866

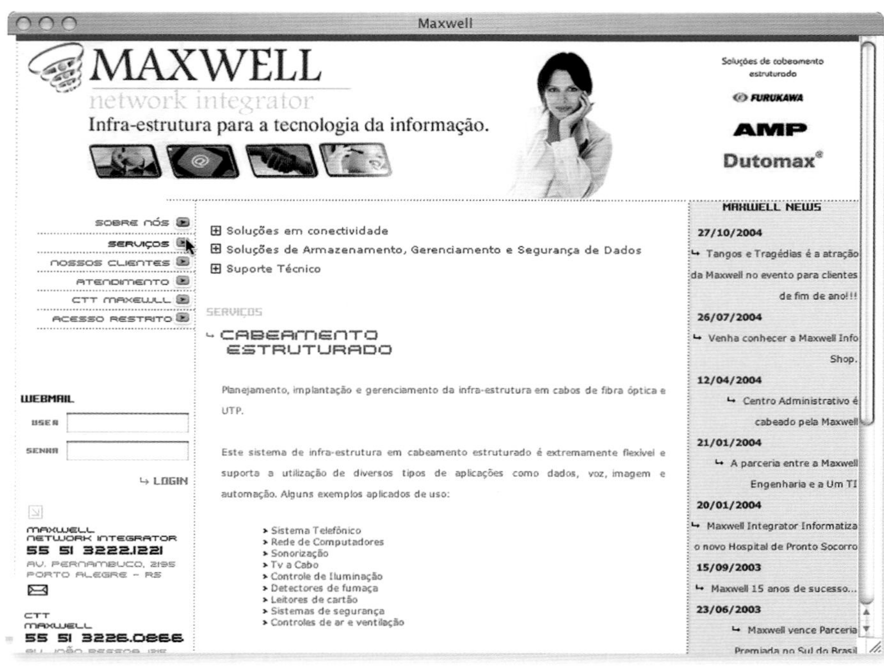
Maxwell
MAXWELL
network integrator
Infra-estrutura para a tecnologia da informação.
Soluções de cabeamento estruturado
FURUKAWA
AMP
Dutomax®
sobre nós
serviços
nossos clientes
atendimento
ctt maxwell
acesso restrito
Soluções em conectividade
Soluções de Armazenamento, Gerenciamento e Segurança de Dados
Suporte Técnico
SERVIÇOS
CABEAMENTO ESTRUTURADO
Planejamento, implantação e gerenciamento da infra-estrutura em cabos de fibra óptica e UTP.
Este sistema de infra-estrutura em cabeamento estruturado é extremamente flexível e suporta a utilização de diversos tipos de aplicações como dados, voz, imagem e automação. Alguns exemplos aplicados de uso:
Sistema Telefônico
Rede de Computadores
Sonorização
Tv a Cabo
Controle de Iluminação
Detectores de fumaça
Leitores de cartão
Sistemas de segurança
Controles de ar e ventilação
MAXWELL NEWS
27/10/2004
Tangos e Tragédias é a atração da Maxwell no evento para clientes de fim de ano!!!
26/07/2004
Venha conhecer a Maxwell Info Shop.
12/04/2004
Centro Administrativo é cabeado pela Maxwell
21/01/2004
A parceria entre a Maxwell Engenharia e a Um TI
20/01/2004
Maxwell Integrator Informatiza o novo Hospital de Pronto Socorro
15/09/2003
Maxwell 15 anos de sucesso...
23/06/2003
Maxwell vence Parceria Premiada no Sul do Brasil
WEBMAIL
USER
SENHA
LOGIN
maxwell network integrator
55 51 3222.1221
av. pernambuco, 2195
porto alegre - rs
ctt maxwell
55 51 3226.0866

www.maxwell.com.br
D: leonardo rafael schneider **C:** dante blauth
A: dbsites **M:** leomega@superig.com.br

prairie inet®
prairieinet
For home
Service that offers freedom and convenience.
A tool for learning.
Make working from home easier.
01 BUSINESS SOLUTIONS
02 RESIDENTIAL SOLUTIONS
03 CUSTOMER SUPPORT
04 ABOUT PRAIRIE INET®
05 CONTACT PRAIRIE INET®
Business Solutions
From small businesses to large companies, Prairie iNet offers broadband Internet access, web hosting, private line and business continuity solutions customized to your business.
LEARN MORE
Residential Solutions
Learn more about Internet access products for your home. Free up your phone line by using a Prairie iNet high-speed, always-on Internet connection.
LEARN MORE
Customer Support
Helpful information for our customers. Access your account online, find answers to common questions and learn how to contact Prairie iNet.
LEARN MORE
Satisfaction Guarantee
Switch your business Internet access to Prairie iNet broadband and receive a 60-day money back guarantee. Available with all business class products.
LEARN MORE
Sign up
Sign up online
or call now
(877) 794-6224 x 2
LEARN MORE

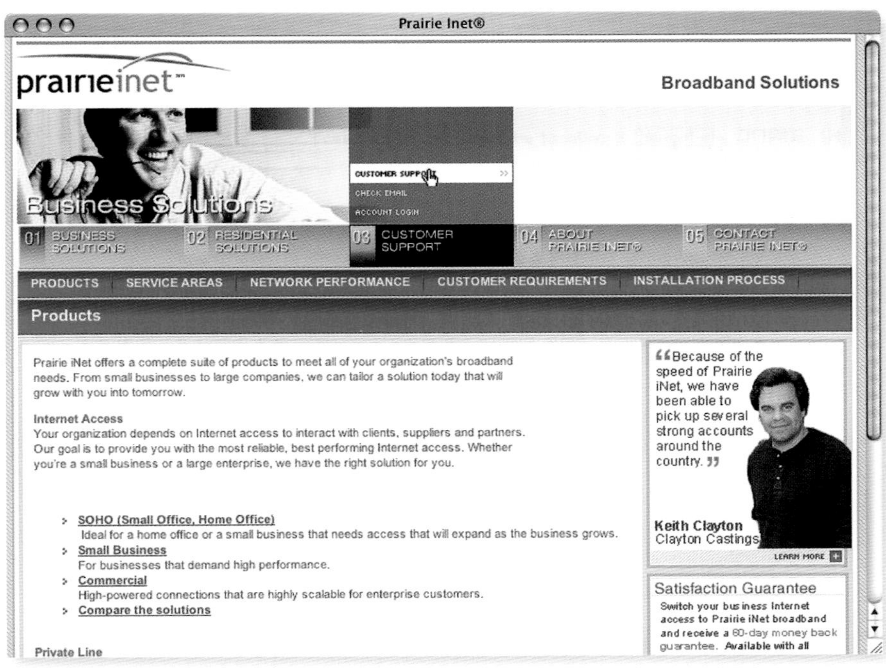
Prairie Inet®
prairieinet
Broadband Solutions
CUSTOMER SUPPORT
CHECK EMAIL
ACCOUNT LOGIN
Business Solutions
01 BUSINESS SOLUTIONS
02 RESIDENTIAL SOLUTIONS
03 CUSTOMER SUPPORT
04 ABOUT PRAIRIE INET®
05 CONTACT PRAIRIE INET®
PRODUCTS
SERVICE AREAS
NETWORK PERFORMANCE
CUSTOMER REQUIREMENTS
INSTALLATION PROCESS
Products
Prairie iNet offers a complete suite of products to meet all of your organization's broadband needs. From small businesses to large companies, we can tailor a solution today that will grow with you into tomorrow.
Internet Access
Your organization depends on Internet access to interact with clients, suppliers and partners. Our goal is to provide you with the most reliable, best performing Internet access. Whether you're a small business or a large enterprise, we have the right solution for you.
SOHO (Small Office, Home Office)
Ideal for a home office or a small business that needs access that will expand as the business grows.
Small Business
For businesses that demand high performance.
Commercial
High-powered connections that are highly scalable for enterprise customers.
Compare the solutions
Private Line
“Because of the speed of Prairie iNet, we have been able to pick up several strong accounts around the country.”
Keith Clayton
Clayton Castings
LEARN MORE
Satisfaction Guarantee
Switch your business Internet access to Prairie iNet broadband and receive a 60-day money back guarantee. Available with all

www.prairieinet.com

D: dan noe **C:** dan noe **P:** screenscape studios

A: screenscape studios **M:** dan@screenscapestudios.com

Capital ID: Brand Management | Interaction Design | Commerce Applications

Capital ID

Over Capital ID | Referenties | Meer informatie | Selecteer uw taal:

success.

ID manager

Internetsofware voor Brand & Identity Management en Brand Asset Management.

> Alles over ID manager
> Client cases
> Meer informatie

ID interactive

Consultancy op het gebied & het gebruik van interactieve kanalen in relatie tot de merk- en huisstijl.

> Alles over ID interactive
> Client cases
> Meer informatie

ID commerce

Web applicaties voor o,.a. Purchasing / Procurement, e-Shop en Intranet.

> Alles over ID Commerce
> Client cases
> Meer informatie

Lees hoe Randstad "ID manager" toepast

Randstad is bezig met een internationale uitrol van ID manager software. De ambities om alle marketingcommunicatie te automatiseren gaan ver. ID manager software helpt ze hierbij.....
Lees verder

Capital ID: Brand Management | Interaction Design | Commerce Applications
Capital ID
Over Capital ID | Referenties | Meer informatie | Selecteer uw taal:
control.
Homepage >> Over Capital ID

> Algemeen
> Management
> Bezoekadres
> Partners
> Meer informatie

Over Capital ID

Capital ID concentreert zich op een drietal activiteiten:

Het ontwikkelen en implementeren van een internetportal waarmee ondernemingen hun huisstijl en marketingactiviteiten kunnen automatiseren door middel van standaard applicaties
ID manager

Het ontwikkelen en implementeren van zogenaamde 'commerce' applicaties voor onder andere procurement / purchasing, intranet, webshop en het automatiseren van instore marketing
ID commerce

Het leveren van diensten rondom online marketing en interaction design
ID interactive

De software van Capital ID is ontwikkeld op het Microsoft .NET framework en wordt toegepast door tientallen nationale en internationale ondernemingen.
Meer info

De consultants van Capital ID hebben jarenlange ervaring op het gebied van ICT en marketing.

Capital ID wordt geleid door: Dennis Steen, Marc van Ballegooijen en Andrey Prins.
Meer info

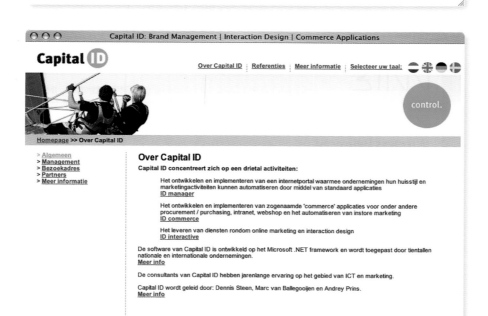

www.capitalid.nl
D: max schrevelius **C:** arnout schutte **P:** dennis steen
A: id interactive **M:** m.schrevelius@capitalid.nl

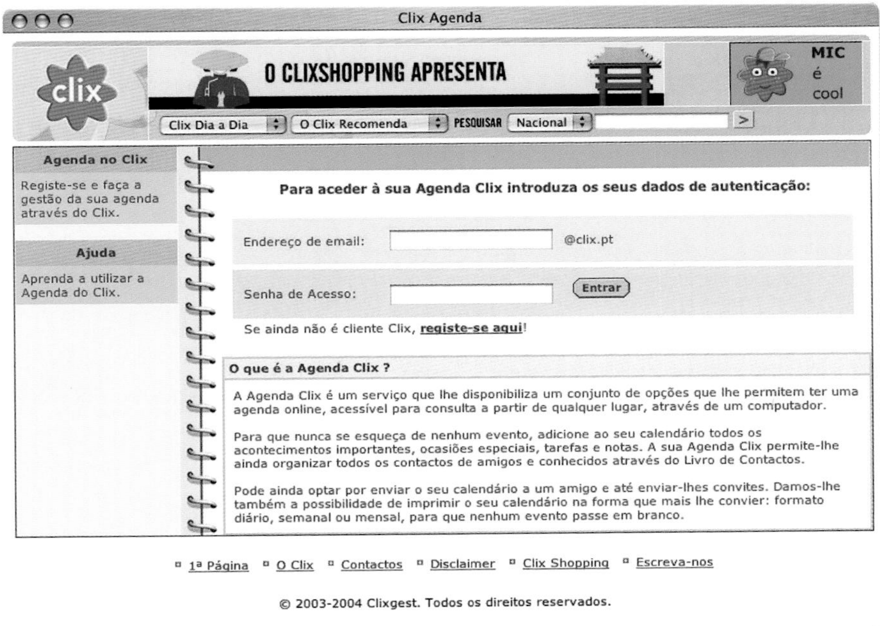
Clix Agenda
clix
O CLIXSHOPPING APRESENTA
MIC é cool
Clix Dia a Dia
O Clix Recomenda
PESQUISAR
Nacional
Agenda no Clix
Registe-se e faça a gestão da sua agenda através do Clix.
Ajuda
Aprenda a utilizar a Agenda do Clix.
Para aceder à sua Agenda Clix introduza os seus dados de autenticação:
Endereço de email:
@clix.pt
Senha de Acesso:
Entrar
Se ainda não é cliente Clix, registe-se aqui!
O que é a Agenda Clix ?
A Agenda Clix é um serviço que lhe disponibiliza um conjunto de opções que lhe permitem ter uma agenda online, acessível para consulta a partir de qualquer lugar, através de um computador.
Para que nunca se esqueça de nenhum evento, adicione ao seu calendário todos os acontecimentos importantes, ocasiões especiais, tarefas e notas. A sua Agenda Clix permite-lhe ainda organizar todos os contactos de amigos e conhecidos através do Livro de Contactos.
Pode ainda optar por enviar o seu calendário a um amigo e até enviar-lhes convites. Damos-lhe também a possibilidade de imprimir o seu calendário na forma que mais lhe convier: formato diário, semanal ou mensal, para que nenhum evento passe em branco.
1ª Página
O Clix
Contactos
Disclaimer
Clix Shopping
Escreva-nos
© 2003-2004 Clixgest. Todos os direitos reservados.

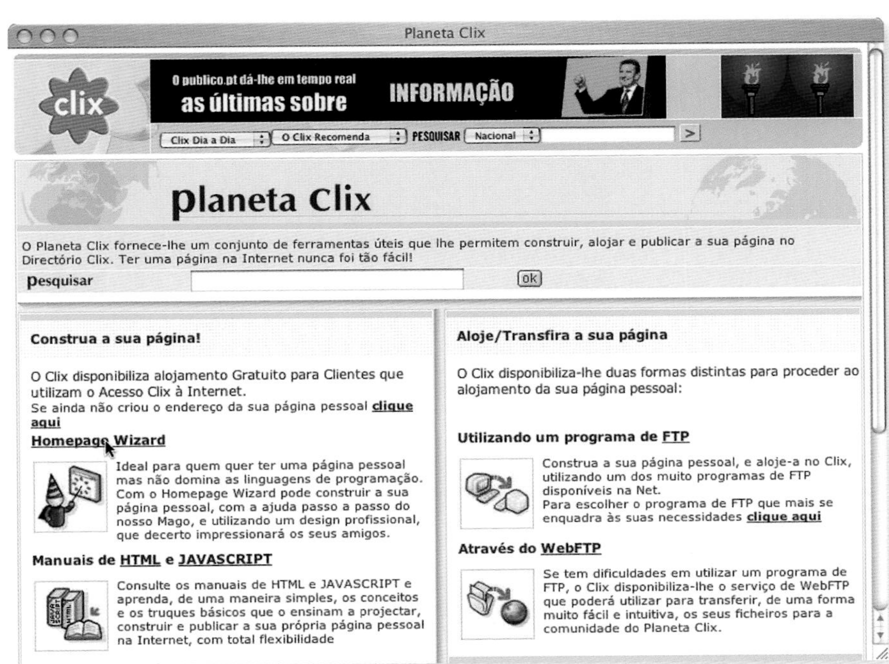
Planeta Clix
clix
O publico.pt dá-lhe em tempo real
as últimas sobre
INFORMAÇÃO
Clix Dia a Dia
O Clix Recomenda
PESQUISAR
Nacional
planeta Clix
O Planeta Clix fornece-lhe um conjunto de ferramentas úteis que lhe permitem construir, alojar e publicar a sua página no Directório Clix. Ter uma página na Internet nunca foi tão fácil!
pesquisar
ok
Construa a sua página!
O Clix disponibiliza alojamento Gratuito para Clientes que utilizam o Acesso Clix à Internet.
Se ainda não criou o endereço da sua página pessoal clique aqui
Homepage Wizard
Ideal para quem quer ter uma página pessoal mas não domina as linguagens de programação. Com o Homepage Wizard pode construir a sua página pessoal, com a ajuda passo a passo do nosso Mago, e utilizando um design profissional, que decerto impressionará os seus amigos.
Manuais de HTML e JAVASCRIPT
Consulte os manuais de HTML e JAVASCRIPT e aprenda, de uma maneira simples, os conceitos e os truques básicos que o ensinam a projectar, construir e publicar a sua própria página pessoal na Internet, com total flexibilidade
Aloje/Transfira a sua página
O Clix disponibiliza-lhe duas formas distintas para proceder ao alojamento da sua página pessoal:
Utilizando um programa de FTP
Construa a sua página pessoal, e aloje-a no Clix, utilizando um dos muito programas de FTP disponíveis na Net.
Para escolher o programa de FTP que mais se enquadra às suas necessidades clique aqui
Através do WebFTP
Se tem dificuldades em utilizar um programa de FTP, o Clix disponibiliza-lhe o serviço de WebFTP que poderá utilizar para transferir, de uma forma muito fácil e intuitiva, os seus ficheiros para a comunidade do Planeta Clix.

superfoto.planetaclix.pt
D: gustavo roscito
A: cgr design **M:** cgr@cgrdesign.com

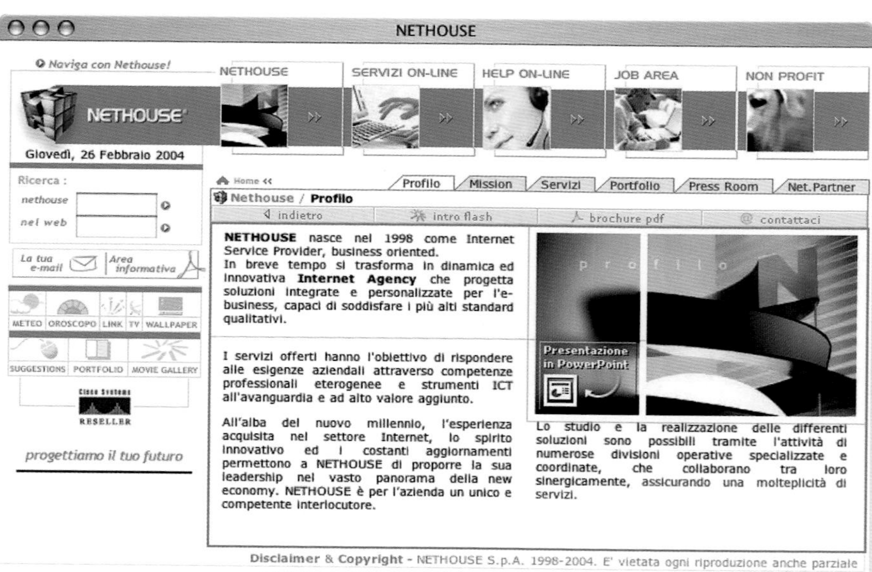
NETHOUSE
Naviga con Nethouse!
NETHOUSE
SERVIZI ON-LINE
HELP ON-LINE
JOB AREA
NON PROFIT
Giovedì, 26 Febbraio 2004
Ricerca :
nethouse
nel web
La tua e-mail
Area informativa
METEO OROSCOPO LINK TV WALLPAPER
SUGGESTIONS PORTFOLIO MOVIE GALLERY
RESELLER
progettiamo il tuo futuro
Home
Profilo
Mission
Servizi
Portfolio
Press Room
Net.Partner
Nethouse / Profilo
indietro
intro flash
brochure pdf
contattaci
NETHOUSE nasce nel 1998 come Internet Service Provider, business oriented.
In breve tempo si trasforma in dinamica ed innovativa Internet Agency che progetta soluzioni integrate e personalizzate per l'e-business, capaci di soddisfare i più alti standard qualitativi.
I servizi offerti hanno l'obiettivo di rispondere alle esigenze aziendali attraverso competenze professionali eterogenee e strumenti ICT all'avanguardia e ad alto valore aggiunto.
All'alba del nuovo millennio, l'esperienza acquisita nel settore Internet, lo spirito innovativo ed i costanti aggiornamenti permettono a NETHOUSE di proporre la sua leadership nel vasto panorama della new economy. NETHOUSE è per l'azienda un unico e competente interlocutore.
Presentazione in PowerPoint
Lo studio e la realizzazione delle differenti soluzioni sono possibili tramite l'attività di numerose divisioni operative specializzate e coordinate, che collaborano tra loro sinergicamente, assicurando una molteplicità di servizi.
Disclaimer & Copyright - NETHOUSE S.p.A. 1998-2004. E' vietata ogni riproduzione anche parziale
Corso Re Umberto I, 57 - 10128 Torino (Italia) Tel: (+39) 011.227.227 Fax: (+39) 011.227.228

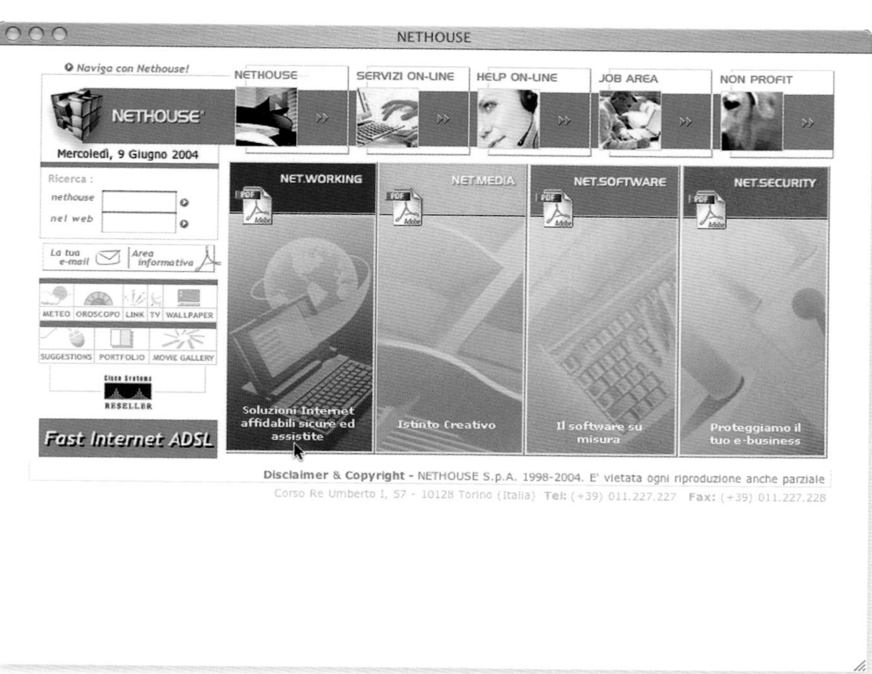
NETHOUSE
Naviga con Nethouse!
NETHOUSE
SERVIZI ON-LINE
HELP ON-LINE
JOB AREA
NON PROFIT
Mercoledì, 9 Giugno 2004
Ricerca :
nethouse
nel web
La tua e-mail
Area informativa
METEO OROSCOPO LINK TV WALLPAPER
SUGGESTIONS PORTFOLIO MOVIE GALLERY
RESELLER
Fast Internet ADSL
NET.WORKING
NET.MEDIA
NET.SOFTWARE
NET.SECURITY
Soluzioni Internet affidabili sicure ed assistite
Istinto Creativo
Il software su misura
Proteggiamo il tuo e-business
Disclaimer & Copyright - NETHOUSE S.p.A. 1998-2004. E' vietata ogni riproduzione anche parziale
Corso Re Umberto I, 57 - 10128 Torino (Italia) Tel: (+39) 011.227.227 Fax: (+39) 011.227.228

www.nethouse.it
D: cristina borgarelli
A: nethouse srl **M:** relazioni.esterne@nethouse.it

Normad1 > Qui sommes-nous ?

NORMAD1
Enjeux d'adresse

ISO 9001

01.NORMAD1 02.ENJEUX D'ADRESSE 03.REFERENTIELS 04.SOLUTIONS 05.HOMOLOGATION 06.VALIDEZ VOS ADRESSES 07.LETTRE INFO

01.NORMAD1

- Certification Iso
- Homologation
- Contactez-nous

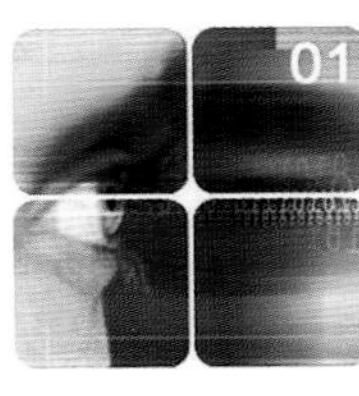
01

En savoir +

- Nos partenaires
- Intégrateurs "Normad1"

HISTORIQUE

NORMAD1 S.A. a été créée le 2 février 1993, deux ans après la conception du premier progiciel (Restructuration, Normalisation, Validation Postale) dont elle tire son nom.

L'activité principale est le développement de progiciels de traitement de l'adresse. Les premiers ont été écrits en ASSEMBLEUR 370 (NORMAD1-2-3) et ne peuvent s'exécuter que sur GROS SYSTEMES IBM® (MVS/VSE/VM). Pour permettre aux produits de fonctionner sur n'importe quel type de calculateur, nous les avons portés en langage C ANSI.

AUJOURD'HUI

Aujourd'hui, toute machine octet 32 bits ou plus disposant d'un compilateur C ANSI peut supporter les versions BATCH des progiciels ; cela concerne donc WINDOWS® (32 Bits), tous les systèmes UNIX, mais aussi d'autres systèmes d'exploitation comme GCOS7 de BULL®. Les versions INTERACTIVES ont été conçues de manière à fonctionner sur WINDOWS® (32 bits).

Situé en région bordelaise, notre centre de développement dispose de toute l'infrastructure matérielle nécessaire : plusieurs machines IBM® fonctionnant sous VM, VSE, MVS, OS/390 et z/OS, un AS/400®, un SUN® Solaris 8 ainsi que différents PC sous WINDOWS® 9x/NT/2000/XP® et LINUX.

Normad1 > Accueil

NORMAD1
Enjeux d'adresse

ISO 9001

01.NORMAD1 02.ENJEUX D'ADRESSE 03.REFERENTIELS 04.SOLUTIONS 05.HOMOLOGATION 06.VALIDEZ VOS ADRESSES 07.LETTRE INFO

ACCUEIL

- Partenaires
- Plan du site
- Téléchargements
- Contactez-nous

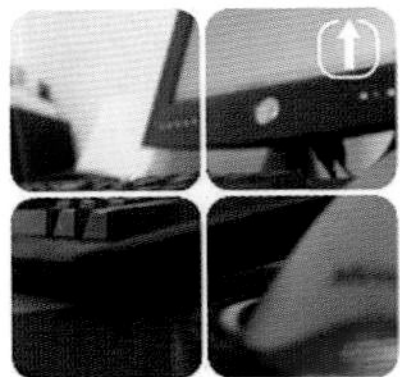

BIENVENUE

NORMAD1 S.A est une entreprise spécialisée dans le développement et la commercialisation de progiciels de traitement d'adresses françaises et européennes, n'hésitez pas à consulter notre gamme de solutions.

En savoir +

EN CE MOMENT

Validez vos adresses en ligne avec les référentiels de Avril 2004.

En savoir +

ACCES DIRECT

Docs 04 Infos sur les versions
Intégrateurs Actualités

ACTUALITES

Avril 2004 : Normad5 homologué sur AS/400!

Après les systèmes Windows®, UNIX et mainframes IBM®, c'est à présent sur systèmes AS/400® que NORMAD5 est homologué par La Poste...

En savoir +

Mars 2004 : Deux nouvelles rubriques !

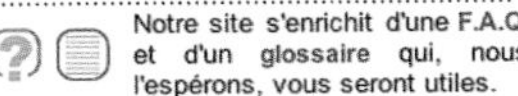

Notre site s'enrichit d'une F.A.Q. et d'un glossaire qui, nous l'espérons, vous seront utiles.

Mars 2004 : Nouvelle lettre d'information !

La lettre d'information n°8 de février est désormais disponible sur ce site...

En savoir +

www.normad1.fr
D: stéphane segura
A: normad1 M: stephane@activelab.net

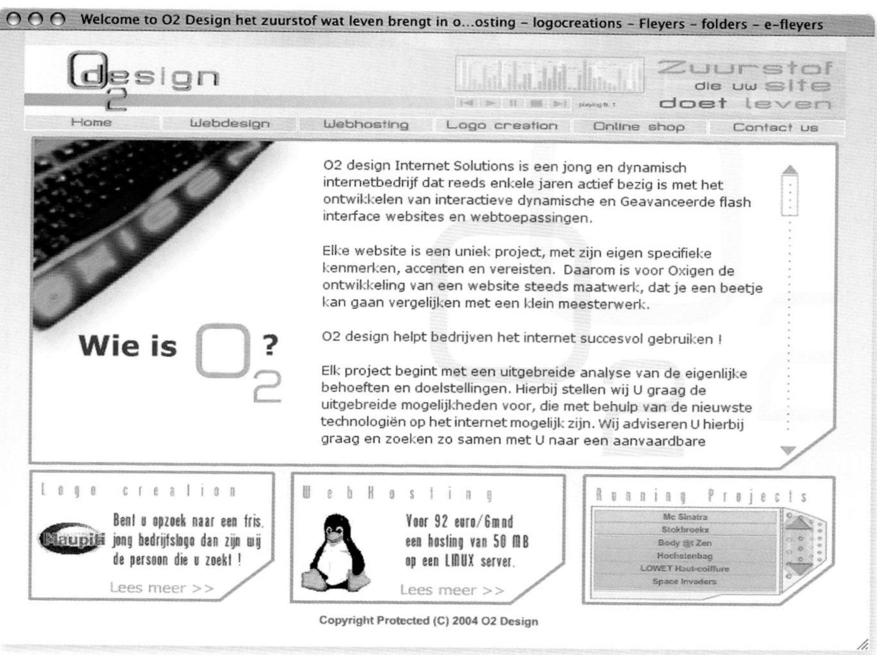
Welcome to O2 Design het zuurstof wat leven brengt in o...osting - logocreations - Fleyers - folders - e-fleyers
design
Zuurstof die uw site doet leven
Home
Webdesign
Webhosting
Logo creation
Online shop
Contact us
O2 design Internet Solutions is een jong en dynamisch internetbedrijf dat reeds enkele jaren actief bezig is met het ontwikkelen van interactieve dynamische en Geavanceerde flash interface websites en webtoepassingen.
Elke website is een uniek project, met zijn eigen specifieke kenmerken, accenten en vereisten. Daarom is voor Oxigen de ontwikkeling van een website steeds maatwerk, dat je een beetje kan gaan vergelijken met een klein meesterwerk.
O2 design helpt bedrijven het internet succesvol gebruiken !
Elk project begint met een uitgebreide analyse van de eigenlijke behoeften en doelstellingen. Hierbij stellen wij U graag de uitgebreide mogelijkheden voor, die met behulp van de nieuwste technologiën op het internet mogelijk zijn. Wij adviseren U hierbij graag en zoeken zo samen met U naar een aanvaardbare
Wie is O2 ?
Logo creation
Bent u opzoek naar een fris, jong bedrijfslogo dan zijn wij de persoon die u zoekt !
Lees meer >>
WebHosting
Voor 92 euro/6mnd een hosting van 50 MB op een LINUX server.
Lees meer >>
Running Projects
Mc Sinatra
Stokbroekx
Body @t Zen
Hochstenbag
LOWET Haut-coiffure
Space Invaders
Copyright Protected (C) 2004 O2 Design

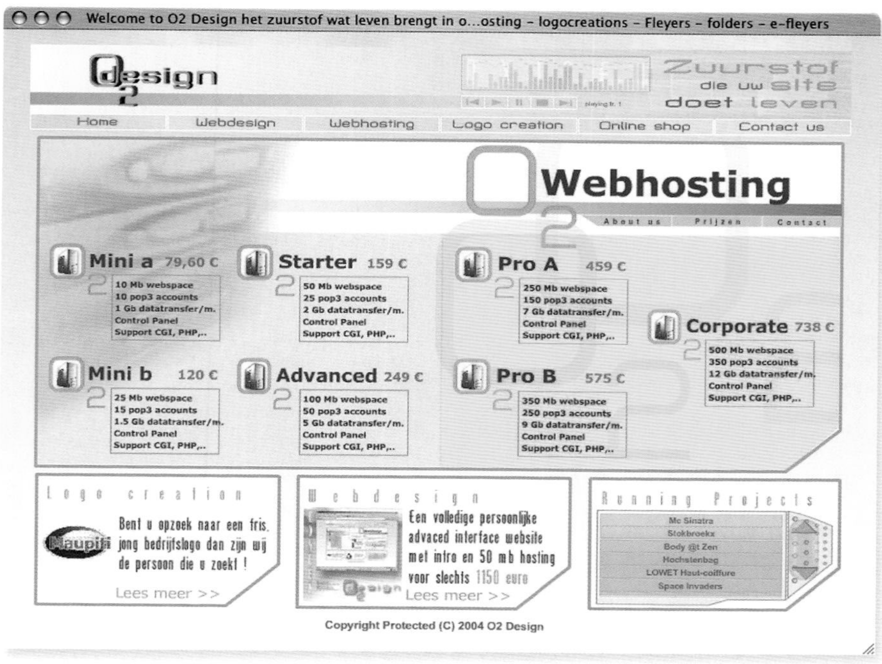
Welcome to O2 Design het zuurstof wat leven brengt in o...osting - logocreations - Fleyers - folders - e-fleyers
design
Zuurstof die uw site doet leven
Home
Webdesign
Webhosting
Logo creation
Online shop
Contact us
Webhosting
About us
Prijzen
Contact
Mini a 79,60 €
10 Mb webspace
10 pop3 accounts
1 Gb datatransfer/m.
Control Panel
Support CGI, PHP,..
Starter 159 €
50 Mb webspace
25 pop3 accounts
2 Gb datatransfer/m.
Control Panel
Support CGI, PHP,..
Pro A 459 €
250 Mb webspace
150 pop3 accounts
7 Gb datatransfer/m.
Control Panel
Support CGI, PHP,..
Corporate 738 €
500 Mb webspace
350 pop3 accounts
12 Gb datatransfer/m.
Control Panel
Support CGI, PHP,..
Mini b 120 €
25 Mb webspace
15 pop3 accounts
1.5 Gb datatransfer/m.
Control Panel
Support CGI, PHP,..
Advanced 249 €
100 Mb webspace
50 pop3 accounts
5 Gb datatransfer/m.
Control Panel
Support CGI, PHP,..
Pro B 575 €
350 Mb webspace
250 pop3 accounts
9 Gb datatransfer/m.
Control Panel
Support CGI, PHP,..
Logo creation
Bent u opzoek naar een fris, jong bedrijfslogo dan zijn wij de persoon die u zoekt !
Lees meer >>
Webdesign
Een volledige persoonlijke advaced interface website met intro en 50 mb hosting voor slechts 1150 euro
Lees meer >>
Running Projects
Mc Sinatra
Stokbroekx
Body @t Zen
Hochstenbag
LOWET Haut-coiffure
Space Invaders
Copyright Protected (C) 2004 O2 Design

www.o2-design.be
D: jeroen hochstenbag
A: o2 design **M:** info@o2-design.be

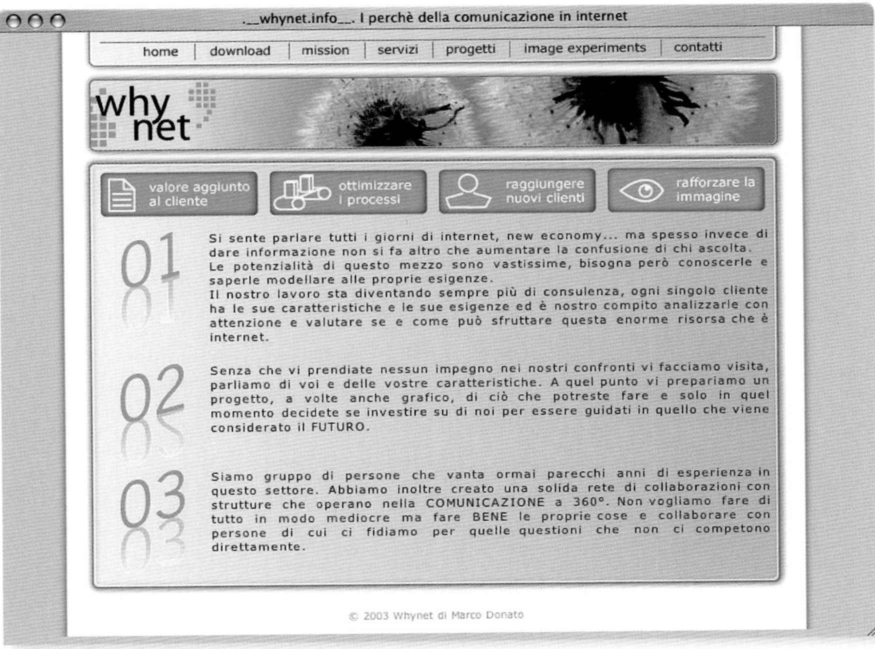
.__whynet.info__. I perchè della comunicazione in internet
home | download | mission | servizi | progetti | image experiments | contatti
why net
valore aggiunto al cliente
ottimizzare i processi
raggiungere nuovi clienti
rafforzare la immagine
01
Si sente parlare tutti i giorni di internet, new economy... ma spesso invece di dare informazione non si fa altro che aumentare la confusione di chi ascolta.
Le potenzialità di questo mezzo sono vastissime, bisogna però conoscerle e saperle modellare alle proprie esigenze.
Il nostro lavoro sta diventando sempre più di consulenza, ogni singolo cliente ha le sue caratteristiche e le sue esigenze ed è nostro compito analizzarle con attenzione e valutare se e come può sfruttare questa enorme risorsa che è internet.
02
Senza che vi prendiate nessun impegno nei nostri confronti vi facciamo visita, parliamo di voi e delle vostre caratteristiche. A quel punto vi prepariamo un progetto, a volte anche grafico, di ciò che potreste fare e solo in quel momento decidete se investire su di noi per essere guidati in quello che viene considerato il FUTURO.
03
Siamo gruppo di persone che vanta ormai parecchi anni di esperienza in questo settore. Abbiamo inoltre creato una solida rete di collaborazioni con strutture che operano nella COMUNICAZIONE a 360°. Non vogliamo fare di tutto in modo mediocre ma fare BENE le proprie cose e collaborare con persone di cui ci fidiamo per quelle questioni che non ci competono direttamente.
© 2003 Whynet di Marco Donato

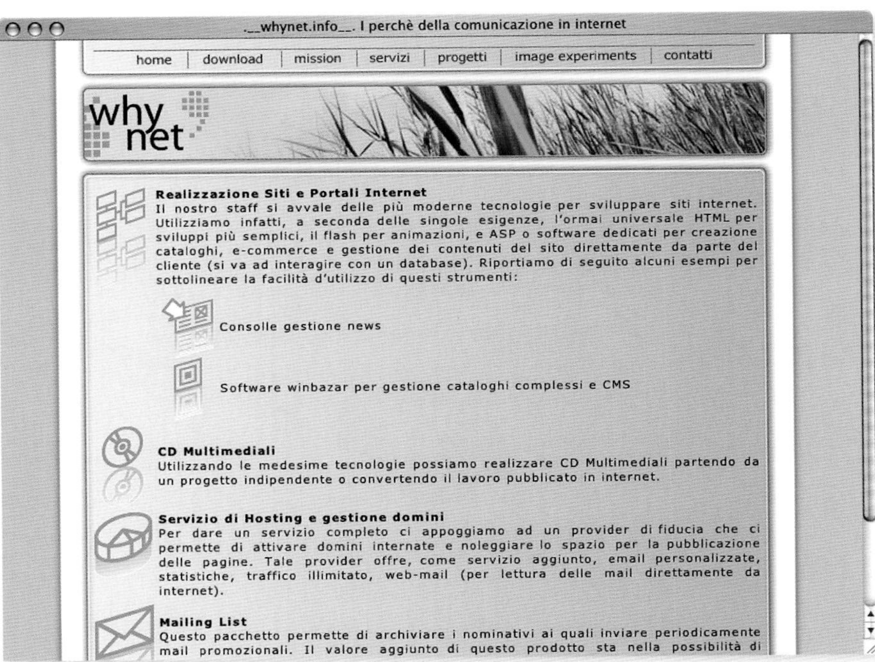
.__whynet.info__. I perchè della comunicazione in internet
home | download | mission | servizi | progetti | image experiments | contatti
why net
Realizzazione Siti e Portali Internet
Il nostro staff si avvale delle più moderne tecnologie per sviluppare siti internet. Utilizziamo infatti, a seconda delle singole esigenze, l'ormai universale HTML per sviluppi più semplici, il flash per animazioni, e ASP o software dedicati per creazione cataloghi, e-commerce e gestione dei contenuti del sito direttamente da parte del cliente (si va ad interagire con un database). Riportiamo di seguito alcuni esempi per sottolineare la facilità d'utilizzo di questi strumenti:
Consolle gestione news
Software winbazar per gestione cataloghi complessi e CMS
CD Multimediali
Utilizzando le medesime tecnologie possiamo realizzare CD Multimediali partendo da un progetto indipendente o convertendo il lavoro pubblicato in internet.
Servizio di Hosting e gestione domini
Per dare un servizio completo ci appoggiamo ad un provider di fiducia che ci permette di attivare domini internate e noleggiare lo spazio per la pubblicazione delle pagine. Tale provider offre, come servizio aggiunto, email personalizzate, statistiche, traffico illimitato, web-mail (per lettura delle mail direttamente da internet).
Mailing List
Questo pacchetto permette di archiviare i nominativi ai quali inviare periodicamente mail promozionali. Il valore aggiunto di questo prodotto sta nella possibilità di

www.whynet.info
D: davide g. aquini
M: info@whynet.info

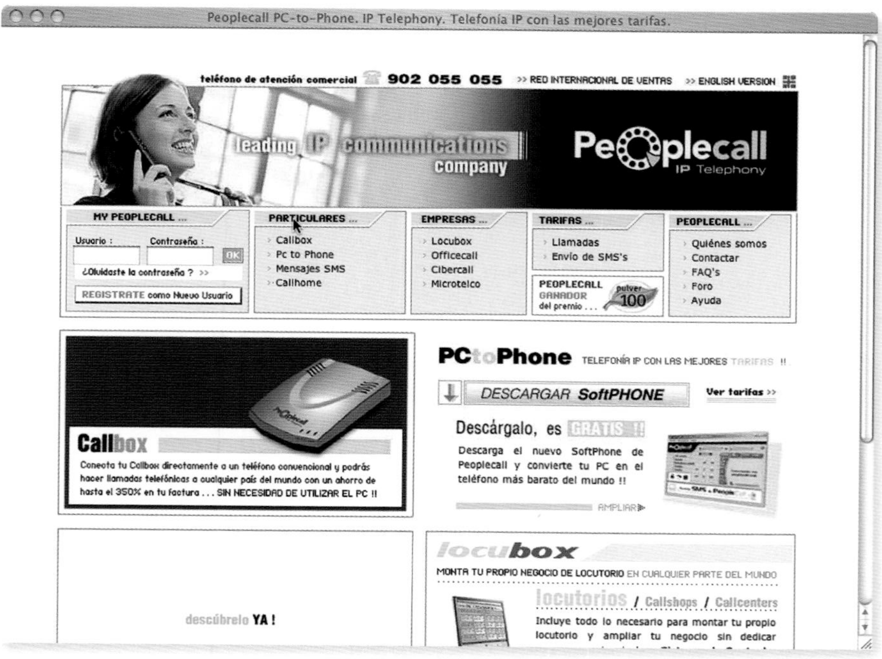
Peoplecall PC-to-Phone. IP Telephony. Telefonía IP con las mejores tarifas.
teléfono de atención comercial 902 055 055
>> RED INTERNACIONAL DE VENTAS >> ENGLISH VERSION
leading IP communications company
Peoplecall IP Telephony
MY PEOPLECALL ...
Usuario : Contraseña :
OK
¿Olvidaste la contraseña ? >>
REGISTRATE como Nuevo Usuario
PARTICULARES ...
Callbox
Pc to Phone
Mensajes SMS
Callhome
EMPRESAS ...
Locubox
Officecall
Cibercall
Microtelco
TARIFAS ...
Llamadas
Envío de SMS's
PEOPLECALL GANADOR del premio ...
PEOPLECALL ...
Quiénes somos
Contactar
FAQ's
Foro
Ayuda
Callbox
Conecta tu Callbox directamente a un teléfono convencional y podrás hacer llamadas telefónicas a cualquier país del mundo con un ahorro de hasta el 350% en tu factura . . . SIN NECESIDAD DE UTILIZAR EL PC !!
PCtoPhone TELEFONÍA IP CON LAS MEJORES TARIFAS !!
DESCARGAR SoftPHONE
Ver tarifas >>
Descárgalo, es GRATIS !!
Descarga el nuevo SoftPhone de Peoplecall y convierte tu PC en el teléfono más barato del mundo !!
AMPLIAR
descúbrelo YA !
locubox
MONTA TU PROPIO NEGOCIO DE LOCUTORIO EN CUALQUIER PARTE DEL MUNDO
locutorios / Callshops / Callcenters
Incluye todo lo necesario para montar tu propio locutorio y ampliar tu negocio sin dedicar

Peoplecall PC-to-Phone. IP Telephony. Telefonía IP con las mejores tarifas.
teléfono de atención comercial 902 055 055
>> RED INTERNACIONAL DE VENTAS >> ENGLISH VERSION
leading IP communications company
Peoplecall IP Telephony
Particulares
· Callbox
· PC to Phone
· Mensajes SMS
· Callhome
Empresas
Tarifas
MyPeoplecall
Sobre Peoplecall
Si tienes ADSL ó CABLE
tienes 1 línea telefónica adicional !!
Callbox
más de 20.000 Callbox instalados en todo el mundo !
OFERTA 135€ +I.V.A. ESPECIAL
10€ en llamadas + 1 línea adicional e independiente + 350% AHORRO
OFERTA 250€ +I.V.A. ESPECIAL
packDUO
EL PACK INCLUYE
· GATEWAY VOIP 1 LINEA
· MANUAL DE INSTALACION
· 10 EUROS EN LLAMADAS
OFERTA ESPECIAL: 135 EUROS
COMPRAR >>
TARIFAS
Siempre las mejores tarifas :
UK
VER RESTO TARIFAS >>

www.peoplecall.com
D: miguel romanillos **C:** hamadi housami **P:** javier de miguel
A: dreamsite **M:** info@dreamsite.es

esfera
home | mi esfera | servicios | productos | desarrollo | quienes somos |
esfera
comunicaciones
Usuarios Mi Esfera:
username
password
entrar
| perdiste tu clave? | registro para nuevos usuarios | contacto

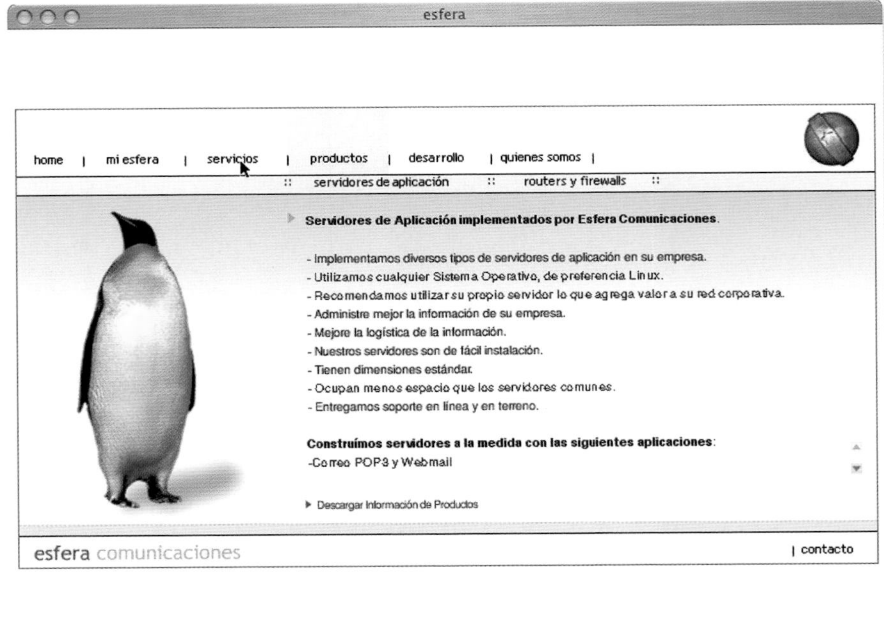
esfera
home | mi esfera | servicios | productos | desarrollo | quienes somos |
:: servidores de aplicación :: routers y firewalls ::
Servidores de Aplicación implementados por Esfera Comunicaciones.
- Implementamos diversos tipos de servidores de aplicación en su empresa.
- Utilizamos cualquier Sistema Operativo, de preferencia Linux.
- Recomendamos utilizar su propio servidor lo que agrega valor a su red corporativa.
- Administre mejor la información de su empresa.
- Mejore la logística de la información.
- Nuestros servidores son de fácil instalación.
- Tienen dimensiones estándar.
- Ocupan menos espacio que los servidores comunes.
- Entregamos soporte en línea y en terreno.
Construímos servidores a la medida con las siguientes aplicaciones:
-Correo POP3 y Webmail
Descargar Información de Productos
esfera comunicaciones
| contacto

www.esfera.cl
D: felipe alvarado
A: think project **M:** felipealvarado@manquehue.net

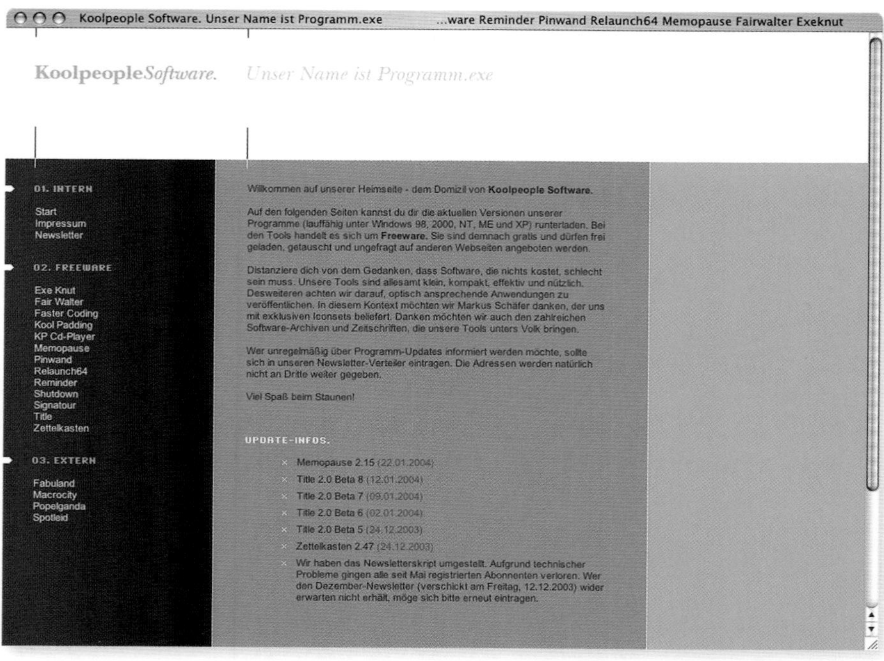
Koolpeople Software. Unser Name ist Programm.exe
...ware Reminder Pinwand Relaunch64 Memopause Fairwalter Exeknut
KoolpeopleSoftware.
Unser Name ist Programm.exe
01. INTERN
Start
Impressum
Newsletter
02. FREEWARE
Exe Knut
Fair Walter
Faster Coding
Kool Padding
KP Cd-Player
Memopause
Pinwand
Relaunch64
Reminder
Shutdown
Signatour
Title
Zettelkasten
03. EXTERN
Fabuland
Macrocity
Popelganda
Spotleid
Willkommen auf unserer Heimseite - dem Domizil von Koolpeople Software.
Auf den folgenden Seiten kannst du dir die aktuellen Versionen unserer Programme (lauffähig unter Windows 98, 2000, NT, ME und XP) runterladen. Bei den Tools handelt es sich um Freeware. Sie sind demnach gratis und dürfen frei geladen, getauscht und ungefragt auf anderen Webseiten angeboten werden.
Distanziere dich von dem Gedanken, dass Software, die nichts kostet, schlecht sein muss. Unsere Tools sind allesamt klein, kompakt, effektiv und nützlich. Desweiteren achten wir darauf, optisch ansprechende Anwendungen zu veröffentlichen. In diesem Kontext möchten wir Markus Schäfer danken, der uns mit exklusiven Iconsets beliefert. Danken möchten wir auch den zahlreichen Software-Archiven und Zeitschriften, die unsere Tools unters Volk bringen.
Wer unregelmäßig über Programm-Updates informiert werden möchte, sollte sich in unseren Newsletter-Verteiler eintragen. Die Adressen werden natürlich nicht an Dritte weiter gegeben.
Viel Spaß beim Staunen!
UPDATE-INFOS.
Memopause 2.15 (22.01.2004)
Title 2.0 Beta 8 (12.01.2004)
Title 2.0 Beta 7 (09.01.2004)
Title 2.0 Beta 6 (02.01.2004)
Title 2.0 Beta 5 (24.12.2003)
Zettelkasten 2.47 (24.12.2003)
Wir haben das Newsletterskript umgestellt. Aufgrund technischer Probleme gingen alle seit Mai registrierten Abonnenten verloren. Wer den Dezember-Newsletter (verschickt am Freitag, 12.12.2003) wider erwarten nicht erhält, möge sich bitte erneut eintragen.

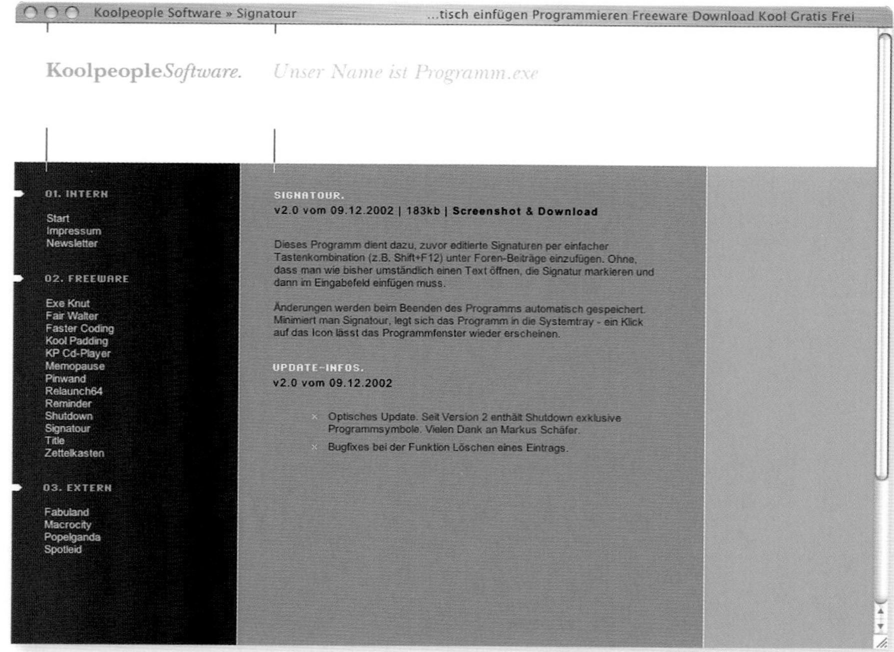
Koolpeople Software » Signatour
...tisch einfügen Programmieren Freeware Download Kool Gratis Frei
KoolpeopleSoftware.
Unser Name ist Programm.exe
01. INTERN
Start
Impressum
Newsletter
02. FREEWARE
Exe Knut
Fair Walter
Faster Coding
Kool Padding
KP Cd-Player
Memopause
Pinwand
Relaunch64
Reminder
Shutdown
Signatour
Title
Zettelkasten
03. EXTERN
Fabuland
Macrocity
Popelganda
Spotleid
SIGNATOUR.
v2.0 vom 09.12.2002 | 183kb | Screenshot & Download
Dieses Programm dient dazu, zuvor editierte Signaturen per einfacher Tastenkombination (z.B. Shift+F12) unter Foren-Beiträge einzufügen. Ohne, dass man wie bisher umständlich einen Text öffnen, die Signatur markieren und dann im Eingabefeld einfügen muss.
Änderungen werden beim Beenden des Programms automatisch gespeichert. Minimiert man Signatour, legt sich das Programm in die Systemtray - ein Klick auf das Icon lässt das Programmfenster wieder erscheinen.
UPDATE-INFOS.
v2.0 vom 09.12.2002
Optisches Update. Seit Version 2 enthält Shutdown exklusive Programmsymbole. Vielen Dank an Markus Schäfer.
Bugfixes bei der Funktion Löschen eines Eintrags.

www.koolpeople.de
D: fabu **C:** daniel lüdecke
M: fabu@wahnsignal.de

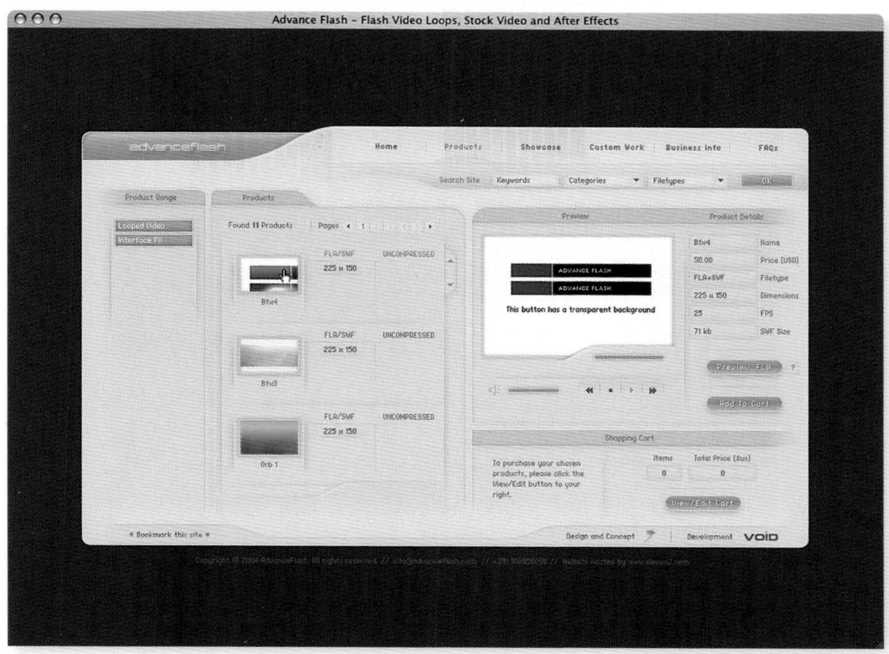
Advance Flash - Flash Video Loops, Stock Video and After Effects
advanceflash
Home
Products
Showcase
Custom Work
Business Info
FAQs
Product Range
Products
Preview
Product Details
This button has a transparent background
Shopping Cart
To purchase your chosen products, please click the View/Edit button to your right.
Design and Concept
Development
VOID

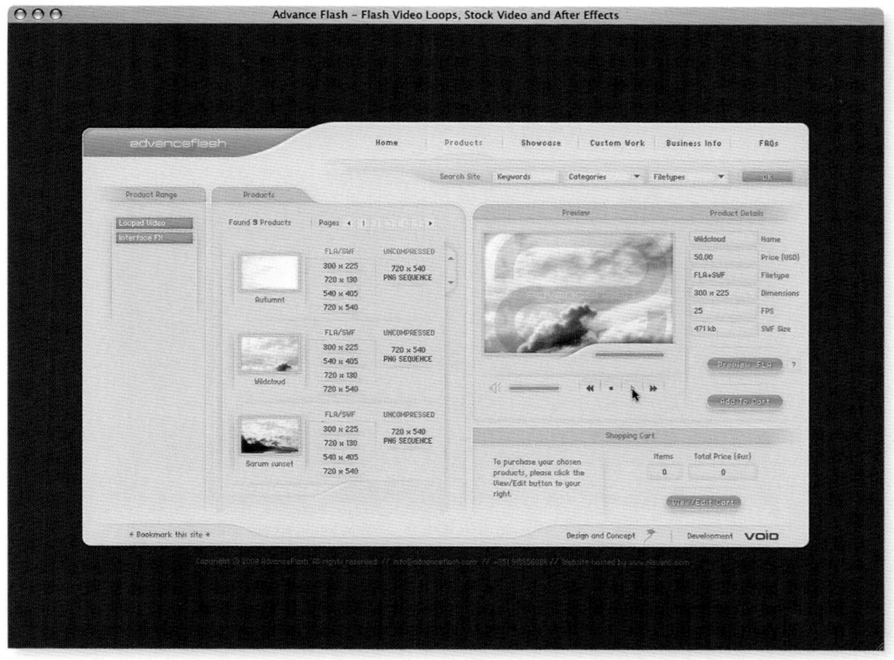
Advance Flash - Flash Video Loops, Stock Video and After Effects
advanceflash
Home
Products
Showcase
Custom Work
Business Info
FAQs
Product Range
Products
Preview
Product Details
Shopping Cart
To purchase your chosen products, please click the View/Edit button to your right.
Design and Concept
Development
VOID

www.advanceflash.com
D: jay birch
A: www.jaybirch.com

Joensen critical software
NEWS
SERVICES | COMPANY PROFILE | PRODUCTS | WHITE PAPERS | LINKS |
Safety Critical Software
Applications...
JOENSEN
CRITICALSOFTWARE
Civilingeniør - Jørleif Joensen
Mobil: 4089 7737 - Tlf: 4390 1957
Mosede Engvej 30 - 2670 Greve
Jorleif.Joensen@joensen-critical.dk
Safety integrity level - common cause failures
This article describes the effects of common cause failures on safety systems with high integrity
>> read more

Joensen critical software
NEWS
SERVICES | COMPANY PROFILE | PRODUCTS | WHITE PAPERS | LINKS |
Design Verification...
JOENSEN
CRITICALSOFTWARE
Civilingeniør - Jørleif Joensen
Mobil: 4089 7737 - Tlf: 4390 1957
Mosede Engvej 30 - 2670 Greve
Jorleif.Joensen@joensen-critical.dk
Safety integrity level - common cause failures
This article describes the effects of common cause failures on safety systems with high integrity
>> read more

www.joensen-critical.dk
D: marianne mickelborg **C:** christian ranum zohnesen **P:** anders weile
M: info@it-art.dk

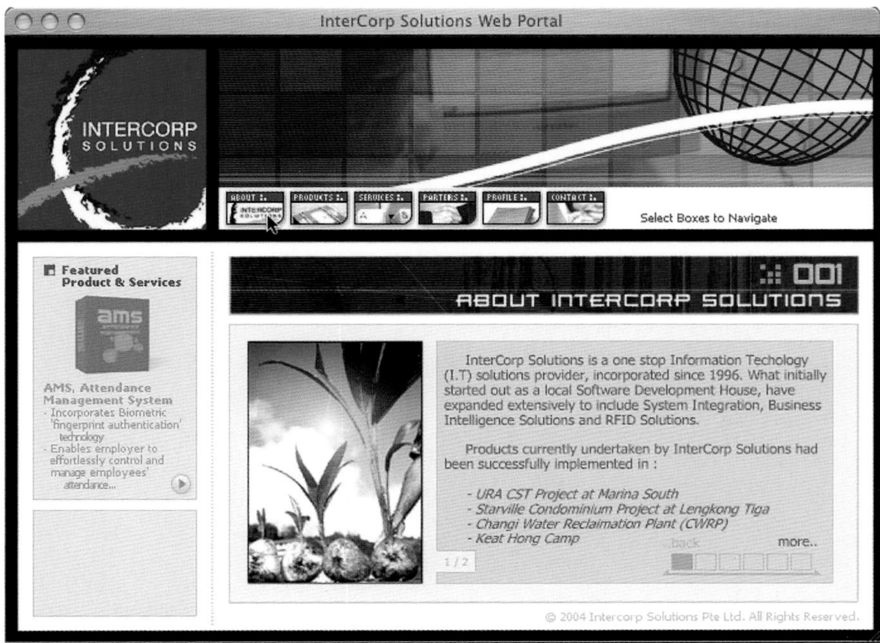
InterCorp Solutions Web Portal
INTERCORP SOLUTIONS
ABOUT PRODUCTS SERVICES PARTERS PROFILE CONTACT
Select Boxes to Navigate
Featured Product & Services
AMS, Attendance Management System
- Incorporates Biometric 'fingerprint authentication' technology
- Enables employer to effortlessly control and manage employees' attendance...
001 ABOUT INTERCORP SOLUTIONS
InterCorp Solutions is a one stop Information Techology (I.T) solutions provider, incorporated since 1996. What initially started out as a local Software Development House, have expanded extensively to include System Integration, Business Intelligence Solutions and RFID Solutions.
Products currently undertaken by InterCorp Solutions had been successfully implemented in :
- URA CST Project at Marina South
- Starville Condominium Project at Lengkong Tiga
- Changi Water Reclaimation Plant (CWRP)
- Keat Hong Camp
..back more..
1 / 2
© 2004 Intercorp Solutions Pte Ltd. All Rights Reserved.

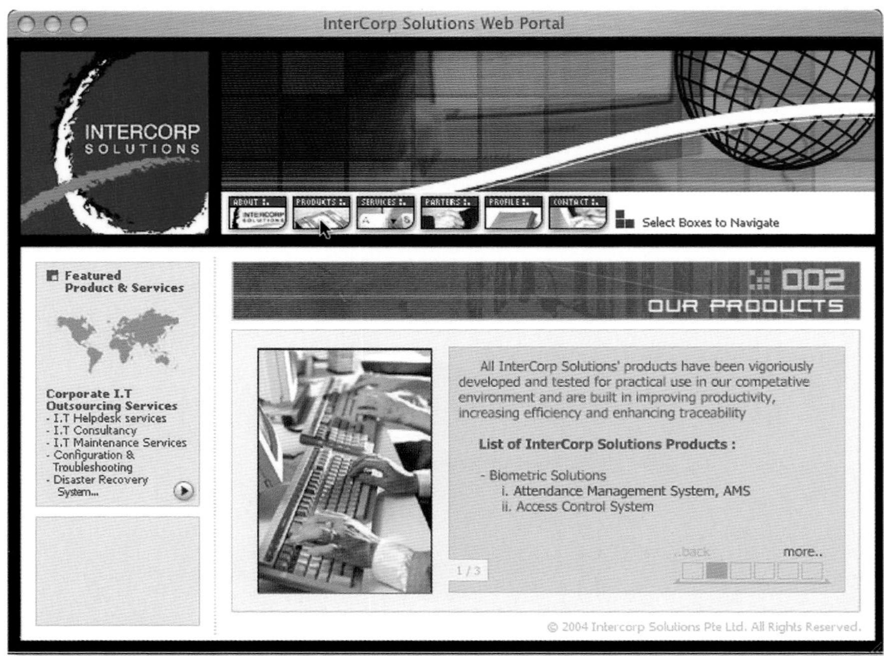
InterCorp Solutions Web Portal
INTERCORP SOLUTIONS
ABOUT PRODUCTS SERVICES PARTERS PROFILE CONTACT
Select Boxes to Navigate
Featured Product & Services
Corporate I.T Outsourcing Services
- I.T Helpdesk services
- I.T Consultancy
- I.T Maintenance Services
- Configuration & Troubleshooting
- Disaster Recovery System...
002 OUR PRODUCTS
All InterCorp Solutions' products have been vigoriously developed and tested for practical use in our competative environment and are built in improving productivity, increasing efficiency and enhancing traceability
List of InterCorp Solutions Products :
- Biometric Solutions
i. Attendance Management System, AMS
ii. Access Control System
..back more..
1 / 3
© 2004 Intercorp Solutions Pte Ltd. All Rights Reserved.

www.intercorpsolutions.com
D: kelvin koh
A: flashwerks **M:** flashwerks@flashwerks.com

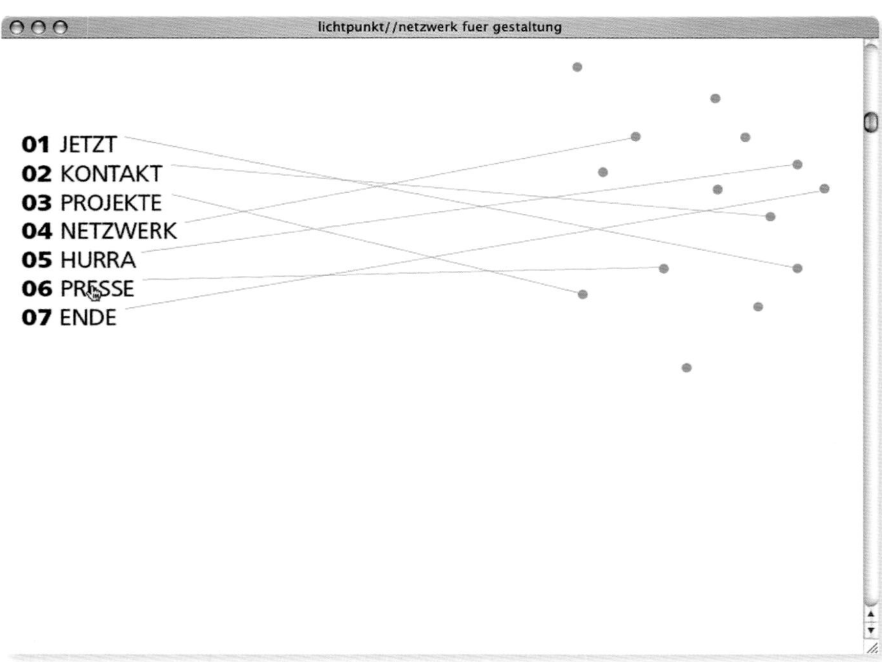
lichtpunkt//netzwerk fuer gestaltung
01 JETZT
02 KONTAKT
03 PROJEKTE
04 NETZWERK
05 HURRA
06 PRESSE
07 ENDE

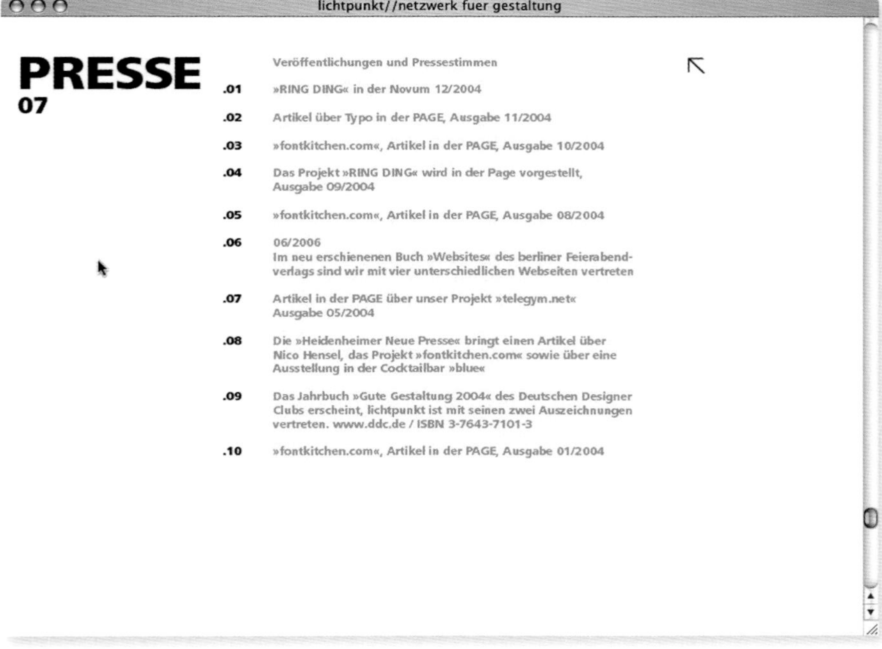
lichtpunkt//netzwerk fuer gestaltung
PRESSE
07
Veröffentlichungen und Pressestimmen
.01 »RING DING« in der Novum 12/2004
.02 Artikel über Typo in der PAGE, Ausgabe 11/2004
.03 »fontkitchen.com«, Artikel in der PAGE, Ausgabe 10/2004
.04 Das Projekt »RING DING« wird in der Page vorgestellt, Ausgabe 09/2004
.05 »fontkitchen.com«, Artikel in der PAGE, Ausgabe 08/2004
.06 06/2006 Im neu erschienenen Buch »Websites« des berliner Feierabend-verlags sind wir mit vier unterschiedlichen Webseiten vertreten
.07 Artikel in der PAGE über unser Projekt »telegym.net« Ausgabe 05/2004
.08 Die »Heidenheimer Neue Presse« bringt einen Artikel über Nico Hensel, das Projekt »fontkitchen.com« sowie über eine Ausstellung in der Cocktailbar »blue«
.09 Das Jahrbuch »Gute Gestaltung 2004« des Deutschen Designer Clubs erscheint, lichtpunkt ist mit seinen zwei Auszeichnungen vertreten. www.ddc.de / ISBN 3-7643-7101-3
.10 »fontkitchen.com«, Artikel in der PAGE, Ausgabe 01/2004

lichtpunkt.biz
D: nico hensel, marc engenhart
A: lichtpunkt // netzwerk für gestaltung **M:** nh@lichtpunkt.biz

Endbox Design

Tens jeito?

TORNA-TE UM HOMEM!!

Na endbox trabalhamos com pessoas nas áreas de Design, Comunicação e Programação

Envia-nos o teu Currículo/Portfolio para rh@endbox.com

Tudo esclarecido? Então pronto, clique na caixa só mais uma vez s.f.f.

design ENDBOX

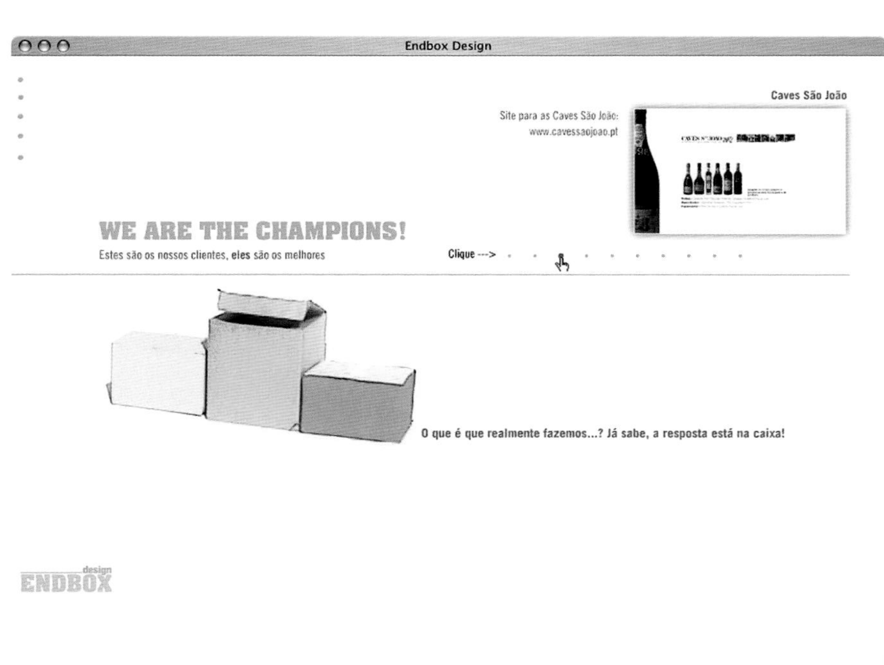
Endbox Design
Caves São João
Site para as Caves São João:
www.cavessaojoao.pt
WE ARE THE CHAMPIONS!
Estes são os nossos clientes, eles são os melhores
Clique --->
O que é que realmente fazemos...? Já sabe, a resposta está na caixa!
design ENDBOX

www.endbox.com

D: rogério machado **C:** rogério machado **P:** joão cardoso

A: endbox design **M:** geral@endbox.com

DIGITARIA - About Us - San Diego Web Development, Multimedia and Online Marketing

digitaria
DIGITAL BRAND MIGRATION™

ABOUT US | NEWS
SERVICES | INTERFACE DESIGN | WEB SITE DEVELOPMENT | APPLICATION DEVELOPMENT | ONLINE MARKETING | MULTIMEDIA DEVELOPMENT
CLIENTS | CASE STUDIES
CONTACT

Digitaria is a flexible, energetic interactive agency dedicated to helping your company achieve its business goals. Clients come to Digitaria when they need new ideas, strategy, and an informed perspective to communicate their brand and reach customers.

We think and create for business.

Although Digitaria Interactive is over five years old, the name Digitaria was used to describe a star over 5,000 years ago by the Dogon, a tribe in Mali, West Africa. According to Dogon tradition, the star Sirius has a companion star, which is invisible to the human eye. This companion star has a 50-year elliptical orbit around the visible Sirius and was named Digitaria (or Sirius B). Though not photographed until 1970, Digitaria has taken its name from this star, a long-standing symbol of foresight and intelligence.

Today the symbolic origins of Digitaria's name, foresight and intelligence, remain the guiding principles behind our organization. We strive to constantly innovate and develop new ideas to allow our clients to take full advantage of digital communications.

DIGITARIA - Services - Web Design, Multimedia Demos, Search Engine Marketing, Media Planning

digitaria
DIGITAL BRAND MIGRATION™

ABOUT US | NEWS
SERVICES
CLIENTS | CASE STUDIES
CONTACT

Combining strategy, creative and technology solutions, Digitaria creates digital media that can be monetized and leveraged across multiple communication channels, including website development, product launches, interactive demos, retail kiosks, banners, multimedia presentations, micro sites, copywriting, usability testing and online tracking reports/analytics. To learn more about our work, view our case studies.

Online Strategy

- Customer Profiling
- Information Architecture
- Online Marketing
- Online Campaigns
- User Surveys

Usability

- User Interviews and Observations
- Clickstream Analysis
- Card Sorting
- Usability Testing

Online Marketing

Creative & Design

- Creative Platforms
- User Interface Design
- Web Design
- Marketing Collateral
- Photography and Art Direction
- Copywriting

Multimedia

- Flash Design and Development
- CD-Roms / DVD
- 3D Graphic Design
- Video
- Kiosk
- Original Sound Design

See Multimedia Samples

www.digitaria.com
D: daiga atvara, gunnar lockwood **C:** matt kardos **P:** ryan o'leary
A: digitaria interactive **M:** daiga@digitaria.com

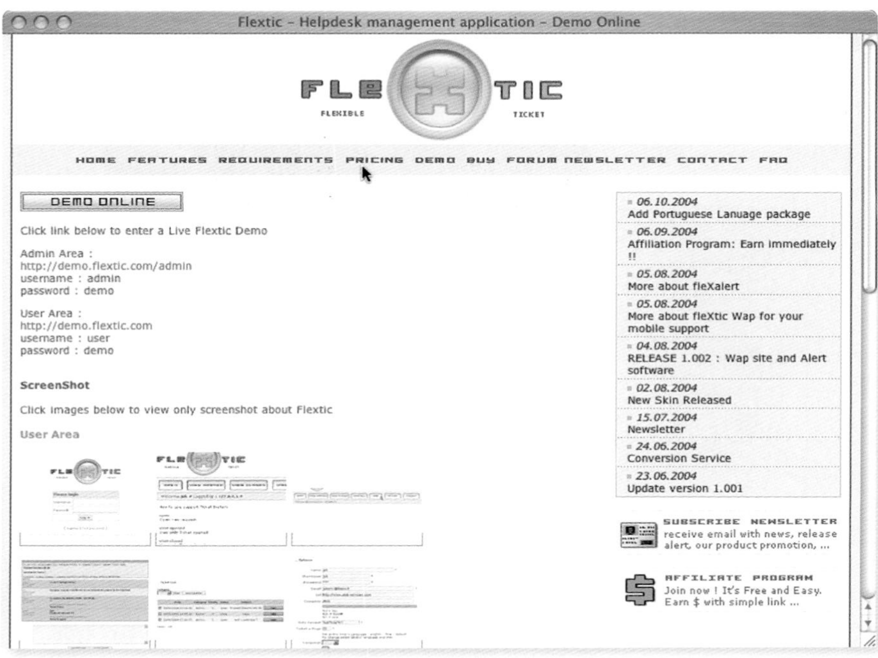
Flextic - Helpdesk management application - Demo Online
FLEXTIC
FLEXIBLE TICKET
HOME FEATURES REQUIREMENTS PRICING DEMO BUY FORUM NEWSLETTER CONTACT FAQ
DEMO ONLINE
Click link below to enter a Live Flextic Demo
Admin Area :
http://demo.flextic.com/admin
username : admin
password : demo
User Area :
http://demo.flextic.com
username : user
password : demo
ScreenShot
Click images below to view only screenshot about Flextic
User Area
06.10.2004
Add Portuguese Lanuage package
06.09.2004
Affiliation Program: Earn immediately !!
05.08.2004
More about fleXalert
05.08.2004
More about fleXtic Wap for your mobile support
04.08.2004
RELEASE 1.002 : Wap site and Alert software
02.08.2004
New Skin Released
15.07.2004
Newsletter
24.06.2004
Conversion Service
23.06.2004
Update version 1.001
SUBSCRIBE NEWSLETTER
receive email with news, release alert, our product promotion, ...
AFFILIATE PROGRAM
Join now ! It's Free and Easy.
Earn $ with simple link ...

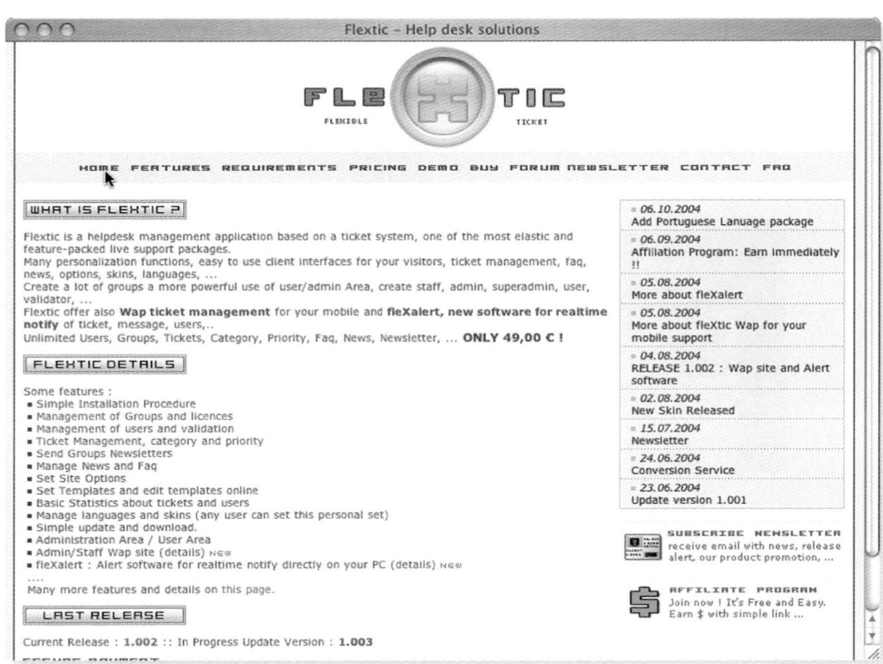
Flextic - Help desk solutions
FLEXTIC
FLEXIBLE TICKET
HOME FEATURES REQUIREMENTS PRICING DEMO BUY FORUM NEWSLETTER CONTACT FAQ
WHAT IS FLEXTIC ?
Flextic is a helpdesk management application based on a ticket system, one of the most elastic and feature-packed live support packages.
Many personalization functions, easy to use client interfaces for your visitors, ticket management, faq, news, options, skins, languages, ...
Create a lot of groups a more powerful use of user/admin Area, create staff, admin, superadmin, user, validator, ...
Flextic offer also Wap ticket management for your mobile and fleXalert, new software for realtime notify of ticket, message, users,..
Unlimited Users, Groups, Tickets, Category, Priority, Faq, News, Newsletter, ... ONLY 49,00 € !
FLEXTIC DETAILS
Some features :
Simple Installation Procedure
Management of Groups and licences
Management of users and validation
Ticket Management, category and priority
Send Groups Newsletters
Manage News and Faq
Set Site Options
Set Templates and edit templates online
Basic Statistics about tickets and users
Manage languages and skins (any user can set this personal set)
Simple update and download.
Administration Area / User Area
Admin/Staff Wap site (details) NEW
fleXalert : Alert software for realtime notify directly on your PC (details) NEW
....
Many more features and details on this page.
LAST RELEASE
Current Release : 1.002 :: In Progress Update Version : 1.003
06.10.2004
Add Portuguese Lanuage package
06.09.2004
Affiliation Program: Earn immediately !!
05.08.2004
More about fleXalert
05.08.2004
More about fleXtic Wap for your mobile support
04.08.2004
RELEASE 1.002 : Wap site and Alert software
02.08.2004
New Skin Released
15.07.2004
Newsletter
24.06.2004
Conversion Service
23.06.2004
Update version 1.001
SUBSCRIBE NEWSLETTER
receive email with news, release alert, our product promotion, ...
AFFILIATE PROGRAM
Join now ! It's Free and Easy.
Earn $ with simple link ...

www.flextic.com
D: simone casaliggi
M: simone@casaliggi.com

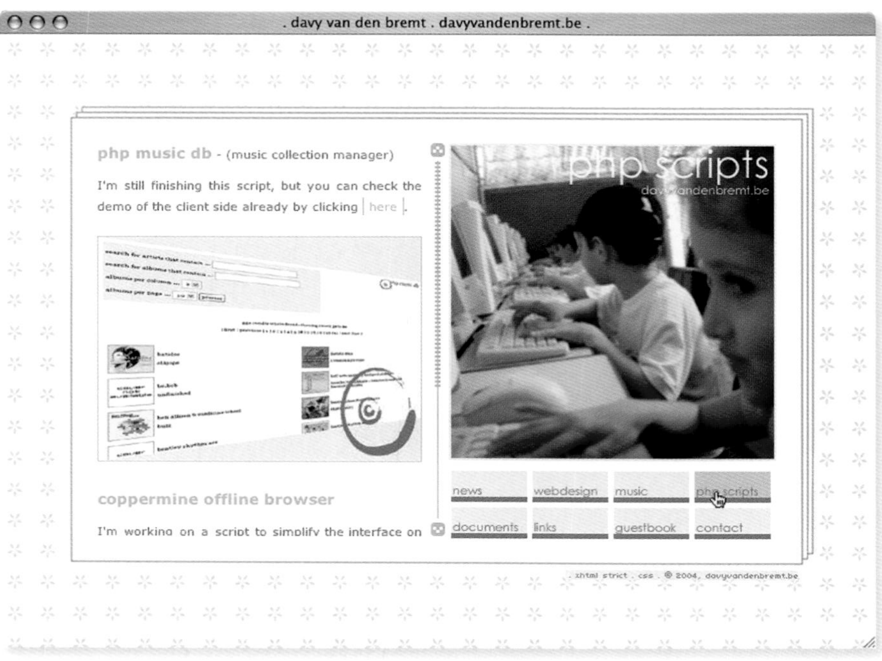
. davy van den bremt . davyvandenbremt.be .
php music db - (music collection manager)
I'm still finishing this script, but you can check the demo of the client side already by clicking | here |.
coppermine offline browser
I'm working on a script to simplify the interface on
php scripts
davyvandenbremt.be
news
webdesign
music
php scripts
documents
links
guestbook
contact
. xhtml strict . css . © 2004, davyvandenbremt.be

. davy van den bremt . davyvandenbremt.be .
http://www.dero.be/
dero.be
who? Dero is a construction firm in Zele (Belgium).
webdesign
davyvandenbremt.be
news
webdesign
music
php scripts
documents
links
guestbook
contact
. xhtml strict . css . © 2004, davyvandenbremt.be

www.davyvandenbremt.be
D: davy van den bremt
M: webmaster@davyvandenbremt.be

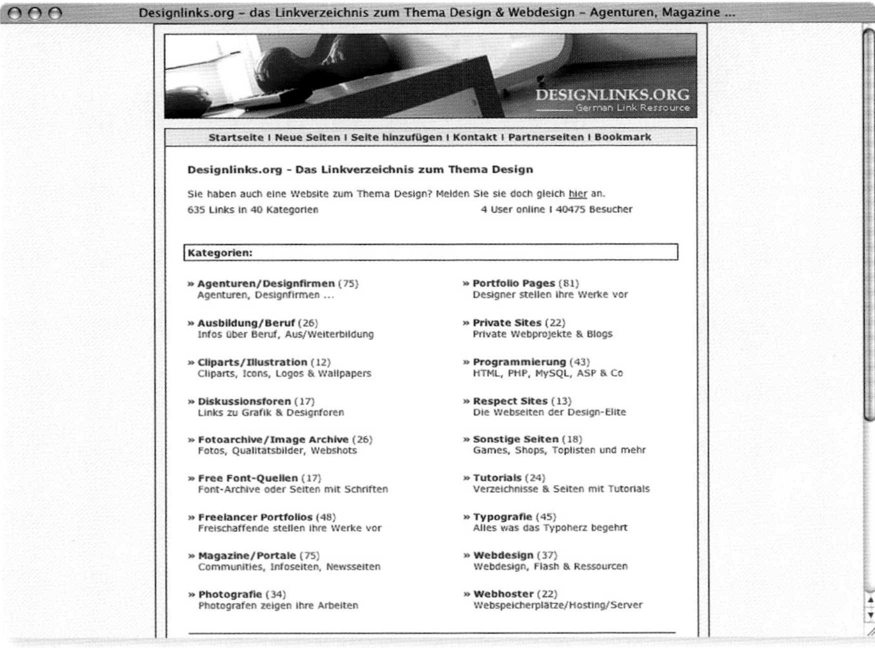
Designlinks.org - das Linkverzeichnis zum Thema Design & Webdesign - Agenturen, Magazine ...
DESIGNLINKS.ORG
German Link Ressource
Startseite | Neue Seiten | Seite hinzufügen | Kontakt | Partnerseiten | Bookmark
Designlinks.org - Das Linkverzeichnis zum Thema Design
Sie haben auch eine Website zum Thema Design? Melden Sie sie doch gleich hier an.
635 Links in 40 Kategorien
4 User online | 40475 Besucher
Kategorien:
» Agenturen/Designfirmen (75)
Agenturen, Designfirmen ...
» Ausbildung/Beruf (26)
Infos über Beruf, Aus/Weiterbildung
» Cliparts/Illustration (12)
Cliparts, Icons, Logos & Wallpapers
» Diskussionsforen (17)
Links zu Grafik & Designforen
» Fotoarchive/Image Archive (26)
Fotos, Qualitätsbilder, Webshots
» Free Font-Quellen (17)
Font-Archive oder Seiten mit Schriften
» Freelancer Portfolios (48)
Freischaffende stellen ihre Werke vor
» Magazine/Portale (75)
Communities, Infoseiten, Newsseiten
» Photografie (34)
Photografen zeigen ihre Arbeiten
» Portfolio Pages (81)
Designer stellen ihre Werke vor
» Private Sites (22)
Private Webprojekte & Blogs
» Programmierung (43)
HTML, PHP, MySQL, ASP & Co
» Respect Sites (13)
Die Webseiten der Design-Elite
» Sonstige Seiten (18)
Games, Shops, Toplisten und mehr
» Tutorials (24)
Verzeichnisse & Seiten mit Tutorials
» Typografie (45)
Alles was das Typoherz begehrt
» Webdesign (37)
Webdesign, Flash & Ressourcen
» Webhoster (22)
Webspeicherplätze/Hosting/Server

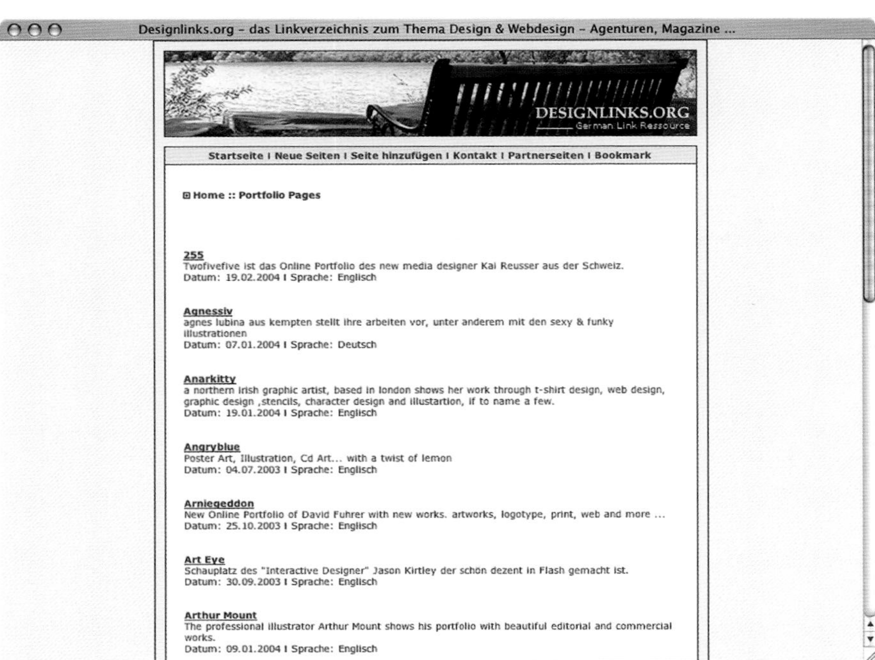
Designlinks.org - das Linkverzeichnis zum Thema Design & Webdesign - Agenturen, Magazine ...
DESIGNLINKS.ORG
German Link Ressource
Startseite | Neue Seiten | Seite hinzufügen | Kontakt | Partnerseiten | Bookmark
Home :: Portfolio Pages
255
Twofivefive ist das Online Portfolio des new media designer Kai Reusser aus der Schweiz.
Datum: 19.02.2004 | Sprache: Englisch
Agnessiv
agnes lubina aus kempten stellt ihre arbeiten vor, unter anderem mit den sexy & funky illustrationen
Datum: 07.01.2004 | Sprache: Deutsch
Anarkitty
a northern irish graphic artist, based in london shows her work through t-shirt design, web design, graphic design ,stencils, character design and illustartion, if to name a few.
Datum: 19.01.2004 | Sprache: Englisch
Angryblue
Poster Art, Illustration, Cd Art... with a twist of lemon
Datum: 04.07.2003 | Sprache: Englisch
Arniegeddon
New Online Portfolio of David Fuhrer with new works. artworks, logotype, print, web and more ...
Datum: 25.10.2003 | Sprache: Englisch
Art Eye
Schauplatz des "Interactive Designer" Jason Kirtley der schön dezent in Flash gemacht ist.
Datum: 30.09.2003 | Sprache: Englisch
Arthur Mount
The professional illustrator Arthur Mount shows his portfolio with beautiful editorial and commercial works.
Datum: 09.01.2004 | Sprache: Englisch

www.designlinks.org
D: marco petzold
M: kontakt@designlinks.org

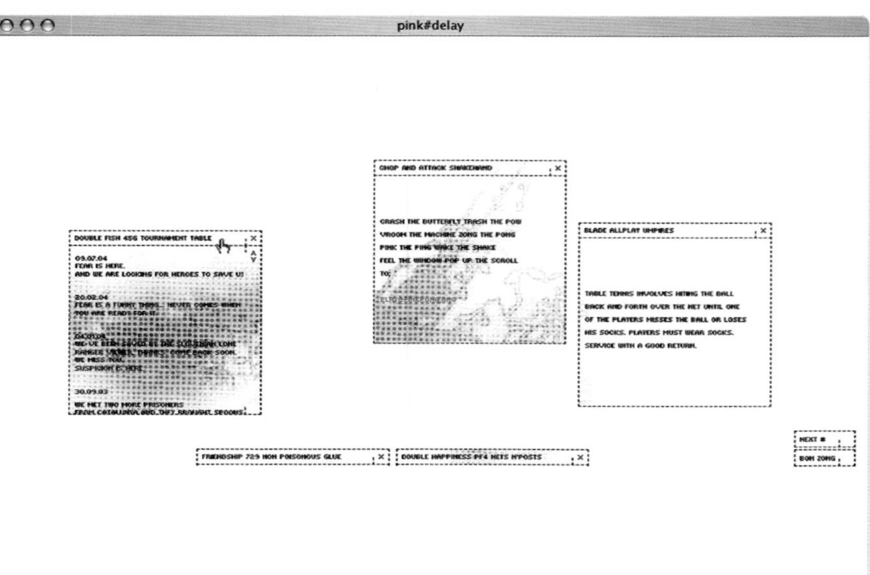
pink#delay
DOUBLE FISH 456 TOURNAMENT TABLE
09.07.04
FEAR IS HERE.
AND WE ARE LOOKING FOR HEROES TO SAVE US
20.02.04
30.09.03
WE MET TWO MORE PRISONERS
CHOP AND ATTACK SHAKEHAND
CRASH THE BUTTERFLY TRASH THE POW
VROOM THE MACHINE ZONG THE PONG
PINK THE PING WAKE THE SHAKE
FEEL THE WINDOW POP UP THE SCROLL
TO:
BLADE ALLPLAY UMPIRES
TABLE TENNIS INVOLVES HITTING THE BALL
BACK AND FORTH OVER THE NET UNTIL ONE
OF THE PLAYERS MISSES THE BALL OR LOSES
HIS SOCKS. PLAYERS MUST WEAR SOCKS.
SERVICE WITH A GOOD RETURN.
FRIENDSHIP 729 NON POISONOUS GLUE
DOUBLE HAPPINESS PF4 NETS N'POSTS
NEXT #
BON ZONG

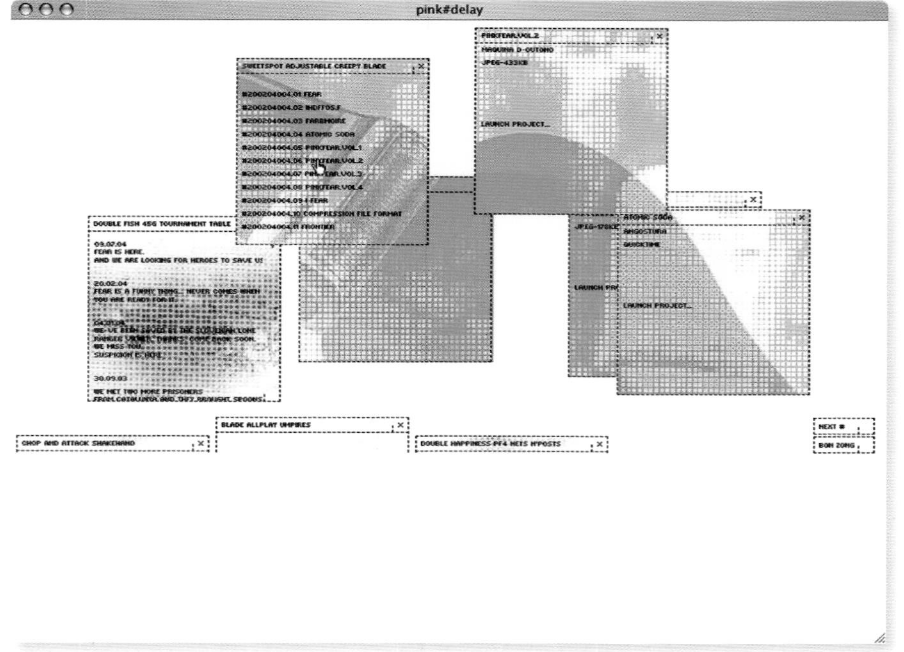
pink#delay
SWEETSPOT ADJUSTABLE CREEPY BLADE
#200204004.01 FEAR
#200204004.03 FARBMOIRE
#200204004.04 ATOMIC SODA
#200204004.05 PINKFEAR.VOL.1
#200204004.06 PINKFEAR.VOL.2
#200204004.08 PINKFEAR.VOL.4
#200204004.10 COMPRESSION FILE FORMAT
#200204004.11 FRONTIER
PINKFEAR.VOL.2
MAQUINA D-OUTONO
JPEG-433KB
LAUNCH PROJECT...
ATOMIC SODA
ANGOSTURA
QUICKTIME
LAUNCH PROJECT...
DOUBLE FISH 456 TOURNAMENT TABLE
09.07.04
FEAR IS HERE.
AND WE ARE LOOKING FOR HEROES TO SAVE US
CHOP AND ATTACK SHAKEHAND
BLADE ALLPLAY UMPIRES
DOUBLE HAPPINESS PF4 NETS N'POSTS
NEXT #
BON ZONG

www.pinkpong.org

D: luis sarmento **C:** aulo carvalho

A: pinkpong **M:** luissarmento@adsl.xl.pt

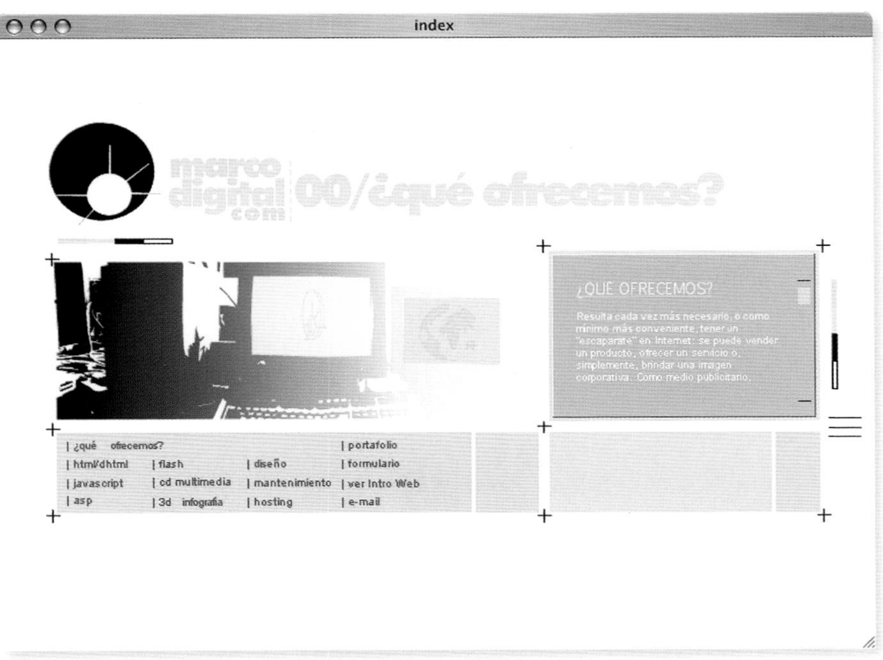
index
marco digital com
00/¿qué ofrecemos?
¿QUE OFRECEMOS?
Resulta cada vez más necesario, o como mínimo más conveniente, tener un "escaparate" en Internet: se puede vender un producto, ofrecer un servicio o, simplemente, brindar una imagen corporativa. Como medio publicitario,
| ¿qué ofrecemos?
| portafolio
| html/dhtml
| flash
| diseño
| formulario
| javascript
| cd multimedia
| mantenimiento
| ver Intro Web
| asp
| 3d infografía
| hosting
| e-mail

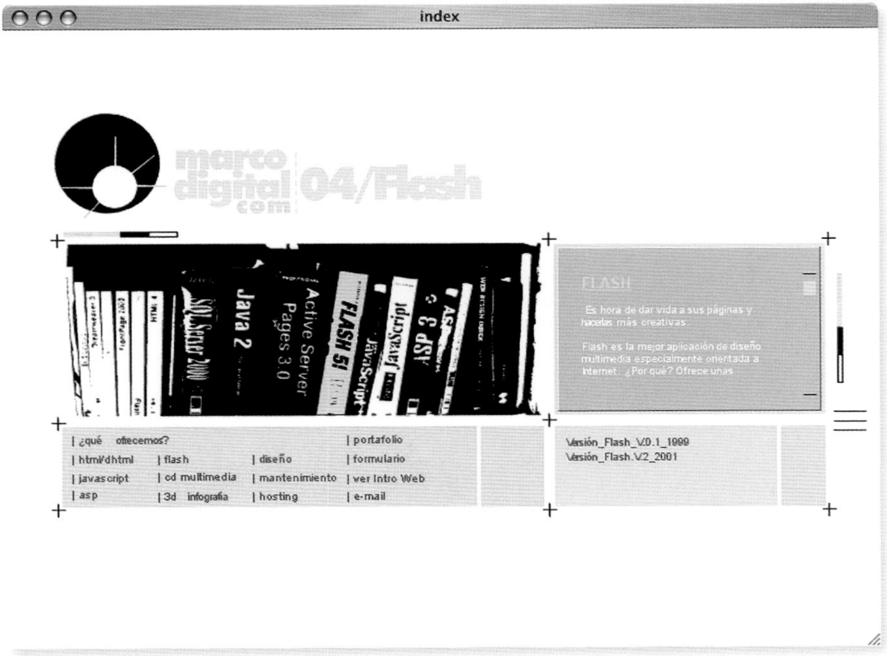
index
marco digital com
04/Flash
Active Server Pages 3.0
Java 2
SQL Server 2000
FLASH 5!
JavaScript
ASP 3
FLASH
Es hora de dar vida a sus páginas y hacerlas más creativas.
Flash es la mejor aplicación de diseño multimedia especialmente orientada a Internet. ¿Por qué? Ofrece unas
| ¿qué ofrecemos?
| portafolio
| html/dhtml
| flash
| diseño
| formulario
| javascript
| cd multimedia
| mantenimiento
| ver Intro Web
| asp
| 3d infografía
| hosting
| e-mail
Versión_Flash_V.0.1_1999
Versión_Flash.V2_2001

www.marcodigital.com
D: pedro j. saavedra macías **C:** curro perez
A: marco digital **M:** marcodigital@marcodigital.com

FORISURgroup | Global Business Solutions | (c) 2003 web site design

.com

Search

e-commerce portales & autogestores

Search

MEDIANTE LA PUBLICACIÓN PERIÓDICA DE NOTICIAS O NOVEDADES EN UN BOLETÍN AL QUE SE SUCRIBEN SUS CLIENTES, CONSEGUIRÁ REFORZAR LA IMAGEN DE SU MARCA MEDIANTE IMPACTOS QUE MENSUALMENTE SERÁN ENVIADOS POR MAIL. DE ESTE MODO AHORRARÁ EN CAMPAÑAS DE MAILING Y ENVÍOS MASIVOS POR FAX. DISPONDRÁ DE UN MÓDULO DE ESTADÍSTICAS QUE LE INFORMARÁ DE LAS VISITAS QUE RECIBE SU PÁGINA WEB Y LE PERMITIRÁ ANALIZAR LAS SECCIONES QUE SON MÁS INTERESANTES PARA LOS USUARIOS.

PODRÁ INCLUIR UN COMPLETO CATÁLOGO DE PRODUCTOS ACTUALIZABLE EN CUALQUIER MOMENTO, Y SI LO CONSIDERA OPORTUNO INCORPORAR UNA PASARELA DE PAGO PARA PODER CERRAR LA VENTA AUTOMÁTICAMENTE.

www.forisur.com
forisur@forisur.com
Server Arsys
www.arsys.es

FORISURgroup
GLOBAL SOLUTIONS BUSINESS

FORISURgroup
T+ 93 2098338 // F+ 93 2097389
Via Augusta, 115-1°2ª 08006
BARCELONA(Spain)

FORISURgroup | Global Business Solutions | (c) 2003 web site design

.com

Search

e-commerce hosting - registro

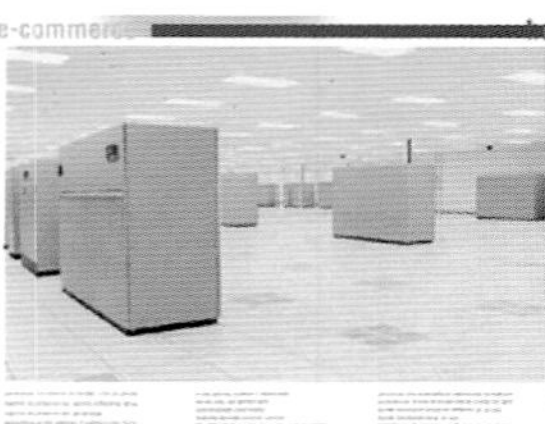

BUSQUEDA Y SELECCION DE DISTRIBUIDORES
BUSQUEDA Y SELECCION DE PROVEEDORES
CREACION, MANTENIMIENTO Y PROMOCION DE PAGINAS WEB COMERCIALES
MARKETING Y COMUNICACION
TRANSPORTES INTERNACIONALES
ADUANAS/ ALMACENAMIENTO Y DISTRIBUCION.
ASESORIA LEGAL MERCANTIL
BUSQUEDA DE PERSONAL ESPECIALIZADO EN COMERCIO EXTERIOR.
FABRICACION Y CONTROL CALIDAD EN CHINA VIETNAM Y BANGLADESH.

www.forisur.com
forisur@forisur.com
Server Arsys
www.arsys.es

FORISURgroup
GLOBAL SOLUTIONS BUSINESS

FORISURgroup
T+ 93 2098338 // F+ 93 2097389
Via Augusta, 115-1°2ª 08006
BARCELONA(Spain)

www.forisur.com
D: julio lozano
A: forisur **M:** jl@forisur.com

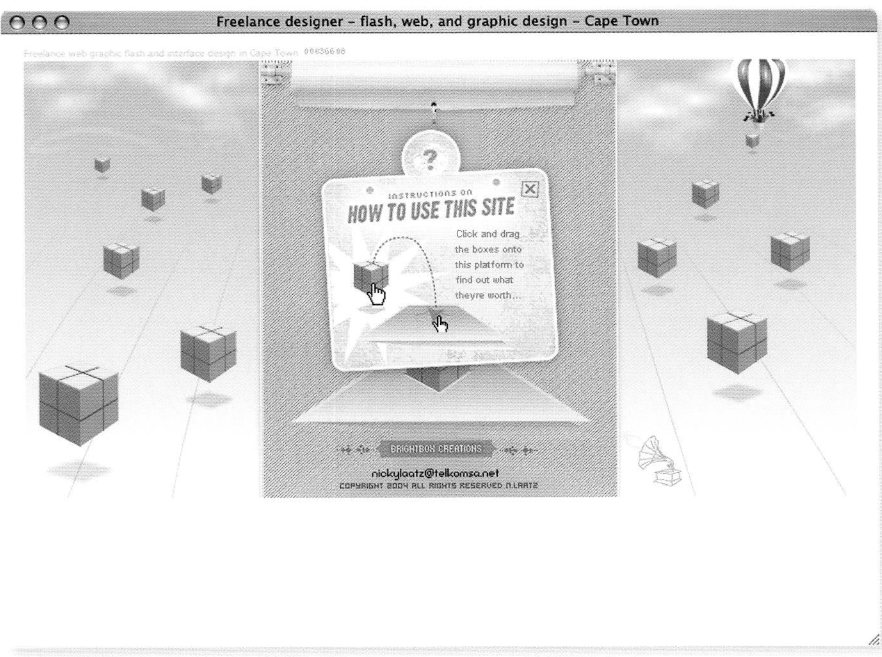
Freelance designer - flash, web, and graphic design - Cape Town
INSTRUCTIONS ON
HOW TO USE THIS SITE
Click and drag the boxes onto this platform to find out what theyre worth...
BRIGHTBOX CREATIONS
nickylaatz@telkomsa.net
COPYRIGHT 2004 ALL RIGHTS RESERVED N.LAATZ

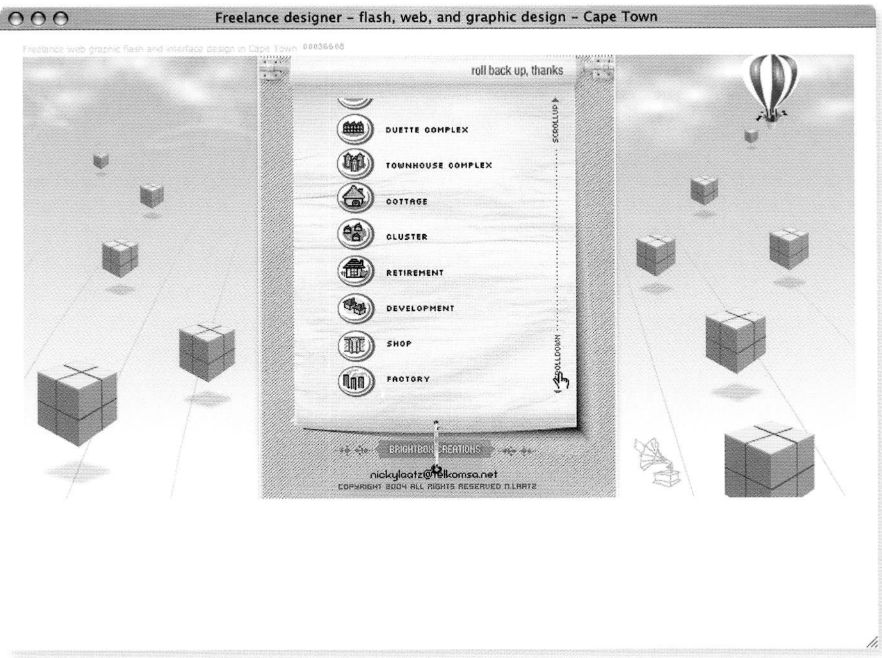
Freelance designer - flash, web, and graphic design - Cape Town
roll back up, thanks
DUETTE COMPLEX
TOWNHOUSE COMPLEX
COTTAGE
CLUSTER
RETIREMENT
DEVELOPMENT
SHOP
FACTORY
BRIGHTBOX CREATIONS
COPYRIGHT 2004 ALL RIGHTS RESERVED N.LAATZ

www.brightbox.co.za
D: nicky laatz
A: brightbox **M:** nickylaatz@telkomsa.net

COLOR IN MOTION
las ESTRELLAS
SELECCIONE UNA ESTRELLA O FOLDER
INSTRUCCIONES
MENU
SALIR

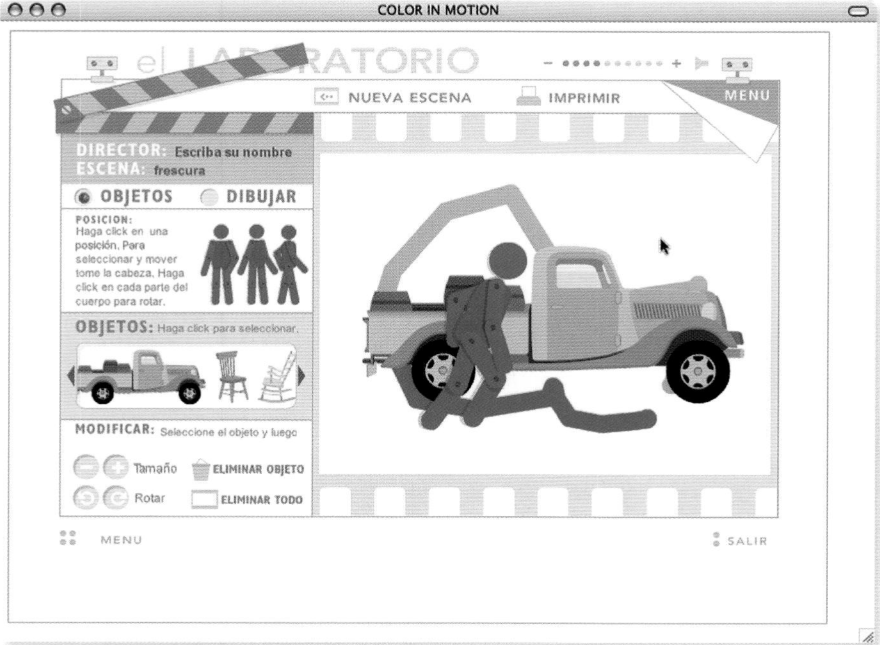
COLOR IN MOTION
NUEVA ESCENA
IMPRIMIR
MENU
DIRECTOR: Escriba su nombre
ESCENA: frescura
OBJETOS
DIBUJAR
POSICION:
Haga click en una posición. Para seleccionar y mover tome la cabeza. Haga click en cada parte del cuerpo para rotar.
OBJETOS: Haga click para seleccionar.
MODIFICAR: Seleccione el objeto y luego
Tamaño
ELIMINAR OBJETO
Rotar
ELIMINAR TODO
MENU
SALIR

www.mariaclaudiacortes.com
D: maria claudia cortes
M: cortesclau@hotmail.com

Female Persuasion
FEMALEPERSUASION.NET
FOUNDED FOR UPCOMING + PROVOCATIVE FEMALE ARTISTS
HOME VISION ARTISTS GALLERY CONTRIBUTORS CONTACT FORUM
GIRLCRUSH
NEW ARTISTS ::
FRESH ::
MILA STERLING: PAINTING
Born in NYC, raised in LA, lived in SF for ten years and Madrid for one, think of them ALL as my hometown
CAROL EG: MIXED MEDIA
I have been reclaiming a form of pattern making by incorporating cut paper, sometimes fabric and
ENID CROW: PHOTOGRAPHY
I take photographs of fake disasters with myself as the main character playing the tragic, screaming female
3.30.2005
So what I'm wondering is why no one is talking about the real Schiavo story...the fact that the REASON she's brain dead is because she had a heart attack as a result of bulimia---and that the ultimate irony is that she's being kept alive through a feeding tube???
.posted by ak @10:54 AM
3.21.2005
In NY?
Maura Reilly, (curator at the Sackler Center for Feminist Art) juried and curated the 6th Biennial Exhibition at A.I.R. Gallery.
March 8 - April 2, 2005
Tuesdays - Saturdays, 11:00 am - 6:00 pm
A.I.R. Gallery: 511 W. 25th Street, 3rd Floor (between 10th Ave. and 11th Ave.),
Chelsea, NYC
www.airnyc.org
212.255.6651
info@airnyc.org
48 women artists: including our own Enid Crow
.posted by ak @11:1 AM
3.17.2005
FEATURED: LUCY MACLEOD
WWW.LUCYMACLEOD.COM
READ INTERVIEW
"IN MY HEART, I THINK A WOMAN HAS TWO CHOICES: EITHER SHE'S A FEMINIST OR A MASOCHIST."
—GLORIA STEINEM
ROCK THE t-shirt
& SUPPORT NARAL.ORG. LOOK HOT WHILE YOU PROTEST!
CHOICE
FRIENDS OF FEMALEPERSUASION
go visit...

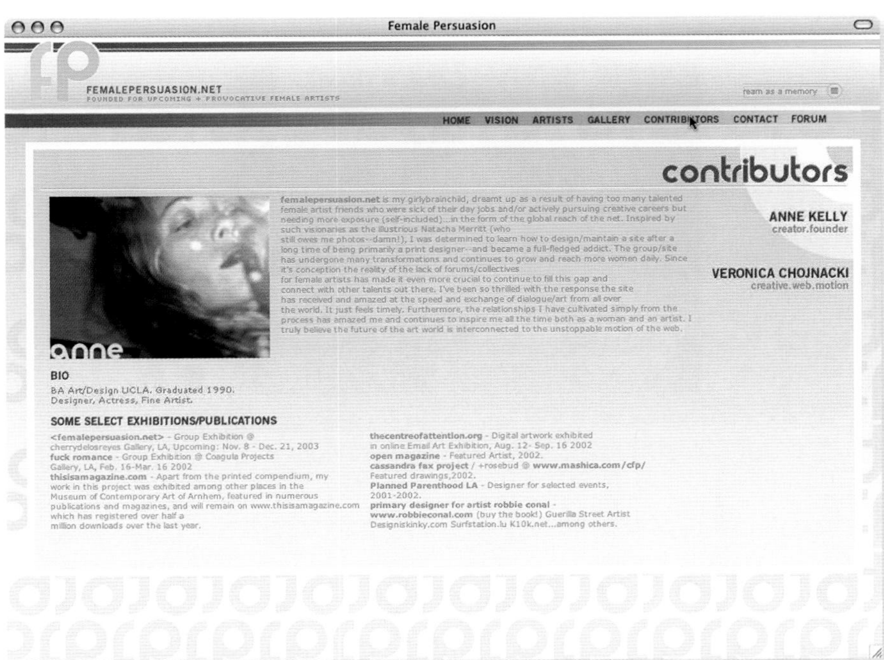
Female Persuasion
FEMALEPERSUASION.NET
FOUNDED FOR UPCOMING + PROVOCATIVE FEMALE ARTISTS
HOME VISION ARTISTS GALLERY CONTRIBUTORS CONTACT FORUM
contributors
femalepersuasion.net is my girlybrainchild, dreamt up as a result of having too many talented female artist friends who were sick of their day jobs and/or actively pursuing creative careers but needing more exposure (self-included)...in the form of the global reach of the net. Inspired by such visionaries as the illustrious Natacha Merritt (who still owes me photos--damn!), I was determined to learn how to design/maintain a site after a long time of being primarily a print designer--and became a full-fledged addict. The group/site has undergone many transformations and continues to grow and reach more women daily. Since it's conception the reality of the lack of forums/collectives for female artists has made it even more crucial to continue to fill this gap and connect with other talents out there. I've been so thrilled with the response the site has received and amazed at the speed and exchange of dialogue/art from all over the world. It just feels timely. Furthermore, the relationships I have cultivated simply from the process has amazed me and continues to inspire me all the time both as a woman and an artist. I truly believe the future of the art world is interconnected to the unstoppable motion of the web.
ANNE KELLY
creator.founder
VERONICA CHOJNACKI
creative.web.motion
anne
BIO
BA Art/Design UCLA. Graduated 1990.
Designer, Actress, Fine Artist.
SOME SELECT EXHIBITIONS/PUBLICATIONS
<femalepersuasion.net> - Group Exhibition @ cherrydelosreyes Gallery, LA, Upcoming: Nov. 8 - Dec. 21, 2003
fuck romance - Group Exhibition @ Coagula Projects Gallery, LA, Feb. 16-Mar. 16 2002
thisisamagazine.com - Apart from the printed compendium, my work in this project was exhibited among other places in the Museum of Contemporary Art of Arnhem, featured in numerous publications and magazines, and will remain on www.thisisamagazine.com which has registered over half a million downloads over the last year.
thecentreofattention.org - Digital artwork exhibited in online Email Art Exhibition, Aug. 12- Sep. 16 2002
open magazine - Featured Artist, 2002.
cassandra fax project / +rosebud @ www.mashica.com/cfp/ Featured drawings,2002.
Planned Parenthood LA - Designer for selected events, 2001-2002.
primary designer for artist robbie conal - www.robbieconal.com (buy the book!) Guerilla Street Artist
Designiskinky.com Surfstation.lu K10k.net...among others.

www.femalepersuasion.net
D: veronica chojnacki, alfredo silva **C:** chapley watson,
A: www.nulinegraphics.com **M:** info@nulinegraphics.com

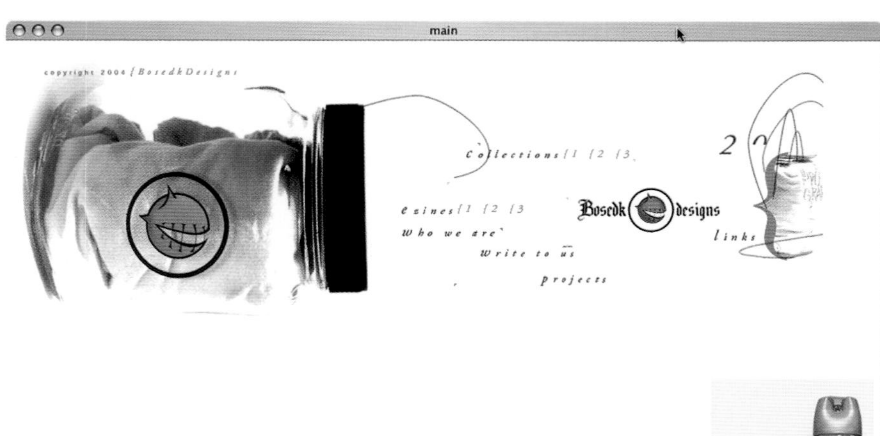
main
copyright 2004 [BosedkDesigns
Collections[1 [2 [3
ezines[1 [2 [3
who we are`
write to us
projects
Bosedk designs
links
Mortein
ALL INSECT KILLER
KILLS MOSQUITOES. AND OTHER INSECTS.

Bosedk Designs-projects
copyright 2004 [BosedkDesigns
projects`
1] ←next→
2]
3]
4]
DISTRESSED
links
Collections[1 [2 [3
write to us
ezines[1 [2 [3

www.bosedkdesigns.com
D: jiten thukral **C:** sumir tagra
A: bosedkdesigns **M:** bosedkdesigns@yahoo.co.inc

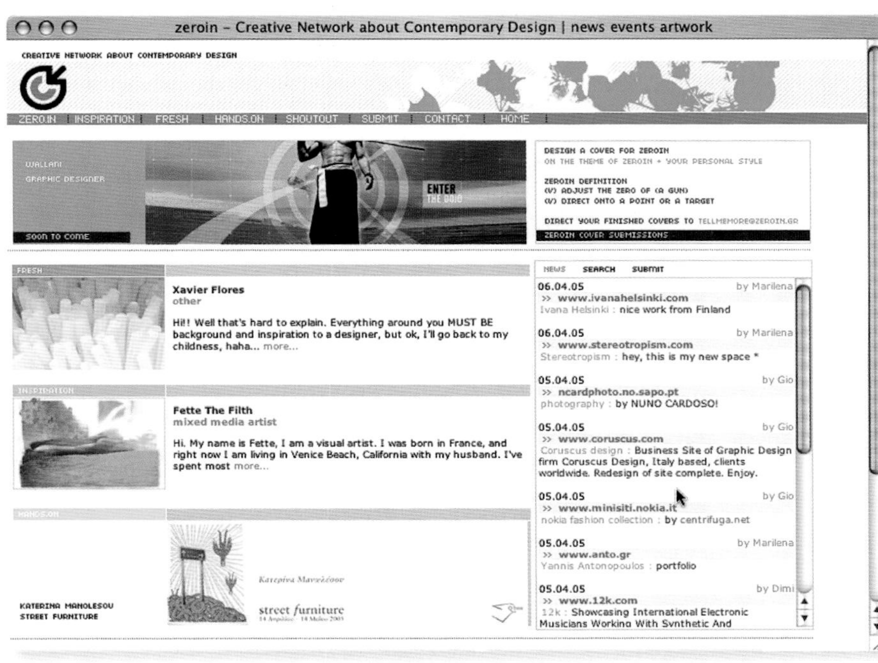
zeroin - Creative Network about Contemporary Design | news events artwork
CREATIVE NETWORK ABOUT CONTEMPORARY DESIGN
ZERO.IN | INSPIRATION | FRESH | HANDS.ON | SHOUTOUT | SUBMIT | CONTACT | HOME
WALLANI
GRAPHIC DESIGNER
ENTER
soon to come
DESIGN A COVER FOR ZEROIN
ON THE THEME OF ZEROIN + YOUR PERSONAL STYLE
ZEROIN DEFINITION
(V) ADJUST THE ZERO OF (A GUN)
(V) DIRECT ONTO A POINT OR A TARGET
DIRECT YOUR FINISHED COVERS TO TELLMEMORE@ZEROIN.GR
ZEROIN COVER SUBMISSIONS
FRESH
Xavier Flores
other
Hi!! Well that's hard to explain. Everything around you MUST BE background and inspiration to a designer, but ok, I'll go back to my childness, haha... more...
INSPIRATION
Fette The Filth
mixed media artist
Hi. My name is Fette, I am a visual artist. I was born in France, and right now I am living in Venice Beach, California with my husband. I've spent most more...
HANDS.ON
KATERINA MANOLESOU
STREET FURNITURE
street furniture
NEWS SEARCH SUBMIT
06.04.05 by Marilena
» www.ivanahelsinki.com
Ivana Helsinki : nice work from Finland
06.04.05 by Marilena
» www.stereotropism.com
Stereotropism : hey, this is my new space *
05.04.05 by Gio
» ncardphoto.no.sapo.pt
photography : by NUNO CARDOSO!
05.04.05 by Gio
» www.coruscus.com
Coruscus design : Business Site of Graphic Design firm Coruscus Design, Italy based, clients worldwide. Redesign of site complete. Enjoy.
05.04.05 by Gio
» www.minisiti.nokia.it
nokia fashion collection : by centrifuga.net
05.04.05 by Marilena
» www.anto.gr
Yannis Antonopoulos : portfolio
05.04.05 by Dimi
» www.12k.com
12k : Showcasing International Electronic Musicians Working With Synthetic And

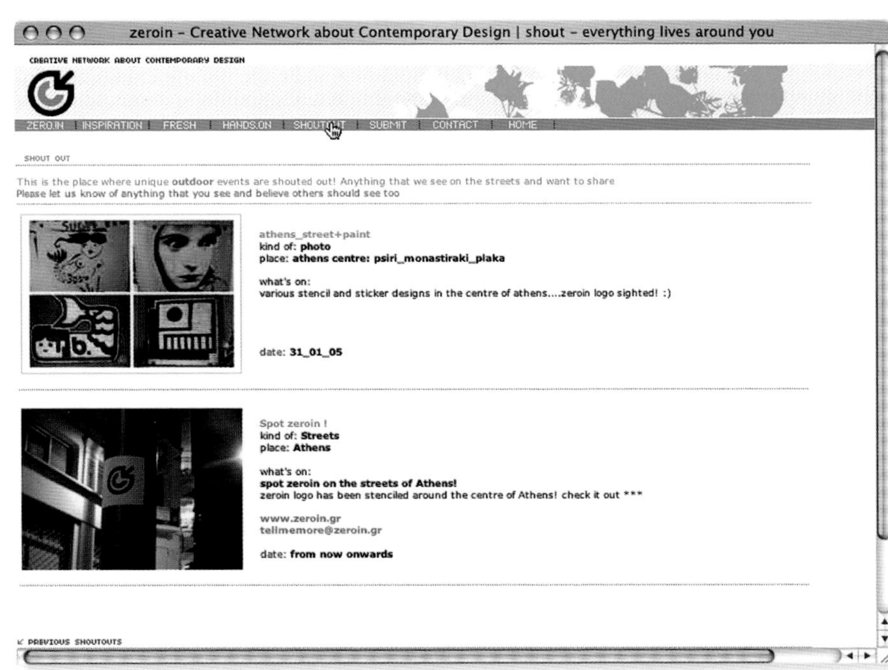
zeroin - Creative Network about Contemporary Design | shout - everything lives around you
CREATIVE NETWORK ABOUT CONTEMPORARY DESIGN
ZERO.IN | INSPIRATION | FRESH | HANDS.ON | SHOUTOUT | SUBMIT | CONTACT | HOME
SHOUT OUT
This is the place where unique outdoor events are shouted out! Anything that we see on the streets and want to share
Please let us know of anything that you see and believe others should see too
athens_street+paint
kind of: photo
place: athens centre: psiri_monastiraki_plaka
what's on:
various stencil and sticker designs in the centre of athens....zeroin logo sighted! :)
date: 31_01_05
Spot zeroin !
kind of: Streets
place: Athens
what's on:
spot zeroin on the streets of Athens!
zeroin logo has been stenciled around the centre of Athens! check it out ***
www.zeroin.gr
tellmemore@zeroin.gr
date: from now onwards
PREVIOUS SHOUTOUTS

www.zeroin.gr
D: marilena zografidi **C:** giorgos grispos
A: zeroin **M:** info@giorgos.info

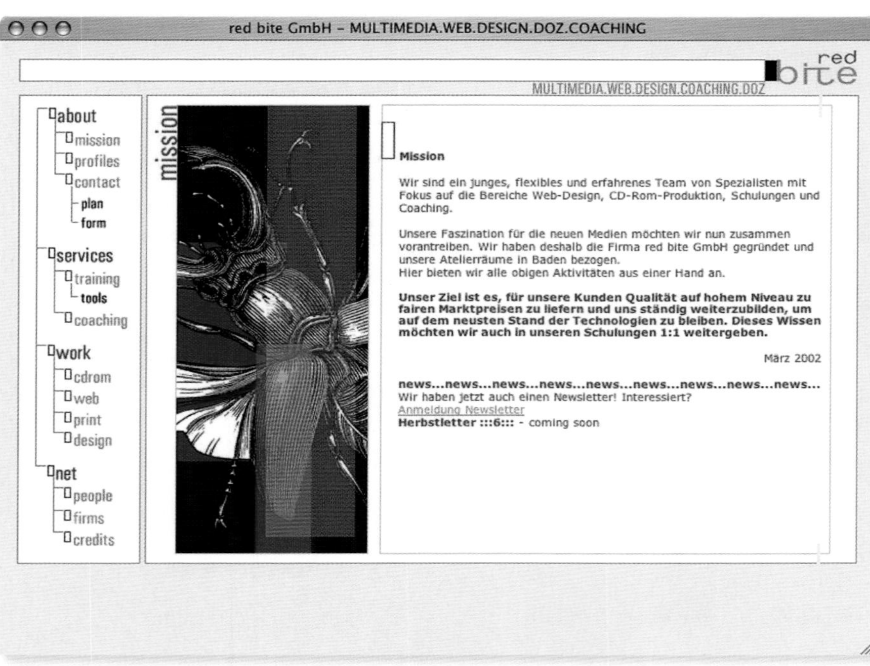
red bite GmbH – MULTIMEDIA.WEB.DESIGN.DOZ.COACHING
red bite
MULTIMEDIA.WEB.DESIGN.COACHING.DOZ
about
mission
profiles
contact
plan
form
services
training
tools
coaching
work
cdrom
web
print
design
net
people
firms
credits
mission
Mission
Wir sind ein junges, flexibles und erfahrenes Team von Spezialisten mit Fokus auf die Bereiche Web-Design, CD-Rom-Produktion, Schulungen und Coaching.
Unsere Faszination für die neuen Medien möchten wir nun zusammen vorantreiben. Wir haben deshalb die Firma red bite GmbH gegründet und unsere Atelierräume in Baden bezogen.
Hier bieten wir alle obigen Aktivitäten aus einer Hand an.
Unser Ziel ist es, für unsere Kunden Qualität auf hohem Niveau zu fairen Marktpreisen zu liefern und uns ständig weiterzubilden, um auf dem neusten Stand der Technologien zu bleiben. Dieses Wissen möchten wir auch in unseren Schulungen 1:1 weitergeben.
März 2002
news...news...news...news...news...news...news...news...news...
Wir haben jetzt auch einen Newsletter! Interessiert?
Anmeldung Newsletter
Herbstletter :::6::: - coming soon

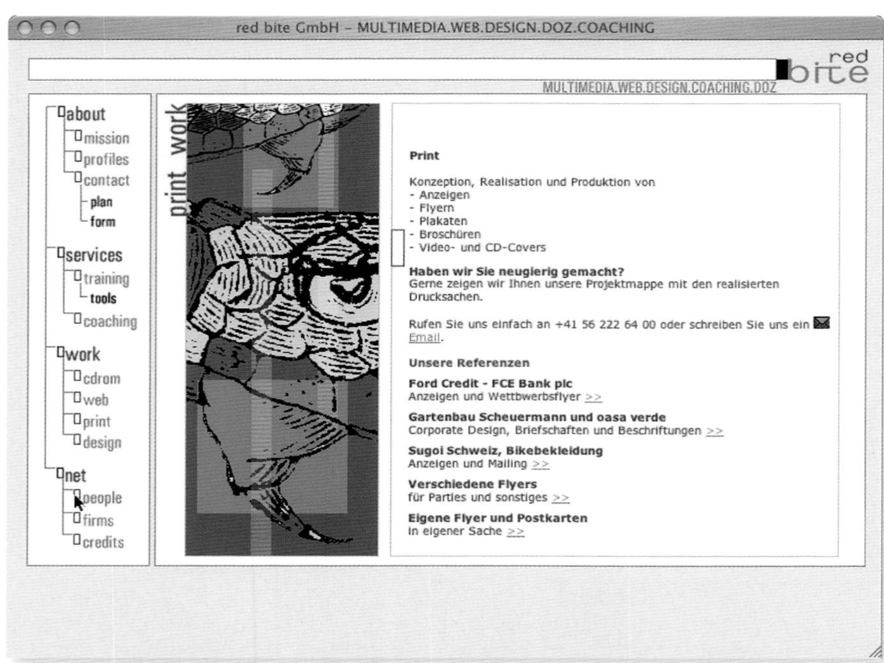
red bite GmbH – MULTIMEDIA.WEB.DESIGN.DOZ.COACHING
red bite
MULTIMEDIA.WEB.DESIGN.COACHING.DOZ
about
mission
profiles
contact
plan
form
services
training
tools
coaching
work
cdrom
web
print
design
net
people
firms
credits
print work
Print
Konzeption, Realisation und Produktion von
- Anzeigen
- Flyern
- Plakaten
- Broschüren
- Video- und CD-Covers
Haben wir Sie neugierig gemacht?
Gerne zeigen wir Ihnen unsere Projektmappe mit den realisierten Drucksachen.
Rufen Sie uns einfach an +41 56 222 64 00 oder schreiben Sie uns ein Email.
Unsere Referenzen
Ford Credit - FCE Bank plc
Anzeigen und Wettbwerbsflyer >>
Gartenbau Scheuermann und oasa verde
Corporate Design, Briefschaften und Beschriftungen >>
Sugoi Schweiz, Bikebekleidung
Anzeigen und Mailing >>
Verschiedene Flyers
für Parties und sonstiges >>
Eigene Flyer und Postkarten
in eigener Sache >>

www.redbite.ch
D: corinne schiess **C:** thomas brenner
A: red bite **M:** cschiess@redbite.ch

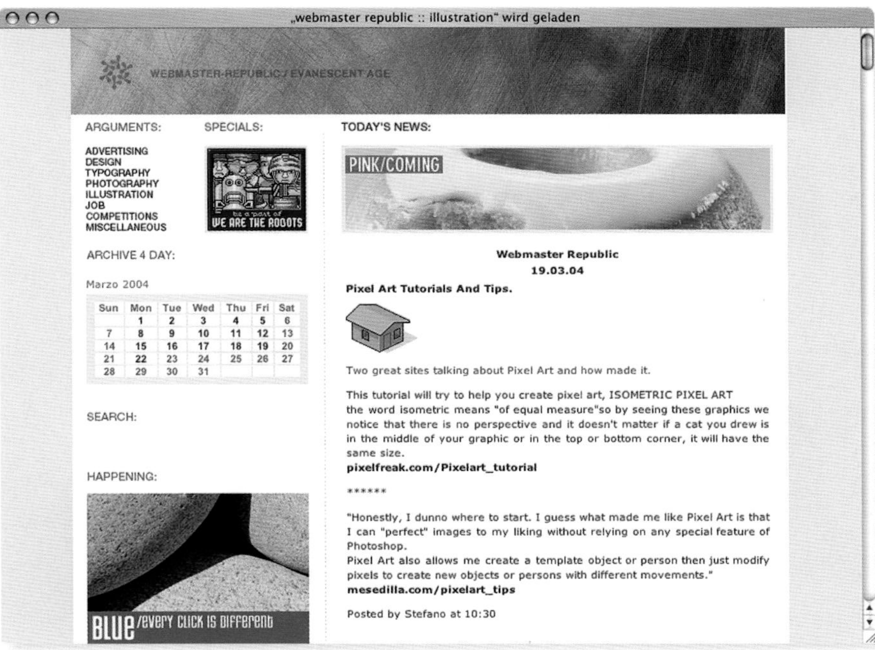
„webmaster republic :: illustration" wird geladen
WEBMASTER-REPUBLIC / EVANESCENT AGE
ARGUMENTS:
SPECIALS:
TODAY'S NEWS:
ADVERTISING
DESIGN
TYPOGRAPHY
PHOTOGRAPHY
ILLUSTRATION
JOB
COMPETITIONS
MISCELLANEOUS
WE ARE THE ROOOTS
PINK/COMING
ARCHIVE 4 DAY:
Marzo 2004
Webmaster Republic
19.03.04
Pixel Art Tutorials And Tips.
Two great sites talking about Pixel Art and how made it.
This tutorial will try to help you create pixel art, ISOMETRIC PIXEL ART
the word isometric means "of equal measure"so by seeing these graphics we notice that there is no perspective and it doesn't matter if a cat you drew is in the middle of your graphic or in the top or bottom corner, it will have the same size.
pixelfreak.com/Pixelart_tutorial
******
"Honestly, I dunno where to start. I guess what made me like Pixel Art is that I can "perfect" images to my liking without relying on any special feature of Photoshop.
Pixel Art also allows me create a template object or person then just modify pixels to create new objects or persons with different movements."
mesedilla.com/pixelart_tips
Posted by Stefano at 10:30
SEARCH:
HAPPENING:
BLUE/every click is different

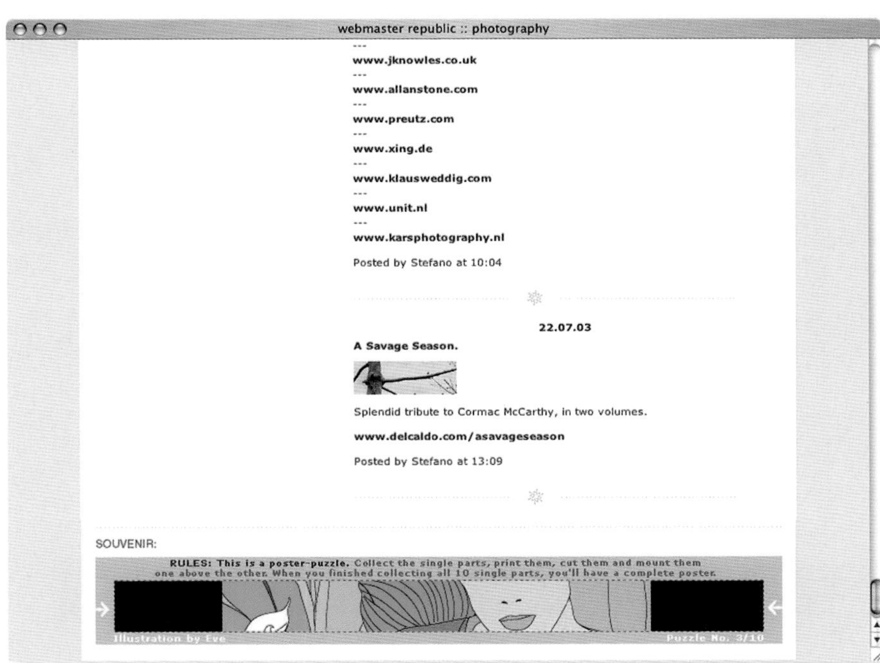
webmaster republic :: photography
www.jknowles.co.uk
www.allanstone.com
www.preutz.com
www.xing.de
www.klausweddig.com
www.unit.nl
www.karsphotography.nl
Posted by Stefano at 10:04
22.07.03
A Savage Season.
Splendid tribute to Cormac McCarthy, in two volumes.
www.delcaldo.com/asavageseason
Posted by Stefano at 13:09
SOUVENIR:
RULES: This is a poster-puzzle. Collect the single parts, print them, cut them and mount them one above the other. When you finished collecting all 10 single parts, you'll have a complete poster.
Illustration by Eve
Puzzle No. 3/10

www.webmaster-republic.it
D: stefano marini, romina raffaelli **C:** emilio vanni
A: winkler & noah **M:** info@winkler-noah.it

mooch v2
mooch for creative living
SPONSORED LINKS
AIR FRANCE
New York £299 rtn. Paris £65 rtn. Havana from £523 rtn or the piste from £80 rtn
SONY ERICSSON
Great deals on phones and accessories including Bluetooth Headsets
BRITART.COM
Buy great contemporary art
DABS.COM
Great prices on iPod, MP3, Palm, cameras, games, consoles, Hifi and more.
EXPEDIA
Its never been cheaper to treat yourself. Fights, hotels, car hire.
BOL.COM
60% off best sellers and free postage on DVD and Videos
101CD.COM
Chart Cds from £7.99, Cds, DVDs, merchandising and Video Games – over 2 million titles
Click here to advertise with us
LIVE
An online magazine bringing the very latest lifestyle and creative news; culture, films, technology, fashion and travel. Continually updated.
CHOICE
From the millions of websites out there, Mooch makes a discriminating choice. Everything you need in life, refined down to the few.
AT A GLANCE
For those in a hurry, the essential websites to view on a single page; from news, sports and culture – fast, simple, and comprehensive.
about us | contact us | content & privacy | design | disclaimer
Newsletter sign up: enter your e-mail submit

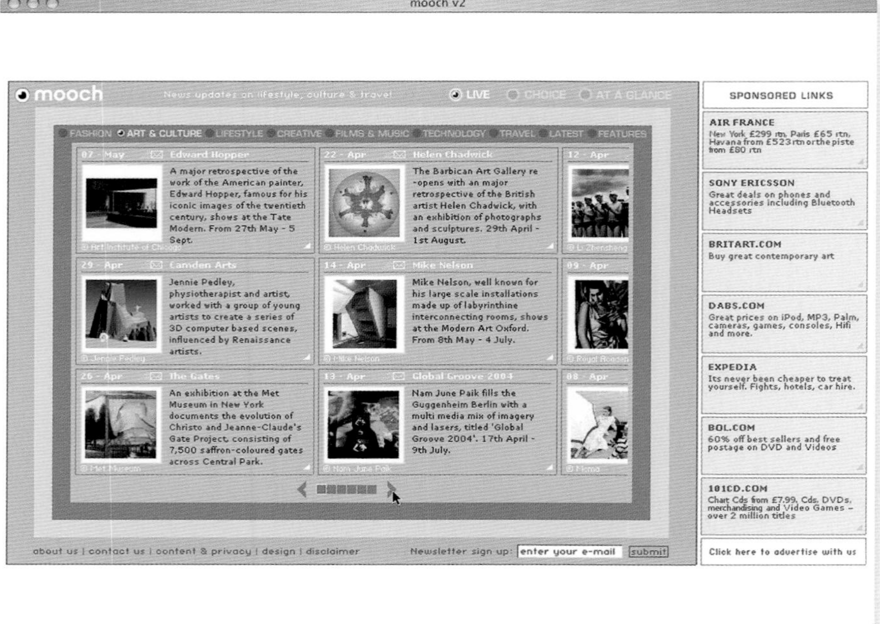
mooch v2
mooch News updates on lifestyle, culture & travel
LIVE CHOICE AT A GLANCE
FASHION ART & CULTURE LIFESTYLE CREATIVE FILMS & MUSIC TECHNOLOGY TRAVEL LATEST FEATURES
07 - May Edward Hopper
A major retrospective of the work of the American painter, Edward Hopper, famous for his iconic images of the twentieth century, shows at the Tate Modern. From 27th May - 5 Sept.
22 - Apr Helen Chadwick
The Barbican Art Gallery re-opens with an major retrospective of the British artist Helen Chadwick, with an exhibition of photographs and sculptures. 29th April - 1st August.
29 - Apr Camden Arts
Jennie Pedley, physiotherapist and artist, worked with a group of young artists to create a series of 3D computer based scenes, influenced by Renaissance artists.
14 - Apr Mike Nelson
Mike Nelson, well known for his large scale installations made up of labyrinthine interconnecting rooms, shows at the Modern Art Oxford. From 8th May - 4 July.
26 - Apr The Gates
An exhibition at the Met Museum in New York documents the evolution of Christo and Jeanne-Claude's Gate Project, consisting of 7,500 saffron-coloured gates across Central Park.
13 - Apr Global Groove 2004
Nam June Paik fills the Guggenheim Berlin with a multi media mix of imagery and lasers, titled 'Global Groove 2004'. 17th April - 9th July.
SPONSORED LINKS
AIR FRANCE
New York £299 rtn. Paris £65 rtn. Havana from £523 rtn or the piste from £80 rtn
SONY ERICSSON
Great deals on phones and accessories including Bluetooth Headsets
BRITART.COM
Buy great contemporary art
DABS.COM
Great prices on iPod, MP3, Palm, cameras, games, consoles, Hifi and more.
EXPEDIA
Its never been cheaper to treat yourself. Fights, hotels, car hire.
BOL.COM
60% off best sellers and free postage on DVD and Videos
101CD.COM
Chart Cds from £7.99, Cds, DVDs, merchandising and Video Games – over 2 million titles
Click here to advertise with us
about us | contact us | content & privacy | design | disclaimer
Newsletter sign up: enter your e-mail submit

www.mooch.info
D: farid chaouki **C:** herve **P:** gee thomson
A: blue-goo **M:** alex@mooch.info

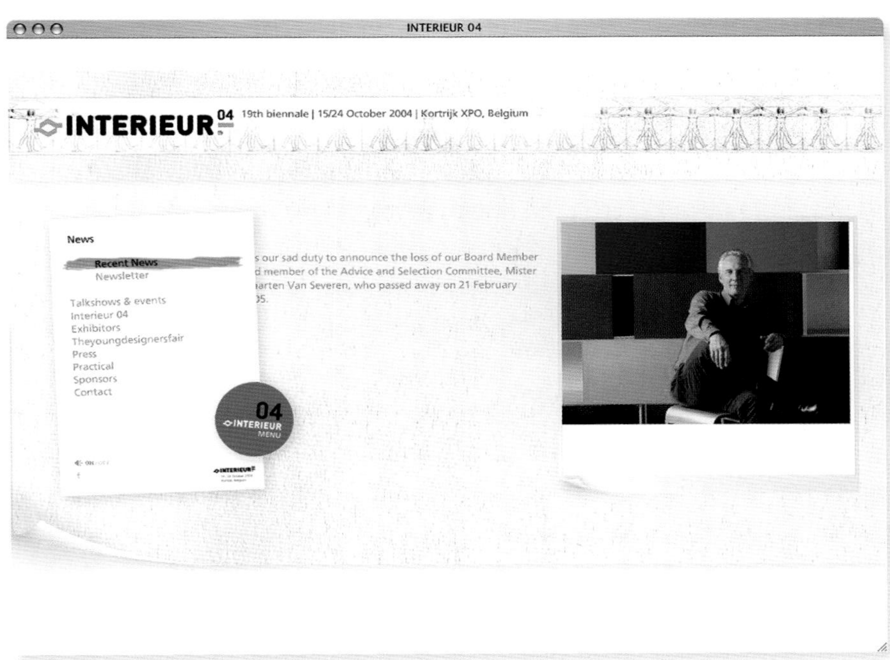
INTERIEUR 04
INTERIEUR 04
19th biennale | 15/24 October 2004 | Kortrijk XPO, Belgium
News
Recent News
Newsletter
Talkshows & events
Interieur 04
Exhibitors
Theyoungdesignersfair
Press
Practical
Sponsors
Contact
s our sad duty to announce the loss of our Board Member
d member of the Advice and Selection Committee, Mister
iarten Van Severen, who passed away on 21 February
)5.
04 INTERIEUR MENU

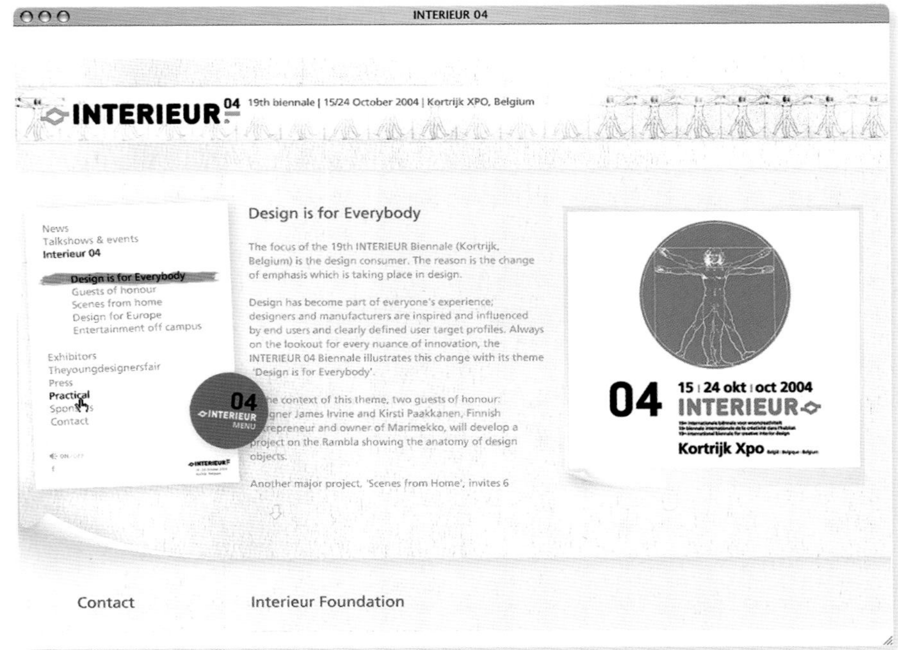
INTERIEUR 04
INTERIEUR 04
19th biennale | 15/24 October 2004 | Kortrijk XPO, Belgium
News
Talkshows & events
Interieur 04
Design is for Everybody
Guests of honour
Scenes from home
Design for Europe
Entertainment off campus
Exhibitors
Theyoungdesignersfair
Press
Practical
Sponsors
Contact
Design is for Everybody
The focus of the 19th INTERIEUR Biennale (Kortrijk, Belgium) is the design consumer. The reason is the change of emphasis which is taking place in design.
Design has become part of everyone's experience; designers and manufacturers are inspired and influenced by end users and clearly defined user target profiles. Always on the lookout for every nuance of innovation, the INTERIEUR 04 Biennale illustrates this change with its theme 'Design is for Everybody'.
he context of this theme, two guests of honour: igner James Irvine and Kirsti Paakkanen, Finnish repreneur and owner of Marimekko, will develop a project on the Rambla showing the anatomy of design objects.
Another major project, 'Scenes from Home', invites 6
04 INTERIEUR MENU
04 15 | 24 okt | oct 2004
INTERIEUR
Kortrijk Xpo
Contact
Interieur Foundation

www.interieur.be

D: thomas baert **C:** jeroen de pelsmaeker **P:** ludwig van den meersschaut
A: fahrenheit 04 **M:** ludwig@fahrenheit04.com

firstborn

firstborn
WHO WE ARE
WHAT WE DO
WHY US
OUR PORTFOLIO
OUR NEWS
CONTACT US
NEWS GALLERY

WATER-TIGHT.

DASANI: MAKE YOUR MOUTH WATER WEBSITE

When up-and-coming ad agency Anomaly needed a company to execute their website vision for the updated Dasani brand, they knew Firstborn was just the team to do so. Working closely and collectively on a daily basis, Firstborn enhanced the overall look of the website, designed all interior pages, and used our robust action scripting skills to bring the entire design to life. Complete with grand, scalable images, not seen on TV commercials, behind the scenes story telling, and cheeky copy, the Dasani website clearly positions the brand in a new, fun, irreverent, mouth-watering way.

CLICK→TO LAUNCH CLICK→FOR MORE NEWS

OUR NEWSFEED

He's back. He's bald. This time around, Ving Rhames is Kojak. The new Kojak TV series from USA Network airs in March and the website just launched! Click here to check it out.

firstborn

firstborn
WHO WE ARE
WHAT WE DO
WHY US
OUR PORTFOLIO
OUR NEWS
CONTACT US
THE DIFFERENCE
THE RECOGNITION

Why us? Because no one else will provide you with a more satisfying experience or superior results. Firstborn is a dedicated team of professionals whose objectives are to create groundbreaking work that always exceeds our client's expectations. If our clients are not happy, then we are not happy.

Still not convinced? We understand that words alone can not be persuasive enough. But know this: Firstborn is genuinely different from the rest of the agencies out there. We are committed to providing our clients with the best possible working experience and product imaginable, and we never settle for second best. The difference is in the way we work, both internally and externally. We work harmoniously with our clients in an effort to deliver design solutions that both teams feel very proud of. We are here to prove to our prospective clients that we are worth their choice.

CURRENT NUMBER OF VISITORS (INCLUDING YOU): 18
LOCAL TIME: 17:19:58

www.firstbornmultimedia.com
D: vas sloutchevsky **C:** shea gonyo, gicheol lee **P:** jeremy berg
A: firstborn **M:** info@firstbornmultimedia.com

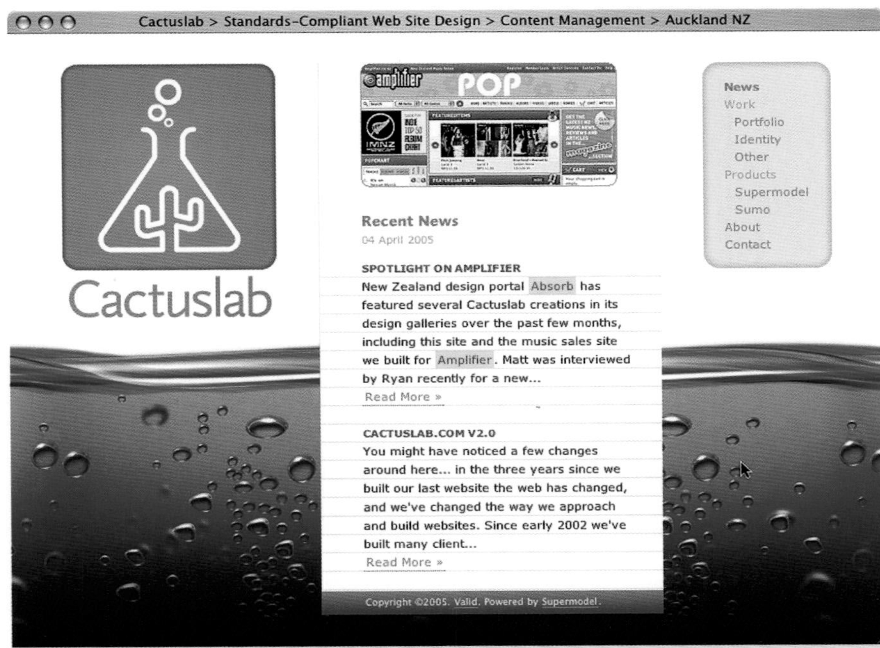
Cactuslab > Standards-Compliant Web Site Design > Content Management > Auckland NZ
Cactuslab
Recent News
04 April 2005
SPOTLIGHT ON AMPLIFIER
New Zealand design portal Absorb has featured several Cactuslab creations in its design galleries over the past few months, including this site and the music sales site we built for Amplifier. Matt was interviewed by Ryan recently for a new...
Read More »
CACTUSLAB.COM V2.0
You might have noticed a few changes around here... in the three years since we built our last website the web has changed, and we've changed the way we approach and build websites. Since early 2002 we've built many client...
Read More »
Copyright ©2005. Valid. Powered by Supermodel.
News
Work
Portfolio
Identity
Other
Products
Supermodel
Sumo
About
Contact

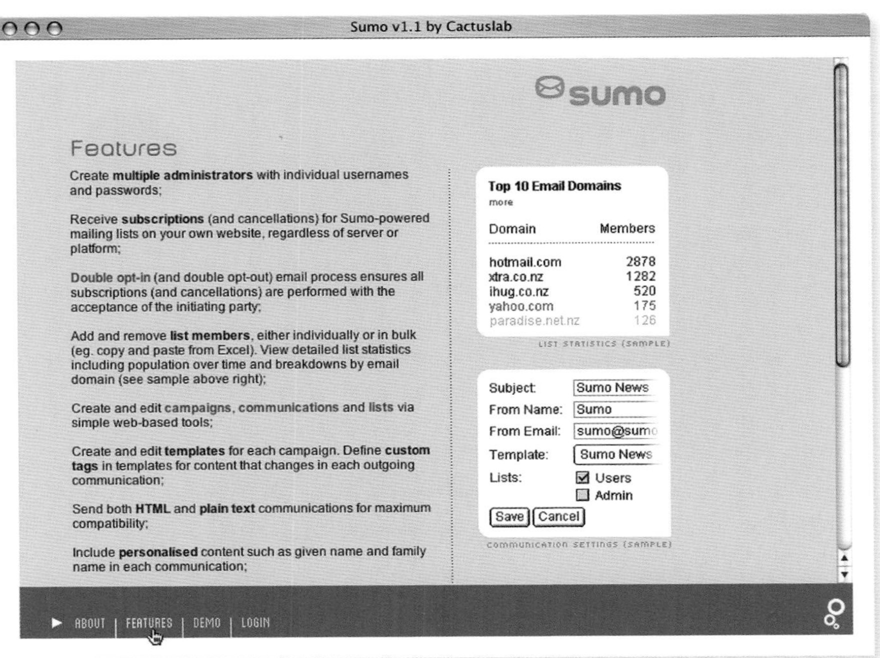
Sumo v1.1 by Cactuslab
sumo
Features
Create multiple administrators with individual usernames and passwords;
Receive subscriptions (and cancellations) for Sumo-powered mailing lists on your own website, regardless of server or platform;
Double opt-in (and double opt-out) email process ensures all subscriptions (and cancellations) are performed with the acceptance of the initiating party;
Add and remove list members, either individually or in bulk (eg. copy and paste from Excel). View detailed list statistics including population over time and breakdowns by email domain (see sample above right);
Create and edit campaigns, communications and lists via simple web-based tools;
Create and edit templates for each campaign. Define custom tags in templates for content that changes in each outgoing communication;
Send both HTML and plain text communications for maximum compatibility;
Include personalised content such as given name and family name in each communication;
Top 10 Email Domains
more
Domain Members
hotmail.com 2878
xtra.co.nz 1282
ihug.co.nz 520
yahoo.com 175
paradise.net.nz 126
LIST STATISTICS (SAMPLE)
Subject: Sumo News
From Name: Sumo
From Email: sumo@sumo
Template: Sumo News
Lists: Users
Admin
Save Cancel
COMMUNICATION SETTINGS (SAMPLE)
ABOUT | FEATURES | DEMO | LOGIN

www.cactuslab.com
D: matthew buchanan **C:** karl von randow
A: cactuslab limited **M:** ouch@cactuslab.com

Currículum vitae de Julián Rojo Soria (III)
Datos personales
Nombre y apellidos: Julián Rojo Soria.
Fecha y lugar de nacimiento: 9 de febrero de 1974. Madrid.
D.N.I.: 01923347.
Domicilio: c/ San Andrés 19. 5º C. 28004 - Madrid.
Teléfono: 91 593 33 14.
Dirección de e-mail: julianrojos@yahoo.es
Currículum vitae
¿Quieres cambiar este currículum? ¡Hay varios modelos! < 1 2 3 4 5 6 7 8 9 >

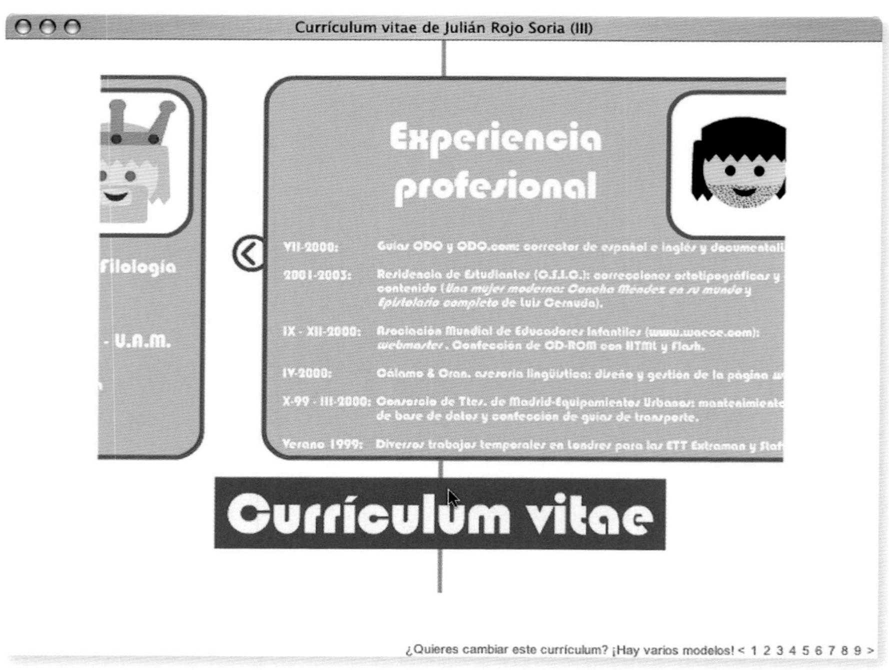
Currículum vitae de Julián Rojo Soria (III)
Filología
U.A.M.
Experiencia profesional
VII-2000: Guías CDC y CDC.com: corrector de español e inglés y documentali
2001-2003: Residencia de Estudiantes (C.S.I.C.): correcciones ortotipográficas y contenido (Una mujer moderna: Concha Méndez en su mundo y Epistolario completo de Luis Cernuda).
IX - XII-2000: Asociación Mundial de Educadores Infantiles (www.waece.com): webmaster. Confección de CD-ROM con HTML y Flash.
IV-2000: Cálamo & Cran. asesoría lingüística: diseño y gestión de la página
X-99 - III-2000: Consorcio de Ttes. de Madrid-Equipamientos Urbanos: mantenimiento de base de datos y confección de guías de transporte.
Verano 1999: Diversos trabajos temporales en Londres para las ETT Extraman y Staf
Currículum vitae
¿Quieres cambiar este currículum? ¡Hay varios modelos! < 1 2 3 4 5 6 7 8 9 >

www.mundofree.com/rojoh/cv2/cv.htm
D: julián rojo soria
M: julianrojos@yahoo.es

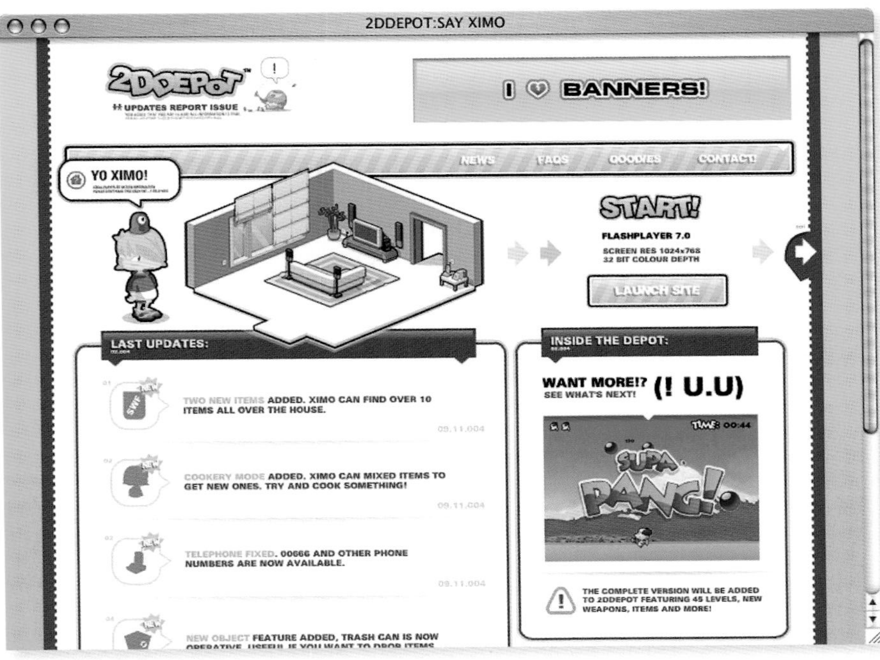
2DDEPOT:SAY XIMO
2DDEPOT
UPDATES REPORT ISSUE
I ♥ BANNERS!
NEWS
FAQS
GOODIES
CONTACT!
YO XIMO!
START!
FLASHPLAYER 7.0
SCREEN RES 1024x768
32 BIT COLOUR DEPTH
LAUNCH SITE
LAST UPDATES:
TWO NEW ITEMS ADDED. XIMO CAN FIND OVER 10 ITEMS ALL OVER THE HOUSE.
09.11.004
COOKERY MODE ADDED. XIMO CAN MIXED ITEMS TO GET NEW ONES. TRY AND COOK SOMETHING!
09.11.004
TELEPHONE FIXED. 00666 AND OTHER PHONE NUMBERS ARE NOW AVAILABLE.
09.11.004
NEW OBJECT FEATURE ADDED, TRASH CAN IS NOW
INSIDE THE DEPOT:
WANT MORE!? (! U.U)
SEE WHAT'S NEXT!
TIME: 00:44
SUPA PANG!
THE COMPLETE VERSION WILL BE ADDED TO 2DDEPOT FEATURING 45 LEVELS, NEW WEAPONS, ITEMS AND MORE!

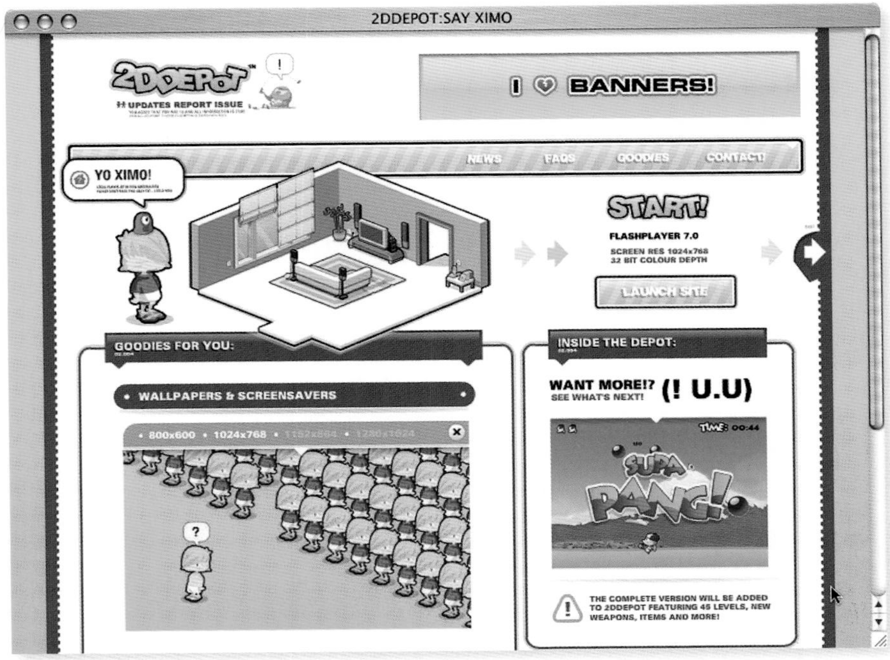
2DDEPOT:SAY XIMO
2DDEPOT
UPDATES REPORT ISSUE
I ♥ BANNERS!
NEWS
FAQS
GOODIES
CONTACT!
YO XIMO!
START!
FLASHPLAYER 7.0
SCREEN RES 1024x768
32 BIT COLOUR DEPTH
LAUNCH SITE
GOODIES FOR YOU:
WALLPAPERS & SCREENSAVERS
800x600 • 1024x768 • 1152x864 • 1280x1024
?
INSIDE THE DEPOT:
WANT MORE!? (! U.U)
SEE WHAT'S NEXT!
TIME: 00:44
SUPA PANG!
THE COMPLETE VERSION WILL BE ADDED TO 2DDEPOT FEATURING 45 LEVELS, NEW WEAPONS, ITEMS AND MORE!

www.2ddepot.com
D: daniel pilar gallego
M: ximo@2ddepot.com

mi3dot.org :: Vijesti
VIJESTI TUTORIALI GALERIJE WWW.DIR INTERVIEWS KOLUMNE UTILS PRIJATELJI RADIONICA MI3 FAQ
VIJESTI
MI3 FEAT. VISITORS
Desktop sat za typofile
BLU DOT Desktop Clock (5 i nešto MB) — svaka minuta ima svoju sličicu.
maratz prije 18h:27min
COIII
Sjećam ga se još od prve, a sada je Conclave Obscurum dogurao do treće verzije.
che.UP prije 1 dan, 0h:38min
Filtriranje galerija
Uvođenje kategorije lomografija i povećanje broja korisnika ponosnih imaoca digitalnih fotoaparata je za sobom donjelo i povećanu količinu smeć.. - radova upitne kvalitete. It's a free country (or so they say), pa nećemo uvoditi moderaciju, nego smo se odlučili za ovaj feature. Od sada pa nadalje i ubuduće svaki korisnik može poklikati koje kategorije radova želi pregledavati, a listu odabranih kategorija može spremiti i u svoj profil. HF
mi3.crew prije 1 dan, 0h:54min
Posljednji pozdrav
Umro je papa Ivan Pavao II
Počivao u miru
mi3.crew prije 7 dana, 20h
Happy Birthday Che!!!1
Sve najbolje!1 20ti, majkemi!!
mi3.crew prije 8 dana, 6h
NEW FORUM MI3DOT.ORG
Latest forum activity...
Novi izgled pinkyyyy.atspace.com
Kada "webdizajner" poludi
besplatni hosting
iPod softver
<b> i <strong>
UTVS
komp i laptop u mreži
Sticky - now playing -
To the forum...
POŠALJI PRIJATELJU
SVJEŽI SADRŽAJ
CSS image hover efekt
Izvedba višejezičnog sajta: gettext i php

mi3dot.org :: Tutorijali - Najnoviji
TUTORIALI
LEARN
Najnoviji tutorijali
Svi tutoriali zahtjevaju određeno predznanje dotičnog softvera i/ili područja jer nisu pisani za totalne početnike, dakle snalaženje unutar programa i poznavanje osnovnih komandi i/ili termina je neophodno. Ukoliko ste totalni početnik kupite knjigu Photoshop Biblija (ili tako nekako) i upoznajte se s osnovnim funkcijama programa.
« povratak
CSS image hover efekt
U tutorialu Poboljšanje sitea uz pomoć CSS-a (autor retro_one) uredno je opisana dobro strukturirana navigacija i pokazano je kako je urediti u CSS-u. No ponekad obični fontovi i ograničenje samo na boje pozadina i 'bordera' elemenata ozbiljnom dizajneru nisu dovoljne za ostvarenje zamišljenog izgleda. Metode za IR (image replacement) u CSS-u već su dugo s nama, neke bolje a neke lošije, primarno zbog potrebe da ljudi na web stranici vide fontove koje je dizajner i namijenio. Idealni IR bi bio takav da zamijeni tekst iz nekog HTML elementa sa slikom — CSS background-image — bez korištenja dodanih tagova (u većini slučajeva nested span elementa), a da očuva tekst tako da ih screen readeri čitaju. Jedan takav blizu idealnog je Accessible Image Replacement (Mike Rundle). Njegovu metodu koristim u ovom tutorialu.
HTML
15.02.2005 20:36
Izvedba višejezičnog sajta: gettext i php
Gettext je odličan u situacijama gdje postoji puno različitih riječi odnosno fraza koje treba prevesti. Držanje prevodljivih fraza u ovakvim ili onakvim arrayima postaje komplicirano kad njihova ukupna količina naraste.
Programiranje - PHP
NEW FORUM MI3DOT.ORG
Latest forum activity...
To the forum...
POŠALJI PRIJATELJU
KATEGORIJE TUTORIALA
Flash (2)
Freehand (3)
HTML (4)

www.mi3dot.org
D: marko kröul **C:** tomaö trkulja
A: mi3dot **M:** emptyhead@mi3dot.org

DeLaROCA Medical Web Desing Trabajos
DeLaROCA™
Connecting People...Connecting Business
delaroca@interior10.net
Inicio Empresa Trabajos Servicios Contacto Noticias
trabajos
(c) www.interior10.net
Portafolio Web...
DeLaROCA Medical Web Solutions tiene una amplia experiencia en el desarrollo y rediseño de sitios web para sociedades científico-sanitarias. A continuación detallamos algunos ejemplos:
sgaic.org
"La funcionalidad y calidad visual de los sitios web que verá en nuestro portafolio le brindará un claro panorama de la importancia de la imagen"

DeLaROCA Medical Web Desing Servicios
DeLaROCA™
Connecting People...Connecting Business
delaroca@interior10.net
Inicio Empresa Trabajos Servicios Contacto Noticias
servicios
(c) www.interior10.net
En Delaroca Medical Web Solutions, aplicamos nuestra experiencia y soluciones para generar una presencia exitosa en Internet.
Producimos sitios Web que atraigan a los pacientes y profesionales, para ello es necesario desarrollar estrategias y soluciones especializadas, por lo que cada uno de nuestros diseños representa una creacion personalizada.
Diseño Web+Marketing Médico
- Páginas Web que enfatizan su contenido para visitantes especificos.
- Páginas que permitan multiplicar la información y con ello sus visitantes.
- Rediseño de Imagen Corporativa.
Nuestos servicios de Diseño Web y Marketing...
Diseño de Sitios Web
Rediseño
Alojamiento
Dominios

www.interior10.net/delaroca/mwd
D: carlos mosquera lópez
M: info@interior10.net

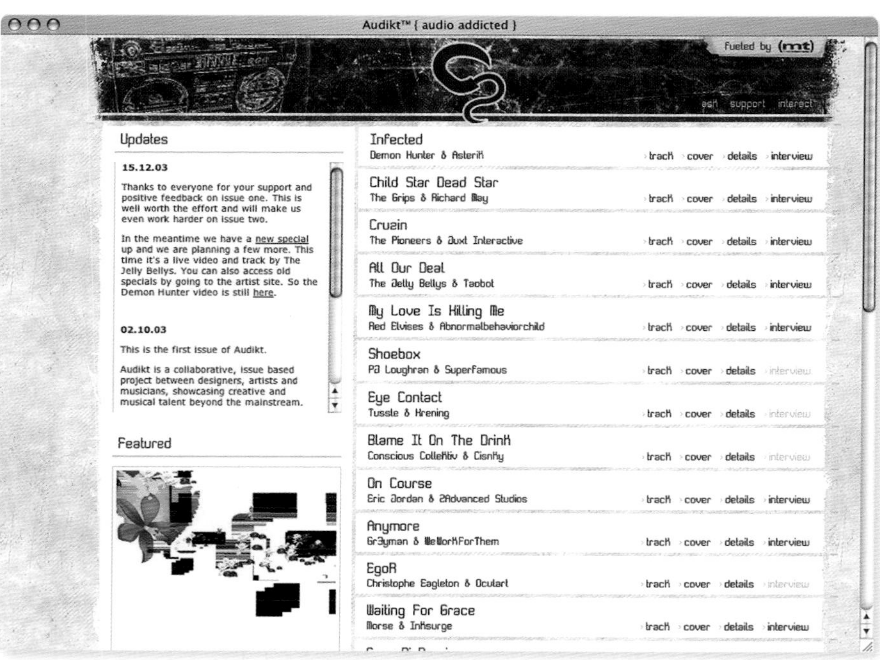
Audikt™ { audio addicted }
Fueled by (mt)
ask support interact
Updates
15.12.03
Thanks to everyone for your support and positive feedback on issue one. This is well worth the effort and will make us even work harder on issue two.
In the meantime we have a new special up and we are planning a few more. This time it's a live video and track by The Jelly Bellys. You can also access old specials by going to the artist site. So the Demon Hunter video is still here.
02.10.03
This is the first issue of Audikt.
Audikt is a collaborative, issue based project between designers, artists and musicians, showcasing creative and musical talent beyond the mainstream.
Featured
Infected
Demon Hunter & Asterik
Child Star Dead Star
The Grips & Richard May
Cruzin
The Pioneers & Juxt Interactive
All Our Deal
The Jelly Bellys & Taobot
My Love Is Killing Me
Red Elvises & Abnormalbehaviorchild
Shoebox
PJ Loughran & Superfamous
Eye Contact
Tussle & Krening
Blame It On The Drink
Conscious Collektiv & Cisnky
On Course
Eric Jordan & 2Advanced Studios
Anymore
Gr3yman & WeWorkForThem
EgoR
Christophe Eagleton & Ocularl
Waiting For Grace
Morse & Inksurge
track cover details interview

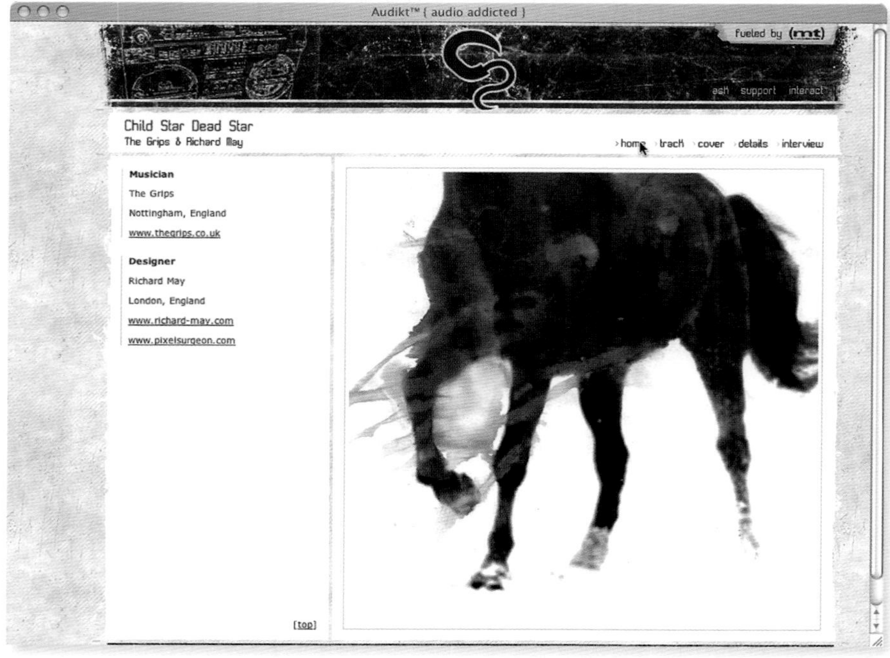
Audikt™ { audio addicted }
Fueled by (mt)
ask support interact
Child Star Dead Star
The Grips & Richard May
home track cover details interview
Musician
The Grips
Nottingham, England
www.thegrips.co.uk
Designer
Richard May
London, England
www.richard-may.com
www.pixelsurgeon.com
[top]

www.audikt.com
D: danny franzreb
A: taobot **M:** danny@taobot.com

WHAT WHAT: ....WHATEVER....

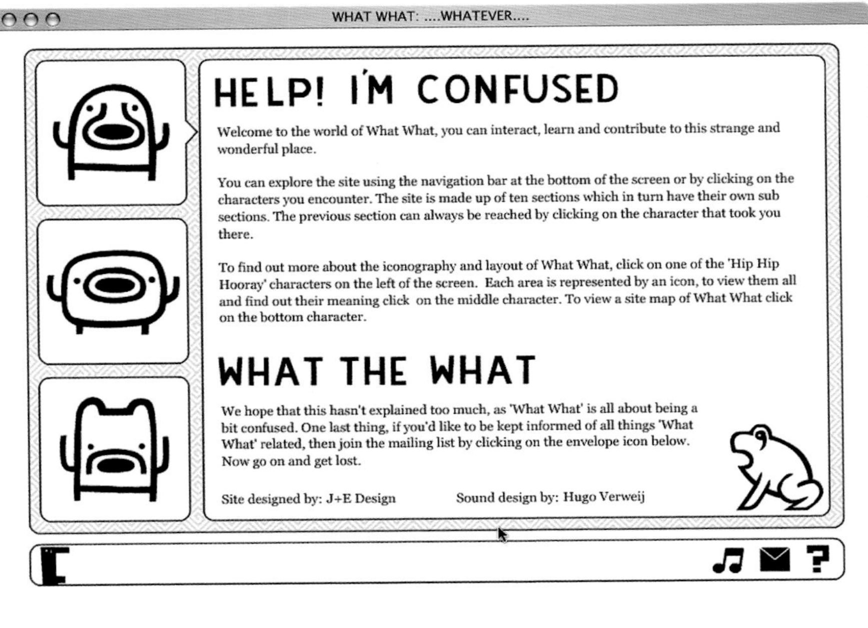
WHAT WHAT: ....WHATEVER....
HELP! I'M CONFUSED
Welcome to the world of What What, you can interact, learn and contribute to this strange and wonderful place.
You can explore the site using the navigation bar at the bottom of the screen or by clicking on the characters you encounter. The site is made up of ten sections which in turn have their own sub sections. The previous section can always be reached by clicking on the character that took you there.
To find out more about the iconography and layout of What What, click on one of the 'Hip Hip Hooray' characters on the left of the screen. Each area is represented by an icon, to view them all and find out their meaning click on the middle character. To view a site map of What What click on the bottom character.
WHAT THE WHAT
We hope that this hasn't explained too much, as 'What What' is all about being a bit confused. One last thing, if you'd like to be kept informed of all things 'What What' related, then join the mailing list by clicking on the envelope icon below. Now go on and get lost.
Site designed by: J+E Design
Sound design by: Hugo Verweij

www.whatwhat.co.uk
D: john and edward harrison **C:** john and edward harrison
A: j+e design **M:** what@whatwhat.co.uk

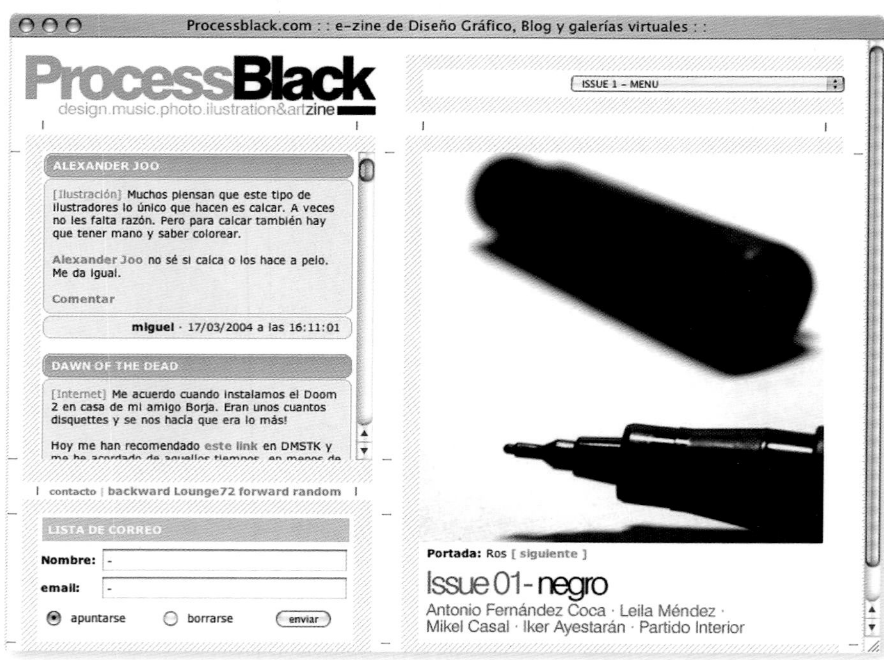
Processblack.com : : e-zine de Diseño Gráfico, Blog y galerías virtuales : :
ProcessBlack
design.music.photo.ilustration&artzine
ISSUE 1 - MENU
ALEXANDER JOO
[Ilustración] Muchos piensan que este tipo de ilustradores lo único que hacen es calcar. A veces no les falta razón. Pero para calcar también hay que tener mano y saber colorear.
Alexander Joo no sé si calca o los hace a pelo. Me da igual.
Comentar
miguel · 17/03/2004 a las 16:11:01
DAWN OF THE DEAD
[Internet] Me acuerdo cuando instalamos el Doom 2 en casa de mi amigo Borja. Eran unos cuantos disquettes y se nos hacía que era lo más!
Hoy me han recomendado este link en DMSTK y
contacto | backward Lounge72 forward random
LISTA DE CORREO
Nombre: -
email: -
apuntarse
borrarse
enviar
Portada: Ros [siguiente]
Issue 01- negro
Antonio Fernández Coca · Leila Méndez · Mikel Casal · Iker Ayestarán · Partido Interior

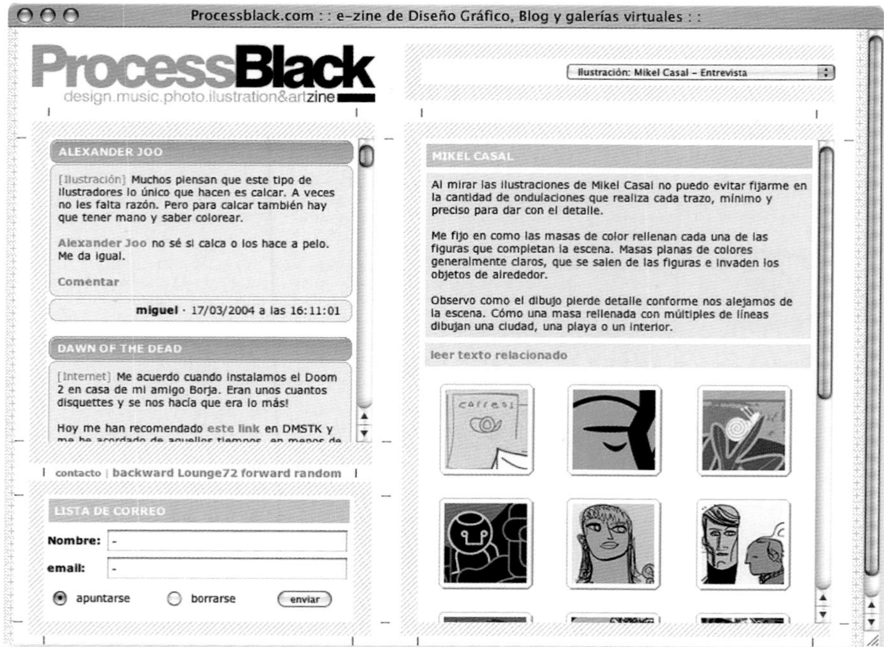
Processblack.com : : e-zine de Diseño Gráfico, Blog y galerías virtuales : :
ProcessBlack
design.music.photo.ilustration&artzine
Ilustración: Mikel Casal - Entrevista
ALEXANDER JOO
[Ilustración] Muchos piensan que este tipo de ilustradores lo único que hacen es calcar. A veces no les falta razón. Pero para calcar también hay que tener mano y saber colorear.
Alexander Joo no sé si calca o los hace a pelo. Me da igual.
Comentar
miguel · 17/03/2004 a las 16:11:01
DAWN OF THE DEAD
[Internet] Me acuerdo cuando instalamos el Doom 2 en casa de mi amigo Borja. Eran unos cuantos disquettes y se nos hacía que era lo más!
Hoy me han recomendado este link en DMSTK y
contacto | backward Lounge72 forward random
LISTA DE CORREO
Nombre: -
email: -
apuntarse
borrarse
enviar
MIKEL CASAL
Al mirar las ilustraciones de Mikel Casal no puedo evitar fijarme en la cantidad de ondulaciones que realiza cada trazo, mínimo y preciso para dar con el detalle.
Me fijo en como las masas de color rellenan cada una de las figuras que completan la escena. Masas planas de colores generalmente claros, que se salen de las figuras e invaden los objetos de alrededor.
Observo como el dibujo pierde detalle conforme nos alejamos de la escena. Cómo una masa rellenada con múltiples de líneas dibujan una ciudad, una playa o un interior.
leer texto relacionado

www.processblack.com
D: miguel garcía
M: miguel@processblack.com

!WE'RE BACK!

2098©

NOW SUPPORTED BY:
SU.COM WEBDIS AGRO

2005-03-20 05:55:32

resist!

HTTP://
213.169.107.13

Archive

2098:
2098 IST EINE GRUPPE OHNE IDEOLOGIE.
SIE WURDE ZUM ZWECK GEMEINSAMEN AUSTAUSCHS GEGRÜNDET.
SIE IST FÜR JEDEN EINZELNEN ALS EXPERIMENTELLE PLATTFORM ZU BETRACHTEN, WO KEIN BESTIMMTES ZIEL VORGEGEBEN IST.
SIE UNTERLIEGT KEINEN BESTIMMTEN REGELN.
DIE AKTIVITÄTEN ERSTRECKEN SICH NICHT NUR AUF DAS INTERNET, WELCHES LEDIGLICH DAS VERBINDENDE MEDIUM DARSTELLT.

PROJEKTE

-2098 STEREO.07.2001

2098-DIE OFFIZIELLE CI ZUR NEUEN SAISON
ALLES AUF EINEN BLICK.

-CAEN.25.05.2001

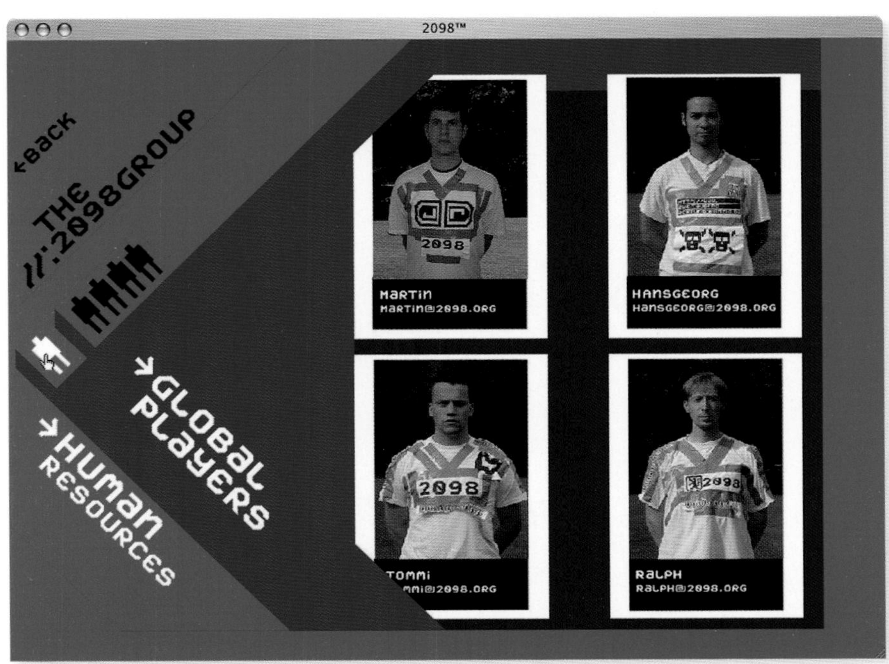
2098™
←BACK
THE //:2098GROUP
→GLOBAL PLAYERS
→HUMAN RESOURCES
MARTIN
MARTIN@2098.ORG
HANSGEORG
HANSGEORG@2098.ORG
TOMMI
RALPH
RALPH@2098.ORG

www.2098.org
D: thomas eberwein, hansgeorg schwarz, ralph heinsohn, martin hesselmeier
A: 2098 **M:** info@2098.org

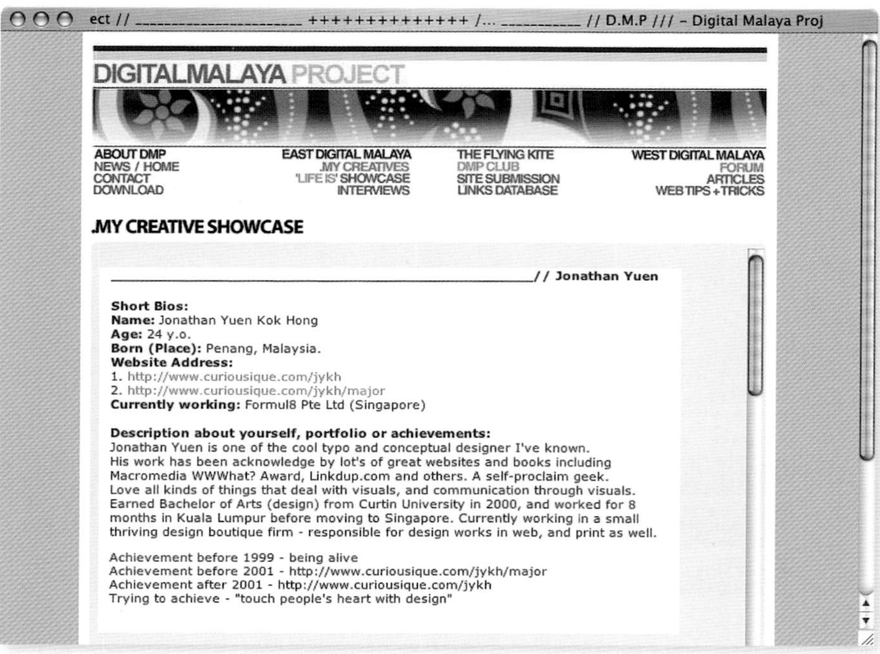
ect // ______________________ ++++++++++++++ /... __________ // D.M.P /// - Digital Malaya Proj
DIGITALMALAYA PROJECT
ABOUT DMP
NEWS / HOME
CONTACT
DOWNLOAD
EAST DIGITAL MALAYA
.MY CREATIVES
'LIFE IS' SHOWCASE
INTERVIEWS
THE FLYING KITE
DMP CLUB
SITE SUBMISSION
LINKS DATABASE
WEST DIGITAL MALAYA
FORUM
ARTICLES
WEB TIPS + TRICKS
.MY CREATIVE SHOWCASE
// Jonathan Yuen
Short Bios:
Name: Jonathan Yuen Kok Hong
Age: 24 y.o.
Born (Place): Penang, Malaysia.
Website Address:
1. http://www.curiousique.com/jykh
2. http://www.curiousique.com/jykh/major
Currently working: Formul8 Pte Ltd (Singapore)
Description about yourself, portfolio or achievements:
Jonathan Yuen is one of the cool typo and conceptual designer I've known.
His work has been acknowledge by lot's of great websites and books including
Macromedia WWWhat? Award, Linkdup.com and others. A self-proclaim geek.
Love all kinds of things that deal with visuals, and communication through visuals.
Earned Bachelor of Arts (design) from Curtin University in 2000, and worked for 8
months in Kuala Lumpur before moving to Singapore. Currently working in a small
thriving design boutique firm - responsible for design works in web, and print as well.
Achievement before 1999 - being alive
Achievement before 2001 - http://www.curiousique.com/jykh/major
Achievement after 2001 - http://www.curiousique.com/jykh
Trying to achieve - "touch people's heart with design"

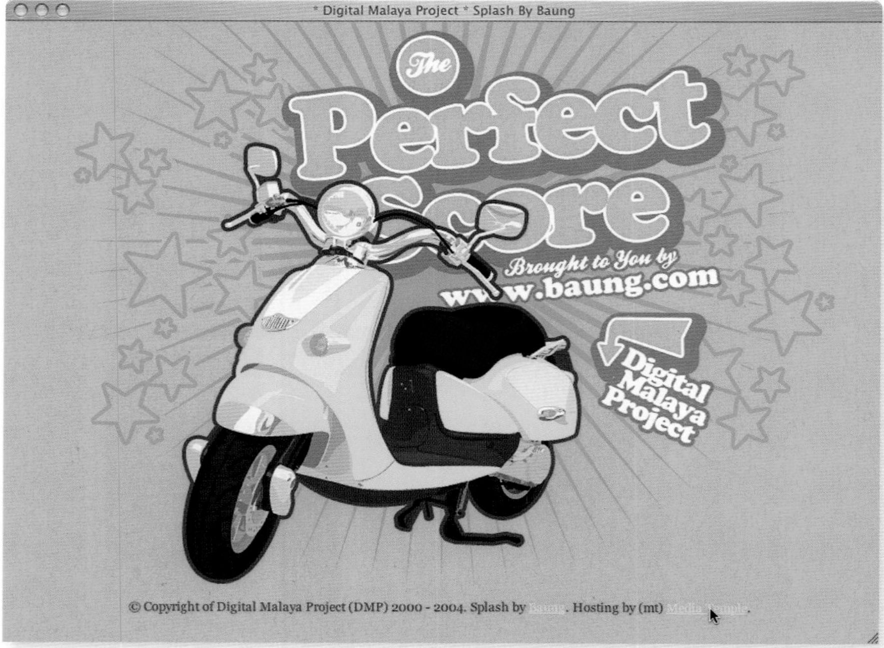
* Digital Malaya Project * Splash By Baung
The
Perfect
Score
Brought to You by
www.baung.com
Digital
Malaya
Project
© Copyright of Digital Malaya Project (DMP) 2000 - 2004. Splash by Baung. Hosting by (mt) Media Temple.

www.digitalmalaya.com
D: muid
A: digital malaya project **M:** muid@digitalmalaya.com

TheFlush::::::::::OnlinePlayground
TheFlush
summer edition
PLAY
STOP
news
AUG 2003
29 AUG. 2003
I uploaded a new picture to my virtual art directory. it's the blue one at the bottom right. I hope you like it.
27 AUG. 2003
Check out the Afterlife project of Jonathan Clark. His photographs of the cemetery are truly amazing. creepy yet peaceful. (and I love the sound)
music
finish them so stay tuned for more!!
To play you'll need realplayer, to download: use rightclick and save target as.
01 - BACK ON TRACK -- play / download
If the links above don't work you can download the music from my garageband page.
If you want to listen to my older music: check out my mp3.com pages.
www.mp3.com/flush
www.mp3.com/theflush

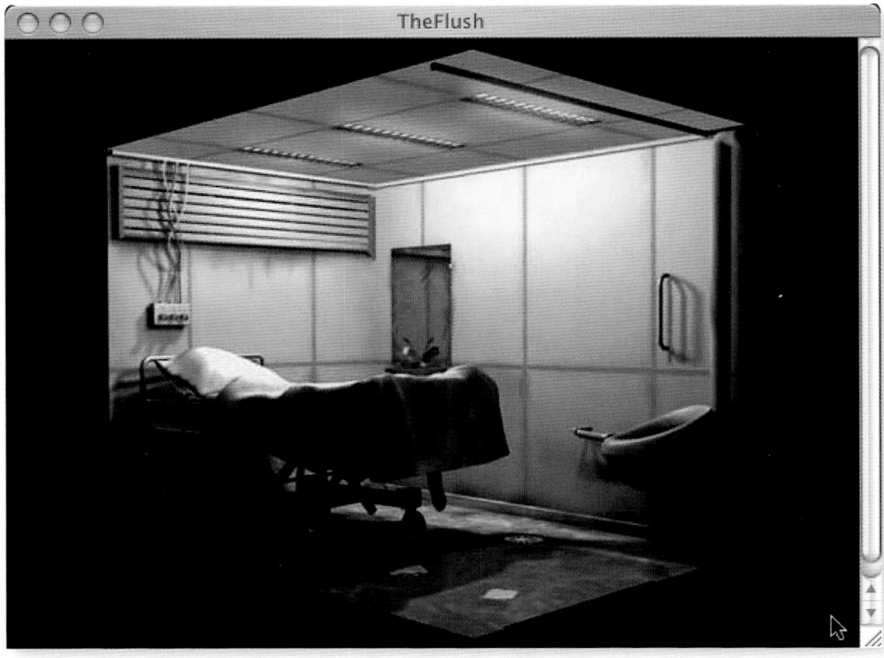
TheFlush

www.theflush.com
D: roel tuerlings
A: theflush **M:** roel@theflush.com

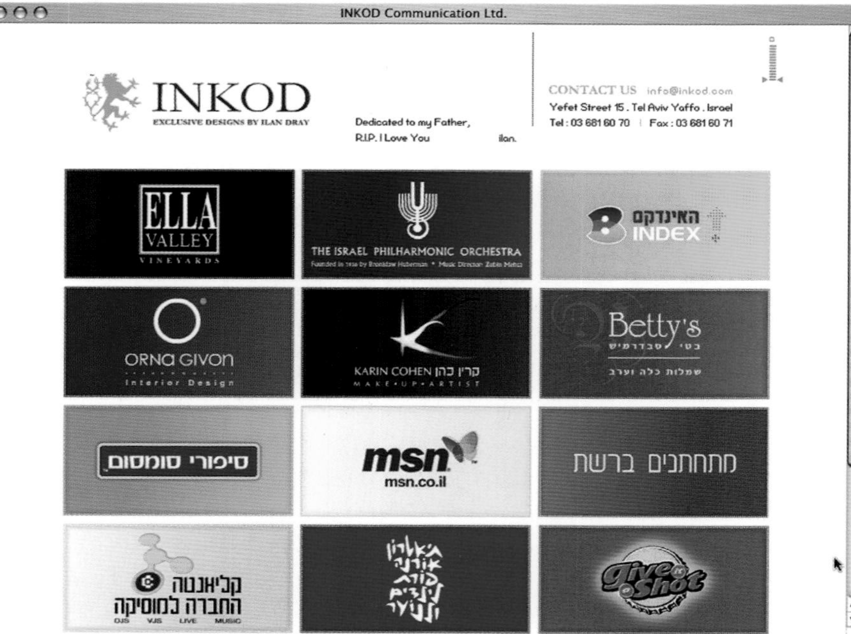
INKOD Communication Ltd.
INKOD
EXCLUSIVE DESIGNS BY ILAN DRAY
Dedicated to my Father,
R.I.P. I Love You ilan.
CONTACT US info@inkod.com
Yefet Street 15 . Tel Aviv Yaffo . Israel
Tel : 03 681 60 70 | Fax : 03 681 60 71
ELLA VALLEY VINEYARDS
THE ISRAEL PHILHARMONIC ORCHESTRA
האינדקס INDEX
ORNA GIVON Interior Design
KARIN COHEN קרין כהן MAKE•UP•ARTIST
Betty's
msn msn.co.il
give a Shot

INKOD Communication Ltd.
INKOD
EXCLUSIVE DESIGNS BY ILAN DRAY
MIX
PORTFOLIO
CONTACT
KID.co.il
THE ISRAEL CANCER ASSOCIATION
Art direction, concept, design & Flash integration.
Launch Kid Website
kid.org.il
The website follows the journey of 3 extraterestrials on Planet Earth, where they get to see for the first time sun and smoke.
The website holds a variety of games, stories and animations, all developed with Macromedia Flash.

www.inkod.com
D: ilan dray **C:** nir givon **P:** roni nizri
A: inkod communication ltd. **M:** ilan@inkod.com

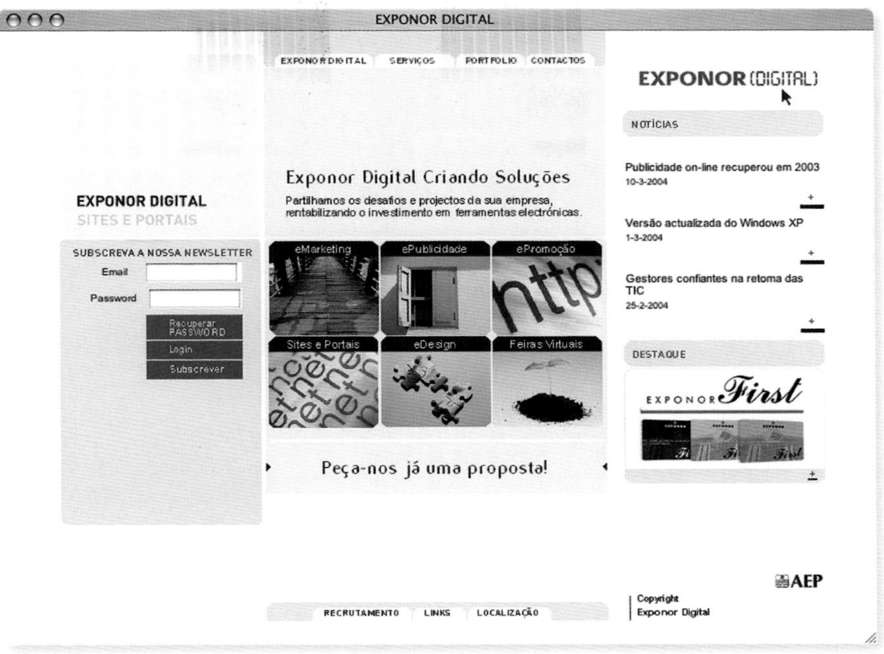
EXPONOR DIGITAL
EXPONOR DIGITAL
SERVIÇOS
PORTFOLIO
CONTACTOS
EXPONOR DIGITAL
NOTÍCIAS
Exponor Digital Criando Soluções
Partilhamos os desafios e projectos da sua empresa, rentabilizando o investimento em ferramentas electrónicas.
EXPONOR DIGITAL
SITES E PORTAIS
Publicidade on-line recuperou em 2003
10-3-2004
Versão actualizada do Windows XP
1-3-2004
Gestores confiantes na retoma das TIC
25-2-2004
SUBSCREVA A NOSSA NEWSLETTER
Email
Password
Recuperar PASSWORD
Login
Subscrever
eMarketing
ePublicidade
ePromoção
Sites e Portais
eDesign
Feiras Virtuais
DESTAQUE
EXPONOR First
Peça-nos já uma proposta!
AEP
RECRUTAMENTO
LINKS
LOCALIZAÇÃO
Copyright
Exponor Digital

EXPONOR DIGITAL
EXPONOR DIGITAL
SERVIÇOS
PORTFOLIO
CONTACTOS
EXPONOR DIGITAL
eMarketing
EXPONOR DIGITAL
ePROMOÇÃO
DESTAQUE
SERVIÇOS
EXPONOR First
eMarketing
Sites e Portais
ePromoção
ePublicidade
eDesign
Design
Suporte e Manutenção
Feiras Virtuais
Uso de recursos interactivos e digitais, como a Internet ou a TV interactiva, de forma a promover comportamentos favoráveis à realização dos objectivos de Marketing.
A grande vantagem do e-Marketing em relação ao Marketing tradicional é a possibilidade de gerir negócios destinados a nichos de mercado, de forma menos dispendiosa e abrangendo grandes áreas geográficas.
Serviço de consultadoria em e-marketing
A EXPONOR DIGITAL apresenta soluções de marketing para a Internet com base na análise e diagnóstico da estratégia global de marketing da sua empresa.
Os seus Negócios em Primeiro Lugar
Desenvolvido pela EXPONOR DIGITAL, o site do programa EXPONOR First apresenta-se como o principal interface entre a comunidade EXPONOR e o programa de fidelização.
Peça-nos já uma proposta!
eMarketing
ePublicidade
ePromoção
Sites e Portais
eDesign
Feiras Virtuais
SUBSCREVA A NOSSA NEWSLETTER
Email
Password
Recuperar PASSWORD
Login

www.exponordigital.com
D: paulo mesquita **C:** josé henrique fernandes **P:** andré pereira
M: paulo.mesquita@exponordigital.com

Chat italiana gratuita!
PUNTO CHAT
Bellissime on-line - Catalogo Video e Foto
Accedi all'archivio video delle HOT CELEBRITY
Apri
CERCA
NEWSLETTER
PROFILI:
TUTTO DA RIFARE !!!
Purtroppo il database ha crashato e con lui tutti i 300 profili e foto dei chatteroni e delle chatterine di Puntochat.
Siamo mortificati davvero ... ma per fortuna rimettere la propria foto online è un gioco da ragazzi!
CHATTA SUBITO!
Entra in chat! C'è un sacco di gente che ti aspetta e che ti vuole conoscere.
HOME
Entra in Chat
Forum
Foto di Chat
Faccia a Faccia
Raduni
DAL MURO DI PUNTOCHAT:
- 10 CoMaNdAmEnTi...
- tranquifunky :D...
- aho !...
- Pittori di strada...
- Vivo per lei...
- CaraBBinieri...
IL FORUM
Un luogo sacro per chi chatta. Nel muro puoi scrivere di tutto... entra ora.
» LA MIA INUTILE CATARSI
.compagni_di_viaggio. è come se non avessi scelta... e davvero non mi riesce di spiegare nient'altro che...
» Il sapore di un ricordo
.compagni_di_viaggio.
Quella...
GENTE DI CHAT
Chi si nasconde dietro il monitor? Detto fatto, ecco le facce più 'fuori' di tutto il web!
» vorrei
.compagni_di_viaggio. Vorrei addormentarmi ogni notte al fianco della persona che amo Vorrei liberare la mia...
» tensioni
.compagni_di_viaggio.
bianche mani sottili
segnate dal tempo
accarezzano il mio...

Punto Chat - Sei nel Canale compagni_di_viaggio
PUNTO CHAT
CERCA
NEWSLETTER
Canale » compagni_di_viaggio
LA MIA INUTILE CATARSI
di uhedra@yahoo.it
è come se non avessi scelta... e davvero non mi riesce di spiegare nient'altro che questo, una sensazione di insofferenza o in certi momenti il panico.Certa gente mi mette soggezione e in quei momenti posso riuscire ad estraniarmi anche dal mio stato fisico,continuando a...
LEGGI TUTTO
VORREI
di rainbow
Vorrei addormentarmi ogni notte al fianco della persona che amo Vorrei liberare la mia testa dai troppi pensieri che mi seguono da altrettanto troppo tempo Vorrei che il mondo non fosse basato sui soldi ma su ben altri valori Vorrei tornare a sentire mia una casa Vorrei non...
LEGGI TUTTO
IL SAPORE DI UN RICORDO
di Laura
Quella notte furono tante le urla che riecheggiavano in quel corridoio apparentemente vuoto ma carico di mille emozioni..
LEGGI TUTTO
TENSIONI
di Lofai
bianche mani sottili
segnate dal tempo
accarezzano il mio viso
CHATTA SUBITO!
Entra in chat! C'è un sacco di gente che ti aspetta e che ti vuole conoscere.
IL FORUM
Un luogo sacro per chi chatta. Nel muro puoi scrivere di tutto... entra ora.
GENTE DI CHAT
Chi si nasconde dietro il monitor? Detto fatto, ecco le facce più 'fuori' di tutto il web!

www.puntochat.it
D: valeria rippa
A: format c **M:** valeria@formatc.it

Auto belgique occasion actualite auto
VROOM.be
Votre voiture est-elle propre?
Rouler économe... un plus pour la nature et pour votre portefeuille!
FR
NL
ACCUEIL
L'ACTUALITÉ
LES OCCASIONS
PRATIQUE
DISCUSSIONS
ANNUAIRE AUTO-MOTO
Toutes les langues
» RECHERCHER
AUTO
» L'actualité auto
» Les essais auto
» Les occasions auto
» Occasions du jour
» Dépose ton annonce
» Forum auto
» Forum auto-bazar
» Forum tuning auto
» Forum ancêtres
» Tout sur le tuning
» Galeries photos
» Prix véhicules neufs
PUBLICITE
John Car
MOTO
» L'actualité moto
» Les essais moto
» Les occasions moto
» Dépose ton annonce
» Occasions du jour
» Forum moto
» Forum moto-bazar
» Les balades à moto!
» Forum tuning moto
PUBLICITÉ
Annonces Goooooogle
Voiture Neuve et Occasion
NOS ESSAIS AUTO
tous nos essais
Toyota RAV4 D-4D
Quel est le secret du succès du RAV4 ? Nous avons voulu le savoir en prenant le volant de la version 5 portes Diesel D-4D 2 litres à ...
» Lire l'essai
Jaguar XK8
Très légèrement restylée, la XK 2004 ressemble à s'y méprendre à l'ancienne version. En 2003, Jaguar avait boosté la motorisation et ...
» Lire l'essai
DERNIÈRES NOUVELLES
toutes les nouveautés
Samsung SM7 : Renault en Corée
Développée par le centre de R&D Renault Samsung Motors, la SM7 est une berline spacieuse au design « sophistiqué » destiné au ...
» Lire l'article
Qu'est-ce qui va à 315 km/h et qui est vert ? - Réponse : le bolide de IdéeVerte Compétition, un projet soutenu par l'Agence Spatiale Européenne (ESA). ...
» Lire l'article
Conduire en hiver - La marque de pneumatiques Continental vient de publier une étude qui montre que le comportement des ...
» Lire l'article
CONCOURS
Un PDA avec GPS intégré à gagner!
valeur 500€
LES DERNIERES OCCASIONS
Aujourd'hui, 13 nouvelles occasions!
» YAMAHA 900 DIVERSION.S - 2002
» VOLKSWAGEN TRANSPORTEUR - 1990
» TOYOTA LAND CRUISER - 2004
» FIAT PUNTO - 2004
» FIAT PUNTO - 2001
» MITSUBISHI SPACE GEAR - 1997
» NISSAN TERRANO 2 - 1998
» VOLKSWAGEN GOLF IV - 2002
Tu n'as pas trouvé l'occasion que tu cherches ? Utilise notre "Occasion Messenger", il t'avertira dès qu'une occasion répond à tes critères de recherches !
» Dépose ta petite annonce auto
» Dépose ta petite annonce moto
ASSURANCE ETHIAS
ASSISTANCE
ALL INCLUSIVE POUR 70 EUR/ANS ?
ASSISTANCE
ALL INCLUSIVE POUR 70 EUR/AN ?

Actualité automobile
VROOM.be
Votre voiture est-elle propre?
Rouler économe... un plus pour la nature et pour votre portefeuille!
FR
NL
ACCUEIL
L'ACTUALITÉ
LES OCCASIONS
PRATIQUE
DISCUSSIONS
ANNUAIRE AUTO-MOTO
Toutes les langues
» RECHERCHER
AUTO
» L'actualité auto
» Les essais auto
» Les occasions auto
» Occasions du jour
» Dépose ton annonce
» Forum auto
» Forum auto-bazar
» Forum tuning auto
» Forum ancêtres
» Tout sur le tuning
» Galeries photos
» Prix véhicules neufs
PUBLICITE
FORD DEALER
MOTO
» L'actualité moto
» Les essais moto
» Les occasions moto
» Dépose ton annonce
» Occasions du jour
» Forum moto
» Forum moto-bazar
» Les balades à moto!
» Forum tuning moto
PUBLICITÉ
Annonces Goooooogle
Voiture Neuve et Occasion
L'ACTUALITE AUTOMOBILE
[retour]
RECHERCHER DANS LES NEWS:
Recherche
Samsung SM7 : Renault en Corée
Développée par le centre de R&D Renault Samsung Motors, la SM7 est une berline spacieuse au design « sophistiqué » destiné au marché coréen. Elle est équipée des moteurs V6 Neo VQ 3.5 et 2.3, issus de l'Alliance Renault Nissan. Elle a un look statutaire qui ressemble fort à ce que peuvent faire les constructeurs coréens. Apparemment ce marché asiatique aime bien ce type de véhicule. Mais surtout, elle applique en exclusivité la nouvelle identité visuelle de la face avant des véhicules Renault Samsung Motors. La SM7 est également équipée de technologies de pointe exclusives sur le marché coréen telles qu'une caméra de rétrovision ou la carte mains libres. En matière de sécurité, la SM7 intègre des développements tels que « the Smart Airbag System » qui comprend des airbags frontaux autoadaptatifs, latéraux et rideau, et tels que l'ABS avec répartiteur de freinage électronique (EBD) et l'amplificateur ... (> lire plus)
Qu'est-ce qui va à 315 km/h et qui est vert ?
Réponse : le bolide de IdéeVerte Compétition, un projet soutenu par l'Agence Spatiale Européenne (ESA). Cette voiture roule au GPL, l'un des carburants les moins polluants. Elle est également est lubrifiée à l'huile de tournesol, tout en étant protégée contre les risques d'incendie par des matériaux spatiaux. Le 4 novembre dernier, à Brétigny-sur-Orge, celle-ci a établi un nouveau record de vitesse à 315 km/h. IdéeVerte Compétition a été fondée
DERNIERS TITRES
> TOUTES LES NEWS
Samsung SM7 : Renault en Corée
Qu'est-ce qui va à 315 km/h et qui est vert ?
Conduire en hiver
Opel Tigra TwinTop : en Diesel... aussi
Saab 9-5 BioPower : rouler à l'alcool
EuroNCAP : les derniers résultats sont rassurants
Range Rover Sport : plébiscite ?
Ferrari Superamerica : le toit sur le coffre
Volkswagen Bora : l'Amérique en primeur
Hyundai Santa Fe : opération lifting
est-elle propre?

www.vroom.be
D: hermans lionel
M: lionel@vroom.be

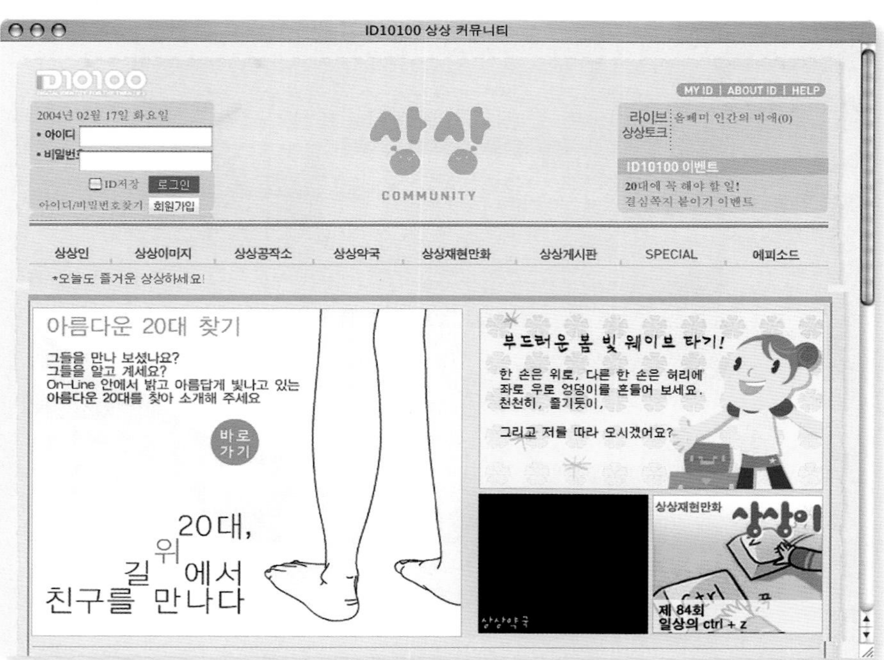

ID10100 상상 커뮤니티
MY ID | ABOUT ID | HELP
2004년 02월 17일 화요일
• 아이디
• 비밀번호
ID저장
로그인
아이디/비밀번호찾기
회원가입
상상
COMMUNITY
라이브 상상토크
ID10100 이벤트
20대에 꼭 해야 할 일!
결심쪽지 붙이기 이벤트
상상인
상상이미지
상상공작소
상상약국
상상재현만화
상상게시판
SPECIAL
에피소드
*오늘도 즐거운 상상하세요!
아름다운 20대 찾기
그들을 만나 보셨나요?
그들을 알고 계세요?
On-Line 안에서 밝고 아름답게 빛나고 있는
아름다운 20대를 찾아 소개해 주세요
바로 가기
20대,
길 위에서
친구를 만나다
부드러운 봄 빛 웨이브 타기!
한 손은 위로, 다른 한 손은 허리에
좌로 우로 엉덩이를 흔들어 보세요.
천천히, 즐기듯이,
그리고 저를 따라 오시겠어요?
상상재현만화
상상이
제 84회
일상의 ctrl + z

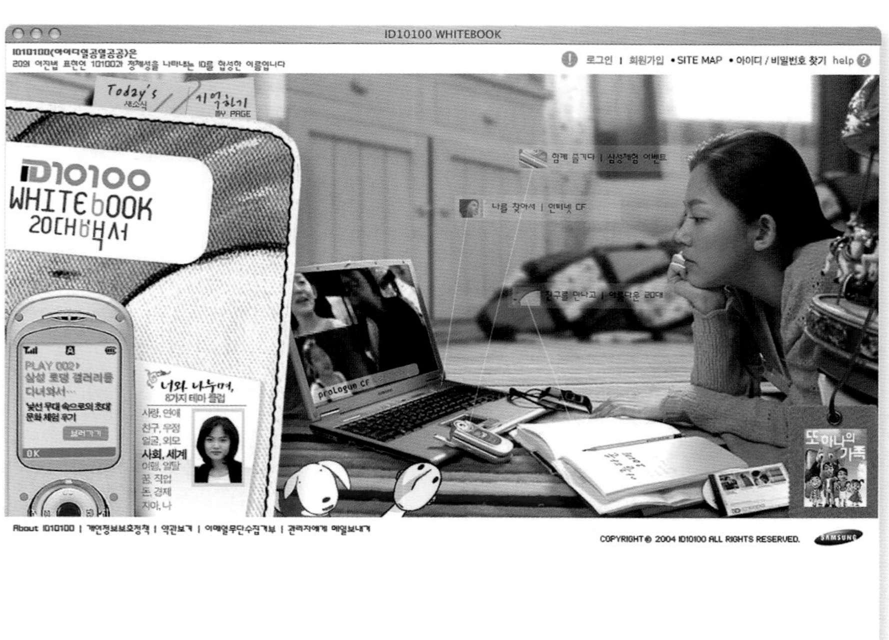

ID10100 WHITEBOOK
로그인 | 회원가입 • SITE MAP • 아이디 / 비밀번호 찾기 help
Today's
ID10100
WHITEbOOK
20대백서
너와 나누며,
사랑, 연애
친구, 우정
사회, 세계
도하나의 가족
COPYRIGHT © 2004 ID10100 ALL RIGHTS RESERVED.
SAMSUNG

id10100.samsung.com
D: ki-young park **P:** cheil communications
A: sugarcube **M:** ivory@samsung.co.kr

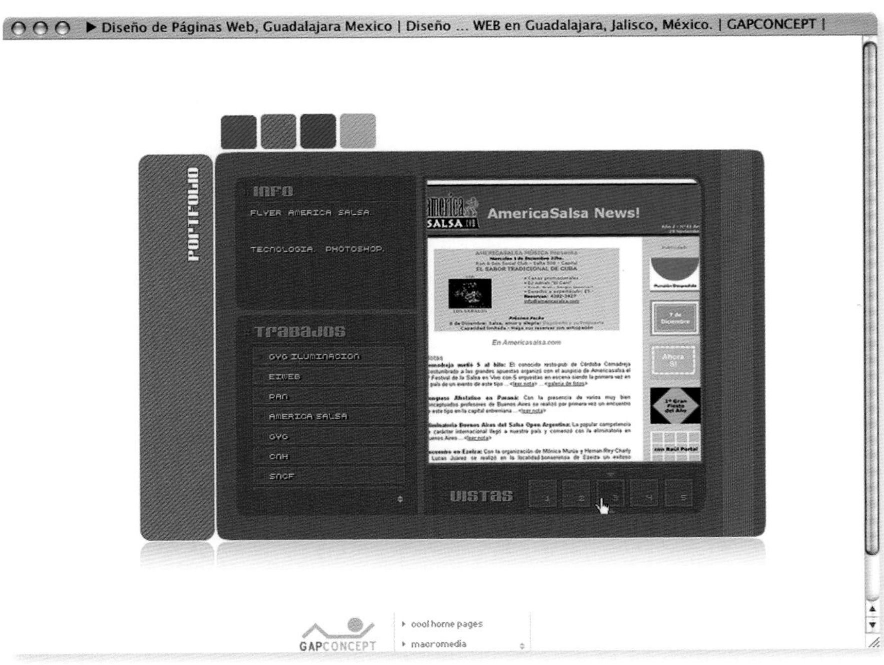

Diseño de Páginas Web, Guadalajara Mexico | Diseño ... WEB en Guadalajara, Jalisco, México. | GAPCONCEPT |
PORTFOLIO
INFO
FLYER AMERICA SALSA
TECNOLOGIA: PHOTOSHOP.
TRABAJOS
GVG ILUMINACION
EIWEB
PAN
AMERICA SALSA
GVG
CNH
SNCF
AmericaSalsa News!
VISTAS
1
2
3
4
5
GAPCONCEPT
cool home pages
macromedia

Diseño de Páginas Web, Guadalajara Mexico | Diseño ... WEB en Guadalajara, Jalisco, México. | GAPCONCEPT |
PROYECTO
INFO
BOCETO QUALITY DESIGN CENTER I
EXPERIMENTOS
QUALITY DESIGN I
QUALITY DESIGN II
QUALITY DESIGN III
GAPCONCEPT
LOGO QUALITY DESIGN
DAVID PRECIADO
que hacemos
como lo hacemos
GAPCONCEPT
cool home pages
macromedia

www.gapconcept.com.mx

D: gabriel alberto pascuariello **C:** gabriel alberto pascuariello

A: gapconcept **M:** info@gapconcept.com.mx

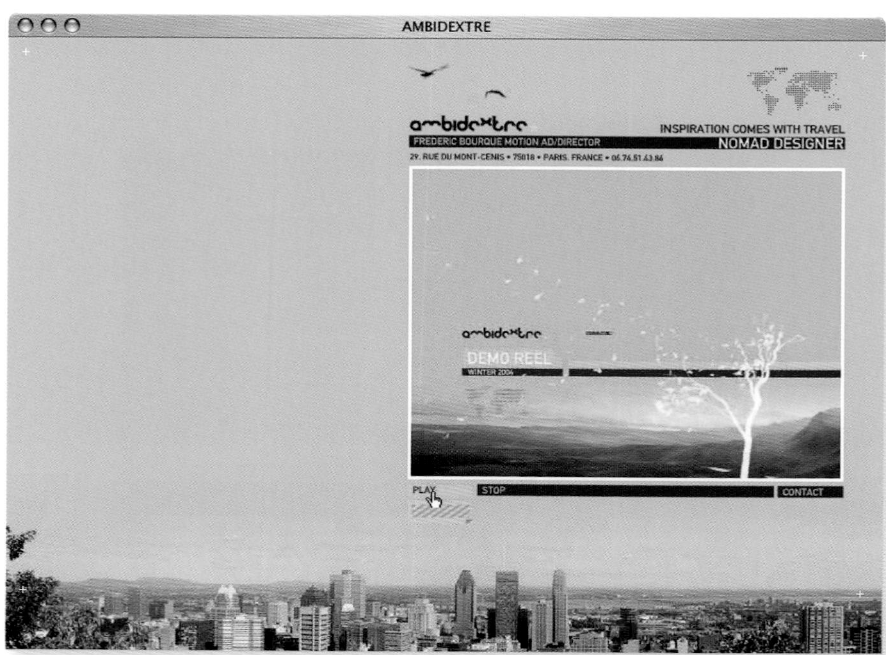
AMBIDEXTRE
ambidextre
INSPIRATION COMES WITH TRAVEL
FREDERIC BOURQUE MOTION AD/DIRECTOR
NOMAD DESIGNER
29, RUE DU MONT-CENIS • 75018 • PARIS, FRANCE • 06.74.51.43.86
ambidextre
DEMO REEL
WINTER 2004
PLAY
STOP
CONTACT

AMBIDEXTRE
ambidextre
INSPIRATION COMES WITH TRAVEL
FREDERIC BOURQUE MOTION AD/DIRECTOR
NOMAD DESIGNER
29, RUE DU MONT-CENIS • 75018 • PARIS, FRANCE • 06.74.51.43.86
EUROP ASSISTANCE
n'a eu de cesse d'anticiper les évolutions de la société
PLAY
STOP
CONTACT

www.ambidextre.com
D: frédéric bourque
A: ambidextre **M:** fred@ambidextre.com

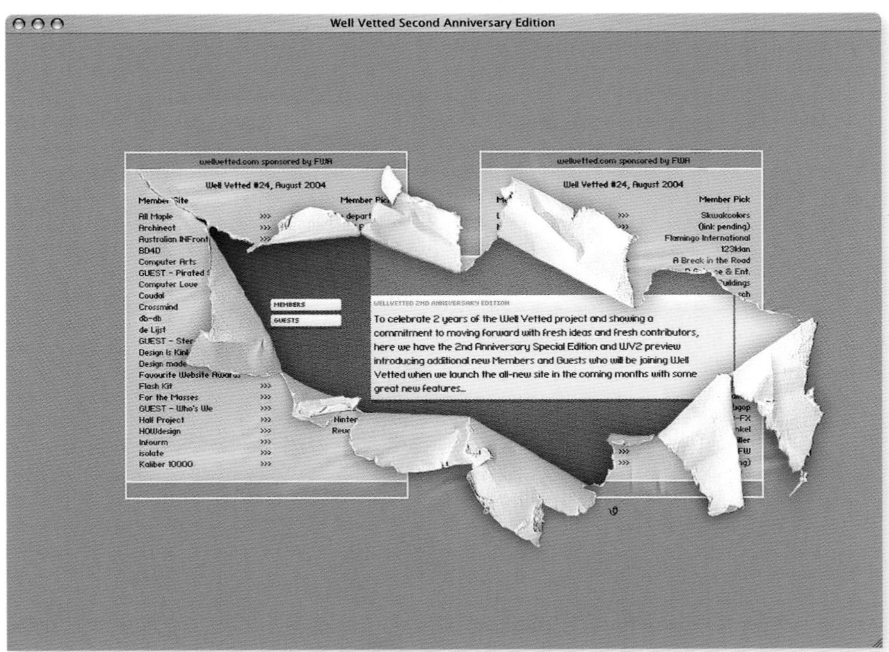
Well Vetted Second Anniversary Edition
wellvetted.com sponsored by FWA
Well Vetted #24, August 2004
WELLVETTED 2ND ANNIVERSARY EDITION
To celebrate 2 years of the Well Vetted project and showing a commitment to moving forward with fresh ideas and fresh contributors, here we have the 2nd Anniversary Special Edition and WV2 preview introducing additional new Members and Guests who will be joining Well Vetted when we launch the all-new site in the coming months with some great new features...

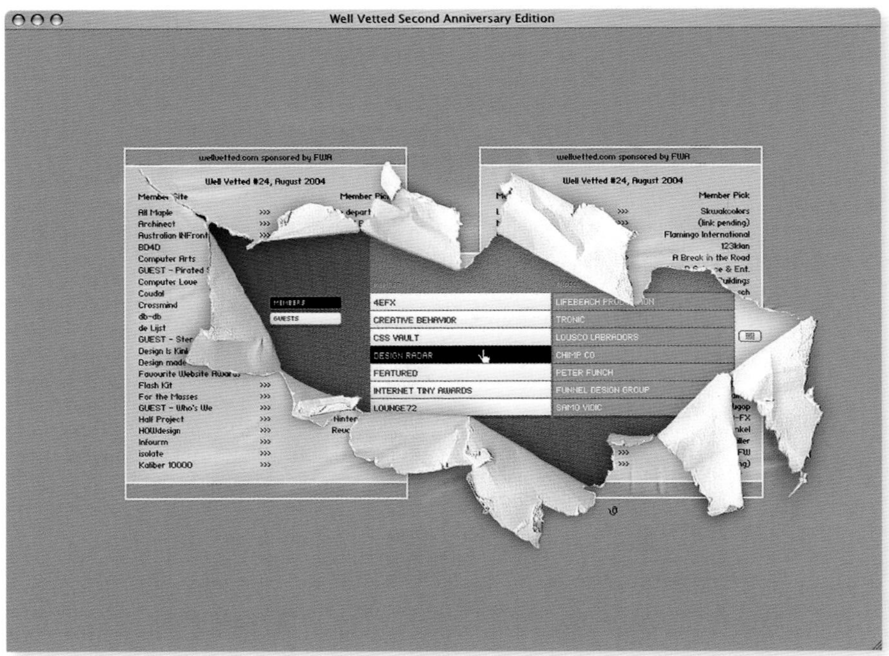
Well Vetted Second Anniversary Edition
wellvetted.com sponsored by FWA
Well Vetted #24, August 2004
4EFX
CREATIVE BEHAVIOR
CSS VAULT
DESIGN RADAR
FEATURED
INTERNET TINY AWARDS
LOUNGE72
TRONIC
LOUSCO LABRADORS
CHIMP CO
PETER FUNCH
FUNNEL DESIGN GROUP
SAMO VIDIC

www.wellvetted.com/wv2/
D: group94 + ingo ramin **C:** group94 **P:** rob ford (fwa)
A: group94 **M:** team@favouritewebsiteawards.com

ZOOBIES
PRESS 1 TO 9
TO CHOOSE
BRUSH SIZE.
0X000000
PRESS 'SPACE' TO CLEAR.
DRAW

ZOOBIES

www.zoobies.net
D: pascal kehl **C:** john lyons
A: inteam graphics **M:** me@herkocoomans.net

:::: Stephane Guillot - Webdesigner Flash ::::
Stephane Guillot
Web Designer

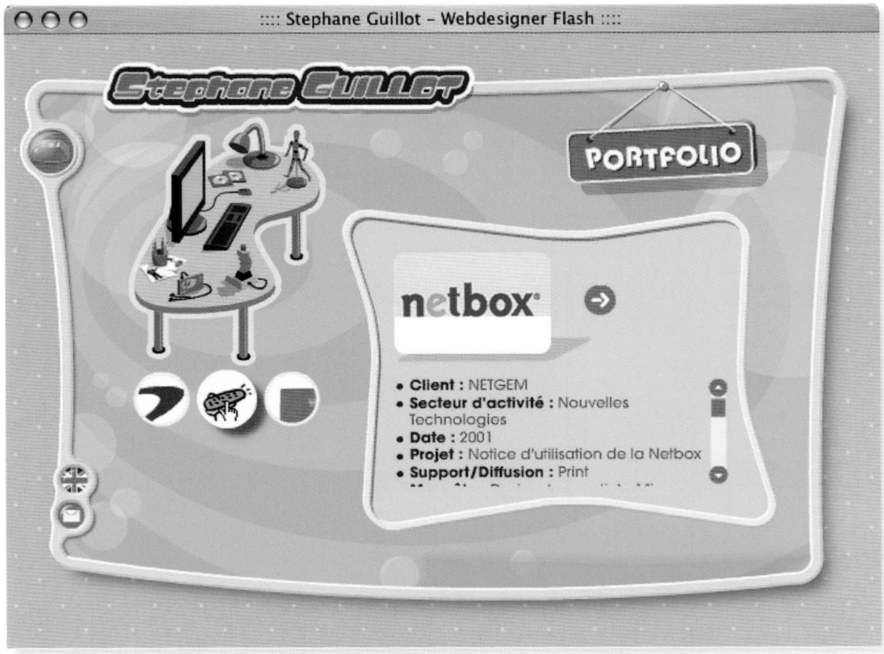
:::: Stephane Guillot - Webdesigner Flash ::::
Stephane Guillot
Portfolio
netbox
• Client : NETGEM
• Secteur d'activité : Nouvelles Technologies
• Date : 2001
• Projet : Notice d'utilisation de la Netbox
• Support/Diffusion : Print

www.stephaneguillot.com
D: stephane guillot
M: postmaster@stephaneguillot.com

Summer Base ****
INIT NAV
LOGIN
Nickname :
Wachtwoord :
LOGIN
NEW USER
ADVERTISING
Win een Sony Playstation 2
chello gamezone
COMMUNITY
321.287 ID's
Nieuwste ID met foto: CAT-WOMAN1
NOW ON TMF
Nu: 15:26u
Interactive Charts
Straks: 16:00u
Play
POLL
Hoeveel geef jij uit aan een Sinterklaas
NEWS
VADER GEZOCHT
Geri Halliwell heeft zichzelf een deadline gesteld om moeder te worden.
LEES MEER
STOP AIDS NOW!
Werk mee aan een wereld zonder Aids
GO
ARTIST TOP 10
Deze week de lekkerste nummers van tien DJ's.
GO
Rate that VJ
GEEF JE OP!
Altijd al je 'one minute of fame' willen hebben?
GO
Who cares?
GAMES REVIEWS
Geef je mening over de
FF CONTACT
Wil jij ook een videoboodschap
LIVE GAMEN
Check de uitslagen van Need
ADVERTISING
ID
Maak er dan nu snel een
HOME CONTACT LEGAL HELP

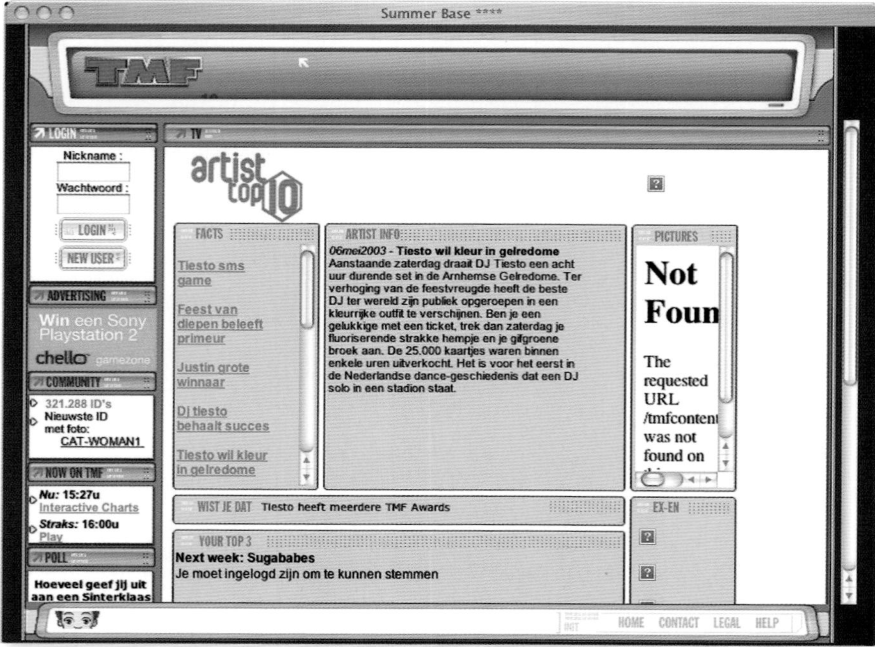
Summer Base ****
TMF
LOGIN
Nickname :
Wachtwoord :
LOGIN
NEW USER
ADVERTISING
Win een Sony Playstation 2
chello gamezone
COMMUNITY
321.288 ID's
Nieuwste ID met foto: CAT-WOMAN1
NOW ON TMF
Nu: 15:27u
Interactive Charts
Straks: 16:00u
Play
POLL
Hoeveel geef jij uit aan een Sinterklaas
TV
artist top 10
FACTS
Tiesto sms game
Feest van diepen beleeft primeur
Justin grote winnaar
Dj tiesto behaalt succes
Tiesto wil kleur in gelredome
ARTIST INFO
06mei2003 - Tiesto wil kleur in gelredome
Aanstaande zaterdag draait DJ Tiesto een acht uur durende set in de Arnhemse Gelredome. Ter verhoging van de feestvreugde heeft de beste DJ ter wereld zijn publiek opgeroepen in een kleurrijke outfit te verschijnen. Ben je een gelukkige met een ticket, trek dan zaterdag je fluoriserende strakke hempje en je gifgroene broek aan. De 25.000 kaartjes waren binnen enkele uren uitverkocht. Het is voor het eerst in de Nederlandse dance-geschiedenis dat een DJ solo in een stadion staat.
PICTURES
Not Foun
The requested URL /tmfcontent was not found on
WIST JE DAT Tiesto heeft meerdere TMF Awards
YOUR TOP 3
Next week: Sugababes
Je moet ingelogd zijn om te kunnen stemmen
EX-EN
HOME CONTACT LEGAL HELP

www.fanta.nl
D: urriaan van bokhoven **C:** neil young **P:** marc maas
A: clockwork **M:** jurriaan@clockwork.nl

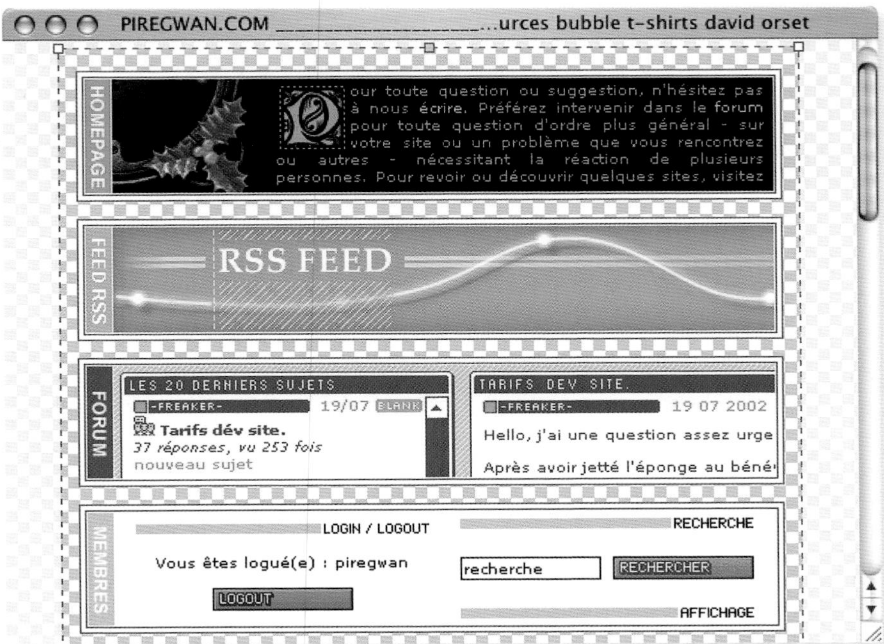
PIREGWAN.COM ...urces bubble t-shirts david orset
HOMEPAGE
our toute question ou suggestion, n'hésitez pas à nous écrire. Préférez intervenir dans le forum pour toute question d'ordre plus général - sur votre site ou un problème que vous rencontrez ou autres - nécessitant la réaction de plusieurs personnes. Pour revoir ou découvrir quelques sites, visitez
FEED RSS
RSS FEED
FORUM
LES 20 DERNIERS SUJETS
-FREAKER- 19/07
Tarifs dév site.
37 réponses, vu 253 fois
nouveau sujet
TARIFS DEV SITE.
-FREAKER- 19 07 2002
Hello, j'ai une question assez urge
Après avoir jetté l'éponge au béné
MEMBRES
LOGIN / LOGOUT
Vous êtes logué(e) : piregwan
LOGOUT
RECHERCHE
recherche
RECHERCHER
AFFICHAGE

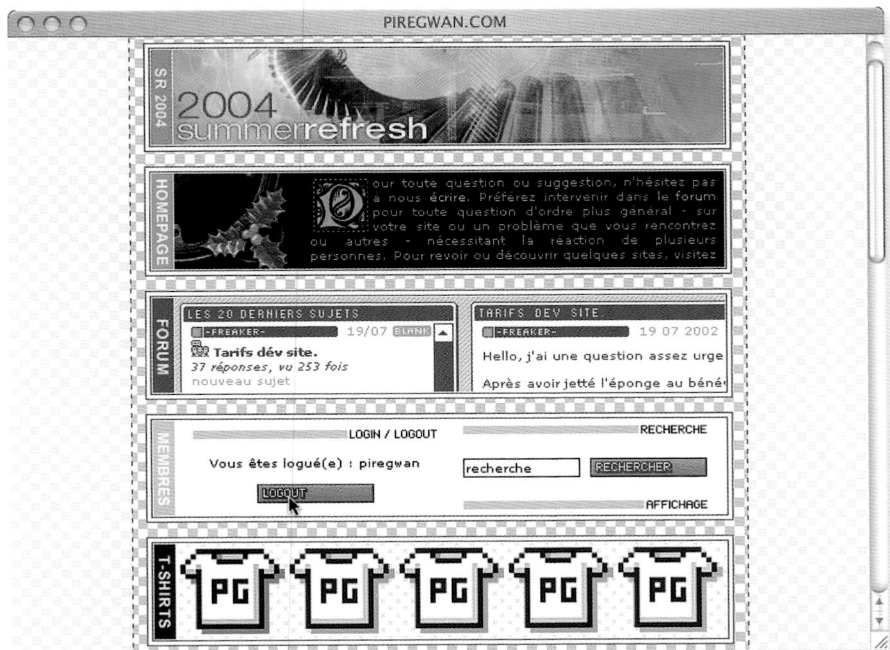
PIREGWAN.COM
SR 2004
2004 summerrefresh
HOMEPAGE
FORUM
MEMBRES
T-SHIRTS
PG

www.piregwan.com
D: david orset
M: webmaster@piregwan.com

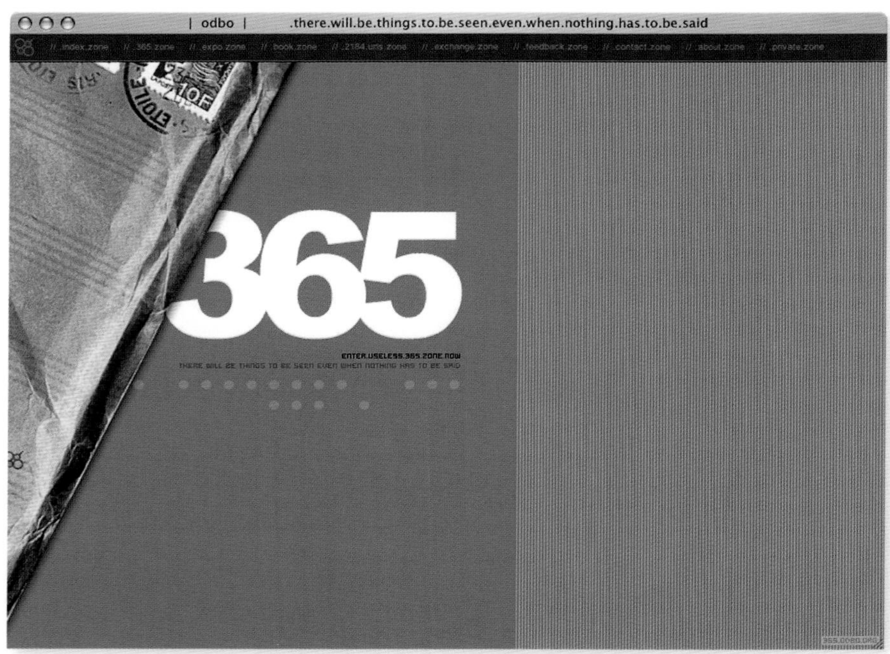
| odbo | .there.will.be.things.to.be.seen.even.when.nothing.has.to.be.said
// .index.zone // .365.zone // .expo.zone // .book.zone // .2184.urls.zone // .exchange.zone // .feedback.zone // .contact.zone // .about.zone // .private.zone
365
ENTER.USELESS.365.ZONE.NOW
THERE WILL BE THINGS TO BE SEEN EVEN WHEN NOTHING HAS TO BE SAID

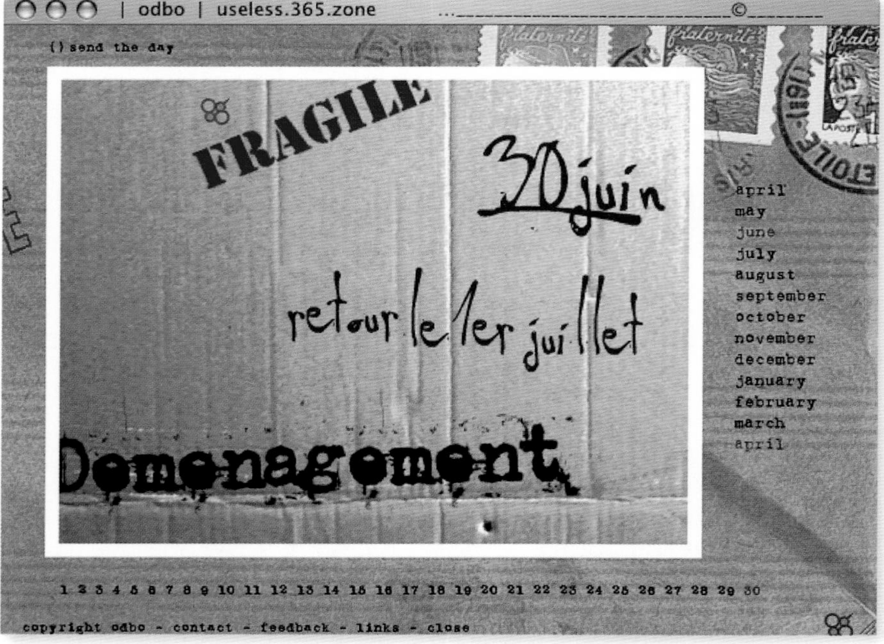
| odbo | useless.365.zone
() send the day
FRAGILE
30 juin
retour le 1er juillet
Demenagement
april
may
june
july
august
september
october
november
december
january
february
march
april
1 2 3 4 5 6 7 8 9 10 11 12 13 14 15 16 17 18 19 20 21 22 23 24 25 26 27 28 29 30
copyright odbo - contact - feedback - links - close

odbo.org
D: julien grandclement
M: odbo@odbo.org

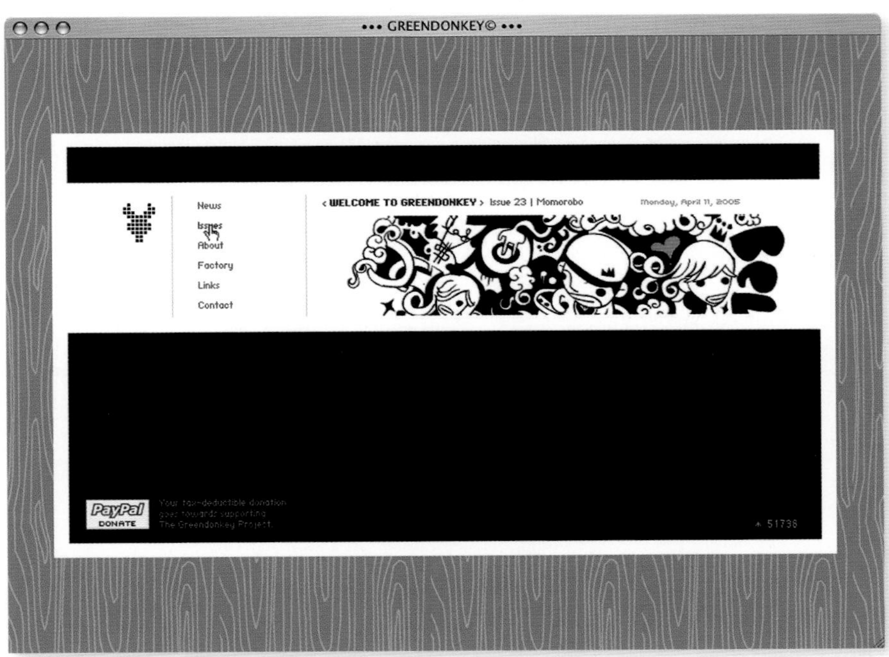
••• GREENDONKEY© •••
News
Issues
About
Factory
Links
Contact
‹ WELCOME TO GREENDONKEY › Issue 23 | Momorobo
Monday, April 11, 2005
PayPal DONATE
Your tax-deductible donation goes towards supporting The Greendonkey Project.
51736

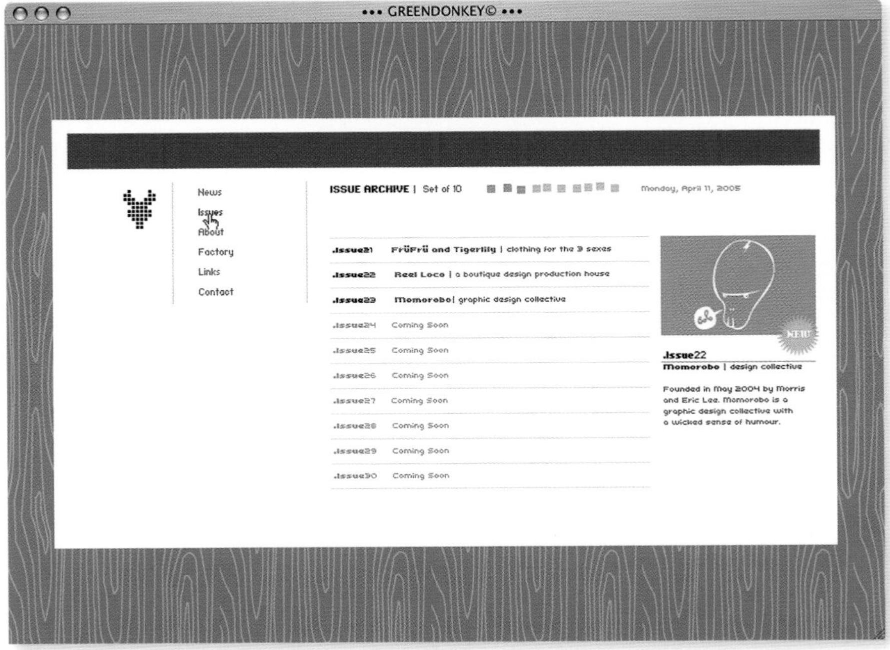
••• GREENDONKEY© •••
News
Issues
About
Factory
Links
Contact
ISSUE ARCHIVE | Set of 10
Monday, April 11, 2005
.issue21 FrüFrü and Tigerlily | clothing for the 3 sexes
.issue22 Reel Loco | a boutique design production house
.issue23 Momorobo | graphic design collective
.issue24 Coming Soon
.issue25 Coming Soon
.issue26 Coming Soon
.issue27 Coming Soon
.issue28 Coming Soon
.issue29 Coming Soon
.issue30 Coming Soon
NEW
.issue22
Momorobo | design collective
Founded in May 2004 by Morris and Eric Lee. Momorobo is a graphic design collective with a wicked sense of humour.

www.greendonkey.info
D: gerard tan
A: junkflea **M:** info@junkflea.com

www.virtual-nights.com
D: jakob schwermer **C:** johannes dieckmann **P:** kai brökelmeier
M: kai.broekelmeier@virtual-nights.de

Art Fart – Documenting street art
Art Fart.
Documenting street art
Navigate p01 -
LEN
This shite is random, anonymous, public and uncategorized. Please
commercial work on this site or
your own work.
© 2004 by

Art Fart – Documenting street art
Art Fart.
Documenting street art
Navigate p01 -
This shite is random, anonymous, public and uncategorized. Please
commercial work on this site or
your own work.
© 2004 by

www.artfart.nl

D: joost olsthoorn **C:** jeroen bekker

M: fart@artfart.nl

Ocio Digital, suplemento de cine, dvd, música y videojuegos - Metro
OCIO DIGITAL
ESTRENOS CINE
NOVEDADES DVD
NOVEDADES MÚSICA
NOVEDADES VIDEOJUEGOS
Últimos estrenos de cine
estrenos
ESTRENOS CINE
>> VOLVER A PORTADA
FAVORITOS
PÁGINA DE INICIO
>> El Lobo
La apasionante historia real de un hombre infiltrado en la cúpula de ETA
MAS CINE
ALTA TENSIÓN
Marie decide convencer a su amiga Álex para pasar el fin de semana en casa ...
ALIENS VS PREDATOR
Alien o Depredador, ¿quién ganará? La apuesta está servida, ¡atrévanse a pu...
SUPER SIZE ME
El promotor de la cruzada contra la denominada comida basura es Morgan
SILVER CITY
A George W. Bush le crecen los enanos en su camino a la reelección como pre...
SIGUIENTE >>
QUIERES ESTE REGALO?
TOP 10
01 BRIDGET JONES
02 ALIEN VS PRED...
03 EL LOBO
04 ¿BAILAMOS?
05 DI QUE SI
06 2 COLGAOS MUY...
07 EL MENSAJERO...
08 CELLULAR
09 RESIDENT EVIL 2
10 MELINDA Y ME...
Top 10 taquilla en la península
metro
© 2004 ACCIÓN MEDIA POWERED BY EDISSENY.COM· TODOS LOS DERECHOS RESERVADOS
POLÍTICA DE PRIVACIDAD | ANÚNCIATE!

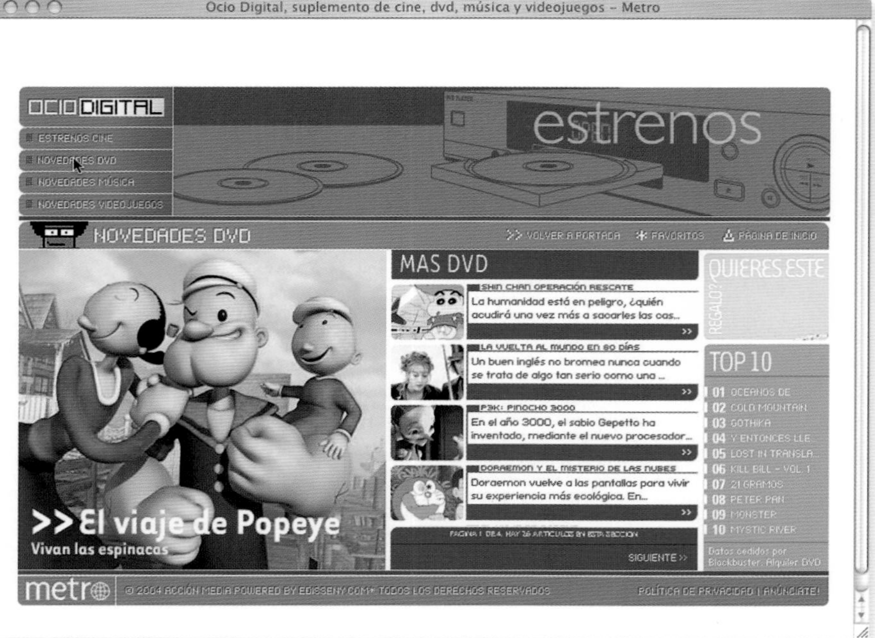
Ocio Digital, suplemento de cine, dvd, música y videojuegos - Metro
OCIO DIGITAL
ESTRENOS CINE
NOVEDADES DVD
NOVEDADES MÚSICA
NOVEDADES VIDEOJUEGOS
estrenos
NOVEDADES DVD
>> VOLVER A PORTADA
FAVORITOS
PÁGINA DE INICIO
MAS DVD
SHIN CHAN OPERACIÓN RESCATE
La humanidad está en peligro, ¿quién acudirá una vez más a sacarles las cas...
LA VUELTA AL MUNDO EN 80 DÍAS
Un buen inglés no bromea nunca cuando se trata de algo tan serio como una ...
P3K: PINOCHO 3000
En el año 3000, el sabio Gepetto ha inventado, mediante el nuevo procesador...
DORAEMON Y EL MISTERIO DE LAS NUBES
Doraemon vuelve a las pantallas para vivir su experiencia más ecológica. En...
SIGUIENTE >>
>> El viaje de Popeye
Vivan las espinacas
QUIERES ESTE REGALO?
TOP 10
01 OCEANOS DE
02 COLD MOUNTAIN
03 GOTHIKA
04 Y ENTONCES LLE
05 LOST IN TRANSLA
06 KILL BILL - VOL. 1
07 21 GRAMOS
08 PETER PAN
09 MONSTER
10 MYSTIC RIVER
Datos cedidos por Blockbuster. Alquiler DVD
metro
© 2004 ACCIÓN MEDIA POWERED BY EDISSENY.COM· TODOS LOS DERECHOS RESERVADOS
POLÍTICA DE PRIVACIDAD | ANÚNCIATE!

www.masociodigital.com
D: emilio garcia vaz
A: edisseny **M:** emilio@edisseny.com

247 MEDIA STUDIOS :: flash webdesign | internet | multimedia | crossmedia ::
reproduction in whole or in part without permission is welcome
Ingo J.Ramin
247 MEDIA STUDIOS The whole truth
SERVICES
PORTFOLIO Clients and Works or the meaning of Life
E.MAIL
THE FIRST CONTACT
"Attention to Detail"
ART OF COMMUNICATION
INTERNET MULTIMEDIA CROSSMEDIA
247 MediaStudios
"Don't give up listening to the voices in your head, they might stop talking"
1007162 Mysterious by Yuko Ohigashi
downloads
friends

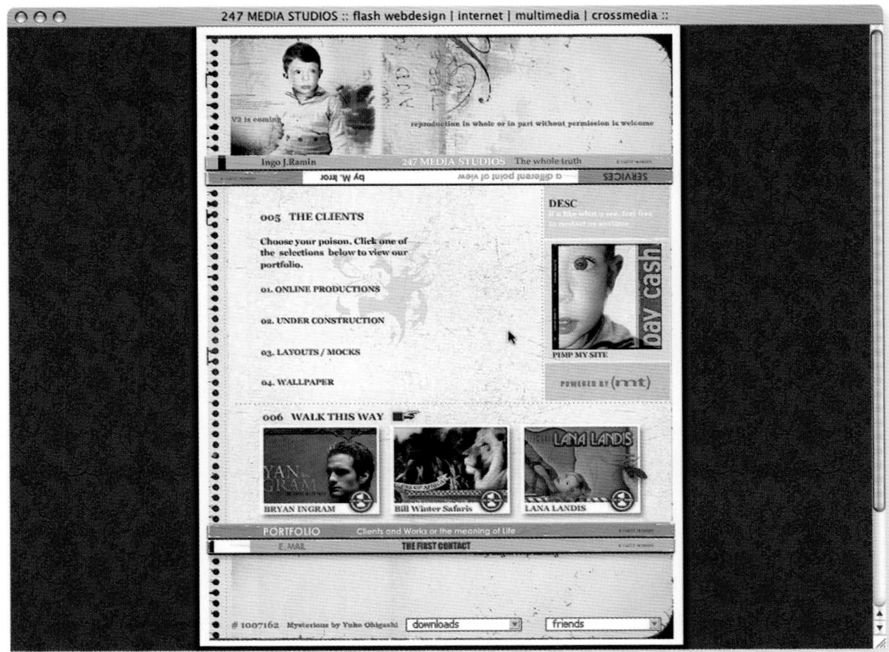
247 MEDIA STUDIOS :: flash webdesign | internet | multimedia | crossmedia ::
reproduction in whole or in part without permission is welcome
Ingo J.Ramin
247 MEDIA STUDIOS The whole truth
SERVICES
005 THE CLIENTS
Choose your poison. Click one of the selections below to view our portfolio.
01. ONLINE PRODUCTIONS
02. UNDER CONSTRUCTION
03. LAYOUTS / MOCKS
04. WALLPAPER
DESC
PIMP MY SITE
006 WALK THIS WAY
BRYAN INGRAM
Bill Winter Safaris
LANA LANDIS
PORTFOLIO Clients and Works or the meaning of Life
E.MAIL
THE FIRST CONTACT
1007162 Mysterious by Yuko Ohigashi
downloads
friends

www.24-7media.de
D: ingo j. ramin
A: 247 mediastudios **M:** info@24-7media.de

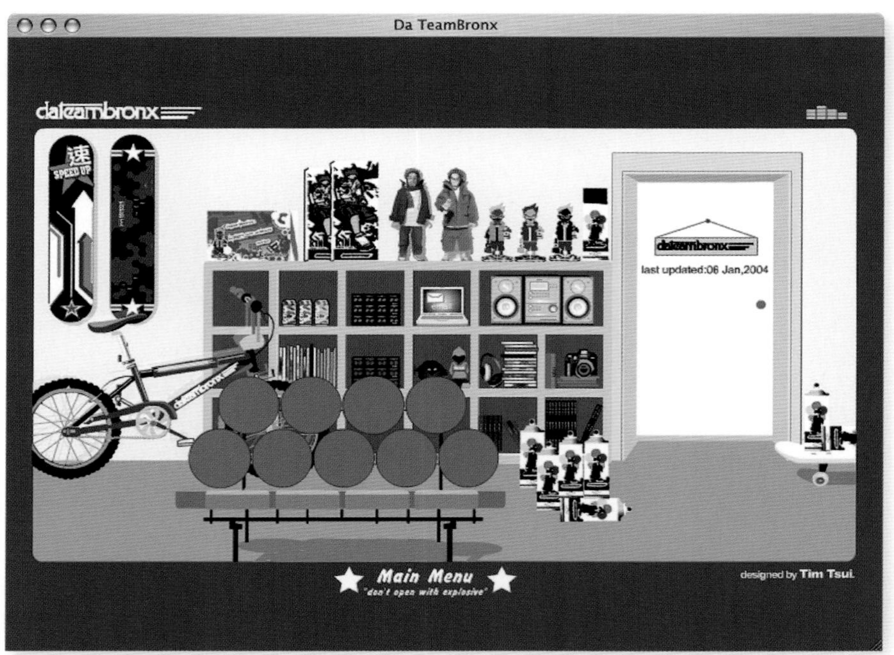
Da TeamBronx
dateambronx
last updated:06 Jan,2004
Main Menu
"don't open with explosive"
designed by Tim Tsui.

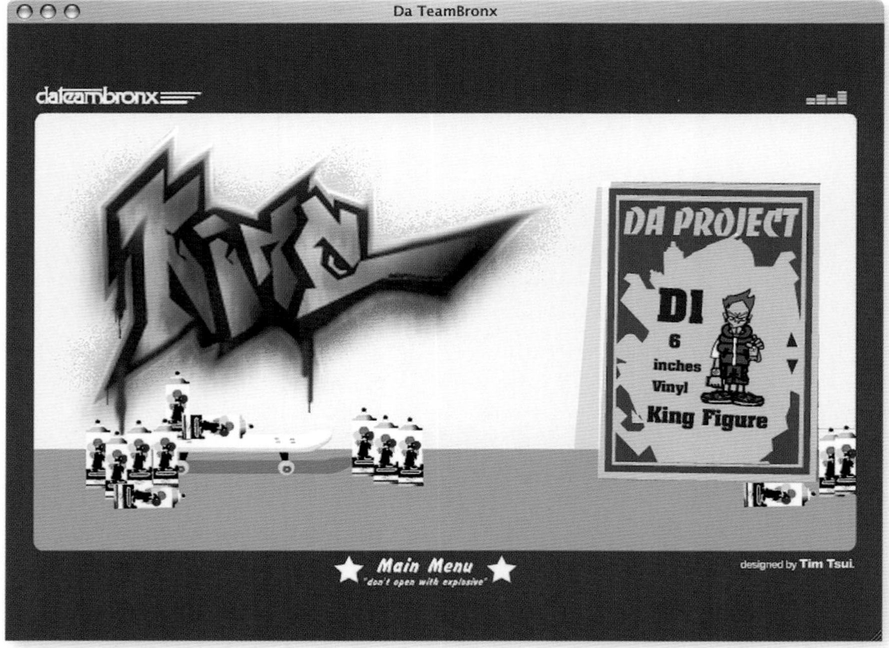
Da TeamBronx
dateambronx
DA PROJECT
DI
6
inches
Vinyl
King Figure
Main Menu
"don't open with explosive"
designed by Tim Tsui.

www.teamzero.com.hk
D: tim tsui
A: da teambronx **M:** info@teamzero.com.hk

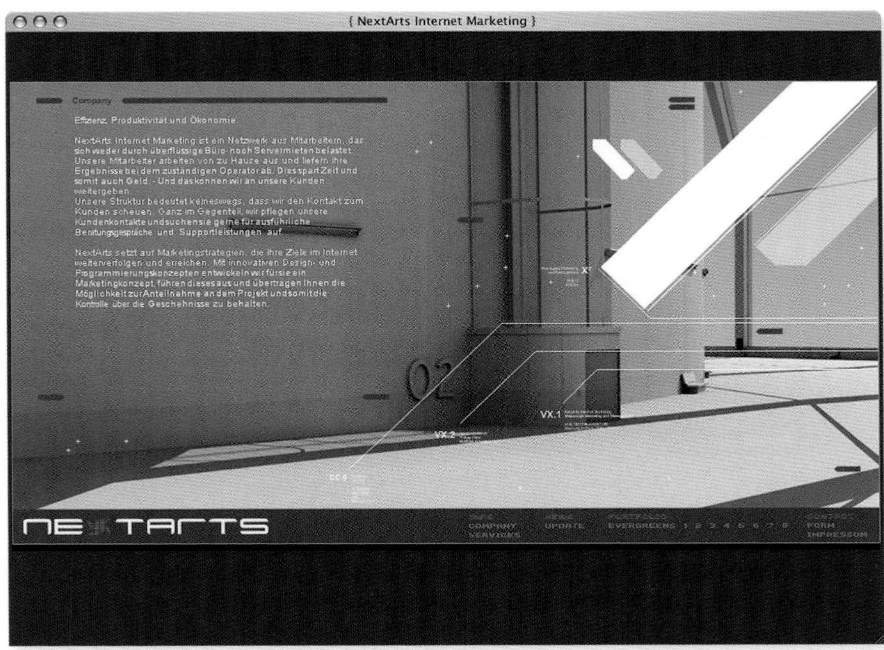
{ NextArts Internet Marketing }
Company
Effizienz, Produktivität und Ökonomie.
NextArts Internet Marketing ist ein Netzwerk aus Mitarbeitern, das sich weder durch überflüssige Büro- noch Servermieten belastet. Unsere Mitarbeiter arbeiten von zu Hause aus und liefern ihre Ergebnisse bei dem zuständigen Operator ab. Dies spart Zeit und somit auch Geld. - Und das können wir an unsere Kunden weitergeben.
Unsere Struktur bedeutet keineswegs, dass wir den Kontakt zum Kunden scheuen. Ganz im Gegenteil, wir pflegen unsere Kundenkontakte und suchen sie gerne für ausführliche Beratungsgespräche und Supportleistungen auf.
NextArts setzt auf Marketingstrategien, die Ihre Ziele im Internet weiterverfolgen und erreichen. Mit innovativen Design- und Programmierungskonzepten entwickeln wir für sie ein Marketingkonzept, führen dieses aus und übertragen Ihnen die Möglichkeit zur Anteilnahme an dem Projekt und somit die Kontrolle über die Geschehnisse zu behalten.
02
X3
VX.1
VX.2
COMPANY
SERVICES
UPDATE
EVERGREENS 1 2 3 4 5 6 7 8
FORM
IMPRESSUM

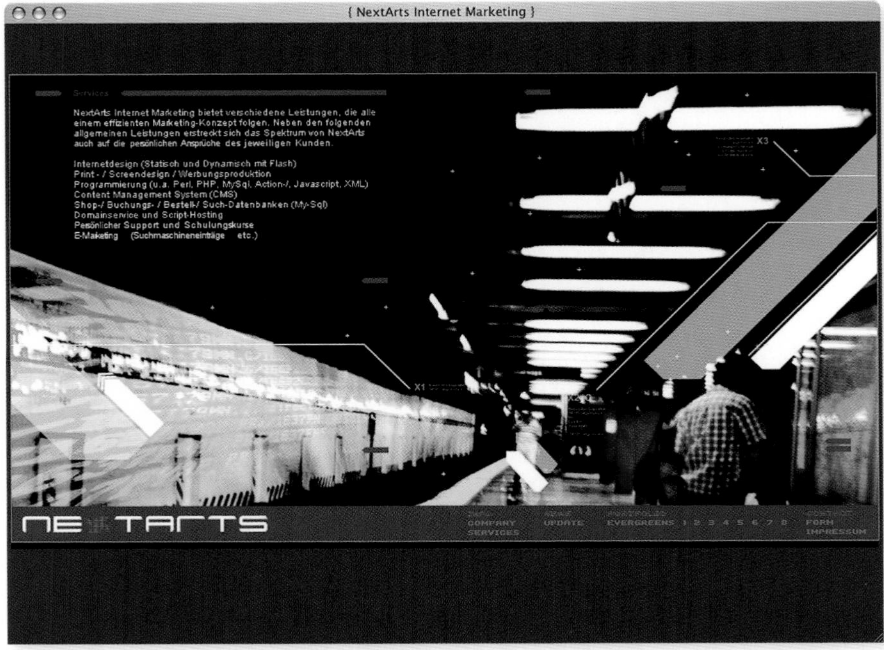
{ NextArts Internet Marketing }
Services
NextArts Internet Marketing bietet verschiedene Leistungen, die alle einem effizienten Marketing-Konzept folgen. Neben den folgenden allgemeinen Leistungen erstreckt sich das Spektrum von NextArts auch auf die persönlichen Ansprüche des jeweiligen Kunden.
Internetdesign (Statisch und Dynamisch mit Flash)
Print - / Screendesign / Werbungsproduktion
Programmierung (u.a. Perl, PHP, MySql, Action-/, Javascript, XML)
Content Management System (CMS)
Shop-/ Buchungs- / Bestell-/ Such-Datenbanken (My-Sql)
Domainservice und Script-Hosting
Persönlicher Support und Schulungskurse
E-Maketing (Suchmaschineneinträge etc.)
X3
X1
COMPANY
SERVICES
UPDATE
EVERGREENS 1 2 3 4 5 6 7 8
FORM
IMPRESSUM

www.nextarts.de
D: philipp dietz
A: nextarts **M:** info@nextarts.de

h-aze.com
[H]aze
[enter]
I'm not a photographer
Just someone who sometimes sees beyond the haze
|| Photos, Web and Graphic Design Agnès Zenko © 2003 All rights reserved ||
|| Flash Player 7 required || These series are regularly updated... ||

h-aze.com
gallery
guests
contact
links
series 01
series 02
series 03
series 04
series 05
series 06
series 07
series 08
[H]aze
|| Photos, Web and Graphic Design Agnès Zenko © 2003 All rights reserved ||
|| Flash Player 7 required || These series are regularly updated... ||

www.h-aze.com
D: agnès zenko
A: haze **M:** aze@h-aze.com

Big Fat Institute for Advanced Interactive Experiences
Big Fat Institute FOR ADVANCED INTERACTIVE EXPERIENCES
A New Brand Experience.
Welcome, friend, to the future of brand-building: advanced interactive experiences that deeply connect with consumers and create bonds that last a lifetime. Get a brief overview to the site by clicking here, or dive right in with an important Public Service Announcement via the television set below.
World of WEBNDER
A brief overview of Advanced Interactive Experiences
Study Buddy.
Take a peek at one of our current cases and see how they are building deeper, more meaningful relationships with their consumers.
Join Us!
One of us.
Receive important news correspondence and swell site updates.
Disclaim to Fame.
We're proud to be held responsible for almost everything we do.
PUBLIC SERVICE Announcements
click to enlarge and play

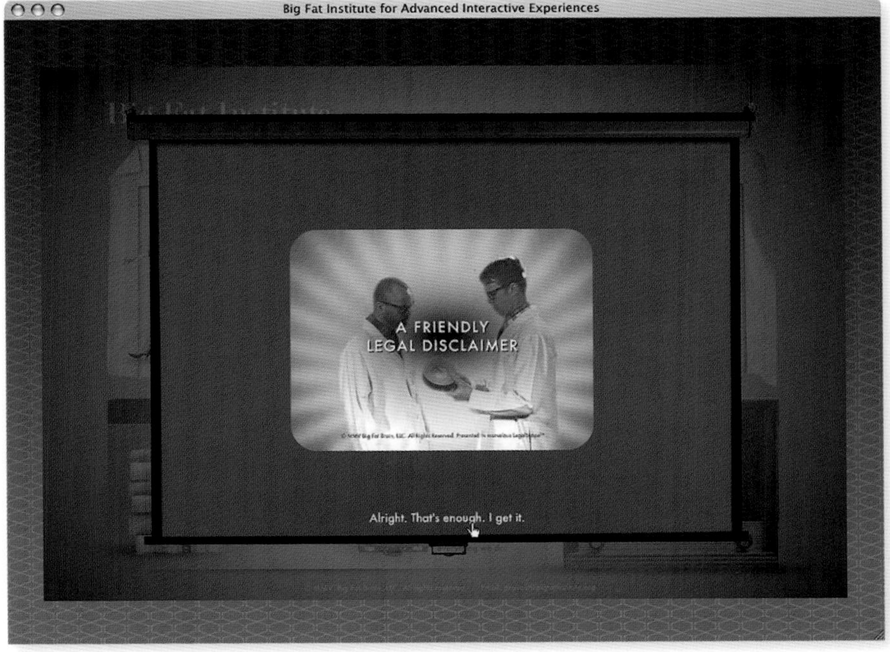
Big Fat Institute for Advanced Interactive Experiences
A FRIENDLY LEGAL DISCLAIMER
Alright. That's enough. I get it.

www.bigfatinstitute.org
D: troy hitch
A: big fat brain **M:** troy@bigfatbraincreative.com

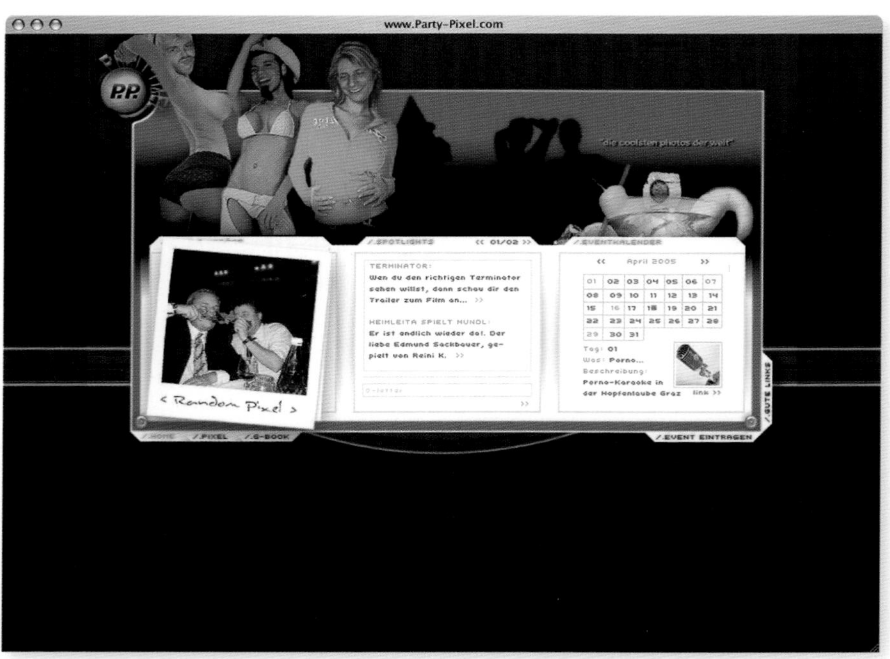

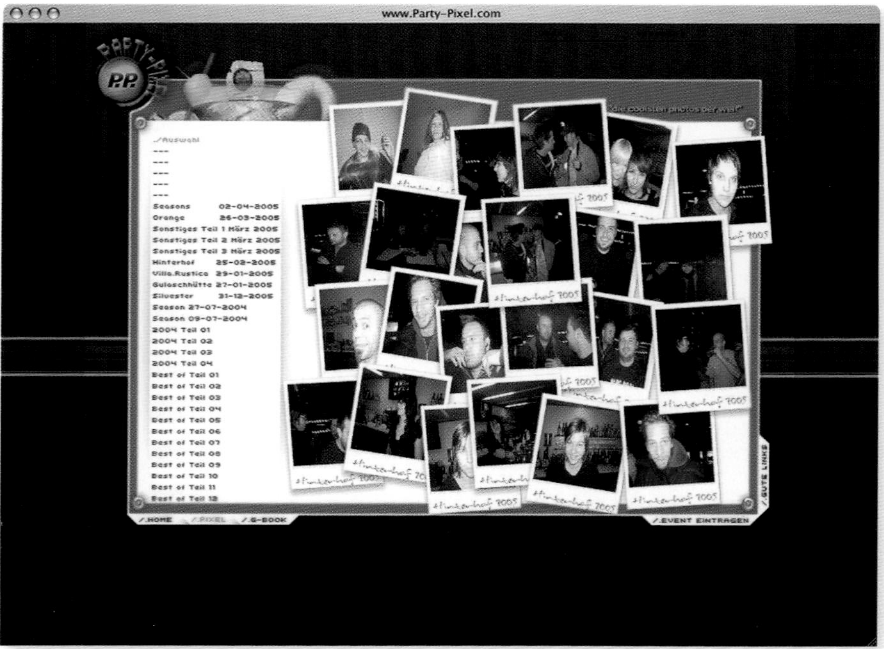

www.party-pixel.com
D: richard hudeczek **C:** richard hudeczek
A: mouse media - digital design **M:** info@mouse-media.net

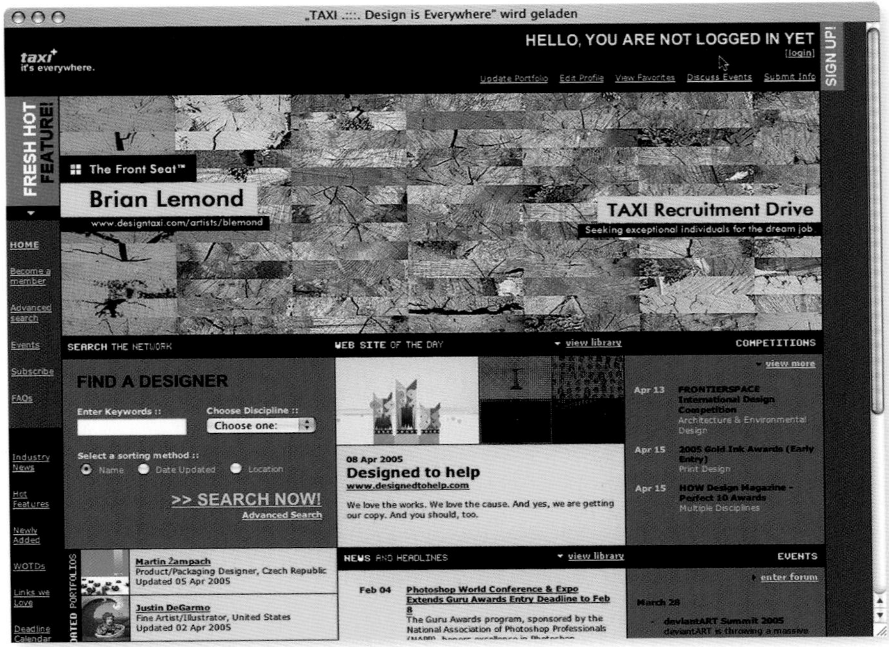
„TAXI .::::. Design is Everywhere" wird geladen
taxi+ it's everywhere.
HELLO, YOU ARE NOT LOGGED IN YET
[login]
Update Portfolio Edit Profile View Favorites Discuss Events Submit Info
SIGN UP!
FRESH HOT FEATURE!
The Front Seat™
Brian Lemond
www.designtaxi.com/artists/blemond
TAXI Recruitment Drive
Seeking exceptional individuals for the dream job
HOME
Become a member
Advanced search
Events
Subscribe
FAQs
SEARCH THE NETWORK
WEB SITE OF THE DAY
view library
COMPETITIONS
view more
FIND A DESIGNER
Enter Keywords ::
Choose Discipline ::
Choose one:
Select a sorting method ::
Name Date Updated Location
>> SEARCH NOW!
Advanced Search
08 Apr 2005
Designed to help
www.designedtohelp.com
We love the works. We love the cause. And yes, we are getting our copy. And you should, too.
Apr 13 FRONTIERSPACE International Design Competition
Architecture & Environmental Design
Apr 15 2005 Gold Ink Awards (Early Entry)
Print Design
Apr 15 HOW Design Magazine - Perfect 10 Awards
Multiple Disciplines
Industry News
Hot Features
Newly Added
WOTDs
Links we Love
Deadline Calendar
Martin Žampach
Product/Packaging Designer, Czech Republic
Updated 05 Apr 2005
Justin DeGarmo
Fine Artist/Illustrator, United States
Updated 02 Apr 2005
NEWS AND HEADLINES
view library
EVENTS
enter forum
Feb 04 Photoshop World Conference & Expo Extends Guru Awards Entry Deadline to Feb 8
The Guru Awards program, sponsored by the National Association of Photoshop Professionals
March 28
deviantART Summit 2005

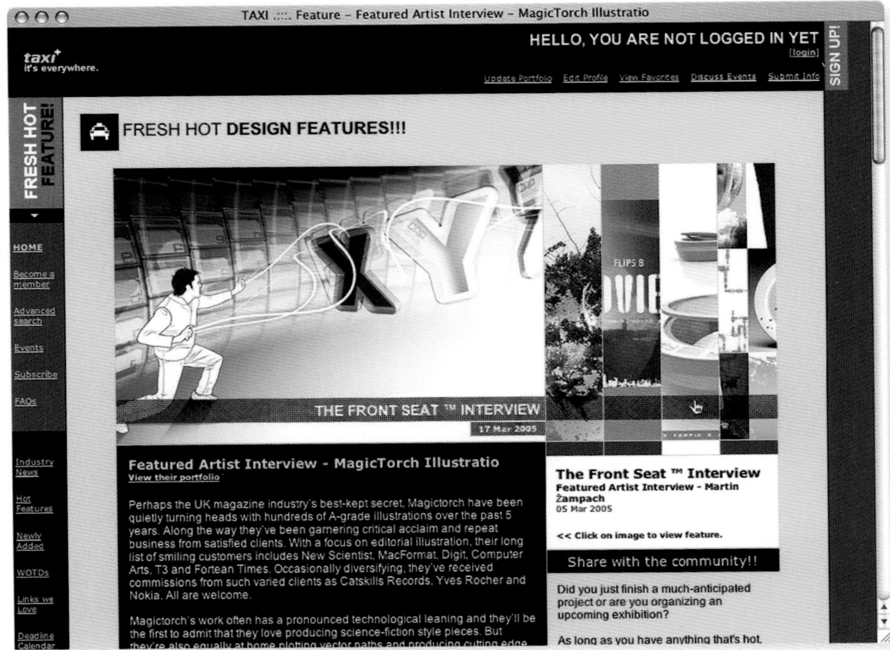
TAXI .::::. Feature – Featured Artist Interview – MagicTorch Illustratio
taxi+ it's everywhere.
HELLO, YOU ARE NOT LOGGED IN YET
[login]
Update Portfolio Edit Profile View Favorites Discuss Events Submit Info
SIGN UP!
FRESH HOT FEATURE!
FRESH HOT DESIGN FEATURES!!!
HOME
Become a member
Advanced search
Events
Subscribe
FAQs
Industry News
Hot Features
Newly Added
WOTDs
Links we Love
Deadline Calendar
THE FRONT SEAT ™ INTERVIEW
17 Mar 2005
Featured Artist Interview - MagicTorch Illustratio
View their portfolio
Perhaps the UK magazine industry's best-kept secret, Magictorch have been quietly turning heads with hundreds of A-grade illustrations over the past 5 years. Along the way they've been garnering critical acclaim and repeat business from satisfied clients. With a focus on editorial illustration, their long list of smiling customers includes New Scientist, MacFormat, Digit, Computer Arts, T3 and Fortean Times. Occasionally diversifying, they've received commissions from such varied clients as Catskills Records, Yves Rocher and Nokia. All are welcome.
Magictorch's work often has a pronounced technological leaning and they'll be the first to admit that they love producing science-fiction style pieces. But
The Front Seat ™ Interview
Featured Artist Interview - Martin Žampach
05 Mar 2005
<< Click on image to view feature.
Share with the community!!
Did you just finish a much-anticipated project or are you organizing an upcoming exhibition?
As long as you have anything that's hot

www.designtaxi.com
D: alex goh k.c. **C:** ting zien lee **P:** hills creative arts
A: hills creative arts **M:** friends@asterik.net

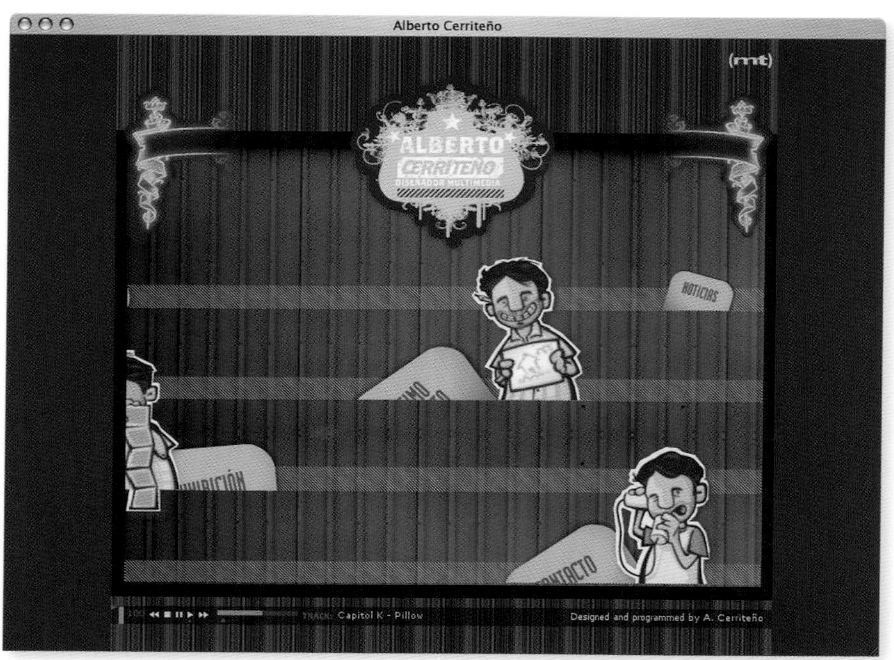
Alberto Cerriteño
(mt)
ALBERTO
CERRITEÑO
DISEÑADOR MULTIMEDIA
NOTICIAS
TRACK: Capitol K - Pillow
Designed and programmed by A. Cerriteño

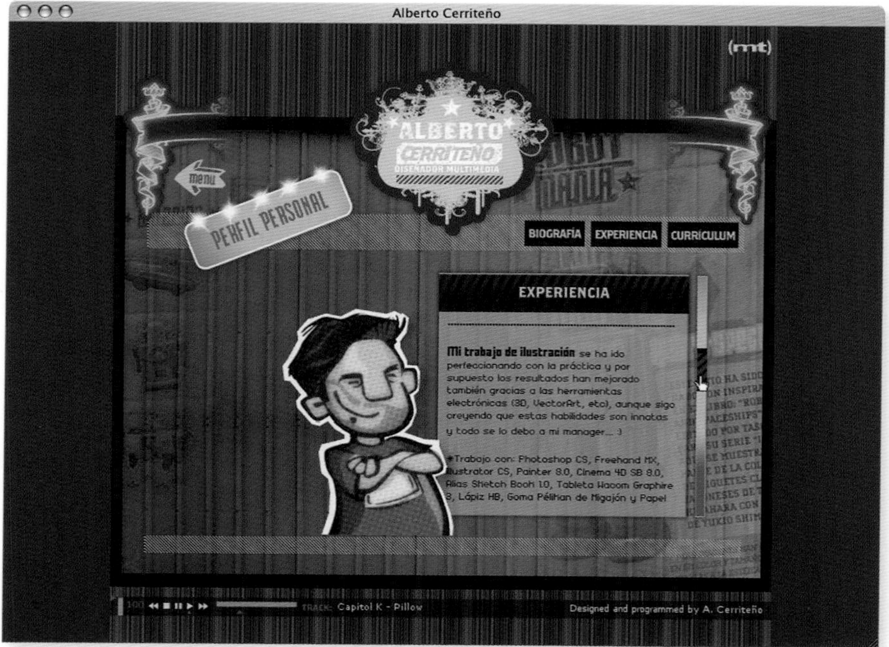
Alberto Cerriteño
(mt)
ALBERTO
CERRITEÑO
DISEÑADOR MULTIMEDIA
menu
PERFIL PERSONAL
BIOGRAFÍA
EXPERIENCIA
CURRÍCULUM
EXPERIENCIA
Mi trabajo de ilustración se ha ido perfeccionando con la práctica y por supuesto los resultados han mejorado también gracias a las herramientas electrónicas (3D, VectorArt, etc), aunque sigo creyendo que estas habilidades son innatas y todo se lo debo a mi manager... :)
*Trabajo con: Photoshop CS, Freehand MX, Illustrator CS, Painter 8.0, Cinema 4D SB 8.0, Alias Shetch Book 1.0, Tableta Wacom Graphire 3, Lápiz HB, Goma Pélikan de Migajón y Papel
TRACK: Capitol K - Pillow
Designed and programmed by A. Cerriteño

www.albertocerriteno.com
D: alberto cerriteño
A: alberto cerriteño multimedia designer **M:** al@albertocerriteno.com

Pixel Gasoline
PIXEL
GASOLINE
REG. T. M.
THE CONTACT
THE SERVICES
THE HISTORY
THE SAMPLES
THE RETURN TO THE BEGINNING

Pixel Gasoline
PIXEL
GASOLINE
REG. T. M.
HISTORY
Pixel Gasoline is the prime production company for web 3D, CD and DVD-rom interfaces, logo and graphic design. Our professional team posesses the best of abilities in order to perfectly produce your content, from the simplest project to the most complex production. With over 6 years of experience in professional 3D, our ultimate goal is to create the highest quality images. Put us to the test.
Founded by Simon Tessier, Pixel Gasoline is the logical result of an insatiable imagination and his thirst to conquer new challenges. The charismatic businessman posesses an impressive bagage of experience and numerous international contacts in professional 3D.
Established in Montreal for many years, is one of the original co-founders of a large 3D animation and special effects firm still active today.
His engine: Passion for the trade and the appetite for perfection.
THE CONTACT
THE SERVICES
THE HISTORY
THE SAMPLES
THE RETURN TO THE BEGINNING

www.pixelgasoline.com
D: simon tessier **C:** simon tessier
A: pixel gasoline **M:** info@pixelgasoline.com

[tronic]
_TRONIC: 2004
PROJECT DESCRIPTION
REEL SPRING 2004
Music: A Touch of Class
fuse
INFINITI
tronic
COLLECTION
SPRING 2004
WINTER 2004
FALL 2003
VISA
All you need.
BEHIND THE MUSIC
THE FUTURE OF

[tronic]
tronic
[ABOUT
[MISSION]
CONTACT
BIOS
Sound Design for Tronic Studio by:
DAVID LAWRENCE
musegarden@earthlink.net

www.tronicstudio.com
D: rei inamoto, jesse seppi, vivian rosenthal, michael foronda
A: tronic studio **M:** info@tronicstudio.com

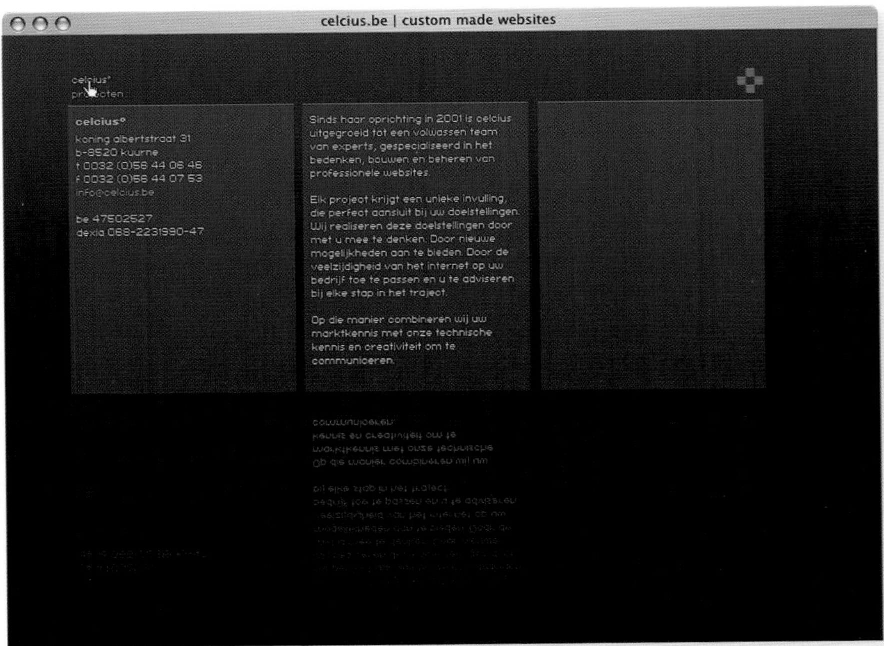
celcius.be | custom made websites
celcius°
projecten
celcius°
koning albertstraat 31
b-8520 kuurne
t 0032 (0)56 44 06 46
f 0032 (0)56 44 07 53
info@celcius.be
be 47502527
dexia 068-2231990-47
Sinds haar oprichting in 2001 is celcius uitgegroeid tot een volwassen team van experts, gespecialiseerd in het bedenken, bouwen en beheren van professionele websites.
Elk project krijgt een unieke invulling, die perfect aansluit bij uw doelstellingen. Wij realiseren deze doelstellingen door met u mee te denken. Door nieuwe mogelijkheden aan te bieden. Door de veelzijdigheid van het internet op uw bedrijf toe te passen en u te adviseren bij elke stap in het traject.
Op die manier combineren wij uw marktkennis met onze technische kennis en creativiteit om te communiceren.

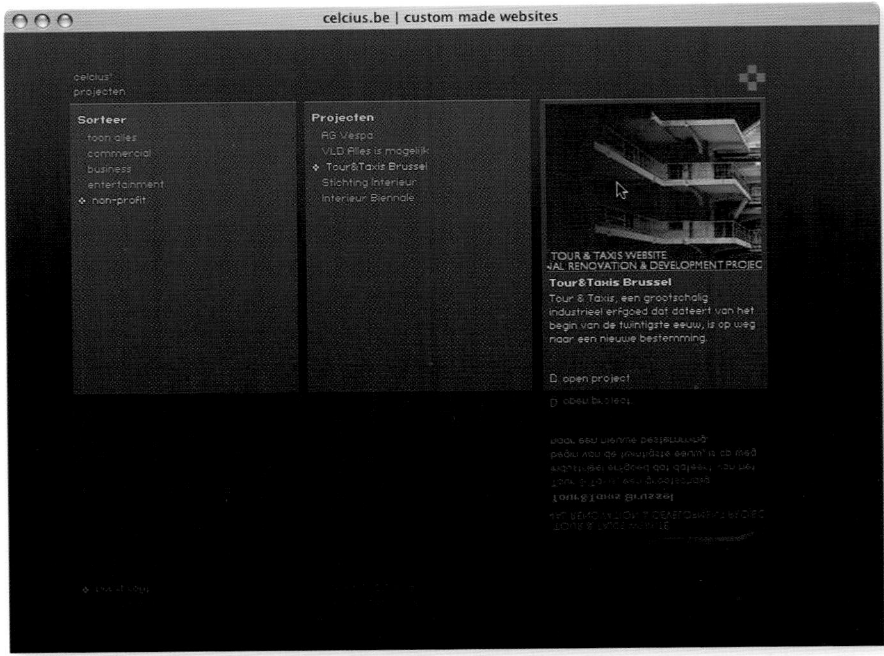
celcius.be | custom made websites
celcius°
projecten
Sorteer
toon alles
commercial
business
entertainment
non-profit
Projecten
AG Vespa
VLD Alles is mogelijk
Tour&Taxis Brussel
Stichting Interieur
Interieur Biennale
TOUR & TAXIS WEBSITE
Tour&Taxis Brussel
Tour & Taxis, een grootschalig industrieel erfgoed dat dateert van het begin van de twintigste eeuw, is op weg naar een nieuwe bestemming.
open project

www.celcius.be
D: sam windey **C:** youri de smet
A: celcius **M:** info@celcius.be

Bienvenue sur AngstProd.com
angst
prod
Forum | Label | Radio

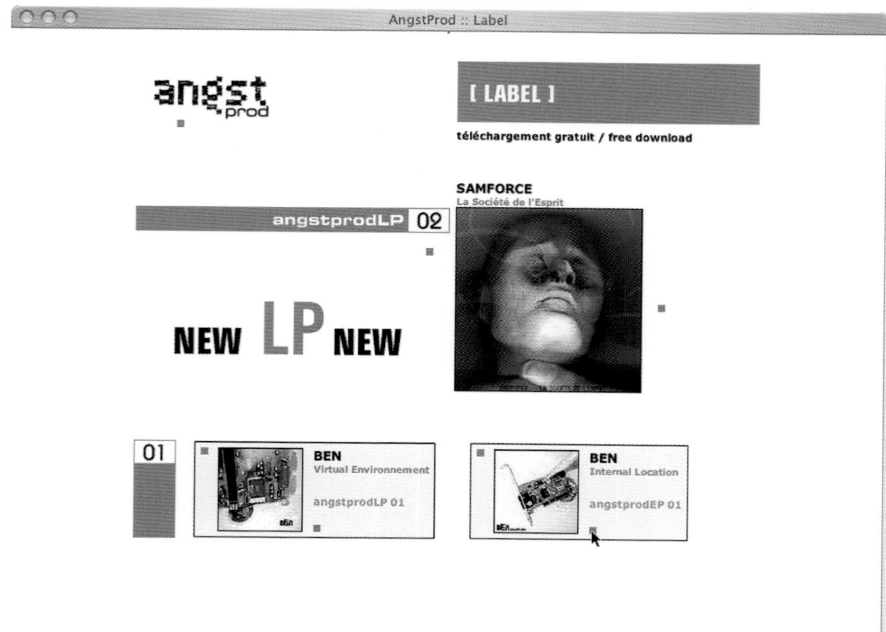
AngstProd :: Label
angst
prod
[LABEL]
téléchargement gratuit / free download
SAMFORCE
La Société de l'Esprit
angstprodLP 02
NEW LP NEW
01
BEN
Virtual Environnement
angstprodLP 01
BEN
Internal Location
angstprodEP 01

www.angstprod.com
D: alexandre dupuy
A: alexdupuy@altern.org **M:** alexdupuy@altern.org

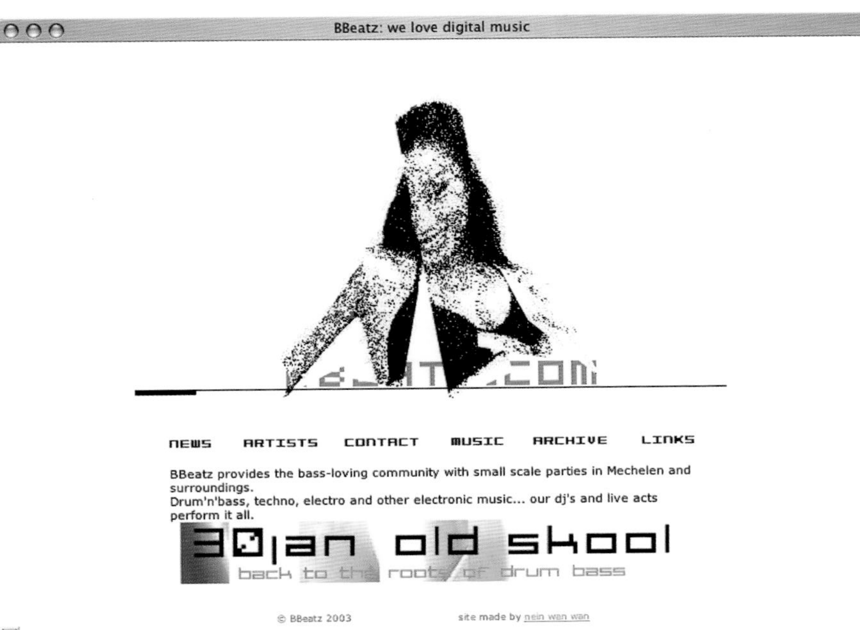
BBeatz: we love digital music
NEWS ARTISTS CONTACT MUSIC ARCHIVE LINKS
BBeatz provides the bass-loving community with small scale parties in Mechelen and surroundings.
Drum'n'bass, techno, electro and other electronic music... our dj's and live acts perform it all.
30|jan old skool
back to the roots of drum bass
© BBeatz 2003
site made by nein wan wan

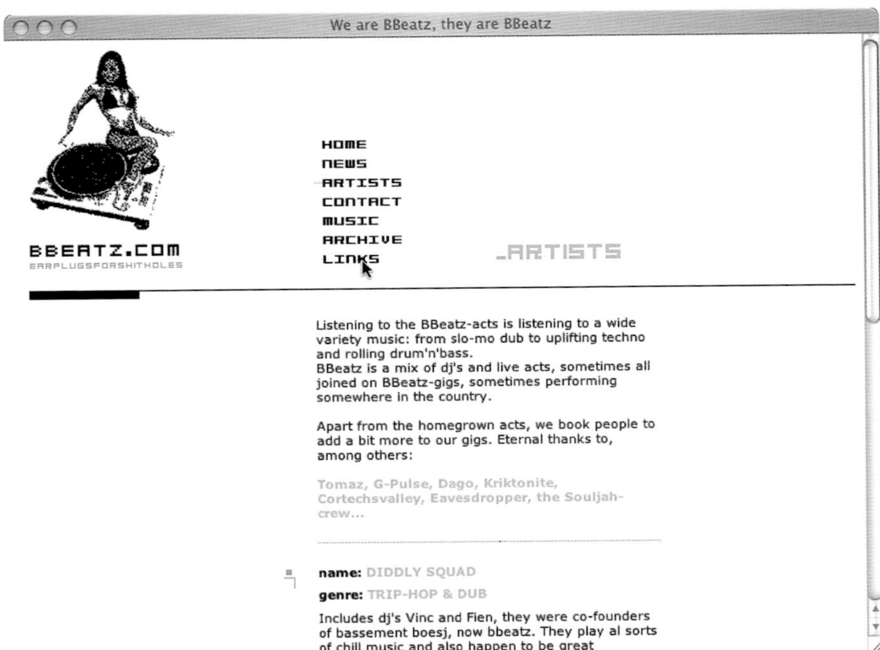
We are BBeatz, they are BBeatz
HOME
NEWS
ARTISTS
CONTACT
MUSIC
ARCHIVE
LINKS
BBEATZ.COM
EARPLUGSFORSHITHOLES
_ARTISTS
Listening to the BBeatz-acts is listening to a wide variety music: from slo-mo dub to uplifting techno and rolling drum'n'bass.
BBeatz is a mix of dj's and live acts, sometimes all joined on BBeatz-gigs, sometimes performing somewhere in the country.
Apart from the homegrown acts, we book people to add a bit more to our gigs. Eternal thanks to, among others:
Tomaz, G-Pulse, Dago, Kriktonite, Cortechsvalley, Eavesdropper, the Souljah-crew...
name: DIDDLY SQUAD
genre: TRIP-HOP & DUB
Includes dj's Vinc and Fien, they were co-founders of bassement boesj, now bbeatz. They play al sorts of chill music and also happen to be great

www.bbeatz.com
D: carl de mey
A: nein wan wan **M:** carl@neinwanwan.com

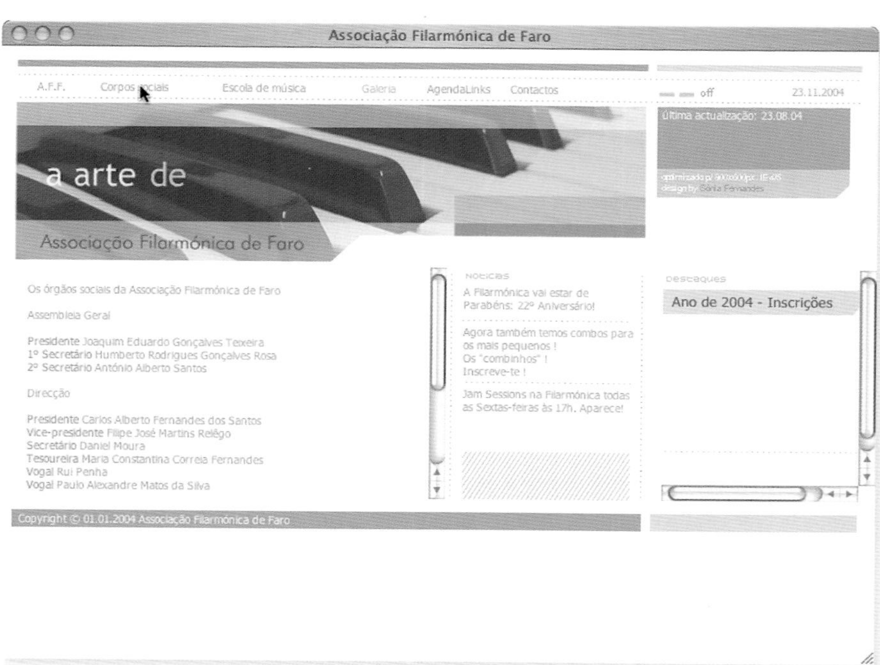
Associação Filarmónica de Faro
A.F.F.
Corpos sociais
Escola de música
Galeria
AgendaLinks
Contactos
off
23.11.2004
última actualização: 23.08.04
a arte de
Associação Filarmónica de Faro
Os órgãos sociais da Associação Filarmónica de Faro
Assembleia Geral
Presidente Joaquim Eduardo Gonçalves Teixeira
1º Secretário Humberto Rodrigues Gonçalves Rosa
2º Secretário António Alberto Santos
Direcção
Presidente Carlos Alberto Fernandes dos Santos
Vice-presidente Filipe José Martins Relêgo
Secretário Daniel Moura
Tesoureira Maria Constantina Correia Fernandes
Vogal Rui Penha
Vogal Paulo Alexandre Matos da Silva
Notícias
A Filarmónica vai estar de Parabéns: 22º Aniversário!
Agora também temos combos para os mais pequenos !
Os "combinhos" !
Inscreve-te !
Jam Sessions na Filarmónica todas as Sextas-feiras às 17h. Aparece!
Destaques
Ano de 2004 - Inscrições
Copyright © 01.01.2004 Associação Filarmónica de Faro

Associação Filarmónica de Faro
A.F.F.
Corpos sociais
Escola de música
Galeria
AgendaLinks
Contactos
off
23.11.2004
última actualização: 23.08.04
música
Associação Filarmónica de Faro
Escola de Música
Reside aqui a nossa maior aposta, após uma remodelação de todo o processo pedagógico da nossa Escola.
É assim que facultamos aos nossos alunos, após a sua inscrição no instrumento que desejam aprender, as disciplinas colectivas de Teoria Musical; Classes Conjunto e Combos, inovação na nossa escola à semelhança das escolas de música Moderna espalhadas pelo mundo inteiro.
Tabela de preços:
Iniciação - até 12 anos - € 25
Guitarra Nível 1 - € 30
Baixo eléctrico - € 30
Trompete - € 30
Saxofone Nível 1 - € 30
Professores
Jon Lavieri
saxofone
Constantina Fernandes
Inic. musical
Carlos Santos
Trompete & Guitarra
Victor Afonso
Trombone
Paulo Silva
Baixo eléctrico
Pedro Gil
Guitarra
Carlos "Cacum" Vieira
Bateria & Percussão
Destaques
Ano de 2004 - Inscrições
Copyright © 01.01.2004 Associação Filarmónica de Faro

www.assoc-filarmonica-faro.com
D: sónia fernandes
M: designercriativa@clix.pt

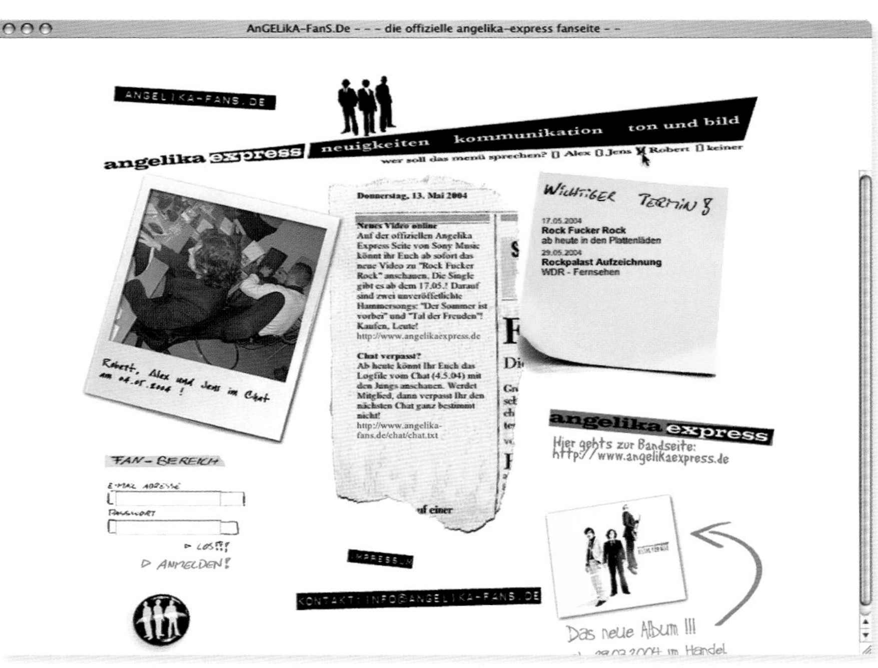
AnGELikA-FanS.De - - - die offizielle angelika-express fanseite - -
ANGELIKA-FANS.DE
neuigkeiten
kommunikation
ton und bild
angelika express
wer soll das menü sprechen? Alex Jens Robert keiner
Donnerstag, 13. Mai 2004
Neues Video online
Auf der offiziellen Angelika Express Seite von Sony Music könnt ihr Euch ab sofort das neue Video zu "Rock Fucker Rock" anschauen. Die Single gibt es ab dem 17.05.! Darauf sind zwei unveröffentlichte Hammersongs: "Der Sommer ist vorbei" und "Tal der Freuden"! Kaufen, Leute!
http://www.angelikaexpress.de
Chat verpasst?
Ab heute könnt Ihr Euch das Logfile vom Chat (4.5.04) mit den Jungs anschauen. Werdet Mitglied, dann verpasst Ihr den nächsten Chat ganz bestimmt nicht!
http://www.angelika-fans.de/chat/chat.txt
Robert, Alex und Jens im Chat am 04.05.2004 !
WICHTIGER TERMIN !
17.05.2004
Rock Fucker Rock
ab heute in den Plattenläden
29.05.2004
Rockpalast Aufzeichnung
WDR - Fernsehen
angelika express
Hier gehts zur Bandseite:
http://www.angelikaexpress.de
FAN-BEREICH
E-MAIL ADRESSE
PASSWORT
LOS!!!
ANMELDEN!
IMPRESSUM
KONTAKT: INFO@ANGELIKA-FANS.DE
Das neue Album !!!

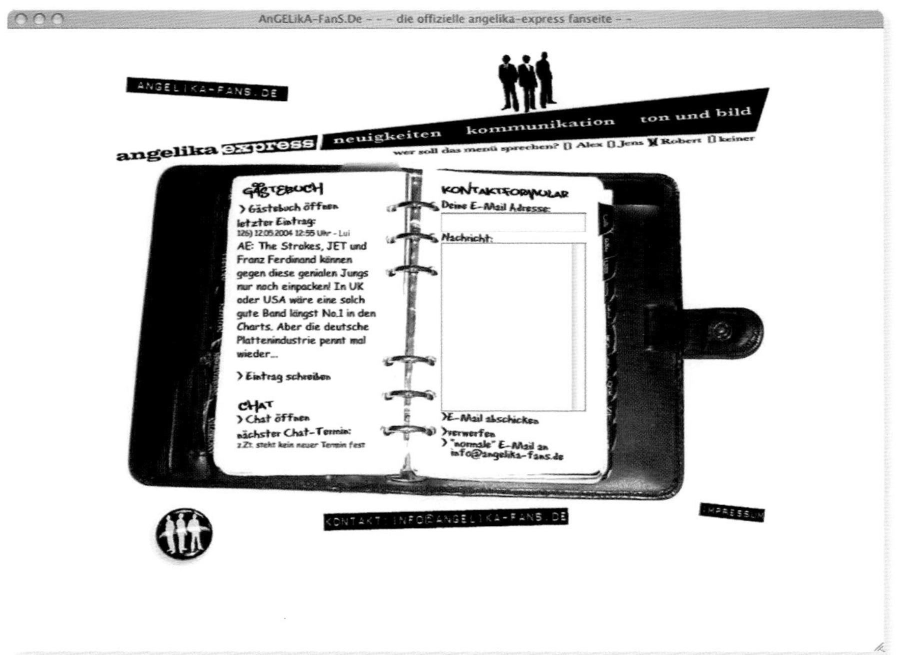
AnGELikA-FanS.De - - - die offizielle angelika-express fanseite - -
ANGELIKA-FANS.DE
neuigkeiten
kommunikation
ton und bild
angelika express
wer soll das menü sprechen? Alex Jens Robert keiner
GÄSTEBUCH
› Gästebuch öffnen
letzter Eintrag:
126) 12.05.2004 12:55 Uhr - Lui
AE: The Strokes, JET und Franz Ferdinand können gegen diese genialen Jungs nur noch einpacken! In UK oder USA wäre eine solch gute Band längst No.1 in den Charts. Aber die deutsche Plattenindustrie pennt mal wieder...
› Eintrag schreiben
CHAT
› Chat öffnen
nächster Chat-Termin:
z.Zt. steht kein neuer Termin fest
KONTAKTFORMULAR
Deine E-Mail Adresse:
Nachricht:
›E-Mail abschicken
›verwerfen
› "normale" E-Mail an info@angelika-fans.de
KONTAKT: INFO@ANGELIKA-FANS.DE
IMPRESSUM

www.angelika-fans.de
D: jörn gahrmann **C:** christian spatz
A: engine-productions **M:** gahrmann@engine-productions.de

la-boum | indi-pop-perlen

la boum start | infos | audio | shop | galerie | klatsch | kontakt | • englisch

ein kleiner (1,1 MB) Trailer über la-boum (Flash-Player erforderlich)

Bandbattle
Do. 6. Mai
in der Rakete, Nürnberg

Bandbattle 2004

Vergesst alle Casting-Shows – hier kommt der original Bandbattle! Zwei Bands in einem Club, die abwechselnd auf einer Riesenbühne ihre Songs zum Besten geben. Ein Wettkampf der Bandgiganten mit krassen Contest Einlagen vom Schlagzeuger-Duell bis zum Covern gegnerischer Musikstücke. Ihr könnt abstimmen, anfeuern und auspfeifen, denn ihr bestimmt wer gewinnt!!
Seid dabei, wenn es heißt „la-boum" gegen die „Smul Meier Band"

Donnerstag, 06.05.2004, 21.00
Rakete Nürnberg
Vogelweiherstr. 64
mehr Infos >>

Erstmal hallo hier...

„für alle Neulinge und „Erstbesucher" –

dies ist die Homepage der Nürnberger Band la-boum. Wir machen Indi-Gitarrenpop oder sowas, einen Eindruck davon kann man sich in unserem Trailer oder unter dem Bereich „audio" verschaffen. Viel Spaß auf unseren Seiten.

Kostenlos downloaden...

Für unseren Trailer und zum Anhören unserer Songs wird das Flash-Plugin benötigt.

GET SHOCKWAVE FLASH

la-boum | Geschichte

la boum start | infos | audio | shop | galerie | klatsch | kontakt | • englisch

News / Konzerte
Geschichte
Newsletter
Pressepaket

Biographie

Gegründet im Sommer 1994, als Schülerband angefangen folgten bald grössere Konzerte (z.B. Vorprogramm von „Mr. Ed jumps the gun").

Anfang **1996** erste CD „multiloop" aufgenommen und damit bei der Musikindustrie beworben.

2 Jahre unter **Vertrag** bei Produzententrio Michael Holm, J. Walter, R. Pospichal

1998 Vertragsauflösung und Rückkehr zur Eigenständigkeit

Seitdem wird Booking, CD-Produktion und Management von der Band selbst ausgeführt, einzig die grafische Umsetzung und der Internetauftritt wird von der Agentur **instant-graphics** betreut.

Wettbewerbe

1998: 1. Preis beim Check`n`Play Wettbewerb, veranstaltet von der Musikzentrale Nürnberg.

1999: Bei der Teilnahme am deutschlandweiten Bandcontest von TV Spielfilm, boxman.de, new yorker records und Billboardtalentnet wurde la boum im November 1999 auf Platz 2 gewählt, woraufhin die Einladung zu einem Auftritt in der UCI Kinowelt Potsdam erfolgte, welcher live über die TV Spielfilm Homepage verfolgt werden konnte.

la-boum stellt sich vor...

Die Nürnberger Band la-boum heißt wie der französische Kult-Teeniefilm aus den Achziger Jahren. Als die 5 Jungs im Sommer 1994 die Band gründeten, war es darum auch ihr Motto jedes Konzert wie eine „Fete" zu organisieren und dem Publikum mit tanzbarer Independent Musik eine Mischung aus Konzert und Party zu präsentieren. Mittlerweile hat la-boum in Deutschland und Österreich schon über 100 Konzerte gegeben und bis jetzt 4 CD`s veröffentlicht. Die Musik der Band ist eine Mischung aus Britpop und Gitarren-Indi - mit manchmal SKA und ELECTRO Elementen.
Es ist eben wie bei einer guten Party: Die Musik ist bunt gemischt - hat aber immer Ohrwurmgarantie und lädt zum Abfeiern ein.

Discographie

1996 CD „Multiloop"

1999 CD „in the supermarket"

2000 CD „the remixes"

2003 Akustik CD „mas i mas"

Konzerte etc.

Mit dem **Akustikprojekt** gab es Konzerte in Deutschland, Frankreich, Italien und Spanien, wobei von Konzerten auf Vernissagen, Strassenmusik, Hochzeitsfeiern bis zu Festivals schon alles dabei war...

In der **elektrischen** Version tourte la-boum bisher durch Deutschland und Österreich, und spielte hauptsächlich bei Open Air Konzerten, Clubgigs und Kneipenfestivals.

www.la-boum.de
D: matthias hauer
A: instant-graphics

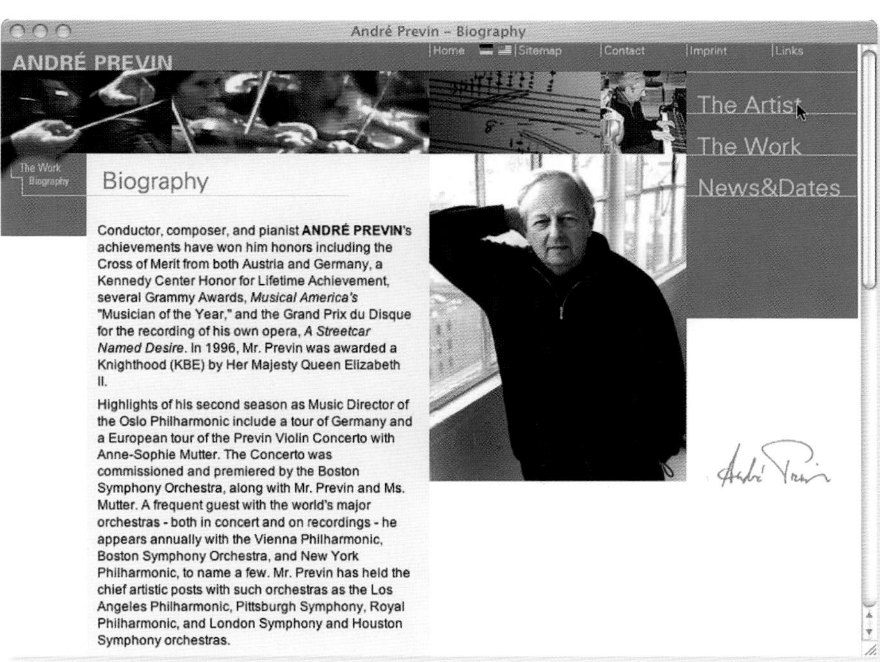
André Previn – Biography
ANDRÉ PREVIN
|Home |Sitemap |Contact |Imprint |Links
The Artist
The Work
News&Dates
The Work
Biography
Biography
Conductor, composer, and pianist ANDRÉ PREVIN's achievements have won him honors including the Cross of Merit from both Austria and Germany, a Kennedy Center Honor for Lifetime Achievement, several Grammy Awards, Musical America's "Musician of the Year," and the Grand Prix du Disque for the recording of his own opera, A Streetcar Named Desire. In 1996, Mr. Previn was awarded a Knighthood (KBE) by Her Majesty Queen Elizabeth II.
Highlights of his second season as Music Director of the Oslo Philharmonic include a tour of Germany and a European tour of the Previn Violin Concerto with Anne-Sophie Mutter. The Concerto was commissioned and premiered by the Boston Symphony Orchestra, along with Mr. Previn and Ms. Mutter. A frequent guest with the world's major orchestras - both in concert and on recordings - he appears annually with the Vienna Philharmonic, Boston Symphony Orchestra, and New York Philharmonic, to name a few. Mr. Previn has held the chief artistic posts with such orchestras as the Los Angeles Philharmonic, Pittsburgh Symphony, Royal Philharmonic, and London Symphony and Houston Symphony orchestras.

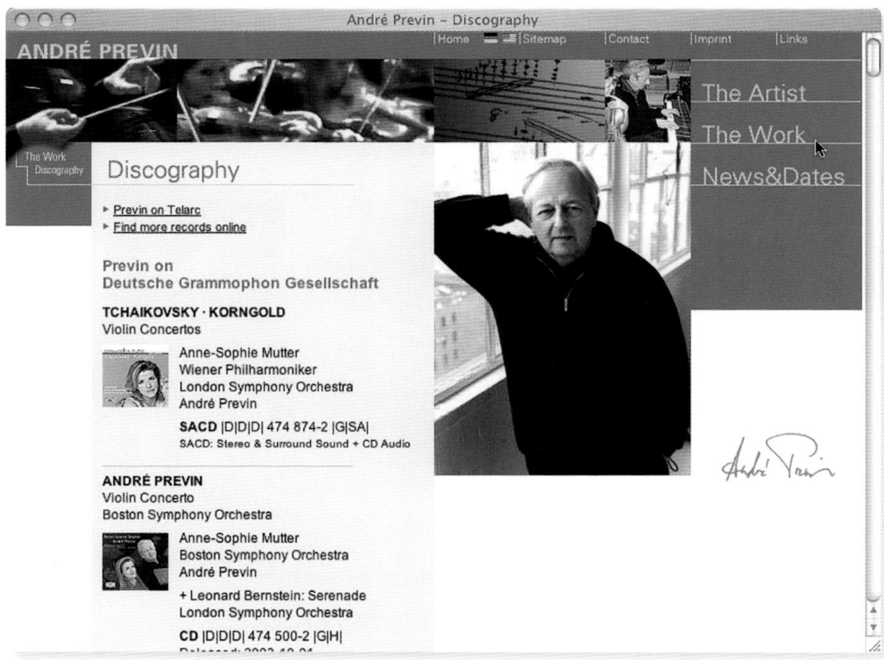
André Previn – Discography
ANDRÉ PREVIN
|Home |Sitemap |Contact |Imprint |Links
The Artist
The Work
News&Dates
The Work
Discography
Discography
Previn on Telarc
Find more records online
Previn on
Deutsche Grammophon Gesellschaft
TCHAIKOVSKY · KORNGOLD
Violin Concertos
Anne-Sophie Mutter
Wiener Philharmoniker
London Symphony Orchestra
André Previn
SACD |D|D|D| 474 874-2 |G|SA|
SACD: Stereo & Surround Sound + CD Audio
ANDRÉ PREVIN
Violin Concerto
Boston Symphony Orchestra
Anne-Sophie Mutter
Boston Symphony Orchestra
André Previn
+ Leonard Bernstein: Serenade
London Symphony Orchestra
CD |D|D|D| 474 500-2 |G|H|

www.andre-previn.com
D: stephan schmidt **C:** peter morgner
A: farbe8 **M:** schmidt@farbe8.com

[micaela carosi official web site]
Micaela Carosi
soprano
official web site
biografia, fotografie. appuntamenti, recensioni, contatti, credits
La TRAVIATA, Opera di Verdi
Atto 1° Scena 3°

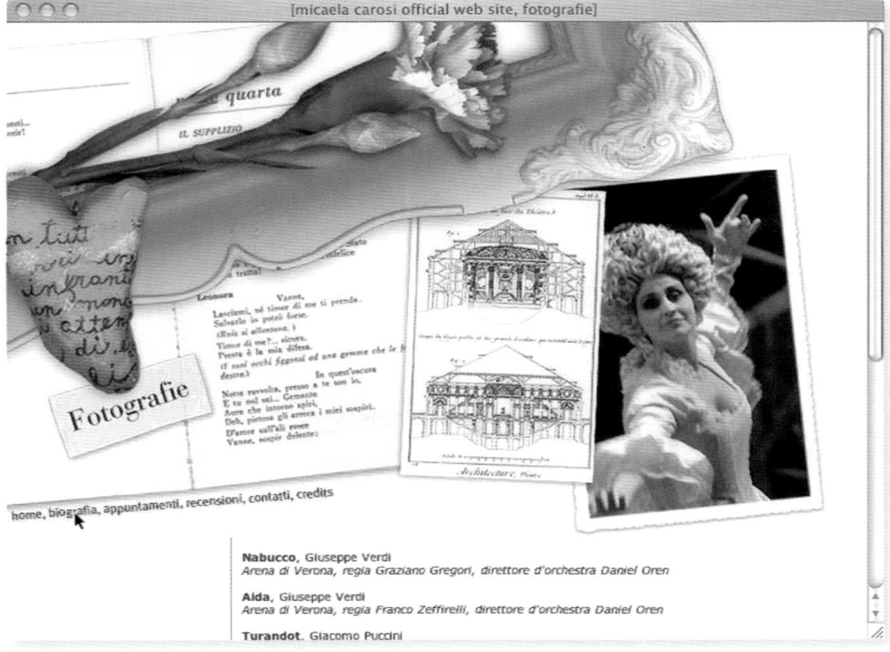
[micaela carosi official web site, fotografie]
quarta
IL SUPPLIZIO
Fotografie
home, biografia, appuntamenti, recensioni, contatti, credits
Nabucco, Giuseppe Verdi
Arena di Verona, regia Graziano Gregori, direttore d'orchestra Daniel Oren
Aida, Giuseppe Verdi
Arena di Verona, regia Franco Zeffirelli, direttore d'orchestra Daniel Oren
Turandot, Giacomo Puccini

www.micaelacarosi.it
D: andrea massimiani
A: interzona **M:** andrea@interzona.it

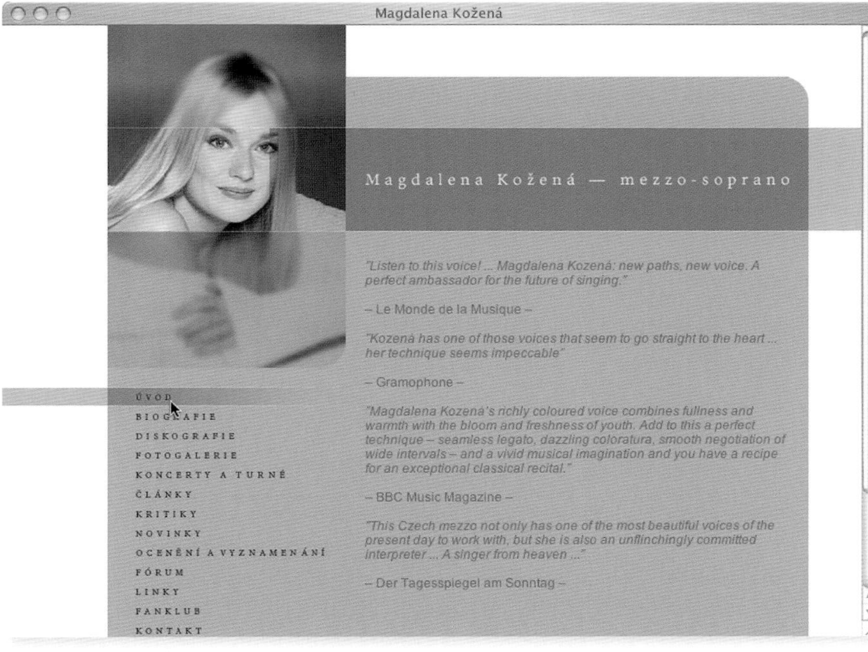
Magdalena Kožená
Magdalena Kožená — mezzo-soprano
"Listen to this voice! ... Magdalena Kozena: new paths, new voice. A perfect ambassador for the future of singing."
– Le Monde de la Musique –
"Kozena has one of those voices that seem to go straight to the heart ... her technique seems impeccable"
– Gramophone –
"Magdalena Kozena's richly coloured voice combines fullness and warmth with the bloom and freshness of youth. Add to this a perfect technique – seamless legato, dazzling coloratura, smooth negotiation of wide intervals – and a vivid musical imagination and you have a recipe for an exceptional classical recital."
– BBC Music Magazine –
"This Czech mezzo not only has one of the most beautiful voices of the present day to work with, but she is also an unflinchingly committed interpreter ... A singer from heaven ..."
– Der Tagesspiegel am Sonntag –
ÚVOD
BIOGRAFIE
DISKOGRAFIE
FOTOGALERIE
KONCERTY A TURNÉ
ČLÁNKY
KRITIKY
NOVINKY
OCENĚNÍ A VYZNAMENÁNÍ
FÓRUM
LINKY
FANKLUB
KONTAKT

Magdalena Kožená
Magdalena Kožená — mezzo-soprano
Magdalena Kožená patří mezi nejuznávanější pěvkyně současnosti. Je žádaným hostem předních světových operních i koncertních pódií. Její pozici jedné z nejvyhledávanějších a nejvýraznějších mezzosopranistek dokládá řada ocenění, které během své kariéry získala v České republice a v zahraničí i exkluzivní smlouva s nahrávací společností Deutsche Grammophon.
Magdalena Kožená se narodila v Brně, kde také studovala na konzervatoři u Něvy Megové. Ve studiu pokračovala u profesorky Evy Blahové na Vysoké škole múzických umění v Bratislavě. Již v průběhu studií zvítězila v řadě soutěží, z nichž nejvýznamnější byla 6. mezinárodní soutěž W. A. Mozarta v Salcburku, na které byla vyhlášena absolutní vítězkou.
Je zvána na nejprestižnější domácí i světové festivaly (Salzburger Festspiele, Glyndebourne Festival, Festival d´Aix-en-Provence, Pražské jaro, Concentus Moraviae, etc...). Pravidelně spolupracuje s předními dirigenty, orchestry a sólisty, jako jsou např. Marc Minkowski a orchestr Les Musiciens du Louvre, Sir Simon Rattle a Berlínští filharmonici, Nicolas Harnoncourt, Vídeňská filharmonie a Concentus musicus Wien, Michel Swierczewski a Pražská komorní filharmonie, Musica Antiqua Köln, klavíristé Malcolm Martineau, Graham Johnson, Karel Košárek a další.
Nahrávky Magdaleny Kožené zahrnují recitál z Bachových árií, Händelova římská moteta, italské kantáty s Marcem Minkowskim pro
ÚVOD
BIOGRAFIE
DISKOGRAFIE
FOTOGALERIE
KONCERTY A TURNÉ
ČLÁNKY
KRITIKY
NOVINKY
OCENĚNÍ A VYZNAMENÁNÍ
FÓRUM
LINKY
FANKLUB
KONTAKT

www.kozena.cz
D: tomáö brousil **C:** radek zigler
A: aluminium **M:** info@aluminium.cz

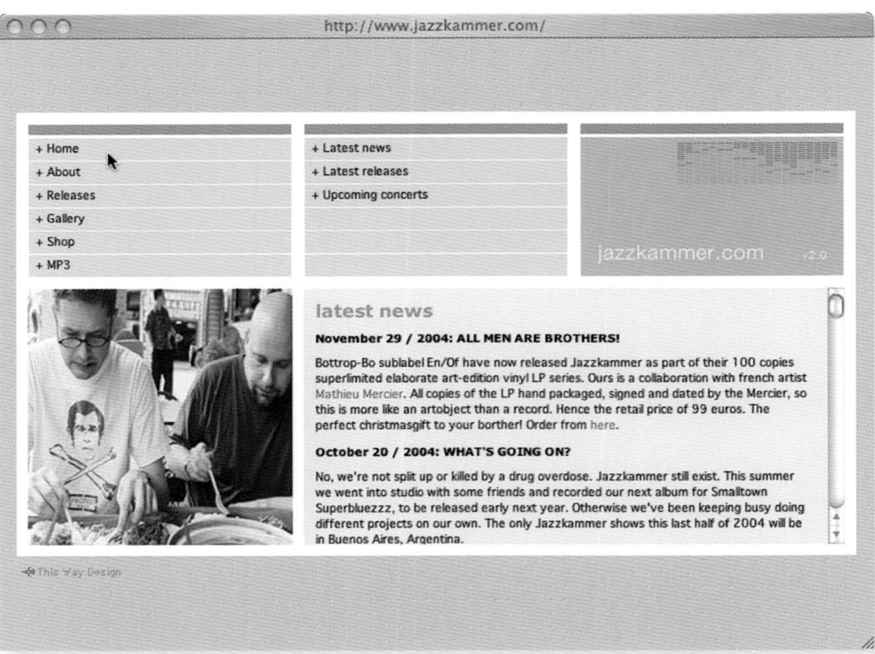
http://www.jazzkammer.com/
+ Home
+ About
+ Releases
+ Gallery
+ Shop
+ MP3
+ Latest news
+ Latest releases
+ Upcoming concerts
jazzkammer.com v2.0
latest news
November 29 / 2004: ALL MEN ARE BROTHERS!
Bottrop-Bo sublabel En/Of have now released Jazzkammer as part of their 100 copies superlimited elaborate art-edition vinyl LP series. Ours is a collaboration with french artist Mathieu Mercier. All copies of the LP hand packaged, signed and dated by the Mercier, so this is more like an artobject than a record. Hence the retail price of 99 euros. The perfect christmasgift to your borther! Order from here.
October 20 / 2004: WHAT'S GOING ON?
No, we're not split up or killed by a drug overdose. Jazzkammer still exist. This summer we went into studio with some friends and recorded our next album for Smalltown Superbluezzz, to be released early next year. Otherwise we've been keeping busy doing different projects on our own. The only Jazzkammer shows this last half of 2004 will be in Buenos Aires, Argentina.
This Way Design

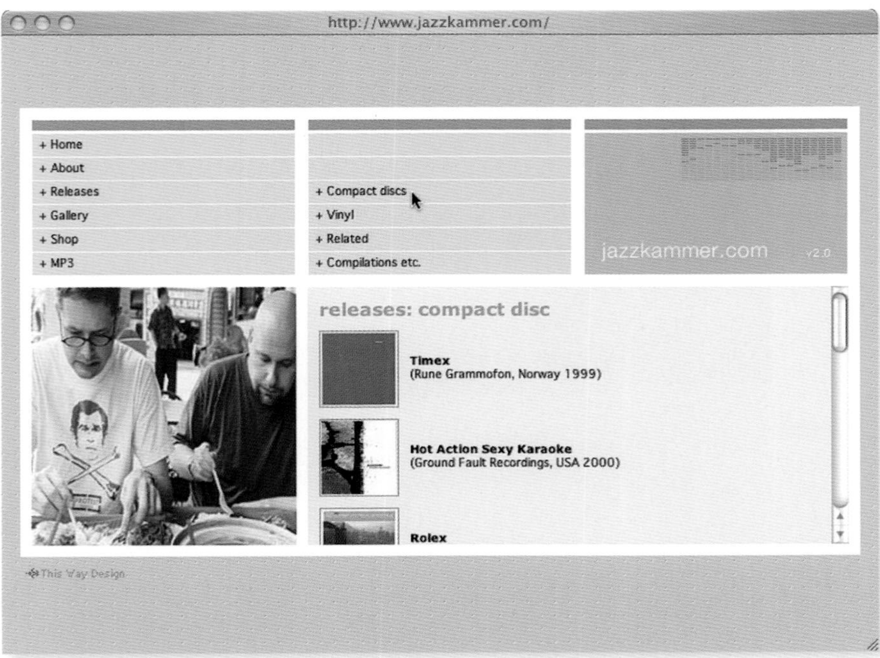
http://www.jazzkammer.com/
+ Home
+ About
+ Releases
+ Gallery
+ Shop
+ MP3
+ Compact discs
+ Vinyl
+ Related
+ Compilations etc.
jazzkammer.com v2.0
releases: compact disc
Timex
(Rune Grammofon, Norway 1999)
Hot Action Sexy Karaoke
(Ground Fault Recordings, USA 2000)
Rolex
This Way Design

www.jazzkammer.com
D: håvard gjelseth
A: this way design **M:** havardg@klapp.no

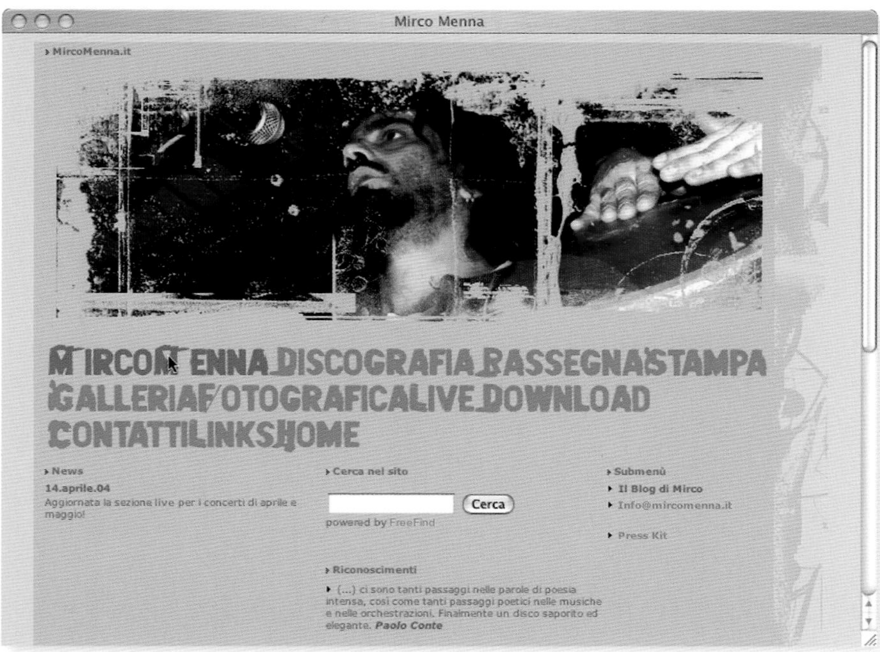
Mirco Menna
MircoMenna.it
MIRCOMENNA DISCOGRAFIA RASSEGNA STAMPA
GALLERIA FOTOGRAFICA LIVE DOWNLOAD
CONTATTI LINKS HOME
News
14.aprile.04
Aggiornata la sezione live per i concerti di aprile e maggio!
Cerca nel sito
Cerca
powered by FreeFind
Submenù
Il Blog di Mirco
Info@mircomenna.it
Press Kit
Riconoscimenti
(...) ci sono tanti passaggi nelle parole di poesia intensa, così come tanti passaggi poetici nelle musiche e nelle orchestrazioni. Finalmente un disco saporito ed elegante. Paolo Conte

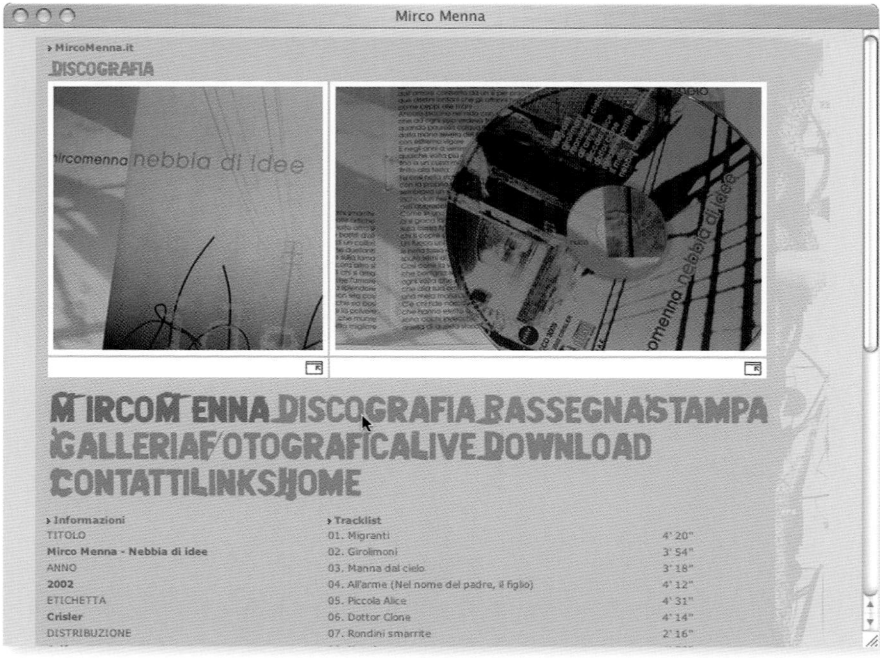
Mirco Menna
MircoMenna.it
DISCOGRAFIA
mircomenna nebbia di idee
MIRCOMENNA DISCOGRAFIA RASSEGNA STAMPA
GALLERIA FOTOGRAFICA LIVE DOWNLOAD
CONTATTI LINKS HOME
Informazioni
TITOLO
Mirco Menna - Nebbia di idee
ANNO
2002
ETICHETTA
Crisler
DISTRIBUZIONE
Tracklist
01. Migranti 4' 20"
02. Girolimoni 3' 54"
03. Manna dal cielo 3' 18"
04. All'arme (Nel nome del padre, il figlio) 4' 12"
05. Piccola Alice 4' 31"
06. Dottor Clone 4' 14"
07. Rondini smarrite 2' 16"

www.mircomenna.it
D: giovanni paletta **C:** mirco menna
A: krghettojuice **M:** mircomenna@libero.it

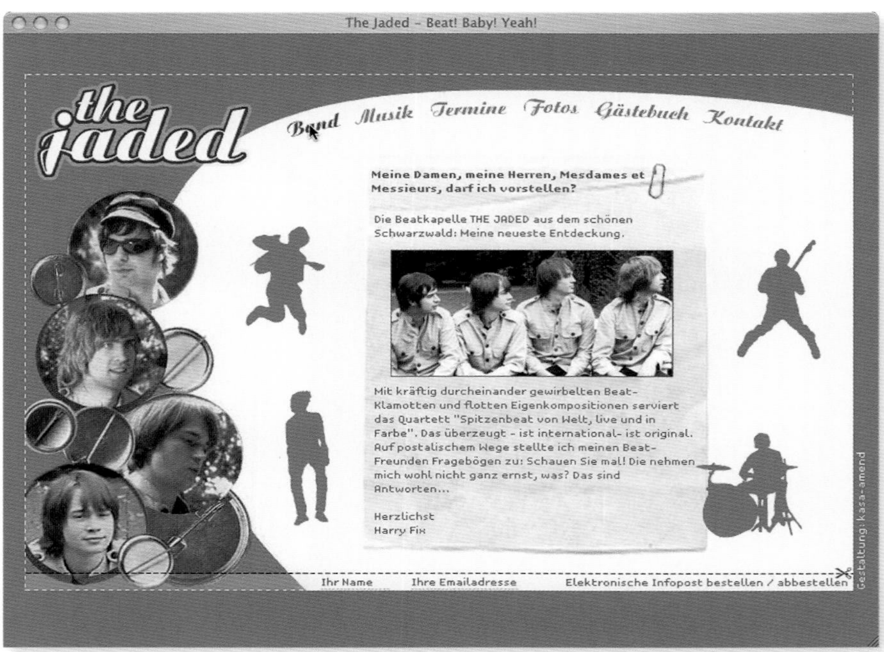
The Jaded - Beat! Baby! Yeah!
the jaded
Band Musik Termine Fotos Gästebuch Kontakt
Meine Damen, meine Herren, Mesdames et Messieurs, darf ich vorstellen?
Die Beatkapelle THE JADED aus dem schönen Schwarzwald: Meine neueste Entdeckung.
Mit kräftig durcheinander gewirbelten Beat-Klamotten und flotten Eigenkompositionen serviert das Quartett "Spitzenbeat von Welt, live und in Farbe". Das überzeugt - ist international- ist original. Auf postalischem Wege stellte ich meinen Beat-Freunden Fragebögen zu: Schauen Sie mal! Die nehmen mich wohl nicht ganz ernst, was? Das sind Antworten...
Herzlichst
Harry Fix
Ihr Name
Ihre Emailadresse
Elektronische Infopost bestellen / abbestellen
Gestaltung: kasa-amend

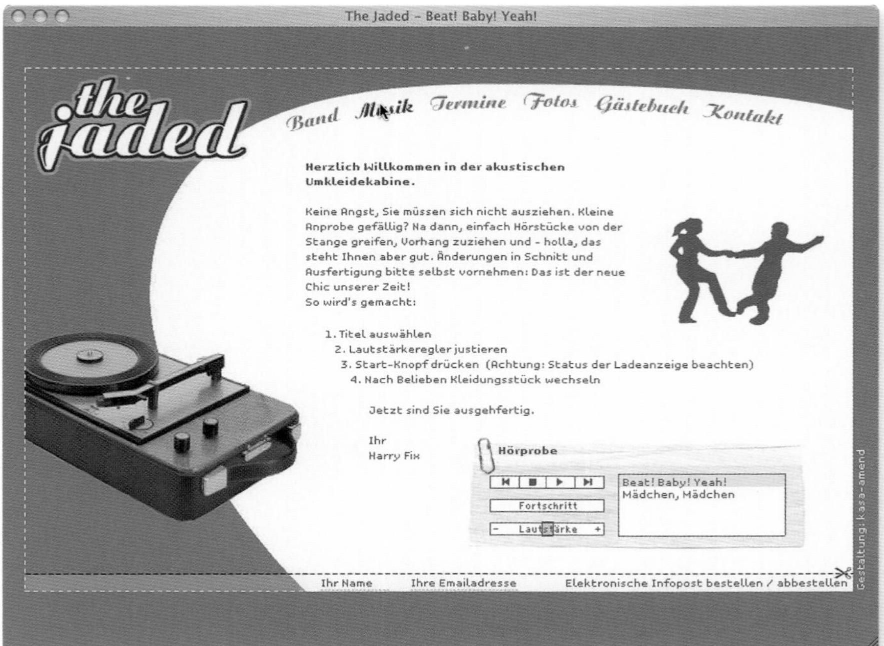
The Jaded - Beat! Baby! Yeah!
the jaded
Band Musik Termine Fotos Gästebuch Kontakt
Herzlich Willkommen in der akustischen Umkleidekabine.
Keine Angst, Sie müssen sich nicht ausziehen. Kleine Anprobe gefällig? Na dann, einfach Hörstücke von der Stange greifen, Vorhang zuziehen und - holla, das steht Ihnen aber gut. Änderungen in Schnitt und Ausfertigung bitte selbst vornehmen: Das ist der neue Chic unserer Zeit!
So wird's gemacht:
1. Titel auswählen
2. Lautstärkeregler justieren
3. Start-Knopf drücken (Achtung: Status der Ladeanzeige beachten)
4. Nach Belieben Kleidungsstück wechseln
Jetzt sind Sie ausgehfertig.
Ihr
Harry Fix
Hörprobe
Fortschritt
Lautstärke
Beat! Baby! Yeah!
Mädchen, Mädchen
Ihr Name
Ihre Emailadresse
Elektronische Infopost bestellen / abbestellen
Gestaltung: kasa-amend

www.thejaded.de
D: kathrin-sarah amend
M: mail@kasa-amend.com

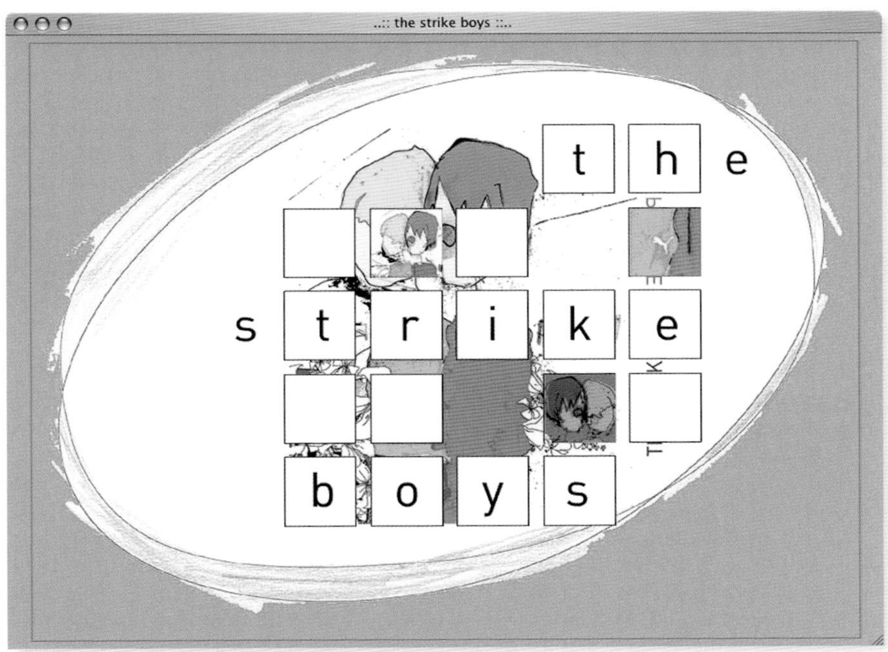
..:: the strike boys ::..
the
strike
boys

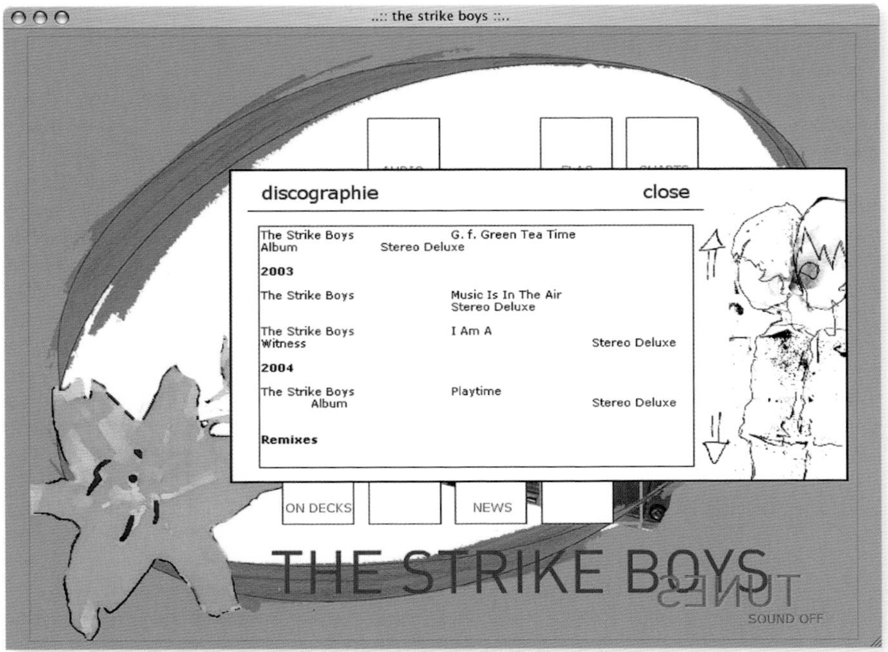
..:: the strike boys ::..
discographie
close
The Strike Boys G. f. Green Tea Time
Album Stereo Deluxe
2003
The Strike Boys Music Is In The Air
Stereo Deluxe
The Strike Boys I Am A
Witness Stereo Deluxe
2004
The Strike Boys Playtime
Album Stereo Deluxe
Remixes
ON DECKS
NEWS
THE STRIKE BOYS
TUNES
SOUND OFF

thestrikeboys.com
D: 2elemente
A: 2elemente **M:** winkler@2elemente.de

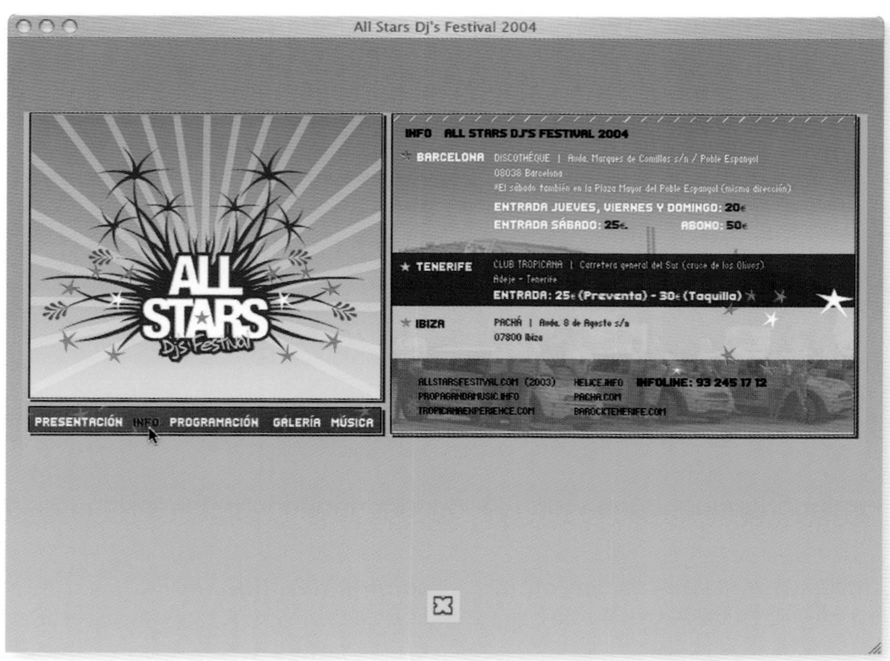
All Stars Dj's Festival 2004
ALL STARS Djs Festival
PRESENTACIÓN INFO PROGRAMACIÓN GALERÍA MÚSICA
INFO ALL STARS DJ'S FESTIVAL 2004
BARCELONA DISCOTHÉQUE | Avda. Marques de Comillas s/n / Poble Espanyol
08038 Barcelona
*El sábado también en la Plaza Mayor del Poble Espanyol (misma dirección)
ENTRADA JUEVES, VIERNES Y DOMINGO: 20€
ENTRADA SÁBADO: 25€. ABONO: 50€
TENERIFE CLUB TROPICANA | Carretera general del Sur (cruce de los Olivos)
Adeje - Tenerife
ENTRADA: 25€ (Preventa) - 30€ (Taquilla)
IBIZA PACHÁ | Avda. 8 de Agosto s/n
07800 Ibiza
ALLSTARSFESTIVAL.COM (2003) HELICE.INFO INFOLINE: 93 245 17 12
PROPAGANDAMUSIC.INFO PACHA.COM
TROPICANAEXPERIENCE.COM BAROCKTENERIFE.COM

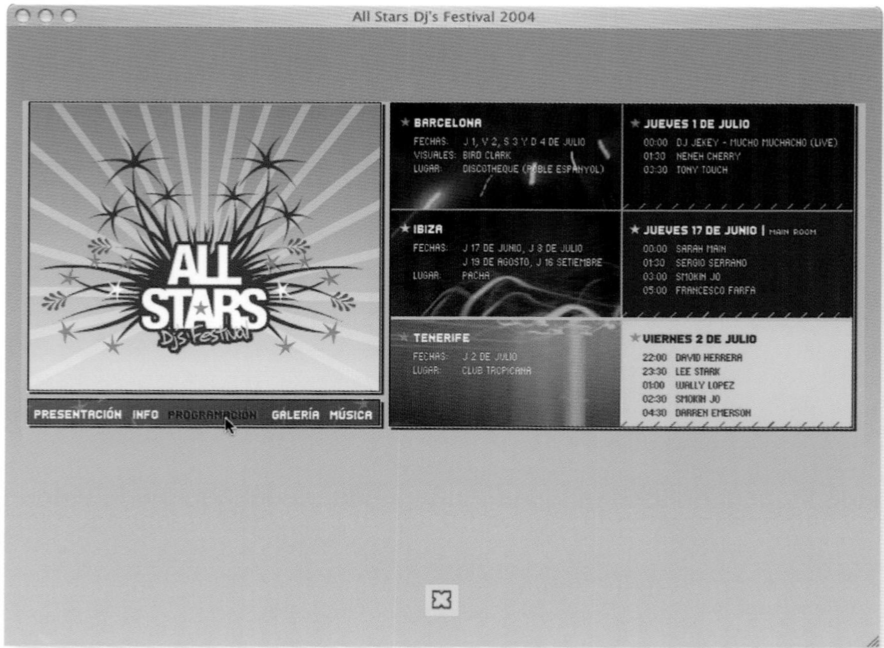
All Stars Dj's Festival 2004
ALL STARS Djs Festival
PRESENTACIÓN INFO PROGRAMACIÓN GALERÍA MÚSICA
BARCELONA
FECHAS: J 1, V 2, S 3 Y D 4 DE JULIO
VISUALES: BIRD CLARK
LUGAR: DISCOTHEQUE (POBLE ESPANYOL)
JUEVES 1 DE JULIO
00:00 DJ JEKEY - MUCHO MUCHACHO (LIVE)
01:30 NENEH CHERRY
03:30 TONY TOUCH
IBIZA
FECHAS: J 17 DE JUNIO, J 8 DE JULIO
J 19 DE AGOSTO, J 16 SETIEMBRE
LUGAR: PACHA
JUEVES 17 DE JUNIO | MAIN ROOM
00:00 SARAH MAIN
01:30 SERGIO SERRANO
03:00 SMOKIN JO
05:00 FRANCESCO FARFA
TENERIFE
FECHAS: J 2 DE JULIO
LUGAR: CLUB TROPICANA
VIERNES 2 DE JULIO
22:00 DAVID HERRERA
23:30 LEE STARK
01:00 WALLY LOPEZ
02:30 SMOKIN JO
04:30 DARREN EMERSON

www.allstarsfestival.com
D: xavi royo **P:** helice management
A: xafdesign **M:** info@xafdesign.com

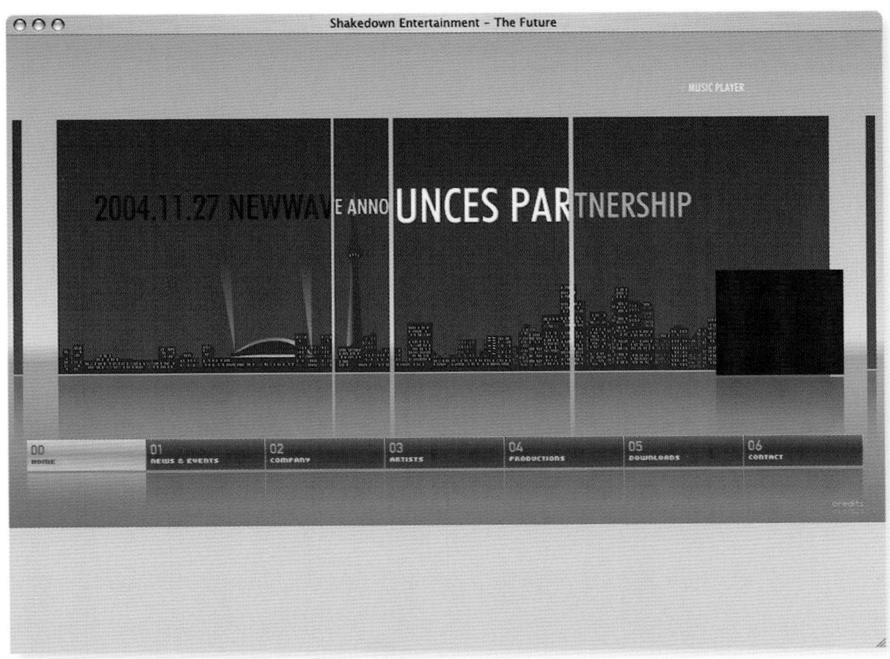
Shakedown Entertainment - The Future
MUSIC PLAYER
2004.11.27 NEWWAVE ANNOUNCES PARTNERSHIP
00 HOME
01 NEWS & EVENTS
02 COMPANY
03 ARTISTS
04 PRODUCTIONS
05 DOWNLOADS
06 CONTACT
credits

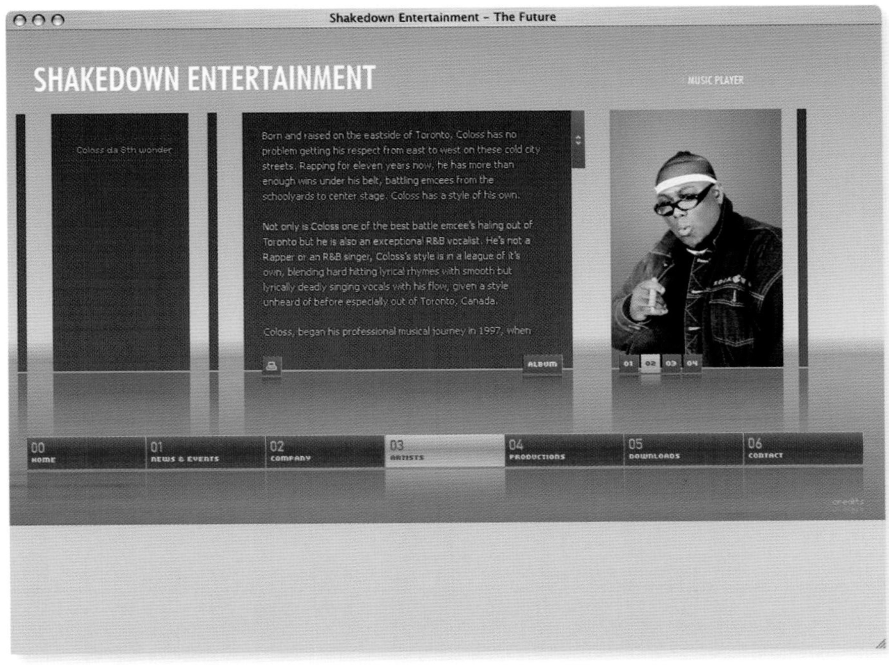
Shakedown Entertainment - The Future
SHAKEDOWN ENTERTAINMENT
MUSIC PLAYER
Coloss da 8th wonder
Born and raised on the eastside of Toronto, Coloss has no problem getting his respect from east to west on these cold city streets. Rapping for eleven years now, he has more than enough wins under his belt, battling emcees from the schoolyards to center stage. Coloss has a style of his own.
Not only is Coloss one of the best battle emcee's haling out of Toronto but he is also an exceptional R&B vocalist. He's not a Rapper or an R&B singer, Coloss's style is in a league of it's own, blending hard hitting lyrical rhymes with smooth but lyrically deadly singing vocals with his flow, given a style unheard of before especially out of Toronto, Canada.
Coloss, began his professional musical journey in 1997, when
ALBUM
01 02 03 04
00 HOME
01 NEWS & EVENTS
02 COMPANY
03 ARTISTS
04 PRODUCTIONS
05 DOWNLOADS
06 CONTACT
credits

www.shakedown-ent.com
D: parque creative **C:** parque creative **P:** newwave marketing
A: newwave marketing

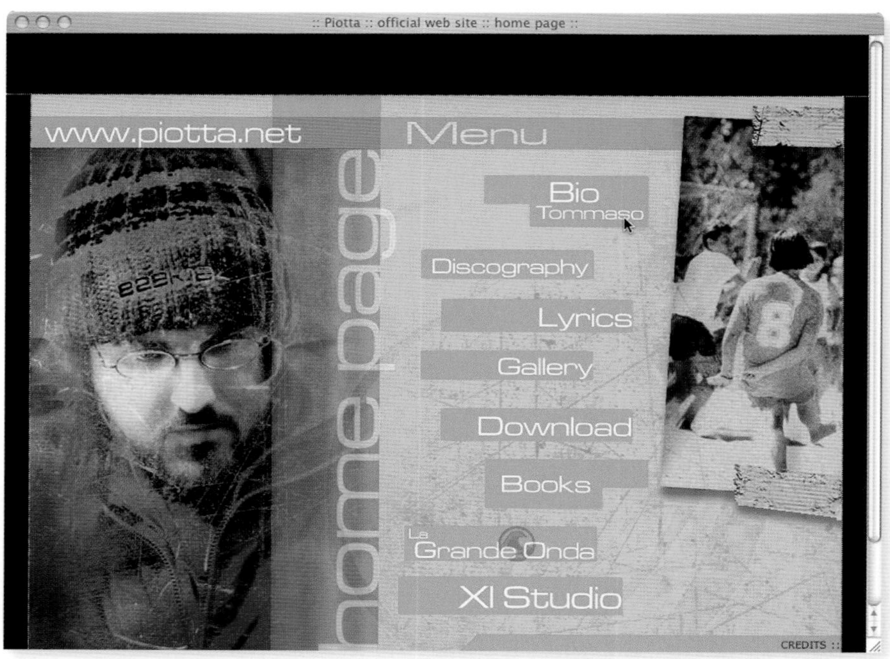
:: Piotta :: official web site :: home page ::
www.piotta.net
Menu
home page
Bio
Tommaso
Discography
Lyrics
Gallery
Download
Books
La
Grande Onda
XI Studio
CREDITS ::

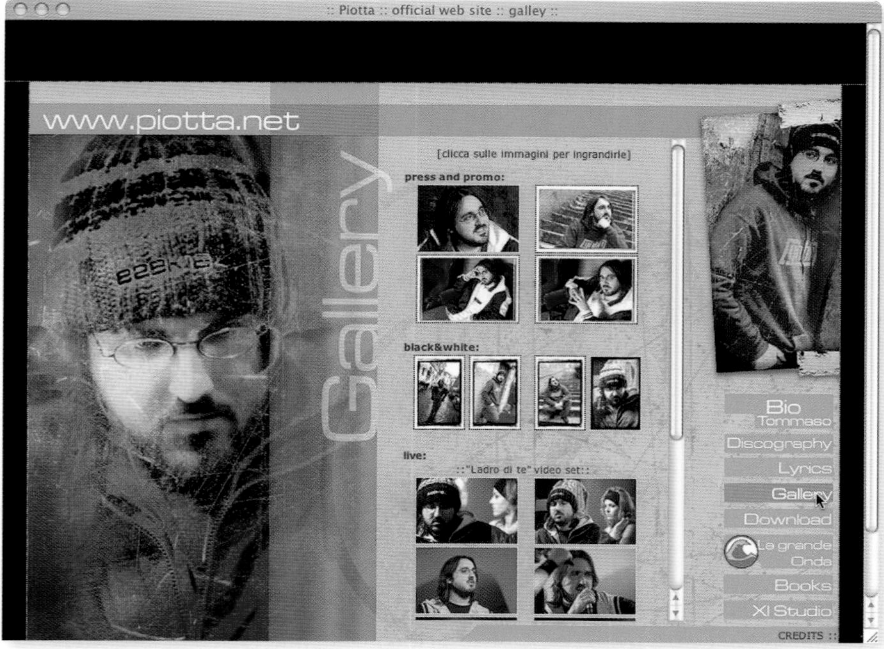
:: Piotta :: official web site :: galley ::
www.piotta.net
Gallery
[clicca sulle immagini per ingrandirle]
press and promo:
black&white:
live:
:: "Ladro di te" video set ::
Bio
Tommaso
Discography
Lyrics
Gallery
Download
La grande
Onda
Books
XI Studio
CREDITS ::

www.piotta.net
D: gianluca spiridigliozzi **C:** villa alfredo
M: gianluca@pubblicittasrl.it

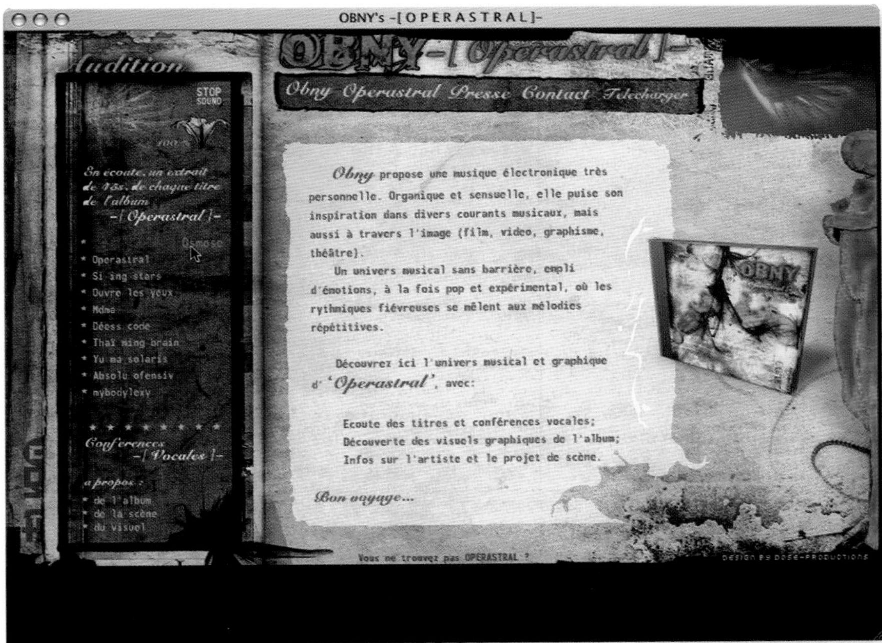
OBNY's -[OPERASTRAL]-
OBNY -[Operastral]-
Obny Operastral Presse Contact Telecharger
Audition
STOP SOUND
100%
En ecoute, un extrait de 45s. de chaque titre de l'album -[Operastral]-
Osmose
Operastral
Si ing stars
Ouvre les yeux
Mdma
Déess code
Thaï ming brain
Yu ma solaris
Absolu ofensiv
mybodylexy
Conférences -[Vocales]-
a propos :
de l'album
de la scène
du visuel
Obny propose une musique électronique très personnelle. Organique et sensuelle, elle puise son inspiration dans divers courants musicaux, mais aussi à travers l'image (film, video, graphisme, théâtre).
Un univers musical sans barrière, empli d'émotions, à la fois pop et expérimental, où les rythmiques fiévreuses se mêlent aux mélodies répétitives.
Découvrez ici l'univers musical et graphique d' 'Operastral', avec:
Ecoute des titres et conférences vocales;
Découverte des visuels graphiques de l'album;
Infos sur l'artiste et le projet de scène.
Bon voyage...
Vous ne trouvez pas OPERASTRAL ?
DESIGN BY DOSE-PRODUCTIONS

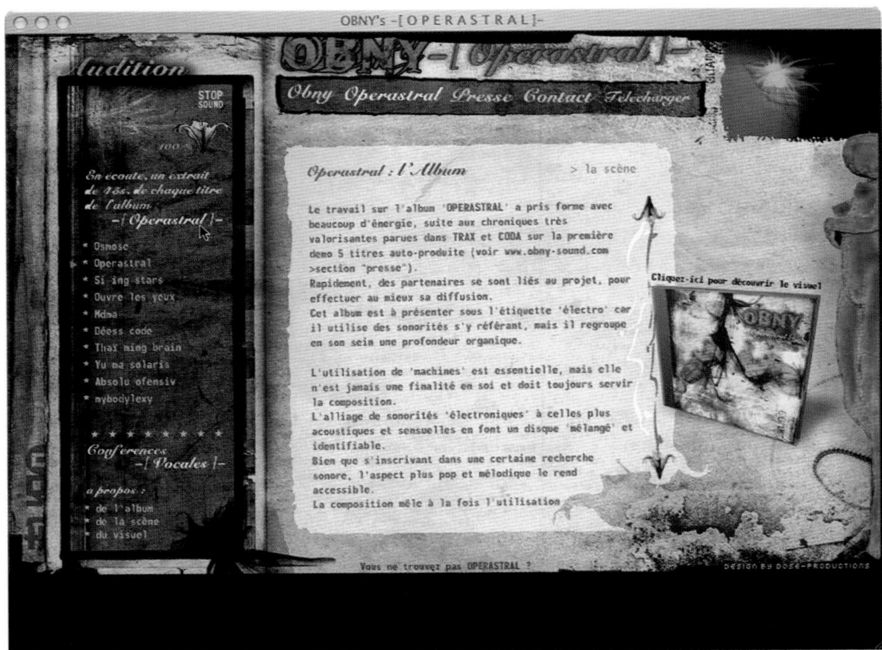
OBNY's -[OPERASTRAL]-
OBNY -[Operastral]-
Obny Operastral Presse Contact Telecharger
Audition
STOP SOUND
100%
En ecoute, un extrait de 45s. de chaque titre de l'album -[Operastral]-
Osmose
Operastral
Si ing stars
Ouvre les yeux
Mdma
Déess code
Thaï ming brain
Yu ma solaris
Absolu ofensiv
mybodylexy
Conférences -[Vocales]-
a propos :
de l'album
de la scène
du visuel
Operastral : l'Album
> la scène
Le travail sur l'album 'OPERASTRAL' a pris forme avec beaucoup d'énergie, suite aux chroniques très valorisantes parues dans TRAX et CODA sur la première demo 5 titres auto-produite (voir www.obny-sound.com >section "presse").
Rapidement, des partenaires se sont liés au projet, pour effectuer au mieux sa diffusion.
Cet album est à présenter sous l'étiquette 'électro' car il utilise des sonorités s'y référant, mais il regroupe en son sein une profondeur organique.
L'utilisation de 'machines' est essentielle, mais elle n'est jamais une finalité en soi et doit toujours servir la composition.
L'alliage de sonorités 'électroniques' à celles plus acoustiques et sensuelles en font un disque 'mélangé' et identifiable.
Bien que s'inscrivant dans une certaine recherche sonore, l'aspect plus pop et mélodique le rend accessible.
La composition mêle à la fois l'utilisation
Cliquez-ici pour découvrir le visuel
Vous ne trouvez pas OPERASTRAL ?
DESIGN BY DOSE-PRODUCTIONS

www.operastral.com
D: sam hayles
A: dose-productions **M:** sam@dose-productions.com

STILL HERE?YESSSSSSSSSS
none of them
CUSTOM GAUGE ROUNDWOUND
BASS STRINGS 2835 MADE IN USA
WWW.NONEOFTHEM.IT
FIVE GUYS, A DREAM & ONLY A LIFE!!
CHI SIAMO
NEWS
MP3
FOTO
FORUM
GUEST BOOK
LINKS
CONTATTI
NONE OF THEM: DEMO '99
TDK
NONE OF TH
LOBO SPECIAL

none of them is able to rock
none of them.
Siamo stufi di ripetere sempre le stesse cose, ma se non vedi i due mozziconi al centro di questa pagina significa che non hai installata la plug-in di Flash, e senza quella non andrai tanto lontano.
Noi che nonostante tutto ti abbiamo ripetuto per tre anni le stesse cose, ti diamo la possibilità di scaricarla cliccando qui .
Il download è gratuito e durerà circa due minuti. poi clicca sulla freccia a destra per entrare nel sito.
ShinyStat
P.viste tot 6566
Record p.v. 45
GO!

www.noneofthem.it/index2.htm
D: francesco dal santo
M: cescl@libero.it

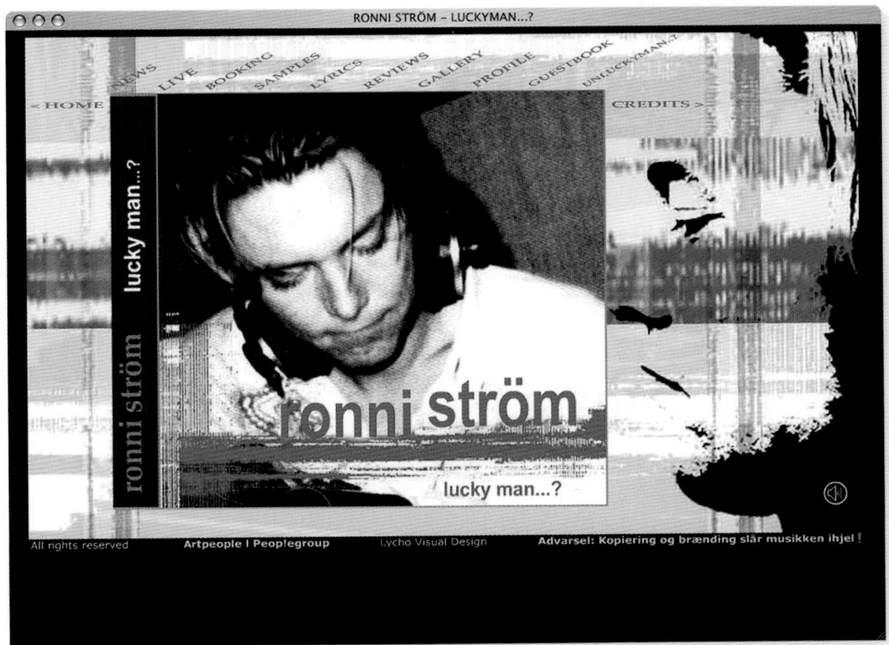
RONNI STRÖM - LUCKYMAN...?
NEWS
LIVE
BOOKING
SAMPLES
LYRICS
REVIEWS
GALLERY
PROFILE
GUESTBOOK
UNLUCKYMAN..?
< HOME
CREDITS >
lucky man...?
ronni ström
ronni ström
lucky man...?
All rights reserved
Artpeople I Peop!egroup
Lycho Visual Design
Advarsel: Kopiering og brænding slår musikken ihjel !

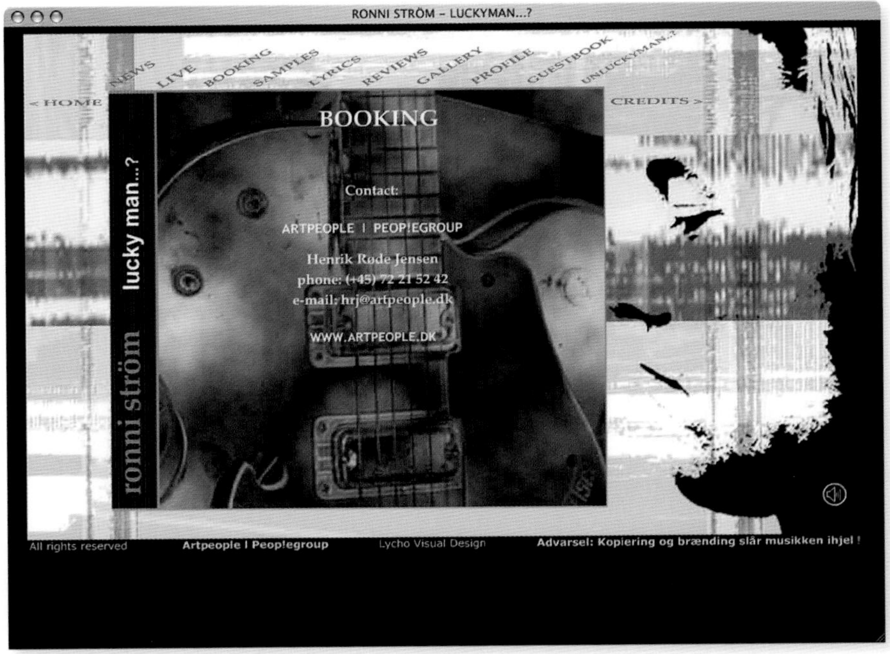
RONNI STRÖM - LUCKYMAN...?
NEWS
LIVE
BOOKING
SAMPLES
LYRICS
REVIEWS
GALLERY
PROFILE
GUESTBOOK
UNLUCKYMAN..?
< HOME
CREDITS >
lucky man...?
ronni ström
BOOKING
Contact:
ARTPEOPLE I PEOP!EGROUP
Henrik Røde Jensen
phone: (+45) 72 21 52 42
e-mail: hrj@artpeople.dk
WWW.ARTPEOPLE.DK
All rights reserved
Artpeople I Peop!egroup
Lycho Visual Design
Advarsel: Kopiering og brænding slår musikken ihjel !

www.ronniluckyman.dk
D: kristian falkenberg, anders bach larsen
A: lycho i/s **M:** kristian@lycho.dk

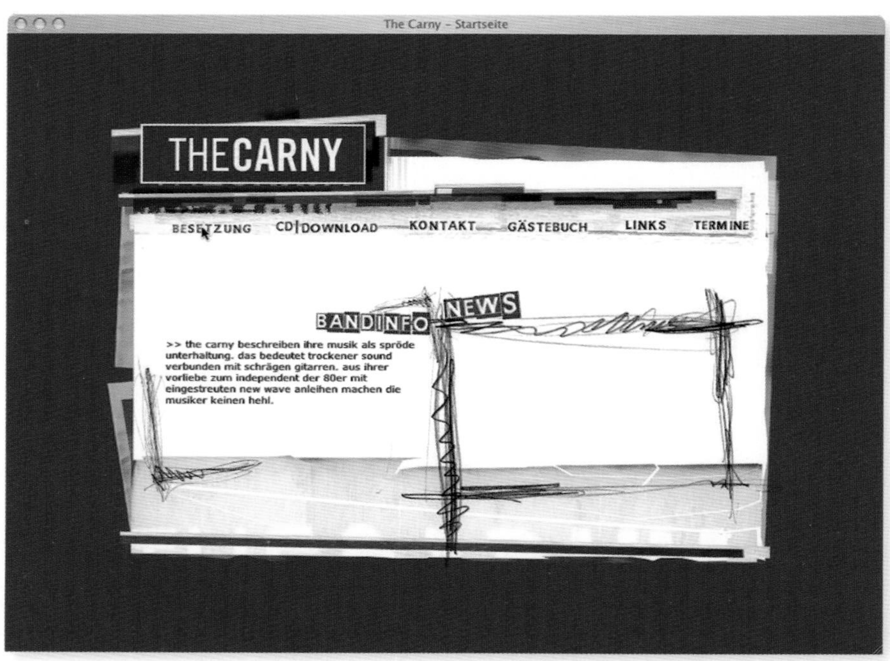
The Carny – Startseite
THECARNY
BESETZUNG
CD|DOWNLOAD
KONTAKT
GÄSTEBUCH
LINKS
TERMINE
BANDINFO
NEWS
>> the carny beschreiben ihre musik als spröde unterhaltung. das bedeutet trockener sound verbunden mit schrägen gitarren. aus ihrer vorliebe zum independent der 80er mit eingestreuten new wave anleihen machen die musiker keinen hehl.

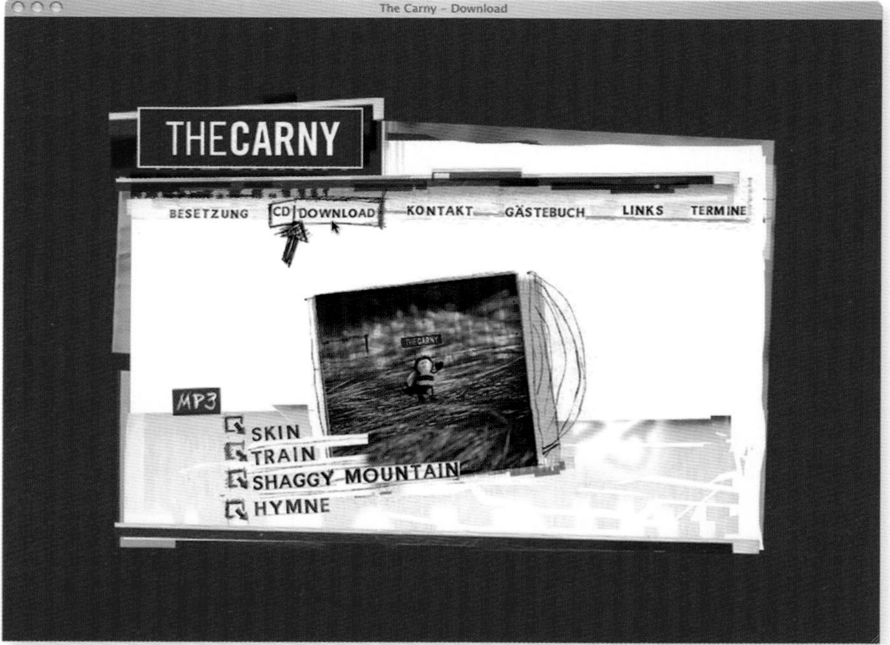
The Carny – Download
THECARNY
BESETZUNG
CD DOWNLOAD
KONTAKT
GÄSTEBUCH
LINKS
TERMINE
MP3
SKIN
TRAIN
SHAGGY MOUNTAIN
HYMNE

www.the-carny.de
D: michael steinert **C:** stefan matthäus
A: grafikstudio steinert **M:** contact@steinert-design.com

.......:: The Rhythm Junks :::.....
The Rhythm Junks

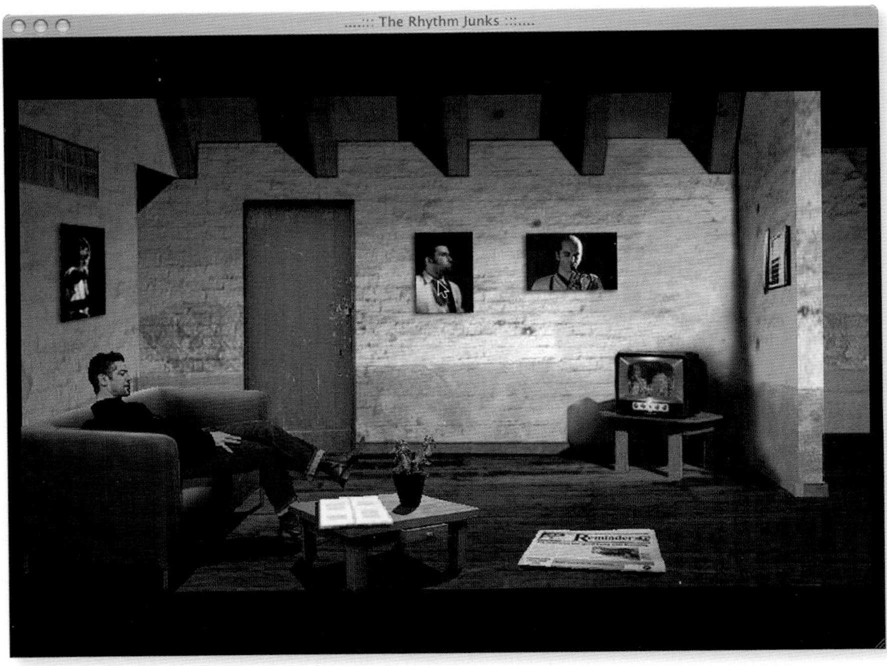
.......:: The Rhythm Junks :::.....

www.stevendebruyn.com
D: tom maebe
A: shivliz **M:** om@shivliz.com

ESTHETIC EDUCATION
FEEDBACK/EMAIL
ESTHETIC EDUCATION
© Copyright 2004 Esthetic Education. All Rights Reserved.
Artwork by Boris Beaucarne.
This site is KELDESIGNED.

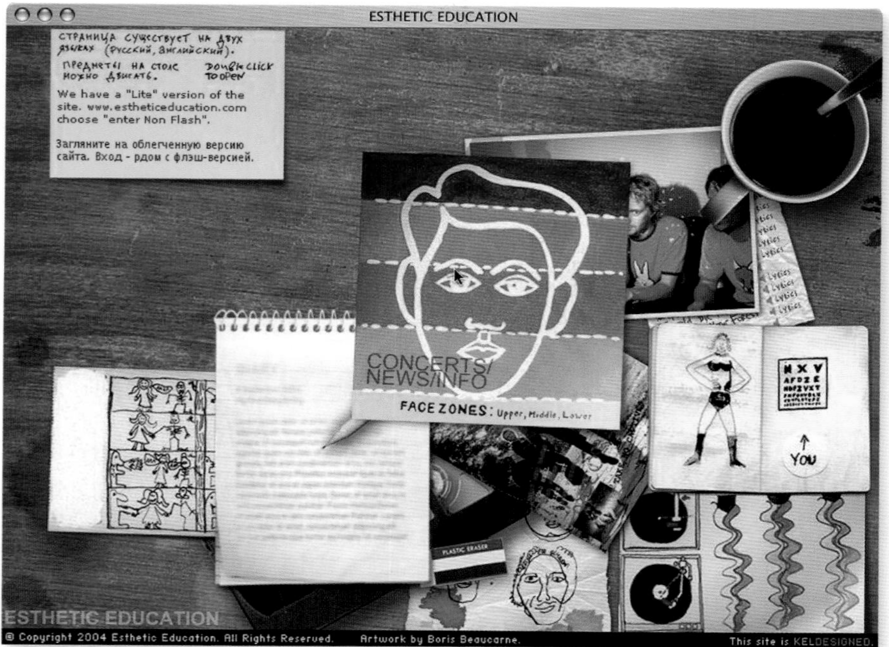
ESTHETIC EDUCATION
We have a "Lite" version of the site. www.estheticeducation.com choose "enter Non Flash".
Загляните на облегченную версию сайта. Вход - рдом с флэш-версией.
CONCERTS/ NEWS/INFO
FACE ZONES: Upper, Middle, Lower
ESTHETIC EDUCATION
© Copyright 2004 Esthetic Education. All Rights Reserved.
Artwork by Boris Beaucarne.
This site is KELDESIGNED.

www.estheticeducation.com
D: keith edward leyson **C:** keith edward leyson
A: keldesigns **M:** www.keldesigned.com

bostich official website
286
VALLE VERDE
BOSTICH
BIO
MUSIC
CONTACT
DOWNLOADS
NEWS
BOSTICH & NORTEC COLLECTIVE RELATED PRESS KIT DOWNLOADABLE PDF'S
FOR UPCOMING LIVE PERFORMANCES / PROXIMAS PRESENTACIONES EN VIVO
PLEASE VISIT > VISITA >
WWW.MILRECORDS.COM

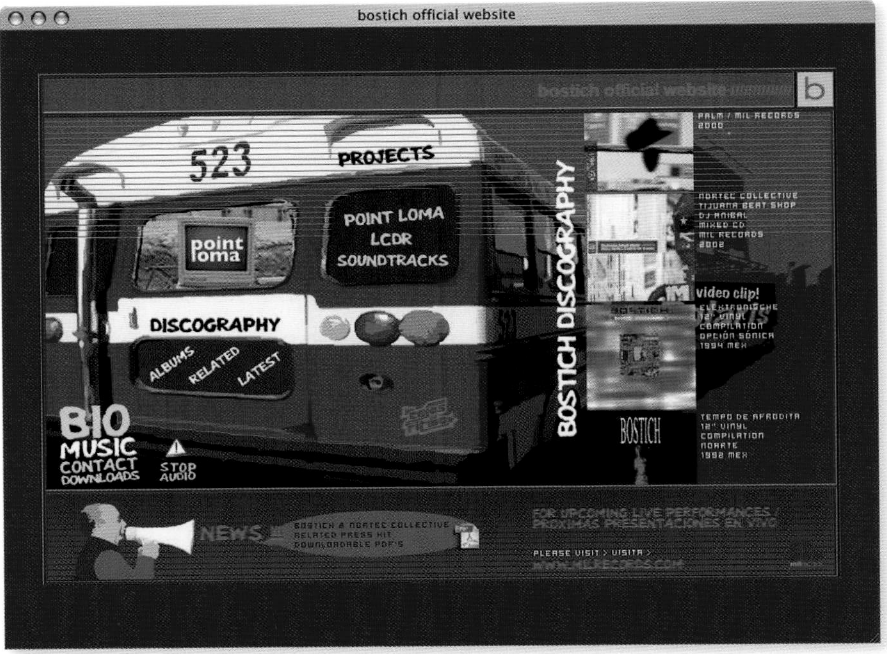
bostich official website
523
PROJECTS
POINT LOMA
LCDR
SOUNDTRACKS
point loma
DISCOGRAPHY
ALBUMS
RELATED
LATEST
BIO
MUSIC
CONTACT
DOWNLOADS
STOP AUDIO
BOSTICH DISCOGRAPHY
PALM / MIL RECORDS 2000
NORTEC COLLECTIVE TIJUANA BEAT SHOP DJ ANIBAL MIXED CD MIL RECORDS 2002
video clip!
TEMPO DE AFRODITA 12" VINYL COMPILATION NORARTE 1992 MEX
BOSTICH
NEWS
BOSTICH & NORTEC COLLECTIVE RELATED PRESS KIT DOWNLOADABLE PDF'S
FOR UPCOMING LIVE PERFORMANCES / PROXIMAS PRESENTACIONES EN VIVO
PLEASE VISIT > VISITA >
WWW.MILRECORDS.COM

www.bostich.org
D: angeles moreno
A: anaimation **M:** naima@anaimation.com

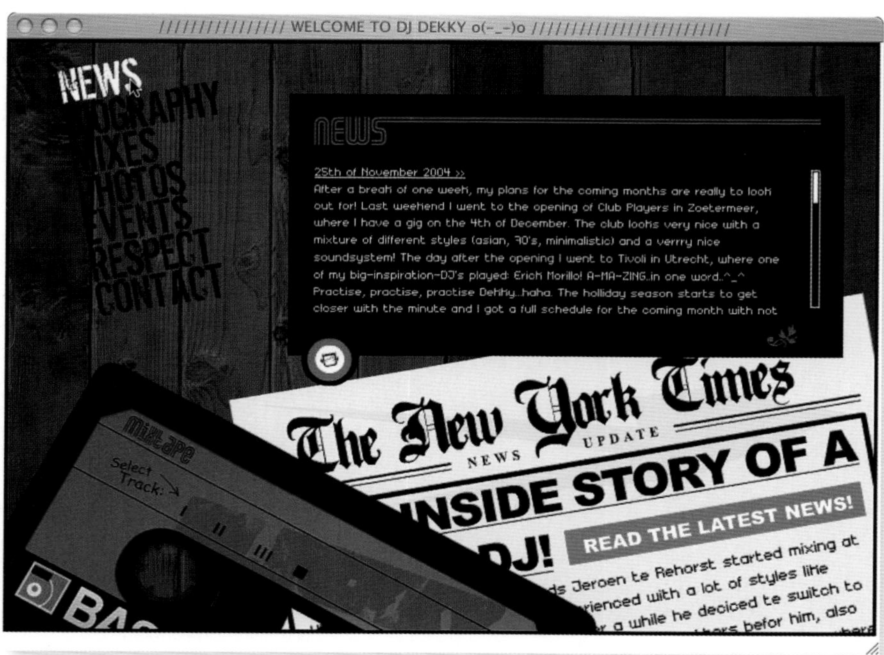
////////////////// WELCOME TO DJ DEKKY o(-_-)o ///////////////////////////
NEWS
CONTACT
NEWS
25th of November 2004 >>
After a break of one week, my plans for the coming months are really to look out for! Last weekend I went to the opening of Club Players in Zoetermeer, where I have a gig on the 4th of December. The club looks very nice with a mixture of different styles (asian, 70's, minimalistic) and a verrry nice soundsystem! The day after the opening I went to Tivoli in Utrecht, where one of my big-inspiration-DJ's played: Erick Morillo! A-MA-ZING..in one word..^_^ Practise, practise, practise Dekky...haha. The holliday season starts to get closer with the minute and I got a full schedule for the coming month with not
The New York Times
NEWS UPDATE
INSIDE STORY OF A
DJ!
READ THE LATEST NEWS!
Select Track:

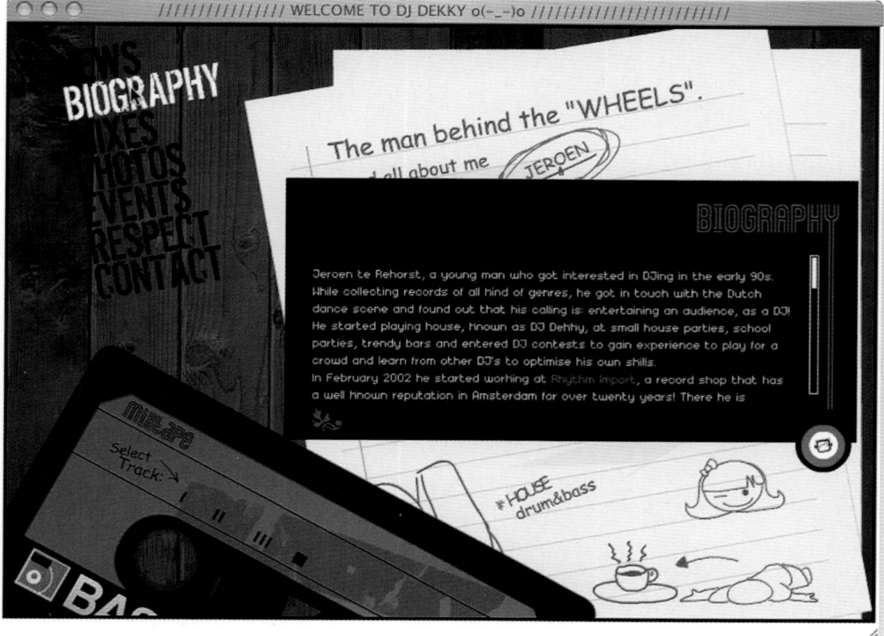
////////////////// WELCOME TO DJ DEKKY o(-_-)o ///////////////////////////
BIOGRAPHY
CONTACT
The man behind the "WHEELS".
JEROEN
BIOGRAPHY
Jeroen te Rekorst, a young man who got interested in DJing in the early 90s. While collecting records of all kind of genres, he got in touch with the Dutch dance scene and found out that his calling is: entertaining an audience, as a DJ! He started playing house, known as DJ Dekky, at small house parties, school parties, trendy bars and entered DJ contests to gain experience to play for a crowd and learn from other DJ's to optimise his own skills.
In February 2002 he started working at Rhythm Import, a record shop that has a well known reputation in Amsterdam for over twenty years! There he is
HOUSE
drum&bass
Select Track:

www.djdekky.com
D: glenn leming **C:** steve tirbeni
A: bureau lift **M:** info@liftyourself.nl

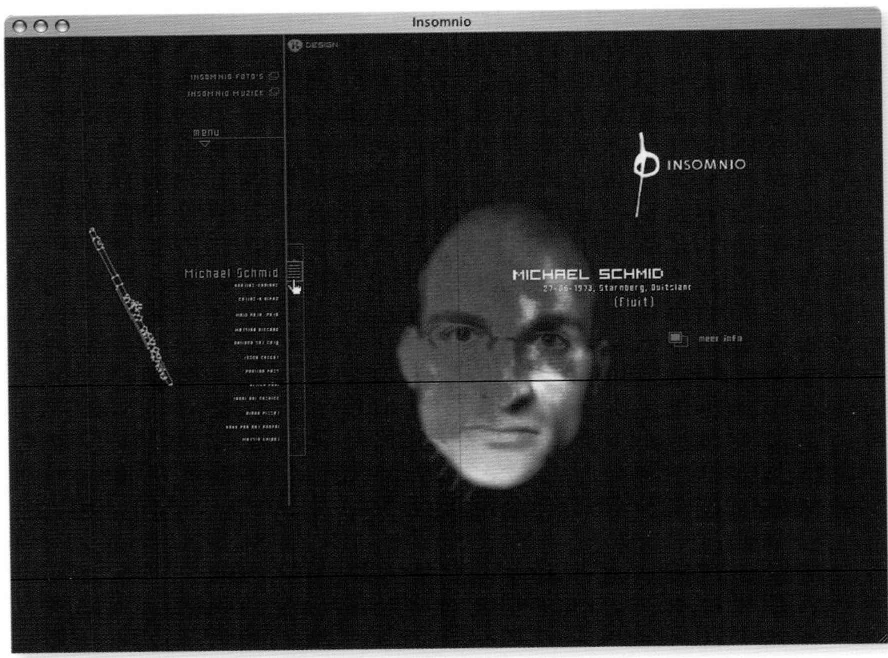
Insomnio
INSOMNIO
Michael Schmid
MICHAEL SCHMID
(Fluit)
meer info

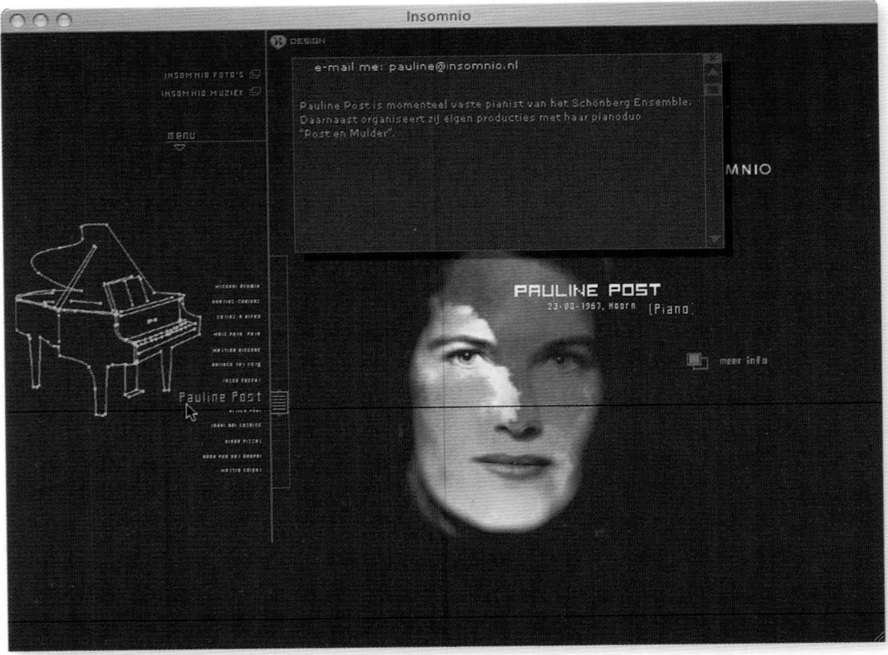
Insomnio
e-mail me: pauline@insomnio.nl
Pauline Post is momenteel vaste pianist van het Schönberg Ensemble.
Daarnaast organiseert zij eigen producties met haar pianoduo
"Post en Mulder".
menu
Pauline Post
PAULINE POST
(Piano)
meer info

www.insomnio.nl
D: hermes jeroen
A: kwatta ontwerpers **M:** jeroen@kwatta.com

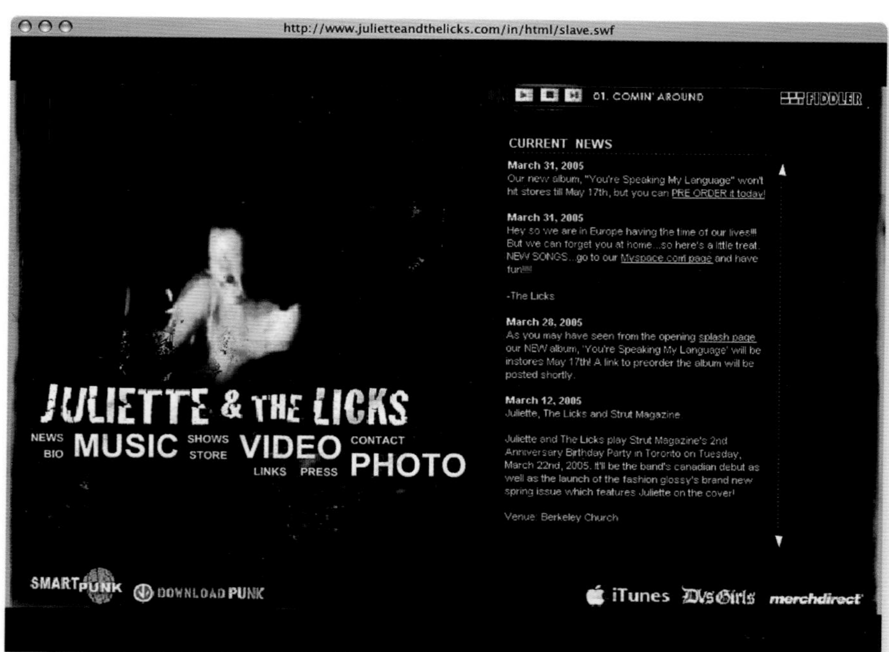
http://www.julietteandthelicks.com/in/html/slave.swf
01. COMIN' AROUND
FIDDLER
CURRENT NEWS
March 31, 2005
Our new album, "You're Speaking My Language" won't hit stores till May 17th, but you can PRE ORDER it today!
March 31, 2005
Hey so we are in Europe having the time of our lives!!! But we can forget you at home...so here's a little treat. NEW SONGS...go to our Myspace.com page and have fun!!!!
-The Licks
March 28, 2005
As you may have seen from the opening splash page our NEW album, 'You're Speaking My Language' will be instores May 17th! A link to preorder the album will be posted shortly.
March 12, 2005
Juliette, The Licks and Strut Magazine
Juliette and The Licks play Strut Magazine's 2nd Anniversary Birthday Party in Toronto on Tuesday, March 22nd, 2005. It'll be the band's canadian debut as well as the launch of the fashion glossy's brand new spring issue which features Juliette on the cover!
Venue: Berkeley Church
JULIETTE & THE LICKS
NEWS
BIO
MUSIC
SHOWS
STORE
VIDEO
LINKS
PRESS
CONTACT
PHOTO
SMARTPUNK
DOWNLOAD PUNK
iTunes
DVS Girls
merchdirect

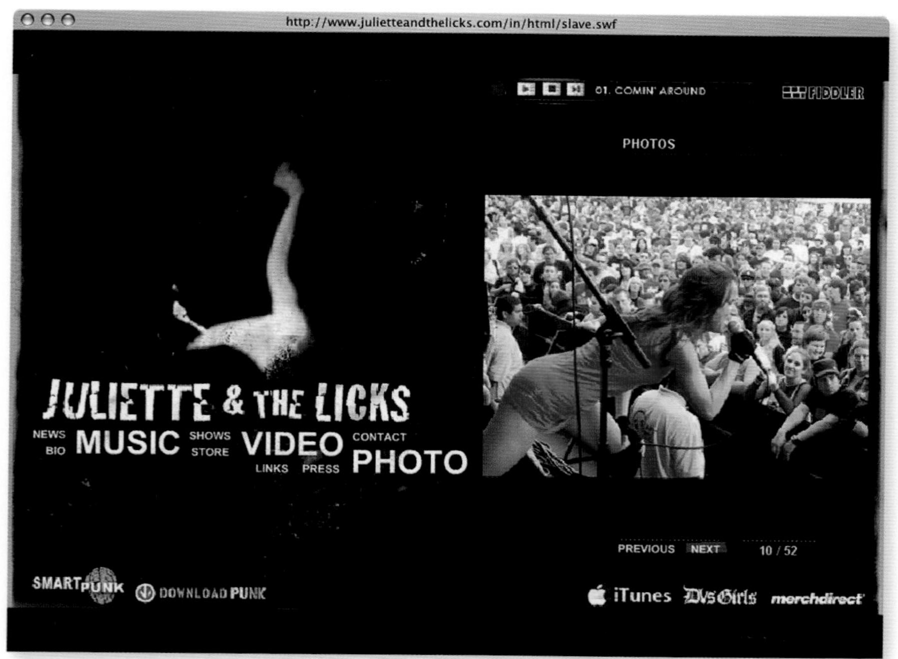
http://www.julietteandthelicks.com/in/html/slave.swf
01. COMIN' AROUND
FIDDLER
PHOTOS
JULIETTE & THE LICKS
NEWS
BIO
MUSIC
SHOWS
STORE
VIDEO
LINKS
PRESS
CONTACT
PHOTO
PREVIOUS
NEXT
10 / 52
SMARTPUNK
DOWNLOAD PUNK
iTunes
DVS Girls
merchdirect

www.julietteandthelicks.com
D: jaymz todd
M: todd_jaymz@hotmail.com

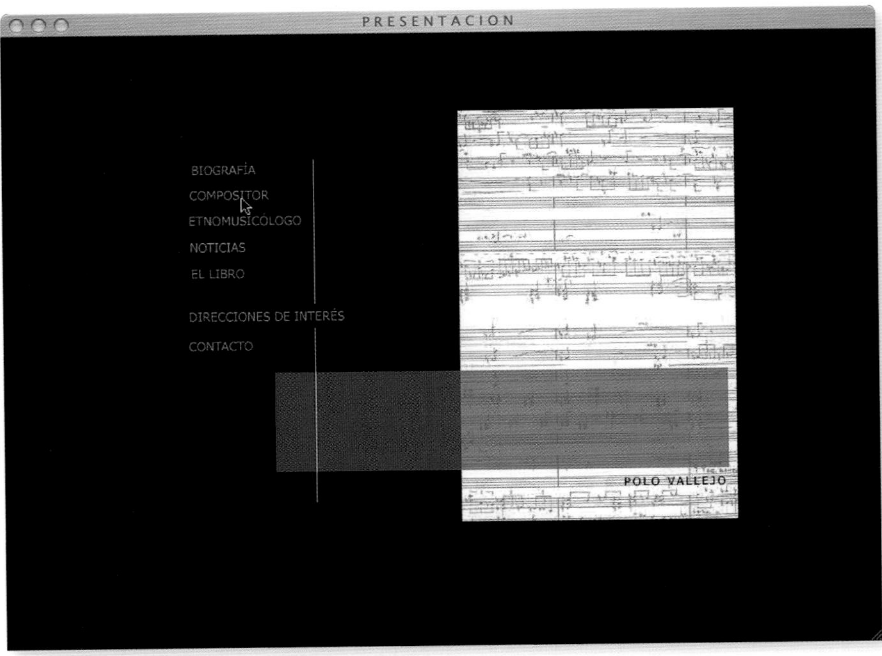
PRESENTACION
BIOGRAFÍA
COMPOSITOR
ETNOMUSICÓLOGO
NOTICIAS
EL LIBRO
DIRECCIONES DE INTERÉS
CONTACTO
POLO VALLEJO

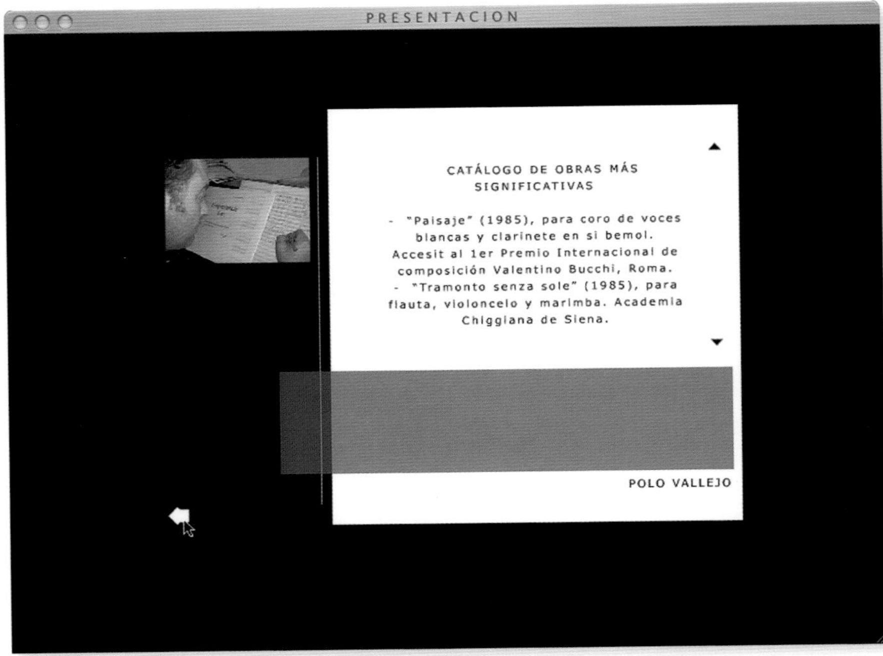
PRESENTACION
CATÁLOGO DE OBRAS MÁS SIGNIFICATIVAS
- "Paisaje" (1985), para coro de voces blancas y clarinete en si bemol. Accesit al 1er Premio Internacional de composición Valentino Bucchi, Roma.
- "Tramonto senza sole" (1985), para flauta, violoncelo y marimba. Academia Chiggiana de Siena.
POLO VALLEJO

www.polovallejo.com
D: carmen triviño barros
M: carmentrivino@wanadoo.es

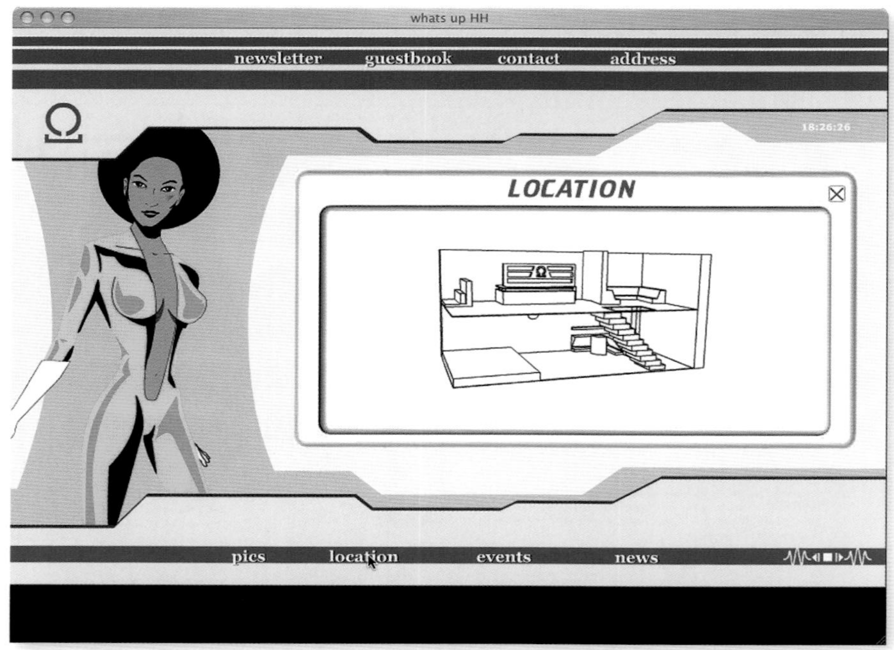
whats up HH
newsletter
guestbook
contact
address
18:26:26
LOCATION
pics
location
events
news

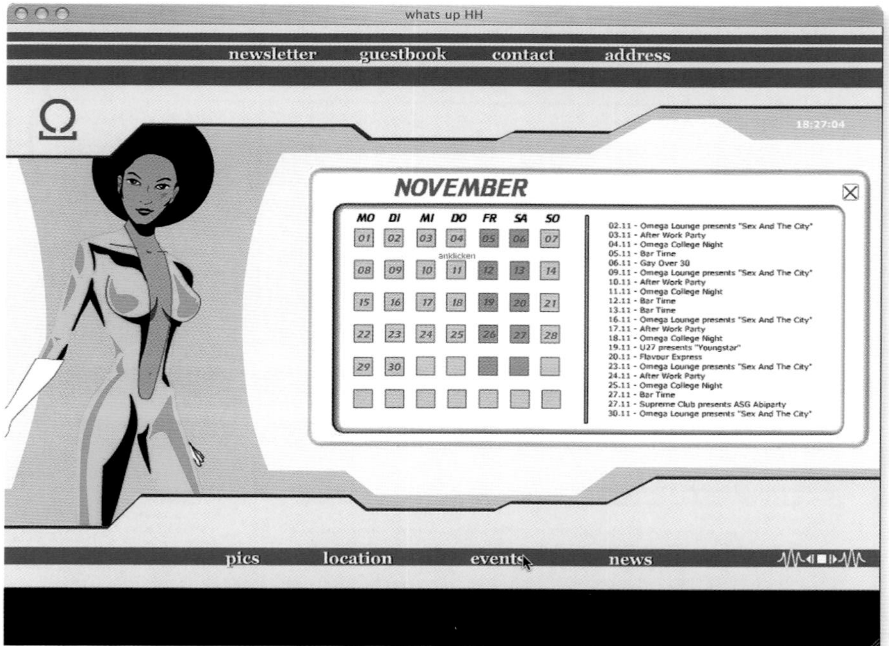
whats up HH
newsletter
guestbook
contact
address
18:27:04
NOVEMBER
MO DI MI DO FR SA SO
01 02 03 04 05 06 07
anklicken
08 09 10 11 12 13 14
15 16 17 18 19 20 21
22 23 24 25 26 27 28
29 30
02.11 - Omega Lounge presents "Sex And The City"
03.11 - After Work Party
04.11 - Omega College Night
05.11 - Bar Time
06.11 - Gay Over 30
09.11 - Omega Lounge presents "Sex And The City"
10.11 - After Work Party
11.11 - Omega College Night
12.11 - Bar Time
13.11 - Bar Time
16.11 - Omega Lounge presents "Sex And The City"
17.11 - After Work Party
18.11 - Omega College Night
19.11 - U27 presents "Youngstar"
20.11 - Flavour Express
23.11 - Omega Lounge presents "Sex And The City"
24.11 - After Work Party
25.11 - Omega College Night
27.11 - Bar Time
27.11 - Supreme Club presents ASG Abiparty
30.11 - Omega Lounge presents "Sex And The City"
pics
location
events
news

www.omega-lounge.de
D: philipp raczek **P:** omega-lounge
M: info@affenkralle.de

VITAMONDANA realizzazione eventi
VITAMONDANA
agenzia
club
informazioni
contatti
02A.GALLERIA EVENTI

VITAMONDANA realizzazione eventi
VITAMONDANA
agenzia
club
informazioni
contatti
01.AGENZIA
01A.GALLERIA STAFF
01B.PRESS AREA
in collaborazione con Qaraj'

www.vitamondana.com
D: alessio papi **P:** vitamondana
A: nextopen **M:** alessio@nextopen.it

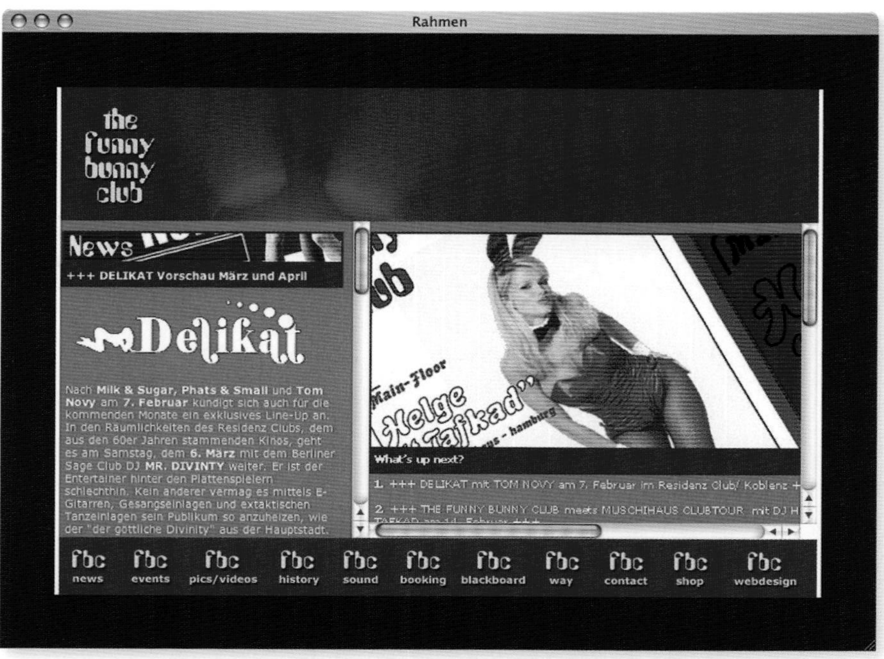
Rahmen
the funny bunny club
News
+++ DELIKAT Vorschau März und April
Delikat
Nach Milk & Sugar, Phats & Small und Tom Novy am 7. Februar kündigt sich auch für die kommenden Monate ein exklusives Line-Up an. In den Räumlichkeiten des Residenz Clubs, dem aus den 60er Jahren stammenden Kinos, geht es am Samstag, dem 6. März mit dem Berliner Sage Club DJ MR. DIVINTY weiter. Er ist der Entertainer hinter den Plattenspielern schlechthin. Kein anderer vermag es mittels E-Gitarren, Gesangseinlagen und extaktischen Tanzeinlagen sein Publikum so anzuheizen, wie der "der göttliche Divinity" aus der Hauptstadt.
Main-Floor
Helge "Tafkad"
What's up next?
1. +++ DELIKAT mit TOM NOVY am 7. Februar im Residenz Club/ Koblenz +
2. +++ THE FUNNY BUNNY CLUB meets MUSCHIHAUS CLUBTOUR mit DJ H
fbc news
fbc events
fbc pics/videos
fbc history
fbc sound
fbc booking
fbc blackboard
fbc way
fbc contact
fbc shop
fbc webdesign

The Funny Bunny Club – Nightfllight Productions Heiko Gemei...emein, Ulf Weber und Lutz Leurs GbR aus Remagen – – Events
the funny bunny club
Delikat
what's next
• 03.07.2004 - DELIKAT mit DJ TONKA
• 10.07.2004 - THE FUNNY BUNNY CLUB - Saison Closing
Home
News
- Events
Newsletter
Pics
Sounds
Gästebuch
History
Kontakt
Impressum
• DELIKAT mit DJ TONKA (03.07.2004)
Delikat immer am ersten Samstag im Monat statt!
„Get entertained by DJ TONKA"
Nach der heißen Nacht mit den Tune Brothers wird am 3. Juli DJ TONKA die Regie an den „Tellern die, die Welt bedeuten" übernehmen. Als Produzent und DJ gilt er als alter Hase in der internationalen DJ-Szene. Mit den Clubhits „She knows you", „Security" oder „Don't be afraid (let your self go)" (Platz 1 DDC) empfahl sich der Mainzer als Remixer für z.B. Bootsy Collins oder Jimmy Sommerville. Seine enge Freundschaft zu Ian Pooley und seine Vorleibe für Achtziger-Sounds schlagen sich ausdrucksvoll in seinem musikalischen Schaffen wieder, das TONKA nun auf seinem aktuellen Album „84" in Langspielformat gebracht hat. Mit seinem Label Vievienne
NEWS INHALT:
+++ Nachmieter gesucht
+++ neue Fotos online
+++ Neue DJ-Sets online
+++ Gewinnt Gästelistenplätze
+++ Nachmieter gesucht
Sehr schöne Wohnung in Sinzig zu vermieten: Nähe Ahr/ Rhein, 2 Gehminuten bis Bahnhof, sehr gut geschnittene 65 qm, 2 ZKDB, Abstellraum, 1. Untergeschoss (sehr hell, 3 Balkontüren), 15 qm Terrasse (Sonnenseite), komplett Laminat oder Fliesen, WG-tauglich, sehr ruhig, Trocknermitbenutzung, Stellplatz (wenn gewünscht) ca. 400 € warm, ab 1. August zu vermieten, Telefon 0177/8378460
+++ neue Fotos online
NEU!!: Fotos von der DELIKAT mit den TUNE BROTHERS (Juni)
+++ Neue DJ-Sets online
Wir haben es geschafft, folgende neuen DJ-Sets sind jetzt online:
+ DELIKAT mit TOM NOVY
+ DELIKAT mit DJ DIVINITY &

www.funny-bunny-club.de
D: daniel jansen
A: jansen grafik **M:** info@daniel-jansen.de

REPUBLICAunderthestation
republica
underthestation
MUSICA OFF
PROGRAMACION
EQUIPO
FIESTAS
FOTOS
GUESTBOOK
LINKS
LITTLE KRIS
SHARK
COLIN PETERS
(MANUMISSION IBIZA)
BARBIE MALIBÚ
SUBSCRIBETE A LA LISTA DE CORREO
ENVIAR

REPUBLICAunderthestation
republica
underthestation
MUSICA OFF
PROGRAMACION
EQUIPO
FIESTAS
FOTOS
GUESTBOOK
LINKS
INICIO
EN LA NOCHE BARCELONESA DESDE 1993, EVOLUCIONA COMO DJ COMBINANDO MÚSICA DANCE COMERCIAL CON TECHNO POP DE LOS 80, PASANDO POR INNUMERABLES SALAS, COMO UPDOWN PORT, PACHITO, FRITZ MAR, NAYANDEI, WALDEN,...A PARTIR DE 1999, Y YA COMO DJ SHARK SE CONVIERTE EN DJ OFICIAL DEL TRIBAL GROUP, DE LA MANO DE DANI ESTEVE. EN SUS SESIONES MEZCLA SONIDOS TRIBALES, TECHOUSE Y VOCALES, PARA CREAR UN AMBIENTE DIVERTIDO, PERO CONTUNDENTE A LA VEZ.
PINCHO PARA QUE LA GENTE SE DIVIERTA !
SUBSCRIBETE A LA LISTA DE CORREO
ENVIAR

www.republicaunderthestation.com
D: marc torrente cesteros **P:** disco republica
A: sirastudio **M:** sirocus69@hotmail.com

Podiumcafe Plein 79 ´s-Hertogenbosch
Plein 79
Programma
Columns
Links
E-mail
beweeg je muis
Inkijk Plein 79
Podiumcafe
PLEIN 79

Podiumcafe Plein 79 ´s-Hertogenbosch
Plein 79
Programma
Columns
Links
E-mail
Programma
Do 03 JUN DJ TJEU 22.00 uur
Vr 04 JUN DJ LARS 22.00 uur
Za 05 JUN DJ JOZUF 22.00 uur
Do 10 JUN DJ TJEU 22.00 uur
Vr 11 JUN DJ LARS 22.00 uur
Za 12 JUN DJ JOZUF 22.00 uur
Do 17 JUN DJ JOZUF 22.00 uur
Vr 18 JUN DJ NILSON 22.00 uur
Za 19 JUN DJ LARS 22.00 uur
Do 24 JUN DJ TJEU 22.00 uur
Podiumcafe
PLEIN 79

www.plein79.nl
D: leo hamers
A: yaikz! **M:** info@yaikz.nl

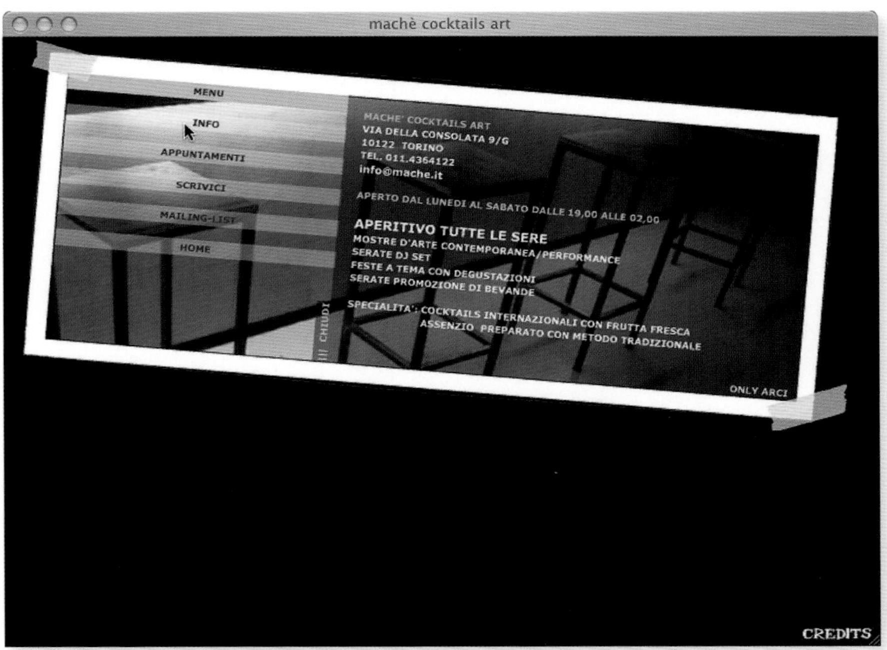
machè cocktails art
MENU
INFO
APPUNTAMENTI
SCRIVICI
MAILING-LIST
HOME
MACHE' COCKTAILS ART
VIA DELLA CONSOLATA 9/G
10122 TORINO
TEL. 011.4364122
info@mache.it
APERTO DAL LUNEDI AL SABATO DALLE 19,00 ALLE 02,00
APERITIVO TUTTE LE SERE
MOSTRE D'ARTE CONTEMPORANEA/PERFORMANCE
SERATE DJ SET
FESTE A TEMA CON DEGUSTAZIONI
SERATE PROMOZIONE DI BEVANDE
SPECIALITA': COCKTAILS INTERNAZIONALI CON FRUTTA FRESCA
ASSENZIO PREPARATO CON METODO TRADIZIONALE
CHIUDI
ONLY ARCI
CREDITS

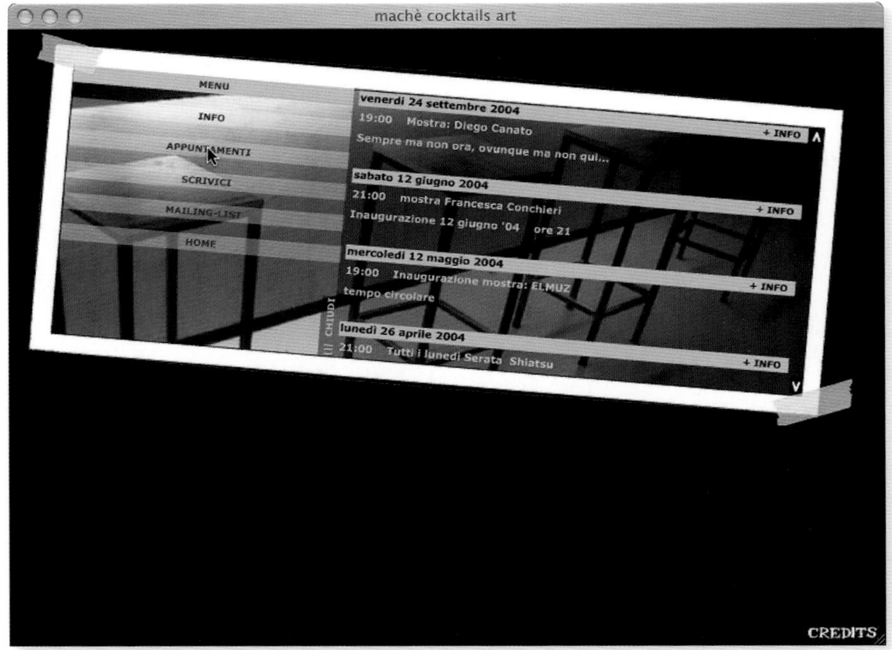
machè cocktails art
MENU
INFO
APPUNTAMENTI
SCRIVICI
MAILING-LIST
HOME
venerdì 24 settembre 2004
19:00 Mostra: Diego Canato
Sempre ma non ora, ovunque ma non qui...
+ INFO
sabato 12 giugno 2004
21:00 mostra Francesca Conchieri
Inaugurazione 12 giugno '04 ore 21
+ INFO
mercoledì 12 maggio 2004
19:00 Inaugurazione mostra: ELMUZ
tempo circolare
+ INFO
lunedì 26 aprile 2004
21:00 Tutti i lunedì Serata Shiatsu
+ INFO
CHIUDI
CREDITS

www.mache.it
D: stefano brizzi
A: tafano **M:** info@tafano.it

du + // designers union hessen – Berufgruppe Grafikdesign und Mediengestaltung in ver.di
ver.di
du designers union hessen
Über uns
Informationen
Links
Kontakt
designers union hessen ist die Berufsgruppe Grafikdesign und Mediengestaltung in ver.di im Rhein-Main-Gebiet und Hessen
Hallo liebe Kolleginnen und Kollegen, sowie Interessierte aus der Medienbranche. Unsere Website ist fast so neu wie designers union als Berufsgruppe in ver.di. Deswegen wird diese Site erst nach und nach mit Inhalten gefüllt.
Bei Interesse eine Mail an: info@du-hessen.info
Aktuelle Termine
6. – 21. Februar 2004
Ausstellungseröffnung »Eulen nach Athentragen«
am 6. Februar im Frankensteiner Hof in Frankfurt/Große Rittergasse 103 ab 19 Uhr.
Nach Athen werden die Arbeiten verschiedener Designer/innen zum Thema »Eulen nach Athen tragen/Emporter des femmes à Paris« nun in Frankfurt gezeigt. Ein Projekt von David Borchers

EMPORTER des femmes à paris

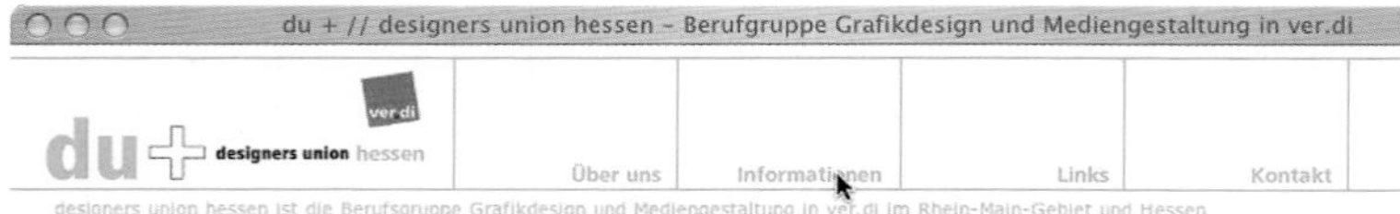
du + // designers union hessen – Berufgruppe Grafikdesign und Mediengestaltung in ver.di
ver.di
du designers union hessen
Über uns
Informationen
Links
Kontakt
designers union hessen ist die Berufsgruppe Grafikdesign und Mediengestaltung in ver.di im Rhein-Main-Gebiet und Hessen

Hier wird nach und nach eine Sammlung von Veranstaltungsberichten, Fachartikeln etc. gesammelt werden.

Veranstaltungsberichte

»Ich lese keine Bücher mit schlechter Typografie!«
Veranstaltung der designers union am 11. Oktober 2003 in Frankfurt

Rund 50 interessierte Kolleg/innen kamen zur ersten Veranstaltung der designers union nach Frankfurt ins Gewerkschaftshaus um den Typonauten und ihren Ausführungen über Buchgestaltung und gute Typografie zu lauschen.

Zu Beginn haben wir kurz einen Überblick über designers union als Berufsgruppe Mediengestaltung und Grafikdesign in verdi gegeben

www.du-hessen.info
D: peter reichard
A: typosition **M:** info@typosition.de

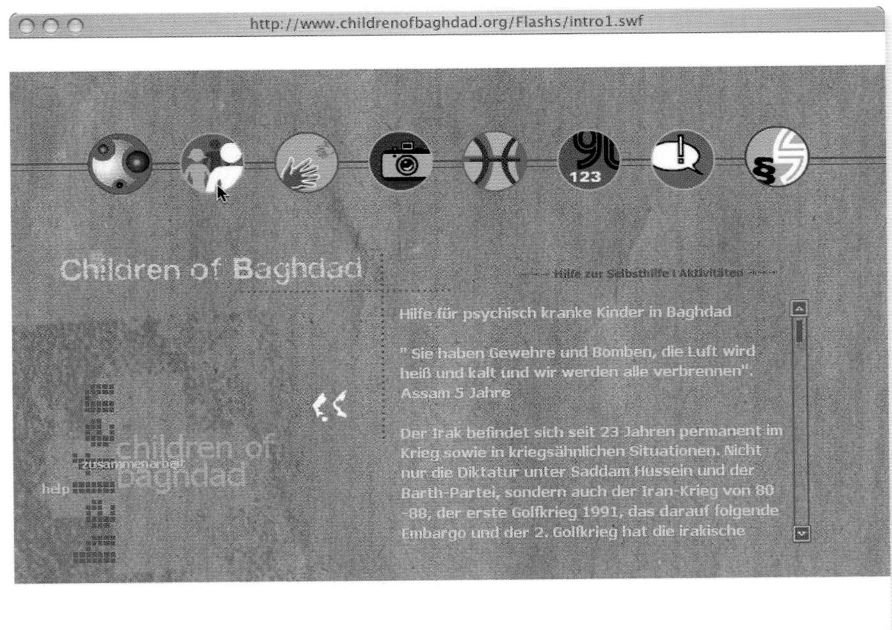
http://www.childrenofbaghdad.org/Flashs/intro1.swf
Children of Baghdad
Hilfe zur Selbsthilfe | Aktivitäten
Hilfe für psychisch kranke Kinder in Baghdad
" Sie haben Gewehre und Bomben, die Luft wird heiß und kalt und wir werden alle verbrennen".
Assam 5 Jahre
Der Irak befindet sich seit 23 Jahren permanent im Krieg sowie in kriegsähnlichen Situationen. Nicht nur die Diktatur unter Saddam Hussein und der Barth-Partei, sondern auch der Iran-Krieg von 80 -88, der erste Golfkrieg 1991, das darauf folgende Embargo und der 2. Golfkrieg hat die irakische
123
zusammenarbeit
help
children of baghdad

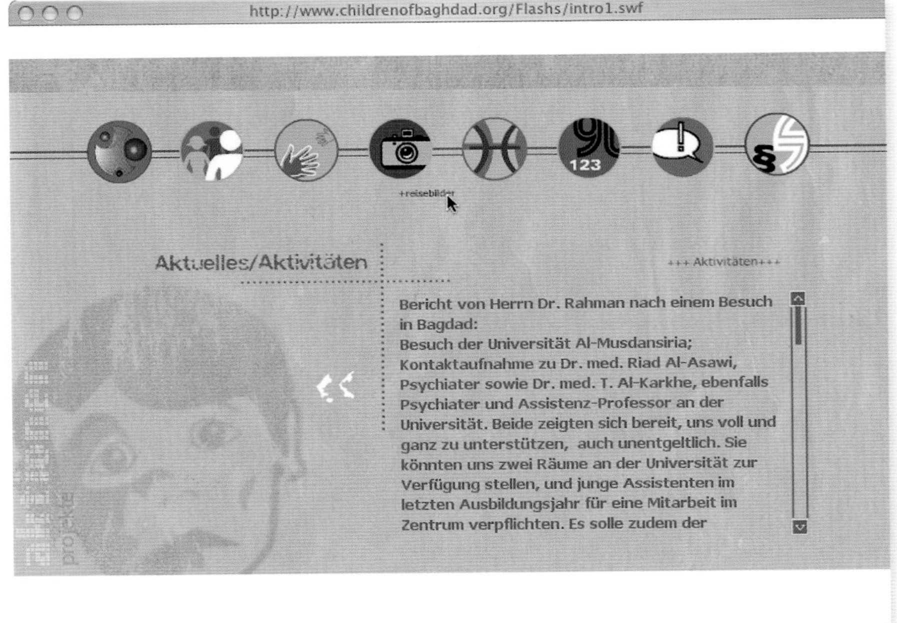
http://www.childrenofbaghdad.org/Flashs/intro1.swf
+reisebilder
Aktuelles/Aktivitäten
+++ Aktivitäten+++
Bericht von Herrn Dr. Rahman nach einem Besuch in Bagdad:
Besuch der Universität Al-Musdansiria;
Kontaktaufnahme zu Dr. med. Riad Al-Asawi, Psychiater sowie Dr. med. T. Al-Karkhe, ebenfalls Psychiater und Assistenz-Professor an der Universität. Beide zeigten sich bereit, uns voll und ganz zu unterstützen, auch unentgeltlich. Sie könnten uns zwei Räume an der Universität zur Verfügung stellen, und junge Assistenten im letzten Ausbildungsjahr für eine Mitarbeit im Zentrum verpflichten. Es solle zudem der
123
projekte

www.childrenofbaghdad.org
D: diane khalik
M: diane_khalik@hotmail.com

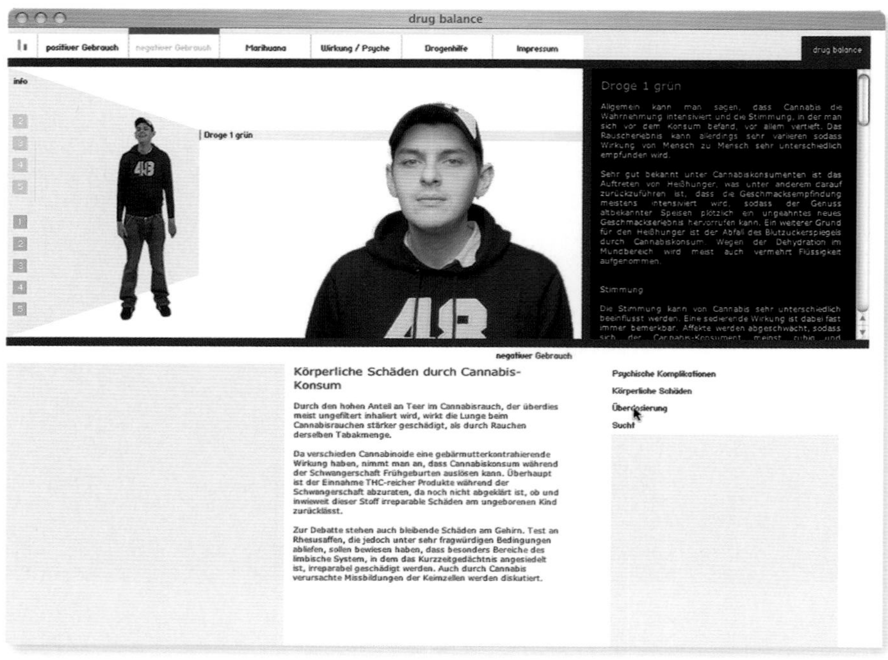
drug balance
positiver Gebrauch
negativer Gebrauch
Marihuana
Wirkung / Psyche
Drogenhilfe
Impressum
drug balance
info
Droge 1 grün
Droge 1 grün
Allgemein kann man sagen, dass Cannabis die Wahrnehmung intensiviert und die Stimmung, in der man sich vor dem Konsum befand, vor allem vertieft. Das Rauscherlebnis kann allerdings sehr variieren sodass Wirkung von Mensch zu Mensch sehr unterschiedlich empfunden wird.
Sehr gut bekannt unter Cannabiskonsumenten ist das Auftreten von Heißhunger, was unter anderem darauf zurückzuführen ist, dass die Geschmacksempfindung meistens intensiviert wird, sodass der Genuss altbekannter Speisen plötzlich ein ungeahntes neues Geschmackserlebnis hervorrufen kann. Ein weiterer Grund für den Heißhunger ist der Abfall des Blutzuckerspiegels durch Cannabiskonsum. Wegen der Dehydration im Mundbereich wird meist auch vermehrt Flüssigkeit aufgenommen.
Stimmung
Die Stimmung kann von Cannabis sehr unterschiedlich beeinflusst werden. Eine sedierende Wirkung ist dabei fast immer bemerkbar. Affekte werden abgeschwächt, sodass
negativer Gebrauch
Körperliche Schäden durch Cannabis-Konsum
Durch den hohen Anteil an Teer im Cannabisrauch, der überdies meist ungefiltert inhaliert wird, wirkt die Lunge beim Cannabisrauchen stärker geschädigt, als durch Rauchen derselben Tabakmenge.
Da verschieden Cannabinoide eine gebärmutterkontrahierende Wirkung haben, nimmt man an, dass Cannabiskonsum während der Schwangerschaft Frühgeburten auslösen kann. Überhaupt ist der Einnahme THC-reicher Produkte während der Schwangerschaft abzuraten, da noch nicht abgeklärt ist, ob und inwieweit dieser Stoff irreparable Schäden am ungeborenen Kind zurücklässt.
Zur Debatte stehen auch bleibende Schäden am Gehirn. Test an Rhesusaffen, die jedoch unter sehr fragwürdigen Bedingungen abliefen, sollen bewiesen haben, dass besonders Bereiche des limbische System, in dem das Kurzzeitgedächtnis angesiedelt ist, irreparabel geschädigt werden. Auch durch Cannabis verursachte Missbildungen der Keimzellen werden diskutiert.
Psychische Komplikationen
Körperliche Schäden
Überdosierung
Sucht

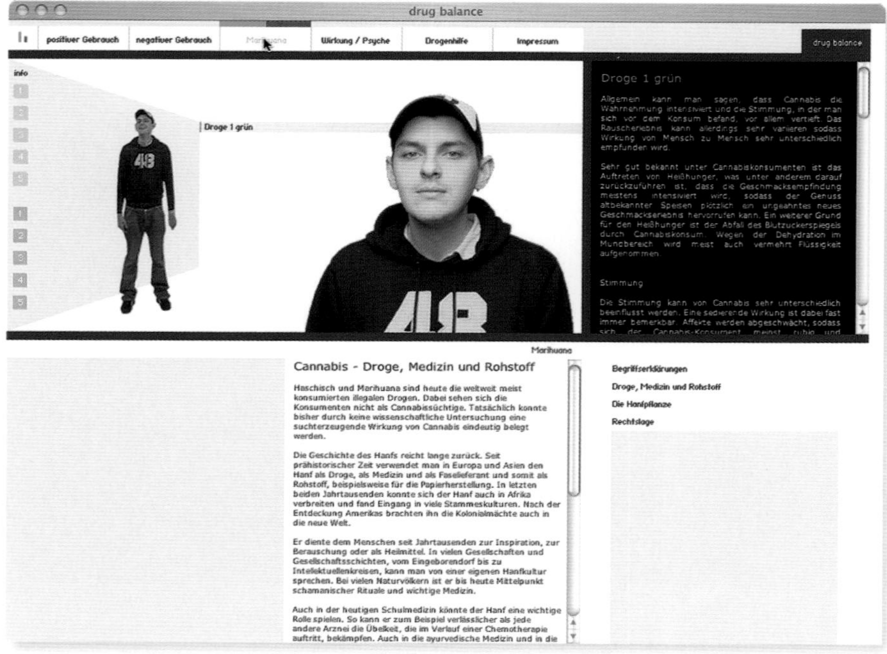
drug balance
positiver Gebrauch
negativer Gebrauch
Wirkung / Psyche
Drogenhilfe
Impressum
drug balance
info
Droge 1 grün
Droge 1 grün
Allgemein kann man sagen, dass Cannabis die Wahrnehmung intensiviert und die Stimmung, in der man sich vor dem Konsum befand, vor allem vertieft. Das Rauscherlebnis kann allerdings sehr variieren sodass Wirkung von Mensch zu Mensch sehr unterschiedlich empfunden wird.
Sehr gut bekannt unter Cannabiskonsumenten ist das Auftreten von Heißhunger, was unter anderem darauf zurückzuführen ist, dass die Geschmacksempfindung meistens intensiviert wird, sodass der Genuss altbekannter Speisen plötzlich ein ungeahntes neues Geschmackserlebnis hervorrufen kann. Ein weiterer Grund für den Heißhunger ist der Abfall des Blutzuckerspiegels durch Cannabiskonsum. Wegen der Dehydration im Mundbereich wird meist auch vermehrt Flüssigkeit aufgenommen.
Stimmung
Die Stimmung kann von Cannabis sehr unterschiedlich beeinflusst werden. Eine sedierende Wirkung ist dabei fast immer bemerkbar. Affekte werden abgeschwächt, sodass
Marihuana
Cannabis - Droge, Medizin und Rohstoff
Haschisch und Marihuana sind heute die weltweit meist konsumierten illegalen Drogen. Dabei sehen sich die Konsumenten nicht als Cannabissüchtige. Tatsächlich konnte bisher durch keine wissenschaftliche Untersuchung eine suchterzeugende Wirkung von Cannabis eindeutig belegt werden.
Die Geschichte des Hanfs reicht lange zurück. Seit prähistorischer Zeit verwendet man in Europa und Asien den Hanf als Droge, als Medizin und als Faselieferant und somit als Rohstoff, beispielsweise für die Papierherstellung. In letzten beiden Jahrtausenden konnte sich der Hanf auch in Afrika verbreiten und fand Eingang in viele Stammeskulturen. Nach der Entdeckung Amerikas brachten ihn die Kolonialmächte auch in die neue Welt.
Er diente dem Menschen seit Jahrtausenden zur Inspiration, zur Berauschung oder als Heilmittel. In vielen Gesellschaften und Gesellschaftsschichten, vom Eingeborendorf bis zu Intellektuellenkreisen, kann man von einer eigenen Hanfkultur sprechen. Bei vielen Naturvölkern ist er bis heute Mittelpunkt schamanischer Rituale und wichtige Medizin.
Auch in der heutigen Schulmedizin könnte der Hanf eine wichtige Rolle spielen. So kann er zum Beispiel verlässlicher als jede andere Arznei die Übelkeit, die im Verlauf einer Chemotherapie auftritt, bekämpfen. Auch in die ayurvedische Medizin und in die
Begriffserklärungen
Droge, Medizin und Rohstoff
Die Hanfpflanze
Rechtslage

www.drug-balance.com
D: dominik welters
M: dominik@domeniceau.de

ilpungolo[punto]com
Martedì, 23 Novembre 104
ilpungolo com
l'eco dei cittadini liberi
"Il mondo è stato fatto dai pazzi perché i saggi vi possano vivere."
(O. Wilde)
Prima Pagina Editoriale Fatti e Commenti Cultura Eventi Recensioni Collabora con noi! Forum Liberbook redazione@ilpungolo.com
Editoriale
LA POLITICA E IL MONDO NUOVO
di Leonardo Raito
Gli sconvolgimenti epocali seguiti agli attacchi dell'11 settembre hanno segnato l'inizio del Mondo Nuovo: un'era di incertezza dove sono stati ribaltati i concetti cardine che avevano guidato l'umanità dalla fine della seconda guerra mondiale; gli stessi concetti che avevano ispirato le teorie di fine della storia come conseguenza del termine della secolare contrapposizione tra i due massimi sistemi politici mondiali, quello capitalistico occidentale incarnato dagli USA e quello socialista incarnato dall'URSS. In
Una scuola - LIBERIA
Fatti e Commenti
I RAPPORTI DI LAVORO SONO RELAZIONI DI MERCATO
di Giorgio Bianco
Cultura
VERO O FALSO ? LE LEGGENDE METROPOLITANE
di Rossano Raspo

ilpungolo[punto]com
Martedì, 23 Novembre 104
ilpungolo com
l'eco dei cittadini liberi
"Il mondo è stato fatto dai pazzi perché i saggi vi possano vivere."
(O. Wilde)
Prima Pagina Editoriale Fatti e Commenti Cultura Eventi Recensioni Collabora con noi! Forum Liberbook redazione@ilpungolo.com
18 Novembre 2004
LA POLITICA E IL MONDO NUOVO
Preoccupa, nel panorama italiano, l'assenza di nuove leve destinate a formare la classe dirigente del domani. Menti nuove per nuovi studi, per nuove soluzioni e prospettive
Leonardo Raito
Gli sconvolgimenti epocali seguiti agli attacchi dell'11 settembre hanno segnato l'inizio del Mondo Nuovo: un'era di incertezza dove sono stati ribaltati i concetti cardine che avevano guidato l'umanità dalla fine della seconda guerra mondiale; gli stessi concetti che avevano ispirato le teorie di fine della storia come conseguenza del termine della secolare contrapposizione tra i due massimi sistemi politici mondiali, quello capitalistico occidentale incarnato dagli USA e quello socialista incarnato dall'URSS. In realtà la storia non è finita ma continua su binari diversi e obbliga i cittadini del mondo globale e globalizzato a riconsiderare le sfide, i programmi, gli stessi presupposti dell'umana esistenza. La politica del XXI secolo ha quindi la necessità di rapportarsi alla nuova realtà in modo innovativo. Nuove soluzioni e nuovi modi di fare politica, nuovi modi di coinvolgere la base popolare.
Preoccupa, nel panorama italiano, l'assenza di nuove leve destinate a formare la classe dirigente del domani. Menti nuove per nuovi studi, per nuove soluzioni e
Editoriale
08 Novembre 2004
IL PAESE DEI PRIVILEGI ANTICHI
di William Longhi
14 Giugno 2004
GUERRE, TORTURE, SPERANZE
di Giovanni Venezia
08 Aprile 2004
L'ITALIA CHE NON C'E'
di Giovanni Venezia
22 Marzo 2004
ORDINAMENTO GIUDIZIARIO: UNA RIFORMA CHE VIAGGIA SU UN TERRENO ACCIDENTATO
di Giovanni Venezia
10 Marzo 2004
LA "FAGLIA" DI HUNTINGTON
di Anna Bono
02 Marzo 2004
POLITICA, POTERE E QUESTIONE MORALE
di Giovanni Venezia
16 Febbraio 2004
LA SOLITA MUSICA PER UNA POLITICA CHE NON SI RINNOVA.....
di Giovanni Venezia
12 Febbraio 2004
MAGISTRATURA E POLITICA: LO SCONTRO INFINITO
di Vagnone di Trofarello

www.ilpungolo.com
D: virgilio venezia
A: mavida snc **M:** virgilio.venezia@mavida.com

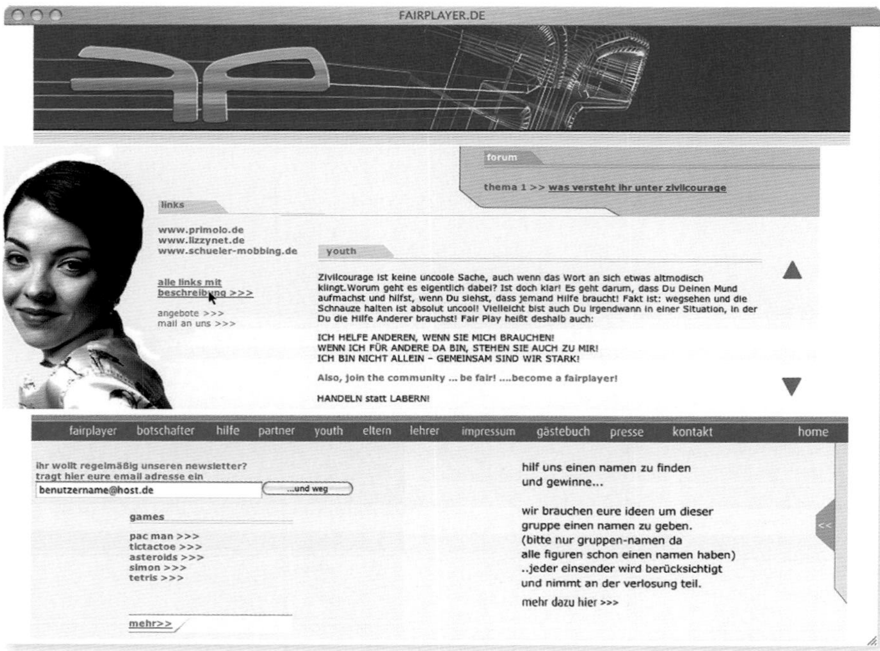
FAIRPLAYER.DE
forum
thema 1 >> was versteht ihr unter zivilcourage
links
www.primolo.de
www.lizzynet.de
www.schueler-mobbing.de
alle links mit beschreibung >>>
angebote >>>
mail an uns >>>
youth
Zivilcourage ist keine uncoole Sache, auch wenn das Wort an sich etwas altmodisch klingt. Worum geht es eigentlich dabei? Ist doch klar! Es geht darum, dass Du Deinen Mund aufmachst und hilfst, wenn Du siehst, dass jemand Hilfe braucht! Fakt ist: wegsehen und die Schnauze halten ist absolut uncool! Vielleicht bist auch Du irgendwann in einer Situation, in der Du die Hilfe Anderer brauchst! Fair Play heißt deshalb auch:
ICH HELFE ANDEREN, WENN SIE MICH BRAUCHEN!
WENN ICH FÜR ANDERE DA BIN, STEHEN SIE AUCH ZU MIR!
ICH BIN NICHT ALLEIN – GEMEINSAM SIND WIR STARK!
Also, join the community ... be fair! ....become a fairplayer!
HANDELN statt LABERN!
fairplayer botschafter hilfe partner youth eltern lehrer impressum gästebuch presse kontakt home
ihr wollt regelmäßig unseren newsletter? tragt hier eure email adresse ein
benutzername@host.de
...und weg
games
pac man >>>
tictactoe >>>
asteroids >>>
simon >>>
tetris >>>
mehr>>
hilf uns einen namen zu finden und gewinne...
wir brauchen eure ideen um dieser gruppe einen namen zu geben. (bitte nur gruppen-namen da alle figuren schon einen namen haben) ..jeder einsender wird berücksichtigt und nimmt an der verlosung teil.
mehr dazu hier >>>

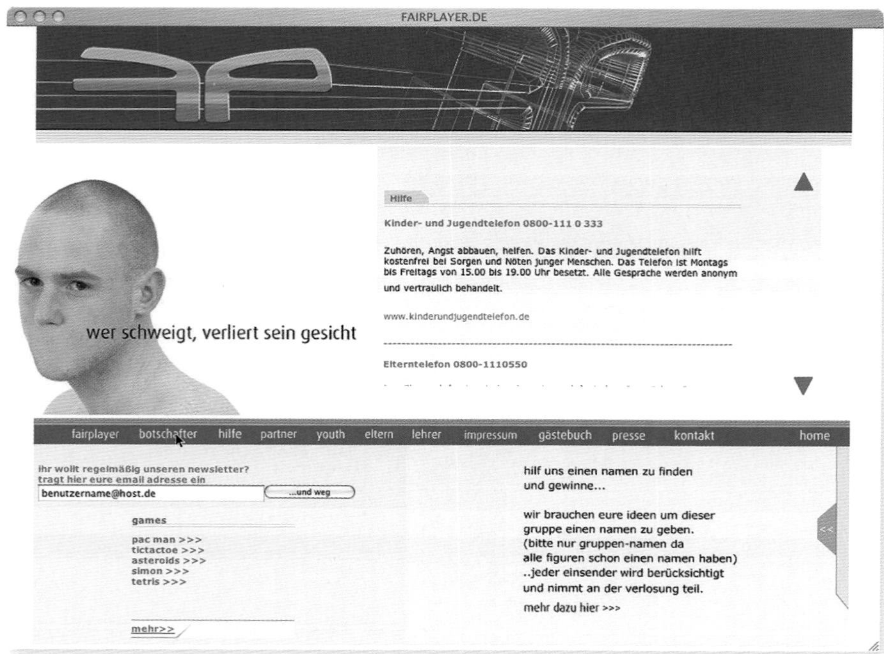
FAIRPLAYER.DE
Hilfe
Kinder- und Jugendtelefon 0800-111 0 333
Zuhören, Angst abbauen, helfen. Das Kinder- und Jugendtelefon hilft kostenfrei bei Sorgen und Nöten junger Menschen. Das Telefon ist Montags bis Freitags von 15.00 bis 19.00 Uhr besetzt. Alle Gespräche werden anonym und vertraulich behandelt.
www.kinderundjugendtelefon.de
Elterntelefon 0800-1110550
wer schweigt, verliert sein gesicht
fairplayer botschafter hilfe partner youth eltern lehrer impressum gästebuch presse kontakt home
ihr wollt regelmäßig unseren newsletter? tragt hier eure email adresse ein
benutzername@host.de
...und weg
games
pac man >>>
tictactoe >>>
asteroids >>>
simon >>>
tetris >>>
mehr>>
hilf uns einen namen zu finden und gewinne...
wir brauchen eure ideen um dieser gruppe einen namen zu geben. (bitte nur gruppen-namen da alle figuren schon einen namen haben) ..jeder einsender wird berücksichtigt und nimmt an der verlosung teil.
mehr dazu hier >>>

www.fairplayer.de
D: martin starke
A: banane design **M:** martin@banane-design.de

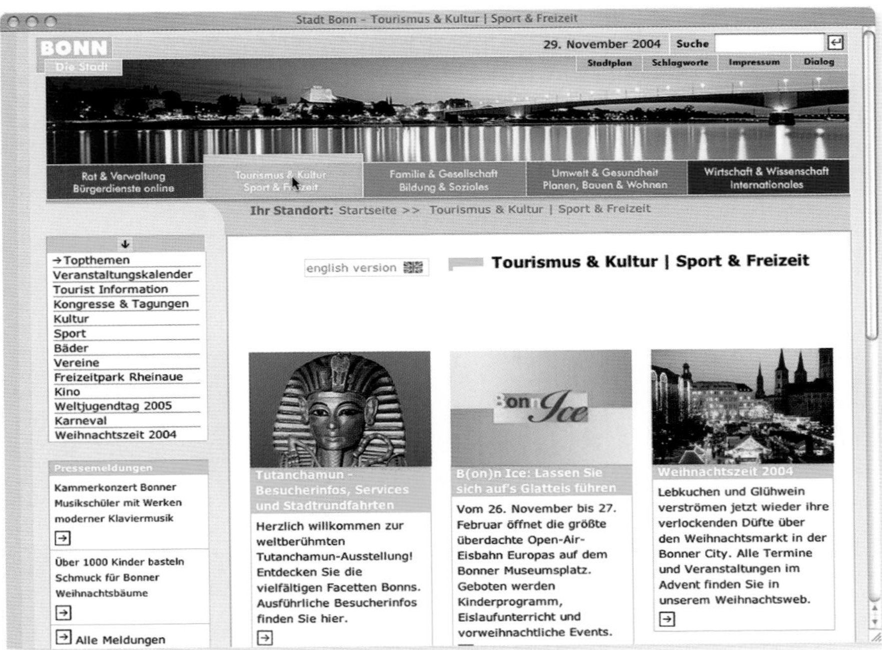
Stadt Bonn - Tourismus & Kultur | Sport & Freizeit
BONN
Die Stadt
29. November 2004
Suche
Stadtplan
Schlagworte
Impressum
Dialog
Rat & Verwaltung
Bürgerdienste online
Tourismus & Kultur
Sport & Freizeit
Familie & Gesellschaft
Bildung & Soziales
Umwelt & Gesundheit
Planen, Bauen & Wohnen
Wirtschaft & Wissenschaft
Internationales
Ihr Standort: Startseite >> Tourismus & Kultur | Sport & Freizeit
→Topthemen
Veranstaltungskalender
Tourist Information
Kongresse & Tagungen
Kultur
Sport
Bäder
Vereine
Freizeitpark Rheinaue
Kino
Weltjugendtag 2005
Karneval
Weihnachtszeit 2004
Pressemeldungen
Kammerkonzert Bonner Musikschüler mit Werken moderner Klaviermusik
Über 1000 Kinder basteln Schmuck für Bonner Weihnachtsbäume
Alle Meldungen
english version
Tourismus & Kultur | Sport & Freizeit
Tutanchamun - Besucherinfos, Services und Stadtrundfahrten
Herzlich willkommen zur weltberühmten Tutanchamun-Ausstellung! Entdecken Sie die vielfältigen Facetten Bonns. Ausführliche Besucherinfos finden Sie hier.
B(on)n Ice: Lassen Sie sich auf's Glatteis führen
Vom 26. November bis 27. Februar öffnet die größte überdachte Open-Air-Eisbahn Europas auf dem Bonner Museumsplatz. Geboten werden Kinderprogramm, Eislaufunterricht und vorweihnachtliche Events.
Weihnachtszeit 2004
Lebkuchen und Glühwein verströmen jetzt wieder ihre verlockenden Düfte über den Weihnachtsmarkt in der Bonner City. Alle Termine und Veranstaltungen im Advent finden Sie in unserem Weihnachtsweb.

Stadt Bonn - Kultur
BONN
Die Stadt
29. November 2004
Suche
Stadtplan
Schlagworte
Impressum
Dialog
Rat & Verwaltung
Bürgerdienste online
Tourismus & Kultur
Sport & Freizeit
Familie & Gesellschaft
Bildung & Soziales
Umwelt & Gesundheit
Planen, Bauen & Wohnen
Wirtschaft & Wissenschaft
Internationales
Ihr Standort: Startseite >> Tourismus & Kultur | Sport & Freizeit >> Kultur
Topthemen
Veranstaltungskalender
Tourist Information
Kongresse & Tagungen
→Kultur
Beethoven
Musik
Theater
Bonner Sommer
Museen
Bildende Kunst
Literatur
Film/Video
Kulturzentren
Kulturlinks
Stadtarchiv
Stadtbibliothek
Sport
Bäder
Vereine
Freizeitpark Rheinaue
Kino
Weltjugendtag 2005
Karneval
Weihnachtszeit 2004
Pressemeldungen
05. Mai 2004
english version
Kultur
Bonn ist Kultur
Zunächst kommt fast jedem die Musik in den Sinn, wenn von der Kulturstadt Bonn die Rede ist. Das Erbe Ludwig van Beethovens, der 1770 hier geboren wurde, verpflichtet. Neben dem jährlich stattfindenden Internationalen Beethovenfest und den Konzerten des Orchesters der Beethovenhalle bietet Bonn eine kulturelle Infrastruktur, die national wie international die Besucher in ihren Bann zieht.
So haben sich etwa die großen Häuser der Museumsmeile zu einem beliebten Publikumsmagneten entwickelt. In der Bonner Innenstadt laden die City-Museen, dicht beieinander liegend und fußläufig erreichbar, ein. Im Norden Bonns haben sich sieben weitere Institutionen im Kunstcarré zusammengeschlossen.
Auf eine lange Tradition bis in die Zeit der Kurfürsten blickt Bonn auch als Theaterstadt zurück. 1826 bauten sich die kunstsinnigen Bürger selbst das erste Schauspielhaus. Auch die private Theaterszene kann sich sehen lassen.
Zu den Highlights des kulturellen Bonns gehört auch die Bonner Biennale , der 1971 aus der Taufe gehobene "Bonner Sommer",

www.bonn.de
D: christine schwarting **C:** tatjana schmalz **P:** peter wafzig
A: seitenbau **M:** wafzig@seitenbau.com

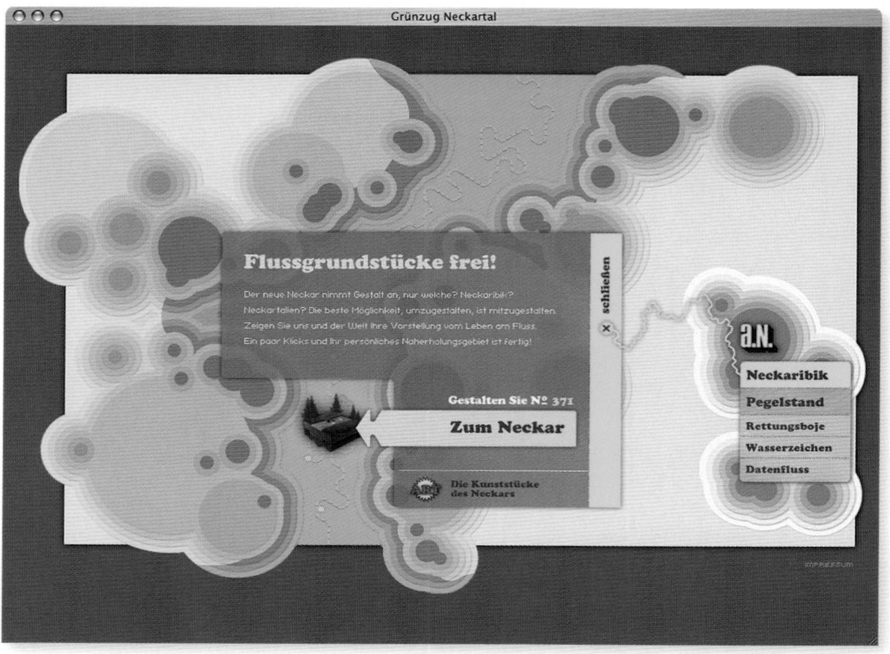
Grünzug Neckartal
Flussgrundstücke frei!
Der neue Neckar nimmt Gestalt an, nur welche? Neckaribik? Neckartalien? Die beste Möglichkeit, umzugestalten, ist mitzugestalten. Zeigen Sie uns und der Welt Ihre Vorstellung vom Leben am Fluss. Ein paar Klicks und Ihr persönliches Naherholungsgebiet ist fertig!
schließen
Gestalten Sie № 371
Zum Neckar
Die Kunststücke des Neckars
a.N.
Neckaribik
Pegelstand
Rettungsboje
Wasserzeichen
Datenfluss

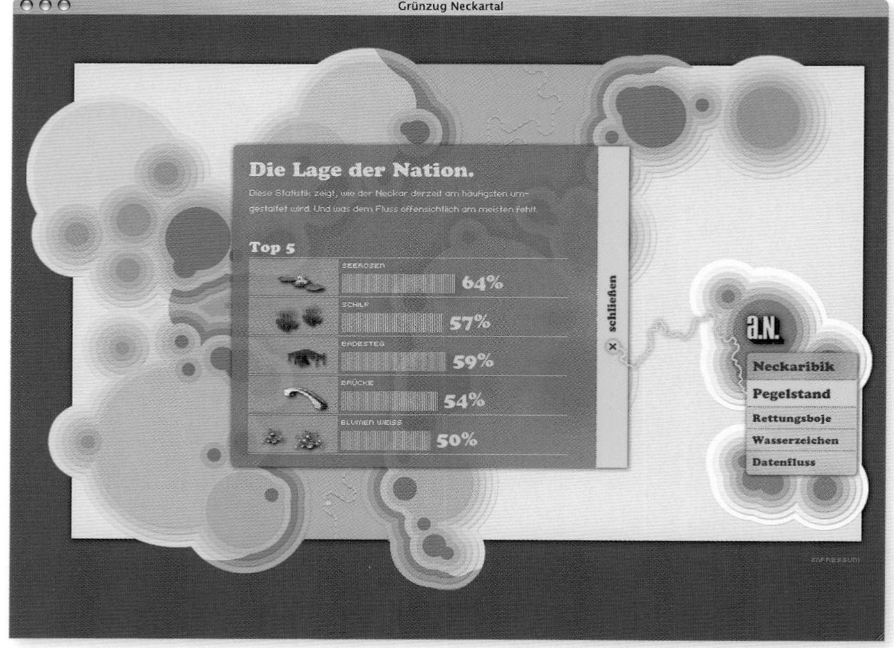
Grünzug Neckartal
Die Lage der Nation.
Diese Statistik zeigt, wie der Neckar derzeit am häufigsten umgestaltet wird. Und was dem Fluss offensichtlich am meisten fehlt.
Top 5
SEEROSEN 64%
SCHILF 57%
BADESTEG 59%
BRÜCKE 54%
BLUMEN WEISS 50%
schließen
a.N.
Neckaribik
Pegelstand
Rettungsboje
Wasserzeichen
Datenfluss

www.am-neckar.de
D: stefan walz **C:** stefanie welker **P:** dorothea feurer, brigitte dingler
A: jung von matt ag **M:** neckar@jvm.de

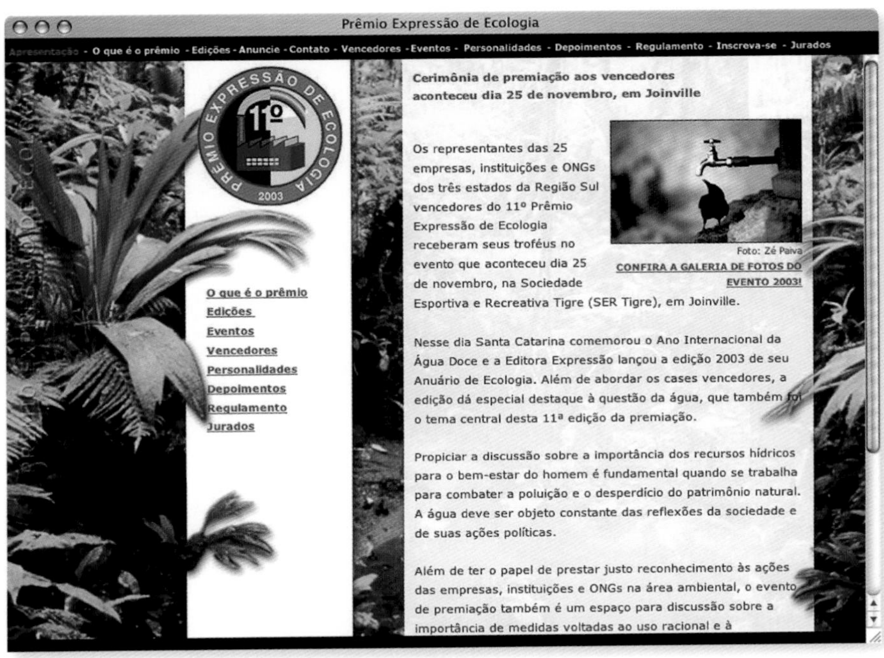
Prêmio Expressão de Ecologia
Apresentação - O que é o prêmio - Edições - Anuncie - Contato - Vencedores - Eventos - Personalidades - Depoimentos - Regulamento - Inscreva-se - Jurados
PRÊMIO EXPRESSÃO DE ECOLOGIA 11º 2003
O que é o prêmio
Edições
Eventos
Vencedores
Personalidades
Depoimentos
Regulamento
Jurados
Cerimônia de premiação aos vencedores aconteceu dia 25 de novembro, em Joinville
Os representantes das 25 empresas, instituições e ONGs dos três estados da Região Sul vencedores do 11º Prêmio Expressão de Ecologia receberam seus troféus no evento que aconteceu dia 25 de novembro, na Sociedade Esportiva e Recreativa Tigre (SER Tigre), em Joinville.
Foto: Zé Paiva
CONFIRA A GALERIA DE FOTOS DO EVENTO 2003!
Nesse dia Santa Catarina comemorou o Ano Internacional da Água Doce e a Editora Expressão lançou a edição 2003 de seu Anuário de Ecologia. Além de abordar os cases vencedores, a edição dá especial destaque à questão da água, que também foi o tema central desta 11ª edição da premiação.
Propiciar a discussão sobre a importância dos recursos hídricos para o bem-estar do homem é fundamental quando se trabalha para combater a poluição e o desperdício do patrimônio natural. A água deve ser objeto constante das reflexões da sociedade e de suas ações políticas.
Além de ter o papel de prestar justo reconhecimento às ações das empresas, instituições e ONGs na área ambiental, o evento de premiação também é um espaço para discussão sobre a importância de medidas voltadas ao uso racional e à

„Prêmio Expressão de Ecologia" wird geladen
Apresentação - O que é o prêmio - Edições - Anuncie - Contato - Vencedores - Eventos - Personalidades - Depoimentos - Regulamento - Inscreva-se - Jurados
PRÊMIO EXPRESSÃO DE ECOLOGIA 12º 2004
2003
2002 - 2001
2000 - 1999
1998 - 1997
1996 - 1995
1994 - 1993
Oportunidade de intercâmbio
Muito mais do que simples cerimônias de entrega de troféus, os eventos de premiação do Prêmio Expressão de Ecologia consolidaram-se, ao longo de dez anos, como oportunidades de encontro e troca de idéias entre empresários, ecologistas, técnicos, especialistas, políticos e ministros de meio ambiente. Reforçando o debate sobre os temas mais atuais.
2003 CONFIRA A GALERIA DE FOTOS!
No dia escolhido como data comemorativa ao Ano Internacional da Água Doce, terça-feira, 25 de novembro, o evento de premiação do 11º Prêmio Expressão de Ecologia evidenciou a preocupação dos setores produtivo e público dos três estados do Sul com o uso racional e a preservação desse recurso fundamental à vida e cujo risco de escassez é cada vez maior. Realizado na sede da Sociedade Esportiva e Recreativa Tigre, em Joinville, o evento reuniu mais de 200 convidados, entre eles os representantes das 25 empresas, instituições e órgãos públicos vencedores da 11ª edição da premiação, na qual o tema mais abordado nos trabalhos inscritos foi exatamente a questão da água.
Representante da ministra do Meio Ambiente, Marina Silva, o secretário nacional de recursos hídricos, João Bosco Senra, destacou em seu discurso as

www.expressao.com.br/ecologia
D: luciano guedes
A: ápice tecnologia **M:** lu75br@yahoo.co.uk

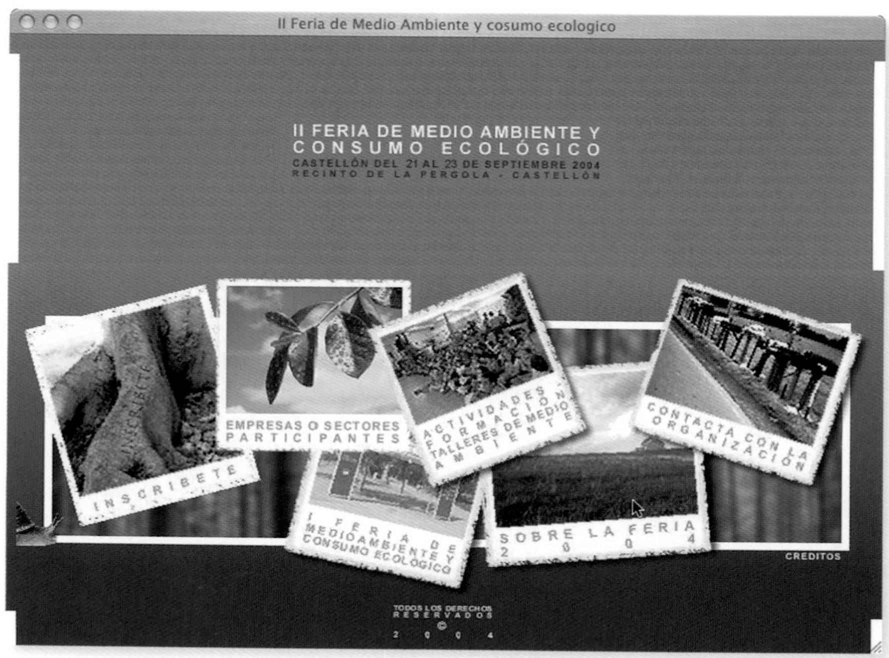
II Feria de Medio Ambiente y cosumo ecologico
II FERIA DE MEDIO AMBIENTE Y
CONSUMO ECOLÓGICO
CASTELLÓN DEL 21 AL 23 DE SEPTIEMBRE 2004
RECINTO DE LA PERGOLA - CASTELLÓN
INSCRIBETE
EMPRESAS O SECTORES PARTICIPANTES
ACTIVIDADES FORMACIÓN TALLERES DE MEDIO AMBIENTE
CONTACTA CON LA ORGANIZACIÓN
I FERIA DE MEDIOAMBIENTE Y CONSUMO ECOLÓGICO
SOBRE LA FERIA 2004
CREDITOS
TODOS LOS DERECHOS RESERVADOS
© 2004

II Feria de Medio Ambiente y cosumo ecologico
II FERIA DE MEDIO AMBIENTE Y
CONSUMO ECOLÓGICO
CASTELLÓN DEL 21 AL 23 DE SEPTIEMBRE 2004
RECINTO DE LA PERGOLA - CASTELLÓN
MENU
SOBRE LA FERIA 2004
La Feria 2004
Circuitos
FCC
FOMENTO DE CONSTRUCCIONES Y CONTRATAS, S.A.
PROMA S.L.
Qué
La II Feria Profesional de Medio Ambiente va a reunir a las principales empresas dedicadas al negocio ambiental (desde el reciclaje de plástico y papel a la depuración de aguas), dedicando también un espacio al consumo ecológico (ropa reciclada, pinturas ecológicas, muebles ergonómicos...).
Se trata de crear un foro de intercambio y contacto entre las firmas que se dedican los servicios medioambientales de la Comunidad Valenciana y las empresas que requieren estas prestaciones. Este foro conseguir· difundir y promocionar servicios industriales
alternativos a los tradicionales, con soluciones que respetan el entorno, tanto en el uso de materias primas como en el consumo de fuentes de
TODOS LOS DERECHOS RESERVADOS
© 2004

www.imorganizacion.com/fm
D: iskiam jara hueso **P:** i+m organizacion
A: iskiamjara **M:** info@iskiamjara.com

Pet Sematary – Friedhof der Kuscheltiere
Pet Sematary
Friedhof der Kuscheltiere
In der Enge der Zuchtkäfige sind stereotype Zwangsbewegungen, Selbstverstümmelung und Kannibalismus unter den Tieren Normalität.
Mehr dazu
Übernehmen Sie eine kostenlose Patenschaft für ein totes Pelztier und zünden Sie eine Grabkerze an.
2024 von 10.000 Gräbern haben bereits einen Paten.
Hintergrundinformationen lesen
Ton aus

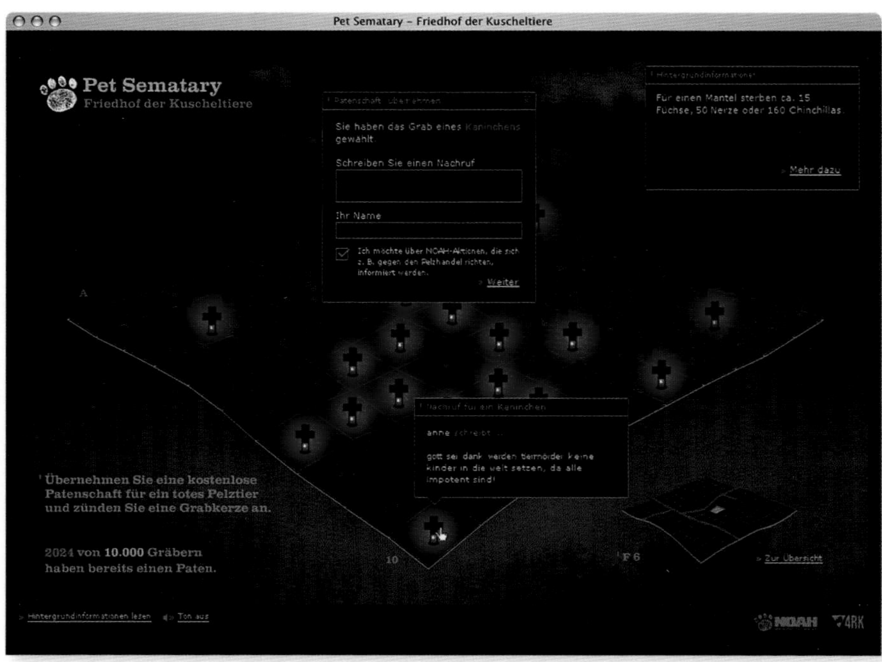

Pet Sematary – Friedhof der Kuscheltiere
Pet Sematary
Friedhof der Kuscheltiere
Sie haben das Grab eines Kaninchens gewählt.
Schreiben Sie einen Nachruf
Ihr Name
Ich möchte über NOAH-Aktionen, die sich z. B. gegen den Pelzhandel richten, informiert werden.
Weiter
Für einen Mantel sterben ca. 15 Füchse, 50 Nerze oder 160 Chinchillas.
Mehr dazu
Nachruf für ein Kaninchen
anne schreibt ...
gott sei dank werden tiermörder keine kinder in die welt setzen, da alle impotent sind!
Zur Übersicht
Übernehmen Sie eine kostenlose Patenschaft für ein totes Pelztier und zünden Sie eine Grabkerze an.
2024 von 10.000 Gräbern haben bereits einen Paten.
Hintergrundinformationen lesen
Ton aus

www.petsematary.de
D: anna mentzel, christophe stoll **C:** florian finke
A: fork unstable media gmbh **M:** hamburg@fork.de

BASTHIES
DAYSHIFT
01 02 03 04 05 06 07 08

CALLA
HOME
DAYSHIFT
NIGHTSHIFT
PEOPLE
TRAVEL
WHATS NEW

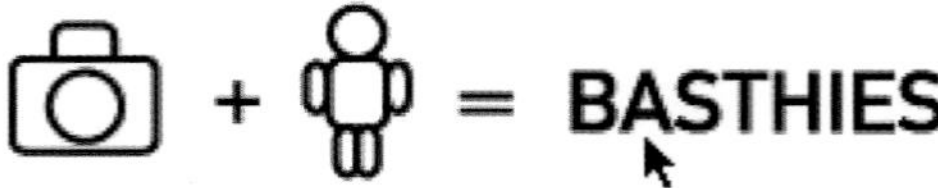
| BASTHIES | PHOTOGRAPHER |
+ = BASTHIES

www.basthies.de/basindex2.html
D: christian brodack
A: bro.design **M:** bro@basthies.de

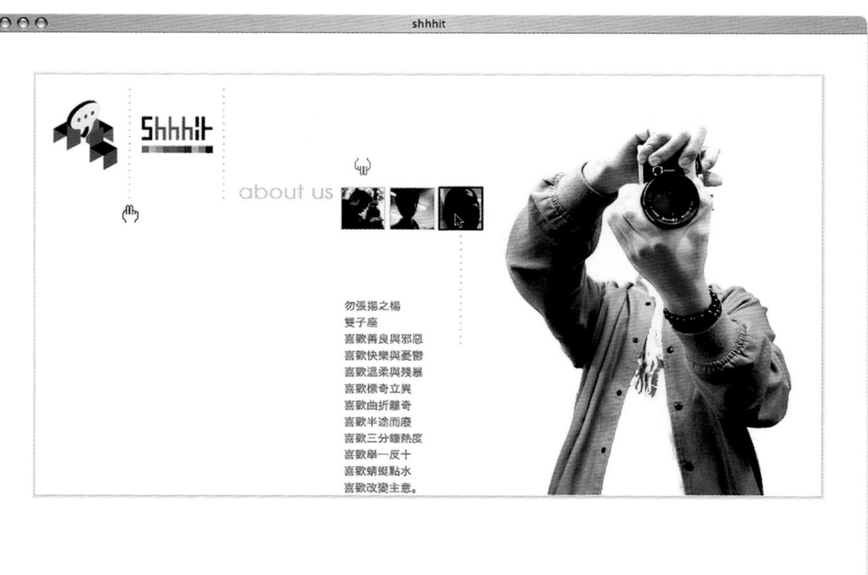
shhhit
Shhhit
about us
勿張揚之楊
雙子座
喜歡善良與邪惡
喜歡快樂與憂鬱
喜歡溫柔與殘暴
喜歡標奇立異
喜歡曲折離奇
喜歡半途而廢
喜歡三分鐘熱度
喜歡舉一反十
喜歡蜻蜓點水
喜歡改變主意。

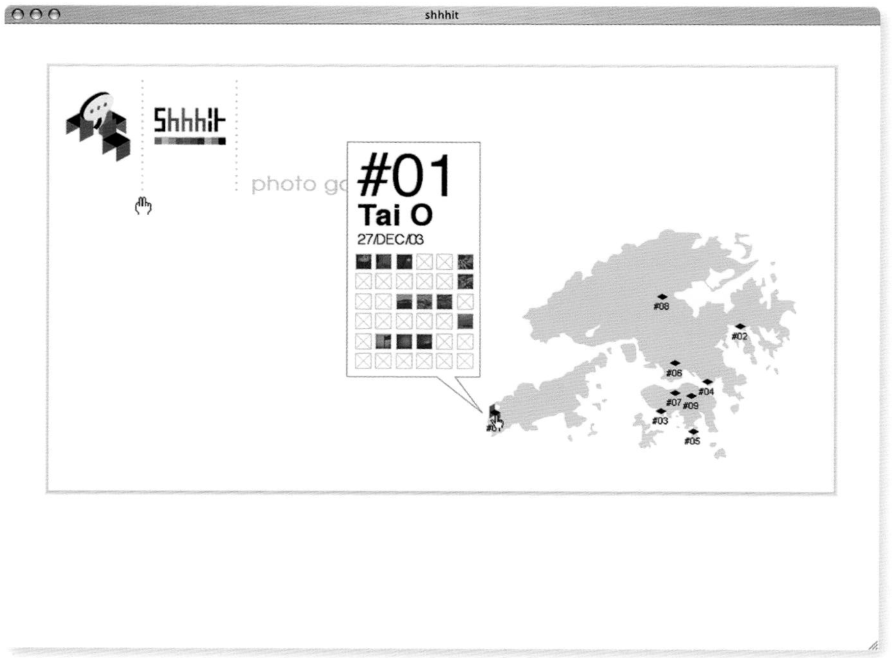
shhhit
Shhhit
photo g
#01
Tai O
27/DEC/03
#08
#02
#06
#04
#07
#09
#03
#05

www.shhhit.com
D: mark
A: shhhit **M:** info@shhhit.com

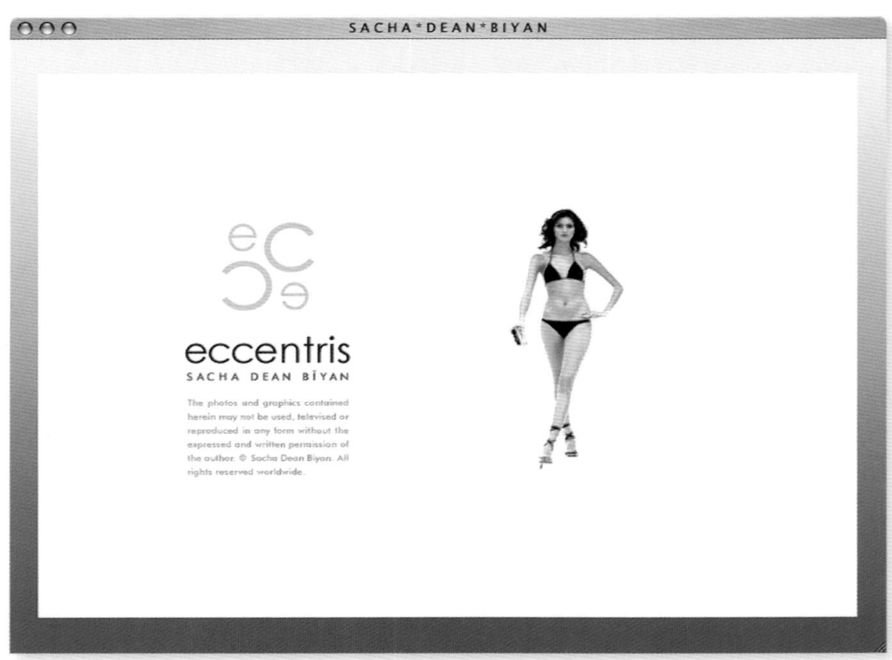
SACHA*DEAN*BIYAN
eccentris
SACHA DEAN BĪYAN
The photos and graphics contained herein may not be used, televised or reproduced in any form without the expressed and written permission of the author. © Sacha Dean Biyan. All rights reserved worldwide.

SACHA*DEAN*BIYAN
BEHIND THE LENS
Every photograph has its own story- not just in the picture but also behind it. Click the boxes below to view some exclusive footage behind the lens. Photos by Roberto Nemanis and Bia Vogt.
ABOUT
PERSPECTIVE
AT WORK
INTERVIEWS
SPIRITUS MUNDI
CONTACT
DOWNLOADS
E-CARDS
SHOP
CREDITS
LEGAL NOTICE
DETOUR

www.eccentris.com
D: vas sloutchevsky **C:** josh ott **P:** jeremy berg
A: firstborn multimedia **M:** www.firstbornmultimedia.com

Samo Vidic - Photography
MARKO GRILC
PEOPLE SNOW/BIKE/WATER ACTION PLACES INFO
LAST UPDATE: 20.08.2004
SET 01 - 02

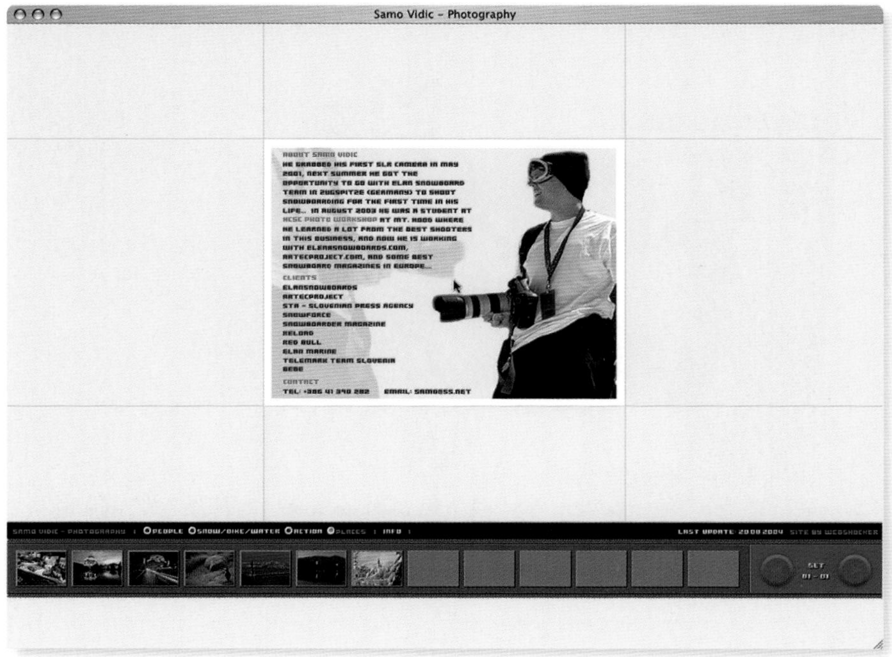
Samo Vidic - Photography
ABOUT SAMO VIDIC
HE GRABBED HIS FIRST SLR CAMERA IN MAY 2001, NEXT SUMMER HE GOT THE OPPORTUNITY TO GO WITH ELAN SNOWBOARD TEAM IN ZUGSPITZE (GERMANY) TO SHOOT SNOWBOARDING FOR THE FIRST TIME IN HIS LIFE... IN AUGUST 2003 HE WAS A STUDENT AT HCSC PHOTO WORKSHOP AT MT. HOOD WHERE HE LEARNED A LOT FROM THE BEST SHOOTERS IN THIS BUSINESS, AND NOW HE IS WORKING WITH ELANSNOWBOARDS.COM, ARTECPROJECT.COM, AND SOME BEST SNOWBOARD MAGAZINES IN EUROPE...
CLIENTS
ELANSNOWBOARDS
ARTECPROJECT
STA - SLOVENIAN PRESS AGENCY
SNOWFORCE
SNOWBOARDER MAGAZINE
RELOAD
RED BULL
ELAN MARINE
TELEMARK TEAM SLOVENIA
BEBE
CONTACT
TEL: +386 41 390 282
PEOPLE SNOW/BIKE/WATER ACTION PLACES INFO
LAST UPDATE: 20.08.2004
SET 01 - 01

www.onlysamo.com
D: matjaz valentar
A: webshocker **M:** www.webshocker.net

.....................:::hello!
UBS
girls issue

.......::: hello: the girls issue
>>
LOVE?

www.hellozine.com
D: lutz erian
M: utz@hellozine.com

MISHA GRAVENOR PHOTOGRAPHY
MISHA GRAVENOR
> OPEN MENU

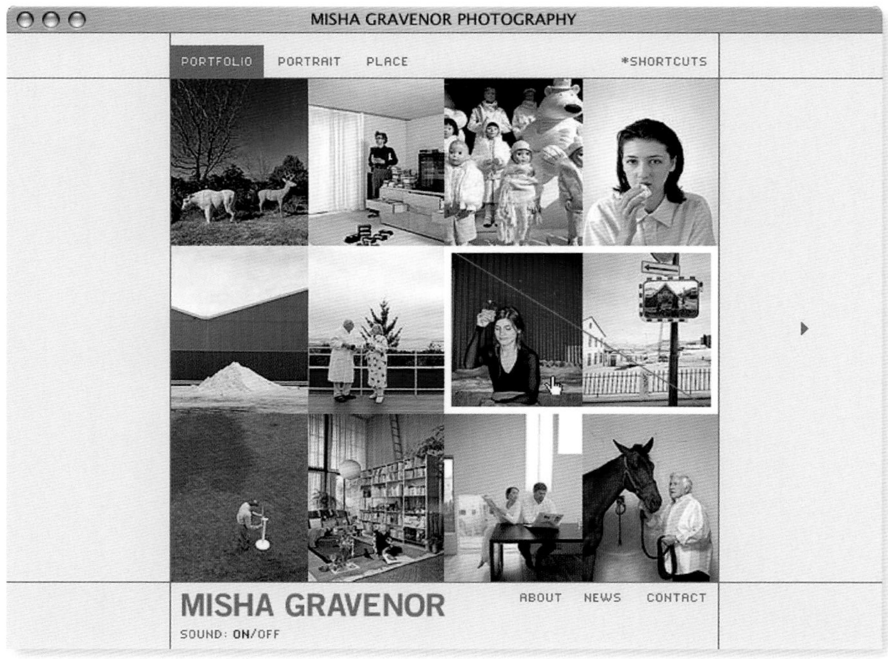
MISHA GRAVENOR PHOTOGRAPHY
PORTFOLIO
PORTRAIT
PLACE
*SHORTCUTS
MISHA GRAVENOR
SOUND: ON/OFF
ABOUT
NEWS
CONTACT

www.mishagravenor.com
D: noah wall
A: knowawall design **M:** www.knowawall.com

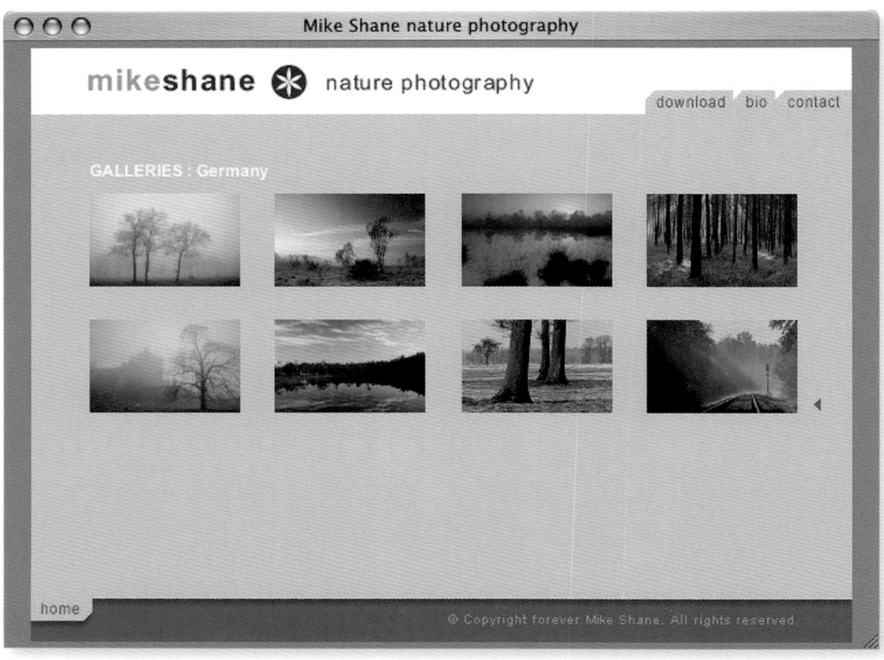
Mike Shane nature photography
mikeshane nature photography
download bio contact
GALLERIES : Germany
home
© Copyright forever Mike Shane. All rights reserved.

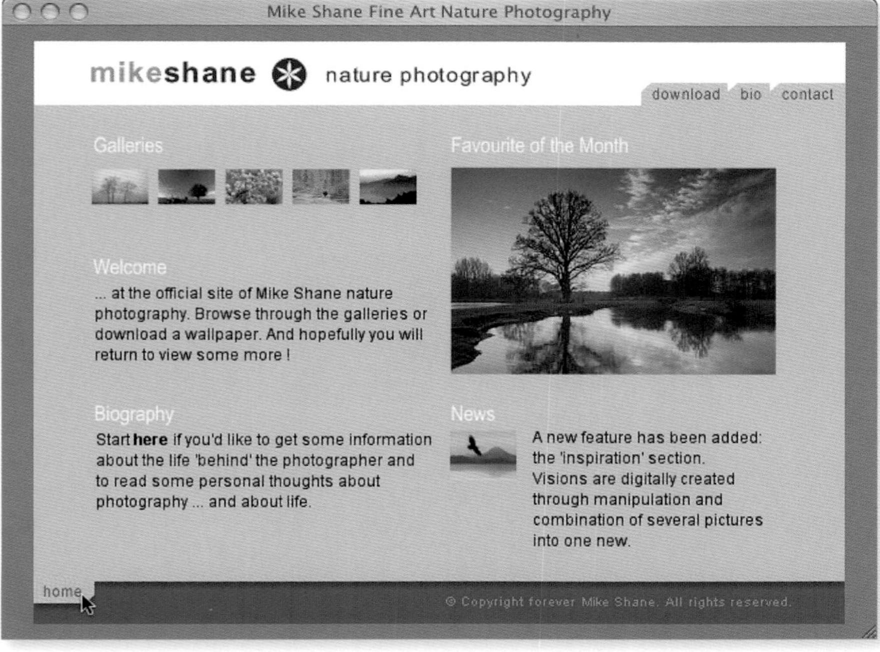
Mike Shane Fine Art Nature Photography
mikeshane nature photography
download bio contact
Galleries
Favourite of the Month
Welcome
... at the official site of Mike Shane nature photography. Browse through the galleries or download a wallpaper. And hopefully you will return to view some more !
Biography
Start here if you'd like to get some information about the life 'behind' the photographer and to read some personal thoughts about photography ... and about life.
News
A new feature has been added: the 'inspiration' section. Visions are digitally created through manipulation and combination of several pictures into one new.
home
© Copyright forever Mike Shane. All rights reserved.

www.omdesign.nl/thehealingpictures/

D: steef hanemaaijer
A: omdesign **M:** s_hanemaaijer@hotmail.com

ku-ku.it
ku-ku
> istanbul
andalusia
austria
barche
favignana
micromondo
Raffle man in Istanbul
info
contact
links

ku-ku.it
ku-ku
Viaggio in Andalusia, Spagna e Portogallo. Estate 2002.
> istanbul
andalusia
austria
barche
favignana
micromondo
beja - vecchio con bimba
Download
tutti i diritti sono riservati

www.ku-ku.it
D: roberta casaligi
A: twirl **M:** roberta@twirl.it

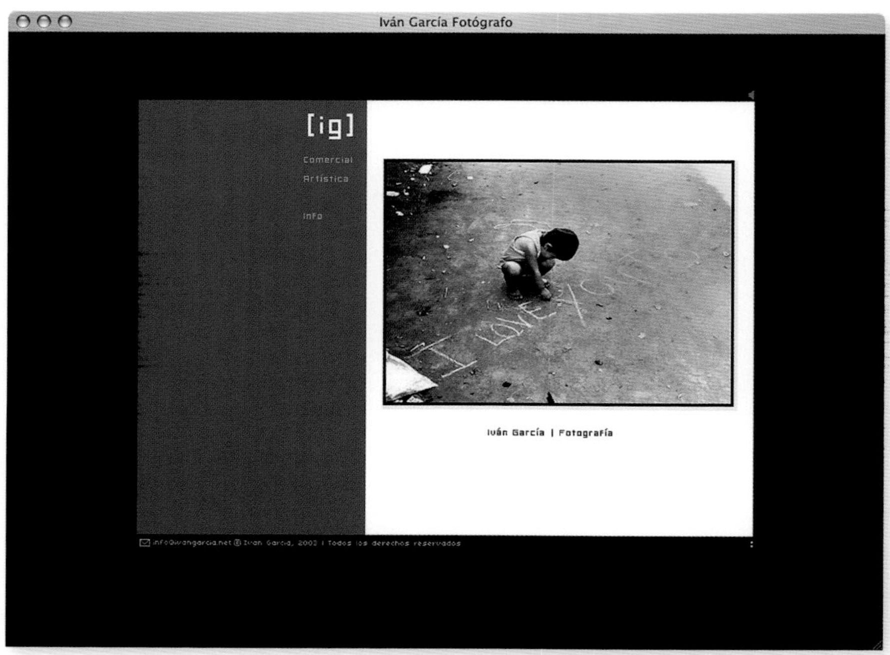
Iván García Fotógrafo
[ig]
Comercial
Artística
Info
Iván García | Fotografía
info@ivangarcia.net © Iván García, 2003 | Todos los derechos reservados

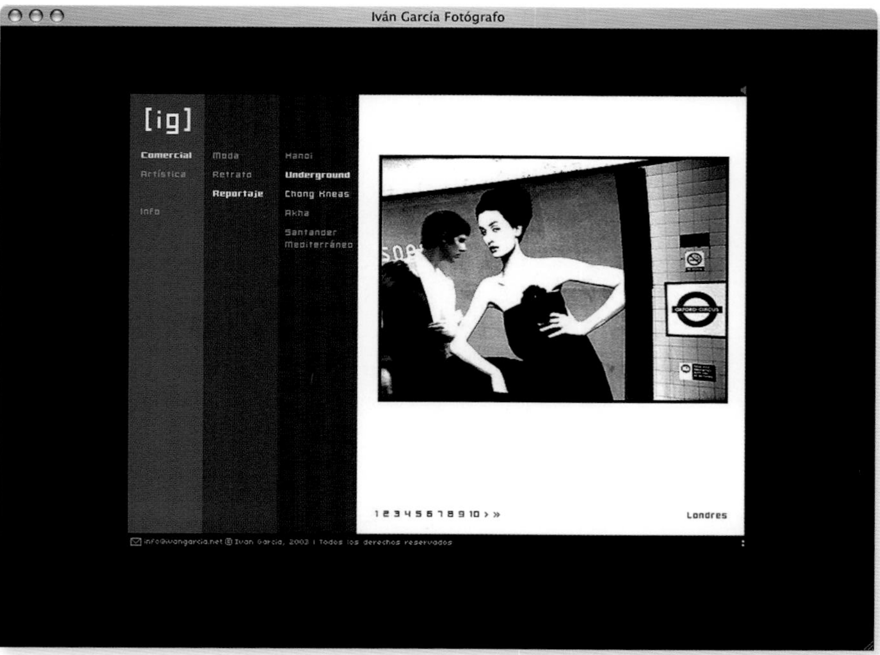
Iván García Fotógrafo
[ig]
Comercial
Artística
Info
Moda
Retrato
Reportaje
Hanoi
Underground
Chong Kneas
Akha
Santander Mediterráneo
1 2 3 4 5 6 7 8 9 10 > »
Londres
info@ivangarcia.net © Iván García, 2003 | Todos los derechos reservados

www.ivangarcia.net
D: miguel ángel moya **C:** cristina muñoz
A: puntoos **M:** info@puntoos.com

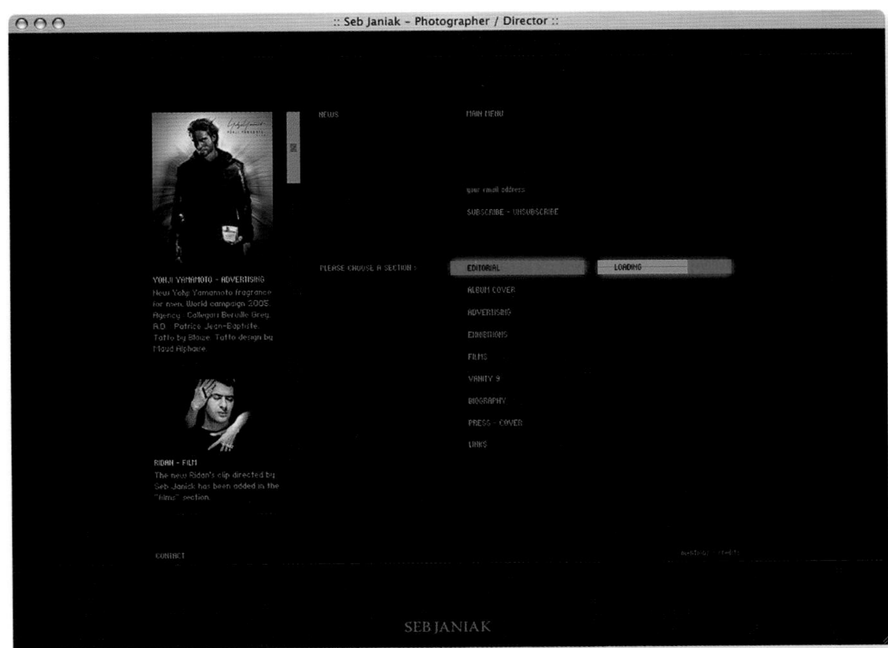
:: Seb Janiak - Photographer / Director ::
NEWS
MAIN MENU
SUBSCRIBE - UNSUBSCRIBE
PLEASE CHOOSE A SECTION :
EDITORIAL
LOADING
ALBUM COVER
ADVERTISING
EXHIBITIONS
FILMS
VANITY 9
BIOGRAPHY
PRESS - COVER
LINKS
YOHJI YAMAMOTO - ADVERTISING
RIDAN - FILM
CONTACT
SEB JANIAK

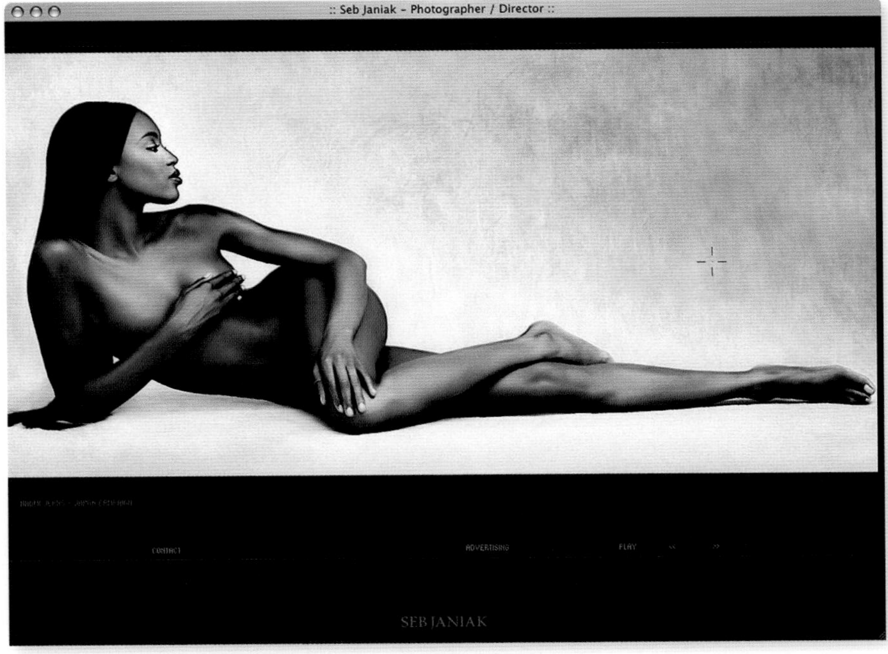
:: Seb Janiak - Photographer / Director ::
CONTACT
ADVERTISING
PLAY
SEB JANIAK

www.sebjaniak.com

D: philippe giuntini **C:** guillaume barbaise **P:** seb janiak, philippe giuntini
A: datakick **M:** philippe@datakick.com

Ronny Knight Photography
RONNY KNIGHT
Menu
Fashion

Ronny Knight Photography
RONNY KNIGHT
Menu
Lifestyle
Fashion
Lifestyle
Editorial
Places
Things
Contact

www.ronnyknight.com
D: destin young **C:** destin young
A: penabrand **M:** pyrogen@mac.com

PICTURESTATION :::::: RECORDING LIFE THROUGH THE LENS
| PICTURESTATION.CO.UK :: THE PHOTOGRAPHERS' WEBSITE
| GALLERY
picturestation
>>> PS - 1.01
>>> PS - 1.02
>>> PS - 1.03
>>> PS - 1.04
>>> PS - 1.05
>>> PS - 1.06
> RECORDING LIFE THROUGH THE LENS. VOLUME 02-2004
> HOME
> ABOUT
FOR PHOTOGRAPHERS
> GET YOUR PORTFOLIO ONLINE :: SIGN-UP TODAY
>>> COLOURS
CLICK HERE TO LAUNCH
> GALLERY 1
> GALLERY 2
> GALLERY 3
> GALLERY 4
> GALLERY 5
> SUBMISSIONS
> LINKS
> ARCHIVE
| PICTUREDESK

PICTURESTATION :::::: RECORDING LIFE THROUGH THE LENS
| PICTURESTATION.CO.UK :: THE PHOTOGRAPHERS' WEBSITE
| GALLERY
PICTURESTATION: THE PHOTOGRAP...
| 0 | 1 | 2 | 3 | 4 | 5 | 6 | 7 | 8 | ABOUT | CONTACT |
picturestation
recording life through the lens
> GALLERY 4
> GALLERY 5
> SUBMISSIONS
> LINKS
> ARCHIVE
| PICTUREDESK

www.picturestation.co.uk
D: jonathan hobson
A: hangar17 new media **M:** info@hangar17.net

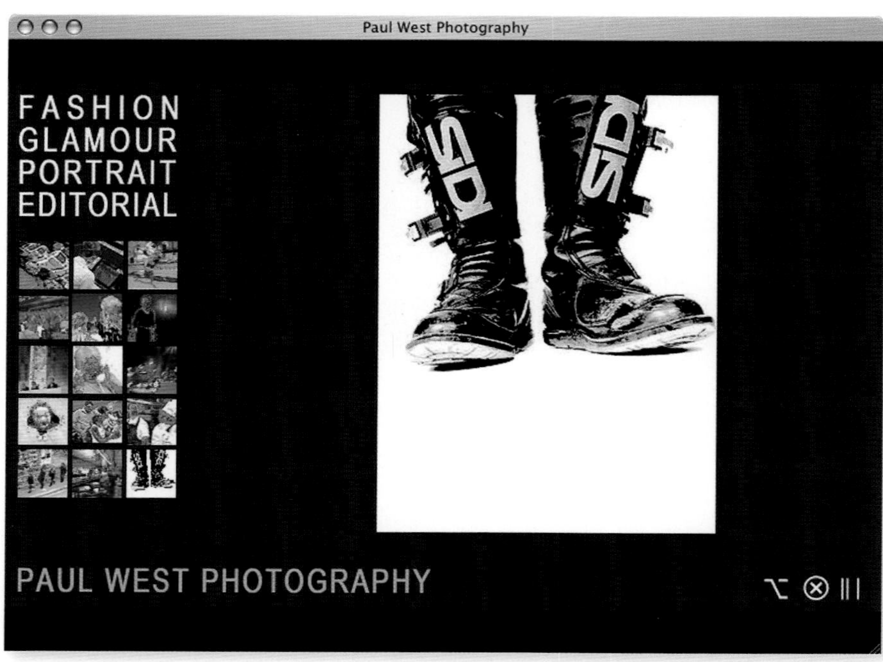
Paul West Photography
FASHION
GLAMOUR
PORTRAIT
EDITORIAL
PAUL WEST PHOTOGRAPHY

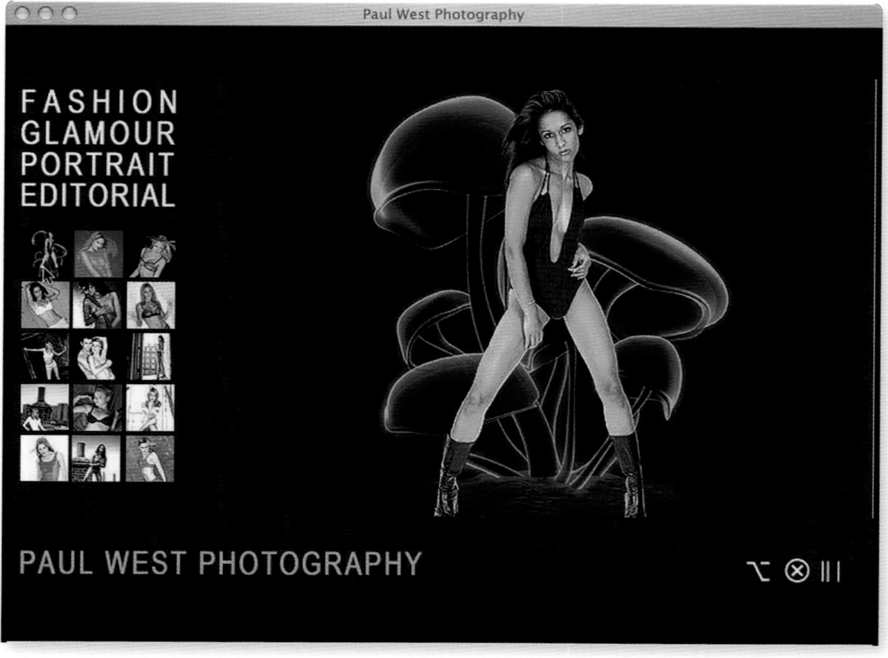
Paul West Photography
FASHION
GLAMOUR
PORTRAIT
EDITORIAL
PAUL WEST PHOTOGRAPHY

www.paulwestphotography.com
D: karl hedner
A: julian **M:** karl@julian.se

Trevor Leighton - Photographer - +44 (0) 7831 220 149
http://www.trevorleighton.com/
TrevorLeightonPhotographer
Introduction 2
Introduction
Beauty
Editorials
Campaigns
Jokers

Trevor Leighton - Photographer - +44 (0) 7831 220 149
http://www.trevorleighton.com/
TrevorLeightonPhotographer
BBC
Introduction
Beauty
Editorials
Campaigns
Jokers
Biography
Contacts

www.trevorleighton.com
D: giorgio finulli
A: natphilosophy **M:** www.fnool.com

Wacoal Company Hong Kong Limited

Wacoal

產品資料 | 關於Wacoal | Wacoal News | 內衣百科全書 | 會員特區 | 主頁 |

Wacoal News
Wacoal銷售地點

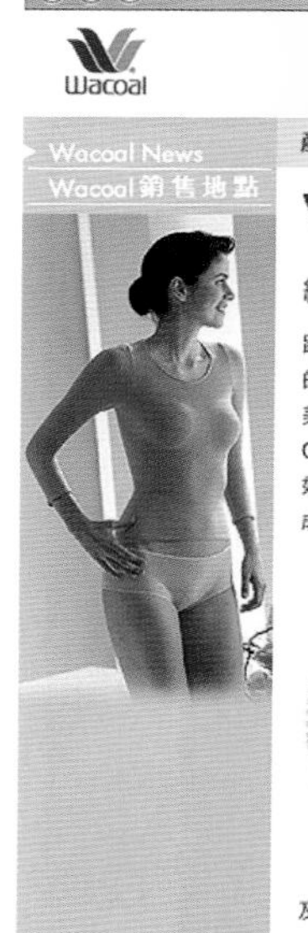

Wacoal News

news16_112003

織麗冬日倩影由Wacoal T-concept內衣為妳塑造

踏入秋冬季，時裝主流仍然圍繞強調曲線衣飾，以往的既厚又臃腫的服飾已被修身剪裁及以展現女性體態美所取代。而既可保暖又能令曲線盡現就非Wacoal T-Concept內衣莫屬！Wacoal T-Concept內衣其簡單設計及如絲細滑的質地，除了能發揮保暖內衣功能外，更可成為現今流行襯衣之百搭服飾！

T-concept™
雙重集中保暖

加厚T位
後

Wacoal T-Concept以T型保暖裁剪，於人體最易流失熱量的背部T位及腰腹部份加厚面積，防止熱量散失，發揮超卓保暖效果。而長袖型的T-Concept更採用一種名為MODAL的天然木漿纖維面料，此物料比棉質有更高吸濕性、透氣性、保濕效果及能減低靜電、耐穿之餘，其柔軟及舒適度更可媲美第二肌膚。

T-Concept的立體成型無側縫設計，與身體更貼服，加上其簡潔的cutting，易於配襯外衣，女士穿著貼身外衣時亦無臃腫感覺。今年，T-Concept備有貼膚色及黑色選擇，個別型號更有長袖型及短袖型設計，可因應外衣款式而隨意配襯。

今個秋冬瀟灑而英氣的打扮仍然係主流，穿上T-Concept配襯妳其他喜愛的服飾，既可保暖更不會令身型變得擁腫，這個冬天妳都可以昂然地瀟灑走一回！

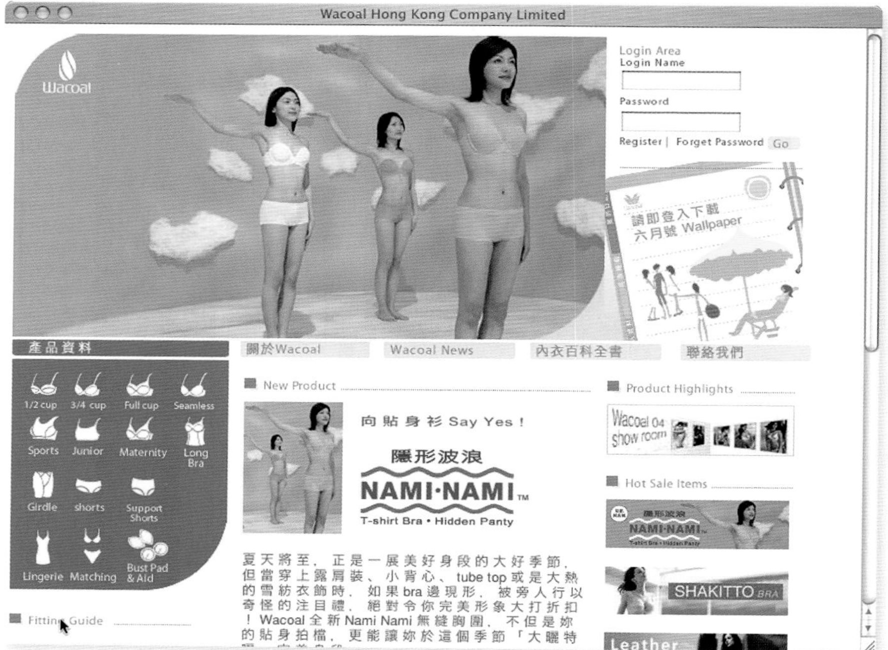
Wacoal Hong Kong Company Limited
Wacoal
Login Area
Login Name
Password
Register | Forget Password Go
請即登入下載
六月號 Wallpaper
產品資料
關於Wacoal
Wacoal News
內衣百科全書
聯絡我們
1/2 cup
3/4 cup
Full cup
Seamless
Sports
Junior
Maternity
Long Bra
Girdle
shorts
Support Shorts
Lingerie
Matching
Bust Pad & Aid
Fitting Guide
New Product
向貼身衫 Say Yes！
隱形波浪
NAMI·NAMI™
T-shirt Bra • Hidden Panty
夏天將至，正是一展美好身段的大好季節，但當穿上露肩裝、小背心、tube top或是大熱的雪紡衣飾時，如果bra邊現形，被旁人行以奇怪的注目禮，絕對令你完美形象大打折扣！Wacoal全新Nami Nami無縫胸圍，不但是妳的貼身拍檔，更能讓妳於這個季節「大曬特
Product Highlights
Wacoal 04 show room
Hot Sale Items
NAMI·NAMI
SHAKITTO BRA
Leather

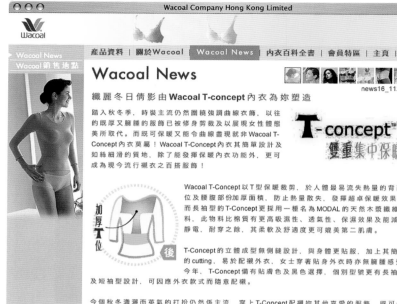

www.wacoal.com.hk
D: yan pang **C:** kenneth ho **P:** kelly sze
A: eureka digital **M:** kelly@eureka-digital.com

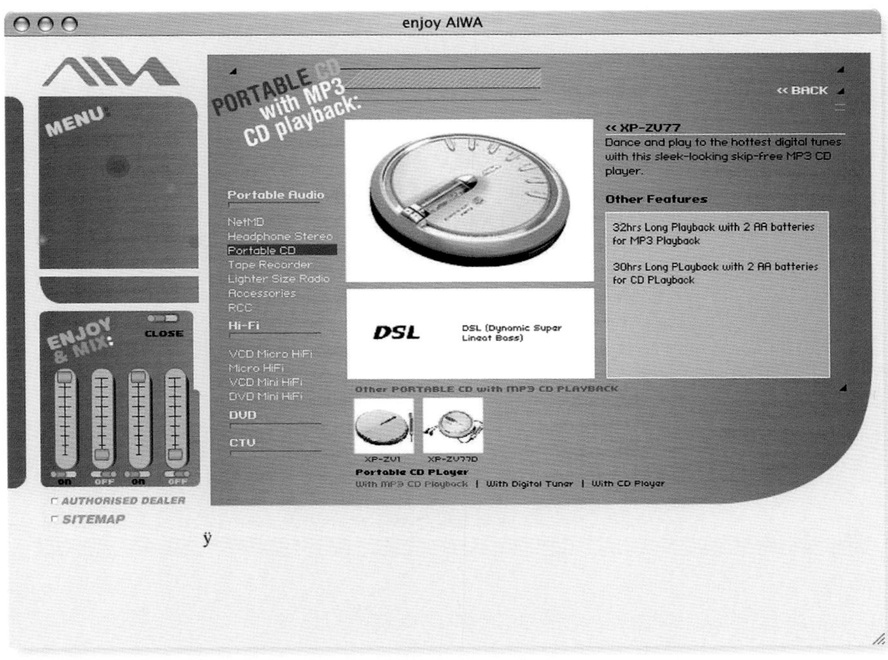
enjoy AIWA
MENU
PORTABLE CD with MP3 CD playback:
<< BACK
<< XP-ZV77
Dance and play to the hottest digital tunes with this sleek-looking skip-free MP3 CD player.
Other Features
32hrs Long Playback with 2 AA batteries for MP3 Playback
30hrs Long PLayback with 2 AA batteries for CD PLayback
DSL
DSL (Dynamic Super Lineat Bass)
Portable Audio
NetMD
Headphone Stereo
Portable CD
Tape Recorder
Lighter Size Radio
Accessories
RCC
Hi-Fi
VCD Micro HiFi
Micro HiFi
VCD Mini HiFi
DVD Mini HiFi
DVD
CTV
ENJOY & MIX:
CLOSE
Other PORTABLE CD with MP3 CD PLAYBACK
XP-ZV1
XP-ZV77D
Portable CD PLayer
With MP3 CD Playback | With Digital Tuner | With CD Player
AUTHORISED DEALER
SITEMAP

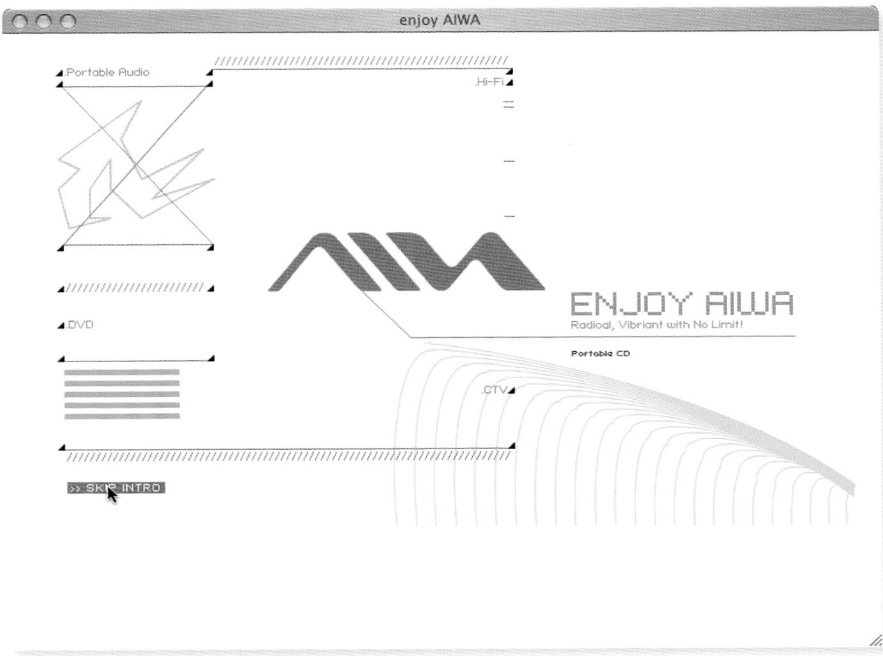
enjoy AIWA
Portable Audio
Hi-Fi
DVD
ENJOY AIWA
Radical, Vibriant with No Limit!
Portable CD
CTV
>> SKIP INTRO

www.aiwa.com.sg
D: tan agnes **P:** aiwa
A: junkflea **M:** info@junkflea.com

+++ TWM - tappi racing e ruote alluminio +++
TWM SPECIAL COMPONENTS
01 HOME
COMEANDRIDEWITHUS
Tappi Racing
Ruote in alluminio
dall'esperienza nelle competizioni alla strada
PRODOTTI
02 AZIENDA
03 PRODOTTI
03.1 TAPPI RACING
03.2 RUOTE ALLUMINIO
04 RACING
05 LA TUA MOTO
06 ADVERTISING
07 CONTATTI
TWM - Via Cappuccini, 50/a - 21013 Gallarate (VA) tel +39.0331.260580 email: info@twmproject.com
credits

+++ TWM - tappi racing e ruote alluminio +++
TWM SPECIAL COMPONENTS
05 La tua moto
COMEANDRIDEWITHUS
Passione
Esperienza
Tecnologia
La tua moto
01 HOME
02 AZIENDA
03 PRODOTTI
03.1 TAPPI RACING
03.2 RUOTE ALLUMINIO
04 RACING
05 LA TUA MOTO
06 ADVERTISING
07 CONTATTI
Se anche tu possiedi una moto equipaggiata con componeti TWM e desideri metterla in mostra sul nostro sito, invia la tua foto con un testo descrittvo all'indirizzo di posta elettonica: info@twmproject.com
Paolo Martinoli
Ermanno Bastianini
Yamaha R1 mod 2000
Accessoriata con tappo e cerchi TWM.
Suzuki SV 650
Preparata da E. Rosboch di Rosmoto.
Monta cerchi TWM.
TWM - Via Cappuccini, 50/a - 21013 Gallarate (VA) tel +39.0331.260580 email: info@twmproject.com
credits

www.twmproject.com
D: logical net
A: logical net **M:** info@logicalnet.it

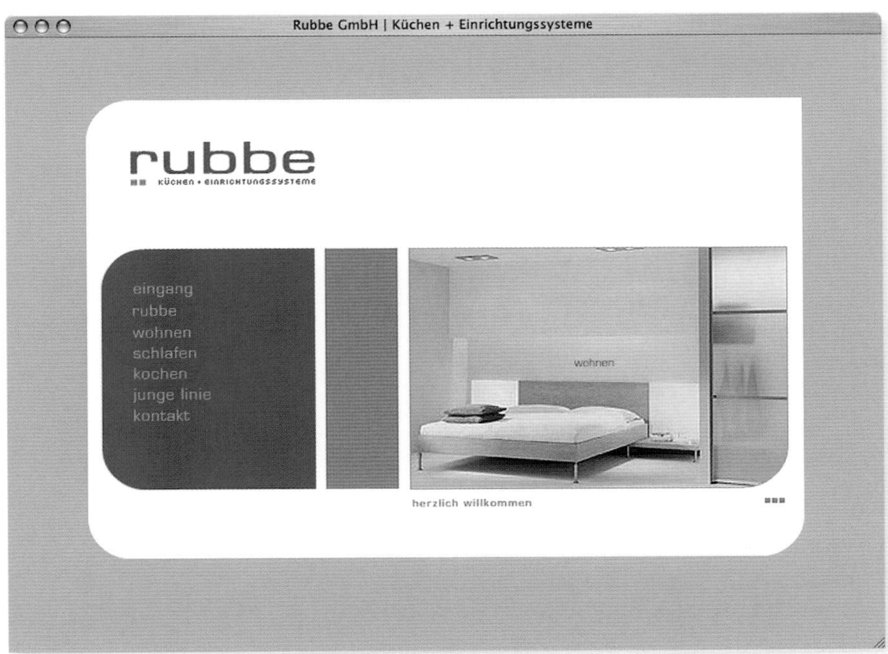
Rubbe GmbH | Küchen + Einrichtungssysteme
rubbe
küchen + einrichtungssysteme
eingang
rubbe
wohnen
schlafen
kochen
junge linie
kontakt
wohnen
herzlich willkommen

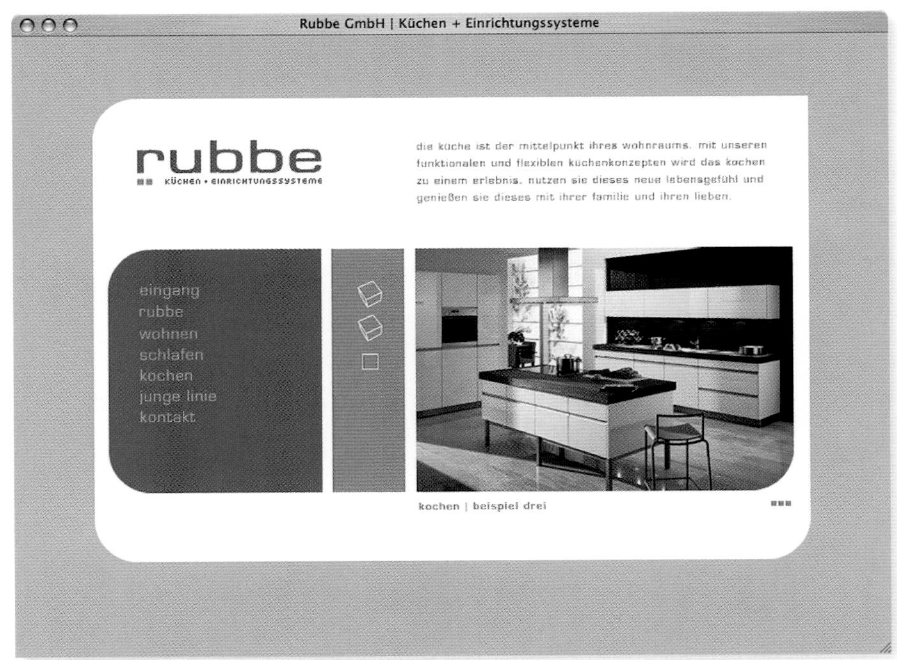
Rubbe GmbH | Küchen + Einrichtungssysteme
rubbe
küchen + einrichtungssysteme
die küche ist der mittelpunkt ihres wohnraums. mit unseren funktionalen und flexiblen küchenkonzepten wird das kochen zu einem erlebnis. nutzen sie dieses neue lebensgefühl und genießen sie dieses mit ihrer familie und ihren lieben.
eingang
rubbe
wohnen
schlafen
kochen
junge linie
kontakt
kochen | beispiel drei

www.rubbe.de
D: marc brautmeier
A: cokoon **M:** mb@cokoon.de

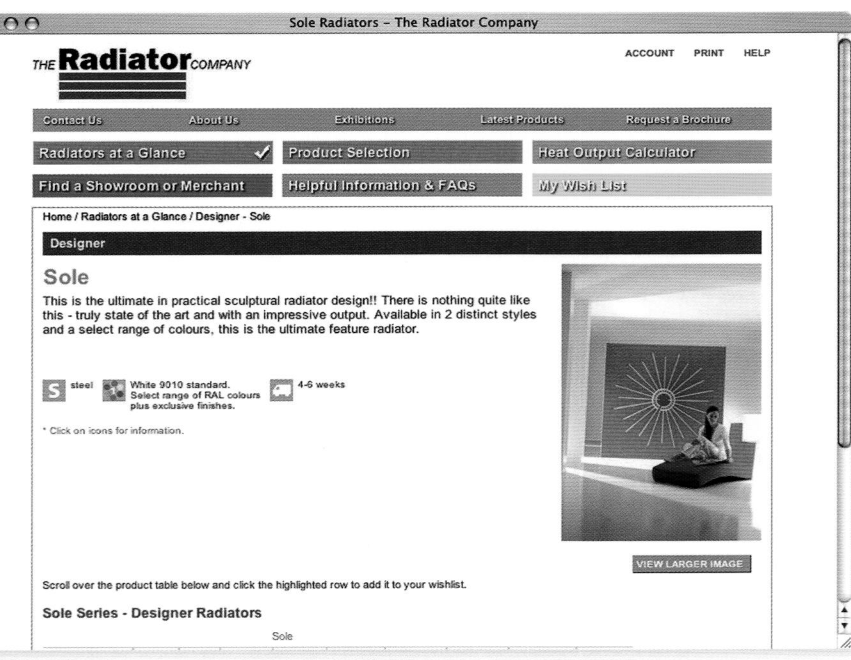
Sole Radiators – The Radiator Company
THE Radiator COMPANY
ACCOUNT PRINT HELP
Contact Us About Us Exhibitions Latest Products Request a Brochure
Radiators at a Glance
Product Selection
Heat Output Calculator
Find a Showroom or Merchant
Helpful Information & FAQs
My Wish List
Home / Radiators at a Glance / Designer - Sole
Designer
Sole
This is the ultimate in practical sculptural radiator design!! There is nothing quite like this - truly state of the art and with an impressive output. Available in 2 distinct styles and a select range of colours, this is the ultimate feature radiator.
steel
White 9010 standard. Select range of RAL colours plus exclusive finishes.
4-6 weeks
* Click on icons for information.
VIEW LARGER IMAGE
Scroll over the product table below and click the highlighted row to add it to your wishlist.
Sole Series - Designer Radiators
Sole

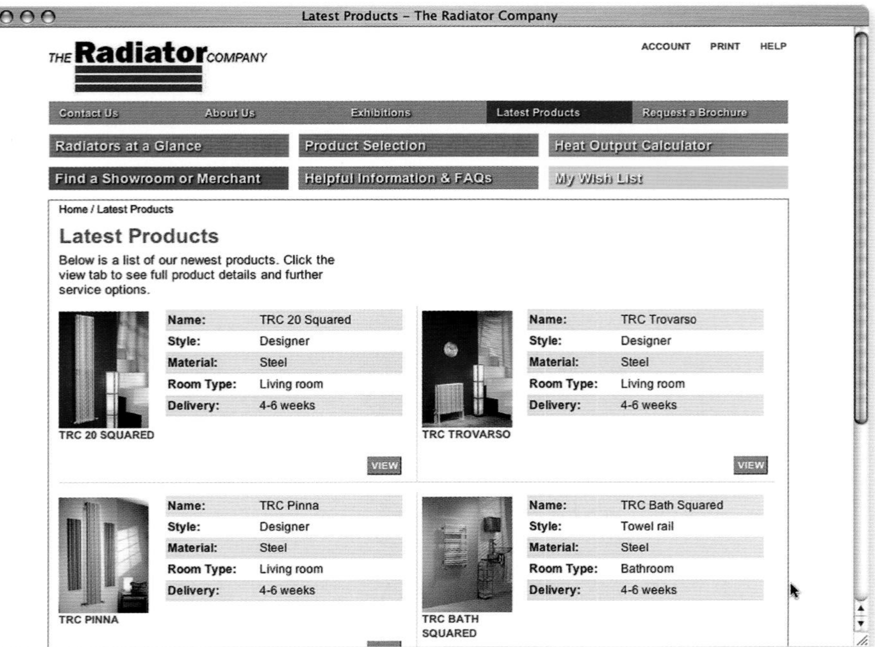
Latest Products – The Radiator Company
THE Radiator COMPANY
ACCOUNT PRINT HELP
Contact Us About Us Exhibitions Latest Products Request a Brochure
Radiators at a Glance
Product Selection
Heat Output Calculator
Find a Showroom or Merchant
Helpful Information & FAQs
My Wish List
Home / Latest Products
Latest Products
Below is a list of our newest products. Click the view tab to see full product details and further service options.
TRC 20 SQUARED
Name: TRC 20 Squared
Style: Designer
Material: Steel
Room Type: Living room
Delivery: 4-6 weeks
VIEW
TRC TROVARSO
Name: TRC Trovarso
Style: Designer
Material: Steel
Room Type: Living room
Delivery: 4-6 weeks
VIEW
TRC PINNA
Name: TRC Pinna
Style: Designer
Material: Steel
Room Type: Living room
Delivery: 4-6 weeks
TRC BATH SQUARED
Name: TRC Bath Squared
Style: Towel rail
Material: Steel
Room Type: Bathroom
Delivery: 4-6 weeks

www.theradiatorcompany.com
D: deep
A: deep llp **M:** deeper@deep.co.uk

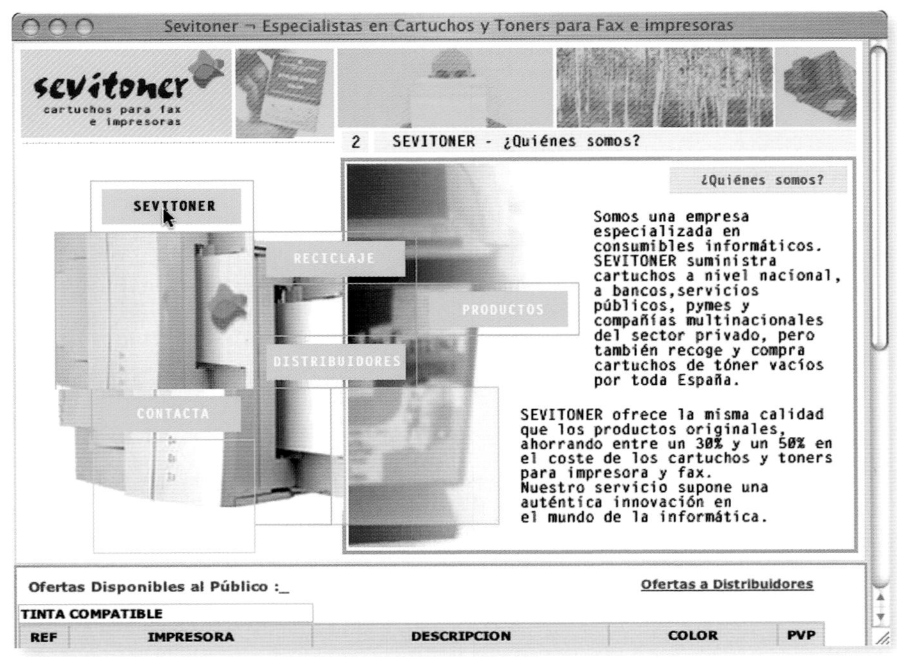
Sevitoner ¬ Especialistas en Cartuchos y Toners para Fax e impresoras
sevitoner
cartuchos para fax e impresoras
2 SEVITONER - ¿Quiénes somos?
¿Quiénes somos?
SEVITONER
RECICLAJE
PRODUCTOS
DISTRIBUIDORES
CONTACTA
Somos una empresa especializada en consumibles informáticos. SEVITONER suministra cartuchos a nivel nacional, a bancos,servicios públicos, pymes y compañías multinacionales del sector privado, pero también recoge y compra cartuchos de tóner vacíos por toda España.
SEVITONER ofrece la misma calidad que los productos originales, ahorrando entre un 30% y un 50% en el coste de los cartuchos y toners para impresora y fax.
Nuestro servicio supone una auténtica innovación en el mundo de la informática.
Ofertas Disponibles al Público :_
Ofertas a Distribuidores
TINTA COMPATIBLE
REF
IMPRESORA
DESCRIPCION
COLOR
PVP

Sevitoner ¬ Productos competitivos : : Cartuchos para Fax e impresoras
sevitoner
cartuchos para fax e impresoras
4 Productos
Elija nuestros productos
SEVITONER
RECICLAJE
PRODUCTOS
DISTRIBUIDORES
CONTACTA
La única diferencia entre un cartucho de tóner original y otro compatible, es que el usuario de éste último tiene que devolver el envase vacío.
El resto la calidad, el rendimiento,el número de copias realizadas, la tonalidad de negros y grises,es exactamente la misma, con la ventaja de que el cartucho de tóner es mucho más económico.
> Elija una opción................
Tinta compatible
Ver
Ofertas Disponibles al Público :_
Ofertas a Distribuidores
TINTA COMPATIBLE
REF
IMPRESORA
DESCRIPCION
COLOR
PVP

www.sevitoner.com
D: javier domínguez
M: jd@javier-dominguez.com

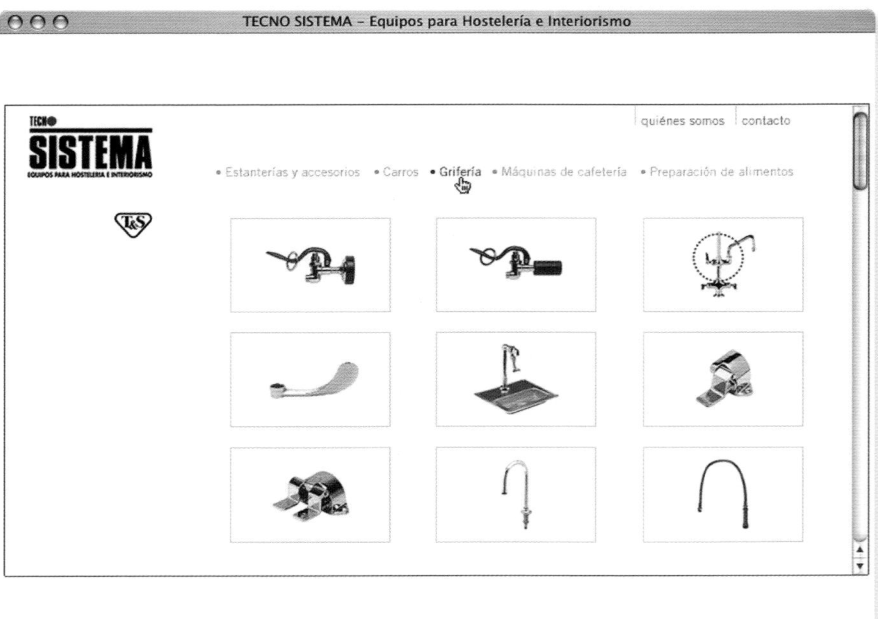
TECNO SISTEMA - Equipos para Hostelería e Interiorismo
TECNO
SISTEMA
EQUIPOS PARA HOSTELERIA E INTERIORISMO
quiénes somos
contacto
• Estanterías y accesorios
• Carros
• Grifería
• Máquinas de cafetería
• Preparación de alimentos

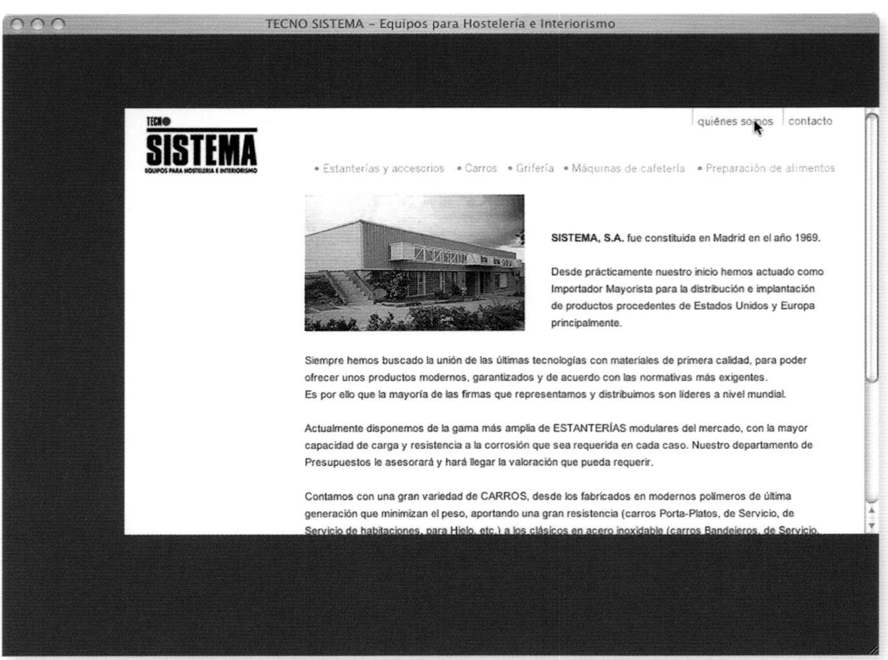
TECNO SISTEMA - Equipos para Hostelería e Interiorismo
TECNO
SISTEMA
EQUIPOS PARA HOSTELERIA E INTERIORISMO
quiénes somos
contacto
• Estanterías y accesorios
• Carros
• Grifería
• Máquinas de cafetería
• Preparación de alimentos
SISTEMA, S.A. fue constituida en Madrid en el año 1969.
Desde prácticamente nuestro inicio hemos actuado como Importador Mayorista para la distribución e implantación de productos procedentes de Estados Unidos y Europa principalmente.
Siempre hemos buscado la unión de las últimas tecnologías con materiales de primera calidad, para poder ofrecer unos productos modernos, garantizados y de acuerdo con las normativas más exigentes.
Es por ello que la mayoría de las firmas que representamos y distribuimos son líderes a nivel mundial.
Actualmente disponemos de la gama más amplia de ESTANTERÍAS modulares del mercado, con la mayor capacidad de carga y resistencia a la corrosión que sea requerida en cada caso. Nuestro departamento de Presupuestos le asesorará y hará llegar la valoración que pueda requerir.
Contamos con una gran variedad de CARROS, desde los fabricados en modernos polímeros de última generación que minimizan el peso, aportando una gran resistencia (carros Porta-Platos, de Servicio, de

www.tecno-sistema.com
D: antonio sanjuán
M: antoniosanjuan@eresmas.com

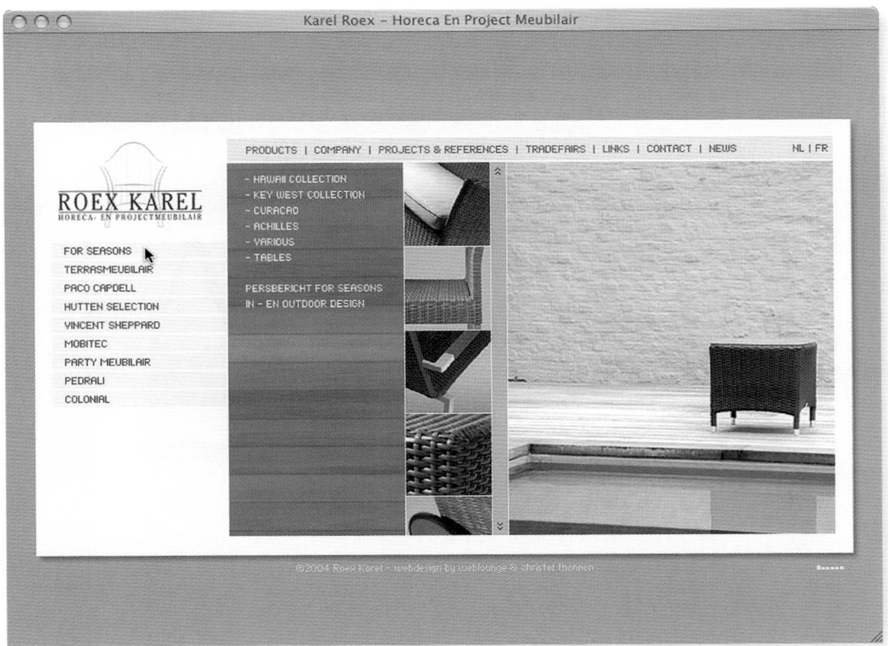
Karel Roex – Horeca En Project Meubilair
ROEX KAREL
HORECA- EN PROJECTMEUBILAIR
PRODUCTS | COMPANY | PROJECTS & REFERENCES | TRADEFAIRS | LINKS | CONTACT | NEWS
NL | FR
FOR SEASONS
TERRASMEUBILAIR
PACO CAPDELL
HUTTEN SELECTION
VINCENT SHEPPARD
MOBITEC
PARTY MEUBILAIR
PEDRALI
COLONIAL
- HAWAII COLLECTION
- KEY WEST COLLECTION
- CURACAO
- ACHILLES
- VARIOUS
- TABLES
PERSBERICHT FOR SEASONS
IN - EN OUTDOOR DESIGN

Karel Roex – Horeca En Project Meubilair
ROEX KAREL
HORECA- EN PROJECTMEUBILAIR
PRODUCTS | COMPANY | PROJECTS & REFERENCES | TRADEFAIRS | LINKS | CONTACT | NEWS
NL | FR
FOR SEASONS
TERRASMEUBILAIR
PACO CAPDELL
HUTTEN SELECTION
VINCENT SHEPPARD
MOBITEC
PARTY MEUBILAIR
PEDRALI
COLONIAL
- STOELEN
- TAFELONDERSTELLEN
- TAFELBLADEN & PARASOLS
- BLOEMBAKKEN
- WINTERSERVICE

www.roex.be
D: kristof van rentergem **C:** jeroen algoet **P:** christel thonnon
A: weblounge **M:** info@weblounge.be

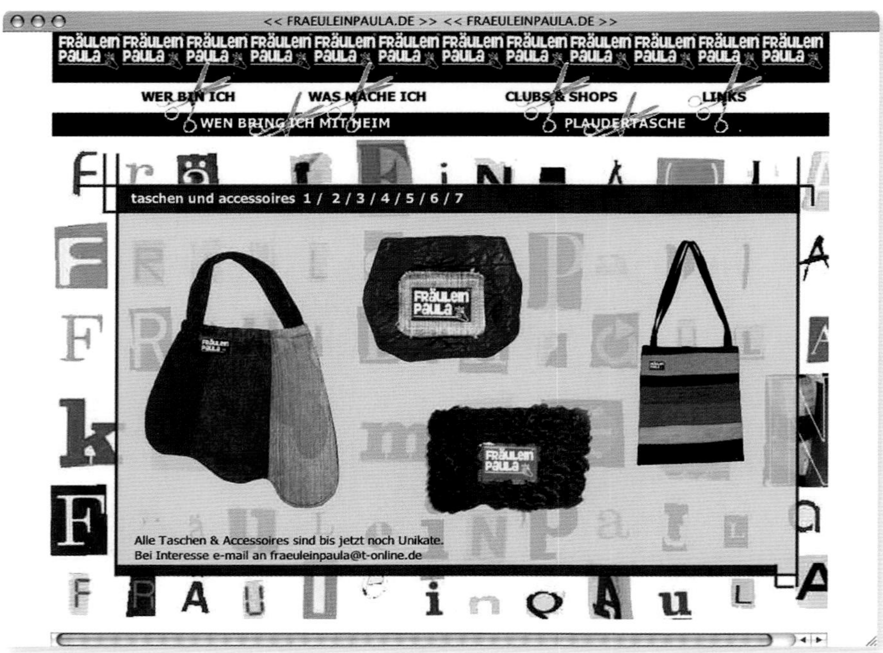

<< FRAEULEINPAULA.DE >> << FRAEULEINPAULA.DE >>
WER BIN ICH
WAS MACHE ICH
CLUBS & SHOPS
LINKS
WEN BRING ICH MIT HEIM
PLAUDERTASCHE
taschen und accessoires 1 / 2 / 3 / 4 / 5 / 6 / 7
Alle Taschen & Accessoires sind bis jetzt noch Unikate.
Bei Interesse e-mail an fraeuleinpaula@t-online.de

<< FRAEULEINPAULA.DE >> << FRAEULEINPAULA.DE >> << FRAEULEINPAULA.DE >> << FRAEULEINPAULA.DE >>

www.fraeuleinpaula.de
D: nina pilsl **C:** freddy freienstein
M: fraeuleinpaula@t-online.de

Creativas Producciones
CREAT!VAS
PRODUCCIONES
Conceptos Creativos
Regalos Corporativos
Automóviles
Deportes Outdoors
Escritorio
Estacional
Juegos
Masivos
Niños
Textil
Vasos y Tazones
Volver a Home
Contacto
Productos destacados
Paletas de Trupan
Morral Tasslan
Ver más +
Gorro Pescador
Ver más +
Otros Productos
Recuerde........
Preparese para la temporada Primavera-Verano con sus promociones

Creativas Producciones
CREAT!VAS
PRODUCCIONES
Conceptos Creativos
Regalos Corporativos
Automóviles
Outdoors
Escritorio
Estacional
Juegos
Masivos
Niños
Textil
Vasos y Tazones
Volver a Home
Contacto
Outdoors
Arco de fútbol colapsable
Binocular
Brújula Jungle
Brújula escritorio
Brújula
Chaqueta aventura
Cooler
Corta pluma
Corta pluma
Corta pluma económica
Corta pluma harley
Corta pluma Suiza
Frazada polar con portafrazada
Frazada polar
Gorro aventure
Balón baby fútbol
Balón fútbol
Balón volleyball
Saco de dormir
Silla arenera de madera
Recuerde........
Preparese para la temporada Primavera-Verano con sus promociones

www.creativas.cl
D: andrés rodríguez
A: dreammaker studios **M:** info@dmstudios.cl

Kuota Österreich >> Home
KUOTA
BICYCLE COMPOSITE TECHNOLOGY
HOME UNTERNEHMEN PRODUKTE KOMPLETTRÄDER HÄNDLER SERVICE KONTAKT NYX
HOME
SITEMAP
NEUHEITEN
NEU
NEWSLETTER
anmelden
© 2004 by Müller GmbH
KUOTA AUSTRIA
SUBSCRIBE AND WIN
PROCYCLING 2004 #11
Kuota Kredo: Aus Freude am Fahren
Auf dem Nürburg-Ring wurde die grandiose Performance des Kuota Kredo ausgetestet. more
IRONMAN HAWAII
Normann Stadler gewinnt auf KUOTA
Auf dem KUOTA Kalibur nimmt er sogar dem ehemaligen Telekom-Profi Hundertmarck neuneinhalb Minuten auf der Raddistanz ab und gewinnt souverän more
PREISLISTE 2005
Version 1.12
Die ersten Preise für die Saison 2005 stehen fest. Jetzt neu mit verbesserter Configurations-Möglichkeit. more
PEZCYCLINGNEWS.COM
Kuota's Light Weight Screamer
Die Story über das Kuota Kredo von Charles Manantan auf PezCyclingNews.com (Englisch). more

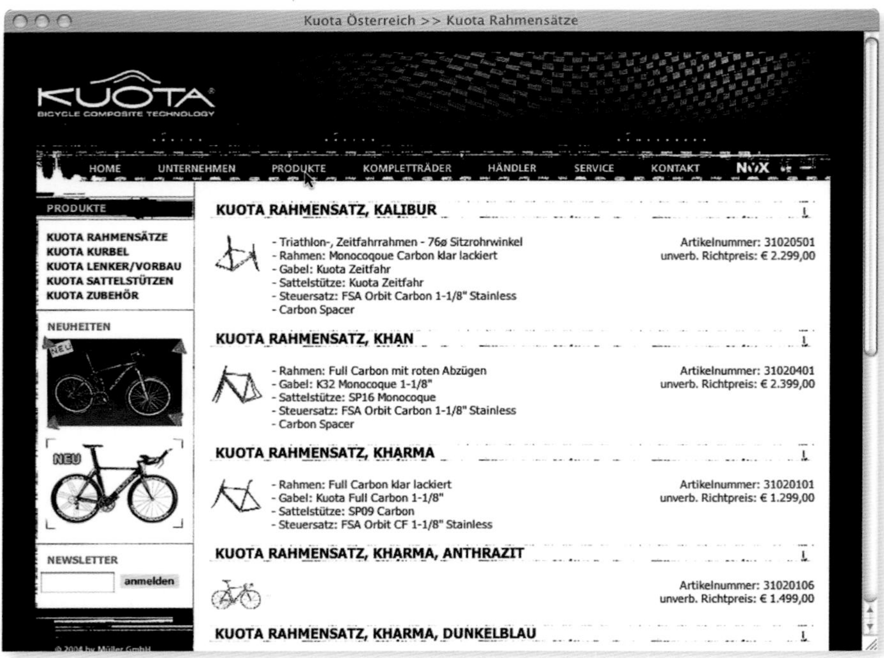
Kuota Österreich >> Kuota Rahmensätze
KUOTA
BICYCLE COMPOSITE TECHNOLOGY
HOME UNTERNEHMEN PRODUKTE KOMPLETTRÄDER HÄNDLER SERVICE KONTAKT NYX
PRODUKTE
KUOTA RAHMENSÄTZE
KUOTA KURBEL
KUOTA LENKER/VORBAU
KUOTA SATTELSTÜTZEN
KUOTA ZUBEHÖR
NEUHEITEN
NEU
NEWSLETTER
anmelden
KUOTA RAHMENSATZ, KALIBUR
- Triathlon-, Zeitfahrrahmen - 76ø Sitzrohrwinkel
- Rahmen: Monocoqoue Carbon klar lackiert
- Gabel: Kuota Zeitfahr
- Sattelstütze: Kuota Zeitfahr
- Steuersatz: FSA Orbit Carbon 1-1/8" Stainless
- Carbon Spacer
Artikelnummer: 31020501
unverb. Richtpreis: € 2.299,00
KUOTA RAHMENSATZ, KHAN
- Rahmen: Full Carbon mit roten Abzügen
- Gabel: K32 Monocoque 1-1/8"
- Sattelstütze: SP16 Monocoque
- Steuersatz: FSA Orbit Carbon 1-1/8" Stainless
- Carbon Spacer
Artikelnummer: 31020401
unverb. Richtpreis: € 2.399,00
KUOTA RAHMENSATZ, KHARMA
- Rahmen: Full Carbon klar lackiert
- Gabel: Kuota Full Carbon 1-1/8"
- Sattelstütze: SP09 Carbon
- Steuersatz: FSA Orbit CF 1-1/8" Stainless
Artikelnummer: 31020101
unverb. Richtpreis: € 1.299,00
KUOTA RAHMENSATZ, KHARMA, ANTHRAZIT
Artikelnummer: 31020106
unverb. Richtpreis: € 1.499,00
KUOTA RAHMENSATZ, KHARMA, DUNKELBLAU

www.kuota.at
D: martin ganglberger P: nyx sportmanagement
A: nopain M: martin@nyx.at

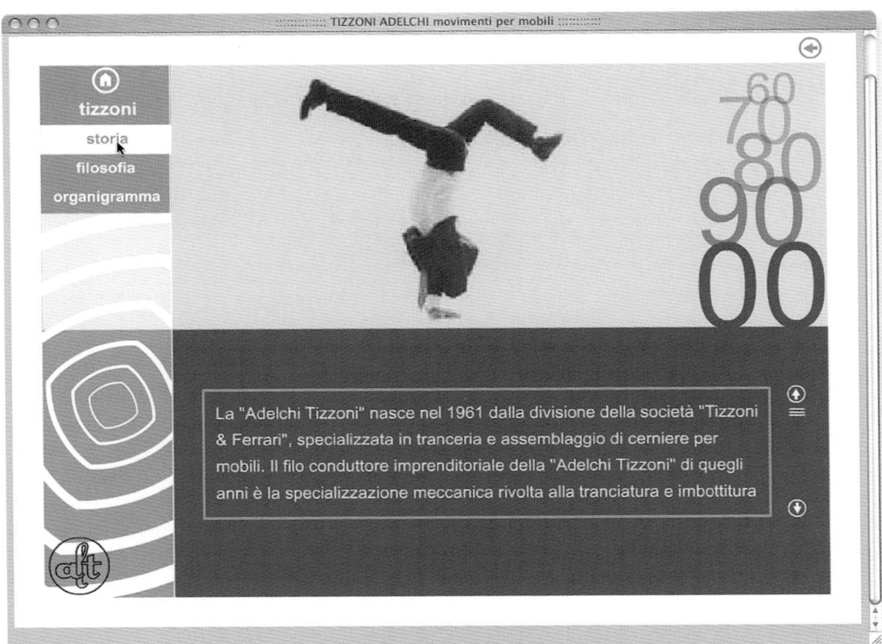
:::::::::::: TIZZONI ADELCHI movimenti per mobili ::::::::::
tizzoni
storia
filosofia
organigramma
60
70
80
90
00
La "Adelchi Tizzoni" nasce nel 1961 dalla divisione della società "Tizzoni & Ferrari", specializzata in tranceria e assemblaggio di cerniere per mobili. Il filo conduttore imprenditoriale della "Adelchi Tizzoni" di quegli anni è la specializzazione meccanica rivolta alla tranciatura e imbottitura

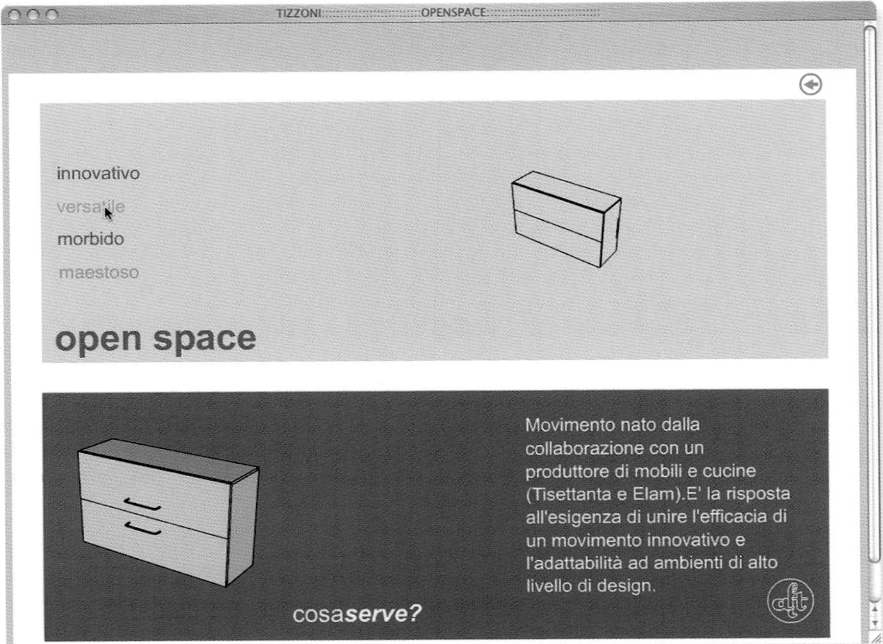
TIZZONI::::::::::::::::::::::::OPENSPACE::::::::::::::::::::::::::
innovativo
versatile
morbido
maestoso
open space
Movimento nato dalla collaborazione con un produttore di mobili e cucine (Tisettanta e Elam).E' la risposta all'esigenza di unire l'efficacia di un movimento innovativo e l'adattabilità ad ambienti di alto livello di design.
cosaserve?

www.tizzoniweb.com
D: vania borozan **C:** massimiliano ambrosini
A: materica **M:** borozan@materica.com

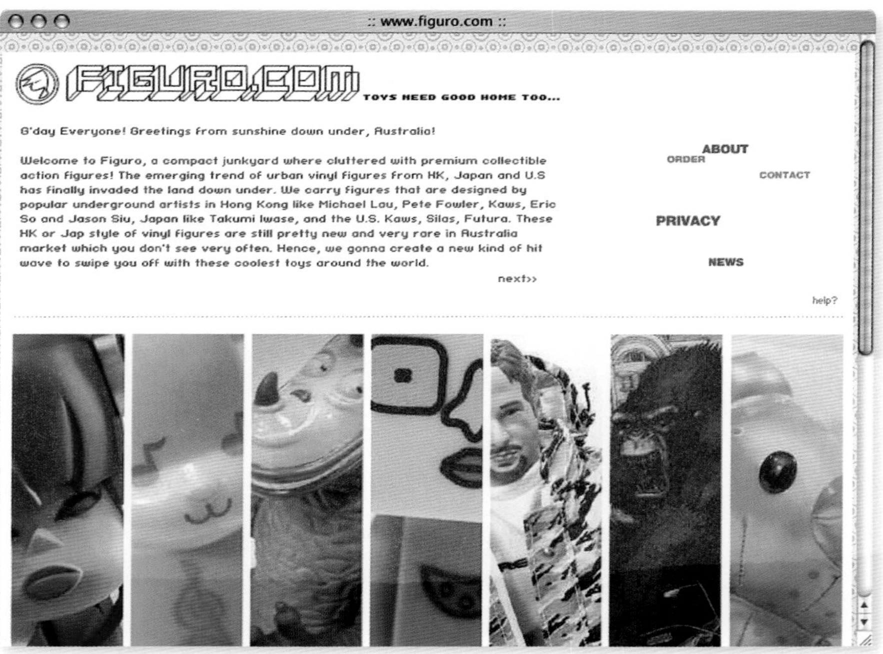
:: www.figuro.com ::
FIGURO.COM
TOYS NEED GOOD HOME TOO...
G'day Everyone! Greetings from sunshine down under, Australia!
Welcome to Figuro, a compact junkyard where cluttered with premium collectible action figures! The emerging trend of urban vinyl figures from HK, Japan and U.S has finally invaded the land down under. We carry figures that are designed by popular underground artists in Hong Kong like Michael Lau, Pete Fowler, Kaws, Eric So and Jason Siu, Japan like Takumi Iwase, and the U.S. Kaws, Silas, Futura. These HK or Jap style of vinyl figures are still pretty new and very rare in Australia market which you don't see very often. Hence, we gonna create a new kind of hit wave to swipe you off with these coolest toys around the world.
next>>
ABOUT
ORDER
CONTACT
PRIVACY
NEWS
help?

:: www.figuro.com ::
figuro
i'm a little wanderer

www.figuro.com
D: billy law
A: figuro M: info@figuro.com

<<<<<<<<<<<< Ôoh de Casa ! >>>>>>>>>...>>>>>>>>>>>>>>>>>>>>>>>>>>>>>>>>>>>>>
Ôoh de casa!
Vila Madalena . São Paulo . SP
Rua Fradique Coutinho . 899
Loja Artesanato Coisas p/casa Presentes Decoração Jardim Novidades
Ôoh de Casa Brindes!
1. Esculturas de caipiras. Matéria-prima: cerâmica.
Contato
e-mail
3812 4934
3815 9577
© copyright Ôoh de Casa!

<<<<<<<<<<<< Ôoh de Casa ! >>>>>>>>>...>>>>>>>>>>>>>>>>>>>>>>>>>>>>>>>>>>>>>
Ôoh de casa!
Vila Madalena . São Paulo . SP
Rua Fradique Coutinho . 899
Loja Artesanato Coisas p/casa Presentes Decoração Jardim Novidades
Ôoh de Casa Brindes!
1. Móbiles de origami. Uma grande variedade para você escolher.
Contato
e-mail
3812 4934
3815 9577
© copyright Ôoh de Casa!

www.oohdecasa.com.br
D: josé waldery pipol
A: hey joe comunicação M: pipol@brinquedosdepalavras.net

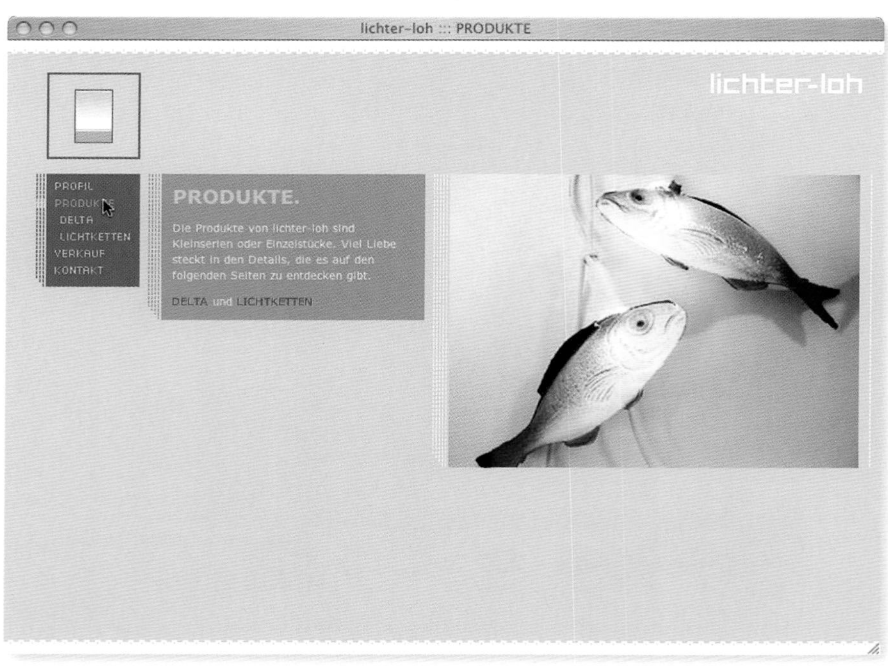
lichter-loh ::: PRODUKTE
lichter-loh
PROFIL
PRODUKTE
DELTA
LICHTKETTEN
VERKAUF
KONTAKT
PRODUKTE.
Die Produkte von lichter-loh sind Kleinserien oder Einzelstücke. Viel Liebe steckt in den Details, die es auf den folgenden Seiten zu entdecken gibt.
DELTA und LICHTKETTEN

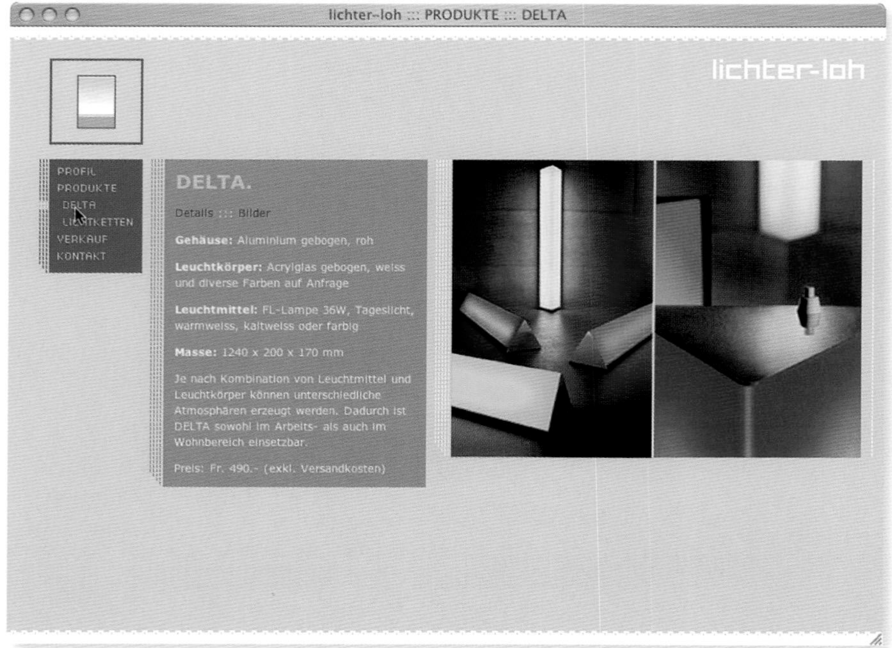
lichter-loh ::: PRODUKTE ::: DELTA
lichter-loh
PROFIL
PRODUKTE
DELTA
LICHTKETTEN
VERKAUF
KONTAKT
DELTA.
Details ::: Bilder
Gehäuse: Aluminium gebogen, roh
Leuchtkörper: Acrylglas gebogen, weiss und diverse Farben auf Anfrage
Leuchtmittel: FL-Lampe 36W, Tageslicht, warmweiss, kaltweiss oder farbig
Masse: 1240 x 200 x 170 mm
Je nach Kombination von Leuchtmittel und Leuchtkörper können unterschiedliche Atmosphären erzeugt werden. Dadurch ist DELTA sowohl im Arbeits- als auch im Wohnbereich einsetzbar.
Preis: Fr. 490.- (exkl. Versandkosten)

www.lichter-loh.ch
D: anita schneeberger **C:** oliver zahorka **P:** lichter-loh
A: out media design **M:** webdesignindex@out.to

Mozilla Firefox
ONE WAY
COLLECTION
05
YRITYS
ONE WAY Sport on nuori ja nopeasti kasvava suomalainen yritys, joka on erikoistunut suunnittelemaan ja tuottamaan kävelysauvoja. Sauvojen erikoisuutena on kaunis ja viimeistelty design. Yrityksen johdolla on vuosien kokemus tuotekehityksestä ja urheilutuotteiden testauksesta. Korkealaatuisesta viimeistelystä ja ainutlaatuisesta designista on tullut yrityksen tavaramerkki.
Yrityksen innovatiivinen lähestymistapa sauvojen designiin, suunnitteluun ja kehitykseen on tehnyt ONE WAY-merkistä nopeasti kasvavan ja helposti tunnistettavan brändin sauvasektorilla.
WE CREATE FASHION
Sound

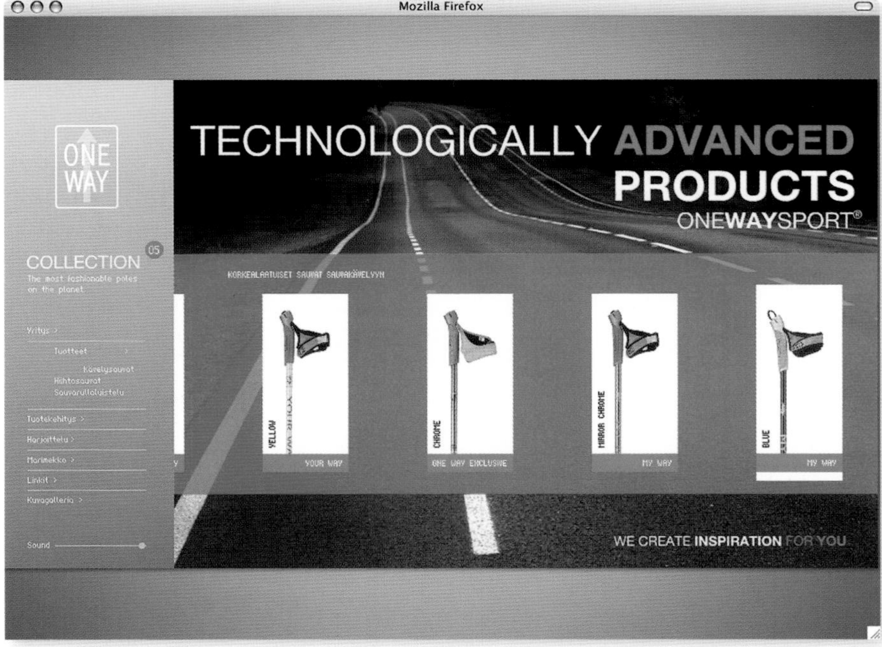
Mozilla Firefox
ONE WAY
COLLECTION
05
TECHNOLOGICALLY ADVANCED PRODUCTS
ONEWAYSPORT®
YELLOW
YOUR WAY
CHROME
ONE WAY EXCLUSIVE
MIRROR CHROME
MY WAY
BLUE
MY WAY
WE CREATE INSPIRATION FOR YOU.
Sound

www.onewaysport.com
D: vladimir morozov **C:** sander sellin **P:** peke eloranta
A: lime creative **M:** www.lime.ee

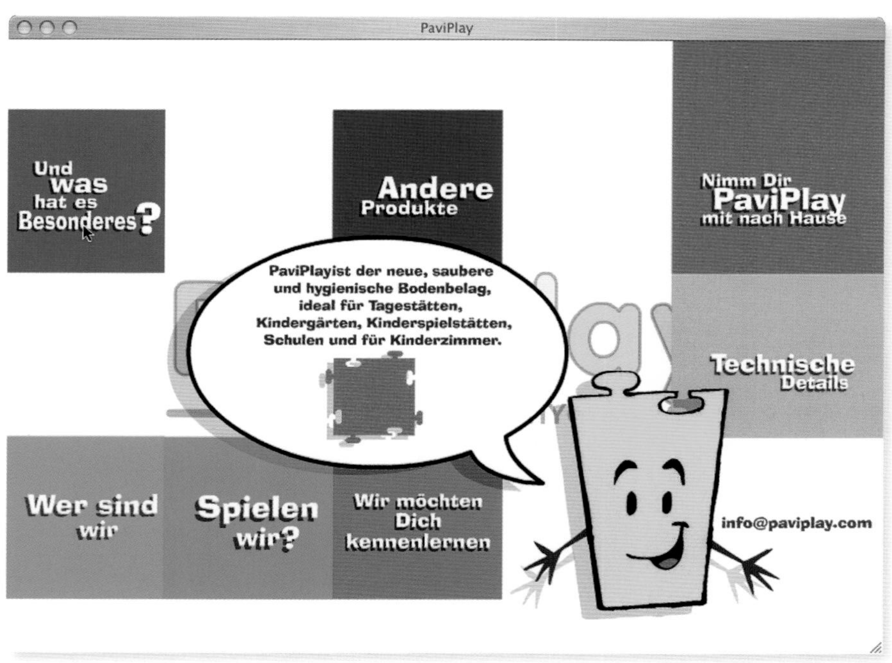
PaviPlay
Und was hat es Besonderes?
Andere Produkte
Nimm Dir PaviPlay mit nach Hause
PaviPlayist der neue, saubere und hygienische Bodenbelag, ideal für Tagestätten, Kindergärten, Kinderspielstätten, Schulen und für Kinderzimmer.
Technische Details
Wer sind wir
Spielen wir?
Wir möchten Dich kennenlernen
info@paviplay.com

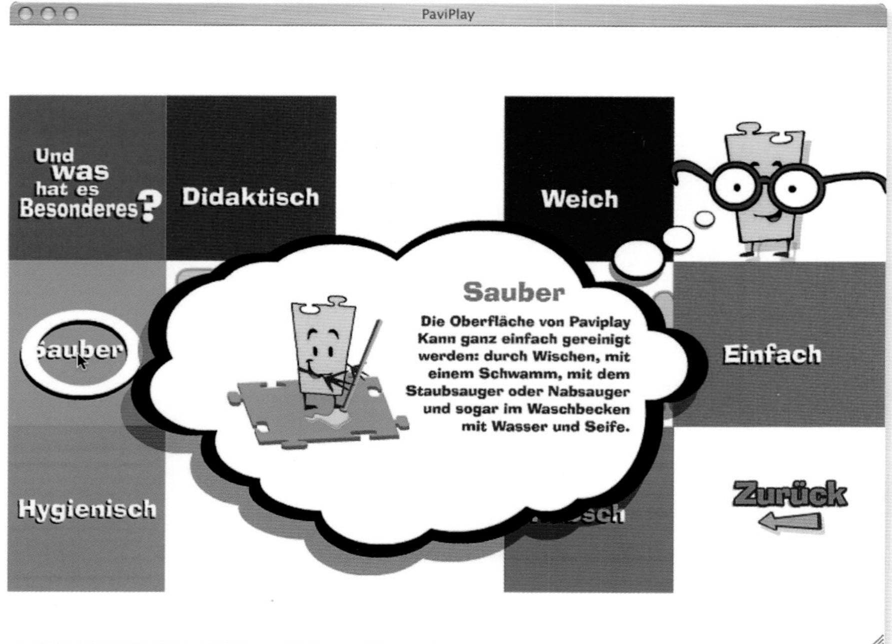
PaviPlay
Und was hat es Besonderes?
Didaktisch
Weich
Sauber
Die Oberfläche von Paviplay Kann ganz einfach gereinigt werden: durch Wischen, mit einem Schwamm, mit dem Staubsauger oder Nabsauger und sogar im Waschbecken mit Wasser und Seife.
Einfach
Hygienisch
Zurück

www.paviplay.com
D: héctor gomis P: paviplay
A: lmental M: info@hectorgomis.com

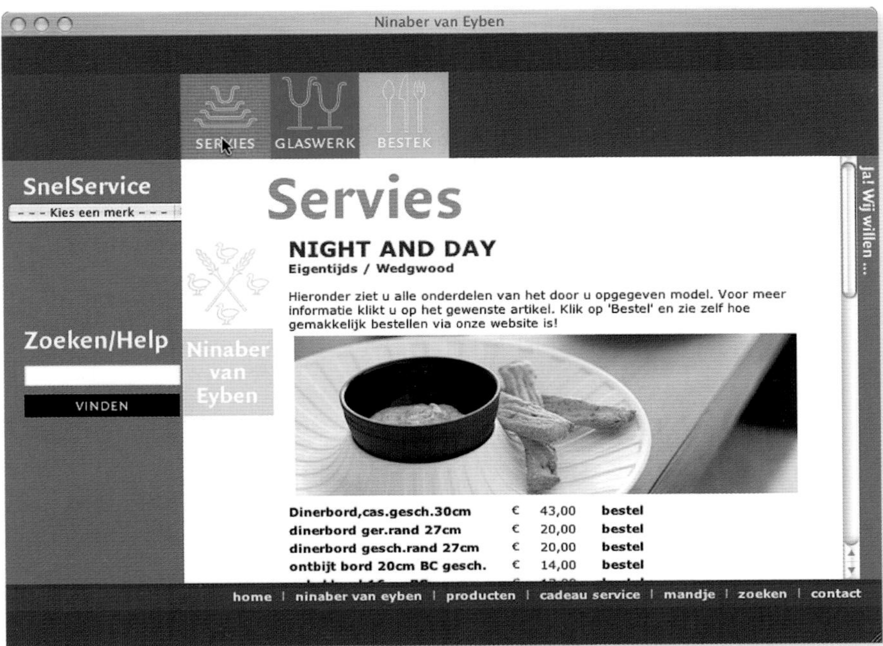
Ninaber van Eyben
SERVIES
GLASWERK
BESTEK
SnelService
--- Kies een merk ---
Zoeken/Help
VINDEN
Ninaber van Eyben
Servies
NIGHT AND DAY
Eigentijds / Wedgwood
Hieronder ziet u alle onderdelen van het door u opgegeven model. Voor meer informatie klikt u op het gewenste artikel. Klik op 'Bestel' en zie zelf hoe gemakkelijk bestellen via onze website is!
Dinerbord,cas.gesch.30cm € 43,00 bestel
dinerbord ger.rand 27cm € 20,00 bestel
dinerbord gesch.rand 27cm € 20,00 bestel
ontbijt bord 20cm BC gesch. € 14,00 bestel
Ja! Wij willen ...
home | ninaber van eyben | producten | cadeau service | mandje | zoeken | contact

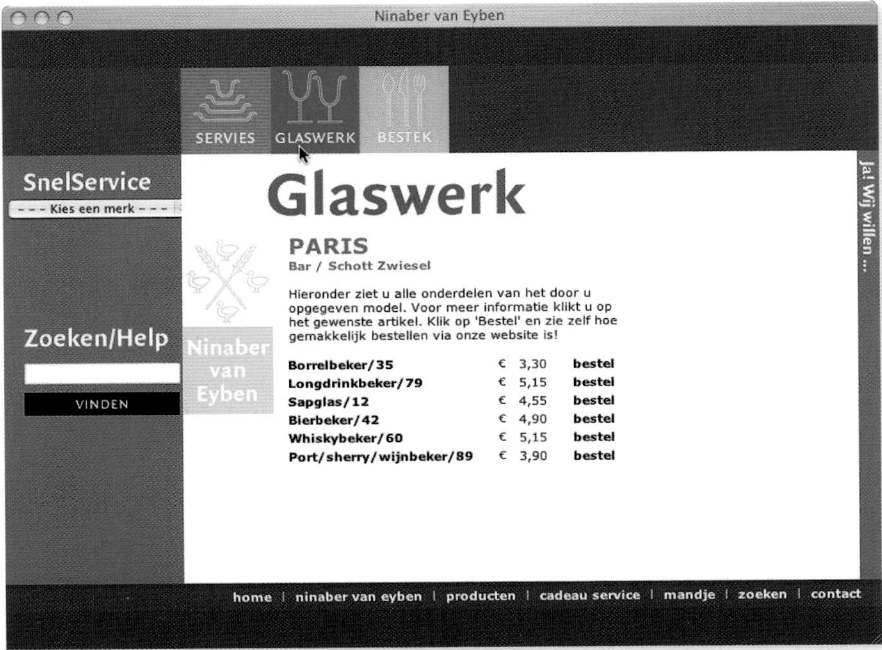
Ninaber van Eyben
SERVIES
GLASWERK
BESTEK
SnelService
--- Kies een merk ---
Zoeken/Help
VINDEN
Ninaber van Eyben
Glaswerk
PARIS
Bar / Schott Zwiesel
Hieronder ziet u alle onderdelen van het door u opgegeven model. Voor meer informatie klikt u op het gewenste artikel. Klik op 'Bestel' en zie zelf hoe gemakkelijk bestellen via onze website is!
Borrelbeker/35 € 3,30 bestel
Longdrinkbeker/79 € 5,15 bestel
Sapglas/12 € 4,55 bestel
Bierbeker/42 € 4,90 bestel
Whiskybeker/60 € 5,15 bestel
Port/sherry/wijnbeker/89 € 3,90 bestel
Ja! Wij willen ...
home | ninaber van eyben | producten | cadeau service | mandje | zoeken | contact

www.ninabervaneyben.nl
D: donald roos
A: otherways souterrain **M:** donald.roos@otherways.nl

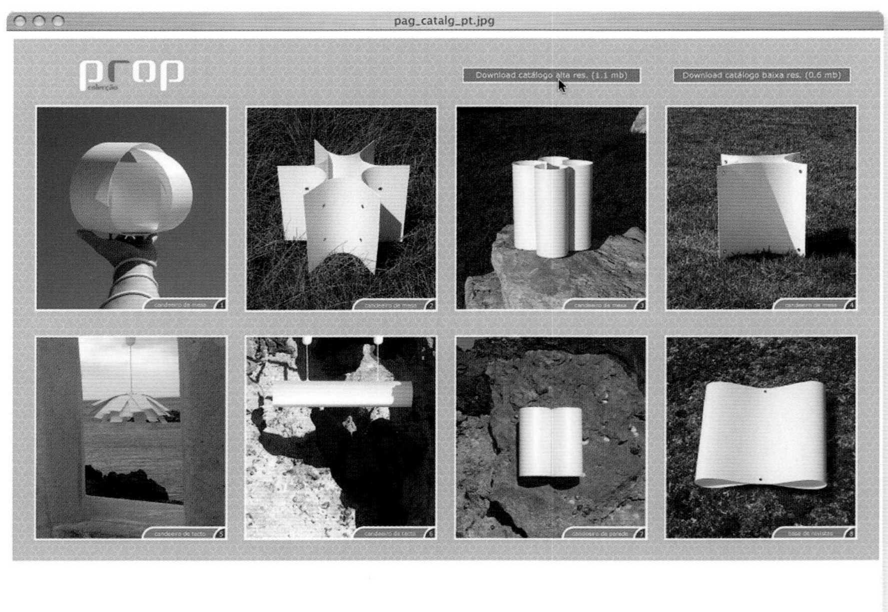
pag_catalg_pt.jpg
prop
Download catálogo alta res. (1.1 mb)
Download catálogo baixa res. (0.6 mb)

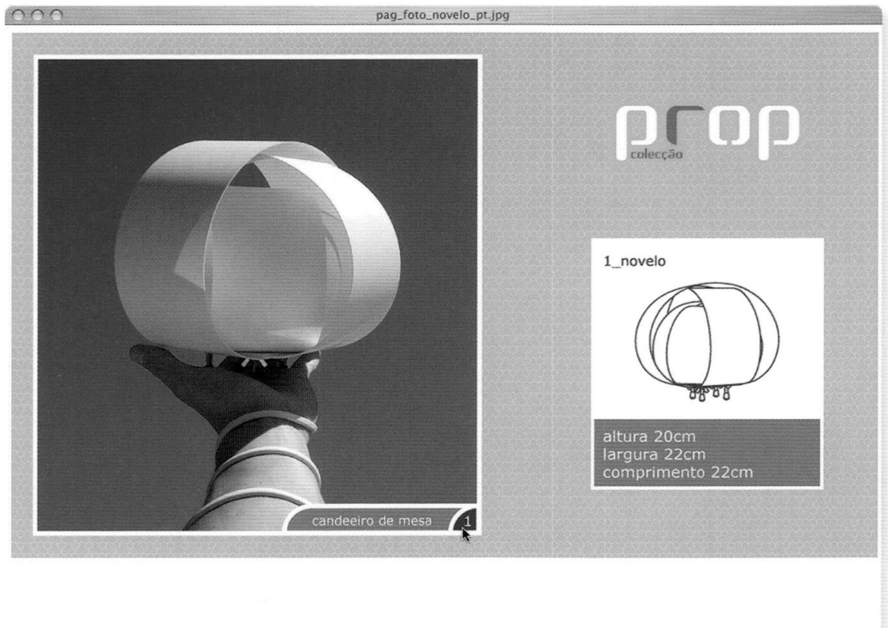
pag_foto_novelo_pt.jpg
candeeiro de mesa
1
prop
colecção
1_novelo
altura 20cm
largura 22cm
comprimento 22cm

prop.com.sapo.pt
D: diogo vital
A: 2design **M:** doisdesign@netcabo.pt

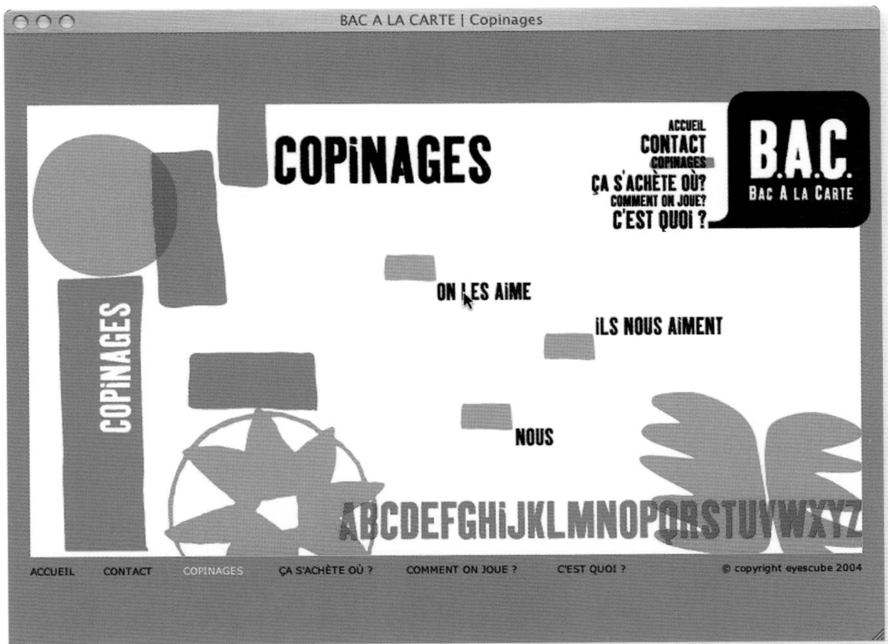
BAC A LA CARTE | Copinages
COPiNAGES
ACCUEIL
CONTACT
COPINAGES
ÇA S'ACHÈTE OÙ?
COMMENT ON JOUE?
C'EST QUOi ?
B.A.C.
BAC A LA CARTE
ON LES AiME
iLS NOUS AiMENT
NOUS
COPiNAGES
ABCDEFGHiJKLMNOPQRSTUVWXYZ
ACCUEIL CONTACT COPINAGES ÇA S'ACHÈTE OÙ ? COMMENT ON JOUE ? C'EST QUOI ?
© copyright eyescube 2004

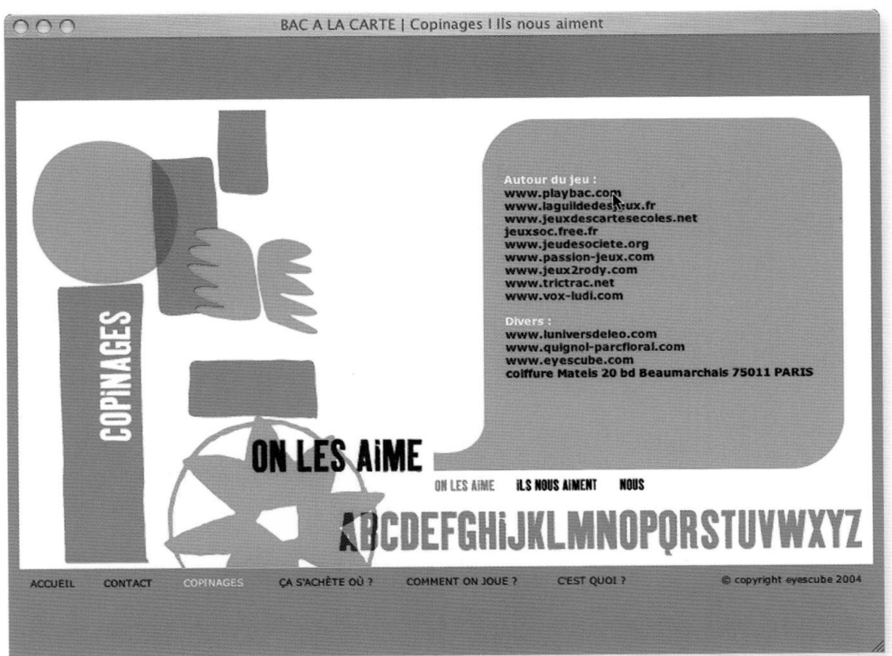
BAC A LA CARTE | Copinages I Ils nous aiment
Autour du jeu :
www.playbac.com
www.laguildedesjeux.fr
www.jeuxdescartesecoles.net
jeuxsoc.free.fr
www.jeudesociete.org
www.passion-jeux.com
www.jeux2rody.com
www.trictrac.net
www.vox-ludi.com
Divers :
www.luniversdeleo.com
www.guignol-parcfloral.com
www.eyescube.com
coiffure Mateis 20 bd Beaumarchais 75011 PARIS
COPiNAGES
ON LES AiME
ON LES AiME iLS NOUS AiMENT NOUS
ABCDEFGHiJKLMNOPQRSTUVWXYZ
ACCUEIL CONTACT COPINAGES ÇA S'ACHÈTE OÙ ? COMMENT ON JOUE ? C'EST QUOI ?
© copyright eyescube 2004

www.bacalacarte.com
D: nicolas pinel **C:** valerie benguerel
A: eyescube **M:** nicolas.pinel@eyescube.com

http://www.stratocucine.com/strato_MX.swf
PRECISION
A FORM
OF
DEVOTION
01
STRATO
CONTACT

http://www.stratocucine.com/strato_MX.swf
Perfection becomes simplicity
The fusion of precious materials with high technological content bears witness to the
incessant research to define exclusive working techniques and new refinement criteria.

www.stratocucine.com
D: group94 **C:** group94 **P:** strato srl italy
A: group94 **M:** info@group94.com

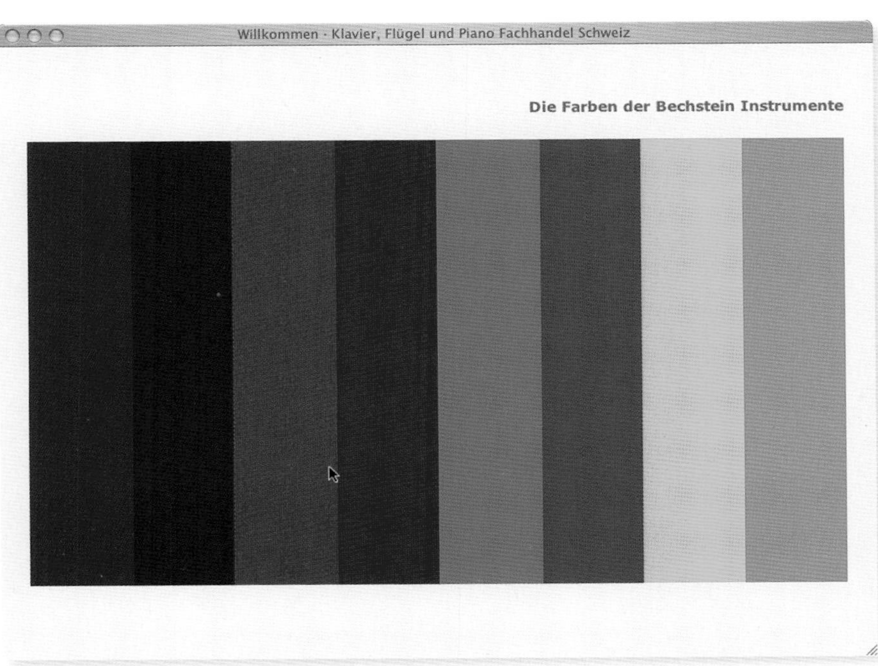
Willkommen - Klavier, Flügel und Piano Fachhandel Schweiz
Die Farben der Bechstein Instrumente

Zimmermann - Klavier, Flügel und Piano Fachhandel Schweiz
Die Farben der Bechstein Instrumente
C.Bechstein
Zimmermann
· Flügel Z 160
· Flügel Z 180
· Flügel Z 190
· Flügel Z 208
· Klavier Z 3
· Klavier Z 2
· Klavier Z 1
W.Hoffmann
Euterpe
Fachhandel
Zimmermann - Flügel Modell Z 180
Eine neue Flügelgeneration für Kenner und Könner, Topmodelle aus der zweiten Linie von Bechstein.
Höhe:
Breite: 150 cm
Tiefe: 180 cm
Farbe: schwarz poliert
schwarz matt
Katalog: ab 1.1.05
Preis: auf Anfrage

www.klavierhandel.ch
D: roger schmid
A: medienwerkstatt **M:** mails@roger-schmid.ch

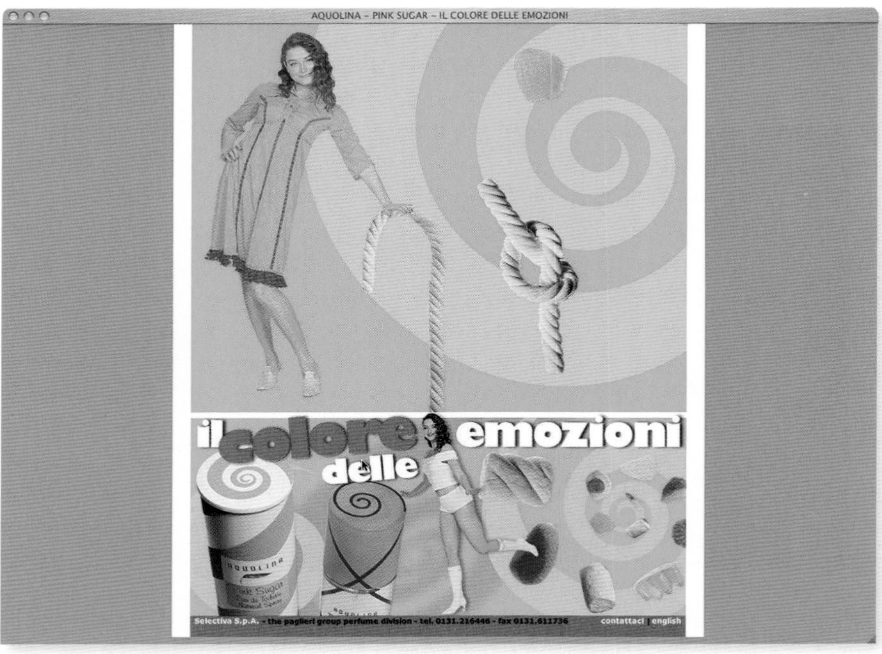
AQUOLINA – PINK SUGAR – IL COLORE DELLE EMOZIONI
il colore delle emozioni
Selectiva S.p.A. – the paglieri group perfume division – tel. 0131.216446 – fax 0131.611736
contattaci | english

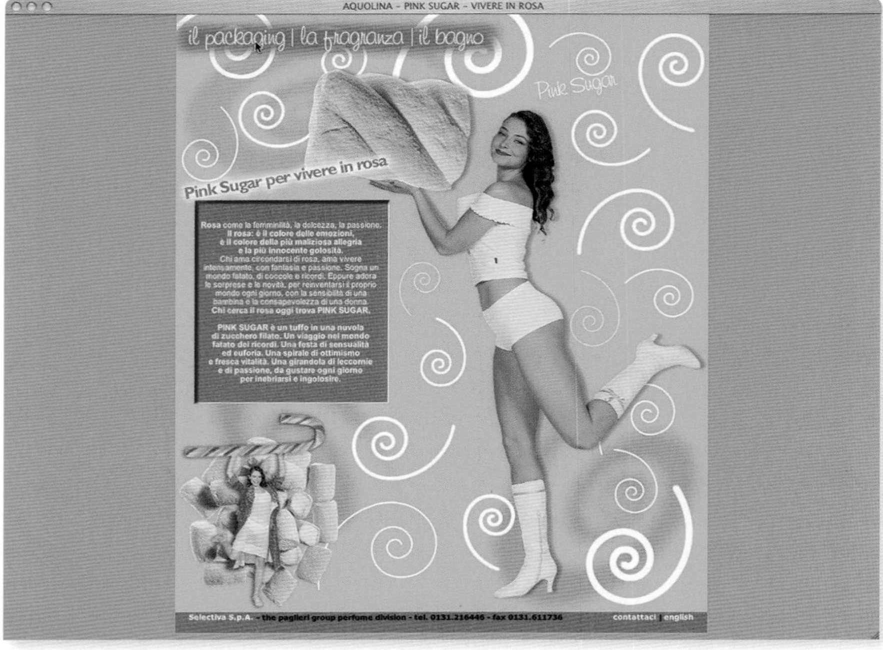
AQUOLINA – PINK SUGAR – VIVERE IN ROSA
il packaging | la fragranza | il bagno
Pink Sugar
Pink Sugar per vivere in rosa
Rosa come la femminilità, la dolcezza, la passione.
Il rosa: è il colore delle emozioni,
è il colore della più maliziosa allegria
e la più innocente golosità.
Chi ama circondarsi di rosa, ama vivere
intensamente, con fantasia e passione. Sogna un
mondo fatato, di coccole e ricordi. Eppure adora
le sorprese e le novità, per reinventarsi il proprio
mondo ogni giorno, con la sensibilità di una
bambina e la consapevolezza di una donna.
Chi cerca il rosa oggi trova PINK SUGAR.
PINK SUGAR è un tuffo in una nuvola
di zucchero filato. Un viaggio nel mondo
fatato dei ricordi. Una festa di sensualità
ed euforia. Una spirale di ottimismo
e fresca vitalità. Una girandola di leccornie
e di passione, da gustare ogni giorno
per inebriarsi e ingolosire.
Selectiva S.p.A. – the paglieri group perfume division – tel. 0131.216446 – fax 0131.611736
contattaci | english

www.selectiva-spa.it/pink_sugar.html
D: andrea tempesta **P:** selectiva
A: studio grafico tempesta **M:** andtemp@tin.it

cd-box.ch – das ideale, kompakte cd-archivsystem
cd-box.ch
das ideale, kompakte cd-archiv-system für den büro- und wohnbe-reich. ein blickfang in jedem raum. modular aufgebaut, einfach und flexi-bel erweiterbar. auf wunsch erhältlich mit untersatz auf rollen. die cd-box ist aus stahlblech, pulver-beschichtet. bietet platz für 100 cds.
home
cd-box
3d-ansicht
daten
impressum
agb
bestellen >>

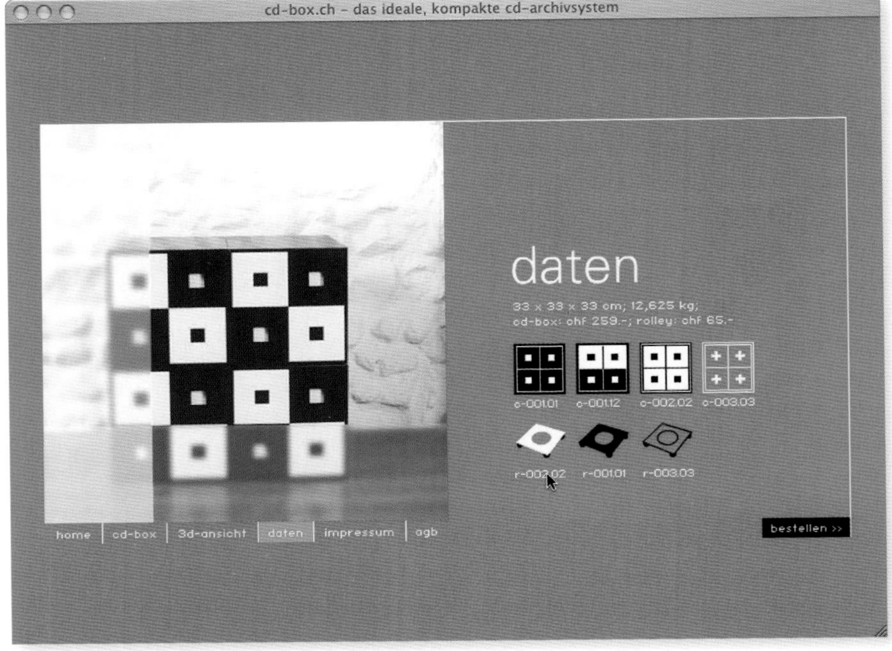
cd-box.ch – das ideale, kompakte cd-archivsystem
daten
33 x 33 x 33 cm; 12,625 kg;
cd-box: chf 259.-; rolley: chf 65.-
c-001.01
c-001.12
c-002.02
c-003.03
r-002.02
r-001.01
r-003.03
home
cd-box
3d-ansicht
daten
impressum
agb
bestellen >>

www.cd-box.ch
D: oliver schmid **P:** albert heer
A: webgarten **M:** oliver.schmid@webgarten.ch

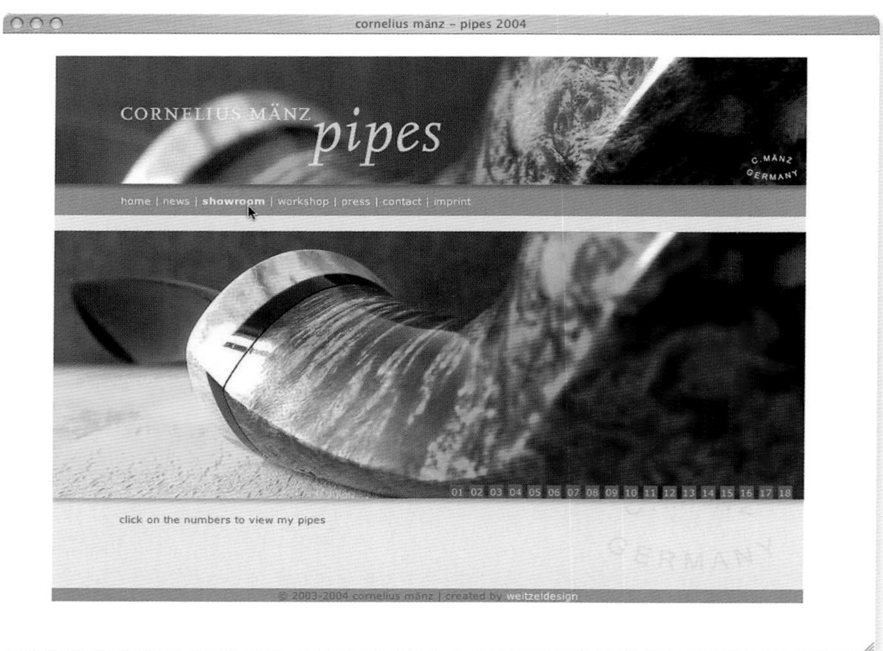
cornelius mänz – pipes 2004
CORNELIUS MÄNZ pipes
C.MÄNZ GERMANY
home | news | showroom | workshop | press | contact | imprint
01 02 03 04 05 06 07 08 09 10 11 12 13 14 15 16 17 18
click on the numbers to view my pipes
© 2003-2004 cornelius mänz | created by weitzeldesign

cornelius mänz – pipes 2004
CORNELIUS MÄNZ pipes
C.MÄNZ GERMANY
home | news | showroom | workshop | press | contact | imprint
pipes 2004
move your mouse over the small images on the right side to enlarge the images.
© 2003-2004 cornelius mänz | created by weitzeldesign

www.corneliusmaenz.com
D: thomas weitzel
A: weitzeldesign **M:** info@weitzeldesign.de

Bontempi | Küche, Küchen, Kücheneinrichtungen,...bel, Kocheinheit, Kocheinheiten, Küchengeräte
DESIGN
Küche
Varenna
BONTEMPI
Albed
Bad
MERATI
Albed
Kontakt
Modell: LK200 System, Design: Bontempi

Bontempi | Küche, Küchen, Kücheneinrichtungen,...bel, Kocheinheit, Kocheinheiten, Küchengeräte
DESIGN
Küche
Varenna
BONTEMPI
Albed
Bad
MERATI
Albed
Kontakt
Modell: LK200 System, Design: Bontempi

www.italdesign.ch
D: patrik steinmann
A: inware **M:** patrik.steinmann@ipaya.com

Brestovac d.o.o.
SOBA ▸
HOTELSKA KUPATILO
GALANTERIJA
design by Heavyform.com

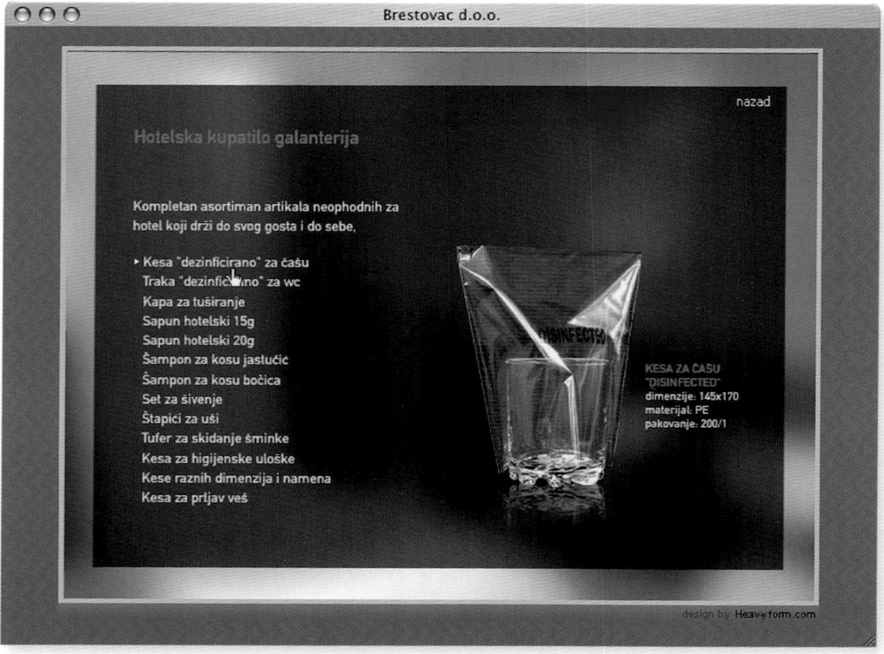
Brestovac d.o.o.
nazad
Hotelska kupatilo galanterija
Kompletan asortiman artikala neophodnih za
hotel koji drži do svog gosta i do sebe,
▸ Kesa "dezinficirano" za čašu
Traka "dezinficirano" za wc
Kapa za tuširanje
Sapun hotelski 15g
Sapun hotelski 20g
Šampon za kosu jastučić
Šampon za kosu bočica
Set za šivenje
Štapići za uši
Tufer za skidanje šminke
Kesa za higijenske uloške
Kese raznih dimenzija i namena
Kesa za prljav veš
DISINFECTED
KESA ZA ČAŠU
"DISINFECTED"
dimenzije: 145x170
materijal: PE
pakovanje: 200/1
design by Heavyform.com

www.brestovac.co.yu
D: nenad bogar **C:** nenad bogar
A: heavyform **M:** nenad@heavyform.com

::TEMAVENTO::
TEMAVENTO
CUSTOM BOARDS
close

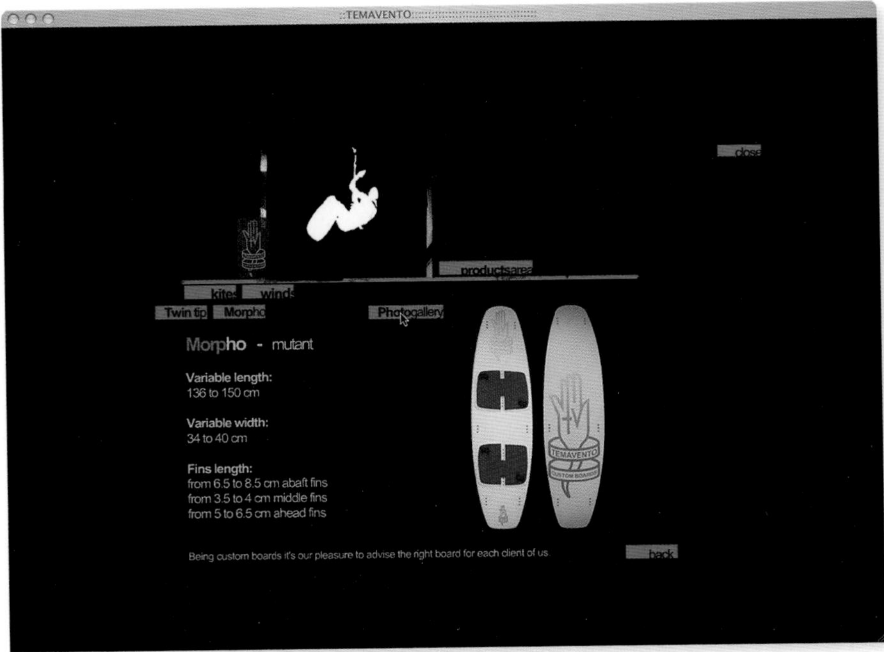
::TEMAVENTO::
close
productsarea
Twin tip
Morpho
Photogallery
Morpho - mutant
Variable length:
136 to 150 cm
Variable width:
34 to 40 cm
Fins length:
from 6.5 to 8.5 cm abaft fins
from 3.5 to 4 cm middle fins
from 5 to 6.5 cm ahead fins
Being custom boards it's our pleasure to advise the right board for each client of us.
back
TEMAVENTO
CUSTOM BOARDS

www.temavento.com
D: alessandro orlandi **C:** luca santinon
A: fishouse **M:** alessandro.orlandi@fishouse.net

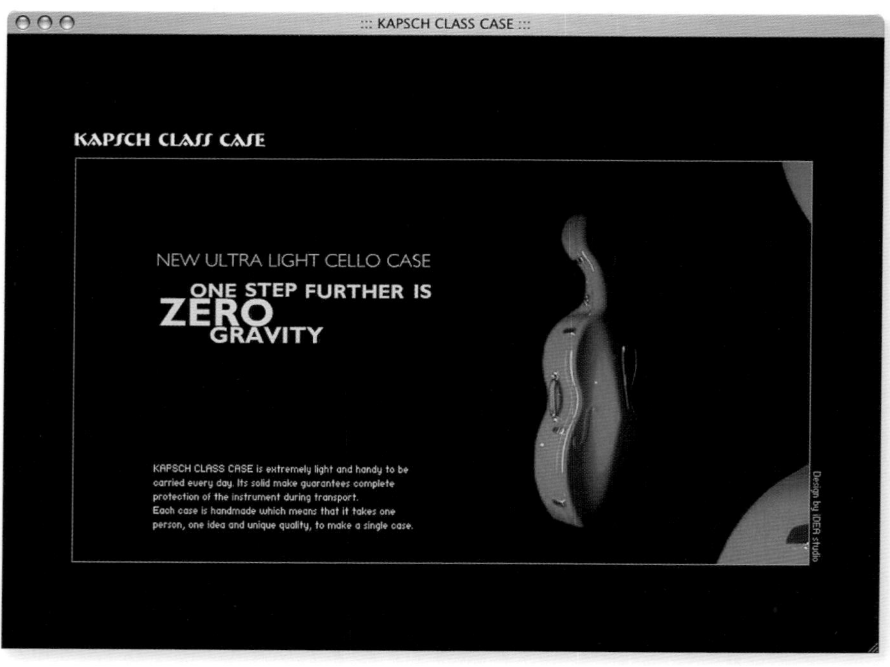
::: KAPSCH CLASS CASE :::
KAPSCH CLASS CASE
NEW ULTRA LIGHT CELLO CASE
ONE STEP FURTHER IS
ZERO
GRAVITY
KAPSCH CLASS CASE is extremely light and handy to be carried every day. Its solid make guarantees complete protection of the instrument during transport.
Each case is handmade which means that it takes one person, one idea and unique quality, to make a single case.
Design by IDEA studio

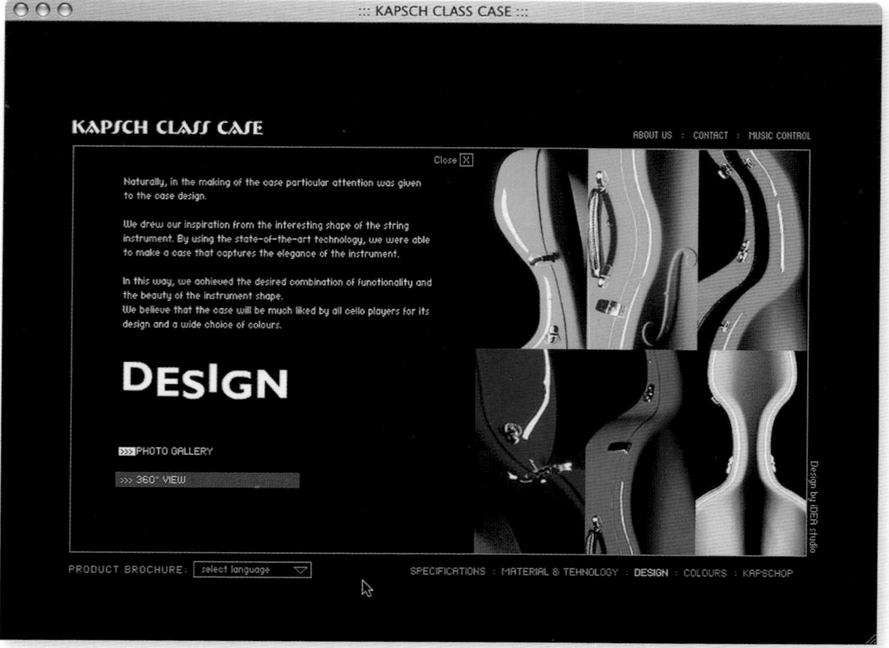
::: KAPSCH CLASS CASE :::
KAPSCH CLASS CASE
ABOUT US : CONTACT : MUSIC CONTROL
Close
Naturally, in the making of the case particular attention was given to the case design.
We drew our inspiration from the interesting shape of the string instrument. By using the state-of-the-art technology, we were able to make a case that captures the elegance of the instrument.
In this way, we achieved the desired combination of functionality and the beauty of the instrument shape.
We believe that the case will be much liked by all cello players for its design and a wide choice of colours.
DESIGN
>>> PHOTO GALLERY
>>> 360° VIEW
PRODUCT BROCHURE: select language
SPECIFICATIONS : MATERIAL & TEHNOLOGY : DESIGN : COLOURS : KAPSCHOP
Design by IDEA studio

www.kapsch.cc
D: boris bengez
A: idea studio **M:** www.idea.hr

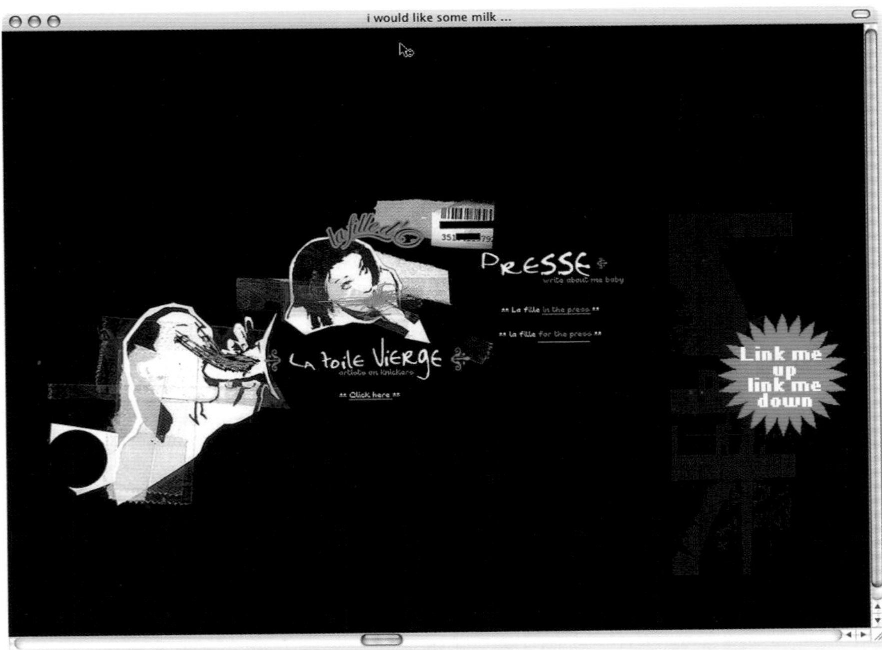
i would like some milk ...
PRESSE
write about me baby
** La fille in the press **
** La fille for the press **
La toile Vierge
artists on knickers
** Click here **
Link me up link me down

i would like some milk ...
Polaroooids
send them to us

www.lafilledo.com

D: pauwels stijn **C:** peter ginneberge **P:** tim siaens

A: www.milkandcookies.be **M:** tim@milkandcookies.be

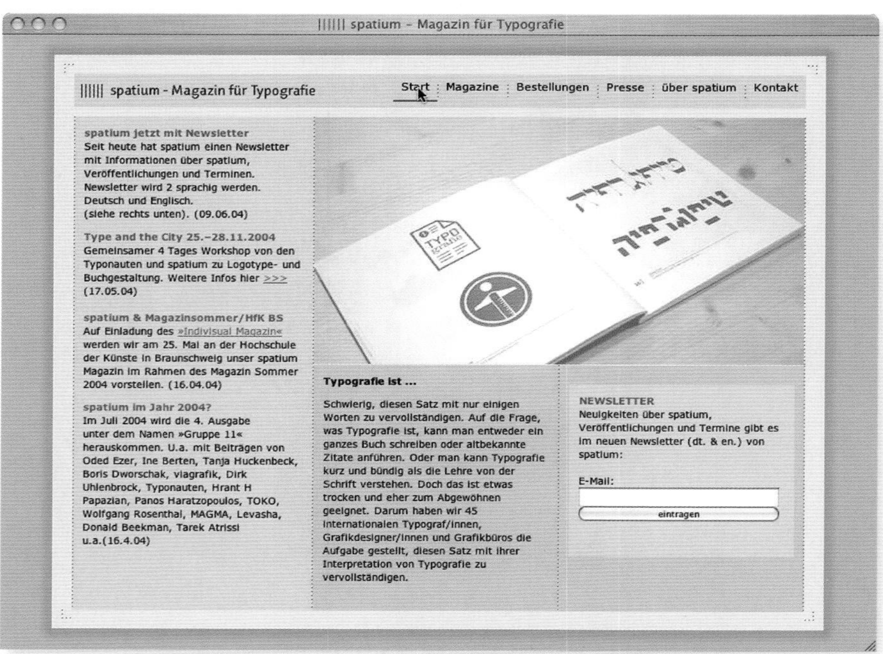
||||| spatium - Magazin für Typografie
||||| spatium - Magazin für Typografie
Start
Magazine
Bestellungen
Presse
über spatium
Kontakt
spatium jetzt mit Newsletter
Seit heute hat spatium einen Newsletter mit Informationen über spatium, Veröffentlichungen und Terminen. Newsletter wird 2 sprachig werden. Deutsch und Englisch. (siehe rechts unten). (09.06.04)
Type and the City 25.–28.11.2004
Gemeinsamer 4 Tages Workshop von den Typonauten und spatium zu Logotype- und Buchgestaltung. Weitere Infos hier >>> (17.05.04)
spatium & Magazinsommer/HfK BS
Auf Einladung des »Indivisual Magazin« werden wir am 25. Mai an der Hochschule der Künste in Braunschweig unser spatium Magazin im Rahmen des Magazin Sommer 2004 vorstellen. (16.04.04)
spatium im Jahr 2004?
Im Juli 2004 wird die 4. Ausgabe unter dem Namen »Gruppe 11« herauskommen. U.a. mit Beiträgen von Oded Ezer, Ine Berten, Tanja Huckenbeck, Boris Dworschak, viagrafik, Dirk Uhlenbrock, Typonauten, Hrant H Papazian, Panos Haratzopoulos, TOKO, Wolfgang Rosenthal, MAGMA, Levasha, Donald Beekman, Tarek Atrissi u.a.(16.4.04)
Typografie ist ...
Schwierig, diesen Satz mit nur einigen Worten zu vervollständigen. Auf die Frage, was Typografie ist, kann man entweder ein ganzes Buch schreiben oder altbekannte Zitate anführen. Oder man kann Typografie kurz und bündig als die Lehre von der Schrift verstehen. Doch das ist etwas trocken und eher zum Abgewöhnen geeignet. Darum haben wir 45 internationalen Typograf/innen, Grafikdesigner/innen und Grafikbüros die Aufgabe gestellt, diesen Satz mit ihrer Interpretation von Typografie zu vervollständigen.
NEWSLETTER
Neuigkeiten über spatium, Veröffentlichungen und Termine gibt es im neuen Newsletter (dt. & en.) von spatium:
E-Mail:
eintragen

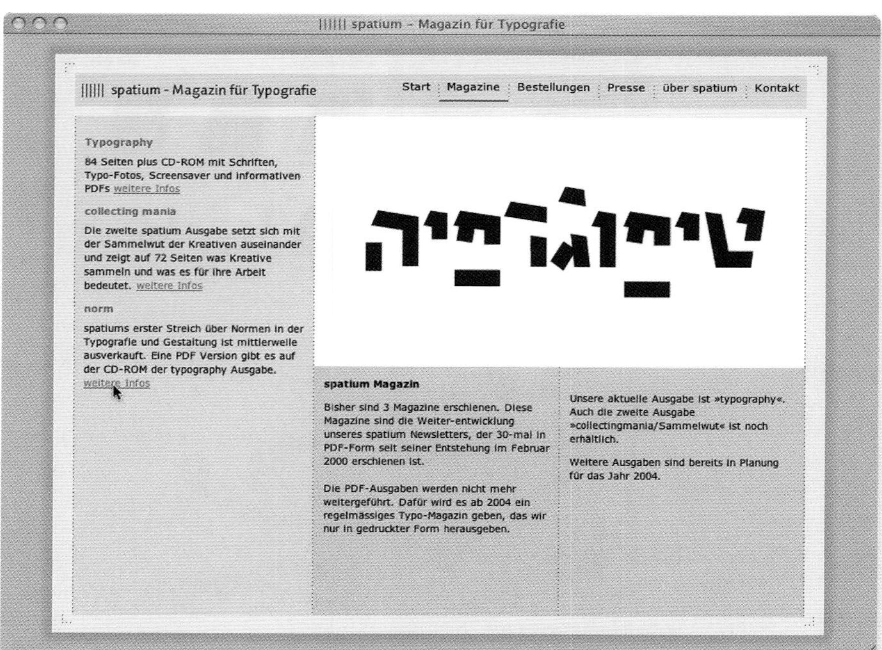
||||| spatium - Magazin für Typografie
||||| spatium - Magazin für Typografie
Start
Magazine
Bestellungen
Presse
über spatium
Kontakt
Typography
84 Seiten plus CD-ROM mit Schriften, Typo-Fotos, Screensaver und informativen PDFs weitere Infos
collecting mania
Die zweite spatium Ausgabe setzt sich mit der Sammelwut der Kreativen auseinander und zeigt auf 72 Seiten was Kreative sammeln und was es für ihre Arbeit bedeutet. weitere Infos
norm
spatiums erster Streich über Normen in der Typografie und Gestaltung ist mittlerweile ausverkauft. Eine PDF Version gibt es auf der CD-ROM der typography Ausgabe. weitere Infos
spatium Magazin
Bisher sind 3 Magazine erschienen. Diese Magazine sind die Weiter-entwicklung unseres spatium Newsletters, der 30-mal in PDF-Form seit seiner Entstehung im Februar 2000 erschienen ist.
Die PDF-Ausgaben werden nicht mehr weitergeführt. Dafür wird es ab 2004 ein regelmässiges Typo-Magazin geben, das wir nur in gedruckter Form herausgeben.
Unsere aktuelle Ausgabe ist »typography«. Auch die zweite Ausgabe »collectingmania/Sammelwut« ist noch erhältlich.
Weitere Ausgaben sind bereits in Planung für das Jahr 2004.

www.spatium-magazin.de
D: jens franke **C:** marcel eichner
M: info@typosition.de

:: EDICIONES FRUTOS DEL TIEMPO ::
EDICIONES
FRUTOS DEL TIEMPO
ASOCIACIÓN CULTURAL
ARTÍCULOS
PUBLICADOS
El Ocaso Del Diccionario
Joaquín Botella (Alicante)
El siguiente artículo se publica con la autorización del diario "El Faro". Aurora Marco, profesora universitaria, ha realizado un estudio sobre el Diccionario de la Real Academia en el que lo tacha de machista. Sabiendo que, por las m..
leer
Un Cuerpo Perfecto
Conchi Izquierdo (Elche)
Después de admirar tu foto en la pared, querida Naomi, después de contemplar la más absoluta perfección en cada curva de tu cuerpo, me miro desnuda en el espejo y me veo gorda, asquerosamente gorda. He perdido 20 kilos en los últimos cinco mese..
leer
La Magia De Nadia
Julio Hermaz (EE.UU)
La Bruja Naddia De artístico figurado, contrasta, rudeza con lo expresivo, áspera la cubierta resalta relieves en el edificio, y donde estaba la campana, está la casa de Naddia, la arpía del municipio. El antiguo campanario se orna con..
leer
Siete Poemas
Juan Antonio Ballesta i Navarro (Alicante)
SI DE MI LUCHA... Si de mi lucha con el tirano no vuelvo... No acudais por mí. ¡Id a por él! MAÑANA TAMBIÉN TENDRAS ROSAS Soy un delincuente.
inicio
historia
actividades
artículos
álbum de fotos
foro
notas de prensa
departamento editorial
contactar
PEDIDOS
LIBROS
» ver pedidos
LIBROS
RECOMENDADOS
examen final

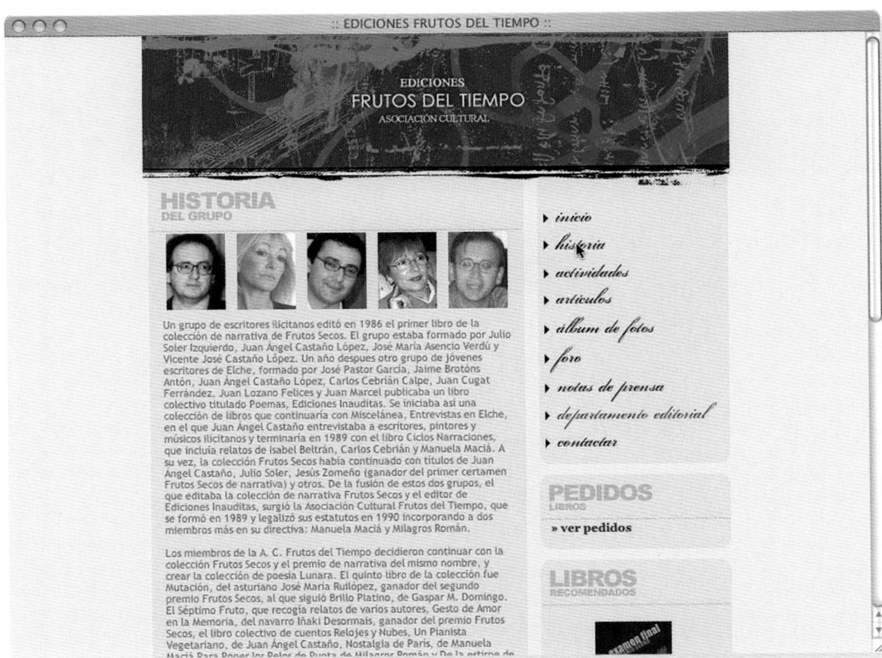
:: EDICIONES FRUTOS DEL TIEMPO ::
EDICIONES
FRUTOS DEL TIEMPO
ASOCIACIÓN CULTURAL
HISTORIA
DEL GRUPO
Un grupo de escritores ilicitanos editó en 1986 el primer libro de la colección de narrativa de Frutos Secos. El grupo estaba formado por Julio Soler Izquierdo, Juan Ángel Castaño López, José María Asencio Verdú y Vicente José Castaño López. Un año despues otro grupo de jóvenes escritores de Elche, formado por José Pastor García, Jaime Brotóns Antón, Juan Ángel Castaño López, Carlos Cebrián Calpe, Juan Cugat Ferrández, Juan Lozano Felices y Juan Marcel publicaba un libro colectivo titulado Poemas, Ediciones Inauditas. Se iniciaba así una colección de libros que continuaría con Miscelánea, Entrevistas en Elche, en el que Juan Ángel Castaño entrevistaba a escritores, pintores y músicos ilicitanos y terminaría en 1989 con el libro Ciclos Narraciones, que incluía relatos de Isabel Beltrán, Carlos Cebrián y Manuela Maciá. A su vez, la colección Frutos Secos había continuado con títulos de Juan Ángel Castaño, Julio Soler, Jesús Zomeño (ganador del primer certamen Frutos Secos de narrativa) y otros. De la fusión de estos dos grupos, el que editaba la colección de narrativa Frutos Secos y el editor de Ediciones Inauditas, surgió la Asociación Cultural Frutos del Tiempo, que se formó en 1989 y legalizó sus estatutos en 1990 incorporando a dos miembros más en su directiva: Manuela Maciá y Milagros Román.
Los miembros de la A. C. Frutos del Tiempo decidieron continuar con la colección Frutos Secos y el premio de narrativa del mismo nombre, y crear la colección de poesía Lunara. El quinto libro de la colección fue Mutación, del asturiano José María Ruilópez, ganador del segundo premio Frutos Secos, al que siguió Brillo Platino, de Gaspar M. Domingo. El Séptimo Fruto, que recogía relatos de varios autores, Gesto de Amor en la Memoria, del navarro Iñaki Desormais, ganador del premio Frutos Secos, el libro colectivo de cuentos Relojes y Nubes, Un Pianista Vegetariano, de Juan Ángel Castaño, Nostalgia de París, de Manuela
inicio
historia
actividades
artículos
álbum de fotos
foro
notas de prensa
departamento editorial
contactar
PEDIDOS
LIBROS
» ver pedidos
LIBROS
RECOMENDADOS
examen final

www.frutosdeltiempo.com
D: josé manuel gonzálvez román **P:** ediciones frutos del tiempo
A: aivlis.net **M:** hologium@aivlis.net

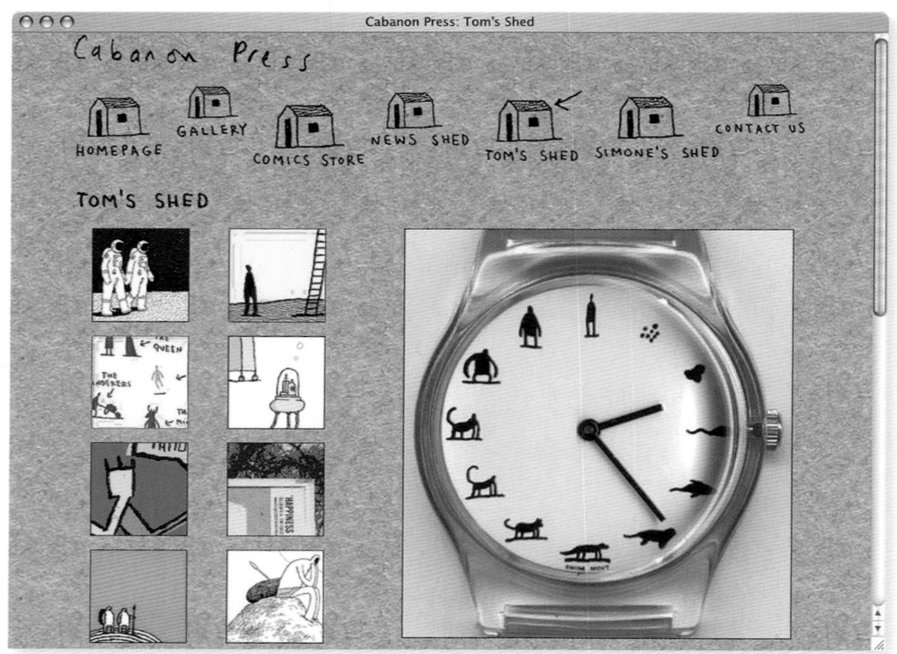
Cabanon Press: Tom's Shed
Cabanon Press
HOMEPAGE
GALLERY
COMICS STORE
NEWS SHED
TOM'S SHED
SIMONE'S SHED
CONTACT US
TOM'S SHED

Cabanon Press
Cabanon Press
HOMEPAGE
GALLERY
COMICS STORE
NEWS SHED
TOM'S SHED
SIMONE'S SHED
CONTACT US
HOME
HELLO
BOTH
bip
bip
bip
© Cabanon Press, Tom Gauld and Simone Lia. 2002 | made by moodia

www.cabanonpress.com
D: tom kerwin
A: moodia **M:** tom@moodia.com

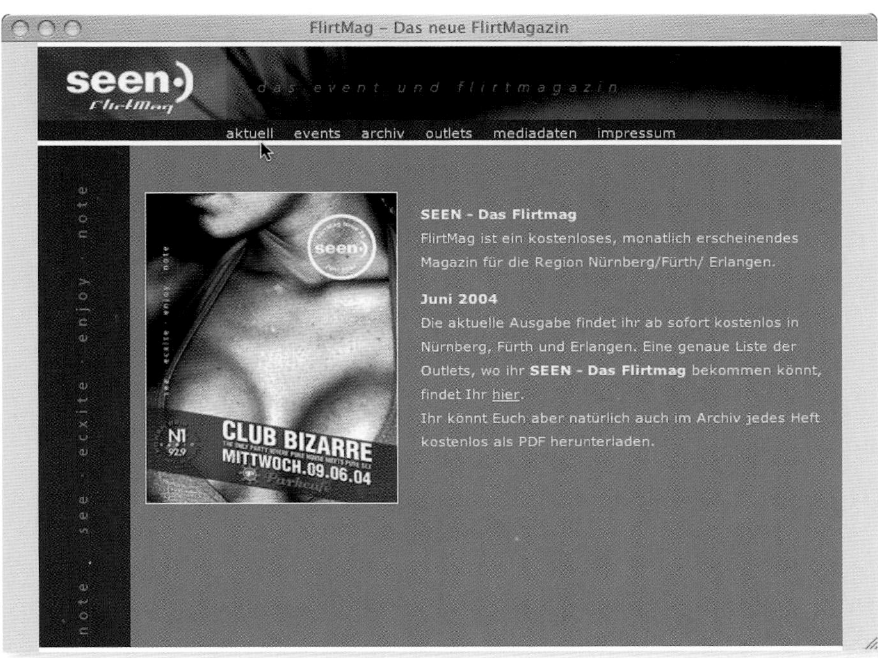
FlirtMag - Das neue FlirtMagazin
seen
das event und flirtmagazin
aktuell events archiv outlets mediadaten impressum
note . see . ecxite . enjoy . note
SEEN - Das Flirtmag
FlirtMag ist ein kostenloses, monatlich erscheinendes Magazin für die Region Nürnberg/Fürth/ Erlangen.
Juni 2004
Die aktuelle Ausgabe findet ihr ab sofort kostenlos in Nürnberg, Fürth und Erlangen. Eine genaue Liste der Outlets, wo ihr SEEN - Das Flirtmag bekommen könnt, findet Ihr hier.
Ihr könnt Euch aber natürlich auch im Archiv jedes Heft kostenlos als PDF herunterladen.
CLUB BIZARRE
MITTWOCH.09.06.04

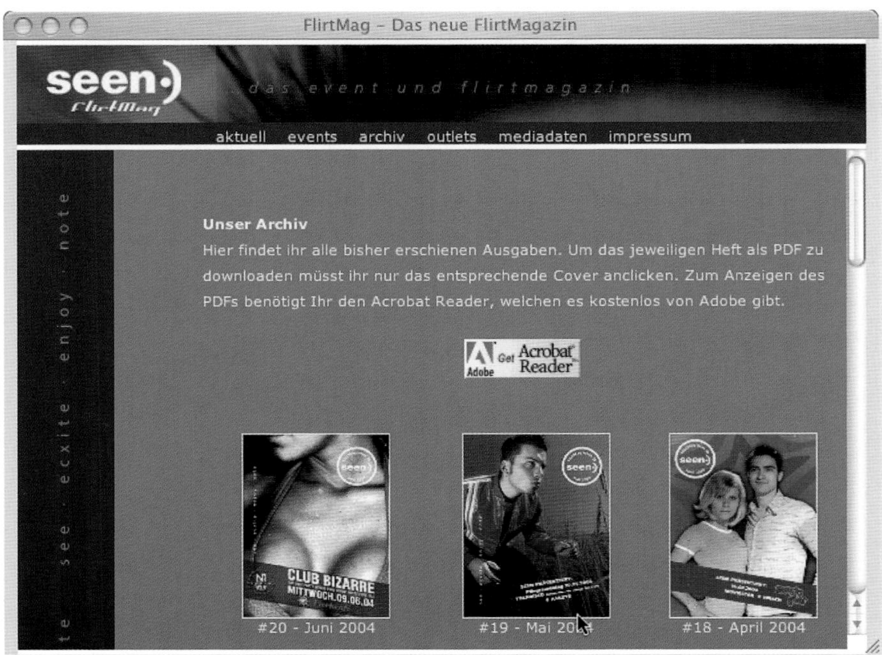
FlirtMag - Das neue FlirtMagazin
seen
das event und flirtmagazin
aktuell events archiv outlets mediadaten impressum
Unser Archiv
Hier findet ihr alle bisher erschienen Ausgaben. Um das jeweiligen Heft als PDF zu downloaden müsst ihr nur das entsprechende Cover anclicken. Zum Anzeigen des PDFs benötigt Ihr den Acrobat Reader, welchen es kostenlos von Adobe gibt.
Get Acrobat Reader
#20 - Juni 2004
#19 - Mai 2004
#18 - April 2004

www.flirtmag.de
D: matthias richter **C:** markus deuerlein
A: project:media **M:** deuerlein@project.de

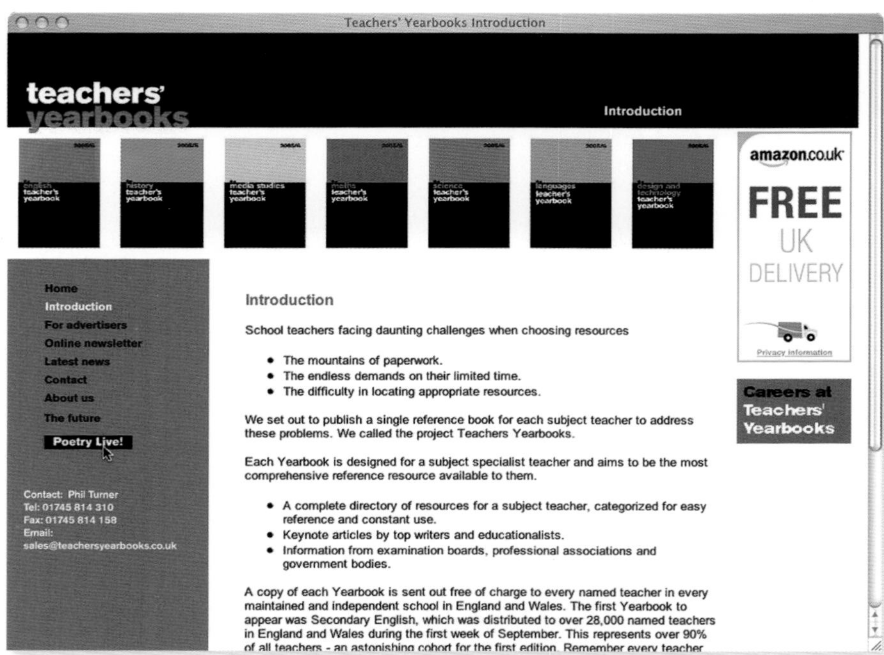
Teachers' Yearbooks Introduction
teachers' yearbooks
Introduction
amazon.co.uk
FREE
UK
DELIVERY
Privacy information
Careers at Teachers' Yearbooks
Home
Introduction
For advertisers
Online newsletter
Latest news
Contact
About us
The future
Poetry Live!
Contact: Phil Turner
Tel: 01745 814 310
Fax: 01745 814 158
Email:
sales@teachersyearbooks.co.uk
Introduction
School teachers facing daunting challenges when choosing resources
The mountains of paperwork.
The endless demands on their limited time.
The difficulty in locating appropriate resources.
We set out to publish a single reference book for each subject teacher to address these problems. We called the project Teachers Yearbooks.
Each Yearbook is designed for a subject specialist teacher and aims to be the most comprehensive reference resource available to them.
A complete directory of resources for a subject teacher, categorized for easy reference and constant use.
Keynote articles by top writers and educationalists.
Information from examination boards, professional associations and government bodies.
A copy of each Yearbook is sent out free of charge to every named teacher in every maintained and independent school in England and Wales. The first Yearbook to appear was Secondary English, which was distributed to over 28,000 named teachers in England and Wales during the first week of September. This represents over 90%

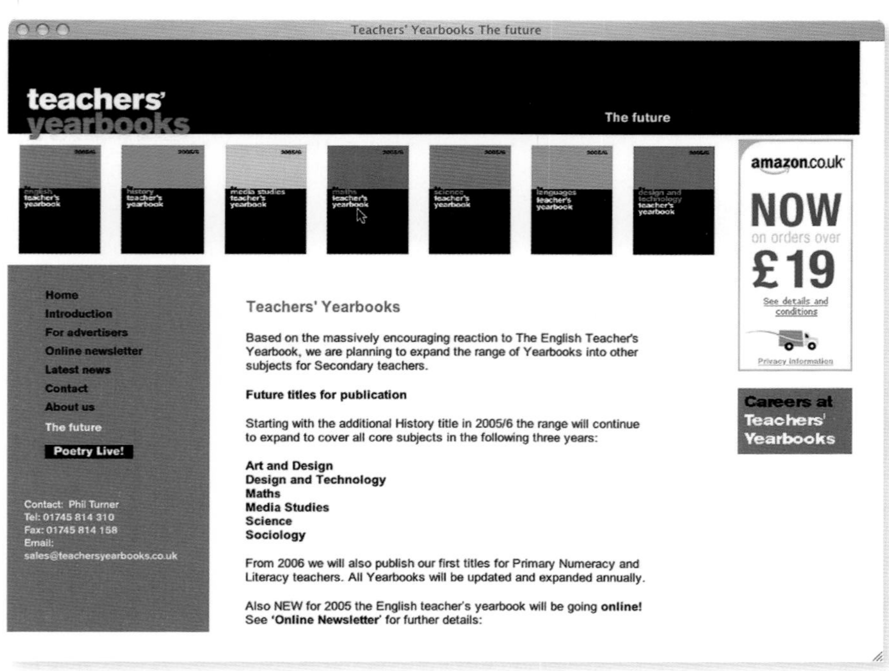
Teachers' Yearbooks The future
teachers' yearbooks
The future
amazon.co.uk
NOW
on orders over
£19
See details and conditions
Privacy information
Careers at Teachers' Yearbooks
Home
Introduction
For advertisers
Online newsletter
Latest news
Contact
About us
The future
Poetry Live!
Contact: Phil Turner
Tel: 01745 814 310
Fax: 01745 814 158
Email:
sales@teachersyearbooks.co.uk
Teachers' Yearbooks
Based on the massively encouraging reaction to The English Teacher's Yearbook, we are planning to expand the range of Yearbooks into other subjects for Secondary teachers.
Future titles for publication
Starting with the additional History title in 2005/6 the range will continue to expand to cover all core subjects in the following three years:
Art and Design
Design and Technology
Maths
Media Studies
Science
Sociology
From 2006 we will also publish our first titles for Primary Numeracy and Literacy teachers. All Yearbooks will be updated and expanded annually.
Also NEW for 2005 the English teacher's yearbook will be going online!
See 'Online Newsletter' for further details:

www.teachersyearbooks.co.uk
D: alice beaven **C:** ed williams
A: positive 2 **M:** contact@positive2.co.uk

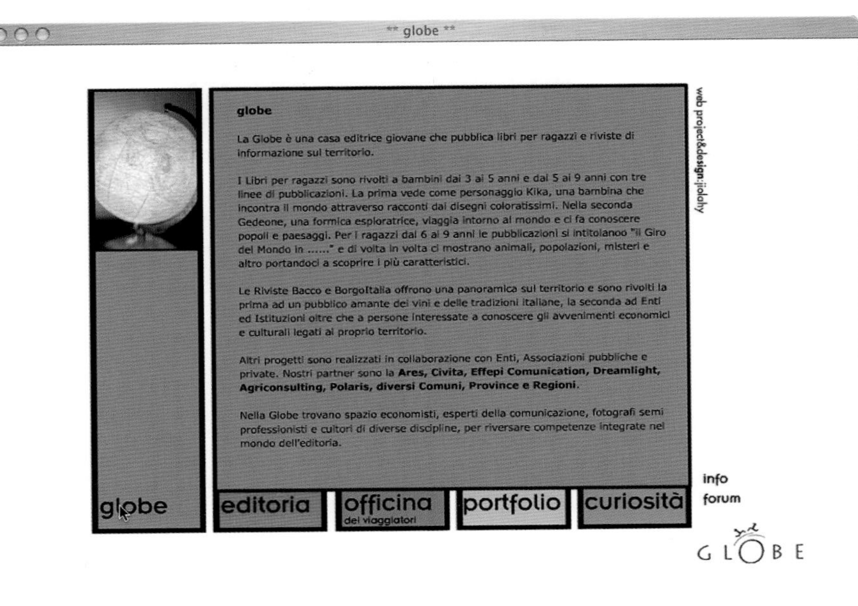
** globe **
globe
La Globe è una casa editrice giovane che pubblica libri per ragazzi e riviste di informazione sul territorio.
I Libri per ragazzi sono rivolti a bambini dai 3 ai 5 anni e dai 5 ai 9 anni con tre linee di pubblicazioni. La prima vede come personaggio Kika, una bambina che incontra il mondo attraverso racconti dai disegni coloratissimi. Nella seconda Gedeone, una formica esploratrice, viaggia intorno al mondo e ci fa conoscere popoli e paesaggi. Per i ragazzi dai 6 ai 9 anni le pubblicazioni si intitolanoo "il Giro del Mondo in ......" e di volta in volta ci mostrano animali, popolazioni, misteri e altro portandoci a scoprire i più caratteristici.
Le Riviste Bacco e BorgoItalia offrono una panoramica sul territorio e sono rivolti la prima ad un pubblico amante dei vini e delle tradizioni italiane, la seconda ad Enti ed Istituzioni oltre che a persone interessate a conoscere gli avvenimenti economici e culturali legati al proprio territorio.
Altri progetti sono realizzati in collaborazione con Enti, Associazioni pubbliche e private. Nostri partner sono la Ares, Civita, Effepi Comunication, Dreamlight, Agriconsulting, Polaris, diversi Comuni, Province e Regioni.
Nella Globe trovano spazio economisti, esperti della comunicazione, fotografi semi professionisti e cultori di diverse discipline, per riversare competenze integrate nel mondo dell'editoria.
web project&design:jiolahy
globe
editoria
officina
dei viaggiatori
portfolio
curiosità
info
forum
GLOBE

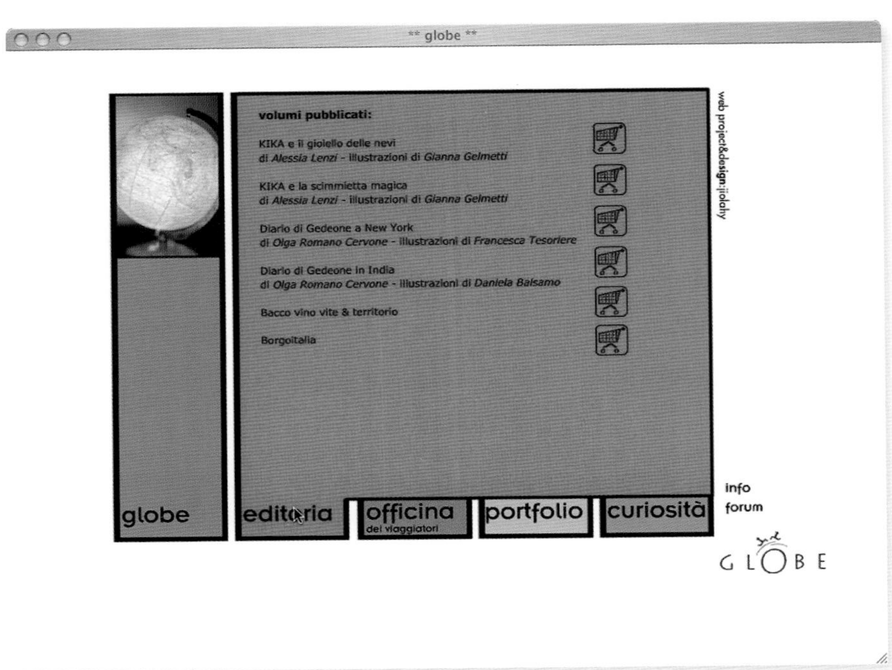
** globe **
volumi pubblicati:
KIKA e il gioiello delle nevi
di Alessia Lenzi - illustrazioni di Gianna Gelmetti
KIKA e la scimmietta magica
di Alessia Lenzi - illustrazioni di Gianna Gelmetti
Diario di Gedeone a New York
di Olga Romano Cervone - illustrazioni di Francesca Tesoriere
Diario di Gedeone in India
di Olga Romano Cervone - illustrazioni di Daniela Balsamo
Bacco vino vite & territorio
BorgoItalia
web project&design:jiolahy
globe
editoria
officina
dei viaggiatori
portfolio
curiosità
info
forum
GLOBE

www.edizioniglobe.it
D: chiara boscotrecase
A: jiolahy **M:** info@jiolahy.it

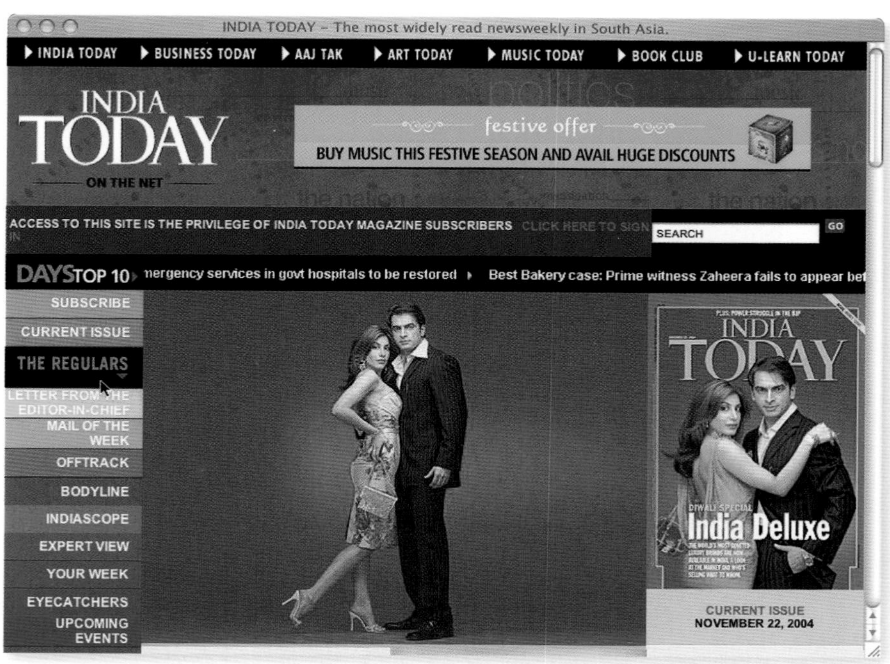
INDIA TODAY – The most widely read newsweekly in South Asia.
INDIA TODAY
BUSINESS TODAY
AAJ TAK
ART TODAY
MUSIC TODAY
BOOK CLUB
U-LEARN TODAY
INDIA TODAY
ON THE NET
festive offer
BUY MUSIC THIS FESTIVE SEASON AND AVAIL HUGE DISCOUNTS
ACCESS TO THIS SITE IS THE PRIVILEGE OF INDIA TODAY MAGAZINE SUBSCRIBERS
SEARCH
GO
DAYSTOP 10
nergency services in govt hospitals to be restored
Best Bakery case: Prime witness Zaheera fails to appear bef
SUBSCRIBE
CURRENT ISSUE
THE REGULARS
LETTER FROM THE EDITOR-IN-CHIEF
MAIL OF THE WEEK
OFFTRACK
BODYLINE
INDIASCOPE
EXPERT VIEW
YOUR WEEK
EYECATCHERS
UPCOMING EVENTS
INDIA TODAY
India Deluxe
CURRENT ISSUE
NOVEMBER 22, 2004

INDIA TODAY – ON THE NET
INDIA TODAY
ON THE NET
festive offer
BUY MUSIC THIS FESTIVE SEASON AND AVAIL HUGE DISCOUNTS
ACCESS TO THIS SITE IS THE PRIVILEGE OF INDIA TODAY MAGAZINE SUBSCRIBERS
SEARCH
GO
DAYSTOP 10
Platinum credit card
Airports Authority of India to raise Rs 5000 crore to upgrade 30 airports: Praful Patel
PRIVILEGED ACCESS TO INDIA TODAY WEB EDITION
To read full versions of articles and exclusive features in this issue of India's most widely read magazine, all you need to do is enter your Subscription ID.
Subscriber Login
Please choose your edition
INDIA EDITION
NORTH AMERICAN EDITION
UK EDITION
GULF EDITION
UAE EDITION
INTERNATIONAL EDITION
TEMPORARY
Enter your subscription ID
Sample Label
Your ID can be found on the address label of the magazine's cover
YOUR SUBSCRIPTION ID
****
41ITI**** 28-01-2002 RGP 27
MR SUDHEER WARRIER
55 PARK DRIVE
THE FARADAY
SINGAPORE 118236
SINGAPORE
Why Subscribe?
INDIA TODAY
AGELESS SUPERSTAR
India Today is the country's most widely read publication-a position it has held for over a decade- with a circulation of 1.4 million every week and a readership in excess of 15 million. Now a subscription to India Today not only helps you make sense of India every week but also gives you privileged access to the web edition. absolutely FREE.
SUBSCRIBE NOW!

www.indiatoday.com
D: kushal grover **C:** kalli purie **P:** india today
M: kgrover@india-today.com

格林繪本網 - 閱讀 To Read
格林繪本網
GrimmPress.com
閱讀
娛樂
活動
格林繪本網 > 閱讀 To Read
閱讀 To Read
新書上架
世界繪本大獎
繪本圖書館
作/畫家故事
繪本講堂
全文檢索
請輸入關鍵字
搜尋
書籍搜尋
請輸入關鍵字
作/ 繪者
書名
當月新書
全部書籍
搜尋
依分類搜尋
閱讀 To Read
哈囉！歡迎來到格林繪本網TO READ單元。在這裡，永遠有數不盡的好書要推薦給您，還有第一手的出版消息要報給您知；我們也將深入介紹世界的繪本以及重要的繪本大獎；而在繪本講堂中，您可以充充電了解繪本是怎麼產生以及如何閱讀繪本……。還在等什麼？Let's go
新書上架
書名 偵探發威
作者 辛西亞．彼得森
繪者 布萊恩．彼得森
出版 2004年12月
簡介 一個發生在狐狸村的有趣故事，藉由畫家彼得森細緻的水彩畫面傳達給各位讀者。威利刺蝟、魯魯兔、和哈維鼠有了大麻煩！…
更多新書
世界繪本大獎
英國聰明書獎
本月主題
主題閱讀—用熱情把愛傳出去
動感書本—用熱情創造奇蹟
繪本講堂—如何替繪本上色？
聖誕老爸--雷蒙布里斯
與精靈合作的人—用熱情來生活與工作
新書上架
偵探發威
消失的寶藏
神秘谷
天國騷動
童話短路2部曲
暢銷排行榜 more
1 聖誕老人餓肚皮
2 聖誕驚喜
3 巴黎人的巴黎
4 奧莉薇

格林繪本網 - 娛樂 To Have Fun
格林繪本網
GrimmPress.com
娛樂
閱讀
活動
格林繪本網 > 娛樂 To Have Fun
動感書本
遊戲
主題閱讀
討論區
電子賀卡
全文檢索
請輸入關鍵字
搜尋
書籍搜尋
請輸入關鍵字
作/ 繪者
書名
當月新書
全部書籍
搜尋
依分類搜尋
娛樂 To Have Fun
動感書本到底怎麼動？小遊戲隱藏著什麼大秘密？不貼郵票就可以向朋友傳達真情意？還有討論區裡大家到底在竊竊私語什麼？好奇吧！快點進入格林繪本網為您準備的To Have Fun區一探究竟！
動感書本
更多動感書本
有熱情就能創造奇蹟
主題 有熱情就能創造奇蹟
日期 2004年12月
簡介 聖誕老人一整年的時間是這麼分配的：他有90天會忙著準備禮物。
遊戲
更多遊戲
色彩大魔力
主題 色彩大魔力
日期 2004年10月
簡介 透過陳雅媛老師所設計的色彩遊戲，看看自己內在的無限潛能，並透過色彩分析，掌握今天的運勢。
本月主題
主題閱讀—用熱情把愛傳出去
動感書本—用熱情創造奇蹟
繪本講堂—如何替繪本上色？
聖誕老爸--雷蒙布里斯
與精靈合作的人—用熱情來生活與工作
新書上架
偵探發威
消失的寶藏
神秘谷
天國騷動
童話短路2部曲
暢銷排行榜 more
1 聖誕老人餓肚皮
2 聖誕驚喜
3 巴黎人的巴黎
4 奧莉薇

www.grimmpress.com.tw
D: ho chung shun **C:** sophie huang **P:** juice wu
A: agenda **M:** lawrenceintaipei@yahoo.com

percoms

**Schlagen Sie Wurzeln,
aber bleiben Sie nicht stehen**

Menschen setzen sich Ziele, privat und beruflich. Vieles lässt sich mit dem vorhandenen Wissen und Können erreichen. Anderes erfordert neue Ansätze, kreative Zugänge, Umdenken. Wer seine psychosozialen Fähigkeiten bewusst einsetzt, besitzt ein starkes Instrument auf dem Weg zur Erreichung seiner Ziele.

Bei Percoms werden diese Fähigkeiten gefördert und vertieft. Das Unternehmen hat sich seit der Gründung durch Mario Müller-Rottmann zu einem Netzwerk aus Spezialisten entwickelt. Sie weisen viele Jahre Erfahrung in verschiedenen Bereichen wie dem Gesundheitswesen, dem öffentlichen Dienst und der Wirtschaft auf. Die Percoms-Stärken sind Führungs- und Kommunikationstrainings, Einzel- und Gruppencoachings, Konfliktberatung und Krisenintervention.

Home
Portrait
Training
Consulting
Coaching
Themen

Termin
Anfrage
Sitemap

percoms:

percoms

Portrait

Seit 1999 positioniert sich Percoms in den Bereichen Personalberatung und -förderung, Psychosoziale Kompetenz, Konfliktmanagement, Krisenintervention und Teamentwicklung.

Im Sinne des Networking – Gedankens arbeiten in den Bereichen Training, Consulting und Coaching verschiedene Fachpersonen an optimalen Lösungen für Firmen und Einzelpersonen.

Home
Portrait
Training
Consulting
Coaching
Themen

Partner
Adresse
Referenzen

percoms:

www.percoms.ch
D: urs buesser
A: *typogestalter **M:** typo@typogestalter.ch

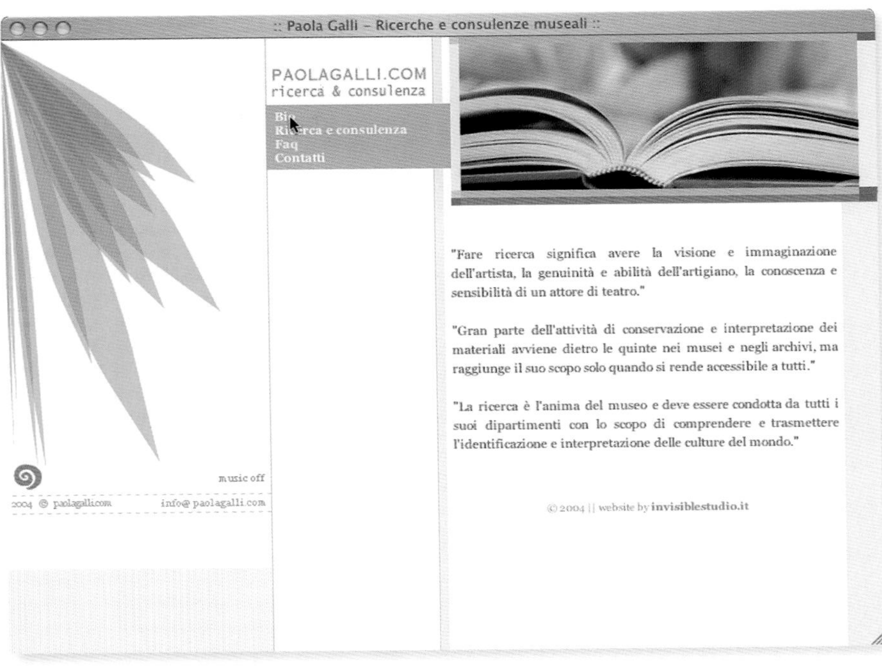
:: Paola Galli - Ricerche e consulenze museali ::
PAOLAGALLI.COM
ricerca & consulenza
Bio
Ricerca e consulenza
Faq
Contatti
"Fare ricerca significa avere la visione e immaginazione dell'artista, la genuinità e abilità dell'artigiano, la conoscenza e sensibilità di un attore di teatro."
"Gran parte dell'attività di conservazione e interpretazione dei materiali avviene dietro le quinte nei musei e negli archivi, ma raggiunge il suo scopo solo quando si rende accessibile a tutti."
"La ricerca è l'anima del museo e deve essere condotta da tutti i suoi dipartimenti con lo scopo di comprendere e trasmettere l'identificazione e interpretazione delle culture del mondo."
music off
2004 © paolagalli.com
info@paolagalli.com
© 2004 || website by invisiblestudio.it

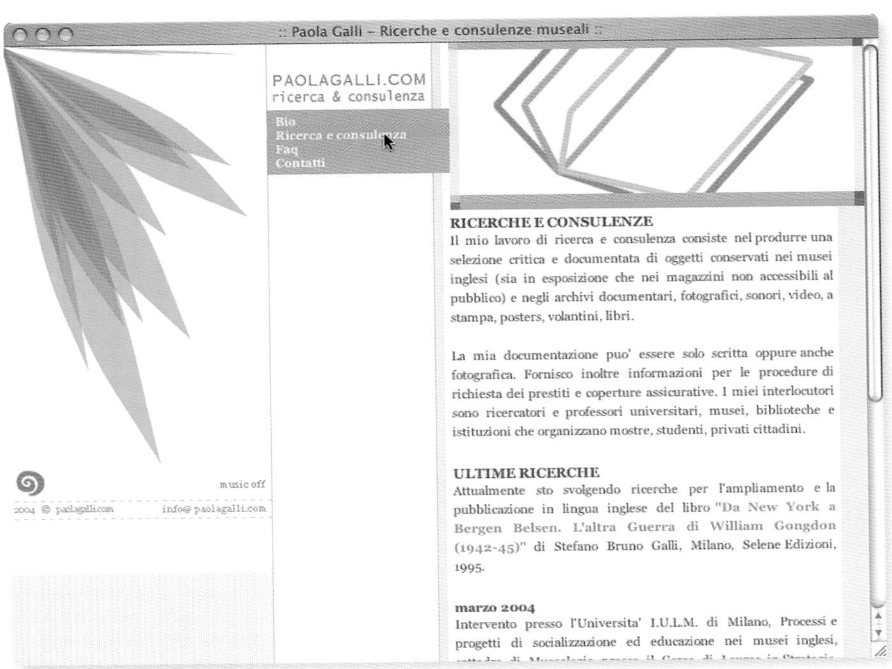
:: Paola Galli - Ricerche e consulenze museali ::
PAOLAGALLI.COM
ricerca & consulenza
Bio
Ricerca e consulenza
Faq
Contatti
RICERCHE E CONSULENZE
Il mio lavoro di ricerca e consulenza consiste nel produrre una selezione critica e documentata di oggetti conservati nei musei inglesi (sia in esposizione che nei magazzini non accessibili al pubblico) e negli archivi documentari, fotografici, sonori, video, a stampa, posters, volantini, libri.
La mia documentazione puo' essere solo scritta oppure anche fotografica. Fornisco inoltre informazioni per le procedure di richiesta dei prestiti e coperture assicurative. I miei interlocutori sono ricercatori e professori universitari, musei, biblioteche e istituzioni che organizzano mostre, studenti, privati cittadini.
ULTIME RICERCHE
Attualmente sto svolgendo ricerche per l'ampliamento e la pubblicazione in lingua inglese del libro "Da New York a Bergen Belsen. L'altra Guerra di William Gongdon (1942-45)" di Stefano Bruno Galli, Milano, Selene Edizioni, 1995.
marzo 2004
Intervento presso l'Universita' I.U.L.M. di Milano, Processi e progetti di socializzazione ed educazione nei musei inglesi,
music off
2004 © paolagalli.com
info@paolagalli.com

www.paolagalli.com
D: stefania boiano **C:** giuliano gaia
A: invisible studio **M:** contact@invisiblestudio.it

:::: MISA PRODUCTION :::: moda e spettacolo
mISa agency
| COMUNICATION | CONTACT |
CHI SIAMO
| CHI SIAMO | DOVE SIAMO | SERVIZI |
mISa communication
La Misa Communication, settore della Misa Agency, si occupa di marketing e pubblicità al servizio delle aziende. Pianifica strategie di marcheting per aziende che vogliono far accrescere, confermare o rilanciare la propria immagine, prodotti o servizi a livello locale, regionale o nazionale. Offriamo un servizio completo, dalla programmazione alla ideazione, alla realizzazione di tutto quello che riguarda il settore marketing e pubblicità. Uno dei punti di forza della nostra azienda è sicuramente la capacità delle nostre figure professionali, addetti ai vari settori e ai collaboratori esterni che svolgono il proprio lavoro con estremo impegno e professionalità.
La COMUNICAZIONE è settore molto vasto, e abbraccia molti campi, dalla Tv, alla radio, agli eventi, alla cartellonistica, al web ecc. La Misa Communication è nata proprio per dare ai clienti un servizio completo di tutte o quasi le forme pubblicitarie esistenti, questo sia direttamente sia indirettamente grazie alle collaborazioni con altre aziende del settore. La cosa che ci contraddistingue, oltre la qualità dei servizi, è la competitività di prezzo e questo è stato possibile grazie alla fiducia che molte aziende hanno riposto nella nostra organizzazione.
Esempi di pubblicità
Eventi pubblicitari dell'azienda, valorizzazione prodotti, presentazione campionari, pubblicità televisiva, radiofonica,
SERVIZI
EVENTI
mISa production
PRODUCTION
LAVORA CON NOI
MODULI
mISa
LAVORA CON NOI
moda
mISa
NEWS
mISa

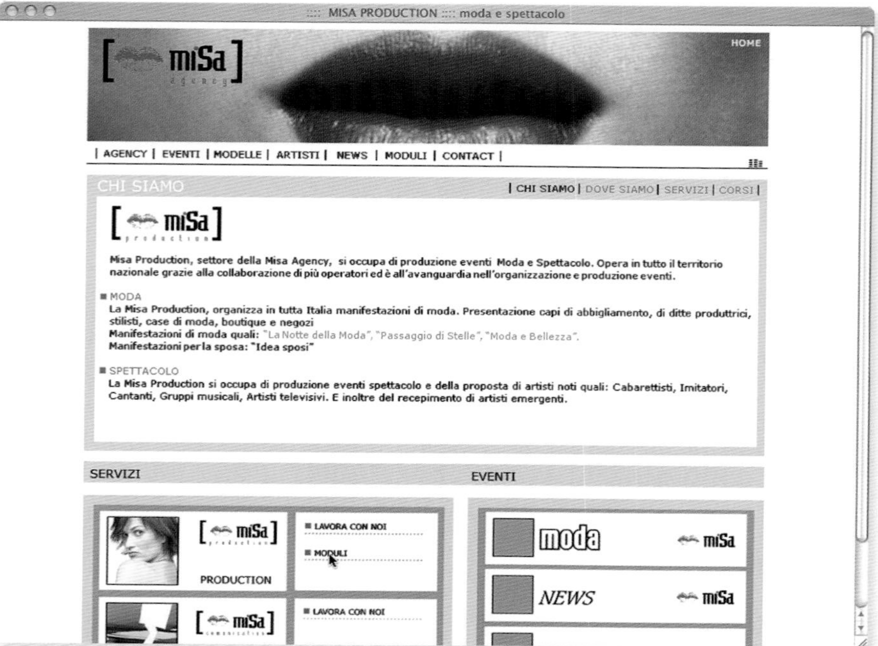
:::: MISA PRODUCTION :::: moda e spettacolo
mISa agency
HOME
| AGENCY | EVENTI | MODELLE | ARTISTI | NEWS | MODULI | CONTACT |
CHI SIAMO
| CHI SIAMO | DOVE SIAMO | SERVIZI | CORSI |
mISa production
Misa Production, settore della Misa Agency, si occupa di produzione eventi Moda e Spettacolo. Opera in tutto il territorio nazionale grazie alla collaborazione di più operatori ed è all'avanguardia nell'organizzazione e produzione eventi.
MODA
La Misa Production, organizza in tutta Italia manifestazioni di moda. Presentazione capi di abbigliamento, di ditte produttrici, stilisti, case di moda, boutique e negozi
Manifestazioni di moda quali: "La Notte della Moda", "Passaggio di Stelle", "Moda e Bellezza".
Manifestazioni per la sposa: "Idea sposi"
SPETTACOLO
La Misa Production si occupa di produzione eventi spettacolo e della proposta di artisti noti quali: Cabarettisti, Imitatori, Cantanti, Gruppi musicali, Artisti televisivi. E inoltre del recepimento di artisti emergenti.
SERVIZI
EVENTI
mISa
PRODUCTION
LAVORA CON NOI
MODULI
mISa
LAVORA CON NOI
moda
mISa
NEWS
mISa

www.misaproduction.com

D: andrea basile **C:** gianfranco losanno **P:** misa production
A: basile advertising **M:** contact@andreabasile.it

::: Programación :::

OUTUBRO						
				1	2	3
4	5	6	7	8	9	10
11	12	13	14	15	16	17
18	19	20	21	22	23	24
25	26	27	28	29	30	31

NOVEMBRO						
1	2	3	4	5	6	7
8	9	10	11	12	13	14
15	16	17	18	19	20	21
22	23	24	25	26	27	28
29	30					

DECEMBRO						
		1	2	3	4	5
6	7	8	9	10	11	12
13	14	15	16	17	18	19
20	21	22	23	24	25	26
27	28	29	30	31		

CURSOS* CHARTER

*realizables cun mínimo de matrículas confirmadas SE QUERES QUE SE FAGAN, APÚNTATE XA

Días 11, 12, 13, 14, 15 **de outubro ● de 11 a 15:00h ● TALLER DE DANZA ●** Cursos Charter

ANDRÉS CORCHERO ● **Barcelona ●** MICROCLIMAS DO CORPO

Imparte: Andrés Corchero (coreógrafo de RARAVIS, Andrés Corchero-Rosa Muñoz) ● Barcelona

Escoitar de maneira global, cos sentidos e os poros da pel abertos, e con sensibilidade, significa prestarnos atención a nós mesmos e prestarlla ós demais e ó que nos rodea. Repetir un adestramento corporal ofrécenos a oportunidade de coñecer os distintos aspectos da nosa estrutura e natureza corporal: os ósos, os músculos, os nervios e tamén a mente e as sensacións. Reexaminar os nosos patróns de movemento, escoitar o mundo exterior desde a nosa pel, reaprender como se produce e o que produce o movemento e, en definitiva, entender o corpo como unha entidade global composta por moitas partes independentes, é un obxectivo deste curso.

::::::::::::::: teatro galán :::::::::

socios

equipo ● infraestructura ● ubicación ● enlaces ● patrocinadores

VANTAXES DE SER SOCIO
Desconto do 20% para socio e acompañante no prezo das entradas.
25% de desconto nos Teatros da Rede Estatal de Teatros Alternativos coa presentación do noso carnet nas taquillas.
Aviso preferente para a realización de cursos con desconto do 20% no prezo das matrículas.

carnet de socio
galán

VANTAXES DE SER SOCIO
Envío preferente da programación trimestral do teatro galán.
Envío do anuario do teatro (Teatro Condensado), publicación que recolle toda a programación por temas e imaxes dos espectáculos.
Invitacións para estreas de carácter especial.

Faite socio dende aquí

+ Información 981 58 51 66 ou teatrogalan@mundo-r.com

www.teatrogalan.com
D: noelia fernandez **C:** carlos fernández
A: desoños **M:** multimedia@desonhos.net

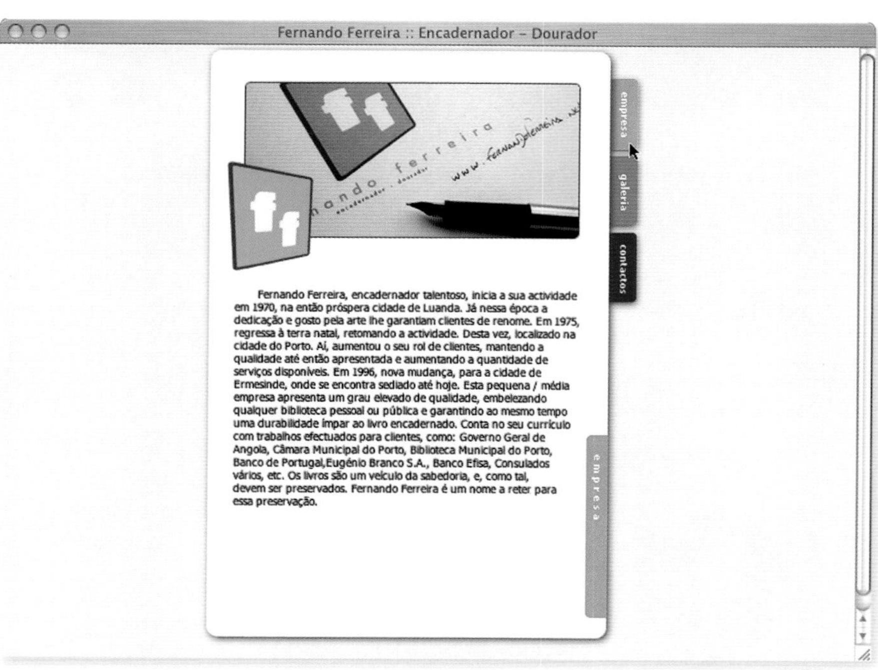
Fernando Ferreira :: Encadernador - Dourador
empresa
galeria
contactos
Fernando Ferreira, encadernador talentoso, inicia a sua actividade em 1970, na então próspera cidade de Luanda. Já nessa época a dedicação e gosto pela arte lhe garantiam clientes de renome. Em 1975, regressa à terra natal, retomando a actividade. Desta vez, localizado na cidade do Porto. Aí, aumentou o seu rol de clientes, mantendo a qualidade até então apresentada e aumentando a quantidade de serviços disponíveis. Em 1996, nova mudança, para a cidade de Ermesinde, onde se encontra sediado até hoje. Esta pequena / média empresa apresenta um grau elevado de qualidade, embelezando qualquer biblioteca pessoal ou pública e garantindo ao mesmo tempo uma durabilidade ímpar ao livro encadernado. Conta no seu currículo com trabalhos efectuados para clientes, como: Governo Geral de Angola, Câmara Municipal do Porto, Biblioteca Municipal do Porto, Banco de Portugal,Eugénio Branco S.A., Banco Efisa, Consulados vários, etc. Os livros são um veículo da sabedoria, e, como tal, devem ser preservados. Fernando Ferreira é um nome a reter para essa preservação.
empresa

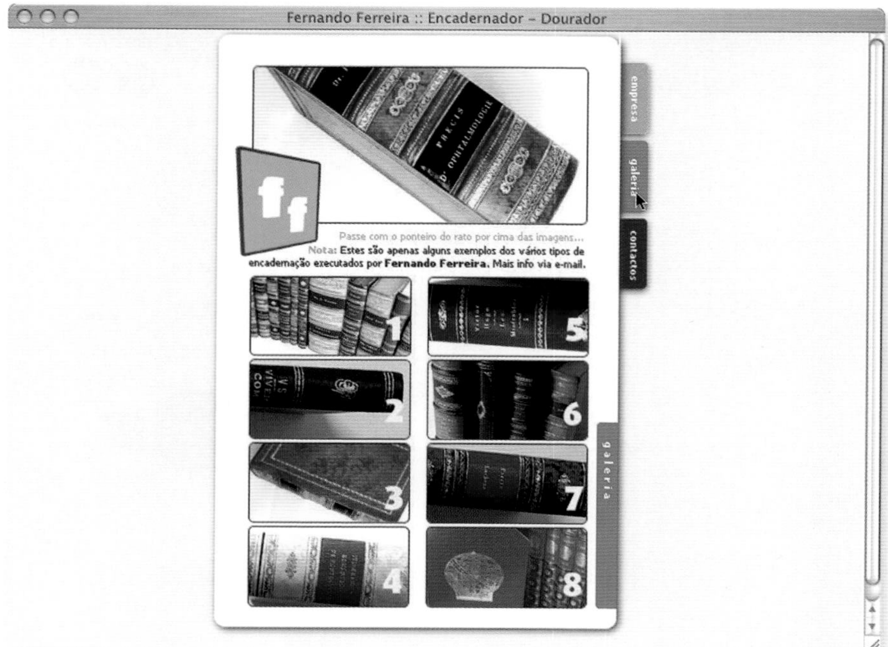
Fernando Ferreira :: Encadernador - Dourador
empresa
galeria
contactos
Passe com o ponteiro do rato por cima das imagens...
Nota: Estes são apenas alguns exemplos dos vários tipos de encademação executados por Fernando Ferreira. Mais info via e-mail.
1
2
3
4
5
6
7
8
galeria

www.fernandoferreira.net
D: ricardo ferreira
M: ricardo_personal@mail.pt

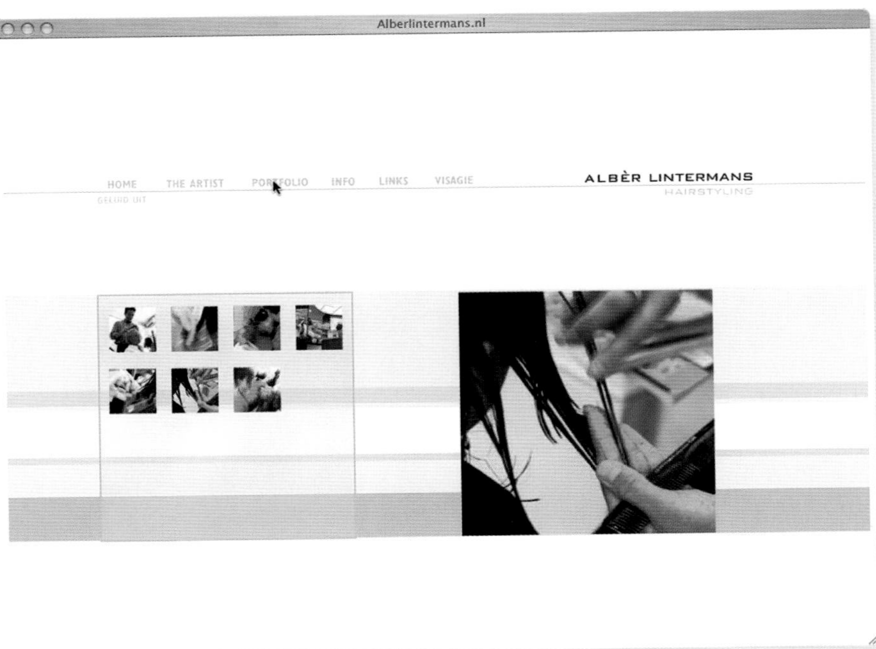
Alberlintermans.nl
HOME
THE ARTIST
PORTFOLIO
INFO
LINKS
VISAGIE
GELUID UIT
ALBÈR LINTERMANS
HAIRSTYLING

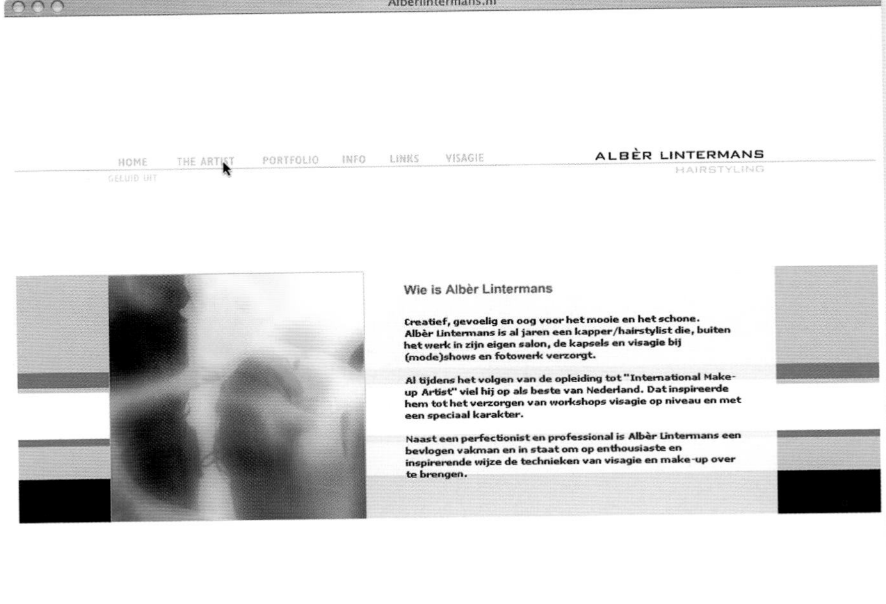
Alberlintermans.nl
HOME
THE ARTIST
PORTFOLIO
INFO
LINKS
VISAGIE
GELUID UIT
ALBÈR LINTERMANS
HAIRSTYLING
Wie is Albèr Lintermans
Creatief, gevoelig en oog voor het mooie en het schone. Albèr Lintermans is al jaren een kapper/hairstylist die, buiten het werk in zijn eigen salon, de kapsels en visagie bij (mode)shows en fotowerk verzorgt.
Al tijdens het volgen van de opleiding tot "International Make-up Artist" viel hij op als beste van Nederland. Dat inspireerde hem tot het verzorgen van workshops visagie op niveau en met een speciaal karakter.
Naast een perfectionist en professional is Albèr Lintermans een bevlogen vakman en in staat om op enthousiaste en inspirerende wijze de technieken van visagie en make-up over te brengen.

www.alberlintermans.nl
D: renate van stiphout **C:** leo hamers
A: yaikz! **M:** info@yaikz.nl

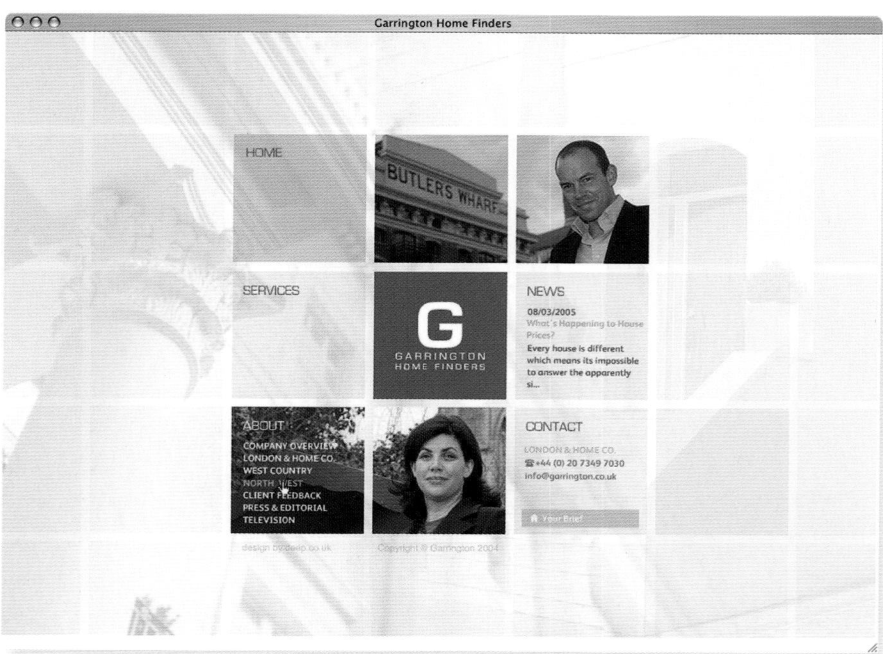
Garrington Home Finders
HOME
BUTLERS WHARF
SERVICES
G
GARRINGTON
HOME FINDERS
NEWS
08/03/2005
What's Happening to House Prices?
Every house is different which means its impossible to answer the apparently si...
ABOUT
COMPANY OVERVIEW
LONDON & HOME CO.
WEST COUNTRY
NORTH WEST
CLIENT FEEDBACK
PRESS & EDITORIAL
TELEVISION
CONTACT
LONDON & HOME CO.
+44 (0) 20 7349 7030
info@garrington.co.uk
Your Brief
design by deep.co.uk
Copyright © Garrington 2004

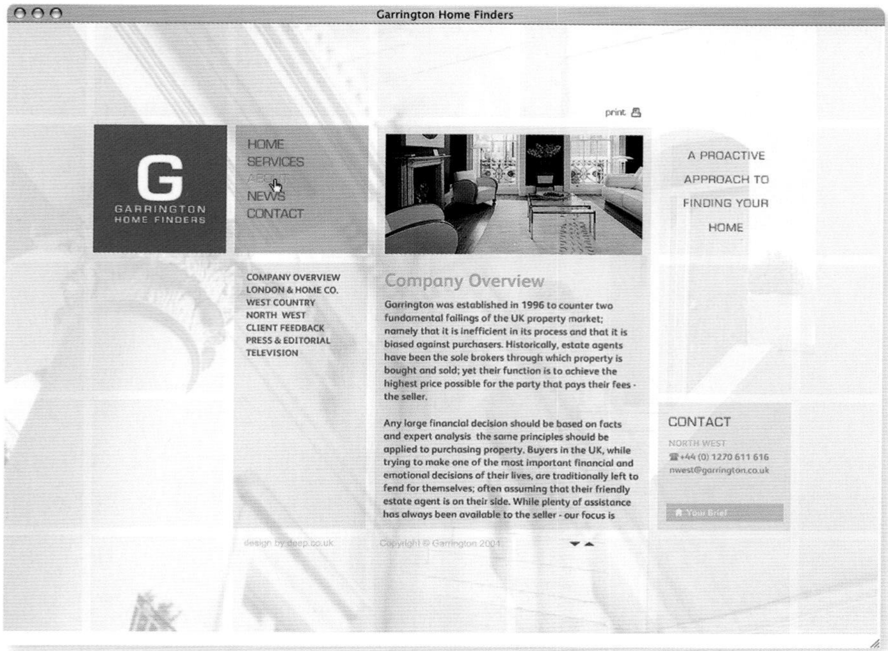
Garrington Home Finders
print
G
GARRINGTON
HOME FINDERS
HOME
SERVICES
ABOUT
NEWS
CONTACT
A PROACTIVE APPROACH TO FINDING YOUR HOME
COMPANY OVERVIEW
LONDON & HOME CO.
WEST COUNTRY
NORTH WEST
CLIENT FEEDBACK
PRESS & EDITORIAL
TELEVISION
Company Overview
Garrington was established in 1996 to counter two fundamental failings of the UK property market; namely that it is inefficient in its process and that it is biased against purchasers. Historically, estate agents have been the sole brokers through which property is bought and sold; yet their function is to achieve the highest price possible for the party that pays their fees - the seller.
Any large financial decision should be based on facts and expert analysis the same principles should be applied to purchasing property. Buyers in the UK, while trying to make one of the most important financial and emotional decisions of their lives, are traditionally left to fend for themselves; often assuming that their friendly estate agent is on their side. While plenty of assistance has always been available to the seller - our focus is
CONTACT
NORTH WEST
+44 (0) 1270 611 616
nwest@garrington.co.uk
Your Brief
design by deep.co.uk
Copyright © Garrington 2004

www.garrington.co.uk
D: deep
A: deep llp **M:** deeper@deep.co.uk

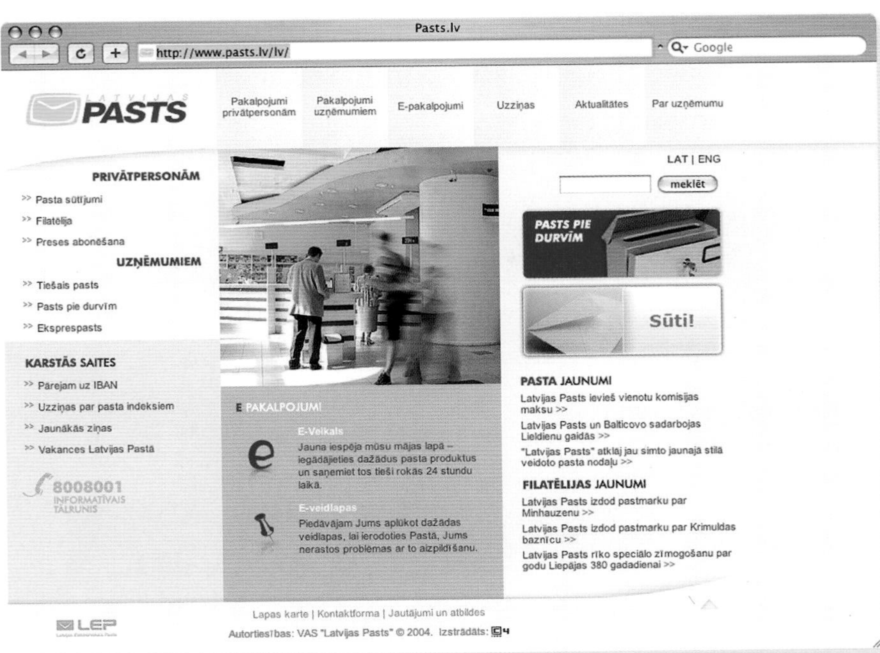

Pasts.lv
http://www.pasts.lv/lv/
Google
LATVIJAS PASTS
Pakalpojumi privātpersonām
Pakalpojumi uzņēmumiem
E-pakalpojumi
Uzziņas
Aktualitātes
Par uzņēmumu
LAT | ENG
meklēt
PRIVĀTPERSONĀM
>> Pasta sūtījumi
>> Filatēlija
>> Preses abonēšana
UZŅĒMUMIEM
>> Tiešais pasts
>> Pasts pie durvīm
>> Ekspresspasts
KARSTĀS SAITES
>> Pārejam uz IBAN
>> Uzziņas par pasta indeksiem
>> Jaunākās ziņas
>> Vakances Latvijas Pastā
8008001
INFORMATĪVAIS TĀLRUNIS
PASTS PIE DURVĪM
Sūti!
E PAKALPOJUMI
E-Veikals
Jauna iespēja mūsu mājas lapā – iegādājieties dažādus pasta produktus un saņemiet tos tieši rokās 24 stundu laikā.
E-veidlapas
Piedāvājam Jums aplūkot dažādas veidlapas, lai ierodoties Pastā, Jums nerastos problēmas ar to aizpildīšanu.
PASTA JAUNUMI
Latvijas Pasts ievieš vienotu komisijas maksu >>
Latvijas Pasts un Balticovo sadarbojas Lieldienu gaidās >>
"Latvijas Pasts" atklāj jau simto jaunajā stilā veidoto pasta nodaļu >>
FILATĒLIJAS JAUNUMI
Latvijas Pasts izdod pastmarku par Minhauzenu >>
Latvijas Pasts izdod pastmarku par Krimuldas baznīcu >>
Latvijas Pasts rīko speciālo zīmogošanu par godu Liepājas 380 gadadienai >>
Lapas karte | Kontaktforma | Jautājumi un atbildes
Autortiesības: VAS "Latvijas Pasts" © 2004. Izstrādāts: C4
LEP

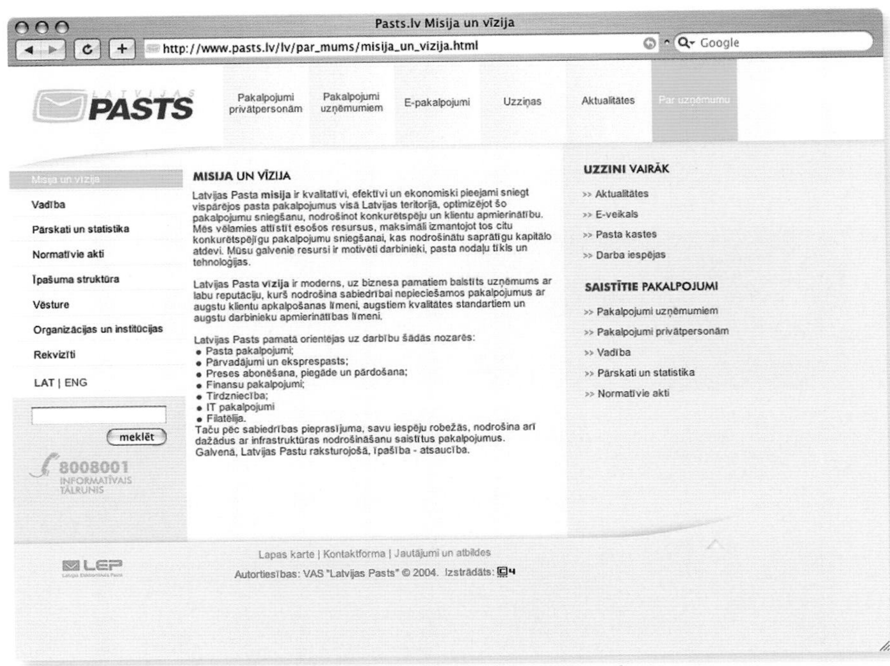

Pasts.lv Misija un vīzija
http://www.pasts.lv/lv/par_mums/misija_un_vizija.html
Google
LATVIJAS PASTS
Pakalpojumi privātpersonām
Pakalpojumi uzņēmumiem
E-pakalpojumi
Uzziņas
Aktualitātes
Par uzņēmumu
Misija un vīzija
Vadība
Pārskati un statistika
Normatīvie akti
Īpašuma struktūra
Vēsture
Organizācijas un institūcijas
Rekvizīti
LAT | ENG
meklēt
8008001
INFORMATĪVAIS TĀLRUNIS
MISIJA UN VĪZIJA
Latvijas Pasta misija ir kvalitatīvi, efektīvi un ekonomiski pieejami sniegt vispārējos pasta pakalpojumus visā Latvijas teritorijā, optimizējot šo pakalpojumu sniegšanu, nodrošinot konkurētspēju un klientu apmierinātību. Mēs vēlamies attīstīt esošos resursus, maksimāli izmantojot tos citu konkurētspējīgu pakalpojumu sniegšanai, kas nodrošinātu saprātīgu kapitālo atdevi. Mūsu galvenie resursi ir motivēti darbinieki, pasta nodaļu tīkls un tehnoloģijas.
Latvijas Pasta vīzija ir moderns, uz biznesa pamatiem balstīts uzņēmums ar labu reputāciju, kurš nodrošina sabiedrībai nepieciešamos pakalpojumus ar augstu klientu apkalpošanas līmeni, augstiem kvalitātes standartiem un augstu darbinieku apmierinātības līmeni.
Latvijas Pasts pamatā orientējas uz darbību šādās nozarēs:
• Pasta pakalpojumi;
• Pārvadājumi un ekspresspasts;
• Preses abonēšana, piegāde un pārdošana;
• Finansu pakalpojumi;
• Tirdzniecība;
• IT pakalpojumi
• Filatēlija.
Taču pēc sabiedrības pieprasījuma, savu iespēju robežās, nodrošina arī dažādus ar infrastruktūras nodrošināšanu saistītus pakalpojumus.
Galvenā, Latvijas Pastu raksturojošā, īpašība - atsaucība.
UZZINI VAIRĀK
>> Aktualitātes
>> E-veikals
>> Pasta kastes
>> Darba iespējas
SAISTĪTIE PAKALPOJUMI
>> Pakalpojumi uzņēmumiem
>> Pakalpojumi privātpersonām
>> Vadība
>> Pārskati un statistika
>> Normatīvie akti
Lapas karte | Kontaktforma | Jautājumi un atbildes
Autortiesības: VAS "Latvijas Pasts" © 2004. Izstrādāts: C4
LEP

www.pasts.lv

D: didzis kalva **C:** arnis stasko, martins kalvans, artis are **P:** sia „c4“
A: rhino design agency co ltd **M:** info@c4.lv

Galleria : wedding planning in Montreal
galleria
event design
Personal planner
Wedding consultation
Wedding styles
Our favorite products
Why Galleria
About us
Contact
Français
English
Wedding planning in just one click
I'm getting married on
Plan my wedding!
dd.mm.yyyy
ourcentreinmontreal
320 Victoria Avenue, Westmount, Montreal, Quebec, Canada H3Z 2M8
Tel.: 514 487-3456
Fax: 514 487-7737
ourpartners
selected from the very best Montreal has to offer
banquet halls, cake creators, caterers, decorators, dj's, entertainers, fashion designers, florists, gift ideas, hotels, invitation designers, limousines, musicians, photographers, restaurants, unique reception venues, videographers, wedding officiants...and more.
weddingconsultation
1 "Selection"
A FREE and unique service offered to future brides and grooms.
2 "À la carte"
Designed for you to pick and choose the important elements to make your wedding unique to your personal style....
3 "Table d'hôte"
This all-inclusive package lets you, your families and your guests fully enjoy your special day.
yourpersonalityyourweddingstyle
Intimate wedding
Who better to share the happiest day of your life than the people that are closest to you?
Fête champêtre
Where better to profess your eternal love than surrounded by the splendors of nature?
Formal wedding
For the couple who truly appreciates fine linen and silverware, formal weddings are a thing of refinement and elegance.
Theme wedding
This is the wedding for the enthusiast couple that wants something different for their special day.

Galleria : wedding styles – intimate wedding
galleria
event design
Personal planner
Wedding consultation
Wedding styles
Our favorite products
Why Galleria
About us
Contact
Français
English
Wedding styles
Intimate wedding
Fête champêtre
Formal wedding
Theme wedding
Intimate wedding
Who better to share the happiest day of your life than the people that are closest to you? It's a fact: while hosting larger weddings, the newlyweds rarely get the chance to spend quality time with their guests. Not only does a smaller wedding give everyone a chance to get acquainted, it is also less stressful for those involved.
The Dress Code:
The dress code will be mainly set by the location of the wedding and will be at most semi-formal. For example, backyard weddings require less formal attire than a wedding reception at a five star restaurant. As for the bride and groom, wear something that you feel comfortable and beautiful in. If you have always dreamed of satin trains and top hats, by all means please indulge, it is your day after all.
The Invitations:
Nothing could be more appropriate than handwritten invitations on handmade paper. Make each invitation personal by writing a brief special note to each of your guests. If this does not appeal to you, find an invitation that is meaningful to you and representative of your relationship.
The Location:
One of the advantages of an intimate wedding is that they can take place where larger weddings simply do not fit. All-time favourite small wedding locations include beautiful backyards, special restaurants, and isolated chalets. But then why not try an original location such as, a museum, a winery or an amusement park? We must also not forget to mention the popular (destination wedding) where you get to exchange your vows while enjoying the exotic beauty of a far-off land.
The Flowers and Centrepieces:
In order to emphasize the intimate atmosphere, it is best to favour small

www.galleriamontreal.com
D: sergei rybakov **P:** anna artamonova-rojansky
A: artefficient **M:** info@artefficient.com

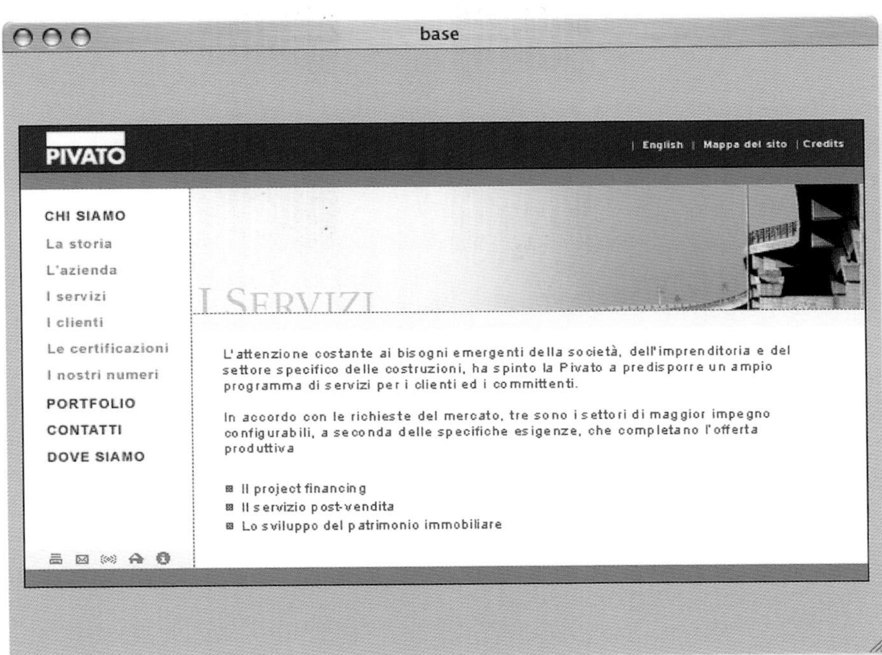
base
PIVATO
| English | Mappa del sito | Credits
CHI SIAMO
La storia
L'azienda
I servizi
I clienti
Le certificazioni
I nostri numeri
PORTFOLIO
CONTATTI
DOVE SIAMO
I SERVIZI
L'attenzione costante ai bisogni emergenti della società, dell'imprenditoria e del settore specifico delle costruzioni, ha spinto la Pivato a predisporre un ampio programma di servizi per i clienti ed i committenti.
In accordo con le richieste del mercato, tre sono i settori di maggior impegno configurabili, a seconda delle specifiche esigenze, che completano l'offerta produttiva
Il project financing
Il servizio post-vendita
Lo sviluppo del patrimonio immobiliare

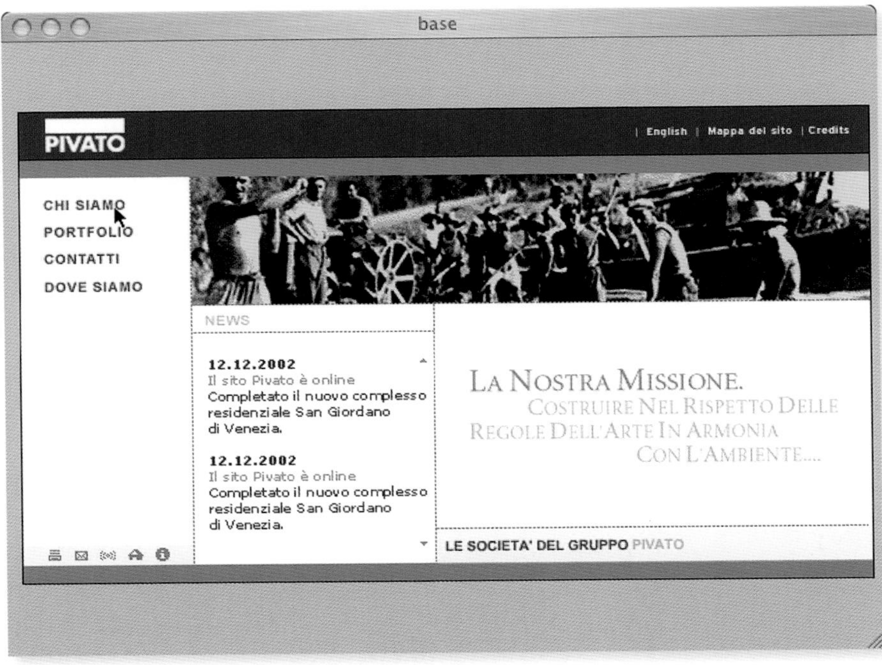
base
PIVATO
| English | Mappa del sito | Credits
CHI SIAMO
PORTFOLIO
CONTATTI
DOVE SIAMO
NEWS
12.12.2002
Il sito Pivato è online
Completato il nuovo complesso residenziale San Giordano di Venezia.
12.12.2002
Il sito Pivato è online
Completato il nuovo complesso residenziale San Giordano di Venezia.
LA NOSTRA MISSIONE.
COSTRUIRE NEL RISPETTO DELLE
REGOLE DELL'ARTE IN ARMONIA
CON L'AMBIENTE....
LE SOCIETA' DEL GRUPPO PIVATO

www.g56.8m.com
D: fabio collet
M: fabio9@freemail.it

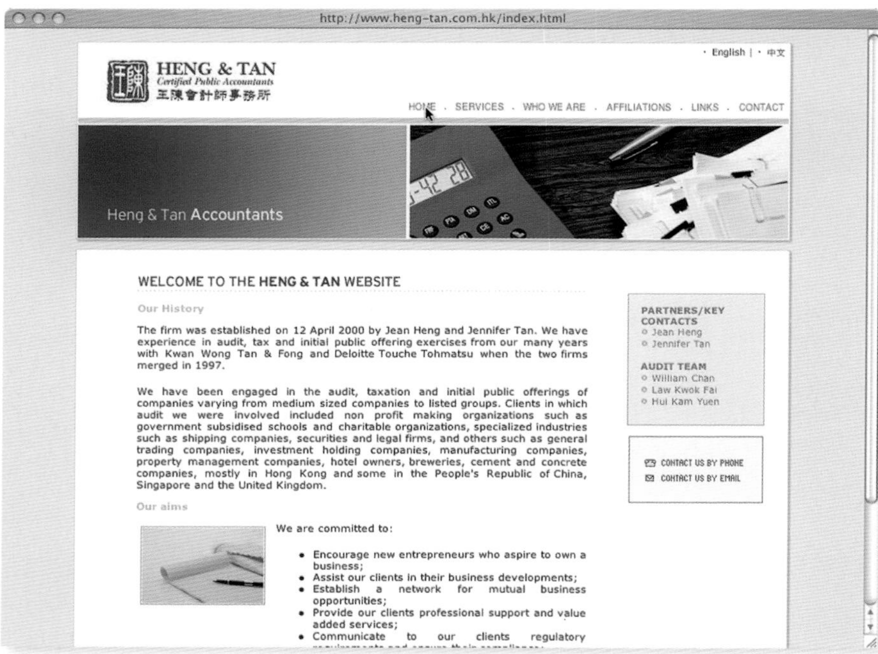
http://www.heng-tan.com.hk/index.html
· English | · 中文
HENG & TAN
Certified Public Accountants
王陳會計師事務所
HOME . SERVICES . WHO WE ARE . AFFILIATIONS . LINKS . CONTACT
Heng & Tan Accountants
WELCOME TO THE HENG & TAN WEBSITE
Our History
The firm was established on 12 April 2000 by Jean Heng and Jennifer Tan. We have experience in audit, tax and initial public offering exercises from our many years with Kwan Wong Tan & Fong and Deloitte Touche Tohmatsu when the two firms merged in 1997.
We have been engaged in the audit, taxation and initial public offerings of companies varying from medium sized companies to listed groups. Clients in which audit we were involved included non profit making organizations such as government subsidised schools and charitable organizations, specialized industries such as shipping companies, securities and legal firms, and others such as general trading companies, investment holding companies, manufacturing companies, property management companies, hotel owners, breweries, cement and concrete companies, mostly in Hong Kong and some in the People's Republic of China, Singapore and the United Kingdom.
Our aims
We are committed to:
Encourage new entrepreneurs who aspire to own a business;
Assist our clients in their business developments;
Establish a network for mutual business opportunities;
Provide our clients professional support and value added services;
Communicate to our clients regulatory
PARTNERS/KEY CONTACTS
Jean Heng
Jennifer Tan
AUDIT TEAM
William Chan
Law Kwok Fai
Hui Kam Yuen
CONTACT US BY PHONE
CONTACT US BY EMAIL

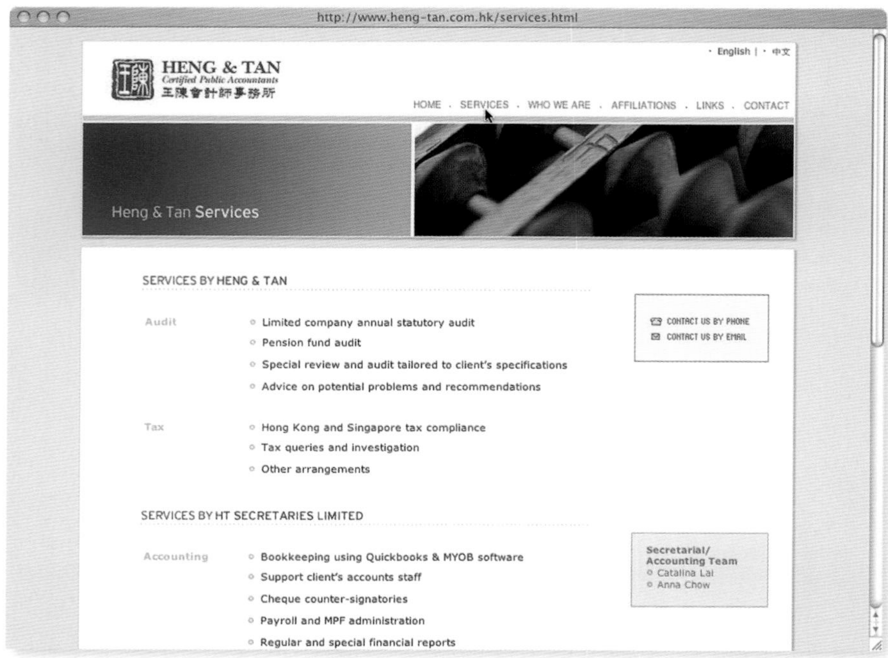
http://www.heng-tan.com.hk/services.html
· English | · 中文
HENG & TAN
Certified Public Accountants
王陳會計師事務所
HOME . SERVICES . WHO WE ARE . AFFILIATIONS . LINKS . CONTACT
Heng & Tan Services
SERVICES BY HENG & TAN
Audit
Limited company annual statutory audit
Pension fund audit
Special review and audit tailored to client's specifications
Advice on potential problems and recommendations
Tax
Hong Kong and Singapore tax compliance
Tax queries and investigation
Other arrangements
SERVICES BY HT SECRETARIES LIMITED
Accounting
Bookkeeping using Quickbooks & MYOB software
Support client's accounts staff
Cheque counter-signatories
Payroll and MPF administration
Regular and special financial reports
CONTACT US BY PHONE
CONTACT US BY EMAIL
Secretarial/ Accounting Team
Catalina Lai
Anna Chow

www.heng-tan.com.hk
D: michael clough **C:** teresa li **P:** ed williams
A: compelite limited **M:** ed@compelite.net

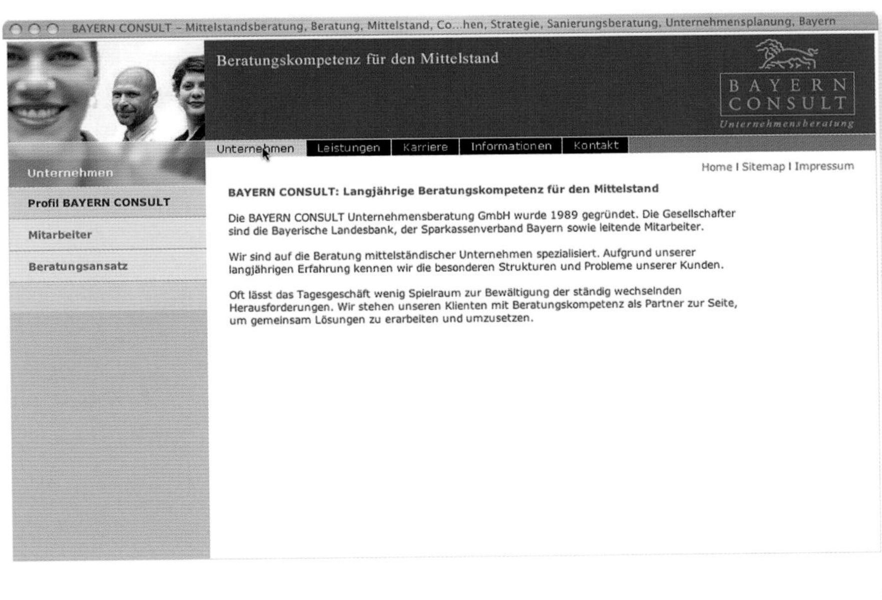
BAYERN CONSULT – Mittelstandsberatung, Beratung, Mittelstand, Co...hen, Strategie, Sanierungsberatung, Unternehmensplanung, Bayern
Beratungskompetenz für den Mittelstand
BAYERN CONSULT
Unternehmensberatung
Unternehmen
Leistungen
Karriere
Informationen
Kontakt
Home | Sitemap | Impressum
Unternehmen
Profil BAYERN CONSULT
Mitarbeiter
Beratungsansatz
BAYERN CONSULT: Langjährige Beratungskompetenz für den Mittelstand
Die BAYERN CONSULT Unternehmensberatung GmbH wurde 1989 gegründet. Die Gesellschafter sind die Bayerische Landesbank, der Sparkassenverband Bayern sowie leitende Mitarbeiter.
Wir sind auf die Beratung mittelständischer Unternehmen spezialisiert. Aufgrund unserer langjährigen Erfahrung kennen wir die besonderen Strukturen und Probleme unserer Kunden.
Oft lässt das Tagesgeschäft wenig Spielraum zur Bewältigung der ständig wechselnden Herausforderungen. Wir stehen unseren Klienten mit Beratungskompetenz als Partner zur Seite, um gemeinsam Lösungen zu erarbeiten und umzusetzen.

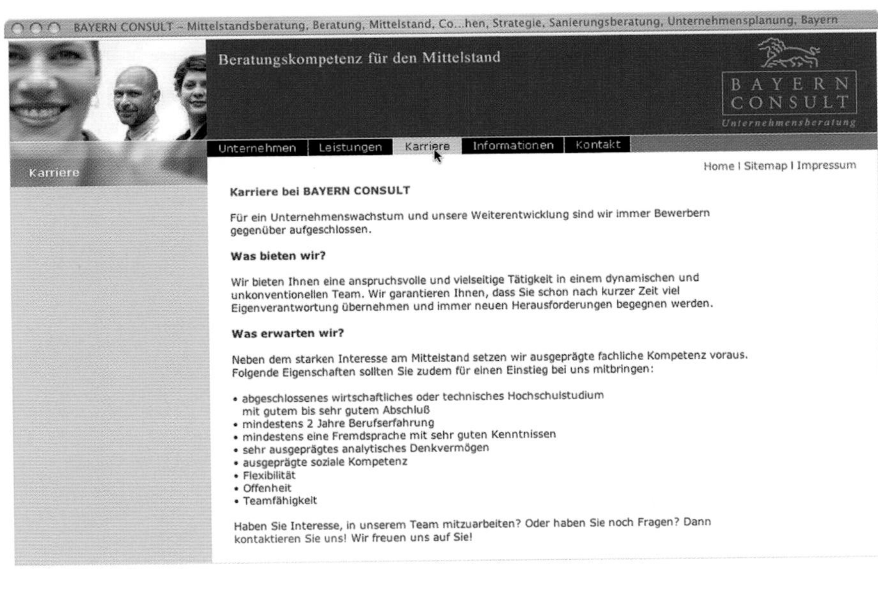
BAYERN CONSULT – Mittelstandsberatung, Beratung, Mittelstand, Co...hen, Strategie, Sanierungsberatung, Unternehmensplanung, Bayern
Beratungskompetenz für den Mittelstand
BAYERN CONSULT
Unternehmensberatung
Unternehmen
Leistungen
Karriere
Informationen
Kontakt
Home | Sitemap | Impressum
Karriere
Karriere bei BAYERN CONSULT
Für ein Unternehmenswachstum und unsere Weiterentwicklung sind wir immer Bewerbern gegenüber aufgeschlossen.
Was bieten wir?
Wir bieten Ihnen eine anspruchsvolle und vielseitige Tätigkeit in einem dynamischen und unkonventionellen Team. Wir garantieren Ihnen, dass Sie schon nach kurzer Zeit viel Eigenverantwortung übernehmen und immer neuen Herausforderungen begegnen werden.
Was erwarten wir?
Neben dem starken Interesse am Mittelstand setzen wir ausgeprägte fachliche Kompetenz voraus. Folgende Eigenschaften sollten Sie zudem für einen Einstieg bei uns mitbringen:
• abgeschlossenes wirtschaftliches oder technisches Hochschulstudium mit gutem bis sehr gutem Abschluß
• mindestens 2 Jahre Berufserfahrung
• mindestens eine Fremdsprache mit sehr guten Kenntnissen
• sehr ausgeprägtes analytisches Denkvermögen
• ausgeprägte soziale Kompetenz
• Flexibilität
• Offenheit
• Teamfähigkeit
Haben Sie Interesse, in unserem Team mitzuarbeiten? Oder haben Sie noch Fragen? Dann kontaktieren Sie uns! Wir freuen uns auf Sie!

www.bayernconsult.de
D: björn hausner
A: mellow design **M:** info@mellowdesign.de

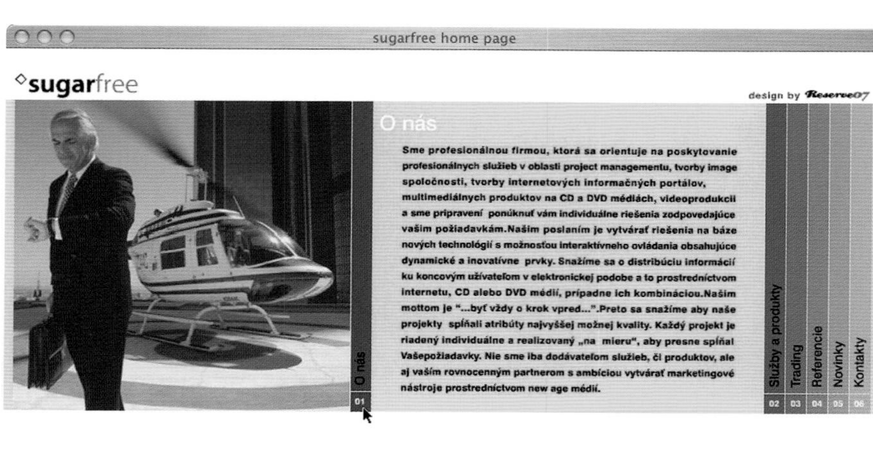
sugarfree home page
sugarfree
design by Reserve07
O nás
Sme profesionálnou firmou, ktorá sa orientuje na poskytovanie profesionálnych služieb v oblasti project managementu, tvorby image spoločnosti, tvorby internetových informačných portálov, multimediálnych produktov na CD a DVD médiách, videoprodukcii a sme pripravení ponúknuť vám individuálne riešenia zodpovedajúce vašim požiadavkám.Našim poslaním je vytvárať riešenia na báze nových technológií s možnosťou interaktívneho ovládania obsahujúce dynamické a inovatívne prvky. Snažíme sa o distribúciu informácií ku koncovým užívateľom v elektronickej podobe a to prostredníctvom internetu, CD alebo DVD médií, prípadne ich kombináciou.Našim mottom je "...byť vždy o krok vpred...".Preto sa snažíme aby naše projekty spĺňali atribúty najvyššej možnej kvality. Každý projekt je riadený individuálne a realizovaný „na mieru", aby presne spĺňal Vašepožiadavky. Nie sme iba dodávateľom služieb, či produktov, ale aj vaším rovnocenným partnerom s ambíciou vytvárať marketingové nástroje prostredníctvom new age médií.
O nás
Služby a produkty
Trading
Referencie
Novinky
Kontakty
01
02
03
04
05
06

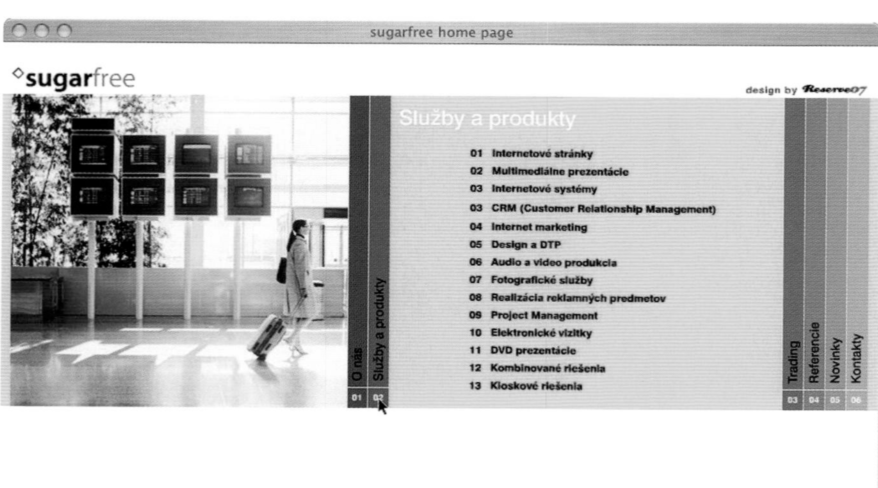
sugarfree home page
sugarfree
design by Reserve07
Služby a produkty
01 Internetové stránky
02 Multimediálne prezentácie
03 Internetové systémy
03 CRM (Customer Relationship Management)
04 Internet marketing
05 Design a DTP
06 Audio a video produkcia
07 Fotografické služby
08 Realizácia reklamných predmetov
09 Project Management
10 Elektronické vizitky
11 DVD prezentácie
12 Kombinované riešenia
13 Kioskové riešenia
O nás
Služby a produkty
Trading
Referencie
Novinky
Kontakty
01
02
03
04
05
06

www.sugarfree.sk

D: robert rozbora **P:** sugar free

A: reserve07 **M:** robert.rozbora@sugarfree.sk

Delphis - solucoes empresariais
Delphis .com.pt
Empresa
Serviços
Internet
Contactos
ConsultoriadeSeguros
comece a poupar nos seus seguros.
Na Delphis temos as mais diversas soluções para que possa encarar aqueles riscos do dia-a-dia sem sobressaltos, e sempre com a melhor relação qualidade-preço. Consulte-nos!
Insira o texto
Na Delphis encontrará as mais variadas soluções, vocacionadas não só para o mercado empresarial, mas também para si que é cliente particular.
Allianz
produtos
Liberty Seguros
totta
promotores
Serviços
Mediação de Seguros
Contabilidade
Assessoria Fiscal e Laboral
Consultoria Financeira
Promoção externa de produtos Banco Totta & Açores (créditos, abertura contas...)
Preenchimento e entrega de declarações de IRS
WebDesign
Alojamento Internet
Registo de Domínios
Através das empresas que representamos, seja nos seguros (Allianz Portugal e Liberty Seguros), ou nos produtos financeiros (Banco Totta & Açores), encontraremos as melhores soluções para o seu caso específico ou para a sua empresa. Faça-nos uma visita e saiba o que podemos fazer por si!
Contacte-nos
Início :: Empresa :: Serviços :: Internet :: Contactos
© Delphis | Política de Privacidade e Condições de Utilização

Delphis - solucoes empresariais
Delphis .com.pt
Empresa
Serviços
Internet
Contactos
ConsultoriaFiscal
saiba como pagar menos impostos
Na Delphis temos as mais diversas soluções para que possa ver reduzida a sua carga fiscal. Visite-nos e saiba o que podemos fazer por si!
Insira o texto
SoluçõesINTERNET
WebDesign
Alojamento
Domínios
Solicite um orçamento gratuito
Visite o nosso portfolio
Conheça os nossos planos de alojamento
Registe o seu domínio nacional ou internacional
Veja se o domínio que pretende está disponível
Início :: Empresa :: Serviços :: Internet :: Contactos
© Delphis | Política de Privacidade e Condições de Utilização

www.delphis.com.pt
D: bruno rodrigues
A: delphis **M:** geral@delphis.com.pt

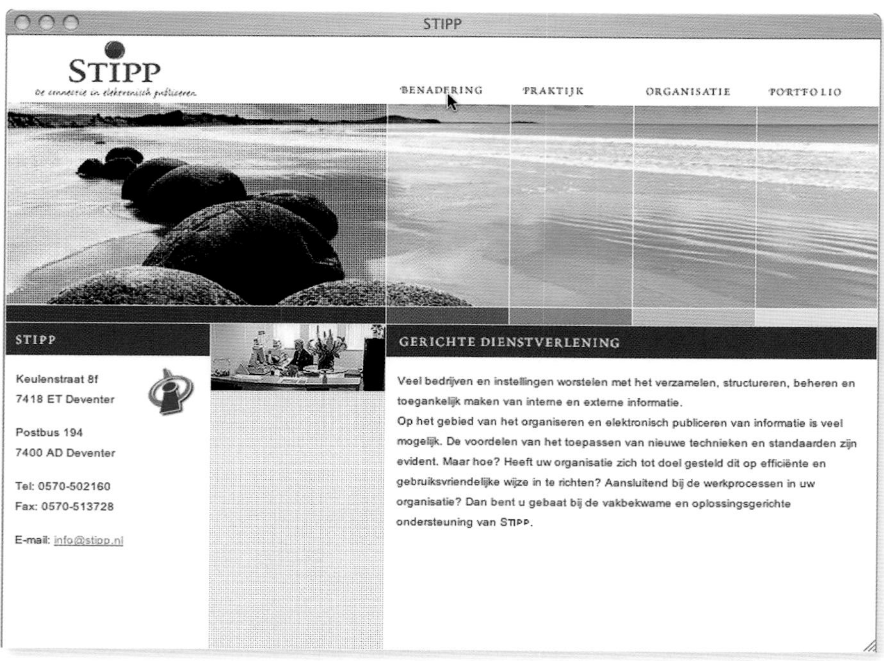
STIPP
STIPP
De connectie in elektronisch publiceren
BENADERING
PRAKTIJK
ORGANISATIE
PORTFOLIO
STIPP
Keulenstraat 8f
7418 ET Deventer
Postbus 194
7400 AD Deventer
Tel: 0570-502160
Fax: 0570-513728
E-mail: info@stipp.nl
GERICHTE DIENSTVERLENING
Veel bedrijven en instellingen worstelen met het verzamelen, structureren, beheren en toegankelijk maken van interne en externe informatie.
Op het gebied van het organiseren en elektronisch publiceren van informatie is veel mogelijk. De voordelen van het toepassen van nieuwe technieken en standaarden zijn evident. Maar hoe? Heeft uw organisatie zich tot doel gesteld dit op efficiënte en gebruiksvriendelijke wijze in te richten? Aansluitend bij de werkprocessen in uw organisatie? Dan bent u gebaat bij de vakbekwame en oplossingsgerichte ondersteuning van STIPP.

STIPP
STIPP
De connectie in elektronisch publiceren
BENADERING
PRAKTIJK
ORGANISATIE
PORTFOLIO
> HOME
STIPP
Keulenstraat 8f
7418 ET Deventer
Postbus 194
7400 AD Deventer
Tel: 0570-502160
Fax: 0570-513728
E-mail: info@stipp.nl
DE PRAKTIJK
Ook binnen uw bedrijf of instelling is veel informatie aanwezig. Of u nu uitgever bent of corporate publisher. Informatie die, mits op de juiste wijze georganiseerd en toegankelijk gemaakt, een aanzienlijke meerwaarde vormt. Die u mogelijkheden biedt om u nadrukkelijk te onderscheiden van uw concurrenten, uw relaties te binden en uw bedrijfsresultaten te verhogen. Die wel vraagt om een op moderne leest geschoeid proces van verwerken en publiceren.
Het opzetten van publicatieprocessen is behoorlijk complex. Het vereist de nodige deskundigheid en vakbekwaamheid met betrekking tot zowel inhoudelijke, technische als organisatorische aspecten.
Corporate publishers, uitgeefwereld, ICT en grafisch en informatieverwerkende bedrijven hebben elkaar daarbij nodig, maar moeten elkaars taal leren spreken. Om vanuit een wederzijds begrip van de probleemstelling tot een effectieve oplossing te komen. STIPP spreekt de talen van deze werelden.

www.stipp.nl
D: danyel weideman
A: puremotion **M:** info@puremotion.nl

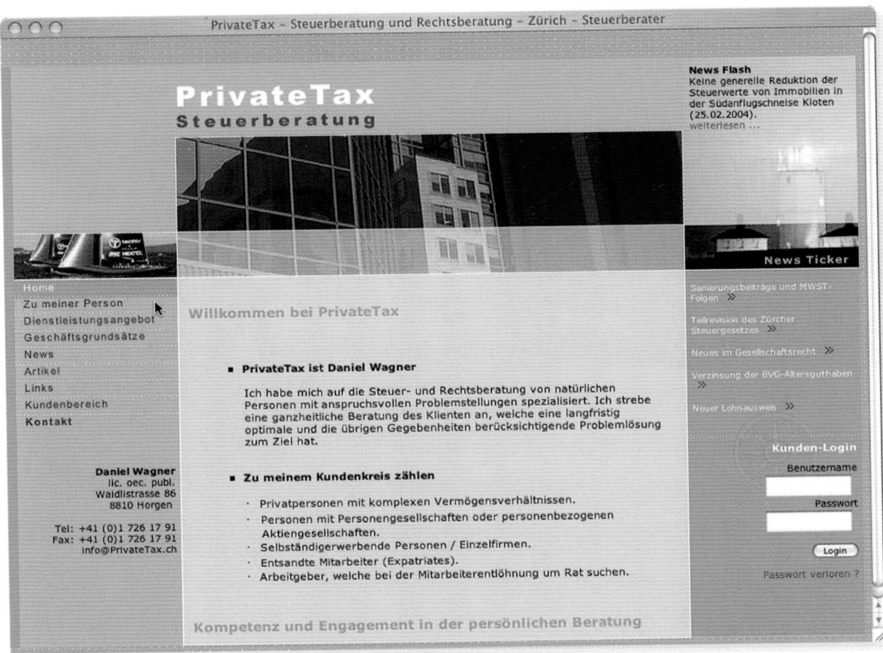
PrivateTax - Steuerberatung und Rechtsberatung - Zürich - Steuerberater
PrivateTax
Steuerberatung
News Flash
Keine generelle Reduktion der Steuerwerte von Immobilien in der Südanflugschneise Kloten (25.02.2004).
weiterlesen ...
News Ticker
Home
Zu meiner Person
Dienstleistungsangebot
Geschäftsgrundsätze
News
Artikel
Links
Kundenbereich
Kontakt
Willkommen bei PrivateTax
PrivateTax ist Daniel Wagner
Ich habe mich auf die Steuer- und Rechtsberatung von natürlichen Personen mit anspruchsvollen Problemstellungen spezialisiert. Ich strebe eine ganzheitliche Beratung des Klienten an, welche eine langfristig optimale und die übrigen Gegebenheiten berücksichtigende Problemlösung zum Ziel hat.
Zu meinem Kundenkreis zählen
Privatpersonen mit komplexen Vermögensverhältnissen.
Personen mit Personengesellschaften oder personenbezogenen Aktiengesellschaften.
Selbständigerwerbende Personen / Einzelfirmen.
Entsandte Mitarbeiter (Expatriates).
Arbeitgeber, welche bei der Mitarbeiterentlöhnung um Rat suchen.
Kompetenz und Engagement in der persönlichen Beratung
Daniel Wagner
lic. oec. publ.
Waldlistrasse 86
8810 Horgen
Tel: +41 (0)1 726 17 91
Fax: +41 (0)1 726 17 91
info@PrivateTax.ch
Kunden-Login
Benutzername
Passwort
Login
Passwort verloren ?

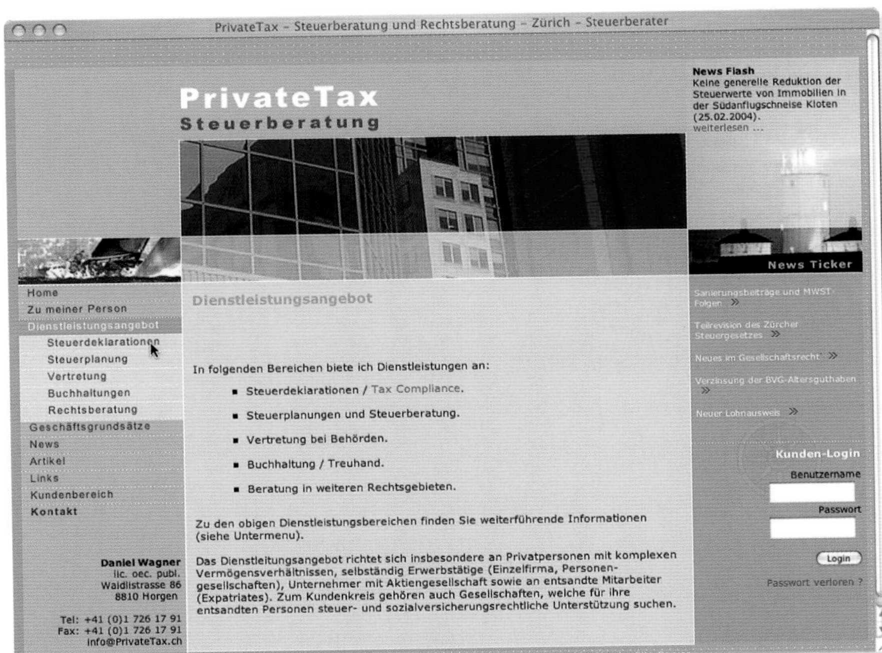
PrivateTax - Steuerberatung und Rechtsberatung - Zürich - Steuerberater
PrivateTax
Steuerberatung
News Flash
Keine generelle Reduktion der Steuerwerte von Immobilien in der Südanflugschneise Kloten (25.02.2004).
weiterlesen ...
News Ticker
Home
Zu meiner Person
Dienstleistungsangebot
Steuerdeklarationen
Steuerplanung
Vertretung
Buchhaltungen
Rechtsberatung
Geschäftsgrundsätze
News
Artikel
Links
Kundenbereich
Kontakt
Dienstleistungsangebot
In folgenden Bereichen biete ich Dienstleistungen an:
Steuerdeklarationen / Tax Compliance.
Steuerplanungen und Steuerberatung.
Vertretung bei Behörden.
Buchhaltung / Treuhand.
Beratung in weiteren Rechtsgebieten.
Zu den obigen Dienstleistungsbereichen finden Sie weiterführende Informationen (siehe Untermenu).
Das Dienstleitungsangebot richtet sich insbesondere an Privatpersonen mit komplexen Vermögensverhältnissen, selbständig Erwerbstätige (Einzelfirma, Personengesellschaften), Unternehmer mit Aktiengesellschaft sowie an entsandte Mitarbeiter (Expatriates). Zum Kundenkreis gehören auch Gesellschaften, welche für ihre entsandten Personen steuer- und sozialversicherungsrechtliche Unterstützung suchen.
Daniel Wagner
lic. oec. publ.
Waldlistrasse 86
8810 Horgen
Tel: +41 (0)1 726 17 91
Fax: +41 (0)1 726 17 91
info@PrivateTax.ch
Kunden-Login
Benutzername
Passwort
Login
Passwort verloren ?

www.privatetax.ch
D: michael janis
A: internetagentur M: info@internetagentur.ch

Rödl Enneking & Partner – Rechtsanwälte und Notar
Rödl Enneking & Partner
Rechtsanwälte und Notar
Home | Impressum und Kontakt | Suche: >> | English
Willkommen bei Rödl Enneking & Partner!
RÖDL ENNEKING & PARTNER ist eine überregional tätige Rechtsanwalt- und Notarkanzlei mit wirtschaftsrechtlicher Ausrichtung.
RÖDL ENNEKING & PARTNER ist hervorgegangen aus einer Kooperation zwischen der an den Standorten Berlin und Düsseldorf agierenden Sozietät Enneking & Partner und der Rödl & Partner Gruppe, die mit ihrem weltweiten Niederlassungsnetz auch internationale Aufgabenstellungen löst.
Wir über uns
Kompetenz
Unser Team
Unsere Standorte
Rödl & Partner
©2004 Rödl Enneking & Partner

Rödl Enneking & Partner – Rechtsanwälte und Notar
Rödl Enneking & Partner
Rechtsanwälte und Notar
Home | Impressum und Kontakt | Suche: >> | English
Wir über uns
RÖDL ENNEKING & PARTNER ist eine überregional tätige Rechtsanwalt- und Notarkanzlei mit wirtschaftsrechtlicher Ausrichtung. RÖDL ENNEKING & PARTNER ist hervorgegangen aus einer Kooperation zwischen der an den Standorten Berlin und Düsseldorf agierenden Sozietät Enneking & Partner und der Rödl & Partner Gruppe, die mit ihrem weltweiten Niederlassungsnetz auch internationale Aufgabenstellungen löst. Wir arbeiten auf allen unternehmensbezogenen Rechtsgebieten und beraten schwerpunktmäßig Unternehmen aller Rechtsformen sowie deren Organe und Gesellschafter.
Arbeitsbereiche von RÖDL ENNEKING & PARTNER sind:
Handels- und Gesellschaftsrecht, Umwandlungsrecht
mergers & acquisitions, private equity, venture capital
Vertragsrecht
Immobilienrecht
Privates Baurecht
Unternehmenssteuerrecht
Steuerstrafrecht
Bankrecht
Arbeitsrecht
Gewerblicher Rechtsschutz
Vergaberecht
Zivilprozessführung / Schiedsgerichtsverfahren
Finanzgerichtsprozess
Unsere Mandantschaft
Wir über uns
Kompetenz
Unser Team
Unsere Standorte
Rödl & Partner
©2004 Rödl Enneking & Partner

www.roedl-enneking.de
D: yilmaz backir **P:** roedl enneking
M: info@backir.de

.. Estudio Jurídico - Santos y Gonzalez-Sierra - Index ..

Santos y Gonzalez-Sierra - **La firma**

SANTOS Y GONZÁLEZ-SIERRA
ESTUDIO JURÍDICO

La firma - Áreas de actuación - Oficinas - Contacto

Santos y González-Sierra es una firma de abogados, con un marcado acento mercantil, definida como estudio jurídico por nuestros clientes y sus necesidades.

La paulatina evolución y adaptación del despacho, a lo largo de los años, a la situación de las empresas, que constituyen el núcleo central de nuestros clientes, ha ido conformando una firma legal que cifra en **la satisfacción del cliente**, en **el asesoramiento previo** y en la **evitación, posible, de los conflictos**, sus señas de identidad.

Al igual que la empresa española ha sufrido en los últimos cincuenta años un cambio profundo en sus estructuras, organización, medios y objetivos; del mismo modo Santos y González-Sierra se ha adaptado a las necesidades que

Nuestra compañía presta servicios de asesoramiento jurídico a entidades mercantiles, de diferentes ramas de actividad, entre las que se encuentran, entre otros:

- Laboratorios Farmacéuticos
- Compañías del sector de las Telecomunicaciones
- Empresas de Nuevas Tecnologías
- Sociedades de Comercio Exterior
- Estudios de Ingeniería
- Empresas de Servicios a la Tercera Edad
- Fabricación de Mobiliario
- Servicios Financieros
- Minería
- Fabricación y distribución de papel

.. Estudio Jurídico - Santos y Gonzalez-Sierra - Areas de actuación ..

Santos y Gonzalez-Sierra - **Areas de Actuación**

SANTOS Y GONZÁLEZ-SIERRA
ESTUDIO JURÍDICO

La firma - Áreas de actuación - Oficinas - Contacto

El núcleo principal de nuestra actividad. Áreas en las que SGS ofrece soluciones jurídicas

Constituyendo la asesoría de empresa el núcleo principal de nuestra actividad, son cuatro las áreas en las que **SGS ABOGADOS** ofrece soluciones jurídicas:

- **Derecho Mercantil:** Asesoramiento a los Órganos de Administración, Modificaciones estatutarias, Fusiones y Adquisiciones, Liquidación y Disolución de Sociedades, Due Dilligence, Compraventa de sociedades, Contratos, Suspensiones de pagos y quiebras.

- **Derecho de las Nuevas Tecnologías :** Contratación Electrónica, Propiedad Intelectual, Protección de Datos

- **Derecho Laboral:** Asesoría laboral a la empresa en plena coordinación con el área de Recursos Humanos de los clientes.

- **Derecho Administrativo :** Asesoramiento en materia de Urbanismo, Derecho de Minas y Farmacéutico así como la defensa ante expedientes administrativos en vía administrativa, económico-administrativa y contencioso-administrativa.

La preparación y experiencia procesal de nuestros profesionales nos permite **ofrecer** en todas las áreas de trabajo, **una defensa cualificada** de los intereses del cliente ante los Tribunales de Justicia en todo el territorio

www.sgsabogados.com
D: norberto del barrio
A: d-noise **M:** nor@d-noise.net

Balatá Beach Properties | Las Terrenas | Dominican Republic

contact us

Balatá Beach Properties

balatá beach properties | lots sales| virtual tour | las terrenas

Untouched by mainstream tourism, this beach is a real jewel. Balatá Beach Properties is located eight kilometers west of the town of Las Terrenas on Playa Cosón and has an extension of 525 mts. (1725 ft.) of beachfront. Playa Cosón has an extension of 8 Kms. (5 miles).

location map ZOOM

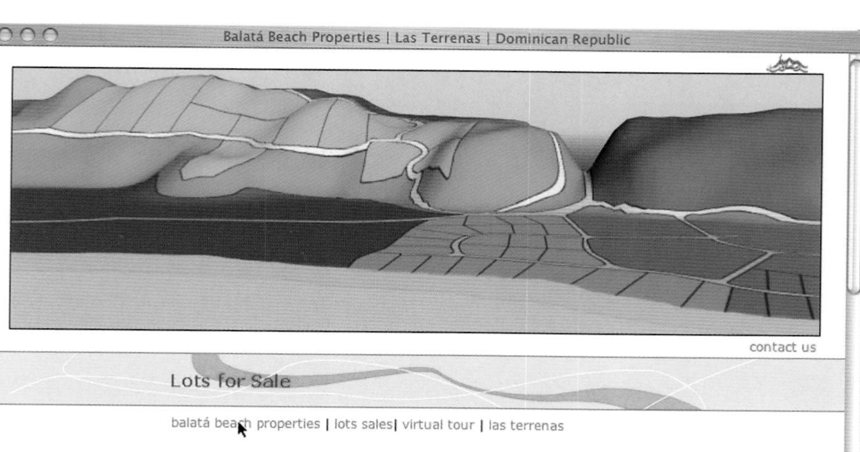
Balatá Beach Properties | Las Terrenas | Dominican Republic
contact us
Lots for Sale
balatá beach properties | lots sales| virtual tour | las terrenas

Move the mouse over the 3D-map above and see size and status of each lot.

choose top view 3Dmap >>

The lots are on average 1850m² (19,888 sqft.) There will be one family villa per lot. Contact for price.

ATLANTICO

www.balatabeachproperties.com
D: martin permantier
A: short cuts **M:** permantier@short-cuts.de

wie buysite vorgeht
was buysite bedeutet.
was buysite bietet.
wie buysite vorgeht.
wie buysite druckt.
die buysite fische.
anfrage/auftrag für buysite.
buysite
vor allem digital.
[Die Datenübernahme]
• Ihre Daten übernehmen wir auf allen aktuellen Datenträgern, via ISDN und Internet.
• Wir verwalten, bearbeiten und speichern Ihre Daten und nutzen sie mehrfach in Ihrem Interesse. Ohne Abhängigkeit von einzelnen Printanbietern.
[Die Vorstufe]
• buysite stellt professionelle Dokumente her und bearbeitet Ihre Daten. QuarkXPress, PageMaker, InDesign, Illustrator und Photoshop stehen als professionelle grafische Programme zur Verfügung.
• Für Print-on-Demand-Lösungen übernehmen wir gerne die Aktualisierungsaufgaben für Ihre Daten.
• Gelieferte Layoutdokumente ergänzen wir mit hochstehenden Bilddaten aus unserem Partnerbetrieb LAC AG.
• Die Leistungsfähigkeit und Professionalität unserer Partnerbetriebe steht Ihnen für die Vorstufe zur Verfügung.

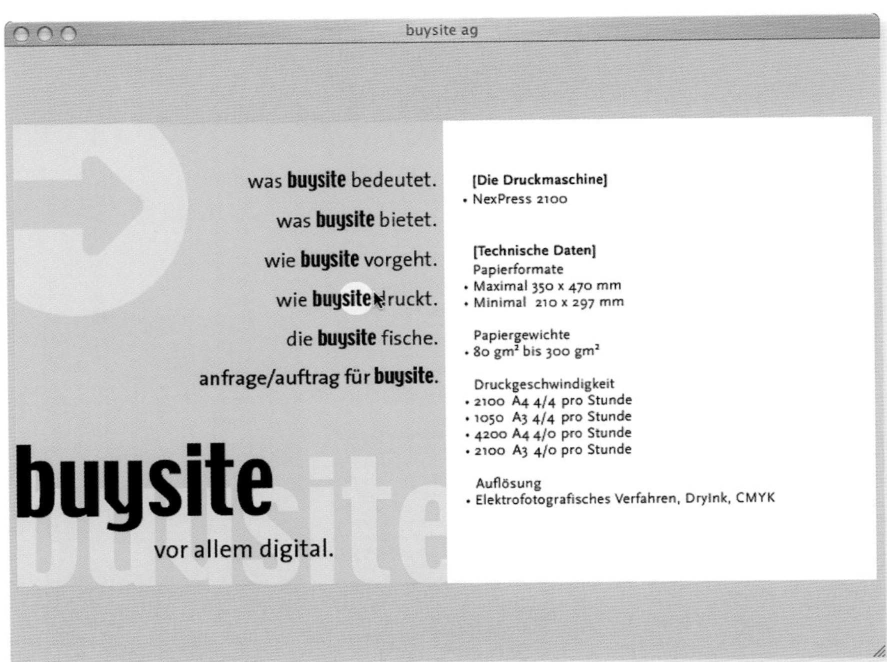
buysite ag
was buysite bedeutet.
was buysite bietet.
wie buysite vorgeht.
wie buysite druckt.
die buysite fische.
anfrage/auftrag für buysite.
buysite
vor allem digital.
[Die Druckmaschine]
• NexPress 2100
[Technische Daten]
Papierformate
• Maximal 350 x 470 mm
• Minimal 210 x 297 mm
Papiergewichte
• 80 gm² bis 300 gm²
Druckgeschwindigkeit
• 2100 A4 4/4 pro Stunde
• 1050 A3 4/4 pro Stunde
• 4200 A4 4/0 pro Stunde
• 2100 A3 4/0 pro Stunde
Auflösung
• Elektrofotografisches Verfahren, DryInk, CMYK

www.buysite.ch

D: michel seeliger

A: chameleon graphics **M:** info@chameleongraphics.ch

Buitenhek & van Doorn Consultancy

BUITENHEK & van DOORN CONSULTANCY

I. Home 2. Bedrijfsprofiel Contact & Route Vacatures & Search 3. Bestuursadvisering Organisatieontwikkeling Personeels- en beloningsmanagement Interim-management Training en coaching 4. Profielen Publicaties Interviews

Welkom

Deze site staat in het teken van persoonlijke ontmoeting en interactie. Zo zet het bedrijfsprofiel onze missie en visie uiteen en schetsen de produktgroepen een beeld van de werkzaamheden. Wij zijn actief op het gebied van bestuursadvisering, organisatieontwikkeling, personeels- en beloningsmanagement, interim-management en training & coaching. Daarnaast delen we middels interviews en publicaties ontwikkelingen binnen onze organisatie en de diverse vakgebieden. Maar het is ook mogelijk persoonlijk contact te leggen met onze medewerkers. Bezoek gerust deze profielen en schroom niet te reageren op de columns. Veel lees- en interactief plezier!

Ed Buitenhek en Rob van Doorn
directie

PRO-ACTIEVE JURIDISCHE BIJSTAND OP HET GEBIED VAN

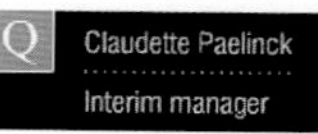
Q
Claudette Paelinck
Interim manager

Profielen

Klik op de banners om de persoonlijke pagina's van onze medewerkers te tonen. En lees meer over hun werkzaamheden, specialisaties en visies.
Overzicht profielen...

Janneke Groen
secretaresse

Interview

"Gezond ondernemerschap en de collectieve ambitie van de medewerkers van Buitenhek & van Doorn Consultancy om een bijdrage te leveren aan de effectieve inrichting van het openbaar bestuur en aan de HRM functie in organisaties binnen de publieke sector, drijft ontwikkelings- en innovatieprocessen."

Dit is de opinie van drs. Meindert Flikkema

Nieuws

Psychologisch onderzoek en assessment

Ons bureau heeft een ultranieuw assessment ontwikkeld op het gebied van (management)teamassessment. Heldere conclusies kunnen getrokken worden gericht op het versterken van het MT als sturend orgaan in moeilijke tijden. Lees verder...
2 november 2004

Wat heb ik als klant aan een full-service bureau?

Het is een bekend streven van ons bureau om een full-service productenpakket aan te bieden. Een dergelijk streven vereist een continu

Buitenhek & van Doorn Consultancy

BUITENHEK & van DOORN CONSULTANCY

I. Home 2. Bedrijfsprofiel Contact & Route Vacatures & Search 3. Bestuursadvisering Organisatieontwikkeling Personeels- en beloningsmanagement Interim-management Training en coaching 4. Profielen Publicaties Interviews

Bedrijfsprofiel

In onze samenleving komt het individu steeds meer voorop te staan en wordt de menselijke factor in organisaties belangrijker. Steeds meer bepaalt de kwaliteit van medewerkers de mate waarin organisaties van hun continuïteit verzekerd zijn. Daarom is een synergie tussen de persoonlijke ambities van medewerkers en de organisatie van groot belang. En vraagt de markt steeds meer om produkten en diensten die daarop aansluiten. En dat is precies wat wij bieden.

Marjan Hartman
office-manager

Andries Knevel
associé

Stefan Sterkenburg
adviseur

Sandra Bakker
secretaresse

Onze kracht

Innovatief en thuis in de wereld van onze klanten

Het optimaal benutten van de bestaande kennis en creativiteit die bij ons en in onze werkkring bestaat, dat is ons uitgangspunt. Een werkwijze die als vanzelf voor draagvlak en een open wijze van communiceren zorgt. Zowel binnen ons eigen bedrijf als de organisatie van de opdrachtgever. Daarbij passen we een geheel eigen werkvorm toe, die op een natuurlijke manier verloopt en een prettige samenwerking bewerkstelligt en bevordert.

Onze cultuur

Betrokken, laagdrempelig, persoonlijk en

Ons unieke aanbod

Geïntegreerde produkt/dienstcombinaties

De perfecte oplossing voor een vraagstuk is nooit zomaar voor handen. Daarom houden we open vizier en bekijken we meerdere invalshoeken. Zo creëren we een vrijheid die ons een dieper inzicht in de situatie verschaft en benutten we de mogelijkheid onze produkten op elk specifiek vraagstuk af te stemmen. Op die wijze heeft ons aanbod een daadwerkelijke meerwaarde voor de opdrachtgever.

Ons ultieme doel

Optimaliseren van de bedrijfsvoering

Als organisatieadviesbureau hebben wij een

benvado.nl
D: bob corporaal **C:** jan glas
A: playcollective **M:** info@reefscape.net

Saybs Sdn Bhd - Products
Syabs Sdn Bhd (485014M)
Financial Consultants
About
Products
Benefits
Careers
Contact
Products & Services
" When you think of me, don't think of Investment, but when you think of Investment, THINK OF ME."
One Stop Centre
• Life Insurance
• Wealth Accumulation
• Personal Accident Insurance
• Education Plan
• Retirement Plan
• Holiday Plan
• Partnership Insurance
• Keyman Insurance
• Workman Compensation
• Group Insurance
• Mortgage Insurance
• Unit Trust
• Bond Business
• Term Insurance
• School Children PA
• Dread Disease Protection
• Fixed Deposit Plan
• Investment Plan
• Low Interest Housing Loan

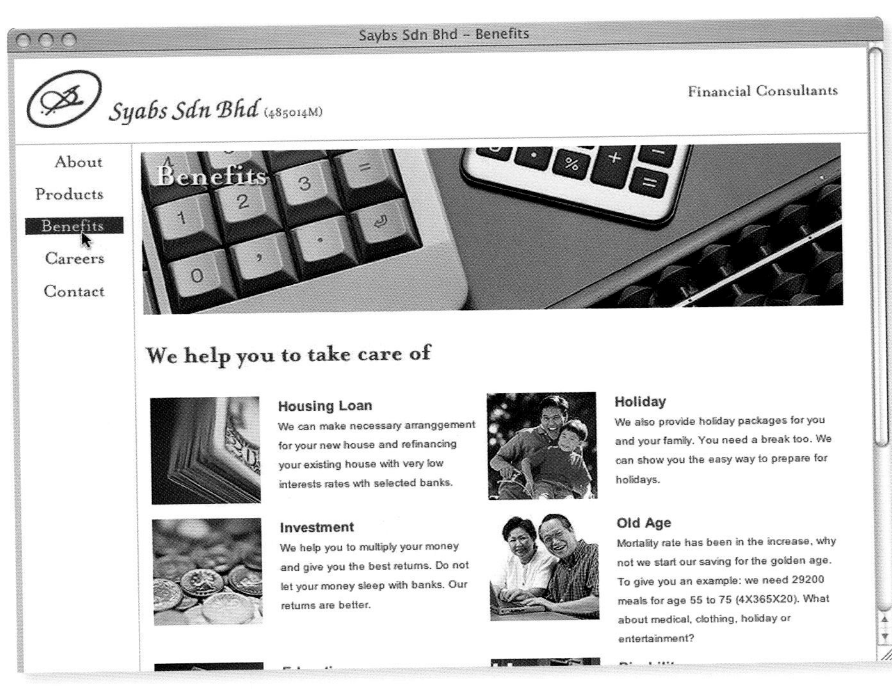
Saybs Sdn Bhd - Benefits
Syabs Sdn Bhd (485014M)
Financial Consultants
About
Products
Benefits
Careers
Contact
Benefits
We help you to take care of
Housing Loan
We can make necessary arranggement for your new house and refinancing your existing house with very low interests rates wth selected banks.
Holiday
We also provide holiday packages for you and your family. You need a break too. We can show you the easy way to prepare for holidays.
Investment
We help you to multiply your money and give you the best returns. Do not let your money sleep with banks. Our returns are better.
Old Age
Mortality rate has been in the increase, why not we start our saving for the golden age. To give you an example: we need 29200 meals for age 55 to 75 (4X365X20). What about medical, clothing, holiday or entertainment?

www.syabs.com.my
D: kerk hwang lok
A: dezain studio **M:** lok@dezainstudio.com

MBB | ontwikkelen&bouwen
Westkanaaldijk 19 - PB 1448
3600 BK Maarssen - Nederland
tel 0346 56 27 44
fax 0346 56 31 82
info@mbb.nl
ONTWIKKELEN&BOUWEN
MBB
WONINGEN IN VERKOOP
WONINGEN IN ONTWIKKELING
BEDRIJFSOBJECTEN
PORTFOLIO SEARCH
projectnaam
plaats
categorie
opleverjaar
opdrachtgever
architect
zoek
MBB
missie / visie
organisatie
vacatures
downloads & links
NIEUWS
laatste nieuws
pers
sponsoring
nieuwsbrief
CONTACT

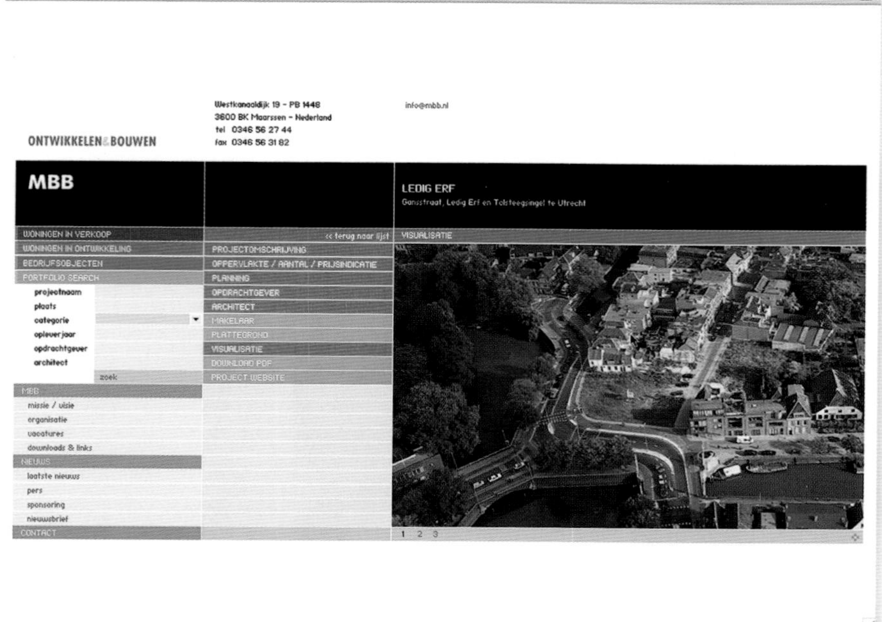
MBB | ontwikkelen&bouwen
Westkanaaldijk 19 - PB 1448
3600 BK Maarssen - Nederland
tel 0346 56 27 44
fax 0346 56 31 82
info@mbb.nl
ONTWIKKELEN&BOUWEN
MBB
LEDIG ERF
VISUALISATIE
PROJECTOMSCHRIJVING
OPPERVLAKTE / AANTAL / PRIJSINDICATIE
PLANNING
OPDRACHTGEVER
ARCHITECT
MAKELAAR
PLATTEGROND
VISUALISATIE
DOWNLOAD PDF
PROJECT WEBSITE

www.mbb.nl
D: sam windey **C:** youri de smet
A: celcius **M:** info@celcius.be

Space Fx
space fx
WHAT WE DO
GALLERY
ABOUT US
CASE STUDIES
FAQs
CONTACT
Security
PRODUCTS:
MULTI-ROOM HIFI
HOME CINEMA
SECURITY
LIGHTING
TELEPHONY
COMPUTER NETWORKING
AUTOMATION
REMOTE OPERATION
AFTER-SALES
Ranging from a simple but clever memorised programme that turns your lights on and off at the same times as you did the previous week, to a comprehensive security system which includes digital CCTV, monitoring, web-viewing of home-cams, access control and fingerprint reading.
We advise and install a security system that suits and exceeds needs and requirements
We design and install for, and have commissioning and servicing agreements with Banham Security.
BANHAM
:: HOME
CREATED BY: LIQUIDCHROME DESIGN

Space Fx
space fx
WHAT WE DO
GALLERY
ABOUT US
CASE STUDIES
FAQs
CONTACT
Case Studies
Case 1
A fully automated apartment, with solar blinds, automatic curtains and clerestory glazing, security, mood-lighting, multi-room hi-fi, and home cinema, all operated by a Crestron integrated system.
CASE 2
:: HOME
CREATED BY: LIQUIDCHROME DESIGN

www.spacefx.co.uk

D: johnny molina

A: liquidchrome design inc. **M:** jm@liquidchrome.net

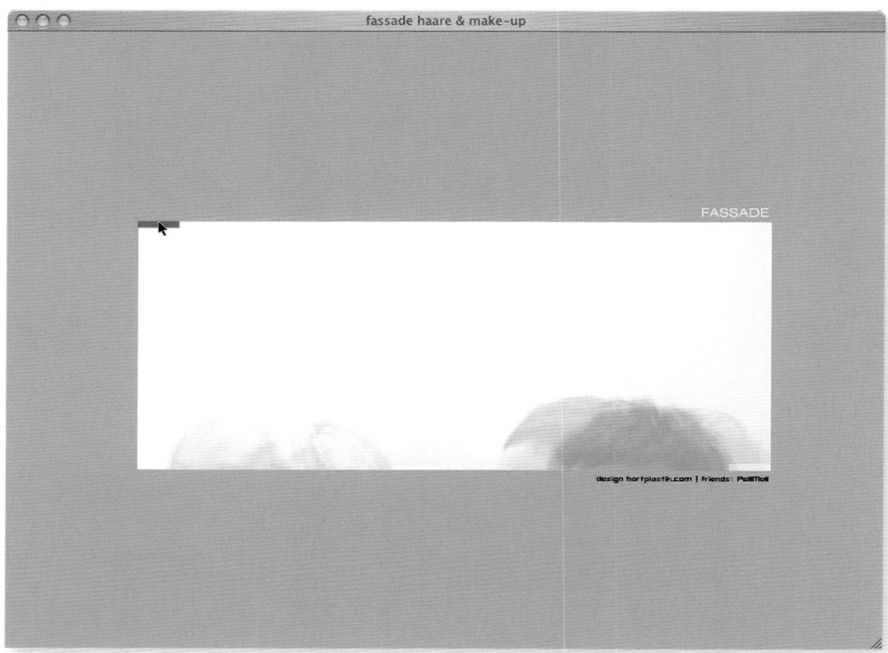
fassade haare & make-up
FASSADE
design hartplastik.com | friends: PeliMoli

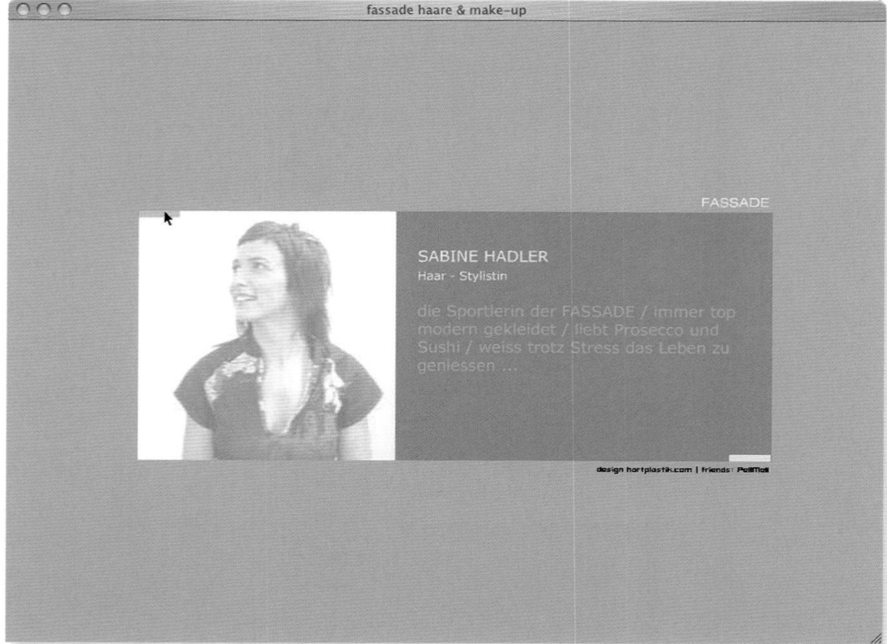
fassade haare & make-up
FASSADE
SABINE HADLER
Haar - Stylistin
die Sportlerin der FASSADE / immer top modern gekleidet / liebt Prosecco und Sushi / weiss trotz Stress das Leben zu geniessen ...
design hartplastik.com | friends: PeliMoli

www.diefassade.at
D: thomas nussmüller
A: hartplastik **M:** mac@hartplastik.com

Quintet- Make Your Home Where Love Grows
The Quintet
Executive Condominium
HOME | PROJECT INFO | SITE PLAN | FLOOR PLANS | CONTACT US
REGISTRATION
"Don't go through life, grow through life." Eric Butterworth
make your home, where love grows.
Experience The Quintet
Copyright © 2003, Centrepoint Properties Ltd. All Rights Reserved. This site is powered by Nxspace.
CENTREPOINT Homes
Where your future begins

Quintet- Make Your Home Where Love Grows
The Quintet
Executive Condominium
HOME | PROJECT INFO | SITE PLAN | FLOOR PLANS | CONTACT US
REGISTRATION
Basketball Court
Tennis Court
Water Feature
Children's Play Pool
Children's Playground
With 459 units in 6 blocks towering 19-22 storeys high, we can take our pick from the 3 and 4-bedroom apartments, and even the exclusive penthouse. Every unit is ever so spacious
Children's Playground
BBQ Pit
Foot Reflexology Area
BBQ Pit
Swimmng Pool
Main Entrance Feature Fountain
Bubble Pool
Jacuzzi
Exercise Station
N
Copyright © 2003, Centrepoint Properties Ltd. All Rights Reserved. This site is powered by Nxspace.
CENTREPOINT Homes
Where your future begins

www.centrepointhomes.com
D: jack lee **P:** david becker
A: nxspace **M:** jack@nxspace.com

Malerbetrieb Gronen

Über uns
Mitarbeiter
Referenzen
Dienst-
leistungen
Kontakt

Über uns
„Handwerkliche Kunst als Synonym für Tradition und Modernität“
Bereits in dritter Generation wird der Malerbetrieb Gronen ausschließlich von der Familie geleitet – nach der Gründung im Jahr 1930 durch Heinrich Gronen, danach durch dessen Nachfolger und Sohn Johannes Gronen, in diesen Tagen von Thomas Gronen, Maler- und

G R O N E N

Malerbetrieb Gronen

Über uns
Mitarbeiter
Referenzen
Dienst-
leistungen
Kontakt

Mitarbeiter
GRONEN

G R O N E N

www.gronen.net
D: jens marquardt **C:** philipp gocht
A: gm medien **M:** info@gm-medien.de

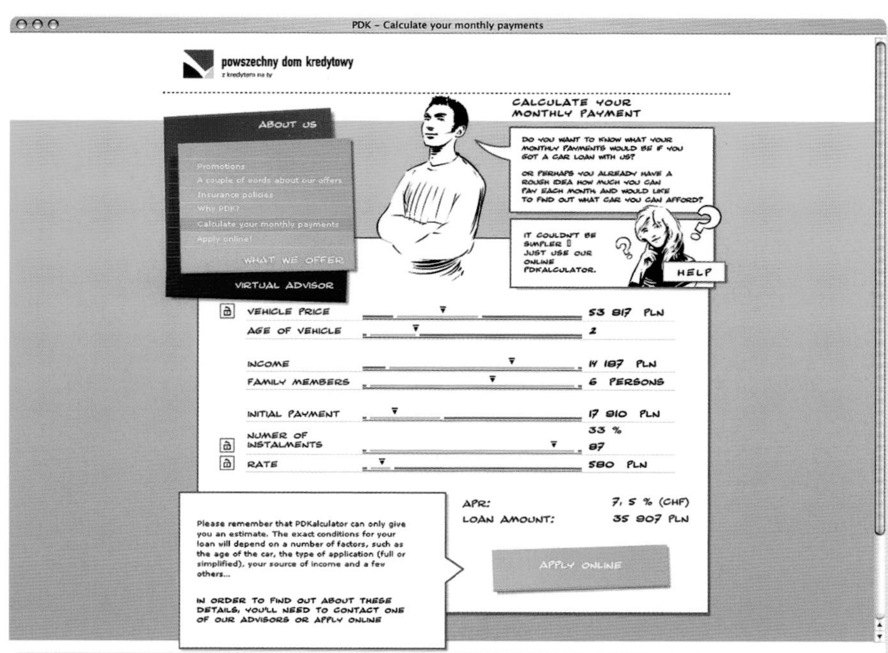
PDK - Calculate your monthly payments
powszechny dom kredytowy
ABOUT US
Promotions
A couple of words about our offers
Insurance policies
Why PDK?
Calculate your monthly payments
Apply online!
WHAT WE OFFER
VIRTUAL ADVISOR
CALCULATE YOUR MONTHLY PAYMENT
DO YOU WANT TO KNOW WHAT YOUR MONTHLY PAYMENTS WOULD BE IF YOU GOT A CAR LOAN WITH US?
OR PERHAPS YOU ALREADY HAVE A ROUGH IDEA HOW MUCH YOU CAN PAY EACH MONTH AND WOULD LIKE TO FIND OUT WHAT CAR YOU CAN AFFORD?
IT COULDN'T BE SIMPLER ! JUST USE OUR ONLINE PDKALCULATOR.
HELP
VEHICLE PRICE 53 817 PLN
AGE OF VEHICLE 2
INCOME 14 187 PLN
FAMILY MEMBERS 6 PERSONS
INITIAL PAYMENT 17 910 PLN
33 %
NUMER OF INSTALMENTS 87
RATE 580 PLN
APR: 7, 5 % (CHF)
LOAN AMOUNT: 35 907 PLN
Please remember that PDKalculator can only give you an estimate. The exact conditions for your loan will depend on a number of factors, such as the age of the car, the type of application (full or simplified), your source of income and a few others...
IN ORDER TO FIND OUT ABOUT THESE DETAILS, YOU'LL NEED TO CONTACT ONE OF OUR ADVISORS OR APPLY ONLINE
APPLY ONLINE

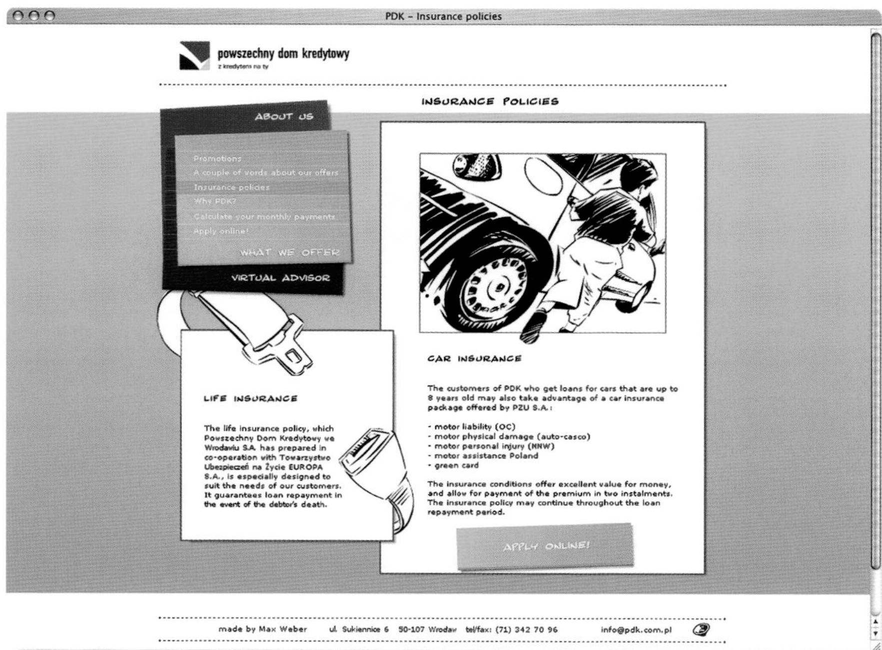
PDK - Insurance policies
powszechny dom kredytowy
INSURANCE POLICIES
ABOUT US
Promotions
A couple of words about our offers
Insurance policies
Why PDK?
Calculate your monthly payments
Apply online!
WHAT WE OFFER
VIRTUAL ADVISOR
LIFE INSURANCE
The life insurance policy, which Powszechny Dom Kredytowy we Wrocławiu S.A. has prepared in co-operation with Towarzystwo Ubezpieczeń na Życie EUROPA S.A., is especially designed to suit the needs of our customers. It guarantees loan repayment in the event of the debtor's death.
CAR INSURANCE
The customers of PDK who get loans for cars that are up to 8 years old may also take advantage of a car insurance package offered by PZU S.A.:
- motor liability (OC)
- motor physical damage (auto-casco)
- motor personal injury (NNW)
- motor assistance Poland
- green card
The insurance conditions offer excellent value for money, and allow for payment of the premium in two instalments. The insurance policy may continue throughout the loan repayment period.
APPLY ONLINE!
made by Max Weber ul. Sukiennice 6 50-107 Wrocław tel/fax: (71) 342 70 96 info@pdk.com.pl

www.pdk.pl/index_feng.html

D: grzegorz mogilewski **C:** lukasz dyszy **P:** malgorzata wozniakowska
A: max weber **M:** max@maxweber.com

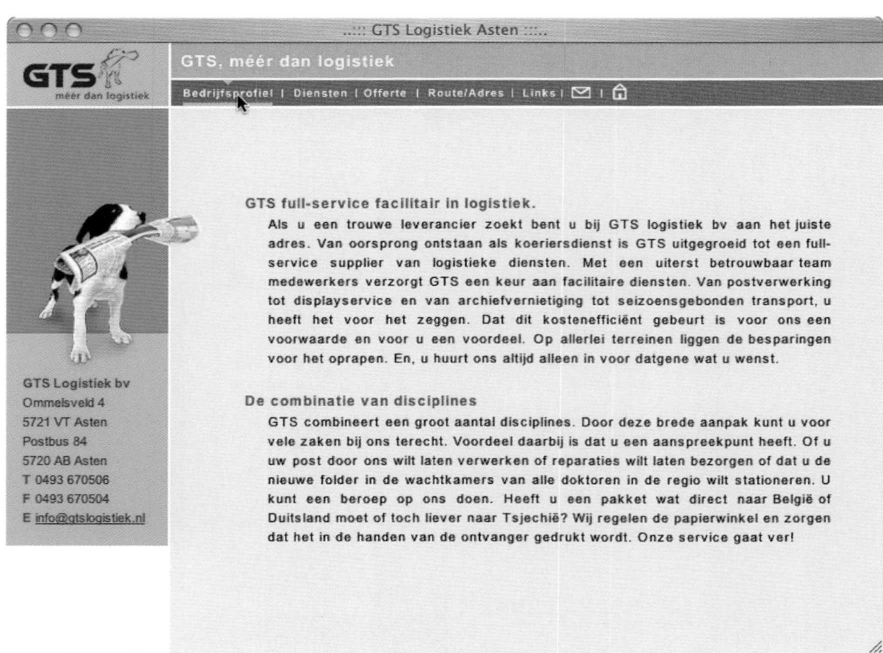
..::: GTS Logistiek Asten :::..
GTS
méér dan logistiek
GTS, méér dan logistiek
Bedrijfsprofiel | Diensten | Offerte | Route/Adres | Links |
GTS full-service facilitair in logistiek.
Als u een trouwe leverancier zoekt bent u bij GTS logistiek bv aan het juiste adres. Van oorsprong ontstaan als koeriersdienst is GTS uitgegroeid tot een full-service supplier van logistieke diensten. Met een uiterst betrouwbaar team medewerkers verzorgt GTS een keur aan facilitaire diensten. Van postverwerking tot displayservice en van archiefvernietiging tot seizoensgebonden transport, u heeft het voor het zeggen. Dat dit kostenefficiënt gebeurt is voor ons een voorwaarde en voor u een voordeel. Op allerlei terreinen liggen de besparingen voor het oprapen. En, u huurt ons altijd alleen in voor datgene wat u wenst.
De combinatie van disciplines
GTS combineert een groot aantal disciplines. Door deze brede aanpak kunt u voor vele zaken bij ons terecht. Voordeel daarbij is dat u een aanspreekpunt heeft. Of u uw post door ons wilt laten verwerken of reparaties wilt laten bezorgen of dat u de nieuwe folder in de wachtkamers van alle doktoren in de regio wilt stationeren. U kunt een beroep op ons doen. Heeft u een pakket wat direct naar België of Duitsland moet of toch liever naar Tsjechië? Wij regelen de papierwinkel en zorgen dat het in de handen van de ontvanger gedrukt wordt. Onze service gaat ver!
GTS Logistiek bv
Ommelsveld 4
5721 VT Asten
Postbus 84
5720 AB Asten
T 0493 670506
F 0493 670504
E info@gtslogistiek.nl

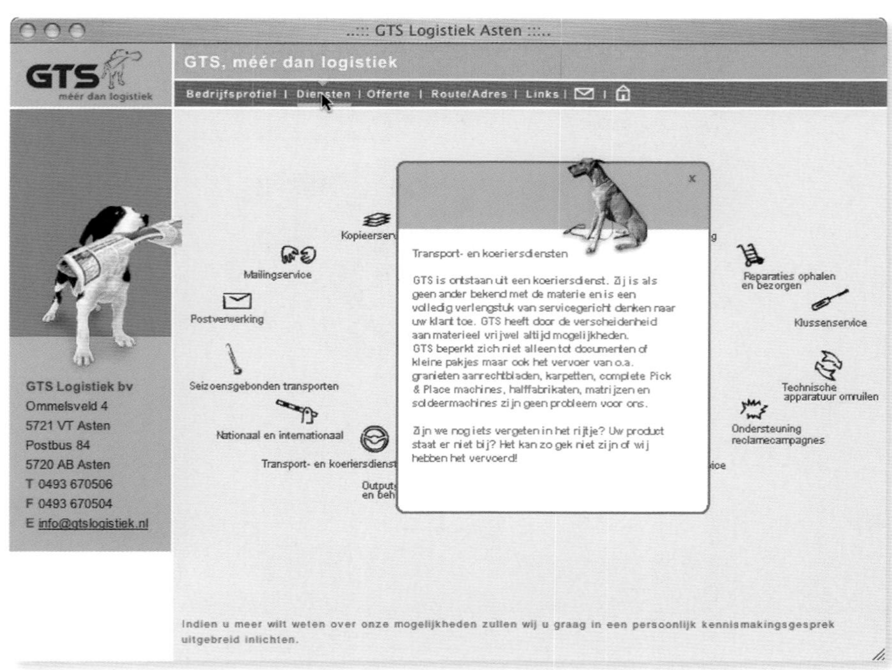
..::: GTS Logistiek Asten :::..
GTS
méér dan logistiek
GTS, méér dan logistiek
Bedrijfsprofiel | Diensten | Offerte | Route/Adres | Links |
Mailingservice
Postverwerking
Seizoensgebonden transporten
Nationaal en internationaal
Reparaties ophalen en bezorgen
Klussenservice
Technische apparatuur omruilen
Ondersteuning reclamecampagnes
Transport- en koeriersdiensten
GTS is ontstaan uit een koeriersdienst. Zij is als geen ander bekend met de materie en is een volledig verlengstuk van servicegericht denken naar uw klant toe. GTS heeft door de verscheidenheid aan materieel vrijwel altijd mogelijkheden.
GTS beperkt zich niet alleen tot documenten of kleine pakjes maar ook het vervoer van o.a. granieten aanrechtbladen, karpetten, complete Pick & Place machines, halffabrikaten, matrijzen en soldeermachines zijn geen probleem voor ons.
Zijn we nog iets vergeten in het rijtje? Uw product staat er niet bij? Het kan zo gek niet zijn of wij hebben het vervoerd!
GTS Logistiek bv
Ommelsveld 4
5721 VT Asten
Postbus 84
5720 AB Asten
T 0493 670506
F 0493 670504
E info@gtslogistiek.nl
Indien u meer wilt weten over onze mogelijkheden zullen wij u graag in een persoonlijk kennismakingsgesprek uitgebreid inlichten.

www.gtslogistiek.nl
D: karlijn schengenga
A: spiegel reclamestudio **M:** karlijn@spiegel.nl

Copias Barquillo
Copias Barquillo
www.copiasbarquillo.com
Home
Impresión Digital
Planos-Plotters
Carteles
Revelado
Servicios
Contacto
planos
#
• Gran producción
• Impresión digital
• Escanea una vez y luego imprime todas las copias de igual manera
• Ploteado a color
• Reducción y ampliación desde 25% hasta 400%

Copias Barquillo
Copias Barquillo
www.copiasbarquillo.com
Home
Impresión Digital
Planos-Plotters
Carteles
Revelado
Servicios
Contacto
carteles
#
• Impresión digital gran formato
• Impresión de todo tipo de carteles
• Gran velocidad
• Distintos tamaños
• Distintos acabados
• Impresión en lona

www.copiasbarquillo.com
D: luis jordá lópez **C:** roberto fernandez
A: ryesoft **M:** luis@ryesoft.com

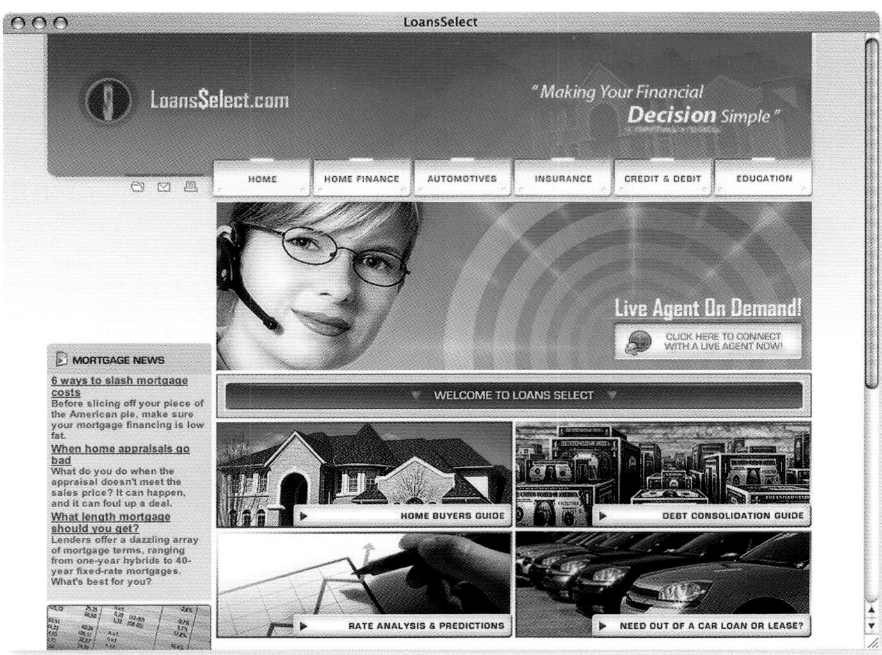
LoansSelect
LoansSelect.com
"Making Your Financial Decision Simple"
HOME
HOME FINANCE
AUTOMOTIVES
INSURANCE
CREDIT & DEBIT
EDUCATION
Live Agent On Demand!
CLICK HERE TO CONNECT WITH A LIVE AGENT NOW!
MORTGAGE NEWS
6 ways to slash mortgage costs
Before slicing off your piece of the American pie, make sure your mortgage financing is low fat.
When home appraisals go bad
What do you do when the appraisal doesn't meet the sales price? It can happen, and it can foul up a deal.
What length mortgage should you get?
Lenders offer a dazzling array of mortgage terms, ranging from one-year hybrids to 40-year fixed-rate mortgages. What's best for you?
WELCOME TO LOANS SELECT
HOME BUYERS GUIDE
DEBT CONSOLIDATION GUIDE
RATE ANALYSIS & PREDICTIONS
NEED OUT OF A CAR LOAN OR LEASE?

LoansSelect
LoansSelect.com
"Making Your Financial Decision Simple"
HOME
HOME FINANCE
AUTOMOTIVES
INSURANCE
CREDIT & DEBIT
EDUCATION
CHAT WITH A LIVE AGENT
HOME BUYERS GUIDE
DEBT CONSOLIDATION GUIDE
ANALYSIS & PREDICTIONS
NEED OUT OF A LOAN?
ENTER FOR CHANCE TO WIN!
DREAM VACATION ON US
SEMINARS AND EVENTS
TOOLS
FREE CREDIT REPORT
PRELOADING VIDEO. PLEASE WAIT
CREDIT & DEBT
JOIN OUR NEWSLETTER
ENTER YOUR EMAIL BELOW
SUBMIT
DEBT MANAGEMENT
STEP 1
STEP 2
STEP 3
Debt Management Application
STEP 1 OF 3
Monthly Net Income*
$ .00
Debt Amount*
$ .00
Number of Creditors*
--Select--
Client ID (Optional)

www.loansselect.com
A: flashlevel.com **M:** info@flashlevel.com

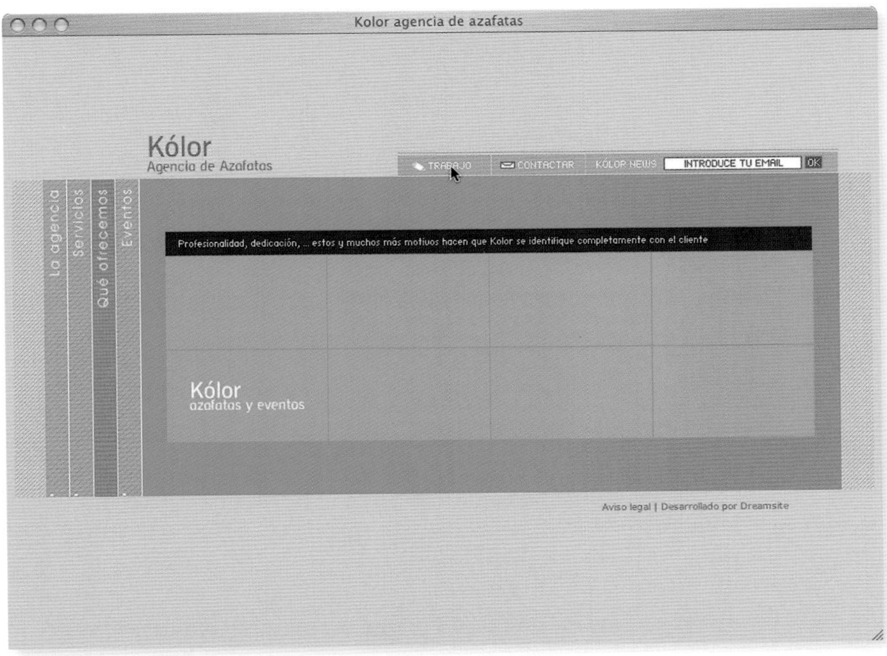
Kolor agencia de azafatas
Kólor
Agencia de Azafatas
TRABAJO
CONTACTAR
KOLOR NEWS
INTRODUCE TU EMAIL
OK
La agencia
Servicios
Qué ofrecemos
Eventos
Profesionalidad, dedicación, ... estos y muchos más motivos hacen que Kolor se identifique completamente con el cliente
Kólor
azafatas y eventos
Aviso legal | Desarrollado por Dreamsite

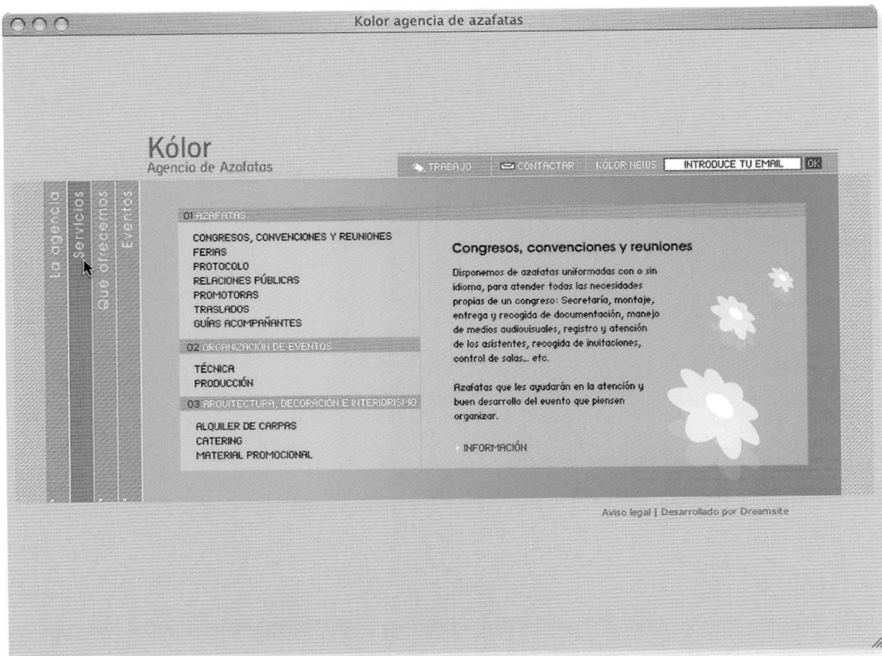
Kolor agencia de azafatas
Kólor
Agencia de Azafatas
TRABAJO
CONTACTAR
KOLOR NEWS
INTRODUCE TU EMAIL
OK
La agencia
Servicios
Qué ofrecemos
Eventos
01 AZAFATAS
CONGRESOS, CONVENCIONES Y REUNIONES
FERIAS
PROTOCOLO
RELACIONES PÚBLICAS
PROMOTORAS
TRASLADOS
GUÍAS ACOMPAÑANTES
02 ORGANIZACIÓN DE EVENTOS
TÉCNICA
PRODUCCIÓN
03 ARQUITECTURA, DECORACIÓN E INTERIORISMO
ALQUILER DE CARPAS
CATERING
MATERIAL PROMOCIONAL
Congresos, convenciones y reuniones
Disponemos de azafatas uniformadas con o sin idioma, para atender todas las necesidades propias de un congreso: Secretaría, montaje, entrega y recogida de documentación, manejo de medios audiovisuales, registro y atención de los asistentes, recogida de invitaciones, control de salas... etc.
Azafatas que les ayudarán en la atención y buen desarrollo del evento que piensen organizar.
INFORMACIÓN
Aviso legal | Desarrollado por Dreamsite

www.agenciakolor.com
D: hamadi housami **C:** javier de miguel
A: dreamsite **M:** info@dreamsite.es

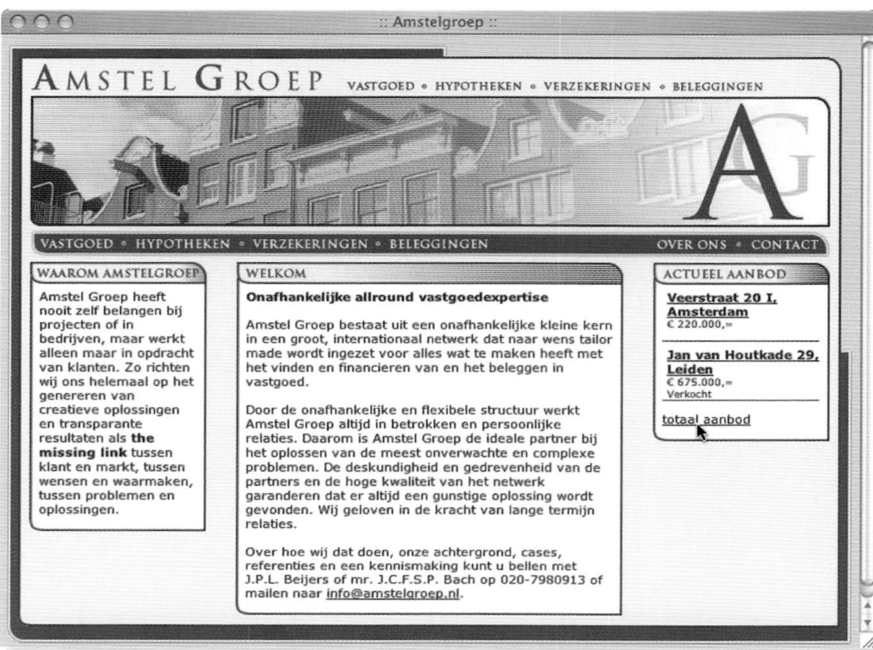
:: Amstelgroep ::
AMSTEL GROEP
VASTGOED • HYPOTHEKEN • VERZEKERINGEN • BELEGGINGEN
VASTGOED • HYPOTHEKEN • VERZEKERINGEN • BELEGGINGEN
OVER ONS • CONTACT
WAAROM AMSTELGROEP
Amstel Groep heeft nooit zelf belangen bij projecten of in bedrijven, maar werkt alleen maar in opdracht van klanten. Zo richten wij ons helemaal op het genereren van creatieve oplossingen en transparante resultaten als the missing link tussen klant en markt, tussen wensen en waarmaken, tussen problemen en oplossingen.
WELKOM
Onafhankelijke allround vastgoedexpertise
Amstel Groep bestaat uit een onafhankelijke kleine kern in een groot, internationaal netwerk dat naar wens tailor made wordt ingezet voor alles wat te maken heeft met het vinden en financieren van en het beleggen in vastgoed.
Door de onafhankelijke en flexibele structuur werkt Amstel Groep altijd in betrokken en persoonlijke relaties. Daarom is Amstel Groep de ideale partner bij het oplossen van de meest onverwachte en complexe problemen. De deskundigheid en gedrevenheid van de partners en de hoge kwaliteit van het netwerk garanderen dat er altijd een gunstige oplossing wordt gevonden. Wij geloven in de kracht van lange termijn relaties.
Over hoe wij dat doen, onze achtergrond, cases, referenties en een kennismaking kunt u bellen met J.P.L. Beijers of mr. J.C.F.S.P. Bach op 020-7980913 of mailen naar info@amstelgroep.nl.
ACTUEEL AANBOD
Veerstraat 20 I, Amsterdam
€ 220.000,=
Jan van Houtkade 29, Leiden
€ 675.000,=
Verkocht
totaal aanbod

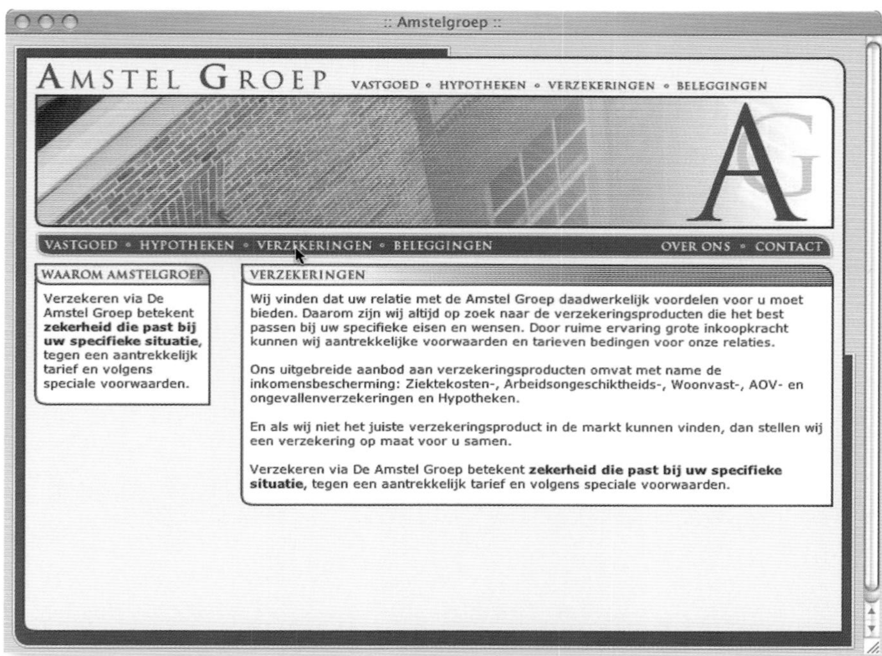
:: Amstelgroep ::
AMSTEL GROEP
VASTGOED • HYPOTHEKEN • VERZEKERINGEN • BELEGGINGEN
VASTGOED • HYPOTHEKEN • VERZEKERINGEN • BELEGGINGEN
OVER ONS • CONTACT
WAAROM AMSTELGROEP
Verzekeren via De Amstel Groep betekent zekerheid die past bij uw specifieke situatie, tegen een aantrekkelijk tarief en volgens speciale voorwaarden.
VERZEKERINGEN
Wij vinden dat uw relatie met de Amstel Groep daadwerkelijk voordelen voor u moet bieden. Daarom zijn wij altijd op zoek naar de verzekeringsproducten die het best passen bij uw specifieke eisen en wensen. Door ruime ervaring grote inkoopkracht kunnen wij aantrekkelijke voorwaarden en tarieven bedingen voor onze relaties.
Ons uitgebreide aanbod aan verzekeringsproducten omvat met name de inkomensbescherming: Ziektekosten-, Arbeidsongeschiktheids-, Woonvast-, AOV- en ongevallenverzekeringen en Hypotheken.
En als wij niet het juiste verzekeringsproduct in de markt kunnen vinden, dan stellen wij een verzekering op maat voor u samen.
Verzekeren via De Amstel Groep betekent zekerheid die past bij uw specifieke situatie, tegen een aantrekkelijk tarief en volgens speciale voorwaarden.

www.amstelgroep.nl
D: nikolai zauber
A: nikolai **M:** info@nikolai.nl

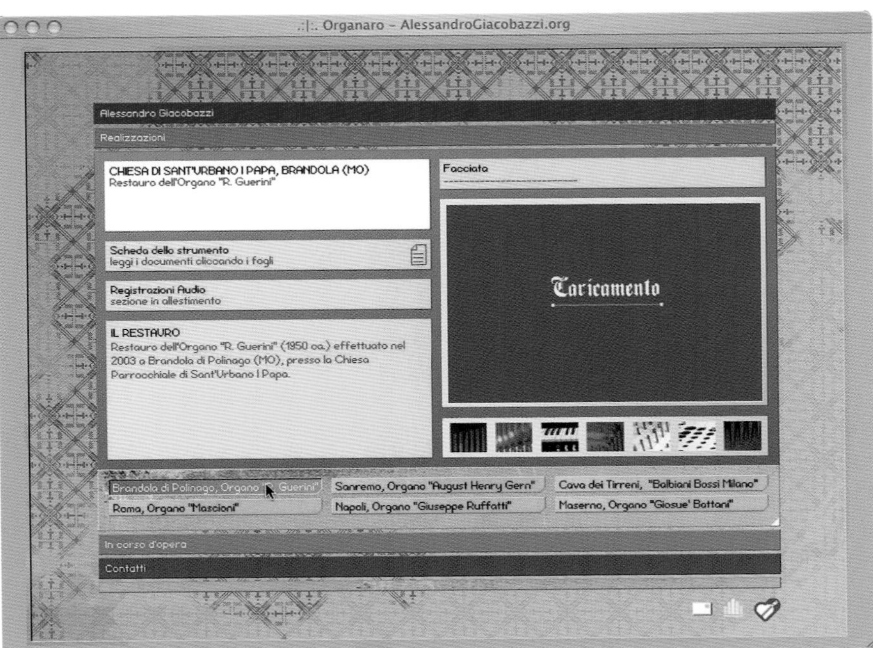
.:|:. Organaro - AlessandroGiacobazzi.org
Alessandro Giacobazzi
Realizzazioni
CHIESA DI SANT'URBANO I PAPA, BRANDOLA (MO)
Restauro dell'Organo "R. Guerini"
Facciata
Scheda dello strumento
leggi i documenti cliccando i fogli
Registrazioni Audio
sezione in allestimento
IL RESTAURO
Restauro dell'Organo "R. Guerini" (1950 ca.) effettuato nel 2003 a Brandola di Polinago (MO), presso la Chiesa Parrocchiale di Sant'Urbano I Papa.
Caricamento
Sanremo, Organo "August Henry Gern"
Cava dei Tirreni, "Balbiani Bossi Milano"
Roma, Organo "Mascioni"
Napoli, Organo "Giuseppe Ruffatti"
Maserno, Organo "Giosue' Battani"
In corso d'opera
Contatti

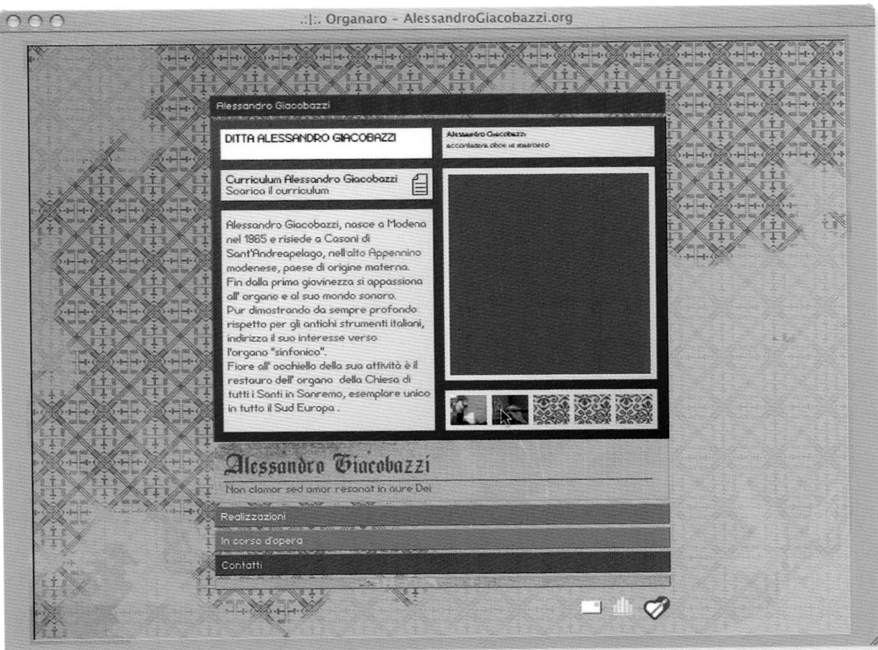
.:|:. Organaro - AlessandroGiacobazzi.org
Alessandro Giacobazzi
DITTA ALESSANDRO GIACOBAZZI
Curriculum Alessandro Giacobazzi
Scarica il curriculum
Alessandro Giacobazzi, nasce a Modena nel 1965 e risiede a Casoni di Sant'Andreapelago, nell'alto Appennino modenese, paese di origine materna.
Fin dalla prima giovinezza si appassiona all' organo e al suo mondo sonoro.
Pur dimostrando da sempre profondo rispetto per gli antichi strumenti italiani, indirizza il suo interesse verso l'organo "sinfonico".
Fiore all' occhiello della sua attività è il restauro dell' organo della Chiesa di tutti i Santi in Sanremo, esemplare unico in tutto il Sud Europa .
Alessandro Giacobazzi
Non clamor sed amor resonat in aure Dei
Realizzazioni
In corso d'opera
Contatti

www.alessandrogiacobazzi.org
D: caroli lorenzo
A: lo zoo di venere **M:** lox@lozoodivenere.it

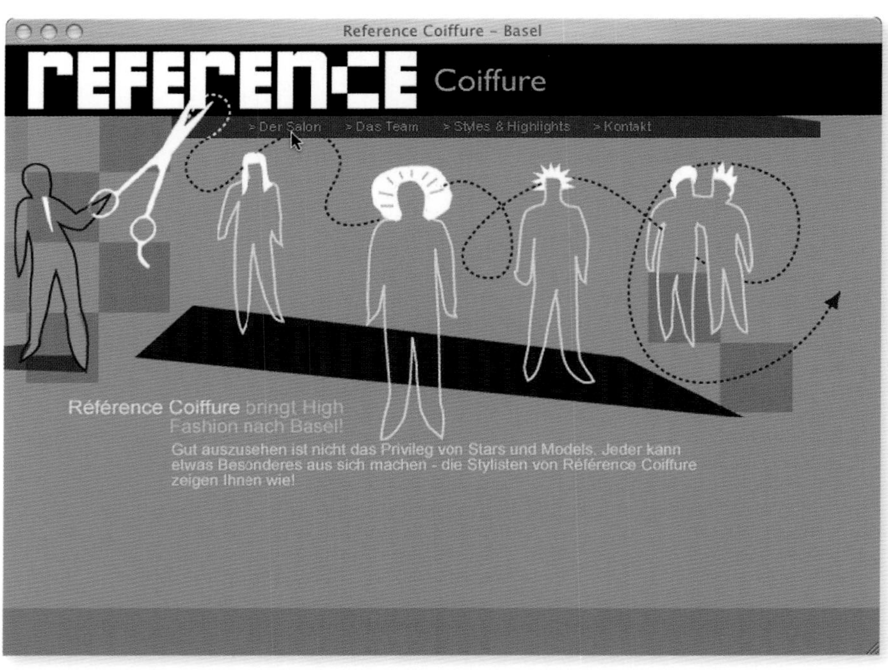
Reference Coiffure - Basel
reference Coiffure
> Der Salon > Das Team > Styles & Highlights > Kontakt
Référence Coiffure bringt High Fashion nach Basel!
Gut auszusehen ist nicht das Privileg von Stars und Models. Jeder kann etwas Besonderes aus sich machen - die Stylisten von Référence Coiffure zeigen Ihnen wie!

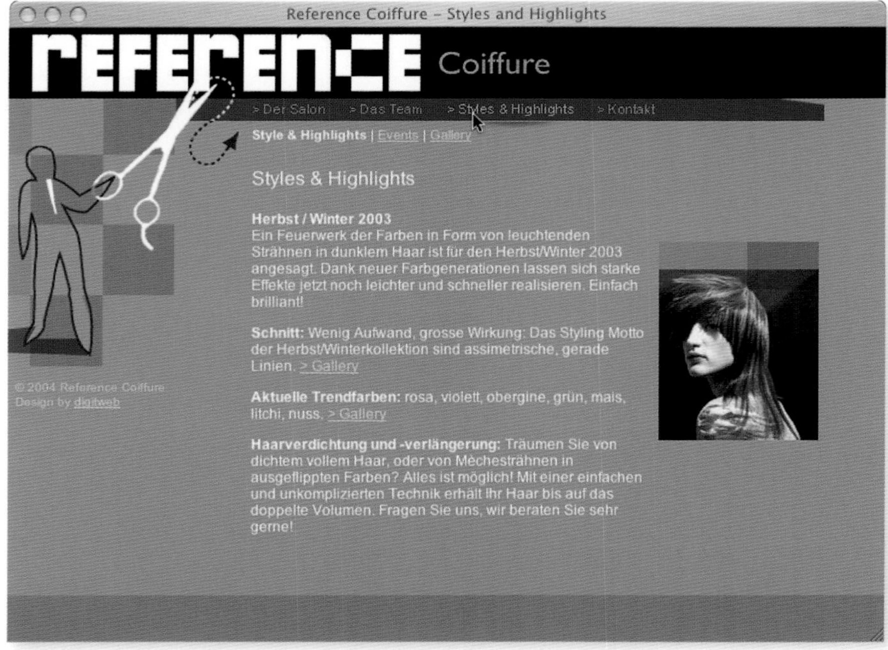
Reference Coiffure - Styles and Highlights
reference Coiffure
> Der Salon > Das Team > Styles & Highlights > Kontakt
Style & Highlights | Events | Gallery
Styles & Highlights
Herbst / Winter 2003
Ein Feuerwerk der Farben in Form von leuchtenden Strähnen in dunklem Haar ist für den Herbst/Winter 2003 angesagt. Dank neuer Farbgenerationen lassen sich starke Effekte jetzt noch leichter und schneller realisieren. Einfach brilliant!
Schnitt: Wenig Aufwand, grosse Wirkung: Das Styling Motto der Herbst/Winterkollektion sind assimetrische, gerade Linien. > Gallery
Aktuelle Trendfarben: rosa, violett, obergine, grün, mais, litchi, nuss. > Gallery
Haarverdichtung und -verlängerung: Träumen Sie von dichtem vollem Haar, oder von Mèchesträhnen in ausgeflippten Farben? Alles ist möglich! Mit einer einfachen und unkomplizierten Technik erhält Ihr Haar bis auf das doppelte Volumen. Fragen Sie uns, wir beraten Sie sehr gerne!
© 2004 Reference Coiffure
Design by digitweb

www.referencecoiffure.ch
D: ben newton
A: digit **M:** ben@digitweb.co.uk

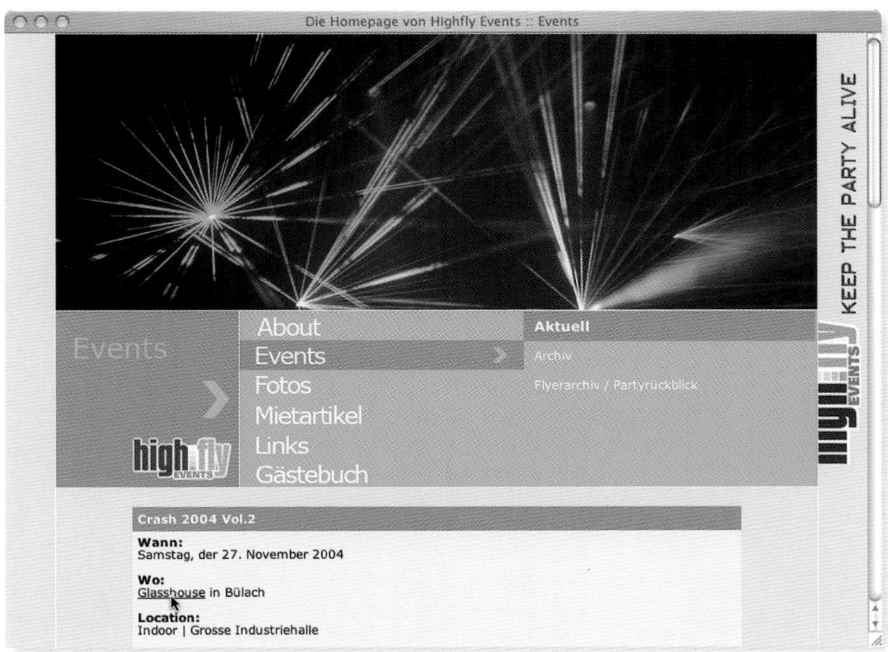
Die Homepage von Highfly Events :: Events
KEEP THE PARTY ALIVE
Events
About
Events
Fotos
Mietartikel
Links
Gästebuch
Aktuell
Archiv
Flyerarchiv / Partyrückblick
Crash 2004 Vol.2
Wann:
Samstag, der 27. November 2004
Wo:
Glasshouse in Bülach
Location:
Indoor | Grosse Industriehalle

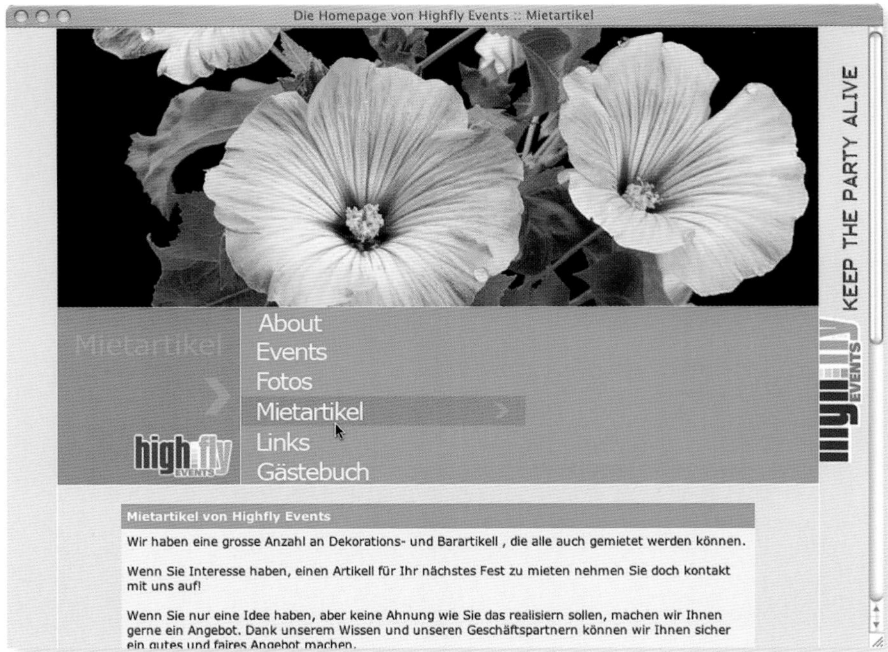
Die Homepage von Highfly Events :: Mietartikel
KEEP THE PARTY ALIVE
Mietartikel
About
Events
Fotos
Mietartikel
Links
Gästebuch
Mietartikel von Highfly Events
Wir haben eine grosse Anzahl an Dekorations- und Barartikell , die alle auch gemietet werden können.
Wenn Sie Interesse haben, einen Artikell für Ihr nächstes Fest zu mieten nehmen Sie doch kontakt mit uns auf!
Wenn Sie nur eine Idee haben, aber keine Ahnung wie Sie das realisiern sollen, machen wir Ihnen gerne ein Angebot. Dank unserem Wissen und unseren Geschäftspartnern können wir Ihnen sicher

www.highfly-events.ch
D: oliver gabor
M: oliver@highfly-events.ch

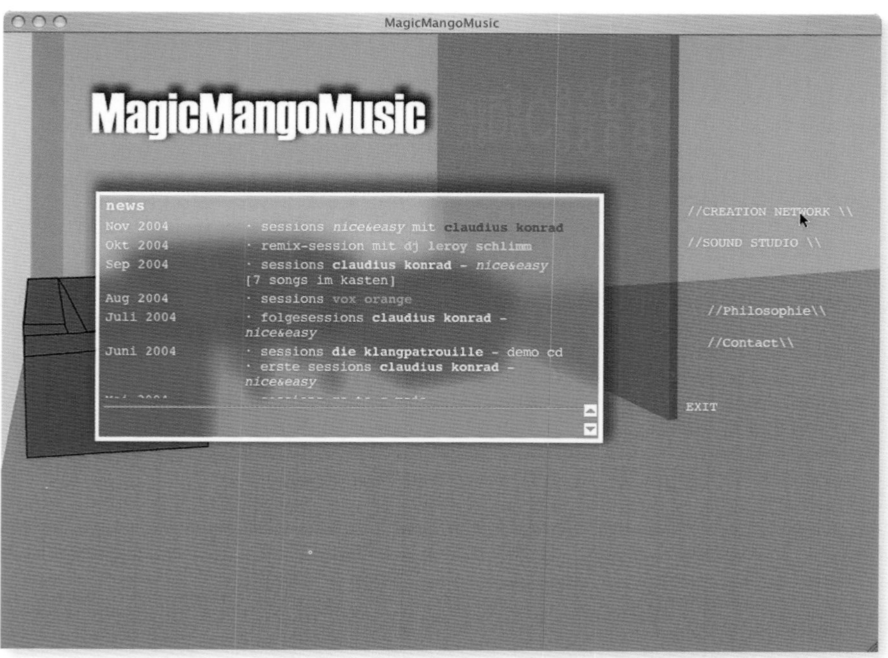
MagicMangoMusic
MagicMangoMusic
news
Nov 2004 · sessions nice&easy mit claudius konrad
Okt 2004 · remix-session mit dj leroy schlimm
Sep 2004 · sessions claudius konrad - nice&easy [7 songs im kasten]
Aug 2004 · sessions vox orange
Juli 2004 · folgesessions claudius konrad - nice&easy
Juni 2004 · sessions die klangpatrouille - demo cd
· erste sessions claudius konrad - nice&easy
//CREATION NETWORK \\
//SOUND STUDIO \\
//Philosophie\\
//Contact\\
EXIT

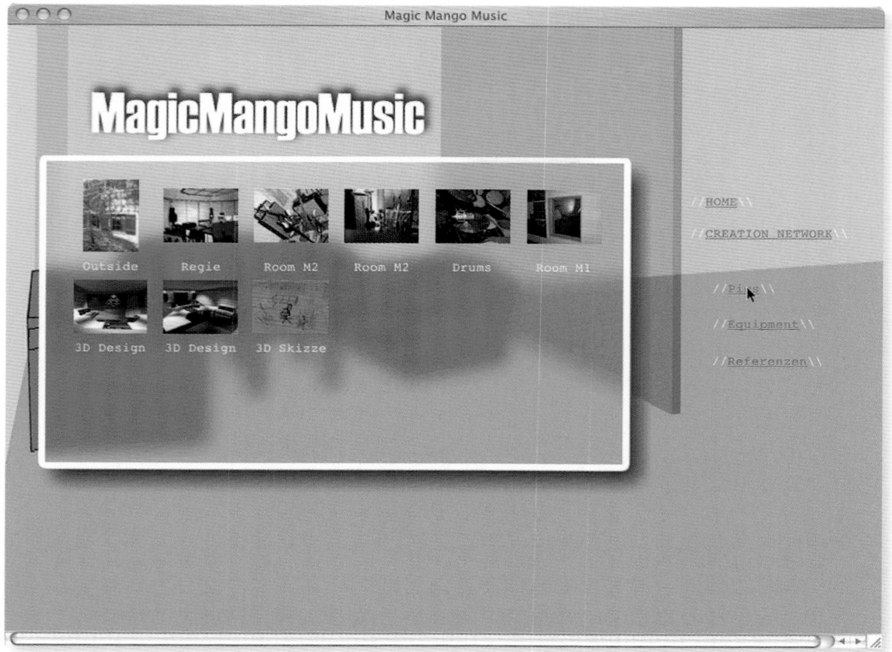
Magic Mango Music
MagicMangoMusic
Outside
Regie
Room M2
Room M2
Drums
Room M1
3D Design
3D Design
3D Skizze
//HOME\\
//CREATION NETWORK\\
//Equipment\\
//Referenzen\\

www.magicmangomusic.de
D: claudius konrad
M: ck@ckonrad.de

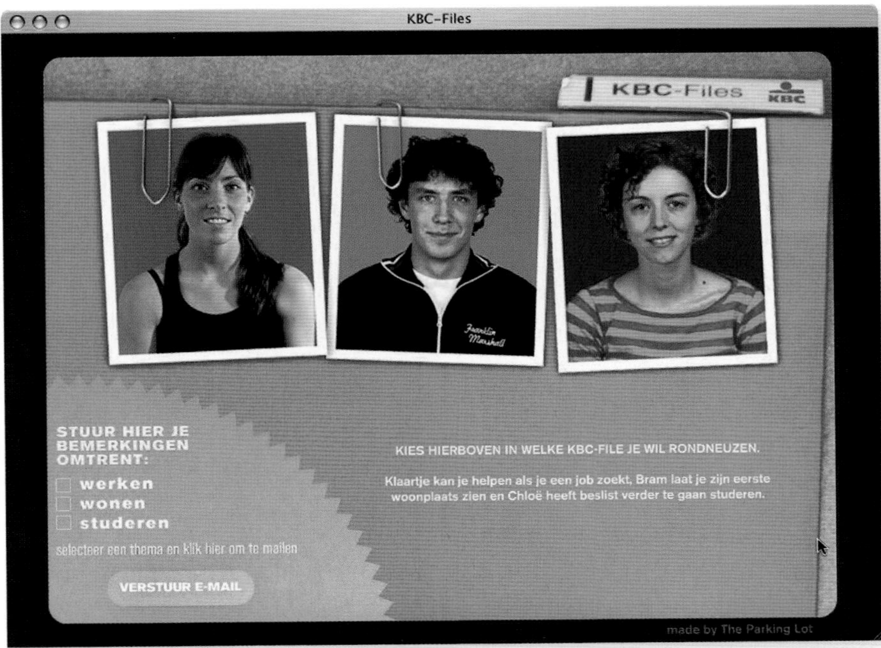
KBC-Files
KBC-Files
STUUR HIER JE BEMERKINGEN OMTRENT:
werken
wonen
studeren
selecteer een thema en klik hier om te mailen
VERSTUUR E-MAIL
KIES HIERBOVEN IN WELKE KBC-FILE JE WIL RONDNEUZEN.
Klaartje kan je helpen als je een job zoekt, Bram laat je zijn eerste woonplaats zien en Chloë heeft beslist verder te gaan studeren.
made by The Parking Lot

KBC-Files
SPAAR TIJD MET HET SNELMENU
Je wilt later een boeiende job met een overschot aan mogelijkheden? Je studiekeuze speelt daar een superbelangrijke rol in. Trek dus ruim de tijd uit om er over na te denken wilt.
made by The Parking Lot

jongeren.kbc.be/kbcfiles
D: miech rolly **C:** kristoffer dams **P:** kbc bank
A: the parking lot **M:** evan@theparkinglot.com

Visage - Frizerski studio i salon za masažu
SA ŠKARAMA TREBA ZNAT!
FRIZERSKI STUDIO I SALON ZA MASAŽU
VISAGE
ŠIROKOBRIŠKA 56/10 000 ZAGREB
HOME
O NAMA
PROIZVODI
MASAŽA
FRIZURE
USLUGE
REFERENCE
IZ MEDIJA
NOVOSTI
KONTAKT
LOKACIJA
Frizure
[SKRATITI VRHOVE?]
VISAGE
Zašto smo drugačiji?
3x
&
Sa škarama treba znati!
Uspješnost našeg posla zasniva se na dugogodišnjem iskustvu, sudjelovanju na mnogobrojnim snimanjima reklamnih i muzičkih spotova i filmova i educiranom osoblju.
Vršimo raznolike tehnike šišanja, bojanja i feniranja. Pružamo tretmane za njegu suhe i masne kose te protiv ispadanja, a uz to kod nas imate mogućnost kupnje proizvoda pomoću kojih te tretmane možete obavljati i kod kuće. Upotrebljavamo visokokvalitetne profesionalne proizvode, kao npr. Schwarzkopf.
Specifičnost naših usluga temelji se na modernom i klasičnom stilu frizura. Jednako kvalitetno pristupamo izradi klasičnih, "otkačenih", revijskih ili svečanih frizura i frizura za svakodnevni look.

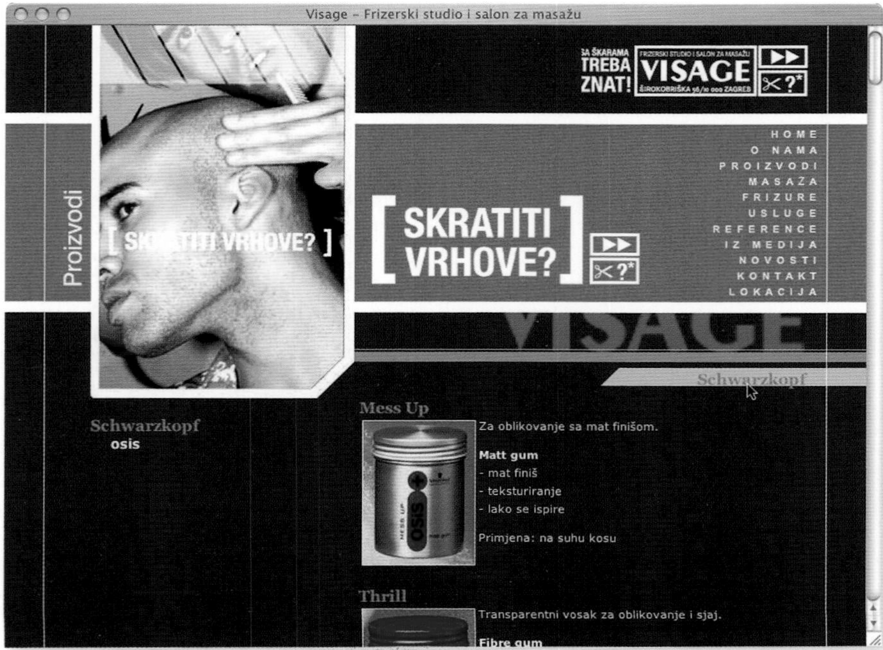
Visage - Frizerski studio i salon za masažu
SA ŠKARAMA TREBA ZNAT!
FRIZERSKI STUDIO I SALON ZA MASAŽU
VISAGE
ŠIROKOBRIŠKA 56/10 000 ZAGREB
HOME
O NAMA
PROIZVODI
MASAŽA
FRIZURE
USLUGE
REFERENCE
IZ MEDIJA
NOVOSTI
KONTAKT
LOKACIJA
Proizvodi
[SKRATITI VRHOVE?]
VISAGE
Schwarzkopf
Schwarzkopf
osis
Mess Up
Za oblikovanje sa mat finišom.
Matt gum
- mat finiš
- teksturiranje
- lako se ispire
Primjena: na suhu kosu
Thrill
Transparentni vosak za oblikovanje i sjaj.
Fibre gum

www.studiovisage.hr
D: robert novak **C:** ivica hrg
A: tramot d.o.o. **M:** nenad@tramot.com

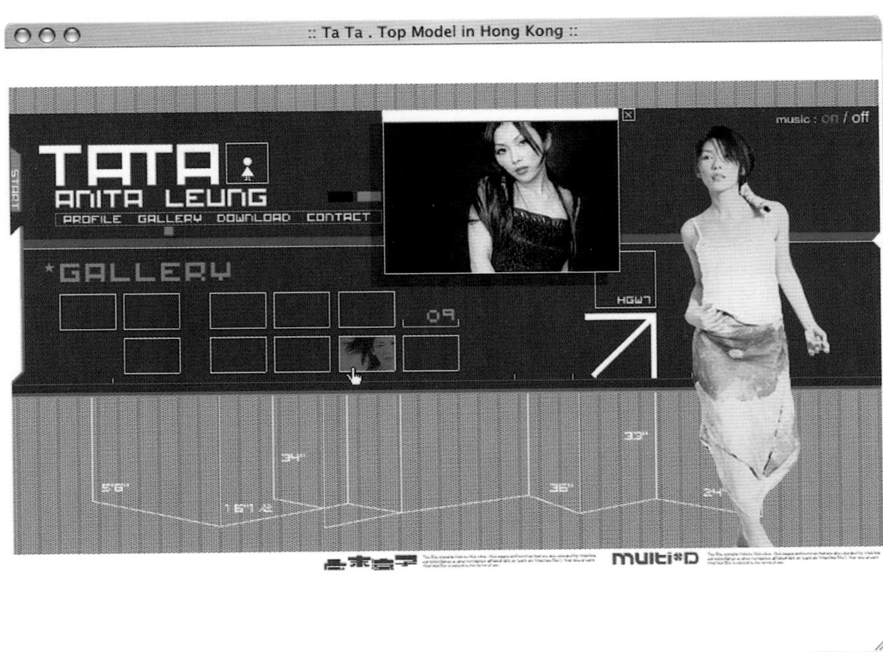
:: Ta Ta . Top Model in Hong Kong ::
TATA
ANITA LEUNG
PROFILE GALLERY DOWNLOAD CONTACT
*GALLERY
music : on / off
multi*D

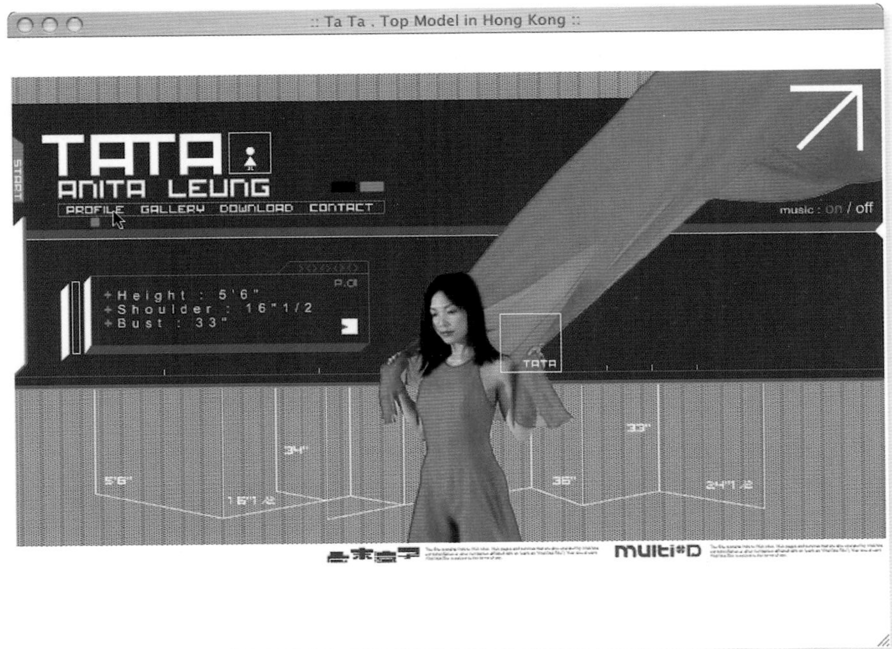
:: Ta Ta . Top Model in Hong Kong ::
TATA
ANITA LEUNG
PROFILE GALLERY DOWNLOAD CONTACT
music : on / off
+Height : 5'6"
+Shoulder : 16"1/2
+Bust : 33"
multi*D

www.anymo.com/model/tata
D: chan adam
A: multi.d **M:** adam@multid.com.hk

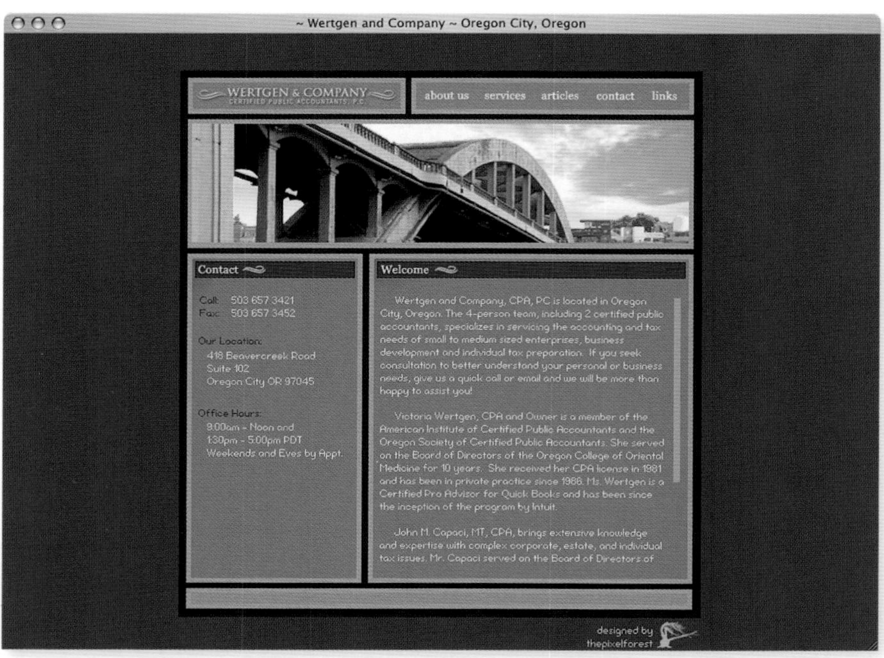
~ Wertgen and Company ~ Oregon City, Oregon
WERTGEN & COMPANY
CERTIFIED PUBLIC ACCOUNTANTS, P.C.
about us services articles contact links
Contact
Call: 503 657 3421
Fax: 503 657 3452
Our Location:
418 Beavercreek Road
Suite 102
Oregon City OR 97045
Office Hours:
8:00am - Noon and
1:30pm - 5:00pm PDT
Weekends and Eves by Appt.
Welcome
Wertgen and Company, CPA, PC is located in Oregon City, Oregon. The 4-person team, including 2 certified public accountants, specializes in servicing the accounting and tax needs of small to medium sized enterprises, business development and individual tax preparation. If you seek consultation to better understand your personal or business needs, give us a quick call or email and we will be more than happy to assist you!
Victoria Wertgen, CPA and Owner is a member of the American Institute of Certified Public Accountants and the Oregon Society of Certified Public Accountants. She served on the Board of Directors of the Oregon College of Oriental Medicine for 10 years. She received her CPA license in 1981 and has been in private practice since 1986. Ms. Wertgen is a Certified Pro Advisor for Quick Books and has been since the inception of the program by Intuit.
John M. Capaci, MT, CPA, brings extensive knowledge and expertise with complex corporate, estate, and individual tax issues. Mr. Capaci served on the Board of Directors of
designed by
thepixelforest

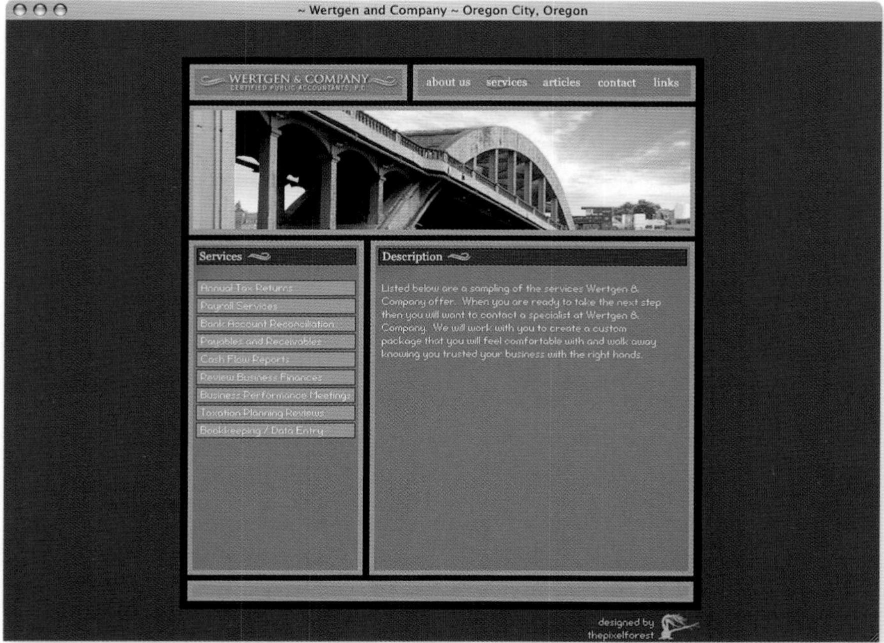
~ Wertgen and Company ~ Oregon City, Oregon
WERTGEN & COMPANY
CERTIFIED PUBLIC ACCOUNTANTS, P.C.
about us services articles contact links
Services
Annual Tax Returns
Payroll Services
Bank Account Reconciliation
Payables and Receivables
Cash Flow Reports
Review Business Finances
Business Performance Meetings
Taxation Planning Reviews
Bookkeeping / Data Entry
Description
Listed below are a sampling of the services Wertgen & Company offer. When you are ready to take the next step then you will want to contact a specialist at Wertgen & Company. We will work with you to create a custom package that you will feel comfortable with and walk away knowing you trusted your business with the right hands.
designed by
thepixelforest

www.wertgen.biz
D: keith mitchell **C:** keith mitchell **P:** keith mitchell
A: thepixelforest **M:** www.thepixelforest.com

~ Ljubov Kravtsova ~
Ljubov Kravtsova
ABOUT
GALLERY
WALLPAPERS
CONTACT
Name: Ljubov Kravtsova
Date of birth: 29.11.1983
Location: Estonia, Tallinn
Height: 171 cm
Weight: 53 kg
Measurements: 84cm-63cm-86cm
Hair: blond
Eyes: green
Dress: 36-38 (eur)
Shoes: 37 (eur)
Spoken languages: Russian/English
Type of modelling: Glamour
Cosmetic
Fitness
GALLERY
ABOUT
WALLPAPERS
CONTACT

~ Ljubov Kravtsova ~
Ljubov Kravtsova
ABOUT
GALLERY
WALLPAPERS
CONTACT
ABOUT
prv. Nxt.
GALLERY
006 / 020
CLICK ON IMAGE TO ZOOM
WALLPAPERS
CONTACT

www.kravtsova.com

A: axiom identiteet oy **M:** info@axiom.ee

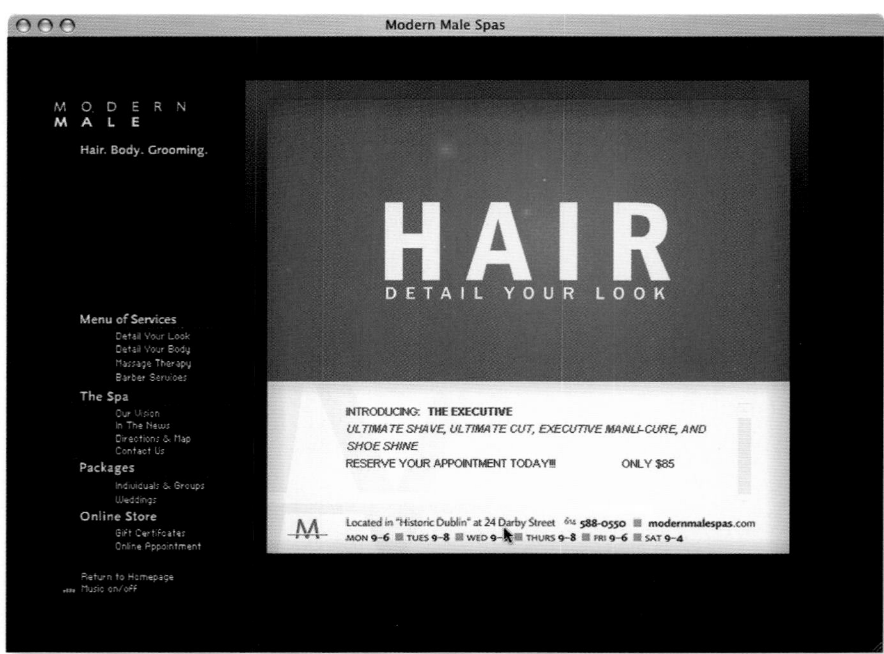
Modern Male Spas
MODERN MALE
Hair. Body. Grooming.
HAIR
DETAIL YOUR LOOK
Menu of Services
Detail Your Look
Detail Your Body
Massage Therapy
Barber Services
The Spa
Our Vision
In The News
Directions & Map
Contact Us
Packages
Individuals & Groups
Weddings
Online Store
Gift Certificates
Online Appointment
Return to Homepage
Music on/off
INTRODUCING: THE EXECUTIVE
ULTIMATE SHAVE, ULTIMATE CUT, EXECUTIVE MANI-CURE, AND SHOE SHINE
RESERVE YOUR APPOINTMENT TODAY!!! ONLY $85
Located in "Historic Dublin" at 24 Darby Street 614 588-0550 modernmalespas.com
MON 9-6 TUES 9-8 WED 9-8 THURS 9-8 FRI 9-6 SAT 9-4

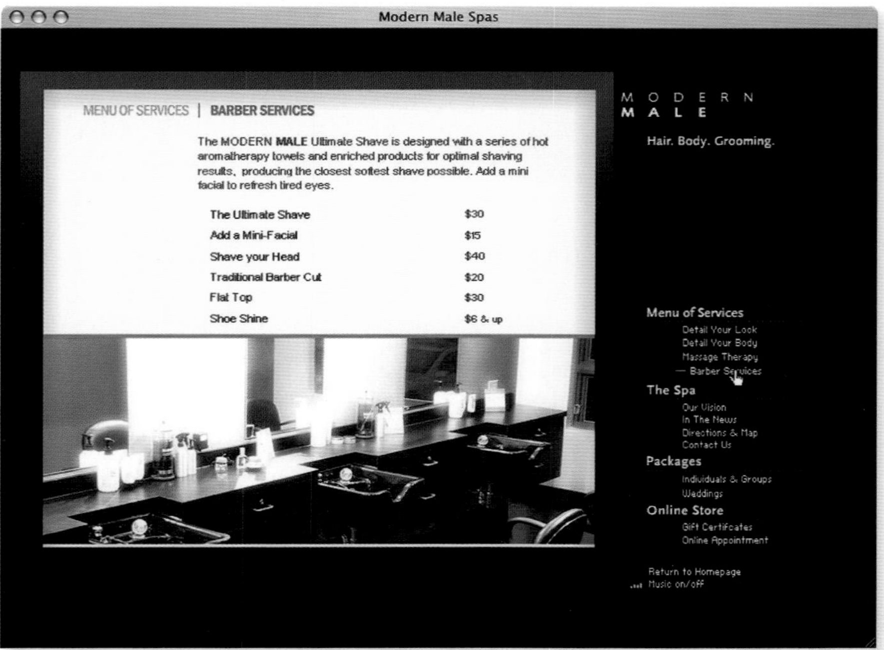
Modern Male Spas
MENU OF SERVICES | BARBER SERVICES
The MODERN MALE Ultimate Shave is designed with a series of hot aromatherapy towels and enriched products for optimal shaving results, producing the closest softest shave possible. Add a mini facial to refresh tired eyes.
The Ultimate Shave $30
Add a Mini-Facial $15
Shave your Head $40
Traditional Barber Cut $20
Flat Top $30
Shoe Shine $6 & up
MODERN MALE
Hair. Body. Grooming.
Menu of Services
Detail Your Look
Detail Your Body
Massage Therapy
Barber Services
The Spa
Our Vision
In The News
Directions & Map
Contact Us
Packages
Individuals & Groups
Weddings
Online Store
Gift Certificates
Online Appointment
Return to Homepage
Music on/off

www.modernmalespas.com
D: giancarlo yerkes **C:** darren cline **P:** stephen lenker
A: noreign studios **M:** www.noreign.com

lifebeach productions | www.lifebeach.ee
X CLOSE WINDOW
lifebeach
productions
Kentmanni 18-41 Tallinn ESTONIA tel +372 6484 902 gsm +372 5263 065 lifebeach@lifebeach.ee
PHOTO PRODUCTIONS
FILM PRODUCTIONS
LIFEBEACH PHOTOGRAPHY
ABOUT THE COMPANY
lifebeach productions
service production company offering
Services for photo and film productions in Estonia
Casting and booking of models and actors to abroad
Photography
local knowledge and contacts to the best Estonian professionals

lifebeach productions | www.lifebeach.ee
Kentmanni 18-41 Tallinn ESTONIA tel +372 6484 902 gsm +372 5263 065 lifebeach@lifebeach.ee
lifebeach
productions
FASHION
COMMERCIAL
PERSONAL
BACK TO MAIN MENU

www.lifebeach.ee
D: vladimir morozov **C:** sander sellin **P:** peke eloranta
A: lime creative **M:** lifebeach@lifebeach.ee

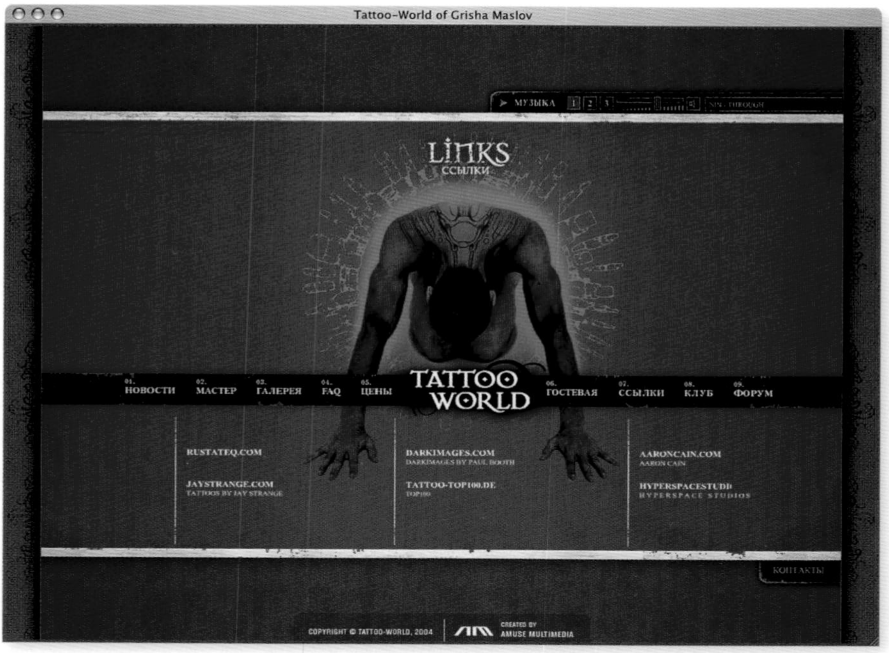
Tattoo-World of Grisha Maslov
МУЗЫКА
LINKS
ССЫЛКИ
01. НОВОСТИ
02. МАСТЕР
03. ГАЛЕРЕЯ
04. FAQ
05. ЦЕНЫ
TATTOO WORLD
06. ГОСТЕВАЯ
07. ССЫЛКИ
08. КЛУБ
09. ФОРУМ
RUSTATEQ.COM
JAYSTRANGE.COM
TATTOOS BY JAY STRANGE
DARKIMAGES.COM
DARKIMAGES BY PAUL BOOTH
TATTOO-TOP100.DE
AARONCAIN.COM
AARON CAIN
HYPERSPACESTUDI
HYPERSPACE STUDIOS
КОНТАКТЫ
COPYRIGHT © TATTOO-WORLD, 2004
CREATED BY
AMUSE MULTIMEDIA

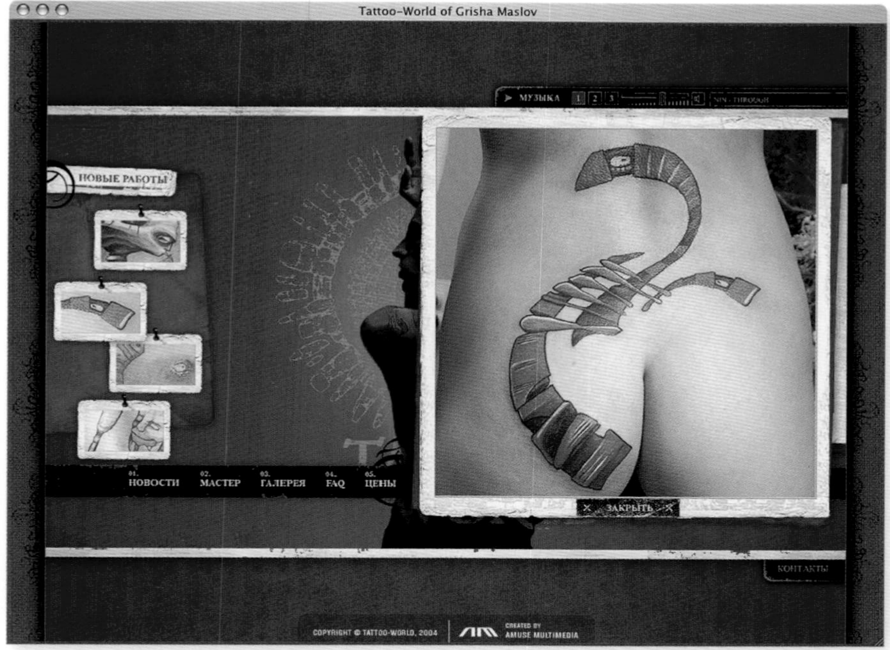
Tattoo-World of Grisha Maslov
МУЗЫКА
НОВЫЕ РАБОТЫ
01. НОВОСТИ
02. МАСТЕР
03. ГАЛЕРЕЯ
04. FAQ
05. ЦЕНЫ
ЗАКРЫТЬ
КОНТАКТЫ
COPYRIGHT © TATTOO-WORLD, 2004
CREATED BY
AMUSE MULTIMEDIA

www.tattoo-world.ru
D: vlad shagov **C:** juriy pishvanov **P:** juriy pishvanov
A: amuse multimedia **M:** info@amusemultimedia.com

Red Italia servizi
red™
home
servizi
annunci
contatti
Red nasce dalla voglia di affiancare sia le singole persone che le aziende, migliorandone l'immagine e rendendone i rapporti e i contatti più efficaci e produttivi. Ti aiuteremo ad espandere le tue conoscenze e le tue attività, qualsiasi sia il punto di partenza e il percorso più adatto da intraprendere.
Licenze: Agenzia Matrimoniale, Agenzia di Pubbliche Relazioni, Interazioni tra Professionisti.
credits

Red Italia servizi
red™
home
servizi
annunci
contatti
Red nasce dalla voglia di affiancare sia le singole persone che le aziende, migliorandone l'immagine e rendendone i rapporti e i contatti più efficaci e produttivi. Ti aiuteremo ad espandere le tue conoscenze e le tue attività, qualsiasi sia il punto di partenza e il percorso più adatto da intraprendere.
Licenze: Agenzia Matrimoniale, Agenzia di Pubbliche Relazioni, Interazioni tra Professionisti.
credits

www.reditalia.it
D: luca bartolini
A: equilibrisospesi **M:** luca@equilibrisospesi.com

.: __ haity.net :. .. ________________
haity
lojas
haity
marcas
contactos
como comprar
catálogo online
noticias
promoções
mailing list
IN ENGLISH?
(C) HAITY.NET
WEBSITE | DESIGN

.: __ haity.net :. .. ________________
loja onlinehaity
haity
home page > haity
A Haity - M. Rosário e Rocha, Lda. - foi fundada a 20 de Dezembro de 1979, com a criação do primeiro estabelecimento na Rua Santa Catarina, N.º 247, na cidade do Porto.
Este primeiro estabelecimento dedicou-se à venda de artigos em couro como carteiras, cintos, marroquinaria e pastas.
Passados seis anos, a 23 de Novembro de 1985, surge um novo estabelecimento situado na mesma rua, permitindo assim oferecer uma maior variedade de produtos.
Desta maneira, a Haity I dedicou-se a carteiras, cintos, lenços, guarda-chuvas e chapéus de senhora, enquanto a Haity II se dedicou à marroquinaria, pastas, gravatas e artigos de viagem.
Com o passar do tempo a Haity sentiu necessidade de se expandir para novos locais, fora do centro da cidade. Daí, surgiram mais 4 lojas situadas num local de eleição: a Foz do Douro.
O primeiro destes novos estabelecimentos foi a Haity III, na Avenida Brasil, Nº 571, a 16 de Junho de 1989.
Mais tarde, a 30 de Outubro de 1994 é criada a Haity IV na Rua do Crasto N.º 41.
Meio ano mais tarde, a 08 de Março de 1995 surge a Haity V, apresentando um novo produto aos clientes: sapatos de Senhora.
Depois de um periodo de três anos no qual não foram criados novos estabelecimentos, surge a Haity VI a 01 de Abril de 1998, aumentado assim as opções dos nossos clientes com a oferta de mais um novo produto: sapatos de Homem.
Mais tarde surge a Haity VII no Aviz dedicada a carteiras, cintos e marroquinaria.
Visite as nossas lojas para conhecer de perto os nossos produtos e marcas representadas.
haity
marcas
lojas
contactos
como comprar
catálogo online
noticias
promoções
página inicial
cesto compras
Itens: 0 = €0,00
finalizar compras
log in
utilizador
Validar
Esqueceu a sua password?
Registe-se aqui para fazer compras.
haity mailing
nome
e-mail
Remover
OK

www.haity.net
D: helder vasconcelos **C:** ricardo machado
A: goweb **M:** helder@goweb.pt

duncan quinn
duncan quinn
LONDON
About
Product
Bespoke
Little Black Book
Contact
Shopping Cart
products
Shirts
Ties
Shoes
Silver Cufflinks
Pocket Squares
Collar Stays
Scarves
Umbrellas
Armadillo Blue $125
Armadillo Cranberry $125
Armadillo Fuchsia $125
Armadillo Pink $125
Armadillo Purple $125
Bubbles Aqua/Green $125
page 1 2 3 4 5 6 7 8 9 10

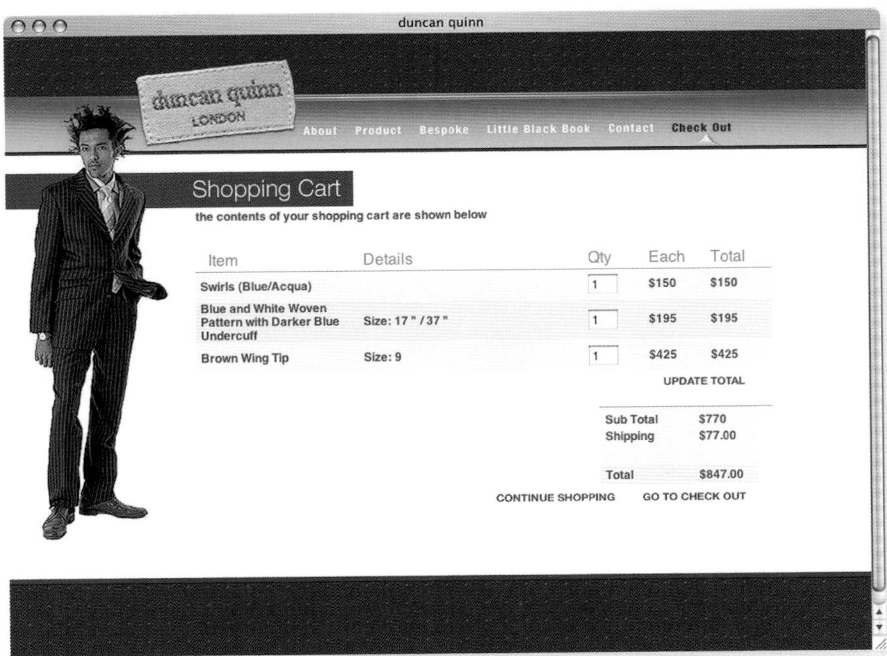
duncan quinn
duncan quinn
LONDON
About
Product
Bespoke
Little Black Book
Contact
Check Out
Shopping Cart
the contents of your shopping cart are shown below
Item
Details
Qty
Each
Total
Swirls (Blue/Acqua)
1
$150
$150
Blue and White Woven Pattern with Darker Blue Undercuff
Size: 17 " / 37 "
1
$195
$195
Brown Wing Tip
Size: 9
1
$425
$425
UPDATE TOTAL
Sub Total
$770
Shipping
$77.00
Total
$847.00
CONTINUE SHOPPING
GO TO CHECK OUT

www.duncanquinn.com
D: brandon ralph, dan gardner **C:** arnie gullov-singh **P:** dave hartt
A: code and theory **M:** www.codeandtheory.com

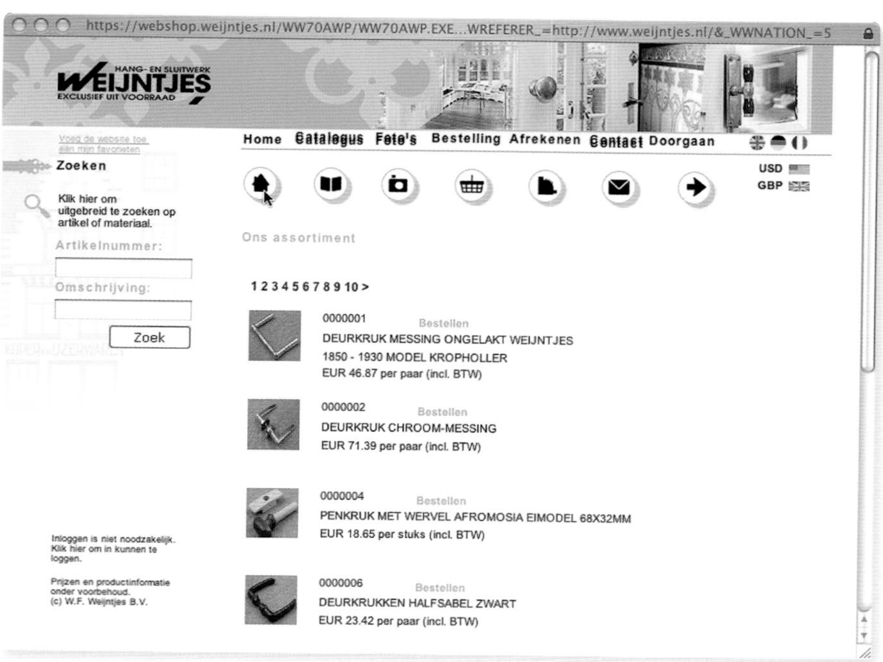
https://webshop.weijntjes.nl/WW70AWP/WW70AWP.EXE...WREFERER_=http://www.weijntjes.nl/&_WWNATION_=5
HANG- EN SLUITWERK WEIJNTJES EXCLUSIEF UIT VOORRAAD
Home Catalogus Foto's Bestelling Afrekenen Contact Doorgaan
USD
GBP
Zoeken
Klik hier om uitgebreid te zoeken op artikel of materiaal.
Artikelnummer:
Omschrijving:
Zoek
Ons assortiment
1 2 3 4 5 6 7 8 9 10 >
0000001 Bestellen
DEURKRUK MESSING ONGELAKT WEIJNTJES
1850 - 1930 MODEL KROPHOLLER
EUR 46.87 per paar (incl. BTW)
0000002 Bestellen
DEURKRUK CHROOM-MESSING
EUR 71.39 per paar (incl. BTW)
0000004 Bestellen
PENKRUK MET WERVEL AFROMOSIA EIMODEL 68X32MM
EUR 18.65 per stuks (incl. BTW)
0000006 Bestellen
DEURKRUKKEN HALFSABEL ZWART
EUR 23.42 per paar (incl. BTW)
Inloggen is niet noodzakelijk. Klik hier om in kunnen te loggen.
Prijzen en productinformatie onder voorbehoud.
(c) W.F. Weijntjes B.V.

https://webshop.weijntjes.nl/WW70AWP/WW70AWP.EXE/CTX_1056-4-yHVWDsVVAo/Articles/SYNC_951184187
HANG- EN SLUITWERK WEIJNTJES EXCLUSIEF UIT VOORRAAD
Home Catalogus Foto's Bestelling Afrekenen Contact Doorgaan
Zoeken
Klik hier om uitgebreid te zoeken op artikel of materiaal.
Artikelnummer:
Omschrijving:
Zoek
Klik op de pagina om de betreffende artikelen weer te geven
1 2 3 4 5 6 7 8 9 10 > >>
Deze pagina downloaden
Inloggen is niet noodzakelijk. Klik hier om in kunnen te loggen.
Prijzen en productinformatie onder voorbehoud.
(c) W.F. Weijntjes B.V.

www.weijntjes.nl
D: debby van dongen
A: conk **M:** webmaster@conk.nl

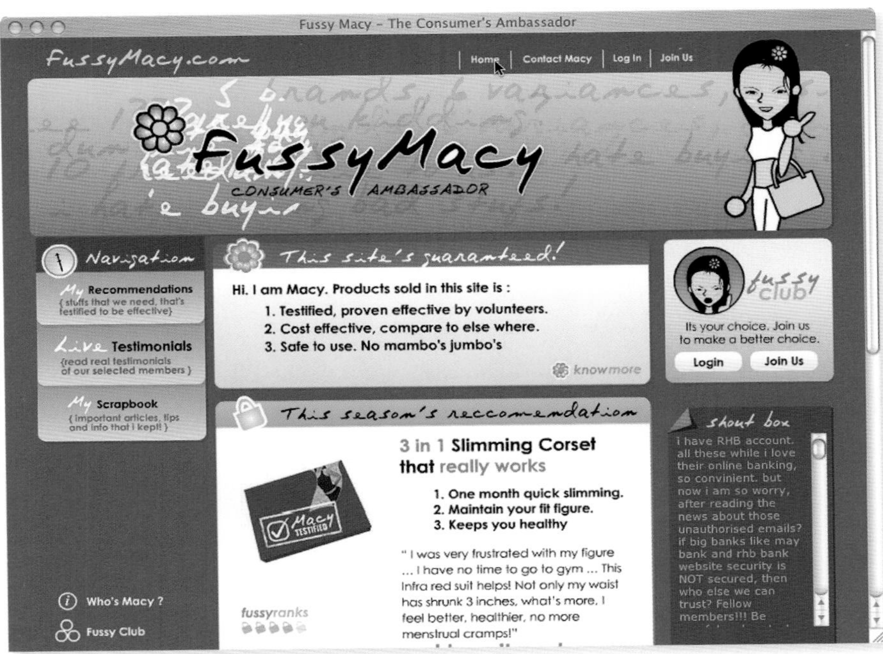
Fussy Macy - The Consumer's Ambassador
FussyMacy.com
Home | Contact Macy | Log In | Join Us
FussyMacy
CONSUMER'S AMBASSADOR
Navigation
My Recommendations
{ stuffs that we need, that's testified to be effective}
Live Testimonials
{read real testimonials of our selected members }
My Scrapbook
{ important articles, tips and info that i kept! }
This site's guaranteed!
Hi. I am Macy. Products sold in this site is :
1. Testified, proven effective by volunteers.
2. Cost effective, compare to else where.
3. Safe to use. No mambo's jumbo's
knowmore
fussy club
Its your choice. Join us to make a better choice.
Login
Join Us
This season's reccomendation
3 in 1 Slimming Corset that really works
1. One month quick slimming.
2. Maintain your fit figure.
3. Keeps you healthy
" I was very frustrated with my figure ... I have no time to go to gym ... This Infra red suit helps! Not only my waist has shrunk 3 inches, what's more, I feel better, healthier, no more menstrual cramps!"
fussyranks
shout box
i have RHB account. all these while i love their online banking, so convinient. but now i am so worry, after reading the news about those unauthorised emails? if big banks like may bank and rhb bank website security is NOT secured, then who else we can trust? Fellow members!!! Be
Who's Macy ?
Fussy Club

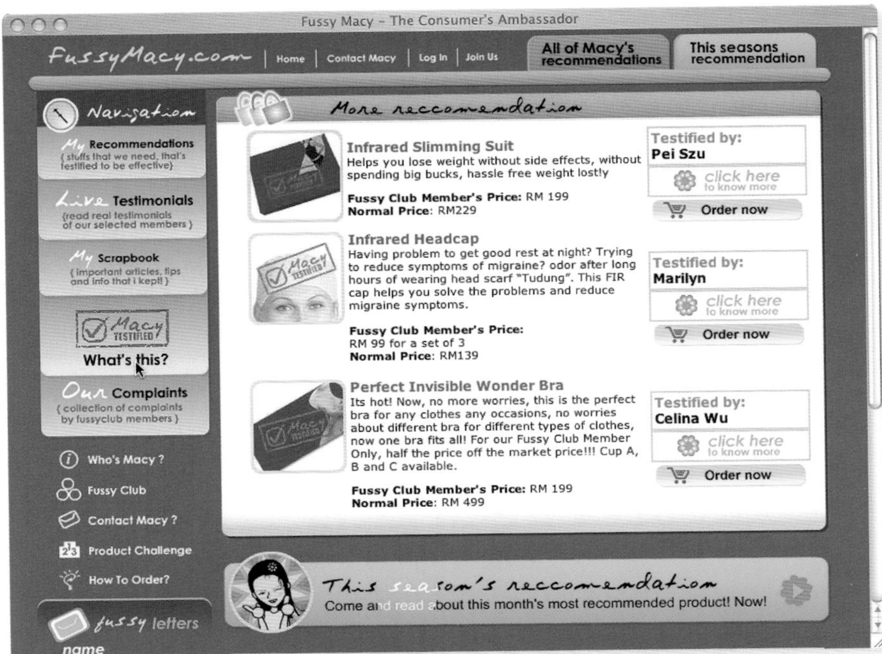
Fussy Macy - The Consumer's Ambassador
FussyMacy.com
Home | Contact Macy | Log In | Join Us
All of Macy's recommendations
This seasons recommendation
Navigation
My Recommendations
{ stuffs that we need, that's testified to be effective}
Live Testimonials
{read real testimonials of our selected members }
My Scrapbook
{ important articles, tips and info that i kept! }
What's this?
Our Complaints
{ collection of complaints by fussyclub members }
Who's Macy ?
Fussy Club
Contact Macy ?
Product Challenge
How To Order?
fussy letters
name
More reccomendation
Infrared Slimming Suit
Helps you lose weight without side effects, without spending big bucks, hassle free weight lostly
Fussy Club Member's Price: RM 199
Normal Price: RM229
Testified by: Pei Szu
click here to know more
Order now
Infrared Headcap
Having problem to get good rest at night? Trying to reduce symptoms of migraine? odor after long hours of wearing head scarf "Tudung". This FIR cap helps you solve the problems and reduce migraine symptoms.
Fussy Club Member's Price: RM 99 for a set of 3
Normal Price: RM139
Testified by: Marilyn
click here to know more
Order now
Perfect Invisible Wonder Bra
Its hot! Now, no more worries, this is the perfect bra for any clothes any occasions, no worries about different bra for different types of clothes, now one bra fits all! For our Fussy Club Member Only, half the price off the market price!!! Cup A, B and C available.
Fussy Club Member's Price: RM 199
Normal Price: RM 499
Testified by: Celina Wu
click here to know more
Order now
This season's reccomendation
Come and read about this month's most recommended product! Now!

www.fussymacy.com
D: yanzer lee
A: fireworks media M: peiszu@fireworksmedia.com

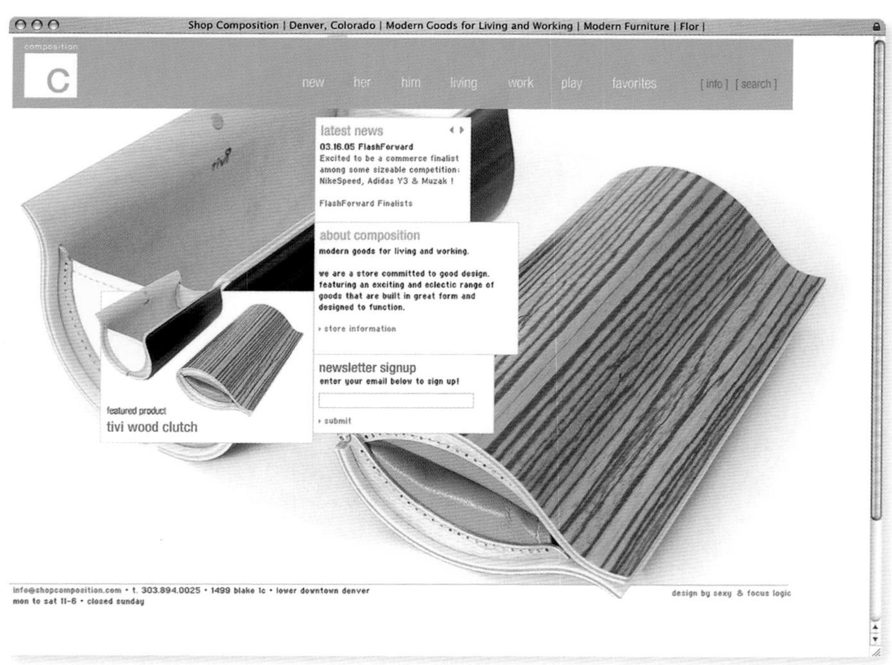
Shop Composition | Denver, Colorado | Modern Goods for Living and Working | Modern Furniture | Flor |
composition
c
new her him living work play favorites
[info] [search]
latest news
03.16.05 FlashForward
Excited to be a commerce finalist among some sizeable competition: NikeSpeed, Adidas Y3 & Muzak !
FlashForward Finalists
about composition
modern goods for living and working.
we are a store committed to good design. featuring an exciting and eclectic range of goods that are built in great form and designed to function.
store information
newsletter signup
enter your email below to sign up!
submit
featured product
tivi wood clutch
info@shopcomposition.com • t. 303.894.0025 • 1499 blake 1c • lower downtown denver
mon to sat 11-6 • closed sunday
design by sexy & focus logic

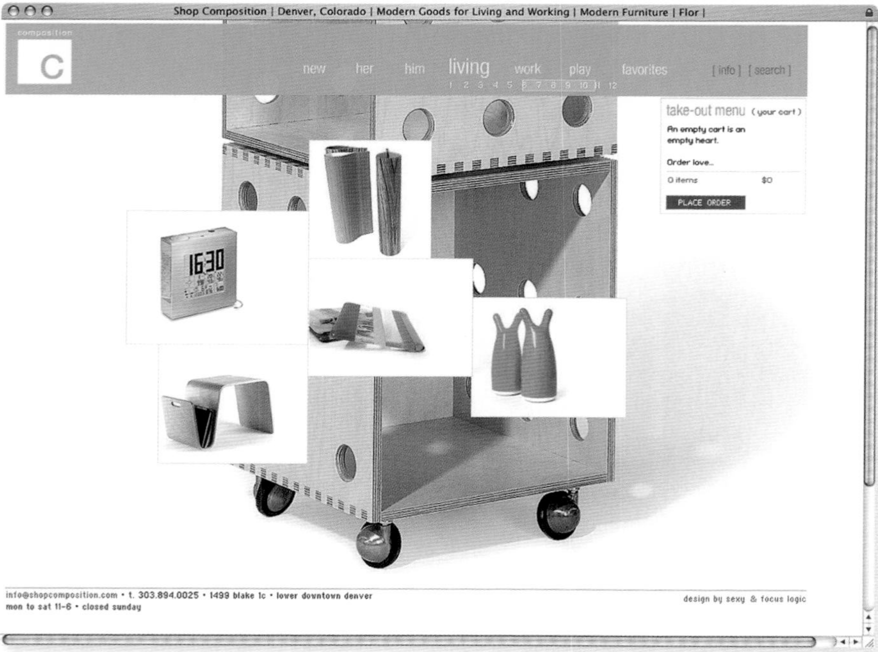
Shop Composition | Denver, Colorado | Modern Goods for Living and Working | Modern Furniture | Flor |
composition
c
new her him living work play favorites
[info] [search]
take-out menu (your cart)
An empty cart is an empty heart.
Order love...
0 items $0
PLACE ORDER
info@shopcomposition.com • t. 303.894.0025 • 1499 blake 1c • lower downtown denver
mon to sat 11-6 • closed sunday
design by sexy & focus logic

www.shopcomposition.com
D: ian coyle **C:** ian coyle
A: hello-sexy **M:** icoyle@hello-sexy.com

EASYSTRAIGHT HAIR STRAIGHTENING SYSTEM
EASYSTRAIGHT™
HAIR STRAIGHTENING SYSTEM
ABOUT EASYSTRAIGHT
EASYSTRAIGHT VS. OTHER STRAIGHTENERS
STEP-BY-STEP INSTRUCTIONS
FAQ'S
ABOUT HAIME MUNOZ
NEW!
Straight & frizz-free for 3 months!
Professional hair straightening at-home!
STRAIGHT, SMOOTH, MANAGEABLE HAIR ... IN UNDER 1 HOUR!
QTY BUY NOW!
Only $29.99 + S&H
HAIME MUNOZ
STRAIGHTENING EXPERT
CONTACT US | NEWS & PRESS | RETAIL PARTNERS | TERMS | PRIVACY | SHIPPING | SPEAK TO A STRAIGHTENING EXPERT AT 1.888.260.5272

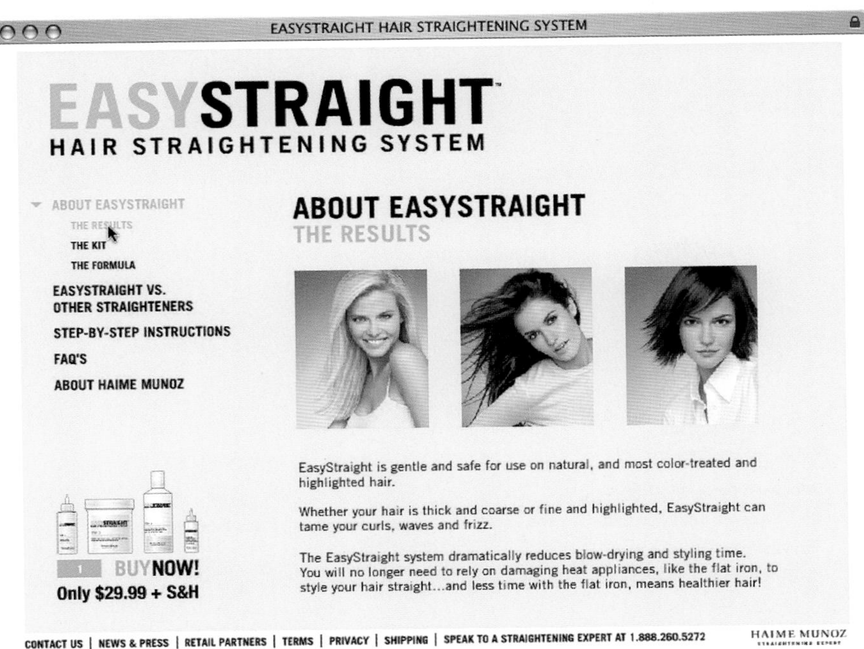
EASYSTRAIGHT HAIR STRAIGHTENING SYSTEM
EASYSTRAIGHT™
HAIR STRAIGHTENING SYSTEM
ABOUT EASYSTRAIGHT
THE RESULTS
THE KIT
THE FORMULA
EASYSTRAIGHT VS. OTHER STRAIGHTENERS
STEP-BY-STEP INSTRUCTIONS
FAQ'S
ABOUT HAIME MUNOZ
ABOUT EASYSTRAIGHT
THE RESULTS
EasyStraight is gentle and safe for use on natural, and most color-treated and highlighted hair.
Whether your hair is thick and coarse or fine and highlighted, EasyStraight can tame your curls, waves and frizz.
The EasyStraight system dramatically reduces blow-drying and styling time. You will no longer need to rely on damaging heat appliances, like the flat iron, to style your hair straight...and less time with the flat iron, means healthier hair!
1 BUY NOW!
Only $29.99 + S&H
CONTACT US | NEWS & PRESS | RETAIL PARTNERS | TERMS | PRIVACY | SHIPPING | SPEAK TO A STRAIGHTENING EXPERT AT 1.888.260.5272
HAIME MUNOZ

www.easystraight.com
D: shea gonyo **C:** shea gonyo **P:** mark ferdman
A: freedom interactive **M:** www.freedominteractivedesign.com

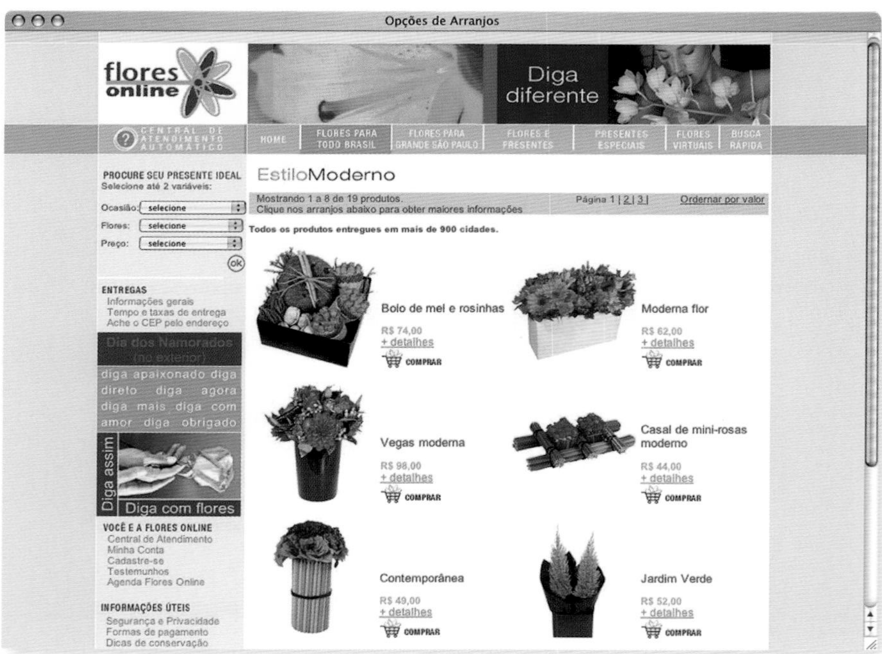
Opções de Arranjos
flores online
Diga diferente
HOME
FLORES PARA TODO BRASIL
FLORES PARA GRANDE SÃO PAULO
FLORES E PRESENTES
PRESENTES ESPECIAIS
FLORES VIRTUAIS
BUSCA RÁPIDA
PROCURE SEU PRESENTE IDEAL
EstiloModerno
Todos os produtos entregues em mais de 900 cidades.
Bolo de mel e rosinhas
Moderna flor
Vegas moderna
Casal de mini-rosas moderno
Contemporânea
Jardim Verde
ENTREGAS
Diga com flores
VOCÊ E A FLORES ONLINE
INFORMAÇÕES ÚTEIS

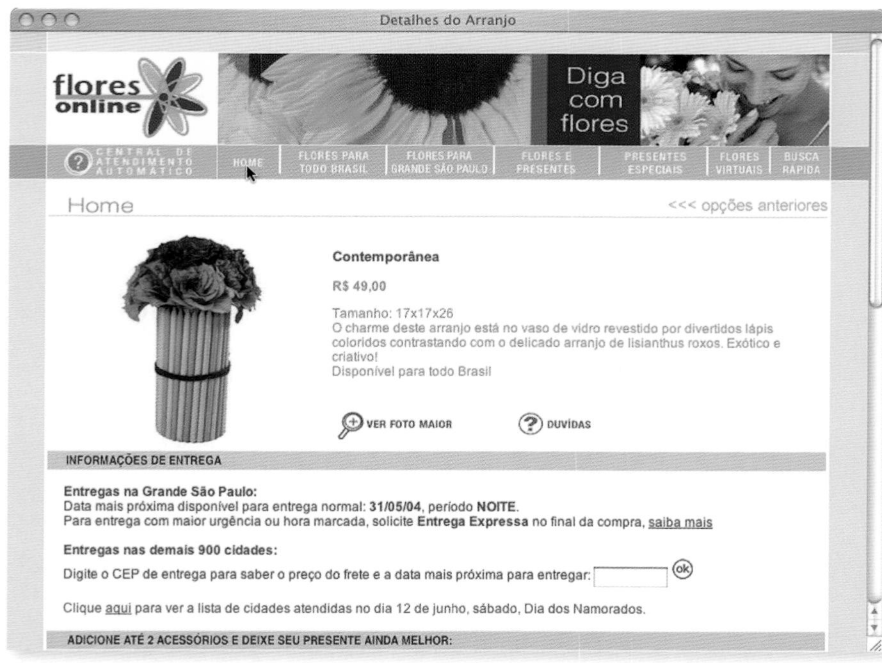
Detalhes do Arranjo
flores online
Diga com flores
Home
<<< opções anteriores
Contemporânea
R$ 49,00
Tamanho: 17x17x26
O charme deste arranjo está no vaso de vidro revestido por divertidos lápis coloridos contrastando com o delicado arranjo de lisianthus roxos. Exótico e criativo!
Disponível para todo Brasil
VER FOTO MAIOR
DÚVIDAS
INFORMAÇÕES DE ENTREGA
Entregas na Grande São Paulo:
Data mais próxima disponível para entrega normal: 31/05/04, período NOITE.
Para entrega com maior urgência ou hora marcada, solicite Entrega Expressa no final da compra, saiba mais
Entregas nas demais 900 cidades:
Digite o CEP de entrega para saber o preço do frete e a data mais próxima para entregar:
Clique aqui para ver a lista de cidades atendidas no dia 12 de junho, sábado, Dia dos Namorados.
ADICIONE ATÉ 2 ACESSÓRIOS E DEIXE SEU PRESENTE AINDA MELHOR:

www.floresonline.com.br
D: ignacio celedon
A: arquimidia M: iggy@arquimidia.com

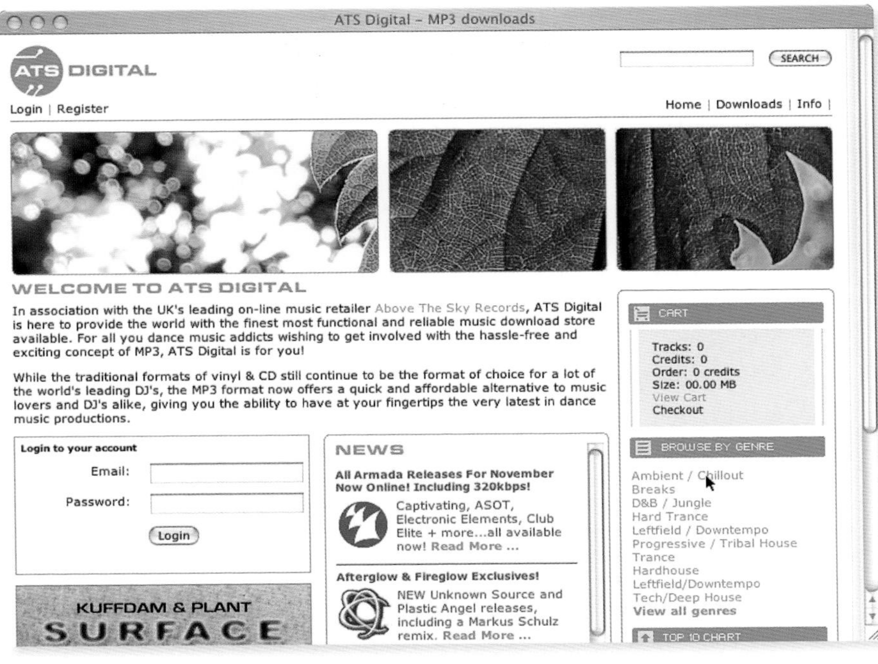
ATS Digital - MP3 downloads
ATS DIGITAL
SEARCH
Login | Register
Home | Downloads | Info |
WELCOME TO ATS DIGITAL
In association with the UK's leading on-line music retailer Above The Sky Records, ATS Digital is here to provide the world with the finest most functional and reliable music download store available. For all you dance music addicts wishing to get involved with the hassle-free and exciting concept of MP3, ATS Digital is for you!
While the traditional formats of vinyl & CD still continue to be the format of choice for a lot of the world's leading DJ's, the MP3 format now offers a quick and affordable alternative to music lovers and DJ's alike, giving you the ability to have at your fingertips the very latest in dance music productions.
Login to your account
Email:
Password:
Login
KUFFDAM & PLANT
SURFACE
NEWS
All Armada Releases For November Now Online! Including 320kbps!
Captivating, ASOT, Electronic Elements, Club Elite + more...all available now! Read More ...
Afterglow & Fireglow Exclusives!
NEW Unknown Source and Plastic Angel releases, including a Markus Schulz remix. Read More ...
CART
Tracks: 0
Credits: 0
Order: 0 credits
Size: 00.00 MB
View Cart
Checkout
BROWSE BY GENRE
Ambient / Chillout
Breaks
D&B / Jungle
Hard Trance
Leftfield / Downtempo
Progressive / Tribal House
Trance
Hardhouse
Leftfield/Downtempo
Tech/Deep House
View all genres
TOP 10 CHART

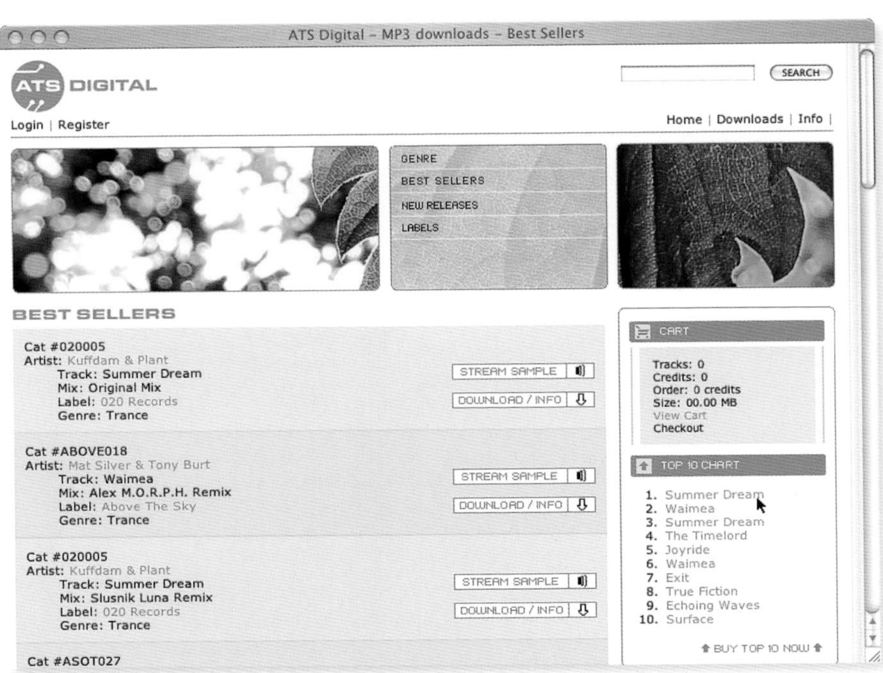
ATS Digital - MP3 downloads - Best Sellers
ATS DIGITAL
SEARCH
Login | Register
Home | Downloads | Info |
GENRE
BEST SELLERS
NEW RELEASES
LABELS
BEST SELLERS
Cat #020005
Artist: Kuffdam & Plant
Track: Summer Dream
Mix: Original Mix
Label: 020 Records
Genre: Trance
STREAM SAMPLE
DOWNLOAD / INFO
Cat #ABOVE018
Artist: Mat Silver & Tony Burt
Track: Waimea
Mix: Alex M.O.R.P.H. Remix
Label: Above The Sky
Genre: Trance
STREAM SAMPLE
DOWNLOAD / INFO
Cat #020005
Artist: Kuffdam & Plant
Track: Summer Dream
Mix: Slusnik Luna Remix
Label: 020 Records
Genre: Trance
STREAM SAMPLE
DOWNLOAD / INFO
Cat #ASOT027
CART
Tracks: 0
Credits: 0
Order: 0 credits
Size: 00.00 MB
View Cart
Checkout
TOP 10 CHART
1. Summer Dream
2. Waimea
3. Summer Dream
4. The Timelord
5. Joyride
6. Waimea
7. Exit
8. True Fiction
9. Echoing Waves
10. Surface
BUY TOP 10 NOW

www.atsdigital.com
D: andrew spooner
M: andrews@flark.net

:::::::::::::: Online Gift Certificate ::::::::::::::
home
my Cart
how it works
terms & conditions
SUNWAY PYRAMID
Your unique Shopping Adventure
EMAIL a gift
Buy gift vouchers online for your loved ones and friends
Shop for the voucher online and make a surprise delivery to your loved ones & friends through the internet! Your recipient has over 30 merchants to choose from!!
Shop Online Now!!
How it works
Interactive Demo
Click here to view the animated demo on how it all works!
1. You choose a Gift Voucher amount and personalize the Gift Voucher with your message.

:::::::::::::::: Email-A-Gift present by Sue ::::::::::::::::
EMAIL a gift
Buy gift vouchers online for your loved ones and friends

www.sunway.com.my/emailagift
D: michael lim **C:** low pk
A: the sunway group **M:** michaellsc@sunway.com.my

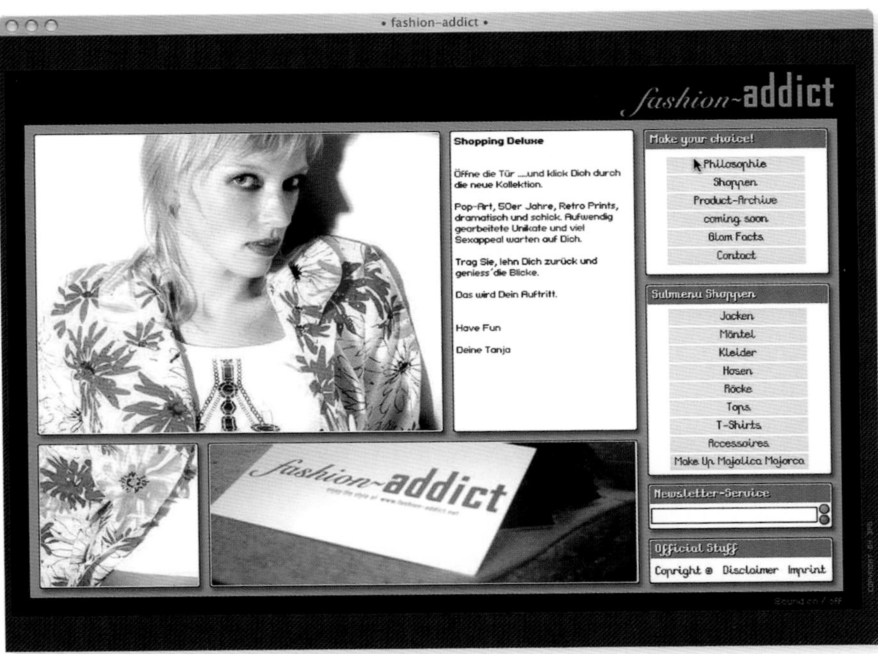
• fashion-addict •
fashion~addict
Shopping Deluxe
Öffne die Tür ....und klick Dich durch die neue Kollektion.
Pop-Art, 50er Jahre, Retro Prints, dramatisch und schick. Aufwendig gearbeitete Unikate und viel Sexappeal warten auf Dich.
Trag Sie, lehn Dich zurück und geniess' die Blicke.
Das wird Dein Auftritt.
Have Fun
Deine Tanja
Make your choice!
Philosophie
Shoppen
Product-Archive
coming soon
Glam Facts
Contact
Submenu Shoppen
Jacken
Mäntel
Kleider
Hosen
Röcke
Tops
T-Shirts
Accessoires
Make Up Majolica Majorca
Newsletter-Service
Official Stuff
Copyright © Disclaimer Imprint

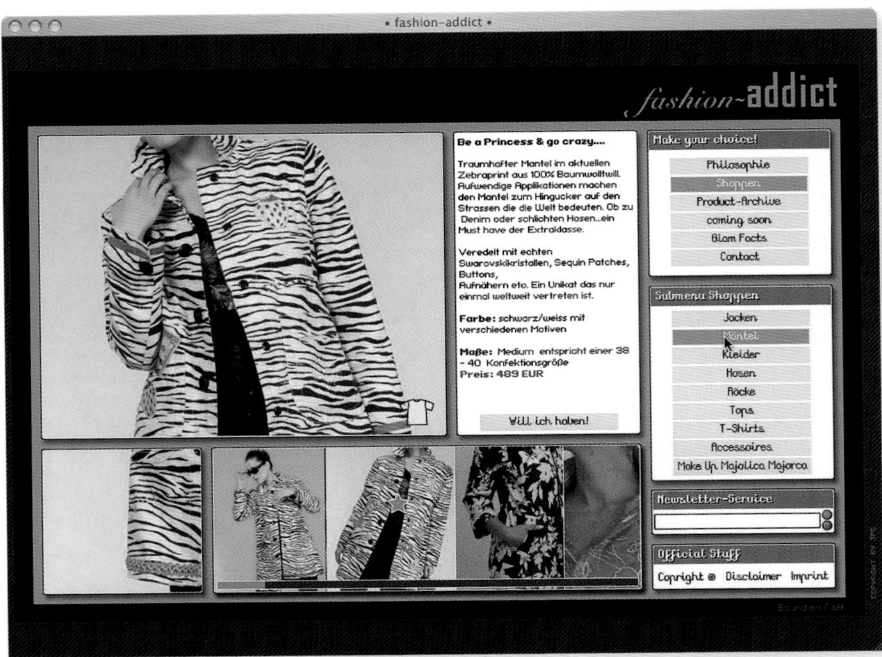
• fashion-addict •
fashion~addict
Be a Princess & go crazy....
Traumhafter Mantel im aktuellen Zebraprint aus 100% Baumwolltwill. Aufwendige Applikationen machen den Mantel zum Hingucker auf den Strassen die die Welt bedeuten. Ob zu Denim oder schlichten Hosen...ein Must have der Extraklasse.
Veredelt mit echten Swarovskikristallen, Sequin Patches, Buttons, Aufnähern etc. Ein Unikat das nur einmal weltweit vertreten ist.
Farbe: schwarz/weiss mit verschiedenen Motiven
Maße: Medium entspricht einer 38 - 40 Konfektionsgröße
Preis: 489 EUR
Will ich haben!
Make your choice!
Philosophie
Shoppen
Product-Archive
coming soon
Glam Facts
Contact
Submenu Shoppen
Jacken
Mäntel
Kleider
Hosen
Röcke
Tops
T-Shirts
Accessoires
Make Up Majolica Majorca
Newsletter-Service
Official Stuff
Copyright © Disclaimer Imprint

www.fashion-addict.net

D: birger dethlefs **C:** martin brecht

M: birger@kix-ass.de

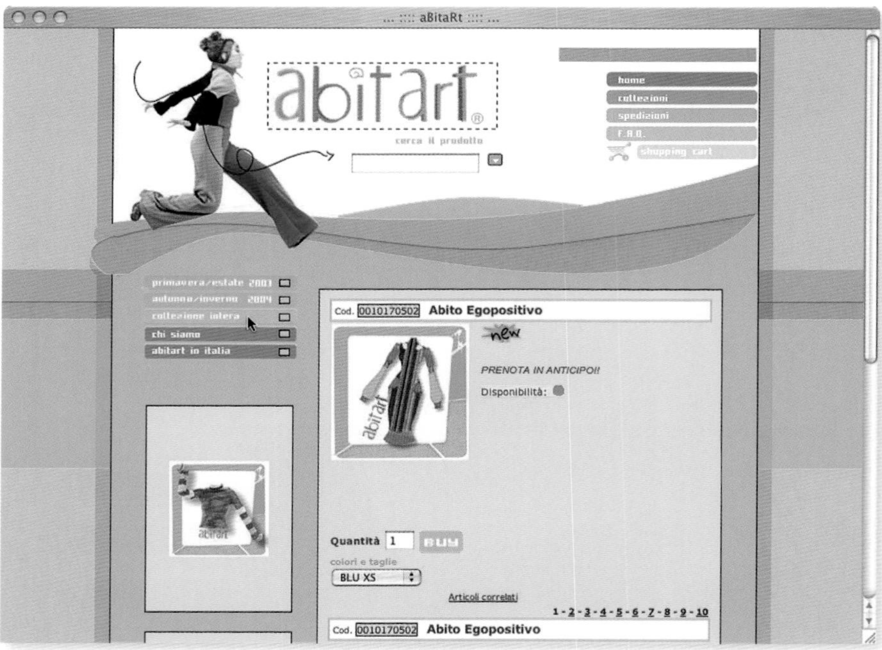
... :::: aBitaRt :::: ...
abitart
cerca il prodotto
home
collezioni
spedizioni
F.A.Q.
shopping cart
primavera/estate 2003
autunno/inverno 2004
collezione intera
chi siamo
abitart in italia
Cod. 0010170502 Abito Egopositivo
new
PRENOTA IN ANTICIPO!!
Disponibilità:
Quantità 1 BUY
colori e taglie
BLU XS
Articoli correlati
1 - 2 - 3 - 4 - 5 - 6 - 7 - 8 - 9 - 10
Cod. 0010170502 Abito Egopositivo

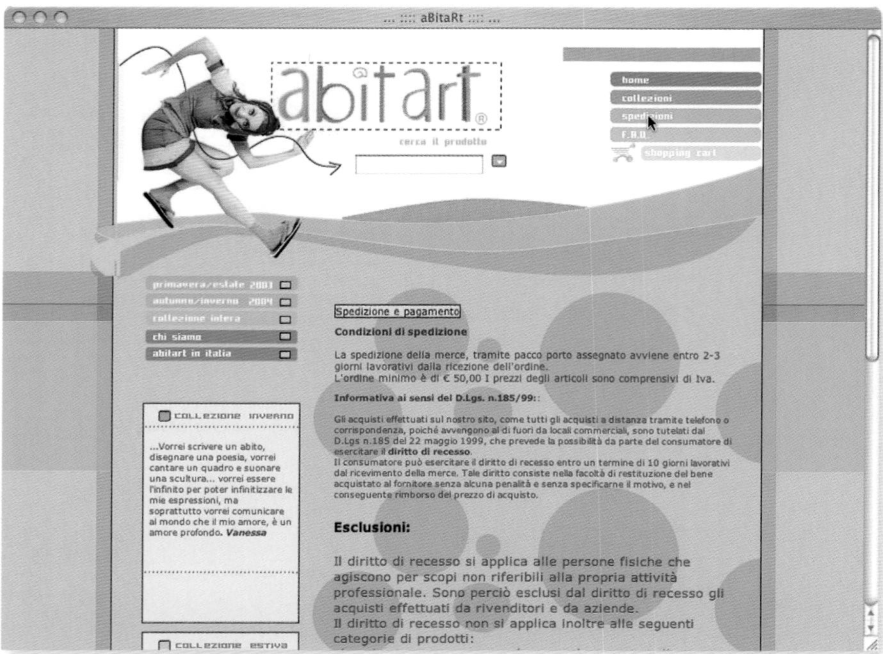
... :::: aBitaRt :::: ...
abitart
cerca il prodotto
home
collezioni
spedizioni
F.A.Q.
shopping cart
primavera/estate 2003
autunno/inverno 2004
collezione intera
chi siamo
abitart in italia
collezione inverno
...Vorrei scrivere un abito, disegnare una poesia, vorrei cantare un quadro e suonare una scultura... vorrei essere l'infinito per poter infinitizzare le mie espressioni, ma soprattutto vorrei comunicare al mondo che il mio amore, è un amore profondo. Vanessa
collezione estiva
Spedizione e pagamento
Condizioni di spedizione
La spedizione della merce, tramite pacco porto assegnato avviene entro 2-3 giorni lavorativi dalla ricezione dell'ordine.
L'ordine minimo è di € 50,00 I prezzi degli articoli sono comprensivi di Iva.
Informativa ai sensi del D.Lgs. n.185/99:
Gli acquisti effettuati sul nostro sito, come tutti gli acquisti a distanza tramite telefono o corrispondenza, poiché avvengono al di fuori da locali commerciali, sono tutelati dal D.Lgs n.185 del 22 maggio 1999, che prevede la possibilità da parte del consumatore di esercitare il diritto di recesso.
Il consumatore può esercitare il diritto di recesso entro un termine di 10 giorni lavorativi dal ricevimento della merce. Tale diritto consiste nella facoltà di restituzione del bene acquistato al fornitore senza alcuna penalità e senza specificarne il motivo, e nel conseguente rimborso del prezzo di acquisto.
Esclusioni:
Il diritto di recesso si applica alle persone fisiche che agiscono per scopi non riferibili alla propria attività professionale. Sono perciò esclusi dal diritto di recesso gli acquisti effettuati da rivenditori e da aziende.
Il diritto di recesso non si applica inoltre alle seguenti categorie di prodotti:

www.abitart.biz
D: gaia zuccaro
A: magadesign **M:** gaia.zuccaro@madesign.net

www.adfreaks.com
D: nazmi kahil
A: marvel chaser inc **M:** naz@marvelchaser.com

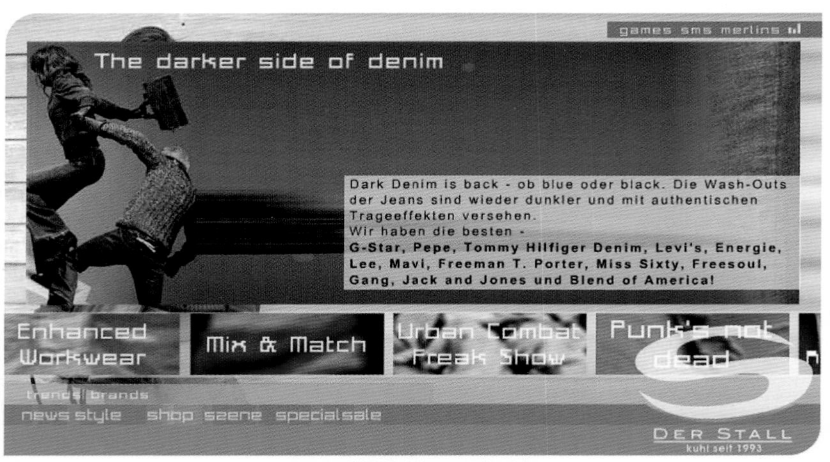
Der Stall – kuhl seit 1993
games sms merlins
The darker side of denim
Dark Denim is back - ob blue oder black. Die Wash-Outs der Jeans sind wieder dunkler und mit authentischen Trageeffekten versehen.
Wir haben die besten -
G-Star, Pepe, Tommy Hilfiger Denim, Levi's, Energie, Lee, Mavi, Freeman T. Porter, Miss Sixty, Freesoul, Gang, Jack and Jones und Blend of America!
Enhanced Workwear
Mix & Match
Urban Combat Freak Show
Punk's not dead
trends brands
news style shop szene specialsale
Der Stall
kuhl seit 1993
Impressum | E-Mail | Produktion: www.querformat.info

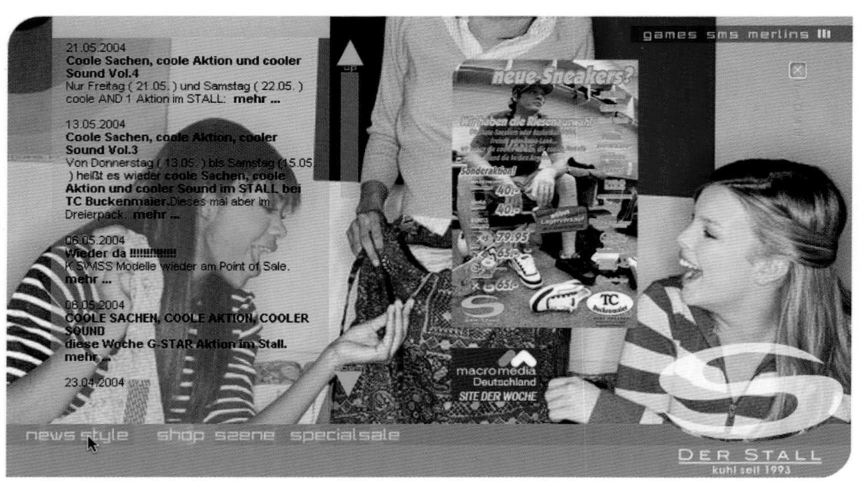
Der Stall – kuhl seit 1993
games sms merlins
21.05.2004
Coole Sachen, coole Aktion und cooler Sound Vol.4
Nur Freitag (21.05.) und Samstag (22.05.) coole AND 1 Aktion im STALL: mehr ...
13.05.2004
Coole Sachen, coole Aktion, cooler Sound Vol.3
Von Donnerstag (13.05.) bis Samstag (15.05.) heißt es wieder coole Sachen, coole Aktion und cooler Sound im STALL bei TC Buckenmaier. Dieses mal aber im Dreierpack. mehr ...
06.05.2004
Wieder da !!!!!!!!!!!
K SWISS Modelle wieder am Point of Sale. mehr ...
06.05.2004
COOLE SACHEN, COOLE AKTION, COOLER SOUND
diese Woche G-STAR Aktion im Stall. mehr ...
23.04.2004
neue Sneakers?
macromedia Deutschland
SITE DER WOCHE
news style shop szene specialsale
Der Stall
kuhl seit 1993
Impressum | E-Mail | Produktion: www.querformat.info

www.derstall.de
D: matthias messerer
A: querformat **M:** messerer@querformat.info

Amadeo Decada
AMADEO DECADA
REINA
SELECT SIZE: S M L
$26.00 >> ADD TO BAG
MEN
WOMEN
ACCESSORIES
VIEW BAG
Total $104.99
AMADEO
REGISTER
SERVICE

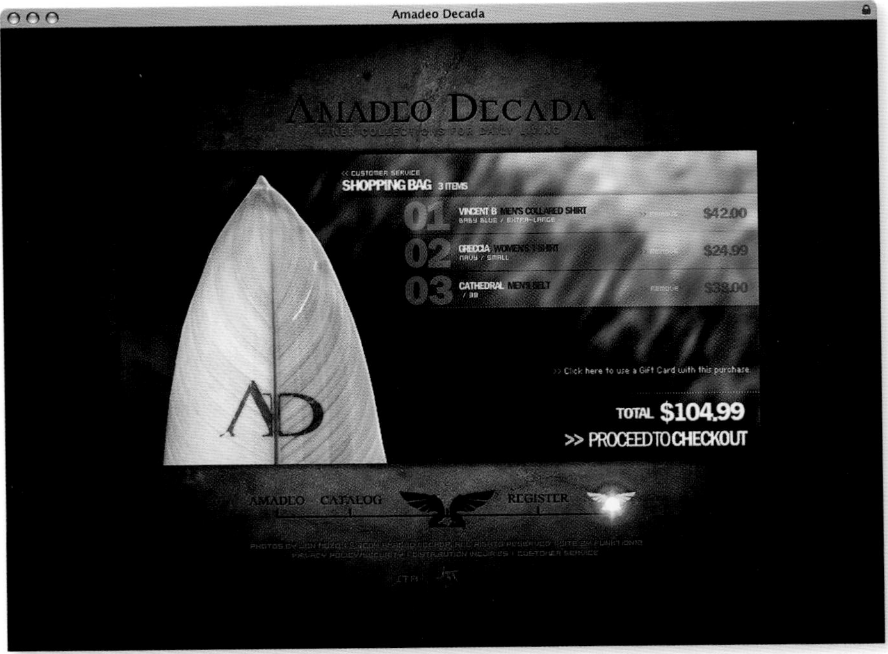
Amadeo Decada
AMADEO DECADA
<< CUSTOMER SERVICE
SHOPPING BAG 3 ITEMS
01 VINCENT B MEN'S COLLARED SHIRT $42.00
02 GRECCIA WOMEN'S T-SHIRT $24.99
03 CATHEDRAL MEN'S BELT $38.00
>> Click here to use a Gift Card with this purchase
TOTAL $104.99
>> PROCEED TO CHECKOUT
AD
AMADEO
CATALOG
REGISTER

www.amadeodecada.com
D: jared kroff **C:** jared kroff
A: funktion12 **M:** funk@funktion12.com

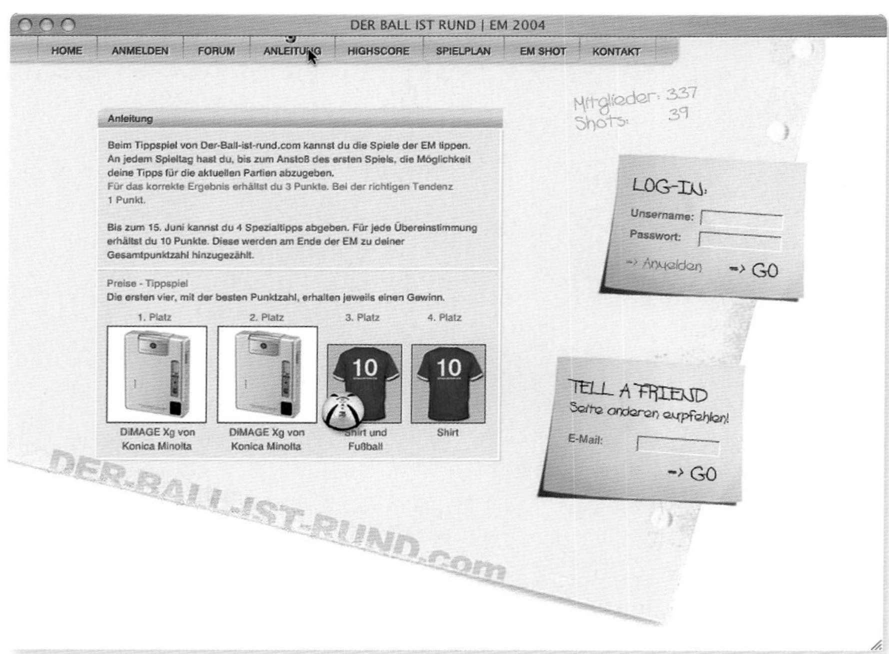
DER BALL IST RUND | EM 2004
HOME
ANMELDEN
FORUM
ANLEITUNG
HIGHSCORE
SPIELPLAN
EM SHOT
KONTAKT
Mitglieder: 337
Shots: 39
Anleitung
Beim Tippspiel von Der-Ball-ist-rund.com kannst du die Spiele der EM tippen.
An jedem Spieltag hast du, bis zum Anstoß des ersten Spiels, die Möglichkeit
deine Tipps für die aktuellen Partien abzugeben.
Für das korrekte Ergebnis erhältst du 3 Punkte. Bei der richtigen Tendenz
1 Punkt.
Bis zum 15. Juni kannst du 4 Spezialtipps abgeben. Für jede Übereinstimmung
erhältst du 10 Punkte. Diese werden am Ende der EM zu deiner
Gesamtpunktzahl hinzugezählt.
Preise - Tippspiel
Die ersten vier, mit der besten Punktzahl, erhalten jeweils einen Gewinn.
1. Platz
2. Platz
3. Platz
4. Platz
DiMAGE Xg von Konica Minolta
DiMAGE Xg von Konica Minolta
Shirt und Fußball
Shirt
LOG-IN:
Username:
Passwort:
Anmelden
GO
TELL A FRIEND
Seite anderen empfehlen!
E-Mail:
GO
DER-BALL-IST-RUND.com

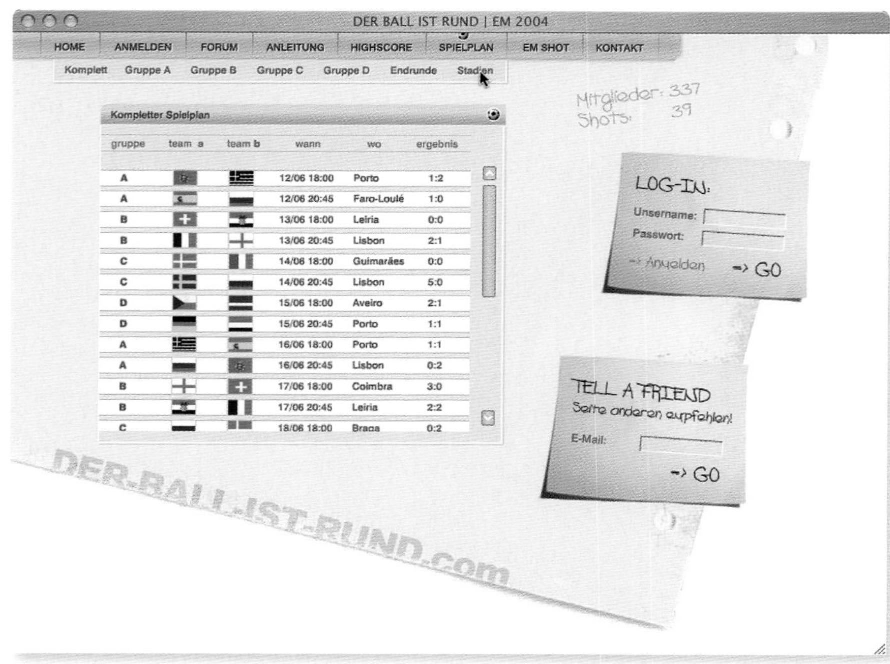
DER BALL IST RUND | EM 2004
HOME
ANMELDEN
FORUM
ANLEITUNG
HIGHSCORE
SPIELPLAN
EM SHOT
KONTAKT
Komplett
Gruppe A
Gruppe B
Gruppe C
Gruppe D
Endrunde
Stadien
Mitglieder: 337
Shots: 39
Kompletter Spielplan
gruppe team a team b wann wo ergebnis
A 12/06 18:00 Porto 1:2
A 12/06 20:45 Faro-Loulé 1:0
B 13/06 18:00 Leiria 0:0
B 13/06 20:45 Lisbon 2:1
C 14/06 18:00 Guimarães 0:0
C 14/06 20:45 Lisbon 5:0
D 15/06 18:00 Aveiro 2:1
D 15/06 20:45 Porto 1:1
A 16/06 18:00 Porto 1:1
A 16/06 20:45 Lisbon 0:2
B 17/06 18:00 Coimbra 3:0
B 17/06 20:45 Leiria 2:2
C 18/06 18:00 Braga 0:2
LOG-IN:
Username:
Passwort:
Anmelden
GO
TELL A FRIEND
Seite anderen empfehlen!
E-Mail:
GO
DER-BALL-IST-RUND.com

www.der-ball-ist-rund.com
D: hannes höß **P:** ali rastagar
A: nockpunkt **M:** info@nockpunkt.com

GIANT BICYCLES 2004
GIANT BICYCLES
http://www.giant.co.jp
WELCOME TO GIANT 2004
Last Up Date : 04. 2.12
HOME
PRODUCTS
RACING COMPONENTS
INFORMATION
WARRANTY
CATALOG
SHOP LIST
GLOBAL SITE
TEAM INFO
TOPICS
GIANT 2004 ラインナップ
revive 2004 ラインナップ
WHAT'S NEW
旧02/03モデル閲覧できるようになりました。[2/12]
2004 GIANTラインナップ掲載しました。[10/31]
2004 GIANTカタログ発売開始しました。[10/24]
revive試乗可能店リスト追加しました。[10/24]
リバイブが東京のパレスサイクリングで試乗できます。[9/17]
TEAM INFOMATION
増田まみ　今期3勝目をあげシリーズチャンピオンに！
全日本MTB選手権大会レポートアップしました。
J-Series 田沢湖大会レポートアップしました。
色川浩樹　田沢湖大会で今期初優勝！
増田まみ　三瓶山でＪシリーズ今期１勝目！
GIANT JAPAN RACING TEAM
TOP NEWS
GIANT2004年モデル発表！
2004 Debut
» 詳細はコチラ
CONTENTS
» 2004 GIANT 製品一覧
» 2004 revive 製品一覧
» 2003 MOSH 製品一覧
» Racing Components一覧
» チームインフォメーション
» カタログ請求方法について
» GIANTショップリスト
» 製品の保証規定について
» 製品リコール情報について
» サービスマニュアル掲載
» GIANTグローバルサイト
CLOSE UP
COPYLIGHT 2003 GIANT CO.,LTD ALL RIGHTS RESERVED

GIANT BICYCLES 2004
GIANT
http://www.giant.co.jp
WELCOME TO GIANT 2004
HOME
PRODUCTS
RACING COMPONENTS
INFORMATION
WARRANTY
CATALOG
SHOP LIST
GLOBAL SITE
TEAM INFO
CATALOG SENDING
2004 GIANT CATALOG
2004 ＧＩＡＮＴ"春"のカタログ発売開始いたしました。
２００４ＧＩＡＮＴカタログをご希望の方は、
下記住所まで送料３００円切手を同封の上、お申し込みください。
ご自宅まで、ご郵送させていただきます。
宛先：
〒230-0054
神奈川県横浜市鶴見区大黒埠頭15-2
株式会社　ジャイアント
2004 ＧＩＡＮＴ春カタログ正誤一覧
ページ 車種 部品 誤 正
P21 VT1 自転車画像下、Photoフレームサイズ：460mm 自転車画像下、Photoフレームサイズ：420mm
P21 VT2 自転車画像下、Photoフレームサイズ：430mm 自転車画像下、Photoフレームサイズ：420mm
COPYLIGHT 2003 GIANT CO.,LTD ALL RIGHTS RESERVED

www.giant.co.jp
D: miho miyadera **C:** yusuke abe
A: creat inc. **M:** miyadera@creat.cc

madridpatina.com
madrid.patina
fomento formación exhibición
home
info
hazte socio
zonas
galerias
contacto
últimas.noticias
galerias!!! |25.11.04|
Hemos subido las fotos del evento de puertas abiertas de Arganzuela del 3 de Octubre y las fotos del último fin de semana. Tenemos pendientes las fotos de la ruta de Delicias.
Muchas gracias a nuestra fotografa, Mari Luz.
27 y 28 noviembre |07.11.04|
Y si el tiempo nos acompaña...:
> El sábado por la mañana estamos en la escuela del patinodromo de Arganzuela con unos 200 alumnos, de todas las edades y niveles.
> A las 17:00 otro emocionante partido de hockey linea, Liga Nacional. Si estás interesado en acudir pidenos más información.
tú, nuestra prioridad
hazte.socio
participa en eventos
pulsa aqui para rellenar el formulario de ingreso
© 2003 asociación sin animo de lucro madridpatina | www.madridpatina.com | info@madridpatina.com | tlf: 6666.317.96

madridpatina.com
madrid.patina
fomento formación exhibición
home
info
zonas
galerias
contacto
info.madridpatina
Índice:
nuestros objetivos
breve historia
memoria 03-04
medios humanos
ser socio de madridpatina
clases de patinaje
¿dónde están las escuelas?
rutas, eventos y actividades
¿quieres colaborar?
patrocinadores
clases para colegios
contrata una exhibición
FAQS (preguntas frecuentes)
¿asociación sin animo de lucro?
¿por qué se cobran algunas rutas?
¿para qué el dinero del ingreso?
¿por qué se cobra por enseñar a patinar?
¿cómo confirmo que quiero clase?
¿tienes que ser socio para clases y rutas?
¿por qué no hacéis las rutas por la carretera?
¿no hay foro en la web?
¿rellené el formulario pero no he recibido confirmación?
¿cuantas clases necesito para saber patinar?
¿tengo que comprarme protecciones?
¿patín línea o patín tradicional?
© 2003 asociación sin animo de lucro madridpatina | www.madridpatina.com | info@madridpatina.com | tlf: 6666.317.96

www.madridpatina.com
D: javier griñán lacaci **C:** fernando bonilla lacaci
A: madridpatina **M:** info@madridpatina.com

GB – Motor Sport

GBmotorsport

L'amore per le automobili e la velocità è qualcosa che ti entra dentro e, probabilmente per tutta la vita, non ti lascerà più. La passione per le curve di una "supercar", l'ansietà nello scoprire tutti quei particolari e quegli accessori destinati a fare nascere un amore ed a creare una leggenda, costituiscono gli elementi fondanti di quel rapporto speciale che si instaura fra un pilota e la sua auto.

le auto...

- BMW 530 Touring
- BMW 645 Ci Cabrio
- Mercedes SLK 2004
- Bentley Continental GT
- Porsche Carrera GT
- e tante altre...

download

Scaricati le nuovissime wallpaper GBmotorsport, oppure invia una cartolina ad un amico...

:: wallpaper :: cartolina

official sponsor...

contact

Via Tuscania 4/6 (Vigna Clara)
00191 Roma
tel: 06 36382021
tel: 06 36382002

info@gbmotorsport.it

© 2004 - GBmotorsport srl home - le auto - download - questo mese - contact designed by kmstudio

GB – Motor Sport

le auto...

Cilindrata cm3: 5439
N° cilindri:
Potenza max: CV 360 a 5500 giri/min
Coppia max:
Velocità max: 320 km\h 100 km\h
N° rapporti: 5 (semiautomatico)
Trazione:
Freni anteriori: in ceramica
Freni posteriori: in ceramica

Lunghezza: 4.56 m
Larghezza: 1.88 m
Altezza: 1.25 m
Peso Kg:
Bagagliaio:
Pneumatici:
Optional: contattare GBmotorsport

Mercedes SRL

:: next

download

Scaricati le nuovissime wallpaper GBmotorsport, oppure invia una cartolina ad un amico...

:: wallpaper :: cartolina

contact

Via Tuscania 4/6 (Vigna Clara)
00191 Roma
tel: 06 36382021
tel: 06 36382002

info@gbmotorsport.it

© 2004 - GBmotorsport srl home - le auto - download - questo mese - contact designed by kmstudio

www.gbmotorsport.it
D: francesco kurhajec **C:** alessandro balasco
A: kmstudio **M:** info@kmstudio.it

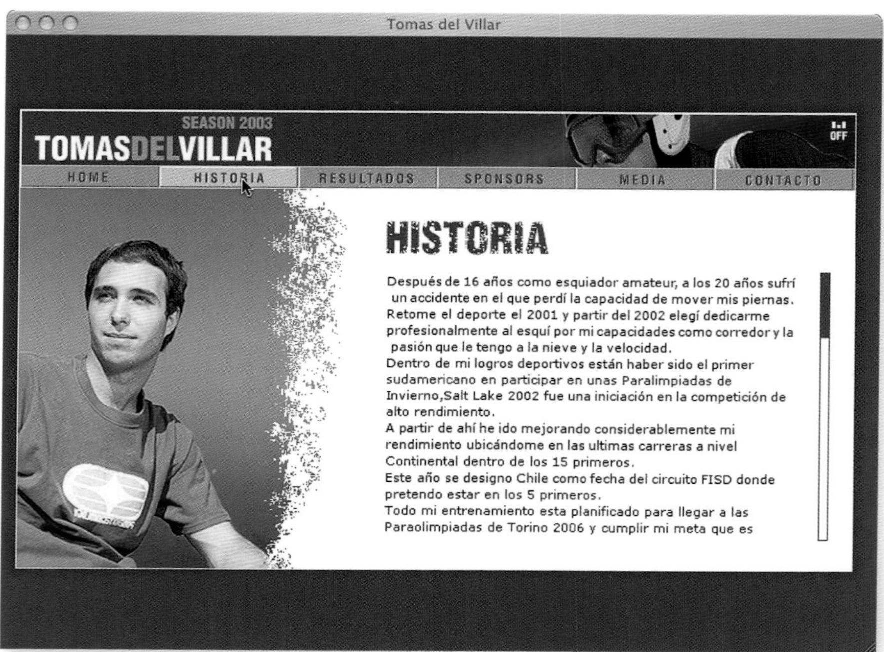
Tomas del Villar
SEASON 2003
TOMASDELVILLAR
HOME
HISTORIA
RESULTADOS
SPONSORS
MEDIA
CONTACTO
HISTORIA
Después de 16 años como esquiador amateur, a los 20 años sufrí un accidente en el que perdí la capacidad de mover mis piernas.
Retome el deporte el 2001 y partir del 2002 elegí dedicarme profesionalmente al esquí por mi capacidades como corredor y la pasión que le tengo a la nieve y la velocidad.
Dentro de mi logros deportivos están haber sido el primer sudamericano en participar en unas Paralimpiadas de Invierno,Salt Lake 2002 fue una iniciación en la competición de alto rendimiento.
A partir de ahí he ido mejorando considerablemente mi rendimiento ubicándome en las ultimas carreras a nivel Continental dentro de los 15 primeros.
Este año se designo Chile como fecha del circuito FISD donde pretendo estar en los 5 primeros.
Todo mi entrenamiento esta planificado para llegar a las Paraolimpiadas de Torino 2006 y cumplir mi meta que es

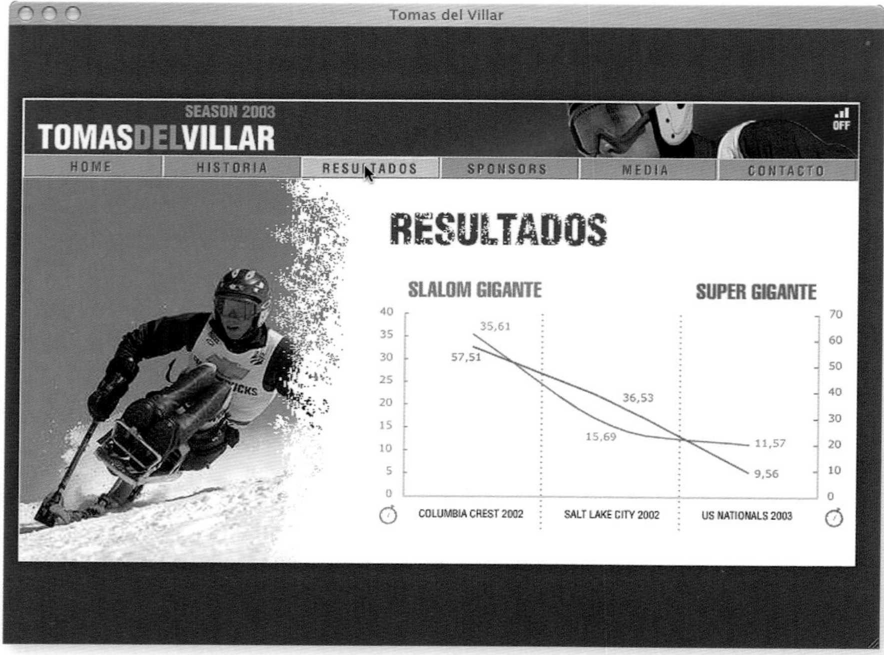
Tomas del Villar
SEASON 2003
TOMASDELVILLAR
HOME
HISTORIA
RESULTADOS
SPONSORS
MEDIA
CONTACTO
RESULTADOS
SLALOM GIGANTE
SUPER GIGANTE
35,61
57,51
36,53
15,69
11,57
9,56
COLUMBIA CREST 2002
SALT LAKE CITY 2002
US NATIONALS 2003

www.tomasdelvillar.cl
D: sebastián jara
A: interactive multimedia M: sjara@interactive.cl

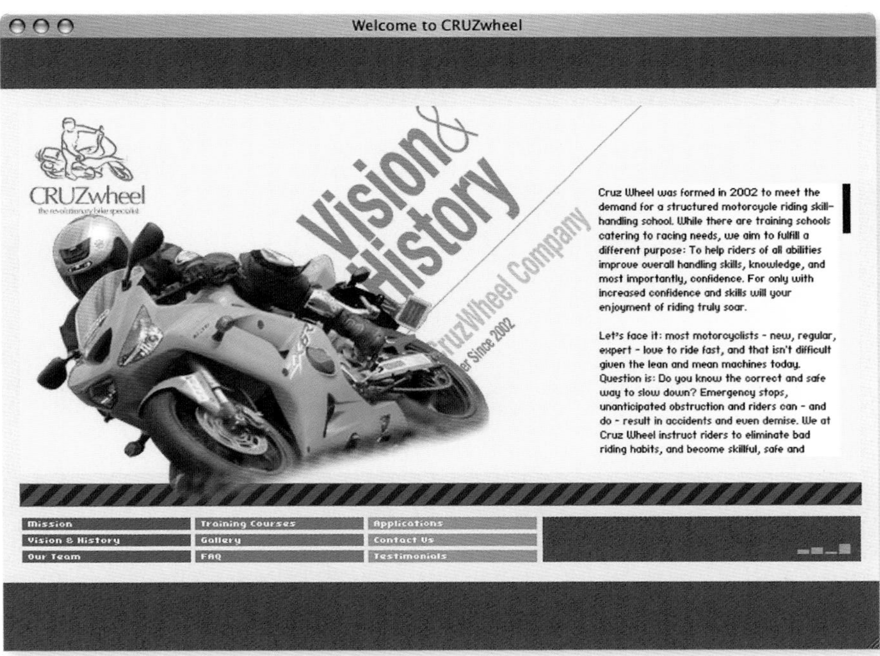
Welcome to CRUZwheel
CRUZwheel
Vision & History
CruzWheel Company
Since 2002
Cruz Wheel was formed in 2002 to meet the demand for a structured motorcycle riding skill-handling school. While there are training schools catering to racing needs, we aim to fulfill a different purpose: To help riders of all abilities improve overall handling skills, knowledge, and most importantly, confidence. For only with increased confidence and skills will your enjoyment of riding truly soar.
Let's face it: most motorcyclists - new, regular, expert - love to ride fast, and that isn't difficult given the lean and mean machines today. Question is: Do you know the correct and safe way to slow down? Emergency stops, unanticipated obstruction and riders can - and do - result in accidents and even demise. We at Cruz Wheel instruct riders to eliminate bad riding habits, and become skillful, safe and
Mission
Vision & History
Our Team
Training Courses
Gallery
FAQ
Applications
Contact Us
Testimonials

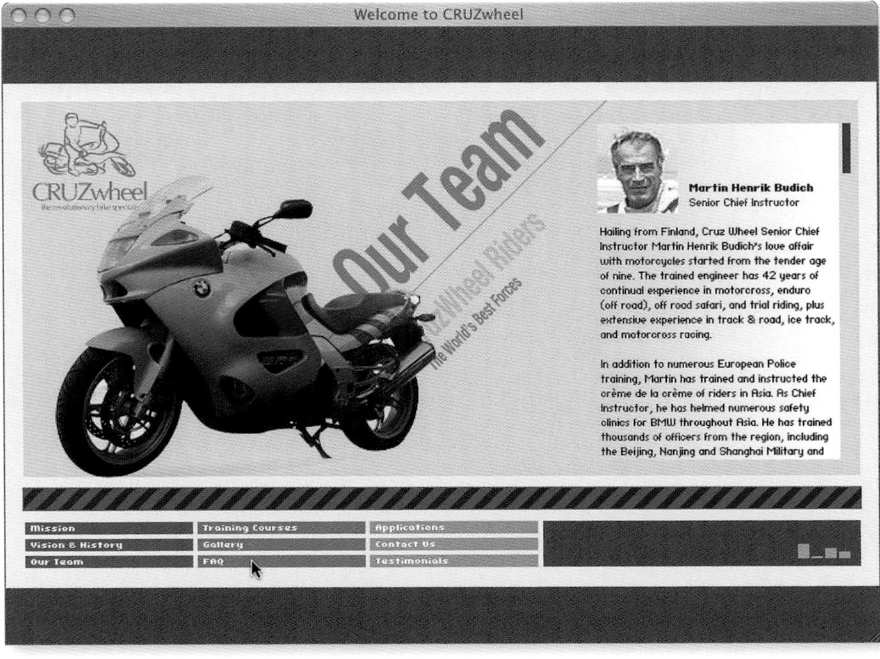
Welcome to CRUZwheel
CRUZwheel
Our Team
The World's Best Forces
Martin Henrik Budich
Senior Chief Instructor
Hailing from Finland, Cruz Wheel Senior Chief Instructor Martin Henrik Budich's love affair with motorcycles started from the tender age of nine. The trained engineer has 42 years of continual experience in motorcross, enduro (off road), off road safari, and trial riding, plus extensive experience in track & road, ice track, and motorcross racing.
In addition to numerous European Police training, Martin has trained and instructed the crème de la crème of riders in Asia. As Chief Instructor, he has helmed numerous safety clinics for BMW throughout Asia. He has trained thousands of officers from the region, including the Beijing, Nanjing and Shanghai Military and
Mission
Vision & History
Our Team
Training Courses
Gallery
FAQ
Applications
Contact Us
Testimonials

www.cruzwheel.com
D: gerard tan
A: junkflea **M:** info@junkflea.com

Sportmuseum Schweiz (SMS) – Basel | Services

ANLÄSSE AUSSTELLUNGEN FÜHRUNGEN VOR
BERATUNG PUBLIKATIONEN ARCHIV
URKUNDEN DEKORATION SAMMLUNGSGUT HOC

SPORTMUSEUM SCHWEIZ // SERVICES // Anlässe

Wir stellen unsere Museumsräume und den Garten für Ihre Anlässe zur Verfügung, kümmern uns um Getränke, Snacks, Service, technische Einrichtungen usw. Neben Führungen und Vorträgen organisieren wir für Sie auch Treffen mit Sportverbänden, Sportlerinnen und Sportlern. So wird Ihr Anlass zum Ereignis!

HOME | MUSEUM | GALERIE | SPORTARTEN | SHOP| E-MAIL

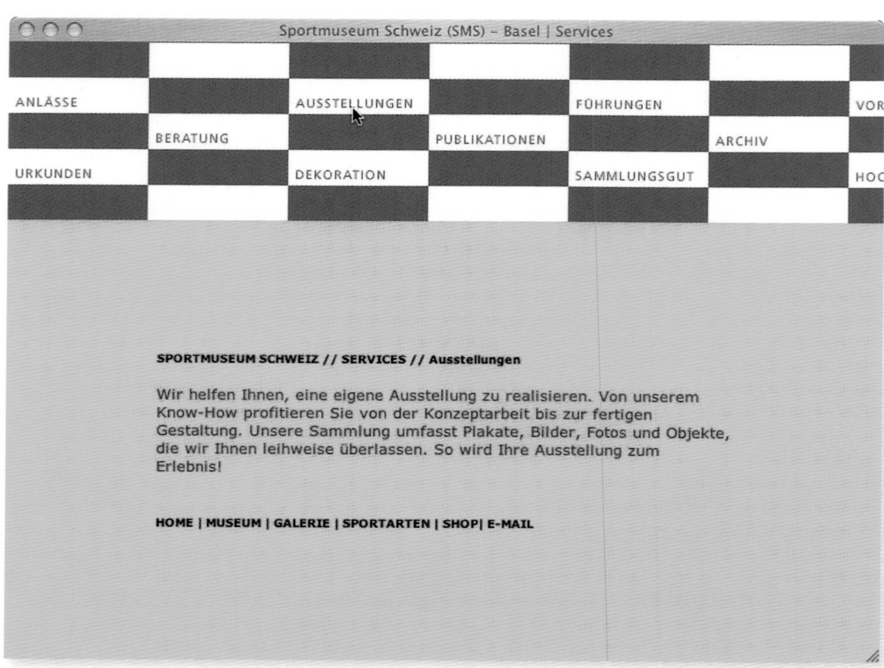
Sportmuseum Schweiz (SMS) – Basel | Services
ANLÄSSE
AUSSTELLUNGEN
FÜHRUNGEN
VOR
BERATUNG
PUBLIKATIONEN
ARCHIV
URKUNDEN
DEKORATION
SAMMLUNGSGUT
HOC
SPORTMUSEUM SCHWEIZ // SERVICES // Ausstellungen
Wir helfen Ihnen, eine eigene Ausstellung zu realisieren. Von unserem Know-How profitieren Sie von der Konzeptarbeit bis zur fertigen Gestaltung. Unsere Sammlung umfasst Plakate, Bilder, Fotos und Objekte, die wir Ihnen leihweise überlassen. So wird Ihre Ausstellung zum Erlebnis!
HOME | MUSEUM | GALERIE | SPORTARTEN | SHOP| E-MAIL

www.swiss-sports-museum.ch
D: sandra leister **C:** alexander schäfer
A: 372dpi **M:** info@372dpi.com

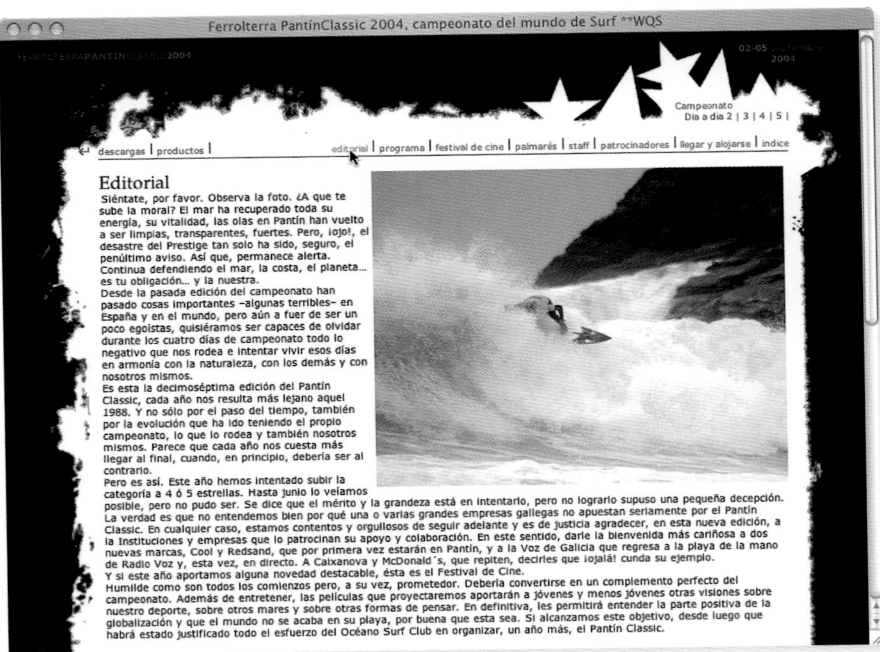
Ferrolterra PantínClassic 2004, campeonato del mundo de Surf **WQS
02-05 septiembre 2004
Campeonato
Dia a dia 2 | 3 | 4 | 5 |
descargas | productos |
editorial | programa | festival de cine | palmarés | staff | patrocinadores | llegar y alojarse | indice
Editorial
Siéntate, por favor. Observa la foto. ¿A que te sube la moral? El mar ha recuperado toda su energía, su vitalidad, las olas en Pantín han vuelto a ser limpias, transparentes, fuertes. Pero, ¡ojo!, el desastre del Prestige tan solo ha sido, seguro, el penúltimo aviso. Así que, permanece alerta. Continua defendiendo el mar, la costa, el planeta... es tu obligación... y la nuestra.
Desde la pasada edición del campeonato han pasado cosas importantes –algunas terribles– en España y en el mundo, pero aún a fuer de ser un poco egoistas, quisiéramos ser capaces de olvidar durante los cuatro días de campeonato todo lo negativo que nos rodea e intentar vivir esos días en armonía con la naturaleza, con los demás y con nosotros mismos.
Es esta la decimoséptima edición del Pantín Classic, cada año nos resulta más lejano aquel 1988. Y no sólo por el paso del tiempo, también por la evolución que ha ido teniendo el propio campeonato, lo que lo rodea y también nosotros mismos. Parece que cada año nos cuesta más llegar al final, cuando, en principio, debería ser al contrario.
Pero es así. Este año hemos intentado subir la categoría a 4 ó 5 estrellas. Hasta junio lo veíamos posible, pero no pudo ser. Se dice que el mérito y la grandeza está en intentarlo, pero no lograrlo supuso una pequeña decepción. La verdad es que no entendemos bien por qué una o varias grandes empresas gallegas no apuestan seriamente por el Pantín Classic. En cualquier caso, estamos contentos y orgullosos de seguir adelante y es de justicia agradecer, en esta nueva edición, a la Instituciones y empresas que lo patrocinan su apoyo y colaboración. En este sentido, darle la bienvenida más cariñosa a dos nuevas marcas, Cool y Redsand, que por primera vez estarán en Pantín, y a la Voz de Galicia que regresa a la playa de la mano de Radio Voz y, esta vez, en directo. A Caixanova y McDonald´s, que repiten, decirles que ¡ojalá! cunda su ejemplo.
Y si este año aportamos alguna novedad destacable, ésta es el Festival de Cine.
Humilde como son todos los comienzos pero, a su vez, prometedor. Debería convertirse en un complemento perfecto del campeonato. Además de entretener, las películas que proyectaremos aportarán a jóvenes y menos jóvenes otras visiones sobre nuestro deporte, sobre otros mares y sobre otras formas de pensar. En definitiva, les permitirá entender la parte positiva de la globalización y que el mundo no se acaba en su playa, por buena que esta sea. Si alcanzamos este objetivo, desde luego que habrá estado justificado todo el esfuerzo del Océano Surf Club en organizar, un año más, el Pantín Classic.

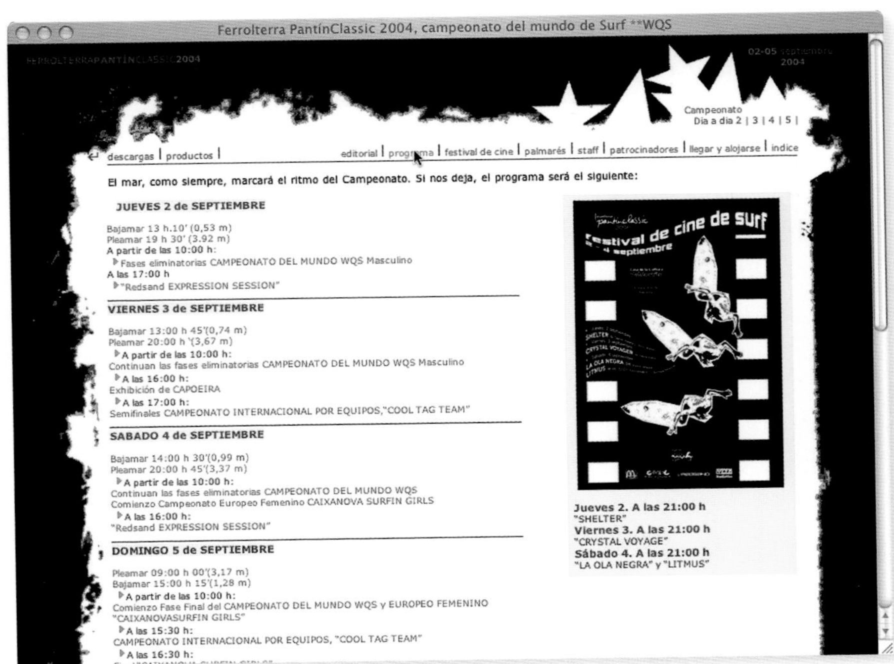
Ferrolterra PantínClassic 2004, campeonato del mundo de Surf **WQS
02-05 septiembre 2004
Campeonato
Dia a dia 2 | 3 | 4 | 5 |
descargas | productos |
editorial | programa | festival de cine | palmarés | staff | patrocinadores | llegar y alojarse | indice
El mar, como siempre, marcará el ritmo del Campeonato. Si nos deja, el programa será el siguiente:
JUEVES 2 de SEPTIEMBRE
Bajamar 13 h.10' (0,53 m)
Pleamar 19 h 30' (3.92 m)
A partir de las 10:00 h:
Fases eliminatorias CAMPEONATO DEL MUNDO WQS Masculino
A las 17:00 h
"Redsand EXPRESSION SESSION"
VIERNES 3 de SEPTIEMBRE
Bajamar 13:00 h 45'(0,74 m)
Pleamar 20:00 h '(3,67 m)
A partir de las 10:00 h:
Continuan las fases eliminatorias CAMPEONATO DEL MUNDO WQS Masculino
A las 16:00 h:
Exhibición de CAPOEIRA
A las 17:00 h:
Semifinales CAMPEONATO INTERNACIONAL POR EQUIPOS,"COOL TAG TEAM"
SABADO 4 de SEPTIEMBRE
Bajamar 14:00 h 30'(0,99 m)
Pleamar 20:00 h 45'(3,37 m)
A partir de las 10:00 h:
Continuan las fases eliminatorias CAMPEONATO DEL MUNDO WQS
Comienzo Campeonato Europeo Femenino CAIXANOVA SURFIN GIRLS
A las 16:00 h:
"Redsand EXPRESSION SESSION"
DOMINGO 5 de SEPTIEMBRE
Pleamar 09:00 h 00'(3,17 m)
Bajamar 15:00 h 15'(1,28 m)
A partir de las 10:00 h:
Comienzo Fase Final del CAMPEONATO DEL MUNDO WQS y EUROPEO FEMENINO "CAIXANOVASURFIN GIRLS"
A las 15:30 h:
CAMPEONATO INTERNACIONAL POR EQUIPOS, "COOL TAG TEAM"
A las 16:30 h:
festival de cine de surf
septiembre
SHELTER
CRYSTAL VOYAGER
LA OLA NEGRA
LITMUS
Jueves 2. A las 21:00 h
"SHELTER"
Viernes 3. A las 21:00 h
"CRYSTAL VOYAGE"
Sábado 4. A las 21:00 h
"LA OLA NEGRA" y "LITMUS"

www.pantinclassic.com
D: daniel ameneiros **P:** oceano surf club
A: octagon! **M:** knox@octagon.cn

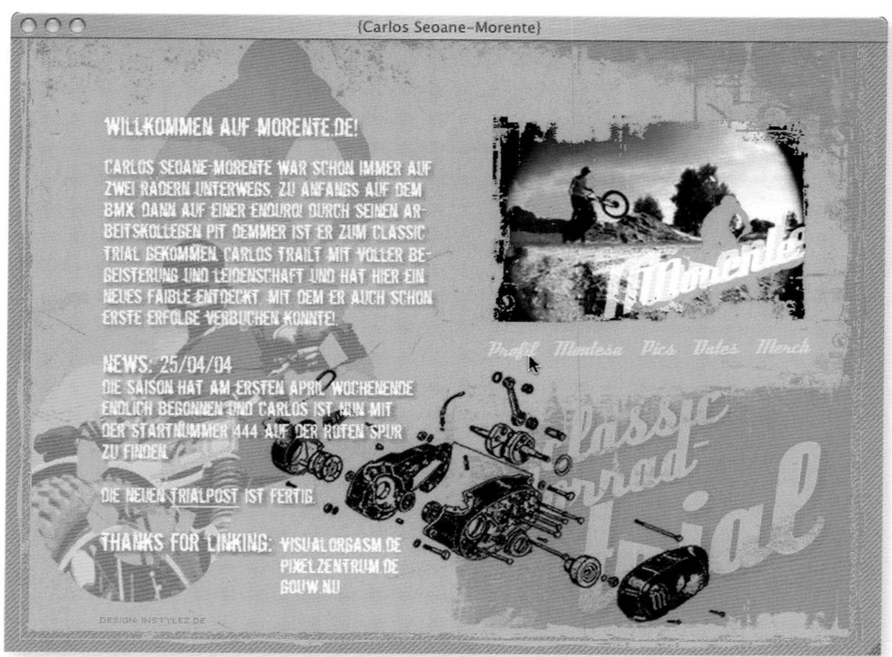
{Carlos Seoane-Morente}
WILLKOMMEN AUF MORENTE.DE!
CARLOS SEOANE-MORENTE WAR SCHON IMMER AUF ZWEI RÄDERN UNTERWEGS. ZU ANFANGS AUF DEM BMX DANN AUF EINER ENDURO! DURCH SEINEN ARBEITSKOLLEGEN PIT DEMMER IST ER ZUM CLASSIC TRIAL GEKOMMEN. CARLOS TRAILT MIT VOLLER BEGEISTERUNG UND LEIDENSCHAFT UND HAT HIER EIN NEUES FAIBLE ENTDECKT, MIT DEM ER AUCH SCHON ERSTE ERFOLGE VERBUCHEN KONNTE!
NEWS: 25/04/04
DIE SAISON HAT AM ERSTEN APRIL WOCHENENDE ENDLICH BEGONNEN UND CARLOS IST NUN MIT DER STARTNUMMER 444 AUF DER ROTEN SPUR ZU FINDEN.
DIE NEUEN TRIALPOST IST FERTIG.
THANKS FOR LINKING: VISUALORGASM.DE
PIXELZENTRUM.DE
GOUW.NU
DESIGN: INSTYLEZ.DE
Morente
Profil Montesa Pics Dates Merch

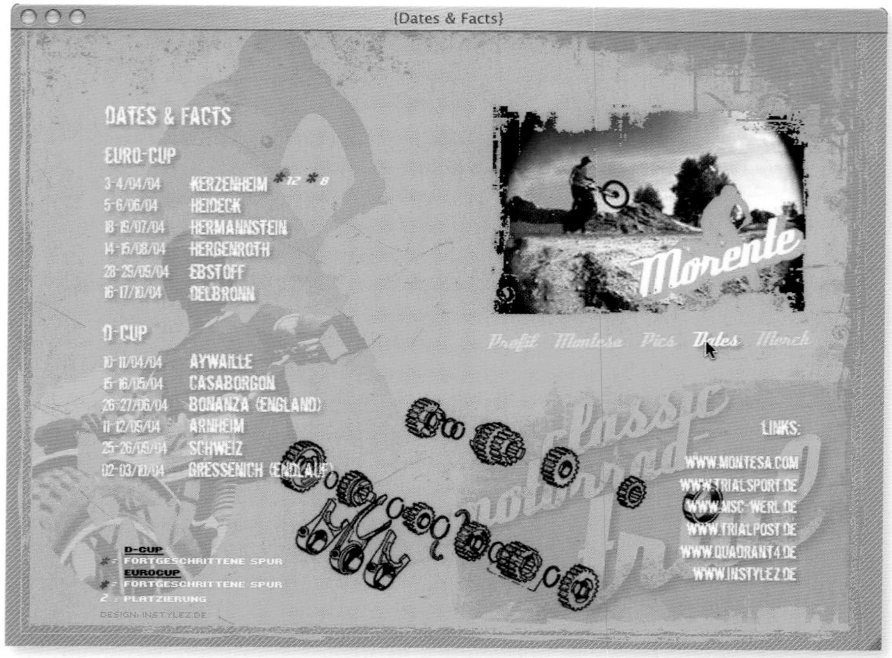
{Dates & Facts}
DATES & FACTS
EURO-CUP
3-4/04/04 KERZENHEIM
5-6/06/04 HEIDECK
18-19/07/04 HERMANNSTEIN
14-15/08/04 HERGENROTH
28-29/09/04 EBSTOFF
16-17/10/04 OELBRONN
D-CUP
10-11/04/04 AYWAILLE
15-16/05/04 CASABORGON
26-27/06/04 BONANZA (ENGLAND)
11-12/05/04 ARNHEIM
25-26/09/04 SCHWEIZ
02-03/10/04 GRESSENICH (ENDLAUF)
D-CUP
FORTGESCHRITTENE SPUR
EUROCUP
FORTGESCHRITTENE SPUR
PLATZIERUNG
DESIGN: INSTYLEZ.DE
Morente
Profil Montesa Pics Dates Merch
LINKS:
WWW.MONTESA.COM
WWW.TRIALSPORT.DE
WWW.MSC-WERL.DE
WWW.TRIALPOST.DE
WWW.QUADRANT4.DE
WWW.INSTYLEZ.DE

www.morente.de
D: michael ziehm
A: instylez **M:** info@instylez.de

:::: BBT :: Buccioni Boxing Team ::::
IL BBT
NASCE A ROMA NEL 2004
SU VOLONTÀ' DEL PRESIDENTE
DAVIDE BUCCIONI.
LA SOCIETÀ HA LO SCOPO DI
RILANCIARE LA "NOBLE ART"
NELLA CAPITALE.
BBT
IN HOC SIGNO VINCES
CHI SIAMO
BB-TEAM
EVENTI
SPONSOR
GALLERY
IN MEMORIA DI
RASSEGNA STAMPA
INFO

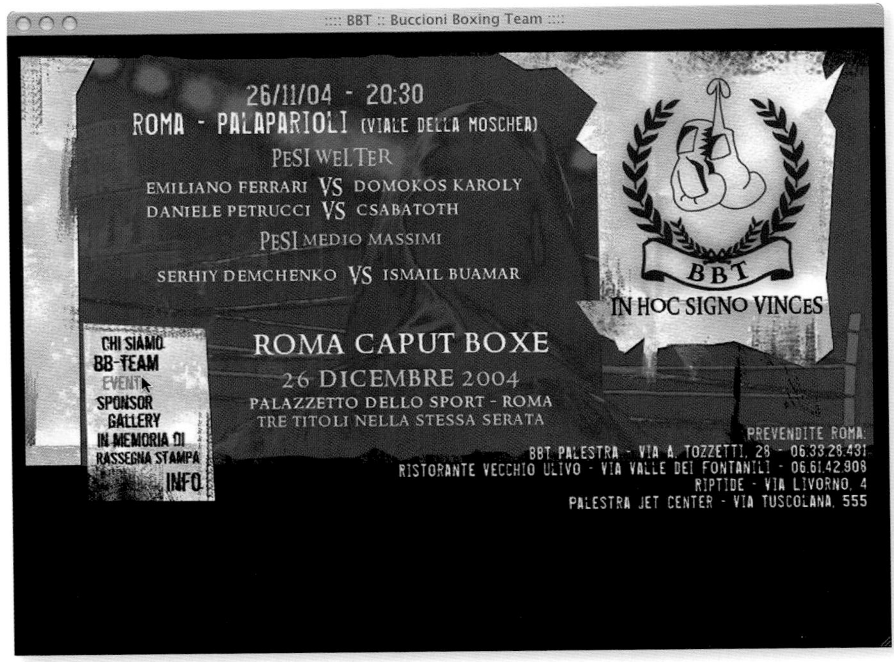
:::: BBT :: Buccioni Boxing Team ::::
26/11/04 - 20:30
ROMA - PALAPARIOLI (VIALE DELLA MOSCHEA)
PESI WELTER
EMILIANO FERRARI VS DOMOKOS KAROLY
DANIELE PETRUCCI VS CSABATOTH
PESI MEDIO MASSIMI
SERHIY DEMCHENKO VS ISMAIL BUAMAR
ROMA CAPUT BOXE
26 DICEMBRE 2004
PALAZZETTO DELLO SPORT - ROMA
TRE TITOLI NELLA STESSA SERATA
PREVENDITE ROMA:
BBT PALESTRA - VIA A. TOZZETTI, 28 - 06.33.28.431
RISTORANTE VECCHIO ULIVO - VIA VALLE DEI FONTANILI - 06.61.42.908
RIPTIDE - VIA LIVORNO, 4
PALESTRA JET CENTER - VIA TUSCOLANA, 555
BBT
IN HOC SIGNO VINCES
CHI SIAMO
BB-TEAM
EVENTI
SPONSOR
GALLERY
IN MEMORIA DI
RASSEGNA STAMPA
INFO

www.buccioniboxingteam.com
D: riccardo pace
A: pufferdesign **M:** info@pufferdesign.com

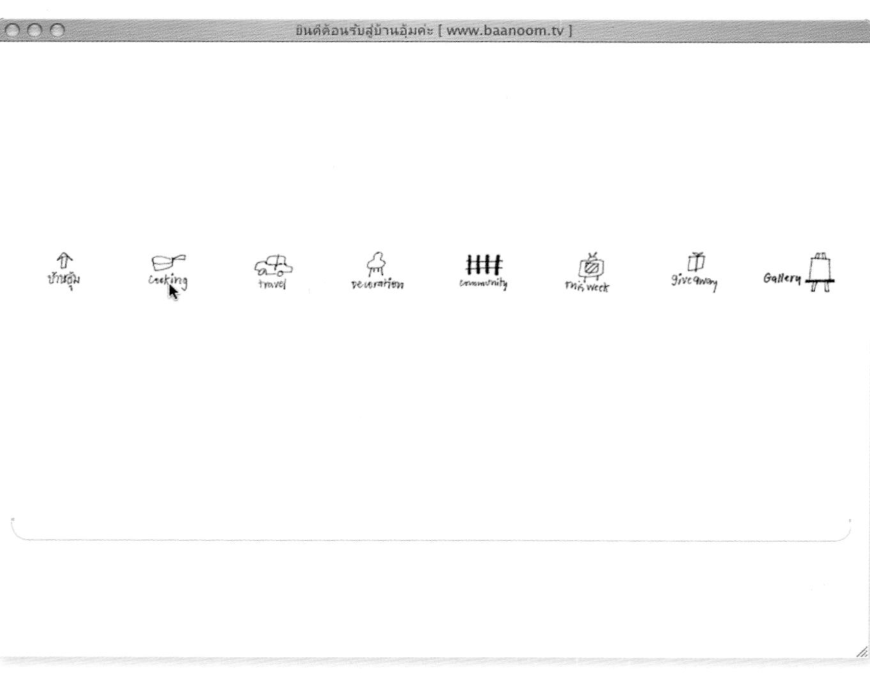
ยินดีต้อนรับสู่บ้านอุ้มค่ะ [www.baanoom.tv]
บ้านอุ้ม
cooking
travel
decoration
community
this week
giveaway
Gallery

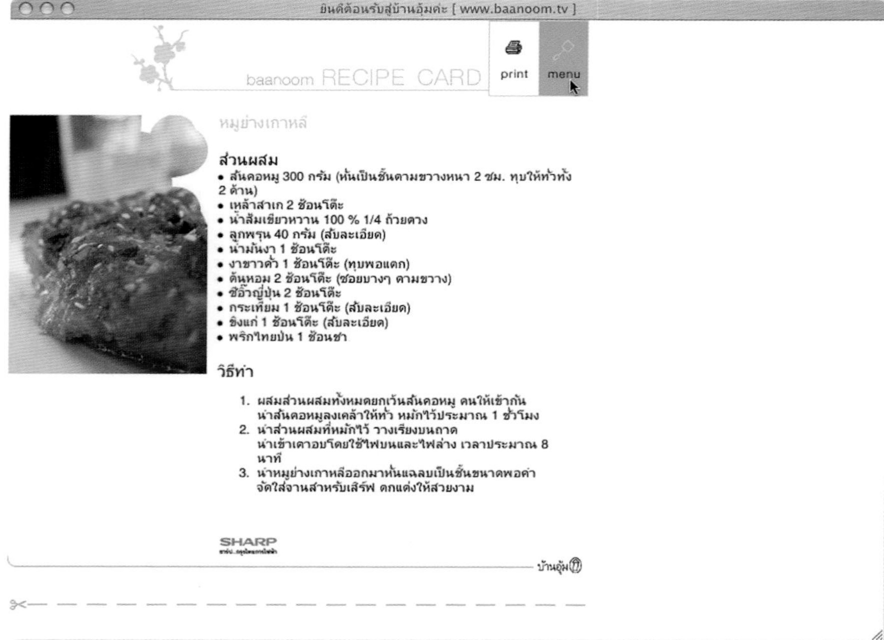
ยินดีต้อนรับสู่บ้านอุ้มค่ะ [www.baanoom.tv]
baanoom RECIPE CARD
print
menu
หมูย่างเกาหลี
ส่วนผสม
• สันคอหมู 300 กรัม (หั่นเป็นชิ้นตามขวางหนา 2 ซม. ทุบให้ทั่วทั้ง 2 ด้าน)
• เหล้าสาเก 2 ช้อนโต๊ะ
• น้ำส้มเขียวหวาน 100 % 1/4 ถ้วยตวง
• ลูกพรุน 40 กรัม (สับละเอียด)
• น้ำมันงา 1 ช้อนโต๊ะ
• งาขาวคั่ว 1 ช้อนโต๊ะ (ทุบพอแตก)
• ต้นหอม 2 ช้อนโต๊ะ (ซอยบางๆ ตามขวาง)
• ซีอิ๊วญี่ปุ่น 2 ช้อนโต๊ะ
• กระเทียม 1 ช้อนโต๊ะ (สับละเอียด)
• ขิงแก่ 1 ช้อนโต๊ะ (สับละเอียด)
• พริกไทยป่น 1 ช้อนชา
วิธีทำ
1. ผสมส่วนผสมทั้งหมดยกเว้นสันคอหมู คนให้เข้ากัน นำสันคอหมูลงเคล้าให้ทั่ว หมักไว้ประมาณ 1 ชั่วโมง
2. นำส่วนผสมที่หมักไว้ วางเรียงบนถาด นำเข้าเตาอบโดยใช้ไฟบนและไฟล่าง เวลาประมาณ 8 นาที
3. นำหมูย่างเกาหลีออกมาหั่นแฉลบเป็นชิ้นขนาดพอคำ จัดใส่จานสำหรับเสิร์ฟ ตกแต่งให้สวยงาม
SHARP
บ้านอุ้ม

www.baanoom.tv
D: suttaporn oudomying **C:** siriyakorn p.
A: kid-ox **M:** pup@kid-ox.com

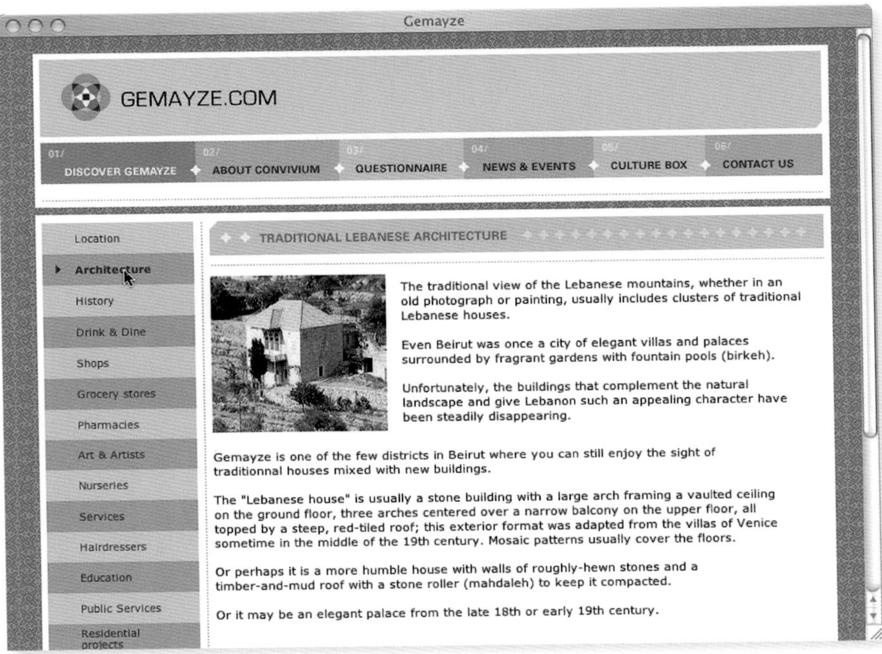
Gemayze
GEMAYZE.COM
01/ DISCOVER GEMAYZE
02/ ABOUT CONVIVIUM
03/ QUESTIONNAIRE
04/ NEWS & EVENTS
05/ CULTURE BOX
06/ CONTACT US
Location
Architecture
History
Drink & Dine
Shops
Grocery stores
Pharmacies
Art & Artists
Nurseries
Services
Hairdressers
Education
Public Services
Residential projects
TRADITIONAL LEBANESE ARCHITECTURE
The traditional view of the Lebanese mountains, whether in an old photograph or painting, usually includes clusters of traditional Lebanese houses.
Even Beirut was once a city of elegant villas and palaces surrounded by fragrant gardens with fountain pools (birkeh).
Unfortunately, the buildings that complement the natural landscape and give Lebanon such an appealing character have been steadily disappearing.
Gemayze is one of the few districts in Beirut where you can still enjoy the sight of traditionnal houses mixed with new buildings.
The "Lebanese house" is usually a stone building with a large arch framing a vaulted ceiling on the ground floor, three arches centered over a narrow balcony on the upper floor, all topped by a steep, red-tiled roof; this exterior format was adapted from the villas of Venice sometime in the middle of the 19th century. Mosaic patterns usually cover the floors.
Or perhaps it is a more humble house with walls of roughly-hewn stones and a timber-and-mud roof with a stone roller (mahdaleh) to keep it compacted.
Or it may be an elegant palace from the late 18th or early 19th century.

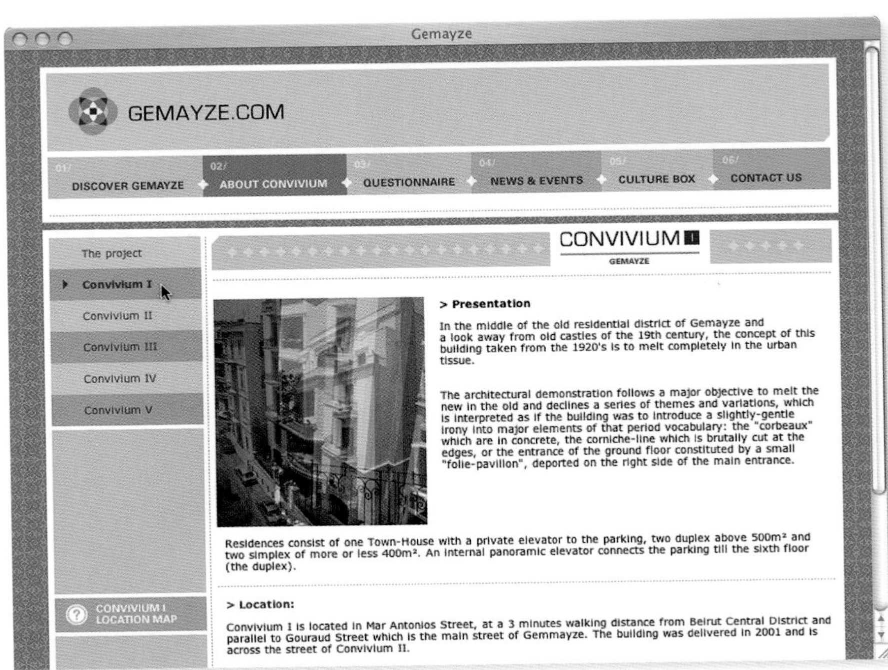
Gemayze
GEMAYZE.COM
01/ DISCOVER GEMAYZE
02/ ABOUT CONVIVIUM
03/ QUESTIONNAIRE
04/ NEWS & EVENTS
05/ CULTURE BOX
06/ CONTACT US
The project
Convivium I
Convivium II
Convivium III
Convivium IV
Convivium V
CONVIVIUM I LOCATION MAP
CONVIVIUM
GEMAYZE
> Presentation
In the middle of the old residential district of Gemayze and a look away from old castles of the 19th century, the concept of this building taken from the 1920's is to melt completely in the urban tissue.
The architectural demonstration follows a major objective to melt the new in the old and declines a series of themes and variations, which is interpreted as if the building was to introduce a slightly-gentle irony into major elements of that period vocabulary: the "corbeaux" which are in concrete, the corniche-line which is brutally cut at the edges, or the entrance of the ground floor constituted by a small "folie-pavillon", deported on the right side of the main entrance.
Residences consist of one Town-House with a private elevator to the parking, two duplex above 500m² and two simplex of more or less 400m². An internal panoramic elevator connects the parking till the sixth floor (the duplex).
> Location:
Convivium I is located in Mar Antonios Street, at a 3 minutes walking distance from Beirut Central District and parallel to Gouraud Street which is the main street of Gemmayze. The building was delivered in 2001 and is across the street of Convivium II.

www.gemayze.com

D: stephanie terroir C: farihan hamdan
M: stephanie@sterroir.com

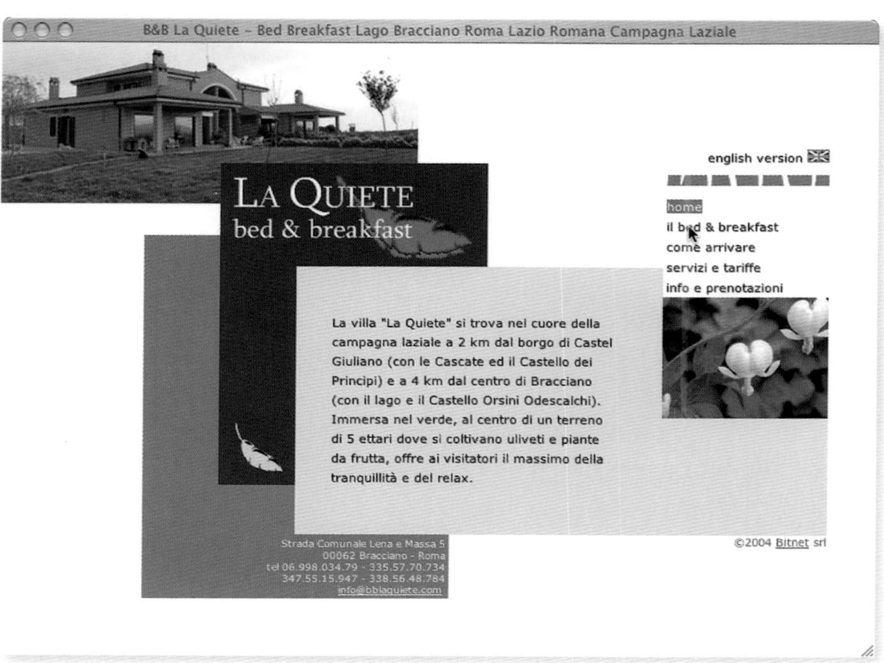
B&B La Quiete - Bed Breakfast Lago Bracciano Roma Lazio Romana Campagna Laziale
english version
home
il bed & breakfast
come arrivare
servizi e tariffe
info e prenotazioni
LA QUIETE
bed & breakfast
La villa "La Quiete" si trova nel cuore della campagna laziale a 2 km dal borgo di Castel Giuliano (con le Cascate ed il Castello dei Principi) e a 4 km dal centro di Bracciano (con il lago e il Castello Orsini Odescalchi). Immersa nel verde, al centro di un terreno di 5 ettari dove si coltivano uliveti e piante da frutta, offre ai visitatori il massimo della tranquillità e del relax.
Strada Comunale Lena e Massa 5
00062 Bracciano - Roma
tel 06.998.034.79 - 335.57.70.734
347.55.15.947 - 338.56.48.784
info@bblaquiete.com
©2004 Bitnet srl

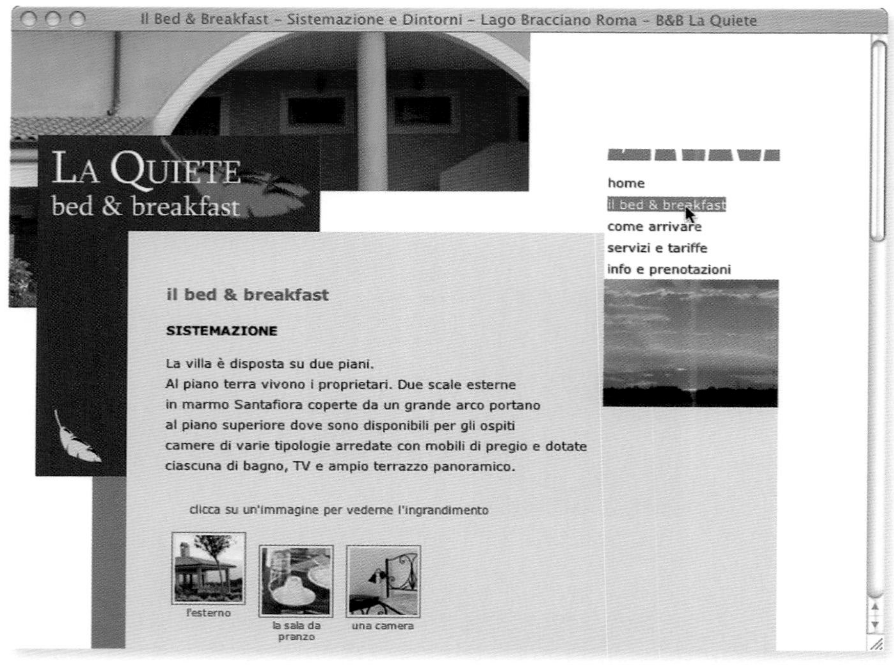
Il Bed & Breakfast - Sistemazione e Dintorni - Lago Bracciano Roma - B&B La Quiete
home
il bed & breakfast
come arrivare
servizi e tariffe
info e prenotazioni
LA QUIETE
bed & breakfast
il bed & breakfast
SISTEMAZIONE
La villa è disposta su due piani.
Al piano terra vivono i proprietari. Due scale esterne in marmo Santafiora coperte da un grande arco portano al piano superiore dove sono disponibili per gli ospiti camere di varie tipologie arredate con mobili di pregio e dotate ciascuna di bagno, TV e ampio terrazzo panoramico.
clicca su un'immagine per vederne l'ingrandimento
l'esterno
la sala da pranzo
una camera

www.bblaquiete.com
D: stefano vitagliano
A: bitnet **M:** info@stefanovitagliano.it

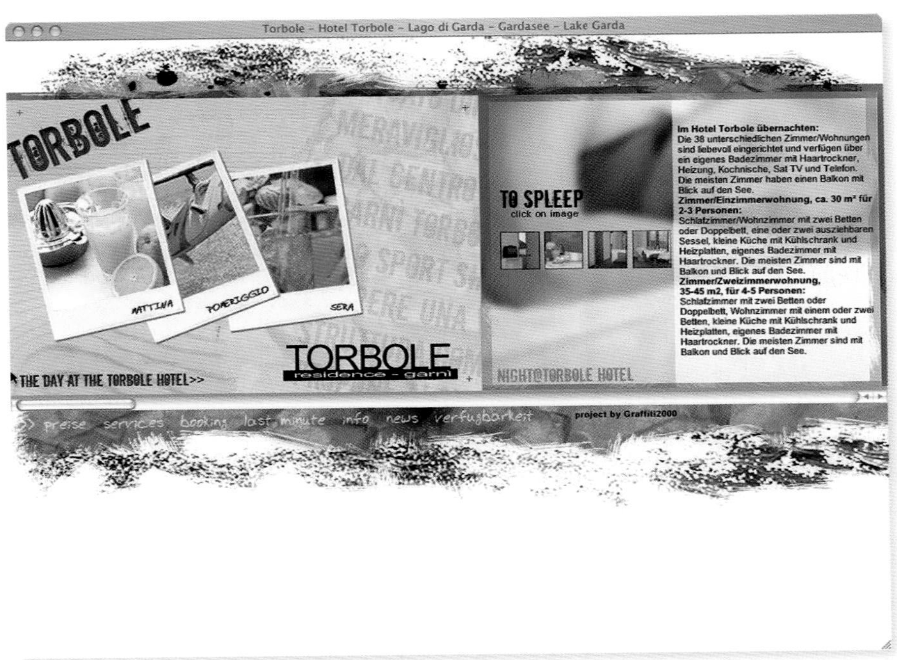
Torbole - Hotel Torbole - Lago di Garda - Gardasee - Lake Garda
TORBOLE
MATTINA
POMERIGGIO
SERA
TORBOLE
residence - garni
THE DAY AT THE TORBOLE HOTEL>>
TO SPLEEP
click on image
NIGHT@TORBOLE HOTEL
Im Hotel Torbole übernachten:
Die 38 unterschiedlichen Zimmer/Wohnungen sind liebevoll eingerichtet und verfügen über ein eigenes Badezimmer mit Haartrockner, Heizung, Kochnische, Sat TV und Telefon. Die meisten Zimmer haben einen Balkon mit Blick auf den See.
Zimmer/Einzimmerwohnung, ca. 30 m² für 2-3 Personen:
Schlafzimmer/Wohnzimmer mit zwei Betten oder Doppelbett, eine oder zwei ausziehbaren Sessel, kleine Küche mit Kühlschrank und Heizplatten, eigenes Badezimmer mit Haartrockner. Die meisten Zimmer sind mit Balkon und Blick auf den See.
Zimmer/Zweizimmerwohnung, 35-45 m2, für 4-5 Personen:
Schlafzimmer mit zwei Betten oder Doppelbett, Wohnzimmer mit einem oder zwei Betten, kleine Küche mit Kühlschrank und Heizplatten, eigenes Badezimmer mit Haartrockner. Die meisten Zimmer sind mit Balkon und Blick auf den See.
preise services booking last minute info news verfugbarkeit
project by Graffiti2000

Torbole - Hotel Torbole - Lago di Garda - Gardasee - Lake Garda
TORBOLE
residence - garni
01.00 PM L'ORA DEL GARDA
13.00 Uhr: Die Stunde der Ora del Garda Gleich nach Mittag beginnt der berühmte Ora-Wind zu blasen, ein thermischer Windder regelmässig von Süden nach Norden bläst, den ganzen See durchquert und seine höchste Intensität genau vor dem Hotel erreicht und damit die besten Voraussetzungen für Freerider und Freestyler bietet.
BEACH
WINDS
1 2 3 4 5 6 7
SELECT THE IMAGE: 02.00 PM ON THE LA
preise services booking last minute info news verfugbarkeit
project by Graffiti2000

www.hoteltorbole.com
D: lorenzo cattoni
A: graffiti2000 **M:** lorenzo.cattoni@graffiti2000.com

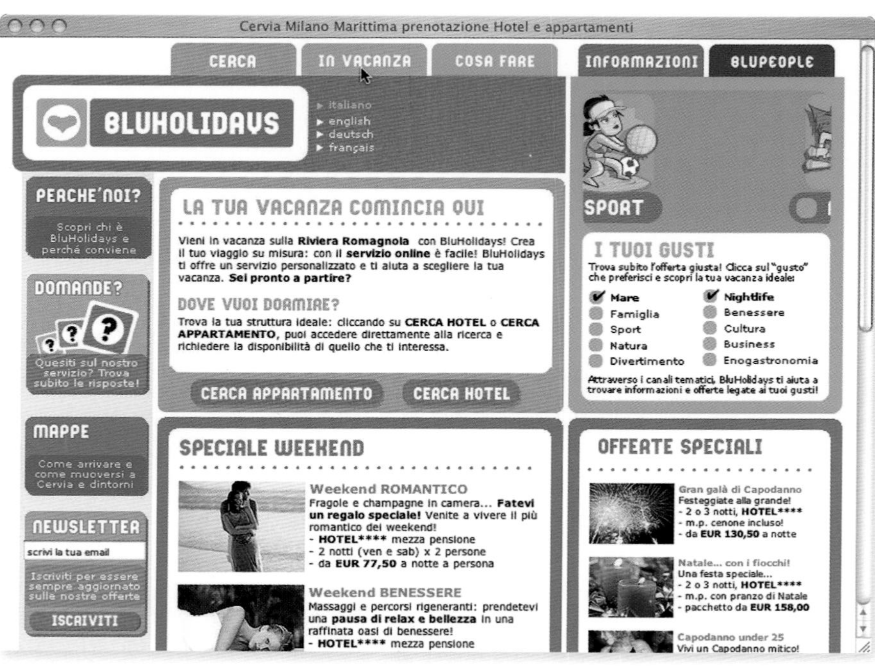

Cervia Milano Marittima prenotazione Hotel e appartamenti
CERCA
IN VACANZA
COSA FARE
INFORMAZIONI
BLUPEOPLE
BLUHOLIDAYS
italiano
english
deutsch
français
PERCHE'NOI?
Scopri chi è BluHolidays e perché conviene
DOMANDE?
Quesiti sul nostro servizio? Trova subito le risposte!
MAPPE
Come arrivare e come muoversi a Cervia e dintorni
NEWSLETTER
scrivi la tua email
Iscriviti per essere sempre aggiornato sulle nostre offerte
ISCRIVITI
LA TUA VACANZA COMINCIA QUI
Vieni in vacanza sulla Riviera Romagnola con BluHolidays! Crea il tuo viaggio su misura: con il servizio online è facile! BluHolidays ti offre un servizio personalizzato e ti aiuta a scegliere la tua vacanza. Sei pronto a partire?
DOVE VUOI DORMIRE?
Trova la tua struttura ideale: cliccando su CERCA HOTEL o CERCA APPARTAMENTO, puoi accedere direttamente alla ricerca e richiedere la disponibilità di quello che ti interessa.
CERCA APPARTAMENTO
CERCA HOTEL
SPORT
I TUOI GUSTI
Trova subito l'offerta giusta! Clicca sul "gusto" che preferisci e scopri la tua vacanza ideale:
Mare
Famiglia
Sport
Natura
Divertimento
Nightlife
Benessere
Cultura
Business
Enogastronomia
Attraverso i canali tematici, BluHolidays ti aiuta a trovare informazioni e offerte legate ai tuoi gusti!
SPECIALE WEEKEND
Weekend ROMANTICO
Fragole e champagne in camera... Fatevi un regalo speciale! Venite a vivere il più romantico dei weekend!
- HOTEL**** mezza pensione
- 2 notti (ven e sab) x 2 persone
- da EUR 77,50 a notte a persona
Weekend BENESSERE
Massaggi e percorsi rigeneranti: prendetevi una pausa di relax e bellezza in una raffinata oasi di benessere!
- HOTEL**** mezza pensione
OFFERTE SPECIALI
Gran galà di Capodanno
Festeggiate alla grande!
- 2 o 3 notti, HOTEL****
- m.p. cenone incluso!
- da EUR 130,50 a notte
Natale... con i fiocchi!
Una festa speciale...
- 2 o 3 notti, HOTEL****
- m.p. con pranzo di Natale
- pacchetto da EUR 158,00
Capodanno under 25
Vivi un Capodanno mitico!

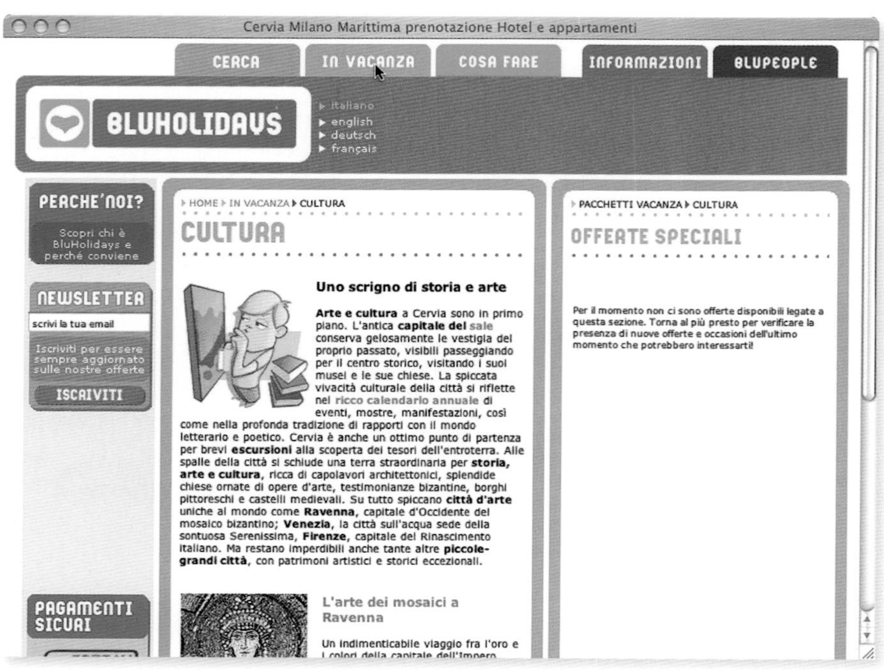

Cervia Milano Marittima prenotazione Hotel e appartamenti
CERCA
IN VACANZA
COSA FARE
INFORMAZIONI
BLUPEOPLE
BLUHOLIDAYS
italiano
english
deutsch
français
PERCHE'NOI?
Scopri chi è BluHolidays e perché conviene
NEWSLETTER
scrivi la tua email
Iscriviti per essere sempre aggiornato sulle nostre offerte
ISCRIVITI
PAGAMENTI SICURI
HOME IN VACANZA CULTURA
CULTURA
Uno scrigno di storia e arte
Arte e cultura a Cervia sono in primo piano. L'antica capitale del sale conserva gelosamente le vestigia del proprio passato, visibili passeggiando per il centro storico, visitando i suoi musei e le sue chiese. La spiccata vivacità culturale della città si riflette nel ricco calendario annuale di eventi, mostre, manifestazioni, così come nella profonda tradizione di rapporti con il mondo letterario e poetico. Cervia è anche un ottimo punto di partenza per brevi escursioni alla scoperta dei tesori dell'entroterra. Alle spalle della città si schiude una terra straordinaria per storia, arte e cultura, ricca di capolavori architettonici, splendide chiese ornate di opere d'arte, testimonianze bizantine, borghi pittoreschi e castelli medievali. Su tutto spiccano città d'arte uniche al mondo come Ravenna, capitale d'Occidente del mosaico bizantino; Venezia, la città sull'acqua sede della sontuosa Serenissima, Firenze, capitale del Rinascimento italiano. Ma restano imperdibili anche tante altre piccole-grandi città, con patrimoni artistici e storici eccezionali.
L'arte dei mosaici a Ravenna
Un indimenticabile viaggio fra l'oro e
PACCHETTI VACANZA CULTURA
OFFERTE SPECIALI
Per il momento non ci sono offerte disponibili legate a questa sezione. Torna al più presto per verificare la presenza di nuove offerte e occasioni dell'ultimo momento che potrebbero interessarti!

www.bluholidays.com
D: antonio moro C: fabio agostini P: giovanni antonioli fantini
A: bluelemon M: a.moro@bluelemon.it

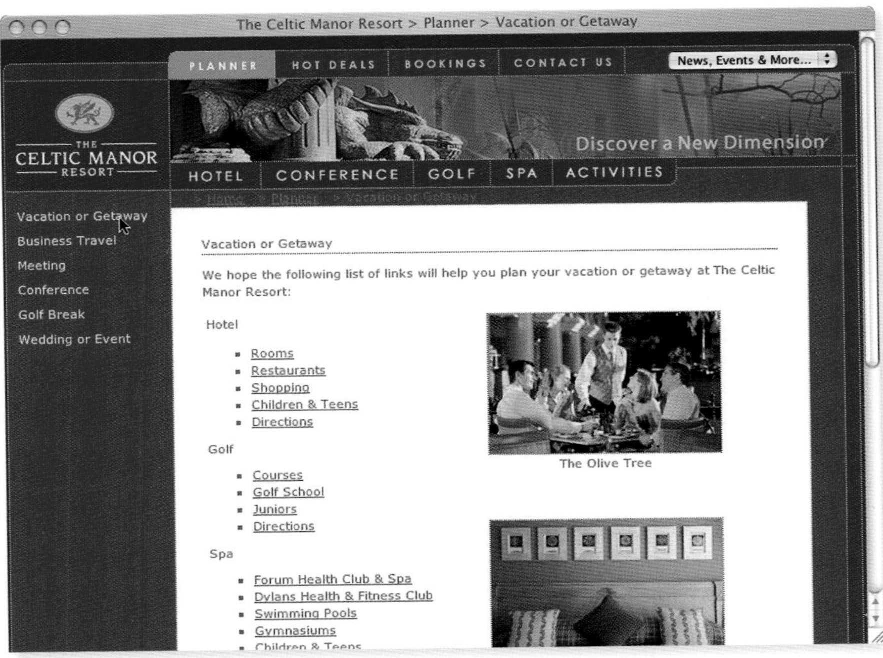
The Celtic Manor Resort > Planner > Vacation or Getaway
PLANNER
HOT DEALS
BOOKINGS
CONTACT US
News, Events & More...
Discover a New Dimension
THE CELTIC MANOR RESORT
HOTEL
CONFERENCE
GOLF
SPA
ACTIVITIES
Vacation or Getaway
Business Travel
Meeting
Conference
Golf Break
Wedding or Event
Vacation or Getaway
We hope the following list of links will help you plan your vacation or getaway at The Celtic Manor Resort:
Hotel
Rooms
Restaurants
Shopping
Children & Teens
Directions
The Olive Tree
Golf
Courses
Golf School
Juniors
Directions
Spa
Forum Health Club & Spa
Dylans Health & Fitness Club
Swimming Pools
Gymnasiums

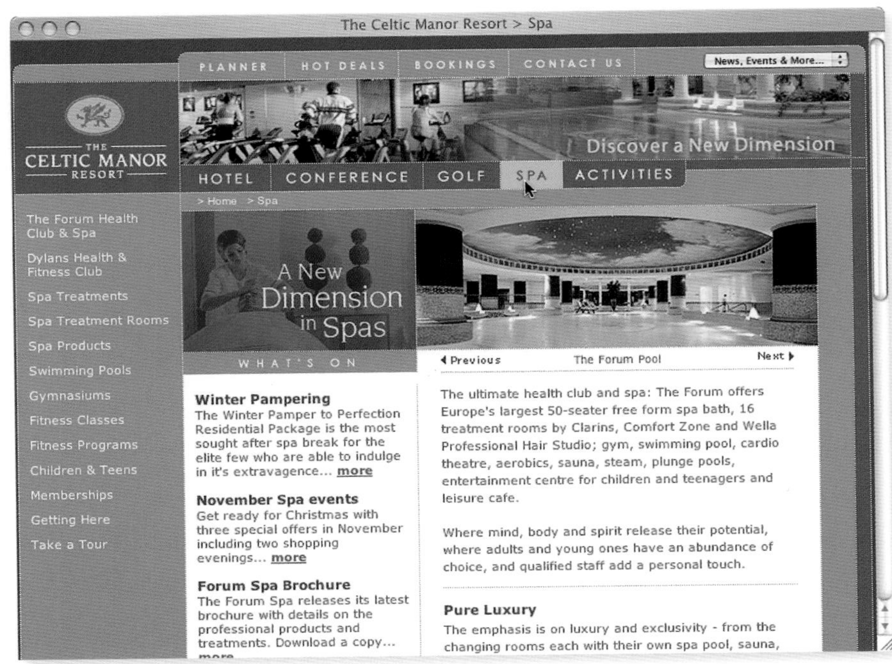
The Celtic Manor Resort > Spa
PLANNER
HOT DEALS
BOOKINGS
CONTACT US
News, Events & More...
Discover a New Dimension
THE CELTIC MANOR RESORT
HOTEL
CONFERENCE
GOLF
SPA
ACTIVITIES
> Home > Spa
The Forum Health Club & Spa
Dylans Health & Fitness Club
Spa Treatments
Spa Treatment Rooms
Spa Products
Swimming Pools
Gymnasiums
Fitness Classes
Fitness Programs
Children & Teens
Memberships
Getting Here
Take a Tour
A New Dimension in Spas
WHAT'S ON
Previous
The Forum Pool
Next
Winter Pampering
The Winter Pamper to Perfection Residential Package is the most sought after spa break for the elite few who are able to indulge in it's extravagence... more
November Spa events
Get ready for Christmas with three special offers in November including two shopping evenings... more
Forum Spa Brochure
The Forum Spa releases its latest brochure with details on the professional products and treatments. Download a copy...
The ultimate health club and spa: The Forum offers Europe's largest 50-seater free form spa bath, 16 treatment rooms by Clarins, Comfort Zone and Wella Professional Hair Studio; gym, swimming pool, cardio theatre, aerobics, sauna, steam, plunge pools, entertainment centre for children and teenagers and leisure cafe.
Where mind, body and spirit release their potential, where adults and young ones have an abundance of choice, and qualified staff add a personal touch.
Pure Luxury
The emphasis is on luxury and exclusivity - from the changing rooms each with their own spa pool, sauna,

www.celtic-manor.com
D: steve gauder **C:** hoejin wang **P:** rick brown
A: gauder design **M:** sgauder@capitalc.net

2 Barcelona Appartementen | Welkom bij 2 Barcelona
Home Appartementen Voorwaarden Contact
Language
2 Barcelona
Welkom bij 2 Barcelona
Home » Welkom bij 2 Barcelona appartementen
Appartement zoeker
2 - 3 personen
tot 75 euro
Zoeken
Bookmark deze pagina
Instellen als homepage
Tell a Friend
2 Barcelona
Appartementen in Barcelona
Gouwe 19
1703 HG Heerhugowaard
info@2barcelona.com
www.2barcelona.com
Najaarsaanbieding
Appartement D een royaal en luxe 6 persoons appartement in de gehele maand november , december en januari voor slechts 60 euro per nacht. (euro 10 p.p.p.n) Een royaal appartement met 3 slaapkamers, een uitgebreide keuken recente badkamer en climate control per kamer. Normale nachtprijs 115 euro nu voor maar 60 euro per nacht (minimaal 4 nachten en excl eenmalig 60 euro schoonmaak en administratiekosten)
klik hier voor alle info
Appartement van de maand
Maria Aguilo - Poble Nou

2 Barcelona Appartementen | Appartement details
Home Appartementen Voorwaarden Contact
Language
2 Barcelona
Appartement details
Home » Appartementen » Appartement details
2 - 3 persoons appartementen
4 - 5 persoons appartementen
6 persoons appartementen
Alle appartementen
H - Plaza Union - Poble Nou
Personen: 3 personen
Prijs per nacht: € 85,-
Plaats: Barcelona
Lokatie: Zie Kaart
Beschikbaar ?: Controleren
Reserveren: Reserveer nu!
Appartement zoeker
2 - 3 personen
tot 75 euro
Zoeken
Volgende afbeelding ›
Wat heeft "Plaza Union - Poble Nou" u te bieden
Wat vroeger een oude en historische plaats was met oude gebouwen uit de 19e eeuw is nu aan het veranderen in een mix tussen oude en nieuwe gebouwen.
Vroeger was er een portier aanwezig bij een appartementencomplex, appartement H is zo'n voormalig portiersverblijf, weliswaar geheel onder handen genomen maar met behoud van details.
Bookmark deze pagina
Instellen als homepage
Tell a Friend
2 Barcelona
Appartementen in Barcelona
Gouwe 19
1703 HG Heerhugowaard
Het is slecht een klein stukje lopen naar de Rambla de Poble Nou. Een lange autovrije promenade die door heel de wijk heenloopt en eindigt bij de Middellandse zee. Naast deze promenade vindt U barretjes en winkeltjes.

www.2barcelona.com
D: mathijs broeks
A: broeksmedia M: info@broeksmedia.nl

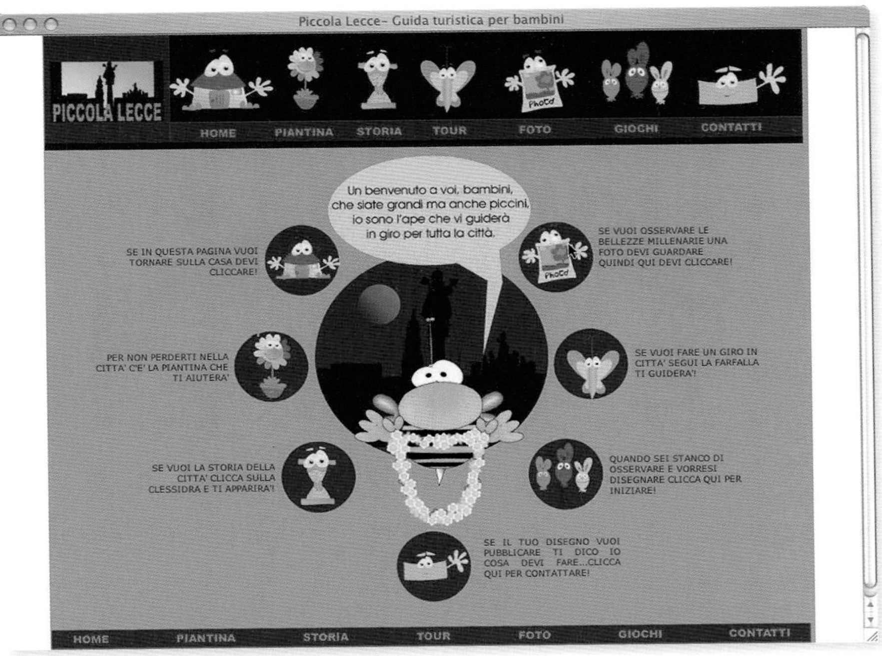
Piccola Lecce- Guida turistica per bambini
PICCOLA LECCE
HOME PIANTINA STORIA TOUR FOTO GIOCHI CONTATTI
Un benvenuto a voi, bambini, che siate grandi ma anche piccini, io sono l'ape che vi guiderà in giro per tutta la città.
SE IN QUESTA PAGINA VUOI TORNARE SULLA CASA DEVI CLICCARE!
SE VUOI OSSERVARE LE BELLEZZE MILLENARIE UNA FOTO DEVI GUARDARE QUINDI QUI DEVI CLICCARE!
PER NON PERDERTI NELLA CITTA' C'E' LA PIANTINA CHE TI AIUTERA'
SE VUOI FARE UN GIRO IN CITTA' SEGUI LA FARFALLA TI GUIDERA'!
SE VUOI LA STORIA DELLA CITTA' CLICCA SULLA CLESSIDRA E TI APPARIRA'!
QUANDO SEI STANCO DI OSSERVARE E VORRESI DISEGNARE CLICCA QUI PER INIZIARE!
SE IL TUO DISEGNO VUOI PUBBLICARE TI DICO IO COSA DEVI FARE...CLICCA QUI PER CONTATTARE!
HOME PIANTINA STORIA TOUR FOTO GIOCHI CONTATTI

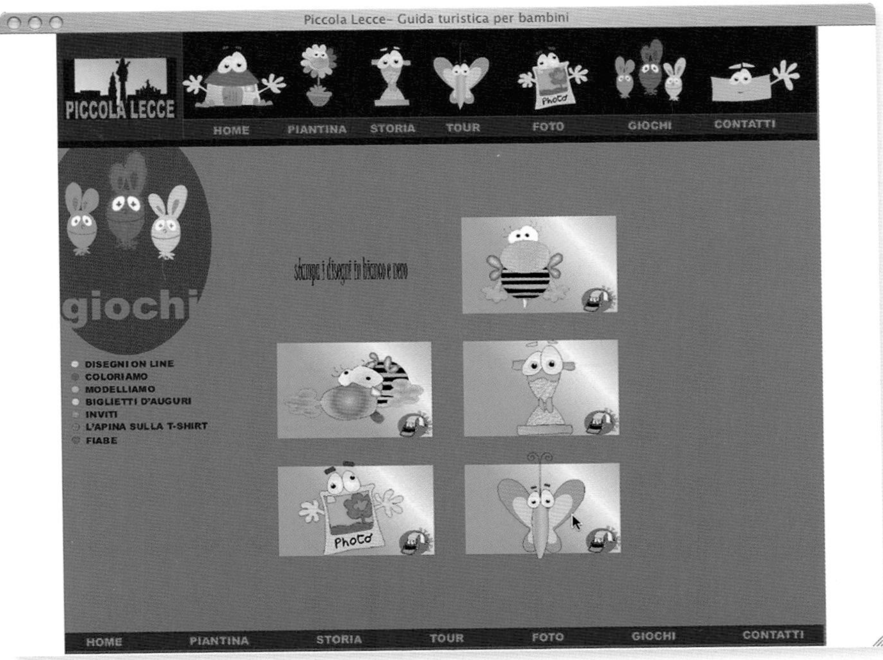
Piccola Lecce- Guida turistica per bambini
PICCOLA LECCE
HOME PIANTINA STORIA TOUR FOTO GIOCHI CONTATTI
giochi
DISEGNI ON LINE
COLORIAMO
MODELLIAMO
BIGLIETTI D'AUGURI
INVITI
L'APINA SULLA T-SHIRT
FIABE
Photo
HOME PIANTINA STORIA TOUR FOTO GIOCHI CONTATTI

www.piccolalecce.it
D: pierpaolo gaballo **P:** piccola lecce
M: pierpaolo.gaballo@clio.it